The Complete Robert Louis Stevenson
Novels, Short Stories, Travels, Non-Fiction, Plays and Poems

Robert Louis Stevenson

GRAPEVINE INDIA

Published by

GRAPEVINE INDIA PUBLISHERS PVT LTD

www.grapevineindia.com
Delhi | Mumbai
email: grapevineindiapublishers@gmail.com

Ordering Information:
Quantity sales: Special discounts are available on quantity purchases by corporations, associations, and others.
For details, reach out to the publisher.

First published by Grapevine India 2023
Copyright © Grapevine 2023
All rights reserved

Treasure Island   p 5

TREASURE ISLAND

To S.L.O., an American gentleman in accordance with whose classic taste the following narrative has been designed, it is now, in return for numerous delightful hours, and with the kindest wishes, dedicated by his affectionate friend, the author.

TO THE HESITATING PURCHASER

If sailor tales to sailor tunes,
Storm and adventure, heat and cold,
If schooners, islands, and maroons,
And buccaneers, and buried gold,
And all the old romance, retold
Exactly in the ancient way,
Can please, as me they pleased of old,
The wiser youngsters of today:

—So be it, and fall on! If not,
If studious youth no longer crave,
His ancient appetites forgot,
Kingston, or Ballantyne the brave,
Or Cooper of the wood and wave:
So be it, also! And may I
And all my pirates share the grave
Where these and their creations lie!

TREASURE ISLAND
PART ONE—The Old Buccaneer

1

The Old Sea-dog at the "Admiral Benbow"

SQUIRE TRELAWNEY, Dr. Livesey, and the rest of these gentlemen having asked me to write down the whole particulars about Treasure Island, from the beginning to the end, keeping nothing back but the bearings of the island, and that only because there is still treasure not yet lifted, I take up my pen in the year of grace 17__ and go back to the time when my father kept the Admiral Benbow inn and the brown old seaman with the sabre cut first took up his lodging under our roof.

I remember him as if it were yesterday, as he came plodding to the inn door, his sea-chest following behind him in a hand-barrow—a tall, strong, heavy, nut-brown man, his tarry pigtail falling over the shoulder of his soiled blue coat, his hands ragged and scarred, with black, broken nails, and the sabre cut across one cheek, a dirty, livid white. I remember him looking round the cove and whistling to himself as he did so, and then breaking out in that old sea-song that he sang so often afterwards:

"Fifteen men on the dead man's chest—
Yo-ho-ho, and a bottle of rum!"

in the high, old tottering voice that seemed to have been tuned and broken at the capstan bars. Then he rapped on the door with a bit of stick like a handspike that he carried, and when my father appeared, called roughly for a glass of rum. This, when it was brought to him, he drank slowly, like a connoisseur, lingering on the taste and still looking about him at the cliffs and up at our signboard.

"This is a handy cove," says he at length; "and a pleasant sittyated grog-shop. Much company, mate?"

My father told him no, very little company, the more was the pity.

"Well, then," said he, "this is the berth for me. Here you, matey," he cried to the man who trundled the barrow; "bring up alongside and help up my chest. I'll stay here a bit," he continued. "I'm a plain man; rum and bacon and eggs is what I want, and that head up there for to watch ships off. What you mought call me? You mought call me captain. Oh, I see what you're at—there"; and he threw down three or four gold pieces on the threshold. "You can tell me when I've worked through that," says he, looking as fierce as a commander.

And indeed bad as his clothes were and coarsely as he spoke, he had none of the appearance of a man who sailed before the mast, but seemed like a mate or skipper accustomed to be obeyed or to strike. The man who came with the barrow told us the mail had set him down the morning before at the Royal George, that he had inquired what inns there were along the coast, and hearing ours well spoken of, I suppose, and described as lonely, had chosen it from the others for his place of residence. And that was all we could learn of our guest.

He was a very silent man by custom. All day he hung round the cove or upon the cliffs with a brass telescope; all evening he sat in a corner of the parlour next the fire and drank rum and water very strong. Mostly he would not speak when spoken to, only look up sudden and fierce and blow through his nose like a fog-horn; and we and the people who came about our house soon learned to let him be. Every day when he came back from his stroll he would ask if any seafaring men had gone by along the road. At first we thought it was the want of company of his own kind that made him ask this question, but at last we began to see he was desirous to avoid them. When a seaman did put up at the Admiral Benbow (as now and then some did, making by the coast road for Bristol) he would look in at him through the curtained door before he entered the parlour; and he was always sure to be as silent as a mouse when any such was present. For me, at least, there was no secret about the matter, for I was, in a way, a sharer in his alarms. He had taken me aside one day and promised me a silver fourpenny on the first of every month if I would only keep my "weather-eye open for a seafaring man with one leg" and let him know the moment he appeared. Often enough when the first of the month came round and I applied to him for my wage, he would only blow through his nose at me and stare me down, but before the week was out he was sure to think better of it, bring me my four-penny piece, and repeat his orders to look out for "the seafaring man with one leg."

How that personage haunted my dreams, I need scarcely tell you. On stormy nights, when the wind shook the four corners of the house and the surf roared along the cove and up the cliffs, I would see him in a thousand forms, and with a thousand diabolical expressions. Now the leg would be cut off at the knee, now at the hip; now he was a monstrous kind of a creature who had never had but the one leg, and that in the middle of his body. To see him leap and run and pursue me over hedge and ditch was the worst of nightmares. And altogether I paid pretty dear for my monthly fourpenny piece, in the shape of these abominable fancies.

But though I was so terrified by the idea of the seafaring man with one leg, I was far less afraid of the captain himself than anybody else who knew him. There were nights when he took a deal more rum and water than his head would carry; and then he would sometimes sit and sing his wicked, old, wild sea-songs, minding nobody; but sometimes he would call for glasses round and force all the trembling company to listen to his stories or bear a chorus to his singing. Often I have heard the house shaking with "Yo-ho-ho, and a bottle of rum," all the neighbours joining in for dear life, with the fear of death upon them, and each singing louder than the other to avoid remark. For in these fits he was the most overriding companion ever known; he would slap his hand on the table for silence all round; he would fly up in a passion of anger at a question, or sometimes because none was put, and so he judged the company was not following his story. Nor would he allow anyone to leave the inn till he had drunk himself sleepy and reeled off to bed.

His stories were what frightened people worst of all. Dreadful stories they were—about hanging, and walking the plank, and storms at sea, and the Dry Tortugas, and wild deeds and places on the Spanish Main. By his own account he must have lived his life among some of the wickedest men that God ever allowed upon the sea, and the language in which he told these stories shocked our plain country people almost as much as the crimes that he described. My father was always saying the inn would be ruined, for people would soon cease coming there to be tyrannized over and put down, and sent shivering to their beds; but I really believe his presence did us good. People were frightened at the time, but on looking back they rather liked it; it was a fine excitement in a quiet country life, and there was even a party of the younger men who pretended to admire him, calling him a "true sea-dog" and a "real old salt" and such like names, and saying there was the sort of man that made England terrible at sea.

In one way, indeed, he bade fair to ruin us, for he kept on staying week after week, and at last month after month, so that all the money had been long exhausted, and still my father never plucked up the heart to insist on having more. If ever he mentioned it, the captain blew through his nose so loudly that you might say he roared, and stared my poor father out of the room. I have seen him wringing his hands after such a rebuff, and I am sure the annoyance and the terror he lived in must have greatly hastened his early and unhappy death.

All the time he lived with us the captain made no change whatever in his dress but to buy some stockings from a hawker. One of the cocks of his hat having fallen down, he let it hang from that day forth, though it was a great annoyance when it blew. I remember the appearance of his coat, which he patched himself upstairs in his room, and which, before the end, was nothing but patches. He never wrote or received a letter, and he never spoke with any but the neighbours, and with these, for the most part, only when drunk on rum. The great sea-chest none of us had ever seen open.

He was only once crossed, and that was towards the end, when my poor father was far gone in a decline that took him off. Dr. Livesey came late one afternoon to see the patient, took a bit of dinner from my mother, and went into the parlour to smoke a pipe until his horse should come down from the hamlet, for we had no stabling at the old Benbow. I followed him in, and I remember observing the contrast the neat, bright doctor, with his powder as white as snow and his bright, black eyes and pleasant manners, made with the coltish country folk, and above all, with that filthy, heavy, bleared scarecrow of a pirate of ours, sitting, far gone in rum, with his arms on the table. Suddenly he—the captain, that is—began to pipe up his eternal song:

"Fifteen men on the dead man's chest—
   Yo-ho-ho, and a bottle of rum!
Drink and the devil had done for the rest—
   Yo-ho-ho, and a bottle of rum!"

At first I had supposed "the dead man's chest" to be that identical big box of his upstairs in the front room, and the thought had been mingled in my nightmares with that of the one-legged seafaring man. But by this time we had all long ceased to pay any particular notice to the song; it was new, that night, to nobody but Dr. Livesey, and on him I observed it did not produce an agreeable effect, for he looked up for a moment quite angrily before he went on with his talk to old Taylor, the gardener, on a new cure for the rheumatics. In the meantime, the captain gradually brightened up at his own music, and at last flapped his hand upon the table before him in a way we all knew to mean silence. The voices stopped at once, all but Dr. Livesey's; he went on as before speaking clear and kind and drawing briskly at his pipe between every word or two. The captain glared at him for a while, flapped his hand again, glared still harder, and at last broke out with a villainous, low oath, "Silence, there, between decks!"

"Were you addressing me, sir?" says the doctor; and when the ruffian had told him, with another oath, that this was so, "I have only one thing to say to you, sir," replies the doctor, "that if you keep on drinking rum, the world will soon be quit of a very dirty scoundrel!"

The old fellow's fury was awful. He sprang to his feet, drew and opened a sailor's clasp-knife, and balancing it open on the palm of his hand, threatened to pin the doctor to the wall.

The doctor never so much as moved. He spoke to him as before, over his shoulder and in the same tone of voice, rather high, so that all the room might hear, but perfectly calm and steady: "If you do not put that knife this instant in your pocket, I promise, upon my honour, you shall hang at the next assizes."

Then followed a battle of looks between them, but the captain soon knuckled under, put up his weapon, and resumed his seat, grumbling like a beaten dog.

"And now, sir," continued the doctor, "since I now know there's such a fellow in my district, you may count I'll have an eye upon you day and night. I'm not a doctor only; I'm a magistrate; and if I catch a breath of complaint against you, if it's only for a piece of incivility like tonight's, I'll take effectual means to have you hunted down and routed out of this. Let that suffice."

Soon after, Dr. Livesey's horse came to the door and he rode away, but the captain held his peace that evening, and for many evenings to come.

2
Black Dog Appears and Disappears

T was not very long after this that there occurred the first of the mysterious events that rid us at last of the captain, though not, as you will see, of his affairs. It was a bitter cold winter, with long, hard frosts and heavy gales; and it was plain from the first that my poor father was little likely to see the spring. He sank daily, and my mother and I had all the inn upon our hands, and were kept busy enough without paying much regard to our unpleasant guest.

It was one January morning, very early—a pinching, frosty morning—the cove all grey with hoar-frost, the ripple lapping softly on the stones, the sun still low and only touching the hilltops and shining far to seaward. The captain had risen earlier than usual and set out down the beach, his cutlass swinging under the broad skirts of the old blue coat, his brass telescope under his arm, his hat tilted back upon his head. I remember his breath hanging like smoke in his wake as he strode off, and the last sound I heard of him as he turned the big rock was a loud snort of indignation, as though his mind was still running upon Dr. Livesey.

Well, mother was upstairs with father and I was laying the breakfast-table against the captain's return when the parlour door opened and a man stepped in on whom I had never set my eyes before. He was a pale, tallowy creature, wanting two fingers of the left hand, and though he wore a cutlass, he did not look much like a fighter. I had always my eye open for seafaring men, with one leg or two, and I remember this one puzzled me. He was not sailorly, and yet he had a smack of the sea about him too.

I asked him what was for his service, and he said he would take rum; but as I was going out of the room to fetch it, he sat down upon a table and motioned me to draw near. I paused where I was, with my napkin in my hand.

"Come here, sonny," says he. "Come nearer here."

I took a step nearer.

"Is this here table for my mate Bill?" he asked with a kind of leer.

I told him I did not know his mate Bill, and this was for a person who stayed in our house whom we called the captain.

"Well," said he, "my mate Bill would be called the captain, as like as not. He has a cut on one cheek and a mighty pleasant way with him, particularly in drink, has my mate Bill. We'll put it, for argument like, that your captain has a cut on one cheek—and we'll put it, if you like, that that cheek's the right one. Ah, well! I told you. Now, is my mate Bill in this here house?"

I told him he was out walking.

"Which way, sonny? Which way is he gone?"

And when I had pointed out the rock and told him how the captain was likely to return, and how soon, and answered a few other questions, "Ah," said he, "this'll be as good as drink to my mate Bill."

The expression of his face as he said these words was not at all pleasant, and I had my own reasons for thinking that the stranger was mistaken, even supposing he meant what he said. But it was no affair of mine, I thought; and besides, it was difficult to know what to do. The stranger kept hanging about just inside the inn door, peering round the corner like a cat waiting for a mouse. Once I stepped out myself into the road, but he immediately called me back, and as I did not obey quick enough for his fancy, a most horrible change came over his tallowy face, and he ordered me in with an oath that made me jump. As soon as I was back again he returned to his former manner, half fawning, half sneering, patted me on the shoulder, told me I was a good boy and he had taken quite a fancy to me. "I have a son of my own," said he, "as like you as two blocks, and he's all the pride of my 'art. But the great thing for boys is discipline, sonny—discipline. Now, if you had sailed along of Bill, you wouldn't have stood there to be spoke to twice—not you. That was never Bill's way, nor the way of sich as sailed with him. And here, sure enough, is my mate Bill, with a spy-glass under his arm, bless his old 'art, to be sure. You and me'll just go back into the parlour, sonny, and get behind the door, and we'll give Bill a little surprise—bless his 'art, I say again."

So saying, the stranger backed along with me into the parlour and put me behind him in the corner so that we were both hidden by the open door. I was very uneasy and alarmed, as you may fancy, and it rather added to my fears to observe that the stranger was certainly frightened himself. He cleared the hilt of his cutlass and loosened the blade in the sheath; and all the time we were waiting there he kept swallowing as if he felt what we used to call a lump in the throat.

At last in strode the captain, slammed the door behind him, without looking to the right or left, and marched straight across the room to where his breakfast awaited him.

"Bill," said the stranger in a voice that I thought he had tried to make bold and big.

The captain spun round on his heel and fronted us; all the brown had gone out of his face, and even his nose was blue; he had the look of a man who sees a ghost, or the evil one, or something worse, if anything can be; and upon my word, I felt sorry to see him all in a moment turn so old and sick.

"Come, Bill, you know me; you know an old shipmate, Bill, surely," said the stranger.

The captain made a sort of gasp.

"Black Dog!" said he.

"And who else?" returned the other, getting more at his ease. "Black Dog as ever was, come for to see his old shipmate Billy, at the Admiral Benbow inn. Ah, Bill, Bill, we have seen a sight of times, us two, since I lost them two talons," holding up his mutilated hand.

"Now, look here," said the captain; "you've run me down; here I am; well, then, speak up; what is it?"

"That's you, Bill," returned Black Dog, "you're in the right of it, Billy. I'll have a glass of rum from this dear child here, as I've took such a liking to; and we'll sit down, if you please, and talk square, like old shipmates."

When I returned with the rum, they were already seated on either side of the captain's breakfast-table—Black Dog next to the door and sitting sideways so as to have one eye on his old shipmate and one, as I thought, on his retreat.

He bade me go and leave the door wide open. "None of your keyholes for me, sonny," he said; and I left them together and retired into the bar.

For a long time, though I certainly did my best to listen, I could hear nothing but a low gattling;

but at last the voices began to grow higher, and I could pick up a word or two, mostly oaths, from the captain.

"No, no, no, no; and an end of it!" he cried once. And again, "If it comes to swinging, swing all, say I."

Then all of a sudden there was a tremendous explosion of oaths and other noises—the chair and table went over in a lump, a clash of steel followed, and then a cry of pain, and the next instant I saw Black Dog in full flight, and the captain hotly pursuing, both with drawn cutlasses, and the former streaming blood from the left shoulder. Just at the door the captain aimed at the fugitive one last tremendous cut, which would certainly have split him to the chine had it not been intercepted by our big signboard of Admiral Benbow. You may see the notch on the lower side of the frame to this day.

That blow was the last of the battle. Once out upon the road, Black Dog, in spite of his wound, showed a wonderful clean pair of heels and disappeared over the edge of the hill in half a minute. The captain, for his part, stood staring at the signboard like a bewildered man. Then he passed his hand over his eyes several times and at last turned back into the house.

"Jim," says he, "rum"; and as he spoke, he reeled a little, and caught himself with one hand against the wall.

"Are you hurt?" cried I.

"Rum," he repeated. "I must get away from here. Rum! Rum!"

I ran to fetch it, but I was quite unsteadied by all that had fallen out, and I broke one glass and fouled the tap, and while I was still getting in my own way, I heard a loud fall in the parlour, and running in, beheld the captain lying full length upon the floor. At the same instant my mother, alarmed by the cries and fighting, came running downstairs to help me. Between us we raised his head. He was breathing very loud and hard, but his eyes were closed and his face a horrible colour.

"Dear, deary me," cried my mother, "what a disgrace upon the house! And your poor father sick!"

In the meantime, we had no idea what to do to help the captain, nor any other thought but that he had got his death-hurt in the scuffle with the stranger. I got the rum, to be sure, and tried to put it down his throat, but his teeth were tightly shut and his jaws as strong as iron. It was a happy relief for us when the door opened and Doctor Livesey came in, on his visit to my father.

"Oh, doctor," we cried, "what shall we do? Where is he wounded?"

"Wounded? A fiddle-stick's end!" said the doctor. "No more wounded than you or I. The man has had a stroke, as I warned him. Now, Mrs. Hawkins, just you run upstairs to your husband and tell him, if possible, nothing about it. For my part, I must do my best to save this fellow's trebly worthless life; Jim, you get me a basin."

When I got back with the basin, the doctor had already ripped up the captain's sleeve and exposed his great sinewy arm. It was tattooed in several places. "Here's luck," "A fair wind," and "Billy Bones his fancy," were very neatly and clearly executed on the forearm; and up near the shoulder there was a sketch of a gallows and a man hanging from it—done, as I thought, with great spirit.

"Prophetic," said the doctor, touching this picture with his finger. "And now, Master Billy

Bones, if that be your name, we'll have a look at the colour of your blood. Jim," he said, "are you afraid of blood?"

"No, sir," said I.

"Well, then," said he, "you hold the basin"; and with that he took his lancet and opened a vein.

A great deal of blood was taken before the captain opened his eyes and looked mistily about him. First he recognized the doctor with an unmistakable frown; then his glance fell upon me, and he looked relieved. But suddenly his colour changed, and he tried to raise himself, crying, "Where's Black Dog?"

"There is no Black Dog here," said the doctor, "except what you have on your own back. You have been drinking rum; you have had a stroke, precisely as I told you; and I have just, very much against my own will, dragged you headforemost out of the grave. Now, Mr. Bones—"

"That's not my name," he interrupted.

"Much I care," returned the doctor. "It's the name of a buccaneer of my acquaintance; and I call you by it for the sake of shortness, and what I have to say to you is this; one glass of rum won't kill you, but if you take one you'll take another and another, and I stake my wig if you don't break off short, you'll die—do you understand that?—die, and go to your own place, like the man in the Bible. Come, now, make an effort. I'll help you to your bed for once."

Between us, with much trouble, we managed to hoist him upstairs, and laid him on his bed, where his head fell back on the pillow as if he were almost fainting.

"Now, mind you," said the doctor, "I clear my conscience—the name of rum for you is death."

And with that he went off to see my father, taking me with him by the arm.

"This is nothing," he said as soon as he had closed the door. "I have drawn blood enough to keep him quiet awhile; he should lie for a week where he is—that is the best thing for him and you; but another stroke would settle him."

3
The Black Spot

ABOUT noon I stopped at the captain's door with some cooling drinks and medicines. He was lying very much as we had left him, only a little higher, and he seemed both weak and excited.

"Jim," he said, "you're the only one here that's worth anything, and you know I've been always good to you. Never a month but I've given you a silver fourpenny for yourself. And now you see, mate, I'm pretty low, and deserted by all; and Jim, you'll bring me one noggin of rum, now, won't you, matey?"

"The doctor—" I began.

But he broke in cursing the doctor, in a feeble voice but heartily. "Doctors is all swabs," he said; "and that doctor there, why, what do he know about seafaring men? I been in places hot as pitch, and mates dropping round with Yellow Jack, and the blessed land a-heaving like the sea with earthquakes—what to the doctor know of lands like that?—and I lived on rum, I tell you. It's been meat and drink, and man and wife, to me; and if I'm not to have my rum now I'm a poor old hulk on a lee shore, my blood'll be on you, Jim, and that doctor swab"; and he ran on again for a while with curses. "Look, Jim, how my fingers fidges," he continued in the pleading tone. "I can't keep 'em still, not I. I haven't had a drop this blessed day. That doctor's a fool, I tell you. If I don't have a dram o' rum, Jim, I'll have the horrors; I seen some on 'em already. I seen old Flint in the corner there, behind you; as plain as print, I seen him; and if I get the horrors, I'm a man that has lived rough, and I'll raise Cain. Your doctor hisself said one glass wouldn't hurt me. I'll give you a golden guinea for a noggin, Jim."

He was growing more and more excited, and this alarmed me for my father, who was very low that day and needed quiet; besides, I was reassured by the doctor's words, now quoted to me, and rather offended by the offer of a bribe.

"I want none of your money," said I, "but what you owe my father. I'll get you one glass, and no more."

When I brought it to him, he seized it greedily and drank it out.

"Aye, aye," said he, "that's some better, sure enough. And now, matey, did that doctor say how long I was to lie here in this old berth?"

"A week at least," said I.

"Thunder!" he cried. "A week! I can't do that; they'd have the black spot on me by then. The lubbers is going about to get the wind of me this blessed moment; lubbers as couldn't keep what they got, and want to nail what is another's. Is that seamanly behaviour, now, I want to know? But I'm a saving soul. I never wasted good money of mine, nor lost it neither; and I'll trick 'em again. I'm not afraid on 'em. I'll shake out another reef, matey, and daddle 'em again."

As he was thus speaking, he had risen from bed with great difficulty, holding to my shoulder with a grip that almost made me cry out, and moving his legs like so much dead weight. His words, spirited as they were in meaning, contrasted sadly with the weakness of the voice in which they were uttered. He paused when he had got into a sitting position on the edge.

"That doctor's done me," he murmured. "My ears is singing. Lay me back."

Before I could do much to help him he had fallen back again to his former place, where he lay for a while silent.

"Jim," he said at length, "you saw that seafaring man today?"

"Black Dog?" I asked.

"Ah! Black Dog," says he. "He's a bad 'un; but there's worse that put him on. Now, if I can't get away nohow, and they tip me the black spot, mind you, it's my old sea-chest they're after; you get on a horse—you can, can't you? Well, then, you get on a horse, and go to—well, yes, I will!—to that eternal doctor swab, and tell him to pipe all hands—magistrates and sich—and he'll lay 'em aboard at the Admiral Benbow—all old Flint's crew, man and boy, all on 'em that's left. I was first mate, I was, old Flint's first mate, and I'm the on'y one as knows the place. He gave it me at Savannah, when he lay a-dying, like as if I was to now, you see. But you won't peach unless they get the black spot on me, or unless you see that Black Dog again or a seafaring man with one leg, Jim—him above all."

"But what is the black spot, captain?" I asked.

"That's a summons, mate. I'll tell you if they get that. But you keep your weather-eye open, Jim, and I'll share with you equals, upon my honour."

He wandered a little longer, his voice growing weaker; but soon after I had given him his medicine, which he took like a child, with the remark, "If ever a seaman wanted drugs, it's me," he fell at last into a heavy, swoon-like sleep, in which I left him. What I should have done had all gone well I do not know. Probably I should have told the whole story to the doctor, for I was in mortal fear lest the captain should repent of his confessions and make an end of me. But as things fell out, my poor father died quite suddenly that evening, which put all other matters on one side. Our natural distress, the visits of the neighbours, the arranging of the funeral, and all the work of the inn to be carried on in the meanwhile kept me so busy that I had scarcely time to think of the captain, far less to be afraid of him.

He got downstairs next morning, to be sure, and had his meals as usual, though he ate little and had more, I am afraid, than his usual supply of rum, for he helped himself out of the bar, scowling and blowing through his nose, and no one dared to cross him. On the night before the funeral he was as drunk as ever; and it was shocking, in that house of mourning, to hear him singing away at his ugly old sea-song; but weak as he was, we were all in the fear of death for him, and the doctor was suddenly taken up with a case many miles away and was never near the house after my father's death. I have said the captain was weak, and indeed he seemed rather to grow weaker than regain his strength. He clambered up and down stairs, and went from the parlour to the bar and back again, and sometimes put his nose out of doors to smell the sea, holding on to the walls as he went for support and breathing hard and fast like a man on a steep mountain. He never particularly addressed me, and it is my belief he had as good as forgotten his confidences; but his temper was more flighty, and allowing for his bodily weakness, more violent than ever. He had an alarming way now when he was drunk of drawing his cutlass and laying it bare before him on the table. But with all that, he minded people less and seemed shut up in his own thoughts and rather wandering. Once, for instance, to our extreme wonder, he piped up to a different air, a kind of country love-song that he must have learned in his youth before he had begun to follow the sea.

So things passed until, the day after the funeral, and about three o'clock of a bitter, foggy, frosty afternoon, I was standing at the door for a moment, full of sad thoughts about my father, when I saw someone drawing slowly near along the road. He was plainly blind, for he tapped before him with a stick and wore a great green shade over his eyes and nose; and he was hunched, as if with age or weakness, and wore a huge old tattered sea-cloak with a hood that made him appear positively deformed. I never saw in my life a more dreadful-looking figure. He stopped a little from the inn, and raising his voice in an odd sing-song, addressed the air in front of him, "Will any kind friend inform a poor blind man, who has lost the precious sight of his eyes in the gracious defence of his native country, England—and God bless King George!—where or in what part of this country he may now be?"

"You are at the Admiral Benbow, Black Hill Cove, my good man," said I.

"I hear a voice," said he, "a young voice. Will you give me your hand, my kind young friend, and lead me in?"

I held out my hand, and the horrible, soft-spoken, eyeless creature gripped it in a moment like a vise. I was so much startled that I struggled to withdraw, but the blind man pulled me close up to him with a single action of his arm.

"Now, boy," he said, "take me in to the captain."

"Sir," said I, "upon my word I dare not."

"Oh," he sneered, "that's it! Take me in straight or I'll break your arm."

And he gave it, as he spoke, a wrench that made me cry out.

"Sir," said I, "it is for yourself I mean. The captain is not what he used to be. He sits with a drawn cutlass. Another gentleman—"

"Come, now, march," interrupted he; and I never heard a voice so cruel, and cold, and ugly as that blind man's. It cowed me more than the pain, and I began to obey him at once, walking straight in at the door and towards the parlour, where our sick old buccaneer was sitting, dazed with rum. The blind man clung close to me, holding me in one iron fist and leaning almost more of his weight on me than I could carry. "Lead me straight up to him, and when I'm in view, cry out, 'Here's a friend for you, Bill.' If you don't, I'll do this," and with that he gave me a twitch that I thought would have made me faint. Between this and that, I was so utterly terrified of the blind beggar that I forgot my terror of the captain, and as I opened the parlour door, cried out the words he had ordered in a trembling voice.

The poor captain raised his eyes, and at one look the rum went out of him and left him staring sober. The expression of his face was not so much of terror as of mortal sickness. He made a movement to rise, but I do not believe he had enough force left in his body.

"Now, Bill, sit where you are," said the beggar. "If I can't see, I can hear a finger stirring. Business is business. Hold out your left hand. Boy, take his left hand by the wrist and bring it near to my right."

We both obeyed him to the letter, and I saw him pass something from the hollow of the hand that held his stick into the palm of the captain's, which closed upon it instantly.

"And now that's done," said the blind man; and at the words he suddenly left hold of me, and with incredible accuracy and nimbleness, skipped out of the parlour and into the road, where, as I still stood motionless, I could hear his stick go tap-tap-tapping into the distance.

It was some time before either I or the captain seemed to gather our senses, but at length, and about at the same moment, I released his wrist, which I was still holding, and he drew in his hand and looked sharply into the palm.

"Ten o'clock!" he cried. "Six hours. We'll do them yet," and he sprang to his feet.

Even as he did so, he reeled, put his hand to his throat, stood swaying for a moment, and then, with a peculiar sound, fell from his whole height face foremost to the floor.

I ran to him at once, calling to my mother. But haste was all in vain. The captain had been struck dead by thundering apoplexy. It is a curious thing to understand, for I had certainly never liked the man, though of late I had begun to pity him, but as soon as I saw that he was dead, I burst into a flood of tears. It was the second death I had known, and the sorrow of the first was still fresh in my heart.

4
The Sea-chest

I LOST no time, of course, in telling my mother all that I knew, and perhaps should have told her long before, and we saw ourselves at once in a difficult and dangerous position. Some of the man's money—if he had any—was certainly due to us, but it was not likely that our captain's shipmates, above all the two specimens seen by me, Black Dog and the blind beggar, would be inclined to give up their booty in payment of the dead man's debts. The captain's order to mount at once and ride for Doctor Livesey would have left my mother alone and unprotected, which was not to be thought of. Indeed, it seemed impossible for either of us to remain much longer in the house; the fall of coals in the kitchen grate, the very ticking of the clock, filled us with alarms. The neighbourhood, to our ears, seemed haunted by approaching footsteps; and what between the dead body of the captain on the parlour floor and the thought of that detestable blind beggar hovering near at hand and ready to return, there were moments when, as the saying goes, I jumped in my skin for terror. Something must speedily be resolved upon, and it occurred to us at last to go forth together and seek help in the neighbouring hamlet. No sooner said than done. Bare-headed as we were, we ran out at once in the gathering evening and the frosty fog.

The hamlet lay not many hundred yards away, though out of view, on the other side of the next cove; and what greatly encouraged me, it was in an opposite direction from that whence the blind man had made his appearance and whither he had presumably returned. We were not many minutes on the road, though we sometimes stopped to lay hold of each other and hearken. But there was no unusual sound—nothing but the low wash of the ripple and the croaking of the inmates of the wood.

It was already candle-light when we reached the hamlet, and I shall never forget how much I was cheered to see the yellow shine in doors and windows; but that, as it proved, was the best of the help we were likely to get in that quarter. For—you would have thought men would have been ashamed of themselves—no soul would consent to return with us to the Admiral Benbow. The more we told of our troubles, the more—man, woman, and child—they clung to the shelter of their houses. The name of Captain Flint, though it was strange to me, was well enough known to some there and carried a great weight of terror. Some of the men who had been to field-work on the far side of the Admiral Benbow remembered, besides, to have seen several strangers on the road, and taking them to be smugglers, to have bolted away; and one at least had seen a little lugger in what we called Kitt's Hole. For that matter, anyone who was a comrade of the captain's was enough to frighten them to death. And the short and the long of the matter was, that while we could get several who were willing enough to ride to Dr. Livesey's, which lay in another direction, not one would help us to defend the inn.

They say cowardice is infectious; but then argument is, on the other hand, a great emboldener; and so when each had said his say, my mother made them a speech. She would not, she declared, lose money that belonged to her fatherless boy; "If none of the rest of you dare," she said, "Jim and I dare. Back we will go, the way we came, and small thanks to you big, hulking, chicken-hearted men. We'll have that chest open, if we die for it. And I'll thank you for that bag, Mrs. Crossley, to bring back our lawful money in."

Of course I said I would go with my mother, and of course they all cried out at our foolhardiness, but even then not a man would go along with us. All they would do was to give me a loaded pistol lest we were attacked, and to promise to have horses ready saddled in case we were pursued on our return, while one lad was to ride forward to the doctor's in search of armed assistance.

My heart was beating finely when we two set forth in the cold night upon this dangerous venture. A full moon was beginning to rise and peered redly through the upper edges of the fog, and this increased our haste, for it was plain, before we came forth again, that all would be as bright as day, and our departure exposed to the eyes of any watchers. We slipped along the hedges, noiseless and swift, nor did we see or hear anything to increase our terrors, till, to our relief, the door of the Admiral Benbow had closed behind us.

I slipped the bolt at once, and we stood and panted for a moment in the dark, alone in the house with the dead captain's body. Then my mother got a candle in the bar, and holding each other's hands, we advanced into the parlour. He lay as we had left him, on his back, with his eyes open and one arm stretched out.

"Draw down the blind, Jim," whispered my mother; "they might come and watch outside. And now," said she when I had done so, "we have to get the key off that; and who's to touch it, I should like to know!" and she gave a kind of sob as she said the words.

I went down on my knees at once. On the floor close to his hand there was a little round of paper, blackened on the one side. I could not doubt that this was the black spot; and taking it up, I found written on the other side, in a very good, clear hand, this short message: "You have till ten tonight."

"He had till ten, Mother," said I; and just as I said it, our old clock began striking. This sudden noise startled us shockingly; but the news was good, for it was only six.

"Now, Jim," she said, "that key."

I felt in his pockets, one after another. A few small coins, a thimble, and some thread and big needles, a piece of pigtail tobacco bitten away at the end, his gully with the crooked handle, a pocket compass, and a tinder box were all that they contained, and I began to despair.

"Perhaps it's round his neck," suggested my mother.

Overcoming a strong repugnance, I tore open his shirt at the neck, and there, sure enough, hanging to a bit of tarry string, which I cut with his own gully, we found the key. At this triumph we were filled with hope and hurried upstairs without delay to the little room where he had slept so long and where his box had stood since the day of his arrival.

It was like any other seaman's chest on the outside, the initial "B" burned on the top of it with a hot iron, and the corners somewhat smashed and broken as by long, rough usage.

"Give me the key," said my mother; and though the lock was very stiff, she had turned it and thrown back the lid in a twinkling.

A strong smell of tobacco and tar rose from the interior, but nothing was to be seen on the top except a suit of very good clothes, carefully brushed and folded. They had never been worn, my mother said. Under that, the miscellany began—a quadrant, a tin canikin, several sticks of tobacco, two brace of very handsome pistols, a piece of bar silver, an old Spanish watch and some other trinkets of little value and mostly of foreign make, a pair of compasses mounted with brass, and five or six curious West Indian shells. I have often wondered since why he should have carried about these shells with him in his wandering, guilty, and hunted life.

In the meantime, we had found nothing of any value but the silver and the trinkets, and neither of these were in our way. Underneath there was an old boat-cloak, whitened with sea-salt on many a harbour-bar. My mother pulled it up with impatience, and there lay before us, the last things in the chest, a bundle tied up in oilcloth, and looking like papers, and a canvas bag that gave forth, at a touch, the jingle of gold.

"I'll show these rogues that I'm an honest woman," said my mother. "I'll have my dues, and not a farthing over. Hold Mrs. Crossley's bag." And she began to count over the amount of the captain's score from the sailor's bag into the one that I was holding.

It was a long, difficult business, for the coins were of all countries and sizes—doubloons, and louis d'ors, and guineas, and pieces of eight, and I know not what besides, all shaken together at random. The guineas, too, were about the scarcest, and it was with these only that my mother knew how to make her count.

When we were about half-way through, I suddenly put my hand upon her arm, for I had heard in the silent frosty air a sound that brought my heart into my mouth—the tap-tapping of the blind man's stick upon the frozen road. It drew nearer and nearer, while we sat holding our breath. Then it struck sharp on the inn door, and then we could hear the handle being turned and the bolt rattling as the wretched being tried to enter; and then there was a long time of silence both within and without. At last the tapping recommenced, and, to our indescribable joy and gratitude, died slowly away again until it ceased to be heard.

"Mother," said I, "take the whole and let's be going," for I was sure the bolted door must have seemed suspicious and would bring the whole hornet's nest about our ears, though how thankful I was that I had bolted it, none could tell who had never met that terrible blind man.

But my mother, frightened as she was, would not consent to take a fraction more than was due to her and was obstinately unwilling to be content with less. It was not yet seven, she said, by a long way; she knew her rights and she would have them; and she was still arguing with me when a little low whistle sounded a good way off upon the hill. That was enough, and more than enough, for both of us.

"I'll take what I have," she said, jumping to her feet.

"And I'll take this to square the count," said I, picking up the oilskin packet.

Next moment we were both groping downstairs, leaving the candle by the empty chest; and the next we had opened the door and were in full retreat. We had not started a moment too soon. The fog was rapidly dispersing; already the moon shone quite clear on the high ground on either side; and it was only in the exact bottom of the dell and round the tavern door that a thin veil still hung unbroken to conceal the first steps of our escape. Far less than half-way to the hamlet, very little beyond the bottom of the hill, we must come forth into the moonlight. Nor was this all, for the sound of several footsteps running came already to our ears, and as we looked back in their direction, a light tossing to and fro and still rapidly advancing showed that one of the newcomers carried a lantern.

"My dear," said my mother suddenly, "take the money and run on. I am going to faint."

This was certainly the end for both of us, I thought. How I cursed the cowardice of the neighbours; how I blamed my poor mother for her honesty and her greed, for her past foolhardiness and present weakness! We were just at the little bridge, by good fortune; and I helped her, tottering as she was, to the edge of the bank, where, sure enough, she gave a sigh and fell on my shoulder. I do not know how I found the strength to do it at all, and I am afraid it was roughly done, but I managed to drag her down the bank and a little way under the arch. Farther I could not move her, for the bridge was too low to let me do more than crawl below it. So there we had to stay— my mother almost entirely exposed and both of us within earshot of the inn.

5

The Last of the Blind Man

MY curiosity, in a sense, was stronger than my fear, for I could not remain where I was, but crept back to the bank again, whence, sheltering my head behind a bush of broom, I might command the road before our door. I was scarcely in position ere my enemies began to arrive, seven or eight of them, running hard, their feet beating out of time along the road and the man with the lantern some paces in front. Three men ran together, hand in hand; and I made out, even through the mist, that the middle man of this trio was the blind beggar. The next moment his voice showed me that I was right.

"Down with the door!" he cried.

"Aye, aye, sir!" answered two or three; and a rush was made upon the Admiral Benbow, the lantern-bearer following; and then I could see them pause, and hear speeches passed in a lower key, as if they were surprised to find the door open. But the pause was brief, for the blind man again issued his commands. His voice sounded louder and higher, as if he were afire with eagerness and rage.

"In, in, in!" he shouted, and cursed them for their delay.

Four or five of them obeyed at once, two remaining on the road with the formidable beggar. There was a pause, then a cry of surprise, and then a voice shouting from the house, "Bill's dead."

But the blind man swore at them again for their delay.

"Search him, some of you shirking lubbers, and the rest of you aloft and get the chest," he cried.

I could hear their feet rattling up our old stairs, so that the house must have shook with it. Promptly afterwards, fresh sounds of astonishment arose; the window of the captain's room was thrown open with a slam and a jingle of broken glass, and a man leaned out into the moonlight, head and shoulders, and addressed the blind beggar on the road below him.

"Pew," he cried, "they've been before us. Someone's turned the chest out alow and aloft."

"Is it there?" roared Pew.

"The money's there."

The blind man cursed the money.

"Flint's fist, I mean," he cried.

"We don't see it here nohow," returned the man.

"Here, you below there, is it on Bill?" cried the blind man again.

At that another fellow, probably him who had remained below to search the captain's body, came to the door of the inn. "Bill's been overhauled a'ready," said he; "nothin' left."

"It's these people of the inn—it's that boy. I wish I had put his eyes out!" cried the blind man, Pew. "There were no time ago—they had the door bolted when I tried it. Scatter, lads, and find 'em."

"Sure enough, they left their glim here," said the fellow from the window.

"Scatter and find 'em! Rout the house out!" reiterated Pew, striking with his stick upon the road.

Then there followed a great to-do through all our old inn, heavy feet pounding to and fro, furniture thrown over, doors kicked in, until the very rocks re-echoed and the men came out again, one after another, on the road and declared that we were nowhere to be found. And just the same whistle that had alarmed my mother and myself over the dead captain's money was once more clearly audible through the night, but this time twice repeated. I had thought it to be the blind man's trumpet, so to speak, summoning his crew to the assault, but I now found that it was a signal from the hillside towards the hamlet, and from its effect upon the buccaneers, a signal to warn them of approaching danger.

"There's Dirk again," said one. "Twice! We'll have to budge, mates."

"Budge, you skulk!" cried Pew. "Dirk was a fool and a coward from the first—you wouldn't mind him. They must be close by; they can't be far; you have your hands on it. Scatter and look for them, dogs! Oh, shiver my soul," he cried, "if I had eyes!"

This appeal seemed to produce some effect, for two of the fellows began to look here and there among the lumber, but half-heartedly, I thought, and with half an eye to their own danger all the time, while the rest stood irresolute on the road.

"You have your hands on thousands, you fools, and you hang a leg! You'd be as rich as kings if you could find it, and you know it's here, and you stand there skulking. There wasn't one of you dared face Bill, and I did it—a blind man! And I'm to lose my chance for you! I'm to be a poor, crawling beggar, sponging for rum, when I might be rolling in a coach! If you had the pluck of a weevil in a biscuit you would catch them still."

"Hang it, Pew, we've got the doubloons!" grumbled one.

"They might have hid the blessed thing," said another. "Take the Georges, Pew, and don't stand here squalling."

Squalling was the word for it; Pew's anger rose so high at these objections till at last, his passion completely taking the upper hand, he struck at them right and left in his blindness and his stick sounded heavily on more than one.

These, in their turn, cursed back at the blind miscreant, threatened him in horrid terms, and tried in vain to catch the stick and wrest it from his grasp.

This quarrel was the saving of us, for while it was still raging, another sound came from the top of the hill on the side of the hamlet—the tramp of horses galloping. Almost at the same time a pistol-shot, flash and report, came from the hedge side. And that was plainly the last signal of danger, for the buccaneers turned at once and ran, separating in every direction, one seaward along the cove, one slant across the hill, and so on, so that in half a minute not a sign of them remained but Pew. Him they had deserted, whether in sheer panic or out of revenge for his ill words and blows I know not; but there he remained behind, tapping up and down the road in a frenzy, and groping and calling for his comrades. Finally he took a wrong turn and ran a few steps past me, towards the hamlet, crying, "Johnny, Black Dog, Dirk," and other names, "you won't leave old Pew, mates—not old Pew!"

Just then the noise of horses topped the rise, and four or five riders came in sight in the moonlight and swept at full gallop down the slope.

At this Pew saw his error, turned with a scream, and ran straight for the ditch, into which he rolled. But he was on his feet again in a second and made another dash, now utterly bewildered, right under the nearest of the coming horses.

The rider tried to save him, but in vain. Down went Pew with a cry that rang high into the night; and the four hoofs trampled and spurned him and passed by. He fell on his side, then gently collapsed upon his face and moved no more.

I leaped to my feet and hailed the riders. They were pulling up, at any rate, horrified at the accident; and I soon saw what they were. One, tailing out behind the rest, was a lad that had gone from the hamlet to Dr. Livesey's; the rest were revenue officers, whom he had met by the way, and with whom he had had the intelligence to return at once. Some news of the lugger in Kitt's Hole had found its way to Supervisor Dance and set him forth that night in our direction, and to that circumstance my mother and I owed our preservation from death.

Pew was dead, stone dead. As for my mother, when we had carried her up to the hamlet, a little cold water and salts and that soon brought her back again, and she was none the worse for her terror, though she still continued to deplore the balance of the money. In the meantime the supervisor rode on, as fast as he could, to Kitt's Hole; but his men had to dismount and grope down the dingle, leading, and sometimes supporting, their horses, and in continual fear of ambushes; so it was no great matter for surprise that when they got down to the Hole the lugger was already under way, though still close in. He hailed her. A voice replied, telling him to keep out of the moonlight or he would get some lead in him, and at the same time a bullet whistled close by his arm. Soon after, the lugger doubled the point and disappeared. Mr. Dance stood there, as he said, "like a fish out of water," and all he could do was to dispatch a man to B—— to warn the cutter. "And that," said he, "is just about as good as nothing. They've got off clean, and there's an end. Only," he added, "I'm glad I trod on Master Pew's corns," for by this time he had heard my story.

I went back with him to the Admiral Benbow, and you cannot imagine a house in such a state of smash; the very clock had been thrown down by these fellows in their furious hunt after my mother and myself; and though nothing had actually been taken away except the captain's money-bag and a little silver from the till, I could see at once that we were ruined. Mr. Dance could make nothing of the scene.

"They got the money, you say? Well, then, Hawkins, what in fortune were they after? More money, I suppose?"

"No, sir; not money, I think," replied I. "In fact, sir, I believe I have the thing in my breast pocket; and to tell you the truth, I should like to get it put in safety."

"To be sure, boy; quite right," said he. "I'll take it, if you like."

"I thought perhaps Dr. Livesey—" I began.

"Perfectly right," he interrupted very cheerily, "perfectly right—a gentleman and a magistrate. And, now I come to think of it, I might as well ride round there myself and report to him or squire. Master Pew's dead, when all's done; not that I regret it, but he's dead, you see, and people will make it out against an officer of his Majesty's revenue, if make it out they can. Now, I'll tell you, Hawkins, if you like, I'll take you along."

I thanked him heartily for the offer, and we walked back to the hamlet where the horses were. By the time I had told mother of my purpose they were all in the saddle.

"Dogger," said Mr. Dance, "you have a good horse; take up this lad behind you."

As soon as I was mounted, holding on to Dogger's belt, the supervisor gave the word, and the party struck out at a bouncing trot on the road to Dr. Livesey's house.

6
The Captain's Papers

WE rode hard all the way till we drew up before Dr. Livesey's door. The house was all dark to the front.

Mr. Dance told me to jump down and knock, and Dogger gave me a stirrup to descend by. The door was opened almost at once by the maid.

"Is Dr. Livesey in?" I asked.

No, she said, he had come home in the afternoon but had gone up to the hall to dine and pass the evening with the squire.

"So there we go, boys," said Mr. Dance.

This time, as the distance was short, I did not mount, but ran with Dogger's stirrup-leather to the lodge gates and up the long, leafless, moonlit avenue to where the white line of the hall buildings looked on either hand on great old gardens. Here Mr. Dance dismounted, and taking me along with him, was admitted at a word into the house.

The servant led us down a matted passage and showed us at the end into a great library, all lined with bookcases and busts upon the top of them, where the squire and Dr. Livesey sat, pipe in hand, on either side of a bright fire.

I had never seen the squire so near at hand. He was a tall man, over six feet high, and broad in proportion, and he had a bluff, rough-and-ready face, all roughened and reddened and lined in his long travels. His eyebrows were very black, and moved readily, and this gave him a look of some temper, not bad, you would say, but quick and high.

"Come in, Mr. Dance," says he, very stately and condescending.

"Good evening, Dance," says the doctor with a nod. "And good evening to you, friend Jim. What good wind brings you here?"

The supervisor stood up straight and stiff and told his story like a lesson; and you should have seen how the two gentlemen leaned forward and looked at each other, and forgot to smoke in their surprise and interest. When they heard how my mother went back to the inn, Dr. Livesey fairly slapped his thigh, and the squire cried "Bravo!" and broke his long pipe against the grate. Long before it was done, Mr. Trelawney (that, you will remember, was the squire's name) had got up from his seat and was striding about the room, and the doctor, as if to hear the better, had taken off his powdered wig and sat there looking very strange indeed with his own close-cropped black poll.

At last Mr. Dance finished the story.

"Mr. Dance," said the squire, "you are a very noble fellow. And as for riding down that black, atrocious miscreant, I regard it as an act of virtue, sir, like stamping on a cockroach. This lad Hawkins is a trump, I perceive. Hawkins, will you ring that bell? Mr. Dance must have some ale."

"And so, Jim," said the doctor, "you have the thing that they were after, have you?"

"Here it is, sir," said I, and gave him the oilskin packet.

The doctor looked it all over, as if his fingers were itching to open it; but instead of doing that, he put it quietly in the pocket of his coat.

"Squire," said he, "when Dance has had his ale he must, of course, be off on his Majesty's service; but I mean to keep Jim Hawkins here to sleep at my house, and with your permission, I propose we should have up the cold pie and let him sup."

"As you will, Livesey," said the squire; "Hawkins has earned better than cold pie."

So a big pigeon pie was brought in and put on a sidetable, and I made a hearty supper, for I was as hungry as a hawk, while Mr. Dance was further complimented and at last dismissed.

"And now, squire," said the doctor.

"And now, Livesey," said the squire in the same breath.

"One at a time, one at a time," laughed Dr. Livesey. "You have heard of this Flint, I suppose?"

"Heard of him!" cried the squire. "Heard of him, you say! He was the bloodthirstiest buccaneer that sailed. Blackbeard was a child to Flint. The Spaniards were so prodigiously afraid of him that, I tell you, sir, I was sometimes proud he was an Englishman. I've seen his top-sails with these eyes, off Trinidad, and the cowardly son of a rum-puncheon that I sailed with put back—put back, sir, into Port of Spain."

"Well, I've heard of him myself, in England," said the doctor. "But the point is, had he money?"

"Money!" cried the squire. "Have you heard the story? What were these villains after but money? What do they care for but money? For what would they risk their rascal carcasses but money?"

"That we shall soon know," replied the doctor. "But you are so confoundedly hot-headed and exclamatory that I cannot get a word in. What I want to know is this: Supposing that I have here in my pocket some clue to where Flint buried his treasure, will that treasure amount to much?"

"Amount, sir!" cried the squire. "It will amount to this: If we have the clue you talk about, I fit out a ship in Bristol dock, and take you and Hawkins here along, and I'll have that treasure if I search a year."

"Very well," said the doctor. "Now, then, if Jim is agreeable, we'll open the packet"; and he laid it before him on the table.

The bundle was sewn together, and the doctor had to get out his instrument case and cut the stitches with his medical scissors. It contained two things—a book and a sealed paper.

"First of all we'll try the book," observed the doctor.

The squire and I were both peering over his shoulder as he opened it, for Dr. Livesey had kindly motioned me to come round from the side-table, where I had been eating, to enjoy the sport of the search. On the first page there were only some scraps of writing, such as a man with a pen in his hand might make for idleness or practice. One was the same as the tattoo mark, "Billy Bones his fancy"; then there was "Mr. W. Bones, mate," "No more rum," "Off Palm Key he got itt," and some other snatches, mostly single words and unintelligible. I could not help wondering who it was that had "got itt," and what "itt" was that he got. A knife in his back as like as not.

"Not much instruction there," said Dr. Livesey as he passed on.

The next ten or twelve pages were filled with a curious series of entries. There was a date at one end of the line and at the other a sum of money, as in common account-books, but instead of explanatory writing, only a varying number of crosses between the two. On the 12th of June, 1745, for instance, a sum of seventy pounds had plainly become due to someone, and there was nothing but six crosses to explain the cause. In a few cases, to be sure, the name of a place would be added, as "Offe Caraccas," or a mere entry of latitude and longitude, as "62° 17' 20", 19° 2' 40"."

The record lasted over nearly twenty years, the amount of the separate entries growing larger as time went on, and at the end a grand total had been made out after five or six wrong additions, and these words appended, "Bones, his pile."

"I can't make head or tail of this," said Dr. Livesey.

"The thing is as clear as noonday," cried the squire. "This is the black-hearted hound's account-book. These crosses stand for the names of ships or towns that they sank or plundered. The sums are the scoundrel's share, and where he feared an ambiguity, you see he added something clearer. 'Offe Caraccas,' now; you see, here was some unhappy vessel boarded off that coast. God help the poor souls that manned her—coral long ago."

"Right!" said the doctor. "See what it is to be a traveller. Right! And the amounts increase, you see, as he rose in rank."

There was little else in the volume but a few bearings of places noted in the blank leaves towards the end and a table for reducing French, English, and Spanish moneys to a common value.

"Thrifty man!" cried the doctor. "He wasn't the one to be cheated."

"And now," said the squire, "for the other." The paper had been sealed in several places with a thimble by way of seal; the very thimble, perhaps, that I had found in the captain's pocket. The doctor opened the seals with great care, and there fell out the map of an island, with latitude and longitude, soundings, names of hills and bays and inlets, and every particular that would be needed to bring a ship to a safe anchorage upon its shores. It was about nine miles long and five across, shaped, you might say, like a fat dragon standing up, and had two fine land-locked harbours, and a hill in the centre part marked "The Spy-glass." There were several additions of a later date, but above all, three crosses of red ink—two on the north part of the island, one in the southwest—and beside this last, in the same red ink, and in a small, neat hand, very different from the captain's tottery characters, these words: "Bulk of treasure here."

Over on the back the same hand had written this further information:

Tall tree, Spy-glass shoulder, bearing a point to the N. of N.N.E.

Skeleton Island E.S.E. and by E.

Ten feet.

The bar silver is in the north cache; you can find it by the trend of the east hummock, ten fathoms south of the black crag with the face on it.

The arms are easy found, in the sand-hill, N. point of north inlet cape, bearing E. and a quarter N.

J.F.

That was all; but brief as it was, and to me incomprehensible, it filled the squire and Dr. Livesey with delight.

"Livesey," said the squire, "you will give up this wretched practice at once. Tomorrow I start for Bristol. In three weeks' time—three weeks!—two weeks—ten days—we'll have the best ship, sir, and the choicest crew in England. Hawkins shall come as cabin-boy. You'll make a famous cabin-boy, Hawkins. You, Livesey, are ship's doctor; I am admiral. We'll take Redruth, Joyce, and Hunter. We'll have favourable winds, a quick passage, and not the least difficulty in finding the spot, and money to eat, to roll in, to play duck and drake with ever after."

"Trelawney," said the doctor, "I'll go with you; and I'll go bail for it, so will Jim, and be a credit to the undertaking. There's only one man I'm afraid of."

"And who's that?" cried the squire. "Name the dog, sir!"

"You," replied the doctor; "for you cannot hold your tongue. We are not the only men who know of this paper. These fellows who attacked the inn tonight—bold, desperate blades, for sure—and the rest who stayed aboard that lugger, and more, I dare say, not far off, are, one and all, through thick and thin, bound that they'll get that money. We must none of us go alone till we get to sea. Jim and I shall stick together in the meanwhile; you'll take Joyce and Hunter when you ride to Bristol, and from first to last, not one of us must breathe a word of what we've found."

"Livesey," returned the squire, "you are always in the right of it. I'll be as silent as the grave."

PART TWO—The Sea-cook

7

I Go to Bristol

IT was longer than the squire imagined ere we were ready for the sea, and none of our first plans—not even Dr. Livesey's, of keeping me beside him—could be carried out as we intended. The doctor had to go to London for a physician to take charge of his practice; the squire was hard at work at Bristol; and I lived on at the hall under the charge of old Redruth, the gamekeeper, almost a prisoner, but full of sea-dreams and the most charming anticipations of strange islands and adventures. I brooded by the hour together over the map, all the details of which I well remembered. Sitting by the fire in the housekeeper's room, I approached that island in my fancy from every possible direction; I explored every acre of its surface; I climbed a thousand times to that tall hill they call the Spy-glass, and from the top enjoyed the most wonderful and changing prospects. Sometimes the isle was thick with savages, with whom we fought, sometimes full of dangerous animals that hunted us, but in all my fancies nothing occurred to me so strange and tragic as our actual adventures.

So the weeks passed on, till one fine day there came a letter addressed to Dr. Livesey, with this addition, "To be opened, in the case of his absence, by Tom Redruth or young Hawkins." Obeying this order, we found, or rather I found—for the gamekeeper was a poor hand at reading anything but print—the following important news:

Old Anchor Inn, Bristol, March 1, 17—

Dear Livesey—As I do not know whether you are at the hall or still in London, I send this in double to both places.

The ship is bought and fitted. She lies at anchor, ready for sea. You never imagined a sweeter schooner—a child might sail her—two hundred tons; name, Hispaniola.

I got her through my old friend, Blandly, who has proved himself throughout the most surprising trump. The admirable fellow literally slaved in my interest, and so, I may say, did everyone in Bristol, as soon as they got wind of the port we sailed for—treasure, I mean.

"Redruth," said I, interrupting the letter, "Dr. Livesey will not like that. The squire has been talking, after all."

"Well, who's a better right?" growled the gamekeeper. "A pretty rum go if squire ain't to talk for Dr. Livesey, I should think."

At that I gave up all attempts at commentary and read straight on:

Blandly himself found the Hispaniola, and by the most admirable management got her for the merest trifle. There is a class of men in Bristol monstrously prejudiced against Blandly. They go the length of declaring that this honest creature would do anything for money, that the Hispaniola belonged to him, and that he sold it me absurdly high—the most transparent calumnies. None of them dare, however, to deny the merits of the ship.

So far there was not a hitch. The workpeople, to be sure—riggers and what not—were most annoyingly slow; but time cured that. It was the crew that troubled me.

I wished a round score of men—in case of natives, buccaneers, or the odious French—and I had the worry of the deuce itself to find so much as half a dozen, till the most remarkable stroke of fortune brought me the very man that I required.

I was standing on the dock, when, by the merest accident, I fell in talk with him. I found he was an old sailor, kept a public-house, knew all the seafaring men in Bristol, had lost his health ashore, and wanted a good berth as cook to get to sea again. He had hobbled down there that morning, he said, to get a smell of the salt.

I was monstrously touched—so would you have been—and, out of pure pity, I engaged him on the spot to be ship's cook. Long John Silver, he is called, and has lost a leg; but that I regarded as a recommendation, since he lost it in his country's service, under the immortal Hawke. He has no pension, Livesey. Imagine the abominable age we live in!

Well, sir, I thought I had only found a cook, but it was a crew I had discovered. Between Silver and myself we got together in a few days a company of the toughest old salts imaginable—not pretty to look at, but fellows, by their faces, of the most indomitable spirit. I declare we could fight a frigate.

Long John even got rid of two out of the six or seven I had already engaged. He showed me in a moment that they were just the sort of fresh-water swabs we had to fear in an adventure of importance.

I am in the most magnificent health and spirits, eating like a bull, sleeping like a tree, yet I shall not enjoy a moment till I hear my old tarpaulins tramping round the capstan. Seaward, ho! Hang the treasure! It's the glory of the sea that has turned my head. So now, Livesey, come post; do not lose an hour, if you respect me.

Let young Hawkins go at once to see his mother, with Redruth for a guard; and then both come full speed to Bristol.

John Trelawney

Postscript—I did not tell you that Blandly, who, by the way, is to send a consort after us if we don't turn up by the end of August, had found an admirable fellow for sailing master—a stiff man, which I regret, but in all other respects a treasure. Long John Silver unearthed a very competent man for a mate, a man named Arrow. I have a boatswain who pipes, Livesey; so things shall go man-o'-war fashion on board the good ship Hispaniola.

I forgot to tell you that Silver is a man of substance; I know of my own knowledge that he has a banker's account, which has never been overdrawn. He leaves his wife to manage the inn; and as she is a woman of colour, a pair of old bachelors like you and I may be excused for guessing that it is the wife, quite as much as the health, that sends him back to roving.

J. T.

P.P.S.—Hawkins may stay one night with his mother.

J. T.

You can fancy the excitement into which that letter put me. I was half beside myself with glee; and if ever I despised a man, it was old Tom Redruth, who could do nothing but grumble and lament. Any of the under-gamekeepers would gladly have changed places with him; but such was not the squire's pleasure, and the squire's pleasure was like law among them all. Nobody but old Redruth would have dared so much as even to grumble.

The next morning he and I set out on foot for the Admiral Benbow, and there I found my mother in good health and spirits. The captain, who had so long been a cause of so much discomfort, was gone where the wicked cease from troubling. The squire had had everything repaired, and the public rooms and the sign repainted, and had added some furniture—above all a beautiful armchair for mother in the bar. He had found her a boy as an apprentice also so that she should not want help while I was gone.

It was on seeing that boy that I understood, for the first time, my situation. I had thought up to that moment of the adventures before me, not at all of the home that I was leaving; and now, at sight of this clumsy stranger, who was to stay here in my place beside my mother, I had my first attack of tears. I am afraid I led that boy a dog's life, for as he was new to the work, I had a hundred opportunities of setting him right and putting him down, and I was not slow to profit by them.

The night passed, and the next day, after dinner, Redruth and I were afoot again and on the road. I said good-bye to Mother and the cove where I had lived since I was born, and the dear old Admiral Benbow—since he was repainted, no longer quite so dear. One of my last thoughts was of the captain, who had so often strode along the beach with his cocked hat, his sabre-cut cheek, and his old brass telescope. Next moment we had turned the corner and my home was out of sight.

The mail picked us up about dusk at the Royal George on the heath. I was wedged in between Redruth and a stout old gentleman, and in spite of the swift motion and the cold night air, I must have dozed a great deal from the very first, and then slept like a log up hill and down dale through stage after stage, for when I was awakened at last it was by a punch in the ribs, and I opened my eyes to find that we were standing still before a large building in a city street and that the day had already broken a long time.

"Where are we?" I asked.

"Bristol," said Tom. "Get down."

Mr. Trelawney had taken up his residence at an inn far down the docks to superintend the work upon the schooner. Thither we had now to walk, and our way, to my great delight, lay along the quays and beside the great multitude of ships of all sizes and rigs and nations. In one, sailors were singing at their work, in another there were men aloft, high over my head, hanging to threads that seemed no thicker than a spider's. Though I had lived by the shore all my life, I seemed never to have been near the sea till then. The smell of tar and salt was something new. I saw the most wonderful figureheads, that had all been far over the ocean. I saw, besides, many old sailors, with rings in their ears, and whiskers curled in ringlets, and tarry pigtails, and their swaggering, clumsy sea-walk; and if I had seen as many kings or archbishops I could not have been more delighted.

And I was going to sea myself, to sea in a schooner, with a piping boatswain and pig-tailed singing seamen, to sea, bound for an unknown island, and to seek for buried treasure!

While I was still in this delightful dream, we came suddenly in front of a large inn and met Squire Trelawney, all dressed out like a sea-officer, in stout blue cloth, coming out of the door with a smile on his face and a capital imitation of a sailor's walk.

"Here you are," he cried, "and the doctor came last night from London. Bravo! The ship's company complete!"

"Oh, sir," cried I, "when do we sail?"

"Sail!" says he. "We sail tomorrow!"

8
At the Sign of the Spy-glass

WHEN I had done breakfasting the squire gave me a note addressed to John Silver, at the sign of the Spy-glass, and told me I should easily find the place by following the line of the docks and keeping a bright lookout for a little tavern with a large brass telescope for sign. I set off, overjoyed at this opportunity to see some more of the ships and seamen, and picked my way among a great crowd of people and carts and bales, for the dock was now at its busiest, until I found the tavern in question.

It was a bright enough little place of entertainment. The sign was newly painted; the windows had neat red curtains; the floor was cleanly sanded. There was a street on each side and an open door on both, which made the large, low room pretty clear to see in, in spite of clouds of tobacco smoke.

The customers were mostly seafaring men, and they talked so loudly that I hung at the door, almost afraid to enter.

As I was waiting, a man came out of a side room, and at a glance I was sure he must be Long John. His left leg was cut off close by the hip, and under the left shoulder he carried a crutch, which he managed with wonderful dexterity, hopping about upon it like a bird. He was very tall and strong, with a face as big as a ham—plain and pale, but intelligent and smiling. Indeed, he seemed in the most cheerful spirits, whistling as he moved about among the tables, with a merry word or a slap on the shoulder for the more favoured of his guests.

Now, to tell you the truth, from the very first mention of Long John in Squire Trelawney's letter I had taken a fear in my mind that he might prove to be the very one-legged sailor whom I had watched for so long at the old Benbow. But one look at the man before me was enough. I had seen the captain, and Black Dog, and the blind man, Pew, and I thought I knew what a buccaneer was like—a very different creature, according to me, from this clean and pleasant-tempered landlord.

I plucked up courage at once, crossed the threshold, and walked right up to the man where he stood, propped on his crutch, talking to a customer.

"Mr. Silver, sir?" I asked, holding out the note.

"Yes, my lad," said he; "such is my name, to be sure. And who may you be?" And then as he saw the squire's letter, he seemed to me to give something almost like a start.

"Oh!" said he, quite loud, and offering his hand. "I see. You are our new cabin-boy; pleased I am to see you."

And he took my hand in his large firm grasp.

Just then one of the customers at the far side rose suddenly and made for the door. It was close by him, and he was out in the street in a moment. But his hurry had attracted my notice, and I recognized him at glance. It was the tallow-faced man, wanting two fingers, who had come first to the Admiral Benbow.

"Oh," I cried, "stop him! It's Black Dog!"

"I don't care two coppers who he is," cried Silver. "But he hasn't paid his score. Harry, run and catch him."

One of the others who was nearest the door leaped up and started in pursuit.

"If he were Admiral Hawke he shall pay his score," cried Silver; and then, relinquishing my hand, "Who did you say he was?" he asked. "Black what?"

"Dog, sir," said I. "Has Mr. Trelawney not told you of the buccaneers? He was one of them."

"So?" cried Silver. "In my house! Ben, run and help Harry. One of those swabs, was he? Was that you drinking with him, Morgan? Step up here."

The man whom he called Morgan—an old, grey-haired, mahogany-faced sailor—came forward pretty sheepishly, rolling his quid.

"Now, Morgan," said Long John very sternly, "you never clapped your eyes on that Black—Black Dog before, did you, now?"

"Not I, sir," said Morgan with a salute.

"You didn't know his name, did you?"

"No, sir."

"By the powers, Tom Morgan, it's as good for you!" exclaimed the landlord. "If you had been mixed up with the like of that, you would never have put another foot in my house, you may lay to that. And what was he saying to you?"

"I don't rightly know, sir," answered Morgan.

"Do you call that a head on your shoulders, or a blessed dead-eye?" cried Long John. "Don't rightly know, don't you! Perhaps you don't happen to rightly know who you was speaking to, perhaps? Come, now, what was he jawing—v'yages, cap'ns, ships? Pipe up! What was it?"

"We was a-talkin' of keel-hauling," answered Morgan.

"Keel-hauling, was you? And a mighty suitable thing, too, and you may lay to that. Get back to your place for a lubber, Tom."

And then, as Morgan rolled back to his seat, Silver added to me in a confidential whisper that was very flattering, as I thought, "He's quite an honest man, Tom Morgan, on'y stupid. And now," he ran on again, aloud, "let's see—Black Dog? No, I don't know the name, not I. Yet I kind of think I've—yes, I've seen the swab. He used to come here with a blind beggar, he used."

"That he did, you may be sure," said I. "I knew that blind man too. His name was Pew."

"It was!" cried Silver, now quite excited. "Pew! That were his name for certain. Ah, he looked a shark, he did! If we run down this Black Dog, now, there'll be news for Cap'n Trelawney! Ben's a good runner; few seamen run better than Ben. He should run him down, hand over hand, by the powers! He talked o' keel-hauling, did he? I'll keel-haul him!"

All the time he was jerking out these phrases he was stumping up and down the tavern on his crutch, slapping tables with his hand, and giving such a show of excitement as would have convinced an Old Bailey judge or a Bow Street runner. My suspicions had been thoroughly reawakened on finding Black Dog at the Spy-glass, and I watched the cook narrowly. But he was too deep, and too ready, and too clever for me, and by the time the two men had come back out of breath and confessed that they had lost the track in a crowd, and been scolded like thieves, I would have gone bail for the innocence of Long John Silver.

"See here, now, Hawkins," said he, "here's a blessed hard thing on a man like me, now, ain't it? There's Cap'n Trelawney—what's he to think? Here I have this confounded son of a Dutchman sitting in my own house drinking of my own rum! Here you comes and tells me of it plain; and here I let him give us all the slip before my blessed deadlights! Now, Hawkins, you do me justice with the cap'n. You're a lad, you are, but you're as smart as paint. I see that when you first come in. Now, here it is: What could I do, with this old timber I hobble on? When I was an A B master mariner I'd have come up alongside of him, hand over hand, and broached him to in a brace of old shakes, I would; but now—"

And then, all of a sudden, he stopped, and his jaw dropped as though he had remembered something.

"The score!" he burst out. "Three goes o' rum! Why, shiver my timbers, if I hadn't forgotten my score!"

And falling on a bench, he laughed until the tears ran down his cheeks. I could not help joining, and we laughed together, peal after peal, until the tavern rang again.

"Why, what a precious old sea-calf I am!" he said at last, wiping his cheeks. "You and me should get on well, Hawkins, for I'll take my davy I should be rated ship's boy. But come now, stand by to go about. This won't do. Dooty is dooty, messmates. I'll put on my old cockerel hat, and step along of you to Cap'n Trelawney, and report this here affair. For mind you, it's serious, young Hawkins; and neither you nor me's come out of it with what I should make so bold as to call credit. Nor you neither, says you; not smart—none of the pair of us smart. But dash my buttons! That was a good un about my score."

And he began to laugh again, and that so heartily, that though I did not see the joke as he did, I was again obliged to join him in his mirth.

On our little walk along the quays, he made himself the most interesting companion, telling me about the different ships that we passed by, their rig, tonnage, and nationality, explaining the work that was going forward—how one was discharging, another taking in cargo, and a third making ready for sea—and every now and then telling me some little anecdote of ships or seamen or repeating a nautical phrase till I had learned it perfectly. I began to see that here was one of the best of possible shipmates.

When we got to the inn, the squire and Dr. Livesey were seated together, finishing a quart of ale with a toast in it, before they should go aboard the schooner on a visit of inspection.

Long John told the story from first to last, with a great deal of spirit and the most perfect truth. "That was how it were, now, weren't it, Hawkins?" he would say, now and again, and I could always bear him entirely out.

The two gentlemen regretted that Black Dog had got away, but we all agreed there was nothing to be done, and after he had been complimented, Long John took up his crutch and departed.

"All hands aboard by four this afternoon," shouted the squire after him.

"Aye, aye, sir," cried the cook, in the passage.

"Well, squire," said Dr. Livesey, "I don't put much faith in your discoveries, as a general thing;

but I will say this, John Silver suits me."

"The man's a perfect trump," declared the squire.

"And now," added the doctor, "Jim may come on board with us, may he not?"

"To be sure he may," says squire. "Take your hat, Hawkins, and we'll see the ship."

9

Powder and Arms

THE Hispaniola lay some way out, and we went under the figureheads and round the sterns of many other ships, and their cables sometimes grated underneath our keel, and sometimes swung above us. At last, however, we got alongside, and were met and saluted as we stepped aboard by the mate, Mr. Arrow, a brown old sailor with earrings in his ears and a squint. He and the squire were very thick and friendly, but I soon observed that things were not the same between Mr. Trelawney and the captain.

This last was a sharp-looking man who seemed angry with everything on board and was soon to tell us why, for we had hardly got down into the cabin when a sailor followed us.

"Captain Smollett, sir, axing to speak with you," said he.

"I am always at the captain's orders. Show him in," said the squire.

The captain, who was close behind his messenger, entered at once and shut the door behind him.

"Well, Captain Smollett, what have you to say? All well, I hope; all shipshape and seaworthy?"

"Well, sir," said the captain, "better speak plain, I believe, even at the risk of offence. I don't like this cruise; I don't like the men; and I don't like my officer. That's short and sweet."

"Perhaps, sir, you don't like the ship?" inquired the squire, very angry, as I could see.

"I can't speak as to that, sir, not having seen her tried," said the captain. "She seems a clever craft; more I can't say."

"Possibly, sir, you may not like your employer, either?" says the squire.

But here Dr. Livesey cut in.

"Stay a bit," said he, "stay a bit. No use of such questions as that but to produce ill feeling. The captain has said too much or he has said too little, and I'm bound to say that I require an explanation of his words. You don't, you say, like this cruise. Now, why?"

"I was engaged, sir, on what we call sealed orders, to sail this ship for that gentleman where he should bid me," said the captain. "So far so good. But now I find that every man before the mast knows more than I do. I don't call that fair, now, do you?"

"No," said Dr. Livesey, "I don't."

"Next," said the captain, "I learn we are going after treasure—hear it from my own hands, mind you. Now, treasure is ticklish work; I don't like treasure voyages on any account, and I don't like them, above all, when they are secret and when (begging your pardon, Mr. Trelawney) the secret has been told to the parrot."

"Silver's parrot?" asked the squire.

"It's a way of speaking," said the captain. "Blabbed, I mean. It's my belief neither of you gentlemen know what you are about, but I'll tell you my way of it—life or death, and a close run."

"That is all clear, and, I dare say, true enough," replied Dr. Livesey. "We take the risk, but we are not so ignorant as you believe us. Next, you say you don't like the crew. Are they not good seamen?"

"I don't like them, sir," returned Captain Smollett. "And I think I should have had the choosing of my own hands, if you go to that."

"Perhaps you should," replied the doctor. "My friend should, perhaps, have taken you along with him; but the slight, if there be one, was unintentional. And you don't like Mr. Arrow?"

"I don't, sir. I believe he's a good seaman, but he's too free with the crew to be a good officer. A mate should keep himself to himself—shouldn't drink with the men before the mast!"

"Do you mean he drinks?" cried the squire.

"No, sir," replied the captain, "only that he's too familiar."

"Well, now, and the short and long of it, captain?" asked the doctor. "Tell us what you want."

"Well, gentlemen, are you determined to go on this cruise?"

"Like iron," answered the squire.

"Very good," said the captain. "Then, as you've heard me very patiently, saying things that I could not prove, hear me a few words more. They are putting the powder and the arms in the fore hold. Now, you have a good place under the cabin; why not put them there?—first point. Then, you are bringing four of your own people with you, and they tell me some of them are to be berthed forward. Why not give them the berths here beside the cabin?—second point."

"Any more?" asked Mr. Trelawney.

"One more," said the captain. "There's been too much blabbing already."

"Far too much," agreed the doctor.

"I'll tell you what I've heard myself," continued Captain Smollett: "that you have a map of an island, that there's crosses on the map to show where treasure is, and that the island lies—" And then he named the latitude and longitude exactly.

"I never told that," cried the squire, "to a soul!"

"The hands know it, sir," returned the captain.

"Livesey, that must have been you or Hawkins," cried the squire.

"It doesn't much matter who it was," replied the doctor. And I could see that neither he nor the captain paid much regard to Mr. Trelawney's protestations. Neither did I, to be sure, he was so loose a talker; yet in this case I believe he was really right and that nobody had told the situation of the island.

"Well, gentlemen," continued the captain, "I don't know who has this map; but I make it a point, it shall be kept secret even from me and Mr. Arrow. Otherwise I would ask you to let me resign."

"I see," said the doctor. "You wish us to keep this matter dark and to make a garrison of the stern part of the ship, manned with my friend's own people, and provided with all the arms and powder on board. In other words, you fear a mutiny."

"Sir," said Captain Smollett, "with no intention to take offence, I deny your right to put words into my mouth. No captain, sir, would be justified in going to sea at all if he had ground enough to say that. As for Mr. Arrow, I believe him thoroughly honest; some of the men are the same; all may be for what I know. But I am responsible for the ship's safety and the life of every man Jack aboard of her. I see things going, as I think, not quite right. And I ask you to take certain precautions or let me resign my berth. And that's all."

"Captain Smollett," began the doctor with a smile, "did ever you hear the fable of the mountain and the mouse? You'll excuse me, I dare say, but you remind me of that fable. When you came in here, I'll stake my wig, you meant more than this."

"Doctor," said the captain, "you are smart. When I came in here I meant to get discharged. I had no thought that Mr. Trelawney would hear a word."

"No more I would," cried the squire. "Had Livesey not been here I should have seen you to the deuce. As it is, I have heard you. I will do as you desire, but I think the worse of you."

"That's as you please, sir," said the captain. "You'll find I do my duty."

And with that he took his leave.

"Trelawney," said the doctor, "contrary to all my notions, I believed you have managed to get two honest men on board with you—that man and John Silver."

"Silver, if you like," cried the squire; "but as for that intolerable humbug, I declare I think his conduct unmanly, unsailorly, and downright un-English."

"Well," says the doctor, "we shall see."

When we came on deck, the men had begun already to take out the arms and powder, yo-ho-ing at their work, while the captain and Mr. Arrow stood by superintending.

The new arrangement was quite to my liking. The whole schooner had been overhauled; six berths had been made astern out of what had been the after-part of the main hold; and this set of cabins was only joined to the galley and forecastle by a sparred passage on the port side. It had been originally meant that the captain, Mr. Arrow, Hunter, Joyce, the doctor, and the squire were to occupy these six berths. Now Redruth and I were to get two of them and Mr. Arrow and the captain were to sleep on deck in the companion, which had been enlarged on each side till you might almost have called it a round-house. Very low it was still, of course; but there was room to swing two hammocks, and even the mate seemed pleased with the arrangement. Even he, perhaps, had been doubtful as to the crew, but that is only guess, for as you shall hear, we had not long the benefit of his opinion.

We were all hard at work, changing the powder and the berths, when the last man or two, and Long John along with them, came off in a shore-boat.

The cook came up the side like a monkey for cleverness, and as soon as he saw what was doing, "So ho, mates!" says he. "What's this?"

"We're a-changing of the powder, Jack," answers one.

"Why, by the powers," cried Long John, "if we do, we'll miss the morning tide!"

"My orders!" said the captain shortly. "You may go below, my man. Hands will want supper."

"Aye, aye, sir," answered the cook, and touching his forelock, he disappeared at once in the direction of his galley.

"That's a good man, captain," said the doctor.

"Very likely, sir," replied Captain Smollett. "Easy with that, men—easy," he ran on, to the fellows who were shifting the powder; and then suddenly observing me examining the swivel we carried amidships, a long brass nine, "Here you, ship's boy," he cried, "out o' that! Off with you to the cook and get some work."

And then as I was hurrying off I heard him say, quite loudly, to the doctor, "I'll have no favourites on my ship."

I assure you I was quite of the squire's way of thinking, and hated the captain deeply.

10

The Voyage

ALL that night we were in a great bustle getting things stowed in their place, and boatfuls of the squire's friends, Mr. Blandly and the like, coming off to wish him a good voyage and a safe return. We never had a night at the Admiral Benbow when I had half the work; and I was dog-tired when, a little before dawn, the boatswain sounded his pipe and the crew began to man the capstan-bars. I might have been twice as weary, yet I would not have left the deck, all was so new and interesting to me—the brief commands, the shrill note of the whistle, the men bustling to their places in the glimmer of the ship's lanterns.

"Now, Barbecue, tip us a stave," cried one voice.

"The old one," cried another.

"Aye, aye, mates," said Long John, who was standing by, with his crutch under his arm, and at once broke out in the air and words I knew so well:

"Fifteen men on the dead man's chest—"

And then the whole crew bore chorus:—

"Yo-ho-ho, and a bottle of rum!"

And at the third "Ho!" drove the bars before them with a will.

Even at that exciting moment it carried me back to the old Admiral Benbow in a second, and I seemed to hear the voice of the captain piping in the chorus. But soon the anchor was short up; soon it was hanging dripping at the bows; soon the sails began to draw, and the land and shipping to flit by on either side; and before I could lie down to snatch an hour of slumber the Hispaniola had begun her voyage to the Isle of Treasure.

I am not going to relate that voyage in detail. It was fairly prosperous. The ship proved to be a good ship, the crew were capable seamen, and the captain thoroughly understood his business. But before we came the length of Treasure Island, two or three things had happened which require to be known.

Mr. Arrow, first of all, turned out even worse than the captain had feared. He had no command among the men, and people did what they pleased with him. But that was by no means the worst of it, for after a day or two at sea he began to appear on deck with hazy eye, red cheeks, stuttering tongue, and other marks of drunkenness. Time after time he was ordered below in disgrace. Sometimes he fell and cut himself; sometimes he lay all day long in his little bunk at one side of the companion; sometimes for a day or two he would be almost sober and attend to his work at least passably.

In the meantime, we could never make out where he got the drink. That was the ship's mystery. Watch him as we pleased, we could do nothing to solve it; and when we asked him to his face, he would only laugh if he were drunk, and if he were sober deny solemnly that he ever tasted anything but water.

He was not only useless as an officer and a bad influence amongst the men, but it was plain that at this rate he must soon kill himself outright, so nobody was much surprised, nor very sorry, when one dark night, with a head sea, he disappeared entirely and was seen no more.

"Overboard!" said the captain. "Well, gentlemen, that saves the trouble of putting him in irons."

But there we were, without a mate; and it was necessary, of course, to advance one of the men. The boatswain, Job Anderson, was the likeliest man aboard, and though he kept his old title, he served in a way as mate. Mr. Trelawney had followed the sea, and his knowledge made him very useful, for he often took a watch himself in easy weather. And the coxswain, Israel Hands, was a careful, wily, old, experienced seaman who could be trusted at a pinch with almost anything.

He was a great confidant of Long John Silver, and so the mention of his name leads me on to speak of our ship's cook, Barbecue, as the men called him.

Aboard ship he carried his crutch by a lanyard round his neck, to have both hands as free as possible. It was something to see him wedge the foot of the crutch against a bulkhead, and propped against it, yielding to every movement of the ship, get on with his cooking like someone safe ashore. Still more strange was it to see him in the heaviest of weather cross the deck. He had a line or two rigged up to help him across the widest spaces—Long John's earrings, they were called; and he would hand himself from one place to another, now using the crutch, now trailing it alongside by the lanyard, as quickly as another man could walk. Yet some of the men who had sailed with him before expressed their pity to see him so reduced.

"He's no common man, Barbecue," said the coxswain to me. "He had good schooling in his young days and can speak like a book when so minded; and brave—a lion's nothing alongside of Long John! I seen him grapple four and knock their heads together—him unarmed."

All the crew respected and even obeyed him. He had a way of talking to each and doing everybody some particular service. To me he was unweariedly kind, and always glad to see me in the galley, which he kept as clean as a new pin, the dishes hanging up burnished and his parrot in a cage in one corner.

"Come away, Hawkins," he would say; "come and have a yarn with John. Nobody more welcome than yourself, my son. Sit you down and hear the news. Here's Cap'n Flint—I calls my parrot Cap'n Flint, after the famous buccaneer—here's Cap'n Flint predicting success to our v'yage. Wasn't you, cap'n?"

And the parrot would say, with great rapidity, "Pieces of eight! Pieces of eight! Pieces of eight!" till you wondered that it was not out of breath, or till John threw his handkerchief over the cage.

"Now, that bird," he would say, "is, maybe, two hundred years old, Hawkins—they live forever mostly; and if anybody's seen more wickedness, it must be the devil himself. She's sailed with England, the great Cap'n England, the pirate. She's been at Madagascar, and at Malabar, and Surinam, and Providence, and Portobello. She was at the fishing up of the wrecked plate ships. It's there she learned 'Pieces of eight,' and little wonder; three hundred and fifty thousand of 'em, Hawkins! She was at the boarding of the viceroy of the Indies out of Goa, she was; and to look at her you would think she was a babby. But you smelt powder—didn't you, cap'n?"

"Stand by to go about," the parrot would scream.

"Ah, she's a handsome craft, she is," the cook would say, and give her sugar from his pocket, and then the bird would peck at the bars and swear straight on, passing belief for wickedness. "There," John would add, "you can't touch pitch and not be mucked, lad. Here's this poor old innocent bird o' mine swearing blue fire, and none the wiser, you may lay to that. She would swear the same, in a manner of speaking, before chaplain." And John would touch his forelock with a solemn way he had that made me think he was the best of men.

In the meantime, the squire and Captain Smollett were still on pretty distant terms with one another. The squire made no bones about the matter; he despised the captain. The captain, on his part, never spoke but when he was spoken to, and then sharp and short and dry, and not a word wasted. He owned, when driven into a corner, that he seemed to have been wrong about the crew, that some of them were as brisk as he wanted to see and all had behaved fairly well. As for the ship, he had taken a downright fancy to her. "She'll lie a point nearer the wind than a man has a right to expect of his own married wife, sir. But," he would add, "all I say is, we're not home again, and I don't like the cruise."

The squire, at this, would turn away and march up and down the deck, chin in air.

"A trifle more of that man," he would say, "and I shall explode."

We had some heavy weather, which only proved the qualities of the Hispaniola. Every man on board seemed well content, and they must have been hard to please if they had been otherwise, for it is my belief there was never a ship's company so spoiled since Noah put to sea. Double grog was going on the least excuse; there was duff on odd days, as, for instance, if the squire heard it was any man's birthday, and always a barrel of apples standing broached in the waist for anyone to help himself that had a fancy.

"Never knew good come of it yet," the captain said to Dr. Livesey. "Spoil forecastle hands, make devils. That's my belief."

But good did come of the apple barrel, as you shall hear, for if it had not been for that, we should have had no note of warning and might all have perished by the hand of treachery.

This was how it came about.

We had run up the trades to get the wind of the island we were after—I am not allowed to be more plain—and now we were running down for it with a bright lookout day and night. It was about the last day of our outward voyage by the largest computation; some time that night, or at latest before noon of the morrow, we should sight the Treasure Island. We were heading S.S.W. and had a steady breeze abeam and a quiet sea. The Hispaniola rolled steadily, dipping her bowsprit now and then with a whiff of spray. All was drawing alow and aloft; everyone was in the bravest spirits because we were now so near an end of the first part of our adventure.

Now, just after sundown, when all my work was over and I was on my way to my berth, it occurred to me that I should like an apple. I ran on deck. The watch was all forward looking out for the island. The man at the helm was watching the luff of the sail and whistling away gently to himself, and that was the only sound excepting the swish of the sea against the bows and around the sides of the ship.

In I got bodily into the apple barrel, and found there was scarce an apple left; but sitting down there in the dark, what with the sound of the waters and the rocking movement of the ship, I had either fallen asleep or was on the point of doing so when a heavy man sat down with rather a clash close by. The barrel shook as he leaned his shoulders against it, and I was just about to jump up when the man began to speak. It was Silver's voice, and before I had heard a dozen words, I would not have shown myself for all the world, but lay there, trembling and listening, in the extreme of fear and curiosity, for from these dozen words I understood that the lives of all the honest men aboard depended upon me alone.

11

What I Heard in the Apple Barrel

NO, not I," said Silver. "Flint was cap'n; I was quartermaster, along of my timber leg. The same broadside I lost my leg, old Pew lost his deadlights. It was a master surgeon, him that ampytated me—out of college and all—Latin by the bucket, and what not; but he was hanged like a dog, and sun-dried like the rest, at Corso Castle. That was Roberts' men, that was, and comed of changing names to their ships—Royal Fortune and so on. Now, what a ship was christened, so let her stay, I says. So it was with the Cassandra, as brought us all safe home from Malabar, after England took the viceroy of the Indies; so it was with the old Walrus, Flint's old ship, as I've seen amuck with the red blood and fit to sink with gold."

"Ah!" cried another voice, that of the youngest hand on board, and evidently full of admiration. "He was the flower of the flock, was Flint!"

"Davis was a man too, by all accounts," said Silver. "I never sailed along of him; first with England, then with Flint, that's my story; and now here on my own account, in a manner of speaking. I laid by nine hundred safe, from England, and two thousand after Flint. That ain't bad for a man before the mast—all safe in bank. 'Tain't earning now, it's saving does it, you may lay to that. Where's all England's men now? I dunno. Where's Flint's? Why, most on 'em aboard here, and glad to get the duff—been begging before that, some on 'em. Old Pew, as had lost his sight, and might have thought shame, spends twelve hundred pound in a year, like a lord in Parliament. Where is he now? Well, he's dead now and under hatches; but for two year before that, shiver my timbers, the man was starving! He begged, and he stole, and he cut throats, and starved at that, by the powers!"

"Well, it ain't much use, after all," said the young seaman.

"'Tain't much use for fools, you may lay to it—that, nor nothing," cried Silver. "But now, you look here: you're young, you are, but you're as smart as paint. I see that when I set my eyes on you, and I'll talk to you like a man."

You may imagine how I felt when I heard this abominable old rogue addressing another in the very same words of flattery as he had used to myself. I think, if I had been able, that I would have killed him through the barrel. Meantime, he ran on, little supposing he was overheard.

"Here it is about gentlemen of fortune. They lives rough, and they risk swinging, but they eat and drink like fighting-cocks, and when a cruise is done, why, it's hundreds of pounds instead of hundreds of farthings in their pockets. Now, the most goes for rum and a good fling, and to sea again in their shirts. But that's not the course I lay. I puts it all away, some here, some there, and none too much anywheres, by reason of suspicion. I'm fifty, mark you; once back from this cruise, I set up gentleman in earnest. Time enough too, says you. Ah, but I've lived easy in the meantime, never denied myself o' nothing heart desires, and slep' soft and ate dainty all my days but when at sea. And how did I begin? Before the mast, like you!"

"Well," said the other, "but all the other money's gone now, ain't it? You daren't show face in Bristol after this."

"Why, where might you suppose it was?" asked Silver derisively.

"At Bristol, in banks and places," answered his companion.

"It were," said the cook; "it were when we weighed anchor. But my old missis has it all by now. And the Spy-glass is sold, lease and goodwill and rigging; and the old girl's off to meet me. I would tell you where, for I trust you, but it'd make jealousy among the mates."

"And can you trust your missis?" asked the other.

"Gentlemen of fortune," returned the cook, "usually trusts little among themselves, and right they are, you may lay to it. But I have a way with me, I have. When a mate brings a slip on his cable—one as knows me, I mean—it won't be in the same world with old John. There was some that was feared of Pew, and some that was feared of Flint; but Flint his own self was feared of me. Feared he was, and proud. They was the roughest crew afloat, was Flint's; the devil himself would have been feared to go to sea with them. Well now, I tell you, I'm not a boasting man, and you seen yourself how easy I keep company, but when I was quartermaster, lambs wasn't the word for Flint's old buccaneers. Ah, you may be sure of yourself in old John's ship."

"Well, I tell you now," replied the lad, "I didn't half a quarter like the job till I had this talk with you, John; but there's my hand on it now."

"And a brave lad you were, and smart too," answered Silver, shaking hands so heartily that all the barrel shook, "and a finer figurehead for a gentleman of fortune I never clapped my eyes on."

By this time I had begun to understand the meaning of their terms. By a "gentleman of fortune" they plainly meant neither more nor less than a common pirate, and the little scene that I had overheard was the last act in the corruption of one of the honest hands—perhaps of the last one left aboard. But on this point I was soon to be relieved, for Silver giving a little whistle, a third man strolled up and sat down by the party.

"Dick's square," said Silver.

"Oh, I know'd Dick was square," returned the voice of the coxswain, Israel Hands. "He's no fool, is Dick." And he turned his quid and spat. "But look here," he went on, "here's what I want to know, Barbecue: how long are we a-going to stand off and on like a blessed bumboat? I've had a'most enough o' Cap'n Smollett; he's hazed me long enough, by thunder! I want to go into that cabin, I do. I want their pickles and wines, and that."

"Israel," said Silver, "your head ain't much account, nor ever was. But you're able to hear, I reckon; leastways, your ears is big enough. Now, here's what I say: you'll berth forward, and you'll live hard, and you'll speak soft, and you'll keep sober till I give the word; and you may lay to that, my son."

"Well, I don't say no, do I?" growled the coxswain. "What I say is, when? That's what I say."

"When! By the powers!" cried Silver. "Well now, if you want to know, I'll tell you when. The last moment I can manage, and that's when. Here's a first-rate seaman, Cap'n Smollett, sails the blessed ship for us. Here's this squire and doctor with a map and such—I don't know where it is, do I? No more do you, says you. Well then, I mean this squire and doctor shall find the stuff, and help us to get it aboard, by the powers. Then we'll see. If I was sure of you all, sons of double Dutchmen, I'd have Cap'n Smollett navigate us half-way back again before I struck."

"Why, we're all seamen aboard here, I should think," said the lad Dick.

"We're all forecastle hands, you mean," snapped Silver. "We can steer a course, but who's to set one? That's what all you gentlemen split on, first and last. If I had my way, I'd have Cap'n Smollett work us back into the trades at least; then we'd have no blessed miscalculations and a spoonful of water a day. But I know the sort you are. I'll finish with 'em at the island, as soon's the blunt's on board, and a pity it is. But you're never happy till you're drunk. Split my sides, I've a sick heart to sail with the likes of you!"

"Easy all, Long John," cried Israel. "Who's a-crossin' of you?"

"Why, how many tall ships, think ye, now, have I seen laid aboard? And how many brisk lads drying in the sun at Execution Dock?" cried Silver. "And all for this same hurry and hurry and hurry. You hear me? I seen a thing or two at sea, I have. If you would on'y lay your course, and a p'int to windward, you would ride in carriages, you would. But not you! I know you. You'll have your mouthful of rum tomorrow, and go hang."

"Everybody knowed you was a kind of a chapling, John; but there's others as could hand and steer as well as you," said Israel. "They liked a bit o' fun, they did. They wasn't so high and dry, nohow, but took their fling, like jolly companions every one."

"So?" says Silver. "Well, and where are they now? Pew was that sort, and he died a beggar-man. Flint was, and he died of rum at Savannah. Ah, they was a sweet crew, they was! On'y, where are they?"

"But," asked Dick, "when we do lay 'em athwart, what are we to do with 'em, anyhow?"

"There's the man for me!" cried the cook admiringly. "That's what I call business. Well, what would you think? Put 'em ashore like maroons? That would have been England's way. Or cut 'em down like that much pork? That would have been Flint's, or Billy Bones's."

"Billy was the man for that," said Israel. "'Dead men don't bite,' says he. Well, he's dead now hisself; he knows the long and short on it now; and if ever a rough hand come to port, it was Billy."

"Right you are," said Silver; "rough and ready. But mark you here, I'm an easy man—I'm quite the gentleman, says you; but this time it's serious. Dooty is dooty, mates. I give my vote—death. When I'm in Parlyment and riding in my coach, I don't want none of these sea-lawyers in the cabin a-coming home, unlooked for, like the devil at prayers. Wait is what I say; but when the time comes, why, let her rip!"

"John," cries the coxswain, "you're a man!"

"You'll say so, Israel when you see," said Silver. "Only one thing I claim—I claim Trelawney. I'll wring his calf's head off his body with these hands, Dick!" he added, breaking off. "You just jump up, like a sweet lad, and get me an apple, to wet my pipe like."

You may fancy the terror I was in! I should have leaped out and run for it if I had found the strength, but my limbs and heart alike misgave me. I heard Dick begin to rise, and then someone seemingly stopped him, and the voice of Hands exclaimed, "Oh, stow that! Don't you get sucking of that bilge, John. Let's have a go of the rum."

"Dick," said Silver, "I trust you. I've a gauge on the keg, mind. There's the key; you fill a pannikin and bring it up."

Terrified as I was, I could not help thinking to myself that this must have been how Mr. Arrow got the strong waters that destroyed him.

Dick was gone but a little while, and during his absence Israel spoke straight on in the cook's ear. It was but a word or two that I could catch, and yet I gathered some important news, for besides other scraps that tended to the same purpose, this whole clause was audible: "Not another man of them'll jine." Hence there were still faithful men on board.

When Dick returned, one after another of the trio took the pannikin and drank—one "To luck," another with a "Here's to old Flint," and Silver himself saying, in a kind of song, "Here's to ourselves, and hold your luff, plenty of prizes and plenty of duff."

Just then a sort of brightness fell upon me in the barrel, and looking up, I found the moon had risen and was silvering the mizzen-top and shining white on the luff of the fore-sail; and almost at the same time the voice of the lookout shouted, "Land ho!"

12

Council of War

THERE was a great rush of feet across the deck. I could hear people tumbling up from the cabin and the forecastle, and slipping in an instant outside my barrel, I dived behind the fore-sail, made a double towards the stern, and came out upon the open deck in time to join Hunter and Dr. Livesey in the rush for the weather bow.

There all hands were already congregated. A belt of fog had lifted almost simultaneously with the appearance of the moon. Away to the south-west of us we saw two low hills, about a couple of miles apart, and rising behind one of them a third and higher hill, whose peak was still buried in the fog. All three seemed sharp and conical in figure.

So much I saw, almost in a dream, for I had not yet recovered from my horrid fear of a minute or two before. And then I heard the voice of Captain Smollett issuing orders. The Hispaniola was laid a couple of points nearer the wind and now sailed a course that would just clear the island on the east.

"And now, men," said the captain, when all was sheeted home, "has any one of you ever seen that land ahead?"

"I have, sir," said Silver. "I've watered there with a trader I was cook in."

"The anchorage is on the south, behind an islet, I fancy?" asked the captain.

"Yes, sir; Skeleton Island they calls it. It were a main place for pirates once, and a hand we had on board knowed all their names for it. That hill to the nor'ard they calls the Fore-mast Hill; there are three hills in a row running south'ard—fore, main, and mizzen, sir. But the main—that's the big un, with the cloud on it—they usually calls the Spy-glass, by reason of a lookout they kept when they was in the anchorage cleaning, for it's there they cleaned their ships, sir, asking your pardon."

"I have a chart here," says Captain Smollett. "See if that's the place."

Long John's eyes burned in his head as he took the chart, but by the fresh look of the paper I knew he was doomed to disappointment. This was not the map we found in Billy Bones's chest, but an accurate copy, complete in all things—names and heights and soundings—with the single exception of the red crosses and the written notes. Sharp as must have been his annoyance, Silver had the strength of mind to hide it.

"Yes, sir," said he, "this is the spot, to be sure, and very prettily drawn out. Who might have done that, I wonder? The pirates were too ignorant, I reckon. Aye, here it is: 'Capt. Kidd's Anchorage'—just the name my shipmate called it. There's a strong current runs along the south, and then away nor'ard up the west coast. Right you was, sir," says he, "to haul your wind and keep the weather of the island. Leastways, if such was your intention as to enter and careen, and there ain't no better place for that in these waters."

"Thank you, my man," says Captain Smollett. "I'll ask you later on to give us a help. You may go."

I was surprised at the coolness with which John avowed his knowledge of the island, and I own I was half-frightened when I saw him drawing nearer to myself. He did not know, to be sure, that I had overheard his council from the apple barrel, and yet I had by this time taken such a horror of his cruelty, duplicity, and power that I could scarce conceal a shudder when he laid his hand upon my arm.

"Ah," says he, "this here is a sweet spot, this island—a sweet spot for a lad to get ashore on. You'll bathe, and you'll climb trees, and you'll hunt goats, you will; and you'll get aloft on them hills like a goat yourself. Why, it makes me young again. I was going to forget my timber leg, I was. It's a pleasant thing to be young and have ten toes, and you may lay to that. When you want to go a bit of exploring, you just ask old John, and he'll put up a snack for you to take along."

And clapping me in the friendliest way upon the shoulder, he hobbled off forward and went below.

Captain Smollett, the squire, and Dr. Livesey were talking together on the quarter-deck, and anxious as I was to tell them my story, I durst not interrupt them openly. While I was still casting about in my thoughts to find some probable excuse, Dr. Livesey called me to his side. He had left his pipe below, and being a slave to tobacco, had meant that I should fetch it; but as soon as I was near enough to speak and not to be overheard, I broke immediately, "Doctor, let me speak. Get the captain and squire down to the cabin, and then make some pretence to send for me. I have terrible news."

The doctor changed countenance a little, but next moment he was master of himself.

"Thank you, Jim," said he quite loudly, "that was all I wanted to know," as if he had asked me a question.

And with that he turned on his heel and rejoined the other two. They spoke together for a little, and though none of them started, or raised his voice, or so much as whistled, it was plain enough that Dr. Livesey had communicated my request, for the next thing that I heard was the captain giving an order to Job Anderson, and all hands were piped on deck.

"My lads," said Captain Smollett, "I've a word to say to you. This land that we have sighted is the place we have been sailing for. Mr. Trelawney, being a very open-handed gentleman, as we all know, has just asked me a word or two, and as I was able to tell him that every man on board had done his duty, alow and aloft, as I never ask to see it done better, why, he and I and the doctor are going below to the cabin to drink your health and luck, and you'll have grog served out for you to drink our health and luck. I'll tell you what I think of this: I think it handsome. And if you think as I do, you'll give a good sea-cheer for the gentleman that does it."

The cheer followed—that was a matter of course; but it rang out so full and hearty that I confess I could hardly believe these same men were plotting for our blood.

"One more cheer for Cap'n Smollett," cried Long John when the first had subsided.

And this also was given with a will.

On the top of that the three gentlemen went below, and not long after, word was sent forward that Jim Hawkins was wanted in the cabin.

I found them all three seated round the table, a bottle of Spanish wine and some raisins before them, and the doctor smoking away, with his wig on his lap, and that, I knew, was a sign that he was agitated. The stern window was open, for it was a warm night, and you could see the moon shining behind on the ship's wake.

"Now, Hawkins," said the squire, "you have something to say. Speak up."

I did as I was bid, and as short as I could make it, told the whole details of Silver's conversation. Nobody interrupted me till I was done, nor did any one of the three of them make so much as a movement, but they kept their eyes upon my face from first to last.

"Jim," said Dr. Livesey, "take a seat."

And they made me sit down at table beside them, poured me out a glass of wine, filled my hands with raisins, and all three, one after the other, and each with a bow, drank my good health, and their service to me, for my luck and courage.

"Now, captain," said the squire, "you were right, and I was wrong. I own myself an ass, and I await your orders."

"No more an ass than I, sir," returned the captain. "I never heard of a crew that meant to mutiny but what showed signs before, for any man that had an eye in his head to see the mischief and take steps according. But this crew," he added, "beats me."

"Captain," said the doctor, "with your permission, that's Silver. A very remarkable man."

"He'd look remarkably well from a yard-arm, sir," returned the captain. "But this is talk; this don't lead to anything. I see three or four points, and with Mr. Trelawney's permission, I'll name them."

"You, sir, are the captain. It is for you to speak," says Mr. Trelawney grandly.

"First point," began Mr. Smollett. "We must go on, because we can't turn back. If I gave the word to go about, they would rise at once. Second point, we have time before us—at least until this treasure's found. Third point, there are faithful hands. Now, sir, it's got to come to blows sooner or later, and what I propose is to take time by the forelock, as the saying is, and come to blows some fine day when they least expect it. We can count, I take it, on your own home servants, Mr. Trelawney?"

"As upon myself," declared the squire.

"Three," reckoned the captain; "ourselves make seven, counting Hawkins here. Now, about the honest hands?"

"Most likely Trelawney's own men," said the doctor; "those he had picked up for himself before he lit on Silver."

"Nay," replied the squire. "Hands was one of mine."

"I did think I could have trusted Hands," added the captain.

"And to think that they're all Englishmen!" broke out the squire. "Sir, I could find it in my heart to blow the ship up."

"Well, gentlemen," said the captain, "the best that I can say is not much. We must lay to, if you please, and keep a bright lookout. It's trying on a man, I know. It would be pleasanter to come to blows. But there's no help for it till we know our men. Lay to, and whistle for a wind, that's my view."

"Jim here," said the doctor, "can help us more than anyone. The men are not shy with him, and Jim is a noticing lad."

"Hawkins, I put prodigious faith in you," added the squire.

I began to feel pretty desperate at this, for I felt altogether helpless; and yet, by an odd train of circumstances, it was indeed through me that safety came. In the meantime, talk as we pleased, there were only seven out of the twenty-six on whom we knew we could rely; and out of these seven one was a boy, so that the grown men on our side were six to their nineteen.

PART THREE—My Shore Adventure

13

How My Shore Adventure Began

THE appearance of the island when I came on deck next morning was altogether changed. Although the breeze had now utterly ceased, we had made a great deal of way during the night and were now lying becalmed about half a mile to the south-east of the low eastern coast. Grey-coloured woods covered a large part of the surface. This even tint was indeed broken up by streaks of yellow sand-break in the lower lands, and by many tall trees of the pine family, out-topping the others—some singly, some in clumps; but the general colouring was uniform and sad. The hills ran up clear above the vegetation in spires of naked rock. All were strangely shaped, and the Spy-glass, which was by three or four hundred feet the tallest on the island, was likewise the strangest in configuration, running up sheer from almost every side and then suddenly cut off at the top like a pedestal to put a statue on.

The Hispaniola was rolling scuppers under in the ocean swell. The booms were tearing at the blocks, the rudder was banging to and fro, and the whole ship creaking, groaning, and jumping like a manufactory. I had to cling tight to the backstay, and the world turned giddily before my eyes, for though I was a good enough sailor when there was way on, this standing still and being rolled about like a bottle was a thing I never learned to stand without a qualm or so, above all in the morning, on an empty stomach.

Perhaps it was this—perhaps it was the look of the island, with its grey, melancholy woods, and wild stone spires, and the surf that we could both see and hear foaming and thundering on the steep beach—at least, although the sun shone bright and hot, and the shore birds were fishing and crying all around us, and you would have thought anyone would have been glad to get to land after being so long at sea, my heart sank, as the saying is, into my boots; and from the first look onward, I hated the very thought of Treasure Island.

We had a dreary morning's work before us, for there was no sign of any wind, and the boats had to be got out and manned, and the ship warped three or four miles round the corner of the island and up the narrow passage to the haven behind Skeleton Island. I volunteered for one of the boats, where I had, of course, no business. The heat was sweltering, and the men grumbled fiercely over their work. Anderson was in command of my boat, and instead of keeping the crew in order, he grumbled as loud as the worst.

"Well," he said with an oath, "it's not forever."

I thought this was a very bad sign, for up to that day the men had gone briskly and willingly about their business; but the very sight of the island had relaxed the cords of discipline.

All the way in, Long John stood by the steersman and conned the ship. He knew the passage like the palm of his hand, and though the man in the chains got everywhere more water than was down in the chart, John never hesitated once.

"There's a strong scour with the ebb," he said, "and this here passage has been dug out, in a manner of speaking, with a spade."

We brought up just where the anchor was in the chart, about a third of a mile from each shore, the mainland on one side and Skeleton Island on the other. The bottom was clean sand. The plunge of our anchor sent up clouds of birds wheeling and crying over the woods, but in less than a minute they were down again and all was once more silent.

The place was entirely land-locked, buried in woods, the trees coming right down to high-water mark, the shores mostly flat, and the hilltops standing round at a distance in a sort of amphitheatre, one here, one there. Two little rivers, or rather two swamps, emptied out into this pond, as you might call it; and the foliage round that part of the shore had a kind of poisonous brightness. From the ship we could see nothing of the house or stockade, for they were quite buried among trees; and if it had not been for the chart on the companion, we might have been the first that had ever anchored there since the island arose out of the seas.

There was not a breath of air moving, nor a sound but that of the surf booming half a mile away along the beaches and against the rocks outside. A peculiar stagnant smell hung over the anchorage—a smell of sodden leaves and rotting tree trunks. I observed the doctor sniffing and sniffing, like someone tasting a bad egg.

"I don't know about treasure," he said, "but I'll stake my wig there's fever here."

If the conduct of the men had been alarming in the boat, it became truly threatening when they had come aboard. They lay about the deck growling together in talk. The slightest order was received with a black look and grudgingly and carelessly obeyed. Even the honest hands must have caught the infection, for there was not one man aboard to mend another. Mutiny, it was plain, hung over us like a thunder-cloud.

And it was not only we of the cabin party who perceived the danger. Long John was hard at work going from group to group, spending himself in good advice, and as for example no man could have shown a better. He fairly outstripped himself in willingness and civility; he was all smiles to everyone. If an order were given, John would be on his crutch in an instant, with the cheeriest "Aye, aye, sir!" in the world; and when there was nothing else to do, he kept up one song after another, as if to conceal the discontent of the rest.

Of all the gloomy features of that gloomy afternoon, this obvious anxiety on the part of Long John appeared the worst.

We held a council in the cabin.

"Sir," said the captain, "if I risk another order, the whole ship'll come about our ears by the run. You see, sir, here it is. I get a rough answer, do I not? Well, if I speak back, pikes will be going in two shakes; if I don't, Silver will see there's something under that, and the game's up. Now, we've only one man to rely on."

"And who is that?" asked the squire.

"Silver, sir," returned the captain; "he's as anxious as you and I to smother things up. This is a tiff; he'd soon talk 'em out of it if he had the chance, and what I propose to do is to give him the chance. Let's allow the men an afternoon ashore. If they all go, why we'll fight the ship. If they none of them go, well then, we hold the cabin, and God defend the right. If some go, you mark my words, sir, Silver'll bring 'em aboard again as mild as lambs."

It was so decided; loaded pistols were served out to all the sure men; Hunter, Joyce, and Redruth were taken into our confidence and received the news with less surprise and a better spirit than we had looked for, and then the captain went on deck and addressed the crew.

"My lads," said he, "we've had a hot day and are all tired and out of sorts. A turn ashore'll hurt nobody—the boats are still in the water; you can take the gigs, and as many as please may go ashore for the afternoon. I'll fire a gun half an hour before sundown."

I believe the silly fellows must have thought they would break their shins over treasure as soon as they were landed, for they all came out of their sulks in a moment and gave a cheer that started the echo in a faraway hill and sent the birds once more flying and squalling round the anchorage.

The captain was too bright to be in the way. He whipped out of sight in a moment, leaving Silver to arrange the party, and I fancy it was as well he did so. Had he been on deck, he could no longer so much as have pretended not to understand the situation. It was as plain as day. Silver was the captain, and a mighty rebellious crew he had of it. The honest hands—and I was soon to see it proved that there were such on board—must have been very stupid fellows. Or rather, I suppose the truth was this, that all hands were disaffected by the example of the ringleaders—only some more, some less; and a few, being good fellows in the main, could neither be led nor driven any further. It is one thing to be idle and skulk and quite another to take a ship and murder a number of innocent men.

At last, however, the party was made up. Six fellows were to stay on board, and the remaining thirteen, including Silver, began to embark.

Then it was that there came into my head the first of the mad notions that contributed so much to save our lives. If six men were left by Silver, it was plain our party could not take and fight the ship; and since only six were left, it was equally plain that the cabin party had no present need of my assistance. It occurred to me at once to go ashore. In a jiffy I had slipped over the side and curled up in the fore-sheets of the nearest boat, and almost at the same moment she shoved off.

No one took notice of me, only the bow oar saying, "Is that you, Jim? Keep your head down." But Silver, from the other boat, looked sharply over and called out to know if that were me; and from that moment I began to regret what I had done.

The crews raced for the beach, but the boat I was in, having some start and being at once the lighter and the better manned, shot far ahead of her consort, and the bow had struck among the shore-side trees and I had caught a branch and swung myself out and plunged into the nearest thicket while Silver and the rest were still a hundred yards behind.

"Jim, Jim!" I heard him shouting.

But you may suppose I paid no heed; jumping, ducking, and breaking through, I ran straight before my nose till I could run no longer.

14

The First Blow

I WAS so pleased at having given the slip to Long John that I began to enjoy myself and look around me with some interest on the strange land that I was in.

I had crossed a marshy tract full of willows, bulrushes, and odd, outlandish, swampy trees; and I had now come out upon the skirts of an open piece of undulating, sandy country, about a mile long, dotted with a few pines and a great number of contorted trees, not unlike the oak in growth, but pale in the foliage, like willows. On the far side of the open stood one of the hills, with two quaint, craggy peaks shining vividly in the sun.

I now felt for the first time the joy of exploration. The isle was uninhabited; my shipmates I had left behind, and nothing lived in front of me but dumb brutes and fowls. I turned hither and thither among the trees. Here and there were flowering plants, unknown to me; here and there I saw snakes, and one raised his head from a ledge of rock and hissed at me with a noise not unlike the spinning of a top. Little did I suppose that he was a deadly enemy and that the noise was the famous rattle.

Then I came to a long thicket of these oaklike trees—live, or evergreen, oaks, I heard afterwards they should be called—which grew low along the sand like brambles, the boughs curiously twisted, the foliage compact, like thatch. The thicket stretched down from the top of one of the sandy knolls, spreading and growing taller as it went, until it reached the margin of the broad, reedy fen, through which the nearest of the little rivers soaked its way into the anchorage. The marsh was steaming in the strong sun, and the outline of the Spy-glass trembled through the haze.

All at once there began to go a sort of bustle among the bulrushes; a wild duck flew up with a quack, another followed, and soon over the whole surface of the marsh a great cloud of birds hung screaming and circling in the air. I judged at once that some of my shipmates must be drawing near along the borders of the fen. Nor was I deceived, for soon I heard the very distant and low tones of a human voice, which, as I continued to give ear, grew steadily louder and nearer.

This put me in a great fear, and I crawled under cover of the nearest live-oak and squatted there, hearkening, as silent as a mouse.

Another voice answered, and then the first voice, which I now recognized to be Silver's, once more took up the story and ran on for a long while in a stream, only now and again interrupted by the other. By the sound they must have been talking earnestly, and almost fiercely; but no distinct word came to my hearing.

At last the speakers seemed to have paused and perhaps to have sat down, for not only did they cease to draw any nearer, but the birds themselves began to grow more quiet and to settle again to their places in the swamp.

And now I began to feel that I was neglecting my business, that since I had been so foolhardy as to come ashore with these desperadoes, the least I could do was to overhear them at their councils, and that my plain and obvious duty was to draw as close as I could manage, under the favourable ambush of the crouching trees.

I could tell the direction of the speakers pretty exactly, not only by the sound of their voices but by the behaviour of the few birds that still hung in alarm above the heads of the intruders.

Crawling on all fours, I made steadily but slowly towards them, till at last, raising my head to an aperture among the leaves, I could see clear down into a little green dell beside the marsh, and closely set about with trees, where Long John Silver and another of the crew stood face to face in conversation.

The sun beat full upon them. Silver had thrown his hat beside him on the ground, and his great, smooth, blond face, all shining with heat, was lifted to the other man's in a kind of appeal.

"Mate," he was saying, "it's because I thinks gold dust of you—gold dust, and you may lay to that! If I hadn't took to you like pitch, do you think I'd have been here a-warning of you? All's up—you can't make nor mend; it's to save your neck that I'm a-speaking, and if one of the wild uns knew it, where'd I be, Tom—now, tell me, where'd I be?"

"Silver," said the other man—and I observed he was not only red in the face, but spoke as hoarse as a crow, and his voice shook too, like a taut rope—"Silver," says he, "you're old, and you're honest, or has the name for it; and you've money too, which lots of poor sailors hasn't; and you're brave, or I'm mistook. And will you tell me you'll let yourself be led away with that kind of a mess of swabs? Not you! As sure as God sees me, I'd sooner lose my hand. If I turn agin my dooty—"

And then all of a sudden he was interrupted by a noise. I had found one of the honest hands—well, here, at that same moment, came news of another. Far away out in the marsh there arose, all of a sudden, a sound like the cry of anger, then another on the back of it; and then one horrid, long-drawn scream. The rocks of the Spy-glass re-echoed it a score of times; the whole troop of marsh-birds rose again, darkening heaven, with a simultaneous whirr; and long after that death yell was still ringing in my brain, silence had re-established its empire, and only the rustle of the redescending birds and the boom of the distant surges disturbed the languor of the afternoon.

Tom had leaped at the sound, like a horse at the spur, but Silver had not winked an eye. He stood where he was, resting lightly on his crutch, watching his companion like a snake about to spring.

"John!" said the sailor, stretching out his hand.

"Hands off!" cried Silver, leaping back a yard, as it seemed to me, with the speed and security of a trained gymnast.

"Hands off, if you like, John Silver," said the other. "It's a black conscience that can make you feared of me. But in heaven's name, tell me, what was that?"

"That?" returned Silver, smiling away, but warier than ever, his eye a mere pin-point in his big face, but gleaming like a crumb of glass. "That? Oh, I reckon that'll be Alan."

And at this point Tom flashed out like a hero.

"Alan!" he cried. "Then rest his soul for a true seaman! And as for you, John Silver, long you've been a mate of mine, but you're mate of mine no more. If I die like a dog, I'll die in my dooty. You've killed Alan, have you? Kill me too, if you can. But I defies you."

And with that, this brave fellow turned his back directly on the cook and set off walking for the beach. But he was not destined to go far. With a cry John seized the branch of a tree, whipped the crutch out of his armpit, and sent that uncouth missile hurtling through the air. It struck poor Tom, point foremost, and with stunning violence, right between the shoulders in the middle of his back. His hands flew up, he gave a sort of gasp, and fell.

Whether he were injured much or little, none could ever tell. Like enough, to judge from the sound, his back was broken on the spot. But he had no time given him to recover. Silver, agile as a monkey even without leg or crutch, was on the top of him next moment and had twice buried his knife up to the hilt in that defenceless body. From my place of ambush, I could hear him pant aloud as he struck the blows.

I do not know what it rightly is to faint, but I do know that for the next little while the whole world swam away from before me in a whirling mist; Silver and the birds, and the tall Spy-glass hilltop, going round and round and topsy-turvy before my eyes, and all manner of bells ringing and distant voices shouting in my ear.

When I came again to myself the monster had pulled himself together, his crutch under his arm, his hat upon his head. Just before him Tom lay motionless upon the sward; but the murderer minded him not a whit, cleansing his blood-stained knife the while upon a wisp of grass. Everything else was unchanged, the sun still shining mercilessly on the steaming marsh and the tall pinnacle of the mountain, and I could scarce persuade myself that murder had been actually done and a human life cruelly cut short a moment since before my eyes.

But now John put his hand into his pocket, brought out a whistle, and blew upon it several modulated blasts that rang far across the heated air. I could not tell, of course, the meaning of the signal, but it instantly awoke my fears. More men would be coming. I might be discovered. They had already slain two of the honest people; after Tom and Alan, might not I come next?

Instantly I began to extricate myself and crawl back again, with what speed and silence I could manage, to the more open portion of the wood. As I did so, I could hear hails coming and going between the old buccaneer and his comrades, and this sound of danger lent me wings. As soon as I was clear of the thicket, I ran as I never ran before, scarce minding the direction of my flight, so long as it led me from the murderers; and as I ran, fear grew and grew upon me until it turned into a kind of frenzy.

Indeed, could anyone be more entirely lost than I? When the gun fired, how should I dare to go down to the boats among those fiends, still smoking from their crime? Would not the first of them who saw me wring my neck like a snipe's? Would not my absence itself be an evidence to them of my alarm, and therefore of my fatal knowledge? It was all over, I thought. Good-bye to the Hispaniola; good-bye to the squire, the doctor, and the captain! There was nothing left for me but death by starvation or death by the hands of the mutineers.

All this while, as I say, I was still running, and without taking any notice, I had drawn near to the foot of the little hill with the two peaks and had got into a part of the island where the live-oaks grew more widely apart and seemed more like forest trees in their bearing and dimensions. Mingled with these were a few scattered pines, some fifty, some nearer seventy, feet high. The air too smelt more freshly than down beside the marsh.

And here a fresh alarm brought me to a standstill with a thumping heart.

15

The Man of the Island

FROM the side of the hill, which was here steep and stony, a spout of gravel was dislodged and fell rattling and bounding through the trees. My eyes turned instinctively in that direction, and I saw a figure leap with great rapidity behind the trunk of a pine. What it was, whether bear or man or monkey, I could in no wise tell. It seemed dark and shaggy; more I knew not. But the terror of this new apparition brought me to a stand.

I was now, it seemed, cut off upon both sides; behind me the murderers, before me this lurking nondescript. And immediately I began to prefer the dangers that I knew to those I knew not. Silver himself appeared less terrible in contrast with this creature of the woods, and I turned on my heel, and looking sharply behind me over my shoulder, began to retrace my steps in the direction of the boats.

Instantly the figure reappeared, and making a wide circuit, began to head me off. I was tired, at any rate; but had I been as fresh as when I rose, I could see it was in vain for me to contend in speed with such an adversary. From trunk to trunk the creature flitted like a deer, running manlike on two legs, but unlike any man that I had ever seen, stooping almost double as it ran. Yet a man it was, I could no longer be in doubt about that.

I began to recall what I had heard of cannibals. I was within an ace of calling for help. But the mere fact that he was a man, however wild, had somewhat reassured me, and my fear of Silver began to revive in proportion. I stood still, therefore, and cast about for some method of escape; and as I was so thinking, the recollection of my pistol flashed into my mind. As soon as I remembered I was not defenceless, courage glowed again in my heart and I set my face resolutely for this man of the island and walked briskly towards him.

He was concealed by this time behind another tree trunk; but he must have been watching me closely, for as soon as I began to move in his direction he reappeared and took a step to meet me. Then he hesitated, drew back, came forward again, and at last, to my wonder and confusion, threw himself on his knees and held out his clasped hands in supplication.

At that I once more stopped.

"Who are you?" I asked.

"Ben Gunn," he answered, and his voice sounded hoarse and awkward, like a rusty lock. "I'm poor Ben Gunn, I am; and I haven't spoke with a Christian these three years."

I could now see that he was a white man like myself and that his features were even pleasing. His skin, wherever it was exposed, was burnt by the sun; even his lips were black, and his fair eyes looked quite startling in so dark a face. Of all the beggar-men that I had seen or fancied, he was the chief for raggedness. He was clothed with tatters of old ship's canvas and old sea-cloth, and this extraordinary patchwork was all held together by a system of the most various and incongruous fastenings, brass buttons, bits of stick, and loops of tarry gaskin. About his waist he wore an old brass-buckled leather belt, which was the one thing solid in his whole accoutrement.

"Three years!" I cried. "Were you shipwrecked?"

"Nay, mate," said he; "marooned."

I had heard the word, and I knew it stood for a horrible kind of punishment common enough among the buccaneers, in which the offender is put ashore with a little powder and shot and left behind on some desolate and distant island.

"Marooned three years agone," he continued, "and lived on goats since then, and berries, and oysters. Wherever a man is, says I, a man can do for himself. But, mate, my heart is sore for Christian diet. You mightn't happen to have a piece of cheese about you, now? No? Well, many's the long night I've dreamed of cheese—toasted, mostly—and woke up again, and here I were."

"If ever I can get aboard again," said I, "you shall have cheese by the stone."

All this time he had been feeling the stuff of my jacket, smoothing my hands, looking at my boots, and generally, in the intervals of his speech, showing a childish pleasure in the presence of a fellow creature. But at my last words he perked up into a kind of startled slyness.

"If ever you can get aboard again, says you?" he repeated. "Why, now, who's to hinder you?"

"Not you, I know," was my reply.

"And right you was," he cried. "Now you—what do you call yourself, mate?"

"Jim," I told him.

"Jim, Jim," says he, quite pleased apparently. "Well, now, Jim, I've lived that rough as you'd be ashamed to hear of. Now, for instance, you wouldn't think I had had a pious mother—to look at me?" he asked.

"Why, no, not in particular," I answered.

"Ah, well," said he, "but I had—remarkable pious. And I was a civil, pious boy, and could rattle off my catechism that fast, as you couldn't tell one word from another. And here's what it come to, Jim, and it begun with chuck-farthen on the blessed grave-stones! That's what it begun with, but it went further'n that; and so my mother told me, and predicked the whole, she did, the pious woman! But it were Providence that put me here. I've thought it all out in this here lonely island, and I'm back on piety. You don't catch me tasting rum so much, but just a thimbleful for luck, of course, the first chance I have. I'm bound I'll be good, and I see the way to. And, Jim"—looking all round him and lowering his voice to a whisper—"I'm rich."

I now felt sure that the poor fellow had gone crazy in his solitude, and I suppose I must have shown the feeling in my face, for he repeated the statement hotly: "Rich! Rich! I says. And I'll tell you what: I'll make a man of you, Jim. Ah, Jim, you'll bless your stars, you will, you was the first that found me!"

And at this there came suddenly a lowering shadow over his face, and he tightened his grasp upon my hand and raised a forefinger threateningly before my eyes.

"Now, Jim, you tell me true: that ain't Flint's ship?" he asked.

At this I had a happy inspiration. I began to believe that I had found an ally, and I answered him at once.

"It's not Flint's ship, and Flint is dead; but I'll tell you true, as you ask me—there are some of Flint's hands aboard; worse luck for the rest of us."

"Not a man—with one—leg?" he gasped.

"Silver?" I asked.

"Ah, Silver!" says he. "That were his name."

"He's the cook, and the ringleader too."

He was still holding me by the wrist, and at that he give it quite a wring.

"If you was sent by Long John," he said, "I'm as good as pork, and I know it. But where was you, do you suppose?"

I had made my mind up in a moment, and by way of answer told him the whole story of our voyage and the predicament in which we found ourselves. He heard me with the keenest interest, and when I had done he patted me on the head.

"You're a good lad, Jim," he said; "and you're all in a clove hitch, ain't you? Well, you just put your trust in Ben Gunn—Ben Gunn's the man to do it. Would you think it likely, now, that your squire would prove a liberal-minded one in case of help—him being in a clove hitch, as you remark?"

I told him the squire was the most liberal of men.

"Aye, but you see," returned Ben Gunn, "I didn't mean giving me a gate to keep, and a suit of livery clothes, and such; that's not my mark, Jim. What I mean is, would he be likely to come down to the toon of, say one thousand pounds out of money that's as good as a man's own already?"

"I am sure he would," said I. "As it was, all hands were to share."

"And a passage home?" he added with a look of great shrewdness.

"Why," I cried, "the squire's a gentleman. And besides, if we got rid of the others, we should want you to help work the vessel home."

"Ah," said he, "so you would." And he seemed very much relieved.

"Now, I'll tell you what," he went on. "So much I'll tell you, and no more. I were in Flint's ship when he buried the treasure; he and six along—six strong seamen. They was ashore nigh on a week, and us standing off and on in the old Walrus. One fine day up went the signal, and here come Flint by himself in a little boat, and his head done up in a blue scarf. The sun was getting up, and mortal white he looked about the cutwater. But, there he was, you mind, and the six all dead—dead and buried. How he done it, not a man aboard us could make out. It was battle, murder, and sudden death, leastways—him against six. Billy Bones was the mate; Long John, he was quartermaster; and they asked him where the treasure was. 'Ah,' says he, 'you can go ashore, if you like, and stay,' he says; 'but as for the ship, she'll beat up for more, by thunder!' That's what he said.

"Well, I was in another ship three years back, and we sighted this island. 'Boys,' said I, 'here's Flint's treasure; let's land and find it.' The cap'n was displeased at that, but my messmates were all of a mind and landed. Twelve days they looked for it, and every day they had the worse word for me, until one fine morning all hands went aboard. 'As for you, Benjamin Gunn,' says they, 'here's a musket,' they says, 'and a spade, and pick-axe. You can stay here and find Flint's money for yourself,' they says.

"Well, Jim, three years have I been here, and not a bite of Christian diet from that day to this. But now, you look here; look at me. Do I look like a man before the mast? No, says you. Nor I weren't, neither, I says."

And with that he winked and pinched me hard.

"Just you mention them words to your squire, Jim," he went on. "Nor he weren't, neither—that's the words. Three years he were the man of this island, light and dark, fair and rain; and sometimes he would maybe think upon a prayer (says you), and sometimes he would maybe think of his old mother, so be as she's alive (you'll say); but the most part of Gunn's time (this is what you'll say)—the most part of his time was took up with another matter. And then you'll give him a nip, like I do."

And he pinched me again in the most confidential manner.

"Then," he continued, "then you'll up, and you'll say this: Gunn is a good man (you'll say), and he puts a precious sight more confidence—a precious sight, mind that—in a gen'leman born than in these gen'leman of fortune, having been one hisself."

"Well," I said, "I don't understand one word that you've been saying. But that's neither here nor there; for how am I to get on board?"

"Ah," said he, "that's the hitch, for sure. Well, there's my boat, that I made with my two hands. I keep her under the white rock. If the worst come to the worst, we might try that after dark. Hi!" he broke out. "What's that?"

For just then, although the sun had still an hour or two to run, all the echoes of the island awoke and bellowed to the thunder of a cannon.

"They have begun to fight!" I cried. "Follow me."

And I began to run towards the anchorage, my terrors all forgotten, while close at my side the marooned man in his goatskins trotted easily and lightly.

"Left, left," says he; "keep to your left hand, mate Jim! Under the trees with you! Theer's where I killed my first goat. They don't come down here now; they're all mastheaded on them mountings for the fear of Benjamin Gunn. Ah! And there's the cetemery"—cemetery, he must have meant. "You see the mounds? I come here and prayed, nows and thens, when I thought maybe a Sunday would be about doo. It weren't quite a chapel, but it seemed more solemn like; and then, says you, Ben Gunn was short-handed—no chapling, nor so much as a Bible and a flag, you says."

So he kept talking as I ran, neither expecting nor receiving any answer.

The cannon-shot was followed after a considerable interval by a volley of small arms.

Another pause, and then, not a quarter of a mile in front of me, I beheld the Union Jack flutter in the air above a wood.

PART FOUR—The Stockade

16

Narrative Continued by the Doctor: How the Ship Was Abandoned

IT was about half past one—three bells in the sea phrase—that the two boats went ashore from the Hispaniola. The captain, the squire, and I were talking matters over in the cabin. Had there been a breath of wind, we should have fallen on the six mutineers who were left aboard with us, slipped our cable, and away to sea. But the wind was wanting; and to complete our helplessness, down came Hunter with the news that Jim Hawkins had slipped into a boat and was gone ashore with the rest.

It never occurred to us to doubt Jim Hawkins, but we were alarmed for his safety. With the men in the temper they were in, it seemed an even chance if we should see the lad again. We ran on deck. The pitch was bubbling in the seams; the nasty stench of the place turned me sick; if ever a man smelt fever and dysentery, it was in that abominable anchorage. The six scoundrels were sitting grumbling under a sail in the forecastle; ashore we could see the gigs made fast and a man sitting in each, hard by where the river runs in. One of them was whistling "Lillibullero."

Waiting was a strain, and it was decided that Hunter and I should go ashore with the jolly-boat in quest of information.

The gigs had leaned to their right, but Hunter and I pulled straight in, in the direction of the stockade upon the chart. The two who were left guarding their boats seemed in a bustle at our appearance; "Lillibullero" stopped off, and I could see the pair discussing what they ought to do. Had they gone and told Silver, all might have turned out differently; but they had their orders, I suppose, and decided to sit quietly where they were and hark back again to "Lillibullero."

There was a slight bend in the coast, and I steered so as to put it between us; even before we landed we had thus lost sight of the gigs. I jumped out and came as near running as I durst, with a big silk handkerchief under my hat for coolness' sake and a brace of pistols ready primed for safety.

I had not gone a hundred yards when I reached the stockade.

This was how it was: a spring of clear water rose almost at the top of a knoll. Well, on the knoll, and enclosing the spring, they had clapped a stout loghouse fit to hold two score of people on a pinch and loopholed for musketry on either side. All round this they had cleared a wide space, and then the thing was completed by a paling six feet high, without door or opening, too strong to pull down without time and labour and too open to shelter the besiegers. The people in the log-house had them in every way; they stood quiet in shelter and shot the others like partridges. All they wanted was a good watch and food; for, short of a complete surprise, they might have held the place against a regiment.

What particularly took my fancy was the spring. For though we had a good enough place of it in the cabin of the Hispaniola, with plenty of arms and ammunition, and things to eat, and excellent wines, there had been one thing overlooked—we had no water. I was thinking this over when there came ringing over the island the cry of a man at the point of death. I was not new to violent death—I have served his Royal Highness the Duke of Cumberland, and got a wound myself at Fontenoy—but I know my pulse went dot and carry one. "Jim Hawkins is gone," was my first thought.

It is something to have been an old soldier, but more still to have been a doctor. There is no time to dilly-dally in our work. And so now I made up my mind instantly, and with no time lost returned to the shore and jumped on board the jolly-boat.

By good fortune Hunter pulled a good oar. We made the water fly, and the boat was soon alongside and I aboard the schooner.

I found them all shaken, as was natural. The squire was sitting down, as white as a sheet, thinking of the harm he had led us to, the good soul! And one of the six forecastle hands was little better.

"There's a man," says Captain Smollett, nodding towards him, "new to this work. He came nigh-hand fainting, doctor, when he heard the cry. Another touch of the rudder and that man would join us."

I told my plan to the captain, and between us we settled on the details of its accomplishment.

We put old Redruth in the gallery between the cabin and the forecastle, with three or four loaded muskets and a mattress for protection. Hunter brought the boat round under the stern-port, and Joyce and I set to work loading her with powder tins, muskets, bags of biscuits, kegs of pork, a cask of cognac, and my invaluable medicine chest.

In the meantime, the squire and the captain stayed on deck, and the latter hailed the coxswain, who was the principal man aboard.

"Mr. Hands," he said, "here are two of us with a brace of pistols each. If any one of you six make a signal of any description, that man's dead."

They were a good deal taken aback, and after a little consultation one and all tumbled down the fore companion, thinking no doubt to take us on the rear. But when they saw Redruth waiting for them in the sparred galley, they went about ship at once, and a head popped out again on deck.

"Down, dog!" cries the captain.

And the head popped back again; and we heard no more, for the time, of these six very faint-hearted seamen.

By this time, tumbling things in as they came, we had the jolly-boat loaded as much as we dared. Joyce and I got out through the stern-port, and we made for shore again as fast as oars could take us.

This second trip fairly aroused the watchers along shore. "Lillibullero" was dropped again; and just before we lost sight of them behind the little point, one of them whipped ashore and disappeared. I had half a mind to change my plan and destroy their boats, but I feared that Silver and the others might be close at hand, and all might very well be lost by trying for too much.

We had soon touched land in the same place as before and set to provision the block house. All three made the first journey, heavily laden, and tossed our stores over the palisade. Then, leaving Joyce to guard them—one man, to be sure, but with half a dozen muskets—Hunter and I returned to the jolly-boat and loaded ourselves once more. So we proceeded without pausing to take breath, till the whole cargo was bestowed, when the two servants took up their position in the block house, and I, with all my power, sculled back to the Hispaniola.

That we should have risked a second boat load seems more daring than it really was. They had the advantage of numbers, of course, but we had the advantage of arms. Not one of the men ashore had a musket, and before they could get within range for pistol shooting, we flattered ourselves we should be able to give a good account of a half-dozen at least.

The squire was waiting for me at the stern window, all his faintness gone from him. He caught the painter and made it fast, and we fell to loading the boat for our very lives. Pork, powder, and biscuit was the cargo, with only a musket and a cutlass apiece for the squire and me and Redruth and the captain. The rest of the arms and powder we dropped overboard in two fathoms and a half of water, so that we could see the bright steel shining far below us in the sun, on the clean, sandy bottom.

By this time the tide was beginning to ebb, and the ship was swinging round to her anchor. Voices were heard faintly halloaing in the direction of the two gigs; and though this reassured us for Joyce and Hunter, who were well to the eastward, it warned our party to be off.

Redruth retreated from his place in the gallery and dropped into the boat, which we then brought round to the ship's counter, to be handier for Captain Smollett.

"Now, men," said he, "do you hear me?"

There was no answer from the forecastle.

"It's to you, Abraham Gray—it's to you I am speaking."

Still no reply.

"Gray," resumed Mr. Smollett, a little louder, "I am leaving this ship, and I order you to follow your captain. I know you are a good man at bottom, and I dare say not one of the lot of you's as bad as he makes out. I have my watch here in my hand; I give you thirty seconds to join me in."

There was a pause.

"Come, my fine fellow," continued the captain; "don't hang so long in stays. I'm risking my life and the lives of these good gentlemen every second."

There was a sudden scuffle, a sound of blows, and out burst Abraham Gray with a knife cut on the side of the cheek, and came running to the captain like a dog to the whistle.

"I'm with you, sir," said he.

And the next moment he and the captain had dropped aboard of us, and we had shoved off and given way.

We were clear out of the ship, but not yet ashore in our stockade.

17

Narrative Continued by the Doctor: The Jolly-boat's Last Trip

THIS fifth trip was quite different from any of the others. In the first place, the little gallipot of a boat that we were in was gravely overloaded. Five grown men, and three of them—Trelawney, Redruth, and the captain—over six feet high, was already more than she was meant to carry. Add to that the powder, pork, and bread-bags. The gunwale was lipping astern. Several times we shipped a little water, and my breeches and the tails of my coat were all soaking wet before we had gone a hundred yards.

The captain made us trim the boat, and we got her to lie a little more evenly. All the same, we were afraid to breathe.

In the second place, the ebb was now making—a strong rippling current running westward through the basin, and then south'ard and seaward down the straits by which we had entered in the morning. Even the ripples were a danger to our overloaded craft, but the worst of it was that we were swept out of our true course and away from our proper landing-place behind the point. If we let the current have its way we should come ashore beside the gigs, where the pirates might appear at any moment.

"I cannot keep her head for the stockade, sir," said I to the captain. I was steering, while he and Redruth, two fresh men, were at the oars. "The tide keeps washing her down. Could you pull a little stronger?"

"Not without swamping the boat," said he. "You must bear up, sir, if you please—bear up until you see you're gaining."

I tried and found by experiment that the tide kept sweeping us westward until I had laid her head due east, or just about right angles to the way we ought to go.

"We'll never get ashore at this rate," said I.

"If it's the only course that we can lie, sir, we must even lie it," returned the captain. "We must keep upstream. You see, sir," he went on, "if once we dropped to leeward of the landing-place, it's hard to say where we should get ashore, besides the chance of being boarded by the gigs; whereas, the way we go the current must slacken, and then we can dodge back along the shore."

"The current's less a'ready, sir," said the man Gray, who was sitting in the fore-sheets; "you can ease her off a bit."

"Thank you, my man," said I, quite as if nothing had happened, for we had all quietly made up our minds to treat him like one of ourselves.

Suddenly the captain spoke up again, and I thought his voice was a little changed.

"The gun!" said he.

"I have thought of that," said I, for I made sure he was thinking of a bombardment of the fort. "They could never get the gun ashore, and if they did, they could never haul it through the woods."

"Look astern, doctor," replied the captain.

We had entirely forgotten the long nine; and there, to our horror, were the five rogues busy about her, getting off her jacket, as they called the stout tarpaulin cover under which she sailed. Not only that, but it flashed into my mind at the same moment that the round-shot and the powder for the gun had been left behind, and a stroke with an axe would put it all into the possession of the evil ones abroad.

"Israel was Flint's gunner," said Gray hoarsely.

At any risk, we put the boat's head direct for the landing-place. By this time we had got so far out of the run of the current that we kept steerage way even at our necessarily gentle rate of rowing, and I could keep her steady for the goal. But the worst of it was that with the course I now held we turned our broadside instead of our stern to the Hispaniola and offered a target like a barn door.

I could hear as well as see that brandy-faced rascal Israel Hands plumping down a round-shot on the deck.

"Who's the best shot?" asked the captain.

"Mr. Trelawney, out and away," said I.

"Mr. Trelawney, will you please pick me off one of these men, sir? Hands, if possible," said the captain.

Trelawney was as cool as steel. He looked to the priming of his gun.

"Now," cried the captain, "easy with that gun, sir, or you'll swamp the boat. All hands stand by to trim her when he aims."

The squire raised his gun, the rowing ceased, and we leaned over to the other side to keep the balance, and all was so nicely contrived that we did not ship a drop.

They had the gun, by this time, slewed round upon the swivel, and Hands, who was at the muzzle with the rammer, was in consequence the most exposed. However, we had no luck, for just as Trelawney fired, down he stooped, the ball whistled over him, and it was one of the other four who fell.

The cry he gave was echoed not only by his companions on board but by a great number of voices from the shore, and looking in that direction I saw the other pirates trooping out from among the trees and tumbling into their places in the boats.

"Here come the gigs, sir," said I.

"Give way, then," cried the captain. "We mustn't mind if we swamp her now. If we can't get ashore, all's up."

"Only one of the gigs is being manned, sir," I added; "the crew of the other most likely going round by shore to cut us off."

"They'll have a hot run, sir," returned the captain. "Jack ashore, you know. It's not them I mind; it's the round-shot. Carpet bowls! My lady's maid couldn't miss. Tell us, squire, when you see the match, and we'll hold water."

In the meanwhile we had been making headway at a good pace for a boat so overloaded, and we had shipped but little water in the process. We were now close in; thirty or forty strokes and we should beach her, for the ebb had already disclosed a narrow belt of sand below the clustering trees. The gig was no longer to be feared; the little point had already concealed it from our eyes. The ebb-tide, which had so cruelly delayed us, was now making reparation and delaying our assailants. The one source of danger was the gun.

"If I durst," said the captain, "I'd stop and pick off another man."

But it was plain that they meant nothing should delay their shot. They had never so much as looked at their fallen comrade, though he was not dead, and I could see him trying to crawl away.

"Ready!" cried the squire.

"Hold!" cried the captain, quick as an echo.

And he and Redruth backed with a great heave that sent her stern bodily under water. The report fell in at the same instant of time. This was the first that Jim heard, the sound of the squire's shot not having reached him. Where the ball passed, not one of us precisely knew, but I fancy it must have been over our heads and that the wind of it may have contributed to our disaster.

At any rate, the boat sank by the stern, quite gently, in three feet of water, leaving the captain and myself, facing each other, on our feet. The other three took complete headers, and came up again drenched and bubbling.

So far there was no great harm. No lives were lost, and we could wade ashore in safety. But there were all our stores at the bottom, and to make things worse, only two guns out of five remained in a state for service. Mine I had snatched from my knees and held over my head, by a sort of instinct. As for the captain, he had carried his over his shoulder by a bandoleer, and like a wise man, lock uppermost. The other three had gone down with the boat.

To add to our concern, we heard voices already drawing near us in the woods along shore, and we had not only the danger of being cut off from the stockade in our half-crippled state but the fear before us whether, if Hunter and Joyce were attacked by half a dozen, they would have the sense and conduct to stand firm. Hunter was steady, that we knew; Joyce was a doubtful case—a pleasant, polite man for a valet and to brush one's clothes, but not entirely fitted for a man of war.

With all this in our minds, we waded ashore as fast as we could, leaving behind us the poor jolly-boat and a good half of all our powder and provisions.

18

Narrative Continued by the Doctor:
End of the First Day's Fighting

WE made our best speed across the strip of wood that now divided us from the stockade, and at every step we took the voices of the buccaneers rang nearer. Soon we could hear their footfalls as they ran and the cracking of the branches as they breasted across a bit of thicket.

I began to see we should have a brush for it in earnest and looked to my priming.

"Captain," said I, "Trelawney is the dead shot. Give him your gun; his own is useless."

They exchanged guns, and Trelawney, silent and cool as he had been since the beginning of the bustle, hung a moment on his heel to see that all was fit for service. At the same time, observing Gray to be unarmed, I handed him my cutlass. It did all our hearts good to see him spit in his hand, knit his brows, and make the blade sing through the air. It was plain from every line of his body that our new hand was worth his salt.

Forty paces farther we came to the edge of the wood and saw the stockade in front of us. We struck the enclosure about the middle of the south side, and almost at the same time, seven mutineers—Job Anderson, the boatswain, at their head—appeared in full cry at the southwestern corner.

They paused as if taken aback, and before they recovered, not only the squire and I, but Hunter and Joyce from the block house, had time to fire. The four shots came in rather a scattering volley, but they did the business: one of the enemy actually fell, and the rest, without hesitation, turned and plunged into the trees.

After reloading, we walked down the outside of the palisade to see to the fallen enemy. He was stone dead—shot through the heart.

We began to rejoice over our good success when just at that moment a pistol cracked in the bush, a ball whistled close past my ear, and poor Tom Redruth stumbled and fell his length on the ground. Both the squire and I returned the shot, but as we had nothing to aim at, it is probable we only wasted powder. Then we reloaded and turned our attention to poor Tom.

The captain and Gray were already examining him, and I saw with half an eye that all was over.

I believe the readiness of our return volley had scattered the mutineers once more, for we were suffered without further molestation to get the poor old gamekeeper hoisted over the stockade and carried, groaning and bleeding, into the log-house.

Poor old fellow, he had not uttered one word of surprise, complaint, fear, or even acquiescence from the very beginning of our troubles till now, when we had laid him down in the log-house to die. He had lain like a Trojan behind his mattress in the gallery; he had followed every order silently, doggedly, and well; he was the oldest of our party by a score of years; and now, sullen, old, serviceable servant, it was he that was to die.

The squire dropped down beside him on his knees and kissed his hand, crying like a child.

"Be I going, doctor?" he asked.

"Tom, my man," said I, "you're going home."

"I wish I had had a lick at them with the gun first," he replied.

"Tom," said the squire, "say you forgive me, won't you?"

"Would that be respectful like, from me to you, squire?" was the answer. "Howsoever, so be it, amen!"

After a little while of silence, he said he thought somebody might read a prayer. "It's the custom, sir," he added apologetically. And not long after, without another word, he passed away.

In the meantime the captain, whom I had observed to be wonderfully swollen about the chest and pockets, had turned out a great many various stores—the British colours, a Bible, a coil of stoutish rope, pen, ink, the log-book, and pounds of tobacco. He had found a longish fir-tree lying felled and trimmed in the enclosure, and with the help of Hunter he had set it up at the corner of the log-house where the trunks crossed and made an angle. Then, climbing on the roof, he had with his own hand bent and run up the colours.

This seemed mightily to relieve him. He re-entered the log-house and set about counting up the stores as if nothing else existed. But he had an eye on Tom's passage for all that, and as soon as all was over, came forward with another flag and reverently spread it on the body.

"Don't you take on, sir," he said, shaking the squire's hand. "All's well with him; no fear for a hand that's been shot down in his duty to captain and owner. It mayn't be good divinity, but it's a fact."

Then he pulled me aside.

"Dr. Livesey," he said, "in how many weeks do you and squire expect the consort?"

I told him it was a question not of weeks but of months, that if we were not back by the end of August Blandly was to send to find us, but neither sooner nor later. "You can calculate for yourself," I said.

"Why, yes," returned the captain, scratching his head; "and making a large allowance, sir, for all the gifts of Providence, I should say we were pretty close hauled."

"How do you mean?" I asked.

"It's a pity, sir, we lost that second load. That's what I mean," replied the captain. "As for powder and shot, we'll do. But the rations are short, very short—so short, Dr. Livesey, that we're perhaps as well without that extra mouth."

And he pointed to the dead body under the flag.

Just then, with a roar and a whistle, a round-shot passed high above the roof of the log-house and plumped far beyond us in the wood.

"Oho!" said the captain. "Blaze away! You've little enough powder already, my lads."

At the second trial, the aim was better, and the ball descended inside the stockade, scattering a cloud of sand but doing no further damage.

"Captain," said the squire, "the house is quite invisible from the ship. It must be the flag they are aiming at. Would it not be wiser to take it in?"

"Strike my colours!" cried the captain. "No, sir, not I"; and as soon as he had said the words, I think we all agreed with him. For it was not only a piece of stout, seamanly, good feeling; it was good policy besides and showed our enemies that we despised their cannonade.

All through the evening they kept thundering away. Ball after ball flew over or fell short or kicked up the sand in the enclosure, but they had to fire so high that the shot fell dead and buried itself in the soft sand. We had no ricochet to fear, and though one popped in through the roof of the log-house and out again through the floor, we soon got used to that sort of horse-play and minded it no more than cricket.

"There is one good thing about all this," observed the captain; "the wood in front of us is likely clear. The ebb has made a good while; our stores should be uncovered. Volunteers to go and bring in pork."

Gray and Hunter were the first to come forward. Well armed, they stole out of the stockade, but it proved a useless mission. The mutineers were bolder than we fancied or they put more trust in Israel's gunnery. For four or five of them were busy carrying off our stores and wading out with them to one of the gigs that lay close by, pulling an oar or so to hold her steady against the current. Silver was in the stern-sheets in command; and every man of them was now provided with a musket from some secret magazine of their own.

The captain sat down to his log, and here is the beginning of the entry:

Alexander Smollett, master; David Livesey, ship's doctor; Abraham Gray, carpenter's mate; John Trelawney, owner; John Hunter and Richard Joyce, owner's servants, landsmen—being all that is left faithful of the ship's company—with stores for ten days at short rations, came ashore this day and flew British colours on the log-house in Treasure Island. Thomas Redruth, owner's servant, landsman, shot by the mutineers; James Hawkins, cabin-boy—

And at the same time, I was wondering over poor Jim Hawkins' fate.

A hail on the land side.

"Somebody hailing us," said Hunter, who was on guard.

"Doctor! Squire! Captain! Hullo, Hunter, is that you?" came the cries.

And I ran to the door in time to see Jim Hawkins, safe and sound, come climbing over the stockade.

19

Narrative Resumed by Jim Hawkins:
The Garrison in the Stockade

AS soon as Ben Gunn saw the colours he came to a halt, stopped me by the arm, and sat down.

"Now," said he, "there's your friends, sure enough."

"Far more likely it's the mutineers," I answered.

"That!" he cried. "Why, in a place like this, where nobody puts in but gen'lemen of fortune, Silver would fly the Jolly Roger, you don't make no doubt of that. No, that's your friends. There's been blows too, and I reckon your friends has had the best of it; and here they are ashore in the old stockade, as was made years and years ago by Flint. Ah, he was the man to have a headpiece, was Flint! Barring rum, his match were never seen. He were afraid of none, not he; on'y Silver—Silver was that genteel."

"Well," said I, "that may be so, and so be it; all the more reason that I should hurry on and join my friends."

"Nay, mate," returned Ben, "not you. You're a good boy, or I'm mistook; but you're on'y a boy, all told. Now, Ben Gunn is fly. Rum wouldn't bring me there, where you're going—not rum wouldn't, till I see your born gen'leman and gets it on his word of honour. And you won't forget my words; 'A precious sight (that's what you'll say), a precious sight more confidence'—and then nips him."

And he pinched me the third time with the same air of cleverness.

"And when Ben Gunn is wanted, you know where to find him, Jim. Just wheer you found him today. And him that comes is to have a white thing in his hand, and he's to come alone. Oh! And you'll say this: 'Ben Gunn,' says you, 'has reasons of his own.'"

"Well," said I, "I believe I understand. You have something to propose, and you wish to see the squire or the doctor, and you're to be found where I found you. Is that all?"

"And when? says you," he added. "Why, from about noon observation to about six bells."

"Good," said I, "and now may I go?"

"You won't forget?" he inquired anxiously. "Precious sight, and reasons of his own, says you. Reasons of his own; that's the mainstay; as between man and man. Well, then"—still holding me—"I reckon you can go, Jim. And, Jim, if you was to see Silver, you wouldn't go for to sell Ben Gunn? Wild horses wouldn't draw it from you? No, says you. And if them pirates camp ashore, Jim, what would you say but there'd be widders in the morning?"

Here he was interrupted by a loud report, and a cannonball came tearing through the trees and pitched in the sand not a hundred yards from where we two were talking. The next moment each of us had taken to his heels in a different direction.

For a good hour to come frequent reports shook the island, and balls kept crashing through the woods. I moved from hiding-place to hiding-place, always pursued, or so it seemed to me, by these terrifying missiles. But towards the end of the bombardment, though still I durst not venture in the direction of the stockade, where the balls fell oftenest, I had begun, in a manner, to pluck up my heart again, and after a long detour to the east, crept down among the shore-side trees.

The sun had just set, the sea breeze was rustling and tumbling in the woods and ruffling the grey surface of the anchorage; the tide, too, was far out, and great tracts of sand lay uncovered; the air, after the heat of the day, chilled me through my jacket.

The Hispaniola still lay where she had anchored; but, sure enough, there was the Jolly Roger—the black flag of piracy—flying from her peak. Even as I looked, there came another red flash and another report that sent the echoes clattering, and one more round-shot whistled through the air. It was the last of the cannonade.

I lay for some time watching the bustle which succeeded the attack. Men were demolishing something with axes on the beach near the stockade—the poor jolly-boat, I afterwards discovered. Away, near the mouth of the river, a great fire was glowing among the trees, and between that point and the ship one of the gigs kept coming and going, the men, whom I had seen so gloomy, shouting at the oars like children. But there was a sound in their voices which suggested rum.

At length I thought I might return towards the stockade. I was pretty far down on the low, sandy spit that encloses the anchorage to the east, and is joined at half-water to Skeleton Island; and now, as I rose to my feet, I saw, some distance further down the spit and rising from among low bushes, an isolated rock, pretty high, and peculiarly white in colour. It occurred to me that this might be the white rock of which Ben Gunn had spoken and that some day or other a boat might be wanted and I should know where to look for one.

Then I skirted among the woods until I had regained the rear, or shoreward side, of the stockade, and was soon warmly welcomed by the faithful party.

I had soon told my story and began to look about me. The log-house was made of unsquared trunks of pine—roof, walls, and floor. The latter stood in several places as much as a foot or a foot and a half above the surface of the sand. There was a porch at the door, and under this porch the little spring welled up into an artificial basin of a rather odd kind—no other than a great ship's kettle of iron, with the bottom knocked out, and sunk "to her bearings," as the captain said, among the sand.

Little had been left besides the framework of the house, but in one corner there was a stone slab laid down by way of hearth and an old rusty iron basket to contain the fire.

The slopes of the knoll and all the inside of the stockade had been cleared of timber to build the house, and we could see by the stumps what a fine and lofty grove had been destroyed. Most of the soil had been washed away or buried in drift after the removal of the trees; only where the streamlet ran down from the kettle a thick bed of moss and some ferns and little creeping bushes were still green among the sand. Very close around the stockade—too close for defence, they said—the wood still flourished high and dense, all of fir on the land side, but towards the sea with a large admixture of live-oaks.

The cold evening breeze, of which I have spoken, whistled through every chink of the rude building and sprinkled the floor with a continual rain of fine sand. There was sand in our eyes, sand in our teeth, sand in our suppers, sand dancing in the spring at the bottom of the kettle, for all the world like porridge beginning to boil. Our chimney was a square hole in the roof; it was but a little part of the smoke that found its way out, and the rest eddied about the house and kept us coughing and piping the eye.

Add to this that Gray, the new man, had his face tied up in a bandage for a cut he had got in breaking away from the mutineers and that poor old Tom Redruth, still unburied, lay along the wall, stiff and stark, under the Union Jack.

If we had been allowed to sit idle, we should all have fallen in the blues, but Captain Smollett was never the man for that. All hands were called up before him, and he divided us into watches. The doctor and Gray and I for one; the squire, Hunter, and Joyce upon the other. Tired though we all were, two were sent out for firewood; two more were set to dig a grave for Redruth; the doctor was named cook; I was put sentry at the door; and the captain himself went from one to another, keeping up our spirits and lending a hand wherever it was wanted.

From time to time the doctor came to the door for a little air and to rest his eyes, which were almost smoked out of his head, and whenever he did so, he had a word for me.

"That man Smollett," he said once, "is a better man than I am. And when I say that it means a deal, Jim."

Another time he came and was silent for a while. Then he put his head on one side, and looked at me.

"Is this Ben Gunn a man?" he asked.

"I do not know, sir," said I. "I am not very sure whether he's sane."

"If there's any doubt about the matter, he is," returned the doctor. "A man who has been three years biting his nails on a desert island, Jim, can't expect to appear as sane as you or me. It doesn't lie in human nature. Was it cheese you said he had a fancy for?"

"Yes, sir, cheese," I answered.

"Well, Jim," says he, "just see the good that comes of being dainty in your food. You've seen my snuff-box, haven't you? And you never saw me take snuff, the reason being that in my snuff-box I carry a piece of Parmesan cheese—a cheese made in Italy, very nutritious. Well, that's for Ben Gunn!"

Before supper was eaten we buried old Tom in the sand and stood round him for a while bareheaded in the breeze. A good deal of firewood had been got in, but not enough for the captain's fancy, and he shook his head over it and told us we "must get back to this tomorrow rather livelier." Then, when we had eaten our pork and each had a good stiff glass of brandy grog, the three chiefs got together in a corner to discuss our prospects.

It appears they were at their wits' end what to do, the stores being so low that we must have been starved into surrender long before help came. But our best hope, it was decided, was to kill off the buccaneers until they either hauled down their flag or ran away with the Hispaniola. From nineteen they were already reduced to fifteen, two others were wounded, and one at least—the man shot beside the gun—severely wounded, if he were not dead. Every time we had a crack at them, we were to take it, saving our own lives, with the extremest care. And besides that, we had two able allies—rum and the climate.

As for the first, though we were about half a mile away, we could hear them roaring and singing late into the night; and as for the second, the doctor staked his wig that, camped where they were in the marsh and unprovided with remedies, the half of them would be on their backs before a week.

"So," he added, "if we are not all shot down first they'll be glad to be packing in the schooner.

It's always a ship, and they can get to buccaneering again, I suppose."

"First ship that ever I lost," said Captain Smollett.

I was dead tired, as you may fancy; and when I got to sleep, which was not till after a great deal of tossing, I slept like a log of wood.

The rest had long been up and had already breakfasted and increased the pile of firewood by about half as much again when I was wakened by a bustle and the sound of voices.

"Flag of truce!" I heard someone say; and then, immediately after, with a cry of surprise, "Silver himself!"

And at that, up I jumped, and rubbing my eyes, ran to a loophole in the wall.

20
Silver's Embassy

SURE enough, there were two men just outside the stockade, one of them waving a white cloth, the other, no less a person than Silver himself, standing placidly by.

It was still quite early, and the coldest morning that I think I ever was abroad in—a chill that pierced into the marrow. The sky was bright and cloudless overhead, and the tops of the trees shone rosily in the sun. But where Silver stood with his lieutenant, all was still in shadow, and they waded knee-deep in a low white vapour that had crawled during the night out of the morass. The chill and the vapour taken together told a poor tale of the island. It was plainly a damp, feverish, unhealthy spot.

"Keep indoors, men," said the captain. "Ten to one this is a trick."

Then he hailed the buccaneer.

"Who goes? Stand, or we fire."

"Flag of truce," cried Silver.

The captain was in the porch, keeping himself carefully out of the way of a treacherous shot, should any be intended. He turned and spoke to us, "Doctor's watch on the lookout. Dr. Livesey take the north side, if you please; Jim, the east; Gray, west. The watch below, all hands to load muskets. Lively, men, and careful."

And then he turned again to the mutineers.

"And what do you want with your flag of truce?" he cried.

This time it was the other man who replied.

"Cap'n Silver, sir, to come on board and make terms," he shouted.

"Cap'n Silver! Don't know him. Who's he?" cried the captain. And we could hear him adding to himself, "Cap'n, is it? My heart, and here's promotion!"

Long John answered for himself. "Me, sir. These poor lads have chosen me cap'n, after your desertion, sir"—laying a particular emphasis upon the word "desertion." "We're willing to submit, if we can come to terms, and no bones about it. All I ask is your word, Cap'n Smollett, to let me safe and sound out of this here stockade, and one minute to get out o' shot before a gun is fired."

"My man," said Captain Smollett, "I have not the slightest desire to talk to you. If you wish to talk to me, you can come, that's all. If there's any treachery, it'll be on your side, and the Lord help you."

"That's enough, cap'n," shouted Long John cheerily. "A word from you's enough. I know a gentleman, and you may lay to that."

We could see the man who carried the flag of truce attempting to hold Silver back. Nor was that wonderful, seeing how cavalier had been the captain's answer. But Silver laughed at him aloud and slapped him on the back as if the idea of alarm had been absurd. Then he advanced to the stockade, threw over his crutch, got a leg up, and with great vigour and skill succeeded in surmounting the fence and dropping safely to the other side.

I will confess that I was far too much taken up with what was going on to be of the slightest use as sentry; indeed, I had already deserted my eastern loophole and crept up behind the captain, who had now seated himself on the threshold, with his elbows on his knees, his head in his hands, and his eyes fixed on the water as it bubbled out of the old iron kettle in the sand. He was whistling "Come, Lasses and Lads."

Silver had terrible hard work getting up the knoll. What with the steepness of the incline, the thick tree stumps, and the soft sand, he and his crutch were as helpless as a ship in stays. But he stuck to it like a man in silence, and at last arrived before the captain, whom he saluted in the handsomest style. He was tricked out in his best; an immense blue coat, thick with brass buttons, hung as low as to his knees, and a fine laced hat was set on the back of his head.

"Here you are, my man," said the captain, raising his head. "You had better sit down."

"You ain't a-going to let me inside, cap'n?" complained Long John. "It's a main cold morning, to be sure, sir, to sit outside upon the sand."

"Why, Silver," said the captain, "if you had pleased to be an honest man, you might have been sitting in your galley. It's your own doing. You're either my ship's cook—and then you were treated handsome—or Cap'n Silver, a common mutineer and pirate, and then you can go hang!"

"Well, well, cap'n," returned the sea-cook, sitting down as he was bidden on the sand, "you'll have to give me a hand up again, that's all. A sweet pretty place you have of it here. Ah, there's Jim! The top of the morning to you, Jim. Doctor, here's my service. Why, there you all are together like a happy family, in a manner of speaking."

"If you have anything to say, my man, better say it," said the captain.

"Right you were, Cap'n Smollett," replied Silver. "Dooty is dooty, to be sure. Well now, you look here, that was a good lay of yours last night. I don't deny it was a good lay. Some of you pretty handy with a handspike-end. And I'll not deny neither but what some of my people was shook—maybe all was shook; maybe I was shook myself; maybe that's why I'm here for terms. But you mark me, cap'n, it won't do twice, by thunder! We'll have to do sentry-go and ease off a point or so on the rum. Maybe you think we were all a sheet in the wind's eye. But I'll tell you I was sober; I was on'y dog tired; and if I'd awoke a second sooner, I'd 'a caught you at the act, I would. He wasn't dead when I got round to him, not he."

"Well?" says Captain Smollett as cool as can be.

All that Silver said was a riddle to him, but you would never have guessed it from his tone. As for me, I began to have an inkling. Ben Gunn's last words came back to my mind. I began to suppose that he had paid the buccaneers a visit while they all lay drunk together round their fire, and I reckoned up with glee that we had only fourteen enemies to deal with.

"Well, here it is," said Silver. "We want that treasure, and we'll have it—that's our point! You would just as soon save your lives, I reckon; and that's yours. You have a chart, haven't you?"

"That's as may be," replied the captain.

"Oh, well, you have, I know that," returned Long John. "You needn't be so husky with a man; there ain't a particle of service in that, and you may lay to it. What I mean is, we want your chart. Now, I never meant you no harm, myself."

"That won't do with me, my man," interrupted the captain. "We know exactly what you meant to do, and we don't care, for now, you see, you can't do it."

And the captain looked at him calmly and proceeded to fill a pipe.

"If Abe Gray—" Silver broke out.

"Avast there!" cried Mr. Smollett. "Gray told me nothing, and I asked him nothing; and what's more, I would see you and him and this whole island blown clean out of the water into blazes first. So there's my mind for you, my man, on that."

This little whiff of temper seemed to cool Silver down. He had been growing nettled before, but now he pulled himself together.

"Like enough," said he. "I would set no limits to what gentlemen might consider shipshape, or might not, as the case were. And seein' as how you are about to take a pipe, cap'n, I'll make so free as do likewise."

And he filled a pipe and lighted it; and the two men sat silently smoking for quite a while, now looking each other in the face, now stopping their tobacco, now leaning forward to spit. It was as good as the play to see them.

"Now," resumed Silver, "here it is. You give us the chart to get the treasure by, and drop shooting poor seamen and stoving of their heads in while asleep. You do that, and we'll offer you a choice. Either you come aboard along of us, once the treasure shipped, and then I'll give you my affy-davy, upon my word of honour, to clap you somewhere safe ashore. Or if that ain't to your fancy, some of my hands being rough and having old scores on account of hazing, then you can stay here, you can. We'll divide stores with you, man for man; and I'll give my affy-davy, as before to speak the first ship I sight, and send 'em here to pick you up. Now, you'll own that's talking. Handsomer you couldn't look to get, now you. And I hope"—raising his voice—"that all hands in this here block house will overhaul my words, for what is spoke to one is spoke to all."

Captain Smollett rose from his seat and knocked out the ashes of his pipe in the palm of his left hand.

"Is that all?" he asked.

"Every last word, by thunder!" answered John. "Refuse that, and you've seen the last of me but musket-balls."

"Very good," said the captain. "Now you'll hear me. If you'll come up one by one, unarmed, I'll engage to clap you all in irons and take you home to a fair trial in England. If you won't, my name is Alexander Smollett, I've flown my sovereign's colours, and I'll see you all to Davy Jones. You can't find the treasure. You can't sail the ship—there's not a man among you fit to sail the ship. You can't fight us—Gray, there, got away from five of you. Your ship's in irons, Master Silver; you're on a lee shore, and so you'll find. I stand here and tell you so; and they're the last good words you'll get from me, for in the name of heaven, I'll put a bullet in your back when next I meet you. Tramp, my lad. Bundle out of this, please, hand over hand, and double quick."

Silver's face was a picture; his eyes started in his head with wrath. He shook the fire out of his pipe.

"Give me a hand up!" he cried.

"Not I," returned the captain.

"Who'll give me a hand up?" he roared.

Not a man among us moved. Growling the foulest imprecations, he crawled along the sand till he got hold of the porch and could hoist himself again upon his crutch. Then he spat into the spring.

"There!" he cried. "That's what I think of ye. Before an hour's out, I'll stove in your old block house like a rum puncheon. Laugh, by thunder, laugh! Before an hour's out, ye'll laugh upon the other side. Them that die'll be the lucky ones."

And with a dreadful oath he stumbled off, ploughed down the sand, was helped across the stockade, after four or five failures, by the man with the flag of truce, and disappeared in an instant afterwards among the trees.

21

The Attack

AS soon as Silver disappeared, the captain, who had been closely watching him, turned towards the interior of the house and found not a man of us at his post but Gray. It was the first time we had ever seen him angry.

"Quarters!" he roared. And then, as we all slunk back to our places, "Gray," he said, "I'll put your name in the log; you've stood by your duty like a seaman. Mr. Trelawney, I'm surprised at you, sir. Doctor, I thought you had worn the king's coat! If that was how you served at Fontenoy, sir, you'd have been better in your berth."

The doctor's watch were all back at their loopholes, the rest were busy loading the spare muskets, and everyone with a red face, you may be certain, and a flea in his ear, as the saying is.

The captain looked on for a while in silence. Then he spoke.

"My lads," said he, "I've given Silver a broadside. I pitched it in red-hot on purpose; and before the hour's out, as he said, we shall be boarded. We're outnumbered, I needn't tell you that, but we fight in shelter; and a minute ago I should have said we fought with discipline. I've no manner of doubt that we can drub them, if you choose."

Then he went the rounds and saw, as he said, that all was clear.

On the two short sides of the house, east and west, there were only two loopholes; on the south side where the porch was, two again; and on the north side, five. There was a round score of muskets for the seven of us; the firewood had been built into four piles—tables, you might say—one about the middle of each side, and on each of these tables some ammunition and four loaded muskets were laid ready to the hand of the defenders. In the middle, the cutlasses lay ranged.

"Toss out the fire," said the captain; "the chill is past, and we mustn't have smoke in our eyes."

The iron fire-basket was carried bodily out by Mr. Trelawney, and the embers smothered among sand.

"Hawkins hasn't had his breakfast. Hawkins, help yourself, and back to your post to eat it," continued Captain Smollett. "Lively, now, my lad; you'll want it before you've done. Hunter, serve out a round of brandy to all hands."

And while this was going on, the captain completed, in his own mind, the plan of the defence.

"Doctor, you will take the door," he resumed. "See, and don't expose yourself; keep within, and fire through the porch. Hunter, take the east side, there. Joyce, you stand by the west, my man. Mr. Trelawney, you are the best shot—you and Gray will take this long north side, with the five loopholes; it's there the danger is. If they can get up to it and fire in upon us through our own ports, things would begin to look dirty. Hawkins, neither you nor I are much account at the shooting; we'll stand by to load and bear a hand."

As the captain had said, the chill was past. As soon as the sun had climbed above our girdle of trees, it fell with all its force upon the clearing and drank up the vapours at a draught. Soon the sand was baking and the resin melting in the logs of the block house. Jackets and coats were flung aside, shirts thrown open at the neck and rolled up to the shoulders; and we stood there, each at his post, in a fever of heat and anxiety.

An hour passed away.

"Hang them!" said the captain. "This is as dull as the doldrums. Gray, whistle for a wind."

And just at that moment came the first news of the attack.

"If you please, sir," said Joyce, "if I see anyone, am I to fire?"

"I told you so!" cried the captain.

"Thank you, sir," returned Joyce with the same quiet civility.

Nothing followed for a time, but the remark had set us all on the alert, straining ears and eyes—the musketeers with their pieces balanced in their hands, the captain out in the middle of the block house with his mouth very tight and a frown on his face.

So some seconds passed, till suddenly Joyce whipped up his musket and fired. The report had scarcely died away ere it was repeated and repeated from without in a scattering volley, shot behind shot, like a string of geese, from every side of the enclosure. Several bullets struck the log-house, but not one entered; and as the smoke cleared away and vanished, the stockade and the woods around it looked as quiet and empty as before. Not a bough waved, not the gleam of a musket-barrel betrayed the presence of our foes.

"Did you hit your man?" asked the captain.

"No, sir," replied Joyce. "I believe not, sir."

"Next best thing to tell the truth," muttered Captain Smollett. "Load his gun, Hawkins. How many should say there were on your side, doctor?"

"I know precisely," said Dr. Livesey. "Three shots were fired on this side. I saw the three flashes—two close together—one farther to the west."

"Three!" repeated the captain. "And how many on yours, Mr. Trelawney?"

But this was not so easily answered. There had come many from the north—seven by the squire's computation, eight or nine according to Gray. From the east and west only a single shot had been fired. It was plain, therefore, that the attack would be developed from the north and that on the other three sides we were only to be annoyed by a show of hostilities. But Captain Smollett made no change in his arrangements. If the mutineers succeeded in crossing the stockade, he argued, they would take possession of any unprotected loophole and shoot us down like rats in our own stronghold.

Nor had we much time left to us for thought. Suddenly, with a loud huzza, a little cloud of pirates leaped from the woods on the north side and ran straight on the stockade. At the same moment, the fire was once more opened from the woods, and a rifle ball sang through the doorway and knocked the doctor's musket into bits.

The boarders swarmed over the fence like monkeys. Squire and Gray fired again and yet again; three men fell, one forwards into the enclosure, two back on the outside. But of these, one was evidently more frightened than hurt, for he was on his feet again in a crack and instantly disappeared among the trees.

Two had bit the dust, one had fled, four had made good their footing inside our defences, while from the shelter of the woods seven or eight men, each evidently supplied with several muskets, kept up a hot though useless fire on the log-house.

The four who had boarded made straight before them for the building, shouting as they ran, and the men among the trees shouted back to encourage them. Several shots were fired, but such was the hurry of the marksmen that not one appears to have taken effect. In a moment, the four pirates had swarmed up the mound and were upon us.

The head of Job Anderson, the boatswain, appeared at the middle loophole.

"At 'em, all hands—all hands!" he roared in a voice of thunder.

At the same moment, another pirate grasped Hunter's musket by the muzzle, wrenched it from his hands, plucked it through the loophole, and with one stunning blow, laid the poor fellow senseless on the floor. Meanwhile a third, running unharmed all around the house, appeared suddenly in the doorway and fell with his cutlass on the doctor.

Our position was utterly reversed. A moment since we were firing, under cover, at an exposed enemy; now it was we who lay uncovered and could not return a blow.

The log-house was full of smoke, to which we owed our comparative safety. Cries and confusion, the flashes and reports of pistol-shots, and one loud groan rang in my ears.

"Out, lads, out, and fight 'em in the open! Cutlasses!" cried the captain.

I snatched a cutlass from the pile, and someone, at the same time snatching another, gave me a cut across the knuckles which I hardly felt. I dashed out of the door into the clear sunlight. Someone was close behind, I knew not whom. Right in front, the doctor was pursuing his assailant down the hill, and just as my eyes fell upon him, beat down his guard and sent him sprawling on his back with a great slash across the face.

"Round the house, lads! Round the house!" cried the captain; and even in the hurly-burly, I perceived a change in his voice.

Mechanically, I obeyed, turned eastwards, and with my cutlass raised, ran round the corner of the house. Next moment I was face to face with Anderson. He roared aloud, and his hanger went up above his head, flashing in the sunlight. I had not time to be afraid, but as the blow still hung impending, leaped in a trice upon one side, and missing my foot in the soft sand, rolled headlong down the slope.

When I had first sallied from the door, the other mutineers had been already swarming up the palisade to make an end of us. One man, in a red night-cap, with his cutlass in his mouth, had even got upon the top and thrown a leg across. Well, so short had been the interval that when I found my feet again all was in the same posture, the fellow with the red night-cap still half-way over, another still just showing his head above the top of the stockade. And yet, in this breath of time, the fight was over and the victory was ours.

Gray, following close behind me, had cut down the big boatswain ere he had time to recover from his last blow. Another had been shot at a loophole in the very act of firing into the house and now lay in agony, the pistol still smoking in his hand. A third, as I had seen, the doctor had disposed of at a blow. Of the four who had scaled the palisade, one only remained unaccounted for, and he, having left his cutlass on the field, was now clambering out again with the fear of death upon him.

"Fire—fire from the house!" cried the doctor. "And you, lads, back into cover."

But his words were unheeded, no shot was fired, and the last boarder made good his escape and disappeared with the rest into the wood. In three seconds nothing remained of the attacking party but the five who had fallen, four on the inside and one on the outside of the palisade.

The doctor and Gray and I ran full speed for shelter. The survivors would soon be back where they had left their muskets, and at any moment the fire might recommence.

The house was by this time somewhat cleared of smoke, and we saw at a glance the price we had paid for victory. Hunter lay beside his loophole, stunned; Joyce by his, shot through the head, never to move again; while right in the centre, the squire was supporting the captain, one as pale as the other.

"The captain's wounded," said Mr. Trelawney.

"Have they run?" asked Mr. Smollett.

"All that could, you may be bound," returned the doctor; "but there's five of them will never run again."

"Five!" cried the captain. "Come, that's better. Five against three leaves us four to nine. That's better odds than we had at starting. We were seven to nineteen then, or thought we were, and that's as bad to bear." *

*The mutineers were soon only eight in number, for the man shot by Mr. Trelawney on board the schooner died that same evening of his wound. But this was, of course, not known till after by the faithful party.

PART FIVE—My Sea Adventure

22

How My Sea Adventure Began

THERE was no return of the mutineers—not so much as another shot out of the woods. They had "got their rations for that day," as the captain put it, and we had the place to ourselves and a quiet time to overhaul the wounded and get dinner. Squire and I cooked outside in spite of the danger, and even outside we could hardly tell what we were at, for horror of the loud groans that reached us from the doctor's patients.

Out of the eight men who had fallen in the action, only three still breathed—that one of the pirates who had been shot at the loophole, Hunter, and Captain Smollett; and of these, the first two were as good as dead; the mutineer indeed died under the doctor's knife, and Hunter, do what we could, never recovered consciousness in this world. He lingered all day, breathing loudly like the old buccaneer at home in his apoplectic fit, but the bones of his chest had been crushed by the blow and his skull fractured in falling, and some time in the following night, without sign or sound, he went to his Maker.

As for the captain, his wounds were grievous indeed, but not dangerous. No organ was fatally injured. Anderson's ball—for it was Job that shot him first—had broken his shoulder-blade and touched the lung, not badly; the second had only torn and displaced some muscles in the calf. He was sure to recover, the doctor said, but in the meantime, and for weeks to come, he must not walk nor move his arm, nor so much as speak when he could help it.

My own accidental cut across the knuckles was a flea-bite. Doctor Livesey patched it up with plaster and pulled my ears for me into the bargain.

After dinner the squire and the doctor sat by the captain's side awhile in consultation; and when they had talked to their hearts' content, it being then a little past noon, the doctor took up his hat and pistols, girt on a cutlass, put the chart in his pocket, and with a musket over his shoulder crossed the palisade on the north side and set off briskly through the trees.

Gray and I were sitting together at the far end of the block house, to be out of earshot of our officers consulting; and Gray took his pipe out of his mouth and fairly forgot to put it back again, so thunder-struck he was at this occurrence.

"Why, in the name of Davy Jones," said he, "is Dr. Livesey mad?"

"Why no," says I. "He's about the last of this crew for that, I take it."

"Well, shipmate," said Gray, "mad he may not be; but if he's not, you mark my words, I am."

"I take it," replied I, "the doctor has his idea; and if I am right, he's going now to see Ben Gunn."

I was right, as appeared later; but in the meantime, the house being stifling hot and the little patch of sand inside the palisade ablaze with midday sun, I began to get another thought into my head, which was not by any means so right. What I began to do was to envy the doctor walking in the cool shadow of the woods with the birds about him and the pleasant smell of the pines, while I sat grilling, with my clothes stuck to the hot resin, and so much blood about me and so many poor dead bodies lying all around that I took a disgust of the place that was almost as strong as fear.

All the time I was washing out the block house, and then washing up the things from dinner, this disgust and envy kept growing stronger and stronger, till at last, being near a bread-bag, and no one then observing me, I took the first step towards my escapade and filled both pockets of my coat with biscuit.

I was a fool, if you like, and certainly I was going to do a foolish, over-bold act; but I was determined to do it with all the precautions in my power. These biscuits, should anything befall me, would keep me, at least, from starving till far on in the next day.

The next thing I laid hold of was a brace of pistols, and as I already had a powder-horn and bullets, I felt myself well supplied with arms.

As for the scheme I had in my head, it was not a bad one in itself. I was to go down the sandy spit that divides the anchorage on the east from the open sea, find the white rock I had observed last evening, and ascertain whether it was there or not that Ben Gunn had hidden his boat, a thing quite worth doing, as I still believe. But as I was certain I should not be allowed to leave the enclosure, my only plan was to take French leave and slip out when nobody was watching, and that was so bad a way of doing it as made the thing itself wrong. But I was only a boy, and I had made my mind up.

Well, as things at last fell out, I found an admirable opportunity. The squire and Gray were busy helping the captain with his bandages, the coast was clear, I made a bolt for it over the stockade and into the thickest of the trees, and before my absence was observed I was out of cry of my companions.

This was my second folly, far worse than the first, as I left but two sound men to guard the house; but like the first, it was a help towards saving all of us.

I took my way straight for the east coast of the island, for I was determined to go down the sea side of the spit to avoid all chance of observation from the anchorage. It was already late in the afternoon, although still warm and sunny. As I continued to thread the tall woods, I could hear from far before me not only the continuous thunder of the surf, but a certain tossing of foliage and grinding of boughs which showed me the sea breeze had set in higher than usual. Soon cool draughts of air began to reach me, and a few steps farther I came forth into the open borders of the grove, and saw the sea lying blue and sunny to the horizon and the surf tumbling and tossing its foam along the beach.

I have never seen the sea quiet round Treasure Island. The sun might blaze overhead, the air be without a breath, the surface smooth and blue, but still these great rollers would be running along all the external coast, thundering and thundering by day and night; and I scarce believe there is one spot in the island where a man would be out of earshot of their noise.

I walked along beside the surf with great enjoyment, till, thinking I was now got far enough to the south, I took the cover of some thick bushes and crept warily up to the ridge of the spit.

Behind me was the sea, in front the anchorage. The sea breeze, as though it had the sooner blown itself out by its unusual violence, was already at an end; it had been succeeded by light, variable airs from the south and south-east, carrying great banks of fog; and the anchorage, under lee of Skeleton Island, lay still and leaden as when first we entered it. The Hispaniola, in that unbroken mirror, was exactly portrayed from the truck to the waterline, the Jolly Roger hanging from her peak.

Alongside lay one of the gigs, Silver in the stern-sheets—him I could always recognize—while a couple of men were leaning over the stern bulwarks, one of them with a red cap—the very rogue that I had seen some hours before stride-legs upon the palisade. Apparently they were talking and laughing, though at that distance—upwards of a mile—I could, of course, hear no word of what was said. All at once there began the most horrid, unearthly screaming, which at first startled me badly, though I had soon remembered the voice of Captain Flint and even thought I could make out the bird by her bright plumage as she sat perched upon her master's wrist.

Soon after, the jolly-boat shoved off and pulled for shore, and the man with the red cap and his comrade went below by the cabin companion.

Just about the same time, the sun had gone down behind the Spy-glass, and as the fog was collecting rapidly, it began to grow dark in earnest. I saw I must lose no time if I were to find the boat that evening.

The white rock, visible enough above the brush, was still some eighth of a mile further down the spit, and it took me a goodish while to get up with it, crawling, often on all fours, among the scrub. Night had almost come when I laid my hand on its rough sides. Right below it there was an exceedingly small hollow of green turf, hidden by banks and a thick underwood about knee-deep, that grew there very plentifully; and in the centre of the dell, sure enough, a little tent of goat-skins, like what the gipsies carry about with them in England.

I dropped into the hollow, lifted the side of the tent, and there was Ben Gunn's boat—home-made if ever anything was home-made; a rude, lop-sided framework of tough wood, and stretched upon that a covering of goat-skin, with the hair inside. The thing was extremely small, even for me, and I can hardly imagine that it could have floated with a full-sized man. There was one thwart set as low as possible, a kind of stretcher in the bows, and a double paddle for propulsion.

I had not then seen a coracle, such as the ancient Britons made, but I have seen one since, and I can give you no fairer idea of Ben Gunn's boat than by saying it was like the first and the worst coracle ever made by man. But the great advantage of the coracle it certainly possessed, for it was exceedingly light and portable.

Well, now that I had found the boat, you would have thought I had had enough of truantry for once, but in the meantime I had taken another notion and become so obstinately fond of it that I would have carried it out, I believe, in the teeth of Captain Smollett himself. This was to slip out under cover of the night, cut the Hispaniola adrift, and let her go ashore where she fancied. I had quite made up my mind that the mutineers, after their repulse of the morning, had nothing nearer their hearts than to up anchor and away to sea; this, I thought, it would be a fine thing to prevent, and now that I had seen how they left their watchmen unprovided with a boat, I thought it might be done with little risk.

Down I sat to wait for darkness, and made a hearty meal of biscuit. It was a night out of ten thousand for my purpose. The fog had now buried all heaven. As the last rays of daylight dwindled and disappeared, absolute blackness settled down on Treasure Island. And when, at last, I shouldered the coracle and groped my way stumblingly out of the hollow where I had supped, there were but two points visible on the whole anchorage.

One was the great fire on shore, by which the defeated pirates lay carousing in the swamp. The other, a mere blur of light upon the darkness, indicated the position of the anchored ship. She had swung round to the ebb—her bow was now towards me—the only lights on board were in the cabin, and what I saw was merely a reflection on the fog of the strong rays that flowed from the stern window.

The ebb had already run some time, and I had to wade through a long belt of swampy sand, where I sank several times above the ankle, before I came to the edge of the retreating water, and wading a little way in, with some strength and dexterity, set my coracle, keel downwards, on the surface.

23

The Ebb-tide Runs

THE coracle—as I had ample reason to know before I was done with her—was a very safe boat for a person of my height and weight, both buoyant and clever in a seaway; but she was the most cross-grained, lop-sided craft to manage. Do as you pleased, she always made more leeway than anything else, and turning round and round was the manoeuvre she was best at. Even Ben Gunn himself has admitted that she was "queer to handle till you knew her way."

Certainly I did not know her way. She turned in every direction but the one I was bound to go; the most part of the time we were broadside on, and I am very sure I never should have made the ship at all but for the tide. By good fortune, paddle as I pleased, the tide was still sweeping me down; and there lay the Hispaniola right in the fairway, hardly to be missed.

First she loomed before me like a blot of something yet blacker than darkness, then her spars and hull began to take shape, and the next moment, as it seemed (for, the farther I went, the brisker grew the current of the ebb), I was alongside of her hawser and had laid hold.

The hawser was as taut as a bowstring, and the current so strong she pulled upon her anchor. All round the hull, in the blackness, the rippling current bubbled and chattered like a little mountain stream. One cut with my sea-gully and the Hispaniola would go humming down the tide.

So far so good, but it next occurred to my recollection that a taut hawser, suddenly cut, is a thing as dangerous as a kicking horse. Ten to one, if I were so foolhardy as to cut the Hispaniola from her anchor, I and the coracle would be knocked clean out of the water.

This brought me to a full stop, and if fortune had not again particularly favoured me, I should have had to abandon my design. But the light airs which had begun blowing from the south-east and south had hauled round after nightfall into the south-west. Just while I was meditating, a puff came, caught the Hispaniola, and forced her up into the current; and to my great joy, I felt the hawser slacken in my grasp, and the hand by which I held it dip for a second under water.

With that I made my mind up, took out my gully, opened it with my teeth, and cut one strand after another, till the vessel swung only by two. Then I lay quiet, waiting to sever these last when the strain should be once more lightened by a breath of wind.

All this time I had heard the sound of loud voices from the cabin, but to say truth, my mind had been so entirely taken up with other thoughts that I had scarcely given ear. Now, however, when I had nothing else to do, I began to pay more heed.

One I recognized for the coxswain's, Israel Hands, that had been Flint's gunner in former days. The other was, of course, my friend of the red night-cap. Both men were plainly the worse of drink, and they were still drinking, for even while I was listening, one of them, with a drunken cry, opened the stern window and threw out something, which I divined to be an empty bottle. But they were not only tipsy; it was plain that they were furiously angry. Oaths flew like hailstones, and every now and then there came forth such an explosion as I thought was sure to end in blows. But each time the quarrel passed off and the voices grumbled lower for a while, until the next crisis came and in its turn passed away without result.

On shore, I could see the glow of the great camp-fire burning warmly through the shore-side trees. Someone was singing, a dull, old, droning sailor's song, with a droop and a quaver at the end of every verse, and seemingly no end to it at all but the patience of the singer. I had heard it on the voyage more than once and remembered these words:

"But one man of her crew alive,
What put to sea with seventy-five."

And I thought it was a ditty rather too dolefully appropriate for a company that had met such cruel losses in the morning. But, indeed, from what I saw, all these buccaneers were as callous as the sea they sailed on.

At last the breeze came; the schooner sidled and drew nearer in the dark; I felt the hawser slacken once more, and with a good, tough effort, cut the last fibres through.

The breeze had but little action on the coracle, and I was almost instantly swept against the bows of the Hispaniola. At the same time, the schooner began to turn upon her heel, spinning slowly, end for end, across the current.

I wrought like a fiend, for I expected every moment to be swamped; and since I found I could not push the coracle directly off, I now shoved straight astern. At length I was clear of my dangerous neighbour, and just as I gave the last impulsion, my hands came across a light cord that was trailing overboard across the stern bulwarks. Instantly I grasped it.

Why I should have done so I can hardly say. It was at first mere instinct, but once I had it in my hands and found it fast, curiosity began to get the upper hand, and I determined I should have one look through the cabin window.

I pulled in hand over hand on the cord, and when I judged myself near enough, rose at infinite risk to about half my height and thus commanded the roof and a slice of the interior of the cabin.

By this time the schooner and her little consort were gliding pretty swiftly through the water; indeed, we had already fetched up level with the camp-fire. The ship was talking, as sailors say, loudly, treading the innumerable ripples with an incessant weltering splash; and until I got my eye above the window-sill I could not comprehend why the watchmen had taken no alarm. One glance, however, was sufficient; and it was only one glance that I durst take from that unsteady skiff. It showed me Hands and his companion locked together in deadly wrestle, each with a hand upon the other's throat.

I dropped upon the thwart again, none too soon, for I was near overboard. I could see nothing for the moment but these two furious, encrimsoned faces swaying together under the smoky lamp, and I shut my eyes to let them grow once more familiar with the darkness.

The endless ballad had come to an end at last, and the whole diminished company about the camp-fire had broken into the chorus I had heard so often:

"Fifteen men on the dead man's chest—
    Yo-ho-ho, and a bottle of rum!
Drink and the devil had done for the rest—
    Yo-ho-ho, and a bottle of rum!"

I was just thinking how busy drink and the devil were at that very moment in the cabin of the Hispaniola, when I was surprised by a sudden lurch of the coracle. At the same moment, she yawed sharply and seemed to change her course. The speed in the meantime had strangely increased.

I opened my eyes at once. All round me were little ripples, combing over with a sharp, bristling sound and slightly phosphorescent. The Hispaniola herself, a few yards in whose wake I was still being whirled along, seemed to stagger in her course, and I saw her spars toss a little against the blackness of the night; nay, as I looked longer, I made sure she also was wheeling to the southward.

I glanced over my shoulder, and my heart jumped against my ribs. There, right behind me, was the glow of the camp-fire. The current had turned at right angles, sweeping round along with it the tall schooner and the little dancing coracle; ever quickening, ever bubbling higher, ever muttering louder, it went spinning through the narrows for the open sea.

Suddenly the schooner in front of me gave a violent yaw, turning, perhaps, through twenty degrees; and almost at the same moment one shout followed another from on board; I could hear feet pounding on the companion ladder and I knew that the two drunkards had at last been interrupted in their quarrel and awakened to a sense of their disaster.

I lay down flat in the bottom of that wretched skiff and devoutly recommended my spirit to its Maker. At the end of the straits, I made sure we must fall into some bar of raging breakers, where all my troubles would be ended speedily; and though I could, perhaps, bear to die, I could not bear to look upon my fate as it approached.

So I must have lain for hours, continually beaten to and fro upon the billows, now and again wetted with flying sprays, and never ceasing to expect death at the next plunge. Gradually weariness grew upon me; a numbness, an occasional stupor, fell upon my mind even in the midst of my terrors, until sleep at last supervened and in my sea-tossed coracle I lay and dreamed of home and the old Admiral Benbow.

24
The Cruise of the Coracle

IT was broad day when I awoke and found myself tossing at the south-west end of Treasure Island. The sun was up but was still hid from me behind the great bulk of the Spy-glass, which on this side descended almost to the sea in formidable cliffs.

Haulbowline Head and Mizzen-mast Hill were at my elbow, the hill bare and dark, the head bound with cliffs forty or fifty feet high and fringed with great masses of fallen rock. I was scarce a quarter of a mile to seaward, and it was my first thought to paddle in and land.

That notion was soon given over. Among the fallen rocks the breakers spouted and bellowed; loud reverberations, heavy sprays flying and falling, succeeded one another from second to second; and I saw myself, if I ventured nearer, dashed to death upon the rough shore or spending my strength in vain to scale the beetling crags.

Nor was that all, for crawling together on flat tables of rock or letting themselves drop into the sea with loud reports I beheld huge slimy monsters—soft snails, as it were, of incredible bigness—two or three score of them together, making the rocks to echo with their barkings.

I have understood since that they were sea lions, and entirely harmless. But the look of them, added to the difficulty of the shore and the high running of the surf, was more than enough to disgust me of that landing-place. I felt willing rather to starve at sea than to confront such perils.

In the meantime I had a better chance, as I supposed, before me. North of Haulbowline Head, the land runs in a long way, leaving at low tide a long stretch of yellow sand. To the north of that, again, there comes another cape—Cape of the Woods, as it was marked upon the chart—buried in tall green pines, which descended to the margin of the sea.

I remembered what Silver had said about the current that sets northward along the whole west coast of Treasure Island, and seeing from my position that I was already under its influence, I preferred to leave Haulbowline Head behind me and reserve my strength for an attempt to land upon the kindlier-looking Cape of the Woods.

There was a great, smooth swell upon the sea. The wind blowing steady and gentle from the south, there was no contrariety between that and the current, and the billows rose and fell unbroken.

Had it been otherwise, I must long ago have perished; but as it was, it is surprising how easily and securely my little and light boat could ride. Often, as I still lay at the bottom and kept no more than an eye above the gunwale, I would see a big blue summit heaving close above me; yet the coracle would but bounce a little, dance as if on springs, and subside on the other side into the trough as lightly as a bird.

I began after a little to grow very bold and sat up to try my skill at paddling. But even a small change in the disposition of the weight will produce violent changes in the behaviour of a coracle. And I had hardly moved before the boat, giving up at once her gentle dancing movement, ran straight down a slope of water so steep that it made me giddy, and struck her nose, with a spout of spray, deep into the side of the next wave.

I was drenched and terrified, and fell instantly back into my old position, whereupon the coracle seemed to find her head again and led me as softly as before among the billows. It was plain she was not to be interfered with, and at that rate, since I could in no way influence her course, what hope had I left of reaching land?

I began to be horribly frightened, but I kept my head, for all that. First, moving with all care, I gradually baled out the coracle with my sea-cap; then, getting my eye once more above the gunwale, I set myself to study how it was she managed to slip so quietly through the rollers.

I found each wave, instead of the big, smooth glossy mountain it looks from shore or from a vessel's deck, was for all the world like any range of hills on dry land, full of peaks and smooth places and valleys. The coracle, left to herself, turning from side to side, threaded, so to speak, her way through these lower parts and avoided the steep slopes and higher, toppling summits of the wave.

"Well, now," thought I to myself, "it is plain I must lie where I am and not disturb the balance; but it is plain also that I can put the paddle over the side and from time to time, in smooth places, give her a shove or two towards land." No sooner thought upon than done. There I lay on my elbows in the most trying attitude, and every now and again gave a weak stroke or two to turn her head to shore.

It was very tiring and slow work, yet I did visibly gain ground; and as we drew near the Cape of the Woods, though I saw I must infallibly miss that point, I had still made some hundred yards of easting. I was, indeed, close in. I could see the cool green tree-tops swaying together in the breeze, and I felt sure I should make the next promontory without fail.

It was high time, for I now began to be tortured with thirst. The glow of the sun from above, its thousandfold reflection from the waves, the sea-water that fell and dried upon me, caking my very lips with salt, combined to make my throat burn and my brain ache. The sight of the trees so near at hand had almost made me sick with longing, but the current had soon carried me past the point, and as the next reach of sea opened out, I beheld a sight that changed the nature of my thoughts.

Right in front of me, not half a mile away, I beheld the Hispaniola under sail. I made sure, of course, that I should be taken; but I was so distressed for want of water that I scarce knew whether to be glad or sorry at the thought, and long before I had come to a conclusion, surprise had taken entire possession of my mind and I could do nothing but stare and wonder.

The Hispaniola was under her main-sail and two jibs, and the beautiful white canvas shone in the sun like snow or silver. When I first sighted her, all her sails were drawing; she was lying a course about north-west, and I presumed the men on board were going round the island on their way back to the anchorage. Presently she began to fetch more and more to the westward, so that I thought they had sighted me and were going about in chase. At last, however, she fell right into the wind's eye, was taken dead aback, and stood there awhile helpless, with her sails shivering.

"Clumsy fellows," said I; "they must still be drunk as owls." And I thought how Captain Smollett would have set them skipping.

Meanwhile the schooner gradually fell off and filled again upon another tack, sailed swiftly for a minute or so, and brought up once more dead in the wind's eye. Again and again was this repeated. To and fro, up and down, north, south, east, and west, the Hispaniola sailed by swoops and dashes, and at each repetition ended as she had begun, with idly flapping canvas. It became plain to me that nobody was steering. And if so, where were the men? Either they were dead drunk or had deserted her, I thought, and perhaps if I could get on board I might return the vessel to her captain.

The current was bearing coracle and schooner southward at an equal rate. As for the latter's sailing, it was so wild and intermittent, and she hung each time so long in irons, that she certainly gained nothing, if she did not even lose. If only I dared to sit up and paddle, I made sure that I could overhaul her. The scheme had an air of adventure that inspired me, and the thought of the water breaker beside the fore companion doubled my growing courage.

Up I got, was welcomed almost instantly by another cloud of spray, but this time stuck to my purpose and set myself, with all my strength and caution, to paddle after the unsteered Hispaniola. Once I shipped a sea so heavy that I had to stop and bail, with my heart fluttering like a bird, but gradually I got into the way of the thing and guided my coracle among the waves, with only now and then a blow upon her bows and a dash of foam in my face.

I was now gaining rapidly on the schooner; I could see the brass glisten on the tiller as it banged about, and still no soul appeared upon her decks. I could not choose but suppose she was deserted. If not, the men were lying drunk below, where I might batten them down, perhaps, and do what I chose with the ship.

For some time she had been doing the worse thing possible for me—standing still. She headed nearly due south, yawing, of course, all the time. Each time she fell off, her sails partly filled, and these brought her in a moment right to the wind again. I have said this was the worst thing possible for me, for helpless as she looked in this situation, with the canvas cracking like cannon and the blocks trundling and banging on the deck, she still continued to run away from me, not only with the speed of the current, but by the whole amount of her leeway, which was naturally great.

But now, at last, I had my chance. The breeze fell for some seconds, very low, and the current gradually turning her, the Hispaniola revolved slowly round her centre and at last presented me her stern, with the cabin window still gaping open and the lamp over the table still burning on into the day. The main-sail hung drooped like a banner. She was stock-still but for the current.

For the last little while I had even lost, but now redoubling my efforts, I began once more to overhaul the chase.

I was not a hundred yards from her when the wind came again in a clap; she filled on the port tack and was off again, stooping and skimming like a swallow.

My first impulse was one of despair, but my second was towards joy. Round she came, till she was broadside on to me—round still till she had covered a half and then two thirds and then three quarters of the distance that separated us. I could see the waves boiling white under her forefoot. Immensely tall she looked to me from my low station in the coracle.

And then, of a sudden, I began to comprehend. I had scarce time to think—scarce time to act and save myself. I was on the summit of one swell when the schooner came stooping over the next. The bowsprit was over my head. I sprang to my feet and leaped, stamping the coracle under water. With one hand I caught the jib-boom, while my foot was lodged between the stay and the brace; and as I still clung there panting, a dull blow told me that the schooner had charged down upon and struck the coracle and that I was left without retreat on the Hispaniola.

25

I Strike the Jolly Roger

HAD scarce gained a position on the bowsprit when the flying jib flapped and filled upon the other tack, with a report like a gun. The schooner trembled to her keel under the reverse, but next moment, the other sails still drawing, the jib flapped back again and hung idle.

This had nearly tossed me off into the sea; and now I lost no time, crawled back along the bowsprit, and tumbled head foremost on the deck.

I was on the lee side of the forecastle, and the mainsail, which was still drawing, concealed from me a certain portion of the after-deck. Not a soul was to be seen. The planks, which had not been swabbed since the mutiny, bore the print of many feet, and an empty bottle, broken by the neck, tumbled to and fro like a live thing in the scuppers.

Suddenly the Hispaniola came right into the wind. The jibs behind me cracked aloud, the rudder slammed to, the whole ship gave a sickening heave and shudder, and at the same moment the main-boom swung inboard, the sheet groaning in the blocks, and showed me the lee after-deck.

There were the two watchmen, sure enough: red-cap on his back, as stiff as a handspike, with his arms stretched out like those of a crucifix and his teeth showing through his open lips; Israel Hands propped against the bulwarks, his chin on his chest, his hands lying open before him on the deck, his face as white, under its tan, as a tallow candle.

For a while the ship kept bucking and sidling like a vicious horse, the sails filling, now on one tack, now on another, and the boom swinging to and fro till the mast groaned aloud under the strain. Now and again too there would come a cloud of light sprays over the bulwark and a heavy blow of the ship's bows against the swell; so much heavier weather was made of it by this great rigged ship than by my home-made, lop-sided coracle, now gone to the bottom of the sea.

At every jump of the schooner, red-cap slipped to and fro, but—what was ghastly to behold—neither his attitude nor his fixed teeth-disclosing grin was anyway disturbed by this rough usage. At every jump too, Hands appeared still more to sink into himself and settle down upon the deck, his feet sliding ever the farther out, and the whole body canting towards the stern, so that his face became, little by little, hid from me; and at last I could see nothing beyond his ear and the frayed ringlet of one whisker.

At the same time, I observed, around both of them, splashes of dark blood upon the planks and began to feel sure that they had killed each other in their drunken wrath.

While I was thus looking and wondering, in a calm moment, when the ship was still, Israel Hands turned partly round and with a low moan writhed himself back to the position in which I had seen him first. The moan, which told of pain and deadly weakness, and the way in which his jaw hung open went right to my heart. But when I remembered the talk I had overheard from the apple barrel, all pity left me.

I walked aft until I reached the main-mast.

"Come aboard, Mr. Hands," I said ironically.

He rolled his eyes round heavily, but he was too far gone to express surprise. All he could do was to utter one word, "Brandy."

It occurred to me there was no time to lose, and dodging the boom as it once more lurched across the deck, I slipped aft and down the companion stairs into the cabin.

It was such a scene of confusion as you can hardly fancy. All the lockfast places had been broken open in quest of the chart. The floor was thick with mud where ruffians had sat down to drink or consult after wading in the marshes round their camp. The bulkheads, all painted in clear white and beaded round with gilt, bore a pattern of dirty hands. Dozens of empty bottles clinked together in corners to the rolling of the ship. One of the doctor's medical books lay open on the table, half of the leaves gutted out, I suppose, for pipelights. In the midst of all this the lamp still cast a smoky glow, obscure and brown as umber.

I went into the cellar; all the barrels were gone, and of the bottles a most surprising number had been drunk out and thrown away. Certainly, since the mutiny began, not a man of them could ever have been sober.

Foraging about, I found a bottle with some brandy left, for Hands; and for myself I routed out some biscuit, some pickled fruits, a great bunch of raisins, and a piece of cheese. With these I came on deck, put down my own stock behind the rudder head and well out of the coxswain's reach, went forward to the water-breaker, and had a good deep drink of water, and then, and not till then, gave Hands the brandy.

He must have drunk a gill before he took the bottle from his mouth.

"Aye," said he, "by thunder, but I wanted some o' that!"

I had sat down already in my own corner and begun to eat.

"Much hurt?" I asked him.

He grunted, or rather, I might say, he barked.

"If that doctor was aboard," he said, "I'd be right enough in a couple of turns, but I don't have no manner of luck, you see, and that's what's the matter with me. As for that swab, he's good and dead, he is," he added, indicating the man with the red cap. "He warn't no seaman anyhow. And where mought you have come from?"

"Well," said I, "I've come aboard to take possession of this ship, Mr. Hands; and you'll please regard me as your captain until further notice."

He looked at me sourly enough but said nothing. Some of the colour had come back into his cheeks, though he still looked very sick and still continued to slip out and settle down as the ship banged about.

"By the by," I continued, "I can't have these colours, Mr. Hands; and by your leave, I'll strike 'em. Better none than these."

And again dodging the boom, I ran to the colour lines, handed down their cursed black flag, and chucked it overboard.

"God save the king!" said I, waving my cap. "And there's an end to Captain Silver!"

He watched me keenly and slyly, his chin all the while on his breast.

"I reckon," he said at last, "I reckon, Cap'n Hawkins, you'll kind of want to get ashore now. S'pose we talks."

"Why, yes," says I, "with all my heart, Mr. Hands. Say on." And I went back to my meal with a good appetite.

"This man," he began, nodding feebly at the corpse "—O'Brien were his name, a rank Irelander—this man and me got the canvas on her, meaning for to sail her back. Well, he's dead now, he is—as dead as bilge; and who's to sail this ship, I don't see. Without I gives you a hint, you ain't that man, as far's I can tell. Now, look here, you gives me food and drink and a old scarf or ankecher to tie my wound up, you do, and I'll tell you how to sail her, and that's about square all round, I take it."

"I'll tell you one thing," says I: "I'm not going back to Captain Kidd's anchorage. I mean to get into North Inlet and beach her quietly there."

"To be sure you did," he cried. "Why, I ain't sich an infernal lubber after all. I can see, can't I? I've tried my fling, I have, and I've lost, and it's you has the wind of me. North Inlet? Why, I haven't no ch'ice, not I! I'd help you sail her up to Execution Dock, by thunder! So I would."

Well, as it seemed to me, there was some sense in this. We struck our bargain on the spot. In three minutes I had the Hispaniola sailing easily before the wind along the coast of Treasure Island, with good hopes of turning the northern point ere noon and beating down again as far as North Inlet before high water, when we might beach her safely and wait till the subsiding tide permitted us to land.

Then I lashed the tiller and went below to my own chest, where I got a soft silk handkerchief of my mother's. With this, and with my aid, Hands bound up the great bleeding stab he had received in the thigh, and after he had eaten a little and had a swallow or two more of the brandy, he began to pick up visibly, sat straighter up, spoke louder and clearer, and looked in every way another man.

The breeze served us admirably. We skimmed before it like a bird, the coast of the island flashing by and the view changing every minute. Soon we were past the high lands and bowling beside low, sandy country, sparsely dotted with dwarf pines, and soon we were beyond that again and had turned the corner of the rocky hill that ends the island on the north.

I was greatly elated with my new command, and pleased with the bright, sunshiny weather and these different prospects of the coast. I had now plenty of water and good things to eat, and my conscience, which had smitten me hard for my desertion, was quieted by the great conquest I had made. I should, I think, have had nothing left me to desire but for the eyes of the coxswain as they followed me derisively about the deck and the odd smile that appeared continually on his face. It was a smile that had in it something both of pain and weakness—a haggard old man's smile; but there was, besides that, a grain of derision, a shadow of treachery, in his expression as he craftily watched, and watched, and watched me at my work.

26
Israel Hands

THE wind, serving us to a desire, now hauled into the west. We could run so much the easier from the north-east corner of the island to the mouth of the North Inlet. Only, as we had no power to anchor and dared not beach her till the tide had flowed a good deal farther, time hung on our hands. The coxswain told me how to lay the ship to; after a good many trials I succeeded, and we both sat in silence over another meal.

"Cap'n," said he at length with that same uncomfortable smile, "here's my old shipmate, O'Brien; s'pose you was to heave him overboard. I ain't partic'lar as a rule, and I don't take no blame for settling his hash, but I don't reckon him ornamental now, do you?"

"I'm not strong enough, and I don't like the job; and there he lies, for me," said I.

"This here's an unlucky ship, this Hispaniola, Jim," he went on, blinking. "There's a power of men been killed in this Hispaniola—a sight o' poor seamen dead and gone since you and me took ship to Bristol. I never seen sich dirty luck, not I. There was this here O'Brien now—he's dead, ain't he? Well now, I'm no scholar, and you're a lad as can read and figure, and to put it straight, do you take it as a dead man is dead for good, or do he come alive again?"

"You can kill the body, Mr. Hands, but not the spirit; you must know that already," I replied. "O'Brien there is in another world, and may be watching us."

"Ah!" says he. "Well, that's unfort'nate—appears as if killing parties was a waste of time. Howsomever, sperrits don't reckon for much, by what I've seen. I'll chance it with the sperrits, Jim. And now, you've spoke up free, and I'll take it kind if you'd step down into that there cabin and get me a—well, a—shiver my timbers! I can't hit the name on 't; well, you get me a bottle of wine, Jim—this here brandy's too strong for my head."

Now, the coxswain's hesitation seemed to be unnatural, and as for the notion of his preferring wine to brandy, I entirely disbelieved it. The whole story was a pretext. He wanted me to leave the deck—so much was plain; but with what purpose I could in no way imagine. His eyes never met mine; they kept wandering to and fro, up and down, now with a look to the sky, now with a flitting glance upon the dead O'Brien. All the time he kept smiling and putting his tongue out in the most guilty, embarrassed manner, so that a child could have told that he was bent on some deception. I was prompt with my answer, however, for I saw where my advantage lay and that with a fellow so densely stupid I could easily conceal my suspicions to the end.

"Some wine?" I said. "Far better. Will you have white or red?"

"Well, I reckon it's about the blessed same to me, shipmate," he replied; "so it's strong, and plenty of it, what's the odds?"

"All right," I answered. "I'll bring you port, Mr. Hands. But I'll have to dig for it."

With that I scuttled down the companion with all the noise I could, slipped off my shoes, ran quietly along the sparred gallery, mounted the forecastle ladder, and popped my head out of the fore companion. I knew he would not expect to see me there, yet I took every precaution possible, and certainly the worst of my suspicions proved too true.

He had risen from his position to his hands and knees, and though his leg obviously hurt him pretty sharply when he moved—for I could hear him stifle a groan—yet it was at a good, rattling rate that he trailed himself across the deck. In half a minute he had reached the port scuppers and picked, out of a coil of rope, a long knife, or rather a short dirk, discoloured to the hilt with blood. He looked upon it for a moment, thrusting forth his under jaw, tried the point upon his hand, and then, hastily concealing it in the bosom of his jacket, trundled back again into his old place against the bulwark.

This was all that I required to know. Israel could move about, he was now armed, and if he had been at so much trouble to get rid of me, it was plain that I was meant to be the victim. What he would do afterwards—whether he would try to crawl right across the island from North Inlet to the camp among the swamps or whether he would fire Long Tom, trusting that his own comrades might come first to help him—was, of course, more than I could say.

Yet I felt sure that I could trust him in one point, since in that our interests jumped together, and that was in the disposition of the schooner. We both desired to have her stranded safe enough, in a sheltered place, and so that, when the time came, she could be got off again with as little labour and danger as might be; and until that was done I considered that my life would certainly be spared.

While I was thus turning the business over in my mind, I had not been idle with my body. I had stolen back to the cabin, slipped once more into my shoes, and laid my hand at random on a bottle of wine, and now, with this for an excuse, I made my reappearance on the deck.

Hands lay as I had left him, all fallen together in a bundle and with his eyelids lowered as though he were too weak to bear the light. He looked up, however, at my coming, knocked the neck off the bottle like a man who had done the same thing often, and took a good swig, with his favourite toast of "Here's luck!" Then he lay quiet for a little, and then, pulling out a stick of tobacco, begged me to cut him a quid.

"Cut me a junk o' that," says he, "for I haven't no knife and hardly strength enough, so be as I had. Ah, Jim, Jim, I reckon I've missed stays! Cut me a quid, as'll likely be the last, lad, for I'm for my long home, and no mistake."

"Well," said I, "I'll cut you some tobacco, but if I was you and thought myself so badly, I would go to my prayers like a Christian man."

"Why?" said he. "Now, you tell me why."

"Why?" I cried. "You were asking me just now about the dead. You've broken your trust; you've lived in sin and lies and blood; there's a man you killed lying at your feet this moment, and you ask me why! For God's mercy, Mr. Hands, that's why."

I spoke with a little heat, thinking of the bloody dirk he had hidden in his pocket and designed, in his ill thoughts, to end me with. He, for his part, took a great draught of the wine and spoke with the most unusual solemnity.

"For thirty years," he said, "I've sailed the seas and seen good and bad, better and worse, fair weather and foul, provisions running out, knives going, and what not. Well, now I tell you, I never seen good come o' goodness yet. Him as strikes first is my fancy; dead men don't bite; them's my views—amen, so be it. And now, you look here," he added, suddenly changing his tone, "we've had about enough of this foolery. The tide's made good enough by now. You just take my orders, Cap'n Hawkins, and we'll sail slap in and be done with it."

All told, we had scarce two miles to run; but the navigation was delicate, the entrance to this northern anchorage was not only narrow and shoal, but lay east and west, so that the schooner must be nicely handled to be got in. I think I was a good, prompt subaltern, and I am very sure that Hands was an excellent pilot, for we went about and about and dodged in, shaving the banks, with a certainty and a neatness that were a pleasure to behold.

Scarcely had we passed the heads before the land closed around us. The shores of North Inlet were as thickly wooded as those of the southern anchorage, but the space was longer and narrower and more like, what in truth it was, the estuary of a river. Right before us, at the southern end, we saw the wreck of a ship in the last stages of dilapidation. It had been a great vessel of three masts but had lain so long exposed to the injuries of the weather that it was hung about with great webs of dripping seaweed, and on the deck of it shore bushes had taken root and now flourished thick with flowers. It was a sad sight, but it showed us that the anchorage was calm.

"Now," said Hands, "look there; there's a pet bit for to beach a ship in. Fine flat sand, never a cat's paw, trees all around of it, and flowers a-blowing like a garding on that old ship."

"And once beached," I inquired, "how shall we get her off again?"

"Why, so," he replied: "you take a line ashore there on the other side at low water, take a turn about one of them big pines; bring it back, take a turn around the capstan, and lie to for the tide. Come high water, all hands take a pull upon the line, and off she comes as sweet as natur'. And now, boy, you stand by. We're near the bit now, and she's too much way on her. Starboard a little—so—steady—starboard—larboard a little—steady—steady!"

So he issued his commands, which I breathlessly obeyed, till, all of a sudden, he cried, "Now, my hearty, luff!" And I put the helm hard up, and the Hispaniola swung round rapidly and ran stem on for the low, wooded shore.

The excitement of these last manoeuvres had somewhat interfered with the watch I had kept hitherto, sharply enough, upon the coxswain. Even then I was still so much interested, waiting for the ship to touch, that I had quite forgot the peril that hung over my head and stood craning over the starboard bulwarks and watching the ripples spreading wide before the bows. I might have fallen without a struggle for my life had not a sudden disquietude seized upon me and made me turn my head. Perhaps I had heard a creak or seen his shadow moving with the tail of my eye; perhaps it was an instinct like a cat's; but, sure enough, when I looked round, there was Hands, already half-way towards me, with the dirk in his right hand.

We must both have cried out aloud when our eyes met, but while mine was the shrill cry of terror, his was a roar of fury like a charging bully's. At the same instant, he threw himself forward and I leapt sideways towards the bows. As I did so, I let go of the tiller, which sprang sharp to leeward, and I think this saved my life, for it struck Hands across the chest and stopped him, for the moment, dead.

Before he could recover, I was safe out of the corner where he had me trapped, with all the deck to dodge about. Just forward of the main-mast I stopped, drew a pistol from my pocket, took a cool aim, though he had already turned and was once more coming directly after me, and drew the trigger. The hammer fell, but there followed neither flash nor sound; the priming was useless with sea-water. I cursed myself for my neglect. Why had not I, long before, reprimed and reloaded my only weapons? Then I should not have been as now, a mere fleeing sheep before this butcher.

Wounded as he was, it was wonderful how fast he could move, his grizzled hair tumbling over his face, and his face itself as red as a red ensign with his haste and fury. I had no time to try my other pistol, nor indeed much inclination, for I was sure it would be useless. One thing I saw plainly: I must not simply retreat before him, or he would speedily hold me boxed into the bows, as a moment since he had so nearly boxed me in the stern. Once so caught, and nine or ten inches of the blood-stained dirk would be my last experience on this side of eternity. I placed my palms against the main-mast, which was of a goodish bigness, and waited, every nerve upon the stretch.

Seeing that I meant to dodge, he also paused; and a moment or two passed in feints on his part and corresponding movements upon mine. It was such a game as I had often played at home about the rocks of Black Hill Cove, but never before, you may be sure, with such a wildly beating heart as now. Still, as I say, it was a boy's game, and I thought I could hold my own at it against an elderly seaman with a wounded thigh. Indeed my courage had begun to rise so high that I allowed myself a few darting thoughts on what would be the end of the affair, and while I saw certainly that I could spin it out for long, I saw no hope of any ultimate escape.

Well, while things stood thus, suddenly the Hispaniola struck, staggered, ground for an instant in the sand, and then, swift as a blow, canted over to the port side till the deck stood at an angle of forty-five degrees and about a puncheon of water splashed into the scupper holes and lay, in a pool, between the deck and bulwark.

We were both of us capsized in a second, and both of us rolled, almost together, into the scuppers, the dead red-cap, with his arms still spread out, tumbling stiffly after us. So near were we, indeed, that my head came against the coxswain's foot with a crack that made my teeth rattle. Blow and all, I was the first afoot again, for Hands had got involved with the dead body. The sudden canting of the ship had made the deck no place for running on; I had to find some new way of escape, and that upon the instant, for my foe was almost touching me. Quick as thought, I sprang into the mizzen shrouds, rattled up hand over hand, and did not draw a breath till I was seated on the cross-trees.

I had been saved by being prompt; the dirk had struck not half a foot below me as I pursued my upward flight; and there stood Israel Hands with his mouth open and his face upturned to mine, a perfect statue of surprise and disappointment.

Now that I had a moment to myself, I lost no time in changing the priming of my pistol, and then, having one ready for service, and to make assurance doubly sure, I proceeded to draw the load of the other and recharge it afresh from the beginning.

My new employment struck Hands all of a heap; he began to see the dice going against him, and after an obvious hesitation, he also hauled himself heavily into the shrouds, and with the dirk in his teeth, began slowly and painfully to mount. It cost him no end of time and groans to haul his wounded leg behind him, and I had quietly finished my arrangements before he was much more than a third of the way up. Then, with a pistol in either hand, I addressed him.

"One more step, Mr. Hands," said I, "and I'll blow your brains out! Dead men don't bite, you know," I added with a chuckle.

He stopped instantly. I could see by the working of his face that he was trying to think, and the process was so slow and laborious that, in my new-found security, I laughed aloud. At last, with a swallow or two, he spoke, his face still wearing the same expression of extreme perplexity. In order to speak he had to take the dagger from his mouth, but in all else he remained unmoved.

"Jim," says he, "I reckon we're fouled, you and me, and we'll have to sign articles. I'd have had you but for that there lurch, but I don't have no luck, not I; and I reckon I'll have to strike, which comes hard, you see, for a master mariner to a ship's younker like you, Jim."

I was drinking in his words and smiling away, as conceited as a cock upon a wall, when, all in a breath, back went his right hand over his shoulder. Something sang like an arrow through the air; I felt a blow and then a sharp pang, and there I was pinned by the shoulder to the mast. In the horrid pain and surprise of the moment—I scarce can say it was by my own volition, and I am sure it was without a conscious aim—both my pistols went off, and both escaped out of my hands. They did not fall alone; with a choked cry, the coxswain loosed his grasp upon the shrouds and plunged head first into the water.

27
"Pieces of Eight"

OWING to the cant of the vessel, the masts hung far out over the water, and from my perch on the cross-trees I had nothing below me but the surface of the bay. Hands, who was not so far up, was in consequence nearer to the ship and fell between me and the bulwarks. He rose once to the surface in a lather of foam and blood and then sank again for good. As the water settled, I could see him lying huddled together on the clean, bright sand in the shadow of the vessel's sides. A fish or two whipped past his body. Sometimes, by the quivering of the water, he appeared to move a little, as if he were trying to rise. But he was dead enough, for all that, being both shot and drowned, and was food for fish in the very place where he had designed my slaughter.

I was no sooner certain of this than I began to feel sick, faint, and terrified. The hot blood was running over my back and chest. The dirk, where it had pinned my shoulder to the mast, seemed to burn like a hot iron; yet it was not so much these real sufferings that distressed me, for these, it seemed to me, I could bear without a murmur; it was the horror I had upon my mind of falling from the cross-trees into that still green water, beside the body of the coxswain.

I clung with both hands till my nails ached, and I shut my eyes as if to cover up the peril. Gradually my mind came back again, my pulses quieted down to a more natural time, and I was once more in possession of myself.

It was my first thought to pluck forth the dirk, but either it stuck too hard or my nerve failed me, and I desisted with a violent shudder. Oddly enough, that very shudder did the business. The knife, in fact, had come the nearest in the world to missing me altogether; it held me by a mere pinch of skin, and this the shudder tore away. The blood ran down the faster, to be sure, but I was my own master again and only tacked to the mast by my coat and shirt.

These last I broke through with a sudden jerk, and then regained the deck by the starboard shrouds. For nothing in the world would I have again ventured, shaken as I was, upon the overhanging port shrouds from which Israel had so lately fallen.

I went below and did what I could for my wound; it pained me a good deal and still bled freely, but it was neither deep nor dangerous, nor did it greatly gall me when I used my arm. Then I looked around me, and as the ship was now, in a sense, my own, I began to think of clearing it from its last passenger—the dead man, O'Brien.

He had pitched, as I have said, against the bulwarks, where he lay like some horrible, ungainly sort of puppet, life-size, indeed, but how different from life's colour or life's comeliness! In that position I could easily have my way with him, and as the habit of tragical adventures had worn off almost all my terror for the dead, I took him by the waist as if he had been a sack of bran and with one good heave, tumbled him overboard. He went in with a sounding plunge; the red cap came off and remained floating on the surface; and as soon as the splash subsided, I could see him and Israel lying side by side, both wavering with the tremulous movement of the water. O'Brien, though still quite a young man, was very bald. There he lay, with that bald head across the knees of the man who had killed him and the quick fishes steering to and fro over both.

I was now alone upon the ship; the tide had just turned. The sun was within so few degrees of setting that already the shadow of the pines upon the western shore began to reach right across the anchorage and fall in patterns on the deck. The evening breeze had sprung up, and though it was well warded off by the hill with the two peaks upon the east, the cordage had begun to sing a little softly to itself and the idle sails to rattle to and fro.

I began to see a danger to the ship. The jibs I speedily doused and brought tumbling to the deck, but the main-sail was a harder matter. Of course, when the schooner canted over, the boom had swung out-board, and the cap of it and a foot or two of sail hung even under water. I thought this made it still more dangerous; yet the strain was so heavy that I half feared to meddle. At last I got my knife and cut the halyards. The peak dropped instantly, a great belly of loose canvas floated broad upon the water, and since, pull as I liked, I could not budge the downhall, that was the extent of what I could accomplish. For the rest, the Hispaniola must trust to luck, like myself.

By this time the whole anchorage had fallen into shadow—the last rays, I remember, falling through a glade of the wood and shining bright as jewels on the flowery mantle of the wreck. It began to be chill; the tide was rapidly fleeting seaward, the schooner settling more and more on her beam-ends.

I scrambled forward and looked over. It seemed shallow enough, and holding the cut hawser in both hands for a last security, I let myself drop softly overboard. The water scarcely reached my waist; the sand was firm and covered with ripple marks, and I waded ashore in great spirits, leaving the Hispaniola on her side, with her main-sail trailing wide upon the surface of the bay. About the same time, the sun went fairly down and the breeze whistled low in the dusk among the tossing pines.

At least, and at last, I was off the sea, nor had I returned thence empty-handed. There lay the schooner, clear at last from buccaneers and ready for our own men to board and get to sea again. I had nothing nearer my fancy than to get home to the stockade and boast of my achievements. Possibly I might be blamed a bit for my truantry, but the recapture of the Hispaniola was a clenching answer, and I hoped that even Captain Smollett would confess I had not lost my time.

So thinking, and in famous spirits, I began to set my face homeward for the block house and my companions. I remembered that the most easterly of the rivers which drain into Captain Kidd's anchorage ran from the two-peaked hill upon my left, and I bent my course in that direction that I might pass the stream while it was small. The wood was pretty open, and keeping along the lower spurs, I had soon turned the corner of that hill, and not long after waded to the mid-calf across the watercourse.

This brought me near to where I had encountered Ben Gunn, the maroon; and I walked more circumspectly, keeping an eye on every side. The dusk had come nigh hand completely, and as I opened out the cleft between the two peaks, I became aware of a wavering glow against the sky, where, as I judged, the man of the island was cooking his supper before a roaring fire. And yet I wondered, in my heart, that he should show himself so careless. For if I could see this radiance, might it not reach the eyes of Silver himself where he camped upon the shore among the marshes?

Gradually the night fell blacker; it was all I could do to guide myself even roughly towards my destination; the double hill behind me and the Spy-glass on my right hand loomed faint and fainter; the stars were few and pale; and in the low ground where I wandered I kept tripping among bushes and rolling into sandy pits.

Suddenly a kind of brightness fell about me. I looked up; a pale glimmer of moonbeams had alighted on the summit of the Spy-glass, and soon after I saw something broad and silvery moving low down behind the trees, and knew the moon had risen.

With this to help me, I passed rapidly over what remained to me of my journey, and sometimes walking, sometimes running, impatiently drew near to the stockade. Yet, as I began to thread the grove that lies before it, I was not so thoughtless but that I slacked my pace and went a trifle warily. It would have been a poor end of my adventures to get shot down by my own party in mistake.

The moon was climbing higher and higher, its light began to fall here and there in masses through the more open districts of the wood, and right in front of me a glow of a different colour appeared among the trees. It was red and hot, and now and again it was a little darkened—as it were, the embers of a bonfire smouldering.

For the life of me I could not think what it might be.

At last I came right down upon the borders of the clearing. The western end was already steeped in moonshine; the rest, and the block house itself, still lay in a black shadow chequered with long silvery streaks of light. On the other side of the house an immense fire had burned itself into clear embers and shed a steady, red reverberation, contrasted strongly with the mellow paleness of the moon. There was not a soul stirring nor a sound beside the noises of the breeze.

I stopped, with much wonder in my heart, and perhaps a little terror also. It had not been our way to build great fires; we were, indeed, by the captain's orders, somewhat niggardly of firewood, and I began to fear that something had gone wrong while I was absent.

I stole round by the eastern end, keeping close in shadow, and at a convenient place, where the darkness was thickest, crossed the palisade.

To make assurance surer, I got upon my hands and knees and crawled, without a sound, towards the corner of the house. As I drew nearer, my heart was suddenly and greatly lightened. It is not a pleasant noise in itself, and I have often complained of it at other times, but just then it was like music to hear my friends snoring together so loud and peaceful in their sleep. The sea-cry of the watch, that beautiful "All's well," never fell more reassuringly on my ear.

In the meantime, there was no doubt of one thing; they kept an infamous bad watch. If it had been Silver and his lads that were now creeping in on them, not a soul would have seen daybreak. That was what it was, thought I, to have the captain wounded; and again I blamed myself sharply for leaving them in that danger with so few to mount guard.

By this time I had got to the door and stood up. All was dark within, so that I could distinguish nothing by the eye. As for sounds, there was the steady drone of the snorers and a small occasional noise, a flickering or pecking that I could in no way account for.

With my arms before me I walked steadily in. I should lie down in my own place (I thought with a silent chuckle) and enjoy their faces when they found me in the morning.

My foot struck something yielding—it was a sleeper's leg; and he turned and groaned, but without awaking.

And then, all of a sudden, a shrill voice broke forth out of the darkness:

"Pieces of eight! Pieces of eight! Pieces of eight! Pieces of eight! Pieces of eight!" and so forth, without pause or change, like the clacking of a tiny mill.

Silver's green parrot, Captain Flint! It was she whom I had heard pecking at a piece of bark; it was she, keeping better watch than any human being, who thus announced my arrival with her wearisome refrain.

I had no time left me to recover. At the sharp, clipping tone of the parrot, the sleepers awoke and sprang up; and with a mighty oath, the voice of Silver cried, "Who goes?"

I turned to run, struck violently against one person, recoiled, and ran full into the arms of a second, who for his part closed upon and held me tight.

"Bring a torch, Dick," said Silver when my capture was thus assured.

And one of the men left the log-house and presently returned with a lighted brand.

PART SIX—Captain Silver

28

In the Enemy's Camp

THE red glare of the torch, lighting up the interior of the block house, showed me the worst of my apprehensions realized. The pirates were in possession of the house and stores: there was the cask of cognac, there were the pork and bread, as before, and what tenfold increased my horror, not a sign of any prisoner. I could only judge that all had perished, and my heart smote me sorely that I had not been there to perish with them.

There were six of the buccaneers, all told; not another man was left alive. Five of them were on their feet, flushed and swollen, suddenly called out of the first sleep of drunkenness. The sixth had only risen upon his elbow; he was deadly pale, and the blood-stained bandage round his head told that he had recently been wounded, and still more recently dressed. I remembered the man who had been shot and had run back among the woods in the great attack, and doubted not that this was he.

The parrot sat, preening her plumage, on Long John's shoulder. He himself, I thought, looked somewhat paler and more stern than I was used to. He still wore the fine broadcloth suit in which he had fulfilled his mission, but it was bitterly the worse for wear, daubed with clay and torn with the sharp briers of the wood.

"So," said he, "here's Jim Hawkins, shiver my timbers! Dropped in, like, eh? Well, come, I take that friendly."

And thereupon he sat down across the brandy cask and began to fill a pipe.

"Give me a loan of the link, Dick," said he; and then, when he had a good light, "That'll do, lad," he added; "stick the glim in the wood heap; and you, gentlemen, bring yourselves to! You needn't stand up for Mr. Hawkins; he'll excuse you, you may lay to that. And so, Jim"—stopping the tobacco—"here you were, and quite a pleasant surprise for poor old John. I see you were smart when first I set my eyes on you, but this here gets away from me clean, it do."

To all this, as may be well supposed, I made no answer. They had set me with my back against the wall, and I stood there, looking Silver in the face, pluckily enough, I hope, to all outward appearance, but with black despair in my heart.

Silver took a whiff or two of his pipe with great composure and then ran on again.

"Now, you see, Jim, so be as you are here," says he, "I'll give you a piece of my mind. I've always liked you, I have, for a lad of spirit, and the picter of my own self when I was young and handsome. I always wanted you to jine and take your share, and die a gentleman, and now, my cock, you've got to. Cap'n Smollett's a fine seaman, as I'll own up to any day, but stiff on discipline. 'Dooty is dooty,' says he, and right he is. Just you keep clear of the cap'n. The doctor himself is gone dead again you—'ungrateful scamp' was what he said; and the short and the long of the whole story is about here: you can't go back to your own lot, for they won't have you; and without you start a third ship's company all by yourself, which might be lonely, you'll have to jine with Cap'n Silver."

So far so good. My friends, then, were still alive, and though I partly believed the truth of Silver's statement, that the cabin party were incensed at me for my desertion, I was more relieved than distressed by what I heard.

"I don't say nothing as to your being in our hands," continued Silver, "though there you are, and you may lay to it. I'm all for argyment; I never seen good come out o' threatening. If you like the service, well, you'll jine; and if you don't, Jim, why, you're free to answer no—free and welcome, shipmate; and if fairer can be said by mortal seaman, shiver my sides!"

"Am I to answer, then?" I asked with a very tremulous voice. Through all this sneering talk, I was made to feel the threat of death that overhung me, and my cheeks burned and my heart beat painfully in my breast.

"Lad," said Silver, "no one's a-pressing of you. Take your bearings. None of us won't hurry you, mate; time goes so pleasant in your company, you see."

"Well," says I, growing a bit bolder, "if I'm to choose, I declare I have a right to know what's what, and why you're here, and where my friends are."

"Wot's wot?" repeated one of the buccaneers in a deep growl. "Ah, he'd be a lucky one as knowed that!"

"You'll perhaps batten down your hatches till you're spoke to, my friend," cried Silver truculently to this speaker. And then, in his first gracious tones, he replied to me, "Yesterday morning, Mr. Hawkins," said he, "in the dog-watch, down came Doctor Livesey with a flag of truce. Says he, 'Cap'n Silver, you're sold out. Ship's gone.' Well, maybe we'd been taking a glass, and a song to help it round. I won't say no. Leastways, none of us had looked out. We looked out, and by thunder, the old ship was gone! I never seen a pack o' fools look fishier; and you may lay to that, if I tells you that looked the fishiest. 'Well,' says the doctor, 'let's bargain.' We bargained, him and I, and here we are: stores, brandy, block house, the firewood you was thoughtful enough to cut, and in a manner of speaking, the whole blessed boat, from cross-trees to kelson. As for them, they've tramped; I don't know where's they are."

He drew again quietly at his pipe.

"And lest you should take it into that head of yours," he went on, "that you was included in the treaty, here's the last word that was said: 'How many are you,' says I, 'to leave?' 'Four,' says he; 'four, and one of us wounded. As for that boy, I don't know where he is, confound him,' says he, 'nor I don't much care. We're about sick of him.' These was his words."

"Is that all?" I asked.

"Well, it's all that you're to hear, my son," returned Silver.

"And now I am to choose?"

"And now you are to choose, and you may lay to that," said Silver.

"Well," said I, "I am not such a fool but I know pretty well what I have to look for. Let the worst come to the worst, it's little I care. I've seen too many die since I fell in with you. But there's a thing or two I have to tell you," I said, and by this time I was quite excited; "and the first is this: here you are, in a bad way—ship lost, treasure lost, men lost, your whole business gone to wreck; and if you want to know who did it—it was I! I was in the apple barrel the night we sighted land, and I heard you, John, and you, Dick Johnson, and Hands, who is now at the bottom of the sea, and told every word you said before the hour was out. And as for the schooner, it was I who cut her cable, and it was I that killed the men you had aboard of her, and it was I who brought her where you'll never see her more, not one of you. The laugh's on my side; I've had the top of this business from the first; I no more fear you than I fear a fly. Kill me, if you please, or spare me. But one thing I'll say, and no more; if you spare me, bygones are bygones, and when you fellows are in court for piracy, I'll save you all I can. It is for you to choose. Kill another and do yourselves no good, or spare me and keep a witness to save you from the gallows."

I stopped, for, I tell you, I was out of breath, and to my wonder, not a man of them moved, but all sat staring at me like as many sheep. And while they were still staring, I broke out again, "And now, Mr. Silver," I said, "I believe you're the best man here, and if things go to the worst, I'll take it kind of you to let the doctor know the way I took it."

"I'll bear it in mind," said Silver with an accent so curious that I could not, for the life of me, decide whether he were laughing at my request or had been favourably affected by my courage.

"I'll put one to that," cried the old mahogany-faced seaman—Morgan by name—whom I had seen in Long John's public-house upon the quays of Bristol. "It was him that knowed Black Dog."

"Well, and see here," added the sea-cook. "I'll put another again to that, by thunder! For it was this same boy that faked the chart from Billy Bones. First and last, we've split upon Jim Hawkins!"

"Then here goes!" said Morgan with an oath.

And he sprang up, drawing his knife as if he had been twenty.

"Avast, there!" cried Silver. "Who are you, Tom Morgan? Maybe you thought you was cap'n here, perhaps. By the powers, but I'll teach you better! Cross me, and you'll go where many a good man's gone before you, first and last, these thirty year back—some to the yard-arm, shiver my timbers, and some by the board, and all to feed the fishes. There's never a man looked me between the eyes and seen a good day a'terwards, Tom Morgan, you may lay to that."

Morgan paused, but a hoarse murmur rose from the others.

"Tom's right," said one.

"I stood hazing long enough from one," added another. "I'll be hanged if I'll be hazed by you, John Silver."

"Did any of you gentlemen want to have it out with me?" roared Silver, bending far forward from his position on the keg, with his pipe still glowing in his right hand. "Put a name on what you're at; you ain't dumb, I reckon. Him that wants shall get it. Have I lived this many years, and a son of a rum puncheon cock his hat athwart my hawse at the latter end of it? You know the way; you're all gentlemen o' fortune, by your account. Well, I'm ready. Take a cutlass, him that dares, and I'll see the colour of his inside, crutch and all, before that pipe's empty."

Not a man stirred; not a man answered.

"That's your sort, is it?" he added, returning his pipe to his mouth. "Well, you're a gay lot to look at, anyway. Not much worth to fight, you ain't. P'r'aps you can understand King George's English. I'm cap'n here by 'lection. I'm cap'n here because I'm the best man by a long sea-mile. You won't fight, as gentlemen o' fortune should; then, by thunder, you'll obey, and you may lay to it! I like that boy, now; I never seen a better boy than that. He's more a man than any pair of rats of you in this here house, and what I say is this: let me see him that'll lay a hand on him—that's what I say, and you may lay to it."

There was a long pause after this. I stood straight up against the wall, my heart still going like a sledge-hammer, but with a ray of hope now shining in my bosom. Silver leant back against the wall, his arms crossed, his pipe in the corner of his mouth, as calm as though he had been in church; yet his eye kept wandering furtively, and he kept the tail of it on his unruly followers. They, on their part, drew gradually together towards the far end of the block house, and the low hiss of their whispering sounded in my ear continuously, like a stream. One after another, they would look up, and the red light of the torch would fall for a second on their nervous faces; but it was not towards me, it was towards Silver that they turned their eyes.

"You seem to have a lot to say," remarked Silver, spitting far into the air. "Pipe up and let me hear it, or lay to."

"Ax your pardon, sir," returned one of the men; "you're pretty free with some of the rules; maybe you'll kindly keep an eye upon the rest. This crew's dissatisfied; this crew don't vally bullying a marlin-spike; this crew has its rights like other crews, I'll make so free as that; and by your own rules, I take it we can talk together. I ax your pardon, sir, acknowledging you for to be captaing at this present; but I claim my right, and steps outside for a council."

And with an elaborate sea-salute, this fellow, a long, ill-looking, yellow-eyed man of five and thirty, stepped coolly towards the door and disappeared out of the house. One after another the rest followed his example, each making a salute as he passed, each adding some apology. "According to rules," said one. "Forecastle council," said Morgan. And so with one remark or another all marched out and left Silver and me alone with the torch.

The sea-cook instantly removed his pipe.

"Now, look you here, Jim Hawkins," he said in a steady whisper that was no more than audible, "you're within half a plank of death, and what's a long sight worse, of torture. They're going to throw me off. But, you mark, I stand by you through thick and thin. I didn't mean to; no, not till you spoke up. I was about desperate to lose that much blunt, and be hanged into the bargain. But I see you was the right sort. I says to myself, you stand by Hawkins, John, and Hawkins'll stand by you. You're his last card, and by the living thunder, John, he's yours! Back to back, says I. You save your witness, and he'll save your neck!"

I began dimly to understand.

"You mean all's lost?" I asked.

"Aye, by gum, I do!" he answered. "Ship gone, neck gone—that's the size of it. Once I looked into that bay, Jim Hawkins, and seen no schooner—well, I'm tough, but I gave out. As for that lot and their council, mark me, they're outright fools and cowards. I'll save your life—if so be as I can—from them. But, see here, Jim—tit for tat—you save Long John from swinging."

I was bewildered; it seemed a thing so hopeless he was asking—he, the old buccaneer, the ringleader throughout.

"What I can do, that I'll do," I said.

"It's a bargain!" cried Long John. "You speak up plucky, and by thunder, I've a chance!"

He hobbled to the torch, where it stood propped among the firewood, and took a fresh light to his pipe.

"Understand me, Jim," he said, returning. "I've a head on my shoulders, I have. I'm on squire's side now. I know you've got that ship safe somewheres. How you done it, I don't know, but safe it is. I guess Hands and O'Brien turned soft. I never much believed in neither of them. Now you mark me. I ask no questions, nor I won't let others. I know when a game's up, I do; and I know a lad that's staunch. Ah, you that's young—you and me might have done a power of good together!"

He drew some cognac from the cask into a tin cannikin.

"Will you taste, messmate?" he asked; and when I had refused: "Well, I'll take a dram myself, Jim," said he. "I need a caulker, for there's trouble on hand. And talking o' trouble, why did that doctor give me the chart, Jim?"

My face expressed a wonder so unaffected that he saw the needlessness of further questions.

"Ah, well, he did, though," said he. "And there's something under that, no doubt—something, surely, under that, Jim—bad or good."

And he took another swallow of the brandy, shaking his great fair head like a man who looks forward to the worst.

29

The Black Spot Again

THE council of buccaneers had lasted some time, when one of them re-entered the house, and with a repetition of the same salute, which had in my eyes an ironical air, begged for a moment's loan of the torch. Silver briefly agreed, and this emissary retired again, leaving us together in the dark.

"There's a breeze coming, Jim," said Silver, who had by this time adopted quite a friendly and familiar tone.

I turned to the loophole nearest me and looked out. The embers of the great fire had so far burned themselves out and now glowed so low and duskily that I understood why these conspirators desired a torch. About half-way down the slope to the stockade, they were collected in a group; one held the light, another was on his knees in their midst, and I saw the blade of an open knife shine in his hand with varying colours in the moon and torchlight. The rest were all somewhat stooping, as though watching the manoeuvres of this last. I could just make out that he had a book as well as a knife in his hand, and was still wondering how anything so incongruous had come in their possession when the kneeling figure rose once more to his feet and the whole party began to move together towards the house.

"Here they come," said I; and I returned to my former position, for it seemed beneath my dignity that they should find me watching them.

"Well, let 'em come, lad—let 'em come," said Silver cheerily. "I've still a shot in my locker."

The door opened, and the five men, standing huddled together just inside, pushed one of their number forward. In any other circumstances it would have been comical to see his slow advance, hesitating as he set down each foot, but holding his closed right hand in front of him.

"Step up, lad," cried Silver. "I won't eat you. Hand it over, lubber. I know the rules, I do; I won't hurt a depytation."

Thus encouraged, the buccaneer stepped forth more briskly, and having passed something to Silver, from hand to hand, slipped yet more smartly back again to his companions.

The sea-cook looked at what had been given him.

"The black spot! I thought so," he observed. "Where might you have got the paper? Why, hillo! Look here, now; this ain't lucky! You've gone and cut this out of a Bible. What fool's cut a Bible?"

"Ah, there!" said Morgan. "There! Wot did I say? No good'll come o' that, I said."

"Well, you've about fixed it now, among you," continued Silver. "You'll all swing now, I reckon. What soft-headed lubber had a Bible?"

"It was Dick," said one.

"Dick, was it? Then Dick can get to prayers," said Silver. "He's seen his slice of luck, has Dick, and you may lay to that."

But here the long man with the yellow eyes struck in.

"Belay that talk, John Silver," he said. "This crew has tipped you the black spot in full council, as in dooty bound; just you turn it over, as in dooty bound, and see what's wrote there. Then you can talk."

"Thanky, George," replied the sea-cook. "You always was brisk for business, and has the rules by heart, George, as I'm pleased to see. Well, what is it, anyway? Ah! 'Deposed'—that's it, is it? Very pretty wrote, to be sure; like print, I swear. Your hand o' write, George? Why, you was gettin' quite a leadin' man in this here crew. You'll be cap'n next, I shouldn't wonder. Just oblige me with that torch again, will you? This pipe don't draw."

"Come, now," said George, "you don't fool this crew no more. You're a funny man, by your account; but you're over now, and you'll maybe step down off that barrel and help vote."

"I thought you said you knowed the rules," returned Silver contemptuously. "Leastways, if you don't, I do; and I wait here—and I'm still your cap'n, mind—till you outs with your grievances and I reply; in the meantime, your black spot ain't worth a biscuit. After that, we'll see."

"Oh," replied George, "you don't be under no kind of apprehension; we're all square, we are. First, you've made a hash of this cruise—you'll be a bold man to say no to that. Second, you let the enemy out o' this here trap for nothing. Why did they want out? I dunno, but it's pretty plain they wanted it. Third, you wouldn't let us go at them upon the march. Oh, we see through you, John Silver; you want to play booty, that's what's wrong with you. And then, fourth, there's this here boy."

"Is that all?" asked Silver quietly.

"Enough, too," retorted George. "We'll all swing and sun-dry for your bungling."

"Well now, look here, I'll answer these four p'ints; one after another I'll answer 'em. I made a hash o' this cruise, did I? Well now, you all know what I wanted, and you all know if that had been done that we'd 'a been aboard the Hispaniola this night as ever was, every man of us alive, and fit, and full of good plum-duff, and the treasure in the hold of her, by thunder! Well, who crossed me? Who forced my hand, as was the lawful cap'n? Who tipped me the black spot the day we landed and began this dance? Ah, it's a fine dance—I'm with you there—and looks mighty like a hornpipe in a rope's end at Execution Dock by London town, it does. But who done it? Why, it was Anderson, and Hands, and you, George Merry! And you're the last above board of that same meddling crew; and you have the Davy Jones's insolence to up and stand for cap'n over me—you, that sank the lot of us! By the powers! But this tops the stiffest yarn to nothing."

Silver paused, and I could see by the faces of George and his late comrades that these words had not been said in vain.

"That's for number one," cried the accused, wiping the sweat from his brow, for he had been talking with a vehemence that shook the house. "Why, I give you my word, I'm sick to speak to you. You've neither sense nor memory, and I leave it to fancy where your mothers was that let you come to sea. Sea! Gentlemen o' fortune! I reckon tailors is your trade."

"Go on, John," said Morgan. "Speak up to the others."

"Ah, the others!" returned John. "They're a nice lot, ain't they? You say this cruise is bungled. Ah! By gum, if you could understand how bad it's bungled, you would see! We're that near the gibbet that my neck's stiff with thinking on it. You've seen 'em, maybe, hanged in chains, birds about 'em, seamen p'inting 'em out as they go down with the tide. 'Who's that?' says one.

'That! Why, that's John Silver. I knowed him well,' says another. And you can hear the chains a-jangle as you go about and reach for the other buoy. Now, that's about where we are, every mother's son of us, thanks to him, and Hands, and Anderson, and other ruination fools of you. And if you want to know about number four, and that boy, why, shiver my timbers, isn't he a hostage? Are we a-going to waste a hostage? No, not us; he might be our last chance, and I shouldn't wonder. Kill that boy? Not me, mates! And number three? Ah, well, there's a deal to say to number three. Maybe you don't count it nothing to have a real college doctor to see you every day—you, John, with your head broke—or you, George Merry, that had the ague shakes upon you not six hours agone, and has your eyes the colour of lemon peel to this same moment on the clock? And maybe, perhaps, you didn't know there was a consort coming either? But there is, and not so long till then; and we'll see who'll be glad to have a hostage when it comes to that. And as for number two, and why I made a bargain—well, you came crawling on your knees to me to make it—on your knees you came, you was that downhearted—and you'd have starved too if I hadn't—but that's a trifle! You look there—that's why!"

And he cast down upon the floor a paper that I instantly recognized—none other than the chart on yellow paper, with the three red crosses, that I had found in the oilcloth at the bottom of the captain's chest. Why the doctor had given it to him was more than I could fancy.

But if it were inexplicable to me, the appearance of the chart was incredible to the surviving mutineers. They leaped upon it like cats upon a mouse. It went from hand to hand, one tearing it from another; and by the oaths and the cries and the childish laughter with which they accompanied their examination, you would have thought, not only they were fingering the very gold, but were at sea with it, besides, in safety.

"Yes," said one, "that's Flint, sure enough. J. F., and a score below, with a clove hitch to it; so he done ever."

"Mighty pretty," said George. "But how are we to get away with it, and us no ship."

Silver suddenly sprang up, and supporting himself with a hand against the wall: "Now I give you warning, George," he cried. "One more word of your sauce, and I'll call you down and fight you. How? Why, how do I know? You had ought to tell me that—you and the rest, that lost me my schooner, with your interference, burn you! But not you, you can't; you hain't got the invention of a cockroach. But civil you can speak, and shall, George Merry, you may lay to that."

"That's fair enow," said the old man Morgan.

"Fair! I reckon so," said the sea-cook. "You lost the ship; I found the treasure. Who's the better man at that? And now I resign, by thunder! Elect whom you please to be your cap'n now; I'm done with it."

"Silver!" they cried. "Barbecue forever! Barbecue for cap'n!"

"So that's the toon, is it?" cried the cook. "George, I reckon you'll have to wait another turn, friend; and lucky for you as I'm not a revengeful man. But that was never my way. And now, shipmates, this black spot? 'Tain't much good now, is it? Dick's crossed his luck and spoiled his Bible, and that's about all."

"It'll do to kiss the book on still, won't it?" growled Dick, who was evidently uneasy at the curse he had brought upon himself.

"A Bible with a bit cut out!" returned Silver derisively. "Not it. It don't bind no more'n a ballad-book."

"Don't it, though?" cried Dick with a sort of joy. "Well, I reckon that's worth having too."

"Here, Jim—here's a cur'osity for you," said Silver, and he tossed me the paper.

It was around about the size of a crown piece. One side was blank, for it had been the last leaf; the other contained a verse or two of Revelation—these words among the rest, which struck sharply home upon my mind: "Without are dogs and murderers." The printed side had been blackened with wood ash, which already began to come off and soil my fingers; on the blank side had been written with the same material the one word "Depposed." I have that curiosity beside me at this moment, but not a trace of writing now remains beyond a single scratch, such as a man might make with his thumb-nail.

That was the end of the night's business. Soon after, with a drink all round, we lay down to sleep, and the outside of Silver's vengeance was to put George Merry up for sentinel and threaten him with death if he should prove unfaithful.

It was long ere I could close an eye, and heaven knows I had matter enough for thought in the man whom I had slain that afternoon, in my own most perilous position, and above all, in the remarkable game that I saw Silver now engaged upon—keeping the mutineers together with one hand and grasping with the other after every means, possible and impossible, to make his peace and save his miserable life. He himself slept peacefully and snored aloud, yet my heart was sore for him, wicked as he was, to think on the dark perils that environed and the shameful gibbet that awaited him.

30

On Parole

I WAS wakened—indeed, we were all wakened, for I could see even the sentinel shake himself together from where he had fallen against the door-post—by a clear, hearty voice hailing us from the margin of the wood:

"Block house, ahoy!" it cried. "Here's the doctor."

And the doctor it was. Although I was glad to hear the sound, yet my gladness was not without admixture. I remembered with confusion my insubordinate and stealthy conduct, and when I saw where it had brought me—among what companions and surrounded by what dangers—I felt ashamed to look him in the face.

He must have risen in the dark, for the day had hardly come; and when I ran to a loophole and looked out, I saw him standing, like Silver once before, up to the mid-leg in creeping vapour.

"You, doctor! Top o' the morning to you, sir!" cried Silver, broad awake and beaming with good nature in a moment. "Bright and early, to be sure; and it's the early bird, as the saying goes, that gets the rations. George, shake up your timbers, son, and help Dr. Livesey over the ship's side. All a-doin' well, your patients was—all well and merry."

So he pattered on, standing on the hilltop with his crutch under his elbow and one hand upon the side of the log-house—quite the old John in voice, manner, and expression.

"We've quite a surprise for you too, sir," he continued. "We've a little stranger here—he! he! A noo boarder and lodger, sir, and looking fit and taut as a fiddle; slep' like a supercargo, he did, right alongside of John—stem to stem we was, all night."

Dr. Livesey was by this time across the stockade and pretty near the cook, and I could hear the alteration in his voice as he said, "Not Jim?"

"The very same Jim as ever was," says Silver.

The doctor stopped outright, although he did not speak, and it was some seconds before he seemed able to move on.

"Well, well," he said at last, "duty first and pleasure afterwards, as you might have said yourself, Silver. Let us overhaul these patients of yours."

A moment afterwards he had entered the block house and with one grim nod to me proceeded with his work among the sick. He seemed under no apprehension, though he must have known that his life, among these treacherous demons, depended on a hair; and he rattled on to his patients as if he were paying an ordinary professional visit in a quiet English family. His manner, I suppose, reacted on the men, for they behaved to him as if nothing had occurred, as if he were still ship's doctor and they still faithful hands before the mast.

"You're doing well, my friend," he said to the fellow with the bandaged head, "and if ever any person had a close shave, it was you; your head must be as hard as iron. Well, George, how goes it? You're a pretty colour, certainly; why, your liver, man, is upside down. Did you take that medicine? Did he take that medicine, men?"

"Aye, aye, sir, he took it, sure enough," returned Morgan.

"Because, you see, since I am mutineers' doctor, or prison doctor as I prefer to call it," says Doctor Livesey in his pleasantest way, "I make it a point of honour not to lose a man for King George (God bless him!) and the gallows."

The rogues looked at each other but swallowed the home-thrust in silence.

"Dick don't feel well, sir," said one.

"Don't he?" replied the doctor. "Well, step up here, Dick, and let me see your tongue. No, I should be surprised if he did! The man's tongue is fit to frighten the French. Another fever."

"Ah, there," said Morgan, "that comed of sp'iling Bibles."

"That comes—as you call it—of being arrant asses," retorted the doctor, "and not having sense enough to know honest air from poison, and the dry land from a vile, pestiferous slough. I think it most probable—though of course it's only an opinion—that you'll all have the deuce to pay before you get that malaria out of your systems. Camp in a bog, would you? Silver, I'm surprised at you. You're less of a fool than many, take you all round; but you don't appear to me to have the rudiments of a notion of the rules of health.

"Well," he added after he had dosed them round and they had taken his prescriptions, with really laughable humility, more like charity schoolchildren than blood-guilty mutineers and pirates—"well, that's done for today. And now I should wish to have a talk with that boy, please."

And he nodded his head in my direction carelessly.

George Merry was at the door, spitting and spluttering over some bad-tasted medicine; but at the first word of the doctor's proposal he swung round with a deep flush and cried "No!" and swore.

Silver struck the barrel with his open hand.

"Si-lence!" he roared and looked about him positively like a lion. "Doctor," he went on in his usual tones, "I was a-thinking of that, knowing as how you had a fancy for the boy. We're all humbly grateful for your kindness, and as you see, puts faith in you and takes the drugs down like that much grog. And I take it I've found a way as'll suit all. Hawkins, will you give me your word of honour as a young gentleman—for a young gentleman you are, although poor born—your word of honour not to slip your cable?"

I readily gave the pledge required.

"Then, doctor," said Silver, "you just step outside o' that stockade, and once you're there I'll bring the boy down on the inside, and I reckon you can yarn through the spars. Good day to you, sir, and all our dooties to the squire and Cap'n Smollett."

The explosion of disapproval, which nothing but Silver's black looks had restrained, broke out immediately the doctor had left the house. Silver was roundly accused of playing double—of trying to make a separate peace for himself, of sacrificing the interests of his accomplices and victims, and, in one word, of the identical, exact thing that he was doing. It seemed to me so obvious, in this case, that I could not imagine how he was to turn their anger. But he was twice the man the rest were, and his last night's victory had given him a huge preponderance on their minds. He called them all the fools and dolts you can imagine, said it was necessary I should talk to the doctor, fluttered the chart in their faces, asked them if they could afford to break the treaty the very day they were bound a-treasure-hunting.

"No, by thunder!" he cried. "It's us must break the treaty when the time comes; and till then I'll gammon that doctor, if I have to ile his boots with brandy."

And then he bade them get the fire lit, and stalked out upon his crutch, with his hand on my shoulder, leaving them in a disarray, and silenced by his volubility rather than convinced.

"Slow, lad, slow," he said. "They might round upon us in a twinkle of an eye if we was seen to hurry."

Very deliberately, then, did we advance across the sand to where the doctor awaited us on the other side of the stockade, and as soon as we were within easy speaking distance Silver stopped.

"You'll make a note of this here also, doctor," says he, "and the boy'll tell you how I saved his life, and were deposed for it too, and you may lay to that. Doctor, when a man's steering as near the wind as me—playing chuck-farthing with the last breath in his body, like—you wouldn't think it too much, mayhap, to give him one good word? You'll please bear in mind it's not my life only now—it's that boy's into the bargain; and you'll speak me fair, doctor, and give me a bit o' hope to go on, for the sake of mercy."

Silver was a changed man once he was out there and had his back to his friends and the block house; his cheeks seemed to have fallen in, his voice trembled; never was a soul more dead in earnest.

"Why, John, you're not afraid?" asked Dr. Livesey.

"Doctor, I'm no coward; no, not I—not so much!" and he snapped his fingers. "If I was I wouldn't say it. But I'll own up fairly, I've the shakes upon me for the gallows. You're a good man and a true; I never seen a better man! And you'll not forget what I done good, not any more than you'll forget the bad, I know. And I step aside—see here—and leave you and Jim alone. And you'll put that down for me too, for it's a long stretch, is that!"

So saying, he stepped back a little way, till he was out of earshot, and there sat down upon a tree-stump and began to whistle, spinning round now and again upon his seat so as to command a sight, sometimes of me and the doctor and sometimes of his unruly ruffians as they went to and fro in the sand between the fire—which they were busy rekindling—and the house, from which they brought forth pork and bread to make the breakfast.

"So, Jim," said the doctor sadly, "here you are. As you have brewed, so shall you drink, my boy. Heaven knows, I cannot find it in my heart to blame you, but this much I will say, be it kind or unkind: when Captain Smollett was well, you dared not have gone off; and when he was ill and couldn't help it, by George, it was downright cowardly!"

I will own that I here began to weep. "Doctor," I said, "you might spare me. I have blamed myself enough; my life's forfeit anyway, and I should have been dead by now if Silver hadn't stood for me; and doctor, believe this, I can die—and I dare say I deserve it—but what I fear is torture. If they come to torture me—"

"Jim," the doctor interrupted, and his voice was quite changed, "Jim, I can't have this. Whip over, and we'll run for it."

"Doctor," said I, "I passed my word."

"I know, I know," he cried. "We can't help that, Jim, now. I'll take it on my shoulders, holus bolus, blame and shame, my boy; but stay here, I cannot let you. Jump! One jump, and you're out, and we'll run for it like antelopes."

"No," I replied; "you know right well you wouldn't do the thing yourself—neither you nor squire nor captain; and no more will I. Silver trusted me; I passed my word, and back I go. But, doctor, you did not let me finish. If they come to torture me, I might let slip a word of where the ship is, for I got the ship, part by luck and part by risking, and she lies in North Inlet, on the southern beach, and just below high water. At half tide she must be high and dry."

"The ship!" exclaimed the doctor.

Rapidly I described to him my adventures, and he heard me out in silence.

"There is a kind of fate in this," he observed when I had done. "Every step, it's you that saves our lives; and do you suppose by any chance that we are going to let you lose yours? That would be a poor return, my boy. You found out the plot; you found Ben Gunn—the best deed that ever you did, or will do, though you live to ninety. Oh, by Jupiter, and talking of Ben Gunn! Why, this is the mischief in person. Silver!" he cried. "Silver! I'll give you a piece of advice," he continued as the cook drew near again; "don't you be in any great hurry after that treasure."

"Why, sir, I do my possible, which that ain't," said Silver. "I can only, asking your pardon, save my life and the boy's by seeking for that treasure; and you may lay to that."

"Well, Silver," replied the doctor, "if that is so, I'll go one step further: look out for squalls when you find it."

"Sir," said Silver, "as between man and man, that's too much and too little. What you're after, why you left the block house, why you given me that there chart, I don't know, now, do I? And yet I done your bidding with my eyes shut and never a word of hope! But no, this here's too much. If you won't tell me what you mean plain out, just say so and I'll leave the helm."

"No," said the doctor musingly; "I've no right to say more; it's not my secret, you see, Silver, or, I give you my word, I'd tell it you. But I'll go as far with you as I dare go, and a step beyond, for I'll have my wig sorted by the captain or I'm mistaken! And first, I'll give you a bit of hope; Silver, if we both get alive out of this wolf-trap, I'll do my best to save you, short of perjury."

Silver's face was radiant. "You couldn't say more, I'm sure, sir, not if you was my mother," he cried.

"Well, that's my first concession," added the doctor. "My second is a piece of advice: keep the boy close beside you, and when you need help, halloo. I'm off to seek it for you, and that itself will show you if I speak at random. Good-bye, Jim."

And Dr. Livesey shook hands with me through the stockade, nodded to Silver, and set off at a brisk pace into the wood.

31

The Treasure-hunt—Flint's Pointer

JIM," said Silver when we were alone, "if I saved your life, you saved mine; and I'll not forget it. I seen the doctor waving you to run for it—with the tail of my eye, I did; and I seen you say no, as plain as hearing. Jim, that's one to you. This is the first glint of hope I had since the attack failed, and I owe it you. And now, Jim, we're to go in for this here treasure-hunting, with sealed orders too, and I don't like it; and you and me must stick close, back to back like, and we'll save our necks in spite o' fate and fortune."

Just then a man hailed us from the fire that breakfast was ready, and we were soon seated here and there about the sand over biscuit and fried junk. They had lit a fire fit to roast an ox, and it was now grown so hot that they could only approach it from the windward, and even there not without precaution. In the same wasteful spirit, they had cooked, I suppose, three times more than we could eat; and one of them, with an empty laugh, threw what was left into the fire, which blazed and roared again over this unusual fuel. I never in my life saw men so careless of the morrow; hand to mouth is the only word that can describe their way of doing; and what with wasted food and sleeping sentries, though they were bold enough for a brush and be done with it, I could see their entire unfitness for anything like a prolonged campaign.

Even Silver, eating away, with Captain Flint upon his shoulder, had not a word of blame for their recklessness. And this the more surprised me, for I thought he had never shown himself so cunning as he did then.

"Aye, mates," said he, "it's lucky you have Barbecue to think for you with this here head. I got what I wanted, I did. Sure enough, they have the ship. Where they have it, I don't know yet; but once we hit the treasure, we'll have to jump about and find out. And then, mates, us that has the boats, I reckon, has the upper hand."

Thus he kept running on, with his mouth full of the hot bacon; thus he restored their hope and confidence, and, I more than suspect, repaired his own at the same time.

"As for hostage," he continued, "that's his last talk, I guess, with them he loves so dear. I've got my piece o' news, and thanky to him for that; but it's over and done. I'll take him in a line when we go treasure-hunting, for we'll keep him like so much gold, in case of accidents, you mark, and in the meantime. Once we got the ship and treasure both and off to sea like jolly companions, why then we'll talk Mr. Hawkins over, we will, and we'll give him his share, to be sure, for all his kindness."

It was no wonder the men were in a good humour now. For my part, I was horribly cast down. Should the scheme he had now sketched prove feasible, Silver, already doubly a traitor, would not hesitate to adopt it. He had still a foot in either camp, and there was no doubt he would prefer wealth and freedom with the pirates to a bare escape from hanging, which was the best he had to hope on our side.

Nay, and even if things so fell out that he was forced to keep his faith with Dr. Livesey, even then what danger lay before us! What a moment that would be when the suspicions of his followers turned to certainty and he and I should have to fight for dear life—he a cripple and I a boy—against five strong and active seamen!

Add to this double apprehension the mystery that still hung over the behaviour of my friends, their unexplained desertion of the stockade, their inexplicable cession of the chart, or harder still to understand, the doctor's last warning to Silver, "Look out for squalls when you find it," and you will readily believe how little taste I found in my breakfast and with how uneasy a heart I set forth behind my captors on the quest for treasure.

We made a curious figure, had anyone been there to see us—all in soiled sailor clothes and all but me armed to the teeth. Silver had two guns slung about him—one before and one behind—besides the great cutlass at his waist and a pistol in each pocket of his square-tailed coat. To complete his strange appearance, Captain Flint sat perched upon his shoulder and gabbling odds and ends of purposeless sea-talk. I had a line about my waist and followed obediently after the sea-cook, who held the loose end of the rope, now in his free hand, now between his powerful teeth. For all the world, I was led like a dancing bear.

The other men were variously burthened, some carrying picks and shovels—for that had been the very first necessary they brought ashore from the Hispaniola—others laden with pork, bread, and brandy for the midday meal. All the stores, I observed, came from our stock, and I could see the truth of Silver's words the night before. Had he not struck a bargain with the doctor, he and his mutineers, deserted by the ship, must have been driven to subsist on clear water and the proceeds of their hunting. Water would have been little to their taste; a sailor is not usually a good shot; and besides all that, when they were so short of eatables, it was not likely they would be very flush of powder.

Well, thus equipped, we all set out—even the fellow with the broken head, who should certainly have kept in shadow—and straggled, one after another, to the beach, where the two gigs awaited us. Even these bore trace of the drunken folly of the pirates, one in a broken thwart, and both in their muddy and unbailed condition. Both were to be carried along with us for the sake of safety; and so, with our numbers divided between them, we set forth upon the bosom of the anchorage.

As we pulled over, there was some discussion on the chart. The red cross was, of course, far too large to be a guide; and the terms of the note on the back, as you will hear, admitted of some ambiguity. They ran, the reader may remember, thus:

Tall tree, Spy-glass shoulder, bearing a point to the N. of N.N.E.

Skeleton Island E.S.E. and by E.

Ten feet.

A tall tree was thus the principal mark. Now, right before us the anchorage was bounded by a plateau from two to three hundred feet high, adjoining on the north the sloping southern shoulder of the Spy-glass and rising again towards the south into the rough, cliffy eminence called the Mizzen-mast Hill. The top of the plateau was dotted thickly with pine-trees of varying height. Every here and there, one of a different species rose forty or fifty feet clear above its neighbours, and which of these was the particular "tall tree" of Captain Flint could only be decided on the spot, and by the readings of the compass.

Yet, although that was the case, every man on board the boats had picked a favourite of his own ere we were half-way over, Long John alone shrugging his shoulders and bidding them wait till they were there.

We pulled easily, by Silver's directions, not to weary the hands prematurely, and after quite a long passage, landed at the mouth of the second river—that which runs down a woody cleft of the Spy-glass. Thence, bending to our left, we began to ascend the slope towards the plateau.

At the first outset, heavy, miry ground and a matted, marish vegetation greatly delayed our progress; but by little and little the hill began to steepen and become stony under foot, and the wood to change its character and to grow in a more open order. It was, indeed, a most pleasant portion of the island that we were now approaching. A heavy-scented broom and many flowering shrubs had almost taken the place of grass. Thickets of green nutmeg-trees were dotted here and there with the red columns and the broad shadow of the pines; and the first mingled their spice with the aroma of the others. The air, besides, was fresh and stirring, and this, under the sheer sunbeams, was a wonderful refreshment to our senses.

The party spread itself abroad, in a fan shape, shouting and leaping to and fro. About the centre, and a good way behind the rest, Silver and I followed—I tethered by my rope, he ploughing, with deep pants, among the sliding gravel. From time to time, indeed, I had to lend him a hand, or he must have missed his footing and fallen backward down the hill.

We had thus proceeded for about half a mile and were approaching the brow of the plateau when the man upon the farthest left began to cry aloud, as if in terror. Shout after shout came from him, and the others began to run in his direction.

"He can't 'a found the treasure," said old Morgan, hurrying past us from the right, "for that's clean a-top."

Indeed, as we found when we also reached the spot, it was something very different. At the foot of a pretty big pine and involved in a green creeper, which had even partly lifted some of the smaller bones, a human skeleton lay, with a few shreds of clothing, on the ground. I believe a chill struck for a moment to every heart.

"He was a seaman," said George Merry, who, bolder than the rest, had gone up close and was examining the rags of clothing. "Leastways, this is good sea-cloth."

"Aye, aye," said Silver; "like enough; you wouldn't look to find a bishop here, I reckon. But what sort of a way is that for bones to lie? 'Tain't in natur'."

Indeed, on a second glance, it seemed impossible to fancy that the body was in a natural position. But for some disarray (the work, perhaps, of the birds that had fed upon him or of the slow-growing creeper that had gradually enveloped his remains) the man lay perfectly straight—his feet pointing in one direction, his hands, raised above his head like a diver's, pointing directly in the opposite.

"I've taken a notion into my old numbskull," observed Silver. "Here's the compass; there's the tip-top p'int o' Skeleton Island, stickin' out like a tooth. Just take a bearing, will you, along the line of them bones."

It was done. The body pointed straight in the direction of the island, and the compass read duly E.S.E. and by E.

"I thought so," cried the cook; "this here is a p'inter. Right up there is our line for the Pole Star and the jolly dollars. But, by thunder! If it don't make me cold inside to think of Flint. This is one of his jokes, and no mistake. Him and these six was alone here; he killed 'em, every man; and this one he hauled here and laid down by compass, shiver my timbers! They're long bones, and the hair's been yellow. Aye, that would be Allardyce. You mind Allardyce, Tom Morgan?"

"Aye, aye," returned Morgan; "I mind him; he owed me money, he did, and took my knife ashore with him."

"Speaking of knives," said another, "why don't we find his'n lying round? Flint warn't the man to pick a seaman's pocket; and the birds, I guess, would leave it be."

"By the powers, and that's true!" cried Silver.

"There ain't a thing left here," said Merry, still feeling round among the bones; "not a copper doit nor a baccy box. It don't look nat'ral to me."

"No, by gum, it don't," agreed Silver; "not nat'ral, nor not nice, says you. Great guns! Messmates, but if Flint was living, this would be a hot spot for you and me. Six they were, and six are we; and bones is what they are now."

"I saw him dead with these here deadlights," said Morgan. "Billy took me in. There he laid, with penny-pieces on his eyes."

"Dead—aye, sure enough he's dead and gone below," said the fellow with the bandage; "but if ever sperrit walked, it would be Flint's. Dear heart, but he died bad, did Flint!"

"Aye, that he did," observed another; "now he raged, and now he hollered for the rum, and now he sang. 'Fifteen Men' were his only song, mates; and I tell you true, I never rightly liked to hear it since. It was main hot, and the windy was open, and I hear that old song comin' out as clear as clear—and the death-haul on the man already."

"Come, come," said Silver; "stow this talk. He's dead, and he don't walk, that I know; leastways, he won't walk by day, and you may lay to that. Care killed a cat. Fetch ahead for the doubloons."

We started, certainly; but in spite of the hot sun and the staring daylight, the pirates no longer ran separate and shouting through the wood, but kept side by side and spoke with bated breath. The terror of the dead buccaneer had fallen on their spirits.

32

The Treasure-hunt—The Voice Among the Trees

PARTLY from the damping influence of this alarm, partly to rest Silver and the sick folk, the whole party sat down as soon as they had gained the brow of the ascent.

The plateau being somewhat tilted towards the west, this spot on which we had paused commanded a wide prospect on either hand. Before us, over the tree-tops, we beheld the Cape of the Woods fringed with surf; behind, we not only looked down upon the anchorage and Skeleton Island, but saw—clear across the spit and the eastern lowlands—a great field of open sea upon the east. Sheer above us rose the Spyglass, here dotted with single pines, there black with precipices. There was no sound but that of the distant breakers, mounting from all round, and the chirp of countless insects in the brush. Not a man, not a sail, upon the sea; the very largeness of the view increased the sense of solitude.

Silver, as he sat, took certain bearings with his compass.

"There are three 'tall trees'" said he, "about in the right line from Skeleton Island. 'Spy-glass shoulder,' I take it, means that lower p'int there. It's child's play to find the stuff now. I've half a mind to dine first."

"I don't feel sharp," growled Morgan. "Thinkin' o' Flint—I think it were—as done me."

"Ah, well, my son, you praise your stars he's dead," said Silver.

"He were an ugly devil," cried a third pirate with a shudder; "that blue in the face too!"

"That was how the rum took him," added Merry. "Blue! Well, I reckon he was blue. That's a true word."

Ever since they had found the skeleton and got upon this train of thought, they had spoken lower and lower, and they had almost got to whispering by now, so that the sound of their talk hardly interrupted the silence of the wood. All of a sudden, out of the middle of the trees in front of us, a thin, high, trembling voice struck up the well-known air and words:

"Fifteen men on the dead man's chest—
   Yo-ho-ho, and a bottle of rum!"

I never have seen men more dreadfully affected than the pirates. The colour went from their six faces like enchantment; some leaped to their feet, some clawed hold of others; Morgan grovelled on the ground.

"It's Flint, by ——!" cried Merry.

The song had stopped as suddenly as it began—broken off, you would have said, in the middle of a note, as though someone had laid his hand upon the singer's mouth. Coming through the clear, sunny atmosphere among the green tree-tops, I thought it had sounded airily and sweetly; and the effect on my companions was the stranger.

"Come," said Silver, struggling with his ashen lips to get the word out; "this won't do. Stand by to go about. This is a rum start, and I can't name the voice, but it's someone skylarking—someone that's flesh and blood, and you may lay to that."

His courage had come back as he spoke, and some of the colour to his face along with it. Already the others had begun to lend an ear to this encouragement and were coming a little to themselves, when the same voice broke out again—not this time singing, but in a faint distant hail that echoed yet fainter among the clefts of the Spy-glass.

"Darby M'Graw," it wailed—for that is the word that best describes the sound—"Darby M'Graw! Darby M'Graw!" again and again and again; and then rising a little higher, and with an oath that I leave out: "Fetch aft the rum, Darby!"

The buccaneers remained rooted to the ground, their eyes starting from their heads. Long after the voice had died away they still stared in silence, dreadfully, before them.

"That fixes it!" gasped one. "Let's go."

"They was his last words," moaned Morgan, "his last words above board."

Dick had his Bible out and was praying volubly. He had been well brought up, had Dick, before he came to sea and fell among bad companions.

Still Silver was unconquered. I could hear his teeth rattle in his head, but he had not yet surrendered.

"Nobody in this here island ever heard of Darby," he muttered; "not one but us that's here." And then, making a great effort: "Shipmates," he cried, "I'm here to get that stuff, and I'll not be beat by man or devil. I never was feared of Flint in his life, and, by the powers, I'll face him dead. There's seven hundred thousand pound not a quarter of a mile from here. When did ever a gentleman o' fortune show his stern to that much dollars for a boozy old seaman with a blue mug—and him dead too?"

But there was no sign of reawakening courage in his followers, rather, indeed, of growing terror at the irreverence of his words.

"Belay there, John!" said Merry. "Don't you cross a sperrit."

And the rest were all too terrified to reply. They would have run away severally had they dared; but fear kept them together, and kept them close by John, as if his daring helped them. He, on his part, had pretty well fought his weakness down.

"Sperrit? Well, maybe," he said. "But there's one thing not clear to me. There was an echo. Now, no man ever seen a sperrit with a shadow; well then, what's he doing with an echo to him, I should like to know? That ain't in natur', surely?"

This argument seemed weak enough to me. But you can never tell what will affect the superstitious, and to my wonder, George Merry was greatly relieved.

"Well, that's so," he said. "You've a head upon your shoulders, John, and no mistake. 'Bout ship, mates! This here crew is on a wrong tack, I do believe. And come to think on it, it was like Flint's voice, I grant you, but not just so clear-away like it, after all. It was liker somebody else's voice now—it was liker—"

"By the powers, Ben Gunn!" roared Silver.

"Aye, and so it were," cried Morgan, springing on his knees. "Ben Gunn it were!"

"It don't make much odds, do it, now?" asked Dick. "Ben Gunn's not here in the body any more'n Flint."

But the older hands greeted this remark with scorn.

"Why, nobody minds Ben Gunn," cried Merry; "dead or alive, nobody minds him."

It was extraordinary how their spirits had returned and how the natural colour had revived in their faces. Soon they were chatting together, with intervals of listening; and not long after, hearing no further sound, they shouldered the tools and set forth again, Merry walking first with Silver's compass to keep them on the right line with Skeleton Island. He had said the truth: dead or alive, nobody minded Ben Gunn.

Dick alone still held his Bible, and looked around him as he went, with fearful glances; but he found no sympathy, and Silver even joked him on his precautions.

"I told you," said he—"I told you you had sp'iled your Bible. If it ain't no good to swear by, what do you suppose a sperrit would give for it? Not that!" and he snapped his big fingers, halting a moment on his crutch.

But Dick was not to be comforted; indeed, it was soon plain to me that the lad was falling sick; hastened by heat, exhaustion, and the shock of his alarm, the fever, predicted by Dr. Livesey, was evidently growing swiftly higher.

It was fine open walking here, upon the summit; our way lay a little downhill, for, as I have said, the plateau tilted towards the west. The pines, great and small, grew wide apart; and even between the clumps of nutmeg and azalea, wide open spaces baked in the hot sunshine. Striking, as we did, pretty near north-west across the island, we drew, on the one hand, ever nearer under the shoulders of the Spy-glass, and on the other, looked ever wider over that western bay where I had once tossed and trembled in the coracle.

The first of the tall trees was reached, and by the bearings proved the wrong one. So with the second. The third rose nearly two hundred feet into the air above a clump of underwood—a giant of a vegetable, with a red column as big as a cottage, and a wide shadow around in which a company could have manoeuvred. It was conspicuous far to sea both on the east and west and might have been entered as a sailing mark upon the chart.

But it was not its size that now impressed my companions; it was the knowledge that seven hundred thousand pounds in gold lay somewhere buried below its spreading shadow. The thought of the money, as they drew nearer, swallowed up their previous terrors. Their eyes burned in their heads; their feet grew speedier and lighter; their whole soul was bound up in that fortune, that whole lifetime of extravagance and pleasure, that lay waiting there for each of them.

Silver hobbled, grunting, on his crutch; his nostrils stood out and quivered; he cursed like a madman when the flies settled on his hot and shiny countenance; he plucked furiously at the line that held me to him and from time to time turned his eyes upon me with a deadly look. Certainly he took no pains to hide his thoughts, and certainly I read them like print. In the immediate nearness of the gold, all else had been forgotten: his promise and the doctor's warning were both things of the past, and I could not doubt that he hoped to seize upon the treasure, find and board the Hispaniola under cover of night, cut every honest throat about that island, and sail away as he had at first intended, laden with crimes and riches.

Shaken as I was with these alarms, it was hard for me to keep up with the rapid pace of the treasure-hunters. Now and again I stumbled, and it was then that Silver plucked so roughly at the rope and launched at me his murderous glances. Dick, who had dropped behind us and now brought up the rear, was babbling to himself both prayers and curses as his fever kept rising.

This also added to my wretchedness, and to crown all, I was haunted by the thought of the tragedy that had once been acted on that plateau, when that ungodly buccaneer with the blue face—he who died at Savannah, singing and shouting for drink—had there, with his own hand, cut down his six accomplices. This grove that was now so peaceful must then have rung with cries, I thought; and even with the thought I could believe I heard it ringing still.

We were now at the margin of the thicket.

"Huzza, mates, all together!" shouted Merry; and the foremost broke into a run.

And suddenly, not ten yards further, we beheld them stop. A low cry arose. Silver doubled his pace, digging away with the foot of his crutch like one possessed; and next moment he and I had come also to a dead halt.

Before us was a great excavation, not very recent, for the sides had fallen in and grass had sprouted on the bottom. In this were the shaft of a pick broken in two and the boards of several packing-cases strewn around. On one of these boards I saw, branded with a hot iron, the name Walrus—the name of Flint's ship.

All was clear to probation. The cache had been found and rifled; the seven hundred thousand pounds were gone!

33

The Fall of a Chieftain

THERE never was such an overturn in this world. Each of these six men was as though he had been struck. But with Silver the blow passed almost instantly. Every thought of his soul had been set full-stretch, like a racer, on that money; well, he was brought up, in a single second, dead; and he kept his head, found his temper, and changed his plan before the others had had time to realize the disappointment.

"Jim," he whispered, "take that, and stand by for trouble."

And he passed me a double-barrelled pistol.

At the same time, he began quietly moving northward, and in a few steps had put the hollow between us two and the other five. Then he looked at me and nodded, as much as to say, "Here is a narrow corner," as, indeed, I thought it was. His looks were not quite friendly, and I was so revolted at these constant changes that I could not forbear whispering, "So you've changed sides again."

There was no time left for him to answer in. The buccaneers, with oaths and cries, began to leap, one after another, into the pit and to dig with their fingers, throwing the boards aside as they did so. Morgan found a piece of gold. He held it up with a perfect spout of oaths. It was a two-guinea piece, and it went from hand to hand among them for a quarter of a minute.

"Two guineas!" roared Merry, shaking it at Silver. "That's your seven hundred thousand pounds, is it? You're the man for bargains, ain't you? You're him that never bungled nothing, you wooden-headed lubber!"

"Dig away, boys," said Silver with the coolest insolence; "you'll find some pig-nuts and I shouldn't wonder."

"Pig-nuts!" repeated Merry, in a scream. "Mates, do you hear that? I tell you now, that man there knew it all along. Look in the face of him and you'll see it wrote there."

"Ah, Merry," remarked Silver, "standing for cap'n again? You're a pushing lad, to be sure."

But this time everyone was entirely in Merry's favour. They began to scramble out of the excavation, darting furious glances behind them. One thing I observed, which looked well for us: they all got out upon the opposite side from Silver.

Well, there we stood, two on one side, five on the other, the pit between us, and nobody screwed up high enough to offer the first blow. Silver never moved; he watched them, very upright on his crutch, and looked as cool as ever I saw him. He was brave, and no mistake.

At last Merry seemed to think a speech might help matters.

"Mates," says he, "there's two of them alone there; one's the old cripple that brought us all here and blundered us down to this; the other's that cub that I mean to have the heart of. Now, mates—"

He was raising his arm and his voice, and plainly meant to lead a charge. But just then—crack! crack! crack!—three musket-shots flashed out of the thicket. Merry tumbled head foremost into the excavation; the man with the bandage spun round like a teetotum and fell all his length upon his side, where he lay dead, but still twitching; and the other three turned and ran for it with all their might.

Before you could wink, Long John had fired two barrels of a pistol into the struggling Merry, and as the man rolled up his eyes at him in the last agony, "George," said he, "I reckon I settled you."

At the same moment, the doctor, Gray, and Ben Gunn joined us, with smoking muskets, from among the nutmeg-trees.

"Forward!" cried the doctor. "Double quick, my lads. We must head 'em off the boats."

And we set off at a great pace, sometimes plunging through the bushes to the chest.

I tell you, but Silver was anxious to keep up with us. The work that man went through, leaping on his crutch till the muscles of his chest were fit to burst, was work no sound man ever equalled; and so thinks the doctor. As it was, he was already thirty yards behind us and on the verge of strangling when we reached the brow of the slope.

"Doctor," he hailed, "see there! No hurry!"

Sure enough there was no hurry. In a more open part of the plateau, we could see the three survivors still running in the same direction as they had started, right for Mizzenmast Hill. We were already between them and the boats; and so we four sat down to breathe, while Long John, mopping his face, came slowly up with us.

"Thank ye kindly, doctor," says he. "You came in in about the nick, I guess, for me and Hawkins. And so it's you, Ben Gunn!" he added. "Well, you're a nice one, to be sure."

"I'm Ben Gunn, I am," replied the maroon, wriggling like an eel in his embarrassment. "And," he added, after a long pause, "how do, Mr. Silver? Pretty well, I thank ye, says you."

"Ben, Ben," murmured Silver, "to think as you've done me!"

The doctor sent back Gray for one of the pick-axes deserted, in their flight, by the mutineers, and then as we proceeded leisurely downhill to where the boats were lying, related in a few words what had taken place. It was a story that profoundly interested Silver; and Ben Gunn, the half-idiot maroon, was the hero from beginning to end.

Ben, in his long, lonely wanderings about the island, had found the skeleton—it was he that had rifled it; he had found the treasure; he had dug it up (it was the haft of his pick-axe that lay broken in the excavation); he had carried it on his back, in many weary journeys, from the foot of the tall pine to a cave he had on the two-pointed hill at the north-east angle of the island, and there it had lain stored in safety since two months before the arrival of the Hispaniola.

When the doctor had wormed this secret from him on the afternoon of the attack, and when next morning he saw the anchorage deserted, he had gone to Silver, given him the chart, which was now useless—given him the stores, for Ben Gunn's cave was well supplied with goats' meat salted by himself—given anything and everything to get a chance of moving in safety from the stockade to the two-pointed hill, there to be clear of malaria and keep a guard upon the money.

"As for you, Jim," he said, "it went against my heart, but I did what I thought best for those who had stood by their duty; and if you were not one of these, whose fault was it?"

That morning, finding that I was to be involved in the horrid disappointment he had prepared for the mutineers, he had run all the way to the cave, and leaving the squire to guard the captain, had taken Gray and the maroon and started, making the diagonal across the island to be at hand beside the pine. Soon, however, he saw that our party had the start of him; and Ben Gunn, being fleet of foot, had been dispatched in front to do his best alone. Then it had occurred to him to work upon the superstitions of his former shipmates, and he was so far successful that Gray and the doctor had come up and were already ambushed before the arrival of the treasure-hunters.

"Ah," said Silver, "it were fortunate for me that I had Hawkins here. You would have let old John be cut to bits, and never given it a thought, doctor."

"Not a thought," replied Dr. Livesey cheerily.

And by this time we had reached the gigs. The doctor, with the pick-axe, demolished one of them, and then we all got aboard the other and set out to go round by sea for North Inlet.

This was a run of eight or nine miles. Silver, though he was almost killed already with fatigue, was set to an oar, like the rest of us, and we were soon skimming swiftly over a smooth sea. Soon we passed out of the straits and doubled the south-east corner of the island, round which, four days ago, we had towed the Hispaniola.

As we passed the two-pointed hill, we could see the black mouth of Ben Gunn's cave and a figure standing by it, leaning on a musket. It was the squire, and we waved a handkerchief and gave him three cheers, in which the voice of Silver joined as heartily as any.

Three miles farther, just inside the mouth of North Inlet, what should we meet but the Hispaniola, cruising by herself? The last flood had lifted her, and had there been much wind or a strong tide current, as in the southern anchorage, we should never have found her more, or found her stranded beyond help. As it was, there was little amiss beyond the wreck of the main-sail. Another anchor was got ready and dropped in a fathom and a half of water. We all pulled round again to Rum Cove, the nearest point for Ben Gunn's treasure-house; and then Gray, single-handed, returned with the gig to the Hispaniola, where he was to pass the night on guard.

A gentle slope ran up from the beach to the entrance of the cave. At the top, the squire met us. To me he was cordial and kind, saying nothing of my escapade either in the way of blame or praise. At Silver's polite salute he somewhat flushed.

"John Silver," he said, "you're a prodigious villain and imposter—a monstrous imposter, sir. I am told I am not to prosecute you. Well, then, I will not. But the dead men, sir, hang about your neck like mill-stones."

"Thank you kindly, sir," replied Long John, again saluting.

"I dare you to thank me!" cried the squire. "It is a gross dereliction of my duty. Stand back."

And thereupon we all entered the cave. It was a large, airy place, with a little spring and a pool of clear water, overhung with ferns. The floor was sand. Before a big fire lay Captain Smollett; and in a far corner, only duskily flickered over by the blaze, I beheld great heaps of coin and quadrilaterals built of bars of gold. That was Flint's treasure that we had come so far to seek and that had cost already the lives of seventeen men from the Hispaniola. How many it had cost in the amassing, what blood and sorrow, what good ships scuttled on the deep, what brave men walking the plank blindfold, what shot of cannon, what shame and lies and cruelty, perhaps no man alive could tell. Yet there were still three upon that island—Silver, and old Morgan, and Ben Gunn—who had each taken his share in these crimes, as each had hoped in vain to share in the reward.

"Come in, Jim," said the captain. "You're a good boy in your line, Jim, but I don't think you and me'll go to sea again. You're too much of the born favourite for me. Is that you, John Silver? What brings you here, man?"

"Come back to my dooty, sir," returned Silver.

"Ah!" said the captain, and that was all he said.

What a supper I had of it that night, with all my friends around me; and what a meal it was, with Ben Gunn's salted goat and some delicacies and a bottle of old wine from the Hispaniola. Never, I am sure, were people gayer or happier. And there was Silver, sitting back almost out of the firelight, but eating heartily, prompt to spring forward when anything was wanted, even joining quietly in our laughter—the same bland, polite, obsequious seaman of the voyage out.

34

And Last

THE next morning we fell early to work, for the transportation of this great mass of gold near a mile by land to the beach, and thence three miles by boat to the Hispaniola, was a considerable task for so small a number of workmen. The three fellows still abroad upon the island did not greatly trouble us; a single sentry on the shoulder of the hill was sufficient to ensure us against any sudden onslaught, and we thought, besides, they had had more than enough of fighting.

Therefore the work was pushed on briskly. Gray and Ben Gunn came and went with the boat, while the rest during their absences piled treasure on the beach. Two of the bars, slung in a rope's end, made a good load for a grown man—one that he was glad to walk slowly with. For my part, as I was not much use at carrying, I was kept busy all day in the cave packing the minted money into bread-bags.

It was a strange collection, like Billy Bones's hoard for the diversity of coinage, but so much larger and so much more varied that I think I never had more pleasure than in sorting them. English, French, Spanish, Portuguese, Georges, and Louises, doubloons and double guineas and moidores and sequins, the pictures of all the kings of Europe for the last hundred years, strange Oriental pieces stamped with what looked like wisps of string or bits of spider's web, round pieces and square pieces, and pieces bored through the middle, as if to wear them round your neck—nearly every variety of money in the world must, I think, have found a place in that collection; and for number, I am sure they were like autumn leaves, so that my back ached with stooping and my fingers with sorting them out.

Day after day this work went on; by every evening a fortune had been stowed aboard, but there was another fortune waiting for the morrow; and all this time we heard nothing of the three surviving mutineers.

At last—I think it was on the third night—the doctor and I were strolling on the shoulder of the hill where it overlooks the lowlands of the isle, when, from out the thick darkness below, the wind brought us a noise between shrieking and singing. It was only a snatch that reached our ears, followed by the former silence.

"Heaven forgive them," said the doctor; "'tis the mutineers!"

"All drunk, sir," struck in the voice of Silver from behind us.

Silver, I should say, was allowed his entire liberty, and in spite of daily rebuffs, seemed to regard himself once more as quite a privileged and friendly dependent. Indeed, it was remarkable how well he bore these slights and with what unwearying politeness he kept on trying to ingratiate himself with all. Yet, I think, none treated him better than a dog, unless it was Ben Gunn, who was still terribly afraid of his old quartermaster, or myself, who had really something to thank him for; although for that matter, I suppose, I had reason to think even worse of him than anybody else, for I had seen him meditating a fresh treachery upon the plateau. Accordingly, it was pretty gruffly that the doctor answered him.

"Drunk or raving," said he.

"Right you were, sir," replied Silver; "and precious little odds which, to you and me."

"I suppose you would hardly ask me to call you a humane man," returned the doctor with a sneer, "and so my feelings may surprise you, Master Silver. But if I were sure they were raving—as I am morally certain one, at least, of them is down with fever—I should leave this camp, and at whatever risk to my own carcass, take them the assistance of my skill."

"Ask your pardon, sir, you would be very wrong," quoth Silver. "You would lose your precious life, and you may lay to that. I'm on your side now, hand and glove; and I shouldn't wish for to see the party weakened, let alone yourself, seeing as I know what I owes you. But these men down there, they couldn't keep their word—no, not supposing they wished to; and what's more, they couldn't believe as you could."

"No," said the doctor. "You're the man to keep your word, we know that."

Well, that was about the last news we had of the three pirates. Only once we heard a gunshot a great way off and supposed them to be hunting. A council was held, and it was decided that we must desert them on the island—to the huge glee, I must say, of Ben Gunn, and with the strong approval of Gray. We left a good stock of powder and shot, the bulk of the salt goat, a few medicines, and some other necessaries, tools, clothing, a spare sail, a fathom or two of rope, and by the particular desire of the doctor, a handsome present of tobacco.

That was about our last doing on the island. Before that, we had got the treasure stowed and had shipped enough water and the remainder of the goat meat in case of any distress; and at last, one fine morning, we weighed anchor, which was about all that we could manage, and stood out of North Inlet, the same colours flying that the captain had flown and fought under at the palisade.

The three fellows must have been watching us closer than we thought for, as we soon had proved. For coming through the narrows, we had to lie very near the southern point, and there we saw all three of them kneeling together on a spit of sand, with their arms raised in supplication. It went to all our hearts, I think, to leave them in that wretched state; but we could not risk another mutiny; and to take them home for the gibbet would have been a cruel sort of kindness. The doctor hailed them and told them of the stores we had left, and where they were to find them. But they continued to call us by name and appeal to us, for God's sake, to be merciful and not leave them to die in such a place.

At last, seeing the ship still bore on her course and was now swiftly drawing out of earshot, one of them—I know not which it was—leapt to his feet with a hoarse cry, whipped his musket to his shoulder, and sent a shot whistling over Silver's head and through the main-sail.

After that, we kept under cover of the bulwarks, and when next I looked out they had disappeared from the spit, and the spit itself had almost melted out of sight in the growing distance. That was, at least, the end of that; and before noon, to my inexpressible joy, the highest rock of Treasure Island had sunk into the blue round of sea.

We were so short of men that everyone on board had to bear a hand—only the captain lying on a mattress in the stern and giving his orders, for though greatly recovered he was still in want of quiet. We laid her head for the nearest port in Spanish America, for we could not risk the voyage home without fresh hands; and as it was, what with baffling winds and a couple of fresh gales, we were all worn out before we reached it.

It was just at sundown when we cast anchor in a most beautiful land-locked gulf, and were immediately surrounded by shore boats full of Negroes and Mexican Indians and half-bloods selling fruits and vegetables and offering to dive for bits of money. The sight of so many good-humoured faces (especially the blacks), the taste of the tropical fruits, and above all the lights that began to shine in the town made a most charming contrast to our dark and bloody sojourn on the island; and the doctor and the squire, taking me along with them, went ashore to pass the early part of the night. Here they met the captain of an English man-of-war, fell in talk with him, went on board his ship, and, in short, had so agreeable a time that day was breaking when we came alongside the Hispaniola.

Ben Gunn was on deck alone, and as soon as we came on board he began, with wonderful contortions, to make us a confession. Silver was gone. The maroon had connived at his escape in a shore boat some hours ago, and he now assured us he had only done so to preserve our lives, which would certainly have been forfeit if "that man with the one leg had stayed aboard." But this was not all. The sea-cook had not gone empty-handed. He had cut through a bulkhead unobserved and had removed one of the sacks of coin, worth perhaps three or four hundred guineas, to help him on his further wanderings.

I think we were all pleased to be so cheaply quit of him.

Well, to make a long story short, we got a few hands on board, made a good cruise home, and the Hispaniola reached Bristol just as Mr. Blandly was beginning to think of fitting out her consort. Five men only of those who had sailed returned with her. "Drink and the devil had done for the rest," with a vengeance, although, to be sure, we were not quite in so bad a case as that other ship they sang about:

With one man of her crew alive,
What put to sea with seventy-five.

All of us had an ample share of the treasure and used it wisely or foolishly, according to our natures. Captain Smollett is now retired from the sea. Gray not only saved his money, but being suddenly smit with the desire to rise, also studied his profession, and he is now mate and part owner of a fine full-rigged ship, married besides, and the father of a family. As for Ben Gunn, he got a thousand pounds, which he spent or lost in three weeks, or to be more exact, in nineteen days, for he was back begging on the twentieth. Then he was given a lodge to keep, exactly as he had feared upon the island; and he still lives, a great favourite, though something of a butt, with the country boys, and a notable singer in church on Sundays and saints' days.

Of Silver we have heard no more. That formidable seafaring man with one leg has at last gone clean out of my life; but I dare say he met his old Negress, and perhaps still lives in comfort with her and Captain Flint. It is to be hoped so, I suppose, for his chances of comfort in another world are very small.

The bar silver and the arms still lie, for all that I know, where Flint buried them; and certainly they shall lie there for me. Oxen and wain-ropes would not bring me back again to that accursed island; and the worst dreams that ever I have are when I hear the surf booming about its coasts or start upright in bed with the sharp voice of Captain Flint still ringing in my ears: "Pieces of eight! Pieces of eight!"

KIDNAPPED

CHAPTER I
I SET OFF UPON MY JOURNEY TO THE HOUSE OF SHAWS

iwill begin the story of my adventures with a certain morning early in the month of June, the year of grace 1751, when I took the key for the last time out of the door of my father's house. The sun began to shine upon the summit of the hills as I went down the road; and by the time I had come as far as the manse, the blackbirds were whistling in the garden lilacs, and the mist that hung around the valley in the time of the dawn was beginning to arise and die away.

Mr. Campbell, the minister of Essendean, was waiting for me by the garden gate, good man! He asked me if I had breakfasted; and hearing that I lacked for nothing, he took my hand in both of his and clapped it kindly under his arm.

"Well, Davie, lad," said he, "I will go with you as far as the ford, to set you on the way." And we began to walk forward in silence.

"Are ye sorry to leave Essendean?" said he, after awhile.

"Why, sir," said I, "if I knew where I was going, or what was likely to become of me, I would tell you candidly. Essendean is a good place indeed, and I have been very happy there; but then I have never been anywhere else. My father and mother, since they are both dead, I shall be no nearer to in Essendean than in the Kingdom of Hungary, and, to speak truth, if I thought I had a chance to better myself where I was going I would go with a good will."

"Ay?" said Mr. Campbell. "Very well, Davie. Then it behoves me to tell your fortune; or so far as I may. When your mother was gone, and your father (the worthy, Christian man) began to sicken for his end, he gave me in charge a certain letter, which he said was your inheritance. 'So soon,' says he, 'as I am gone, and the house is redd up and the gear disposed of' (all which, Davie, hath been done), 'give my boy this letter into his hand, and start him off to the house of Shaws, not far from Cramond. That is the place I came from,' he said, 'and it's where it befits that my boy should return. He is a steady lad,' your father said, 'and a canny goer; and I doubt not he will come safe, and be well lived where he goes.'"

"The house of Shaws!" I cried. "What had my poor father to do with the house of Shaws?"

"Nay," said Mr. Campbell, "who can tell that for a surety? But the name of that family, Davie, boy, is the name you bear—Balfours of Shaws: an ancient, honest, reputable house, peradventure in these latter days decayed. Your father, too, was a man of learning as befitted his position; no man more plausibly conducted school; nor had he the manner or the speech of a common dominie; but (as ye will yourself remember) I took aye a pleasure to have him to the manse to meet the gentry; and those of my own house, Campbell of Kilrennet, Campbell of Dunswire, Campbell of Minch, and others, all well-kenned gentlemen, had pleasure in his society. Lastly, to put all the elements of this affair before you, here is the testamentary letter itself, superscrived by the own hand of our departed brother."

He gave me the letter, which was addressed in these words: "To the hands of Ebenezer Balfour, Esquire, of Shaws, in his house of Shaws, these will be delivered by my son, David Balfour."

My heart was beating hard at this great prospect now suddenly opening before a lad of seventeen years of age, the son of a poor country dominie in the Forest of Ettrick.

"Mr. Campbell," I stammered, "and if you were in my shoes, would you go?"

"Of a surety," said the minister, "that would I, and without pause. A pretty lad like you should get to Cramond (which is near in by Edinburgh) in two days of walk. If the worst came to the worst, and your high relations (as I cannot but suppose them to be somewhat of your blood) should put you to the door, ye can but walk the two days back again and risp at the manse door. But I would rather hope that ye shall be well received, as your poor father forecast for you, and for anything that I ken come to be a great man in time. And here, Davie, laddie," he resumed, "it lies near upon my conscience to improve this parting, and set you on the right guard against the dangers of the world."

Here he cast about for a comfortable seat, lighted on a big boulder under a birch by the trackside, sate down upon it with a very long, serious upper lip, and the sun now shining in upon us between two peaks, put his pocket-handkerchief over his cocked hat to shelter him. There, then, with uplifted forefinger, he first put me on my guard against a considerable number of heresies, to which I had no temptation, and urged upon me to be instant in my prayers and reading of the Bible. That done, he drew a picture of the great house that I was bound to, and how I should conduct myself with its inhabitants.

"Be soople, Davie, in things immaterial," said he. "Bear ye this in mind, that, though gentle born, ye have had a country rearing. Dinnae shame us, Davie, dinnae shame us! In yon great, muckle house, with all these domestics, upper and under, show yourself as nice, as circumspect, as quick at the conception, and as slow of speech as any. As for the laird—remember he's the laird; I say no more: honour to whom honour. It's a pleasure to obey a laird; or should be, to the young."

"Well, sir," said I, "it may be; and I'll promise you I'll try to make it so."

"Why, very well said," replied Mr. Campbell, heartily. "And now to come to the material, or (to make a quibble) to the immaterial. I have here a little packet which contains four things." He tugged it, as he spoke, and with some great difficulty, from the skirt pocket of his coat. "Of these four things, the first is your legal due: the little pickle money for your father's books and plenishing, which I have bought (as I have explained from the first) in the design of re-selling at a profit to the incoming dominie. The other three are gifties that Mrs. Campbell and myself would be blithe of your acceptance. The first, which is round, will likely please ye best at the first off-go; but, O Davie, laddie, it's but a drop of water in the sea; it'll help you but a step, and vanish like the morning. The second, which is flat and square and written upon, will stand by you through life, like a good staff for the road, and a good pillow to your head in sickness. And as for the last, which is cubical, that'll see you, it's my prayerful wish, into a better land."

With that he got upon his feet, took off his hat, and prayed a little while aloud, and in affecting terms, for a young man setting out into the world; then suddenly took me in his arms and embraced me very hard; then held me at arm's length, looking at me with his face all working with sorrow; and then whipped about, and crying good-bye to me, set off backward by the way that we had come at a sort of jogging run. It might have been laughable to another; but I was in no mind to laugh. I watched him as long as he was in sight; and he never stopped hurrying, nor once looked back. Then it came in upon my mind that this was all his sorrow at my departure; and my conscience smote me hard and fast, because I, for my part, was overjoyed to get away out of that quiet country-side, and go to a great, busy house, among rich and respected gentlefolk of my own name and blood.

"Davie, Davie," I thought, "was ever seen such black ingratitude? Can you forget old favours and old friends at the mere whistle of a name? Fie, fie; think shame."

And I sat down on the boulder the good man had just left, and opened the parcel to see the nature of my gifts. That which he had called cubical, I had never had much doubt of; sure enough it was a little Bible, to carry in a plaid-neuk. That which he had called round, I found to be a shilling piece; and the third, which was to help me so wonderfully both in health and sickness all the days of my life, was a little piece of coarse yellow paper, written upon thus in red ink:

"TO MAKE LILLY OF THE VALLEY WATER.—Take the flowers of lilly of the valley and distil them in sack, and drink a spooneful or two as there is occasion. It restores speech to those that have the dumb palsey. It is good against the Gout; it comforts the heart and strengthens the memory; and the flowers, put into a Glasse, close stopt, and set into ane hill of ants for a month, then take it out, and you will find a liquor which comes from the flowers, which keep in a vial; it is good, ill or well, and whether man or woman."

And then, in the minister's own hand, was added:

"Likewise for sprains, rub it in; and for the cholic, a great spooneful in the hour."

To be sure, I laughed over this; but it was rather tremulous laughter; and I was glad to get my bundle on my staff's end and set out over the ford and up the hill upon the farther side; till, just as I came on the green drove-road running wide through the heather, I took my last look of Kirk Essendean, the trees about the manse, and the big rowans in the kirkyard where my father and my mother lay.

CHAPTER II
I COME TO MY JOURNEY'S END

In the forenoon of the second day, coming to the top of a hill, I saw all the country fall away before me down to the sea; and in the midst of this descent, on a long ridge, the city of Edinburgh smoking like a kiln. There was a flag upon the castle, and ships moving or lying anchored in the firth; both of which, for as far away as they were, I could distinguish clearly; and both brought my country heart into my mouth.

Presently after, I came by a house where a shepherd lived, and got a rough direction for the neighbourhood of Cramond; and so, from one to another, worked my way to the westward of the capital by Colinton, till I came out upon the Glasgow road. And there, to my great pleasure and wonder, I beheld a regiment marching to the fifes, every foot in time; an old red-faced general on a grey horse at the one end, and at the other the company of Grenadiers, with their Pope's-hats. The pride of life seemed to mount into my brain at the sight of the red coats and the hearing of that merry music.

A little farther on, and I was told I was in Cramond parish, and began to substitute in my inquiries the name of the house of Shaws. It was a word that seemed to surprise those of whom I sought my way. At first I thought the plainness of my appearance, in my country habit, and that all dusty from the road, consorted ill with the greatness of the place to which I was bound. But after two, or maybe three, had given me the same look and the same answer, I began to take it in my head there was something strange about the Shaws itself.

The better to set this fear at rest, I changed the form of my inquiries; and spying an honest fellow coming along a lane on the shaft of his cart, I asked him if he had ever heard tell of a house they called the house of Shaws.

He stopped his cart and looked at me, like the others.

"Ay" said he. "What for?"

"It's a great house?" I asked.

"Doubtless," says he. "The house is a big, muckle house."

"Ay," said I, "but the folk that are in it?"

"Folk?" cried he. "Are ye daft? There's nae folk there—to call folk."

"What?" say I; "not Mr. Ebenezer?"

"Ou, ay" says the man; "there's the laird, to be sure, if it's him you're wanting. What'll like be your business, mannie?"

"I was led to think that I would get a situation," I said, looking as modest as I could.

"What?" cries the carter, in so sharp a note that his very horse started; and then, "Well, mannie," he added, "it's nane of my affairs; but ye seem a decent-spoken lad; and if ye'll take a word from me, ye'll keep clear of the Shaws."

The next person I came across was a dapper little man in a beautiful white wig, whom I saw to be a barber on his rounds; and knowing well that barbers were great gossips, I asked him plainly what sort of a man was Mr. Balfour of the Shaws.

"Hoot, hoot, hoot," said the barber, "nae kind of a man, nae kind of a man at all;" and began to ask me very shrewdly what my business was; but I was more than a match for him at that, and he went on to his next customer no wiser than he came.

I cannot well describe the blow this dealt to my illusions. The more indistinct the accusations were, the less I liked them, for they left the wider field to fancy. What kind of a great house was this, that all the parish should start and stare to be asked the way to it? or what sort of a gentleman, that his ill-fame should be thus current on the wayside? If an hour's walking would have brought me back to Essendean, I had left my adventure then and there, and returned to Mr. Campbell's. But when I had come so far a way already, mere shame would not suffer me to desist till I had put the matter to the touch of proof; I was bound, out of mere self-respect, to carry it through; and little as I liked the sound of what I heard, and slow as I began to travel, I still kept asking my way and still kept advancing.

It was drawing on to sundown when I met a stout, dark, sour-looking woman coming trudging down a hill; and she, when I had put my usual question, turned sharp about, accompanied me back to the summit she had just left, and pointed to a great bulk of building standing very bare upon a green in the bottom of the next valley. The country was pleasant round about, running in low hills, pleasantly watered and wooded, and the crops, to my eyes, wonderfully good; but the house itself appeared to be a kind of ruin; no road led up to it; no smoke arose from any of the chimneys; nor was there any semblance of a garden. My heart sank. "That!" I cried.

The woman's face lit up with a malignant anger. "That is the house of Shaws!" she cried. "Blood built it; blood stopped the building of it; blood shall bring it down. See here!" she cried again—"I spit upon the ground, and crack my thumb at it! Black be its fall! If ye see the laird, tell him what ye hear; tell him this makes the twelve hunner and nineteen time that Jennet Clouston has called down the curse on him and his house, byre and stable, man, guest, and master, wife, miss, or bairn—black, black be their fall!"

And the woman, whose voice had risen to a kind of eldritch sing-song, turned with a skip, and was gone. I stood where she left me, with my hair on end. In those days folk still believed in witches and trembled at a curse; and this one, falling so pat, like a wayside omen, to arrest me ere I carried out my purpose, took the pith out of my legs.

I sat me down and stared at the house of Shaws. The more I looked, the pleasanter that countryside appeared; being all set with hawthorn bushes full of flowers; the fields dotted with sheep; a fine flight of rooks in the sky; and every sign of a kind soil and climate; and yet the barrack in the midst of it went sore against my fancy.

Country folk went by from the fields as I sat there on the side of the ditch, but I lacked the spirit to give them a good-e'en. At last the sun went down, and then, right up against the yellow sky, I saw a scroll of smoke go mounting, not much thicker, as it seemed to me, than the smoke of a candle; but still there it was, and meant a fire, and warmth, and cookery, and some living inhabitant that must have lit it; and this comforted my heart.

So I set forward by a little faint track in the grass that led in my direction. It was very faint indeed to be the only way to a place of habitation; yet I saw no other. Presently it brought me to stone uprights, with an unroofed lodge beside them, and coats of arms upon the top. A main entrance it was plainly meant to be, but never finished; instead of gates of wrought iron, a pair of hurdles were tied across with a straw rope; and as there were no park walls, nor any sign of avenue, the track that I was following passed on the right hand of the pillars, and went wandering on toward the house.

The nearer I got to that, the drearier it appeared. It seemed like the one wing of a house that had never been finished. What should have been the inner end stood open on the upper floors, and showed against the sky with steps and stairs of uncompleted masonry. Many of the windows were unglazed, and bats flew in and out like doves out of a dove-cote.

The night had begun to fall as I got close; and in three of the lower windows, which were very high up and narrow, and well barred, the changing light of a little fire began to glimmer. Was this the palace I had been coming to? Was it within these walls that I was to seek new friends and begin great fortunes? Why, in my father's house on Essen-Waterside, the fire and the bright lights would show a mile away, and the door open to a beggar's knock!

I came forward cautiously, and giving ear as I came, heard some one rattling with dishes, and a little dry, eager cough that came in fits; but there was no sound of speech, and not a dog barked.

The door, as well as I could see it in the dim light, was a great piece of wood all studded with nails; and I lifted my hand with a faint heart under my jacket, and knocked once. Then I stood and waited. The house had fallen into a dead silence; a whole minute passed away, and nothing stirred but the bats overhead. I knocked again, and hearkened again. By this time my ears had grown so accustomed to the quiet, that I could hear the ticking of the clock inside as it slowly counted out the seconds; but whoever was in that house kept deadly still, and must have held his breath.

I was in two minds whether to run away; but anger got the upper hand, and I began instead to rain kicks and buffets on the door, and to shout out aloud for Mr. Balfour. I was in full career, when I heard the cough right overhead, and jumping back and looking up, beheld a man's head in a tall nightcap, and the bell mouth of a blunderbuss, at one of the first-storey windows.

"It's loaded," said a voice.

"I have come here with a letter," I said, "to Mr. Ebenezer Balfour of Shaws. Is he here?"

"From whom is it?" asked the man with the blunderbuss.

"That is neither here nor there," said I, for I was growing very wroth.

"Well," was the reply, "ye can put it down upon the doorstep, and be off with ye."

"I will do no such thing," I cried. "I will deliver it into Mr. Balfour's hands, as it was meant I should. It is a letter of introduction."

"A what?" cried the voice, sharply.

I repeated what I had said.

"Who are ye, yourself?" was the next question, after a considerable pause.

"I am not ashamed of my name," said I. "They call me David Balfour."

At that, I made sure the man started, for I heard the blunderbuss rattle on the window-sill; and it was after quite a long pause, and with a curious change of voice, that the next question followed:

"Is your father dead?"

I was so much surprised at this, that I could find no voice to answer, but stood staring.

"Ay," the man resumed, "he'll be dead, no doubt; and that'll be what brings ye chapping to my door." Another pause, and then defiantly, "Well, man," he said, "I'll let ye in;" and he disappeared from the window.

CHAPTER III

I MAKE ACQUAINTANCE OF MY UNCLE

Presently there came a great rattling of chains and bolts, and the door was cautiously opened and shut to again behind me as soon as I had passed.

"Go into the kitchen and touch naething," said the voice; and while the person of the house set himself to replacing the defences of the door, I groped my way forward and entered the kitchen.

The fire had burned up fairly bright, and showed me the barest room I think I ever put my eyes on. Half-a-dozen dishes stood upon the shelves; the table was laid for supper with a bowl of porridge, a horn spoon, and a cup of small beer. Besides what I have named, there was not another thing in that great, stone-vaulted, empty chamber but lockfast chests arranged along the wall and a corner cupboard with a padlock.

As soon as the last chain was up, the man rejoined me. He was a mean, stooping, narrow-shouldered, clay-faced creature; and his age might have been anything between fifty and seventy. His nightcap was of flannel, and so was the nightgown that he wore, instead of coat and waistcoat, over his ragged shirt. He was long unshaved; but what most distressed and even daunted me, he would neither take his eyes away from me nor look me fairly in the face. What he was, whether by trade or birth, was more than I could fathom; but he seemed most like an old, unprofitable serving-man, who should have been left in charge of that big house upon board wages.

"Are ye sharp-set?" he asked, glancing at about the level of my knee. "Ye can eat that drop parritch?"

I said I feared it was his own supper.

"O," said he, "I can do fine wanting it. I'll take the ale, though, for it slockens (moistens) my cough." He drank the cup about half out, still keeping an eye upon me as he drank; and then suddenly held out his hand. "Let's see the letter," said he.

I told him the letter was for Mr. Balfour; not for him.

"And who do ye think I am?" says he. "Give me Alexander's letter."

"You know my father's name?"

"It would be strange if I didnae," he returned, "for he was my born brother; and little as ye seem to like either me or my house, or my good parritch, I'm your born uncle, Davie, my man, and you my born nephew. So give us the letter, and sit down and fill your kyte."

If I had been some years younger, what with shame, weariness, and disappointment, I believe I had burst into tears. As it was, I could find no words, neither black nor white, but handed him the letter, and sat down to the porridge with as little appetite for meat as ever a young man had.

Meanwhile, my uncle, stooping over the fire, turned the letter over and over in his hands.

"Do ye ken what's in it?" he asked, suddenly.

"You see for yourself, sir," said I, "that the seal has not been broken."

"Ay," said he, "but what brought you here?"

"To give the letter," said I.

"No," says he, cunningly, "but ye'll have had some hopes, nae doubt?"

"I confess, sir," said I, "when I was told that I had kinsfolk well-to-do, I did indeed indulge the hope that they might help me in my life. But I am no beggar; I look for no favours at your hands, and I want none that are not freely given. For as poor as I appear, I have friends of my own that will be blithe to help me."

"Hoot-toot!" said Uncle Ebenezer, "dinnae fly up in the snuff at me. We'll agree fine yet. And, Davie, my man, if you're done with that bit parritch, I could just take a sup of it myself. Ay," he continued, as soon as he had ousted me from the stool and spoon, "they're fine, halesome food—they're grand food, parritch." He murmured a little grace to himself and fell to. "Your father was very fond of his meat, I mind; he was a hearty, if not a great eater; but as for me, I could never do mair than pyke at food." He took a pull at the small beer, which probably reminded him of hospitable duties, for his next speech ran thus: "If ye're dry ye'll find water behind the door."

To this I returned no answer, standing stiffly on my two feet, and looking down upon my uncle with a mighty angry heart. He, on his part, continued to eat like a man under some pressure of time, and to throw out little darting glances now at my shoes and now at my home-spun stockings. Once only, when he had ventured to look a little higher, our eyes met; and no thief taken with a hand in a man's pocket could have shown more lively signals of distress. This set me in a muse, whether his timidity arose from too long a disuse of any human company; and whether perhaps, upon a little trial, it might pass off, and my uncle change into an altogether different man. From this I was awakened by his sharp voice.

"Your father's been long dead?" he asked.

"Three weeks, sir," said I.

"He was a secret man, Alexander—a secret, silent man," he continued. "He never said muckle when he was young. He'll never have spoken muckle of me?"

"I never knew, sir, till you told it me yourself, that he had any brother."

"Dear me, dear me!" said Ebenezer. "Nor yet of Shaws, I dare say?"

"Not so much as the name, sir," said I.

"To think o' that!" said he. "A strange nature of a man!" For all that, he seemed singularly satisfied, but whether with himself, or me, or with this conduct of my father's, was more than I could read. Certainly, however, he seemed to be outgrowing that distaste, or ill-will, that he had conceived at first against my person; for presently he jumped up, came across the room behind me, and hit me a smack upon the shoulder. "We'll agree fine yet!" he cried. "I'm just as glad I let you in. And now come awa' to your bed."

To my surprise, he lit no lamp or candle, but set forth into the dark passage, groped his way, breathing deeply, up a flight of steps, and paused before a door, which he unlocked. I was close upon his heels, having stumbled after him as best I might; and then he bade me go in, for that was my chamber. I did as he bid, but paused after a few steps, and begged a light to go to bed with.

"Hoot-toot!" said Uncle Ebenezer, "there's a fine moon."

"Neither moon nor star, sir, and pit-mirk,"* said I. "I cannae see the bed."

   * Dark as the pit.

"Hoot-toot, hoot-toot!" said he. "Lights in a house is a thing I dinnae agree with. I'm unco feared of fires. Good-night to ye, Davie, my man." And before I had time to add a further protest, he pulled the door to, and I heard him lock me in from the outside.

I did not know whether to laugh or cry. The room was as cold as a well, and the bed, when I had found my way to it, as damp as a peat-hag; but by good fortune I had caught up my bundle and my plaid, and rolling myself in the latter, I lay down upon the floor under lee of the big bedstead, and fell speedily asleep.

With the first peep of day I opened my eyes, to find myself in a great chamber, hung with stamped leather, furnished with fine embroidered furniture, and lit by three fair windows. Ten years ago, or perhaps twenty, it must have been as pleasant a room to lie down or to awake in as a man could wish; but damp, dirt, disuse, and the mice and spiders had done their worst since then. Many of the window-panes, besides, were broken; and indeed this was so common a feature in that house, that I believe my uncle must at some time have stood a siege from his indignant neighbours—perhaps with Jennet Clouston at their head.

Meanwhile the sun was shining outside; and being very cold in that miserable room, I knocked and shouted till my gaoler came and let me out. He carried me to the back of the house, where was a draw-well, and told me to "wash my face there, if I wanted;" and when that was done, I made the best of my own way back to the kitchen, where he had lit the fire and was making the porridge. The table was laid with two bowls and two horn spoons, but the same single measure of small beer. Perhaps my eye rested on this particular with some surprise, and perhaps my uncle observed it; for he spoke up as if in answer to my thought, asking me if I would like to drink ale—for so he called it.

I told him such was my habit, but not to put himself about.

"Na, na," said he; "I'll deny you nothing in reason."

He fetched another cup from the shelf; and then, to my great surprise, instead of drawing more beer, he poured an accurate half from one cup to the other. There was a kind of nobleness in this that took my breath away; if my uncle was certainly a miser, he was one of that thorough breed that goes near to make the vice respectable.

When we had made an end of our meal, my uncle Ebenezer unlocked a drawer, and drew out of it a clay pipe and a lump of tobacco, from which he cut one fill before he locked it up again. Then he sat down in the sun at one of the windows and silently smoked. From time to time his eyes came coasting round to me, and he shot out one of his questions. Once it was, "And your mother?" and when I had told him that she, too, was dead, "Ay, she was a bonnie lassie!" Then, after another long pause, "Whae were these friends o' yours?"

I told him they were different gentlemen of the name of Campbell; though, indeed, there was only one, and that the minister, that had ever taken the least note of me; but I began to think my uncle made too light of my position, and finding myself all alone with him, I did not wish him to suppose me helpless.

He seemed to turn this over in his mind; and then, "Davie, my man," said he, "ye've come to the right bit when ye came to your uncle Ebenezer. I've a great notion of the family, and I mean to do the right by you; but while I'm taking a bit think to mysel' of what's the best thing to put you to—whether the law, or the meenistry, or maybe the army, whilk is what boys are fondest of—I wouldnae like the Balfours to be humbled before a wheen Hieland Campbells, and I'll ask you to keep your tongue within your teeth. Nae letters; nae messages; no kind of word to onybody; or else—there's my door."

"Uncle Ebenezer," said I, "I've no manner of reason to suppose you mean anything but well by me. For all that, I would have you to know that I have a pride of my own. It was by no will of mine that I came seeking you; and if you show me your door again, I'll take you at the word."

He seemed grievously put out. "Hoots-toots," said he, "ca' cannie, man—ca' cannie! Bide a day or two. I'm nae warlock, to find a fortune for you in the bottom of a parritch bowl; but just you give me a day or two, and say naething to naebody, and as sure as sure, I'll do the right by you."

"Very well," said I, "enough said. If you want to help me, there's no doubt but I'll be glad of it, and none but I'll be grateful."

It seemed to me (too soon, I dare say) that I was getting the upper hand of my uncle; and I began next to say that I must have the bed and bedclothes aired and put to sun-dry; for nothing would make me sleep in such a pickle.

"Is this my house or yours?" said he, in his keen voice, and then all of a sudden broke off. "Na, na," said he, "I didnae mean that. What's mine is yours, Davie, my man, and what's yours is mine. Blood's thicker than water; and there's naebody but you and me that ought the name." And then on he rambled about the family, and its ancient greatness, and his father that began to enlarge the house, and himself that stopped the building as a sinful waste; and this put it in my head to give him Jennet Clouston's message.

"The limmer!" he cried. "Twelve hunner and fifteen—that's every day since I had the limmer rowpit!* Dod, David, I'll have her roasted on red peats before I'm by with it! A witch—a proclaimed witch! I'll aff and see the session clerk."

   * Sold up.

And with that he opened a chest, and got out a very old and well-preserved blue coat and waistcoat, and a good enough beaver hat, both without lace. These he threw on any way, and taking a staff from the cupboard, locked all up again, and was for setting out, when a thought arrested him.

"I cannae leave you by yoursel' in the house," said he. "I'll have to lock you out."

The blood came to my face. "If you lock me out," I said, "it'll be the last you'll see of me in friendship."

He turned very pale, and sucked his mouth in.

"This is no the way," he said, looking wickedly at a corner of the floor—"this is no the way to win my favour, David."

"Sir," says I, "with a proper reverence for your age and our common blood, I do not value your favour at a boddle's purchase. I was brought up to have a good conceit of myself; and if you were all the uncle, and all the family, I had in the world ten times over, I wouldn't buy your liking at such prices."

Uncle Ebenezer went and looked out of the window for awhile. I could see him all trembling and twitching, like a man with palsy. But when he turned round, he had a smile upon his face.

"Well, well," said he, "we must bear and forbear. I'll no go; that's all that's to be said of it."

"Uncle Ebenezer," I said, "I can make nothing out of this. You use me like a thief; you hate to have me in this house; you let me see it, every word and every minute: it's not possible that you can like me; and as for me, I've spoken to you as I never thought to speak to any man. Why do you seek to keep me, then? Let me gang back—let me gang back to the friends I have, and that like me!"

"Na, na; na, na," he said, very earnestly. "I like you fine; we'll agree fine yet; and for the honour of the house I couldnae let you leave the way ye came. Bide here quiet, there's a good lad; just you bide here quiet a bittie, and ye'll find that we agree."

"Well, sir," said I, after I had thought the matter out in silence, "I'll stay awhile. It's more just I should be helped by my own blood than strangers; and if we don't agree, I'll do my best it shall be through no fault of mine."

CHAPTER IV

I RUN A GREAT DANGER IN THE HOUSE OF SHAWS

For a day that was begun so ill, the day passed fairly well. We had the porridge cold again at noon, and hot porridge at night; porridge and small beer was my uncle's diet. He spoke but little, and that in the same way as before, shooting a question at me after a long silence; and when I sought to lead him to talk about my future, slipped out of it again. In a room next door to the kitchen, where he suffered me to go, I found a great number of books, both Latin and English, in which I took great pleasure all the afternoon. Indeed, the time passed so lightly in this good company, that I began to be almost reconciled to my residence at Shaws; and nothing but the sight of my uncle, and his eyes playing hide and seek with mine, revived the force of my distrust.

One thing I discovered, which put me in some doubt. This was an entry on the fly-leaf of a chap-book (one of Patrick Walker's) plainly written by my father's hand and thus conceived: "To my brother Ebenezer on his fifth birthday." Now, what puzzled me was this: That, as my father was of course the younger brother, he must either have made some strange error, or he must have written, before he was yet five, an excellent, clear manly hand of writing.

I tried to get this out of my head; but though I took down many interesting authors, old and new, history, poetry, and story-book, this notion of my father's hand of writing stuck to me; and when at length I went back into the kitchen, and sat down once more to porridge and small beer, the first thing I said to Uncle Ebenezer was to ask him if my father had not been very quick at his book.

"Alexander? No him!" was the reply. "I was far quicker mysel'; I was a clever chappie when I was young. Why, I could read as soon as he could."

This puzzled me yet more; and a thought coming into my head, I asked if he and my father had been twins.

He jumped upon his stool, and the horn spoon fell out of his hand upon the floor. "What gars ye ask that?" he said, and he caught me by the breast of the jacket, and looked this time straight into my eyes: his own were little and light, and bright like a bird's, blinking and winking strangely.

"What do you mean?" I asked, very calmly, for I was far stronger than he, and not easily frightened. "Take your hand from my jacket. This is no way to behave."

My uncle seemed to make a great effort upon himself. "Dod man, David," he said, "ye should-nae speak to me about your father. That's where the mistake is." He sat awhile and shook, blinking in his plate: "He was all the brother that ever I had," he added, but with no heart in his voice; and then he caught up his spoon and fell to supper again, but still shaking.

Now this last passage, this laying of hands upon my person and sudden profession of love for my dead father, went so clean beyond my comprehension that it put me into both fear and hope. On the one hand, I began to think my uncle was perhaps insane and might be dangerous; on the other, there came up into my mind (quite unbidden by me and even discouraged) a story like some ballad I had heard folk singing, of a poor lad that was a rightful heir and a wicked kinsman that tried to keep him from his own. For why should my uncle play a part with a relative that came, almost a beggar, to his door, unless in his heart he had some cause to fear him?

With this notion, all unacknowledged, but nevertheless getting firmly settled in my head, I now began to imitate his covert looks; so that we sat at table like a cat and a mouse, each stealthily observing the other. Not another word had he to say to me, black or white, but was busy turning something secretly over in his mind; and the longer we sat and the more I looked at him, the more certain I became that the something was unfriendly to myself.

When he had cleared the platter, he got out a single pipeful of tobacco, just as in the morning, turned round a stool into the chimney corner, and sat awhile smoking, with his back to me.

"Davie," he said, at length, "I've been thinking;" then he paused, and said it again. "There's a wee bit siller that I half promised ye before ye were born," he continued; "promised it to your father. O, naething legal, ye understand; just gentlemen daffing at their wine. Well, I keepit that bit money separate—it was a great expense, but a promise is a promise—and it has grown by now to be a matter of just precisely—just exactly"—and here he paused and stumbled—"of just exactly forty pounds!" This last he rapped out with a sidelong glance over his shoulder; and the next moment added, almost with a scream, "Scots!"

The pound Scots being the same thing as an English shilling, the difference made by this second thought was considerable; I could see, besides, that the whole story was a lie, invented with some end which it puzzled me to guess; and I made no attempt to conceal the tone of raillery in which I answered—

"O, think again, sir! Pounds sterling, I believe!"

"That's what I said," returned my uncle: "pounds sterling! And if you'll step out-by to the door a minute, just to see what kind of a night it is, I'll get it out to ye and call ye in again."

I did his will, smiling to myself in my contempt that he should think I was so easily to be deceived. It was a dark night, with a few stars low down; and as I stood just outside the door, I heard a hollow moaning of wind far off among the hills. I said to myself there was something thundery and changeful in the weather, and little knew of what a vast importance that should prove to me before the evening passed.

When I was called in again, my uncle counted out into my hand seven and thirty golden guinea pieces; the rest was in his hand, in small gold and silver; but his heart failed him there, and he crammed the change into his pocket.

"There," said he, "that'll show you! I'm a queer man, and strange wi' strangers; but my word is my bond, and there's the proof of it."

Now, my uncle seemed so miserly that I was struck dumb by this sudden generosity, and could find no words in which to thank him.

"No a word!" said he. "Nae thanks; I want nae thanks. I do my duty. I'm no saying that everybody would have done it; but for my part (though I'm a careful body, too) it's a pleasure to me to do the right by my brother's son; and it's a pleasure to me to think that now we'll agree as such near friends should."

I spoke him in return as handsomely as I was able; but all the while I was wondering what would come next, and why he had parted with his precious guineas; for as to the reason he had given, a baby would have refused it.

Presently he looked towards me sideways.

"And see here," says he, "tit for tat."

I told him I was ready to prove my gratitude in any reasonable degree, and then waited, looking for some monstrous demand. And yet, when at last he plucked up courage to speak, it was only to tell me (very properly, as I thought) that he was growing old and a little broken, and that he would expect me to help him with the house and the bit garden.

I answered, and expressed my readiness to serve.

"Well," he said, "let's begin." He pulled out of his pocket a rusty key. "There," says he, "there's the key of the stair-tower at the far end of the house. Ye can only win into it from the outside, for that part of the house is no finished. Gang ye in there, and up the stairs, and bring me down the chest that's at the top. There's papers in't," he added.

"Can I have a light, sir?" said I.

"Na," said he, very cunningly. "Nae lights in my house."

"Very well, sir," said I. "Are the stairs good?"

"They're grand," said he; and then, as I was going, "Keep to the wall," he added; "there's nae bannisters. But the stairs are grand underfoot."

Out I went into the night. The wind was still moaning in the distance, though never a breath of it came near the house of Shaws. It had fallen blacker than ever; and I was glad to feel along the wall, till I came the length of the stairtower door at the far end of the unfinished wing. I had got the key into the keyhole and had just turned it, when all upon a sudden, without sound of wind or thunder, the whole sky lighted up with wild fire and went black again. I had to put my hand over my eyes to get back to the colour of the darkness; and indeed I was already half blinded when I stepped into the tower.

It was so dark inside, it seemed a body could scarce breathe; but I pushed out with foot and hand, and presently struck the wall with the one, and the lowermost round of the stair with the other. The wall, by the touch, was of fine hewn stone; the steps too, though somewhat steep and narrow, were of polished masonwork, and regular and solid underfoot. Minding my uncle's word about the bannisters, I kept close to the tower side, and felt my way in the pitch darkness with a beating heart.

The house of Shaws stood some five full storeys high, not counting lofts. Well, as I advanced, it seemed to me the stair grew airier and a thought more lightsome; and I was wondering what might be the cause of this change, when a second blink of the summer lightning came and went. If I did not cry out, it was because fear had me by the throat; and if I did not fall, it was more by Heaven's mercy than my own strength. It was not only that the flash shone in on every side through breaches in the wall, so that I seemed to be clambering aloft upon an open scaffold, but the same passing brightness showed me the steps were of unequal length, and that one of my feet rested that moment within two inches of the well.

This was the grand stair! I thought; and with the thought, a gust of a kind of angry courage came into my heart. My uncle had sent me here, certainly to run great risks, perhaps to die. I swore I would settle that "perhaps," if I should break my neck for it; got me down upon my hands and knees; and as slowly as a snail, feeling before me every inch, and testing the solidity of every stone, I continued to ascend the stair. The darkness, by contrast with the flash, appeared to have redoubled; nor was that all, for my ears were now troubled and my mind confounded by a great stir of bats in the top part of the tower, and the foul beasts, flying downwards, sometimes beat about my face and body.

The tower, I should have said, was square; and in every corner the step was made of a great stone of a different shape to join the flights. Well, I had come close to one of these turns, when, feeling forward as usual, my hand slipped upon an edge and found nothing but emptiness beyond it. The stair had been carried no higher; to set a stranger mounting it in the darkness was to send him straight to his death; and (although, thanks to the lightning and my own precautions, I was safe enough) the mere thought of the peril in which I might have stood, and the dreadful height I might have fallen from, brought out the sweat upon my body and relaxed my joints.

But I knew what I wanted now, and turned and groped my way down again, with a wonderful anger in my heart. About half-way down, the wind sprang up in a clap and shook the tower, and died again; the rain followed; and before I had reached the ground level it fell in buckets. I put out my head into the storm, and looked along towards the kitchen. The door, which I had shut behind me when I left, now stood open, and shed a little glimmer of light; and I thought I could see a figure standing in the rain, quite still, like a man hearkening. And then there came a blinding flash, which showed me my uncle plainly, just where I had fancied him to stand; and hard upon the heels of it, a great tow-row of thunder.

Now, whether my uncle thought the crash to be the sound of my fall, or whether he heard in it God's voice denouncing murder, I will leave you to guess. Certain it is, at least, that he was seized on by a kind of panic fear, and that he ran into the house and left the door open behind him. I followed as softly as I could, and, coming unheard into the kitchen, stood and watched him.

He had found time to open the corner cupboard and bring out a great case bottle of aqua vitae, and now sat with his back towards me at the table. Ever and again he would be seized with a fit of deadly shuddering and groan aloud, and carrying the bottle to his lips, drink down the raw spirits by the mouthful.

I stepped forward, came close behind him where he sat, and suddenly clapping my two hands down upon his shoulders—"Ah!" cried I.

My uncle gave a kind of broken cry like a sheep's bleat, flung up his arms, and tumbled to the floor like a dead man. I was somewhat shocked at this; but I had myself to look to first of all, and did not hesitate to let him lie as he had fallen. The keys were hanging in the cupboard; and it was my design to furnish myself with arms before my uncle should come again to his senses and the power of devising evil. In the cupboard were a few bottles, some apparently of medicine; a great many bills and other papers, which I should willingly enough have rummaged, had I had the time; and a few necessaries that were nothing to my purpose. Thence I turned to the chests. The first was full of meal; the second of moneybags and papers tied into sheaves; in the third, with many other things (and these for the most part clothes) I found a rusty, ugly-looking Highland dirk without the scabbard. This, then, I concealed inside my waistcoat, and turned to my uncle.

He lay as he had fallen, all huddled, with one knee up and one arm sprawling abroad; his face had a strange colour of blue, and he seemed to have ceased breathing. Fear came on me that he was dead; then I got water and dashed it in his face; and with that he seemed to come a little to himself, working his mouth and fluttering his eyelids. At last he looked up and saw me, and there came into his eyes a terror that was not of this world.

"Come, come," said I; "sit up."

"Are ye alive?" he sobbed. "O man, are ye alive?"

"That am I," said I. "Small thanks to you!"

He had begun to seek for his breath with deep sighs. "The blue phial," said he—"in the aumry—the blue phial." His breath came slower still.

I ran to the cupboard, and, sure enough, found there a blue phial of medicine, with the dose written on it on a paper, and this I administered to him with what speed I might.

"It's the trouble," said he, reviving a little; "I have a trouble, Davie. It's the heart."

I set him on a chair and looked at him. It is true I felt some pity for a man that looked so sick, but I was full besides of righteous anger; and I numbered over before him the points on which I wanted explanation: why he lied to me at every word; why he feared that I should leave him; why he disliked it to be hinted that he and my father were twins—"Is that because it is true?" I asked; why he had given me money to which I was convinced I had no claim; and, last of all, why he had tried to kill me. He heard me all through in silence; and then, in a broken voice, begged me to let him go to bed.

"I'll tell ye the morn," he said; "as sure as death I will."

And so weak was he that I could do nothing but consent. I locked him into his room, however, and pocketed the key, and then returning to the kitchen, made up such a blaze as had not shone there for many a long year, and wrapping myself in my plaid, lay down upon the chests and fell asleep.

CHAPTER V
I GO TO THE QUEEN'S FERRY

Much rain fell in the night; and the next morning there blew a bitter wintry wind out of the north-west, driving scattered clouds. For all that, and before the sun began to peep or the last of the stars had vanished, I made my way to the side of the burn, and had a plunge in a deep whirling pool. All aglow from my bath, I sat down once more beside the fire, which I replenished, and began gravely to consider my position.

There was now no doubt about my uncle's enmity; there was no doubt I carried my life in my hand, and he would leave no stone unturned that he might compass my destruction. But I was young and spirited, and like most lads that have been country-bred, I had a great opinion of my shrewdness. I had come to his door no better than a beggar and little more than a child; he had met me with treachery and violence; it would be a fine consummation to take the upper hand, and drive him like a herd of sheep.

I sat there nursing my knee and smiling at the fire; and I saw myself in fancy smell out his secrets one after another, and grow to be that man's king and ruler. The warlock of Essendean, they say, had made a mirror in which men could read the future; it must have been of other stuff than burning coal; for in all the shapes and pictures that I sat and gazed at, there was never a ship, never a seaman with a hairy cap, never a big bludgeon for my silly head, or the least sign of all those tribulations that were ripe to fall on me.

Presently, all swollen with conceit, I went up-stairs and gave my prisoner his liberty. He gave me good-morning civilly; and I gave the same to him, smiling down upon him, from the heights of my sufficiency. Soon we were set to breakfast, as it might have been the day before.

"Well, sir," said I, with a jeering tone, "have you nothing more to say to me?" And then, as he made no articulate reply, "It will be time, I think, to understand each other," I continued. "You took me for a country Johnnie Raw, with no more mother-wit or courage than a porridge-stick. I took you for a good man, or no worse than others at the least. It seems we were both wrong. What cause you have to fear me, to cheat me, and to attempt my life—"

He murmured something about a jest, and that he liked a bit of fun; and then, seeing me smile, changed his tone, and assured me he would make all clear as soon as we had breakfasted. I saw by his face that he had no lie ready for me, though he was hard at work preparing one; and I think I was about to tell him so, when we were interrupted by a knocking at the door.

Bidding my uncle sit where he was, I went to open it, and found on the doorstep a half-grown boy in sea-clothes. He had no sooner seen me than he began to dance some steps of the sea-hornpipe (which I had never before heard of far less seen), snapping his fingers in the air and footing it right cleverly. For all that, he was blue with the cold; and there was something in his face, a look between tears and laughter, that was highly pathetic and consisted ill with this gaiety of manner.

"What cheer, mate?" says he, with a cracked voice.

I asked him soberly to name his pleasure.

"O, pleasure!" says he; and then began to sing:

"For it's my delight, of a shiny night,

In the season of the year."

"Well," said I, "if you have no business at all, I will even be so unmannerly as to shut you out."

"Stay, brother!" he cried. "Have you no fun about you? or do you want to get me thrashed? I've brought a letter from old Heasyoasy to Mr. Belflower." He showed me a letter as he spoke. "And I say, mate," he added, "I'm mortal hungry."

"Well," said I, "come into the house, and you shall have a bite if I go empty for it."

With that I brought him in and set him down to my own place, where he fell-to greedily on the remains of breakfast, winking to me between whiles, and making many faces, which I think the poor soul considered manly. Meanwhile, my uncle had read the letter and sat thinking; then, suddenly, he got to his feet with a great air of liveliness, and pulled me apart into the farthest corner of the room.

"Read that," said he, and put the letter in my hand.

Here it is, lying before me as I write:

"The Hawes Inn, at the Queen's Ferry.

"Sir,—I lie here with my hawser up and down, and send my cabin-boy to informe. If you have any further commands for over-seas, to-day will be the last occasion, as the wind will serve us well out of the firth. I will not seek to deny that I have had crosses with your doer,* Mr. Rankeillor; of which, if not speedily redd up, you may looke to see some losses follow. I have drawn a bill upon you, as per margin, and am, sir, your most obedt., humble servant, "ELIAS HOSEASON." * Agent.

"You see, Davie," resumed my uncle, as soon as he saw that I had done, "I have a venture with this man Hoseason, the captain of a trading brig, the Covenant, of Dysart. Now, if you and me was to walk over with yon lad, I could see the captain at the Hawes, or maybe on board the Covenant if there was papers to be signed; and so far from a loss of time, we can jog on to the lawyer, Mr. Rankeillor's. After a' that's come and gone, ye would be swier* to believe me upon my naked word; but ye'll believe Rankeillor. He's factor to half the gentry in these parts; an auld man, forby: highly respeckit, and he kenned your father."

* Unwilling.

I stood awhile and thought. I was going to some place of shipping, which was doubtless populous, and where my uncle durst attempt no violence, and, indeed, even the society of the cabin-boy so far protected me. Once there, I believed I could force on the visit to the lawyer, even if my uncle were now insincere in proposing it; and, perhaps, in the bottom of my heart, I wished a nearer view of the sea and ships. You are to remember I had lived all my life in the inland hills, and just two days before had my first sight of the firth lying like a blue floor, and the sailed ships moving on the face of it, no bigger than toys. One thing with another, I made up my mind.

"Very well," says I, "let us go to the Ferry."

My uncle got into his hat and coat, and buckled an old rusty cutlass on; and then we trod the fire out, locked the door, and set forth upon our walk.

The wind, being in that cold quarter the north-west, blew nearly in our faces as we went. It was the month of June; the grass was all white with daisies, and the trees with blossom; but, to judge by our blue nails and aching wrists, the time might have been winter and the whiteness a December frost.

Uncle Ebenezer trudged in the ditch, jogging from side to side like an old ploughman coming home from work. He never said a word the whole way; and I was thrown for talk on the cabin-boy. He told me his name was Ransome, and that he had followed the sea since he was nine, but could not say how old he was, as he had lost his reckoning. He showed me tattoo marks, baring his breast in the teeth of the wind and in spite of my remonstrances, for I thought it was enough to kill him; he swore horribly whenever he remembered, but more like a silly schoolboy than a man; and boasted of many wild and bad things that he had done: stealthy thefts, false accusations, ay, and even murder; but all with such a dearth of likelihood in the details, and such a weak and crazy swagger in the delivery, as disposed me rather to pity than to believe him.

I asked him of the brig (which he declared was the finest ship that sailed) and of Captain Hoseason, in whose praises he was equally loud. Heasyoasy (for so he still named the skipper) was a man, by his account, that minded for nothing either in heaven or earth; one that, as people said, would "crack on all sail into the day of judgment;" rough, fierce, unscrupulous, and brutal; and all this my poor cabin-boy had taught himself to admire as something seamanlike and manly. He would only admit one flaw in his idol. "He ain't no seaman," he admitted. "That's Mr. Shuan that navigates the brig; he's the finest seaman in the trade, only for drink; and I tell you I believe it! Why, look'ere;" and turning down his stocking he showed me a great, raw, red wound that made my blood run cold. "He done that—Mr. Shuan done it," he said, with an air of pride.

"What!" I cried, "do you take such savage usage at his hands? Why, you are no slave, to be so handled!"

"No," said the poor moon-calf, changing his tune at once, "and so he'll find. See'ere;" and he showed me a great case-knife, which he told me was stolen. "O," says he, "let me see him try; I dare him to; I'll do for him! O, he ain't the first!" And he confirmed it with a poor, silly, ugly oath.

I have never felt such pity for any one in this wide world as I felt for that half-witted creature, and it began to come over me that the brig Covenant (for all her pious name) was little better than a hell upon the seas.

"Have you no friends?" said I.

He said he had a father in some English seaport, he forgot which.

"He was a fine man, too," he said, "but he's dead."

"In Heaven's name," cried I, "can you find no reputable life on shore?"

"O, no," says he, winking and looking very sly, "they would put me to a trade. I know a trick worth two of that, I do!"

I asked him what trade could be so dreadful as the one he followed, where he ran the continual peril of his life, not alone from wind and sea, but by the horrid cruelty of those who were his masters. He said it was very true; and then began to praise the life, and tell what a pleasure it was to get on shore with money in his pocket, and spend it like a man, and buy apples, and swagger, and surprise what he called stick-in-the-mud boys. "And then it's not all as bad as that," says he;

"there's worse off than me: there's the twenty-pounders. O, laws! you should see them taking on. Why, I've seen a man as old as you, I dessay"—(to him I seemed old)—"ah, and he had a beard, too—well, and as soon as we cleared out of the river, and he had the drug out of his head—my! how he cried and carried on! I made a fine fool of him, I tell you! And then there's little uns, too: oh, little by me! I tell you, I keep them in order. When we carry little uns, I have a rope's end of my own to wollop'em." And so he ran on, until it came in on me what he meant by twenty-pounders were those unhappy criminals who were sent over-seas to slavery in North America, or the still more unhappy innocents who were kidnapped or trepanned (as the word went) for private interest or vengeance.

Just then we came to the top of the hill, and looked down on the Ferry and the Hope. The Firth of Forth (as is very well known) narrows at this point to the width of a good-sized river, which makes a convenient ferry going north, and turns the upper reach into a landlocked haven for all manner of ships. Right in the midst of the narrows lies an islet with some ruins; on the south shore they have built a pier for the service of the Ferry; and at the end of the pier, on the other side of the road, and backed against a pretty garden of holly-trees and hawthorns, I could see the building which they called the Hawes Inn.

The town of Queensferry lies farther west, and the neighbourhood of the inn looked pretty lonely at that time of day, for the boat had just gone north with passengers. A skiff, however, lay beside the pier, with some seamen sleeping on the thwarts; this, as Ransome told me, was the brig's boat waiting for the captain; and about half a mile off, and all alone in the anchorage, he showed me the Covenant herself. There was a sea-going bustle on board; yards were swinging into place; and as the wind blew from that quarter, I could hear the song of the sailors as they pulled upon the ropes. After all I had listened to upon the way, I looked at that ship with an extreme abhorrence; and from the bottom of my heart I pitied all poor souls that were condemned to sail in her.

We had all three pulled up on the brow of the hill; and now I marched across the road and addressed my uncle. "I think it right to tell you, sir," says I, "there's nothing that will bring me on board that Covenant."

He seemed to waken from a dream. "Eh?" he said. "What's that?"

I told him over again.

"Well, well," he said, "we'll have to please ye, I suppose. But what are we standing here for? It's perishing cold; and if I'm no mistaken, they're busking the Covenant for sea."

CHAPTER VI
WHAT BEFELL AT THE QUEEN'S FERRY

As soon as we came to the inn, Ransome led us up the stair to a small room, with a bed in it, and heated like an oven by a great fire of coal. At a table hard by the chimney, a tall, dark, sober-looking man sat writing. In spite of the heat of the room, he wore a thick sea-jacket, buttoned to the neck, and a tall hairy cap drawn down over his ears; yet I never saw any man, not even a judge upon the bench, look cooler, or more studious and self-possessed, than this ship-captain.

He got to his feet at once, and coming forward, offered his large hand to Ebenezer. "I am proud to see you, Mr. Balfour," said he, in a fine deep voice, "and glad that ye are here in time. The wind's fair, and the tide upon the turn; we'll see the old coal-bucket burning on the Isle of May before to-night."

"Captain Hoseason," returned my uncle, "you keep your room unco hot."

"It's a habit I have, Mr. Balfour," said the skipper. "I'm a cold-rife man by my nature; I have a cold blood, sir. There's neither fur, nor flannel—no, sir, nor hot rum, will warm up what they call the temperature. Sir, it's the same with most men that have been carbonadoed, as they call it, in the tropic seas."

"Well, well, captain," replied my uncle, "we must all be the way we're made."

But it chanced that this fancy of the captain's had a great share in my misfortunes. For though I had promised myself not to let my kinsman out of sight, I was both so impatient for a nearer look of the sea, and so sickened by the closeness of the room, that when he told me to "run down-stairs and play myself awhile," I was fool enough to take him at his word.

Away I went, therefore, leaving the two men sitting down to a bottle and a great mass of papers; and crossing the road in front of the inn, walked down upon the beach. With the wind in that quarter, only little wavelets, not much bigger than I had seen upon a lake, beat upon the shore. But the weeds were new to me—some green, some brown and long, and some with little bladders that crackled between my fingers. Even so far up the firth, the smell of the sea-water was exceedingly salt and stirring; the Covenant, besides, was beginning to shake out her sails, which hung upon the yards in clusters; and the spirit of all that I beheld put me in thoughts of far voyages and foreign places.

I looked, too, at the seamen with the skiff—big brown fellows, some in shirts, some with jackets, some with coloured handkerchiefs about their throats, one with a brace of pistols stuck into his pockets, two or three with knotty bludgeons, and all with their case-knives. I passed the time of day with one that looked less desperate than his fellows, and asked him of the sailing of the brig. He said they would get under way as soon as the ebb set, and expressed his gladness to be out of a port where there were no taverns and fiddlers; but all with such horrifying oaths, that I made haste to get away from him.

This threw me back on Ransome, who seemed the least wicked of that gang, and who soon came out of the inn and ran to me, crying for a bowl of punch. I told him I would give him no such thing, for neither he nor I was of an age for such indulgences. "But a glass of ale you may have, and welcome," said I. He mopped and mowed at me, and called me names; but he was glad to get the ale, for all that; and presently we were set down at a table in the front room of the inn, and both eating and drinking with a good appetite.

Here it occurred to me that, as the landlord was a man of that county, I might do well to make a friend of him. I offered him a share, as was much the custom in those days; but he was far too great a man to sit with such poor customers as Ransome and myself, and he was leaving the room, when I called him back to ask if he knew Mr. Rankeillor.

"Hoot, ay," says he, "and a very honest man. And, O, by-the-by," says he, "was it you that came in with Ebenezer?" And when I had told him yes, "Ye'll be no friend of his?" he asked, meaning, in the Scottish way, that I would be no relative.

I told him no, none.

"I thought not," said he, "and yet ye have a kind of gliff* of Mr. Alexander."

   * Look.

I said it seemed that Ebenezer was ill-seen in the country.

"Nae doubt," said the landlord. "He's a wicked auld man, and there's many would like to see him girning in the tow*. Jennet Clouston and mony mair that he has harried out of house and hame. And yet he was ance a fine young fellow, too. But that was before the sough** gaed abroad about Mr. Alexander, that was like the death of him."

   * Rope.

   ** Report.

"And what was it?" I asked.

"Ou, just that he had killed him," said the landlord. "Did ye never hear that?"

"And what would he kill him for?" said I.

"And what for, but just to get the place," said he.

"The place?" said I. "The Shaws?"

"Nae other place that I ken," said he.

"Ay, man?" said I. "Is that so? Was my—was Alexander the eldest son?"

"'Deed was he," said the landlord. "What else would he have killed him for?"

And with that he went away, as he had been impatient to do from the beginning.

Of course, I had guessed it a long while ago; but it is one thing to guess, another to know; and I sat stunned with my good fortune, and could scarce grow to believe that the same poor lad who had trudged in the dust from Ettrick Forest not two days ago, was now one of the rich of the earth, and had a house and broad lands, and might mount his horse tomorrow. All these pleasant things, and a thousand others, crowded into my mind, as I sat staring before me out of the inn window, and paying no heed to what I saw; only I remember that my eye lighted on Captain Hoseason down on the pier among his seamen, and speaking with some authority. And presently he came marching back towards the house, with no mark of a sailor's clumsiness, but carrying his fine, tall figure with a manly bearing, and still with the same sober, grave expression on his face. I wondered if it was possible that Ransome's stories could be true, and half disbelieved them; they fitted so ill with the man's looks. But indeed, he was neither so good as I supposed him, nor quite so bad as Ransome did; for, in fact, he was two men, and left the better one behind as soon as he set foot on board his vessel.

The next thing, I heard my uncle calling me, and found the pair in the road together. It was the captain who addressed me, and that with an air (very flattering to a young lad) of grave equality.

"Sir," said he, "Mr. Balfour tells me great things of you; and for my own part, I like your looks. I wish I was for longer here, that we might make the better friends; but we'll make the most of what we have. Ye shall come on board my brig for half an hour, till the ebb sets, and drink a bowl with me."

Now, I longed to see the inside of a ship more than words can tell; but I was not going to put myself in jeopardy, and I told him my uncle and I had an appointment with a lawyer.

"Ay, ay," said he, "he passed me word of that. But, ye see, the boat'll set ye ashore at the town pier, and that's but a penny stonecast from Rankeillor's house." And here he suddenly leaned down and whispered in my ear: "Take care of the old tod;* he means mischief. Come aboard till I can get a word with ye." And then, passing his arm through mine, he continued aloud, as he set off towards his boat: "But, come, what can I bring ye from the Carolinas? Any friend of Mr. Balfour's can command. A roll of tobacco? Indian feather-work? a skin of a wild beast? a stone pipe? the mocking-bird that mews for all the world like a cat? the cardinal bird that is as red as blood?—take your pick and say your pleasure."

* Fox.

By this time we were at the boat-side, and he was handing me in. I did not dream of hanging back; I thought (the poor fool!) that I had found a good friend and helper, and I was rejoiced to see the ship. As soon as we were all set in our places, the boat was thrust off from the pier and began to move over the waters: and what with my pleasure in this new movement and my surprise at our low position, and the appearance of the shores, and the growing bigness of the brig as we drew near to it, I could hardly understand what the captain said, and must have answered him at random.

As soon as we were alongside (where I sat fairly gaping at the ship's height, the strong humming of the tide against its sides, and the pleasant cries of the seamen at their work) Hoseason, declaring that he and I must be the first aboard, ordered a tackle to be sent down from the main-yard. In this I was whipped into the air and set down again on the deck, where the captain stood ready waiting for me, and instantly slipped back his arm under mine. There I stood some while, a little dizzy with the unsteadiness of all around me, perhaps a little afraid, and yet vastly pleased with these strange sights; the captain meanwhile pointing out the strangest, and telling me their names and uses.

"But where is my uncle?" said I suddenly.

"Ay," said Hoseason, with a sudden grimness, "that's the point."

I felt I was lost. With all my strength, I plucked myself clear of him and ran to the bulwarks. Sure enough, there was the boat pulling for the town, with my uncle sitting in the stern. I gave a piercing cry—"Help, help! Murder!"—so that both sides of the anchorage rang with it, and my uncle turned round where he was sitting, and showed me a face full of cruelty and terror.

It was the last I saw. Already strong hands had been plucking me back from the ship's side; and now a thunderbolt seemed to strike me; I saw a great flash of fire, and fell senseless.

CHAPTER VII
I GO TO SEA IN THE BRIG "COVENANT" OF DYSART

I came to myself in darkness, in great pain, bound hand and foot, and deafened by many unfamiliar noises. There sounded in my ears a roaring of water as of a huge mill-dam, the thrashing of heavy sprays, the thundering of the sails, and the shrill cries of seamen. The whole world now heaved giddily up, and now rushed giddily downward; and so sick and hurt was I in body, and my mind so much confounded, that it took me a long while, chasing my thoughts up and down, and ever stunned again by a fresh stab of pain, to realise that I must be lying somewhere bound in the belly of that unlucky ship, and that the wind must have strengthened to a gale. With the clear perception of my plight, there fell upon me a blackness of despair, a horror of remorse at my own folly, and a passion of anger at my uncle, that once more bereft me of my senses.

When I returned again to life, the same uproar, the same confused and violent movements, shook and deafened me; and presently, to my other pains and distresses, there was added the sickness of an unused landsman on the sea. In that time of my adventurous youth, I suffered many hardships; but none that was so crushing to my mind and body, or lit by so few hopes, as these first hours aboard the brig.

I heard a gun fire, and supposed the storm had proved too strong for us, and we were firing signals of distress. The thought of deliverance, even by death in the deep sea, was welcome to me. Yet it was no such matter; but (as I was afterwards told) a common habit of the captain's, which I here set down to show that even the worst man may have his kindlier side. We were then passing, it appeared, within some miles of Dysart, where the brig was built, and where old Mrs. Hoseason, the captain's mother, had come some years before to live; and whether outward or inward bound, the Covenant was never suffered to go by that place by day, without a gun fired and colours shown.

I had no measure of time; day and night were alike in that ill-smelling cavern of the ship's bowels where I lay; and the misery of my situation drew out the hours to double. How long, therefore, I lay waiting to hear the ship split upon some rock, or to feel her reel head foremost into the depths of the sea, I have not the means of computation. But sleep at length stole from me the consciousness of sorrow.

I was awakened by the light of a hand-lantern shining in my face. A small man of about thirty, with green eyes and a tangle of fair hair, stood looking down at me.

"Well," said he, "how goes it?"

I answered by a sob; and my visitor then felt my pulse and temples, and set himself to wash and dress the wound upon my scalp.

"Ay," said he, "a sore dunt*. What, man? Cheer up! The world's no done; you've made a bad start of it but you'll make a better. Have you had any meat?"

   * Stroke.

I said I could not look at it: and thereupon he gave me some brandy and water in a tin pannikin, and left me once more to myself.

The next time he came to see me, I was lying betwixt sleep and waking, my eyes wide open in the darkness, the sickness quite departed, but succeeded by a horrid giddiness and swimming that was almost worse to bear. I ached, besides, in every limb, and the cords that bound me seemed to be of fire. The smell of the hole in which I lay seemed to have become a part of me; and during the long interval since his last visit I had suffered tortures of fear, now from the scurrying of the ship's rats, that sometimes pattered on my very face, and now from the dismal imaginings that haunt the bed of fever.

The glimmer of the lantern, as a trap opened, shone in like the heaven's sunlight; and though it only showed me the strong, dark beams of the ship that was my prison, I could have cried aloud for gladness. The man with the green eyes was the first to descend the ladder, and I noticed that he came somewhat unsteadily. He was followed by the captain. Neither said a word; but the first set to and examined me, and dressed my wound as before, while Hoseason looked me in my face with an odd, black look.

"Now, sir, you see for yourself," said the first: "a high fever, no appetite, no light, no meat: you see for yourself what that means."

"I am no conjurer, Mr. Riach," said the captain.

"Give me leave, sir," said Riach; "you've a good head upon your shoulders, and a good Scotch tongue to ask with; but I will leave you no manner of excuse; I want that boy taken out of this hole and put in the forecastle."

"What ye may want, sir, is a matter of concern to nobody but yoursel'," returned the captain; "but I can tell ye that which is to be. Here he is; here he shall bide."

"Admitting that you have been paid in a proportion," said the other, "I will crave leave humbly to say that I have not. Paid I am, and none too much, to be the second officer of this old tub, and you ken very well if I do my best to earn it. But I was paid for nothing more."

"If ye could hold back your hand from the tin-pan, Mr. Riach, I would have no complaint to make of ye," returned the skipper; "and instead of asking riddles, I make bold to say that ye would keep your breath to cool your porridge. We'll be required on deck," he added, in a sharper note, and set one foot upon the ladder.

But Mr. Riach caught him by the sleeve.

"Admitting that you have been paid to do a murder——" he began.

Hoseason turned upon him with a flash.

"What's that?" he cried. "What kind of talk is that?"

"It seems it is the talk that you can understand," said Mr. Riach, looking him steadily in the face.

"Mr. Riach, I have sailed with ye three cruises," replied the captain. "In all that time, sir, ye should have learned to know me: I'm a stiff man, and a dour man; but for what ye say the now—fie, fie!—it comes from a bad heart and a black conscience. If ye say the lad will die——"

"Ay, will he!" said Mr. Riach.

"Well, sir, is not that enough?" said Hoseason. "Flit him where ye please!"

Thereupon the captain ascended the ladder; and I, who had lain silent throughout this strange conversation, beheld Mr. Riach turn after him and bow as low as to his knees in what was plainly a spirit of derision. Even in my then state of sickness, I perceived two things: that the mate was touched with liquor, as the captain hinted, and that (drunk or sober) he was like to prove a valuable friend.

Five minutes afterwards my bonds were cut, I was hoisted on a man's back, carried up to the forecastle, and laid in a bunk on some sea-blankets; where the first thing that I did was to lose my senses.

It was a blessed thing indeed to open my eyes again upon the daylight, and to find myself in the society of men. The forecastle was a roomy place enough, set all about with berths, in which the men of the watch below were seated smoking, or lying down asleep. The day being calm and the wind fair, the scuttle was open, and not only the good daylight, but from time to time (as the ship rolled) a dusty beam of sunlight shone in, and dazzled and delighted me. I had no sooner moved, moreover, than one of the men brought me a drink of something healing which Mr. Riach had prepared, and bade me lie still and I should soon be well again. There were no bones broken, he explained: "A clour* on the head was naething. Man," said he, "it was me that gave it ye!"

* Blow.

Here I lay for the space of many days a close prisoner, and not only got my health again, but came to know my companions. They were a rough lot indeed, as sailors mostly are: being men rooted out of all the kindly parts of life, and condemned to toss together on the rough seas, with masters no less cruel. There were some among them that had sailed with the pirates and seen things it would be a shame even to speak of; some were men that had run from the king's ships, and went with a halter round their necks, of which they made no secret; and all, as the saying goes, were "at a word and a blow" with their best friends. Yet I had not been many days shut up with them before I began to be ashamed of my first judgment, when I had drawn away from them at the Ferry pier, as though they had been unclean beasts. No class of man is altogether bad, but each has its own faults and virtues; and these shipmates of mine were no exception to the rule. Rough they were, sure enough; and bad, I suppose; but they had many virtues. They were kind when it occurred to them, simple even beyond the simplicity of a country lad like me, and had some glimmerings of honesty.

There was one man, of maybe forty, that would sit on my berthside for hours and tell me of his wife and child. He was a fisher that had lost his boat, and thus been driven to the deep-sea voyaging. Well, it is years ago now: but I have never forgotten him. His wife (who was "young by him," as he often told me) waited in vain to see her man return; he would never again make the fire for her in the morning, nor yet keep the bairn when she was sick. Indeed, many of these poor fellows (as the event proved) were upon their last cruise; the deep seas and cannibal fish received them; and it is a thankless business to speak ill of the dead.

Among other good deeds that they did, they returned my money, which had been shared among them; and though it was about a third short, I was very glad to get it, and hoped great good from it in the land I was going to. The ship was bound for the Carolinas; and you must not suppose that I was going to that place merely as an exile. The trade was even then much depressed; since that, and with the rebellion of the colonies and the formation of the United States, it has, of course, come to an end; but in those days of my youth, white men were still sold into slavery on the plantations, and that was the destiny to which my wicked uncle had condemned me.

The cabin-boy Ransome (from whom I had first heard of these atrocities) came in at times from the round-house, where he berthed and served, now nursing a bruised limb in silent agony, now raving against the cruelty of Mr. Shuan. It made my heart bleed; but the men had a great respect for the chief mate, who was, as they said, "the only seaman of the whole jing-bang, and none such a bad man when he was sober." Indeed, I found there was a strange peculiarity about our two mates: that Mr. Riach was sullen, unkind, and harsh when he was sober, and Mr. Shuan would not hurt a fly except when he was drinking. I asked about the captain; but I was told drink made no difference upon that man of iron.

I did my best in the small time allowed me to make some thing like a man, or rather I should say something like a boy, of the poor creature, Ransome. But his mind was scarce truly human. He could remember nothing of the time before he came to sea; only that his father had made clocks, and had a starling in the parlour, which could whistle "The North Countrie;" all else had been blotted out in these years of hardship and cruelties. He had a strange notion of the dry land, picked up from sailor's stories: that it was a place where lads were put to some kind of slavery called a trade, and where apprentices were continually lashed and clapped into foul prisons. In a town, he thought every second person a decoy, and every third house a place in which seamen would be drugged and murdered. To be sure, I would tell him how kindly I had myself been used upon that dry land he was so much afraid of, and how well fed and carefully taught both by my friends and my parents: and if he had been recently hurt, he would weep bitterly and swear to run away; but if he was in his usual crackbrain humour, or (still more) if he had had a glass of spirits in the roundhouse, he would deride the notion.

It was Mr. Riach (Heaven forgive him!) who gave the boy drink; and it was, doubtless, kindly meant; but besides that it was ruin to his health, it was the pitifullest thing in life to see this unhappy, unfriended creature staggering, and dancing, and talking he knew not what. Some of the men laughed, but not all; others would grow as black as thunder (thinking, perhaps, of their own childhood or their own children) and bid him stop that nonsense, and think what he was doing. As for me, I felt ashamed to look at him, and the poor child still comes about me in my dreams.

All this time, you should know, the Covenant was meeting continual head-winds and tumbling up and down against head-seas, so that the scuttle was almost constantly shut, and the forecastle lighted only by a swinging lantern on a beam. There was constant labour for all hands; the sails had to be made and shortened every hour; the strain told on the men's temper; there was a growl of quarrelling all day long from berth to berth; and as I was never allowed to set my foot on deck, you can picture to yourselves how weary of my life I grew to be, and how impatient for a change.

And a change I was to get, as you shall hear; but I must first tell of a conversation I had with Mr. Riach, which put a little heart in me to bear my troubles. Getting him in a favourable stage of drink (for indeed he never looked near me when he was sober), I pledged him to secrecy, and told him my whole story.

He declared it was like a ballad; that he would do his best to help me; that I should have paper, pen, and ink, and write one line to Mr. Campbell and another to Mr. Rankeillor; and that if I had told the truth, ten to one he would be able (with their help) to pull me through and set me in my rights.

"And in the meantime," says he, "keep your heart up. You're not the only one, I'll tell you that. There's many a man hoeing tobacco over-seas that should be mounting his horse at his own door at home; many and many! And life is all a variorum, at the best. Look at me: I'm a laird's son and more than half a doctor, and here I am, man-Jack to Hoseason!"

I thought it would be civil to ask him for his story.

He whistled loud.

"Never had one," said he. "I like fun, that's all." And he skipped out of the forecastle.

CHAPTER VIII
THE ROUND-HOUSE

One night, about eleven o'clock, a man of Mr. Riach's watch (which was on deck) came below for his jacket; and instantly there began to go a whisper about the forecastle that "Shuan had done for him at last." There was no need of a name; we all knew who was meant; but we had scarce time to get the idea rightly in our heads, far less to speak of it, when the scuttle was again flung open, and Captain Hoseason came down the ladder. He looked sharply round the bunks in the tossing light of the lantern; and then, walking straight up to me, he addressed me, to my surprise, in tones of kindness.

"My man," said he, "we want ye to serve in the round-house. You and Ransome are to change berths. Run away aft with ye."

Even as he spoke, two seamen appeared in the scuttle, carrying Ransome in their arms; and the ship at that moment giving a great sheer into the sea, and the lantern swinging, the light fell direct on the boy's face. It was as white as wax, and had a look upon it like a dreadful smile. The blood in me ran cold, and I drew in my breath as if I had been struck.

"Run away aft; run away aft with ye!" cried Hoseason.

And at that I brushed by the sailors and the boy (who neither spoke nor moved), and ran up the ladder on deck.

The brig was sheering swiftly and giddily through a long, cresting swell. She was on the starboard tack, and on the left hand, under the arched foot of the foresail, I could see the sunset still quite bright. This, at such an hour of the night, surprised me greatly; but I was too ignorant to draw the true conclusion—that we were going north-about round Scotland, and were now on the high sea between the Orkney and Shetland Islands, having avoided the dangerous currents of the Pentland Firth. For my part, who had been so long shut in the dark and knew nothing of head-winds, I thought we might be half-way or more across the Atlantic. And indeed (beyond that I wondered a little at the lateness of the sunset light) I gave no heed to it, and pushed on across the decks, running between the seas, catching at ropes, and only saved from going overboard by one of the hands on deck, who had been always kind to me.

The round-house, for which I was bound, and where I was now to sleep and serve, stood some six feet above the decks, and considering the size of the brig, was of good dimensions. Inside were a fixed table and bench, and two berths, one for the captain and the other for the two mates, turn and turn about. It was all fitted with lockers from top to bottom, so as to stow away the officers' belongings and a part of the ship's stores; there was a second store-room underneath, which you entered by a hatchway in the middle of the deck; indeed, all the best of the meat and drink and the whole of the powder were collected in this place; and all the firearms, except the two pieces of brass ordnance, were set in a rack in the aftermost wall of the round-house. The most of the cutlasses were in another place.

A small window with a shutter on each side, and a skylight in the roof, gave it light by day; and after dark there was a lamp always burning. It was burning when I entered, not brightly, but enough to show Mr. Shuan sitting at the table, with the brandy bottle and a tin pannikin in front of him. He was a tall man, strongly made and very black; and he stared before him on the table like one stupid.

He took no notice of my coming in; nor did he move when the captain followed and leant on the berth beside me, looking darkly at the mate. I stood in great fear of Hoseason, and had my reasons for it; but something told me I need not be afraid of him just then; and I whispered in his ear: "How is he?" He shook his head like one that does not know and does not wish to think, and his face was very stern.

Presently Mr. Riach came in. He gave the captain a glance that meant the boy was dead as plain as speaking, and took his place like the rest of us; so that we all three stood without a word, staring down at Mr. Shuan, and Mr. Shuan (on his side) sat without a word, looking hard upon the table.

All of a sudden he put out his hand to take the bottle; and at that Mr. Riach started forward and caught it away from him, rather by surprise than violence, crying out, with an oath, that there had been too much of this work altogether, and that a judgment would fall upon the ship. And as he spoke (the weather sliding-doors standing open) he tossed the bottle into the sea.

Mr. Shuan was on his feet in a trice; he still looked dazed, but he meant murder, ay, and would have done it, for the second time that night, had not the captain stepped in between him and his victim.

"Sit down!" roars the captain. "Ye sot and swine, do ye know what ye've done? Ye've murdered the boy!"

Mr. Shuan seemed to understand; for he sat down again, and put up his hand to his brow.

"Well," he said, "he brought me a dirty pannikin!"

At that word, the captain and I and Mr. Riach all looked at each other for a second with a kind of frightened look; and then Hoseason walked up to his chief officer, took him by the shoulder, led him across to his bunk, and bade him lie down and go to sleep, as you might speak to a bad child. The murderer cried a little, but he took off his sea-boots and obeyed.

"Ah!" cried Mr. Riach, with a dreadful voice, "ye should have interfered long syne. It's too late now."

"Mr. Riach," said the captain, "this night's work must never be kennt in Dysart. The boy went overboard, sir; that's what the story is; and I would give five pounds out of my pocket it was true!" He turned to the table. "What made ye throw the good bottle away?" he added. "There was nae sense in that, sir. Here, David, draw me another. They're in the bottom locker;" and he tossed me a key. "Ye'll need a glass yourself, sir," he added to Riach. "Yon was an ugly thing to see."

So the pair sat down and hob-a-nobbed; and while they did so, the murderer, who had been lying and whimpering in his berth, raised himself upon his elbow and looked at them and at me.

That was the first night of my new duties; and in the course of the next day I had got well into the run of them. I had to serve at the meals, which the captain took at regular hours, sitting down with the officer who was off duty; all the day through I would be running with a dram to one or other of my three masters; and at night I slept on a blanket thrown on the deck boards at the aftermost end of the round-house, and right in the draught of the two doors. It was a hard and a cold bed; nor was I suffered to sleep without interruption; for some one would be always coming in from deck to get a dram, and when a fresh watch was to be set, two and sometimes all three would sit down and brew a bowl together. How they kept their health, I know not, any more than how I kept my own.

And yet in other ways it was an easy service. There was no cloth to lay; the meals were either of oatmeal porridge or salt junk, except twice a week, when there was duff: and though I was clumsy enough and (not being firm on my sealegs) sometimes fell with what I was bringing them, both Mr. Riach and the captain were singularly patient. I could not but fancy they were making up lee-way with their consciences, and that they would scarce have been so good with me if they had not been worse with Ransome.

As for Mr. Shuan, the drink or his crime, or the two together, had certainly troubled his mind. I cannot say I ever saw him in his proper wits. He never grew used to my being there, stared at me continually (sometimes, I could have thought, with terror), and more than once drew back from my hand when I was serving him. I was pretty sure from the first that he had no clear mind of what he had done, and on my second day in the round-house I had the proof of it. We were alone, and he had been staring at me a long time, when all at once, up he got, as pale as death, and came close up to me, to my great terror. But I had no cause to be afraid of him.

"You were not here before?" he asked.

"No, sir," said I."

"There was another boy?" he asked again; and when I had answered him, "Ah!" says he, "I thought that," and went and sat down, without another word, except to call for brandy.

You may think it strange, but for all the horror I had, I was still sorry for him. He was a married man, with a wife in Leith; but whether or no he had a family, I have now forgotten; I hope not.

Altogether it was no very hard life for the time it lasted, which (as you are to hear) was not long. I was as well fed as the best of them; even their pickles, which were the great dainty, I was allowed my share of; and had I liked I might have been drunk from morning to night, like Mr. Shuan. I had company, too, and good company of its sort. Mr. Riach, who had been to the college, spoke to me like a friend when he was not sulking, and told me many curious things, and some that were informing; and even the captain, though he kept me at the stick's end the most part of the time, would sometimes unbuckle a bit, and tell me of the fine countries he had visited.

The shadow of poor Ransome, to be sure, lay on all four of us, and on me and Mr. Shuan in particular, most heavily. And then I had another trouble of my own. Here I was, doing dirty work for three men that I looked down upon, and one of whom, at least, should have hung upon a gallows; that was for the present; and as for the future, I could only see myself slaving alongside of negroes in the tobacco fields. Mr. Riach, perhaps from caution, would never suffer me to say another word about my story; the captain, whom I tried to approach, rebuffed me like a dog and would not hear a word; and as the days came and went, my heart sank lower and lower, till I was even glad of the work which kept me from thinking.

CHAPTER IX

THE MAN WITH THE BELT OF GOLD

More than a week went by, in which the ill-luck that had hitherto pursued the Covenant upon this voyage grew yet more strongly marked. Some days she made a little way; others, she was driven actually back. At last we were beaten so far to the south that we tossed and tacked to and fro the whole of the ninth day, within sight of Cape Wrath and the wild, rocky coast on either hand of it. There followed on that a council of the officers, and some decision which I did not rightly understand, seeing only the result: that we had made a fair wind of a foul one and were running south.

The tenth afternoon there was a falling swell and a thick, wet, white fog that hid one end of the brig from the other. All afternoon, when I went on deck, I saw men and officers listening hard over the bulwarks—"for breakers," they said; and though I did not so much as understand the word, I felt danger in the air, and was excited.

Maybe about ten at night, I was serving Mr. Riach and the captain at their supper, when the ship struck something with a great sound, and we heard voices singing out. My two masters leaped to their feet.

"She's struck!" said Mr. Riach.

"No, sir," said the captain. "We've only run a boat down."

And they hurried out.

The captain was in the right of it. We had run down a boat in the fog, and she had parted in the midst and gone to the bottom with all her crew but one. This man (as I heard afterwards) had been sitting in the stern as a passenger, while the rest were on the benches rowing. At the moment of the blow, the stern had been thrown into the air, and the man (having his hands free, and for all he was encumbered with a frieze overcoat that came below his knees) had leaped up and caught hold of the brig's bowsprit. It showed he had luck and much agility and unusual strength, that he should have thus saved himself from such a pass. And yet, when the captain brought him into the round-house, and I set eyes on him for the first time, he looked as cool as I did.

He was smallish in stature, but well set and as nimble as a goat; his face was of a good open expression, but sunburnt very dark, and heavily freckled and pitted with the small-pox; his eyes were unusually light and had a kind of dancing madness in them, that was both engaging and alarming; and when he took off his great-coat, he laid a pair of fine silver-mounted pistols on the table, and I saw that he was belted with a great sword. His manners, besides, were elegant, and he pledged the captain handsomely. Altogether I thought of him, at the first sight, that here was a man I would rather call my friend than my enemy.

The captain, too, was taking his observations, but rather of the man's clothes than his person. And to be sure, as soon as he had taken off the great-coat, he showed forth mighty fine for the round-house of a merchant brig: having a hat with feathers, a red waistcoat, breeches of black plush, and a blue coat with silver buttons and handsome silver lace; costly clothes, though somewhat spoiled with the fog and being slept in.

"I'm vexed, sir, about the boat," says the captain.

"There are some pretty men gone to the bottom," said the stranger, "that I would rather see on the dry land again than half a score of boats."

"Friends of yours?" said Hoseason.

"You have none such friends in your country," was the reply. "They would have died for me like dogs."

"Well, sir," said the captain, still watching him, "there are more men in the world than boats to put them in."

"And that's true, too," cried the other, "and ye seem to be a gentleman of great penetration."

"I have been in France, sir," says the captain, so that it was plain he meant more by the words than showed upon the face of them.

"Well, sir," says the other, "and so has many a pretty man, for the matter of that."

"No doubt, sir," says the captain, "and fine coats."

"Oho!" says the stranger, "is that how the wind sets?" And he laid his hand quickly on his pistols.

"Don't be hasty," said the captain. "Don't do a mischief before ye see the need of it. Ye've a French soldier's coat upon your back and a Scotch tongue in your head, to be sure; but so has many an honest fellow in these days, and I dare say none the worse of it."

"So?" said the gentleman in the fine coat: "are ye of the honest party?" (meaning, Was he a Jacobite? for each side, in these sort of civil broils, takes the name of honesty for its own).

"Why, sir," replied the captain, "I am a true-blue Protestant, and I thank God for it." (It was the first word of any religion I had ever heard from him, but I learnt afterwards he was a great church-goer while on shore.) "But, for all that," says he, "I can be sorry to see another man with his back to the wall."

"Can ye so, indeed?" asked the Jacobite. "Well, sir, to be quite plain with ye, I am one of those honest gentlemen that were in trouble about the years forty-five and six; and (to be still quite plain with ye) if I got into the hands of any of the red-coated gentry, it's like it would go hard with me. Now, sir, I was for France; and there was a French ship cruising here to pick me up; but she gave us the go-by in the fog—as I wish from the heart that ye had done yoursel'! And the best that I can say is this: If ye can set me ashore where I was going, I have that upon me will reward you highly for your trouble."

"In France?" says the captain. "No, sir; that I cannot do. But where ye come from—we might talk of that."

And then, unhappily, he observed me standing in my corner, and packed me off to the galley to get supper for the gentleman. I lost no time, I promise you; and when I came back into the round-house, I found the gentleman had taken a money-belt from about his waist, and poured out a guinea or two upon the table. The captain was looking at the guineas, and then at the belt, and then at the gentleman's face; and I thought he seemed excited.

"Half of it," he cried, "and I'm your man!"

The other swept back the guineas into the belt, and put it on again under his waistcoat. "I have told ye sir," said he, "that not one doit of it belongs to me. It belongs to my chieftain," and here he touched his hat, "and while I would be but a silly messenger to grudge some of it that the rest might come safe, I should show myself a hound indeed if I bought my own carcase any too dear. Thirty guineas on the sea-side, or sixty if ye set me on the Linnhe Loch. Take it, if ye will; if not, ye can do your worst."

"Ay," said Hoseason. "And if I give ye over to the soldiers?"

"Ye would make a fool's bargain," said the other. "My chief, let me tell you, sir, is forfeited, like every honest man in Scotland. His estate is in the hands of the man they call King George; and it is his officers that collect the rents, or try to collect them. But for the honour of Scotland, the poor tenant bodies take a thought upon their chief lying in exile; and this money is a part of that very rent for which King George is looking. Now, sir, ye seem to me to be a man that understands things: bring this money within the reach of Government, and how much of it'll come to you?"

"Little enough, to be sure," said Hoseason; and then, "if they knew," he added, drily. "But I think, if I was to try, that I could hold my tongue about it."

"Ah, but I'll begowk* ye there!" cried the gentleman. "Play me false, and I'll play you cunning. If a hand is laid upon me, they shall ken what money it is."

    *Befool.

"Well," returned the captain, "what must be must. Sixty guineas, and done. Here's my hand upon it."

"And here's mine," said the other.

And thereupon the captain went out (rather hurriedly, I thought), and left me alone in the round-house with the stranger.

At that period (so soon after the forty-five) there were many exiled gentlemen coming back at the peril of their lives, either to see their friends or to collect a little money; and as for the Highland chiefs that had been forfeited, it was a common matter of talk how their tenants would stint themselves to send them money, and their clansmen outface the soldiery to get it in, and run the gauntlet of our great navy to carry it across. All this I had, of course, heard tell of; and now I had a man under my eyes whose life was forfeit on all these counts and upon one more, for he was not only a rebel and a smuggler of rents, but had taken service with King Louis of France. And as if all this were not enough, he had a belt full of golden guineas round his loins. Whatever my opinions, I could not look on such a man without a lively interest.

"And so you're a Jacobite?" said I, as I set meat before him.

"Ay," said he, beginning to eat. "And you, by your long face, should be a Whig?" *

    * Whig or Whigamore was the cant name for those who were

      loyal to King George.

"Betwixt and between," said I, not to annoy him; for indeed I was as good a Whig as Mr. Campbell could make me.

"And that's naething," said he. "But I'm saying, Mr. Betwixt-and-Between," he added, "this bottle of yours is dry; and it's hard if I'm to pay sixty guineas and be grudged a dram upon the back of it."

"I'll go and ask for the key," said I, and stepped on deck.

The fog was as close as ever, but the swell almost down. They had laid the brig to, not knowing precisely where they were, and the wind (what little there was of it) not serving well for their true course. Some of the hands were still hearkening for breakers; but the captain and the two officers were in the waist with their heads together. It struck me (I don't know why) that they were after no good; and the first word I heard, as I drew softly near, more than confirmed me.

It was Mr. Riach, crying out as if upon a sudden thought: "Couldn't we wile him out of the round-house?"

"He's better where he is," returned Hoseason; "he hasn't room to use his sword."

"Well, that's true," said Riach; "but he's hard to come at."

"Hut!" said Hoseason. "We can get the man in talk, one upon each side, and pin him by the two arms; or if that'll not hold, sir, we can make a run by both the doors and get him under hand before he has the time to draw."

At this hearing, I was seized with both fear and anger at these treacherous, greedy, bloody men that I sailed with. My first mind was to run away; my second was bolder.

"Captain," said I, "the gentleman is seeking a dram, and the bottle's out. Will you give me the key?"

They all started and turned about.

"Why, here's our chance to get the firearms!"

Riach cried; and then to me: "Hark ye, David," he said, "do ye ken where the pistols are?"

"Ay, ay," put in Hoseason. "David kens; David's a good lad. Ye see, David my man, yon wild Hielandman is a danger to the ship, besides being a rank foe to King George, God bless him!"

I had never been so be-Davided since I came on board: but I said Yes, as if all I heard were quite natural.

"The trouble is," resumed the captain, "that all our firelocks, great and little, are in the round-house under this man's nose; likewise the powder. Now, if I, or one of the officers, was to go in and take them, he would fall to thinking. But a lad like you, David, might snap up a horn and a pistol or two without remark. And if ye can do it cleverly, I'll bear it in mind when it'll be good for you to have friends; and that's when we come to Carolina."

Here Mr. Riach whispered him a little.

"Very right, sir," said the captain; and then to myself: "And see here, David, yon man has a beltful of gold, and I give you my word that you shall have your fingers in it."

I told him I would do as he wished, though indeed I had scarce breath to speak with; and upon that he gave me the key of the spirit locker, and I began to go slowly back to the round-house. What was I to do? They were dogs and thieves; they had stolen me from my own country; they had killed poor Ransome; and was I to hold the candle to another murder? But then, upon the other hand, there was the fear of death very plain before me; for what could a boy and a man, if they were as brave as lions, against a whole ship's company?

I was still arguing it back and forth, and getting no great clearness, when I came into the round-house and saw the Jacobite eating his supper under the lamp; and at that my mind was made up all in a moment. I have no credit by it; it was by no choice of mine, but as if by compulsion, that I walked right up to the table and put my hand on his shoulder.

"Do ye want to be killed?" said I. He sprang to his feet, and looked a question at me as clear as if he had spoken.

"O!" cried I, "they're all murderers here; it's a ship full of them! They've murdered a boy already. Now it's you."

"Ay, ay," said he; "but they have n't got me yet." And then looking at me curiously, "Will ye stand with me?"

"That will I!" said I. "I am no thief, nor yet murderer. I'll stand by you."

"Why, then," said he, "what's your name?"

"David Balfour," said I; and then, thinking that a man with so fine a coat must like fine people, I added for the first time, "of Shaws."

It never occurred to him to doubt me, for a Highlander is used to see great gentlefolk in great poverty; but as he had no estate of his own, my words nettled a very childish vanity he had.

"My name is Stewart," he said, drawing himself up. "Alan Breck, they call me. A king's name is good enough for me, though I bear it plain and have the name of no farm-midden to clap to the hind-end of it."

And having administered this rebuke, as though it were something of a chief importance, he turned to examine our defences.

The round-house was built very strong, to support the breaching of the seas. Of its five apertures, only the skylight and the two doors were large enough for the passage of a man. The doors, besides, could be drawn close: they were of stout oak, and ran in grooves, and were fitted with hooks to keep them either shut or open, as the need arose. The one that was already shut I secured in this fashion; but when I was proceeding to slide to the other, Alan stopped me.

"David," said he—"for I cannae bring to mind the name of your landed estate, and so will make so bold as to call you David—that door, being open, is the best part of my defences."

"It would be yet better shut," says I.

"Not so, David," says he. "Ye see, I have but one face; but so long as that door is open and my face to it, the best part of my enemies will be in front of me, where I would aye wish to find them."

Then he gave me from the rack a cutlass (of which there were a few besides the firearms), choosing it with great care, shaking his head and saying he had never in all his life seen poorer weapons; and next he set me down to the table with a powder-horn, a bag of bullets and all the pistols, which he bade me charge.

"And that will be better work, let me tell you," said he, "for a gentleman of decent birth, than scraping plates and raxing* drams to a wheen tarry sailors."

*Reaching.

Thereupon he stood up in the midst with his face to the door, and drawing his great sword, made trial of the room he had to wield it in.

"I must stick to the point," he said, shaking his head; "and that's a pity, too. It doesn't set my genius, which is all for the upper guard. And, now," said he, "do you keep on charging the pistols, and give heed to me."

I told him I would listen closely. My chest was tight, my mouth dry, the light dark to my eyes; the thought of the numbers that were soon to leap in upon us kept my heart in a flutter: and the sea, which I heard washing round the brig, and where I thought my dead body would be cast ere morning, ran in my mind strangely.

"First of all," said he, "how many are against us?"

I reckoned them up; and such was the hurry of my mind, I had to cast the numbers twice. "Fifteen," said I.

Alan whistled. "Well," said he, "that can't be cured. And now follow me. It is my part to keep this door, where I look for the main battle. In that, ye have no hand. And mind and dinnae fire to this side unless they get me down; for I would rather have ten foes in front of me than one friend like you cracking pistols at my back."

I told him, indeed I was no great shot.

"And that's very bravely said," he cried, in a great admiration of my candour. "There's many a pretty gentleman that wouldnae dare to say it."

"But then, sir," said I, "there is the door behind you, which they may perhaps break in."

"Ay," said he, "and that is a part of your work. No sooner the pistols charged, than ye must climb up into yon bed where ye're handy at the window; and if they lift hand against the door, ye're to shoot. But that's not all. Let's make a bit of a soldier of ye, David. What else have ye to guard?"

"There's the skylight," said I. "But indeed, Mr. Stewart, I would need to have eyes upon both sides to keep the two of them; for when my face is at the one, my back is to the other."

"And that's very true," said Alan. "But have ye no ears to your head?"

"To be sure!" cried I. "I must hear the bursting of the glass!"

"Ye have some rudiments of sense," said Alan, grimly.

CHAPTER X
THE SIEGE OF THE ROUND-HOUSE

But now our time of truce was come to an end. Those on deck had waited for my coming till they grew impatient; and scarce had Alan spoken, when the captain showed face in the open door.

"Stand!" cried Alan, and pointed his sword at him. The captain stood, indeed; but he neither winced nor drew back a foot.

"A naked sword?" says he. "This is a strange return for hospitality."

"Do ye see me?" said Alan. "I am come of kings; I bear a king's name. My badge is the oak. Do ye see my sword? It has slashed the heads off mair Whigamores than you have toes upon your feet. Call up your vermin to your back, sir, and fall on! The sooner the clash begins, the sooner ye'll taste this steel throughout your vitals."

The captain said nothing to Alan, but he looked over at me with an ugly look. "David," said he, "I'll mind this;" and the sound of his voice went through me with a jar.

Next moment he was gone.

"And now," said Alan, "let your hand keep your head, for the grip is coming."

Alan drew a dirk, which he held in his left hand in case they should run in under his sword. I, on my part, clambered up into the berth with an armful of pistols and something of a heavy heart, and set open the window where I was to watch. It was a small part of the deck that I could overlook, but enough for our purpose. The sea had gone down, and the wind was steady and kept the sails quiet; so that there was a great stillness in the ship, in which I made sure I heard the sound of muttering voices. A little after, and there came a clash of steel upon the deck, by which I knew they were dealing out the cutlasses and one had been let fall; and after that, silence again.

I do not know if I was what you call afraid; but my heart beat like a bird's, both quick and little; and there was a dimness came before my eyes which I continually rubbed away, and which continually returned. As for hope, I had none; but only a darkness of despair and a sort of anger against all the world that made me long to sell my life as dear as I was able. I tried to pray, I remember, but that same hurry of my mind, like a man running, would not suffer me to think upon the words; and my chief wish was to have the thing begin and be done with it.

It came all of a sudden when it did, with a rush of feet and a roar, and then a shout from Alan, and a sound of blows and some one crying out as if hurt. I looked back over my shoulder, and saw Mr. Shuan in the doorway, crossing blades with Alan.

"That's him that killed the boy!" I cried.

"Look to your window!" said Alan; and as I turned back to my place, I saw him pass his sword through the mate's body.

It was none too soon for me to look to my own part; for my head was scarce back at the window, before five men, carrying a spare yard for a battering-ram, ran past me and took post to drive the door in. I had never fired with a pistol in my life, and not often with a gun; far less against a fellow-creature. But it was now or never; and just as they swang the yard, I cried out: "Take that!" and shot into their midst.

I must have hit one of them, for he sang out and gave back a step, and the rest stopped as if a little disconcerted. Before they had time to recover, I sent another ball over their heads; and at my third shot (which went as wide as the second) the whole party threw down the yard and ran for it.

Then I looked round again into the deck-house. The whole place was full of the smoke of my own firing, just as my ears seemed to be burst with the noise of the shots. But there was Alan, standing as before; only now his sword was running blood to the hilt, and himself so swelled with triumph and fallen into so fine an attitude, that he looked to be invincible. Right before him on the floor was Mr. Shuan, on his hands and knees; the blood was pouring from his mouth, and he was sinking slowly lower, with a terrible, white face; and just as I looked, some of those from behind caught hold of him by the heels and dragged him bodily out of the round-house. I believe he died as they were doing it.

"There's one of your Whigs for ye!" cried Alan; and then turning to me, he asked if I had done much execution.

I told him I had winged one, and thought it was the captain.

"And I've settled two," says he. "No, there's not enough blood let; they'll be back again. To your watch, David. This was but a dram before meat."

I settled back to my place, re-charging the three pistols I had fired, and keeping watch with both eye and ear.

Our enemies were disputing not far off upon the deck, and that so loudly that I could hear a word or two above the washing of the seas.

"It was Shuan bauchled* it," I heard one say.

 * Bungled.

And another answered him with a "Wheesht, man! He's paid the piper."

After that the voices fell again into the same muttering as before. Only now, one person spoke most of the time, as though laying down a plan, and first one and then another answered him briefly, like men taking orders. By this, I made sure they were coming on again, and told Alan.

"It's what we have to pray for," said he. "Unless we can give them a good distaste of us, and done with it, there'll be nae sleep for either you or me. But this time, mind, they'll be in earnest."

By this, my pistols were ready, and there was nothing to do but listen and wait. While the brush lasted, I had not the time to think if I was frighted; but now, when all was still again, my mind ran upon nothing else. The thought of the sharp swords and the cold steel was strong in me; and presently, when I began to hear stealthy steps and a brushing of men's clothes against the round-house wall, and knew they were taking their places in the dark, I could have found it in my mind to cry out aloud.

All this was upon Alan's side; and I had begun to think my share of the fight was at an end, when I heard some one drop softly on the roof above me.

Then there came a single call on the sea-pipe, and that was the signal. A knot of them made one rush of it, cutlass in hand, against the door; and at the same moment, the glass of the skylight was dashed in a thousand pieces, and a man leaped through and landed on the floor. Before he got his feet, I had clapped a pistol to his back, and might have shot him, too; only at the touch of him (and him alive) my whole flesh misgave me, and I could no more pull the trigger than I could have flown.

He had dropped his cutlass as he jumped, and when he felt the pistol, whipped straight round and laid hold of me, roaring out an oath; and at that either my courage came again, or I grew so much afraid as came to the same thing; for I gave a shriek and shot him in the midst of the body. He gave the most horrible, ugly groan and fell to the floor. The foot of a second fellow, whose legs were dangling through the skylight, struck me at the same time upon the head; and at that I snatched another pistol and shot this one through the thigh, so that he slipped through and tumbled in a lump on his companion's body. There was no talk of missing, any more than there was time to aim; I clapped the muzzle to the very place and fired.

I might have stood and stared at them for long, but I heard Alan shout as if for help, and that brought me to my senses.

He had kept the door so long; but one of the seamen, while he was engaged with others, had run in under his guard and caught him about the body. Alan was dirking him with his left hand, but the fellow clung like a leech. Another had broken in and had his cutlass raised. The door was thronged with their faces. I thought we were lost, and catching up my cutlass, fell on them in flank.

But I had not time to be of help. The wrestler dropped at last; and Alan, leaping back to get his distance, ran upon the others like a bull, roaring as he went. They broke before him like water, turning, and running, and falling one against another in their haste. The sword in his hands flashed like quicksilver into the huddle of our fleeing enemies; and at every flash there came the scream of a man hurt. I was still thinking we were lost, when lo! they were all gone, and Alan was driving them along the deck as a sheep-dog chases sheep.

Yet he was no sooner out than he was back again, being as cautious as he was brave; and meanwhile the seamen continued running and crying out as if he was still behind them; and we heard them tumble one upon another into the forecastle, and clap-to the hatch upon the top.

The round-house was like a shambles; three were dead inside, another lay in his death agony across the threshold; and there were Alan and I victorious and unhurt.

He came up to me with open arms. "Come to my arms!" he cried, and embraced and kissed me hard upon both cheeks. "David," said he, "I love you like a brother. And O, man," he cried in a kind of ecstasy, "am I no a bonny fighter?"

Thereupon he turned to the four enemies, passed his sword clean through each of them, and tumbled them out of doors one after the other. As he did so, he kept humming and singing and whistling to himself, like a man trying to recall an air; only what HE was trying was to make one. All the while, the flush was in his face, and his eyes were as bright as a five-year-old child's with a new toy. And presently he sat down upon the table, sword in hand; the air that he was making all the time began to run a little clearer, and then clearer still; and then out he burst with a great voice into a Gaelic song.

I have translated it here, not in verse (of which I have no skill) but at least in the king's English.

He sang it often afterwards, and the thing became popular; so that I have heard it and had it explained to me, many's the time.

"This is the song of the sword of Alan; The smith made it, The fire set it; Now it shines in the hand of Alan Breck.

"Their eyes were many and bright, Swift were they to behold, Many the hands they guided: The sword was alone.

"The dun deer troop over the hill, They are many, the hill is one; The dun deer vanish, The hill remains.

"Come to me from the hills of heather, Come from the isles of the sea. O far-beholding eagles, Here is your meat."

Now this song which he made (both words and music) in the hour of our victory, is something less than just to me, who stood beside him in the tussle. Mr. Shuan and five more were either killed outright or thoroughly disabled; but of these, two fell by my hand, the two that came by the skylight. Four more were hurt, and of that number, one (and he not the least important) got his hurt from me. So that, altogether, I did my fair share both of the killing and the wounding, and might have claimed a place in Alan's verses. But poets have to think upon their rhymes; and in good prose talk, Alan always did me more than justice.

In the meanwhile, I was innocent of any wrong being done me. For not only I knew no word of the Gaelic; but what with the long suspense of the waiting, and the scurry and strain of our two spirts of fighting, and more than all, the horror I had of some of my own share in it, the thing was no sooner over than I was glad to stagger to a seat. There was that tightness on my chest that I could hardly breathe; the thought of the two men I had shot sat upon me like a nightmare; and all upon a sudden, and before I had a guess of what was coming, I began to sob and cry like any child.

Alan clapped my shoulder, and said I was a brave lad and wanted nothing but a sleep.

"I'll take the first watch," said he. "Ye've done well by me, David, first and last; and I wouldn't lose you for all Appin—no, nor for Breadalbane."

So I made up my bed on the floor; and he took the first spell, pistol in hand and sword on knee, three hours by the captain's watch upon the wall. Then he roused me up, and I took my turn of three hours; before the end of which it was broad day, and a very quiet morning, with a smooth, rolling sea that tossed the ship and made the blood run to and fro on the round-house floor, and a heavy rain that drummed upon the roof. All my watch there was nothing stirring; and by the banging of the helm, I knew they had even no one at the tiller. Indeed (as I learned afterwards) there were so many of them hurt or dead, and the rest in so ill a temper, that Mr. Riach and the captain had to take turn and turn like Alan and me, or the brig might have gone ashore and nobody the wiser. It was a mercy the night had fallen so still, for the wind had gone down as soon as the rain began. Even as it was, I judged by the wailing of a great number of gulls that went crying and fishing round the ship, that she must have drifted pretty near the coast or one of the islands of the Hebrides; and at last, looking out of the door of the round-house, I saw the great stone hills of Skye on the right hand, and, a little more astern, the strange isle of Rum.

CHAPTER XI

THE CAPTAIN KNUCKLES UNDER

Alan and I sat down to breakfast about six of the clock. The floor was covered with broken glass and in a horrid mess of blood, which took away my hunger. In all other ways we were in a situation not only agreeable but merry; having ousted the officers from their own cabin, and having at command all the drink in the ship—both wine and spirits—and all the dainty part of what was eatable, such as the pickles and the fine sort of bread. This, of itself, was enough to set us in good humour, but the richest part of it was this, that the two thirstiest men that ever came out of Scotland (Mr. Shuan being dead) were now shut in the fore-part of the ship and condemned to what they hated most—cold water.

"And depend upon it," Alan said, "we shall hear more of them ere long. Ye may keep a man from the fighting, but never from his bottle."

We made good company for each other. Alan, indeed, expressed himself most lovingly; and taking a knife from the table, cut me off one of the silver buttons from his coat.

"I had them," says he, "from my father, Duncan Stewart; and now give ye one of them to be a keepsake for last night's work. And wherever ye go and show that button, the friends of Alan Breck will come around you."

He said this as if he had been Charlemagne, and commanded armies; and indeed, much as I admired his courage, I was always in danger of smiling at his vanity: in danger, I say, for had I not kept my countenance, I would be afraid to think what a quarrel might have followed.

As soon as we were through with our meal he rummaged in the captain's locker till he found a clothes-brush; and then taking off his coat, began to visit his suit and brush away the stains, with such care and labour as I supposed to have been only usual with women. To be sure, he had no other; and, besides (as he said), it belonged to a king and so behoved to be royally looked after.

For all that, when I saw what care he took to pluck out the threads where the button had been cut away, I put a higher value on his gift.

He was still so engaged when we were hailed by Mr. Riach from the deck, asking for a parley; and I, climbing through the skylight and sitting on the edge of it, pistol in hand and with a bold front, though inwardly in fear of broken glass, hailed him back again and bade him speak out. He came to the edge of the round-house, and stood on a coil of rope, so that his chin was on a level with the roof; and we looked at each other awhile in silence. Mr. Riach, as I do not think he had been very forward in the battle, so he had got off with nothing worse than a blow upon the cheek: but he looked out of heart and very weary, having been all night afoot, either standing watch or doctoring the wounded.

"This is a bad job," said he at last, shaking his head.

"It was none of our choosing," said I.

"The captain," says he, "would like to speak with your friend. They might speak at the window."

"And how do we know what treachery he means?" cried I.

"He means none, David," returned Mr. Riach, "and if he did, I'll tell ye the honest truth, we couldnae get the men to follow."

"Is that so?" said I.

"I'll tell ye more than that," said he. "It's not only the men; it's me. I'm frich'ened, Davie." And he smiled across at me. "No," he continued, "what we want is to be shut of him."

Thereupon I consulted with Alan, and the parley was agreed to and parole given upon either side; but this was not the whole of Mr. Riach's business, and he now begged me for a dram with such instancy and such reminders of his former kindness, that at last I handed him a pannikin with about a gill of brandy. He drank a part, and then carried the rest down upon the deck, to share it (I suppose) with his superior.

A little after, the captain came (as was agreed) to one of the windows, and stood there in the rain, with his arm in a sling, and looking stern and pale, and so old that my heart smote me for having fired upon him.

Alan at once held a pistol in his face.

"Put that thing up!" said the captain. "Have I not passed my word, sir? or do ye seek to affront me?"

"Captain," says Alan, "I doubt your word is a breakable. Last night ye haggled and argle-bargled like an apple-wife; and then passed me your word, and gave me your hand to back it; and ye ken very well what was the upshot. Be damned to your word!" says he.

"Well, well, sir," said the captain, "ye'll get little good by swearing." (And truly that was a fault of which the captain was quite free.) "But we have other things to speak," he continued, bitterly. "Ye've made a sore hash of my brig; I haven't hands enough left to work her; and my first officer (whom I could ill spare) has got your sword throughout his vitals, and passed without speech. There is nothing left me, sir, but to put back into the port of Glasgow after hands; and there (by your leave) ye will find them that are better able to talk to you."

"Ay?" said Alan; "and faith, I'll have a talk with them mysel'! Unless there's naebody speaks English in that town, I have a bonny tale for them. Fifteen tarry sailors upon the one side, and a man and a halfling boy upon the other! O, man, it's peetiful!"

Hoseason flushed red.

"No," continued Alan, "that'll no do. Ye'll just have to set me ashore as we agreed."

"Ay," said Hoseason, "but my first officer is dead—ye ken best how. There's none of the rest of us acquaint with this coast, sir; and it's one very dangerous to ships."

"I give ye your choice," says Alan. "Set me on dry ground in Appin, or Ardgour, or in Morven, or Arisaig, or Morar; or, in brief, where ye please, within thirty miles of my own country; except in a country of the Campbells. That's a broad target. If ye miss that, ye must be as feckless at the sailoring as I have found ye at the fighting. Why, my poor country people in their bit cobles* pass from island to island in all weathers, ay, and by night too, for the matter of that."

   *Coble: a small boat used in fishing.

"A coble's not a ship, sir," said the captain. "It has nae draught of water."

"Well, then, to Glasgow if ye list!" says Alan. "We'll have the laugh of ye at the least."

"My mind runs little upon laughing," said the captain. "But all this will cost money, sir."

"Well, sir," says Alan, "I am nae weathercock. Thirty guineas, if ye land me on the sea-side; and sixty, if ye put me in the Linnhe Loch."

"But see, sir, where we lie, we are but a few hours' sail from Ardnamurchan," said Hoseason. "Give me sixty, and I'll set ye there."

"And I'm to wear my brogues and run jeopardy of the red-coats to please you?" cries Alan. "No, sir; if ye want sixty guineas earn them, and set me in my own country."

"It's to risk the brig, sir," said the captain, "and your own lives along with her."

"Take it or want it," says Alan.

"Could ye pilot us at all?" asked the captain, who was frowning to himself.

"Well, it's doubtful," said Alan. "I'm more of a fighting man (as ye have seen for yoursel') than a sailor-man. But I have been often enough picked up and set down upon this coast, and should ken something of the lie of it."

The captain shook his head, still frowning.

"If I had lost less money on this unchancy cruise," says he, "I would see you in a rope's end before I risked my brig, sir. But be it as ye will. As soon as I get a slant of wind (and there's some coming, or I'm the more mistaken) I'll put it in hand. But there's one thing more. We may meet in with a king's ship and she may lay us aboard, sir, with no blame of mine: they keep the cruisers thick upon this coast, ye ken who for. Now, sir, if that was to befall, ye might leave the money."

"Captain," says Alan, "if ye see a pennant, it shall be your part to run away. And now, as I hear you're a little short of brandy in the fore-part, I'll offer ye a change: a bottle of brandy against two buckets of water."

That was the last clause of the treaty, and was duly executed on both sides; so that Alan and I could at last wash out the round-house and be quit of the memorials of those whom we had slain, and the captain and Mr. Riach could be happy again in their own way, the name of which was drink.

CHAPTER XII

I HEAR OF THE "RED FOX"

Before we had done cleaning out the round-house, a breeze sprang up from a little to the east of north. This blew off the rain and brought out the sun.

And here I must explain; and the reader would do well to look at a map. On the day when the fog fell and we ran down Alan's boat, we had been running through the Little Minch. At dawn after the battle, we lay becalmed to the east of the Isle of Canna or between that and Isle Eriska in the chain of the Long Island. Now to get from there to the Linnhe Loch, the straight course was through the narrows of the Sound of Mull. But the captain had no chart; he was afraid to trust his brig so deep among the islands; and the wind serving well, he preferred to go by west of Tiree and come up under the southern coast of the great Isle of Mull.

All day the breeze held in the same point, and rather freshened than died down; and towards afternoon, a swell began to set in from round the outer Hebrides. Our course, to go round about the inner isles, was to the west of south, so that at first we had this swell upon our beam, and were much rolled about. But after nightfall, when we had turned the end of Tiree and began to head more to the east, the sea came right astern.

Meanwhile, the early part of the day, before the swell came up, was very pleasant; sailing, as we were, in a bright sunshine and with many mountainous islands upon different sides. Alan and I sat in the round-house with the doors open on each side (the wind being straight astern), and smoked a pipe or two of the captain's fine tobacco. It was at this time we heard each other's stories, which was the more important to me, as I gained some knowledge of that wild Highland country on which I was so soon to land. In those days, so close on the back of the great rebellion, it was needful a man should know what he was doing when he went upon the heather.

It was I that showed the example, telling him all my misfortune; which he heard with great good-nature. Only, when I came to mention that good friend of mine, Mr. Campbell the minister, Alan fired up and cried out that he hated all that were of that name.

"Why," said I, "he is a man you should be proud to give your hand to."

"I know nothing I would help a Campbell to," says he, "unless it was a leaden bullet. I would hunt all of that name like blackcocks. If I lay dying, I would crawl upon my knees to my chamber window for a shot at one."

"Why, Alan," I cried, "what ails ye at the Campbells?"

"Well," says he, "ye ken very well that I am an Appin Stewart, and the Campbells have long harried and wasted those of my name; ay, and got lands of us by treachery—but never with the sword," he cried loudly, and with the word brought down his fist upon the table. But I paid the less attention to this, for I knew it was usually said by those who have the underhand. "There's more than that," he continued, "and all in the same story: lying words, lying papers, tricks fit for a peddler, and the show of what's legal over all, to make a man the more angry."

"You that are so wasteful of your buttons," said I, "I can hardly think you would be a good judge of business."

"Ah!" says he, falling again to smiling, "I got my wastefulness from the same man I got the buttons from; and that was my poor father, Duncan Stewart, grace be to him! He was the prettiest man of his kindred; and the best swordsman in the Hielands, David, and that is the same as to say, in all the world, I should ken, for it was him that taught me. He was in the Black Watch, when first it was mustered; and, like other gentlemen privates, had a gillie at his back to carry his firelock for him on the march. Well, the King, it appears, was wishful to see Hieland swordsmanship; and my father and three more were chosen out and sent to London town, to let him see it at the best. So they were had into the palace and showed the whole art of the sword for two hours at a stretch, before King George and Queen Carline, and the Butcher Cumberland, and many more of whom I havenae mind. And when they were through, the King (for all he was a rank usurper) spoke them fair and gave each man three guineas in his hand. Now, as they were going out of the palace, they had a porter's lodge to go by; and it came in on my father, as he was perhaps the first private Hieland gentleman that had ever gone by that door, it was right he should give the poor porter a proper notion of their quality. So he gives the King's three guineas into the man's hand, as if it was his common custom; the three others that came behind him did the same; and there they were on the street, never a penny the better for their pains. Some say it was one, that was the first to fee the King's porter; and some say it was another; but the truth of it is, that it was Duncan Stewart, as I am willing to prove with either sword or pistol. And that was the father that I had, God rest him!"

"I think he was not the man to leave you rich," said I.

"And that's true," said Alan. "He left me my breeks to cover me, and little besides. And that was how I came to enlist, which was a black spot upon my character at the best of times, and would still be a sore job for me if I fell among the red-coats."

"What," cried I, "were you in the English army?"

"That was I," said Alan. "But I deserted to the right side at Preston Pans—and that's some comfort."

I could scarcely share this view: holding desertion under arms for an unpardonable fault in honour. But for all I was so young, I was wiser than say my thought. "Dear, dear," says I, "the punishment is death."

"Ay" said he, "if they got hands on me, it would be a short shrift and a lang tow for Alan! But I have the King of France's commission in my pocket, which would aye be some protection."

"I misdoubt it much," said I.

"I have doubts mysel'," said Alan drily.

"And, good heaven, man," cried I, "you that are a condemned rebel, and a deserter, and a man of the French King's—what tempts ye back into this country? It's a braving of Providence."

"Tut!" says Alan, "I have been back every year since forty-six!"

"And what brings ye, man?" cried I.

"Well, ye see, I weary for my friends and country," said he. "France is a braw place, nae doubt; but I weary for the heather and the deer. And then I have bit things that I attend to. Whiles I pick up a few lads to serve the King of France: recruits, ye see; and that's aye a little money. But the heart of the matter is the business of my chief, Ardshiel."

"I thought they called your chief Appin," said I.

"Ay, but Ardshiel is the captain of the clan," said he, which scarcely cleared my mind. "Ye see,

David, he that was all his life so great a man, and come of the blood and bearing the name of kings, is now brought down to live in a French town like a poor and private person. He that had four hundred swords at his whistle, I have seen, with these eyes of mine, buying butter in the market-place, and taking it home in a kale-leaf. This is not only a pain but a disgrace to us of his family and clan. There are the bairns forby, the children and the hope of Appin, that must be learned their letters and how to hold a sword, in that far country. Now, the tenants of Appin have to pay a rent to King George; but their hearts are staunch, they are true to their chief; and what with love and a bit of pressure, and maybe a threat or two, the poor folk scrape up a second rent for Ardshiel. Well, David, I'm the hand that carries it." And he struck the belt about his body, so that the guineas rang.

"Do they pay both?" cried I.

"Ay, David, both," says he.

"What! two rents?" I repeated.

"Ay, David," said he. "I told a different tale to yon captain man; but this is the truth of it. And it's wonderful to me how little pressure is needed. But that's the handiwork of my good kinsman and my father's friend, James of the Glens: James Stewart, that is: Ardshiel's half-brother. He it is that gets the money in, and does the management."

This was the first time I heard the name of that James Stewart, who was afterwards so famous at the time of his hanging. But I took little heed at the moment, for all my mind was occupied with the generosity of these poor Highlanders.

"I call it noble," I cried. "I'm a Whig, or little better; but I call it noble."

"Ay" said he, "ye're a Whig, but ye're a gentleman; and that's what does it. Now, if ye were one of the cursed race of Campbell, ye would gnash your teeth to hear tell of it. If ye were the Red Fox..." And at that name, his teeth shut together, and he ceased speaking. I have seen many a grim face, but never a grimmer than Alan's when he had named the Red Fox.

"And who is the Red Fox?" I asked, daunted, but still curious.

"Who is he?" cried Alan. "Well, and I'll tell you that. When the men of the clans were broken at Culloden, and the good cause went down, and the horses rode over the fetlocks in the best blood of the north, Ardshiel had to flee like a poor deer upon the mountains—he and his lady and his bairns. A sair job we had of it before we got him shipped; and while he still lay in the heather, the English rogues, that couldnae come at his life, were striking at his rights. They stripped him of his powers; they stripped him of his lands; they plucked the weapons from the hands of his clansmen, that had borne arms for thirty centuries; ay, and the very clothes off their backs—so that it's now a sin to wear a tartan plaid, and a man may be cast into a gaol if he has but a kilt about his legs. One thing they couldnae kill. That was the love the clansmen bore their chief. These guineas are the proof of it. And now, in there steps a man, a Campbell, red-headed Colin of Glenure——"

"Is that him you call the Red Fox?" said I.

"Will ye bring me his brush?" cries Alan, fiercely. "Ay, that's the man. In he steps, and gets papers from King George, to be so-called King's factor on the lands of Appin. And at first he sings small, and is hail-fellow-well-met with Sheamus—that's James of the Glens, my chieftain's agent. But by-and-by, that came to his ears that I have just told you; how the poor commons of Appin, the farmers and the crofters and the boumen, were wringing their very plaids to get a second rent, and send it over-seas for Ardshiel and his poor bairns. What was it ye called it, when I told ye?"

"I called it noble, Alan," said I.

"And you little better than a common Whig!" cries Alan. "But when it came to Colin Roy, the black Campbell blood in him ran wild. He sat gnashing his teeth at the wine table. What! should a Stewart get a bite of bread, and him not be able to prevent it? Ah! Red Fox, if ever I hold you at a gun's end, the Lord have pity upon ye!" (Alan stopped to swallow down his anger.) "Well, David, what does he do? He declares all the farms to let. And, thinks he, in his black heart, 'I'll soon get other tenants that'll overbid these Stewarts, and Maccolls, and Macrobs' (for these are all names in my clan, David); 'and then,' thinks he, 'Ardshiel will have to hold his bonnet on a French roadside.'"

"Well," said I, "what followed?"

Alan laid down his pipe, which he had long since suffered to go out, and set his two hands upon his knees.

"Ay," said he, "ye'll never guess that! For these same Stewarts, and Maccolls, and Macrobs (that had two rents to pay, one to King George by stark force, and one to Ardshiel by natural kindness) offered him a better price than any Campbell in all broad Scotland; and far he sent seeking them—as far as to the sides of Clyde and the cross of Edinburgh—seeking, and fleeching, and begging them to come, where there was a Stewart to be starved and a red-headed hound of a Campbell to be pleasured!"

"Well, Alan," said I, "that is a strange story, and a fine one, too. And Whig as I may be, I am glad the man was beaten."

"Him beaten?" echoed Alan. "It's little ye ken of Campbells, and less of the Red Fox. Him beaten? No: nor will be, till his blood's on the hillside! But if the day comes, David man, that I can find time and leisure for a bit of hunting, there grows not enough heather in all Scotland to hide him from my vengeance!"

"Man Alan," said I, "ye are neither very wise nor very Christian to blow off so many words of anger. They will do the man ye call the Fox no harm, and yourself no good. Tell me your tale plainly out. What did he next?"

"And that's a good observe, David," said Alan. "Troth and indeed, they will do him no harm; the more's the pity! And barring that about Christianity (of which my opinion is quite otherwise, or I would be nae Christian), I am much of your mind."

"Opinion here or opinion there," said I, "it's a kent thing that Christianity forbids revenge."

"Ay" said he, "it's well seen it was a Campbell taught ye! It would be a convenient world for them and their sort, if there was no such a thing as a lad and a gun behind a heather bush! But that's nothing to the point. This is what he did."

"Ay" said I, "come to that."

"Well, David," said he, "since he couldnae be rid of the loyal commons by fair means, he swore he would be rid of them by foul. Ardshiel was to starve: that was the thing he aimed at. And since them that fed him in his exile wouldnae be bought out—right or wrong, he would drive them out. Therefore he sent for lawyers, and papers, and red-coats to stand at his back. And the kindly folk of that country must all pack and tramp, every father's son out of his father's house, and out of the place where he was bred and fed, and played when he was a callant. And who are to succeed them? Bare-leggit beggars! King George is to whistle for his rents; he maun dow with less; he can spread his butter thinner: what cares Red Colin? If he can hurt Ardshiel, he has his wish; if he can pluck the meat from my chieftain's table, and the bit toys out of his children's hands, he will gang hame singing to Glenure!"

"Let me have a word," said I. "Be sure, if they take less rents, be sure Government has a finger in the pie. It's not this Campbell's fault, man—it's his orders. And if ye killed this Colin tomorrow, what better would ye be? There would be another factor in his shoes, as fast as spur can drive."

"Ye're a good lad in a fight," said Alan; "but, man! ye have Whig blood in ye!"

He spoke kindly enough, but there was so much anger under his contempt that I thought it was wise to change the conversation. I expressed my wonder how, with the Highlands covered with troops, and guarded like a city in a siege, a man in his situation could come and go without arrest.

"It's easier than ye would think," said Alan. "A bare hillside (ye see) is like all one road; if there's a sentry at one place, ye just go by another. And then the heather's a great help. And everywhere there are friends' houses and friends' byres and haystacks. And besides, when folk talk of a country covered with troops, it's but a kind of a byword at the best. A soldier covers nae mair of it than his boot-soles. I have fished a water with a sentry on the other side of the brae, and killed a fine trout; and I have sat in a heather bush within six feet of another, and learned a real bonny tune from his whistling. This was it," said he, and whistled me the air.

"And then, besides," he continued, "it's no sae bad now as it was in forty-six. The Hielands are what they call pacified. Small wonder, with never a gun or a sword left from Cantyre to Cape Wrath, but what tenty* folk have hidden in their thatch! But what I would like to ken, David, is just how long? Not long, ye would think, with men like Ardshiel in exile and men like the Red Fox sitting birling the wine and oppressing the poor at home. But it's a kittle thing to decide what folk'll bear, and what they will not. Or why would Red Colin be riding his horse all over my poor country of Appin, and never a pretty lad to put a bullet in him?"

 * Careful.

And with this Alan fell into a muse, and for a long time sate very sad and silent.

I will add the rest of what I have to say about my friend, that he was skilled in all kinds of music, but principally pipe-music; was a well-considered poet in his own tongue; had read several books both in French and English; was a dead shot, a good angler, and an excellent fencer with the small sword as well as with his own particular weapon. For his faults, they were on his face, and I now knew them all. But the worst of them, his childish propensity to take offence and to pick quarrels, he greatly laid aside in my case, out of regard for the battle of the round-house. But whether it was because I had done well myself, or because I had been a witness of his own much greater prowess, is more than I can tell. For though he had a great taste for courage in other men, yet he admired it most in Alan Breck.

CHAPTER XIII
THE LOSS OF THE BRIG

It was already late at night, and as dark as it ever would be at that season of the year (and that is to say, it was still pretty bright), when Hoseason clapped his head into the round-house door.

"Here," said he, "come out and see if ye can pilot."

"Is this one of your tricks?" asked Alan.

"Do I look like tricks?" cries the captain. "I have other things to think of—my brig's in danger!"

By the concerned look of his face, and, above all, by the sharp tones in which he spoke of his brig, it was plain to both of us he was in deadly earnest; and so Alan and I, with no great fear of treachery, stepped on deck.

The sky was clear; it blew hard, and was bitter cold; a great deal of daylight lingered; and the moon, which was nearly full, shone brightly. The brig was close hauled, so as to round the southwest corner of the Island of Mull, the hills of which (and Ben More above them all, with a wisp of mist upon the top of it) lay full upon the lar-board bow. Though it was no good point of sailing for the Covenant, she tore through the seas at a great rate, pitching and straining, and pursued by the westerly swell.

Altogether it was no such ill night to keep the seas in; and I had begun to wonder what it was that sat so heavily upon the captain, when the brig rising suddenly on the top of a high swell, he pointed and cried to us to look. Away on the lee bow, a thing like a fountain rose out of the moonlit sea, and immediately after we heard a low sound of roaring.

"What do ye call that?" asked the captain, gloomily.

"The sea breaking on a reef," said Alan. "And now ye ken where it is; and what better would ye have?"

"Ay," said Hoseason, "if it was the only one."

And sure enough, just as he spoke there came a second fountain farther to the south.

"There!" said Hoseason. "Ye see for yourself. If I had kent of these reefs, if I had had a chart, or if Shuan had been spared, it's not sixty guineas, no, nor six hundred, would have made me risk my brig in sic a stoneyard! But you, sir, that was to pilot us, have ye never a word?"

"I'm thinking," said Alan, "these'll be what they call the Torran Rocks."

"Are there many of them?" says the captain.

"Truly, sir, I am nae pilot," said Alan; "but it sticks in my mind there are ten miles of them."

Mr. Riach and the captain looked at each other.

"There's a way through them, I suppose?" said the captain.

"Doubtless," said Alan, "but where? But it somehow runs in my mind once more that it is clearer under the land."

"So?" said Hoseason. "We'll have to haul our wind then, Mr. Riach; we'll have to come as near in about the end of Mull as we can take her, sir; and even then we'll have the land to kep the wind off us, and that stoneyard on our lee. Well, we're in for it now, and may as well crack on."

With that he gave an order to the steersman, and sent Riach to the foretop. There were only five men on deck, counting the officers; these being all that were fit (or, at least, both fit and willing) for their work. So, as I say, it fell to Mr. Riach to go aloft, and he sat there looking out and hailing the deck with news of all he saw.

"The sea to the south is thick," he cried; and then, after a while, "it does seem clearer in by the land."

"Well, sir," said Hoseason to Alan, "we'll try your way of it. But I think I might as well trust to a blind fiddler. Pray God you're right."

"Pray God I am!" says Alan to me. "But where did I hear it? Well, well, it will be as it must."

As we got nearer to the turn of the land the reefs began to be sown here and there on our very path; and Mr. Riach sometimes cried down to us to change the course. Sometimes, indeed, none too soon; for one reef was so close on the brig's weather board that when a sea burst upon it the lighter sprays fell upon her deck and wetted us like rain.

The brightness of the night showed us these perils as clearly as by day, which was, perhaps, the more alarming. It showed me, too, the face of the captain as he stood by the steersman, now on one foot, now on the other, and sometimes blowing in his hands, but still listening and looking and as steady as steel. Neither he nor Mr. Riach had shown well in the fighting; but I saw they were brave in their own trade, and admired them all the more because I found Alan very white.

"Ochone, David," says he, "this is no the kind of death I fancy!"

"What, Alan!" I cried, "you're not afraid?"

"No," said he, wetting his lips, "but you'll allow, yourself, it's a cold ending."

By this time, now and then sheering to one side or the other to avoid a reef, but still hugging the wind and the land, we had got round Iona and begun to come alongside Mull. The tide at the tail of the land ran very strong, and threw the brig about. Two hands were put to the helm, and Hoseason himself would sometimes lend a help; and it was strange to see three strong men throw their weight upon the tiller, and it (like a living thing) struggle against and drive them back. This would have been the greater danger had not the sea been for some while free of obstacles. Mr. Riach, besides, announced from the top that he saw clear water ahead.

"Ye were right," said Hoseason to Alan. "Ye have saved the brig, sir. I'll mind that when we come to clear accounts." And I believe he not only meant what he said, but would have done it; so high a place did the Covenant hold in his affections.

But this is matter only for conjecture, things having gone otherwise than he forecast.

"Keep her away a point," sings out Mr. Riach. "Reef to windward!"

And just at the same time the tide caught the brig, and threw the wind out of her sails. She came round into the wind like a top, and the next moment struck the reef with such a dunch as threw us all flat upon the deck, and came near to shake Mr. Riach from his place upon the mast.

I was on my feet in a minute. The reef on which we had struck was close in under the southwest end of Mull, off a little isle they call Earraid, which lay low and black upon the larboard. Sometimes the swell broke clean over us; sometimes it only ground the poor brig upon the reef, so that we could hear her beat herself to pieces; and what with the great noise of the sails, and the singing of the wind, and the flying of the spray in the moonlight, and the sense of danger, I think my head must have been partly turned, for I could scarcely understand the things I saw.

Presently I observed Mr. Riach and the seamen busy round the skiff, and, still in the same blank, ran over to assist them; and as soon as I set my hand to work, my mind came clear again. It was no very easy task, for the skiff lay amidships and was full of hamper, and the breaking of the heavier seas continually forced us to give over and hold on; but we all wrought like horses while we could.

Meanwhile such of the wounded as could move came clambering out of the fore-scuttle and began to help; while the rest that lay helpless in their bunks harrowed me with screaming and begging to be saved.

The captain took no part. It seemed he was struck stupid. He stood holding by the shrouds, talking to himself and groaning out aloud whenever the ship hammered on the rock. His brig was like wife and child to him; he had looked on, day by day, at the mishandling of poor Ransome; but when it came to the brig, he seemed to suffer along with her.

All the time of our working at the boat, I remember only one other thing: that I asked Alan, looking across at the shore, what country it was; and he answered, it was the worst possible for him, for it was a land of the Campbells.

We had one of the wounded men told off to keep a watch upon the seas and cry us warning. Well, we had the boat about ready to be launched, when this man sang out pretty shrill: "For God's sake, hold on!" We knew by his tone that it was something more than ordinary; and sure enough, there followed a sea so huge that it lifted the brig right up and canted her over on her beam. Whether the cry came too late, or my hold was too weak, I know not; but at the sudden tilting of the ship I was cast clean over the bulwarks into the sea.

I went down, and drank my fill, and then came up, and got a blink of the moon, and then down again. They say a man sinks a third time for good. I cannot be made like other folk, then; for I would not like to write how often I went down, or how often I came up again. All the while, I was being hurled along, and beaten upon and choked, and then swallowed whole; and the thing was so distracting to my wits, that I was neither sorry nor afraid.

Presently, I found I was holding to a spar, which helped me somewhat. And then all of a sudden I was in quiet water, and began to come to myself.

It was the spare yard I had got hold of, and I was amazed to see how far I had travelled from the brig. I hailed her, indeed; but it was plain she was already out of cry. She was still holding together; but whether or not they had yet launched the boat, I was too far off and too low down to see.

While I was hailing the brig, I spied a tract of water lying between us where no great waves came, but which yet boiled white all over and bristled in the moon with rings and bubbles. Sometimes the whole tract swung to one side, like the tail of a live serpent; sometimes, for a glimpse, it would all disappear and then boil up again. What it was I had no guess, which for the time increased my fear of it; but I now know it must have been the roost or tide race, which had carried me away so fast and tumbled me about so cruelly, and at last, as if tired of that play, had flung out me and the spare yard upon its landward margin.

I now lay quite becalmed, and began to feel that a man can die of cold as well as of drowning. The shores of Earraid were close in; I could see in the moonlight the dots of heather and the sparkling of the mica in the rocks.

"Well," thought I to myself, "if I cannot get as far as that, it's strange!"

I had no skill of swimming, Essen Water being small in our neighbourhood; but when I laid hold upon the yard with both arms, and kicked out with both feet, I soon begun to find that I was moving. Hard work it was, and mortally slow; but in about an hour of kicking and splashing, I had got well in between the points of a sandy bay surrounded by low hills.

The sea was here quite quiet; there was no sound of any surf; the moon shone clear; and I thought in my heart I had never seen a place so desert and desolate. But it was dry land; and when at last it grew so shallow that I could leave the yard and wade ashore upon my feet, I cannot tell if I was more tired or more grateful. Both, at least, I was: tired as I never was before that night; and grateful to God as I trust I have been often, though never with more cause.

CHAPTER XIV
THE ISLET

With my stepping ashore I began the most unhappy part of my adventures. It was half-past twelve in the morning, and though the wind was broken by the land, it was a cold night. I dared not sit down (for I thought I should have frozen), but took off my shoes and walked to and fro upon the sand, bare-foot, and beating my breast with infinite weariness. There was no sound of man or cattle; not a cock crew, though it was about the hour of their first waking; only the surf broke outside in the distance, which put me in mind of my perils and those of my friend. To walk by the sea at that hour of the morning, and in a place so desert-like and lonesome, struck me with a kind of fear.

As soon as the day began to break I put on my shoes and climbed a hill—the ruggedest scramble I ever undertook—falling, the whole way, between big blocks of granite, or leaping from one to another. When I got to the top the dawn was come. There was no sign of the brig, which must have lifted from the reef and sunk. The boat, too, was nowhere to be seen. There was never a sail upon the ocean; and in what I could see of the land was neither house nor man.

I was afraid to think what had befallen my shipmates, and afraid to look longer at so empty a scene. What with my wet clothes and weariness, and my belly that now began to ache with hunger, I had enough to trouble me without that. So I set off eastward along the south coast, hoping to find a house where I might warm myself, and perhaps get news of those I had lost. And at the worst, I considered the sun would soon rise and dry my clothes.

After a little, my way was stopped by a creek or inlet of the sea, which seemed to run pretty deep into the land; and as I had no means to get across, I must needs change my direction to go about the end of it. It was still the roughest kind of walking; indeed the whole, not only of Earraid, but of the neighbouring part of Mull (which they call the Ross) is nothing but a jumble of granite rocks with heather in among. At first the creek kept narrowing as I had looked to see; but presently to my surprise it began to widen out again. At this I scratched my head, but had still no notion of the truth: until at last I came to a rising ground, and it burst upon me all in a moment that I was cast upon a little barren isle, and cut off on every side by the salt seas.

Instead of the sun rising to dry me, it came on to rain, with a thick mist; so that my case was lamentable.

I stood in the rain, and shivered, and wondered what to do, till it occurred to me that perhaps the creek was fordable. Back I went to the narrowest point and waded in. But not three yards from shore, I plumped in head over ears; and if ever I was heard of more, it was rather by God's grace than my own prudence. I was no wetter (for that could hardly be), but I was all the colder for this mishap; and having lost another hope was the more unhappy.

And now, all at once, the yard came in my head. What had carried me through the roost would surely serve me to cross this little quiet creek in safety. With that I set off, undaunted, across the top of the isle, to fetch and carry it back. It was a weary tramp in all ways, and if hope had not buoyed me up, I must have cast myself down and given up. Whether with the sea salt, or because I was growing fevered, I was distressed with thirst, and had to stop, as I went, and drink the peaty water out of the hags.

I came to the bay at last, more dead than alive; and at the first glance, I thought the yard was something farther out than when I left it. In I went, for the third time, into the sea. The sand was smooth and firm, and shelved gradually down, so that I could wade out till the water was almost to my neck and the little waves splashed into my face. But at that depth my feet began to leave me, and I durst venture in no farther. As for the yard, I saw it bobbing very quietly some twenty feet beyond.

I had borne up well until this last disappointment; but at that I came ashore, and flung myself down upon the sands and wept.

The time I spent upon the island is still so horrible a thought to me, that I must pass it lightly over. In all the books I have read of people cast away, they had either their pockets full of tools, or a chest of things would be thrown upon the beach along with them, as if on purpose. My case was very different. I had nothing in my pockets but money and Alan's silver button; and being inland bred, I was as much short of knowledge as of means.

I knew indeed that shell-fish were counted good to eat; and among the rocks of the isle I found a great plenty of limpets, which at first I could scarcely strike from their places, not knowing quickness to be needful. There were, besides, some of the little shells that we call buckies; I think periwinkle is the English name. Of these two I made my whole diet, devouring them cold and raw as I found them; and so hungry was I, that at first they seemed to me delicious.

Perhaps they were out of season, or perhaps there was something wrong in the sea about my island. But at least I had no sooner eaten my first meal than I was seized with giddiness and retching, and lay for a long time no better than dead. A second trial of the same food (indeed I had no other) did better with me, and revived my strength. But as long as I was on the island, I never knew what to expect when I had eaten; sometimes all was well, and sometimes I was thrown into a miserable sickness; nor could I ever distinguish what particular fish it was that hurt me.

All day it streamed rain; the island ran like a sop, there was no dry spot to be found; and when I lay down that night, between two boulders that made a kind of roof, my feet were in a bog.

The second day I crossed the island to all sides. There was no one part of it better than another; it was all desolate and rocky; nothing living on it but game birds which I lacked the means to kill, and the gulls which haunted the outlying rocks in a prodigious number. But the creek, or strait, that cut off the isle from the main-land of the Ross, opened out on the north into a bay, and the bay again opened into the Sound of Iona; and it was the neighbourhood of this place that I chose to be my home; though if I had thought upon the very name of home in such a spot, I must have burst out weeping.

I had good reasons for my choice. There was in this part of the isle a little hut of a house like a pig's hut, where fishers used to sleep when they came there upon their business; but the turf roof of it had fallen entirely in; so that the hut was of no use to me, and gave me less shelter than my rocks. What was more important, the shell-fish on which I lived grew there in great plenty; when the tide was out I could gather a peck at a time: and this was doubtless a convenience. But the other reason went deeper. I had become in no way used to the horrid solitude of the isle, but still looked round me on all sides (like a man that was hunted), between fear and hope that I might see some human creature coming. Now, from a little up the hillside over the bay, I could catch a sight of the great, ancient church and the roofs of the people's houses in Iona. And on the other hand, over the low country of the Ross, I saw smoke go up, morning and evening, as if from a homestead in a hollow of the land.

I used to watch this smoke, when I was wet and cold, and had my head half turned with loneliness; and think of the fireside and the company, till my heart burned. It was the same with the roofs of Iona. Altogether, this sight I had of men's homes and comfortable lives, although it put a point on my own sufferings, yet it kept hope alive, and helped me to eat my raw shell-fish (which had soon grown to be a disgust), and saved me from the sense of horror I had whenever I was quite alone with dead rocks, and fowls, and the rain, and the cold sea.

I say it kept hope alive; and indeed it seemed impossible that I should be left to die on the shores of my own country, and within view of a church-tower and the smoke of men's houses. But the second day passed; and though as long as the light lasted I kept a bright look-out for boats on the Sound or men passing on the Ross, no help came near me. It still rained, and I turned in to sleep, as wet as ever, and with a cruel sore throat, but a little comforted, perhaps, by having said good-night to my next neighbours, the people of Iona.

Charles the Second declared a man could stay outdoors more days in the year in the climate of England than in any other. This was very like a king, with a palace at his back and changes of dry clothes. But he must have had better luck on his flight from Worcester than I had on that miserable isle. It was the height of the summer; yet it rained for more than twenty-four hours, and did not clear until the afternoon of the third day.

This was the day of incidents. In the morning I saw a red deer, a buck with a fine spread of antlers, standing in the rain on the top of the island; but he had scarce seen me rise from under my rock, before he trotted off upon the other side. I supposed he must have swum the strait; though what should bring any creature to Earraid, was more than I could fancy.

A little after, as I was jumping about after my limpets, I was startled by a guinea-piece, which fell upon a rock in front of me and glanced off into the sea. When the sailors gave me my money again, they kept back not only about a third of the whole sum, but my father's leather purse; so that from that day out, I carried my gold loose in a pocket with a button. I now saw there must be a hole, and clapped my hand to the place in a great hurry. But this was to lock the stable door after the steed was stolen. I had left the shore at Queensferry with near on fifty pounds; now I found no more than two guinea-pieces and a silver shilling.

It is true I picked up a third guinea a little after, where it lay shining on a piece of turf. That made a fortune of three pounds and four shillings, English money, for a lad, the rightful heir of an estate, and now starving on an isle at the extreme end of the wild Highlands.

This state of my affairs dashed me still further; and, indeed my plight on that third morning was truly pitiful. My clothes were beginning to rot; my stockings in particular were quite worn through, so that my shanks went naked; my hands had grown quite soft with the continual soaking; my throat was very sore, my strength had much abated, and my heart so turned against the horrid stuff I was condemned to eat, that the very sight of it came near to sicken me.

And yet the worst was not yet come.

There is a pretty high rock on the northwest of Earraid, which (because it had a flat top and overlooked the Sound) I was much in the habit of frequenting; not that ever I stayed in one place, save when asleep, my misery giving me no rest. Indeed, I wore myself down with continual and aimless goings and comings in the rain.

As soon, however, as the sun came out, I lay down on the top of that rock to dry myself. The comfort of the sunshine is a thing I cannot tell. It set me thinking hopefully of my deliverance, of which I had begun to despair; and I scanned the sea and the Ross with a fresh interest. On the south of my rock, a part of the island jutted out and hid the open ocean, so that a boat could thus come quite near me upon that side, and I be none the wiser.

Well, all of a sudden, a coble with a brown sail and a pair of fishers aboard of it, came flying round that corner of the isle, bound for Iona. I shouted out, and then fell on my knees on the rock and reached up my hands and prayed to them. They were near enough to hear—I could even see the colour of their hair; and there was no doubt but they observed me, for they cried out in the Gaelic tongue, and laughed. But the boat never turned aside, and flew on, right before my eyes, for Iona.

I could not believe such wickedness, and ran along the shore from rock to rock, crying on them piteously even after they were out of reach of my voice, I still cried and waved to them; and when they were quite gone, I thought my heart would have burst. All the time of my troubles I wept only twice. Once, when I could not reach the yard, and now, the second time, when these fishers turned a deaf ear to my cries. But this time I wept and roared like a wicked child, tearing up the turf with my nails, and grinding my face in the earth. If a wish would kill men, those two fishers would never have seen morning, and I should likely have died upon my island.

When I was a little over my anger, I must eat again, but with such loathing of the mess as I could now scarce control. Sure enough, I should have done as well to fast, for my fishes poisoned me again. I had all my first pains; my throat was so sore I could scarce swallow; I had a fit of strong shuddering, which clucked my teeth together; and there came on me that dreadful sense of illness, which we have no name for either in Scotch or English. I thought I should have died, and made my peace with God, forgiving all men, even my uncle and the fishers; and as soon as I had thus made up my mind to the worst, clearness came upon me; I observed the night was falling dry; my clothes were dried a good deal; truly, I was in a better case than ever before, since I had landed on the isle; and so I got to sleep at last, with a thought of gratitude.

The next day (which was the fourth of this horrible life of mine) I found my bodily strength run very low. But the sun shone, the air was sweet, and what I managed to eat of the shell-fish agreed well with me and revived my courage.

I was scarce back on my rock (where I went always the first thing after I had eaten) before I observed a boat coming down the Sound, and with her head, as I thought, in my direction.

I began at once to hope and fear exceedingly; for I thought these men might have thought better of their cruelty and be coming back to my assistance. But another disappointment, such as yesterday's, was more than I could bear. I turned my back, accordingly, upon the sea, and did not look again till I had counted many hundreds. The boat was still heading for the island. The next time I counted the full thousand, as slowly as I could, my heart beating so as to hurt me. And then it was out of all question. She was coming straight to Earraid!

I could no longer hold myself back, but ran to the seaside and out, from one rock to another, as far as I could go. It is a marvel I was not drowned; for when I was brought to a stand at last, my legs shook under me, and my mouth was so dry, I must wet it with the sea-water before I was able to shout.

All this time the boat was coming on; and now I was able to perceive it was the same boat and the same two men as yesterday. This I knew by their hair, which the one had of a bright yellow and the other black. But now there was a third man along with them, who looked to be of a better class.

As soon as they were come within easy speech, they let down their sail and lay quiet. In spite of my supplications, they drew no nearer in, and what frightened me most of all, the new man tee-hee'd with laughter as he talked and looked at me.

Then he stood up in the boat and addressed me a long while, speaking fast and with many wavings of his hand. I told him I had no Gaelic; and at this he became very angry, and I began to suspect he thought he was talking English. Listening very close, I caught the word "whateffer" several times; but all the rest was Gaelic and might have been Greek and Hebrew for me.

"Whatever," said I, to show him I had caught a word.

"Yes, yes—yes, yes," says he, and then he looked at the other men, as much as to say, "I told you I spoke English," and began again as hard as ever in the Gaelic.

This time I picked out another word, "tide." Then I had a flash of hope. I remembered he was always waving his hand towards the mainland of the Ross.

"Do you mean when the tide is out—?" I cried, and could not finish.

"Yes, yes," said he. "Tide."

At that I turned tail upon their boat (where my adviser had once more begun to tee-hee with laughter), leaped back the way I had come, from one stone to another, and set off running across the isle as I had never run before. In about half an hour I came out upon the shores of the creek; and, sure enough, it was shrunk into a little trickle of water, through which I dashed, not above my knees, and landed with a shout on the main island.

A sea-bred boy would not have stayed a day on Earraid; which is only what they call a tidal islet, and except in the bottom of the neaps, can be entered and left twice in every twenty-four hours, either dry-shod, or at the most by wading. Even I, who had the tide going out and in before me in the bay, and even watched for the ebbs, the better to get my shellfish—even I (I say) if I had sat down to think, instead of raging at my fate, must have soon guessed the secret, and got free. It was no wonder the fishers had not understood me. The wonder was rather that they had ever guessed my pitiful illusion, and taken the trouble to come back. I had starved with cold and hunger on that island for close upon one hundred hours. But for the fishers, I might have left my bones there, in pure folly. And even as it was, I had paid for it pretty dear, not only in past sufferings, but in my present case; being clothed like a beggar-man, scarce able to walk, and in great pain of my sore throat.

I have seen wicked men and fools, a great many of both; and I believe they both get paid in the end; but the fools first.

CHAPTER XV
THE LAD WITH THE SILVER BUTTON:
THROUGH THE ISLE OF MULL

The Ross of Mull, which I had now got upon, was rugged and trackless, like the isle I had just left; being all bog, and brier, and big stone. There may be roads for them that know that country well; but for my part I had no better guide than my own nose, and no other landmark than Ben More.

I aimed as well as I could for the smoke I had seen so often from the island; and with all my great weariness and the difficulty of the way came upon the house in the bottom of a little hollow about five or six at night. It was low and longish, roofed with turf and built of unmortared stones; and on a mound in front of it, an old gentleman sat smoking his pipe in the sun.

With what little English he had, he gave me to understand that my shipmates had got safe ashore, and had broken bread in that very house on the day after.

"Was there one," I asked, "dressed like a gentleman?"

He said they all wore rough great-coats; but to be sure, the first of them, the one that came alone, wore breeches and stockings, while the rest had sailors' trousers.

"Ah," said I, "and he would have a feathered hat?"

He told me, no, that he was bareheaded like myself.

At first I thought Alan might have lost his hat; and then the rain came in my mind, and I judged it more likely he had it out of harm's way under his great-coat. This set me smiling, partly because my friend was safe, partly to think of his vanity in dress.

And then the old gentleman clapped his hand to his brow, and cried out that I must be the lad with the silver button.

"Why, yes!" said I, in some wonder.

"Well, then," said the old gentleman, "I have a word for you, that you are to follow your friend to his country, by Torosay."

He then asked me how I had fared, and I told him my tale. A south-country man would certainly have laughed; but this old gentleman (I call him so because of his manners, for his clothes were dropping off his back) heard me all through with nothing but gravity and pity. When I had done, he took me by the hand, led me into his hut (it was no better) and presented me before his wife, as if she had been the Queen and I a duke.

The good woman set oat-bread before me and a cold grouse, patting my shoulder and smiling to me all the time, for she had no English; and the old gentleman (not to be behind) brewed me a strong punch out of their country spirit. All the while I was eating, and after that when I was drinking the punch, I could scarce come to believe in my good fortune; and the house, though it was thick with the peat-smoke and as full of holes as a colander, seemed like a palace.

The punch threw me in a strong sweat and a deep slumber; the good people let me lie; and it was near noon of the next day before I took the road, my throat already easier and my spirits quite restored by good fare and good news. The old gentleman, although I pressed him hard, would take no money, and gave me an old bonnet for my head; though I am free to own I was no sooner out of view of the house than I very jealously washed this gift of his in a wayside fountain.

Thought I to myself: "If these are the wild Highlanders, I could wish my own folk wilder."

I not only started late, but I must have wandered nearly half the time. True, I met plenty of people, grubbing in little miserable fields that would not keep a cat, or herding little kine about the bigness of asses. The Highland dress being forbidden by law since the rebellion, and the people condemned to the Lowland habit, which they much disliked, it was strange to see the variety of their array. Some went bare, only for a hanging cloak or great-coat, and carried their trousers on their backs like a useless burthen: some had made an imitation of the tartan with little parti-coloured stripes patched together like an old wife's quilt; others, again, still wore the Highland philabeg, but by putting a few stitches between the legs transformed it into a pair of trousers like a Dutchman's. All those makeshifts were condemned and punished, for the law was harshly applied, in hopes to break up the clan spirit; but in that out-of-the-way, sea-bound isle, there were few to make remarks and fewer to tell tales.

They seemed in great poverty; which was no doubt natural, now that rapine was put down, and the chiefs kept no longer an open house; and the roads (even such a wandering, country by-track as the one I followed) were infested with beggars. And here again I marked a difference from my own part of the country. For our Lowland beggars—even the gownsmen themselves, who beg by patent—had a louting, flattering way with them, and if you gave them a plaek and asked change, would very civilly return you a boddle. But these Highland beggars stood on their dignity, asked alms only to buy snuff (by their account) and would give no change.

To be sure, this was no concern of mine, except in so far as it entertained me by the way. What was much more to the purpose, few had any English, and these few (unless they were of the brotherhood of beggars) not very anxious to place it at my service. I knew Torosay to be my destination, and repeated the name to them and pointed; but instead of simply pointing in reply, they would give me a screed of the Gaelic that set me foolish; so it was small wonder if I went out of my road as often as I stayed in it.

At last, about eight at night, and already very weary, I came to a lone house, where I asked admittance, and was refused, until I bethought me of the power of money in so poor a country, and held up one of my guineas in my finger and thumb. Thereupon, the man of the house, who had hitherto pretended to have no English, and driven me from his door by signals, suddenly began to speak as clearly as was needful, and agreed for five shillings to give me a night's lodging and guide me the next day to Torosay.

I slept uneasily that night, fearing I should be robbed; but I might have spared myself the pain; for my host was no robber, only miserably poor and a great cheat. He was not alone in his poverty; for the next morning, we must go five miles about to the house of what he called a rich man to have one of my guineas changed. This was perhaps a rich man for Mull; he would have scarce been thought so in the south; for it took all he had—the whole house was turned upside down, and a neighbour brought under contribution, before he could scrape together twenty shillings in silver. The odd shilling he kept for himself, protesting he could ill afford to have so great a sum of money lying "locked up." For all that he was very courteous and well spoken, made us both sit down with his family to dinner, and brewed punch in a fine china bowl, over which my rascal guide grew so merry that he refused to start.

I was for getting angry, and appealed to the rich man (Hector Maclean was his name), who had been a witness to our bargain and to my payment of the five shillings. But Maclean had taken his share of the punch, and vowed that no gentleman should leave his table after the bowl was brewed; so there was nothing for it but to sit and hear Jacobite toasts and Gaelic songs, till all were tipsy and staggered off to the bed or the barn for their night's rest.

Next day (the fourth of my travels) we were up before five upon the clock; but my rascal guide got to the bottle at once, and it was three hours before I had him clear of the house, and then (as you shall hear) only for a worse disappointment.

As long as we went down a heathery valley that lay before Mr. Maclean's house, all went well; only my guide looked constantly over his shoulder, and when I asked him the cause, only grinned at me. No sooner, however, had we crossed the back of a hill, and got out of sight of the house windows, than he told me Torosay lay right in front, and that a hill-top (which he pointed out) was my best landmark.

"I care very little for that," said I, "since you are going with me."

The impudent cheat answered me in the Gaelic that he had no English.

"My fine fellow," I said, "I know very well your English comes and goes. Tell me what will bring it back? Is it more money you wish?"

"Five shillings mair," said he, "and hersel' will bring ye there."

I reflected awhile and then offered him two, which he accepted greedily, and insisted on having in his hands at once "for luck," as he said, but I think it was rather for my misfortune.

The two shillings carried him not quite as many miles; at the end of which distance, he sat down upon the wayside and took off his brogues from his feet, like a man about to rest.

I was now red-hot. "Ha!" said I, "have you no more English?"

He said impudently, "No."

At that I boiled over, and lifted my hand to strike him; and he, drawing a knife from his rags, squatted back and grinned at me like a wildcat. At that, forgetting everything but my anger, I ran in upon him, put aside his knife with my left, and struck him in the mouth with the right. I was a strong lad and very angry, and he but a little man; and he went down before me heavily. By good luck, his knife flew out of his hand as he fell.

I picked up both that and his brogues, wished him a good morning, and set off upon my way, leaving him barefoot and disarmed. I chuckled to myself as I went, being sure I was done with that rogue, for a variety of reasons. First, he knew he could have no more of my money; next, the brogues were worth in that country only a few pence; and, lastly, the knife, which was really a dagger, it was against the law for him to carry.

In about half an hour of walk, I overtook a great, ragged man, moving pretty fast but feeling before him with a staff. He was quite blind, and told me he was a catechist, which should have put me at my ease. But his face went against me; it seemed dark and dangerous and secret; and presently, as we began to go on alongside, I saw the steel butt of a pistol sticking from under the flap of his coat-pocket. To carry such a thing meant a fine of fifteen pounds sterling upon a first offence, and transportation to the colonies upon a second. Nor could I quite see why a religious teacher should go armed, or what a blind man could be doing with a pistol.

I told him about my guide, for I was proud of what I had done, and my vanity for once got the heels of my prudence. At the mention of the five shillings he cried out so loud that I made up my mind I should say nothing of the other two, and was glad he could not see my blushes.

"Was it too much?" I asked, a little faltering.

"Too much!" cries he. "Why, I will guide you to Torosay myself for a dram of brandy. And give you the great pleasure of my company (me that is a man of some learning) in the bargain."

I said I did not see how a blind man could be a guide; but at that he laughed aloud, and said his stick was eyes enough for an eagle.

"In the Isle of Mull, at least," says he, "where I know every stone and heather-bush by mark of head. See, now," he said, striking right and left, as if to make sure, "down there a burn is running; and at the head of it there stands a bit of a small hill with a stone cocked upon the top of that; and it's hard at the foot of the hill, that the way runs by to Torosay; and the way here, being for droves, is plainly trodden, and will show grassy through the heather."

I had to own he was right in every feature, and told my wonder.

"Ha!" says he, "that's nothing. Would ye believe me now, that before the Act came out, and when there were weepons in this country, I could shoot? Ay, could I!" cries he, and then with a leer: "If ye had such a thing as a pistol here to try with, I would show ye how it's done."

I told him I had nothing of the sort, and gave him a wider berth. If he had known, his pistol stuck at that time quite plainly out of his pocket, and I could see the sun twinkle on the steel of the butt. But by the better luck for me, he knew nothing, thought all was covered, and lied on in the dark.

He then began to question me cunningly, where I came from, whether I was rich, whether I could change a five-shilling piece for him (which he declared he had that moment in his sporran), and all the time he kept edging up to me and I avoiding him. We were now upon a sort of green cattle-track which crossed the hills towards Torosay, and we kept changing sides upon that like dancers in a reel. I had so plainly the upper-hand that my spirits rose, and indeed I took a pleasure in this game of blindman's buff; but the catechist grew angrier and angrier, and at last began to swear in Gaelic and to strike for my legs with his staff.

Then I told him that, sure enough, I had a pistol in my pocket as well as he, and if he did not strike across the hill due south I would even blow his brains out.

He became at once very polite, and after trying to soften me for some time, but quite in vain, he cursed me once more in Gaelic and took himself off. I watched him striding along, through bog and brier, tapping with his stick, until he turned the end of a hill and disappeared in the next hollow. Then I struck on again for Torosay, much better pleased to be alone than to travel with that man of learning. This was an unlucky day; and these two, of whom I had just rid myself, one after the other, were the two worst men I met with in the Highlands.

At Torosay, on the Sound of Mull and looking over to the mainland of Morven, there was an inn with an innkeeper, who was a Maclean, it appeared, of a very high family; for to keep an inn is thought even more genteel in the Highlands than it is with us, perhaps as partaking of hospitality, or perhaps because the trade is idle and drunken. He spoke good English, and finding me to be something of a scholar, tried me first in French, where he easily beat me, and then in the Latin, in which I don't know which of us did best. This pleasant rivalry put us at once upon friendly terms; and I sat up and drank punch with him (or to be more correct, sat up and watched him drink it), until he was so tipsy that he wept upon my shoulder.

I tried him, as if by accident, with a sight of Alan's button; but it was plain he had never seen or heard of it. Indeed, he bore some grudge against the family and friends of Ardshiel, and before he was drunk he read me a lampoon, in very good Latin, but with a very ill meaning, which he had made in elegiac verses upon a person of that house.

When I told him of my catechist, he shook his head, and said I was lucky to have got clear off. "That is a very dangerous man," he said; "Duncan Mackiegh is his name; he can shoot by the ear at several yards, and has been often accused of highway robberies, and once of murder."

"The cream of it is," says I, "that he called himself a catechist."

"And why should he not?" says he, "when that is what he is. It was Maclean of Duart gave it to him because he was blind. But perhaps it was a peety," says my host, "for he is always on the road, going from one place to another to hear the young folk say their religion; and, doubtless, that is a great temptation to the poor man."

At last, when my landlord could drink no more, he showed me to a bed, and I lay down in very good spirits; having travelled the greater part of that big and crooked Island of Mull, from Earraid to Torosay, fifty miles as the crow flies, and (with my wanderings) much nearer a hundred, in four days and with little fatigue. Indeed I was by far in better heart and health of body at the end of that long tramp than I had been at the beginning.

CHAPTER XVI
THE LAD WITH THE SILVER BUTTON:
ACROSS MORVEN

There is a regular ferry from Torosay to Kinlochaline on the mainland. Both shores of the Sound are in the country of the strong clan of the Macleans, and the people that passed the ferry with me were almost all of that clan. The skipper of the boat, on the other hand, was called Neil Roy Macrob; and since Macrob was one of the names of Alan's clansmen, and Alan himself had sent me to that ferry, I was eager to come to private speech of Neil Roy.

In the crowded boat this was of course impossible, and the passage was a very slow affair. There was no wind, and as the boat was wretchedly equipped, we could pull but two oars on one side, and one on the other. The men gave way, however, with a good will, the passengers taking spells to help them, and the whole company giving the time in Gaelic boat-songs. And what with the songs, and the sea-air, and the good-nature and spirit of all concerned, and the bright weather, the passage was a pretty thing to have seen.

But there was one melancholy part. In the mouth of Loch Aline we found a great sea-going ship at anchor; and this I supposed at first to be one of the King's cruisers which were kept along that coast, both summer and winter, to prevent communication with the French. As we got a little nearer, it became plain she was a ship of merchandise; and what still more puzzled me, not only her decks, but the sea-beach also, were quite black with people, and skiffs were continually plying to and fro between them. Yet nearer, and there began to come to our ears a great sound of mourning, the people on board and those on the shore crying and lamenting one to another so as to pierce the heart.

Then I understood this was an emigrant ship bound for the American colonies.

We put the ferry-boat alongside, and the exiles leaned over the bulwarks, weeping and reaching out their hands to my fellow-passengers, among whom they counted some near friends. How long this might have gone on I do not know, for they seemed to have no sense of time: but at last the captain of the ship, who seemed near beside himself (and no great wonder) in the midst of this crying and confusion, came to the side and begged us to depart.

Thereupon Neil sheered off; and the chief singer in our boat struck into a melancholy air, which was presently taken up both by the emigrants and their friends upon the beach, so that it sounded from all sides like a lament for the dying. I saw the tears run down the cheeks of the men and women in the boat, even as they bent at the oars; and the circumstances and the music of the song (which is one called "Lochaber no more") were highly affecting even to myself.

At Kinlochaline I got Neil Roy upon one side on the beach, and said I made sure he was one of Appin's men.

"And what for no?" said he.

"I am seeking somebody," said I; "and it comes in my mind that you will have news of him. Alan Breck Stewart is his name." And very foolishly, instead of showing him the button, I sought to pass a shilling in his hand.

At this he drew back. "I am very much affronted," he said; "and this is not the way that one shentleman should behave to another at all. The man you ask for is in France; but if he was in my sporran," says he, "and your belly full of shillings, I would not hurt a hair upon his body."

I saw I had gone the wrong way to work, and without wasting time upon apologies, showed him the button lying in the hollow of my palm.

"Aweel, aweel," said Neil; "and I think ye might have begun with that end of the stick, whatever! But if ye are the lad with the silver button, all is well, and I have the word to see that ye come safe. But if ye will pardon me to speak plainly," says he, "there is a name that you should never take into your mouth, and that is the name of Alan Breck; and there is a thing that ye would never do, and that is to offer your dirty money to a Hieland shentleman."

It was not very easy to apologise; for I could scarce tell him (what was the truth) that I had never dreamed he would set up to be a gentleman until he told me so. Neil on his part had no wish to prolong his dealings with me, only to fulfil his orders and be done with it; and he made haste to give me my route. This was to lie the night in Kinlochaline in the public inn; to cross Morven the next day to Ardgour, and lie the night in the house of one John of the Claymore, who was warned that I might come; the third day, to be set across one loch at Corran and another at Balachulish, and then ask my way to the house of James of the Glens, at Aucharn in Duror of Appin. There was a good deal of ferrying, as you hear; the sea in all this part running deep into the mountains and winding about their roots. It makes the country strong to hold and difficult to travel, but full of prodigious wild and dreadful prospects.

I had some other advice from Neil: to speak with no one by the way, to avoid Whigs, Campbells, and the "red-soldiers;" to leave the road and lie in a bush if I saw any of the latter coming, "for it was never chancy to meet in with them;" and in brief, to conduct myself like a robber or a Jacobite agent, as perhaps Neil thought me.

The inn at Kinlochaline was the most beggarly vile place that ever pigs were styed in, full of smoke, vermin, and silent Highlanders. I was not only discontented with my lodging, but with myself for my mismanagement of Neil, and thought I could hardly be worse off. But very wrongly, as I was soon to see; for I had not been half an hour at the inn (standing in the door most of the time, to ease my eyes from the peat smoke) when a thunderstorm came close by, the springs broke in a little hill on which the inn stood, and one end of the house became a running water. Places of public entertainment were bad enough all over Scotland in those days; yet it was a wonder to myself, when I had to go from the fireside to the bed in which I slept, wading over the shoes.

Early in my next day's journey I overtook a little, stout, solemn man, walking very slowly with his toes turned out, sometimes reading in a book and sometimes marking the place with his finger, and dressed decently and plainly in something of a clerical style.

This I found to be another catechist, but of a different order from the blind man of Mull: being indeed one of those sent out by the Edinburgh Society for Propagating Christian Knowledge, to evangelise the more savage places of the Highlands. His name was Henderland; he spoke with the broad south-country tongue, which I was beginning to weary for the sound of; and besides common countryship, we soon found we had a more particular bond of interest. For my good friend, the minister of Essendean, had translated into the Gaelic in his by-time a number of hymns and pious books which Henderland used in his work, and held in great esteem. Indeed, it was one of these he was carrying and reading when we met.

We fell in company at once, our ways lying together as far as to Kingairloch. As we went, he stopped and spoke with all the wayfarers and workers that we met or passed; and though of course I could not tell what they discoursed about, yet I judged Mr. Henderland must be well liked in the countryside, for I observed many of them to bring out their mulls and share a pinch of snuff with him.

I told him as far in my affairs as I judged wise; as far, that is, as they were none of Alan's; and gave Balachulish as the place I was travelling to, to meet a friend; for I thought Aucharn, or even Duror, would be too particular, and might put him on the scent.

On his part, he told me much of his work and the people he worked among, the hiding priests and Jacobites, the Disarming Act, the dress, and many other curiosities of the time and place. He seemed moderate; blaming Parliament in several points, and especially because they had framed the Act more severely against those who wore the dress than against those who carried weapons.

This moderation put it in my mind to question him of the Red Fox and the Appin tenants; questions which, I thought, would seem natural enough in the mouth of one travelling to that country.

He said it was a bad business. "It's wonderful," said he, "where the tenants find the money, for their life is mere starvation. (Ye don't carry such a thing as snuff, do ye, Mr. Balfour? No. Well, I'm better wanting it.) But these tenants (as I was saying) are doubtless partly driven to it. James Stewart in Duror (that's him they call James of the Glens) is half-brother to Ardshiel, the captain of the clan; and he is a man much looked up to, and drives very hard. And then there's one they call Alan Breck—"

"Ah!" I cried, "what of him?"

"What of the wind that bloweth where it listeth?" said Henderland. "He's here and awa; here to-day and gone to-morrow: a fair heather-cat. He might be glowering at the two of us out of yon whin-bush, and I wouldnae wonder! Ye'll no carry such a thing as snuff, will ye?"

I told him no, and that he had asked the same thing more than once.

"It's highly possible," said he, sighing. "But it seems strange ye shouldnae carry it. However, as I was saying, this Alan Breck is a bold, desperate customer, and well kent to be James's right hand. His life is forfeit already; he would boggle at naething; and maybe, if a tenant-body was to hang back he would get a dirk in his wame."

"You make a poor story of it all, Mr. Henderland," said I. "If it is all fear upon both sides, I care to hear no more of it."

"Na," said Mr. Henderland, "but there's love too, and self-denial that should put the like of you and me to shame. There's something fine about it; no perhaps Christian, but humanly fine. Even Alan Breck, by all that I hear, is a chield to be respected. There's many a lying sneck-draw sits close in kirk in our own part of the country, and stands well in the world's eye, and maybe is a far worse man, Mr. Balfour, than yon misguided shedder of man's blood. Ay, ay, we might take a lesson by them.—Ye'll perhaps think I've been too long in the Hielands?" he added, smiling to me.

I told him not at all; that I had seen much to admire among the Highlanders; and if he came to that, Mr. Campbell himself was a Highlander.

"Ay," said he, "that's true. It's a fine blood."

"And what is the King's agent about?" I asked.

"Colin Campbell?" says Henderland. "Putting his head in a bees' byke!"

"He is to turn the tenants out by force, I hear?" said I.

"Yes," says he, "but the business has gone back and forth, as folk say. First, James of the Glens rode to Edinburgh, and got some lawyer (a Stewart, nae doubt—they all hing together like bats in a steeple) and had the proceedings stayed. And then Colin Campbell cam' in again, and had the upper-hand before the Barons of Exchequer. And now they tell me the first of the tenants are to flit to-morrow. It's to begin at Duror under James's very windows, which doesnae seem wise by my humble way of it."

"Do you think they'll fight?" I asked.

"Well," says Henderland, "they're disarmed—or supposed to be—for there's still a good deal of cold iron lying by in quiet places. And then Colin Campbell has the sogers coming. But for all that, if I was his lady wife, I wouldnae be well pleased till I got him home again. They're queer customers, the Appin Stewarts."

I asked if they were worse than their neighbours.

"No they," said he. "And that's the worst part of it. For if Colin Roy can get his business done in Appin, he has it all to begin again in the next country, which they call Mamore, and which is one of the countries of the Camerons. He's King's Factor upon both, and from both he has to drive out the tenants; and indeed, Mr. Balfour (to be open with ye), it's my belief that if he escapes the one lot, he'll get his death by the other."

So we continued talking and walking the great part of the day; until at last, Mr. Henderland after expressing his delight in my company, and satisfaction at meeting with a friend of Mr. Campbell's ("whom," says he, "I will make bold to call that sweet singer of our covenanted Zion"), proposed that I should make a short stage, and lie the night in his house a little beyond Kingairloch. To say truth, I was overjoyed; for I had no great desire for John of the Claymore, and since my double misadventure, first with the guide and next with the gentleman skipper, I stood in some fear of any Highland stranger. Accordingly we shook hands upon the bargain, and came in the afternoon to a small house, standing alone by the shore of the Linnhe Loch. The sun was already gone from the desert mountains of Ardgour upon the hither side, but shone on those of Appin on the farther; the loch lay as still as a lake, only the gulls were crying round the sides of it; and the whole place seemed solemn and uncouth.

We had no sooner come to the door of Mr. Henderland's dwelling, than to my great surprise (for I was now used to the politeness of Highlanders) he burst rudely past me, dashed into the room, caught up a jar and a small horn-spoon, and began ladling snuff into his nose in most excessive quantities. Then he had a hearty fit of sneezing, and looked round upon me with a rather silly smile.

"It's a vow I took," says he. "I took a vow upon me that I wouldnae carry it. Doubtless it's a great privation; but when I think upon the martyrs, not only to the Scottish Covenant but to other points of Christianity, I think shame to mind it."

As soon as we had eaten (and porridge and whey was the best of the good man's diet) he took a grave face and said he had a duty to perform by Mr. Campbell, and that was to inquire into my state of mind towards God. I was inclined to smile at him since the business of the snuff; but he had not spoken long before he brought the tears into my eyes. There are two things that men should never weary of, goodness and humility; we get none too much of them in this rough world among cold, proud people; but Mr. Henderland had their very speech upon his tongue. And though I was a good deal puffed up with my adventures and with having come off, as the saying is, with flying colours; yet he soon had me on my knees beside a simple, poor old man, and both proud and glad to be there.

Before we went to bed he offered me sixpence to help me on my way, out of a scanty store he kept in the turf wall of his house; at which excess of goodness I knew not what to do. But at last he was so earnest with me that I thought it the more mannerly part to let him have his way, and so left him poorer than myself.

CHAPTER XVII
THE DEATH OF THE RED FOX

The next day Mr. Henderland found for me a man who had a boat of his own and was to cross the Linnhe Loch that afternoon into Appin, fishing. Him he prevailed on to take me, for he was one of his flock; and in this way I saved a long day's travel and the price of the two public ferries I must otherwise have passed.

It was near noon before we set out; a dark day with clouds, and the sun shining upon little patches. The sea was here very deep and still, and had scarce a wave upon it; so that I must put the water to my lips before I could believe it to be truly salt. The mountains on either side were high, rough and barren, very black and gloomy in the shadow of the clouds, but all silver-laced with little watercourses where the sun shone upon them. It seemed a hard country, this of Appin, for people to care as much about as Alan did.

There was but one thing to mention. A little after we had started, the sun shone upon a little moving clump of scarlet close in along the water-side to the north. It was much of the same red as soldiers' coats; every now and then, too, there came little sparks and lightnings, as though the sun had struck upon bright steel.

I asked my boatman what it should be, and he answered he supposed it was some of the red soldiers coming from Fort William into Appin, against the poor tenantry of the country. Well, it was a sad sight to me; and whether it was because of my thoughts of Alan, or from something prophetic in my bosom, although this was but the second time I had seen King George's troops, I had no good will to them.

At last we came so near the point of land at the entering in of Loch Leven that I begged to be set on shore. My boatman (who was an honest fellow and mindful of his promise to the catechist) would fain have carried me on to Balachulish; but as this was to take me farther from my secret destination, I insisted, and was set on shore at last under the wood of Lettermore (or Lettervore, for I have heard it both ways) in Alan's country of Appin.

This was a wood of birches, growing on a steep, craggy side of a mountain that overhung the loch. It had many openings and ferny howes; and a road or bridle track ran north and south through the midst of it, by the edge of which, where was a spring, I sat down to eat some oat-bread of Mr. Henderland's and think upon my situation.

Here I was not only troubled by a cloud of stinging midges, but far more by the doubts of my mind. What I ought to do, why I was going to join myself with an outlaw and a would-be murderer like Alan, whether I should not be acting more like a man of sense to tramp back to the south country direct, by my own guidance and at my own charges, and what Mr. Campbell or even Mr. Henderland would think of me if they should ever learn my folly and presumption: these were the doubts that now began to come in on me stronger than ever.

As I was so sitting and thinking, a sound of men and horses came to me through the wood; and presently after, at a turning of the road, I saw four travellers come into view. The way was in this part so rough and narrow that they came single and led their horses by the reins. The first was a great, red-headed gentleman, of an imperious and flushed face, who carried his hat in his hand and fanned himself, for he was in a breathing heat. The second, by his decent black garb and white wig, I correctly took to be a lawyer. The third was a servant, and wore some part of his clothes in tartan, which showed that his master was of a Highland family, and either an outlaw or else in singular good odour with the Government, since the wearing of tartan was against the Act. If I had been better versed in these things, I would have known the tartan to be of the Argyle (or Campbell) colours. This servant had a good-sized portmanteau strapped on his horse, and a net of lemons (to brew punch with) hanging at the saddle-bow; as was often enough the custom with luxurious travellers in that part of the country.

As for the fourth, who brought up the tail, I had seen his like before, and knew him at once to be a sheriff's officer.

I had no sooner seen these people coming than I made up my mind (for no reason that I can tell) to go through with my adventure; and when the first came alongside of me, I rose up from the bracken and asked him the way to Aucharn.

He stopped and looked at me, as I thought, a little oddly; and then, turning to the lawyer, "Mungo," said he, "there's many a man would think this more of a warning than two pyats. Here am I on my road to Duror on the job ye ken; and here is a young lad starts up out of the bracken, and speers if I am on the way to Aucharn."

"Glenure," said the other, "this is an ill subject for jesting."

These two had now drawn close up and were gazing at me, while the two followers had halted about a stone-cast in the rear.

"And what seek ye in Aucharn?" said Colin Roy Campbell of Glenure, him they called the Red Fox; for he it was that I had stopped.

"The man that lives there," said I.

"James of the Glens," says Glenure, musingly; and then to the lawyer: "Is he gathering his people, think ye?"

"Anyway," says the lawyer, "we shall do better to bide where we are, and let the soldiers rally us."

"If you are concerned for me," said I, "I am neither of his people nor yours, but an honest subject of King George, owing no man and fearing no man."

"Why, very well said," replies the Factor. "But if I may make so bold as ask, what does this honest man so far from his country? and why does he come seeking the brother of Ardshiel? I have power here, I must tell you. I am King's Factor upon several of these estates, and have twelve files of soldiers at my back."

"I have heard a waif word in the country," said I, a little nettled, "that you were a hard man to drive."

He still kept looking at me, as if in doubt.

"Well," said he, at last, "your tongue is bold; but I am no unfriend to plainness. If ye had asked me the way to the door of James Stewart on any other day but this, I would have set ye right and bidden ye God speed. But to-day—eh, Mungo?" And he turned again to look at the lawyer.

But just as he turned there came the shot of a firelock from higher up the hill; and with the very sound of it Glenure fell upon the road.

"O, I am dead!" he cried, several times over.

The lawyer had caught him up and held him in his arms, the servant standing over and clasping his hands. And now the wounded man looked from one to another with scared eyes, and there was a change in his voice, that went to the heart.

"Take care of yourselves," says he. "I am dead."

He tried to open his clothes as if to look for the wound, but his fingers slipped on the buttons. With that he gave a great sigh, his head rolled on his shoulder, and he passed away.

The lawyer said never a word, but his face was as sharp as a pen and as white as the dead man's; the servant broke out into a great noise of crying and weeping, like a child; and I, on my side, stood staring at them in a kind of horror. The sheriff's officer had run back at the first sound of the shot, to hasten the coming of the soldiers.

At last the lawyer laid down the dead man in his blood upon the road, and got to his own feet with a kind of stagger.

I believe it was his movement that brought me to my senses; for he had no sooner done so than I began to scramble up the hill, crying out, "The murderer! the murderer!"

So little a time had elapsed, that when I got to the top of the first steepness, and could see some part of the open mountain, the murderer was still moving away at no great distance. He was a big man, in a black coat, with metal buttons, and carried a long fowling-piece.

"Here!" I cried. "I see him!"

At that the murderer gave a little, quick look over his shoulder, and began to run. The next moment he was lost in a fringe of birches; then he came out again on the upper side, where I could see him climbing like a jackanapes, for that part was again very steep; and then he dipped behind a shoulder, and I saw him no more.

All this time I had been running on my side, and had got a good way up, when a voice cried upon me to stand.

I was at the edge of the upper wood, and so now, when I halted and looked back, I saw all the open part of the hill below me.

The lawyer and the sheriff's officer were standing just above the road, crying and waving on me to come back; and on their left, the red-coats, musket in hand, were beginning to struggle singly out of the lower wood.

"Why should I come back?" I cried. "Come you on!"

"Ten pounds if ye take that lad!" cried the lawyer. "He's an accomplice. He was posted here to hold us in talk."

At that word (which I could hear quite plainly, though it was to the soldiers and not to me that he was crying it) my heart came in my mouth with quite a new kind of terror. Indeed, it is one thing to stand the danger of your life, and quite another to run the peril of both life and character. The thing, besides, had come so suddenly, like thunder out of a clear sky, that I was all amazed and helpless.

The soldiers began to spread, some of them to run, and others to put up their pieces and cover me; and still I stood.

"Jouk* in here among the trees," said a voice close by.

* Duck.

Indeed, I scarce knew what I was doing, but I obeyed; and as I did so, I heard the firelocks bang and the balls whistle in the birches.

Just inside the shelter of the trees I found Alan Breck standing, with a fishing-rod. He gave me no salutation; indeed it was no time for civilities; only "Come!" says he, and set off running along the side of the mountain towards Balachulish; and I, like a sheep, to follow him.

Now we ran among the birches; now stooping behind low humps upon the mountain-side; now crawling on all fours among the heather. The pace was deadly: my heart seemed bursting against my ribs; and I had neither time to think nor breath to speak with. Only I remember seeing with wonder, that Alan every now and then would straighten himself to his full height and look back; and every time he did so, there came a great far-away cheering and crying of the soldiers.

Quarter of an hour later, Alan stopped, clapped down flat in the heather, and turned to me.

"Now," said he, "it's earnest. Do as I do, for your life."

And at the same speed, but now with infinitely more precaution, we traced back again across the mountain-side by the same way that we had come, only perhaps higher; till at last Alan threw himself down in the upper wood of Lettermore, where I had found him at the first, and lay, with his face in the bracken, panting like a dog.

My own sides so ached, my head so swam, my tongue so hung out of my mouth with heat and dryness, that I lay beside him like one dead.

CHAPTER XVIII
I TALK WITH ALAN IN THE WOOD OF LETTERMORE

Alan was the first to come round. He rose, went to the border of the wood, peered out a little, and then returned and sat down.

"Well," said he, "yon was a hot burst, David."

I said nothing, nor so much as lifted my face. I had seen murder done, and a great, ruddy, jovial gentleman struck out of life in a moment; the pity of that sight was still sore within me, and yet that was but a part of my concern. Here was murder done upon the man Alan hated; here was Alan skulking in the trees and running from the troops; and whether his was the hand that fired or only the head that ordered, signified but little. By my way of it, my only friend in that wild country was blood-guilty in the first degree; I held him in horror; I could not look upon his face; I would have rather lain alone in the rain on my cold isle, than in that warm wood beside a murderer.

"Are ye still wearied?" he asked again.

"No," said I, still with my face in the bracken; "no, I am not wearied now, and I can speak. You and me must twine," * I said. "I liked you very well, Alan, but your ways are not mine, and they're not God's: and the short and the long of it is just that we must twine."

    * Part.

"I will hardly twine from ye, David, without some kind of reason for the same," said Alan, mighty gravely. "If ye ken anything against my reputation, it's the least thing that ye should do, for old acquaintance' sake, to let me hear the name of it; and if ye have only taken a distaste to my society, it will be proper for me to judge if I'm insulted."

"Alan," said I, "what is the sense of this? Ye ken very well yon Campbell-man lies in his blood upon the road."

He was silent for a little; then says he, "Did ever ye hear tell of the story of the Man and the Good People?"—by which he meant the fairies.

"No," said I, "nor do I want to hear it."

"With your permission, Mr. Balfour, I will tell it you, whatever," says Alan. "The man, ye should ken, was cast upon a rock in the sea, where it appears the Good People were in use to come and rest as they went through to Ireland. The name of this rock is called the Skerryvore, and it's not far from where we suffered ship-wreck. Well, it seems the man cried so sore, if he could just see his little bairn before he died! that at last the king of the Good People took peety upon him, and sent one flying that brought back the bairn in a poke* and laid it down beside the man where he lay sleeping. So when the man woke, there was a poke beside him and something into the inside of it that moved. Well, it seems he was one of these gentry that think aye the worst of things; and for greater security, he stuck his dirk throughout that poke before he opened it, and there was his bairn dead. I am thinking to myself, Mr. Balfour, that you and the man are very much alike."

    * Bag.

"Do you mean you had no hand in it?" cried I, sitting up.

"I will tell you first of all, Mr. Balfour of Shaws, as one friend to another," said Alan, "that if I were going to kill a gentleman, it would not be in my own country, to bring trouble on my clan; and I would not go wanting sword and gun, and with a long fishing-rod upon my back."

"Well," said I, "that's true!"

"And now," continued Alan, taking out his dirk and laying his hand upon it in a certain manner, "I swear upon the Holy Iron I had neither art nor part, act nor thought in it."

"I thank God for that!" cried I, and offered him my hand.

He did not appear to see it.

"And here is a great deal of work about a Campbell!" said he. "They are not so scarce, that I ken!"

"At least," said I, "you cannot justly blame me, for you know very well what you told me in the brig. But the temptation and the act are different, I thank God again for that. We may all be tempted; but to take a life in cold blood, Alan!" And I could say no more for the moment. "And do you know who did it?" I added. "Do you know that man in the black coat?"

"I have nae clear mind about his coat," said Alan cunningly, "but it sticks in my head that it was blue."

"Blue or black, did ye know him?" said I.

"I couldnae just conscientiously swear to him," says Alan. "He gaed very close by me, to be sure, but it's a strange thing that I should just have been tying my brogues."

"Can you swear that you don't know him, Alan?" I cried, half angered, half in a mind to laugh at his evasions.

"Not yet," says he; "but I've a grand memory for forgetting, David."

"And yet there was one thing I saw clearly," said I; "and that was, that you exposed yourself and me to draw the soldiers."

"It's very likely," said Alan; "and so would any gentleman. You and me were innocent of that transaction."

"The better reason, since we were falsely suspected, that we should get clear," I cried. "The innocent should surely come before the guilty."

"Why, David," said he, "the innocent have aye a chance to get assoiled in court; but for the lad that shot the bullet, I think the best place for him will be the heather. Them that havenae dipped their hands in any little difficulty, should be very mindful of the case of them that have. And that is the good Christianity. For if it was the other way round about, and the lad whom I couldnae just clearly see had been in our shoes, and we in his (as might very well have been), I think we would be a good deal obliged to him oursel's if he would draw the soldiers."

When it came to this, I gave Alan up. But he looked so innocent all the time, and was in such clear good faith in what he said, and so ready to sacrifice himself for what he deemed his duty, that my mouth was closed. Mr. Henderland's words came back to me: that we ourselves might take a lesson by these wild Highlanders. Well, here I had taken mine. Alan's morals were all tail-first; but he was ready to give his life for them, such as they were.

"Alan," said I, "I'll not say it's the good Christianity as I understand it, but it's good enough. And here I offer ye my hand for the second time."

Whereupon he gave me both of his, saying surely I had cast a spell upon him, for he could forgive me anything. Then he grew very grave, and said we had not much time to throw away, but must both flee that country: he, because he was a deserter, and the whole of Appin would now be searched like a chamber, and every one obliged to give a good account of himself; and I, because I was certainly involved in the murder.

"O!" says I, willing to give him a little lesson, "I have no fear of the justice of my country."

"As if this was your country!" said he. "Or as if ye would be tried here, in a country of Stewarts!"

"It's all Scotland," said I.

"Man, I whiles wonder at ye," said Alan. "This is a Campbell that's been killed. Well, it'll be tried in Inverara, the Campbells' head place; with fifteen Campbells in the jury-box and the biggest Campbell of all (and that's the Duke) sitting cocking on the bench. Justice, David? The same justice, by all the world, as Glenure found awhile ago at the roadside."

This frightened me a little, I confess, and would have frightened me more if I had known how nearly exact were Alan's predictions; indeed it was but in one point that he exaggerated, there being but eleven Campbells on the jury; though as the other four were equally in the Duke's dependence, it mattered less than might appear. Still, I cried out that he was unjust to the Duke of Argyle, who (for all he was a Whig) was yet a wise and honest nobleman.

"Hoot!" said Alan, "the man's a Whig, nae doubt; but I would never deny he was a good chieftain to his clan. And what would the clan think if there was a Campbell shot, and naebody hanged, and their own chief the Justice General? But I have often observed," says Alan, "that you Low-country bodies have no clear idea of what's right and wrong."

At this I did at last laugh out aloud, when to my surprise, Alan joined in, and laughed as merrily as myself.

"Na, na," said he, "we're in the Hielands, David; and when I tell ye to run, take my word and run. Nae doubt it's a hard thing to skulk and starve in the Heather, but it's harder yet to lie shackled in a red-coat prison."

I asked him whither we should flee; and as he told me "to the Lowlands," I was a little better inclined to go with him; for, indeed, I was growing impatient to get back and have the upper-hand of my uncle. Besides, Alan made so sure there would be no question of justice in the matter, that I began to be afraid he might be right. Of all deaths, I would truly like least to die by the gallows; and the picture of that uncanny instrument came into my head with extraordinary clearness (as I had once seen it engraved at the top of a pedlar's ballad) and took away my appetite for courts of justice.

"I'll chance it, Alan," said I. "I'll go with you."

"But mind you," said Alan, "it's no small thing. Ye maun lie bare and hard, and brook many an empty belly. Your bed shall be the moorcock's, and your life shall be like the hunted deer's, and ye shall sleep with your hand upon your weapons. Ay, man, ye shall taigle many a weary foot, or we get clear! I tell ye this at the start, for it's a life that I ken well. But if ye ask what other chance ye have, I answer: Nane. Either take to the heather with me, or else hang."

"And that's a choice very easily made," said I; and we shook hands upon it. "And now let's take another peek at the red-coats," says Alan, and he led me to the north-eastern fringe of the wood.

Looking out between the trees, we could see a great side of mountain, running down exceeding steep into the waters of the loch. It was a rough part, all hanging stone, and heather, and big scrogs of birchwood; and away at the far end towards Balachulish, little wee red soldiers were dipping up and down over hill and howe, and growing smaller every minute. There was no cheering now, for I think they had other uses for what breath was left them; but they still stuck to the trail, and doubtless thought that we were close in front of them.

Alan watched them, smiling to himself.

"Ay," said he, "they'll be gey weary before they've got to the end of that employ! And so you and me, David, can sit down and eat a bite, and breathe a bit longer, and take a dram from my bottle. Then we'll strike for Aucharn, the house of my kinsman, James of the Glens, where I must get my clothes, and my arms, and money to carry us along; and then, David, we'll cry, 'Forth, Fortune!' and take a cast among the heather."

So we sat again and ate and drank, in a place whence we could see the sun going down into a field of great, wild, and houseless mountains, such as I was now condemned to wander in with my companion. Partly as we so sat, and partly afterwards, on the way to Aucharn, each of us narrated his adventures; and I shall here set down so much of Alan's as seems either curious or needful.

It appears he ran to the bulwarks as soon as the wave was passed; saw me, and lost me, and saw me again, as I tumbled in the roost; and at last had one glimpse of me clinging on the yard. It was this that put him in some hope I would maybe get to land after all, and made him leave those clues and messages which had brought me (for my sins) to that unlucky country of Appin.

In the meanwhile, those still on the brig had got the skiff launched, and one or two were on board of her already, when there came a second wave greater than the first, and heaved the brig out of her place, and would certainly have sent her to the bottom, had she not struck and caught on some projection of the reef. When she had struck first, it had been bows-on, so that the stern had hitherto been lowest. But now her stern was thrown in the air, and the bows plunged under the sea; and with that, the water began to pour into the fore-scuttle like the pouring of a mill-dam.

It took the colour out of Alan's face, even to tell what followed. For there were still two men lying impotent in their bunks; and these, seeing the water pour in and thinking the ship had foundered, began to cry out aloud, and that with such harrowing cries that all who were on deck tumbled one after another into the skiff and fell to their oars. They were not two hundred yards away, when there came a third great sea; and at that the brig lifted clean over the reef; her canvas filled for a moment, and she seemed to sail in chase of them, but settling all the while; and presently she drew down and down, as if a hand was drawing her; and the sea closed over the Covenant of Dysart.

Never a word they spoke as they pulled ashore, being stunned with the horror of that screaming; but they had scarce set foot upon the beach when Hoseason woke up, as if out of a muse, and bade them lay hands upon Alan. They hung back indeed, having little taste for the employment; but Hoseason was like a fiend, crying that Alan was alone, that he had a great sum about him, that he had been the means of losing the brig and drowning all their comrades, and that here was both revenge and wealth upon a single cast. It was seven against one; in that part of the shore there was no rock that Alan could set his back to; and the sailors began to spread out and come behind him.

"And then," said Alan, "the little man with the red head—I havenae mind of the name that he is called."

"Riach," said I.

"Ay" said Alan, "Riach! Well, it was him that took up the clubs for me, asked the men if they werenae feared of a judgment, and, says he 'Dod, I'll put my back to the Hielandman's mysel'.' That's none such an entirely bad little man, yon little man with the red head," said Alan. "He has some spunks of decency."

"Well," said I, "he was kind to me in his way."

"And so he was to Alan," said he; "and by my troth, I found his way a very good one! But ye see, David, the loss of the ship and the cries of these poor lads sat very ill upon the man; and I'm thinking that would be the cause of it."

"Well, I would think so," says I; "for he was as keen as any of the rest at the beginning. But how did Hoseason take it?"

"It sticks in my mind that he would take it very ill," says Alan. "But the little man cried to me to run, and indeed I thought it was a good observe, and ran. The last that I saw they were all in a knot upon the beach, like folk that were not agreeing very well together."

"What do you mean by that?" said I.

"Well, the fists were going," said Alan; "and I saw one man go down like a pair of breeks. But I thought it would be better no to wait. Ye see there's a strip of Campbells in that end of Mull, which is no good company for a gentleman like me. If it hadnae been for that I would have waited and looked for ye mysel', let alone giving a hand to the little man." (It was droll how Alan dwelt on Mr. Riach's stature, for, to say the truth, the one was not much smaller than the other.) "So," says he, continuing, "I set my best foot forward, and whenever I met in with any one I cried out there was a wreck ashore. Man, they didnae stop to fash with me! Ye should have seen them linking for the beach! And when they got there they found they had had the pleasure of a run, which is aye good for a Campbell. I'm thinking it was a judgment on the clan that the brig went down in the lump and didnae break. But it was a very unlucky thing for you, that same; for if any wreck had come ashore they would have hunted high and low, and would soon have found ye."

CHAPTER XIX
THE HOUSE OF FEAR

Night fell as we were walking, and the clouds, which had broken up in the afternoon, settled in and thickened, so that it fell, for the season of the year, extremely dark. The way we went was over rough mountainsides; and though Alan pushed on with an assured manner, I could by no means see how he directed himself.

At last, about half-past ten of the clock, we came to the top of a brae, and saw lights below us. It seemed a house door stood open and let out a beam of fire and candle-light; and all round the house and steading five or six persons were moving hurriedly about, each carrying a lighted brand.

"James must have tint his wits," said Alan. "If this was the soldiers instead of you and me, he would be in a bonny mess. But I dare say he'll have a sentry on the road, and he would ken well enough no soldiers would find the way that we came."

Hereupon he whistled three times, in a particular manner. It was strange to see how, at the first sound of it, all the moving torches came to a stand, as if the bearers were affrighted; and how, at the third, the bustle began again as before.

Having thus set folks' minds at rest, we came down the brae, and were met at the yard gate (for this place was like a well-doing farm) by a tall, handsome man of more than fifty, who cried out to Alan in the Gaelic.

"James Stewart," said Alan, "I will ask ye to speak in Scotch, for here is a young gentleman with me that has nane of the other. This is him," he added, putting his arm through mine, "a young gentleman of the Lowlands, and a laird in his country too, but I am thinking it will be the better for his health if we give his name the go-by."

James of the Glens turned to me for a moment, and greeted me courteously enough; the next he had turned to Alan.

"This has been a dreadful accident," he cried. "It will bring trouble on the country." And he wrung his hands.

"Hoots!" said Alan, "ye must take the sour with the sweet, man. Colin Roy is dead, and be thankful for that!"

"Ay" said James, "and by my troth, I wish he was alive again! It's all very fine to blow and boast beforehand; but now it's done, Alan; and who's to bear the wyte* of it? The accident fell out in Appin—mind ye that, Alan; it's Appin that must pay; and I am a man that has a family."

   * Blame.

While this was going on I looked about me at the servants. Some were on ladders, digging in the thatch of the house or the farm buildings, from which they brought out guns, swords, and different weapons of war; others carried them away; and by the sound of mattock blows from somewhere farther down the brae, I suppose they buried them. Though they were all so busy, there prevailed no kind of order in their efforts; men struggled together for the same gun and ran into each other with their burning torches; and James was continually turning about from his talk with Alan, to cry out orders which were apparently never understood. The faces in the torchlight were like those of people overborne with hurry and panic; and though none spoke above his breath, their speech sounded both anxious and angry.

It was about this time that a lassie came out of the house carrying a pack or bundle; and it has often made me smile to think how Alan's instinct awoke at the mere sight of it.

"What's that the lassie has?" he asked.

"We're just setting the house in order, Alan," said James, in his frightened and somewhat fawning way. "They'll search Appin with candles, and we must have all things straight. We're digging the bit guns and swords into the moss, ye see; and these, I am thinking, will be your ain French clothes. We'll be to bury them, I believe."

"Bury my French clothes!" cried Alan. "Troth, no!" And he laid hold upon the packet and retired into the barn to shift himself, recommending me in the meanwhile to his kinsman.

James carried me accordingly into the kitchen, and sat down with me at table, smiling and talking at first in a very hospitable manner. But presently the gloom returned upon him; he sat frowning and biting his fingers; only remembered me from time to time; and then gave me but a word or two and a poor smile, and back into his private terrors. His wife sat by the fire and wept, with her face in her hands; his eldest son was crouched upon the floor, running over a great mass of papers and now and again setting one alight and burning it to the bitter end; all the while a servant lass with a red face was rummaging about the room, in a blind hurry of fear, and whimpering as she went; and every now and again one of the men would thrust in his face from the yard, and cry for orders.

At last James could keep his seat no longer, and begged my permission to be so unmannerly as walk about. "I am but poor company altogether, sir," says he, "but I can think of nothing but this dreadful accident, and the trouble it is like to bring upon quite innocent persons."

A little after he observed his son burning a paper which he thought should have been kept; and at that his excitement burst out so that it was painful to witness. He struck the lad repeatedly.

"Are you gone gyte?" * he cried. "Do you wish to hang your father?" and forgetful of my presence, carried on at him a long time together in the Gaelic, the young man answering nothing; only the wife, at the name of hanging, throwing her apron over her face and sobbing out louder than before.

* Mad.

This was all wretched for a stranger like myself to hear and see; and I was right glad when Alan returned, looking like himself in his fine French clothes, though (to be sure) they were now grown almost too battered and withered to deserve the name of fine. I was then taken out in my turn by another of the sons, and given that change of clothing of which I had stood so long in need, and a pair of Highland brogues made of deer-leather, rather strange at first, but after a little practice very easy to the feet.

By the time I came back Alan must have told his story; for it seemed understood that I was to fly with him, and they were all busy upon our equipment. They gave us each a sword and pistols, though I professed my inability to use the former; and with these, and some ammunition, a bag of oatmeal, an iron pan, and a bottle of right French brandy, we were ready for the heather. Money, indeed, was lacking. I had about two guineas left; Alan's belt having been despatched by another hand, that trusty messenger had no more than seventeen-pence to his whole fortune; and as for James, it appears he had brought himself so low with journeys to Edinburgh and legal expenses on behalf of the tenants, that he could only scrape together three-and-five-pence-halfpenny, the most of it in coppers.

"This'll no do," said Alan.

"Ye must find a safe bit somewhere near by," said James, "and get word sent to me. Ye see, ye'll have to get this business prettily off, Alan. This is no time to be stayed for a guinea or two. They're sure to get wind of ye, sure to seek ye, and by my way of it, sure to lay on ye the wyte of this day's accident. If it falls on you, it falls on me that am your near kinsman and harboured ye while ye were in the country. And if it comes on me——" he paused, and bit his fingers, with a white face. "It would be a painful thing for our friends if I was to hang," said he.

"It would be an ill day for Appin," says Alan.

"It's a day that sticks in my throat," said James. "O man, man, man—man Alan! you and me have spoken like two fools!" he cried, striking his hand upon the wall so that the house rang again.

"Well, and that's true, too," said Alan; "and my friend from the Lowlands here" (nodding at me) "gave me a good word upon that head, if I would only have listened to him."

"But see here," said James, returning to his former manner, "if they lay me by the heels, Alan, it's then that you'll be needing the money. For with all that I have said and that you have said, it will look very black against the two of us; do ye mark that? Well, follow me out, and ye'll, I'll see that I'll have to get a paper out against ye mysel'; have to offer a reward for ye; ay, will I! It's a sore thing to do between such near friends; but if I get the dirdum* of this dreadful accident, I'll have to fend for myself, man. Do ye see that?"

    * Blame.

He spoke with a pleading earnestness, taking Alan by the breast of the coat.

"Ay" said Alan, "I see that."

"And ye'll have to be clear of the country, Alan—ay, and clear of Scotland—you and your friend from the Lowlands, too. For I'll have to paper your friend from the Lowlands. Ye see that, Alan—say that ye see that!"

I thought Alan flushed a bit. "This is unco hard on me that brought him here, James," said he, throwing his head back. "It's like making me a traitor!"

"Now, Alan, man!" cried James. "Look things in the face! He'll be papered anyway; Mungo Campbell'll be sure to paper him; what matters if I paper him too? And then, Alan, I am a man that has a family." And then, after a little pause on both sides, "And, Alan, it'll be a jury of Campbells," said he.

"There's one thing," said Alan, musingly, "that naebody kens his name."

"Nor yet they shallnae, Alan! There's my hand on that," cried James, for all the world as if he had really known my name and was foregoing some advantage. "But just the habit he was in, and what he looked like, and his age, and the like? I couldnae well do less."

"I wonder at your father's son," cried Alan, sternly. "Would ye sell the lad with a gift? Would ye change his clothes and then betray him?"

"No, no, Alan," said James. "No, no: the habit he took off—the habit Mungo saw him in." But I thought he seemed crestfallen; indeed, he was clutching at every straw, and all the time, I dare say, saw the faces of his hereditary foes on the bench, and in the jury-box, and the gallows in the background.

"Well, sir," says Alan, turning to me, "what say ye to that? Ye are here under the safeguard of my honour; and it's my part to see nothing done but what shall please you."

"I have but one word to say," said I; "for to all this dispute I am a perfect stranger. But the plain common-sense is to set the blame where it belongs, and that is on the man who fired the shot. Paper him, as ye call it, set the hunt on him; and let honest, innocent folk show their faces in safety." But at this both Alan and James cried out in horror; bidding me hold my tongue, for that was not to be thought of; and asking me what the Camerons would think? (which confirmed me, it must have been a Cameron from Mamore that did the act) and if I did not see that the lad might be caught? "Ye havenae surely thought of that?" said they, with such innocent earnestness, that my hands dropped at my side and I despaired of argument.

"Very well, then," said I, "paper me, if you please, paper Alan, paper King George! We're all three innocent, and that seems to be what's wanted. But at least, sir," said I to James, recovering from my little fit of annoyance, "I am Alan's friend, and if I can be helpful to friends of his, I will not stumble at the risk."

I thought it best to put a fair face on my consent, for I saw Alan troubled; and, besides (thinks I to myself), as soon as my back is turned, they will paper me, as they call it, whether I consent or not. But in this I saw I was wrong; for I had no sooner said the words, than Mrs. Stewart leaped out of her chair, came running over to us, and wept first upon my neck and then on Alan's, blessing God for our goodness to her family.

"As for you, Alan, it was no more than your bounden duty," she said. "But for this lad that has come here and seen us at our worst, and seen the goodman fleeching like a suitor, him that by rights should give his commands like any king—as for you, my lad," she says, "my heart is wae not to have your name, but I have your face; and as long as my heart beats under my bosom, I will keep it, and think of it, and bless it." And with that she kissed me, and burst once more into such sobbing, that I stood abashed.

"Hoot, hoot," said Alan, looking mighty silly. "The day comes unco soon in this month of July; and to-morrow there'll be a fine to-do in Appin, a fine riding of dragoons, and crying of 'Cruachan!' * and running of red-coats; and it behoves you and me to the sooner be gone."

* The rallying-word of the Campbells.

Thereupon we said farewell, and set out again, bending somewhat eastwards, in a fine mild dark night, and over much the same broken country as before.

CHAPTER XX

THE FLIGHT IN THE HEATHER: THE ROCKS

Sometimes we walked, sometimes ran; and as it drew on to morning, walked ever the less and ran the more. Though, upon its face, that country appeared to be a desert, yet there were huts and houses of the people, of which we must have passed more than twenty, hidden in quiet places of the hills. When we came to one of these, Alan would leave me in the way, and go himself and rap upon the side of the house and speak awhile at the window with some sleeper awakened. This was to pass the news; which, in that country, was so much of a duty that Alan must pause to attend to it even while fleeing for his life; and so well attended to by others, that in more than half of the houses where we called they had heard already of the murder. In the others, as well as I could make out (standing back at a distance and hearing a strange tongue), the news was received with more of consternation than surprise.

For all our hurry, day began to come in while we were still far from any shelter. It found us in a prodigious valley, strewn with rocks and where ran a foaming river. Wild mountains stood around it; there grew there neither grass nor trees; and I have sometimes thought since then, that it may have been the valley called Glencoe, where the massacre was in the time of King William. But for the details of our itinerary, I am all to seek; our way lying now by short cuts, now by great detours; our pace being so hurried, our time of journeying usually by night; and the names of such places as I asked and heard being in the Gaelic tongue and the more easily forgotten.

The first peep of morning, then, showed us this horrible place, and I could see Alan knit his brow.

"This is no fit place for you and me," he said. "This is a place they're bound to watch."

And with that he ran harder than ever down to the water-side, in a part where the river was split in two among three rocks. It went through with a horrid thundering that made my belly quake; and there hung over the lynn a little mist of spray. Alan looked neither to the right nor to the left, but jumped clean upon the middle rock and fell there on his hands and knees to check himself, for that rock was small and he might have pitched over on the far side. I had scarce time to measure the distance or to understand the peril before I had followed him, and he had caught and stopped me.

So there we stood, side by side upon a small rock slippery with spray, a far broader leap in front of us, and the river dinning upon all sides. When I saw where I was, there came on me a deadly sickness of fear, and I put my hand over my eyes. Alan took me and shook me; I saw he was speaking, but the roaring of the falls and the trouble of my mind prevented me from hearing; only I saw his face was red with anger, and that he stamped upon the rock. The same look showed me the water raging by, and the mist hanging in the air: and with that I covered my eyes again and shuddered.

The next minute Alan had set the brandy bottle to my lips, and forced me to drink about a gill, which sent the blood into my head again. Then, putting his hands to his mouth, and his mouth to my ear, he shouted, "Hang or drown!" and turning his back upon me, leaped over the farther branch of the stream, and landed safe.

I was now alone upon the rock, which gave me the more room; the brandy was singing in my ears; I had this good example fresh before me, and just wit enough to see that if I did not leap at once, I should never leap at all. I bent low on my knees and flung myself forth, with that kind of anger of despair that has sometimes stood me in stead of courage. Sure enough, it was but my hands that reached the full length; these slipped, caught again, slipped again; and I was sliddering back into the lynn, when Alan seized me, first by the hair, then by the collar, and with a great strain dragged me into safety.

Never a word he said, but set off running again for his life, and I must stagger to my feet and run after him. I had been weary before, but now I was sick and bruised, and partly drunken with the brandy; I kept stumbling as I ran, I had a stitch that came near to overmaster me; and when at last Alan paused under a great rock that stood there among a number of others, it was none too soon for David Balfour.

A great rock I have said; but by rights it was two rocks leaning together at the top, both some twenty feet high, and at the first sight inaccessible. Even Alan (though you may say he had as good as four hands) failed twice in an attempt to climb them; and it was only at the third trial, and then by standing on my shoulders and leaping up with such force as I thought must have broken my collar-bone, that he secured a lodgment. Once there, he let down his leathern girdle; and with the aid of that and a pair of shallow footholds in the rock, I scrambled up beside him.

Then I saw why we had come there; for the two rocks, being both somewhat hollow on the top and sloping one to the other, made a kind of dish or saucer, where as many as three or four men might have lain hidden.

All this while Alan had not said a word, and had run and climbed with such a savage, silent frenzy of hurry, that I knew that he was in mortal fear of some miscarriage. Even now we were on the rock he said nothing, nor so much as relaxed the frowning look upon his face; but clapped flat down, and keeping only one eye above the edge of our place of shelter scouted all round the compass. The dawn had come quite clear; we could see the stony sides of the valley, and its bottom, which was bestrewed with rocks, and the river, which went from one side to another, and made white falls; but nowhere the smoke of a house, nor any living creature but some eagles screaming round a cliff.

Then at last Alan smiled.

"Ay" said he, "now we have a chance;" and then looking at me with some amusement, "Ye're no very gleg* at the jumping," said he.

 * Brisk.

At this I suppose I coloured with mortification, for he added at once, "Hoots! small blame to ye! To be feared of a thing and yet to do it, is what makes the prettiest kind of a man. And then there was water there, and water's a thing that dauntons even me. No, no," said Alan, "it's no you that's to blame, it's me."

I asked him why.

"Why," said he, "I have proved myself a gomeral this night. For first of all I take a wrong road, and that in my own country of Appin; so that the day has caught us where we should never have been; and thanks to that, we lie here in some danger and mair discomfort. And next (which is the worst of the two, for a man that has been so much among the heather as myself) I have come wanting a water-bottle, and here we lie for a long summer's day with naething but neat spirit. Ye may think that a small matter; but before it comes night, David, ye'll give me news of it."

I was anxious to redeem my character, and offered, if he would pour out the brandy, to run down and fill the bottle at the river.

"I wouldnae waste the good spirit either," says he. "It's been a good friend to you this night; or in my poor opinion, ye would still be cocking on yon stone. And what's mair," says he, "ye may have observed (you that's a man of so much penetration) that Alan Breck Stewart was perhaps walking quicker than his ordinar'."

"You!" I cried, "you were running fit to burst."

"Was I so?" said he. "Well, then, ye may depend upon it, there was nae time to be lost. And now here is enough said; gang you to your sleep, lad, and I'll watch."

Accordingly, I lay down to sleep; a little peaty earth had drifted in between the top of the two rocks, and some bracken grew there, to be a bed to me; the last thing I heard was still the crying of the eagles.

I dare say it would be nine in the morning when I was roughly awakened, and found Alan's hand pressed upon my mouth.

"Wheesht!" he whispered. "Ye were snoring."

"Well," said I, surprised at his anxious and dark face, "and why not?"

He peered over the edge of the rock, and signed to me to do the like.

It was now high day, cloudless, and very hot. The valley was as clear as in a picture. About half a mile up the water was a camp of red-coats; a big fire blazed in their midst, at which some were cooking; and near by, on the top of a rock about as high as ours, there stood a sentry, with the sun sparkling on his arms. All the way down along the river-side were posted other sentries; here near together, there widelier scattered; some planted like the first, on places of command, some on the ground level and marching and counter-marching, so as to meet half-way. Higher up the glen, where the ground was more open, the chain of posts was continued by horse-soldiers, whom we could see in the distance riding to and fro. Lower down, the infantry continued; but as the stream was suddenly swelled by the confluence of a considerable burn, they were more widely set, and only watched the fords and stepping-stones.

I took but one look at them, and ducked again into my place. It was strange indeed to see this valley, which had lain so solitary in the hour of dawn, bristling with arms and dotted with the red coats and breeches.

"Ye see," said Alan, "this was what I was afraid of, Davie: that they would watch the burn-side. They began to come in about two hours ago, and, man! but ye're a grand hand at the sleeping! We're in a narrow place. If they get up the sides of the hill, they could easy spy us with a glass; but if they'll only keep in the foot of the valley, we'll do yet. The posts are thinner down the water; and, come night, we'll try our hand at getting by them."

"And what are we to do till night?" I asked.

"Lie here," says he, "and birstle."

That one good Scotch word, "birstle," was indeed the most of the story of the day that we had now to pass. You are to remember that we lay on the bare top of a rock, like scones upon a girdle; the sun beat upon us cruelly; the rock grew so heated, a man could scarce endure the touch of it; and the little patch of earth and fern, which kept cooler, was only large enough for one at a time. We took turn about to lie on the naked rock, which was indeed like the position of that saint that was martyred on a gridiron; and it ran in my mind how strange it was, that in the same climate and at only a few days' distance, I should have suffered so cruelly, first from cold upon my island and now from heat upon this rock.

All the while we had no water, only raw brandy for a drink, which was worse than nothing; but we kept the bottle as cool as we could, burying it in the earth, and got some relief by bathing our breasts and temples.

The soldiers kept stirring all day in the bottom of the valley, now changing guard, now in patrolling parties hunting among the rocks. These lay round in so great a number, that to look for men among them was like looking for a needle in a bottle of hay; and being so hopeless a task, it was gone about with the less care. Yet we could see the soldiers pike their bayonets among the heather, which sent a cold thrill into my vitals; and they would sometimes hang about our rock, so that we scarce dared to breathe.

It was in this way that I first heard the right English speech; one fellow as he went by actually clapping his hand upon the sunny face of the rock on which we lay, and plucking it off again with an oath. "I tell you it's 'ot," says he; and I was amazed at the clipping tones and the odd sing-song in which he spoke, and no less at that strange trick of dropping out the letter "h." To be sure, I had heard Ransome; but he had taken his ways from all sorts of people, and spoke so imperfectly at the best, that I set down the most of it to childishness. My surprise was all the greater to hear that manner of speaking in the mouth of a grown man; and indeed I have never grown used to it; nor yet altogether with the English grammar, as perhaps a very critical eye might here and there spy out even in these memoirs.

The tediousness and pain of these hours upon the rock grew only the greater as the day went on; the rock getting still the hotter and the sun fiercer. There were giddiness, and sickness, and sharp pangs like rheumatism, to be supported. I minded then, and have often minded since, on the lines in our Scotch psalm:—

"The moon by night thee shall not smite,

Nor yet the sun by day;"

and indeed it was only by God's blessing that we were neither of us sun-smitten.

At last, about two, it was beyond men's bearing, and there was now temptation to resist, as well as pain to thole. For the sun being now got a little into the west, there came a patch of shade on the east side of our rock, which was the side sheltered from the soldiers.

"As well one death as another," said Alan, and slipped over the edge and dropped on the ground on the shadowy side.

I followed him at once, and instantly fell all my length, so weak was I and so giddy with that long exposure. Here, then, we lay for an hour or two, aching from head to foot, as weak as water, and lying quite naked to the eye of any soldier who should have strolled that way. None came, however, all passing by on the other side; so that our rock continued to be our shield even in this new position.

Presently we began again to get a little strength; and as the soldiers were now lying closer along the river-side, Alan proposed that we should try a start. I was by this time afraid of but one thing in the world; and that was to be set back upon the rock; anything else was welcome to me; so we got ourselves at once in marching order, and began to slip from rock to rock one after the other, now crawling flat on our bellies in the shade, now making a run for it, heart in mouth.

The soldiers, having searched this side of the valley after a fashion, and being perhaps somewhat sleepy with the sultriness of the afternoon, had now laid by much of their vigilance, and stood dozing at their posts or only kept a look-out along the banks of the river; so that in this way, keeping down the valley and at the same time towards the mountains, we drew steadily away from their neighbourhood. But the business was the most wearing I had ever taken part in. A man had need of a hundred eyes in every part of him, to keep concealed in that uneven country and within cry of so many and scattered sentries. When we must pass an open place, quickness was not all, but a swift judgment not only of the lie of the whole country, but of the solidity of every stone on which we must set foot; for the afternoon was now fallen so breathless that the rolling of a pebble sounded abroad like a pistol shot, and would start the echo calling among the hills and cliffs.

By sundown we had made some distance, even by our slow rate of progress, though to be sure the sentry on the rock was still plainly in our view. But now we came on something that put all fears out of season; and that was a deep rushing burn, that tore down, in that part, to join the glen river. At the sight of this we cast ourselves on the ground and plunged head and shoulders in the water; and I cannot tell which was the more pleasant, the great shock as the cool stream went over us, or the greed with which we drank of it.

We lay there (for the banks hid us), drank again and again, bathed our chests, let our wrists trail in the running water till they ached with the chill; and at last, being wonderfully renewed, we got out the meal-bag and made drammach in the iron pan. This, though it is but cold water mingled with oatmeal, yet makes a good enough dish for a hungry man; and where there are no means of making fire, or (as in our case) good reason for not making one, it is the chief stand-by of those who have taken to the heather.

As soon as the shadow of the night had fallen, we set forth again, at first with the same caution, but presently with more boldness, standing our full height and stepping out at a good pace of walking. The way was very intricate, lying up the steep sides of mountains and along the brows of cliffs; clouds had come in with the sunset, and the night was dark and cool; so that I walked without much fatigue, but in continual fear of falling and rolling down the mountains, and with no guess at our direction.

The moon rose at last and found us still on the road; it was in its last quarter, and was long beset with clouds; but after awhile shone out and showed me many dark heads of mountains, and was reflected far underneath us on the narrow arm of a sea-loch.

At this sight we both paused: I struck with wonder to find myself so high and walking (as it seemed to me) upon clouds; Alan to make sure of his direction.

Seemingly he was well pleased, and he must certainly have judged us out of ear-shot of all our enemies; for throughout the rest of our night-march he beguiled the way with whistling of many tunes, warlike, merry, plaintive; reel tunes that made the foot go faster; tunes of my own south country that made me fain to be home from my adventures; and all these, on the great, dark, desert mountains, making company upon the way.

CHAPTER XXI
THE FLIGHT IN THE HEATHER:
THE HEUGH OF CORRYNAKIEGH

Early as day comes in the beginning of July, it was still dark when we reached our destination, a cleft in the head of a great mountain, with a water running through the midst, and upon the one hand a shallow cave in a rock. Birches grew there in a thin, pretty wood, which a little farther on was changed into a wood of pines. The burn was full of trout; the wood of cushat-doves; on the open side of the mountain beyond, whaups would be always whistling, and cuckoos were plentiful. From the mouth of the cleft we looked down upon a part of Mamore, and on the sea-loch that divides that country from Appin; and this from so great a height as made it my continual wonder and pleasure to sit and behold them.

The name of the cleft was the Heugh of Corrynakiegh; and although from its height and being so near upon the sea, it was often beset with clouds, yet it was on the whole a pleasant place, and the five days we lived in it went happily.

We slept in the cave, making our bed of heather bushes which we cut for that purpose, and covering ourselves with Alan's great-coat. There was a low concealed place, in a turning of the glen, where we were so bold as to make fire: so that we could warm ourselves when the clouds set in, and cook hot porridge, and grill the little trouts that we caught with our hands under the stones and overhanging banks of the burn. This was indeed our chief pleasure and business; and not only to save our meal against worse times, but with a rivalry that much amused us, we spent a great part of our days at the water-side, stripped to the waist and groping about or (as they say) guddling for these fish. The largest we got might have been a quarter of a pound; but they were of good flesh and flavour, and when broiled upon the coals, lacked only a little salt to be delicious.

In any by-time Alan must teach me to use my sword, for my ignorance had much distressed him; and I think besides, as I had sometimes the upper-hand of him in the fishing, he was not sorry to turn to an exercise where he had so much the upper-hand of me. He made it somewhat more of a pain than need have been, for he stormed at me all through the lessons in a very violent manner of scolding, and would push me so close that I made sure he must run me through the body. I was often tempted to turn tail, but held my ground for all that, and got some profit of my lessons; if it was but to stand on guard with an assured countenance, which is often all that is required. So, though I could never in the least please my master, I was not altogether displeased with myself.

In the meanwhile, you are not to suppose that we neglected our chief business, which was to get away.

"It will be many a long day," Alan said to me on our first morning, "before the red-coats think upon seeking Corrynakiegh; so now we must get word sent to James, and he must find the siller for us."

"And how shall we send that word?" says I. "We are here in a desert place, which yet we dare not leave; and unless ye get the fowls of the air to be your messengers, I see not what we shall be able to do."

"Ay?" said Alan. "Ye're a man of small contrivance, David."

Thereupon he fell in a muse, looking in the embers of the fire; and presently, getting a piece of wood, he fashioned it in a cross, the four ends of which he blackened on the coals. Then he looked at me a little shyly.

"Could ye lend me my button?" says he. "It seems a strange thing to ask a gift again, but I own I am laith to cut another."

I gave him the button; whereupon he strung it on a strip of his great-coat which he had used to bind the cross; and tying in a little sprig of birch and another of fir, he looked upon his work with satisfaction.

"Now," said he, "there is a little clachan" (what is called a hamlet in the English) "not very far from Corrynakiegh, and it has the name of Koalisnacoan. There there are living many friends of mine whom I could trust with my life, and some that I am no just so sure of. Ye see, David, there will be money set upon our heads; James himsel' is to set money on them; and as for the Campbells, they would never spare siller where there was a Stewart to be hurt. If it was otherwise, I would go down to Koalisnacoan whatever, and trust my life into these people's hands as lightly as I would trust another with my glove."

"But being so?" said I.

"Being so," said he, "I would as lief they didnae see me. There's bad folk everywhere, and what's far worse, weak ones. So when it comes dark again, I will steal down into that clachan, and set this that I have been making in the window of a good friend of mine, John Breck Maccoll, a bouman* of Appin's."

> *A bouman is a tenant who takes stock from the landlord and
>
> shares with him the increase.

"With all my heart," says I; "and if he finds it, what is he to think?"

"Well," says Alan, "I wish he was a man of more penetration, for by my troth I am afraid he will make little enough of it! But this is what I have in my mind. This cross is something in the nature of the crosstarrie, or fiery cross, which is the signal of gathering in our clans; yet he will know well enough the clan is not to rise, for there it is standing in his window, and no word with it. So he will say to himsel', THE CLAN IS NOT TO RISE, BUT THERE IS SOMETHING. Then he will see my button, and that was Duncan Stewart's. And then he will say to himsel', THE SON OF DUNCAN IS IN THE HEATHER, AND HAS NEED OF ME."

"Well," said I, "it may be. But even supposing so, there is a good deal of heather between here and the Forth."

"And that is a very true word," says Alan. "But then John Breck will see the sprig of birch and the sprig of pine; and he will say to himsel' (if he is a man of any penetration at all, which I misdoubt), ALAN WILL BE LYING IN A WOOD WHICH IS BOTH OF PINES AND BIRCHES. Then he will think to himsel', THAT IS NOT SO VERY RIFE HEREABOUT; and then he will come and give us a look up in Corrynakiegh. And if he does not, David, the devil may fly away with him, for what I care; for he will no be worth the salt to his porridge."

"Eh, man," said I, drolling with him a little, "you're very ingenious! But would it not be simpler for you to write him a few words in black and white?"

"And that is an excellent observe, Mr. Balfour of Shaws," says Alan, drolling with me; "and it would certainly be much simpler for me to write to him, but it would be a sore job for John

Breck to read it. He would have to go to the school for two-three years; and it's possible we might be wearied waiting on him."

So that night Alan carried down his fiery cross and set it in the bouman's window. He was troubled when he came back; for the dogs had barked and the folk run out from their houses; and he thought he had heard a clatter of arms and seen a red-coat come to one of the doors. On all accounts we lay the next day in the borders of the wood and kept a close look-out, so that if it was John Breck that came we might be ready to guide him, and if it was the red-coats we should have time to get away.

About noon a man was to be spied, straggling up the open side of the mountain in the sun, and looking round him as he came, from under his hand. No sooner had Alan seen him than he whistled; the man turned and came a little towards us: then Alan would give another "peep!" and the man would come still nearer; and so by the sound of whistling, he was guided to the spot where we lay.

He was a ragged, wild, bearded man, about forty, grossly disfigured with the small pox, and looked both dull and savage. Although his English was very bad and broken, yet Alan (according to his very handsome use, whenever I was by) would suffer him to speak no Gaelic. Perhaps the strange language made him appear more backward than he really was; but I thought he had little good-will to serve us, and what he had was the child of terror.

Alan would have had him carry a message to James; but the bouman would hear of no message. "She was forget it," he said in his screaming voice; and would either have a letter or wash his hands of us.

I thought Alan would be gravelled at that, for we lacked the means of writing in that desert.

But he was a man of more resources than I knew; searched the wood until he found the quill of a cushat-dove, which he shaped into a pen; made himself a kind of ink with gunpowder from his horn and water from the running stream; and tearing a corner from his French military commission (which he carried in his pocket, like a talisman to keep him from the gallows), he sat down and wrote as follows:

"DEAR KINSMAN,—Please send the money by the bearer to the place he kens of.

"Your affectionate cousin,

"A. S."

This he intrusted to the bouman, who promised to make what manner of speed he best could, and carried it off with him down the hill.

He was three full days gone, but about five in the evening of the third, we heard a whistling in the wood, which Alan answered; and presently the bouman came up the water-side, looking for us, right and left. He seemed less sulky than before, and indeed he was no doubt well pleased to have got to the end of such a dangerous commission.

He gave us the news of the country; that it was alive with red-coats; that arms were being found, and poor folk brought in trouble daily; and that James and some of his servants were already clapped in prison at Fort William, under strong suspicion of complicity. It seemed it was noised on all sides that Alan Breck had fired the shot; and there was a bill issued for both him and me, with one hundred pounds reward.

This was all as bad as could be; and the little note the bouman had carried us from Mrs. Stewart was of a miserable sadness. In it she besought Alan not to let himself be captured, assuring him, if he fell in the hands of the troops, both he and James were no better than dead men. The money she had sent was all that she could beg or borrow, and she prayed heaven we could be doing with it. Lastly, she said, she enclosed us one of the bills in which we were described.

This we looked upon with great curiosity and not a little fear, partly as a man may look in a mirror, partly as he might look into the barrel of an enemy's gun to judge if it be truly aimed. Alan was advertised as "a small, pock-marked, active man of thirty-five or thereby, dressed in a feathered hat, a French side-coat of blue with silver buttons, and lace a great deal tarnished, a red waistcoat and breeches of black, shag;" and I as "a tall strong lad of about eighteen, wearing an old blue coat, very ragged, an old Highland bonnet, a long homespun waistcoat, blue breeches; his legs bare, low-country shoes, wanting the toes; speaks like a Lowlander, and has no beard."

Alan was well enough pleased to see his finery so fully remembered and set down; only when he came to the word tarnish, he looked upon his lace like one a little mortified. As for myself, I thought I cut a miserable figure in the bill; and yet was well enough pleased too, for since I had changed these rags, the description had ceased to be a danger and become a source of safety.

"Alan," said I, "you should change your clothes."

"Na, troth!" said Alan, "I have nae others. A fine sight I would be, if I went back to France in a bonnet!"

This put a second reflection in my mind: that if I were to separate from Alan and his tell-tale clothes I should be safe against arrest, and might go openly about my business. Nor was this all; for suppose I was arrested when I was alone, there was little against me; but suppose I was taken in company with the reputed murderer, my case would begin to be grave. For generosity's sake I dare not speak my mind upon this head; but I thought of it none the less.

I thought of it all the more, too, when the bouman brought out a green purse with four guineas in gold, and the best part of another in small change. True, it was more than I had. But then Alan, with less than five guineas, had to get as far as France; I, with my less than two, not beyond Queensferry; so that taking things in their proportion, Alan's society was not only a peril to my life, but a burden on my purse.

But there was no thought of the sort in the honest head of my companion. He believed he was serving, helping, and protecting me. And what could I do but hold my peace, and chafe, and take my chance of it?

"It's little enough," said Alan, putting the purse in his pocket, "but it'll do my business. And now, John Breck, if ye will hand me over my button, this gentleman and me will be for taking the road."

But the bouman, after feeling about in a hairy purse that hung in front of him in the Highland manner (though he wore otherwise the Lowland habit, with sea-trousers), began to roll his eyes strangely, and at last said, "Her nainsel will loss it," meaning he thought he had lost it.

"What!" cried Alan, "you will lose my button, that was my father's before me? Now I will tell you what is in my mind, John Breck: it is in my mind this is the worst day's work that ever ye did since ye was born."

And as Alan spoke, he set his hands on his knees and looked at the bouman with a smiling mouth, and that dancing light in his eyes that meant mischief to his enemies.

Perhaps the bouman was honest enough; perhaps he had meant to cheat and then, finding himself alone with two of us in a desert place, cast back to honesty as being safer; at least, and all at once, he seemed to find that button and handed it to Alan.

"Well, and it is a good thing for the honour of the Maccolls," said Alan, and then to me, "Here is my button back again, and I thank you for parting with it, which is of a piece with all your friendships to me." Then he took the warmest parting of the bouman. "For," says he, "ye have done very well by me, and set your neck at a venture, and I will always give you the name of a good man."

Lastly, the bouman took himself off by one way; and Alan and I (getting our chattels together) struck into another to resume our flight.

CHAPTER XXII

THE FLIGHT IN THE HEATHER: THE MOOR

Some seven hours' incessant, hard travelling brought us early in the morning to the end of a range of mountains. In front of us there lay a piece of low, broken, desert land, which we must now cross. The sun was not long up, and shone straight in our eyes; a little, thin mist went up from the face of the moorland like a smoke; so that (as Alan said) there might have been twenty squadron of dragoons there and we none the wiser.

We sat down, therefore, in a howe of the hill-side till the mist should have risen, and made ourselves a dish of drammach, and held a council of war.

"David," said Alan, "this is the kittle bit. Shall we lie here till it comes night, or shall we risk it, and stave on ahead?"

"Well," said I, "I am tired indeed, but I could walk as far again, if that was all."

"Ay, but it isnae," said Alan, "nor yet the half. This is how we stand: Appin's fair death to us. To the south it's all Campbells, and no to be thought of. To the north; well, there's no muckle to be gained by going north; neither for you, that wants to get to Queensferry, nor yet for me, that wants to get to France. Well, then, we'll can strike east."

"East be it!" says I, quite cheerily; but I was thinking in to myself: "O, man, if you would only take one point of the compass and let me take any other, it would be the best for both of us."

"Well, then, east, ye see, we have the muirs," said Alan. "Once there, David, it's mere pitch-and-toss. Out on yon bald, naked, flat place, where can a body turn to? Let the red-coats come over a hill, they can spy you miles away; and the sorrow's in their horses' heels, they would soon ride you down. It's no good place, David; and I'm free to say, it's worse by daylight than by dark."

"Alan," said I, "hear my way of it. Appin's death for us; we have none too much money, nor yet meal; the longer they seek, the nearer they may guess where we are; it's all a risk; and I give my word to go ahead until we drop."

Alan was delighted. "There are whiles," said he, "when ye are altogether too canny and Whiggish to be company for a gentleman like me; but there come other whiles when ye show yoursel' a mettle spark; and it's then, David, that I love ye like a brother."

The mist rose and died away, and showed us that country lying as waste as the sea; only the moorfowl and the pewees crying upon it, and far over to the east, a herd of deer, moving like dots. Much of it was red with heather; much of the rest broken up with bogs and hags and peaty pools; some had been burnt black in a heath fire; and in another place there was quite a forest of dead firs, standing like skeletons. A wearier-looking desert man never saw; but at least it was clear of troops, which was our point.

We went down accordingly into the waste, and began to make our toilsome and devious travel towards the eastern verge. There were the tops of mountains all round (you are to remember) from whence we might be spied at any moment; so it behoved us to keep in the hollow parts of the moor, and when these turned aside from our direction to move upon its naked face with infinite care. Sometimes, for half an hour together, we must crawl from one heather bush to another, as hunters do when they are hard upon the deer. It was a clear day again, with a blazing sun; the water in the brandy bottle was soon gone; and altogether, if I had guessed what it would be to crawl half the time upon my belly and to walk much of the rest stooping nearly to the knees, I should certainly have held back from such a killing enterprise.

Toiling and resting and toiling again, we wore away the morning; and about noon lay down in a thick bush of heather to sleep. Alan took the first watch; and it seemed to me I had scarce closed my eyes before I was shaken up to take the second. We had no clock to go by; and Alan stuck a sprig of heath in the ground to serve instead; so that as soon as the shadow of the bush should fall so far to the east, I might know to rouse him. But I was by this time so weary that I could have slept twelve hours at a stretch; I had the taste of sleep in my throat; my joints slept even when my mind was waking; the hot smell of the heather, and the drone of the wild bees, were like possets to me; and every now and again I would give a jump and find I had been dozing.

The last time I woke I seemed to come back from farther away, and thought the sun had taken a great start in the heavens. I looked at the sprig of heath, and at that I could have cried aloud: for I saw I had betrayed my trust. My head was nearly turned with fear and shame; and at what I saw, when I looked out around me on the moor, my heart was like dying in my body. For sure enough, a body of horse-soldiers had come down during my sleep, and were drawing near to us from the south-east, spread out in the shape of a fan and riding their horses to and fro in the deep parts of the heather.

When I waked Alan, he glanced first at the soldiers, then at the mark and the position of the sun, and knitted his brows with a sudden, quick look, both ugly and anxious, which was all the reproach I had of him.

"What are we to do now?" I asked.

"We'll have to play at being hares," said he. "Do ye see yon mountain?" pointing to one on the north-eastern sky.

"Ay," said I.

"Well, then," says he, "let us strike for that. Its name is Ben Alder. it is a wild, desert mountain full of hills and hollows, and if we can win to it before the morn, we may do yet."

"But, Alan," cried I, "that will take us across the very coming of the soldiers!"

"I ken that fine," said he; "but if we are driven back on Appin, we are two dead men. So now, David man, be brisk!"

With that he began to run forward on his hands and knees with an incredible quickness, as though it were his natural way of going. All the time, too, he kept winding in and out in the lower parts of the moorland where we were the best concealed. Some of these had been burned or at least scathed with fire; and there rose in our faces (which were close to the ground) a blinding, choking dust as fine as smoke. The water was long out; and this posture of running on the hands and knees brings an overmastering weakness and weariness, so that the joints ache and the wrists faint under your weight.

Now and then, indeed, where was a big bush of heather, we lay awhile, and panted, and putting aside the leaves, looked back at the dragoons. They had not spied us, for they held straight on; a half-troop, I think, covering about two miles of ground, and beating it mighty thoroughly as they went. I had awakened just in time; a little later, and we must have fled in front of them, instead of escaping on one side. Even as it was, the least misfortune might betray us; and now and again, when a grouse rose out of the heather with a clap of wings, we lay as still as the dead and were afraid to breathe.

The aching and faintness of my body, the labouring of my heart, the soreness of my hands, and the smarting of my throat and eyes in the continual smoke of dust and ashes, had soon grown to be so unbearable that I would gladly have given up. Nothing but the fear of Alan lent me enough of a false kind of courage to continue. As for himself (and you are to bear in mind that he was cumbered with a great-coat) he had first turned crimson, but as time went on the redness began to be mingled with patches of white; his breath cried and whistled as it came; and his voice, when he whispered his observations in my ear during our halts, sounded like nothing human. Yet he seemed in no way dashed in spirits, nor did he at all abate in his activity, so that I was driven to marvel at the man's endurance.

At length, in the first gloaming of the night, we heard a trumpet sound, and looking back from among the heather, saw the troop beginning to collect. A little after, they had built a fire and camped for the night, about the middle of the waste.

At this I begged and besought that we might lie down and sleep.

"There shall be no sleep the night!" said Alan. "From now on, these weary dragoons of yours will keep the crown of the muirland, and none will get out of Appin but winged fowls. We got through in the nick of time, and shall we jeopard what we've gained? Na, na, when the day comes, it shall find you and me in a fast place on Ben Alder."

"Alan," I said, "it's not the want of will: it's the strength that I want. If I could, I would; but as sure as I'm alive I cannot."

"Very well, then," said Alan. "I'll carry ye."

I looked to see if he were jesting; but no, the little man was in dead earnest; and the sight of so much resolution shamed me.

"Lead away!" said I. "I'll follow."

He gave me one look as much as to say, "Well done, David!" and off he set again at his top speed.

It grew cooler and even a little darker (but not much) with the coming of the night. The sky was cloudless; it was still early in July, and pretty far north; in the darkest part of that night, you would have needed pretty good eyes to read, but for all that, I have often seen it darker in a winter mid-day. Heavy dew fell and drenched the moor like rain; and this refreshed me for a while. When we stopped to breathe, and I had time to see all about me, the clearness and sweetness of the night, the shapes of the hills like things asleep, and the fire dwindling away behind us, like a bright spot in the midst of the moor, anger would come upon me in a clap that I must still drag myself in agony and eat the dust like a worm.

By what I have read in books, I think few that have held a pen were ever really wearied, or they would write of it more strongly. I had no care of my life, neither past nor future, and I scarce remembered there was such a lad as David Balfour. I did not think of myself, but just of each fresh step which I was sure would be my last, with despair—and of Alan, who was the cause of it, with hatred. Alan was in the right trade as a soldier; this is the officer's part to make men continue to do things, they know not wherefore, and when, if the choice was offered, they would lie down where they were and be killed. And I dare say I would have made a good enough private; for in these last hours it never occurred to me that I had any choice but just to obey as long as I was able, and die obeying.

Day began to come in, after years, I thought; and by that time we were past the greatest danger, and could walk upon our feet like men, instead of crawling like brutes. But, dear heart have mercy! what a pair we must have made, going double like old grandfathers, stumbling like babes, and as white as dead folk. Never a word passed between us; each set his mouth and kept his eyes in front of him, and lifted up his foot and set it down again, like people lifting weights at a country play;* all the while, with the moorfowl crying "peep!" in the heather, and the light coming slowly clearer in the east.

   * Village fair.

I say Alan did as I did. Not that ever I looked at him, for I had enough ado to keep my feet; but because it is plain he must have been as stupid with weariness as myself, and looked as little where we were going, or we should not have walked into an ambush like blind men.

It fell in this way. We were going down a heathery brae, Alan leading and I following a pace or two behind, like a fiddler and his wife; when upon a sudden the heather gave a rustle, three or four ragged men leaped out, and the next moment we were lying on our backs, each with a dirk at his throat.

I don't think I cared; the pain of this rough handling was quite swallowed up by the pains of which I was already full; and I was too glad to have stopped walking to mind about a dirk. I lay looking up in the face of the man that held me; and I mind his face was black with the sun, and his eyes very light, but I was not afraid of him. I heard Alan and another whispering in the Gaelic; and what they said was all one to me.

Then the dirks were put up, our weapons were taken away, and we were set face to face, sitting in the heather.

"They are Cluny's men," said Alan. "We couldnae have fallen better. We're just to bide here with these, which are his out-sentries, till they can get word to the chief of my arrival."

Now Cluny Macpherson, the chief of the clan Vourich, had been one of the leaders of the great rebellion six years before; there was a price on his life; and I had supposed him long ago in France, with the rest of the heads of that desperate party. Even tired as I was, the surprise of what I heard half wakened me.

"What," I cried, "is Cluny still here?"

"Ay, is he so!" said Alan. "Still in his own country and kept by his own clan. King George can do no more."

I think I would have asked farther, but Alan gave me the put-off. "I am rather wearied," he said, "and I would like fine to get a sleep." And without more words, he rolled on his face in a deep heather bush, and seemed to sleep at once.

There was no such thing possible for me. You have heard grasshoppers whirring in the grass in the summer time? Well, I had no sooner closed my eyes, than my body, and above all my head, belly, and wrists, seemed to be filled with whirring grasshoppers; and I must open my eyes again at once, and tumble and toss, and sit up and lie down; and look at the sky which dazzled me, or at Cluny's wild and dirty sentries, peering out over the top of the brae and chattering to each other in the Gaelic.

That was all the rest I had, until the messenger returned; when, as it appeared that Cluny would be glad to receive us, we must get once more upon our feet and set forward. Alan was in excellent good spirits, much refreshed by his sleep, very hungry, and looking pleasantly forward to a dram and a dish of hot collops, of which, it seems, the messenger had brought him word. For my part, it made me sick to hear of eating. I had been dead-heavy before, and now I felt a kind of dreadful lightness, which would not suffer me to walk. I drifted like a gossamer; the ground seemed to me a cloud, the hills a feather-weight, the air to have a current, like a running burn, which carried me to and fro. With all that, a sort of horror of despair sat on my mind, so that I could have wept at my own helplessness.

I saw Alan knitting his brows at me, and supposed it was in anger; and that gave me a pang of light-headed fear, like what a child may have. I remember, too, that I was smiling, and could not stop smiling, hard as I tried; for I thought it was out of place at such a time. But my good companion had nothing in his mind but kindness; and the next moment, two of the gillies had me by the arms, and I began to be carried forward with great swiftness (or so it appeared to me, although I dare say it was slowly enough in truth), through a labyrinth of dreary glens and hollows and into the heart of that dismal mountain of Ben Alder.

CHAPTER XXIII
CLUNY'S CAGE

We came at last to the foot of an exceeding steep wood, which scrambled up a craggy hillside, and was crowned by a naked precipice.

"It's here," said one of the guides, and we struck up hill.

The trees clung upon the slope, like sailors on the shrouds of a ship, and their trunks were like the rounds of a ladder, by which we mounted.

Quite at the top, and just before the rocky face of the cliff sprang above the foliage, we found that strange house which was known in the country as "Cluny's Cage." The trunks of several trees had been wattled across, the intervals strengthened with stakes, and the ground behind this barricade levelled up with earth to make the floor. A tree, which grew out from the hillside, was the living centre-beam of the roof. The walls were of wattle and covered with moss. The whole house had something of an egg shape; and it half hung, half stood in that steep, hillside thicket, like a wasp's nest in a green hawthorn.

Within, it was large enough to shelter five or six persons with some comfort. A projection of the cliff had been cunningly employed to be the fireplace; and the smoke rising against the face of the rock, and being not dissimilar in colour, readily escaped notice from below.

This was but one of Cluny's hiding-places; he had caves, besides, and underground chambers in several parts of his country; and following the reports of his scouts, he moved from one to another as the soldiers drew near or moved away. By this manner of living, and thanks to the affection of his clan, he had not only stayed all this time in safety, while so many others had fled or been taken and slain: but stayed four or five years longer, and only went to France at last by the express command of his master. There he soon died; and it is strange to reflect that he may have regretted his Cage upon Ben Alder.

When we came to the door he was seated by his rock chimney, watching a gillie about some cookery. He was mighty plainly habited, with a knitted nightcap drawn over his ears, and smoked a foul cutty pipe. For all that he had the manners of a king, and it was quite a sight to see him rise out of his place to welcome us.

"Well, Mr. Stewart, come awa', sir!" said he, "and bring in your friend that as yet I dinna ken the name of."

"And how is yourself, Cluny?" said Alan. "I hope ye do brawly, sir. And I am proud to see ye, and to present to ye my friend the Laird of Shaws, Mr. David Balfour."

Alan never referred to my estate without a touch of a sneer, when we were alone; but with strangers, he rang the words out like a herald.

"Step in by, the both of ye, gentlemen," says Cluny. "I make ye welcome to my house, which is a queer, rude place for certain, but one where I have entertained a royal personage, Mr. Stewart—ye doubtless ken the personage I have in my eye. We'll take a dram for luck, and as soon as this handless man of mine has the collops ready, we'll dine and take a hand at the cartes as gentlemen should. My life is a bit driegh," says he, pouring out the brandy; "I see little company, and sit and twirl my thumbs, and mind upon a great day that is gone by, and weary for another great day that we all hope will be upon the road. And so here's a toast to ye: The Restoration!"

Thereupon we all touched glasses and drank. I am sure I wished no ill to King George; and if he had been there himself in proper person, it's like he would have done as I did. No sooner had I taken out the drain than I felt hugely better, and could look on and listen, still a little mistily perhaps, but no longer with the same groundless horror and distress of mind.

It was certainly a strange place, and we had a strange host. In his long hiding, Cluny had grown to have all manner of precise habits, like those of an old maid. He had a particular place, where no one else must sit; the Cage was arranged in a particular way, which none must disturb; cookery was one of his chief fancies, and even while he was greeting us in, he kept an eye to the collops.

It appears, he sometimes visited or received visits from his wife and one or two of his nearest friends, under the cover of night; but for the more part lived quite alone, and communicated only with his sentinels and the gillies that waited on him in the Cage. The first thing in the morning, one of them, who was a barber, came and shaved him, and gave him the news of the country, of which he was immoderately greedy. There was no end to his questions; he put them as earnestly as a child; and at some of the answers, laughed out of all bounds of reason, and would break out again laughing at the mere memory, hours after the barber was gone.

To be sure, there might have been a purpose in his questions; for though he was thus sequestered, and like the other landed gentlemen of Scotland, stripped by the late Act of Parliament of legal powers, he still exercised a patriarchal justice in his clan. Disputes were brought to him in his hiding-hole to be decided; and the men of his country, who would have snapped their fingers at the Court of Session, laid aside revenge and paid down money at the bare word of this forfeited and hunted outlaw. When he was angered, which was often enough, he gave his commands and breathed threats of punishment like any king; and his gillies trembled and crouched away from him like children before a hasty father. With each of them, as he entered, he ceremoniously shook hands, both parties touching their bonnets at the same time in a military manner. Altogether, I had a fair chance to see some of the inner workings of a Highland clan; and this with a proscribed, fugitive chief; his country conquered; the troops riding upon all sides in quest of him, sometimes within a mile of where he lay; and when the least of the ragged fellows whom he rated and threatened, could have made a fortune by betraying him.

On that first day, as soon as the collops were ready, Cluny gave them with his own hand a squeeze of a lemon (for he was well supplied with luxuries) and bade us draw in to our meal.

"They," said he, meaning the collops, "are such as I gave his Royal Highness in this very house; bating the lemon juice, for at that time we were glad to get the meat and never fashed for kitchen.* Indeed, there were mair dragoons than lemons in my country in the year forty-six."

* Condiment.

I do not know if the collops were truly very good, but my heart rose against the sight of them, and I could eat but little. All the while Cluny entertained us with stories of Prince Charlie's stay in the Cage, giving us the very words of the speakers, and rising from his place to show us where they stood. By these, I gathered the Prince was a gracious, spirited boy, like the son of a race of polite kings, but not so wise as Solomon. I gathered, too, that while he was in the Cage, he was often drunk; so the fault that has since, by all accounts, made such a wreck of him, had even then begun to show itself.

We were no sooner done eating than Cluny brought out an old, thumbed, greasy pack of cards, such as you may find in a mean inn; and his eyes brightened in his face as he proposed that we should fall to playing.

Now this was one of the things I had been brought up to eschew like disgrace; it being held by my father neither the part of a Christian nor yet of a gentleman to set his own livelihood and fish for that of others, on the cast of painted pasteboard. To be sure, I might have pleaded my fatigue, which was excuse enough; but I thought it behoved that I should bear a testimony. I must have got very red in the face, but I spoke steadily, and told them I had no call to be a judge of others, but for my own part, it was a matter in which I had no clearness.

Cluny stopped mingling the cards. "What in deil's name is this?" says he. "What kind of Whiggish, canting talk is this, for the house of Cluny Macpherson?"

"I will put my hand in the fire for Mr. Balfour," says Alan. "He is an honest and a mettle gentleman, and I would have ye bear in mind who says it. I bear a king's name," says he, cocking his hat; "and I and any that I call friend are company for the best. But the gentleman is tired, and should sleep; if he has no mind to the cartes, it will never hinder you and me. And I'm fit and willing, sir, to play ye any game that ye can name."

"Sir," says Cluny, "in this poor house of mine I would have you to ken that any gentleman may follow his pleasure. If your friend would like to stand on his head, he is welcome. And if either he, or you, or any other man, is not preceesely satisfied, I will be proud to step outside with him."

I had no will that these two friends should cut their throats for my sake.

"Sir," said I, "I am very wearied, as Alan says; and what's more, as you are a man that likely has sons of your own, I may tell you it was a promise to my father."

"Say nae mair, say nae mair," said Cluny, and pointed me to a bed of heather in a corner of the Cage. For all that he was displeased enough, looked at me askance, and grumbled when he looked. And indeed it must be owned that both my scruples and the words in which I declared them, smacked somewhat of the Covenanter, and were little in their place among wild Highland Jacobites.

What with the brandy and the venison, a strange heaviness had come over me; and I had scarce lain down upon the bed before I fell into a kind of trance, in which I continued almost the whole time of our stay in the Cage. Sometimes I was broad awake and understood what passed; sometimes I only heard voices, or men snoring, like the voice of a silly river; and the plaids upon the wall dwindled down and swelled out again, like firelight shadows on the roof. I must sometimes have spoken or cried out, for I remember I was now and then amazed at being answered; yet I was conscious of no particular nightmare, only of a general, black, abiding horror—a horror of the place I was in, and the bed I lay in, and the plaids on the wall, and the voices, and the fire, and myself.

The barber-gillie, who was a doctor too, was called in to prescribe for me; but as he spoke in the Gaelic, I understood not a word of his opinion, and was too sick even to ask for a translation. I knew well enough I was ill, and that was all I cared about.

I paid little heed while I lay in this poor pass. But Alan and Cluny were most of the time at the cards, and I am clear that Alan must have begun by winning; for I remember sitting up, and seeing them hard at it, and a great glittering pile of as much as sixty or a hundred guineas on the table. It looked strange enough, to see all this wealth in a nest upon a cliff-side, wattled about growing trees. And even then, I thought it seemed deep water for Alan to be riding, who had no better battle-horse than a green purse and a matter of five pounds.

The luck, it seems, changed on the second day. About noon I was wakened as usual for dinner, and as usual refused to eat, and was given a dram with some bitter infusion which the barber had prescribed. The sun was shining in at the open door of the Cage, and this dazzled and offended me. Cluny sat at the table, biting the pack of cards. Alan had stooped over the bed, and had his face close to my eyes; to which, troubled as they were with the fever, it seemed of the most shocking bigness.

He asked me for a loan of my money.

"What for?" said I.

"O, just for a loan," said he.

"But why?" I repeated. "I don't see."

"Hut, David!" said Alan, "ye wouldnae grudge me a loan?"

I would, though, if I had had my senses! But all I thought of then was to get his face away, and I handed him my money.

On the morning of the third day, when we had been forty-eight hours in the Cage, I awoke with a great relief of spirits, very weak and weary indeed, but seeing things of the right size and with their honest, everyday appearance. I had a mind to eat, moreover, rose from bed of my own movement, and as soon as we had breakfasted, stepped to the entry of the Cage and sat down outside in the top of the wood. It was a grey day with a cool, mild air: and I sat in a dream all morning, only disturbed by the passing by of Cluny's scouts and servants coming with provisions and reports; for as the coast was at that time clear, you might almost say he held court openly.

When I returned, he and Alan had laid the cards aside, and were questioning a gillie; and the chief turned about and spoke to me in the Gaelic.

"I have no Gaelic, sir," said I.

Now since the card question, everything I said or did had the power of annoying Cluny. "Your name has more sense than yourself, then," said he angrily, "for it's good Gaelic. But the point is this. My scout reports all clear in the south, and the question is, have ye the strength to go?"

I saw cards on the table, but no gold; only a heap of little written papers, and these all on Cluny's side. Alan, besides, had an odd look, like a man not very well content; and I began to have a strong misgiving.

"I do not know if I am as well as I should be," said I, looking at Alan; "but the little money we have has a long way to carry us."

Alan took his under-lip into his mouth, and looked upon the ground.

"David," says he at last, "I've lost it; there's the naked truth."

"My money too?" said I.

"Your money too," says Alan, with a groan. "Ye shouldnae have given it me. I'm daft when I get to the cartes."

"Hoot-toot! hoot-toot!" said Cluny. "It was all daffing; it's all nonsense. Of course you'll have your money back again, and the double of it, if ye'll make so free with me. It would be a singular thing for me to keep it. It's not to be supposed that I would be any hindrance to gentlemen in your situation; that would be a singular thing!" cries he, and began to pull gold out of his pocket with a mighty red face.

Alan said nothing, only looked on the ground.

"Will you step to the door with me, sir?" said I.

Cluny said he would be very glad, and followed me readily enough, but he looked flustered and put out.

"And now, sir," says I, "I must first acknowledge your generosity."

"Nonsensical nonsense!" cries Cluny. "Where's the generosity? This is just a most unfortunate affair; but what would ye have me do—boxed up in this bee-skep of a cage of mine—but just set my friends to the cartes, when I can get them? And if they lose, of course, it's not to be supposed——" And here he came to a pause.

"Yes," said I, "if they lose, you give them back their money; and if they win, they carry away yours in their pouches! I have said before that I grant your generosity; but to me, sir, it's a very painful thing to be placed in this position."

There was a little silence, in which Cluny seemed always as if he was about to speak, but said nothing. All the time he grew redder and redder in the face.

"I am a young man," said I, "and I ask your advice. Advise me as you would your son. My friend fairly lost his money, after having fairly gained a far greater sum of yours; can I accept it back again? Would that be the right part for me to play? Whatever I do, you can see for yourself it must be hard upon a man of any pride."

"It's rather hard on me, too, Mr. Balfour," said Cluny, "and ye give me very much the look of a man that has entrapped poor people to their hurt. I wouldnae have my friends come to any house of mine to accept affronts; no," he cried, with a sudden heat of anger, "nor yet to give them!"

"And so you see, sir," said I, "there is something to be said upon my side; and this gambling is a very poor employ for gentlefolks. But I am still waiting your opinion."

I am sure if ever Cluny hated any man it was David Balfour. He looked me all over with a warlike eye, and I saw the challenge at his lips. But either my youth disarmed him, or perhaps his own sense of justice. Certainly it was a mortifying matter for all concerned, and not least Cluny; the more credit that he took it as he did.

"Mr. Balfour," said he, "I think you are too nice and covenanting, but for all that you have the spirit of a very pretty gentleman. Upon my honest word, ye may take this money—it's what I would tell my son—and here's my hand along with it!"

CHAPTER XXIV

THE FLIGHT IN THE HEATHER: THE QUARREL

Alan and I were put across Loch Errocht under cloud of night, and went down its eastern shore to another hiding-place near the head of Loch Rannoch, whither we were led by one of the gillies from the Cage. This fellow carried all our luggage and Alan's great-coat in the bargain, trotting along under the burthen, far less than the half of which used to weigh me to the ground, like a stout hill pony with a feather; yet he was a man that, in plain contest, I could have broken on my knee.

Doubtless it was a great relief to walk disencumbered; and perhaps without that relief, and the consequent sense of liberty and lightness, I could not have walked at all. I was but new risen from a bed of sickness; and there was nothing in the state of our affairs to hearten me for much exertion; travelling, as we did, over the most dismal deserts in Scotland, under a cloudy heaven, and with divided hearts among the travellers.

For long, we said nothing; marching alongside or one behind the other, each with a set countenance: I, angry and proud, and drawing what strength I had from these two violent and sinful feelings; Alan angry and ashamed, ashamed that he had lost my money, angry that I should take it so ill.

The thought of a separation ran always the stronger in my mind; and the more I approved of it, the more ashamed I grew of my approval. It would be a fine, handsome, generous thing, indeed, for Alan to turn round and say to me: "Go, I am in the most danger, and my company only increases yours." But for me to turn to the friend who certainly loved me, and say to him: "You are in great danger, I am in but little; your friendship is a burden; go, take your risks and bear your hardships alone——" no, that was impossible; and even to think of it privily to myself, made my cheeks to burn.

And yet Alan had behaved like a child, and (what is worse) a treacherous child. Wheedling my money from me while I lay half-conscious was scarce better than theft; and yet here he was trudging by my side, without a penny to his name, and by what I could see, quite blithe to sponge upon the money he had driven me to beg. True, I was ready to share it with him; but it made me rage to see him count upon my readiness.

These were the two things uppermost in my mind; and I could open my mouth upon neither without black ungenerosity. So I did the next worst, and said nothing, nor so much as looked once at my companion, save with the tail of my eye.

At last, upon the other side of Loch Errocht, going over a smooth, rushy place, where the walking was easy, he could bear it no longer, and came close to me.

"David," says he, "this is no way for two friends to take a small accident. I have to say that I'm sorry; and so that's said. And now if you have anything, ye'd better say it."

"O," says I, "I have nothing."

He seemed disconcerted; at which I was meanly pleased.

"No," said he, with rather a trembling voice, "but when I say I was to blame?"

"Why, of course, ye were to blame," said I, coolly; "and you will bear me out that I have never reproached you."

"Never," says he; "but ye ken very well that ye've done worse. Are we to part? Ye said so once before. Are ye to say it again? There's hills and heather enough between here and the two seas, David; and I will own I'm no very keen to stay where I'm no wanted."

This pierced me like a sword, and seemed to lay bare my private disloyalty.

"Alan Breck!" I cried; and then: "Do you think I am one to turn my back on you in your chief need? You dursn't say it to my face. My whole conduct's there to give the lie to it. It's true, I fell asleep upon the muir; but that was from weariness, and you do wrong to cast it up to me———"

"Which is what I never did," said Alan.

"But aside from that," I continued, "what have I done that you should even me to dogs by such a supposition? I never yet failed a friend, and it's not likely I'll begin with you. There are things between us that I can never forget, even if you can."

"I will only say this to ye, David," said Alan, very quietly, "that I have long been owing ye my life, and now I owe ye money. Ye should try to make that burden light for me."

This ought to have touched me, and in a manner it did, but the wrong manner. I felt I was behaving badly; and was now not only angry with Alan, but angry with myself in the bargain; and it made me the more cruel.

"You asked me to speak," said I. "Well, then, I will. You own yourself that you have done me a disservice; I have had to swallow an affront: I have never reproached you, I never named the thing till you did. And now you blame me," cried I, "because I cannae laugh and sing as if I was glad to be affronted. The next thing will be that I'm to go down upon my knees and thank you for it! Ye should think more of others, Alan Breck. If ye thought more of others, ye would perhaps speak less about yourself; and when a friend that likes you very well has passed over an offence without a word, you would be blithe to let it lie, instead of making it a stick to break his back with. By your own way of it, it was you that was to blame; then it shouldnae be you to seek the quarrel."

"Aweel," said Alan, "say nae mair."

And we fell back into our former silence; and came to our journey's end, and supped, and lay down to sleep, without another word.

The gillie put us across Loch Rannoch in the dusk of the next day, and gave us his opinion as to our best route. This was to get us up at once into the tops of the mountains: to go round by a circuit, turning the heads of Glen Lyon, Glen Lochay, and Glen Dochart, and come down upon the lowlands by Kippen and the upper waters of the Forth. Alan was little pleased with a route which led us through the country of his blood-foes, the Glenorchy Campbells. He objected that by turning to the east, we should come almost at once among the Athole Stewarts, a race of his own name and lineage, although following a different chief, and come besides by a far easier and swifter way to the place whither we were bound. But the gillie, who was indeed the chief man of Cluny's scouts, had good reasons to give him on all hands, naming the force of troops in every district, and alleging finally (as well as I could understand) that we should nowhere be so little troubled as in a country of the Campbells.

Alan gave way at last, but with only half a heart. "It's one of the dowiest countries in Scotland," said he. "There's naething there that I ken, but heath, and crows, and Campbells. But I see that ye're a man of some penetration; and be it as ye please!"

We set forth accordingly by this itinerary; and for the best part of three nights travelled on eerie mountains and among the well-heads of wild rivers; often buried in mist, almost continually blown and rained upon, and not once cheered by any glimpse of sunshine. By day, we lay and slept in the drenching heather; by night, incessantly clambered upon break-neck hills and among rude crags. We often wandered; we were often so involved in fog, that we must lie quiet till it lightened. A fire was never to be thought of. Our only food was drammach and a portion of cold meat that we had carried from the Cage; and as for drink, Heaven knows we had no want of water.

This was a dreadful time, rendered the more dreadful by the gloom of the weather and the country. I was never warm; my teeth chattered in my head; I was troubled with a very sore throat, such as I had on the isle; I had a painful stitch in my side, which never left me; and when I slept in my wet bed, with the rain beating above and the mud oozing below me, it was to live over again in fancy the worst part of my adventures—to see the tower of Shaws lit by lightning, Ransome carried below on the men's backs, Shuan dying on the round-house floor, or Colin Campbell grasping at the bosom of his coat. From such broken slumbers, I would be aroused in the gloaming, to sit up in the same puddle where I had slept, and sup cold drammach; the rain driving sharp in my face or running down my back in icy trickles; the mist enfolding us like as in a gloomy chamber—or, perhaps, if the wind blew, falling suddenly apart and showing us the gulf of some dark valley where the streams were crying aloud.

The sound of an infinite number of rivers came up from all round. In this steady rain the springs of the mountain were broken up; every glen gushed water like a cistern; every stream was in high spate, and had filled and overflowed its channel. During our night tramps, it was solemn to hear the voice of them below in the valleys, now booming like thunder, now with an angry cry. I could well understand the story of the Water Kelpie, that demon of the streams, who is fabled to keep wailing and roaring at the ford until the coming of the doomed traveller. Alan I saw believed it, or half believed it; and when the cry of the river rose more than usually sharp, I was little surprised (though, of course, I would still be shocked) to see him cross himself in the manner of the Catholics.

During all these horrid wanderings we had no familiarity, scarcely even that of speech. The truth is that I was sickening for my grave, which is my best excuse. But besides that I was of an unforgiving disposition from my birth, slow to take offence, slower to forget it, and now incensed both against my companion and myself. For the best part of two days he was unweariedly kind; silent, indeed, but always ready to help, and always hoping (as I could very well see) that my displeasure would blow by. For the same length of time I stayed in myself, nursing my anger, roughly refusing his services, and passing him over with my eyes as if he had been a bush or a stone.

The second night, or rather the peep of the third day, found us upon a very open hill, so that we could not follow our usual plan and lie down immediately to eat and sleep. Before we had reached a place of shelter, the grey had come pretty clear, for though it still rained, the clouds ran higher; and Alan, looking in my face, showed some marks of concern.

"Ye had better let me take your pack," said he, for perhaps the ninth time since we had parted from the scout beside Loch Rannoch.

"I do very well, I thank you," said I, as cold as ice.

Alan flushed darkly. "I'll not offer it again," he said. "I'm not a patient man, David."

"I never said you were," said I, which was exactly the rude, silly speech of a boy of ten.

Alan made no answer at the time, but his conduct answered for him. Henceforth, it is to be thought, he quite forgave himself for the affair at Cluny's; cocked his hat again, walked jauntily, whistled airs, and looked at me upon one side with a provoking smile.

The third night we were to pass through the western end of the country of Balquhidder. It came clear and cold, with a touch in the air like frost, and a northerly wind that blew the clouds away and made the stars bright. The streams were full, of course, and still made a great noise among the hills; but I observed that Alan thought no more upon the Kelpie, and was in high good spirits. As for me, the change of weather came too late; I had lain in the mire so long that (as the Bible has it) my very clothes "abhorred me." I was dead weary, deadly sick and full of pains and shiverings; the chill of the wind went through me, and the sound of it confused my ears. In this poor state I had to bear from my companion something in the nature of a persecution. He spoke a good deal, and never without a taunt. "Whig" was the best name he had to give me. "Here," he would say, "here's a dub for ye to jump, my Whiggie! I ken you're a fine jumper!" And so on; all the time with a gibing voice and face.

I knew it was my own doing, and no one else's; but I was too miserable to repent. I felt I could drag myself but little farther; pretty soon, I must lie down and die on these wet mountains like a sheep or a fox, and my bones must whiten there like the bones of a beast. My head was light perhaps; but I began to love the prospect, I began to glory in the thought of such a death, alone in the desert, with the wild eagles besieging my last moments. Alan would repent then, I thought; he would remember, when I was dead, how much he owed me, and the remembrance would be torture. So I went like a sick, silly, and bad-hearted schoolboy, feeding my anger against a fellow-man, when I would have been better on my knees, crying on God for mercy. And at each of Alan's taunts, I hugged myself. "Ah!" thinks I to myself, "I have a better taunt in readiness; when I lie down and die, you will feel it like a buffet in your face; ah, what a revenge! ah, how you will regret your ingratitude and cruelty!"

All the while, I was growing worse and worse. Once I had fallen, my leg simply doubling under me, and this had struck Alan for the moment; but I was afoot so briskly, and set off again with such a natural manner, that he soon forgot the incident. Flushes of heat went over me, and then spasms of shuddering. The stitch in my side was hardly bearable. At last I began to feel that I could trail myself no farther: and with that, there came on me all at once the wish to have it out with Alan, let my anger blaze, and be done with my life in a more sudden manner. He had just called me "Whig." I stopped.

"Mr. Stewart," said I, in a voice that quivered like a fiddle-string, "you are older than I am, and should know your manners. Do you think it either very wise or very witty to cast my politics in my teeth? I thought, where folk differed, it was the part of gentlemen to differ civilly; and if I did not, I may tell you I could find a better taunt than some of yours."

Alan had stopped opposite to me, his hat cocked, his hands in his breeches pockets, his head a little on one side. He listened, smiling evilly, as I could see by the starlight; and when I had done he began to whistle a Jacobite air. It was the air made in mockery of General Cope's defeat at Preston Pans:

"Hey, Johnnie Cope, are ye waukin' yet?

And are your drums a-beatin' yet?"

And it came in my mind that Alan, on the day of that battle, had been engaged upon the royal side.

"Why do ye take that air, Mr. Stewart?" said I. "Is that to remind me you have been beaten on both sides?"

The air stopped on Alan's lips. "David!" said he.

"But it's time these manners ceased," I continued; "and I mean you shall henceforth speak civilly of my King and my good friends the Campbells."

"I am a Stewart—" began Alan.

"O!" says I, "I ken ye bear a king's name. But you are to remember, since I have been in the Highlands, I have seen a good many of those that bear it; and the best I can say of them is this, that they would be none the worse of washing."

"Do you know that you insult me?" said Alan, very low.

"I am sorry for that," said I, "for I am not done; and if you distaste the sermon, I doubt the pirliecue* will please you as little. You have been chased in the field by the grown men of my party; it seems a poor kind of pleasure to out-face a boy. Both the Campbells and the Whigs have beaten you; you have run before them like a hare. It behoves you to speak of them as of your betters."

* A second sermon.

Alan stood quite still, the tails of his great-coat clapping behind him in the wind.

"This is a pity," he said at last. "There are things said that cannot be passed over."

"I never asked you to," said I. "I am as ready as yourself."

"Ready?" said he.

"Ready," I repeated. "I am no blower and boaster like some that I could name. Come on!" And drawing my sword, I fell on guard as Alan himself had taught me.

"David!" he cried. "Are ye daft? I cannae draw upon ye, David. It's fair murder."

"That was your look-out when you insulted me," said I.

"It's the truth!" cried Alan, and he stood for a moment, wringing his mouth in his hand like a man in sore perplexity. "It's the bare truth," he said, and drew his sword. But before I could touch his blade with mine, he had thrown it from him and fallen to the ground. "Na, na," he kept saying, "na, na—I cannae, I cannae."

At this the last of my anger oozed all out of me; and I found myself only sick, and sorry, and blank, and wondering at myself. I would have given the world to take back what I had said; but a word once spoken, who can recapture it? I minded me of all Alan's kindness and courage in the past, how he had helped and cheered and borne with me in our evil days; and then recalled my own insults, and saw that I had lost for ever that doughty friend. At the same time, the sickness that hung upon me seemed to redouble, and the pang in my side was like a sword for sharpness. I thought I must have swooned where I stood.

This it was that gave me a thought. No apology could blot out what I had said; it was needless to think of one, none could cover the offence; but where an apology was vain, a mere cry for help might bring Alan back to my side. I put my pride away from me. "Alan!" I said; "if ye cannae help me, I must just die here."

He started up sitting, and looked at me.

"It's true," said I. "I'm by with it. O, let me get into the bield of a house—I'll can die there easier." I had no need to pretend; whether I chose or not, I spoke in a weeping voice that would have melted a heart of stone.

"Can ye walk?" asked Alan.

"No," said I, "not without help. This last hour my legs have been fainting under me; I've a stitch in my side like a red-hot iron; I cannae breathe right. If I die, ye'll can forgive me, Alan? In my heart, I liked ye fine—even when I was the angriest."

"Wheesht, wheesht!" cried Alan. "Dinna say that! David man, ye ken—" He shut his mouth upon a sob. "Let me get my arm about ye," he continued; "that's the way! Now lean upon me hard. Gude kens where there's a house! We're in Balwhidder, too; there should be no want of houses, no, nor friends' houses here. Do ye gang easier so, Davie?"

"Ay," said I, "I can be doing this way;" and I pressed his arm with my hand.

Again he came near sobbing. "Davie," said he, "I'm no a right man at all; I have neither sense nor kindness; I could nae remember ye were just a bairn, I couldnae see ye were dying on your feet; Davie, ye'll have to try and forgive me."

"O man, let's say no more about it!" said I. "We're neither one of us to mend the other—that's the truth! We must just bear and forbear, man Alan. O, but my stitch is sore! Is there nae house?"

"I'll find a house to ye, David," he said, stoutly. "We'll follow down the burn, where there's bound to be houses. My poor man, will ye no be better on my back?"

"O, Alan," says I, "and me a good twelve inches taller?"

"Ye're no such a thing," cried Alan, with a start. "There may be a trifling matter of an inch or two; I'm no saying I'm just exactly what ye would call a tall man, whatever; and I dare say," he added, his voice tailing off in a laughable manner, "now when I come to think of it, I dare say ye'll be just about right. Ay, it'll be a foot, or near hand; or may be even mair!"

It was sweet and laughable to hear Alan eat his words up in the fear of some fresh quarrel. I could have laughed, had not my stitch caught me so hard; but if I had laughed, I think I must have wept too.

"Alan," cried I, "what makes ye so good to me? What makes ye care for such a thankless fellow?"

"'Deed, and I don't know" said Alan. "For just precisely what I thought I liked about ye, was that ye never quarrelled:—and now I like ye better!"

CHAPTER XXV

IN BALQUHIDDER

At the door of the first house we came to, Alan knocked, which was of no very safe enterprise in such a part of the Highlands as the Braes of Balquhidder. No great clan held rule there; it was filled and disputed by small septs, and broken remnants, and what they call "chiefless folk," driven into the wild country about the springs of Forth and Teith by the advance of the Campbells. Here were Stewarts and Maclarens, which came to the same thing, for the Maclarens followed Alan's chief in war, and made but one clan with Appin. Here, too, were many of that old, proscribed, nameless, red-handed clan of the Macgregors. They had always been ill-considered, and now worse than ever, having credit with no side or party in the whole country of Scotland. Their chief, Macgregor of Macgregor, was in exile; the more immediate leader of that part of them about Balquhidder, James More, Rob Roy's eldest son, lay waiting his trial in Edinburgh Castle; they were in ill-blood with Highlander and Lowlander, with the Grahames, the Maclarens, and the Stewarts; and Alan, who took up the quarrel of any friend, however distant, was extremely wishful to avoid them.

Chance served us very well; for it was a household of Maclarens that we found, where Alan was not only welcome for his name's sake but known by reputation. Here then I was got to bed without delay, and a doctor fetched, who found me in a sorry plight. But whether because he was a very good doctor, or I a very young, strong man, I lay bedridden for no more than a week, and before a month I was able to take the road again with a good heart.

All this time Alan would not leave me though I often pressed him, and indeed his foolhardiness in staying was a common subject of outcry with the two or three friends that were let into the secret. He hid by day in a hole of the braes under a little wood; and at night, when the coast was clear, would come into the house to visit me. I need not say if I was pleased to see him; Mrs. Maclaren, our hostess, thought nothing good enough for such a guest; and as Duncan Dhu (which was the name of our host) had a pair of pipes in his house, and was much of a lover of music, this time of my recovery was quite a festival, and we commonly turned night into day.

The soldiers let us be; although once a party of two companies and some dragoons went by in the bottom of the valley, where I could see them through the window as I lay in bed. What was much more astonishing, no magistrate came near me, and there was no question put of whence I came or whither I was going; and in that time of excitement, I was as free of all inquiry as though I had lain in a desert. Yet my presence was known before I left to all the people in Balquhidder and the adjacent parts; many coming about the house on visits and these (after the custom of the country) spreading the news among their neighbours. The bills, too, had now been printed. There was one pinned near the foot of my bed, where I could read my own not very flattering portrait and, in larger characters, the amount of the blood money that had been set upon my life. Duncan Dhu and the rest that knew that I had come there in Alan's company, could have entertained no doubt of who I was; and many others must have had their guess. For though I had changed my clothes, I could not change my age or person; and Lowland boys of eighteen were not so rife in these parts of the world, and above all about that time, that they could fail to put one thing with another, and connect me with the bill. So it was, at least. Other folk keep a secret among two or three near friends, and somehow it leaks out; but among these clansmen, it is told to a whole countryside, and they will keep it for a century.

There was but one thing happened worth narrating; and that is the visit I had of Robin Oig, one of the sons of the notorious Rob Roy. He was sought upon all sides on a charge of carrying a young woman from Balfron and marrying her (as was alleged) by force; yet he stepped about

Balquhidder like a gentleman in his own walled policy. It was he who had shot James Maclaren at the plough stilts, a quarrel never satisfied; yet he walked into the house of his blood enemies as a rider* might into a public inn.* Commercial traveller. </>

Duncan had time to pass me word of who it was; and we looked at one another in concern. You should understand, it was then close upon the time of Alan's coming; the two were little likely to agree; and yet if we sent word or sought to make a signal, it was sure to arouse suspicion in a man under so dark a cloud as the Macgregor.

He came in with a great show of civility, but like a man among inferiors; took off his bonnet to Mrs. Maclaren, but clapped it on his head again to speak to Duncan; and having thus set himself (as he would have thought) in a proper light, came to my bedside and bowed.

"I am given to know, sir," says he, "that your name is Balfour."

"They call me David Balfour," said I, "at your service."

"I would give ye my name in return, sir," he replied, "but it's one somewhat blown upon of late days; and it'll perhaps suffice if I tell ye that I am own brother to James More Drummond or Macgregor, of whom ye will scarce have failed to hear."

"No, sir," said I, a little alarmed; "nor yet of your father, Macgregor-Campbell." And I sat up and bowed in bed; for I thought best to compliment him, in case he was proud of having had an outlaw to his father.

He bowed in return. "But what I am come to say, sir," he went on, "is this. In the year '45, my brother raised a part of the 'Gregara' and marched six companies to strike a stroke for the good side; and the surgeon that marched with our clan and cured my brother's leg when it was broken in the brush at Preston Pans, was a gentleman of the same name precisely as yourself. He was brother to Balfour of Baith; and if you are in any reasonable degree of nearness one of that gentleman's kin, I have come to put myself and my people at your command."

You are to remember that I knew no more of my descent than any cadger's dog; my uncle, to be sure, had prated of some of our high connections, but nothing to the present purpose; and there was nothing left me but that bitter disgrace of owning that I could not tell.

Robin told me shortly he was sorry he had put himself about, turned his back upon me without a sign of salutation, and as he went towards the door, I could hear him telling Duncan that I was "only some kinless loon that didn't know his own father." Angry as I was at these words, and ashamed of my own ignorance, I could scarce keep from smiling that a man who was under the lash of the law (and was indeed hanged some three years later) should be so nice as to the descent of his acquaintances.

Just in the door, he met Alan coming in; and the two drew back and looked at each other like strange dogs. They were neither of them big men, but they seemed fairly to swell out with pride. Each wore a sword, and by a movement of his haunch, thrust clear the hilt of it, so that it might be the more readily grasped and the blade drawn.

"Mr. Stewart, I am thinking," says Robin.

"Troth, Mr. Macgregor, it's not a name to be ashamed of," answered Alan.

"I did not know ye were in my country, sir," says Robin.

"It sticks in my mind that I am in the country of my friends the Maclarens," says Alan.

"That's a kittle point," returned the other. "There may be two words to say to that. But I think I will have heard that you are a man of your sword?"

"Unless ye were born deaf, Mr. Macgregor, ye will have heard a good deal more than that," says Alan. "I am not the only man that can draw steel in Appin; and when my kinsman and captain, Ardshiel, had a talk with a gentleman of your name, not so many years back, I could never hear that the Macgregor had the best of it."

"Do ye mean my father, sir?" says Robin.

"Well, I wouldnae wonder," said Alan. "The gentleman I have in my mind had the ill-taste to clap Campbell to his name."

"My father was an old man," returned Robin.

"The match was unequal. You and me would make a better pair, sir."

"I was thinking that," said Alan.

I was half out of bed, and Duncan had been hanging at the elbow of these fighting cocks, ready to intervene upon the least occasion. But when that word was uttered, it was a case of now or never; and Duncan, with something of a white face to be sure, thrust himself between.

"Gentlemen," said he, "I will have been thinking of a very different matter, whateffer. Here are my pipes, and here are you two gentlemen who are baith acclaimed pipers. It's an auld dispute which one of ye's the best. Here will be a braw chance to settle it."

"Why, sir," said Alan, still addressing Robin, from whom indeed he had not so much as shifted his eyes, nor yet Robin from him, "why, sir," says Alan, "I think I will have heard some sough* of the sort. Have ye music, as folk say? Are ye a bit of a piper?"

   * Rumour.

"I can pipe like a Macrimmon!" cries Robin.

"And that is a very bold word," quoth Alan.

"I have made bolder words good before now," returned Robin, "and that against better adversaries."

"It is easy to try that," says Alan.

Duncan Dhu made haste to bring out the pair of pipes that was his principal possession, and to set before his guests a mutton-ham and a bottle of that drink which they call Athole brose, and which is made of old whiskey, strained honey and sweet cream, slowly beaten together in the right order and proportion. The two enemies were still on the very breach of a quarrel; but down they sat, one upon each side of the peat fire, with a mighty show of politeness. Maclaren pressed them to taste his mutton-ham and "the wife's brose," reminding them the wife was out of Athole and had a name far and wide for her skill in that confection. But Robin put aside these hospitalities as bad for the breath.

"I would have ye to remark, sir," said Alan, "that I havenae broken bread for near upon ten hours, which will be worse for the breath than any brose in Scotland."

"I will take no advantages, Mr. Stewart," replied Robin. "Eat and drink; I'll follow you."

Each ate a small portion of the ham and drank a glass of the brose to Mrs. Maclaren; and then after a great number of civilities, Robin took the pipes and played a little spring in a very ranting manner.

"Ay, ye can blow" said Alan; and taking the instrument from his rival, he first played the same spring in a manner identical with Robin's; and then wandered into variations, which, as he went on, he decorated with a perfect flight of grace-notes, such as pipers love, and call the "warblers."

I had been pleased with Robin's playing, Alan's ravished me.

"That's no very bad, Mr. Stewart," said the rival, "but ye show a poor device in your warblers."

"Me!" cried Alan, the blood starting to his face. "I give ye the lie."

"Do ye own yourself beaten at the pipes, then," said Robin, "that ye seek to change them for the sword?"

"And that's very well said, Mr. Macgregor," returned Alan; "and in the meantime" (laying a strong accent on the word) "I take back the lie. I appeal to Duncan."

"Indeed, ye need appeal to naebody," said Robin. "Ye're a far better judge than any Maclaren in Balquhidder: for it's a God's truth that you're a very creditable piper for a Stewart. Hand me the pipes." Alan did as he asked; and Robin proceeded to imitate and correct some part of Alan's variations, which it seemed that he remembered perfectly.

"Ay, ye have music," said Alan, gloomily.

"And now be the judge yourself, Mr. Stewart," said Robin; and taking up the variations from the beginning, he worked them throughout to so new a purpose, with such ingenuity and sentiment, and with so odd a fancy and so quick a knack in the grace-notes, that I was amazed to hear him.

As for Alan, his face grew dark and hot, and he sat and gnawed his fingers, like a man under some deep affront. "Enough!" he cried. "Ye can blow the pipes—make the most of that." And he made as if to rise.

But Robin only held out his hand as if to ask for silence, and struck into the slow measure of a pibroch. It was a fine piece of music in itself, and nobly played; but it seems, besides, it was a piece peculiar to the Appin Stewarts and a chief favourite with Alan. The first notes were scarce out, before there came a change in his face; when the time quickened, he seemed to grow restless in his seat; and long before that piece was at an end, the last signs of his anger died from him, and he had no thought but for the music.

"Robin Oig," he said, when it was done, "ye are a great piper. I am not fit to blow in the same kingdom with ye. Body of me! ye have mair music in your sporran than I have in my head! And though it still sticks in my mind that I could maybe show ye another of it with the cold steel, I warn ye beforehand—it'll no be fair! It would go against my heart to haggle a man that can blow the pipes as you can!"

Thereupon that quarrel was made up; all night long the brose was going and the pipes changing hands; and the day had come pretty bright, and the three men were none the better for what they had been taking, before Robin as much as thought upon the road.

CHAPTER XXVI
END OF THE FLIGHT: WE PASS THE FORTH

The month, as I have said, was not yet out, but it was already far through August, and beautiful warm weather, with every sign of an early and great harvest, when I was pronounced able for my journey. Our money was now run to so low an ebb that we must think first of all on speed; for if we came not soon to Mr. Rankeillor's, or if when we came there he should fail to help me, we must surely starve. In Alan's view, besides, the hunt must have now greatly slackened; and the line of the Forth and even Stirling Bridge, which is the main pass over that river, would be watched with little interest.

"It's a chief principle in military affairs," said he, "to go where ye are least expected. Forth is our trouble; ye ken the saying, 'Forth bridles the wild Hielandman.' Well, if we seek to creep round about the head of that river and come down by Kippen or Balfron, it's just precisely there that they'll be looking to lay hands on us. But if we stave on straight to the auld Brig of Stirling, I'll lay my sword they let us pass unchallenged."

The first night, accordingly, we pushed to the house of a Maclaren in Strathire, a friend of Duncan's, where we slept the twenty-first of the month, and whence we set forth again about the fall of night to make another easy stage. The twenty-second we lay in a heather bush on the hillside in Uam Var, within view of a herd of deer, the happiest ten hours of sleep in a fine, breathing sunshine and on bone-dry ground, that I have ever tasted. That night we struck Allan Water, and followed it down; and coming to the edge of the hills saw the whole Carse of Stirling underfoot, as flat as a pancake, with the town and castle on a hill in the midst of it, and the moon shining on the Links of Forth.

"Now," said Alan, "I kenna if ye care, but ye're in your own land again. We passed the Hieland Line in the first hour; and now if we could but pass yon crooked water, we might cast our bonnets in the air."

In Allan Water, near by where it falls into the Forth, we found a little sandy islet, overgrown with burdock, butterbur and the like low plants, that would just cover us if we lay flat. Here it was we made our camp, within plain view of Stirling Castle, whence we could hear the drums beat as some part of the garrison paraded. Shearers worked all day in a field on one side of the river, and we could hear the stones going on the hooks and the voices and even the words of the men talking. It behoved to lie close and keep silent. But the sand of the little isle was sun-warm, the green plants gave us shelter for our heads, we had food and drink in plenty; and to crown all, we were within sight of safety.

As soon as the shearers quit their work and the dusk began to fall, we waded ashore and struck for the Bridge of Stirling, keeping to the fields and under the field fences.

The bridge is close under the castle hill, an old, high, narrow bridge with pinnacles along the parapet; and you may conceive with how much interest I looked upon it, not only as a place famous in history, but as the very doors of salvation to Alan and myself. The moon was not yet up when we came there; a few lights shone along the front of the fortress, and lower down a few lighted windows in the town; but it was all mighty still, and there seemed to be no guard upon the passage.

I was for pushing straight across; but Alan was more wary.

"It looks unco' quiet," said he; "but for all that we'll lie down here cannily behind a dyke, and make sure."

So we lay for about a quarter of an hour, whiles whispering, whiles lying still and hearing nothing earthly but the washing of the water on the piers. At last there came by an old, hobbling woman with a crutch stick; who first stopped a little, close to where we lay, and bemoaned herself and the long way she had travelled; and then set forth again up the steep spring of the bridge. The woman was so little, and the night still so dark, that we soon lost sight of her; only heard the sound of her steps, and her stick, and a cough that she had by fits, draw slowly farther away.

"She's bound to be across now," I whispered.

"Na," said Alan, "her foot still sounds boss* upon the bridge."

   * Hollow.

And just then—"Who goes?" cried a voice, and we heard the butt of a musket rattle on the stones. I must suppose the sentry had been sleeping, so that had we tried, we might have passed unseen; but he was awake now, and the chance forfeited.

"This'll never do," said Alan. "This'll never, never do for us, David."

And without another word, he began to crawl away through the fields; and a little after, being well out of eye-shot, got to his feet again, and struck along a road that led to the eastward. I could not conceive what he was doing; and indeed I was so sharply cut by the disappointment, that I was little likely to be pleased with anything. A moment back and I had seen myself knocking at Mr. Rankeillor's door to claim my inheritance, like a hero in a ballad; and here was I back again, a wandering, hunted blackguard, on the wrong side of Forth.

"Well?" said I.

"Well," said Alan, "what would ye have? They're none such fools as I took them for. We have still the Forth to pass, Davie—weary fall the rains that fed and the hillsides that guided it!"

"And why go east?" said I.

"Ou, just upon the chance!" said he. "If we cannae pass the river, we'll have to see what we can do for the firth."

"There are fords upon the river, and none upon the firth," said I.

"To be sure there are fords, and a bridge forbye," quoth Alan; "and of what service, when they are watched?"

"Well," said I, "but a river can be swum."

"By them that have the skill of it," returned he; "but I have yet to hear that either you or me is much of a hand at that exercise; and for my own part, I swim like a stone."

"I'm not up to you in talking back, Alan," I said; "but I can see we're making bad worse. If it's hard to pass a river, it stands to reason it must be worse to pass a sea."

"But there's such a thing as a boat," says Alan, "or I'm the more deceived."

"Ay, and such a thing as money," says I. "But for us that have neither one nor other, they might just as well not have been invented."

"Ye think so?" said Alan.

"I do that," said I.

"David," says he, "ye're a man of small invention and less faith. But let me set my wits upon the hone, and if I cannae beg, borrow, nor yet steal a boat, I'll make one!"

"I think I see ye!" said I. "And what's more than all that: if ye pass a bridge, it can tell no tales; but if we pass the firth, there's the boat on the wrong side—somebody must have brought it—the country-side will all be in a bizz——"

"Man!" cried Alan, "if I make a boat, I'll make a body to take it back again! So deave me with no more of your nonsense, but walk (for that's what you've got to do)—and let Alan think for ye."

All night, then, we walked through the north side of the Carse under the high line of the Ochil mountains; and by Alloa and Clackmannan and Culross, all of which we avoided: and about ten in the morning, mighty hungry and tired, came to the little clachan of Limekilns. This is a place that sits near in by the water-side, and looks across the Hope to the town of the Queensferry. Smoke went up from both of these, and from other villages and farms upon all hands. The fields were being reaped; two ships lay anchored, and boats were coming and going on the Hope. It was altogether a right pleasant sight to me; and I could not take my fill of gazing at these comfortable, green, cultivated hills and the busy people both of the field and sea.

For all that, there was Mr. Rankeillor's house on the south shore, where I had no doubt wealth awaited me; and here was I upon the north, clad in poor enough attire of an outlandish fashion, with three silver shillings left to me of all my fortune, a price set upon my head, and an outlawed man for my sole company.

"O, Alan!" said I, "to think of it! Over there, there's all that heart could want waiting me; and the birds go over, and the boats go over—all that please can go, but just me only! O, man, but it's a heart-break!"

In Limekilns we entered a small change-house, which we only knew to be a public by the wand over the door, and bought some bread and cheese from a good-looking lass that was the servant. This we carried with us in a bundle, meaning to sit and eat it in a bush of wood on the sea-shore, that we saw some third part of a mile in front. As we went, I kept looking across the water and sighing to myself; and though I took no heed of it, Alan had fallen into a muse. At last he stopped in the way.

"Did ye take heed of the lass we bought this of?" says he, tapping on the bread and cheese.

"To be sure," said I, "and a bonny lass she was."

"Ye thought that?" cries he. "Man, David, that's good news."

"In the name of all that's wonderful, why so?" says I. "What good can that do?"

"Well," said Alan, with one of his droll looks, "I was rather in hopes it would maybe get us that boat."

"If it were the other way about, it would be liker it," said I.

"That's all that you ken, ye see," said Alan. "I don't want the lass to fall in love with ye, I want her to be sorry for ye, David; to which end there is no manner of need that she should take you for a beauty. Let me see" (looking me curiously over). "I wish ye were a wee thing paler; but apart from that ye'll do fine for my purpose—ye have a fine, hang-dog, rag-and-tatter, clappermaclaw kind of a look to ye, as if ye had stolen the coat from a potato-bogle. Come; right about, and back to the change-house for that boat of ours."

I followed him, laughing.

"David Balfour," said he, "ye're a very funny gentleman by your way of it, and this is a very funny employ for ye, no doubt. For all that, if ye have any affection for my neck (to say nothing of your own) ye will perhaps be kind enough to take this matter responsibly. I am going to do a bit of play-acting, the bottom ground of which is just exactly as serious as the gallows for the pair of us. So bear it, if ye please, in mind, and conduct yourself according."

"Well, well," said I, "have it as you will."

As we got near the clachan, he made me take his arm and hang upon it like one almost helpless with weariness; and by the time he pushed open the change-house door, he seemed to be half carrying me. The maid appeared surprised (as well she might be) at our speedy return; but Alan had no words to spare for her in explanation, helped me to a chair, called for a tass of brandy with which he fed me in little sips, and then breaking up the bread and cheese helped me to eat it like a nursery-lass; the whole with that grave, concerned, affectionate countenance, that might have imposed upon a judge. It was small wonder if the maid were taken with the picture we presented, of a poor, sick, overwrought lad and his most tender comrade. She drew quite near, and stood leaning with her back on the next table.

"What's like wrong with him?" said she at last.

Alan turned upon her, to my great wonder, with a kind of fury. "Wrong?" cries he. "He's walked more hundreds of miles than he has hairs upon his chin, and slept oftener in wet heather than dry sheets. Wrong, quo' she! Wrong enough, I would think! Wrong, indeed!" and he kept grumbling to himself as he fed me, like a man ill-pleased.

"He's young for the like of that," said the maid.

"Ower young," said Alan, with his back to her.

"He would be better riding," says she.

"And where could I get a horse to him?" cried Alan, turning on her with the same appearance of fury. "Would ye have me steal?"

I thought this roughness would have sent her off in dudgeon, as indeed it closed her mouth for the time. But my companion knew very well what he was doing; and for as simple as he was in some things of life, had a great fund of roguishness in such affairs as these.

"Ye neednae tell me," she said at last—"ye're gentry."

"Well," said Alan, softened a little (I believe against his will) by this artless comment, "and suppose we were? Did ever you hear that gentrice put money in folk's pockets?"

She sighed at this, as if she were herself some disinherited great lady. "No," says she, "that's true indeed."

I was all this while chafing at the part I played, and sitting tongue-tied between shame and merriment; but somehow at this I could hold in no longer, and bade Alan let me be, for I was better already. My voice stuck in my throat, for I ever hated to take part in lies; but my very embarrassment helped on the plot, for the lass no doubt set down my husky voice to sickness and fatigue.

"Has he nae friends?" said she, in a tearful voice.

"That has he so!" cried Alan, "if we could but win to them!—friends and rich friends, beds to lie in, food to eat, doctors to see to him—and here he must tramp in the dubs and sleep in the heather like a beggarman."

"And why that?" says the lass.

"My dear," said Alan, "I cannae very safely say; but I'll tell ye what I'll do instead," says he, "I'll whistle ye a bit tune." And with that he leaned pretty far over the table, and in a mere breath of a whistle, but with a wonderful pretty sentiment, gave her a few bars of "Charlie is my darling."

"Wheesht," says she, and looked over her shoulder to the door.

"That's it," said Alan.

"And him so young!" cries the lass.

"He's old enough to——" and Alan struck his forefinger on the back part of his neck, meaning that I was old enough to lose my head.

"It would be a black shame," she cried, flushing high.

"It's what will be, though," said Alan, "unless we manage the better."

At this the lass turned and ran out of that part of the house, leaving us alone together. Alan in high good humour at the furthering of his schemes, and I in bitter dudgeon at being called a Jacobite and treated like a child.

"Alan," I cried, "I can stand no more of this."

"Ye'll have to sit it then, Davie," said he. "For if ye upset the pot now, ye may scrape your own life out of the fire, but Alan Breck is a dead man."

This was so true that I could only groan; and even my groan served Alan's purpose, for it was overheard by the lass as she came flying in again with a dish of white puddings and a bottle of strong ale.

"Poor lamb!" says she, and had no sooner set the meat before us, than she touched me on the shoulder with a little friendly touch, as much as to bid me cheer up. Then she told us to fall to, and there would be no more to pay; for the inn was her own, or at least her father's, and he was gone for the day to Pittencrieff. We waited for no second bidding, for bread and cheese is but cold comfort and the puddings smelt excellently well; and while we sat and ate, she took up that same place by the next table, looking on, and thinking, and frowning to herself, and drawing the string of her apron through her hand.

"I'm thinking ye have rather a long tongue," she said at last to Alan.

"Ay" said Alan; "but ye see I ken the folk I speak to."

"I would never betray ye," said she, "if ye mean that."

"No," said he, "ye're not that kind. But I'll tell ye what ye would do, ye would help."

"I couldnae," said she, shaking her head. "Na, I couldnae."

"No," said he, "but if ye could?"

She answered him nothing.

"Look here, my lass," said Alan, "there are boats in the Kingdom of Fife, for I saw two (no less) upon the beach, as I came in by your town's end. Now if we could have the use of a boat to pass under cloud of night into Lothian, and some secret, decent kind of a man to bring that boat back again and keep his counsel, there would be two souls saved—mine to all likelihood—his to a dead surety. If we lack that boat, we have but three shillings left in this wide world; and where to go, and how to do, and what other place there is for us except the chains of a gibbet—I give you my naked word, I kenna! Shall we go wanting, lassie? Are ye to lie in your warm bed and think upon us, when the wind gowls in the chimney and the rain tirls on the roof? Are ye to eat your meat by the cheeks of a red fire, and think upon this poor sick lad of mine, biting his finger ends on a blae muir for cauld and hunger? Sick or sound, he must aye be moving; with the death grapple at his throat he must aye be trailing in the rain on the lang roads; and when he gants his last on a rickle of cauld stanes, there will be nae friends near him but only me and God."

At this appeal, I could see the lass was in great trouble of mind, being tempted to help us, and yet in some fear she might be helping malefactors; and so now I determined to step in myself and to allay her scruples with a portion of the truth.

"Did ever you hear," said I, "of Mr. Rankeillor of the Ferry?"

"Rankeillor the writer?" said she. "I daur say that!"

"Well," said I, "it's to his door that I am bound, so you may judge by that if I am an ill-doer; and I will tell you more, that though I am indeed, by a dreadful error, in some peril of my life, King George has no truer friend in all Scotland than myself."

Her face cleared up mightily at this, although Alan's darkened.

"That's more than I would ask," said she. "Mr. Rankeillor is a kennt man." And she bade us finish our meat, get clear of the clachan as soon as might be, and lie close in the bit wood on the sea-beach. "And ye can trust me," says she, "I'll find some means to put you over."

At this we waited for no more, but shook hands with her upon the bargain, made short work of the puddings, and set forth again from Limekilns as far as to the wood. It was a small piece of perhaps a score of elders and hawthorns and a few young ashes, not thick enough to veil us from passersby upon the road or beach. Here we must lie, however, making the best of the brave warm weather and the good hopes we now had of a deliverance, and planing more particularly what remained for us to do.

We had but one trouble all day; when a strolling piper came and sat in the same wood with us; a red-nosed, bleareyed, drunken dog, with a great bottle of whisky in his pocket, and a long story of wrongs that had been done him by all sorts of persons, from the Lord President of the Court of Session, who had denied him justice, down to the Bailies of Inverkeithing who had given him more of it than he desired. It was impossible but he should conceive some suspicion of two men lying all day concealed in a thicket and having no business to allege. As long as he stayed there he kept us in hot water with prying questions; and after he was gone, as he was a man not very likely to hold his tongue, we were in the greater impatience to be gone ourselves.

The day came to an end with the same brightness; the night fell quiet and clear; lights came out in houses and hamlets and then, one after another, began to be put out; but it was past eleven, and we were long since strangely tortured with anxieties, before we heard the grinding of oars upon the rowing-pins. At that, we looked out and saw the lass herself coming rowing to us in a boat. She had trusted no one with our affairs, not even her sweetheart, if she had one; but as soon as her father was asleep, had left the house by a window, stolen a neighbour's boat, and come to our assistance single-handed.

I was abashed how to find expression for my thanks; but she was no less abashed at the thought of hearing them; begged us to lose no time and to hold our peace, saying (very properly) that the heart of our matter was in haste and silence; and so, what with one thing and another, she had set us on the Lothian shore not far from Carriden, had shaken hands with us, and was out again at sea and rowing for Limekilns, before there was one word said either of her service or our gratitude.

Even after she was gone, we had nothing to say, as indeed nothing was enough for such a kindness. Only Alan stood a great while upon the shore shaking his head.

"It is a very fine lass," he said at last. "David, it is a very fine lass." And a matter of an hour later, as we were lying in a den on the sea-shore and I had been already dozing, he broke out again in commendations of her character. For my part, I could say nothing, she was so simple a creature that my heart smote me both with remorse and fear: remorse because we had traded upon her ignorance; and fear lest we should have anyway involved her in the dangers of our situation.

CHAPTER XXVII
I COME TO MR. RANKEILLOR

The next day it was agreed that Alan should fend for himself till sunset; but as soon as it began to grow dark, he should lie in the fields by the roadside near to Newhalls, and stir for naught until he heard me whistling. At first I proposed I should give him for a signal the "Bonnie House of Airlie," which was a favourite of mine; but he objected that as the piece was very commonly known, any ploughman might whistle it by accident; and taught me instead a little fragment of a Highland air, which has run in my head from that day to this, and will likely run in my head when I lie dying. Every time it comes to me, it takes me off to that last day of my uncertainty, with Alan sitting up in the bottom of the den, whistling and beating the measure with a finger, and the grey of the dawn coming on his face.

I was in the long street of Queensferry before the sun was up. It was a fairly built burgh, the houses of good stone, many slated; the town-hall not so fine, I thought, as that of Peebles, nor yet the street so noble; but take it altogether, it put me to shame for my foul tatters.

As the morning went on, and the fires began to be kindled, and the windows to open, and the people to appear out of the houses, my concern and despondency grew ever the blacker. I saw now that I had no grounds to stand upon; and no clear proof of my rights, nor so much as of my own identity. If it was all a bubble, I was indeed sorely cheated and left in a sore pass. Even if things were as I conceived, it would in all likelihood take time to establish my contentions; and what time had I to spare with less than three shillings in my pocket, and a condemned, hunted man upon my hands to ship out of the country? Truly, if my hope broke with me, it might come to the gallows yet for both of us. And as I continued to walk up and down, and saw people looking askance at me upon the street or out of windows, and nudging or speaking one to another with smiles, I began to take a fresh apprehension: that it might be no easy matter even to come to speech of the lawyer, far less to convince him of my story.

For the life of me I could not muster up the courage to address any of these reputable burghers; I thought shame even to speak with them in such a pickle of rags and dirt; and if I had asked for the house of such a man as Mr. Rankeillor, I suppose they would have burst out laughing in my face. So I went up and down, and through the street, and down to the harbour-side, like a dog that has lost its master, with a strange gnawing in my inwards, and every now and then a movement of despair. It grew to be high day at last, perhaps nine in the forenoon; and I was worn with these wanderings, and chanced to have stopped in front of a very good house on the landward side, a house with beautiful, clear glass windows, flowering knots upon the sills, the walls new-harled* and a chase-dog sitting yawning on the step like one that was at home. Well, I was even envying this dumb brute, when the door fell open and there issued forth a shrewd, ruddy, kindly, consequential man in a well-powdered wig and spectacles. I was in such a plight that no one set eyes on me once, but he looked at me again; and this gentleman, as it proved, was so much struck with my poor appearance that he came straight up to me and asked me what I did.

* Newly rough-cast.

I told him I was come to the Queensferry on business, and taking heart of grace, asked him to direct me to the house of Mr. Rankeillor.

"Why," said he, "that is his house that I have just come out of; and for a rather singular chance, I am that very man."

"Then, sir," said I, "I have to beg the favour of an interview."

"I do not know your name," said he, "nor yet your face."

"My name is David Balfour," said I.

"David Balfour?" he repeated, in rather a high tone, like one surprised. "And where have you come from, Mr. David Balfour?" he asked, looking me pretty drily in the face.

"I have come from a great many strange places, sir," said I; "but I think it would be as well to tell you where and how in a more private manner."

He seemed to muse awhile, holding his lip in his hand, and looking now at me and now upon the causeway of the street.

"Yes," says he, "that will be the best, no doubt." And he led me back with him into his house, cried out to some one whom I could not see that he would be engaged all morning, and brought me into a little dusty chamber full of books and documents. Here he sate down, and bade me be seated; though I thought he looked a little ruefully from his clean chair to my muddy rags. "And now," says he, "if you have any business, pray be brief and come swiftly to the point. Nec gemino bellum Trojanum oritur ab ovo—do you understand that?" says he, with a keen look.

"I will even do as Horace says, sir," I answered, smiling, "and carry you in medias res." He nodded as if he was well pleased, and indeed his scrap of Latin had been set to test me. For all that, and though I was somewhat encouraged, the blood came in my face when I added: "I have reason to believe myself some rights on the estate of Shaws."

He got a paper book out of a drawer and set it before him open. "Well?" said he.

But I had shot my bolt and sat speechless.

"Come, come, Mr. Balfour," said he, "you must continue. Where were you born?"

"In Essendean, sir," said I, "the year 1733, the 12th of March."

He seemed to follow this statement in his paper book; but what that meant I knew not. "Your father and mother?" said he.

"My father was Alexander Balfour, schoolmaster of that place," said I, "and my mother Grace Pitarrow; I think her people were from Angus."

"Have you any papers proving your identity?" asked Mr. Rankeillor.

"No, sir," said I, "but they are in the hands of Mr. Campbell, the minister, and could be readily produced. Mr. Campbell, too, would give me his word; and for that matter, I do not think my uncle would deny me."

"Meaning Mr. Ebenezer Balfour?" says he.

"The same," said I.

"Whom you have seen?" he asked.

"By whom I was received into his own house," I answered.

"Did you ever meet a man of the name of Hoseason?" asked Mr. Rankeillor.

"I did so, sir, for my sins," said I; "for it was by his means and the procurement of my uncle, that I was kidnapped within sight of this town, carried to sea, suffered shipwreck and a hundred other hardships, and stand before you to-day in this poor accoutrement."

"You say you were shipwrecked," said Rankeillor; "where was that?"

"Off the south end of the Isle of Mull," said I. "The name of the isle on which I was cast up is the Island Earraid."

"Ah!" says he, smiling, "you are deeper than me in the geography. But so far, I may tell you, this agrees pretty exactly with other informations that I hold. But you say you were kidnapped; in what sense?"

"In the plain meaning of the word, sir," said I. "I was on my way to your house, when I was trepanned on board the brig, cruelly struck down, thrown below, and knew no more of anything till we were far at sea. I was destined for the plantations; a fate that, in God's providence, I have escaped."

"The brig was lost on June the 27th," says he, looking in his book, "and we are now at August the 24th. Here is a considerable hiatus, Mr. Balfour, of near upon two months. It has already caused a vast amount of trouble to your friends; and I own I shall not be very well contented until it is set right."

"Indeed, sir," said I, "these months are very easily filled up; but yet before I told my story, I would be glad to know that I was talking to a friend."

"This is to argue in a circle," said the lawyer. "I cannot be convinced till I have heard you. I cannot be your friend till I am properly informed. If you were more trustful, it would better befit your time of life. And you know, Mr. Balfour, we have a proverb in the country that evil-doers are aye evil-dreaders."

"You are not to forget, sir," said I, "that I have already suffered by my trustfulness; and was shipped off to be a slave by the very man that (if I rightly understand) is your employer?"

All this while I had been gaining ground with Mr. Rankeillor, and in proportion as I gained ground, gaining confidence. But at this sally, which I made with something of a smile myself, he fairly laughed aloud.

"No, no," said he, "it is not so bad as that. Fui, non sum. I was indeed your uncle's man of business; but while you (imberbis juvenis custode remoto) were gallivanting in the west, a good deal of water has run under the bridges; and if your ears did not sing, it was not for lack of being talked about. On the very day of your sea disaster, Mr. Campbell stalked into my office, demanding you from all the winds. I had never heard of your existence; but I had known your father; and from matters in my competence (to be touched upon hereafter) I was disposed to fear the worst. Mr. Ebenezer admitted having seen you; declared (what seemed improbable) that he had given you considerable sums; and that you had started for the continent of Europe, intending to fulfil your education, which was probable and praiseworthy. Interrogated how you had come to send no word to Mr. Campbell, he deponed that you had expressed a great desire to break with your past life. Further interrogated where you now were, protested ignorance, but believed you were in Leyden. That is a close sum of his replies. I am not exactly sure that any one believed him," continued Mr. Rankeillor with a smile; "and in particular he so much disrelished me expressions of mine that (in a word) he showed me to the door. We were then at a full stand; for whatever shrewd suspicions we might entertain, we had no shadow of probation. In the very article, comes Captain Hoseason with the story of your drowning; whereupon all fell through; with no consequences but concern to Mr. Campbell, injury to my pocket, and another blot upon your uncle's character, which could very ill afford it. And now, Mr. Balfour," said he, "you understand the whole process of these matters, and can judge for yourself to what extent I may be trusted."

Indeed he was more pedantic than I can represent him, and placed more scraps of Latin in his speech; but it was all uttered with a fine geniality of eye and manner which went far to conquer my distrust. Moreover, I could see he now treated me as if I was myself beyond a doubt; so that first point of my identity seemed fully granted.

"Sir," said I, "if I tell you my story, I must commit a friend's life to your discretion. Pass me your word it shall be sacred; and for what touches myself, I will ask no better guarantee than just your face."

He passed me his word very seriously. "But," said he, "these are rather alarming prolocutions; and if there are in your story any little jostles to the law, I would beg you to bear in mind that I am a lawyer, and pass lightly."

Thereupon I told him my story from the first, he listening with his spectacles thrust up and his eyes closed, so that I sometimes feared he was asleep. But no such matter! he heard every word (as I found afterward) with such quickness of hearing and precision of memory as often surprised me. Even strange outlandish Gaelic names, heard for that time only, he remembered and would remind me of, years after. Yet when I called Alan Breck in full, we had an odd scene. The name of Alan had of course rung through Scotland, with the news of the Appin murder and the offer of the reward; and it had no sooner escaped me than the lawyer moved in his seat and opened his eyes.

"I would name no unnecessary names, Mr. Balfour," said he; "above all of Highlanders, many of whom are obnoxious to the law."

"Well, it might have been better not," said I, "but since I have let it slip, I may as well continue."

"Not at all," said Mr. Rankeillor. "I am somewhat dull of hearing, as you may have remarked; and I am far from sure I caught the name exactly. We will call your friend, if you please, Mr. Thomson—that there may be no reflections. And in future, I would take some such way with any Highlander that you may have to mention—dead or alive."

By this, I saw he must have heard the name all too clearly, and had already guessed I might be coming to the murder. If he chose to play this part of ignorance, it was no matter of mine; so I smiled, said it was no very Highland-sounding name, and consented. Through all the rest of my story Alan was Mr. Thomson; which amused me the more, as it was a piece of policy after his own heart. James Stewart, in like manner, was mentioned under the style of Mr. Thomson's kinsman; Colin Campbell passed as a Mr. Glen; and to Cluny, when I came to that part of my tale, I gave the name of "Mr. Jameson, a Highland chief." It was truly the most open farce, and I wondered that the lawyer should care to keep it up; but, after all, it was quite in the taste of that age, when there were two parties in the state, and quiet persons, with no very high opinions of their own, sought out every cranny to avoid offence to either.

"Well, well," said the lawyer, when I had quite done, "this is a great epic, a great Odyssey of yours. You must tell it, sir, in a sound Latinity when your scholarship is riper; or in English if you please, though for my part I prefer the stronger tongue. You have rolled much; quae regio in terris—what parish in Scotland (to make a homely translation) has not been filled with your wanderings? You have shown, besides, a singular aptitude for getting into false positions; and, yes, upon the whole, for behaving well in them. This Mr. Thomson seems to me a gentleman of some choice qualities, though perhaps a trifle bloody-minded. It would please me none the worse, if (with all his merits) he were soused in the North Sea, for the man, Mr. David, is a sore embarrassment. But you are doubtless quite right to adhere to him; indubitably, he adhered to you. It comes—we may say—he was your true companion; nor less paribus curis vestigia figit, for I dare say you would both take an orra thought upon the gallows. Well, well, these days are fortunately by; and I think (speaking humanly) that you are near the end of your troubles."

As he thus moralised on my adventures, he looked upon me with so much humour and benignity that I could scarce contain my satisfaction. I had been so long wandering with lawless people, and making my bed upon the hills and under the bare sky, that to sit once more in a clean, covered house, and to talk amicably with a gentleman in broadcloth, seemed mighty elevations. Even as I thought so, my eye fell on my unseemly tatters, and I was once more plunged in confusion. But the lawyer saw and understood me. He rose, called over the stair to lay another plate, for Mr. Balfour would stay to dinner, and led me into a bedroom in the upper part of the house. Here he set before me water and soap, and a comb; and laid out some clothes that belonged to his son; and here, with another apposite tag, he left me to my toilet.

CHAPTER XXVIII
I GO IN QUEST OF MY INHERITANCE

Hmade what change I could in my appearance; and blithe was I to look in the glass and find the beggarman a thing of the past, and David Balfour come to life again. And yet I was ashamed of the change too, and, above all, of the borrowed clothes. When I had done, Mr. Rankeillor caught me on the stair, made me his compliments, and had me again into the cabinet.

"Sit ye down, Mr. David," said he, "and now that you are looking a little more like yourself, let me see if I can find you any news. You will be wondering, no doubt, about your father and your uncle? To be sure it is a singular tale; and the explanation is one that I blush to have to offer you. For," says he, really with embarrassment, "the matter hinges on a love affair."

"Truly," said I, "I cannot very well join that notion with my uncle."

"But your uncle, Mr. David, was not always old," replied the lawyer, "and what may perhaps surprise you more, not always ugly. He had a fine, gallant air; people stood in their doors to look after him, as he went by upon a mettle horse. I have seen it with these eyes, and I ingenuously confess, not altogether without envy; for I was a plain lad myself and a plain man's son; and in those days it was a case of Odi te, qui bellus es, Sabelle."

"It sounds like a dream," said I.

"Ay, ay," said the lawyer, "that is how it is with youth and age. Nor was that all, but he had a spirit of his own that seemed to promise great things in the future. In 1715, what must he do but run away to join the rebels? It was your father that pursued him, found him in a ditch, and brought him back multum gementem; to the mirth of the whole country. However, majora canamus—the two lads fell in love, and that with the same lady. Mr. Ebenezer, who was the admired and the beloved, and the spoiled one, made, no doubt, mighty certain of the victory; and when he found he had deceived himself, screamed like a peacock. The whole country heard of it; now he lay sick at home, with his silly family standing round the bed in tears; now he rode from public-house to public-house, and shouted his sorrows into the lug of Tom, Dick, and Harry. Your father, Mr. David, was a kind gentleman; but he was weak, dolefully weak; took all this folly with a long countenance; and one day—by your leave!—resigned the lady. She was no such fool, however; it's from her you must inherit your excellent good sense; and she refused to be bandied from one to another. Both got upon their knees to her; and the upshot of the matter for that while was that she showed both of them the door. That was in August; dear me! the same year I came from college. The scene must have been highly farcical."

I thought myself it was a silly business, but I could not forget my father had a hand in it. "Surely, sir, it had some note of tragedy," said I.

"Why, no, sir, not at all," returned the lawyer. "For tragedy implies some ponderable matter in dispute, some dignus vindice nodus; and this piece of work was all about the petulance of a young ass that had been spoiled, and wanted nothing so much as to be tied up and soundly belted. However, that was not your father's view; and the end of it was, that from concession to concession on your father's part, and from one height to another of squalling, sentimental selfishness upon your uncle's, they came at last to drive a sort of bargain, from whose ill results you have recently been smarting. The one man took the lady, the other the estate. Now, Mr. David, they talk a great deal of charity and generosity; but in this disputable state of life, I often think the happiest consequences seem to flow when a gentleman consults his lawyer, and takes all the law allows him. Anyhow, this piece of Quixotry on your father's part, as it was unjust in itself, has brought forth a monstrous family of injustices. Your father and mother lived and died poor folk; you were poorly reared; and in the meanwhile, what a time it has been for the tenants on the estate of Shaws! And I might add (if it was a matter I cared much about) what a time for Mr. Ebenezer!"

"And yet that is certainly the strangest part of all," said I, "that a man's nature should thus change."

"True," said Mr. Rankeillor. "And yet I imagine it was natural enough. He could not think that he had played a handsome part. Those who knew the story gave him the cold shoulder; those who knew it not, seeing one brother disappear, and the other succeed in the estate, raised a cry of murder; so that upon all sides he found himself evited. Money was all he got by his bargain; well, he came to think the more of money. He was selfish when he was young, he is selfish now that he is old; and the latter end of all these pretty manners and fine feelings you have seen for yourself."

"Well, sir," said I, "and in all this, what is my position?"

"The estate is yours beyond a doubt," replied the lawyer. "It matters nothing what your father signed, you are the heir of entail. But your uncle is a man to fight the indefensible; and it would be likely your identity that he would call in question. A lawsuit is always expensive, and a family lawsuit always scandalous; besides which, if any of your doings with your friend Mr. Thomson were to come out, we might find that we had burned our fingers. The kidnapping, to be sure, would be a court card upon our side, if we could only prove it. But it may be difficult to prove; and my advice (upon the whole) is to make a very easy bargain with your uncle, perhaps even leaving him at Shaws where he has taken root for a quarter of a century, and contenting yourself in the meanwhile with a fair provision."

I told him I was very willing to be easy, and that to carry family concerns before the public was a step from which I was naturally much averse. In the meantime (thinking to myself) I began to see the outlines of that scheme on which we afterwards acted.

"The great affair," I asked, "is to bring home to him the kidnapping?"

"Surely," said Mr. Rankeillor, "and if possible, out of court. For mark you here, Mr. David: we could no doubt find some men of the Covenant who would swear to your reclusion; but once they were in the box, we could no longer check their testimony, and some word of your friend Mr. Thomson must certainly crop out. Which (from what you have let fall) I cannot think to be desirable."

"Well, sir," said I, "here is my way of it." And I opened my plot to him.

"But this would seem to involve my meeting the man Thomson?" says he, when I had done.

"I think so, indeed, sir," said I.

"Dear doctor!" cries he, rubbing his brow. "Dear doctor! No, Mr. David, I am afraid your scheme is inadmissible. I say nothing against your friend, Mr. Thomson: I know nothing against him; and if I did—mark this, Mr. David!—it would be my duty to lay hands on him. Now I put it to you: is it wise to meet? He may have matters to his charge. He may not have told you all. His name may not be even Thomson!" cries the lawyer, twinkling; "for some of these fellows will pick up names by the roadside as another would gather haws."

"You must be the judge, sir," said I.

But it was clear my plan had taken hold upon his fancy, for he kept musing to himself till we were called to dinner and the company of Mrs. Rankeillor; and that lady had scarce left us again to ourselves and a bottle of wine, ere he was back harping on my proposal. When and where was I to meet my friend Mr. Thomson; was I sure of Mr. T.'s discretion; supposing we could catch the old fox tripping, would I consent to such and such a term of an agreement—these and the like questions he kept asking at long intervals, while he thoughtfully rolled his wine upon his tongue. When I had answered all of them, seemingly to his contentment, he fell into a still deeper muse, even the claret being now forgotten. Then he got a sheet of paper and a pencil, and set to work writing and weighing every word; and at last touched a bell and had his clerk into the chamber.

"Torrance," said he, "I must have this written out fair against to-night; and when it is done, you will be so kind as put on your hat and be ready to come along with this gentleman and me, for you will probably be wanted as a witness."

"What, sir," cried I, as soon as the clerk was gone, "are you to venture it?"

"Why, so it would appear," says he, filling his glass. "But let us speak no more of business. The very sight of Torrance brings in my head a little droll matter of some years ago, when I had made a tryst with the poor oaf at the cross of Edinburgh. Each had gone his proper errand; and when it came four o'clock, Torrance had been taking a glass and did not know his master, and I, who had forgot my spectacles, was so blind without them, that I give you my word I did not know my own clerk." And thereupon he laughed heartily.

I said it was an odd chance, and smiled out of politeness; but what held me all the afternoon in wonder, he kept returning and dwelling on this story, and telling it again with fresh details and laughter; so that I began at last to be quite put out of countenance and feel ashamed for my friend's folly.

Towards the time I had appointed with Alan, we set out from the house, Mr. Rankeillor and I arm in arm, and Torrance following behind with the deed in his pocket and a covered basket in his hand. All through the town, the lawyer was bowing right and left, and continually being button-holed by gentlemen on matters of burgh or private business; and I could see he was one greatly looked up to in the county. At last we were clear of the houses, and began to go along the side of the haven and towards the Hawes Inn and the Ferry pier, the scene of my misfortune. I could not look upon the place without emotion, recalling how many that had been there with me that day were now no more: Ransome taken, I could hope, from the evil to come; Shuan passed where I dared not follow him; and the poor souls that had gone down with the brig in her last plunge. All these, and the brig herself, I had outlived; and come through these hardships and fearful perils without scath. My only thought should have been of gratitude; and yet I could not behold the place without sorrow for others and a chill of recollected fear.

I was so thinking when, upon a sudden, Mr. Rankeillor cried out, clapped his hand to his pockets, and began to laugh.

"Why," he cries, "if this be not a farcical adventure! After all that I said, I have forgot my glasses!"

At that, of course, I understood the purpose of his anecdote, and knew that if he had left his spectacles at home, it had been done on purpose, so that he might have the benefit of Alan's help without the awkwardness of recognising him. And indeed it was well thought upon; for now (suppose things to go the very worst) how could Rankeillor swear to my friend's identity, or how be made to bear damaging evidence against myself? For all that, he had been a long while of finding out his want, and had spoken to and recognised a good few persons as we came through the town; and I had little doubt myself that he saw reasonably well.

As soon as we were past the Hawes (where I recognised the landlord smoking his pipe in the door, and was amazed to see him look no older) Mr. Rankeillor changed the order of march, walking behind with Torrance and sending me forward in the manner of a scout. I went up the hill, whistling from time to time my Gaelic air; and at length I had the pleasure to hear it answered and to see Alan rise from behind a bush. He was somewhat dashed in spirits, having passed a long day alone skulking in the county, and made but a poor meal in an alehouse near Dundas. But at the mere sight of my clothes, he began to brighten up; and as soon as I had told him in what a forward state our matters were and the part I looked to him to play in what remained, he sprang into a new man.

"And that is a very good notion of yours," says he; "and I dare to say that you could lay your hands upon no better man to put it through than Alan Breck. It is not a thing (mark ye) that any one could do, but takes a gentleman of penetration. But it sticks in my head your lawyer-man will be somewhat wearying to see me," says Alan.

Accordingly I cried and waved on Mr. Rankeillor, who came up alone and was presented to my friend, Mr. Thomson.

"Mr. Thomson, I am pleased to meet you," said he. "But I have forgotten my glasses; and our friend, Mr. David here" (clapping me on the shoulder), "will tell you that I am little better than blind, and that you must not be surprised if I pass you by to-morrow."

This he said, thinking that Alan would be pleased; but the Highlandman's vanity was ready to startle at a less matter than that.

"Why, sir," says he, stiffly, "I would say it mattered the less as we are met here for a particular end, to see justice done to Mr. Balfour; and by what I can see, not very likely to have much else in common. But I accept your apology, which was a very proper one to make."

"And that is more than I could look for, Mr. Thomson," said Rankeillor, heartily. "And now as you and I are the chief actors in this enterprise, I think we should come into a nice agreement; to which end, I propose that you should lend me your arm, for (what with the dusk and the want of my glasses) I am not very clear as to the path; and as for you, Mr. David, you will find Torrance a pleasant kind of body to speak with. Only let me remind you, it's quite needless he should hear more of your adventures or those of—ahem—Mr. Thomson."

Accordingly these two went on ahead in very close talk, and Torrance and I brought up the rear.

Night was quite come when we came in view of the house of Shaws. Ten had been gone some time; it was dark and mild, with a pleasant, rustling wind in the south-west that covered the sound of our approach; and as we drew near we saw no glimmer of light in any portion of the building. It seemed my uncle was already in bed, which was indeed the best thing for our arrangements. We made our last whispered consultations some fifty yards away; and then the lawyer and Torrance and I crept quietly up and crouched down beside the corner of the house; and as soon as we were in our places, Alan strode to the door without concealment and began to knock.

CHAPTER XXIX
I COME INTO MY KINGDOM

or some time Alan volleyed upon the door, and his knocking only roused the echoes of the house and neighbourhood. At last, however, I could hear the noise of a window gently thrust up, and knew that my uncle had come to his observatory. By what light there was, he would see Alan standing, like a dark shadow, on the steps; the three witnesses were hidden quite out of his view; so that there was nothing to alarm an honest man in his own house. For all that, he studied his visitor awhile in silence, and when he spoke his voice had a quaver of misgiving.

"What's this?" says he. "This is nae kind of time of night for decent folk; and I hae nae trokings* wi' night-hawks. What brings ye here? I have a blunderbush."

   * Dealings.

"Is that yoursel', Mr. Balfour?" returned Alan, stepping back and looking up into the darkness. "Have a care of that blunderbuss; they're nasty things to burst."

"What brings ye here? and whae are ye?" says my uncle, angrily.

"I have no manner of inclination to rowt out my name to the country-side," said Alan; "but what brings me here is another story, being more of your affair than mine; and if ye're sure it's what ye would like, I'll set it to a tune and sing it to you."

"And what is't?" asked my uncle.

"David," says Alan.

"What was that?" cried my uncle, in a mighty changed voice.

"Shall I give ye the rest of the name, then?" said Alan.

There was a pause; and then, "I'm thinking I'll better let ye in," says my uncle, doubtfully.

"I dare say that," said Alan; "but the point is, Would I go? Now I will tell you what I am thinking. I am thinking that it is here upon this doorstep that we must confer upon this business; and it shall be here or nowhere at all whatever; for I would have you to understand that I am as stiffnecked as yoursel', and a gentleman of better family."

This change of note disconcerted Ebenezer; he was a little while digesting it, and then says he, "Weel, weel, what must be must," and shut the window. But it took him a long time to get down-stairs, and a still longer to undo the fastenings, repenting (I dare say) and taken with fresh claps of fear at every second step and every bolt and bar. At last, however, we heard the creak of the hinges, and it seems my uncle slipped gingerly out and (seeing that Alan had stepped back a pace or two) sate him down on the top doorstep with the blunderbuss ready in his hands.

"And, now" says he, "mind I have my blunderbush, and if ye take a step nearer ye're as good as deid."

"And a very civil speech," says Alan, "to be sure."

"Na," says my uncle, "but this is no a very chanty kind of a proceeding, and I'm bound to be prepared. And now that we understand each other, ye'll can name your business."

"Why," says Alan, "you that are a man of so much understanding, will doubtless have perceived that I am a Hieland gentleman. My name has nae business in my story; but the county of my friends is no very far from the Isle of Mull, of which ye will have heard. It seems there was a ship lost in those parts; and the next day a gentleman of my family was seeking wreck-wood for his fire along the sands, when he came upon a lad that was half drowned. Well, he brought him to; and he and some other gentleman took and clapped him in an auld, ruined castle, where from that day to this he has been a great expense to my friends. My friends are a wee wild-like, and not so particular about the law as some that I could name; and finding that the lad owned some decent folk, and was your born nephew, Mr. Balfour, they asked me to give ye a bit call and confer upon the matter. And I may tell ye at the off-go, unless we can agree upon some terms, ye are little likely to set eyes upon him. For my friends," added Alan, simply, "are no very well off."

My uncle cleared his throat. "I'm no very caring," says he. "He wasnae a good lad at the best of it, and I've nae call to interfere."

"Ay, ay," said Alan, "I see what ye would be at: pretending ye don't care, to make the ransom smaller."

"Na," said my uncle, "it's the mere truth. I take nae manner of interest in the lad, and I'll pay nae ransome, and ye can make a kirk and a mill of him for what I care."

"Hoot, sir," says Alan. "Blood's thicker than water, in the deil's name! Ye cannae desert your brother's son for the fair shame of it; and if ye did, and it came to be kennt, ye wouldnae be very popular in your country-side, or I'm the more deceived."

"I'm no just very popular the way it is," returned Ebenezer; "and I dinnae see how it would come to be kennt. No by me, onyway; nor yet by you or your friends. So that's idle talk, my buckie," says he.

"Then it'll have to be David that tells it," said Alan.

"How that?" says my uncle, sharply.

"Ou, just this way," says Alan. "My friends would doubtless keep your nephew as long as there was any likelihood of siller to be made of it, but if there was nane, I am clearly of opinion they would let him gang where he pleased, and be damned to him!"

"Ay, but I'm no very caring about that either," said my uncle. "I wouldnae be muckle made up with that."

"I was thinking that," said Alan.

"And what for why?" asked Ebenezer.

"Why, Mr. Balfour," replied Alan, "by all that I could hear, there were two ways of it: either ye liked David and would pay to get him back; or else ye had very good reasons for not wanting him, and would pay for us to keep him. It seems it's not the first; well then, it's the second; and blythe am I to ken it, for it should be a pretty penny in my pocket and the pockets of my friends."

"I dinnae follow ye there," said my uncle.

"No?" said Alan. "Well, see here: you dinnae want the lad back; well, what do ye want done with him, and how much will ye pay?"

My uncle made no answer, but shifted uneasily on his seat.

"Come, sir," cried Alan. "I would have you to ken that I am a gentleman; I bear a king's name; I am nae rider to kick my shanks at your hall door. Either give me an answer in civility, and that out of hand; or by the top of Glencoe, I will ram three feet of iron through your vitals."

"Eh, man," cried my uncle, scrambling to his feet, "give me a meenit! What's like wrong with ye? I'm just a plain man and nae dancing master; and I'm tryin to be as ceevil as it's morally possible. As for that wild talk, it's fair disreputable. Vitals, says you! And where would I be with my blunderbush?" he snarled.

"Powder and your auld hands are but as the snail to the swallow against the bright steel in the hands of Alan," said the other. "Before your jottering finger could find the trigger, the hilt would dirl on your breast-bane."

"Eh, man, whae's denying it?" said my uncle. "Pit it as ye please, hae't your ain way; I'll do naething to cross ye. Just tell me what like ye'll be wanting, and ye'll see that we'll can agree fine."

"Troth, sir," said Alan, "I ask for nothing but plain dealing. In two words: do ye want the lad killed or kept?"

"O, sirs!" cried Ebenezer. "O, sirs, me! that's no kind of language!"

"Killed or kept!" repeated Alan.

"O, keepit, keepit!" wailed my uncle. "We'll have nae bloodshed, if you please."

"Well," says Alan, "as ye please; that'll be the dearer."

"The dearer?" cries Ebenezer. "Would ye fyle your hands wi' crime?"

"Hoot!" said Alan, "they're baith crime, whatever! And the killing's easier, and quicker, and surer. Keeping the lad'll be a fashious* job, a fashious, kittle business."

   * Troublesome.

"I'll have him keepit, though," returned my uncle. "I never had naething to do with onything morally wrong; and I'm no gaun to begin to pleasure a wild Hielandman."

"Ye're unco scrupulous," sneered Alan.

"I'm a man o' principle," said Ebenezer, simply; "and if I have to pay for it, I'll have to pay for it. And besides," says he, "ye forget the lad's my brother's son."

"Well, well," said Alan, "and now about the price. It's no very easy for me to set a name upon it; I would first have to ken some small matters. I would have to ken, for instance, what ye gave Hoseason at the first off-go?"

"Hoseason!" cries my uncle, struck aback. "What for?"

"For kidnapping David," says Alan.

"It's a lee, it's a black lee!" cried my uncle. "He was never kidnapped. He leed in his throat that tauld ye that. Kidnapped? He never was!"

"That's no fault of mine nor yet of yours," said Alan; "nor yet of Hoseason's, if he's a man that can be trusted."

"What do ye mean?" cried Ebenezer. "Did Hoseason tell ye?"

"Why, ye donnered auld runt, how else would I ken?" cried Alan. "Hoseason and me are partners; we gang shares; so ye can see for yoursel' what good ye can do leeing. And I must plainly say ye drove a fool's bargain when ye let a man like the sailor-man so far forward in your private matters. But that's past praying for; and ye must lie on your bed the way ye made it. And the point in hand is just this: what did ye pay him?"

"Has he tauld ye himsel'?" asked my uncle.

"That's my concern," said Alan.

"Weel," said my uncle, "I dinnae care what he said, he leed, and the solemn God's truth is this, that I gave him twenty pound. But I'll be perfec'ly honest with ye: forby that, he was to have the selling of the lad in Caroliny, whilk would be as muckle mair, but no from my pocket, ye see."

"Thank you, Mr. Thomson. That will do excellently well," said the lawyer, stepping forward; and then mighty civilly, "Good-evening, Mr. Balfour," said he.

And, "Good-evening, Uncle Ebenezer," said I.

And, "It's a braw nicht, Mr. Balfour," added Torrance.

Never a word said my uncle, neither black nor white; but just sat where he was on the top doorstep and stared upon us like a man turned to stone. Alan filched away his blunderbuss; and the lawyer, taking him by the arm, plucked him up from the doorstep, led him into the kitchen, whither we all followed, and set him down in a chair beside the hearth, where the fire was out and only a rush-light burning.

There we all looked upon him for a while, exulting greatly in our success, but yet with a sort of pity for the man's shame.

"Come, come, Mr. Ebenezer," said the lawyer, "you must not be down-hearted, for I promise you we shall make easy terms. In the meanwhile give us the cellar key, and Torrance shall draw us a bottle of your father's wine in honour of the event." Then, turning to me and taking me by the hand, "Mr. David," says he, "I wish you all joy in your good fortune, which I believe to be deserved." And then to Alan, with a spice of drollery, "Mr. Thomson, I pay you my compliment; it was most artfully conducted; but in one point you somewhat outran my comprehension. Do I understand your name to be James? or Charles? or is it George, perhaps?"

"And why should it be any of the three, sir?" quoth Alan, drawing himself up, like one who smelt an offence.

"Only, sir, that you mentioned a king's name," replied Rankeillor; "and as there has never yet been a King Thomson, or his fame at least has never come my way, I judged you must refer to that you had in baptism."

This was just the stab that Alan would feel keenest, and I am free to confess he took it very ill. Not a word would he answer, but stepped off to the far end of the kitchen, and sat down and sulked; and it was not till I stepped after him, and gave him my hand, and thanked him by title as the chief spring of my success, that he began to smile a bit, and was at last prevailed upon to join our party.

By that time we had the fire lighted, and a bottle of wine uncorked; a good supper came out of the basket, to which Torrance and I and Alan set ourselves down; while the lawyer and my uncle passed into the next chamber to consult. They stayed there closeted about an hour; at the end of which period they had come to a good understanding, and my uncle and I set our hands to the agreement in a formal manner. By the terms of this, my uncle bound himself to satisfy Rankeillor as to his intromissions, and to pay me two clear thirds of the yearly income of Shaws.

So the beggar in the ballad had come home; and when I lay down that night on the kitchen chests, I was a man of means and had a name in the country. Alan and Torrance and Rankeillor slept and snored on their hard beds; but for me who had lain out under heaven and upon dirt and stones, so many days and nights, and often with an empty belly, and in fear of death, this good change in my case unmanned me more than any of the former evil ones; and I lay till dawn, looking at the fire on the roof and planning the future.

CHAPTER XXX
GOOD-BYE

So far as I was concerned myself, I had come to port; but I had still Alan, to whom I was so much beholden, on my hands; and I felt besides a heavy charge in the matter of the murder and James of the Glens. On both these heads I unbosomed to Rankeillor the next morning, walking to and fro about six of the clock before the house of Shaws, and with nothing in view but the fields and woods that had been my ancestors' and were now mine. Even as I spoke on these grave subjects, my eye would take a glad bit of a run over the prospect, and my heart jump with pride.

About my clear duty to my friend, the lawyer had no doubt. I must help him out of the county at whatever risk; but in the case of James, he was of a different mind.

"Mr. Thomson," says he, "is one thing, Mr. Thomson's kinsman quite another. I know little of the facts, but I gather that a great noble (whom we will call, if you like, the D. of A.)* has some concern and is even supposed to feel some animosity in the matter. The D. of A. is doubtless an excellent nobleman; but, Mr. David, timeo qui nocuere deos. If you interfere to balk his vengeance, you should remember there is one way to shut your testimony out; and that is to put you in the dock. There, you would be in the same pickle as Mr. Thomson's kinsman. You will object that you are innocent; well, but so is he. And to be tried for your life before a Highland jury, on a Highland quarrel and with a Highland Judge upon the bench, would be a brief transition to the gallows."

* The Duke of Argyle.

Now I had made all these reasonings before and found no very good reply to them; so I put on all the simplicity I could. "In that case, sir," said I, "I would just have to be hanged—would I not?"

"My dear boy," cries he, "go in God's name, and do what you think is right. It is a poor thought that at my time of life I should be advising you to choose the safe and shameful; and I take it back with an apology. Go and do your duty; and be hanged, if you must, like a gentleman. There are worse things in the world than to be hanged."

"Not many, sir," said I, smiling.

"Why, yes, sir," he cried, "very many. And it would be ten times better for your uncle (to go no farther afield) if he were dangling decently upon a gibbet."

Thereupon he turned into the house (still in a great fervour of mind, so that I saw I had pleased him heartily) and there he wrote me two letters, making his comments on them as he wrote.

"This," says he, "is to my bankers, the British Linen Company, placing a credit to your name. Consult Mr. Thomson, he will know of ways; and you, with this credit, can supply the means. I trust you will be a good husband of your money; but in the affair of a friend like Mr. Thomson, I would be even prodigal. Then for his kinsman, there is no better way than that you should seek the Advocate, tell him your tale, and offer testimony; whether he may take it or not, is quite another matter, and will turn on the D. of A. Now, that you may reach the Lord Advocate well recommended, I give you here a letter to a namesake of your own, the learned Mr. Balfour of Pilrig, a man whom I esteem. It will look better that you should be presented by one of your own name; and the laird of Pilrig is much looked up to in the Faculty and stands well with

Lord Advocate Grant. I would not trouble him, if I were you, with any particulars; and (do you know?) I think it would be needless to refer to Mr. Thomson. Form yourself upon the laird, he is a good model; when you deal with the Advocate, be discreet; and in all these matters, may the Lord guide you, Mr. David!"

Thereupon he took his farewell, and set out with Torrance for the Ferry, while Alan and I turned our faces for the city of Edinburgh. As we went by the footpath and beside the gateposts and the unfinished lodge, we kept looking back at the house of my fathers. It stood there, bare and great and smokeless, like a place not lived in; only in one of the top windows, there was the peak of a nightcap bobbing up and down and back and forward, like the head of a rabbit from a burrow. I had little welcome when I came, and less kindness while I stayed; but at least I was watched as I went away.

Alan and I went slowly forward upon our way, having little heart either to walk or speak. The same thought was uppermost in both, that we were near the time of our parting; and remembrance of all the bygone days sate upon us sorely. We talked indeed of what should be done; and it was resolved that Alan should keep to the county, biding now here, now there, but coming once in the day to a particular place where I might be able to communicate with him, either in my own person or by messenger. In the meanwhile, I was to seek out a lawyer, who was an Appin Stewart, and a man therefore to be wholly trusted; and it should be his part to find a ship and to arrange for Alan's safe embarkation. No sooner was this business done, than the words seemed to leave us; and though I would seek to jest with Alan under the name of Mr. Thomson, and he with me on my new clothes and my estate, you could feel very well that we were nearer tears than laughter.

We came the by-way over the hill of Corstorphine; and when we got near to the place called Rest-and-be-Thankful, and looked down on Corstorphine bogs and over to the city and the castle on the hill, we both stopped, for we both knew without a word said that we had come to where our ways parted. Here he repeated to me once again what had been agreed upon between us: the address of the lawyer, the daily hour at which Alan might be found, and the signals that were to be made by any that came seeking him. Then I gave what money I had (a guinea or two of Rankeillor's) so that he should not starve in the meanwhile; and then we stood a space, and looked over at Edinburgh in silence.

"Well, good-bye," said Alan, and held out his left hand.

THE STRANGE CASE OF DR. JEKYLL AND MR. HYDE

STORY OF THE DOOR

Mr. Utterson the lawyer was a man of a rugged countenance that was never lighted by a smile; cold, scanty and embarrassed in discourse; backward in sentiment; lean, long, dusty, dreary and yet somehow lovable. At friendly meetings, and when the wine was to his taste, something eminently human beaconed from his eye; something indeed which never found its way into his talk, but which spoke not only in these silent symbols of the after-dinner face, but more often and loudly in the acts of his life. He was austere with himself; drank gin when he was alone, to mortify a taste for vintages; and though he enjoyed the theatre, had not crossed the doors of one for twenty years. But he had an approved tolerance for others; sometimes wondering, almost with envy, at the high pressure of spirits involved in their misdeeds; and in any extremity inclined to help rather than to reprove. "I incline to Cain's heresy," he used to say quaintly: "I let my brother go to the devil in his own way." In this character, it was frequently his fortune to be the last reputable acquaintance and the last good influence in the lives of downgoing men. And to such as these, so long as they came about his chambers, he never marked a shade of change in his demeanour.

No doubt the feat was easy to Mr. Utterson; for he was undemonstrative at the best, and even his friendship seemed to be founded in a similar catholicity of good-nature. It is the mark of a modest man to accept his friendly circle ready-made from the hands of opportunity; and that was the lawyer's way. His friends were those of his own blood or those whom he had known the longest; his affections, like ivy, were the growth of time, they implied no aptness in the object. Hence, no doubt the bond that united him to Mr. Richard Enfield, his distant kinsman, the well-known man about town. It was a nut to crack for many, what these two could see in each other, or what subject they could find in common. It was reported by those who encountered them in their Sunday walks, that they said nothing, looked singularly dull and would hail with obvious relief the appearance of a friend. For all that, the two men put the greatest store by these excursions, counted them the chief jewel of each week, and not only set aside occasions of pleasure, but even resisted the calls of business, that they might enjoy them uninterrupted.

It chanced on one of these rambles that their way led them down a by-street in a busy quarter of London. The street was small and what is called quiet, but it drove a thriving trade on the weekdays. The inhabitants were all doing well, it seemed and all emulously hoping to do better still, and laying out the surplus of their grains in coquetry; so that the shop fronts stood along that thoroughfare with an air of invitation, like rows of smiling saleswomen. Even on Sunday, when it veiled its more florid charms and lay comparatively empty of passage, the street shone out in contrast to its dingy neighbourhood, like a fire in a forest; and with its freshly painted shutters, well-polished brasses, and general cleanliness and gaiety of note, instantly caught and pleased the eye of the passenger.

Two doors from one corner, on the left hand going east the line was broken by the entry of a court; and just at that point a certain sinister block of building thrust forward its gable on the street. It was two storeys high; showed no window, nothing but a door on the lower storey and a blind forehead of discoloured wall on the upper; and bore in every feature, the marks of prolonged and sordid negligence. The door, which was equipped with neither bell nor knocker, was blistered and distained. Tramps slouched into the recess and struck matches on the panels; children kept shop upon the steps; the schoolboy had tried his knife on the mouldings; and for close on a generation, no one had appeared to drive away these random visitors or to repair their ravages.

Mr. Enfield and the lawyer were on the other side of the by-street; but when they came abreast of the entry, the former lifted up his cane and pointed.

"Did you ever remark that door?" he asked; and when his companion had replied in the affirmative, "It is connected in my mind," added he, "with a very odd story."

"Indeed?" said Mr. Utterson, with a slight change of voice, "and what was that?"

"Well, it was this way," returned Mr. Enfield: "I was coming home from some place at the end of the world, about three o'clock of a black winter morning, and my way lay through a part of town where there was literally nothing to be seen but lamps. Street after street and all the folks asleep—street after street, all lighted up as if for a procession and all as empty as a church—till at last I got into that state of mind when a man listens and listens and begins to long for the sight of a policeman. All at once, I saw two figures: one a little man who was stumping along eastward at a good walk, and the other a girl of maybe eight or ten who was running as hard as she was able down a cross street. Well, sir, the two ran into one another naturally enough at the corner; and then came the horrible part of the thing; for the man trampled calmly over the child's body and left her screaming on the ground. It sounds nothing to hear, but it was hellish to see. It wasn't like a man; it was like some damned Juggernaut. I gave a few halloa, took to my heels, collared my gentleman, and brought him back to where there was already quite a group about the screaming child. He was perfectly cool and made no resistance, but gave me one look, so ugly that it brought out the sweat on me like running. The people who had turned out were the girl's own family; and pretty soon, the doctor, for whom she had been sent put in his appearance. Well, the child was not much the worse, more frightened, according to the sawbones; and there you might have supposed would be an end to it. But there was one curious circumstance. I had taken a loathing to my gentleman at first sight. So had the child's family, which was only natural. But the doctor's case was what struck me. He was the usual cut and dry apothecary, of no particular age and colour, with a strong Edinburgh accent and about as emotional as a bagpipe. Well, sir, he was like the rest of us; every time he looked at my prisoner, I saw that sawbones turn sick and white with the desire to kill him. I knew what was in his mind, just as he knew what was in mine; and killing being out of the question, we did the next best. We told the man we could and would make such a scandal out of this as should make his name stink from one end of London to the other. If he had any friends or any credit, we undertook that he should lose them. And all the time, as we were pitching it in red hot, we were keeping the women off him as best we could for they were as wild as harpies. I never saw a circle of such hateful faces; and there was the man in the middle, with a kind of black sneering coolness—frightened too, I could see that—but carrying it off, sir, really like Satan. 'If you choose to make capital out of this accident,' said he, 'I am naturally helpless. No gentleman but wishes to avoid a scene,' says he. 'Name your figure.' Well, we screwed him up to a hundred pounds for the child's family; he would have clearly liked to stick out; but there was something about the lot of us that meant mischief, and at last he struck. The next thing was to get the money; and where do you think he carried us but to that place with the door?—whipped out a key, went in, and presently came back with the matter of ten pounds in gold and a cheque for the balance on Coutts's, drawn payable to bearer and signed with a name that I can't mention, though it's one of the points of my story, but it was a name at least very well known and often printed. The figure was stiff; but the signature was good for more than that if it was only genuine. I took the liberty of pointing out to my gentleman that the whole business looked apocryphal, and that a man does not, in real life, walk into a cellar door at four in the morning and come out with another man's cheque for close upon a hundred pounds. But he was quite easy and sneering. 'Set your mind at rest,' says he, 'I will stay with you till the banks open and cash the cheque myself.' So we all set off, the doctor, and the child's father, and our friend and myself, and passed the rest of the night in my chambers; and next day, when we had breakfasted, went in a body to the bank. I gave in the cheque myself, and said I had every reason to believe it was a forgery. Not a bit of it. The cheque was genuine."

"Tut-tut!" said Mr. Utterson.

"I see you feel as I do," said Mr. Enfield. "Yes, it's a bad story. For my man was a fellow that nobody could have to do with, a really damnable man; and the person that drew the cheque is the very pink of the proprieties, celebrated too, and (what makes it worse) one of your fellows who do what they call good. Blackmail, I suppose; an honest man paying through the nose for some of the capers of his youth. Black Mail House is what I call the place with the door, in consequence. Though even that, you know, is far from explaining all," he added, and with the words fell into a vein of musing.

From this he was recalled by Mr. Utterson asking rather suddenly: "And you don't know if the drawer of the cheque lives there?"

"A likely place, isn't it?" returned Mr. Enfield. "But I happen to have noticed his address; he lives in some square or other."

"And you never asked about the—place with the door?" said Mr. Utterson.

"No, sir; I had a delicacy," was the reply. "I feel very strongly about putting questions; it partakes too much of the style of the day of judgment. You start a question, and it's like starting a stone. You sit quietly on the top of a hill; and away the stone goes, starting others; and presently some bland old bird (the last you would have thought of) is knocked on the head in his own back garden and the family have to change their name. No sir, I make it a rule of mine: the more it looks like Queer Street, the less I ask."

"A very good rule, too," said the lawyer.

"But I have studied the place for myself," continued Mr. Enfield. "It seems scarcely a house. There is no other door, and nobody goes in or out of that one but, once in a great while, the gentleman of my adventure. There are three windows looking on the court on the first floor; none below; the windows are always shut but they're clean. And then there is a chimney which is generally smoking; so somebody must live there. And yet it's not so sure; for the buildings are so packed together about the court, that it's hard to say where one ends and another begins."

The pair walked on again for a while in silence; and then "Enfield," said Mr. Utterson, "that's a good rule of yours."

"Yes, I think it is," returned Enfield.

"But for all that," continued the lawyer, "there's one point I want to ask. I want to ask the name of that man who walked over the child."

"Well," said Mr. Enfield, "I can't see what harm it would do. It was a man of the name of Hyde."

"Hm," said Mr. Utterson. "What sort of a man is he to see?"

"He is not easy to describe. There is something wrong with his appearance; something displeasing, something down-right detestable. I never saw a man I so disliked, and yet I scarce know why. He must be deformed somewhere; he gives a strong feeling of deformity, although I couldn't specify the point. He's an extraordinary looking man, and yet I really can name nothing out of the way. No, sir; I can make no hand of it; I can't describe him. And it's not want of memory; for I declare I can see him this moment."

Mr. Utterson again walked some way in silence and obviously under a weight of consideration. "You are sure he used a key?" he inquired at last.

"My dear sir..." began Enfield, surprised out of himself.

"Yes, I know," said Utterson; "I know it must seem strange. The fact is, if I do not ask you the name of the other party, it is because I know it already. You see, Richard, your tale has gone home. If you have been inexact in any point you had better correct it."

"I think you might have warned me," returned the other with a touch of sullenness. "But I have been pedantically exact, as you call it. The fellow had a key; and what's more, he has it still. I saw him use it not a week ago."

Mr. Utterson sighed deeply but said never a word; and the young man presently resumed. "Here is another lesson to say nothing," said he. "I am ashamed of my long tongue. Let us make a bargain never to refer to this again."

"With all my heart," said the lawyer. "I shake hands on that, Richard."

SEARCH FOR MR. HYDE

That evening Mr. Utterson came home to his bachelor house in sombre spirits and sat down to dinner without relish. It was his custom of a Sunday, when this meal was over, to sit close by the fire, a volume of some dry divinity on his reading desk, until the clock of the neighbouring church rang out the hour of twelve, when he would go soberly and gratefully to bed. On this night however, as soon as the cloth was taken away, he took up a candle and went into his business room. There he opened his safe, took from the most private part of it a document endorsed on the envelope as Dr. Jekyll's Will and sat down with a clouded brow to study its contents. The will was holograph, for Mr. Utterson though he took charge of it now that it was made, had refused to lend the least assistance in the making of it; it provided not only that, in case of the decease of Henry Jekyll, M.D., D.C.L., L.L.D., F.R.S., etc., all his possessions were to pass into the hands of his "friend and benefactor Edward Hyde," but that in case of Dr. Jekyll's "disappearance or unexplained absence for any period exceeding three calendar months," the said Edward Hyde should step into the said Henry Jekyll's shoes without further delay and free from any burthen or obligation beyond the payment of a few small sums to the members of the doctor's household. This document had long been the lawyer's eyesore. It offended him both as a lawyer and as a lover of the sane and customary sides of life, to whom the fanciful was the immodest. And hitherto it was his ignorance of Mr. Hyde that had swelled his indignation; now, by a sudden turn, it was his knowledge. It was already bad enough when the name was but a name of which he could learn no more. It was worse when it began to be clothed upon with detestable attributes; and out of the shifting, insubstantial mists that had so long baffled his eye, there leaped up the sudden, definite presentment of a fiend.

"I thought it was madness," he said, as he replaced the obnoxious paper in the safe, "and now I begin to fear it is disgrace."

With that he blew out his candle, put on a greatcoat, and set forth in the direction of Cavendish Square, that citadel of medicine, where his friend, the great Dr. Lanyon, had his house and received his crowding patients. "If anyone knows, it will be Lanyon," he had thought.

The solemn butler knew and welcomed him; he was subjected to no stage of delay, but ushered direct from the door to the dining-room where Dr. Lanyon sat alone over his wine. This was a hearty, healthy, dapper, red-faced gentleman, with a shock of hair prematurely white, and a boisterous and decided manner. At sight of Mr. Utterson, he sprang up from his chair and welcomed him with both hands. The geniality, as was the way of the man, was somewhat theatrical to the eye; but it reposed on genuine feeling. For these two were old friends, old mates both at school and college, both thorough respectors of themselves and of each other, and what does not always follow, men who thoroughly enjoyed each other's company.

After a little rambling talk, the lawyer led up to the subject which so disagreeably preoccupied his mind.

"I suppose, Lanyon," said he, "you and I must be the two oldest friends that Henry Jekyll has?"

"I wish the friends were younger," chuckled Dr. Lanyon. "But I suppose we are. And what of that? I see little of him now."

"Indeed?" said Utterson. "I thought you had a bond of common interest."

"We had," was the reply. "But it is more than ten years since Henry Jekyll became too fanciful for me. He began to go wrong, wrong in mind; and though of course I continue to take an interest in him for old sake's sake, as they say, I see and I have seen devilish little of the man. Such unscientific balderdash," added the doctor, flushing suddenly purple, "would have estranged Damon and Pythias."

This little spirit of temper was somewhat of a relief to Mr. Utterson. "They have only differed on some point of science," he thought; and being a man of no scientific passions (except in the matter of conveyancing), he even added: "It is nothing worse than that!" He gave his friend a few seconds to recover his composure, and then approached the question he had come to put. "Did you ever come across a protégé of his—one Hyde?" he asked.

"Hyde?" repeated Lanyon. "No. Never heard of him. Since my time."

That was the amount of information that the lawyer carried back with him to the great, dark bed on which he tossed to and fro, until the small hours of the morning began to grow large. It was a night of little ease to his toiling mind, toiling in mere darkness and besieged by questions.

Six o'clock struck on the bells of the church that was so conveniently near to Mr. Utterson's dwelling, and still he was digging at the problem. Hitherto it had touched him on the intellectual side alone; but now his imagination also was engaged, or rather enslaved; and as he lay and tossed in the gross darkness of the night and the curtained room, Mr. Enfield's tale went by before his mind in a scroll of lighted pictures. He would be aware of the great field of lamps of a nocturnal city; then of the figure of a man walking swiftly; then of a child running from the doctor's; and then these met, and that human Juggernaut trod the child down and passed on regardless of her screams. Or else he would see a room in a rich house, where his friend lay asleep, dreaming and smiling at his dreams; and then the door of that room would be opened, the curtains of the bed plucked apart, the sleeper recalled, and lo! there would stand by his side a figure to whom power was given, and even at that dead hour, he must rise and do its bidding. The figure in these two phases haunted the lawyer all night; and if at any time he dozed over, it was but to see it glide more stealthily through sleeping houses, or move the more swiftly and still the more swiftly, even to dizziness, through wider labyrinths of lamplighted city, and at every street corner crush a child and leave her screaming. And still the figure had no face by which he might know it; even in his dreams, it had no face, or one that baffled him and melted before his eyes; and thus it was that there sprang up and grew apace in the lawyer's mind a singularly strong, almost an inordinate, curiosity to behold the features of the real Mr. Hyde. If he could but once set eyes on him, he thought the mystery would lighten and perhaps roll altogether away, as was the habit of mysterious things when well examined. He might see a reason for his friend's strange preference or bondage (call it which you please) and even for the startling clause of the will. At least it would be a face worth seeing: the face of a man who was without bowels of mercy: a face which had but to show itself to raise up, in the mind of the unimpressionable Enfield, a spirit of enduring hatred.

From that time forward, Mr. Utterson began to haunt the door in the by-street of shops. In the morning before office hours, at noon when business was plenty and time scarce, at night under the face of the fogged city moon, by all lights and at all hours of solitude or concourse, the lawyer was to be found on his chosen post.

"If he be Mr. Hyde," he had thought, "I shall be Mr. Seek."

And at last his patience was rewarded. It was a fine dry night; frost in the air; the streets as clean as a ballroom floor; the lamps, unshaken by any wind, drawing a regular pattern of light and shadow. By ten o'clock, when the shops were closed, the by-street was very solitary and, in spite of the low growl of London from all round, very silent. Small sounds carried far; domestic sounds out of the houses were clearly audible on either side of the roadway; and the rumour of the approach of any passenger preceded him by a long time. Mr. Utterson had been some minutes at his post, when he was aware of an odd light footstep drawing near. In the course of his nightly patrols, he had long grown accustomed to the quaint effect with which the footfalls of a single person, while he is still a great way off, suddenly spring out distinct from the vast hum and clatter of the city. Yet his attention had never before been so sharply and decisively arrested; and it was with a strong, superstitious prevision of success that he withdrew into the entry of the court.

The steps drew swiftly nearer, and swelled out suddenly louder as they turned the end of the street. The lawyer, looking forth from the entry, could soon see what manner of man he had to deal with. He was small and very plainly dressed and the look of him, even at that distance, went somehow strongly against the watcher's inclination. But he made straight for the door, crossing the roadway to save time; and as he came, he drew a key from his pocket like one approaching home.

Mr. Utterson stepped out and touched him on the shoulder as he passed. "Mr. Hyde, I think?"

Mr. Hyde shrank back with a hissing intake of the breath. But his fear was only momentary; and though he did not look the lawyer in the face, he answered coolly enough: "That is my name. What do you want?"

"I see you are going in," returned the lawyer. "I am an old friend of Dr. Jekyll's—Mr. Utterson of Gaunt Street—you must have heard of my name; and meeting you so conveniently, I thought you might admit me."

"You will not find Dr. Jekyll; he is from home," replied Mr. Hyde, blowing in the key. And then suddenly, but still without looking up, "How did you know me?" he asked.

"On your side," said Mr. Utterson "will you do me a favour?"

"With pleasure," replied the other. "What shall it be?"

"Will you let me see your face?" asked the lawyer.

Mr. Hyde appeared to hesitate, and then, as if upon some sudden reflection, fronted about with an air of defiance; and the pair stared at each other pretty fixedly for a few seconds. "Now I shall know you again," said Mr. Utterson. "It may be useful."

"Yes," returned Mr. Hyde, "It is as well we have met; and à propos, you should have my address." And he gave a number of a street in Soho.

"Good God!" thought Mr. Utterson, "can he, too, have been thinking of the will?" But he kept his feelings to himself and only grunted in acknowledgment of the address.

"And now," said the other, "how did you know me?"

"By description," was the reply.

"Whose description?"

"We have common friends," said Mr. Utterson.

"Common friends," echoed Mr. Hyde, a little hoarsely. "Who are they?"

"Jekyll, for instance," said the lawyer.

"He never told you," cried Mr. Hyde, with a flush of anger. "I did not think you would have lied."

"Come," said Mr. Utterson, "that is not fitting language."

The other snarled aloud into a savage laugh; and the next moment, with extraordinary quickness, he had unlocked the door and disappeared into the house.

The lawyer stood awhile when Mr. Hyde had left him, the picture of disquietude. Then he began slowly to mount the street, pausing every step or two and putting his hand to his brow like a man in mental perplexity. The problem he was thus debating as he walked, was one of a class that is rarely solved. Mr. Hyde was pale and dwarfish, he gave an impression of deformity without any nameable malformation, he had a displeasing smile, he had borne himself to the lawyer with a sort of murderous mixture of timidity and boldness, and he spoke with a husky, whispering and somewhat broken voice; all these were points against him, but not all of these together could explain the hitherto unknown disgust, loathing and fear with which Mr. Utterson regarded him. "There must be something else," said the perplexed gentleman. "There is something more, if I could find a name for it. God bless me, the man seems hardly human! Something troglodytic, shall we say? or can it be the old story of Dr. Fell? or is it the mere radiance of a foul soul that thus transpires through, and transfigures, its clay continent? The last, I think; for, O my poor old Harry Jekyll, if ever I read Satan's signature upon a face, it is on that of your new friend."

Round the corner from the by-street, there was a square of ancient, handsome houses, now for the most part decayed from their high estate and let in flats and chambers to all sorts and conditions of men; map-engravers, architects, shady lawyers and the agents of obscure enterprises. One house, however, second from the corner, was still occupied entire; and at the door of this, which wore a great air of wealth and comfort, though it was now plunged in darkness except for the fanlight, Mr. Utterson stopped and knocked. A well-dressed, elderly servant opened the door.

"Is Dr. Jekyll at home, Poole?" asked the lawyer.

"I will see, Mr. Utterson," said Poole, admitting the visitor, as he spoke, into a large, low-roofed, comfortable hall paved with flags, warmed (after the fashion of a country house) by a bright, open fire, and furnished with costly cabinets of oak. "Will you wait here by the fire, sir? or shall I give you a light in the dining-room?"

"Here, thank you," said the lawyer, and he drew near and leaned on the tall fender. This hall, in which he was now left alone, was a pet fancy of his friend the doctor's; and Utterson himself was wont to speak of it as the pleasantest room in London. But tonight there was a shudder in his blood; the face of Hyde sat heavy on his memory; he felt (what was rare with him) a nausea and distaste of life; and in the gloom of his spirits, he seemed to read a menace in the flickering of the firelight on the polished cabinets and the uneasy starting of the shadow on the roof. He was ashamed of his relief, when Poole presently returned to announce that Dr. Jekyll was gone out.

"I saw Mr. Hyde go in by the old dissecting room, Poole," he said. "Is that right, when Dr. Jekyll is from home?"

"Quite right, Mr. Utterson, sir," replied the servant. "Mr. Hyde has a key."

"Your master seems to repose a great deal of trust in that young man, Poole," resumed the other musingly.

"Yes, sir, he does indeed," said Poole. "We have all orders to obey him."

"I do not think I ever met Mr. Hyde?" asked Utterson.

"O, dear no, sir. He never dines here," replied the butler. "Indeed we see very little of him on this side of the house; he mostly comes and goes by the laboratory."

"Well, good-night, Poole."

"Good-night, Mr. Utterson."

And the lawyer set out homeward with a very heavy heart. "Poor Harry Jekyll," he thought, "my mind misgives me he is in deep waters! He was wild when he was young; a long while ago to be sure; but in the law of God, there is no statute of limitations. Ay, it must be that; the ghost of some old sin, the cancer of some concealed disgrace: punishment coming, pede claudo, years after memory has forgotten and self-love condoned the fault." And the lawyer, scared by the thought, brooded awhile on his own past, groping in all the corners of memory, least by chance some Jack-in-the-Box of an old iniquity should leap to light there. His past was fairly blameless; few men could read the rolls of their life with less apprehension; yet he was humbled to the dust by the many ill things he had done, and raised up again into a sober and fearful gratitude by the many he had come so near to doing yet avoided. And then by a return on his former subject, he conceived a spark of hope. "This Master Hyde, if he were studied," thought he, "must have secrets of his own; black secrets, by the look of him; secrets compared to which poor Jekyll's worst would be like sunshine. Things cannot continue as they are. It turns me cold to think of this creature stealing like a thief to Harry's bedside; poor Harry, what a wakening! And the danger of it; for if this Hyde suspects the existence of the will, he may grow impatient to inherit. Ay, I must put my shoulders to the wheel—if Jekyll will but let me," he added, "if Jekyll will only let me." For once more he saw before his mind's eye, as clear as transparency, the strange clauses of the will.

DR. JEKYLL WAS QUITE AT EASE

A fortnight later, by excellent good fortune, the doctor gave one of his pleasant dinners to some five or six old cronies, all intelligent, reputable men and all judges of good wine; and Mr. Utterson so contrived that he remained behind after the others had departed. This was no new arrangement, but a thing that had befallen many scores of times. Where Utterson was liked, he was liked well. Hosts loved to detain the dry lawyer, when the light-hearted and loose-tongued had already their foot on the threshold; they liked to sit a while in his unobtrusive company, practising for solitude, sobering their minds in the man's rich silence after the expense and strain of gaiety. To this rule, Dr. Jekyll was no exception; and as he now sat on the opposite side of the fire—a large, well-made, smooth-faced man of fifty, with something of a slyish cast perhaps, but every mark of capacity and kindness—you could see by his looks that he cherished for Mr. Utterson a sincere and warm affection.

"I have been wanting to speak to you, Jekyll," began the latter. "You know that will of yours?"

A close observer might have gathered that the topic was distasteful; but the doctor carried it off gaily. "My poor Utterson," said he, "you are unfortunate in such a client. I never saw a man so distressed as you were by my will; unless it were that hide-bound pedant, Lanyon, at what he called my scientific heresies. O, I know he's a good fellow—you needn't frown—an excellent fellow, and I always mean to see more of him; but a hide-bound pedant for all that; an ignorant, blatant pedant. I was never more disappointed in any man than Lanyon."

"You know I never approved of it," pursued Utterson, ruthlessly disregarding the fresh topic.

"My will? Yes, certainly, I know that," said the doctor, a trifle sharply. "You have told me so."

"Well, I tell you so again," continued the lawyer. "I have been learning something of young Hyde."

The large handsome face of Dr. Jekyll grew pale to the very lips, and there came a blackness about his eyes. "I do not care to hear more," said he. "This is a matter I thought we had agreed to drop."

"What I heard was abominable," said Utterson.

"It can make no change. You do not understand my position," returned the doctor, with a certain incoherency of manner. "I am painfully situated, Utterson; my position is a very strange—a very strange one. It is one of those affairs that cannot be mended by talking."

"Jekyll," said Utterson, "you know me: I am a man to be trusted. Make a clean breast of this in confidence; and I make no doubt I can get you out of it."

"My good Utterson," said the doctor, "this is very good of you, this is downright good of you, and I cannot find words to thank you in. I believe you fully; I would trust you before any man alive, ay, before myself, if I could make the choice; but indeed it isn't what you fancy; it is not as bad as that; and just to put your good heart at rest, I will tell you one thing: the moment I choose, I can be rid of Mr. Hyde. I give you my hand upon that; and I thank you again and again; and I will just add one little word, Utterson, that I'm sure you'll take in good part: this is a private matter, and I beg of you to let it sleep."

Utterson reflected a little, looking in the fire.

"I have no doubt you are perfectly right," he said at last, getting to his feet.

"Well, but since we have touched upon this business, and for the last time I hope," continued the doctor, "there is one point I should like you to understand. I have really a very great interest in poor Hyde. I know you have seen him; he told me so; and I fear he was rude. But I do sincerely take a great, a very great interest in that young man; and if I am taken away, Utterson, I wish you to promise me that you will bear with him and get his rights for him. I think you would, if you knew all; and it would be a weight off my mind if you would promise."

"I can't pretend that I shall ever like him," said the lawyer.

"I don't ask that," pleaded Jekyll, laying his hand upon the other's arm; "I only ask for justice; I only ask you to help him for my sake, when I am no longer here."

Utterson heaved an irrepressible sigh. "Well," said he, "I promise."

THE CAREW MURDER CASE

Nearly a year later, in the month of October, 18—, London was startled by a crime of singular ferocity and rendered all the more notable by the high position of the victim. The details were few and startling. A maid servant living alone in a house not far from the river, had gone upstairs to bed about eleven. Although a fog rolled over the city in the small hours, the early part of the night was cloudless, and the lane, which the maid's window overlooked, was brilliantly lit by the full moon. It seems she was romantically given, for she sat down upon her box, which stood immediately under the window, and fell into a dream of musing. Never (she used to say, with streaming tears, when she narrated that experience), never had she felt more at peace with all men or thought more kindly of the world. And as she so sat she became aware of an aged beautiful gentleman with white hair, drawing near along the lane; and advancing to meet him, another and very small gentleman, to whom at first she paid less attention. When they had come within speech (which was just under the maid's eyes) the older man bowed and accosted the other with a very pretty manner of politeness. It did not seem as if the subject of his address were of great importance; indeed, from his pointing, it sometimes appeared as if he were only inquiring his way; but the moon shone on his face as he spoke, and the girl was pleased to watch it, it seemed to breathe such an innocent and old-world kindness of disposition, yet with something high too, as of a well-founded self-content. Presently her eye wandered to the other, and she was surprised to recognise in him a certain Mr. Hyde, who had once visited her master and for whom she had conceived a dislike. He had in his hand a heavy cane, with which he was trifling; but he answered never a word, and seemed to listen with an ill-contained impatience. And then all of a sudden he broke out in a great flame of anger, stamping with his foot, brandishing the cane, and carrying on (as the maid described it) like a madman. The old gentleman took a step back, with the air of one very much surprised and a trifle hurt; and at that Mr. Hyde broke out of all bounds and clubbed him to the earth. And next moment, with ape-like fury, he was trampling his victim under foot and hailing down a storm of blows, under which the bones were audibly shattered and the body jumped upon the roadway. At the horror of these sights and sounds, the maid fainted.

It was two o'clock when she came to herself and called for the police. The murderer was gone long ago; but there lay his victim in the middle of the lane, incredibly mangled. The stick with which the deed had been done, although it was of some rare and very tough and heavy wood, had broken in the middle under the stress of this insensate cruelty; and one splintered half had rolled in the neighbouring gutter—the other, without doubt, had been carried away by the murderer. A purse and gold watch were found upon the victim: but no cards or papers, except a sealed and stamped envelope, which he had been probably carrying to the post, and which bore the name and address of Mr. Utterson.

This was brought to the lawyer the next morning, before he was out of bed; and he had no sooner seen it and been told the circumstances, than he shot out a solemn lip. "I shall say nothing till I have seen the body," said he; "this may be very serious. Have the kindness to wait while I dress." And with the same grave countenance he hurried through his breakfast and drove to the police station, whither the body had been carried. As soon as he came into the cell, he nodded.

"Yes," said he, "I recognise him. I am sorry to say that this is Sir Danvers Carew."

"Good God, sir," exclaimed the officer, "is it possible?" And the next moment his eye lighted up with professional ambition. "This will make a deal of noise," he said. "And perhaps you can help us to the man." And he briefly narrated what the maid had seen, and showed the broken stick.

Mr. Utterson had already quailed at the name of Hyde; but when the stick was laid before him, he could doubt no longer; broken and battered as it was, he recognised it for one that he had himself presented many years before to Henry Jekyll.

"Is this Mr. Hyde a person of small stature?" he inquired.

"Particularly small and particularly wicked-looking, is what the maid calls him," said the officer.

Mr. Utterson reflected; and then, raising his head, "If you will come with me in my cab," he said, "I think I can take you to his house."

It was by this time about nine in the morning, and the first fog of the season. A great chocolate-coloured pall lowered over heaven, but the wind was continually charging and routing these embattled vapours; so that as the cab crawled from street to street, Mr. Utterson beheld a marvelous number of degrees and hues of twilight; for here it would be dark like the back-end of evening; and there would be a glow of a rich, lurid brown, like the light of some strange conflagration; and here, for a moment, the fog would be quite broken up, and a haggard shaft of daylight would glance in between the swirling wreaths. The dismal quarter of Soho seen under these changing glimpses, with its muddy ways, and slatternly passengers, and its lamps, which had never been extinguished or had been kindled afresh to combat this mournful reinvasion of darkness, seemed, in the lawyer's eyes, like a district of some city in a nightmare. The thoughts of his mind, besides, were of the gloomiest dye; and when he glanced at the companion of his drive, he was conscious of some touch of that terror of the law and the law's officers, which may at times assail the most honest.

As the cab drew up before the address indicated, the fog lifted a little and showed him a dingy street, a gin palace, a low French eating house, a shop for the retail of penny numbers and twopenny salads, many ragged children huddled in the doorways, and many women of many different nationalities passing out, key in hand, to have a morning glass; and the next moment the fog settled down again upon that part, as brown as umber, and cut him off from his blackguardly surroundings. This was the home of Henry Jekyll's favourite; of a man who was heir to a quarter of a million sterling.

An ivory-faced and silvery-haired old woman opened the door. She had an evil face, smoothed by hypocrisy: but her manners were excellent. Yes, she said, this was Mr. Hyde's, but he was not at home; he had been in that night very late, but he had gone away again in less than an hour; there was nothing strange in that; his habits were very irregular, and he was often absent; for instance, it was nearly two months since she had seen him till yesterday.

"Very well, then, we wish to see his rooms," said the lawyer; and when the woman began to declare it was impossible, "I had better tell you who this person is," he added. "This is Inspector Newcomen of Scotland Yard."

A flash of odious joy appeared upon the woman's face. "Ah!" said she, "he is in trouble! What has he done?"

Mr. Utterson and the inspector exchanged glances. "He don't seem a very popular character," observed the latter. "And now, my good woman, just let me and this gentleman have a look about us."

In the whole extent of the house, which but for the old woman remained otherwise empty, Mr. Hyde had only used a couple of rooms; but these were furnished with luxury and good taste. A closet was filled with wine; the plate was of silver, the napery elegant; a good picture hung upon the walls, a gift (as Utterson supposed) from Henry Jekyll, who was much of a connoisseur;

and the carpets were of many plies and agreeable in colour. At this moment, however, the rooms bore every mark of having been recently and hurriedly ransacked; clothes lay about the floor, with their pockets inside out; lock-fast drawers stood open; and on the hearth there lay a pile of grey ashes, as though many papers had been burned. From these embers the inspector disinterred the butt end of a green cheque book, which had resisted the action of the fire; the other half of the stick was found behind the door; and as this clinched his suspicions, the officer declared himself delighted. A visit to the bank, where several thousand pounds were found to be lying to the murderer's credit, completed his gratification.

"You may depend upon it, sir," he told Mr. Utterson: "I have him in my hand. He must have lost his head, or he never would have left the stick or, above all, burned the cheque book. Why, money's life to the man. We have nothing to do but wait for him at the bank, and get out the handbills."

This last, however, was not so easy of accomplishment; for Mr. Hyde had numbered few familiars—even the master of the servant maid had only seen him twice; his family could nowhere be traced; he had never been photographed; and the few who could describe him differed widely, as common observers will. Only on one point were they agreed; and that was the haunting sense of unexpressed deformity with which the fugitive impressed his beholders.

INCIDENT OF THE LETTER

It was late in the afternoon, when Mr. Utterson found his way to Dr. Jekyll's door, where he was at once admitted by Poole, and carried down by the kitchen offices and across a yard which had once been a garden, to the building which was indifferently known as the laboratory or dissecting rooms. The doctor had bought the house from the heirs of a celebrated surgeon; and his own tastes being rather chemical than anatomical, had changed the destination of the block at the bottom of the garden. It was the first time that the lawyer had been received in that part of his friend's quarters; and he eyed the dingy, windowless structure with curiosity, and gazed round with a distasteful sense of strangeness as he crossed the theatre, once crowded with eager students and now lying gaunt and silent, the tables laden with chemical apparatus, the floor strewn with crates and littered with packing straw, and the light falling dimly through the foggy cupola. At the further end, a flight of stairs mounted to a door covered with red baize; and through this, Mr. Utterson was at last received into the doctor's cabinet. It was a large room fitted round with glass presses, furnished, among other things, with a cheval-glass and a business table, and looking out upon the court by three dusty windows barred with iron. The fire burned in the grate; a lamp was set lighted on the chimney shelf, for even in the houses the fog began to lie thickly; and there, close up to the warmth, sat Dr. Jekyll, looking deathly sick. He did not rise to meet his visitor, but held out a cold hand and bade him welcome in a changed voice.

"And now," said Mr. Utterson, as soon as Poole had left them, "you have heard the news?"

The doctor shuddered. "They were crying it in the square," he said. "I heard them in my dining-room."

"One word," said the lawyer. "Carew was my client, but so are you, and I want to know what I am doing. You have not been mad enough to hide this fellow?"

"Utterson, I swear to God," cried the doctor, "I swear to God I will never set eyes on him again. I bind my honour to you that I am done with him in this world. It is all at an end. And indeed he does not want my help; you do not know him as I do; he is safe, he is quite safe; mark my words, he will never more be heard of."

The lawyer listened gloomily; he did not like his friend's feverish manner. "You seem pretty sure of him," said he; "and for your sake, I hope you may be right. If it came to a trial, your name might appear."

"I am quite sure of him," replied Jekyll; "I have grounds for certainty that I cannot share with any one. But there is one thing on which you may advise me. I have—I have received a letter; and I am at a loss whether I should show it to the police. I should like to leave it in your hands, Utterson; you would judge wisely, I am sure; I have so great a trust in you."

"You fear, I suppose, that it might lead to his detection?" asked the lawyer.

"No," said the other. "I cannot say that I care what becomes of Hyde; I am quite done with him. I was thinking of my own character, which this hateful business has rather exposed."

Utterson ruminated awhile; he was surprised at his friend's selfishness, and yet relieved by it. "Well," said he, at last, "let me see the letter."

The letter was written in an odd, upright hand and signed "Edward Hyde": and it signified, briefly enough, that the writer's benefactor, Dr. Jekyll, whom he had long so unworthily repaid for a thousand generosities, need labour under no alarm for his safety, as he had means of escape on which he placed a sure dependence. The lawyer liked this letter well enough; it put a better colour on the intimacy than he had looked for; and he blamed himself for some of his past suspicions.

"Have you the envelope?" he asked.

"I burned it," replied Jekyll, "before I thought what I was about. But it bore no postmark. The note was handed in."

"Shall I keep this and sleep upon it?" asked Utterson.

"I wish you to judge for me entirely," was the reply. "I have lost confidence in myself."

"Well, I shall consider," returned the lawyer. "And now one word more: it was Hyde who dictated the terms in your will about that disappearance?"

The doctor seemed seized with a qualm of faintness; he shut his mouth tight and nodded.

"I knew it," said Utterson. "He meant to murder you. You had a fine escape."

"I have had what is far more to the purpose," returned the doctor solemnly: "I have had a lesson—O God, Utterson, what a lesson I have had!" And he covered his face for a moment with his hands.

On his way out, the lawyer stopped and had a word or two with Poole. "By the bye," said he, "there was a letter handed in to-day: what was the messenger like?" But Poole was positive nothing had come except by post; "and only circulars by that," he added.

This news sent off the visitor with his fears renewed. Plainly the letter had come by the laboratory door; possibly, indeed, it had been written in the cabinet; and if that were so, it must be differently judged, and handled with the more caution. The newsboys, as he went, were crying themselves hoarse along the footways: "Special edition. Shocking murder of an M.P." That was the funeral oration of one friend and client; and he could not help a certain apprehension lest the good name of another should be sucked down in the eddy of the scandal. It was, at least, a ticklish decision that he had to make; and self-reliant as he was by habit, he began to cherish a longing for advice. It was not to be had directly; but perhaps, he thought, it might be fished for.

Presently after, he sat on one side of his own hearth, with Mr. Guest, his head clerk, upon the other, and midway between, at a nicely calculated distance from the fire, a bottle of a particular old wine that had long dwelt unsunned in the foundations of his house. The fog still slept on the wing above the drowned city, where the lamps glimmered like carbuncles; and through the muffle and smother of these fallen clouds, the procession of the town's life was still rolling in through the great arteries with a sound as of a mighty wind. But the room was gay with firelight. In the bottle the acids were long ago resolved; the imperial dye had softened with time, as the colour grows richer in stained windows; and the glow of hot autumn afternoons on hillside vineyards, was ready to be set free and to disperse the fogs of London. Insensibly the lawyer melted. There was no man from whom he kept fewer secrets than Mr. Guest; and he was not always sure that he kept as many as he meant. Guest had often been on business to the doctor's; he knew Poole; he could scarce have failed to hear of Mr. Hyde's familiarity about the house; he might draw conclusions: was it not as well, then, that he should see a letter which put that mystery to right? and above all since Guest, being a great student and critic of handwriting, would consider the step natural and obliging? The clerk, besides, was a man of counsel; he could scarce read so strange a document without dropping a remark; and by that remark Mr. Utterson might shape his future course.

"This is a sad business about Sir Danvers," he said.

"Yes, sir, indeed. It has elicited a great deal of public feeling," returned Guest. "The man, of course, was mad."

"I should like to hear your views on that," replied Utterson. "I have a document here in his handwriting; it is between ourselves, for I scarce know what to do about it; it is an ugly business at the best. But there it is; quite in your way: a murderer's autograph."

Guest's eyes brightened, and he sat down at once and studied it with passion. "No sir," he said: "not mad; but it is an odd hand."

"And by all accounts a very odd writer," added the lawyer.

Just then the servant entered with a note.

"Is that from Dr. Jekyll, sir?" inquired the clerk. "I thought I knew the writing. Anything private, Mr. Utterson?"

"Only an invitation to dinner. Why? Do you want to see it?"

"One moment. I thank you, sir;" and the clerk laid the two sheets of paper alongside and sedulously compared their contents. "Thank you, sir," he said at last, returning both; "it's a very interesting autograph."

There was a pause, during which Mr. Utterson struggled with himself. "Why did you compare them, Guest?" he inquired suddenly.

"Well, sir," returned the clerk, "there's a rather singular resemblance; the two hands are in many points identical: only differently sloped."

"Rather quaint," said Utterson.

"It is, as you say, rather quaint," returned Guest.

"I wouldn't speak of this note, you know," said the master.

"No, sir," said the clerk. "I understand."

But no sooner was Mr. Utterson alone that night, than he locked the note into his safe, where it reposed from that time forward. "What!" he thought. "Henry Jekyll forge for a murderer!" And his blood ran cold in his veins.

INCIDENT OF DR. LANYON

Time ran on; thousands of pounds were offered in reward, for the death of Sir Danvers was resented as a public injury; but Mr. Hyde had disappeared out of the ken of the police as though he had never existed. Much of his past was unearthed, indeed, and all disreputable: tales came out of the man's cruelty, at once so callous and violent; of his vile life, of his strange associates, of the hatred that seemed to have surrounded his career; but of his present whereabouts, not a whisper. From the time he had left the house in Soho on the morning of the murder, he was simply blotted out; and gradually, as time drew on, Mr. Utterson began to recover from the hotness of his alarm, and to grow more at quiet with himself. The death of Sir Danvers was, to his way of thinking, more than paid for by the disappearance of Mr. Hyde. Now that that evil influence had been withdrawn, a new life began for Dr. Jekyll. He came out of his seclusion, renewed relations with his friends, became once more their familiar guest and entertainer; and whilst he had always been known for charities, he was now no less distinguished for religion. He was busy, he was much in the open air, he did good; his face seemed to open and brighten, as if with an inward consciousness of service; and for more than two months, the doctor was at peace.

On the 8th of January Utterson had dined at the doctor's with a small party; Lanyon had been there; and the face of the host had looked from one to the other as in the old days when the trio were inseparable friends. On the 12th, and again on the 14th, the door was shut against the lawyer. "The doctor was confined to the house," Poole said, "and saw no one." On the 15th, he tried again, and was again refused; and having now been used for the last two months to see his friend almost daily, he found this return of solitude to weigh upon his spirits. The fifth night he had in Guest to dine with him; and the sixth he betook himself to Dr. Lanyon's.

There at least he was not denied admittance; but when he came in, he was shocked at the change which had taken place in the doctor's appearance. He had his death-warrant written legibly upon his face. The rosy man had grown pale; his flesh had fallen away; he was visibly balder and older; and yet it was not so much these tokens of a swift physical decay that arrested the lawyer's notice, as a look in the eye and quality of manner that seemed to testify to some deep-seated terror of the mind. It was unlikely that the doctor should fear death; and yet that was what Utterson was tempted to suspect. "Yes," he thought; "he is a doctor, he must know his own state and that his days are counted; and the knowledge is more than he can bear." And yet when Utterson remarked on his ill looks, it was with an air of great firmness that Lanyon declared himself a doomed man.

"I have had a shock," he said, "and I shall never recover. It is a question of weeks. Well, life has been pleasant; I liked it; yes, sir, I used to like it. I sometimes think if we knew all, we should be more glad to get away."

"Jekyll is ill, too," observed Utterson. "Have you seen him?"

But Lanyon's face changed, and he held up a trembling hand. "I wish to see or hear no more of Dr. Jekyll," he said in a loud, unsteady voice. "I am quite done with that person; and I beg that you will spare me any allusion to one whom I regard as dead."

"Tut, tut!" said Mr. Utterson; and then after a considerable pause, "Can't I do anything?" he inquired. "We are three very old friends, Lanyon; we shall not live to make others."

"Nothing can be done," returned Lanyon; "ask himself."

"He will not see me," said the lawyer.

"I am not surprised at that," was the reply. "Some day, Utterson, after I am dead, you may perhaps come to learn the right and wrong of this. I cannot tell you. And in the meantime, if you can sit and talk with me of other things, for God's sake, stay and do so; but if you cannot keep clear of this accursed topic, then in God's name, go, for I cannot bear it."

As soon as he got home, Utterson sat down and wrote to Jekyll, complaining of his exclusion from the house, and asking the cause of this unhappy break with Lanyon; and the next day brought him a long answer, often very pathetically worded, and sometimes darkly mysterious in drift. The quarrel with Lanyon was incurable. "I do not blame our old friend," Jekyll wrote, "but I share his view that we must never meet. I mean from henceforth to lead a life of extreme seclusion; you must not be surprised, nor must you doubt my friendship, if my door is often shut even to you. You must suffer me to go my own dark way. I have brought on myself a punishment and a danger that I cannot name. If I am the chief of sinners, I am the chief of sufferers also. I could not think that this earth contained a place for sufferings and terrors so unmanning; and you can do but one thing, Utterson, to lighten this destiny, and that is to respect my silence." Utterson was amazed; the dark influence of Hyde had been withdrawn, the doctor had returned to his old tasks and amities; a week ago, the prospect had smiled with every promise of a cheerful and an honoured age; and now in a moment, friendship, and peace of mind, and the whole tenor of his life were wrecked. So great and unprepared a change pointed to madness; but in view of Lanyon's manner and words, there must lie for it some deeper ground.

A week afterwards Dr. Lanyon took to his bed, and in something less than a fortnight he was dead. The night after the funeral, at which he had been sadly affected, Utterson locked the door of his business room, and sitting there by the light of a melancholy candle, drew out and set before him an envelope addressed by the hand and sealed with the seal of his dead friend. "PRIVATE: for the hands of G. J. Utterson ALONE, and in case of his predecease to be destroyed unread," so it was emphatically superscribed; and the lawyer dreaded to behold the contents. "I have buried one friend to-day," he thought: "what if this should cost me another?" And then he condemned the fear as a disloyalty, and broke the seal. Within there was another enclosure, likewise sealed, and marked upon the cover as "not to be opened till the death or disappearance of Dr. Henry Jekyll." Utterson could not trust his eyes. Yes, it was disappearance; here again, as in the mad will which he had long ago restored to its author, here again were the idea of a disappearance and the name of Henry Jekyll bracketted. But in the will, that idea had sprung from the sinister suggestion of the man Hyde; it was set there with a purpose all too plain and horrible. Written by the hand of Lanyon, what should it mean? A great curiosity came on the trustee, to disregard the prohibition and dive at once to the bottom of these mysteries; but professional honour and faith to his dead friend were stringent obligations; and the packet slept in the inmost corner of his private safe.

It is one thing to mortify curiosity, another to conquer it; and it may be doubted if, from that day forth, Utterson desired the society of his surviving friend with the same eagerness. He thought of him kindly; but his thoughts were disquieted and fearful. He went to call indeed; but he was perhaps relieved to be denied admittance; perhaps, in his heart, he preferred to speak with Poole upon the doorstep and surrounded by the air and sounds of the open city, rather than to be admitted into that house of voluntary bondage, and to sit and speak with its inscrutable recluse. Poole had, indeed, no very pleasant news to communicate. The doctor, it appeared, now more than ever confined himself to the cabinet over the laboratory, where he would sometimes even sleep; he was out of spirits, he had grown very silent, he did not read; it seemed as if he had something on his mind. Utterson became so used to the unvarying character of these reports, that he fell off little by little in the frequency of his visits.

INCIDENT AT THE WINDOW

It chanced on Sunday, when Mr. Utterson was on his usual walk with Mr. Enfield, that their way lay once again through the by-street; and that when they came in front of the door, both stopped to gaze on it.

"Well," said Enfield, "that story's at an end at least. We shall never see more of Mr. Hyde."

"I hope not," said Utterson. "Did I ever tell you that I once saw him, and shared your feeling of repulsion?"

"It was impossible to do the one without the other," returned Enfield. "And by the way, what an ass you must have thought me, not to know that this was a back way to Dr. Jekyll's! It was partly your own fault that I found it out, even when I did."

"So you found it out, did you?" said Utterson. "But if that be so, we may step into the court and take a look at the windows. To tell you the truth, I am uneasy about poor Jekyll; and even outside, I feel as if the presence of a friend might do him good."

The court was very cool and a little damp, and full of premature twilight, although the sky, high up overhead, was still bright with sunset. The middle one of the three windows was half-way open; and sitting close beside it, taking the air with an infinite sadness of mien, like some disconsolate prisoner, Utterson saw Dr. Jekyll.

"What! Jekyll!" he cried. "I trust you are better."

"I am very low, Utterson," replied the doctor drearily, "very low. It will not last long, thank God."

"You stay too much indoors," said the lawyer. "You should be out, whipping up the circulation like Mr. Enfield and me. (This is my cousin—Mr. Enfield—Dr. Jekyll.) Come now; get your hat and take a quick turn with us."

"You are very good," sighed the other. "I should like to very much; but no, no, no, it is quite impossible; I dare not. But indeed, Utterson, I am very glad to see you; this is really a great pleasure; I would ask you and Mr. Enfield up, but the place is really not fit."

"Why, then," said the lawyer, good-naturedly, "the best thing we can do is to stay down here and speak with you from where we are."

"That is just what I was about to venture to propose," returned the doctor with a smile. But the words were hardly uttered, before the smile was struck out of his face and succeeded by an expression of such abject terror and despair, as froze the very blood of the two gentlemen below. They saw it but for a glimpse for the window was instantly thrust down; but that glimpse had been sufficient, and they turned and left the court without a word. In silence, too, they traversed the by-street; and it was not until they had come into a neighbouring thoroughfare, where even upon a Sunday there were still some stirrings of life, that Mr. Utterson at last turned and looked at his companion. They were both pale; and there was an answering horror in their eyes.

"God forgive us, God forgive us," said Mr. Utterson.

But Mr. Enfield only nodded his head very seriously, and walked on once more in silence.

THE LAST NIGHT

Mr. Utterson was sitting by his fireside one evening after dinner, when he was surprised to receive a visit from Poole.

"Bless me, Poole, what brings you here?" he cried; and then taking a second look at him, "What ails you?" he added; "is the doctor ill?"

"Mr. Utterson," said the man, "there is something wrong."

"Take a seat, and here is a glass of wine for you," said the lawyer. "Now, take your time, and tell me plainly what you want."

"You know the doctor's ways, sir," replied Poole, "and how he shuts himself up. Well, he's shut up again in the cabinet; and I don't like it, sir—I wish I may die if I like it. Mr. Utterson, sir, I'm afraid."

"Now, my good man," said the lawyer, "be explicit. What are you afraid of?"

"I've been afraid for about a week," returned Poole, doggedly disregarding the question, "and I can bear it no more."

The man's appearance amply bore out his words; his manner was altered for the worse; and except for the moment when he had first announced his terror, he had not once looked the lawyer in the face. Even now, he sat with the glass of wine untasted on his knee, and his eyes directed to a corner of the floor. "I can bear it no more," he repeated.

"Come," said the lawyer, "I see you have some good reason, Poole; I see there is something seriously amiss. Try to tell me what it is."

"I think there's been foul play," said Poole, hoarsely.

"Foul play!" cried the lawyer, a good deal frightened and rather inclined to be irritated in consequence. "What foul play! What does the man mean?"

"I daren't say, sir," was the answer; "but will you come along with me and see for yourself?"

Mr. Utterson's only answer was to rise and get his hat and greatcoat; but he observed with wonder the greatness of the relief that appeared upon the butler's face, and perhaps with no less, that the wine was still untasted when he set it down to follow.

It was a wild, cold, seasonable night of March, with a pale moon, lying on her back as though the wind had tilted her, and flying wrack of the most diaphanous and lawny texture. The wind made talking difficult, and flecked the blood into the face. It seemed to have swept the streets unusually bare of passengers, besides; for Mr. Utterson thought he had never seen that part of London so deserted. He could have wished it otherwise; never in his life had he been conscious of so sharp a wish to see and touch his fellow-creatures; for struggle as he might, there was borne in upon his mind a crushing anticipation of calamity. The square, when they got there, was full of wind and dust, and the thin trees in the garden were lashing themselves along the railing. Poole, who had kept all the way a pace or two ahead, now pulled up in the middle of the pavement, and in spite of the biting weather, took off his hat and mopped his brow with a red pocket-handkerchief. But for all the hurry of his coming, these were not the dews of exertion that he wiped away, but the moisture of some strangling anguish; for his face was white and his voice, when he spoke, harsh and broken.

"Well, sir," he said, "here we are, and God grant there be nothing wrong."

"Amen, Poole," said the lawyer.

Thereupon the servant knocked in a very guarded manner; the door was opened on the chain; and a voice asked from within, "Is that you, Poole?"

"It's all right," said Poole. "Open the door."

The hall, when they entered it, was brightly lighted up; the fire was built high; and about the hearth the whole of the servants, men and women, stood huddled together like a flock of sheep. At the sight of Mr. Utterson, the housemaid broke into hysterical whimpering; and the cook, crying out "Bless God! it's Mr. Utterson," ran forward as if to take him in her arms.

"What, what? Are you all here?" said the lawyer peevishly. "Very irregular, very unseemly; your master would be far from pleased."

"They're all afraid," said Poole.

Blank silence followed, no one protesting; only the maid lifted her voice and now wept loudly.

"Hold your tongue!" Poole said to her, with a ferocity of accent that testified to his own jangled nerves; and indeed, when the girl had so suddenly raised the note of her lamentation, they had all started and turned towards the inner door with faces of dreadful expectation. "And now," continued the butler, addressing the knife-boy, "reach me a candle, and we'll get this through hands at once." And then he begged Mr. Utterson to follow him, and led the way to the back garden.

"Now, sir," said he, "you come as gently as you can. I want you to hear, and I don't want you to be heard. And see here, sir, if by any chance he was to ask you in, don't go."

Mr. Utterson's nerves, at this unlooked-for termination, gave a jerk that nearly threw him from his balance; but he recollected his courage and followed the butler into the laboratory building through the surgical theatre, with its lumber of crates and bottles, to the foot of the stair. Here Poole motioned him to stand on one side and listen; while he himself, setting down the candle and making a great and obvious call on his resolution, mounted the steps and knocked with a somewhat uncertain hand on the red baize of the cabinet door.

"Mr. Utterson, sir, asking to see you," he called; and even as he did so, once more violently signed to the lawyer to give ear.

A voice answered from within: "Tell him I cannot see anyone," it said complainingly.

"Thank you, sir," said Poole, with a note of something like triumph in his voice; and taking up his candle, he led Mr. Utterson back across the yard and into the great kitchen, where the fire was out and the beetles were leaping on the floor.

"Sir," he said, looking Mr. Utterson in the eyes, "Was that my master's voice?"

"It seems much changed," replied the lawyer, very pale, but giving look for look.

"Changed? Well, yes, I think so," said the butler. "Have I been twenty years in this man's house, to be deceived about his voice? No, sir; master's made away with; he was made away with eight days ago, when we heard him cry out upon the name of God; and who's in there instead of him, and why it stays there, is a thing that cries to Heaven, Mr. Utterson!"

"This is a very strange tale, Poole; this is rather a wild tale my man," said Mr. Utterson, biting his finger. "Suppose it were as you suppose, supposing Dr. Jekyll to have been—well, murdered, what could induce the murderer to stay? That won't hold water; it doesn't commend itself to reason."

"Well, Mr. Utterson, you are a hard man to satisfy, but I'll do it yet," said Poole. "All this last week (you must know) him, or it, whatever it is that lives in that cabinet, has been crying night and day for some sort of medicine and cannot get it to his mind. It was sometimes his way—the master's, that is—to write his orders on a sheet of paper and throw it on the stair. We've had nothing else this week back; nothing but papers, and a closed door, and the very meals left there to be smuggled in when nobody was looking. Well, sir, every day, ay, and twice and thrice in the same day, there have been orders and complaints, and I have been sent flying to all the wholesale chemists in town. Every time I brought the stuff back, there would be another paper telling me to return it, because it was not pure, and another order to a different firm. This drug is wanted bitter bad, sir, whatever for."

"Have you any of these papers?" asked Mr. Utterson.

Poole felt in his pocket and handed out a crumpled note, which the lawyer, bending nearer to the candle, carefully examined. Its contents ran thus: "Dr. Jekyll presents his compliments to Messrs. Maw. He assures them that their last sample is impure and quite useless for his present purpose. In the year 18—, Dr. J. purchased a somewhat large quantity from Messrs. M. He now begs them to search with most sedulous care, and should any of the same quality be left, forward it to him at once. Expense is no consideration. The importance of this to Dr. J. can hardly be exaggerated." So far the letter had run composedly enough, but here with a sudden splutter of the pen, the writer's emotion had broken loose. "For God's sake," he added, "find me some of the old."

"This is a strange note," said Mr. Utterson; and then sharply, "How do you come to have it open?"

"The man at Maw's was main angry, sir, and he threw it back to me like so much dirt," returned Poole.

"This is unquestionably the doctor's hand, do you know?" resumed the lawyer.

"I thought it looked like it," said the servant rather sulkily; and then, with another voice, "But what matters hand of write?" he said. "I've seen him!"

"Seen him?" repeated Mr. Utterson. "Well?"

"That's it!" said Poole. "It was this way. I came suddenly into the theatre from the garden. It seems he had slipped out to look for this drug or whatever it is; for the cabinet door was open, and there he was at the far end of the room digging among the crates. He looked up when I came in, gave a kind of cry, and whipped upstairs into the cabinet. It was but for one minute that I saw him, but the hair stood upon my head like quills. Sir, if that was my master, why had he a mask upon his face? If it was my master, why did he cry out like a rat, and run from me? I have served him long enough. And then..." The man paused and passed his hand over his face.

"These are all very strange circumstances," said Mr. Utterson, "but I think I begin to see daylight. Your master, Poole, is plainly seized with one of those maladies that both torture and deform the sufferer; hence, for aught I know, the alteration of his voice; hence the mask and the avoidance of his friends; hence his eagerness to find this drug, by means of which the poor soul retains some hope of ultimate recovery—God grant that he be not deceived! There is my explanation; it is sad enough, Poole, ay, and appalling to consider; but it is plain and natural, hangs well together, and delivers us from all exorbitant alarms."

"Sir," said the butler, turning to a sort of mottled pallor, "that thing was not my master, and there's the truth. My master"—here he looked round him and began to whisper—"is a tall, fine build of a man, and this was more of a dwarf." Utterson attempted to protest. "O, sir," cried Poole, "do you think I do not know my master after twenty years? Do you think I do not know where his head comes to in the cabinet door, where I saw him every morning of my life? No, sir, that thing in the mask was never Dr. Jekyll—God knows what it was, but it was never Dr. Jekyll; and it is the belief of my heart that there was murder done."

"Poole," replied the lawyer, "if you say that, it will become my duty to make certain. Much as I desire to spare your master's feelings, much as I am puzzled by this note which seems to prove him to be still alive, I shall consider it my duty to break in that door."

"Ah, Mr. Utterson, that's talking!" cried the butler.

"And now comes the second question," resumed Utterson: "Who is going to do it?"

"Why, you and me, sir," was the undaunted reply.

"That's very well said," returned the lawyer; "and whatever comes of it, I shall make it my business to see you are no loser."

"There is an axe in the theatre," continued Poole; "and you might take the kitchen poker for yourself."

The lawyer took that rude but weighty instrument into his hand, and balanced it. "Do you know, Poole," he said, looking up, "that you and I are about to place ourselves in a position of some peril?"

"You may say so, sir, indeed," returned the butler.

"It is well, then that we should be frank," said the other. "We both think more than we have said; let us make a clean breast. This masked figure that you saw, did you recognise it?"

"Well, sir, it went so quick, and the creature was so doubled up, that I could hardly swear to that," was the answer. "But if you mean, was it Mr. Hyde?—why, yes, I think it was! You see, it was much of the same bigness; and it had the same quick, light way with it; and then who else could have got in by the laboratory door? You have not forgot, sir, that at the time of the murder he had still the key with him? But that's not all. I don't know, Mr. Utterson, if you ever met this Mr. Hyde?"

"Yes," said the lawyer, "I once spoke with him."

"Then you must know as well as the rest of us that there was something queer about that gentleman—something that gave a man a turn—I don't know rightly how to say it, sir, beyond this: that you felt in your marrow kind of cold and thin."

"I own I felt something of what you describe," said Mr. Utterson.

"Quite so, sir," returned Poole. "Well, when that masked thing like a monkey jumped from among the chemicals and whipped into the cabinet, it went down my spine like ice. O, I know it's not evidence, Mr. Utterson; I'm book-learned enough for that; but a man has his feelings, and I give you my bible-word it was Mr. Hyde!"

"Ay, ay," said the lawyer. "My fears incline to the same point. Evil, I fear, founded—evil was sure to come—of that connection. Ay truly, I believe you; I believe poor Harry is killed; and I believe his murderer (for what purpose, God alone can tell) is still lurking in his victim's room. Well, let our name be vengeance. Call Bradshaw."

The footman came at the summons, very white and nervous.

"Pull yourself together, Bradshaw," said the lawyer. "This suspense, I know, is telling upon all of you; but it is now our intention to make an end of it. Poole, here, and I are going to force our way into the cabinet. If all is well, my shoulders are broad enough to bear the blame. Meanwhile, lest anything should really be amiss, or any malefactor seek to escape by the back, you and the boy must go round the corner with a pair of good sticks and take your post at the laboratory door. We give you ten minutes to get to your stations."

As Bradshaw left, the lawyer looked at his watch. "And now, Poole, let us get to ours," he said; and taking the poker under his arm, led the way into the yard. The scud had banked over the moon, and it was now quite dark. The wind, which only broke in puffs and draughts into that deep well of building, tossed the light of the candle to and fro about their steps, until they came into the shelter of the theatre, where they sat down silently to wait. London hummed solemnly all around; but nearer at hand, the stillness was only broken by the sounds of a footfall moving to and fro along the cabinet floor.

"So it will walk all day, sir," whispered Poole; "ay, and the better part of the night. Only when a new sample comes from the chemist, there's a bit of a break. Ah, it's an ill conscience that's such an enemy to rest! Ah, sir, there's blood foully shed in every step of it! But hark again, a little closer—put your heart in your ears, Mr. Utterson, and tell me, is that the doctor's foot?"

The steps fell lightly and oddly, with a certain swing, for all they went so slowly; it was different indeed from the heavy creaking tread of Henry Jekyll. Utterson sighed. "Is there never anything else?" he asked.

Poole nodded. "Once," he said. "Once I heard it weeping!"

"Weeping? how that?" said the lawyer, conscious of a sudden chill of horror.

"Weeping like a woman or a lost soul," said the butler. "I came away with that upon my heart, that I could have wept too."

But now the ten minutes drew to an end. Poole disinterred the axe from under a stack of packing straw; the candle was set upon the nearest table to light them to the attack; and they drew near with bated breath to where that patient foot was still going up and down, up and down, in the quiet of the night.

"Jekyll," cried Utterson, with a loud voice, "I demand to see you." He paused a moment, but there came no reply. "I give you fair warning, our suspicions are aroused, and I must and shall see you," he resumed; "if not by fair means, then by foul—if not of your consent, then by brute force!"

"Utterson," said the voice, "for God's sake, have mercy!"

"Ah, that's not Jekyll's voice—it's Hyde's!" cried Utterson. "Down with the door, Poole!"

Poole swung the axe over his shoulder; the blow shook the building, and the red baize door leaped against the lock and hinges. A dismal screech, as of mere animal terror, rang from the cabinet. Up went the axe again, and again the panels crashed and the frame bounded; four times the blow fell; but the wood was tough and the fittings were of excellent workmanship; and it was not until the fifth, that the lock burst and the wreck of the door fell inwards on the carpet.

The besiegers, appalled by their own riot and the stillness that had succeeded, stood back a little and peered in. There lay the cabinet before their eyes in the quiet lamplight, a good fire glowing and chattering on the hearth, the kettle singing its thin strain, a drawer or two open, papers neatly set forth on the business table, and nearer the fire, the things laid out for tea; the quietest room, you would have said, and, but for the glazed presses full of chemicals, the most commonplace that night in London.

Right in the middle there lay the body of a man sorely contorted and still twitching. They drew near on tiptoe, turned it on its back and beheld the face of Edward Hyde. He was dressed in clothes far too large for him, clothes of the doctor's bigness; the cords of his face still moved with a semblance of life, but life was quite gone; and by the crushed phial in the hand and the strong smell of kernels that hung upon the air, Utterson knew that he was looking on the body of a self-destroyer.

"We have come too late," he said sternly, "whether to save or punish. Hyde is gone to his account; and it only remains for us to find the body of your master."

The far greater proportion of the building was occupied by the theatre, which filled almost the whole ground storey and was lighted from above, and by the cabinet, which formed an upper storey at one end and looked upon the court. A corridor joined the theatre to the door on the by-street; and with this the cabinet communicated separately by a second flight of stairs. There were besides a few dark closets and a spacious cellar. All these they now thoroughly examined. Each closet needed but a glance, for all were empty, and all, by the dust that fell from their doors, had stood long unopened. The cellar, indeed, was filled with crazy lumber, mostly dating from the times of the surgeon who was Jekyll's predecessor; but even as they opened the door they were advertised of the uselessness of further search, by the fall of a perfect mat of cobweb which had for years sealed up the entrance. Nowhere was there any trace of Henry Jekyll, dead or alive.

Poole stamped on the flags of the corridor. "He must be buried here," he said, hearkening to the sound.

"Or he may have fled," said Utterson, and he turned to examine the door in the by-street. It was locked; and lying near by on the flags, they found the key, already stained with rust.

"This does not look like use," observed the lawyer.

"Use!" echoed Poole. "Do you not see, sir, it is broken? much as if a man had stamped on it."

"Ay," continued Utterson, "and the fractures, too, are rusty." The two men looked at each other with a scare. "This is beyond me, Poole," said the lawyer. "Let us go back to the cabinet."

They mounted the stair in silence, and still with an occasional awestruck glance at the dead body, proceeded more thoroughly to examine the contents of the cabinet. At one table, there were traces of chemical work, various measured heaps of some white salt being laid on glass saucers, as though for an experiment in which the unhappy man had been prevented.

"That is the same drug that I was always bringing him," said Poole; and even as he spoke, the kettle with a startling noise boiled over.

This brought them to the fireside, where the easy-chair was drawn cosily up, and the tea things stood ready to the sitter's elbow, the very sugar in the cup. There were several books on a shelf; one lay beside the tea things open, and Utterson was amazed to find it a copy of a pious work, for which Jekyll had several times expressed a great esteem, annotated, in his own hand with startling blasphemies.

Next, in the course of their review of the chamber, the searchers came to the cheval-glass, into whose depths they looked with an involuntary horror. But it was so turned as to show them nothing but the rosy glow playing on the roof, the fire sparkling in a hundred repetitions along the glazed front of the presses, and their own pale and fearful countenances stooping to look in.

"This glass has seen some strange things, sir," whispered Poole.

"And surely none stranger than itself," echoed the lawyer in the same tones. "For what did Jekyll"—he caught himself up at the word with a start, and then conquering the weakness—"what could Jekyll want with it?" he said.

"You may say that!" said Poole.

Next they turned to the business table. On the desk, among the neat array of papers, a large envelope was uppermost, and bore, in the doctor's hand, the name of Mr. Utterson. The lawyer unsealed it, and several enclosures fell to the floor. The first was a will, drawn in the same eccentric terms as the one which he had returned six months before, to serve as a testament in case of death and as a deed of gift in case of disappearance; but in place of the name of Edward Hyde, the lawyer, with indescribable amazement read the name of Gabriel John Utterson. He looked at Poole, and then back at the paper, and last of all at the dead malefactor stretched upon the carpet.

"My head goes round," he said. "He has been all these days in possession; he had no cause to like me; he must have raged to see himself displaced; and he has not destroyed this document."

He caught up the next paper; it was a brief note in the doctor's hand and dated at the top. "O Poole!" the lawyer cried, "he was alive and here this day. He cannot have been disposed of in so short a space; he must be still alive, he must have fled! And then, why fled? and how? and in that case, can we venture to declare this suicide? O, we must be careful. I foresee that we may yet involve your master in some dire catastrophe."

"Why don't you read it, sir?" asked Poole.

"Because I fear," replied the lawyer solemnly. "God grant I have no cause for it!" And with that he brought the paper to his eyes and read as follows:

"My dear Utterson,—When this shall fall into your hands, I shall have disappeared, under what circumstances I have not the penetration to foresee, but my instinct and all the circumstances of my nameless situation tell me that the end is sure and must be early. Go then, and first read the narrative which Lanyon warned me he was to place in your hands; and if you care to hear more, turn to the confession of

"Your unworthy and unhappy friend,

"HENRY JEKYLL."

"There was a third enclosure?" asked Utterson.

"Here, sir," said Poole, and gave into his hands a considerable packet sealed in several places.

The lawyer put it in his pocket. "I would say nothing of this paper. If your master has fled or is dead, we may at least save his credit. It is now ten; I must go home and read these documents in quiet; but I shall be back before midnight, when we shall send for the police."

They went out, locking the door of the theatre behind them; and Utterson, once more leaving the servants gathered about the fire in the hall, trudged back to his office to read the two narratives in which this mystery was now to be explained.

DR. LANYON'S NARRATIVE

On the ninth of January, now four days ago, I received by the evening delivery a registered envelope, addressed in the hand of my colleague and old school companion, Henry Jekyll. I was a good deal surprised by this; for we were by no means in the habit of correspondence; I had seen the man, dined with him, indeed, the night before; and I could imagine nothing in our intercourse that should justify formality of registration. The contents increased my wonder; for this is how the letter ran:

"10th December, 18—.

"Dear Lanyon,—You are one of my oldest friends; and although we may have differed at times on scientific questions, I cannot remember, at least on my side, any break in our affection. There was never a day when, if you had said to me, 'Jekyll, my life, my honour, my reason, depend upon you,' I would not have sacrificed my left hand to help you. Lanyon, my life, my honour, my reason, are all at your mercy; if you fail me to-night, I am lost. You might suppose, after this preface, that I am going to ask you for something dishonourable to grant. Judge for yourself.

"I want you to postpone all other engagements for to-night—ay, even if you were summoned to the bedside of an emperor; to take a cab, unless your carriage should be actually at the door; and with this letter in your hand for consultation, to drive straight to my house. Poole, my butler, has his orders; you will find him waiting your arrival with a locksmith. The door of my cabinet is then to be forced; and you are to go in alone; to open the glazed press (letter E) on the left hand, breaking the lock if it be shut; and to draw out, with all its contents as they stand, the fourth drawer from the top or (which is the same thing) the third from the bottom. In my extreme distress of mind, I have a morbid fear of misdirecting you; but even if I am in error, you may know the right drawer by its contents: some powders, a phial and a paper book. This drawer I beg of you to carry back with you to Cavendish Square exactly as it stands.

"That is the first part of the service: now for the second. You should be back, if you set out at once on the receipt of this, long before midnight; but I will leave you that amount of margin, not only in the fear of one of those obstacles that can neither be prevented nor foreseen, but because an hour when your servants are in bed is to be preferred for what will then remain to do. At midnight, then, I have to ask you to be alone in your consulting room, to admit with your own hand into the house a man who will present himself in my name, and to place in his hands the drawer that you will have brought with you from my cabinet. Then you will have played your part and earned my gratitude completely. Five minutes afterwards, if you insist upon an explanation, you will have understood that these arrangements are of capital importance; and that by the neglect of one of them, fantastic as they must appear, you might have charged your conscience with my death or the shipwreck of my reason.

"Confident as I am that you will not trifle with this appeal, my heart sinks and my hand trembles at the bare thought of such a possibility. Think of me at this hour, in a strange place, labouring under a blackness of distress that no fancy can exaggerate, and yet well aware that, if you will but punctually serve me, my troubles will roll away like a story that is told. Serve me, my dear Lanyon and save

"Your friend,

"H.J.

"P.S.—I had already sealed this up when a fresh terror struck upon my soul. It is possible that the post-office may fail me, and this letter not come into your hands until to-morrow morning. In that case, dear Lanyon, do my errand when it shall be most convenient for you in the course of the day; and once more expect my messenger at midnight. It may then already be too late; and if that night passes without event, you will know that you have seen the last of Henry Jekyll."

Upon the reading of this letter, I made sure my colleague was insane; but till that was proved beyond the possibility of doubt, I felt bound to do as he requested. The less I understood of this farrago, the less I was in a position to judge of its importance; and an appeal so worded could not be set aside without a grave responsibility. I rose accordingly from table, got into a hansom, and drove straight to Jekyll's house. The butler was awaiting my arrival; he had received by the same post as mine a registered letter of instruction, and had sent at once for a locksmith and a carpenter. The tradesmen came while we were yet speaking; and we moved in a body to old Dr. Denman's surgical theatre, from which (as you are doubtless aware) Jekyll's private cabinet is most conveniently entered. The door was very strong, the lock excellent; the carpenter avowed he would have great trouble and have to do much damage, if force were to be used; and the locksmith was near despair. But this last was a handy fellow, and after two hour's work, the door stood open. The press marked E was unlocked; and I took out the drawer, had it filled up with straw and tied in a sheet, and returned with it to Cavendish Square.

Here I proceeded to examine its contents. The powders were neatly enough made up, but not with the nicety of the dispensing chemist; so that it was plain they were of Jekyll's private manufacture; and when I opened one of the wrappers I found what seemed to me a simple crystalline salt of a white colour. The phial, to which I next turned my attention, might have been about half full of a blood-red liquor, which was highly pungent to the sense of smell and seemed to me to contain phosphorus and some volatile ether. At the other ingredients I could make no guess. The book was an ordinary version book and contained little but a series of dates. These covered a period of many years, but I observed that the entries ceased nearly a year ago and quite abruptly. Here and there a brief remark was appended to a date, usually no more than a single word: "double" occurring perhaps six times in a total of several hundred entries; and once very early in the list and followed by several marks of exclamation, "total failure!!!" All this, though it whetted my curiosity, told me little that was definite. Here were a phial of some salt, and the record of a series of experiments that had led (like too many of Jekyll's investigations) to no end of practical usefulness. How could the presence of these articles in my house affect either the honour, the sanity, or the life of my flighty colleague? If his messenger could go to one place, why could he not go to another? And even granting some impediment, why was this gentleman to be received by me in secret? The more I reflected the more convinced I grew that I was dealing with a case of cerebral disease; and though I dismissed my servants to bed, I loaded an old revolver, that I might be found in some posture of self-defence.

Twelve o'clock had scarce rung out over London, ere the knocker sounded very gently on the door. I went myself at the summons, and found a small man crouching against the pillars of the portico.

"Are you come from Dr. Jekyll?" I asked.

He told me "yes" by a constrained gesture; and when I had bidden him enter, he did not obey me without a searching backward glance into the darkness of the square. There was a policeman not far off, advancing with his bull's eye open; and at the sight, I thought my visitor started and made greater haste.

These particulars struck me, I confess, disagreeably; and as I followed him into the bright light of the consulting room, I kept my hand ready on my weapon. Here, at last, I had a chance of clearly seeing him. I had never set eyes on him before, so much was certain. He was small, as

I have said; I was struck besides with the shocking expression of his face, with his remarkable combination of great muscular activity and great apparent debility of constitution, and—last but not least—with the odd, subjective disturbance caused by his neighbourhood. This bore some resemblance to incipient rigour, and was accompanied by a marked sinking of the pulse. At the time, I set it down to some idiosyncratic, personal distaste, and merely wondered at the acuteness of the symptoms; but I have since had reason to believe the cause to lie much deeper in the nature of man, and to turn on some nobler hinge than the principle of hatred.

This person (who had thus, from the first moment of his entrance, struck in me what I can only describe as a disgustful curiosity) was dressed in a fashion that would have made an ordinary person laughable; his clothes, that is to say, although they were of rich and sober fabric, were enormously too large for him in every measurement—the trousers hanging on his legs and rolled up to keep them from the ground, the waist of the coat below his haunches, and the collar sprawling wide upon his shoulders. Strange to relate, this ludicrous accoutrement was far from moving me to laughter. Rather, as there was something abnormal and misbegotten in the very essence of the creature that now faced me—something seizing, surprising and revolting—this fresh disparity seemed but to fit in with and to reinforce it; so that to my interest in the man's nature and character, there was added a curiosity as to his origin, his life, his fortune and status in the world.

These observations, though they have taken so great a space to be set down in, were yet the work of a few seconds. My visitor was, indeed, on fire with sombre excitement.

"Have you got it?" he cried. "Have you got it?" And so lively was his impatience that he even laid his hand upon my arm and sought to shake me.

I put him back, conscious at his touch of a certain icy pang along my blood. "Come, sir," said I. "You forget that I have not yet the pleasure of your acquaintance. Be seated, if you please." And I showed him an example, and sat down myself in my customary seat and with as fair an imitation of my ordinary manner to a patient, as the lateness of the hour, the nature of my preoccupations, and the horror I had of my visitor, would suffer me to muster.

"I beg your pardon, Dr. Lanyon," he replied civilly enough. "What you say is very well founded; and my impatience has shown its heels to my politeness. I come here at the instance of your colleague, Dr. Henry Jekyll, on a piece of business of some moment; and I understood..." He paused and put his hand to his throat, and I could see, in spite of his collected manner, that he was wrestling against the approaches of the hysteria—"I understood, a drawer..."

But here I took pity on my visitor's suspense, and some perhaps on my own growing curiosity.

"There it is, sir," said I, pointing to the drawer, where it lay on the floor behind a table and still covered with the sheet.

He sprang to it, and then paused, and laid his hand upon his heart; I could hear his teeth grate with the convulsive action of his jaws; and his face was so ghastly to see that I grew alarmed both for his life and reason.

"Compose yourself," said I.

He turned a dreadful smile to me, and as if with the decision of despair, plucked away the sheet. At sight of the contents, he uttered one loud sob of such immense relief that I sat petrified. And the next moment, in a voice that was already fairly well under control, "Have you a graduated glass?" he asked.

I rose from my place with something of an effort and gave him what he asked.

He thanked me with a smiling nod, measured out a few minims of the red tincture and added one of the powders. The mixture, which was at first of a reddish hue, began, in proportion as the crystals melted, to brighten in colour, to effervesce audibly, and to throw off small fumes of vapour. Suddenly and at the same moment, the ebullition ceased and the compound changed to a dark purple, which faded again more slowly to a watery green. My visitor, who had watched these metamorphoses with a keen eye, smiled, set down the glass upon the table, and then turned and looked upon me with an air of scrutiny.

"And now," said he, "to settle what remains. Will you be wise? will you be guided? will you suffer me to take this glass in my hand and to go forth from your house without further parley? or has the greed of curiosity too much command of you? Think before you answer, for it shall be done as you decide. As you decide, you shall be left as you were before, and neither richer nor wiser, unless the sense of service rendered to a man in mortal distress may be counted as a kind of riches of the soul. Or, if you shall so prefer to choose, a new province of knowledge and new avenues to fame and power shall be laid open to you, here, in this room, upon the instant; and your sight shall be blasted by a prodigy to stagger the unbelief of Satan."

"Sir," said I, affecting a coolness that I was far from truly possessing, "you speak enigmas, and you will perhaps not wonder that I hear you with no very strong impression of belief. But I have gone too far in the way of inexplicable services to pause before I see the end."

"It is well," replied my visitor. "Lanyon, you remember your vows: what follows is under the seal of our profession. And now, you who have so long been bound to the most narrow and material views, you who have denied the virtue of transcendental medicine, you who have derided your superiors—behold!"

He put the glass to his lips and drank at one gulp. A cry followed; he reeled, staggered, clutched at the table and held on, staring with injected eyes, gasping with open mouth; and as I looked there came, I thought, a change—he seemed to swell—his face became suddenly black and the features seemed to melt and alter—and the next moment, I had sprung to my feet and leaped back against the wall, my arms raised to shield me from that prodigy, my mind submerged in terror.

"O God!" I screamed, and "O God!" again and again; for there before my eyes—pale and shaken, and half fainting, and groping before him with his hands, like a man restored from death—there stood Henry Jekyll!

What he told me in the next hour, I cannot bring my mind to set on paper. I saw what I saw, I heard what I heard, and my soul sickened at it; and yet now when that sight has faded from my eyes, I ask myself if I believe it, and I cannot answer. My life is shaken to its roots; sleep has left me; the deadliest terror sits by me at all hours of the day and night; and I feel that my days are numbered, and that I must die; and yet I shall die incredulous. As for the moral turpitude that man unveiled to me, even with tears of penitence, I cannot, even in memory, dwell on it without a start of horror. I will say but one thing, Utterson, and that (if you can bring your mind to credit it) will be more than enough. The creature who crept into my house that night was, on Jekyll's own confession, known by the name of Hyde and hunted for in every corner of the land as the murderer of Carew.

HASTIE LANYON.
HENRY JEKYLL'S FULL STATEMENT OF THE CASE

I was born in the year 18— to a large fortune, endowed besides with excellent parts, inclined by nature to industry, fond of the respect of the wise and good among my fellowmen, and thus, as might have been supposed, with every guarantee of an honourable and distinguished future. And indeed the worst of my faults was a certain impatient gaiety of disposition, such as has made the happiness of many, but such as I found it hard to reconcile with my imperious desire to carry my head high, and wear a more than commonly grave countenance before the public. Hence it came about that I concealed my pleasures; and that when I reached years of reflection, and began to look round me and take stock of my progress and position in the world, I stood already committed to a profound duplicity of life. Many a man would have even blazoned such irregularities as I was guilty of; but from the high views that I had set before me, I regarded and hid them with an almost morbid sense of shame. It was thus rather the exacting nature of my aspirations than any particular degradation in my faults, that made me what I was, and, with even a deeper trench than in the majority of men, severed in me those provinces of good and ill which divide and compound man's dual nature. In this case, I was driven to reflect deeply and inveterately on that hard law of life, which lies at the root of religion and is one of the most plentiful springs of distress. Though so profound a double-dealer, I was in no sense a hypocrite; both sides of me were in dead earnest; I was no more myself when I laid aside restraint and plunged in shame, than when I laboured, in the eye of day, at the furtherance of knowledge or the relief of sorrow and suffering. And it chanced that the direction of my scientific studies, which led wholly towards the mystic and the transcendental, reacted and shed a strong light on this consciousness of the perennial war among my members. With every day, and from both sides of my intelligence, the moral and the intellectual, I thus drew steadily nearer to that truth, by whose partial discovery I have been doomed to such a dreadful shipwreck: that man is not truly one, but truly two. I say two, because the state of my own knowledge does not pass beyond that point. Others will follow, others will outstrip me on the same lines; and I hazard the guess that man will be ultimately known for a mere polity of multifarious, incongruous and independent denizens. I, for my part, from the nature of my life, advanced infallibly in one direction and in one direction only. It was on the moral side, and in my own person, that I learned to recognise the thorough and primitive duality of man; I saw that, of the two natures that contended in the field of my consciousness, even if I could rightly be said to be either, it was only because I was radically both; and from an early date, even before the course of my scientific discoveries had begun to suggest the most naked possibility of such a miracle, I had learned to dwell with pleasure, as a beloved daydream, on the thought of the separation of these elements. If each, I told myself, could be housed in separate identities, life would be relieved of all that was unbearable; the unjust might go his way, delivered from the aspirations and remorse of his more upright twin; and the just could walk steadfastly and securely on his upward path, doing the good things in which he found his pleasure, and no longer exposed to disgrace and penitence by the hands of this extraneous evil. It was the curse of mankind that these incongruous faggots were thus bound together—that in the agonised womb of consciousness, these polar twins should be continuously struggling. How, then were they dissociated?

I was so far in my reflections when, as I have said, a side light began to shine upon the subject from the laboratory table. I began to perceive more deeply than it has ever yet been stated, the trembling immateriality, the mistlike transience, of this seemingly so solid body in which we walk attired. Certain agents I found to have the power to shake and pluck back that fleshly vestment, even as a wind might toss the curtains of a pavilion. For two good reasons, I will not enter deeply into this scientific branch of my confession. First, because I have been made to learn that the doom and burthen of our life is bound for ever on man's shoulders, and when the attempt is made to cast it off, it but returns upon us with more unfamiliar and more awful pressure. Second, because, as my narrative will make, alas! too evident, my discoveries were incomplete. Enough then, that I not only recognised my natural body from the mere aura and effulgence of certain of the powers that made up my spirit, but managed to compound a drug by which these powers should be dethroned from their supremacy, and a second form and countenance substituted, none the less natural to me because they were the expression, and bore the stamp of lower elements in my soul.

I hesitated long before I put this theory to the test of practice. I knew well that I risked death; for any drug that so potently controlled and shook the very fortress of identity, might, by the least scruple of an overdose or at the least inopportunity in the moment of exhibition, utterly blot out that immaterial tabernacle which I looked to it to change. But the temptation of a discovery so singular and profound at last overcame the suggestions of alarm. I had long since prepared my tincture; I purchased at once, from a firm of wholesale chemists, a large quantity of a particular salt which I knew, from my experiments, to be the last ingredient required; and late one accursed night, I compounded the elements, watched them boil and smoke together in the glass, and when the ebullition had subsided, with a strong glow of courage, drank off the potion.

The most racking pangs succeeded: a grinding in the bones, deadly nausea, and a horror of the spirit that cannot be exceeded at the hour of birth or death. Then these agonies began swiftly to subside, and I came to myself as if out of a great sickness. There was something strange in my sensations, something indescribably new and, from its very novelty, incredibly sweet. I felt younger, lighter, happier in body; within I was conscious of a heady recklessness, a current of disordered sensual images running like a millrace in my fancy, a solution of the bonds of obligation, an unknown but not an innocent freedom of the soul. I knew myself, at the first breath of this new life, to be more wicked, tenfold more wicked, sold a slave to my original evil; and the thought, in that moment, braced and delighted me like wine. I stretched out my hands, exulting in the freshness of these sensations; and in the act, I was suddenly aware that I had lost in stature.

There was no mirror, at that date, in my room; that which stands beside me as I write, was brought there later on and for the very purpose of these transformations. The night however, was far gone into the morning—the morning, black as it was, was nearly ripe for the conception of the day—the inmates of my house were locked in the most rigorous hours of slumber; and I determined, flushed as I was with hope and triumph, to venture in my new shape as far as to my bedroom. I crossed the yard, wherein the constellations looked down upon me, I could have thought, with wonder, the first creature of that sort that their unsleeping vigilance had yet disclosed to them; I stole through the corridors, a stranger in my own house; and coming to my room, I saw for the first time the appearance of Edward Hyde.

I must here speak by theory alone, saying not that which I know, but that which I suppose to be most probable. The evil side of my nature, to which I had now transferred the stamping efficacy, was less robust and less developed than the good which I had just deposed. Again, in the course of my life, which had been, after all, nine tenths a life of effort, virtue and control, it had been much less exercised and much less exhausted. And hence, as I think, it came about that Edward Hyde was so much smaller, slighter and younger than Henry Jekyll. Even as good shone upon the countenance of the one, evil was written broadly and plainly on the face of the other. Evil besides (which I must still believe to be the lethal side of man) had left on that body an imprint of deformity and decay. And yet when I looked upon that ugly idol in the glass, I was conscious of no repugnance, rather of a leap of welcome. This, too, was myself. It seemed natural and human. In my eyes it bore a livelier image of the spirit, it seemed more express and single, than the imperfect and divided countenance I had been hitherto accustomed to call mine. And in so far I was doubtless right. I have observed that when I wore the semblance of Edward Hyde, none could come near to me at first without a visible misgiving of the flesh. This, as I take it, was because all human beings, as we meet them, are commingled out of good and evil: and Edward Hyde, alone in the ranks of mankind, was pure evil.

I lingered but a moment at the mirror: the second and conclusive experiment had yet to be attempted; it yet remained to be seen if I had lost my identity beyond redemption and must flee before daylight from a house that was no longer mine; and hurrying back to my cabinet, I once more prepared and drank the cup, once more suffered the pangs of dissolution, and came to myself once more with the character, the stature and the face of Henry Jekyll.

That night I had come to the fatal cross-roads. Had I approached my discovery in a more noble spirit, had I risked the experiment while under the empire of generous or pious aspirations, all must have been otherwise, and from these agonies of death and birth, I had come forth an angel instead of a fiend. The drug had no discriminating action; it was neither diabolical nor divine; it but shook the doors of the prisonhouse of my disposition; and like the captives of Philippi, that which stood within ran forth. At that time my virtue slumbered; my evil, kept awake by ambition, was alert and swift to seize the occasion; and the thing that was projected was Edward Hyde. Hence, although I had now two characters as well as two appearances, one was wholly evil, and the other was still the old Henry Jekyll, that incongruous compound of whose reformation and improvement I had already learned to despair. The movement was thus wholly toward the worse.

Even at that time, I had not conquered my aversions to the dryness of a life of study. I would still be merrily disposed at times; and as my pleasures were (to say the least) undignified, and I was not only well known and highly considered, but growing towards the elderly man, this incoherency of my life was daily growing more unwelcome. It was on this side that my new power tempted me until I fell in slavery. I had but to drink the cup, to doff at once the body of the noted professor, and to assume, like a thick cloak, that of Edward Hyde. I smiled at the notion; it seemed to me at the time to be humourous; and I made my preparations with the most studious care. I took and furnished that house in Soho, to which Hyde was tracked by the police; and engaged as a housekeeper a creature whom I knew well to be silent and unscrupulous. On the other side, I announced to my servants that a Mr. Hyde (whom I described) was to have full liberty and power about my house in the square; and to parry mishaps, I even called and made myself a familiar object, in my second character. I next drew up that will to which you so much objected; so that if anything befell me in the person of Dr. Jekyll, I could enter on that of Edward Hyde without pecuniary loss. And thus fortified, as I supposed, on every side, I began to profit by the strange immunities of my position.

Men have before hired bravos to transact their crimes, while their own person and reputation sat under shelter. I was the first that ever did so for his pleasures. I was the first that could plod in the public eye with a load of genial respectability, and in a moment, like a schoolboy, strip off these lendings and spring headlong into the sea of liberty. But for me, in my impenetrable mantle, the safety was complete. Think of it—I did not even exist! Let me but escape into my laboratory door, give me but a second or two to mix and swallow the draught that I had always standing ready; and whatever he had done, Edward Hyde would pass away like the stain of breath upon a mirror; and there in his stead, quietly at home, trimming the midnight lamp in his study, a man who could afford to laugh at suspicion, would be Henry Jekyll.

The pleasures which I made haste to seek in my disguise were, as I have said, undignified; I would scarce use a harder term. But in the hands of Edward Hyde, they soon began to turn toward the monstrous. When I would come back from these excursions, I was often plunged into a kind of wonder at my vicarious depravity. This familiar that I called out of my own soul, and sent forth alone to do his good pleasure, was a being inherently malign and villainous; his every act and thought centered on self; drinking pleasure with bestial avidity from any degree of torture to another; relentless like a man of stone. Henry Jekyll stood at times aghast before the acts of Edward Hyde; but the situation was apart from ordinary laws, and insidiously relaxed the grasp of conscience. It was Hyde, after all, and Hyde alone, that was guilty. Jekyll was no worse; he woke again to his good qualities seemingly unimpaired; he would even make haste, where it was possible, to undo the evil done by Hyde. And thus his conscience slumbered.

Into the details of the infamy at which I thus connived (for even now I can scarce grant that I committed it) I have no design of entering; I mean but to point out the warnings and the successive steps with which my chastisement approached. I met with one accident which, as it brought on no consequence, I shall no more than mention. An act of cruelty to a child aroused against me the anger of a passer-by, whom I recognised the other day in the person of your kinsman; the doctor and the child's family joined him; there were moments when I feared for my life; and at last, in order to pacify their too just resentment, Edward Hyde had to bring them to the door, and pay them in a cheque drawn in the name of Henry Jekyll. But this danger was easily eliminated from the future, by opening an account at another bank in the name of Edward Hyde himself; and when, by sloping my own hand backward, I had supplied my double with a signature, I thought I sat beyond the reach of fate.

Some two months before the murder of Sir Danvers, I had been out for one of my adventures, had returned at a late hour, and woke the next day in bed with somewhat odd sensations. It was in vain I looked about me; in vain I saw the decent furniture and tall proportions of my room in the square; in vain that I recognised the pattern of the bed curtains and the design of the mahogany frame; something still kept insisting that I was not where I was, that I had not wakened where I seemed to be, but in the little room in Soho where I was accustomed to sleep in the body of Edward Hyde. I smiled to myself, and in my psychological way, began lazily to inquire into the elements of this illusion, occasionally, even as I did so, dropping back into a comfortable morning doze. I was still so engaged when, in one of my more wakeful moments, my eyes fell upon my hand. Now the hand of Henry Jekyll (as you have often remarked) was professional in shape and size; it was large, firm, white and comely. But the hand which I now saw, clearly enough, in the yellow light of a mid-London morning, lying half shut on the bedclothes, was lean, corded, knuckly, of a dusky pallor and thickly shaded with a swart growth of hair. It was the hand of Edward Hyde.

I must have stared upon it for near half a minute, sunk as I was in the mere stupidity of wonder, before terror woke up in my breast as sudden and startling as the crash of cymbals; and bounding from my bed I rushed to the mirror. At the sight that met my eyes, my blood was changed into something exquisitely thin and icy. Yes, I had gone to bed Henry Jekyll, I had awakened Edward Hyde. How was this to be explained? I asked myself; and then, with another bound of terror—how was it to be remedied? It was well on in the morning; the servants were up; all my drugs were in the cabinet—a long journey down two pairs of stairs, through the back passage, across the open court and through the anatomical theatre, from where I was then standing horror-struck. It might indeed be possible to cover my face; but of what use was that, when I was unable to conceal the alteration in my stature? And then with an overpowering sweetness of relief, it came back upon my mind that the servants were already used to the coming and going of my second self. I had soon dressed, as well as I was able, in clothes of my own size: had soon passed through the house, where Bradshaw stared and drew back at seeing Mr. Hyde at such an hour and in such a strange array; and ten minutes later, Dr. Jekyll had returned to his own shape and was sitting down, with a darkened brow, to make a feint of breakfasting.

Small indeed was my appetite. This inexplicable incident, this reversal of my previous experience, seemed, like the Babylonian finger on the wall, to be spelling out the letters of my judgment; and I began to reflect more seriously than ever before on the issues and possibilities of my double existence. That part of me which I had the power of projecting, had lately been much exercised and nourished; it had seemed to me of late as though the body of Edward Hyde had grown in stature, as though (when I wore that form) I were conscious of a more generous tide of blood; and I began to spy a danger that, if this were much prolonged, the balance of my nature might be permanently overthrown, the power of voluntary change be forfeited, and the character of Edward Hyde become irrevocably mine. The power of the drug had not been always equally displayed. Once, very early in my career, it had totally failed me; since then I had been obliged on more than one occasion to double, and once, with infinite risk of death, to treble the amount; and these rare uncertainties had cast hitherto the sole shadow on my contentment. Now, however, and in the light of that morning's accident, I was led to remark that whereas, in the beginning, the difficulty had been to throw off the body of Jekyll, it had of late gradually but decidedly transferred itself to the other side. All things therefore seemed to point to this; that I was slowly losing hold of my original and better self, and becoming slowly incorporated with my second and worse.

Between these two, I now felt I had to choose. My two natures had memory in common, but all other faculties were most unequally shared between them. Jekyll (who was composite) now with the most sensitive apprehensions, now with a greedy gusto, projected and shared in the pleasures and adventures of Hyde; but Hyde was indifferent to Jekyll, or but remembered him as the mountain bandit remembers the cavern in which he conceals himself from pursuit. Jekyll had more than a father's interest; Hyde had more than a son's indifference. To cast in my lot with Jekyll, was to die to those appetites which I had long secretly indulged and had of late begun to pamper. To cast it in with Hyde, was to die to a thousand interests and aspirations, and to become, at a blow and forever, despised and friendless. The bargain might appear unequal; but there was still another consideration in the scales; for while Jekyll would suffer smartingly in the fires of abstinence, Hyde would be not even conscious of all that he had lost. Strange as my circumstances were, the terms of this debate are as old and commonplace as man; much the same inducements and alarms cast the die for any tempted and trembling sinner; and it fell out with me, as it falls with so vast a majority of my fellows, that I chose the better part and was found wanting in the strength to keep to it.

Yes, I preferred the elderly and discontented doctor, surrounded by friends and cherishing honest hopes; and bade a resolute farewell to the liberty, the comparative youth, the light step, leaping impulses and secret pleasures, that I had enjoyed in the disguise of Hyde. I made this choice perhaps with some unconscious reservation, for I neither gave up the house in Soho, nor destroyed the clothes of Edward Hyde, which still lay ready in my cabinet. For two months, however, I was true to my determination; for two months, I led a life of such severity as I had never before attained to, and enjoyed the compensations of an approving conscience. But time began at last to obliterate the freshness of my alarm; the praises of conscience began to grow into a thing of course; I began to be tortured with throes and longings, as of Hyde struggling after freedom; and at last, in an hour of moral weakness, I once again compounded and swallowed the transforming draught.

I do not suppose that, when a drunkard reasons with himself upon his vice, he is once out of five hundred times affected by the dangers that he runs through his brutish, physical insensibility; neither had I, long as I had considered my position, made enough allowance for the complete moral insensibility and insensate readiness to evil, which were the leading characters of Edward Hyde. Yet it was by these that I was punished. My devil had been long caged, he came out roaring. I was conscious, even when I took the draught, of a more unbridled, a more furious propensity to ill. It must have been this, I suppose, that stirred in my soul that tempest of impatience with which I listened to the civilities of my unhappy victim; I declare, at least, before God, no man morally sane could have been guilty of that crime upon so pitiful a provocation;

and that I struck in no more reasonable spirit than that in which a sick child may break a plaything. But I had voluntarily stripped myself of all those balancing instincts by which even the worst of us continues to walk with some degree of steadiness among temptations; and in my case, to be tempted, however slightly, was to fall.

Instantly the spirit of hell awoke in me and raged. With a transport of glee, I mauled the unresisting body, tasting delight from every blow; and it was not till weariness had begun to succeed, that I was suddenly, in the top fit of my delirium, struck through the heart by a cold thrill of terror. A mist dispersed; I saw my life to be forfeit; and fled from the scene of these excesses, at once glorying and trembling, my lust of evil gratified and stimulated, my love of life screwed to the topmost peg. I ran to the house in Soho, and (to make assurance doubly sure) destroyed my papers; thence I set out through the lamplit streets, in the same divided ecstasy of mind, gloating on my crime, light-headedly devising others in the future, and yet still hastening and still hearkening in my wake for the steps of the avenger. Hyde had a song upon his lips as he compounded the draught, and as he drank it, pledged the dead man. The pangs of transformation had not done tearing him, before Henry Jekyll, with streaming tears of gratitude and remorse, had fallen upon his knees and lifted his clasped hands to God. The veil of self-indulgence was rent from head to foot. I saw my life as a whole: I followed it up from the days of childhood, when I had walked with my father's hand, and through the self-denying toils of my professional life, to arrive again and again, with the same sense of unreality, at the damned horrors of the evening. I could have screamed aloud; I sought with tears and prayers to smother down the crowd of hideous images and sounds with which my memory swarmed against me; and still, between the petitions, the ugly face of my iniquity stared into my soul. As the acuteness of this remorse began to die away, it was succeeded by a sense of joy. The problem of my conduct was solved. Hyde was thenceforth impossible; whether I would or not, I was now confined to the better part of my existence; and O, how I rejoiced to think of it! with what willing humility I embraced anew the restrictions of natural life! with what sincere renunciation I locked the door by which I had so often gone and come, and ground the key under my heel!

The next day, came the news that the murder had not been overlooked, that the guilt of Hyde was patent to the world, and that the victim was a man high in public estimation. It was not only a crime, it had been a tragic folly. I think I was glad to know it; I think I was glad to have my better impulses thus buttressed and guarded by the terrors of the scaffold. Jekyll was now my city of refuge; let but Hyde peep out an instant, and the hands of all men would be raised to take and slay him.

I resolved in my future conduct to redeem the past; and I can say with honesty that my resolve was fruitful of some good. You know yourself how earnestly, in the last months of the last year, I laboured to relieve suffering; you know that much was done for others, and that the days passed quietly, almost happily for myself. Nor can I truly say that I wearied of this beneficent and innocent life; I think instead that I daily enjoyed it more completely; but I was still cursed with my duality of purpose; and as the first edge of my penitence wore off, the lower side of me, so long indulged, so recently chained down, began to growl for licence. Not that I dreamed of resuscitating Hyde; the bare idea of that would startle me to frenzy: no, it was in my own person that I was once more tempted to trifle with my conscience; and it was as an ordinary secret sinner that I at last fell before the assaults of temptation.

There comes an end to all things; the most capacious measure is filled at last; and this brief condescension to my evil finally destroyed the balance of my soul. And yet I was not alarmed; the fall seemed natural, like a return to the old days before I had made my discovery. It was a fine, clear, January day, wet under foot where the frost had melted, but cloudless overhead; and the Regent's Park was full of winter chirrupings and sweet with spring odours. I sat in the sun on a bench; the animal within me licking the chops of memory; the spiritual side a little drowsed, promising subsequent penitence, but not yet moved to begin. After all, I reflected, I was like my neighbours; and then I smiled, comparing myself with other men, comparing my active good-will with the lazy cruelty of their neglect. And at the very moment of that vainglorious thought, a qualm came over me, a horrid nausea and the most deadly shuddering. These passed away, and left me faint; and then as in its turn faintness subsided, I began to be aware of a change in the temper of my thoughts, a greater boldness, a contempt of danger, a solution of the bonds of obligation. I looked down; my clothes hung formlessly on my shrunken limbs; the hand that lay on my knee was corded and hairy. I was once more Edward Hyde. A moment before I had been safe of all men's respect, wealthy, beloved—the cloth laying for me in the dining-room at home; and now I was the common quarry of mankind, hunted, houseless, a known murderer, thrall to the gallows.

My reason wavered, but it did not fail me utterly. I have more than once observed that in my second character, my faculties seemed sharpened to a point and my spirits more tensely elastic; thus it came about that, where Jekyll perhaps might have succumbed, Hyde rose to the importance of the moment. My drugs were in one of the presses of my cabinet; how was I to reach them? That was the problem that (crushing my temples in my hands) I set myself to solve. The laboratory door I had closed. If I sought to enter by the house, my own servants would consign me to the gallows. I saw I must employ another hand, and thought of Lanyon. How was he to be reached? how persuaded? Supposing that I escaped capture in the streets, how was I to make my way into his presence? and how should I, an unknown and displeasing visitor, prevail on the famous physician to rifle the study of his colleague, Dr. Jekyll? Then I remembered that of my original character, one part remained to me: I could write my own hand; and once I had conceived that kindling spark, the way that I must follow became lighted up from end to end.

Thereupon, I arranged my clothes as best I could, and summoning a passing hansom, drove to an hotel in Portland Street, the name of which I chanced to remember. At my appearance (which was indeed comical enough, however tragic a fate these garments covered) the driver could not conceal his mirth. I gnashed my teeth upon him with a gust of devilish fury; and the smile withered from his face—happily for him—yet more happily for myself, for in another instant I had certainly dragged him from his perch. At the inn, as I entered, I looked about me with so black a countenance as made the attendants tremble; not a look did they exchange in my presence; but obsequiously took my orders, led me to a private room, and brought me wherewithal to write. Hyde in danger of his life was a creature new to me; shaken with inordinate anger, strung to the pitch of murder, lusting to inflict pain. Yet the creature was astute; mastered his fury with a great effort of the will; composed his two important letters, one to Lanyon and one to Poole; and that he might receive actual evidence of their being posted, sent them out with directions that they should be registered. Thenceforward, he sat all day over the fire in the private room, gnawing his nails; there he dined, sitting alone with his fears, the waiter visibly quailing before his eye; and thence, when the night was fully come, he set forth in the corner of a closed cab, and was driven to and fro about the streets of the city. He, I say—I cannot say, I. That child of Hell had nothing human; nothing lived in him but fear and hatred. And when at last, thinking the driver had begun to grow suspicious, he discharged the cab and ventured on foot, attired in his misfitting clothes, an object marked out for observation, into the midst of the nocturnal passengers, these two base passions raged within him like a tempest. He walked fast, hunted by his fears, chattering to himself, skulking through the less frequented thoroughfares, counting the minutes that still divided him from midnight. Once a woman spoke to him, offering, I think, a box of lights. He smote her in the face, and she fled.

When I came to myself at Lanyon's, the horror of my old friend perhaps affected me somewhat: I do not know; it was at least but a drop in the sea to the abhorrence with which I looked back upon these hours. A change had come over me. It was no longer the fear of the gallows, it was the horror of being Hyde that racked me. I received Lanyon's condemnation partly in a dream;

it was partly in a dream that I came home to my own house and got into bed. I slept after the prostration of the day, with a stringent and profound slumber which not even the nightmares that wrung me could avail to break. I awoke in the morning shaken, weakened, but refreshed. I still hated and feared the thought of the brute that slept within me, and I had not of course forgotten the appalling dangers of the day before; but I was once more at home, in my own house and close to my drugs; and gratitude for my escape shone so strong in my soul that it almost rivalled the brightness of hope.

I was stepping leisurely across the court after breakfast, drinking the chill of the air with pleasure, when I was seized again with those indescribable sensations that heralded the change; and I had but the time to gain the shelter of my cabinet, before I was once again raging and freezing with the passions of Hyde. It took on this occasion a double dose to recall me to myself; and alas! six hours after, as I sat looking sadly in the fire, the pangs returned, and the drug had to be re-administered. In short, from that day forth it seemed only by a great effort as of gymnastics, and only under the immediate stimulation of the drug, that I was able to wear the countenance of Jekyll. At all hours of the day and night, I would be taken with the premonitory shudder; above all, if I slept, or even dozed for a moment in my chair, it was always as Hyde that I awakened. Under the strain of this continually impending doom and by the sleeplessness to which I now condemned myself, ay, even beyond what I had thought possible to man, I became, in my own person, a creature eaten up and emptied by fever, languidly weak both in body and mind, and solely occupied by one thought: the horror of my other self. But when I slept, or when the virtue of the medicine wore off, I would leap almost without transition (for the pangs of transformation grew daily less marked) into the possession of a fancy brimming with images of terror, a soul boiling with causeless hatreds, and a body that seemed not strong enough to contain the raging energies of life. The powers of Hyde seemed to have grown with the sickliness of Jekyll. And certainly the hate that now divided them was equal on each side. With Jekyll, it was a thing of vital instinct. He had now seen the full deformity of that creature that shared with him some of the phenomena of consciousness, and was co-heir with him to death: and beyond these links of community, which in themselves made the most poignant part of his distress, he thought of Hyde, for all his energy of life, as of something not only hellish but inorganic. This was the shocking thing; that the slime of the pit seemed to utter cries and voices; that the amorphous dust gesticulated and sinned; that what was dead, and had no shape, should usurp the offices of life. And this again, that that insurgent horror was knit to him closer than a wife, closer than an eye; lay caged in his flesh, where he heard it mutter and felt it struggle to be born; and at every hour of weakness, and in the confidence of slumber, prevailed against him, and deposed him out of life. The hatred of Hyde for Jekyll was of a different order. His terror of the gallows drove him continually to commit temporary suicide, and return to his subordinate station of a part instead of a person; but he loathed the necessity, he loathed the despondency into which Jekyll was now fallen, and he resented the dislike with which he was himself regarded. Hence the ape-like tricks that he would play me, scrawling in my own hand blasphemies on the pages of my books, burning the letters and destroying the portrait of my father; and indeed, had it not been for his fear of death, he would long ago have ruined himself in order to involve me in the ruin. But his love of life is wonderful; I go further: I, who sicken and freeze at the mere thought of him, when I recall the abjection and passion of this attachment, and when I know how he fears my power to cut him off by suicide, I find it in my heart to pity him.

It is useless, and the time awfully fails me, to prolong this description; no one has ever suffered such torments, let that suffice; and yet even to these, habit brought—no, not alleviation—but a certain callousness of soul, a certain acquiescence of despair; and my punishment might have gone on for years, but for the last calamity which has now fallen, and which has finally severed me from my own face and nature. My provision of the salt, which had never been renewed since the date of the first experiment, began to run low. I sent out for a fresh supply and mixed the draught; the ebullition followed, and the first change of colour, not the second; I drank it and it was without efficiency. You will learn from Poole how I have had London ransacked; it was in vain; and I am now persuaded that my first supply was impure, and that it was that unknown impurity which lent efficacy to the draught.

About a week has passed, and I am now finishing this statement under the influence of the last of the old powders. This, then, is the last time, short of a miracle, that Henry Jekyll can think his own thoughts or see his own face (now how sadly altered!) in the glass. Nor must I delay too long to bring my writing to an end; for if my narrative has hitherto escaped destruction, it has been by a combination of great prudence and great good luck. Should the throes of change take me in the act of writing it, Hyde will tear it in pieces; but if some time shall have elapsed after I have laid it by, his wonderful selfishness and circumscription to the moment will probably save it once again from the action of his ape-like spite. And indeed the doom that is closing on us both has already changed and crushed him. Half an hour from now, when I shall again and forever reindue that hated personality, I know how I shall sit shuddering and weeping in my chair, or continue, with the most strained and fearstruck ecstasy of listening, to pace up and down this room (my last earthly refuge) and give ear to every sound of menace. Will Hyde die upon the scaffold? or will he find courage to release himself at the last moment? God knows; I am careless; this is my true hour of death, and what is to follow concerns another than myself. Here then, as I lay down the pen and proceed to seal up my confession, I bring the life of that unhappy Henry Jekyll to an end.

*** END OF THE PROJECT GUTENBERG EBOOK THE STRANGE CASE OF DR. JEKYLL AND MR. HYDE ***

This file should be named 43-h.htm or 43-h.zip

This and all associated files of various formats will be found in https://www.gutenberg.org/4/43/

Updated editions will replace the previous one—the old editions will be renamed.

Creating the works from print editions not protected by U.S. copyright law means that no one owns a United States copyright in these works, so the Foundation (and you!) can copy and distribute it in the United States without permission and without paying copyright royalties. Special rules, set forth in the General Terms of Use part of this license, apply to copying and distributing Project Gutenberg™ electronic works to protect the PROJECT GUTENBERG™ concept and trademark. Project Gutenberg is a registered trademark, and may not be used if you charge for an eBook, except by following the terms of the trademark license, including paying royalties for use of the Project Gutenberg trademark. If you do not charge anything for copies of this eBook, complying with the trademark license is very easy. You may use this eBook for nearly any purpose such as creation of derivative works, reports, performances and research. Project Gutenberg eBooks may be modified and printed and given away--you may do practically ANYTHING in the United States with eBooks not protected by U.S. copyright law. Redistribution is subject to the trademark license, especially commercial redistribution.

THE WRECKER

BY ROBERT LOUIS STEVENSON
AND LLOYD OSBOURNE

IN THE MARQUESAS.

It was about three o'clock of a winter's afternoon in Tai-o-hae, the French capital and port of entry of the Marquesas Islands. The trades blew strong and squally; the surf roared loud on the shingle beach; and the fifty-ton schooner of war, that carries the flag and influence of France about the islands of the cannibal group, rolled at her moorings under Prison Hill. The clouds hung low and black on the surrounding amphitheatre of mountains; rain had fallen earlier in the day, real tropic rain, a waterspout for violence; and the green and gloomy brow of the mountain was still seamed with many silver threads of torrent.

In these hot and healthy islands winter is but a name. The rain had not refreshed, nor could the wind invigorate, the dwellers of Tai-o-hae: away at one end, indeed, the commandant was directing some changes in the residency garden beyond Prison Hill; and the gardeners, being all convicts, had no choice but to continue to obey. All other folks slumbered and took their rest: Vaekehu, the native queen, in her trim house under the rustling palms; the Tahitian commissary, in his beflagged official residence; the merchants, in their deserted stores; and even the club-servant in the club, his head fallen forward on the bottle-counter, under the map of the world and the cards of navy officers. In the whole length of the single shoreside street, with its scattered board houses looking to the sea, its grateful shade of palms and green jungle of puraos, no moving figure could be seen. Only, at the end of the rickety pier, that once (in the prosperous days of the American rebellion) was used to groan under the cotton of John Hart, there might have been spied upon a pile of lumber the famous tattooed white man, the living curiosity of Tai-o-hae.

His eyes were open, staring down the bay. He saw the mountains droop, as they approached the entrance, and break down in cliffs; the surf boil white round the two sentinel islets; and between, on the narrow bight of blue horizon, Ua-pu upraise the ghost of her pinnacled mountain tops. But his mind would take no account of these familiar features; as he dodged in and out along the frontier line of sleep and waking, memory would serve him with broken fragments of the past: brown faces and white, of skipper and shipmate, king and chief, would arise before his mind and vanish; he would recall old voyages, old landfalls in the hour of dawn; he would hear again the drums beat for a man-eating festival; perhaps he would summon up the form of that island princess for the love of whom he had submitted his body to the cruel hands of the tattooer, and now sat on the lumber, at the pier-end of Tai-o-hae, so strange a figure of a European. Or perhaps from yet further back, sounds and scents of England and his childhood might assail him: the merry clamour of cathedral bells, the broom upon the foreland, the song of the river on the weir.

It is bold water at the mouth of the bay; you can steer a ship about either sentinel, close enough to toss a biscuit on the rocks. Thus it chanced that, as the tattooed man sat dozing and dreaming, he was startled into wakefulness and animation by the appearance of a flying jib beyond the western islet. Two more headsails followed; and before the tattooed man had scrambled to his feet, a topsail schooner, of some hundred tons, had luffed about the sentinel and was standing up the bay, close-hauled.

The sleeping city awakened by enchantment. Natives appeared upon all sides, hailing each other with the magic cry "Ehippy"—ship; the Queen stepped forth on her verandah, shading her eyes under a hand that was a miracle of the fine art of tattooing; the commandant broke from his domestic convicts and ran into the residency for his glass; the harbour master, who was also the gaoler, came speeding down the Prison Hill; the seventeen brown Kanakas and the French boatswain's mate, that make up the complement of the war-schooner, crowded on the forward deck; and the various English, Americans, Germans, Poles, Corsicans, and Scots—the merchants and the clerks of Tai-o-hae—deserted their places of business, and gathered, according to invariable custom, on the road before the club.

So quickly did these dozen whites collect, so short are the distances in Tai-o-hae, that they were already exchanging guesses as to the nationality and business of the strange vessel, before she had gone about upon her second board towards the anchorage. A moment after, English colours were broken out at the main truck.

"I told you she was a Johnny Bull—knew it by her headsails," said an evergreen old salt, still qualified (if he could anywhere have found an owner unacquainted with his story) to adorn another quarter-deck and lose another ship.

"She has American lines, anyway," said the astute Scots engineer of the gin-mill; "it's my belief she's a yacht."

"That's it," said the old salt, "a yacht! look at her davits, and the boat over the stern."

"A yacht in your eye!" said a Glasgow voice. "Look at her red ensign! A yacht! not much she isn't!"

"You can close the store, anyway, Tom," observed a gentlemanly German. "Bon jour, mon Prince!" he added, as a dark, intelligent native cantered by on a neat chestnut. "Vous allez boire un verre de biere?"

But Prince Stanilas Moanatini, the only reasonably busy human creature on the island, was riding hot-spur to view this morning's landslip on the mountain road: the sun already visibly declined; night was imminent; and if he would avoid the perils of darkness and precipice, and the fear of the dead, the haunters of the jungle, he must for once decline a hospitable invitation. Even had he been minded to alight, it presently appeared there would be difficulty as to the refreshment offered.

"Beer!" cried the Glasgow voice. "No such a thing; I tell you there's only eight bottles in the club! Here's the first time I've seen British colours in this port! and the man that sails under them has got to drink that beer."

The proposal struck the public mind as fair, though far from cheering; for some time back, indeed, the very name of beer had been a sound of sorrow in the club, and the evenings had passed in dolorous computation.

"Here is Havens," said one, as if welcoming a fresh topic. "What do you think of her, Havens?"

"I don't think," replied Havens, a tall, bland, cool-looking, leisurely Englishman, attired in spotless duck, and deliberately dealing with a cigarette. "I may say I know. She's consigned to me from Auckland by Donald & Edenborough. I am on my way aboard."

"What ship is she?" asked the ancient mariner.

"Haven't an idea," returned Havens. "Some tramp they have chartered."

With that he placidly resumed his walk, and was soon seated in the stern-sheets of a whaleboat manned by uproarious Kanakas, himself daintily perched out of the way of the least maculation, giving his commands in an unobtrusive, dinner-table tone of voice, and sweeping neatly enough alongside the schooner.

A weather-beaten captain received him at the gangway.

"You are consigned to us, I think," said he. "I am Mr. Havens."

"That is right, sir," replied the captain, shaking hands. "You will find the owner, Mr. Dodd, below. Mind the fresh paint on the house."

Havens stepped along the alley-way, and descended the ladder into the main cabin.

"Mr. Dodd, I believe," said he, addressing a smallish, bearded gentleman, who sat writing at the table. "Why," he cried, "it isn't Loudon Dodd?"

"Myself, my dear fellow," replied Mr. Dodd, springing to his feet with companionable alacrity. "I had a half-hope it might be you, when I found your name on the papers. Well, there's no change in you; still the same placid, fresh-looking Britisher."

"I can't return the compliment; for you seem to have become a Britisher yourself," said Havens.

"I promise you, I am quite unchanged," returned Dodd. "The red tablecloth at the top of the stick is not my flag; it's my partner's. He is not dead, but sleepeth. There he is," he added, pointing to a bust which formed one of the numerous unexpected ornaments of that unusual cabin.

Havens politely studied it. "A fine bust," said he; "and a very nice-looking fellow."

"Yes; he's a good fellow," said Dodd. "He runs me now. It's all his money."

"He doesn't seem to be particularly short of it," added the other, peering with growing wonder round the cabin.

"His money, my taste," said Dodd. "The black-walnut bookshelves are Old English; the books all mine,—mostly Renaissance French. You should see how the beach-combers wilt away when they go round them looking for a change of Seaside Library novels. The mirrors are genuine Venice; that's a good piece in the corner. The daubs are mine—and his; the mudding mine."

"Mudding? What is that?" asked Havens.

"These bronzes," replied Dodd. "I began life as a sculptor."

"Yes; I remember something about that," said the other. "I think, too, you said you were interested in Californian real estate."

"Surely, I never went so far as that," said Dodd. "Interested? I guess not. Involved, perhaps. I was born an artist; I never took an interest in anything but art. If I were to pile up this old schooner to-morrow," he added, "I declare I believe I would try the thing again!"

"Insured?" inquired Havens.

"Yes," responded Dodd. "There's some fool in 'Frisco who insures us, and comes down like a wolf on the fold on the profits; but we'll get even with him some day."

"Well, I suppose it's all right about the cargo," said Havens.

"O, I suppose so!" replied Dodd. "Shall we go into the papers?"

"We'll have all to-morrow, you know," said Havens; "and they'll be rather expecting you at the club. C'est l'heure de l'absinthe. Of course, Loudon, you'll dine with me later on?"

Mr. Dodd signified his acquiescence; drew on his white coat, not without a trifling difficulty, for he was a man of middle age, and well-to-do; arranged his beard and moustaches at one of the Venetian mirrors; and, taking a broad felt hat, led the way through the trade-room into the ship's waist.

The stern boat was waiting alongside,—a boat of an elegant model, with cushions and polished hard-wood fittings.

"You steer," observed Loudon. "You know the best place to land."

"I never like to steer another man's boat," replied Havens.

"Call it my partner's, and cry quits," returned Loudon, getting nonchalantly down the side.

Havens followed and took the yoke lines without further protest. "I am sure I don't know how you make this pay," he said. "To begin with, she is too big for the trade, to my taste; and then you carry so much style."

"I don't know that she does pay," returned Loudon. "I never pretend to be a business man. My partner appears happy; and the money is all his, as I told you—I only bring the want of business habits."

"You rather like the berth, I suppose?" suggested Havens.

"Yes," said Loudon; "it seems odd, but I rather do."

While they were yet on board, the sun had dipped; the sunset gun (a rifle) cracked from the war-schooner, and the colours had been handed down. Dusk was deepening as they came ashore; and the Cercle Internationale (as the club is officially and significantly named) began to shine, from under its low verandas, with the light of many lamps. The good hours of the twenty-four drew on; the hateful, poisonous day-fly of Nukahiva, was beginning to desist from its activity; the land-breeze came in refreshing draughts; and the club men gathered together for the hour of absinthe. To the commandant himself, to the man whom he was then contending with at billiards—a trader from the next island, honorary member of the club, and once carpenter's mate on board a Yankee war-ship—to the doctor of the port, to the Brigadier of Gendarmerie, to the opium farmer, and to all the white men whom the tide of commerce, or the chances of shipwreck and desertion, had stranded on the beach of Tai-o-hae, Mr. Loudon Dodd was formally presented; by all (since he was a man of pleasing exterior, smooth ways, and an unexceptionable flow of talk, whether in French or English) he was excellently well received; and presently, with one of the last eight bottles of beer on a table at his elbow, found himself the rather silent centre-piece of a voluble group on the verandah.

Talk in the South Seas is all upon one pattern; it is a wide ocean, indeed, but a narrow world: you shall never talk long and not hear the name of Bully Hayes, a naval hero whose exploits and deserved extinction left Europe cold; commerce will be touched on, copra, shell, perhaps cotton or fungus; but in a far-away, dilettante fashion, as by men not deeply interested; through all, the names of schooners and their captains, will keep coming and going, thick as may-flies; and news of the last shipwreck will be placidly exchanged and debated. To a stranger, this conversation will at first seem scarcely brilliant; but he will soon catch the tone; and by the time he shall have moved a year or so in the island world, and come across a good number of the schooners so that every captain's name calls up a figure in pyjamas or white duck, and becomes used to a certain laxity of moral tone which prevails (as in memory of Mr. Hayes) on smuggling, ship-scuttling, barratry, piracy, the labour trade, and other kindred fields of human activity, he will find Polynesia no less amusing and no less instructive than Pall Mall or Paris.

Mr. Loudon Dodd, though he was new to the group of the Marquesas, was already an old, salted trader; he knew the ships and the captains; he had assisted, in other islands, at the first steps of some career of which he now heard the culmination, or (vice versa) he had brought with him from further south the end of some story which had begun in Tai-o-hae. Among other matter of interest, like other arrivals in the South Seas, he had a wreck to announce. The John T. Richards, it appeared, had met the fate of other island schooners.

"Dickinson piled her up on Palmerston Island," Dodd announced.

"Who were the owners?" inquired one of the club men.

"O, the usual parties!" returned Loudon,—"Capsicum & Co."

A smile and a glance of intelligence went round the group; and perhaps Loudon gave voice to the general sentiment by remarking, "Talk of good business! I know nothing better than a schooner, a competent captain, and a sound, reliable reef."

"Good business! There's no such a thing!" said the Glasgow man. "Nobody makes anything but the missionaries—dash it!"

"I don't know," said another. "There's a good deal in opium."

"It's a good job to strike a tabooed pearl-island, say, about the fourth year," remarked a third; "skim the whole lagoon on the sly, and up stick and away before the French get wind of you."

"A pig nokket of cold is good," observed a German.

"There's something in wrecks, too," said Havens. "Look at that man in Honolulu, and the ship that went ashore on Waikiki Reef; it was blowing a kona, hard; and she began to break up as soon as she touched. Lloyd's agent had her sold inside an hour; and before dark, when she went to pieces in earnest, the man that bought her had feathered his nest. Three more hours of daylight, and he might have retired from business. As it was, he built a house on Beretania Street, and called it for the ship."

"Yes, there's something in wrecks sometimes," said the Glasgow voice; "but not often."

"As a general rule, there's deuced little in anything," said Havens.

"Well, I believe that's a Christian fact," cried the other. "What I want is a secret; get hold of a rich man by the right place, and make him squeal."

"I suppose you know it's not thought to be the ticket," returned Havens.

"I don't care for that; it's good enough for me," cried the man from Glasgow, stoutly. "The only devil of it is, a fellow can never find a secret in a place like the South Seas: only in London and Paris."

"M'Gibbon's been reading some dime-novel, I suppose," said one club man.

"He's been reading Aurora Floyd," remarked another.

"And what if I have?" cried M'Gibbon. "It's all true. Look at the newspapers! It's just your confounded ignorance that sets you snickering. I tell you, it's as much a trade as underwriting, and a dashed sight more honest."

The sudden acrimony of these remarks called Loudon (who was a man of peace) from his reserve. "It's rather singular," said he, "but I seem to have practised about all these means of livelihood."

"Tit you effer vind a nokket?" inquired the inarticulate German, eagerly.

"No. I have been most kinds of fool in my time," returned Loudon, "but not the gold-digging variety. Every man has a sane spot somewhere."

"Well, then," suggested some one, "did you ever smuggle opium?"

"Yes, I did," said Loudon.

"Was there money in that?"

"All the way," responded Loudon.

"And perhaps you bought a wreck?" asked another.

"Yes, sir," said Loudon.

"How did that pan out?" pursued the questioner.

"Well, mine was a peculiar kind of wreck," replied Loudon. "I don't know, on the whole, that I can recommend that branch of industry."

"Did she break up?" asked some one.

"I guess it was rather I that broke down," says Loudon. "Head not big enough."

"Ever try the blackmail?" inquired Havens.

"Simple as you see me sitting here!" responded Dodd.

"Good business?"

"Well, I'm not a lucky man, you see," returned the stranger. "It ought to have been good."

"You had a secret?" asked the Glasgow man.

"As big as the State of Texas."

"And the other man was rich?"

"He wasn't exactly Jay Gould, but I guess he could buy these islands if he wanted."

"Why, what was wrong, then? Couldn't you get hands on him?"

"It took time, but I had him cornered at last; and then——"

"What then?"

"The speculation turned bottom up. I became the man's bosom friend."

"The deuce you did!"

"He couldn't have been particular, you mean?" asked Dodd pleasantly. "Well, no; he's a man of rather large sympathies."

"If you're done talking nonsense, Loudon," said Havens, "let's be getting to my place for dinner."

Outside, the night was full of the roaring of the surf. Scattered lights glowed in the green thicket. Native women came by twos and threes out of the darkness, smiled and ogled the two whites, perhaps wooed them with a strain of laughter, and went by again, bequeathing to the air a heady perfume of palm-oil and frangipani blossom. From the club to Mr. Havens's residence was but a step or two, and to any dweller in Europe they must have seemed steps in fairyland. If such an one could but have followed our two friends into the wide-verandahed house, sat down with them in the cool trellised room, where the wine shone on the lamp-lighted tablecloth; tasted of their exotic food—the raw fish, the breadfruit, the cooked bananas, the roast pig served with the inimitable miti, and that king of delicacies, palm-tree salad; seen and heard by fits and starts, now peering round the corner of the door, now railing within against invisible assistants, a certain comely young native lady in a sacque, who seemed too modest to be a member of the family, and too imperious to be less; and then if such an one were whisked again through space to Upper Tooting, or wherever else he honored the domestic gods, "I have had a dream," I think he would say, as he sat up, rubbing his eyes, in the familiar chimney-corner chair, "I have had a dream of a place, and I declare I believe it must be heaven." But to Dodd and his entertainer, all this amenity of the tropic night and all these dainties of the island table, were grown things of custom; and they fell to meat like men who were hungry, and drifted into idle talk like men who were a trifle bored.

The scene in the club was referred to.

"I never heard you talk so much nonsense, Loudon," said the host.

"Well, it seemed to me there was sulphur in the air, so I talked for talking," returned the other. "But it was none of it nonsense."

"Do you mean to say it was true?" cried Havens,—"that about the opium and the wreck, and the blackmailing and the man who became your friend?"

"Every last word of it," said Loudon.

"You seem to have been seeing life," returned the other.

"Yes, it's a queer yarn," said his friend; "if you think you would like, I'll tell it you."

Here follows the yarn of Loudon Dodd, not as he told it to his friend, but as he subsequently wrote it.

THE YARN.

CHAPTER I. A SOUND COMMERCIAL EDUCATION.

The beginning of this yarn is my poor father's character. There never was a better man, nor a handsomer, nor (in my view) a more unhappy—unhappy in his business, in his pleasures, in his place of residence, and (I am sorry to say it) in his son. He had begun life as a land-surveyor, soon became interested in real estate, branched off into many other speculations, and had the name of one of the smartest men in the State of Muskegon. "Dodd has a big head," people used to say; but I was never so sure of his capacity. His luck, at least, was beyond doubt for long; his assiduity, always. He fought in that daily battle of money-grubbing, with a kind of sad-eyed loyalty like a martyr's; rose early, ate fast, came home dispirited and over-weary, even from success; grudged himself all pleasure, if his nature was capable of taking any, which I sometimes wondered; and laid out, upon some deal in wheat or corner in aluminium, the essence of which was little better than highway robbery, treasures of conscientiousness and self-denial.

Unluckily, I never cared a cent for anything but art, and never shall. My idea of man's chief end was to enrich the world with things of beauty, and have a fairly good time myself while doing so. I do not think I mentioned that second part, which is the only one I have managed to carry out; but my father must have suspected the suppression, for he branded the whole affair as self-indulgence.

"Well," I remember crying once, "and what is your life? You are only trying to get money, and to get it from other people at that."

He sighed bitterly (which was very much his habit), and shook his poor head at me. "Ah, Loudon, Loudon!" said he, "you boys think yourselves very smart. But, struggle as you please, a man has to work in this world. He must be an honest man or a thief, Loudon."

You can see for yourself how vain it was to argue with my father. The despair that seized upon me after such an interview was, besides, embittered by remorse; for I was at times petulant, but he invariably gentle; and I was fighting, after all, for my own liberty and pleasure, he singly for what he thought to be my good. And all the time he never despaired. "There is good stuff in you, Loudon," he would say; "there is the right stuff in you. Blood will tell, and you will come right in time. I am not afraid my boy will ever disgrace me; I am only vexed he should sometimes talk nonsense." And then he would pat my shoulder or my hand with a kind of motherly way he had, very affecting in a man so strong and beautiful.

As soon as I had graduated from the high school, he packed me off to the Muskegon Commercial Academy. You are a foreigner, and you will have a difficulty in accepting the reality of this seat of education. I assure you before I begin that I am wholly serious. The place really existed, possibly exists to-day: we were proud of it in the State, as something exceptionally nineteenth century and civilized; and my father, when he saw me to the cars, no doubt considered he was putting me in a straight line for the Presidency and the New Jerusalem.

"Loudon," said he, "I am now giving you a chance that Julius Caesar could not have given to his son—a chance to see life as it is, before your own turn comes to start in earnest. Avoid rash speculation, try to behave like a gentleman; and if you will take my advice, confine yourself to a safe, conservative business in railroads. Breadstuffs are tempting, but very dangerous; I would not try breadstuffs at your time of life; but you may feel your way a little in other commodities.

Take a pride to keep your books posted, and never throw good money after bad. There, my dear boy, kiss me good-by; and never forget that you are an only chick, and that your dad watches your career with fond suspense."

The commercial college was a fine, roomy establishment, pleasantly situate among woods. The air was healthy, the food excellent, the premium high. Electric wires connected it (to use the words of the prospectus) with "the various world centres." The reading-room was well supplied with "commercial organs." The talk was that of Wall Street; and the pupils (from fifty to a hundred lads) were principally engaged in rooking or trying to rook one another for nominal sums in what was called "college paper." We had class hours, indeed, in the morning, when we studied German, French, book-keeping, and the like goodly matters; but the bulk of our day and the gist of the education centred in the exchange, where we were taught to gamble in produce and securities. Since not one of the participants possessed a bushel of wheat or a dollar's worth of stock, legitimate business was of course impossible from the beginning. It was cold-drawn gambling, without colour or disguise. Just that which is the impediment and destruction of all genuine commercial enterprise, just that we were taught with every luxury of stage effect. Our simulacrum of a market was ruled by the real markets outside, so that we might experience the course and vicissitude of prices. We must keep books, and our ledgers were overhauled at the month's end by the principal or his assistants. To add a spice of verisimilitude, "college paper" (like poker chips) had an actual marketable value. It was bought for each pupil by anxious parents and guardians at the rate of one cent for the dollar. The same pupil, when his education was complete, resold, at the same figure, so much as was left him to the college; and even in the midst of his curriculum, a successful operator would sometimes realize a proportion of his holding, and stand a supper on the sly in the neighbouring hamlet. In short, if there was ever a worse education, it must have been in that academy where Oliver met Charlie Bates.

When I was first guided into the exchange to have my desk pointed out by one of the assistant teachers, I was overwhelmed by the clamour and confusion. Certain blackboards at the other end of the building were covered with figures continually replaced. As each new set appeared, the pupils swayed to and fro, and roared out aloud with a formidable and to me quite meaningless vociferation; leaping at the same time upon the desks and benches, signalling with arms and heads, and scribbling briskly in note-books. I thought I had never beheld a scene more disagreeable; and when I considered that the whole traffic was illusory, and all the money then upon the market would scarce have sufficed to buy a pair of skates, I was at first astonished, although not for long. Indeed, I had no sooner called to mind how grown-up men and women of considerable estate will lose their temper about half-penny points, than (making an immediate allowance for my fellow-students) I transferred the whole of my astonishment to the assistant teacher, who—poor gentleman—had quite forgot to show me to my desk, and stood in the midst of this hurly-burly, absorbed and seemingly transported.

"Look, look," he shouted in my ear; "a falling market! The bears have had it all their own way since yesterday."

"It can't matter," I replied, making him hear with difficulty, for I was unused to speak in such a babel, "since it is all fun."

"True," said he; "and you must always bear in mind that the real profit is in the book-keeping. I trust, Dodd, to be able to congratulate you upon your books. You are to start in with ten thousand dollars of college paper, a very liberal figure, which should see you through the whole curriculum, if you keep to a safe, conservative business.... Why, what's that?" he broke off, once more attracted by the changing figures on the board. "Seven, four, three! Dodd, you are in luck: this is the most spirited rally we have had this term. And to think that the same scene is now transpiring in New York, Chicago, St. Louis, and rival business centres! For two cents,

I would try a flutter with the boys myself," he cried, rubbing his hands; "only it's against the regulations."

"What would you do, sir?" I asked.

"Do?" he cried, with glittering eyes. "Buy for all I was worth!"

"Would that be a safe, conservative business?" I inquired, as innocent as a lamb.

He looked daggers at me. "See that sandy-haired man in glasses?" he asked, as if to change the subject. "That's Billson, our most prominent undergraduate. We build confidently on Billson's future. You could not do better, Dodd, than follow Billson."

Presently after, in the midst of a still growing tumult, the figures coming and going more busily than ever on the board, and the hall resounding like Pandemonium with the howls of operators, the assistant teacher left me to my own resources at my desk. The next boy was posting up his ledger, figuring his morning's loss, as I discovered later on; and from this ungenial task he was readily diverted by the sight of a new face.

"Say, Freshman," he said, "what's your name? What? Son of Big Head Dodd? What's your figure? Ten thousand? O, you're away up! What a soft-headed clam you must be to touch your books!"

I asked him what else I could do, since the books were to be examined once a month.

"Why, you galoot, you get a clerk!" cries he. "One of our dead beats—that's all they're here for. If you're a successful operator, you need never do a stroke of work in this old college."

The noise had now become deafening; and my new friend, telling me that some one had certainly "gone down," that he must know the news, and that he would bring me a clerk when he returned, buttoned his coat and plunged into the tossing throng. It proved that he was right: some one had gone down; a prince had fallen in Israel; the corner in lard had proved fatal to the mighty; and the clerk who was brought back to keep my books, spare me all work, and get all my share of the education, at a thousand dollars a month, college paper (ten dollars, United States currency) was no other than the prominent Billson whom I could do no better than follow. The poor lad was very unhappy. It's the only good thing I have to say for Muskegon Commercial College, that we were all, even the small fry, deeply mortified to be posted as defaulters; and the collapse of a merchant prince like Billson, who had ridden pretty high in his days of prosperity, was, of course, particularly hard to bear. But the spirit of make-believe conquered even the bitterness of recent shame; and my clerk took his orders, and fell to his new duties, with decorum and civility.

Such were my first impressions in this absurd place of education; and, to be frank, they were far from disagreeable. As long as I was rich, my evenings and afternoons would be my own; the clerk must keep my books, the clerk could do the jostling and bawling in the exchange; and I could turn my mind to landscape-painting and Balzac's novels, which were then my two preoccupations. To remain rich, then, became my problem; or, in other words, to do a safe, conservative line of business. I am looking for that line still; and I believe the nearest thing to it in this imperfect world is the sort of speculation sometimes insidiously proposed to childhood, in the formula, "Heads, I win; tails, you lose." Mindful of my father's parting words, I turned my attention timidly to railroads; and for a month or so maintained a position of inglorious security, dealing for small amounts in the most inert stocks, and bearing (as best I could) the scorn of my hired clerk. One day I had ventured a little further by way of experiment; and, in the sure expectation they would continue to go down, sold several thousand dollars of Pan-Handle Preference (I think it was). I had no sooner made this venture than some fools in New York began to bull the market; Pan-Handles rose like a balloon; and in the inside of half an hour I saw my position compromised. Blood will tell, as my father said; and I stuck to it gallantly: all afternoon I continued selling that infernal stock, all afternoon it continued skying. I suppose I had come (a frail cockle-shell) athwart the hawse of Jay Gould; and, indeed, I think I remember that this vagary in the market proved subsequently to be the first move in a considerable deal. That evening, at least, the name of H. Loudon Dodd held the first rank in our collegiate gazette, and I and Billson (once more thrown upon the world) were competing for the same clerkship. The present object takes the present eye. My disaster, for the moment, was the more conspicuous; and it was I that got the situation. So you see, even in Muskegon Commercial College, there were lessons to be learned.

For my own part, I cared very little whether I lost or won at a game so random, so complex, and so dull; but it was sorry news to write to my poor father, and I employed all the resources of my eloquence. I told him (what was the truth) that the successful boys had none of the education; so that if he wished me to learn, he should rejoice at my misfortune. I went on (not very consistently) to beg him to set me up again, when I would solemnly promise to do a safe business in reliable railroads. Lastly (becoming somewhat carried away), I assured him I was totally unfit for business, and implored him to take me away from this abominable place, and let me go to Paris to study art. He answered briefly, gently, and sadly, telling me the vacation was near at hand, when we could talk things over.

When the time came, he met me at the depot, and I was shocked to see him looking older. He seemed to have no thought but to console me and restore (what he supposed I had lost) my courage. I must not be down-hearted; many of the best men had made a failure in the beginning. I told him I had no head for business, and his kind face darkened. "You must not say that, Loudon," he replied; "I will never believe my son to be a coward."

"But I don't like it," I pleaded. "It hasn't got any interest for me, and art has. I know I could do more in art," and I reminded him that a successful painter gains large sums; that a picture of Meissonier's would sell for many thousand dollars.

"And do you think, Loudon," he replied, "that a man who can paint a thousand dollar picture has not grit enough to keep his end up in the stock market? No, sir; this Mason (of whom you speak) or our own American Bierstadt—if you were to put them down in a wheat pit to-morrow, they would show their mettle. Come, Loudon, my dear; heaven knows I have no thought but your own good, and I will offer you a bargain. I start you again next term with ten thousand dollars; show yourself a man, and double it, and then (if you still wish to go to Paris, which I know you won't) I'll let you go. But to let you run away as if you were whipped, is what I am too proud to do."

My heart leaped at this proposal, and then sank again. It seemed easier to paint a Meissonier on the spot than to win ten thousand dollars on that mimic stock exchange. Nor could I help reflecting on the singularity of such a test for a man's capacity to be a painter. I ventured even to comment on this.

He sighed deeply. "You forget, my dear," said he, "I am a judge of the one, and not of the other. You might have the genius of Bierstadt himself, and I would be none the wiser."

"And then," I continued, "it's scarcely fair. The other boys are helped by their people, who telegraph and give them pointers. There's Jim Costello, who never budges without a word from his father in New York. And then, don't you see, if anybody is to win, somebody must lose?"

"I'll keep you posted," cried my father, with unusual animation; "I did not know it was allowed.

I'll wire you in the office cipher, and we'll make it a kind of partnership business, Loudon:—Dodd & Son, eh?" and he patted my shoulder and repeated, "Dodd & Son, Dodd & Son," with the kindliest amusement.

If my father was to give me pointers, and the commercial college was to be a stepping-stone to Paris, I could look my future in the face. The old boy, too, was so pleased at the idea of our association in this foolery that he immediately plucked up spirit. Thus it befell that those who had met at the depot like a pair of mutes, sat down to table with holiday faces.

And now I have to introduce a new character that never said a word nor wagged a finger, and yet shaped my whole subsequent career. You have crossed the States, so that in all likelihood you have seen the head of it, parcel-gilt and curiously fluted, rising among trees from a wide plain; for this new character was no other than the State capitol of Muskegon, then first projected. My father had embraced the idea with a mixture of patriotism and commercial greed both perfectly genuine. He was of all the committees, he had subscribed a great deal of money, and he was making arrangements to have a finger in most of the contracts. Competitive plans had been sent in; at the time of my return from college my father was deep in their consideration; and as the idea entirely occupied his mind, the first evening did not pass away before he had called me into council. Here was a subject at last into which I could throw myself with pleasurable zeal. Architecture was new to me, indeed; but it was at least an art; and for all the arts I had a taste naturally classical and that capacity to take delighted pains which some famous idiot has supposed to be synonymous with genius. I threw myself headlong into my father's work, acquainted myself with all the plans, their merits and defects, read besides in special books, made myself a master of the theory of strains, studied the current prices of materials, and (in one word) "devilled" the whole business so thoroughly, that when the plans came up for consideration, Big Head Dodd was supposed to have earned fresh laurels. His arguments carried the day, his choice was approved by the committee, and I had the anonymous satisfaction to know that arguments and choice were wholly mine. In the recasting of the plan which followed, my part was even larger; for I designed and cast with my own hand a hot-air grating for the offices, which had the luck or merit to be accepted. The energy and aptitude which I displayed throughout delighted and surprised my father, and I believe, although I say it whose tongue should be tied, that they alone prevented Muskegon capitol from being the eyesore of my native State.

Altogether, I was in a cheery frame of mind when I returned to the commercial college; and my earlier operations were crowned with a full measure of success. My father wrote and wired to me continually. "You are to exercise your own judgment, Loudon," he would say. "All that I do is to give you the figures; but whatever operation you take up must be upon your own responsibility, and whatever you earn will be entirely due to your own dash and forethought." For all that, it was always clear what he intended me to do, and I was always careful to do it. Inside of a month I was at the head of seventeen or eighteen thousand dollars, college paper. And here I fell a victim to one of the vices of the system. The paper (I have already explained) had a real value of one per cent; and cost, and could be sold for, currency. Unsuccessful speculators were thus always selling clothes, books, banjos, and sleeve-links, in order to pay their differences; the successful, on the other hand, were often tempted to realise, and enjoy some return upon their profits. Now I wanted thirty dollars' worth of artist-truck, for I was always sketching in the woods; my allowance was for the time exhausted; I had begun to regard the exchange (with my father's help) as a place where money was to be got for stooping; and in an evil hour I realised three thousand dollars of the college paper and bought my easel.

It was a Wednesday morning when the things arrived, and set me in the seventh heaven of satisfaction. My father (for I can scarcely say myself) was trying at this time a "straddle" in wheat between Chicago and New York; the operation so called is, as you know, one of the most tempting and least safe upon the chess-board of finance. On the Thursday, luck began to turn against my father's calculations; and by the Friday evening, I was posted on the boards as a defaulter for the second time. Here was a rude blow: my father would have taken it ill enough in any case; for however much a man may resent the incapacity of an only son, he will feel his own more sensibly. But it chanced that, in our bitter cup of failure, there was one ingredient that might truly be called poisonous. He had been keeping the run of my position; he missed the three thousand dollars, paper; and in his view, I had stolen thirty dollars, currency. It was an extreme view perhaps; but in some senses, it was just: and my father, although (to my judgment) quite reckless of honesty in the essence of his operations, was the soul of honour as to their details. I had one grieved letter from him, dignified and tender; and during the rest of that wretched term, working as a clerk, selling my clothes and sketches to make futile speculations, my dream of Paris quite vanished. I was cheered by no word of kindness and helped by no hint of counsel from my father.

All the time he was no doubt thinking of little else but his son, and what to do with him. I believe he had been really appalled by what he regarded as my laxity of principle, and began to think it might be well to preserve me from temptation; the architect of the capitol had, besides, spoken obligingly of my design; and while he was thus hanging between two minds, Fortune suddenly stepped in, and Muskegon State capitol reversed my destiny.

"Loudon," said my father, as he met me at the depot, with a smiling countenance, "if you were to go to Paris, how long would it take you to become an experienced sculptor?"

"How do you mean, father?" I cried. "Experienced?"

"A man that could be entrusted with the highest styles," he answered; "the nude, for instance; and the patriotic and emblematical styles."

"It might take three years," I replied.

"You think Paris necessary?" he asked. "There are great advantages in our own country; and that man Prodgers appears to be a very clever sculptor, though I suppose he stands too high to go around giving lessons."

"Paris is the only place," I assured him.

"Well, I think myself it will sound better," he admitted. "A Young Man, a Native of this State, Son of a Leading Citizen, Studies Prosecuted under the Most Experienced Masters in Paris," he added, relishingly.

"But, my dear dad, what is it all about?" I interrupted. "I never even dreamed of being a sculptor."

"Well, here it is," said he. "I took up the statuary contract on our new capitol; I took it up at first as a deal; and then it occurred to me it would be better to keep it in the family. It meets your idea; there's considerable money in the thing; and it's patriotic. So, if you say the word, you shall go to Paris, and come back in three years to decorate the capitol of your native State. It's a big chance for you, Loudon; and I'll tell you what—every dollar you earn, I'll put another alongside of it. But the sooner you go, and the harder you work, the better; for if the first half-dozen statues aren't in a line with public taste in Muskegon, there will be trouble."

CHAPTER II. ROUSSILLON WINE.

My mother's family was Scotch, and it was judged fitting I should pay a visit on my way Paris-ward, to my Uncle Adam Loudon, a wealthy retired grocer of Edinburgh. He was very stiff and very ironical; he fed me well, lodged me sumptuously, and seemed to take it out of me all the time, cent per cent, in secret entertainment which caused his spectacles to glitter and his mouth to twitch. The ground of this ill-suppressed mirth (as well as I could make out) was simply the fact that I was an American. "Well," he would say, drawing out the word to infinity, "and I suppose now in your country, things will be so and so." And the whole group of my cousins would titter joyously. Repeated receptions of this sort must be at the root, I suppose, of what they call the Great American Jest; and I know I was myself goaded into saying that my friends went naked in the summer months, and that the Second Methodist Episcopal Church in Muskegon was decorated with scalps. I cannot say that these flights had any great success; they seemed to awaken little more surprise than the fact that my father was a Republican or that I had been taught in school to spell COLOUR without the U. If I had told them (what was after all the truth) that my father had paid a considerable annual sum to have me brought up in a gambling hell, the tittering and grinning of this dreadful family might perhaps have been excused.

I cannot deny but I was sometimes tempted to knock my Uncle Adam down; and indeed I believe it must have come to a rupture at last, if they had not given a dinner party at which I was the lion. On this occasion, I learned (to my surprise and relief) that the incivility to which I had been subjected was a matter for the family circle and might be regarded almost in the light of an endearment. To strangers I was presented with consideration; and the account given of "my American brother-in-law, poor Janie's man, James K. Dodd, the well-known millionnaire of Muskegon," was calculated to enlarge the heart of a proud son.

An aged assistant of my grandfather's, a pleasant, humble creature with a taste for whiskey, was at first deputed to be my guide about the city. With this harmless but hardly aristocratic companion, I went to Arthur's Seat and the Calton Hill, heard the band play in the Princes Street Gardens, inspected the regalia and the blood of Rizzio, and fell in love with the great castle on its cliff, the innumerable spires of churches, the stately buildings, the broad prospects, and those narrow and crowded lanes of the old town where my ancestors had lived and died in the days before Columbus.

But there was another curiosity that interested me more deeply—my grandfather, Alexander Loudon. In his time, the old gentleman had been a working mason, and had risen from the ranks more, I think, by shrewdness than by merit. In his appearance, speech, and manners, he bore broad marks of his origin, which were gall and wormwood to my Uncle Adam. His nails, in spite of anxious supervision, were often in conspicuous mourning; his clothes hung about him in bags and wrinkles like a ploughman's Sunday coat; his accent was rude, broad, and dragging: take him at his best, and even when he could be induced to hold his tongue, his mere presence in a corner of the drawing-room, with his open-air wrinkles, his scanty hair, his battered hands, and the cheerful craftiness of his expression, advertised the whole gang of us for a self-made family. My aunt might mince and my cousins bridle; but there was no getting over the solid, physical fact of the stonemason in the chimney-corner.

That is one advantage of being an American: it never occurred to me to be ashamed of my grandfather, and the old gentleman was quick to mark the difference. He held my mother in tender memory, perhaps because he was in the habit of daily contrasting her with Uncle Adam, whom he detested to the point of frenzy; and he set down to inheritance from his favourite my own becoming treatment of himself. On our walks abroad, which soon became daily, he would sometimes (after duly warning me to keep the matter dark from "Aadam") skulk into some old familiar pot-house; and there (if he had the luck to encounter any of his veteran cronies) he would present me to the company with manifest pride, casting at the same time a covert slur on the rest of his descendants. "This is my Jeannie's yin," he would say. "He's a fine fallow, him." The purpose of our excursions was not to seek antiquities or to enjoy famous prospects, but to visit one after another a series of doleful suburbs, for which it was the old gentleman's chief claim to renown that he had been the sole contractor, and too often the architect besides. I have rarely seen a more shocking exhibition: the bricks seemed to be blushing in the walls, and the slates on the roof to have turned pale with shame; but I was careful not to communicate these impressions to the aged artificer at my side; and when he would direct my attention to some fresh monstrosity—perhaps with the comment, "There's an idee of mine's: it's cheap and tasty, and had a graand run; the idee was soon stole, and there's whole deestricts near Glesgie with the goathic adeetion and that plunth,"—I would civilly make haste to admire and (what I found particularly delighted him) to inquire into the cost of each adornment. It will be conceived that Muskegon capitol was a frequent and a welcome ground of talk; I drew him all the plans from memory; and he, with the aid of a narrow volume full of figures and tables, which answered (I believe) to the name of Molesworth, and was his constant pocket companion, would draw up rough estimates and make imaginary offers on the various contracts. Our Muskegon builders he pronounced a pack of cormorants; and the congenial subject, together with my knowledge of architectural terms, the theory of strains, and the prices of materials in the States, formed a strong bond of union between what might have been otherwise an ill-assorted pair, and led my grandfather to pronounce me, with emphasis, "a real intalligent kind of a cheild." Thus a second time, as you will presently see, the capitol of my native State had influentially affected the current of my life.

I left Edinburgh, however, with not the least idea that I had done a stroke of excellent business for myself, and singly delighted to escape out of a somewhat dreary house and plunge instead into the rainbow city of Paris. Every man has his own romance; mine clustered exclusively about the practice of the arts, the life of Latin Quarter students, and the world of Paris as depicted by that grimy wizard, the author of the Comedie Humaine. I was not disappointed—I could not have been; for I did not see the facts, I brought them with me ready-made. Z. Marcas lived next door to me in my ungainly, ill-smelling hotel of the Rue Racine; I dined at my villainous restaurant with Lousteau and with Rastignac: if a curricle nearly ran me down at a street-crossing, Maxime de Trailles would be the driver. I dined, I say, at a poor restaurant and lived in a poor hotel; and this was not from need, but sentiment. My father gave me a profuse allowance, and I might have lived (had I chosen) in the Quartier de l'Etoile and driven to my studies daily. Had I done so, the glamour must have fled: I should still have been but Loudon Dodd; whereas now I was a Latin Quarter student, Murger's successor, living in flesh and blood the life of one of those romances I had loved to read, to re-read, and to dream over, among the woods of Muskegon.

At this time we were all a little Murger-mad in the Latin Quarter. The play of the Vie de Boheme (a dreary, snivelling piece) had been produced at the Odeon, had run an unconscionable time—for Paris, and revived the freshness of the legend. The same business, you may say, or there and thereabout, was being privately enacted in consequence in every garret of the neighbourhood, and a good third of the students were consciously impersonating Rodolphe or Schaunard to their own incommunicable satisfaction. Some of us went far, and some farther. I always looked with awful envy (for instance) on a certain countryman of my own who had a studio in the Rue Monsieur le Prince, wore boots, and long hair in a net, and could be seen tramping off, in this guise, to the worst eating-house of the quarter, followed by a Corsican model, his mistress, in the conspicuous costume of her race and calling. It takes some greatness of soul to carry even folly to such heights as these; and for my own part, I had to content myself by pretending very arduously to be poor, by wearing a smoking-cap on the streets, and by pursuing, through a series of misadventures, that extinct mammal, the grisette. The most grievous part was the eating and the drinking. I was born with a dainty tooth and a palate for wine; and only a genuine devotion to romance could have supported me under the cat-civets that I had to swallow, and the red ink of Bercy I must wash them down withal. Every now and again, after a hard day at the studio, where I was steadily and far from unsuccessfully industrious, a wave of distaste would overbear me; I would slink away from my haunts and companions, indemnify myself for weeks of self-denial with fine wines and dainty dishes; seated perhaps on a terrace, perhaps in an arbour in a garden, with a volume of one of my favourite authors propped open in front of me, and now consulted awhile, and now forgotten:—so remain, relishing my situation, till night fell and the lights of the city kindled; and thence stroll homeward by the riverside, under the moon or stars, in a heaven of poetry and digestion.

One such indulgence led me in the course of my second year into an adventure which I must relate: indeed, it is the very point I have been aiming for, since that was what brought me in acquaintance with Jim Pinkerton. I sat down alone to dinner one October day when the rusty leaves were falling and scuttling on the boulevard, and the minds of impressionable men inclined in about an equal degree towards sadness and conviviality. The restaurant was no great place, but boasted a considerable cellar and a long printed list of vintages. This I was perusing with the double zest of a man who is fond of wine and a lover of beautiful names, when my eye fell (near the end of the card) on that not very famous or familiar brand, Roussillon. I remembered it was a wine I had never tasted, ordered a bottle, found it excellent, and when I had discussed the contents, called (according to my habit) for a final pint. It appears they did not keep Roussillon in half-bottles. "All right," said I. "Another bottle." The tables at this eating-house are close together; and the next thing I can remember, I was in somewhat loud conversation with my nearest neighbours. From these I must have gradually extended my attentions; for I have a clear recollection of gazing about a room in which every chair was half turned round and every face turned smilingly to mine. I can even remember what I was saying at the moment; but after twenty years, the embers of shame are still alive; and I prefer to give your imagination the cue, by simply mentioning that my muse was the patriotic. It had been my design to adjourn for coffee in the company of some of these new friends; but I was no sooner on the sidewalk than I found myself unaccountably alone. The circumstance scarce surprised me at the time, much less now; but I was somewhat chagrined a little after to find I had walked into a kiosque. I began to wonder if I were any the worse for my last bottle, and decided to steady myself with coffee and brandy. In the Cafe de la Source, where I went for this restorative, the fountain was playing, and (what greatly surprised me) the mill and the various mechanical figures on the rockery appeared to have been freshly repaired and performed the most enchanting antics. The cafe was extraordinarily hot and bright, with every detail of a conspicuous clearness, from the faces of the guests to the type of the newspapers on the tables, and the whole apartment swang to and fro like a hammock, with an exhilarating motion. For some while I was so extremely pleased with these particulars that I thought I could never be weary of beholding them: then dropped of a sudden into a causeless sadness; and then, with the same swiftness and spontaneity, arrived at the conclusion that I was drunk and had better get to bed.

It was but a step or two to my hotel, where I got my lighted candle from the porter and mounted the four flights to my own room. Although I could not deny that I was drunk, I was at the same time lucidly rational and practical. I had but one preoccupation—to be up in time on the morrow for my work; and when I observed the clock on my chimney-piece to have stopped, I decided to go down stairs again and give directions to the porter. Leaving the candle burning and my door open, to be a guide to me on my return, I set forth accordingly. The house was quite dark; but as there were only the three doors on each landing, it was impossible to wander, and I had nothing to do but descend the stairs until I saw the glimmer of the porter's night light. I counted four flights: no porter. It was possible, of course, that I had reckoned incorrectly; so I went down another and another, and another, still counting as I went, until I had reached the preposterous figure of nine flights. It was now quite clear that I had somehow passed the porter's lodge without remarking it; indeed, I was, at the lowest figure, five pairs of stairs below the street, and plunged in the very bowels of the earth. That my hotel should thus be founded upon catacombs was a discovery of considerable interest; and if I had not been in a frame of mind entirely businesslike, I might have continued to explore all night this subterranean empire. But I was bound I must be up betimes on the next morning, and for that end it was imperative that I should find the porter. I faced about accordingly, and counting with painful care, remounted towards the level of the street. Five, six, and seven flights I climbed, and still there was no porter. I began to be weary of the job, and reflecting that I was now close to my own room, decided I should go to bed. Eight, nine, ten, eleven, twelve, thirteen flights I mounted; and my open door seemed to be as wholly lost to me as the porter and his floating dip. I remembered that the house stood but six stories at its highest point, from which it appeared (on the most moderate computation) I was now three stories higher than the roof. My original sense of amusement was succeeded by a not unnatural irritation. "My room has just GOT to be here," said I, and I stepped towards the door with outspread arms. There was no door and no wall; in place of either there yawned before me a dark corridor, in which I continued to advance for some time without encountering the smallest opposition. And this in a house whose extreme area scantily contained three small rooms, a narrow landing, and the stair! The thing was manifestly nonsense; and you will scarcely be surprised to learn that I now began to lose my temper. At this juncture I perceived a filtering of light along the floor, stretched forth my hand which encountered the knob of a door-handle, and without further ceremony entered a room. A young lady was within; she was going to bed, and her toilet was far advanced, or the other way about, if you prefer.

"I hope you will pardon this intrusion," said I; "but my room is No. 12, and something has gone wrong with this blamed house."

She looked at me a moment; and then, "If you will step outside for a moment, I will take you there," says she.

Thus, with perfect composure on both sides, the matter was arranged. I waited a while outside her door. Presently she rejoined me, in a dressing-gown, took my hand, led me up another flight, which made the fourth above the level of the roof, and shut me into my own room, where (being quite weary after these contraordinary explorations) I turned in, and slumbered like a child.

I tell you the thing calmly, as it appeared to me to pass; but the next day, when I awoke and put memory in the witness-box, I could not conceal from myself that the tale presented a good many improbable features. I had no mind for the studio, after all, and went instead to the Luxembourg gardens, there, among the sparrows and the statues and the falling leaves, to cool and clear my head. It is a garden I have always loved. You sit there in a public place of history and fiction. Barras and Fouche have looked from these windows. Lousteau and de Banville (one as real as the other) have rhymed upon these benches. The city tramples by without the railings to a lively measure; and within and about you, trees rustle, children and sparrows utter their small cries, and the statues look on forever. Here, then, in a seat opposite the gallery entrance, I set to work on the events of the last night, to disengage (if it were possible) truth from fiction.

The house, by daylight, had proved to be six stories high, the same as ever. I could find, with all my architectural experience, no room in its altitude for those interminable stairways, no width between its walls for that long corridor, where I had tramped at night. And there was yet a greater difficulty. I had read somewhere an aphorism that everything may be false to itself save human nature. A house might elongate or enlarge itself—or seem to do so to a gentleman who had been dining. The ocean might dry up, the rocks melt in the sun, the stars fall from heaven like autumn apples; and there was nothing in these incidents to boggle the philosopher. But the case of the young lady stood upon a different foundation. Girls were not good enough, or not good that way, or else they were too good. I was ready to accept any of these views: all pointed to the same conclusion, which I was thus already on the point of reaching, when a fresh argument occurred, and instantly confirmed it. I could remember the exact words we had each said; and I had spoken, and she had replied, in English. Plainly, then, the whole affair was an illusion: catacombs, and stairs, and charitable lady, all were equally the stuff of dreams.

I had just come to this determination, when there blew a flaw of wind through the autumnal gardens; the dead leaves showered down, and a flight of sparrows, thick as a snowfall, wheeled above my head with sudden pipings. This agreeable bustle was the affair of a moment, but it startled me from the abstraction into which I had fallen like a summons. I sat briskly up, and as I did so, my eyes rested on the figure of a lady in a brown jacket and carrying a paint-box. By her side walked a fellow some years older than myself, with an easel under his arm; and alike by their course and cargo I might judge they were bound for the gallery, where the lady was, doubtless, engaged upon some copying. You can imagine my surprise when I recognized in her the heroine of my adventure. To put the matter beyond question, our eyes met, and she, seeing herself remembered and recalling the trim in which I had last beheld her, looked swiftly on the ground with just a shadow of confusion.

I could not tell you to-day if she were plain or pretty; but she had behaved with so much good sense, and I had cut so poor a figure in her presence, that I became instantly fired with the desire to display myself in a more favorable light. The young man besides was possibly her brother; brothers are apt to be hasty, theirs being a part in which it is possible, at a comparatively early age, to assume the dignity of manhood; and it occurred to me it might be wise to forestall all possible complications by an apology.

On this reasoning I drew near to the gallery door, and had hardly got in position before the young man came out. Thus it was that I came face to face with my third destiny; for my career has been entirely shaped by these three elements,—my father, the capitol of Muskegon, and my friend, Jim Pinkerton. As for the young lady with whom my mind was at the moment chiefly occupied, I was never to hear more of her from that day forward: an excellent example of the Blind Man's Buff that we call life.

CHAPTER III. TO INTRODUCE MR. PINKERTON.

The stranger, I have said, was some years older than myself: a man of a good stature, a very lively face, cordial, agitated manners, and a gray eye as active as a fowl's.

"May I have a word with you?" said I.

"My dear sir," he replied, "I don't know what it can be about, but you may have a hundred if you like."

"You have just left the side of a young lady," I continued, "towards whom I was led (very unintentionally) into the appearance of an offence. To speak to herself would be only to renew her embarrassment, and I seize the occasion of making my apology, and declaring my respect, to one of my own sex who is her friend, and perhaps," I added, with a bow, "her natural protector."

"You are a countryman of mine; I know it!" he cried: "I am sure of it by your delicacy to a lady. You do her no more than justice. I was introduced to her the other night at tea, in the apartment of some people, friends of mine; and meeting her again this morning, I could not do less than carry her easel for her. My dear sir, what is your name?"

I was disappointed to find he had so little bond with my young lady; and but that it was I who had sought the acquaintance, might have been tempted to retreat. At the same time, something in the stranger's eye engaged me.

"My name," said I, "is Loudon Dodd; I am a student of sculpture here from Muskegon."

"Of sculpture?" he cried, as though that would have been his last conjecture. "Mine is James Pinkerton; I am delighted to have the pleasure of your acquaintance."

"Pinkerton!" it was now my turn to exclaim. "Are you Broken-Stool Pinkerton?"

He admitted his identity with a laugh of boyish delight; and indeed any young man in the quarter might have been proud to own a sobriquet thus gallantly acquired.

In order to explain the name, I must here digress into a chapter of the history of manners in the nineteenth century, very well worth commemoration for its own sake. In some of the studios at that date, the hazing of new pupils was both barbarous and obscene. Two incidents, following one on the heels of the other tended to produce an advance in civilization by the means (as so commonly happens) of a passing appeal to savage standards. The first was the arrival of a little gentleman from Armenia. He had a fez upon his head and (what nobody counted on) a dagger in his pocket. The hazing was set about in the customary style, and, perhaps in virtue of the victim's head-gear, even more boisterously than usual. He bore it at first with an inviting patience; but upon one of the students proceeding to an unpardonable freedom, plucked out his knife and suddenly plunged it in the belly of the jester. This gentleman, I am pleased to say, passed months upon a bed of sickness, before he was in a position to resume his studies. The second incident was that which had earned Pinkerton his reputation. In a crowded studio, while some very filthy brutalities were being practised on a trembling debutant, a tall, pale fellow sprang from his stool and (without the smallest preface or explanation) sang out, "All English and Americans to clear the shop!" Our race is brutal, but not filthy; and the summons was nobly responded to. Every Anglo-Saxon student seized his stool; in a moment the studio was full of bloody coxcombs, the French fleeing in disorder for the door, the victim liberated and amazed. In this feat of arms, both English-speaking nations covered themselves with glory; but I am proud to claim the author of the whole for an American, and a patriotic American at that, being the same gentleman who had subsequently to be held down in the bottom of a box during a performance of L'Oncle Sam, sobbing at intervals, "My country! O my country!" While yet another (my new acquaintance, Pinkerton) was supposed to have made the most conspicuous figure in the actual battle. At one blow, he had broken his own stool, and sent the largest of his opponents back foremost through what we used to call a "conscientious nude." It appears that, in the continuation of his flight, this fallen warrior issued on the boulevard still framed in the burst canvas.

It will be understood how much talk the incident aroused in the students' quarter, and that I was highly gratified to make the acquaintance of my famous countryman. It chanced I was to see more of the quixotic side of his character before the morning was done; for as we continued to stroll together, I found myself near the studio of a young Frenchman whose work I had promised to examine, and in the fashion of the quarter carried up Pinkerton along with me. Some of my comrades of this date were pretty obnoxious fellows. I could almost always admire and respect the grown-up practitioners of art in Paris; but many of those who were still in a state of pupilage were sorry specimens, so much so that I used often to wonder where the painters came from, and where the brutes of students went to. A similar mystery hangs over the intermediate stages of the medical profession, and must have perplexed the least observant. The ruffian, at least, whom I now carried Pinkerton to visit, was one of the most crapulous in the quarter. He turned out for our delectation a huge "crust" (as we used to call it) of St. Stephen, wallowing in red upon his belly in an exhausted receiver, and a crowd of Hebrews in blue, green, and yellow, pelting him—apparently with buns; and while we gazed upon this contrivance, regaled us with a piece of his own recent biography, of which his mind was still very full, and which he seemed to fancy, represented him in a heroic posture. I was one of those cosmopolitan Americans, who accept the world (whether at home or abroad) as they find it, and whose favourite part is that of the spectator; yet even I was listening with ill-suppressed disgust, when I was aware of a violent plucking at my sleeve.

"Is he saying he kicked her down stairs?" asked Pinkerton, white as St. Stephen.

"Yes," said I: "his discarded mistress; and then he pelted her with stones. I suppose that's what gave him the idea for his picture. He has just been alleging the pathetic excuse that she was old enough to be his mother."

Something like a sob broke from Pinkerton. "Tell him," he gasped—"I can't speak this language, though I understand a little; I never had any proper education—tell him I'm going to punch his head."

"For God's sake, do nothing of the sort!" I cried. "They don't understand that sort of thing here." And I tried to bundle him out.

"Tell him first what we think of him," he objected. "Let me tell him what he looks in the eyes of a pure-minded American"

"Leave that to me," said I, thrusting Pinkerton clear through the door.

"Qu'est-ce qu'il a?" [1] inquired the student.

    [1] "What's the matter with him?"

"Monsieur se sent mal au coeur d'avoir trop regardé votre croute," [2] said I, and made my escape, scarce with dignity, at Pinkerton's heels.

    [2] "The gentleman is sick at his stomach from having looked too long at your daub."

"What did you say to him?" he asked.

"The only thing that he could feel," was my reply.

After this scene, the freedom with which I had ejected my new acquaintance, and the precipitation with which I had followed him, the least I could do was to propose luncheon. I have forgot the name of the place to which I led him, nothing loath; it was on the far side of the Luxembourg at least, with a garden behind, where we were speedily set face to face at table, and began to dig into each other's history and character, like terriers after rabbits, according to the approved fashion of youth.

Pinkerton's parents were from the old country; there too, I incidentally gathered, he had himself been born, though it was a circumstance he seemed prone to forget. Whether he had run away, or his father had turned him out, I never fathomed; but about the age of twelve, he was thrown upon his own resources. A travelling tin-type photographer picked him up, like a haw out of a hedgerow, on a wayside in New Jersey; took a fancy to the urchin; carried him on with him in his wandering life; taught him all he knew himself—to take tin-types (as well as I can make out) and doubt the Scriptures; and died at last in Ohio at the corner of a road. "He was a grand specimen," cried Pinkerton; "I wish you could have seen him, Mr. Dodd. He had an appearance of magnanimity that used to remind me of the patriarchs." On the death of this random protector, the boy inherited the plant and continued the business. "It was a life I could have chosen, Mr. Dodd!" he cried. "I have been in all the finest scenes of that magnificent continent that we were born to be the heirs of. I wish you could see my collection of tin-types; I wish I had them here. They were taken for my own pleasure and to be a memento; and they show Nature in her grandest as well as her gentlest moments." As he tramped the Western States and Territories, taking tin-types, the boy was continually getting hold of books, good, bad, and indifferent, popular and abstruse, from the novels of Sylvanus Cobb to Euclid's Elements, both of which I found (to my almost equal wonder) he had managed to peruse: he was taking stock by the way, of the people, the products, and the country, with an eye unusually observant and a memory unusually retentive; and he was collecting for himself a body of magnanimous and semi-intellectual nonsense, which he supposed to be the natural thoughts and to contain the whole duty of the born American. To be pure-minded, to be patriotic, to get culture and money with both hands and with the same irrational fervour—these appeared to be the chief articles of his creed. In later days (not of course upon this first occasion) I would sometimes ask him why; and he had his answer pat. "To build up the type!" he would cry. "We're all committed to that; we're all under bond to fulfil the American Type! Loudon, the hope of the world is there. If we fail, like these old feudal monarchies, what is left?"

The trade of a tin-typer proved too narrow for the lad's ambition; it was insusceptible of expansion, he explained, it was not truly modern; and by a sudden conversion of front, he became a railroad-scalper. The principles of this trade I never clearly understood; but its essence appears to be to cheat the railroads out of their due fare. "I threw my whole soul into it; I grudged myself food and sleep while I was at it; the most practised hands admitted I had caught on to the idea in a month and revolutionised the practice inside of a year," he said. "And there's interest in it, too. It's amusing to pick out some one going by, make up your mind about his character and tastes, dash out of the office and hit him flying with an offer of the very place he wants to go to. I don't think there was a scalper on the continent made fewer blunders. But I took it only as a stage. I was saving every dollar; I was looking ahead. I knew what I wanted—wealth, education, a refined home, and a conscientious, cultured lady for a wife; for, Mr. Dodd"—this with a formidable outcry—"every man is bound to marry above him: if the woman's not the man's superior, I brand it as mere sensuality. There was my idea, at least. That was what I was saving for; and enough, too! But it isn't every man, I know that—it's far from every man—could do what I did: close up the livest agency in Saint Jo, where he was coining dollars by the pot, set out alone, without a friend or a word of French, and settle down here to spend his capital learning art."

"Was it an old taste?" I asked him, "or a sudden fancy?"

"Neither, Mr. Dodd," he admitted. "Of course I had learned in my tin-typing excursions to glory and exult in the works of God. But it wasn't that. I just said to myself, What is most wanted in my age and country? More culture and more art, I said; and I chose the best place, saved my money, and came here to get them."

The whole attitude of this young man warmed and shamed me. He had more fire in his little toe than I had in my whole carcase; he was stuffed to bursting with the manly virtues; thrift and courage glowed in him; and even if his artistic vocation seemed (to one of my exclusive tenets) not quite clear, who could predict what might be accomplished by a creature so full-blooded and so inspired with animal and intellectual energy? So, when he proposed that I should come and see his work (one of the regular stages of a Latin Quarter friendship), I followed him with interest and hope.

He lodged parsimoniously at the top of a tall house near the Observatory, in a bare room, principally furnished with his own trunks and papered with his own despicable studies. No man has less taste for disagreeable duties than myself; perhaps there is only one subject on which I cannot flatter a man without a blush; but upon that, upon all that touches art, my sincerity is Roman. Once and twice I made the circuit of his walls in silence, spying in every corner for some spark of merit; he, meanwhile, following close at my heels, reading the verdict in my face with furtive glances, presenting some fresh study for my inspection with undisguised anxiety, and (after it had been silently weighed in the balances and found wanting) whisking it away with an open gesture of despair. By the time the second round was completed, we were both extremely depressed.

"O!" he groaned, breaking the long silence, "it's quite unnecessary you should speak!"

"Do you want me to be frank with you? I think you are wasting time," said I.

"You don't see any promise?" he inquired, beguiled by some return of hope, and turning upon me the embarrassing brightness of his eye. "Not in this still-life here, of the melon? One fellow thought it good."

It was the least I could do to give the melon a more particular examination; which, when I had done, I could but shake my head. "I am truly sorry, Pinkerton," said I, "but I can't advise you to persevere."

He seemed to recover his fortitude at the moment, rebounding from disappointment like a man of india-rubber. "Well," said he stoutly, "I don't know that I'm surprised. But I'll go on with the course; and throw my whole soul into it, too. You mustn't think the time is lost. It's all culture; it will help me to extend my relations when I get back home; it may fit me for a position on one of the illustrateds; and then I can always turn dealer," he said, uttering the monstrous proposition, which was enough to shake the Latin Quarter to the dust, with entire simplicity. "It's all experience, besides;" he continued, "and it seems to me there's a tendency to underrate experience, both as net profit and investment. Never mind. That's done with. But it took courage for you to say what you did, and I'll never forget it. Here's my hand, Mr. Dodd. I'm not your equal in culture or talent—"

"You know nothing about that," I interrupted. "I have seen your work, but you haven't seen mine."

"No more I have," he cried; "and let's go see it at once! But I know you are away up. I can feel it here."

To say truth, I was almost ashamed to introduce him to my studio—my work, whether absolutely good or bad, being so vastly superior to his. But his spirits were now quite restored; and he amazed me, on the way, with his light-hearted talk and new projects. So that I began at last to understand how matters lay: that this was not an artist who had been deprived of the practice of his single art; but only a business man of very extended interests, informed (perhaps something of the most suddenly) that one investment out of twenty had gone wrong.

As a matter of fact besides (although I never suspected it) he was already seeking consolation with another of the muses, and pleasing himself with the notion that he would repay me for my sincerity, cement our friendship, and (at one and the same blow) restore my estimation of his talents. Several times already, when I had been speaking of myself, he had pulled out a writing-pad and scribbled a brief note; and now, when we entered the studio, I saw it in his hand again, and the pencil go to his mouth, as he cast a comprehensive glance round the uncomfortable building.

"Are you going to make a sketch of it?" I could not help asking, as I unveiled the Genius of Muskegon.

"Ah, that's my secret," said he. "Never you mind. A mouse can help a lion."

He walked round my statue and had the design explained to him. I had represented Muskegon as a young, almost a stripling, mother, with something of an Indian type; the babe upon her knees was winged, to indicate our soaring future; and her seat was a medley of sculptured fragments, Greek, Roman, and Gothic, to remind us of the older worlds from which we trace our generation.

"Now, does this satisfy you, Mr. Dodd?" he inquired, as soon as I had explained to him the main features of the design.

"Well," I said, "the fellows seem to think it's not a bad bonne femme for a beginner. I don't think it's entirely bad myself. Here is the best point; it builds up best from here. No, it seems to me it has a kind of merit," I admitted; "but I mean to do better."

"Ah, that's the word!" cried Pinkerton. "There's the word I love!" and he scribbled in his pad.

"What in creation ails you?" I inquired. "It's the most commonplace expression in the English language."

"Better and better!" chuckled Pinkerton. "The unconsciousness of genius. Lord, but this is coming in beautiful!" and he scribbled again.

"If you're going to be fulsome," said I, "I'll close the place of entertainment." And I threatened to replace the veil upon the Genius.

"No, no," said he. "Don't be in a hurry. Give me a point or two. Show me what's particularly good."

"I would rather you found that out for yourself," said I.

"The trouble is," said he, "that I've never turned my attention to sculpture, beyond, of course, admiring it, as everybody must who has a soul. So do just be a good fellow, and explain to me what you like in it, and what you tried for, and where the merit comes in. It'll be all education for me."

"Well, in sculpture, you see, the first thing you have to consider is the masses. It's, after all, a kind of architecture," I began, and delivered a lecture on that branch of art, with illustrations from my own masterpiece there present, all of which, if you don't mind, or whether you mind or not, I mean to conscientiously omit. Pinkerton listened with a fiery interest, questioned me with a certain uncultivated shrewdness, and continued to scratch down notes, and tear fresh sheets from his pad. I found it inspiring to have my words thus taken down like a professor's lecture; and having had no previous experience of the press, I was unaware that they were all being taken down wrong. For the same reason (incredible as it must appear in an American) I never entertained the least suspicion that they were destined to be dished up with a sauce of penny-a-lining gossip; and myself, my person, and my works of art butchered to make a holiday for the readers of a Sunday paper. Night had fallen over the Genius of Muskegon before the issue of my theoretic eloquence was stayed, nor did I separate from my new friend without an appointment for the morrow.

I was indeed greatly taken with this first view of my countryman, and continued, on further acquaintance, to be interested, amused, and attracted by him in about equal proportions. I must not say he had a fault, not only because my mouth is sealed by gratitude, but because those he had sprang merely from his education, and you could see he had cultivated and improved them like virtues. For all that, I can never deny he was a troublous friend to me, and the trouble began early.

It may have been a fortnight later that I divined the secret of the writing-pad. My wretch (it leaked out) wrote letters for a paper in the West, and had filled a part of one of them with descriptions of myself. I pointed out to him that he had no right to do so without asking my permission.

"Why, this is just what I hoped!" he exclaimed. "I thought you didn't seem to catch on; only it seemed too good to be true."

"But, my good fellow, you were bound to warn me," I objected.

"I know it's generally considered etiquette," he admitted; "but between friends, and when it was only with a view of serving you, I thought it wouldn't matter. I wanted it (if possible) to come on you as a surprise; I wanted you just to waken, like Lord Byron, and find the papers full of you. You must admit it was a natural thought. And no man likes to boast of a favour beforehand."

"But, heavens and earth! how do you know I think it a favour?" I cried.

He became immediately plunged in despair. "You think it a liberty," said he; "I see that. I would rather have cut off my hand. I would stop it now, only it's too late; it's published by now. And I wrote it with so much pride and pleasure!"

I could think of nothing but how to console him. "O, I daresay it's all right," said I. "I know you meant it kindly, and you would be sure to do it in good taste."

"That you may swear to," he cried. "It's a pure, bright, A number 1 paper; the St. Jo Sunday Herald. The idea of the series was quite my own; I interviewed the editor, put it to him straight; the freshness of the idea took him, and I walked out of that office with the contract in my pocket, and did my first Paris letter that evening in Saint Jo. The editor did no more than glance his eye down the headlines. 'You're the man for us,' said he."

I was certainly far from reassured by this sketch of the class of literature in which I was to make my first appearance; but I said no more, and possessed my soul in patience, until the day came when I received a copy of a newspaper marked in the corner, "Compliments of J.P." I opened it with sensible shrinkings; and there, wedged between an account of a prize-fight and a skittish article upon chiropody—think of chiropody treated with a leer!—I came upon a column and a half in which myself and my poor statue were embalmed. Like the editor with the first of the series, I did but glance my eye down the head-lines and was more than satisfied.

ANOTHER OF PINKERTON'S SPICY CHATS.

ART PRACTITIONERS IN PARIS.

MUSKEGON'S COLUMNED CAPITOL.

SON OF MILLIONAIRE DODD,

PATRIOT AND ARTIST.

"HE MEANS TO DO BETTER."

In the body of the text, besides, my eye caught, as it passed, some deadly expressions: "Figure somewhat fleshy," "bright, intellectual smile," "the unconsciousness of genius," "'Now, Mr. Dodd,' resumed the reporter, 'what would be your idea of a distinctively American quality in sculpture?'" It was true the question had been asked; it was true, alas! that I had answered; and now here was my reply, or some strange hash of it, gibbeted in the cold publicity of type. I thanked God that my French fellow-students were ignorant of English; but when I thought of the British—of Myner (for instance) or the Stennises—I think I could have fallen on Pinkerton and beat him.

To divert my thoughts (if it were possible) from this calamity, I turned to a letter from my father which had arrived by the same post. The envelope contained a strip of newspaper-cutting; and my eye caught again, "Son of Millionaire Dodd—Figure somewhat fleshy," and the rest of the degrading nonsense. What would my father think of it? I wondered, and opened his manuscript. "My dearest boy," it began, "I send you a cutting which has pleased me very much, from a St. Joseph paper of high standing. At last you seem to be coming fairly to the front; and I cannot but reflect with delight and gratitude how very few youths of your age occupy nearly two columns of press-matter all to themselves. I only wish your dear mother had been here to read it over my shoulder; but we will hope she shares my grateful emotion in a better place. Of course I have sent a copy to your grandfather and uncle in Edinburgh; so you can keep the one I enclose. This Jim Pinkerton seems a valuable acquaintance; he has certainly great talent; and it is a good general rule to keep in with pressmen."

I hope it will be set down to the right side of my account, but I had no sooner read these words, so touchingly silly, than my anger against Pinkerton was swallowed up in gratitude. Of all the circumstances of my career, my birth, perhaps, excepted, not one had given my poor father so profound a pleasure as this article in the Sunday Herald. What a fool, then, was I, to be lamenting! when I had at last, and for once, and at the cost of only a few blushes, paid back a fraction of my debt of gratitude. So that, when I next met Pinkerton, I took things very lightly; my father was pleased, and thought the letter very clever, I told him; for my own part, I had no taste for publicity: thought the public had no concern with the artist, only with his art; and though I owned he had handled it with great consideration, I should take it as a favour if he never did it again.

"There it is," he said despondingly. "I've hurt you. You can't deceive me, Loudon. It's the want of tact, and it's incurable." He sat down, and leaned his head upon his hand. "I had no advantages when I was young, you see," he added.

"Not in the least, my dear fellow," said I. "Only the next time you wish to do me a service, just speak about my work; leave my wretched person out, and my still more wretched conversation; and above all," I added, with an irrepressible shudder, "don't tell them how I said it! There's that phrase, now: 'With a proud, glad smile.' Who cares whether I smiled or not?"

"Oh, there now, Loudon, you're entirely wrong," he broke in. "That's what the public likes; that's the merit of the thing, the literary value. It's to call up the scene before them; it's to enable the humblest citizen to enjoy that afternoon the same as I did. Think what it would have been to me when I was tramping around with my tin-types to find a column and a half of real, cultured conversation—an artist, in his studio abroad, talking of his art—and to know how he looked as he did it, and what the room was like, and what he had for breakfast; and to tell myself, eating tinned beans beside a creek, that if all went well, the same sort of thing would, sooner or later, happen to myself: why, Loudon, it would have been like a peephole into heaven!"

"Well, if it gives so much pleasure," I admitted, "the sufferers shouldn't complain. Only give the other fellows a turn."

The end of the matter was to bring myself and the journalist in a more close relation. If I know anything at all of human nature—and the IF is no mere figure of speech, but stands for honest doubt—no series of benefits conferred, or even dangers shared, would have so rapidly confirmed our friendship as this quarrel avoided, this fundamental difference of taste and training accepted and condoned.

CHAPTER IV. IN WHICH I EXPERIENCE EXTREMES OF FORTUNE.

Whether it came from my training and repeated bankruptcy at the commercial college, or by direct inheritance from old Loudon, the Edinburgh mason, there can be no doubt about the fact that I was thrifty. Looking myself impartially over, I believe that is my only manly virtue. During my first two years in Paris I not only made it a point to keep well inside of my allowance, but accumulated considerable savings in the bank. You will say, with my masquerade of living as a penniless student, it must have been easy to do so: I should have had no difficulty, however, in doing the reverse. Indeed, it is wonderful I did not; and early in the third year, or soon after I had known Pinkerton, a singular incident proved it to have been equally wise. Quarter-day came, and brought no allowance. A letter of remonstrance was despatched, and for the first time in my experience, remained unanswered. A cablegram was more effectual; for it brought me at least a promise of attention. "Will write at once," my father telegraphed; but I waited long for his letter. I was puzzled, angry, and alarmed; but thanks to my previous thrift, I cannot say that I was ever practically embarrassed. The embarrassment, the distress, the agony, were all for my unhappy father at home in Muskegon, struggling for life and fortune against untoward chances, returning at night from a day of ill-starred shifts and ventures, to read and perhaps to weep over that last harsh letter from his only child, to which he lacked the courage to reply.

Nearly three months after time, and when my economies were beginning to run low, I received at last a letter with the customary bills of exchange.

"My dearest boy," it ran, "I believe, in the press of anxious business, your letters and even your allowance have been somewhile neglected. You must try to forgive your poor old dad, for he has had a trying time; and now when it is over, the doctor wants me to take my shotgun and go to the Adirondacks for a change. You must not fancy I am sick, only over-driven and under the weather. Many of our foremost operators have gone down: John T. M'Brady skipped to Canada with a trunkful of boodle; Billy Sandwith, Charlie Downs, Joe Kaiser, and many others of our leading men in this city bit the dust. But Big-Head Dodd has again weathered the blizzard, and I think I have fixed things so that we may be richer than ever before autumn.

"Now I will tell you, my dear, what I propose. You say you are well advanced with your first statue; start in manfully and finish it, and if your teacher—I can never remember how to spell his name—will send me a certificate that it is up to market standard, you shall have ten thousand dollars to do what you like with, either at home or in Paris. I suggest, since you say the facilities for work are so much greater in that city, you would do well to buy or build a little home; and the first thing you know, your dad will be dropping in for a luncheon. Indeed, I would come now, for I am beginning to grow old, and I long to see my dear boy; but there are still some operations that want watching and nursing. Tell your friend, Mr. Pinkerton, that I read his letters every week; and though I have looked in vain lately for my Loudon's name, still I learn something of the life he is leading in that strange, old world, depicted by an able pen."

Here was a letter that no young man could possibly digest in solitude. It marked one of those junctures when the confidant is necessary; and the confidant selected was none other than Jim Pinkerton. My father's message may have had an influence in this decision; but I scarce suppose so, for the intimacy was already far advanced. I had a genuine and lively taste for my compatriot; I laughed at, I scolded, and I loved him. He, upon his side, paid me a kind of doglike service of admiration, gazing at me from afar off as at one who had liberally enjoyed those "advantages" which he envied for himself. He followed at heel; his laugh was ready chorus; our friends gave him the nickname of "The Henchman." It was in this insidious form that servitude approached me.

Pinkerton and I read and re-read the famous news: he, I can swear, with an enjoyment as unalloyed and far more vocal than my own. The statue was nearly done: a few days' work sufficed to prepare it for exhibition; the master was approached; he gave his consent; and one cloudless morning of May beheld us gathered in my studio for the hour of trial. The master wore his many-hued rosette; he came attended by two of my French fellow-pupils—friends of mine and both considerable sculptors in Paris at this hour. "Corporal John" (as we used to call him) breaking for once those habits of study and reserve which have since carried him so high in the opinion of the world, had left his easel of a morning to countenance a fellow-countryman in some suspense. My dear old Romney was there by particular request; for who that knew him would think a pleasure quite complete unless he shared it, or not support a mortification more easily if he were present to console? The party was completed by John Myner, the Englishman; by the brothers Stennis,—Stennis-aine and Stennis-frere, as they used to figure on their accounts at Barbizon—a pair of hare-brained Scots; and by the inevitable Jim, as white as a sheet and bedewed with the sweat of anxiety.

I suppose I was little better myself when I unveiled the Genius of Muskegon. The master walked about it seriously; then he smiled.

"It is already not so bad," said he, in that funny English of which he was so proud. "No, already not so bad."

We all drew a deep breath of relief; and Corporal John (as the most considerable junior present) explained to him it was intended for a public building, a kind of prefecture—

"He! Quoi?" cried he, relapsing into French. "Qu'est-ce que vous me chantez la? O, in America," he added, on further information being hastily furnished. "That is anozer sing. O, very good, very good."

The idea of the required certificate had to be introduced to his mind in the light of a pleasantry— the fancy of a nabob little more advanced than the red Indians of "Fennimore Cooperr"; and it took all our talents combined to conceive a form of words that would be acceptable on both sides. One was found, however: Corporal John engrossed it in his undecipherable hand, the master lent it the sanction of his name and flourish, I slipped it into an envelope along with one of the two letters I had ready prepared in my pocket, and as the rest of us moved off along the boulevard to breakfast, Pinkerton was detached in a cab and duly committed it to the post.

The breakfast was ordered at Lavenue's, where no one need be ashamed to entertain even the master; the table was laid in the garden; I had chosen the bill of fare myself; on the wine question we held a council of war with the most fortunate results; and the talk, as soon as the master laid aside his painful English, became fast and furious. There were a few interruptions, indeed, in the way of toasts. The master's health had to be drunk, and he responded in a little well-turned speech, full of neat allusions to my future and to the United States; my health followed; and then my father's must not only be proposed and drunk, but a full report must be despatched to him at once by cablegram—an extravagance which was almost the means of the master's dissolution. Choosing Corporal John to be his confidant (on the ground, I presume, that he was already too good an artist to be any longer an American except in name) he summed up his amazement in one oft-repeated formula—"C'est barbare!" Apart from these genial formalities, we talked, talked of art, and talked of it as only artists can. Here in the South Seas we talk schooners most of the time; in the Quarter we talked art with the like unflagging interest, and perhaps as much result.

Before very long, the master went away; Corporal John (who was already a sort of young master) followed on his heels; and the rank and file were naturally relieved by their departure. We were now among equals; the bottle passed, the conversation sped. I think I can still hear the

Stennis brothers pour forth their copious tirades; Dijon, my portly French fellow-student, drop witticisms well-conditioned like himself; and another (who was weak in foreign languages) dash hotly into the current of talk with some "Je trove que pore oon sontimong de delicacy, Corot ...," or some "Pour moi Corot est le plou ...," and then, his little raft of French foundering at once, scramble silently to shore again. He at least could understand; but to Pinkerton, I think the noise, the wine, the sun, the shadows of the leaves, and the esoteric glory of being seated at a foreign festival, made up the whole available means of entertainment.

We sat down about half past eleven; I suppose it was two when, some point arising and some particular picture being instanced, an adjournment to the Louvre was proposed. I paid the score, and in a moment we were trooping down the Rue de Renne. It was smoking hot; Paris glittered with that superficial brilliancy which is so agreeable to the man in high spirits, and in moods of dejection so depressing; the wine sang in my ears, it danced and brightened in my eyes. The pictures that we saw that afternoon, as we sped briskly and loquaciously through the immortal galleries, appear to me, upon a retrospect, the loveliest of all; the comments we exchanged to have touched the highest mark of criticism, grave or gay.

It was only when we issued again from the museum that a difference of race broke up the party. Dijon proposed an adjournment to a cafe, there to finish the afternoon on beer; the elder Stennis, revolted at the thought, moved for the country, a forest if possible, and a long walk. At once the English speakers rallied to the name of any exercise: even to me, who have been often twitted with my sedentary habits, the thought of country air and stillness proved invincibly attractive. It appeared, upon investigation, we had just time to hail a cab and catch one of the fast trains for Fontainebleau. Beyond the clothes we stood in, all were destitute of what is called (with dainty vagueness) personal effects; and it was earnestly mooted, on the other side, whether we had not time to call upon the way and pack a satchel? But the Stennis boys exclaimed upon our effeminacy. They had come from London, it appeared, a week before with nothing but greatcoats and tooth-brushes. No baggage—there was the secret of existence. It was expensive, to be sure; for every time you had to comb your hair, a barber must be paid, and every time you changed your linen, one shirt must be bought and another thrown away; but anything was better (argued these young gentlemen) than to be the slaves of haversacks. "A fellow has to get rid gradually of all material attachments; that was manhood" (said they); "and as long as you were bound down to anything,—house, umbrella, or portmanteau,—you were still tethered by the umbilical cord." Something engaging in this theory carried the most of us away. The two Frenchmen, indeed, retired, scoffing, to their bock; and Romney, being too poor to join the excursion on his own resources and too proud to borrow, melted unobtrusively away. Meanwhile the remainder of the company crowded the benches of a cab; the horse was urged (as horses have to be) by an appeal to the pocket of the driver; the train caught by the inside of a minute; and in less than an hour and a half we were breathing deep of the sweet air of the forest and stretching our legs up the hill from Fontainebleau octroi, bound for Barbizon. That the leading members of our party covered the distance in fifty-one minutes and a half is (I believe) one of the historic landmarks of the colony; but you will scarce be surprised to learn that I was somewhat in the rear. Myner, a comparatively philosophic Briton, kept me company in my deliberate advance; the glory of the sun's going down, the fall of the long shadows, the inimitable scent and the inspiration of the woods, attuned me more and more to walk in a silence which progressively infected my companion; and I remember that, when at last he spoke, I was startled from a deep abstraction.

"Your father seems to be a pretty good kind of a father," said he. "Why don't he come to see you?" I was ready with some dozen of reasons, and had more in stock; but Myner, with that shrewdness which made him feared and admired, suddenly fixed me with his eye-glass and asked, "Ever press him?"

The blood came in my face. No; I had never pressed him; I had never even encouraged him to come. I was proud of him; proud of his handsome looks, of his kind, gentle ways, of that bright face he could show when others were happy; proud, too (meanly proud, if you like) of his great wealth and startling liberalities. And yet he would have been in the way of my Paris life, of much of which he would have disapproved. I had feared to expose to criticism his innocent remarks on art; I had told myself, I had even partly believed, he did not want to come; I had been (and still am) convinced that he was sure to be unhappy out of Muskegon; in short, I had a thousand reasons, good and bad, not all of which could alter one iota of the fact that I knew he only waited for my invitation.

"Thank you, Myner," said I; "you're a much better fellow than ever I supposed. I'll write tonight."

"O, you're a pretty decent sort yourself," returned Myner, with more than his usual flippancy of manner, but (as I was gratefully aware) not a trace of his occasional irony of meaning.

Well, these were brave days, on which I could dwell forever. Brave, too, were those that followed, when Pinkerton and I walked Paris and the suburbs, viewing and pricing houses for my new establishment, or covered ourselves with dust and returned laden with Chinese gods and brass warming-pans from the dealers in antiquities. I found Pinkerton well up in the situation of these establishments as well as in the current prices, and with quite a smattering of critical judgment; it turned out he was investing capital in pictures and curiosities for the States, and the superficial thoroughness of the creature appeared in the fact, that although he would never be a connoisseur, he was already something of an expert. The things themselves left him as near as may be cold; but he had a joy of his own in understanding how to buy and sell them.

In such engagements the time passed until I might very well expect an answer from my father. Two mails followed each other, and brought nothing. By the third I received a long and almost incoherent letter of remorse, encouragement, consolation, and despair. From this pitiful document, which (with a movement of piety) I burned as soon as I had read it, I gathered that the bubble of my father's wealth was burst, that he was now both penniless and sick; and that I, so far from expecting ten thousand dollars to throw away in juvenile extravagance, must look no longer for the quarterly remittances on which I lived. My case was hard enough; but I had sense enough to perceive, and decency enough to do my duty. I sold my curiosities, or rather I sent Pinkerton to sell them; and he had previously bought and now disposed of them so wisely that the loss was trifling. This, with what remained of my last allowance, left me at the head of no less than five thousand francs. Five hundred I reserved for my own immediate necessities; the rest I mailed inside of the week to my father at Muskegon, where they came in time to pay his funeral expenses.

The news of his death was scarcely a surprise and scarce a grief to me. I could not conceive my father a poor man. He had led too long a life of thoughtless and generous profusion to endure the change; and though I grieved for myself, I was able to rejoice that my father had been taken from the battle. I grieved, I say, for myself; and it is probable there were at the same date many thousands of persons grieving with less cause. I had lost my father; I had lost the allowance; my whole fortune (including what had been returned from Muskegon) scarce amounted to a thousand francs; and to crown my sorrows, the statuary contract had changed hands. The new contractor had a son of his own, or else a nephew; and it was signified to me, with business-like plainness, that I must find another market for my pigs. In the meanwhile I had given up my room, and slept on a truckle-bed in the corner of the studio, where as I read myself to sleep at night, and when I awoke in the morning, that now useless bulk, the Genius of Muskegon, was ever present to my eyes. Poor stone lady! born to be enthroned under the gilded, echoing dome of the new capitol, whither was she now to drift? for what base purposes be ultimately broken up, like an unseaworthy ship? and what should befall her ill-starred artificer, standing, with his thousand francs, on the threshold of a life so hard as that of the unbefriended sculptor?

It was a subject often and earnestly debated by myself and Pinkerton. In his opinion, I should instantly discard my profession. "Just drop it, here and now," he would say. "Come back home with me, and let's throw our whole soul into business. I have the capital; you bring the culture. Dodd & Pinkerton—I never saw a better name for an advertisement; and you can't think, Loudon, how much depends upon a name." On my side, I would admit that a sculptor should possess one of three things—capital, influence, or an energy only to be qualified as hellish. The first two I had now lost; to the third I never had the smallest claim; and yet I wanted the cowardice (or perhaps it was the courage) to turn my back on my career without a fight. I told him, besides, that however poor my chances were in sculpture, I was convinced they were yet worse in business, for which I equally lacked taste and aptitude. But upon this head, he was my father over again; assured me that I spoke in ignorance; that any intelligent and cultured person was Bound to succeed; that I must, besides, have inherited some of my father's fitness; and, at any rate, that I had been regularly trained for that career in the commercial college.

"Pinkerton," I said, "can't you understand that, as long as I was there, I never took the smallest interest in any stricken thing? The whole affair was poison to me."

"It's not possible," he would cry; "it can't be; you couldn't live in the midst of it and not feel the charm; with all your poetry of soul, you couldn't help! Loudon," he would go on, "you drive me crazy. You expect a man to be all broken up about the sunset, and not to care a dime for a place where fortunes are fought for and made and lost all day; or for a career that consists in studying up life till you have it at your finger-ends, spying out every cranny where you can get your hand in and a dollar out, and standing there in the midst—one foot on bankruptcy, the other on a borrowed dollar, and the whole thing spinning round you like a mill—raking in the stamps, in spite of fate and fortune."

To this romance of dickering I would reply with the romance (which is also the virtue) of art: reminding him of those examples of constancy through many tribulations, with which the role of Apollo is illustrated; from the case of Millet, to those of many of our friends and comrades, who had chosen this agreeable mountain path through life, and were now bravely clambering among rocks and brambles, penniless and hopeful.

"You will never understand it, Pinkerton," I would say. "You look to the result, you want to see some profit of your endeavours: that is why you could never learn to paint, if you lived to be Methusalem. The result is always a fizzle: the eyes of the artist are turned in; he lives for a frame of mind. Look at Romney, now. There is the nature of the artist. He hasn't a cent; and if you offered him to-morrow the command of an army, or the presidentship of the United States, he wouldn't take it, and you know he wouldn't."

"I suppose not," Pinkerton would cry, scouring his hair with both his hands; "and I can't see why; I can't see what in fits he would be after, not to; I don't seem to rise to these views. Of course, it's the fault of not having had advantages in early life; but, Loudon, I'm so miserably low that it seems to me silly. The fact is," he might add with a smile, "I don't seem to have the least use for a frame of mind without square meals; and you can't get it out of my head that it's a man's duty to die rich, if he can."

"What for?" I asked him once.

"O, I don't know," he replied. "Why in snakes should anybody want to be a sculptor, if you come to that? I would love to sculp myself. But what I can't see is why you should want to do nothing else. It seems to argue a poverty of nature."

Whether or not he ever came to understand me—and I have been so tossed about since then that I am not very sure I understand myself—he soon perceived that I was perfectly in earnest; and after about ten days of argument, suddenly dropped the subject, and announced that he was wasting capital, and must go home at once. No doubt he should have gone long before, and had already lingered over his intended time for the sake of our companionship and my misfortune; but man is so unjustly minded that the very fact, which ought to have disarmed, only embittered my vexation. I resented his departure in the light of a desertion; I would not say, but doubtless I betrayed it; and something hang-dog in the man's face and bearing led me to believe he was himself remorseful. It is certain at least that, during the time of his preparations, we drew sensibly apart—a circumstance that I recall with shame. On the last day, he had me to dinner at a restaurant which he knew I had formerly frequented, and had only forsworn of late from considerations of economy. He seemed ill at ease; I was myself both sorry and sulky; and the meal passed with little conversation.

"Now, Loudon," said he, with a visible effort, after the coffee was come and our pipes lighted, "you can never understand the gratitude and loyalty I bear you. You don't know what a boon it is to be taken up by a man that stands on the pinnacle of civilization; you can't think how it's refined and purified me, how it's appealed to my spiritual nature; and I want to tell you that I would die at your door like a dog."

I don't know what answer I tried to make, but he cut me short.

"Let me say it out!" he cried. "I revere you for your whole-souled devotion to art; I can't rise to it, but there's a strain of poetry in my nature, Loudon, that responds to it. I want you to carry it out, and I mean to help you."

"Pinkerton, what nonsense is this?" I interrupted.

"Now don't get mad, Loudon; this is a plain piece of business," said he; "it's done every day; it's even typical. How are all those fellows over here in Paris, Henderson, Sumner, Long?—it's all the same story: a young man just plum full of artistic genius on the one side, a man of business on the other who doesn't know what to do with his dollars—"

"But, you fool, you're as poor as a rat," I cried.

"You wait till I get my irons in the fire!" returned Pinkerton. "I'm bound to be rich; and I tell you I mean to have some of the fun as I go along. Here's your first allowance; take it at the hand of a friend; I'm one that holds friendship sacred as you do yourself. It's only a hundred francs; you'll get the same every month, and as soon as my business begins to expand we'll increase it to something fitting. And so far from it's being a favour, just let me handle your statuary for the American market, and I'll call it one of the smartest strokes of business in my life."

It took me a long time, and it had cost us both much grateful and painful emotion, before I had finally managed to refuse his offer and compounded for a bottle of particular wine. He dropped the subject at last suddenly with a "Never mind; that's all done with," nor did he again refer to the subject, though we passed together the rest of the afternoon, and I accompanied him, on his departure; to the doors of the waiting-room at St. Lazare. I felt myself strangely alone; a voice told me that I had rejected both the counsels of wisdom and the helping hand of friendship; and as I passed through the great bright city on my homeward way, I measured it for the first time with the eye of an adversary.

CHAPTER V. IN WHICH I AM DOWN ON MY LUCK IN PARIS.

In no part of the world is starvation an agreeable business; but I believe it is admitted there is no worse place to starve in than this city of Paris. The appearances of life are there so especially gay, it is so much a magnified beer-garden, the houses are so ornate, the theatres so numerous, the very pace of the vehicles is so brisk, that a man in any deep concern of mind or pain of body is constantly driven in upon himself. In his own eyes, he seems the one serious creature moving in a world of horrible unreality; voluble people issuing from a cafe, the queue at theatre doors, Sunday cabfuls of second-rate pleasure-seekers, the bedizened ladies of the pavement, the show in the jewellers' windows—all the familiar sights contributing to flout his own unhappiness, want, and isolation. At the same time, if he be at all after my pattern, he is perhaps supported by a childish satisfaction: this is life at last, he may tell himself, this is the real thing; the bladders on which I was set swimming are now empty, my own weight depends upon the ocean; by my own exertions I must perish or succeed; and I am now enduring in the vivid fact, what I so much delighted to read of in the case of Lonsteau or Lucien, Rodolphe or Schaunard.

Of the steps of my misery, I cannot tell at length. In ordinary times what were politically called "loans" (although they were never meant to be repaid) were matters of constant course among the students, and many a man has partly lived on them for years. But my misfortune befell me at an awkward juncture. Many of my friends were gone; others were themselves in a precarious situation. Romney (for instance) was reduced to tramping Paris in a pair of country sabots, his only suit of clothes so imperfect (in spite of cunningly adjusted pins) that the authorities at the Luxembourg suggested his withdrawal from the gallery. Dijon, too, was on a leeshore, designing clocks and gas-brackets for a dealer; and the most he could do was to offer me a corner of his studio where I might work. My own studio (it will be gathered) I had by that time lost; and in the course of my expulsion the Genius of Muskegon was finally separated from her author. To continue to possess a full-sized statue, a man must have a studio, a gallery, or at least the freedom of a back garden. He cannot carry it about with him, like a satchel, in the bottom of a cab, nor can he cohabit in a garret, ten by fifteen, with so momentous a companion. It was my first idea to leave her behind at my departure. There, in her birthplace, she might lend an inspiration, methought, to my successor. But the proprietor, with whom I had unhappily quarrelled, seized the occasion to be disagreeable, and called upon me to remove my property. For a man in such straits as I now found myself, the hire of a lorry was a consideration; and yet even that I could have faced, if I had had anywhere to drive to after it was hired. Hysterical laughter seized upon me as I beheld (in imagination) myself, the waggoner, and the Genius of Muskegon, standing in the public view of Paris, without the shadow of a destination; perhaps driving at last to the nearest rubbish heap, and dumping there, among the ordures of a city, the beloved child of my invention. From these extremities I was relieved by a seasonable offer, and I parted from the Genius of Muskegon for thirty francs. Where she now stands, under what name she is admired or criticised, history does not inform us; but I like to think she may adorn the shrubbery of some suburban tea-garden, where holiday shop-girls hang their hats upon the mother, and their swains (by way of an approach of gallantry) identify the winged infant with the god of love.

In a certain cabman's eating-house on the outer boulevard I got credit for my midday meal. Supper I was supposed not to require, sitting down nightly to the delicate table of some rich acquaintances. This arrangement was extremely ill-considered. My fable, credible enough at first, and so long as my clothes were in good order, must have seemed worse than doubtful after my coat became frayed about the edges, and my boots began to squelch and pipe along the restaurant floors. The allowance of one meal a day besides, though suitable enough to the state of my finances, agreed poorly with my stomach. The restaurant was a place I had often visited experimentally, to taste the life of students then more unfortunate than myself; and I had never in those days entered it without disgust, or left it without nausea. It was strange to find myself sitting down with avidity, rising up with satisfaction, and counting the hours that divided me from my return to such a table. But hunger is a great magician; and so soon as I had spent my ready cash, and could no longer fill up on bowls of chocolate or hunks of bread, I must depend entirely on that cabman's eating-house, and upon certain rare, long-expected, long-remembered windfalls. Dijon (for instance) might get paid for some of his pot-boiling work, or else an old friend would pass through Paris; and then I would be entertained to a meal after my own soul, and contract a Latin Quarter loan, which would keep me in tobacco and my morning coffee for a fortnight. It might be thought the latter would appear the more important. It might be supposed that a life, led so near the confines of actual famine, should have dulled the nicety of my palate. On the contrary, the poorer a man's diet, the more sharply is he set on dainties. The last of my ready cash, about thirty francs, was deliberately squandered on a single dinner; and a great part of my time when I was alone was passed upon the details of imaginary feasts.

One gleam of hope visited me—an order for a bust from a rich Southerner. He was free-handed, jolly of speech, merry of countenance; kept me in good humour through the sittings, and when they were over, carried me off with him to dinner and the sights of Paris. I ate well; I laid on flesh; by all accounts, I made a favourable likeness of the being, and I confess I thought my future was assured. But when the bust was done, and I had despatched it across the Atlantic, I could never so much as learn of its arrival. The blow felled me; I should have lain down and tried no stroke to right myself, had not the honour of my country been involved. For Dijon improved the opportunity in the European style; informing me (for the first time) of the manners of America: how it was a den of banditti without the smallest rudiment of law or order, and debts could be there only collected with a shotgun. "The whole world knows it," he would say; "you are alone, mon petit Loudon, you are alone to be in ignorance of these facts. The judges of the Supreme Court fought but the other day with stilettos on the bench at Cincinnati. You should read the little book of one of my friends: Le Touriste dans le Far-West; you will see it all there in good French." At last, incensed by days of such discussion, I undertook to prove to him the contrary, and put the affair in the hands of my late father's lawyer. From him I had the gratification of hearing, after a due interval, that my debtor was dead of the yellow fever in Key West, and had left his affairs in some confusion. I suppress his name; for though he treated me with cruel nonchalance, it is probable he meant to deal fairly in the end.

Soon after this a shade of change in my reception at the cabman's eating-house marked the beginning of a new phase in my distress. The first day, I told myself it was but fancy; the next, I made quite sure it was a fact; the third, in mere panic I stayed away, and went for forty-eight hours fasting. This was an act of great unreason; for the debtor who stays away is but the more remarked, and the boarder who misses a meal is sure to be accused of infidelity. On the fourth day, therefore, I returned, inwardly quaking. The proprietor looked askance upon my entrance; the waitresses (who were his daughters) neglected my wants and sniffed at the affected joviality of my salutations; last and most plain, when I called for a suisse (such as was being served to all the other diners) I was bluntly told there were no more. It was obvious I was near the end of my tether; one plank divided me from want, and now I felt it tremble. I passed a sleepless night, and the first thing in the morning took my way to Myner's studio. It was a step I had long meditated and long refrained from; for I was scarce intimate with the Englishman; and though I knew him to possess plenty of money, neither his manner nor his reputation were the least encouraging to beggars.

I found him at work on a picture, which I was able conscientiously to praise, dressed in his usual tweeds, plain, but pretty fresh, and standing out in disagreeable contrast to my own withered and degraded outfit. As we talked, he continued to shift his eyes watchfully between his handiwork and the fat model, who sat at the far end of the studio in a state of nature, with one arm gallantly arched above her head. My errand would have been difficult enough under the best of circumstances: placed between Myner, immersed in his art, and the white, fat, naked female in a ridiculous attitude, I found it quite impossible. Again and again I attempted to approach the point, again and again fell back on commendations of the picture; and it was not until the model had enjoyed an interval of repose, during which she took the conversation in her own hands and regaled us (in a soft, weak voice) with details as to her husband's prosperity, her sister's lamented decline from the paths of virtue, and the consequent wrath of her father, a peasant of stern principles, in the vicinity of Chalons on the Marne;—it was not, I say, until after this was over, and I had once more cleared my throat for the attack, and once more dropped aside into some commonplace about the picture, that Myner himself brought me suddenly and vigorously to the point.

"You didn't come here to talk this rot," said he.

"No," I replied sullenly; "I came to borrow money."

He painted awhile in silence.

"I don't think we were ever very intimate?" he asked.

"Thank you," said I. "I can take my answer," and I made as if to go, rage boiling in my heart.

"Of course you can go if you like," said Myner; "but I advise you to stay and have it out."

"What more is there to say?" I cried. "You don't want to keep me here for a needless humiliation?"

"Look here, Dodd, you must try and command your temper," said he. "This interview is of your own seeking, and not mine; if you suppose it's not disagreeable to me, you're wrong; and if you think I will give you money without knowing thoroughly about your prospects, you take me for a fool. Besides," he added, "if you come to look at it, you've got over the worst of it by now: you have done the asking, and you have every reason to know I mean to refuse. I hold out no false hopes, but it may be worth your while to let me judge."

Thus—I was going to say—encouraged, I stumbled through my story; told him I had credit at the cabman's eating-house, but began to think it was drawing to a close; how Dijon lent me a corner of his studio, where I tried to model ornaments, figures for clocks, Time with the scythe, Leda and the swan, musketeers for candlesticks, and other kickshaws, which had never (up to that day) been honoured with the least approval.

"And your room?" asked Myner.

"O, my room is all right, I think," said I. "She is a very good old lady, and has never even mentioned her bill."

"Because she is a very good old lady, I don't see why she should be fined," observed Myner.

"What do you mean by that?" I cried.

"I mean this," said he. "The French give a great deal of credit amongst themselves; they find it pays on the whole, or the system would hardly be continued; but I can't see where WE come in; I can't see that it's honest of us Anglo-Saxons to profit by their easy ways, and then skip over the Channel or (as you Yankees do) across the Atlantic."

"But I'm not proposing to skip," I objected.

"Exactly," he replied. "And shouldn't you? There's the problem. You seem to me to have a lack of sympathy for the proprietors of cabmen's eating-houses. By your own account you're not getting on: the longer you stay, it'll only be the more out of the pocket of the dear old lady at your lodgings. Now, I'll tell you what I'll do: if you consent to go, I'll pay your passage to New York, and your railway fare and expenses to Muskegon (if I have the name right) where your father lived, where he must have left friends, and where, no doubt, you'll find an opening. I don't seek any gratitude, for of course you'll think me a beast; but I do ask you to pay it back when you are able. At any rate, that's all I can do. It might be different if I thought you a genius, Dodd; but I don't, and I advise you not to."

"I think that was uncalled for, at least," said I.

"I daresay it was," he returned, with the same steadiness. "It seemed to me pertinent; and, besides, when you ask me for money upon no security, you treat me with the liberty of a friend, and it's to be presumed that I can do the like. But the point is, do you accept?"

"No, thank you," said I; "I have another string to my bow."

"All right," says Myner. "Be sure it's honest."

"Honest? honest?" I cried. "What do you mean by calling my honesty in question?"

"I won't, if you don't like it," he replied. "You seem to think honesty as easy as Blind Man's Buff: I don't. It's some difference of definition."

I went straight from this irritating interview, during which Myner had never discontinued painting, to the studio of my old master. Only one card remained for me to play, and I was now resolved to play it: I must drop the gentleman and the frock-coat, and approach art in the workman's tunic.

"Tiens, this little Dodd!" cried the master; and then, as his eye fell on my dilapidated clothing, I thought I could perceive his countenance to darken.

I made my plea in English; for I knew, if he were vain of anything, it was of his achievement of the island tongue. "Master," said I, "will you take me in your studio again? but this time as a workman."

"I sought your fazer was immensely reech," said he.

I explained to him that I was now an orphan and penniless.

He shook his head. "I have betterr workmen waiting at my door," said he, "far betterr workmen."

"You used to think something of my work, sir," I pleaded.

"Somesing, somesing—yes!" he cried; "enough for a son of a reech man—not enough for an orphan. Besides, I sought you might learn to be an artist; I did not sink you might learn to be a workman."

On a certain bench on the outer boulevard, not far from the tomb of Napoleon, a bench shaded at that date by a shabby tree, and commanding a view of muddy roadway and blank wall, I sat down to wrestle with my misery. The weather was cheerless and dark; in three days I had eaten but once; I had no tobacco; my shoes were soaked, my trousers horrid with mire; my humour and all the circumstances of the time and place lugubriously attuned. Here were two men who had both spoken fairly of my work while I was rich and wanted nothing; now that I was poor and lacked all: "no genius," said the one; "not enough for an orphan," the other; and the first offered me my passage like a pauper immigrant, and the second refused me a day's wage as a hewer of stone—plain dealing for an empty belly. They had not been insincere in the past; they were not insincere to-day: change of circumstance had introduced a new criterion: that was all.

But if I acquitted my two Job's comforters of insincerity, I was yet far from admitting them infallible. Artists had been contemned before, and had lived to turn the laugh on their contemners. How old was Corot before he struck the vein of his own precious metal? When had a young man been more derided (or more justly so) than the god of my admiration, Balzac? Or if I required a bolder inspiration, what had I to do but turn my head to where the gold dome of the Invalides glittered against inky squalls, and recall the tale of him sleeping there: from the day when a young artillery-sub could be giggled at and nicknamed Puss-in-Boots by frisky misses; on to the days of so many crowns and so many victories, and so many hundred mouths of cannon, and so many thousand war-hoofs trampling the roadways of astonished Europe eighty miles in front of the grand army? To go back, to give up, to proclaim myself a failure, an ambitious failure, first a rocket, then a stick! I, Loudon Dodd, who had refused all other livelihoods with scorn, and been advertised in the Saint Joseph Sunday Herald as a patriot and an artist, to be returned upon my native Muskegon like damaged goods, and go the circuit of my father's acquaintance, cap in hand, and begging to sweep offices! No, by Napoleon! I would die at my chosen trade; and the two who had that day flouted me should live to envy my success, or to weep tears of unavailing penitence behind my pauper coffin.

Meantime, if my courage was still undiminished, I was none the nearer to a meal. At no great distance my cabman's eating-house stood, at the tail of a muddy cab-rank, on the shores of a wide thoroughfare of mud, offering (to fancy) a face of ambiguous invitation. I might be received, I might once more fill my belly there; on the other hand, it was perhaps this day the bolt was destined to fall, and I might be expelled instead, with vulgar hubbub. It was policy to make the attempt, and I knew it was policy; but I had already, in the course of that one morning, endured too many affronts, and I felt I could rather starve than face another. I had courage and to spare for the future, none left for that day; courage for the main campaign, but not a spark of it for that preliminary skirmish of the cabman's restaurant. I continued accordingly to sit upon my bench, not far from the ashes of Napoleon, now drowsy, now light-headed, now in complete mental obstruction, or only conscious of an animal pleasure in quiescence; and now thinking, planning, and remembering with unexampled clearness, telling myself tales of sudden wealth, and gustfully ordering and greedily consuming imaginary meals: in the course of which I must have dropped asleep.

It was towards dark that I was suddenly recalled to famine by a cold souse of rain, and sprang shivering to my feet. For a moment I stood bewildered: the whole train of my reasoning and dreaming passed afresh through my mind; I was again tempted, drawn as if with cords, by the image of the cabman's eating-house, and again recoiled from the possibility of insult. "Qui dort dîne," thought I to myself; and took my homeward way with wavering footsteps, through rainy streets in which the lamps and the shop-windows now began to gleam; still marshalling imaginary dinners as I went.

"Ah, Monsieur Dodd," said the porter, "there has been a registered letter for you. The facteur will bring it again to-morrow."

A registered letter for me, who had been so long without one? Of what it could possibly contain, I had no vestige of a guess; nor did I delay myself guessing; far less from any conscious plan of dishonesty: the lies flowed from me like a natural secretion.

"O," said I, "my remittance at last! What a bother I should have missed it! Can you lend me a hundred francs until to-morrow?"

I had never attempted to borrow from the porter till that moment: the registered letter was, besides, my warranty; and he gave me what he had—three napoleons and some francs in silver. I pocketed the money carelessly, lingered a while chaffing, strolled leisurely to the door; and then (fast as my trembling legs could carry me) round the corner to the Cafe de Cluny. French waiters are deft and speedy; they were not deft enough for me; and I had scarce decency to let the man set the wine upon the table or put the butter alongside the bread, before my glass and my mouth were filled. Exquisite bread of the Cafe Cluny, exquisite first glass of old Pomard tingling to my wet feet, indescribable first olive culled from the hors d'oeuvre—I suppose, when I come to lie dying, and the lamp begins to grow dim, I shall still recall your savour. Over the rest of that meal, and the rest of the evening, clouds lie thick; clouds perhaps of Burgundy; perhaps, more properly, of famine and repletion.

I remember clearly, at least, the shame, the despair, of the next morning, when I reviewed what I had done, and how I had swindled the poor honest porter; and, as if that were not enough, fairly burnt my ships, and brought bankruptcy home to that last refuge, my garret. The porter would expect his money; I could not pay him; here was scandal in the house; and I knew right well the cause of scandal would have to pack. "What do you mean by calling my honesty in question?" I had cried the day before, turning upon Myner. Ah, that day before! the day before Waterloo, the day before the Flood; the day before I had sold the roof over my head, my future, and my self-respect, for a dinner at the Cafe Cluny!

In the midst of these lamentations the famous registered letter came to my door, with healing under its seals. It bore the postmark of San Francisco, where Pinkerton was already struggling to the neck in multifarious affairs: it renewed the offer of an allowance, which his improved estate permitted him to announce at the figure of two hundred francs a month; and in case I was in some immediate pinch, it enclosed an introductory draft for forty dollars. There are a thousand excellent reasons why a man, in this self-helpful epoch, should decline to be dependent on another; but the most numerous and cogent considerations all bow to a necessity as stern as mine; and the banks were scarce open ere the draft was cashed.

It was early in December that I thus sold myself into slavery; and for six months I dragged a slowly lengthening chain of gratitude and uneasiness. At the cost of some debt I managed to excel myself and eclipse the Genius of Muskegon, in a small but highly patriotic Standard Bearer for the Salon; whither it was duly admitted, where it stood the proper length of days entirely unremarked, and whence it came back to me as patriotic as before. I threw my whole soul (as Pinkerton would have phrased it) into clocks and candlesticks; the devil a candlestick-maker would have anything to say to my designs. Even when Dijon, with his infinite good humour and infinite scorn for all such journey-work, consented to peddle them in indiscriminately with his own, the dealers still detected and rejected mine. Home they returned to me, true as the Standard Bearer; who now, at the head of quite a regiment of lesser idols, began to grow an eyesore in the scanty studio of my friend. Dijon and I have sat by the hour, and gazed upon that company of images. The severe, the frisky, the classical, the Louis Quinze, were there—from Joan of Arc in her soldierly cuirass to Leda with the swan; nay, and God forgive me for a man that knew better! the humorous was represented also. We sat and gazed, I say; we criticised, we turned them hither and thither; even upon the closest inspection they looked quite like statuettes; and yet nobody would have a gift of them!

Vanity dies hard; in some obstinate cases it outlives the man: but about the sixth month, when I already owed near two hundred dollars to Pinkerton, and half as much again in debts scattered about Paris, I awoke one morning with a horrid sentiment of oppression, and found I was alone:

my vanity had breathed her last during the night. I dared not plunge deeper in the bog; I saw no hope in my poor statuary; I owned myself beaten at last; and sitting down in my nightshirt beside the window, whence I had a glimpse of the tree-tops at the corner of the boulevard, and where the music of its early traffic fell agreeably upon my ear, I penned my farewell to Paris, to art, to my whole past life, and my whole former self. "I give in," I wrote. "When the next allowance arrives, I shall go straight out West, where you can do what you like with me."

It is to be understood that Pinkerton had been, in a sense, pressing me to come from the beginning; depicting his isolation among new acquaintances, "who have none of them your culture," he wrote; expressing his friendship in terms so warm that it sometimes embarrassed me to think how poorly I could echo them; dwelling upon his need for assistance; and the next moment turning about to commend my resolution and press me to remain in Paris. "Only remember, Loudon," he would write, "if you ever DO tire of it, there's plenty of work here for you—honest, hard, well-paid work, developing the resources of this practically virgin State. And of course I needn't say what a pleasure it would be to me if we were going at it SHOULDER TO SHOULDER." I marvel (looking back) that I could so long have resisted these appeals, and continue to sink my friend's money in a manner that I knew him to dislike. At least, when I did awake to any sense of my position, I awoke to it entirely; and determined not only to follow his counsel for the future, but even as regards the past, to rectify his losses. For in this juncture of affairs I called to mind that I was not without a possible resource, and resolved, at whatever cost of mortification, to beard the Loudon family in their historic city.

In the excellent Scots' phrase, I made a moonlight flitting, a thing never dignified, but in my case unusually easy. As I had scarce a pair of boots worth portage, I deserted the whole of my effects without a pang. Dijon fell heir to Joan of Arc, the Standard Bearer, and the Musketeers. He was present when I bought and frugally stocked my new portmanteau; and it was at the door of the trunk shop that I took my leave of him, for my last few hours in Paris must be spent alone. It was alone (and at a far higher figure than my finances warranted) that I discussed my dinner; alone that I took my ticket at Saint Lazare; all alone, though in a carriage full of people, that I watched the moon shine on the Seine flood with its tufted islets, on Rouen with her spires, and on the shipping in the harbour of Dieppe. When the first light of the morning called me from troubled slumbers on the deck, I beheld the dawn at first with pleasure; I watched with pleasure the green shores of England rising out of rosy haze; I took the salt air with delight into my nostrils; and then all came back to me; that I was no longer an artist, no longer myself; that I was leaving all I cared for, and returning to all that I detested, the slave of debt and gratitude, a public and a branded failure.

From this picture of my own disgrace and wretchedness, it is not wonderful if my mind turned with relief to the thought of Pinkerton, waiting for me, as I knew, with unwearied affection, and regarding me with a respect that I had never deserved, and might therefore fairly hope that I should never forfeit. The inequality of our relation struck me rudely. I must have been stupid, indeed, if I could have considered the history of that friendship without shame—I, who had given so little, who had accepted and profited by so much. I had the whole day before me in London, and I determined (at least in words) to set the balance somewhat straighter. Seated in the corner of a public place, and calling for sheet after sheet of paper, I poured forth the expression of my gratitude, my penitence for the past, my resolutions for the future. Till now, I told him, my course had been mere selfishness. I had been selfish to my father and to my friend, taking their help, and denying them (which was all they asked) the poor gratification of my company and countenance.

Wonderful are the consolations of literature! As soon as that letter was written and posted, the consciousness of virtue glowed in my veins like some rare vintage.

CHAPTER VI. IN WHICH I GO WEST.

I reached my uncle's door next morning in time to sit down with the family to breakfast. More than three years had intervened almost without mutation in that stationary household, since I had sat there first, a young American freshman, bewildered among unfamiliar dainties, Finnan haddock, kippered salmon, baps and mutton ham, and had wearied my mind in vain to guess what should be under the tea-cosey. If there were any change at all, it seemed that I had risen in the family esteem. My father's death once fittingly referred to, with a ceremonial lengthening of Scotch upper lips and wagging of the female head, the party launched at once (God help me) into the more cheerful topic of my own successes. They had been so pleased to hear such good accounts of me; I was quite a great man now; where was that beautiful statue of the Genius of Something or other? "You haven't it here? not here? Really?" asks the sprightliest of my cousins, shaking curls at me; as though it were likely I had brought it in a cab, or kept it concealed about my person like a birthday surprise. In the bosom of this family, unaccustomed to the tropical nonsense of the West, it became plain the Sunday Herald and poor, blethering Pinkerton had been accepted for their face. It is not possible to invent a circumstance that could have more depressed me; and I am conscious that I behaved all through that breakfast like a whipt schoolboy.

At length, the meal and family prayers being both happily over, I requested the favour of an interview with Uncle Adam on "the state of my affairs." At sound of this ominous expression, the good man's face conspicuously lengthened; and when my grandfather, having had the proposition repeated to him (for he was hard of hearing) announced his intention of being present at the interview, I could not but think that Uncle Adam's sorrow kindled into momentary irritation. Nothing, however, but the usual grim cordiality appeared upon the surface; and we all three passed ceremoniously to the adjoining library, a gloomy theatre for a depressing piece of business. My grandfather charged a clay pipe, and sat tremulously smoking in a corner of the fireless chimney; behind him, although the morning was both chill and dark, the window was partly open and the blind partly down: I cannot depict what an air he had of being out of place, like a man shipwrecked there. Uncle Adam had his station at the business table in the midst. Valuable rows of books looked down upon the place of torture; and I could hear sparrows chirping in the garden, and my sprightly cousin already banging the piano and pouring forth an acid stream of song from the drawing-room overhead.

It was in these circumstances that, with all brevity of speech and a certain boyish sullenness of manner, looking the while upon the floor, I informed my relatives of my financial situation: the amount I owed Pinkerton; the hopelessness of any maintenance from sculpture; the career offered me in the States; and how, before becoming more beholden to a stranger, I had judged it right to lay the case before my family.

"I am only sorry you did not come to me at first," said Uncle Adam. "I take the liberty to say it would have been more decent."

"I think so too, Uncle Adam," I replied; "but you must bear in mind I was ignorant in what light you might regard my application."

"I hope I would never turn my back on my own flesh and blood," he returned with emphasis; but to my anxious ear, with more of temper than affection. "I could never forget you were my sister's son. I regard this as a manifest duty. I have no choice but to accept the entire responsibility of the position you have made."

I did not know what else to do but murmur "thank you."

"Yes," he pursued, "and there is something providential in the circumstance that you come at the right time. In my old firm there is a vacancy; they call themselves Italian Warehousemen now," he continued, regarding me with a twinkle of humour; "so you may think yourself in luck: we were only grocers in my day. I shall place you there to-morrow."

"Stop a moment, Uncle Adam," I broke in. "This is not at all what I am asking. I ask you to pay Pinkerton, who is a poor man. I ask you to clear my feet of debt, not to arrange my life or any part of it."

"If I wished to be harsh, I might remind you that beggars cannot be choosers," said my uncle; "and as to managing your life, you have tried your own way already, and you see what you have made of it. You must now accept the guidance of those older and (whatever you may think of it) wiser than yourself. All these schemes of your friend (of whom I know nothing, by the by) and talk of openings in the West, I simply disregard. I have no idea whatever of your going trekking across a continent on a wild-goose chase. In this situation, which I am fortunately able to place at your disposal, and which many a well-conducted young man would be glad to jump at, you will receive, to begin with, eighteen shillings a week."

"Eighteen shillings a week!" I cried. "Why, my poor friend gave me more than that for nothing!"

"And I think it is this very friend you are now trying to repay?" observed my uncle, with an air of one advancing a strong argument.

"Aadam!" said my grandfather.

"I'm vexed you should be present at this business," quoth Uncle Adam, swinging rather obsequiously towards the stonemason; "but I must remind you it is of your own seeking."

"Aadam!" repeated the old man.

"Well, sir, I am listening," says my uncle.

My grandfather took a puff or two in silence; and then, "Ye're makin' an awfu' poor appearance, Aadam," said he.

My uncle visibly reared at the affront. "I'm sorry you should think so," said he, "and still more sorry you should say so before present company."

"A believe that; A ken that, Aadam," returned old Loudon, dryly; "and the curiis thing is, I'm no very carin'. See here, ma man," he continued, addressing himself to me. "A'm your grandfaither, amn't I not? Never you mind what Aadam says. A'll see justice din ye. A'm rich."

"Father," said Uncle Adam, "I would like one word with you in private."

I rose to go.

"Set down upon your hinderlands," cried my grandfather, almost savagely. "If Aadam has anything to say, let him say it. It's me that has the money here; and by Gravy! I'm goin' to be obeyed."

Upon this scurvy encouragement, it appeared that my uncle had no remark to offer: twice challenged to "speak out and be done with it," he twice sullenly declined; and I may mention that about this period of the engagement, I began to be sorry for him.

"See here, then, Jeannie's yin!" resumed my grandfather. "A'm goin' to give ye a set-off. Your mither was always my fav'rite, for A never could agree with Aadam. A like ye fine yoursel'; there's nae noansense aboot ye; ye've a fine nayteral idee of builder's work; ye've been to France, where they tell me they're grand at the stuccy. A splendid thing for ceilin's, the stuccy! and it's a vaiyable disguise, too; A don't believe there's a builder in Scotland has used more stuccy than me. But as A was sayin', if ye'll follie that trade, with the capital that A'm goin' to give ye, ye may live yet to be as rich as mysel'. Ye see, ye would have always had a share of it when A was gone; it appears ye're needin' it now; well, ye'll get the less, as is only just and proper."

Uncle Adam cleared his throat. "This is very handsome, father," said he; "and I am sure Loudon feels it so. Very handsome, and as you say, very just; but will you allow me to say that it had better, perhaps, be put in black and white?"

The enmity always smouldering between the two men at this ill-judged interruption almost burst in flame. The stonemason turned upon his offspring, his long upper lip pulled down, for all the world, like a monkey's. He stared a while in virulent silence; and then "Get Gregg!" said he.

The effect of these words was very visible. "He will be gone to his office," stammered my uncle.

"Get Gregg!" repeated my grandfather.

"I tell you, he will be gone to his office," reiterated Adam.

"And I tell ye, he's takin' his smoke," retorted the old man.

"Very well, then," cried my uncle, getting to his feet with some alacrity, as upon a sudden change of thought, "I will get him myself."

"Ye will not!" cried my grandfather. "Ye will sit there upon your hinderland."

"Then how the devil am I to get him?" my uncle broke forth, with not unnatural petulance.

My grandfather (having no possible answer) grinned at his son with the malice of a schoolboy; then he rang the bell.

"Take the garden key," said Uncle Adam to the servant; "go over to the garden, and if Mr. Gregg the lawyer is there (he generally sits under the red hawthorn), give him old Mr. Loudon's compliments, and will he step in here for a moment?"

"Mr. Gregg the lawyer!" At once I understood (what had been puzzling me) the significance of my grandfather and the alarm of my poor uncle: the stonemason's will, it was supposed, hung trembling in the balance.

"Look here, grandfather," I said, "I didn't want any of this. All I wanted was a loan of (say) two hundred pounds. I can take care of myself; I have prospects and opportunities, good friends in the States——"

The old man waved me down. "It's me that speaks here," he said curtly; and we waited the coming of the lawyer in a triple silence. He appeared at last, the maid ushering him in—a spectacled, dry, but not ungenial looking man.

"Here, Gregg," cried my grandfather. "Just a question: What has Aadam got to do with my will?"

"I'm afraid I don't quite understand," said the lawyer, staring.

"What has he got to do with it?" repeated the old man, smiting with his fist upon the arm of his chair. "Is my money mine's, or is it Aadam's? Can Aadam interfere?"

"O, I see," said Mr. Gregg. "Certainly not. On the marriage of both of your children a certain sum was paid down and accepted in full of legitim. You have surely not forgotten the circumstance, Mr. Loudon?"

"So that, if I like," concluded my grandfather, hammering out his words, "I can leave every doit I die possessed of to the Great Magunn?"—meaning probably the Great Mogul.

"No doubt of it," replied Gregg, with a shadow of a smile.

"Ye hear that, Aadam?" asked my grandfather.

"I may be allowed to say I had no need to hear it," said my uncle.

"Very well," says my grandfather. "You and Jeannie's yin can go for a bit walk. Me and Gregg has business."

When once I was in the hall alone with Uncle Adam, I turned to him, sick at heart. "Uncle Adam," I said, "you can understand, better than I can say, how very painful all this is to me."

"Yes, I am sorry you have seen your grandfather in so unamiable a light," replied this extraordinary man. "You shouldn't allow it to affect your mind though. He has sterling qualities, quite an extraordinary character; and I have no fear but he means to behave handsomely to you."

His composure was beyond my imitation: the house could not contain me, nor could I even promise to return to it: in concession to which weakness, it was agreed that I should call in about an hour at the office of the lawyer, whom (as he left the library) Uncle Adam should waylay and inform of the arrangement. I suppose there was never a more topsy-turvy situation: you would have thought it was I who had suffered some rebuff, and that iron-sided Adam was a generous conqueror who scorned to take advantage.

It was plain enough that I was to be endowed: to what extent and upon what conditions I was now left for an hour to meditate in the wide and solitary thoroughfares of the new town, taking counsel with street-corner statues of George IV. and William Pitt, improving my mind with the pictures in the window of a music-shop, and renewing my acquaintance with Edinburgh east wind. By the end of the hour I made my way to Mr. Gregg's office, where I was placed, with a few appropriate words, in possession of a cheque for two thousand pounds and a small parcel of architectural works.

"Mr. Loudon bids me add," continued the lawyer, consulting a little sheet of notes, "that although these volumes are very valuable to the practical builder, you must be careful not to lose originality. He tells you also not to be 'hadden doun'—his own expression—by the theory of strains, and that Portland cement, properly sanded, will go a long way."

I smiled, and remarked that I supposed it would.

"I once lived in one of my excellent client's houses," observed the lawyer; "and I was tempted, in that case, to think it had gone far enough."

"Under these circumstances, sir," said I, "you will be rather relieved to hear that I have no intention of becoming a builder."

At this, he fairly laughed; and, the ice being broken, I was able to consult him as to my conduct.

He insisted I must return to the house, at least, for luncheon, and one of my walks with Mr. Loudon. "For the evening, I will furnish you with an excuse, if you please," said he, "by asking you to a bachelor dinner with myself. But the luncheon and the walk are unavoidable. He is an old man, and, I believe, really fond of you; he would naturally feel aggrieved if there were any appearance of avoiding him; and as for Mr. Adam, do you know, I think your delicacy out of place.... And now, Mr. Dodd, what are you to do with this money?"

Ay, there was the question. With two thousand pounds—fifty thousand francs—I might return to Paris and the arts, and be a prince and millionaire in that thrifty Latin Quarter. I think I had the grace, with one corner of my mind, to be glad that I had sent the London letter: I know very well that with the rest and worst of me, I repented bitterly of that precipitate act. On one point, however, my whole multiplex estate of man was unanimous: the letter being gone, there was no help but I must follow. The money was accordingly divided in two unequal shares: for the first, Mr. Gregg got me a bill in the name of Dijon to meet my liabilities in Paris; for the second, as I had already cash in hand for the expenses of my journey, he supplied me with drafts on San Francisco.

The rest of my business in Edinburgh, not to dwell on a very agreeable dinner with the lawyer or the horrors of the family luncheon, took the form of an excursion with the stonemason, who led me this time to no suburb or work of his old hands, but with an impulse both natural and pretty, to that more enduring home which he had chosen for his clay. It was in a cemetery, by some strange chance, immured within the bulwarks of a prison; standing, besides, on the margin of a cliff, crowded with elderly stone memorials, and green with turf and ivy. The east wind (which I thought too harsh for the old man) continually shook the boughs, and the thin sun of a Scottish summer drew their dancing shadows.

"I wanted ye to see the place," said he. "Yon's the stane. Euphemia Ross: that was my goodwife, your grandmither—hoots! I'm wrong; that was my first yin; I had no bairns by her;—yours is the second, Mary Murray, Born 1819, Died 1850: that's her—a fine, plain, decent sort of a creature, tak' her athegether. Alexander Loudon, Born Seventeen Ninety-Twa, Died—and then a hole in the ballant: that's me. Alexander's my name. They ca'd me Ecky when I was a boy. Eh, Ecky! ye're an awfu' auld man!"

I had a second and sadder experience of graveyards at my next alighting-place, the city of Muskegon, now rendered conspicuous by the dome of the new capitol encaged in scaffolding. It was late in the afternoon when I arrived, and raining; and as I walked in great streets, of the very name of which I was quite ignorant—double, treble, and quadruple lines of horse-cars jingling by—hundred-fold wires of telegraph and telephone matting heaven above my head—huge, staring houses, garish and gloomy, flanking me from either hand—the thought of the Rue Racine, ay, and of the cabman's eating-house, brought tears to my eyes. The whole monotonous Babel had grown, or I should rather say swelled, with such a leap since my departure, that I must continually inquire my way; and the very cemetery was brand new. Death, however, had been active; the graves were already numerous, and I must pick my way in the rain, among the tawdry sepulchres of millionnaires, and past the plain black crosses of Hungarian labourers, till chance or instinct led me to the place that was my father's. The stone had been erected (I knew already) "by admiring friends"; I could now judge their taste in monuments; their taste in literature, methought, I could imagine, and I refrained from drawing near enough to read the terms of the inscription. But the name was in larger letters and stared at me—JAMES K. DODD. What a singular thing is a name, I thought; how it clings to a man, and continually misrepresents, and then survives him; and it flashed across my mind, with a mixture of regret and bitter mirth, that I had never known, and now probably never should know, what the K had represented. King, Kilter, Kay, Kaiser, I went, running over names at random, and then stumbled with ludicrous misspelling on Kornelius, and had nearly laughed aloud. I have never been more childish; I suppose (although the deeper voices of my nature seemed all dumb) because I have never been more moved. And at this last incongruous antic of my nerves, I was seized with a panic of remorse and fled the cemetery.

Scarce less funereal was the rest of my experience in Muskegon, where, nevertheless, I lingered, visiting my father's circle, for some days. It was in piety to him I lingered; and I might have spared myself the pain. His memory was already quite gone out. For his sake, indeed, I was made welcome; and for mine the conversation rolled awhile with laborious effort on the virtues of the deceased. His former comrades dwelt, in my company, upon his business talents or his generosity for public purposes; when my back was turned, they remembered him no more. My father had loved me; I had left him alone to live and die among the indifferent; now I returned to find him dead and buried and forgotten. Unavailing penitence translated itself in my thoughts to fresh resolve. There was another poor soul who loved me: Pinkerton. I must not be guilty twice of the same error.

A week perhaps had been thus wasted, nor had I prepared my friend for the delay. Accordingly, when I had changed trains at Council Bluffs, I was aware of a man appearing at the end of the car with a telegram in his hand and inquiring whether there were any one aboard "of the name of LONDON Dodd?" I thought the name near enough, claimed the despatch, and found it was from Pinkerton: "What day do you arrive? Awfully important." I sent him an answer giving day and hour, and at Ogden found a fresh despatch awaiting me: "That will do. Unspeakable relief. Meet you at Sacramento." In Paris days I had a private name for Pinkerton: "The Irrepressible" was what I had called him in hours of bitterness, and the name rose once more on my lips. What mischief was he up to now? What new bowl was my benignant monster brewing for his Frankenstein? In what new imbroglio should I alight on the Pacific coast? My trust in the man was entire, and my distrust perfect. I knew he would never mean amiss; but I was convinced he would almost never (in my sense) do aright.

I suppose these vague anticipations added a shade of gloom to that already gloomy place of travel: Nebraska, Wyoming, Utah, Nevada, scowled in my face at least, and seemed to point me back again to that other native land of mine, the Latin Quarter. But when the Sierras had been climbed, and the train, after so long beating and panting, stretched itself upon the downward track—when I beheld that vast extent of prosperous country rolling seaward from the woods and the blue mountains, that illimitable spread of rippling corn, the trees growing and blowing in the merry weather, the country boys thronging aboard the train with figs and peaches, and the conductors, and the very darky stewards, visibly exulting in the change—up went my soul like a balloon; Care fell from his perch upon my shoulders; and when I spied my Pinkerton among the crowd at Sacramento, I thought of nothing but to shout and wave for him, and grasp him by the hand, like what he was—my dearest friend.

"O Loudon!" he cried. "Man, how I've pined for you! And you haven't come an hour too soon. You're known here and waited for; I've been booming you already; you're billed for a lecture to-morrow night: Student Life in Paris, Grave and Gay: twelve hundred places booked at the last stock! Tut, man, you're looking thin! Here, try a drop of this." And he produced a case bottle, staringly labelled PINKERTON'S THIRTEEN STAR GOLDEN STATE BRANDY, WARRANTED ENTIRE.

"God bless me!" said I, gasping and winking after my first plunge into this fiery fluid. "And what does 'Warranted Entire' mean?"

"Why, Loudon! you ought to know that!" cried Pinkerton. "It's real, copper-bottomed English; you see it on all the old-time wayside hostelries over there."

"But if I'm not mistaken, it means something Warranted Entirely different," said I, "and applies to the public house, and not the beverages sold."

"It's very possible," said Jim, quite unabashed. "It's effective, anyway; and I can tell you, sir, it has boomed that spirit: it goes now by the gross of cases. By the way, I hope you won't mind; I've got your portrait all over San Francisco for the lecture, enlarged from that carte de visite: H. Loudon Dodd, the Americo-Parisienne Sculptor. Here's a proof of the small handbills; the posters are the same, only in red and blue, and the letters fourteen by one."

I looked at the handbill, and my head turned. What was the use of words? why seek to explain to Pinkerton the knotted horrors of "Americo-Parisienne"? He took an early occasion to point it out as "rather a good phrase; gives the two sides at a glance: I wanted the lecture written up to that." Even after we had reached San Francisco, and at the actual physical shock of my own effigy placarded on the streets I had broken forth in petulant words, he never comprehended in the least the ground of my aversion.

"If I had only known you disliked red lettering!" was as high as he could rise. "You are perfectly right: a clear-cut black is preferable, and shows a great deal further. The only thing that pains me is the portrait: I own I thought that a success. I'm dreadfully and truly sorry, my dear fellow: I see now it's not what you had a right to expect; but I did it, Loudon, for the best; and the press is all delighted."

At the moment, sweeping through green tule swamps, I fell direct on the essential. "But, Pinkerton," I cried, "this lecture is the maddest of your madnesses. How can I prepare a lecture in thirty hours?"

"All done, Loudon!" he exclaimed in triumph. "All ready. Trust me to pull a piece of business through. You'll find it all type-written in my desk at home. I put the best talent of San Francisco on the job: Harry Miller, the brightest pressman in the city."

And so he rattled on, beyond reach of my modest protestations, blurting out his complicated interests, crying up his new acquaintances, and ever and again hungering to introduce me to some "whole-souled, grand fellow, as sharp as a needle," from whom, and the very thought of whom, my spirit shrank instinctively.

Well, I was in for it: in for Pinkerton, in for the portrait, in for the type-written lecture. One promise I extorted—that I was never again to be committed in ignorance; even for that, when I saw how its extortion puzzled and depressed the Irrepressible, my soul repented me; and in all else I suffered myself to be led uncomplaining at his chariot wheels. The Irrepressible, did I say? The Irresistible were nigher truth.

But the time to have seen me was when I sat down to Harry Miller's lecture. He was a facetious dog, this Harry Miller; he had a gallant way of skirting the indecent which (in my case) produced physical nausea; and he could be sentimental and even melodramatic about grisettes and starving genius. I found he had enjoyed the benefit of my correspondence with Pinkerton: adventures of my own were here and there horridly misrepresented, sentiments of my own echoed and exaggerated till I blushed to recognise them. I will do Harry Miller justice: he must have had a kind of talent, almost of genius; all attempts to lower his tone proving fruitless, and the Harry-Millerism ineradicable. Nay, the monster had a certain key of style, or want of style, so that certain milder passages, which I sought to introduce, discorded horribly, and impoverished (if that were possible) the general effect.

By an early hour of the numbered evening I might have been observed at the sign of the Poodle Dog, dining with my agent: so Pinkerton delighted to describe himself. Thence, like an ox to the slaughter, he led me to the hall, where I stood presently alone, confronting assembled San

Francisco, with no better allies than a table, a glass of water, and a mass of manuscript and typework, representing Harry Miller and myself. I read the lecture; for I had lacked both time and will to get the trash by heart—read it hurriedly, humbly, and with visible shame. Now and then I would catch in the auditorium an eye of some intelligence, now and then, in the manuscript, would stumble on a richer vein of Harry Miller, and my heart would fail me, and I gabbled. The audience yawned, it stirred uneasily, it muttered, grumbled, and broke forth at last in articulate cries of "Speak up!" and "Nobody can hear!" I took to skipping, and being extremely ill-acquainted with the country, almost invariably cut in again in the unintelligible midst of some new topic. What struck me as extremely ominous, these misfortunes were allowed to pass without a laugh. Indeed, I was beginning to fear the worst, and even personal indignity, when all at once the humour of the thing broke upon me strongly. I could have laughed aloud; and being again summoned to speak up, I faced my patrons for the first time with a smile. "Very well," I said, "I will try, though I don't suppose anybody wants to hear, and I can't see why anybody should." Audience and lecturer laughed together till the tears ran down; vociferous and repeated applause hailed my impromptu sally. Another hit which I made but a little after, as I turned three pages of the copy: "You see, I am leaving out as much as I possibly can," increased the esteem with which my patrons had begun to regard me; and when I left the stage at last, my departing form was cheered with laughter, stamping, shouting, and the waving of hats.

Pinkerton was in the waiting-room, feverishly jotting in his pocket-book. As he saw me enter, he sprang up, and I declare the tears were trickling on his cheeks.

"My dear boy," he cried, "I can never forgive myself, and you can never forgive me. Never mind: I did it for the best. And how nobly you clung on! I dreaded we should have had to return the money at the doors."

"It would have been more honest if we had," said I.

The pressmen followed me, Harry Miller in the front ranks; and I was amazed to find them, on the whole, a pleasant set of lads, probably more sinned against than sinning, and even Harry Miller apparently a gentleman. I had in oysters and champagne—for the receipts were excellent—and being in a high state of nervous tension, kept the table in a roar. Indeed, I was never in my life so well inspired as when I described my vigil over Harry Miller's literature or the series of my emotions as I faced the audience. The lads vowed I was the soul of good company and the prince of lecturers; and—so wonderful an institution is the popular press—if you had seen the notices next day in all the papers, you must have supposed my evening's entertainment an unqualified success.

I was in excellent spirits when I returned home that night, but the miserable Pinkerton sorrowed for us both.

"O, Loudon," he said, "I shall never forgive myself. When I saw you didn't catch on to the idea of the lecture, I should have given it myself!"

CHAPTER VII. IRONS IN THE FIRE.
Opes Strepitumque.

The food of the body differs not so greatly for the fool or the sage, the elephant or the cocksparrow; and similar chemical elements, variously disguised, support all mortals. A brief study of Pinkerton in his new setting convinced me of a kindred truth about that other and mental digestion, by which we extract what is called "fun for our money" out of life. In the same spirit as a schoolboy, deep in Mayne Reid, handles a dummy gun and crawls among imaginary forests, Pinkerton sped through Kearney Street upon his daily business, representing to himself a highly coloured part in life's performance, and happy for hours if he should have chanced to brush against a millionnaire. Reality was his romance; he gloried to be thus engaged; he wallowed in his business. Suppose a man to dig up a galleon on the Coromandel coast, his rakish schooner keeping the while an offing under easy sail, and he, by the blaze of a great fire of wreckwood, to measure ingots by the bucketful on the uproarious beach: such an one might realise a greater material spoil; he should have no more profit of romance than Pinkerton when he cast up his weekly balance-sheet in a bald office. Every dollar gained was like something brought ashore from a mysterious deep; every venture made was like a diver's plunge; and as he thrust his bold hand into the plexus of the money-market, he was delightedly aware of how he shook the pillars of existence, turned out men (as at a battle-cry) to labour in far countries, and set the gold twitching in the drawers of millionnaires.

I could never fathom the full extent of his speculations; but there were five separate businesses which he avowed and carried like a banner. The Thirteen Star Golden State Brandy, Warranted Entire (a very flagrant distillation) filled a great part of his thoughts, and was kept before the public in an eloquent but misleading treatise: Why Drink French Brandy? A Word to the Wise. He kept an office for advertisers, counselling, designing, acting as middleman with printers and bill-stickers, for the inexperienced or the uninspired: the dull haberdasher came to him for ideas, the smart theatrical agent for his local knowledge; and one and all departed with a copy of his pamphlet: How, When, and Where; or, the Advertiser's Vade-Mecum. He had a tug chartered every Saturday afternoon and night, carried people outside the Heads, and provided them with lines and bait for six hours' fishing, at the rate of five dollars a person. I am told that some of them (doubtless adroit anglers) made a profit on the transaction. Occasionally he bought wrecks and condemned vessels; these latter (I cannot tell you how) found their way to sea again under aliases, and continued to stem the waves triumphantly enough under the colours of Bolivia or Nicaragua. Lastly, there was a certain agricultural engine, glorying in a great deal of vermilion and blue paint, and filling (it appeared) a "long-felt want," in which his interest was something like a tenth.

This for the face or front of his concerns. "On the outside," as he phrased it, he was variously and mysteriously engaged. No dollar slept in his possession; rather he kept all simultaneously flying like a conjurer with oranges. My own earnings, when I began to have a share, he would but show me for a moment, and disperse again, like those illusive money gifts which are flashed in the eyes of childhood only to be entombed in the missionary box. And he would come down radiant from a weekly balance-sheet, clap me on the shoulder, declare himself a winner by Gargantuan figures, and prove destitute of a quarter for a drink.

"What on earth have you done with it?" I would ask.

"Into the mill again; all re-invested!" he would cry, with infinite delight. Investment was ever his word. He could not bear what he called gambling. "Never touch stocks, Loudon," he would say; "nothing but legitimate business." And yet, Heaven knows, many an indurated gambler might have drawn back appalled at the first hint of some of Pinkerton's investments! One, which I succeeded in tracking home, and instance for a specimen, was a seventh share in the charter of a certain ill-starred schooner bound for Mexico, to smuggle weapons on the one trip, and cigars upon the other. The latter end of this enterprise, involving (as it did) shipwreck, confiscation, and a lawsuit with the underwriters, was too painful to be dwelt upon at length. "It's proved a disappointment," was as far as my friend would go with me in words; but I knew, from observation, that the fabric of his fortunes tottered. For the rest, it was only by accident I got wind of the transaction; for Pinkerton, after a time, was shy of introducing me to his arcana: the reason you are to hear presently.

The office which was (or should have been) the point of rest for so many evolving dollars stood in the heart of the city: a high and spacious room, with many plate-glass windows. A glazed cabinet of polished redwood offered to the eye a regiment of some two hundred bottles, conspicuously labelled. These were all charged with Pinkerton's Thirteen Star, although from across the room it would have required an expert to distinguish them from the same number of bottles of Courvoisier. I used to twit my friend with this resemblance, and propose a new edition of the pamphlet, with the title thus improved: Why Drink French Brandy, when we give you the same labels? The doors of the cabinet revolved all day upon their hinges; and if there entered any one who was a stranger to the merits of the brand, he departed laden with a bottle. When I used to protest at this extravagance, "My dear Loudon," Pinkerton would cry, "you don't seem to catch on to business principles! The prime cost of the spirit is literally nothing. I couldn't find a cheaper advertisement if I tried." Against the side post of the cabinet there leaned a gaudy umbrella, preserved there as a relic. It appears that when Pinkerton was about to place Thirteen Star upon the market, the rainy season was at hand. He lay dark, almost in penury, awaiting the first shower, at which, as upon a signal, the main thoroughfares became dotted with his agents, vendors of advertisements; and the whole world of San Francisco, from the businessman fleeing for the ferry-boat, to the lady waiting at the corner for her car, sheltered itself under umbrellas with this strange device: Are you wet? Try Thirteen Star. "It was a mammoth boom," said Pinkerton, with a sigh of delighted recollection. "There wasn't another umbrella to be seen. I stood at this window, Loudon, feasting my eyes; and I declare, I felt like Vanderbilt." And it was to this neat application of the local climate that he owed, not only much of the sale of Thirteen Star, but the whole business of his advertising agency.

The large desk (to resume our survey of the office) stood about the middle, knee-deep in stacks of handbills and posters, of Why Drink French Brandy? and The Advertiser's Vade-Mecum. It was flanked upon the one hand by two female type-writers, who rested not between the hours of nine and four, and upon the other by a model of the agricultural machine. The walls, where they were not broken by telephone boxes and a couple of photographs—one representing the wreck of the James L. Moody on a bold and broken coast, the other the Saturday tug alive with amateur fishers—almost disappeared under oil-paintings gaudily framed. Many of these were relics of the Latin Quarter, and I must do Pinkerton the justice to say that none of them were bad, and some had remarkable merit. They went off slowly but for handsome figures; and their places were progressively supplied with the work of local artists. These last it was one of my first duties to review and criticise. Some of them were villainous, yet all were saleable. I said so; and the next moment saw myself, the figure of a miserable renegade, bearing arms in the wrong camp. I was to look at pictures thenceforward, not with the eye of the artist, but the dealer; and I saw the stream widen that divided me from all I loved.

"Now, Loudon," Pinkerton had said, the morning after the lecture, "now Loudon, we can go at it shoulder to shoulder. This is what I have longed for: I wanted two heads and four arms; and now I have 'em. You'll find it's just the same as art—all observation and imagination; only more movement. Just wait till you begin to feel the charm!"

I might have waited long. Perhaps I lack a sense; for our whole existence seemed to me one dreary bustle, and the place we bustled in fitly to be called the Place of Yawning. I slept in a little den behind the office; Pinkerton, in the office itself, stretched on a patent sofa which sometimes collapsed, his slumbers still further menaced by an imminent clock with an alarm. Roused by this diabolical contrivance, we rose early, went forth early to breakfast, and returned by nine to what Pinkerton called work, and I distraction. Masses of letters must be opened, read, and answered; some by me at a subsidiary desk which had been introduced on the morning of my arrival; others by my bright-eyed friend, pacing the room like a caged lion as he dictated to the tinkling type-writers. Masses of wet proof had to be overhauled and scrawled upon with a blue pencil—"rustic"—"six-inch caps"—"bold spacing here"—or sometimes terms more fervid, as for instance this, which I remember Pinkerton to have spirted on the margin of an advertisement of Soothing Syrup: "Throw this all down. Have you never printed an advertisement? I'll be round in half an hour." The ledger and sale-book, besides, we had always with us. Such was the backbone of our occupation, and tolerable enough; but the far greater proportion of our time was consumed by visitors, whole-souled, grand fellows no doubt, and as sharp as a needle, but to me unfortunately not diverting. Some were apparently half-witted, and must be talked over by the hour before they could reach the humblest decision, which they only left the office to return again (ten minutes later) and rescind. Others came with a vast show of hurry and despatch, but I observed it to be principally show. The agricultural model for instance, which was practicable, proved a kind of flypaper for these busybodies. I have seen them blankly turn the crank of it for five minutes at a time, simulating (to nobody's deception) business interest: "Good thing this, Pinkerton? Sell much of it? Ha! Couldn't use it, I suppose, as a medium of advertisement for my article?"—which was perhaps toilet soap. Others (a still worse variety) carried us to neighbouring saloons to dice for cocktails and (after the cocktails were paid) for dollars on a corner of the counter. The attraction of dice for all these people was indeed extraordinary: at a certain club, where I once dined in the character of "my partner, Mr. Dodd," the dice-box came on the table with the wine, an artless substitute for after-dinner wit.

Of all our visitors, I believe I preferred Emperor Norton; the very mention of whose name reminds me I am doing scanty justice to the folks of San Francisco. In what other city would a harmless madman who supposed himself emperor of the two Americas have been so fostered and encouraged? Where else would even the people of the streets have respected the poor soul's illusion? Where else would bankers and merchants have received his visits, cashed his cheques, and submitted to his small assessments? Where else would he have been suffered to attend and address the exhibition days of schools and colleges? where else, in God's green earth, have taken his pick of restaurants, ransacked the bill of fare, and departed scathless? They tell me he was even an exacting patron, threatening to withdraw his custom when dissatisfied; and I can believe it, for his face wore an expression distinctly gastronomical. Pinkerton had received from this monarch a cabinet appointment; I have seen the brevet, wondering mainly at the good nature of the printer who had executed the forms, and I think my friend was at the head either of foreign affairs or education: it mattered, indeed, nothing, the presentation being in all offices identical. It was at a comparatively early date that I saw Jim in the exercise of his public functions. His Majesty entered the office—a portly, rather flabby man, with the face of a gentleman, rendered unspeakably pathetic and absurd by the great sabre at his side and the peacock's feather in his hat.

"I have called to remind you, Mr. Pinkerton, that you are somewhat in arrear of taxes," he said, with old-fashioned, stately courtesy.

"Well, your Majesty, what is the amount?" asked Jim; and when the figure was named (it was generally two or three dollars), paid upon the nail and offered a bonus in the shape of Thirteen Star.

"I am always delighted to patronise native industries," said Norton the First. "San Francisco is public-spirited in what concerns its Emperor; and indeed, sir, of all my domains, it is my favourite city."

"Come," said I, when he was gone, "I prefer that customer to the lot."

"It's really rather a distinction," Jim admitted. "I think it must have been the umbrella racket that attracted him."

We were distinguished under the rose by the notice of other and greater men. There were days when Jim wore an air of unusual capacity and resolve, spoke with more brevity like one pressed for time, and took often on his tongue such phrases as "Longhurst told me so this morning," or "I had it straight from Longhurst himself." It was no wonder, I used to think, that Pinkerton was called to council with such Titans; for the creature's quickness and resource were beyond praise. In the early days when he consulted me without reserve, pacing the room, projecting, ciphering, extending hypothetical interests, trebling imaginary capital, his "engine" (to renew an excellent old word) labouring full steam ahead, I could never decide whether my sense of respect or entertainment were the stronger. But these good hours were destined to curtailment.

"Yes, it's smart enough," I once observed. "But, Pinkerton, do you think it's honest?"

"You don't think it's honest!" he wailed. "O dear me, that ever I should have heard such an expression on your lips!"

At sight of his distress, I plagiarised unblushingly from Myner. "You seem to think honesty as simple as Blind Man's Buff," said I. "It's a more delicate affair than that: delicate as any art."

"O well! at that rate!" he exclaimed, with complete relief. "That's casuistry."

"I am perfectly certain of one thing: that what you propose is dishonest," I returned.

"Well, say no more about it. That's settled," he replied.

Thus, almost at a word, my point was carried. But the trouble was that such differences continued to recur, until we began to regard each other with alarm. If there were one thing Pinkerton valued himself upon, it was his honesty; if there were one thing he clung to, it was my good opinion; and when both were involved, as was the case in these commercial cruces, the man was on the rack. My own position, if you consider how much I owed him, how hateful is the trade of fault-finder, and that yet I lived and fattened on these questionable operations, was perhaps equally distressing. If I had been more sterling or more combative things might have gone extremely far. But, in truth, I was just base enough to profit by what was not forced on my attention, rather than seek scenes: Pinkerton quite cunning enough to avail himself of my weakness; and it was a relief to both when he began to involve his proceedings in a decent mystery.

Our last dispute, which had a most unlooked-for consequence, turned on the refitting of condemned ships. He had bought a miserable hulk, and came, rubbing his hands, to inform me she was already on the slip, under a new name, to be repaired. When first I had heard of this industry I suppose I scarcely comprehended; but much discussion had sharpened my faculties, and now my brow became heavy.

"I can be no party to that, Pinkerton," said I.

He leaped like a man shot. "What next?" he cried. "What ails you, anyway? You seem to me to dislike everything that's profitable."

"This ship has been condemned by Lloyd's agent," said I.

"But I tell you it's a deal. The ship's in splendid condition; there's next to nothing wrong with her but the garboard streak and the sternpost. I tell you Lloyd's is a ring like everybody else; only it's an English ring, and that's what deceives you. If it was American, you would be crying it down all day. It's Anglomania, common Anglomania," he cried, with growing irritation.

"I will not make money by risking men's lives," was my ultimatum.

"Great Caesar! isn't all speculation a risk? Isn't the fairest kind of shipowning to risk men's lives? And mining—how's that for risk? And look at the elevator business—there's danger, if you like! Didn't I take my risk when I bought her? She might have been too far gone; and where would I have been? Loudon," he cried, "I tell you the truth: you're too full of refinement for this world!"

"I condemn you out of your own lips," I replied. "'The fairest kind of shipowning,' says you. If you please, let us only do the fairest kind of business."

The shot told; the Irrepressible was silenced; and I profited by the chance to pour in a broadside of another sort. He was all sunk in money-getting, I pointed out; he never dreamed of anything but dollars. Where were all his generous, progressive sentiments? Where was his culture? I asked. And where was the American Type?

"It's true, Loudon," he cried, striding up and down the room, and wildly scouring at his hair. "You're perfectly right. I'm becoming materialised. O, what a thing to have to say, what a confession to make! Materialised! Me! Loudon, this must go on no longer. You've been a loyal friend to me once more; give me your hand!—you've saved me again. I must do something to rouse the spiritual side; something desperate; study something, something dry and tough. What shall it be? Theology? Algebra? What's Algebra?"

"It's dry and tough enough," said I; "a squared $+ 2ab + b$ squared."

"It's stimulating, though?" he inquired.

I told him I believed so, and that it was considered fortifying to Types.

"Then that's the thing for me. I'll study Algebra," he concluded.

The next day, by application to one of his type-writing women, he got word of a young lady, one Miss Mamie McBride, who was willing and able to conduct him in these bloomless meadows; and, her circumstances being lean, and terms consequently moderate, he and Mamie were soon in agreement for two lessons in the week. He took fire with unexampled rapidity; he seemed unable to tear himself away from the symbolic art; an hour's lesson occupied the whole evening; and the original two was soon increased to four, and then to five. I bade him beware of female blandishments. "The first thing you know, you'll be falling in love with the algebraist," said I.

"Don't say it even in jest," he cried. "She's a lady I revere. I could no more lay a hand upon her than I could upon a spirit. Loudon, I don't believe God ever made a purer-minded woman."

Which appeared to me too fervent to be reassuring.

Meanwhile I had been long expostulating with my friend upon a different matter. "I'm the fifth wheel," I kept telling him. "For any use I am, I might as well be in Senegambia. The letters you give me to attend to might be answered by a sucking child. And I tell you what it is, Pinkerton: either you've got to find me some employment, or I'll have to start in and find it for myself."

This I said with a corner of my eye in the usual quarter, toward the arts, little dreaming what destiny was to provide.

"I've got it, Loudon," Pinkerton at last replied. "Got the idea on the Potrero cars. Found I hadn't a pencil, borrowed one from the conductor, and figured on it roughly all the way in town. I saw it was the thing at last; gives you a real show. All your talents and accomplishments come in. Here's a sketch advertisement. Just run your eye over it. 'Sun, Ozone, and Music! PINKERTON'S HEBDOMADARY PICNICS!' (That's a good, catching phrase, 'hebdomadary,' though it's hard to say. I made a note of it when I was looking in the dictionary how to spell hectagonal. 'Well, you're a boss word,' I said. 'Before you're very much older, I'll have you in type as long as yourself.' And here it is, you see.) 'Five dollars a head, and ladies free. MONSTER OLIO OF ATTRACTIONS.' (How does that strike you?) 'Free luncheon under the greenwood tree. Dance on the elastic sward. Home again in the Bright Evening Hours. Manager and Honorary Steward, H. Loudon Dodd, Esq., the well-known connoisseur.'"

Singular how a man runs from Scylla to Charybdis! I was so intent on securing the disappearance of a single epithet that I accepted the rest of the advertisement and all that it involved without discussion. So it befell that the words "well-known connoisseur" were deleted; but that H. Loudon Dodd became manager and honorary steward of Pinkerton's Hebdomadary Picnics, soon shortened, by popular consent, to the Dromedary.

By eight o'clock, any Sunday morning, I was to be observed by an admiring public on the wharf. The garb and attributes of sacrifice consisted of a black frock coat, rosetted, its pockets bulging with sweetmeats and inferior cigars, trousers of light blue, a silk hat like a reflector, and a varnished wand. A goodly steamer guarded my one flank, panting and throbbing, flags fluttering fore and aft of her, illustrative of the Dromedary and patriotism. My other flank was covered by the ticket-office, strongly held by a trusty character of the Scots persuasion, rosetted like his superior and smoking a cigar to mark the occasion festive. At half-past, having assured myself that all was well with the free luncheons, I lit a cigar myself, and awaited the strains of the "Pioneer Band." I had never to wait long—they were German and punctual—and by a few minutes after the half-hour, I would hear them booming down street with a long military roll of drums, some score of gratuitous asses prancing at the head in bearskin hats and buckskin aprons, and conspicuous with resplendent axes. The band, of course, we paid for; but so strong is the San Franciscan passion for public masquerade, that the asses (as I say) were all gratuitous, pranced for the love of it, and cost us nothing but their luncheon.

The musicians formed up in the bows of my steamer, and struck into a skittish polka; the asses mounted guard upon the gangway and the ticket-office; and presently after, in family parties of father, mother, and children, in the form of duplicate lovers or in that of solitary youth, the public began to descend upon us by the carful at a time; four to six hundred perhaps, with a strong German flavour, and all merry as children. When these had been shepherded on board, and the inevitable belated two or three had gained the deck amidst the cheering of the public, the hawser was cast off, and we plunged into the bay.

And now behold the honorary steward in hour of duty and glory; see me circulate amid crowd, radiating affability and laughter, liberal with my sweetmeats and cigars. I say unblushing things to hobbledehoy girls, tell shy young persons this is the married people's boat, roguishly ask the abstracted if they are thinking of their sweethearts, offer Paterfamilias a cigar, am struck with the beauty and grow curious about the age of mamma's youngest who (I assure her gaily) will be a man before his mother; or perhaps it may occur to me, from the sensible expression of her face, that she is a person of good counsel, and I ask her earnestly if she knows any particularly pleasant place on the Saucelito or San Rafael coast, for the scene of our picnic is always supposed to be uncertain. The next moment I am back at my giddy badinage with the young ladies, wakening laughter as I go, and leaving in my wake applausive comments of "Isn't Mr. Dodd a funny gentleman?" and "O, I think he's just too nice!"

An hour having passed in this airy manner, I start upon my rounds afresh, with a bag full of coloured tickets, all with pins attached, and all with legible inscriptions: "Old Germany," "California," "True Love," "Old Fogies," "La Belle France," "Green Erin," "The Land of Cakes," "Washington," "Blue Jay," "Robin Red-Breast,"—twenty of each denomination; for when it comes to the luncheon, we sit down by twenties. These are distributed with anxious tact—for, indeed, this is the most delicate part of my functions—but outwardly with reckless unconcern, amidst the gayest flutter and confusion; and are immediately after sported upon hats and bonnets, to the extreme diffusion of cordiality, total strangers hailing each other by "the number of their mess"—so we humorously name it—and the deck ringing with cries of, "Here, all Blue Jays to the rescue!" or, "I say, am I alone in this blame' ship? Ain't there no more Californians?"

By this time we are drawing near to the appointed spot. I mount upon the bridge, the observed of all observers.

"Captain," I say, in clear, emphatic tones, heard far and wide, "the majority of the company appear to be in favour of the little cove beyond One Tree Point."

"All right, Mr. Dodd," responds the captain, heartily; "all one to me. I am not exactly sure of the place you mean; but just you stay here and pilot me."

I do, pointing with my wand. I do pilot him, to the inexpressible entertainment of the picnic; for I am (why should I deny it?) the popular man. We slow down off the mouth of a grassy valley, watered by a brook, and set in pines and redwoods. The anchor is let go; the boats are lowered, two of them already packed with the materials of an impromptu bar; and the Pioneer Band, accompanied by the resplendent asses, fill the other, and move shoreward to the inviting strains of Buffalo Gals, won't you come out to-night? It is a part of our programme that one of the asses shall, from sheer clumsiness, in the course of this embarkation, drop a dummy axe into the water, whereupon the mirth of the picnic can hardly be assuaged. Upon one occasion, the dummy axe floated, and the laugh turned rather the wrong way.

In from ten to twenty minutes the boats are along-side again, the messes are marshalled separately on the deck, and the picnic goes ashore, to find the band and the impromptu bar awaiting them. Then come the hampers, which are piled upon the beach, and surrounded by a stern guard of stalwart asses, axe on shoulder. It is here I take my place, note-book in hand, under a banner bearing the legend, "Come here for hampers." Each hamper contains a complete outfit for a separate twenty, cold provender, plates, glasses, knives, forks, and spoons: an agonized printed appeal from the fevered pen of Pinkerton, pasted on the inside of the lid, beseeches that care be taken of the glass and silver. Beer, wine, and lemonade are flowing already from the bar, and the various clans of twenty file away into the woods, with bottles under their arms, and the hampers strung upon a stick. Till one they feast there, in a very moderate seclusion, all being within earshot of the band. From one till four, dancing takes place upon the grass; the bar does a roaring business; and the honorary steward, who has already exhausted himself to bring life into the dullest of the messes, must now indefatigably dance with the plainest of the women. At four a bugle-call is sounded; and by half-past behold us on board again, pioneers, corrugated iron bar, empty bottles, and all; while the honorary steward, free at last, subsides into the captain's cabin over a brandy and soda and a book. Free at last, I say; yet there remains before him the frantic leave-takings at the pier, and a sober journey up to Pinkerton's office with two policemen and the day's takings in a bag.

What I have here sketched was the routine. But we appealed to the taste of San Francisco more distinctly in particular fetes. "Ye Olde Time Pycke-Nycke," largely advertised in handbills beginning "Oyez, Oyez!" and largely frequented by knights, monks, and cavaliers, was drowned out by unseasonable rain, and returned to the city one of the saddest spectacles I ever remember to have witnessed. In pleasing contrast, and certainly our chief success, was "The Gathering of the Clans," or Scottish picnic. So many milk-white knees were never before simultaneously exhibited in public, and to judge by the prevalence of "Royal Stewart" and the number of eagle's feathers, we were a high-born company. I threw forward the Scottish flank of my own ancestry, and passed muster as a clansman with applause. There was, indeed, but one small cloud on this red-letter day. I had laid in a large supply of the national beverage, in the shape of The "Rob Roy MacGregor O" Blend, Warranted Old and Vatted; and this must certainly have been a generous spirit, for I had some anxious work between four and half-past, conveying on board the inanimate forms of chieftains.

To one of our ordinary festivities, where he was the life and soul of his own mess, Pinkerton himself came incognito, bringing the algebraist on his arm. Miss Mamie proved to be a well-enough-looking mouse, with a large, limpid eye, very good manners, and a flow of the most correct expressions I have ever heard upon the human lip. As Pinkerton's incognito was strict, I had little opportunity to cultivate the lady's acquaintance; but I was informed afterwards that she considered me "the wittiest gentleman she had ever met." "The Lord mend your taste in wit!" thought I; but I cannot conceal that such was the general impression. One of my pleasantries even went the round of San Francisco, and I have heard it (myself all unknown) bandied in saloons. To be unknown began at last to be a rare experience; a bustle woke upon my passage; above all, in humble neighbourhoods. "Who's that?" one would ask, and the other would cry, "That! Why, Dromedary Dodd!" or, with withering scorn, "Not know Mr. Dodd of the Picnics? Well!" and indeed I think it marked a rather barren destiny; for our picnics, if a trifle vulgar, were as gay and innocent as the age of gold; I am sure no people divert themselves so easily and so well: and even with the cares of my stewardship, I was often happy to be there.

Indeed, there were but two drawbacks in the least considerable. The first was my terror of the hobbledehoy girls, to whom (from the demands of my situation) I was obliged to lay myself so open. The other, if less momentous, was more mortifying. In early days, at my mother's knee, as a man may say, I had acquired the unenviable accomplishment (which I have never since been able to lose) of singing Just before the Battle. I have what the French call a fillet of voice, my best notes scarce audible about a dinner-table, and the upper register rather to be regarded as a higher power of silence: experts tell me besides that I sing flat; nor, if I were the best singer in the world, does Just before the Battle occur to my mature taste as the song that I would choose to sing. In spite of all which considerations, at one picnic, memorably dull, and after I had exhausted every other art of pleasing, I gave, in desperation, my one song. From that hour my doom was gone forth. Either we had a chronic passenger (though I could never detect him), or the very wood and iron of the steamer must have retained the tradition. At every successive picnic word went round that Mr. Dodd was a singer; that Mr. Dodd sang Just before the Battle, and finally that now was the time when Mr. Dodd sang Just before the Battle; so that the thing became a fixture like the dropping of the dummy axe, and you are to conceive me, Sunday after Sunday, piping up my lamentable ditty and covered, when it was done, with gratuitous applause. It is a beautiful trait in human nature that I was invariably offered an encore.

I was well paid, however, even to sing. Pinkerton and I, after an average Sunday, had five hundred dollars to divide. Nay, and the picnics were the means, although indirectly, of bringing me a singular windfall. This was at the end of the season, after the "Grand Farewell Fancy Dress Gala." Many of the hampers had suffered severely; and it was judged wiser to save storage, dispose of them, and lay in a fresh stock when the campaign re-opened. Among my purchasers was a workingman of the name of Speedy, to whose house, after several unavailing letters, I must proceed in person, wondering to find myself once again on the wrong side, and playing the creditor to some one else's debtor. Speedy was in the belligerent stage of fear. He could not pay. It appeared he had already resold the hampers, and he defied me to do my worst. I did not like to lose my own money; I hated to lose Pinkerton's; and the bearing of my creditor incensed me.

"Do you know, Mr. Speedy, that I can send you to the penitentiary?" said I, willing to read him a lesson.

The dire expression was overheard in the next room. A large, fresh, motherly Irishwoman ran forth upon the instant, and fell to besiege me with caresses and appeals. "Sure now, and ye couldn't have the heart to ut, Mr. Dodd, you, that's so well known to be a pleasant gentleman; and it's a pleasant face ye have, and the picture of me own brother that's dead and gone. It's a truth that he's been drinking. Ye can smell it off of him, more blame to him. But, indade, and there's nothing in the house beyont the furnicher, and Thim Stock. It's the stock that ye'll be taking, dear. A sore penny it has cost me, first and last, and by all tales, not worth an owld tobacco pipe." Thus adjured, and somewhat embarrassed by the stern attitude I had adopted, I suffered myself to be invested with a considerable quantity of what is called wild-cat stock, in which this excellent if illogical female had been squandering her hard-earned gold. It could scarce be said to better my position, but the step quieted the woman; and, on the other hand, I could not think I was taking much risk, for the shares in question (they were those of what I will call the Catamount Silver Mine) had fallen some time before to the bed-rock quotation, and now lay perfectly inert, or were only kicked (like other waste paper) about the kennel of the exchange by bankrupt speculators.

A month or two after, I perceived by the stock-list that Catamount had taken a bound; before afternoon, "thim stock" were worth a quite considerable pot of money; and I learned, upon inquiry, that a bonanza had been found in a condemned lead, and the mine was now expected to do wonders. Remarkable to philosophers how bonanzas are found in condemned leads, and how the stock is always at freezing-point immediately before! By some stroke of chance the, Speedys had held on to the right thing; they had escaped the syndicate; yet a little more, if I had not come to dun them, and Mrs. Speedy would have been buying a silk dress. I could not bear, of course, to profit by the accident, and returned to offer restitution. The house was in a bustle; the neighbours (all stock-gamblers themselves) had crowded to condole; and Mrs. Speedy sat with streaming tears, the centre of a sympathetic group. "For fifteen year I've been at ut," she was lamenting, as I entered, "and grudging the babes the very milk, more shame to me! to pay their dhirty assessments. And now, my dears, I should be a lady, and driving in my coach, if all had their rights; and a sorrow on that man Dodd! As soon as I set eyes on him, I seen the divil was in the house."

It was upon these words that I made my entrance, which was therefore dramatic enough, though nothing to what followed. For when it appeared that I was come to restore the lost fortune, and when Mrs. Speedy (after copiously weeping on my bosom) had refused the restitution, and when Mr. Speedy (summoned to that end from a camp of the Grand Army of the Republic) had added his refusal, and when I had insisted, and they had insisted, and the neighbours had applauded and supported each of us in turn; and when at last it was agreed we were to hold the stock together, and share the proceeds in three parts—one for me, one for Mr. Speedy, and one for his spouse—I will leave you to conceive the enthusiasm that reigned in that small, bare apartment, with the sewing-machine in the one corner, and the babes asleep in the other, and pictures of Garfield and the Battle of Gettysburg on the yellow walls. Port wine was had in by a sympathiser, and we drank it mingled with tears.

"And I dhrink to your health, my dear," sobbed Mrs. Speedy, especially affected by my gallantry in the matter of the third share; "and I'm sure we all dhrink to his health—Mr. Dodd of the picnics, no gentleman better known than him; and it's my prayer, dear, the good God may be long spared to see ye in health and happiness!"

In the end I was the chief gainer; for I sold my third while it was worth five thousand dollars, but the Speedys more adventurously held on until the syndicate reversed the process, when they were happy to escape with perhaps a quarter of that sum. It was just as well; for the bulk of the money was (in Pinkerton's phrase) reinvested; and when next I saw Mrs. Speedy, she was still gorgeously dressed from the proceeds of the late success, but was already moist with tears over the new catastrophe. "We're froze out, me darlin'! All the money we had, dear, and the sewing-machine, and Jim's uniform, was in the Golden West; and the vipers has put on a new assessment."

By the end of the year, therefore, this is how I stood. I had made

By Catamount Silver Mine	$5,000
By the picnics	3,000
By the lecture	600
By profit and loss on capital in Pinkerton's business	1,350

$9,950

to which must be added

What remained of my grandfather's donation	8,500

$18,450

It appears, on the other hand, that

I had spent	4,000

Which thus left me to the good	$14,450

A result on which I am not ashamed to say I looked with gratitude and pride. Some eight thousand (being late conquest) was liquid and actually tractile in the bank; the rest whirled beyond reach and even sight (save in the mirror of a balance-sheet) under the compelling spell of wizard Pinkerton. Dollars of mine were tacking off the shores of Mexico, in peril of the deep and the guarda-costas; they rang on saloon-counters in the city of Tombstone, Arizona; they shone in faro-tents among the mountain diggings; the imagination flagged in following them, so wide were they diffused, so briskly they span to the turning of the wizard's crank. But here, there, or everywhere I could still tell myself it was all mine, and what was more convincing, draw substantial dividends. My fortune, I called it; and it represented, when expressed in dollars, or even British pounds, an honest pot of money; when extended into francs, a veritable fortune. Perhaps I have let the cat out of the bag; perhaps you see already where my hopes were pointing, and begin to blame my inconsistency. But I must first tell you my excuse, and the change that had befallen Pinkerton.

About a week after the picnic to which he escorted Mamie, Pinkerton avowed the state of his affections. From what I had observed on board the steamer, where methought Mamie waited on him with her limpid eyes, I encouraged the bashful lover to proceed; and the very next evening he was carrying me to call on his affianced.

"You must befriend her, Loudon, as you have always befriended me," he said, pathetically.

"By saying disagreeable things? I doubt if that be the way to a young lady's favour," I replied; "and since this picnicking I begin to be a man of some experience."

"Yes, you do nobly there; I can't describe how I admire you," he cried. "Not that she will ever need it; she has had every advantage. God knows what I have done to deserve her. O man, what a responsibility this is for a rough fellow and not always truthful!"

"Brace up, old man, brace up!" said I.

But when we reached Mamie's boarding-house, it was almost with tears that he presented me. "Here is Loudon, Mamie," were his words. "I want you to love him; he has a grand nature."

"You are certainly no stranger to me, Mr. Dodd," was her gracious expression. "James is never weary of descanting on your goodness."

"My dear lady," said I, "when you know our friend a little better, you will make a large allowance for his warm heart. My goodness has consisted in allowing him to feed and clothe and toil for me when he could ill afford it. If I am now alive, it is to him I owe it; no man had a kinder friend. You must take good care of him," I added, laying my hand on his shoulder, "and keep him in good order, for he needs it."

Pinkerton was much affected by this speech, and so, I fear, was Mamie. I admit it was a tactless performance. "When you know our friend a little better," was not happily said; and even "keep him in good order, for he needs it" might be construed into matter of offence; but I lay it before you in all confidence of your acquittal: was the general tone of it "patronising"? Even if such was the verdict of the lady, I cannot but suppose the blame was neither wholly hers nor wholly mine; I cannot but suppose that Pinkerton had already sickened the poor woman of my very name; so that if I had come with the songs of Apollo, she must still have been disgusted.

Here, however, were two finger-posts to Paris. Jim was going to be married, and so had the less need of my society. I had not pleased his bride, and so was, perhaps, better absent. Late one evening I broached the idea to my friend. It had been a great day for me; I had just banked my five thousand catamountain dollars; and as Jim had refused to lay a finger on the stock, risk and profit were both wholly mine, and I was celebrating the event with stout and crackers. I began by telling him that if it caused him any pain or any anxiety about his affairs, he had but to say the word, and he should hear no more of my proposal. He was the truest and best friend I ever had or was ever like to have; and it would be a strange thing if I refused him any favour he was sure he wanted. At the same time I wished him to be sure; for my life was wasting in my hands. I was like one from home; all my true interests summoned me away. I must remind him, besides, that he was now about to marry and assume new interests, and that our extreme familiarity might be even painful to his wife.—"O no, Loudon; I feel you are wrong there," he interjected warmly; "she DOES appreciate your nature."—So much the better, then, I continued; and went on to point out that our separation need not be for long; that, in the way affairs were going, he might join me in two years with a fortune, small, indeed, for the States, but in France almost conspicuous; that we might unite our resources, and have one house in Paris for the winter and a second near Fontainebleau for summer, where we could be as happy as the day was long, and bring up little Pinkertons as practical artistic workmen, far from the money-hunger of the West. "Let me go then," I concluded; "not as a deserter, but as the vanguard, to lead the march of the Pinkerton men."

So I argued and pleaded, not without emotion; my friend sitting opposite, resting his chin upon his hand and (but for that single interjection) silent. "I have been looking for this, Loudon," said he, when I had done. "It does pain me, and that's the fact—I'm so miserably selfish. And I believe it's a death blow to the picnics; for it's idle to deny that you were the heart and soul of them with your wand and your gallant bearing, and wit and humour and chivalry, and throwing that kind of society atmosphere about the thing. But for all that, you're right, and you ought to go. You may count on forty dollars a week; and if Depew City—one of nature's centres for this State—pan out the least as I expect, it may be double. But it's forty dollars anyway; and to think that two years ago you were almost reduced to beggary!"

"I WAS reduced to it," said I.

"Well, the brutes gave you nothing, and I'm glad of it now!" cried Jim. "It's the triumphant return I glory in! Think of the master, and that cold-blooded Myner too! Yes, just let the Depew City boom get on its legs, and you shall go; and two years later, day for day, I'll shake hands with you in Paris, with Mamie on my arm, God bless her!"

We talked in this vein far into the night. I was myself so exultant in my new-found liberty, and Pinkerton so proud of my triumph, so happy in my happiness, in so warm a glow about the gallant little woman of his choice, and the very room so filled with castles in the air and cottages at Fontainebleau, that it was little wonder if sleep fled our eyelids, and three had followed two upon the office clock before Pinkerton unfolded the mechanism of his patent sofa.

CHAPTER VIII. FACES ON THE CITY FRONT.

It is very much the custom to view life as if it were exactly ruled in two, like sleep and waking; the provinces of play and business standing separate. The business side of my career in San Francisco has been now disposed of; I approach the chapter of diversion; and it will be found they had about an equal share in building up the story of the Wrecker—a gentleman whose appearance may be presently expected.

With all my occupations, some six afternoons and two or three odd evenings remained at my disposal every week: a circumstance the more agreeable as I was a stranger in a city singularly picturesque. From what I had once called myself, The Amateur Parisian, I grew (or declined) into a waterside prowler, a lingerer on wharves, a frequenter of shy neighbourhoods, a scraper of acquaintance with eccentric characters. I visited Chinese and Mexican gambling-hells, German secret societies, sailors' boarding-houses, and "dives" of every complexion of the disreputable and dangerous. I have seen greasy Mexican hands pinned to the table with a knife for cheating, seamen (when blood-money ran high) knocked down upon the public street and carried insensible on board short-handed ships, shots exchanged, and the smoke (and the company) dispersing from the doors of the saloon. I have heard cold-minded Polacks debate upon the readiest method of burning San Francisco to the ground, hot-headed working men and women bawl and swear in the tribune at the Sandlot, and Kearney himself open his subscription for a gallows, name the manufacturers who were to grace it with their dangling bodies, and read aloud to the delighted multitude a telegram of adhesion from a member of the State legislature: all which preparations of proletarian war were (in a moment) breathed upon and abolished by the mere name and fame of Mr. Coleman. That lion of the Vigilantes had but to rouse himself and shake his ears, and the whole brawling mob was silenced. I could not but reflect what a strange manner of man this was, to be living unremarked there as a private merchant, and to be so feared by a whole city; and if I was disappointed, in my character of looker-on, to have the matter end ingloriously without the firing of a shot or the hanging of a single millionnaire, philosophy tried to tell me that this sight was truly the more picturesque. In a thousand towns and different epochs I might have had occasion to behold the cowardice and carnage of street fighting; where else, but only there and then, could I have enjoyed a view of Coleman (the intermittent despot) walking meditatively up hill in a quiet part of town, with a very rolling gait, and slapping gently his great thigh?

Minora Canamus. This historic figure stalks silently through a corner of the San Francisco of my memory: the rest is bric-a-brac, the reminiscences of a vagrant sketcher. My delight was much in slums. Little Italy was a haunt of mine; there I would look in at the windows of small eating-shops, transported bodily from Genoa or Naples, with their macaroni, and chianti flasks, and portraits of Garibaldi, and coloured political caricatures; or (entering in) hold high debate with some ear-ringed fisher of the bay as to the designs of "Mr. Owstria" and "Mr. Rooshia." I was often to be observed (had there been any to observe me) in that dis-peopled, hill-side solitude of Little Mexico, with its crazy wooden houses, endless crazy wooden stairs, and perilous mountain goat-paths in the sand. Chinatown by a thousand eccentricities drew and held me; I could never have enough of its ambiguous, interracial atmosphere, as of a vitalised museum; never wonder enough at its outlandish, necromantic-looking vegetables set forth to sell in commonplace American shop-windows, its temple doors open and the scent of the joss-stick streaming forth on the American air, its kites of Oriental fashion hanging fouled in Western telegraph-wires, its flights of paper prayers which the trade-wind hunts and dissipates along Western gutters. I was a frequent wanderer on North Beach, gazing at the straits, and the huge Cape-Horners creeping out to sea, and imminent Tamalpais. Thence, on my homeward way, I might visit that strange and filthy shed, earth-paved and walled with the cages of wild animals and birds, where at a ramshackle counter, amid the yells of monkeys, and a poignant atmosphere of menagerie, forty-rod whiskey was administered by a proprietor as dirty as his beasts. Nor did I even neglect Nob Hill, which is itself a kind of slum, being the habitat of the mere millionnaire. There they dwell upon the hill-top, high raised above man's clamour, and the trade-wind blows between their palaces about deserted streets.

But San Francisco is not herself only. She is not only the most interesting city in the Union, and the hugest smelting-pot of races and the precious metals. She keeps, besides, the doors of the Pacific, and is the port of entry to another world and an earlier epoch in man's history. Nowhere else shall you observe (in the ancient phrase) so many tall ships as here convene from round the Horn, from China, from Sydney, and the Indies; but scarce remarked amid that crowd of deep-sea giants, another class of craft, the Island schooner, circulates: low in the water, with lofty spars and dainty lines, rigged and fashioned like a yacht, manned with brown-skinned, soft-spoken, sweet-eyed native sailors, and equipped with their great double-ender boats that tell a tale of boisterous sea-beaches. These steal out and in again, unnoted by the world or even the newspaper press, save for the line in the clearing column, "Schooner So-and-so for Yap and South Sea Islands"—steal out with nondescript cargoes of tinned salmon, gin, bolts of gaudy cotton stuff, women's hats, and Waterbury watches, to return, after a year, piled as high as to the eaves of the house with copra, or wallowing deep with the shells of the tortoise or the pearl oyster. To me, in my character of the Amateur Parisian, this island traffic, and even the island world, were beyond the bounds of curiosity, and how much more of knowledge. I stood there on the extreme shore of the West and of to-day. Seventeen hundred years ago, and seven thousand miles to the east, a legionary stood, perhaps, upon the wall of Antoninus, and looked northward toward the mountains of the Picts. For all the interval of time and space, I, when I looked from the cliff-house on the broad Pacific, was that man's heir and analogue: each of us standing on the verge of the Roman Empire (or, as we now call it, Western civilization), each of us gazing onward into zones unromanised. But I was dull. I looked rather backward, keeping a kind eye on Paris; and it required a series of converging incidents to change my attitude of nonchalance for one of interest, and even longing, which I little dreamed that I should live to gratify.

The first of these incidents brought me in acquaintance with a certain San Francisco character, who had something of a name beyond the limits of the city, and was known to many lovers of good English. I had discovered a new slum, a place of precarious, sandy cliffs, deep, sandy cuttings, solitary, ancient houses, and the butt-ends of streets. It was already environed. The ranks of the street-lamps threaded it unbroken. The city, upon all sides of it, was tightly packed, and growled with traffic. To-day, I do not doubt the very landmarks are all swept away; but it offered then, within narrow limits, a delightful peace, and (in the morning, when I chiefly went there) a seclusion almost rural. On a steep sand-hill, in this neighbourhood, toppled, on the most insecure foundation, a certain row of houses, each with a bit of garden, and all (I have to presume) inhabited. Thither I used to mount by a crumbling footpath, and in front of the last of the houses, would sit down to sketch. The very first day I saw I was observed, out of the ground-floor window by a youngish, good-looking fellow, prematurely bald, and with an expression both lively and engaging. The second, as we were still the only figures in the landscape, it was no more than natural that we should nod. The third, he came out fairly from his intrenchments, praised my sketch, and with the impromptu cordiality of artists carried me into his apartment; where I sat presently in the midst of a museum of strange objects,—paddles and battle-clubs and baskets, rough-hewn stone images, ornaments of threaded shell, cocoanut bowls, snowy cocoanut plumes—evidences and examples of another earth, another climate, another race, and another (if a ruder) culture. Nor did these objects lack a fitting commentary in the conversation of my new acquaintance. Doubtless you have read his book. You know already how he tramped and starved, and had so fine a profit of living, in his days among the islands; and meeting him, as I did, one artist with another, after months of offices and picnics, you can imagine with what charm he would speak, and with what pleasure I would hear. It was in such talks, which we were both eager to repeat, that I first heard the names—first fell under the spell—of the islands; and it was from one of the first of them that I returned (a happy man) with Omoo under one arm, and my friend's own adventures under the other.

The second incident was more dramatic, and had, besides, a bearing on my future. I was standing, one day, near a boat-landing under Telegraph Hill. A large barque, perhaps of eighteen hundred tons, was coming more than usually close about the point to reach her moorings; and I was observing her with languid inattention, when I observed two men to stride across the bulwarks, drop into a shore boat, and, violently dispossessing the boatman of his oars, pull toward the landing where I stood. In a surprisingly short time they came tearing up the steps; and I could see that both were too well dressed to be foremast hands—the first even with research, and both, and specially the first, appeared under the empire of some strong emotion.

"Nearest police office!" cried the leader.

"This way," said I, immediately falling in with their precipitate pace. "What's wrong? What ship is that?"

"That's the Gleaner," he replied. "I am chief officer, this gentleman's third; and we've to get in our depositions before the crew. You see they might corral us with the captain; and that's no kind of berth for me. I've sailed with some hard cases in my time, and seen pins flying like sand on a squally day—but never a match to our old man. It never let up from the Hook to the Farallones; and the last man was dropped not sixteen hours ago. Packet rats our men were, and as tough a crowd as ever sand-bagged a man's head in; but they looked sick enough when the captain started in with his fancy shooting."

"O, he's done up," observed the other. "He won't go to sea no more."

"You make me tired," retorted his superior. "If he gets ashore in one piece and isn't lynched in the next ten minutes, he'll do yet. The owners have a longer memory than the public; they'll stand by him; they don't find as smart a captain every day in the year."

"O, he's a son of a gun of a fine captain; there ain't no doubt of that," concurred the other, heartily. "Why, I don't suppose there's been no wages paid aboard that Gleaner for three trips."

"No wages?" I exclaimed, for I was still a novice in maritime affairs.

"Not to sailor-men before the mast," agreed the mate. "Men cleared out; wasn't the soft job they maybe took it for. She isn' the first ship that never paid wages."

I could not but observe that our pace was progressively relaxing; and indeed I have often wondered since whether the hurry of the start were not intended for the gallery alone. Certain it is at least, that when we had reached the police office, and the mates had made their deposition, and told their horrid tale of five men murdered, some with savage passion, some with cold brutality, between Sandy Hook and San Francisco, the police were despatched in time to be too late. Before we arrived, the ruffian had slipped out upon the dock, had mingled with the crowd, and found a refuge in the house of an acquaintance; and the ship was only tenanted by his late victims. Well for him that he had been thus speedy. For when word began to go abroad among the shore-side characters, when the last victim was carried by to the hospital, when those who had escaped (as by miracle) from that floating shambles, began to circulate and show their wounds in the crowd, it was strange to witness the agitation that seized and shook that portion of the city. Men shed tears in public; bosses of lodging-houses, long inured to brutality, and above all, brutality to sailors, shook their fists at heaven: if hands could have been laid on the captain of the Gleaner, his shrift would have been short. That night (so gossip reports) he was headed up in a barrel and smuggled across the bay: in two ships already he had braved the penitentiary and the gallows; and yet, by last accounts, he now commands another on the Western Ocean.

As I have said, I was never quite certain whether Mr. Nares (the mate) did not intend that his superior should escape. It would have been like his preference of loyalty to law; it would have been like his prejudice, which was all in favour of the after-guard. But it must remain a matter of conjecture only. Well as I came to know him in the sequel, he was never communicative on that point, nor indeed on any that concerned the voyage of the Gleaner. Doubtless he had some reason for his reticence. Even during our walk to the police office, he debated several times with Johnson, the third officer, whether he ought not to give up himself, as well as to denounce the captain. He had decided in the negative, arguing that "it would probably come to nothing; and even if there was a stink, he had plenty good friends in San Francisco." And to nothing it came; though it must have very nearly come to something, for Mr. Nares disappeared immediately from view and was scarce less closely hidden than his captain.

Johnson, on the other hand, I often met. I could never learn this man's country; and though he himself claimed to be American, neither his English nor his education warranted the claim. In all likelihood he was of Scandinavian birth and blood, long pickled in the forecastles of English and American ships. It is possible that, like so many of his race in similar positions, he had already lost his native tongue. In mind, at least, he was quite denationalised; thought only in English—to call it so; and though by nature one of the mildest, kindest, and most feebly playful of mankind, he had been so long accustomed to the cruelty of sea discipline, that his stories (told perhaps with a giggle) would sometimes turn me chill. In appearance, he was tall, light of weight, bold and high-bred of feature, dusky-haired, and with a face of a clean even brown: the ornament of outdoor men. Seated in a chair, you might have passed him off for a baronet or a military officer; but let him rise, and it was Fo'c's'le Jack that came rolling toward you, crab-like; let him but open his lips, and it was Fo'c's'le Jack that piped and drawled his ungrammatical gibberish. He had sailed (among other places) much among the islands; and after a Cape Horn passage with its snow-squalls and its frozen sheets, he announced his intention of "taking a turn among them Kanakas." I thought I should have lost him soon; but according to the unwritten usage of mariners, he had first to dissipate his wages. "Guess I'll have to paint this town red," was his hyperbolical expression; for sure no man ever embarked upon a milder course of dissipation, most of his days being passed in the little parlour behind Black Tom's public house, with a select corps of old particular acquaintances, all from the South Seas, and all patrons of a long yarn, a short pipe, and glasses round.

Black Tom's, to the front, presented the appearance of a fourth-rate saloon, devoted to Kanaka seamen, dirt, negrohead tobacco, bad cigars, worse gin, and guitars and banjos in a state of decline. The proprietor, a powerful coloured man, was at once a publican, a ward politician, leader of some brigade of "lambs" or "smashers," at the wind of whose clubs the party bosses and the mayor were supposed to tremble, and (what hurt nothing) an active and reliable crimp. His front quarters, then, were noisy, disreputable, and not even safe. I have seen worse frequented saloons where there were fewer scandals; for Tom was often drunk himself; and there is no doubt the Lambs must have been a useful body, or the place would have been closed. I remember one day, not long before an election, seeing a blind man, very well dressed, led up to the counter and remain a long while in consultation with the negro. The pair looked so ill-assorted, and the awe with which the drinkers fell back and left them in the midst of an impromptu privacy was so unusual in such a place, that I turned to my next neighbour with a question. He told me the blind man was a distinguished party boss, called by some the King of San Francisco, but perhaps better known by his picturesque Chinese nickname of the Blind White Devil. "The Lambs must be wanted pretty bad, I guess," my informant added. I have here a sketch of the Blind White Devil leaning on the counter; on the next page, and taken the same hour, a jotting of Black Tom threatening a whole crowd of customers with a long Smith and

Wesson: to such heights and depths we rose and fell in the front parts of the saloon.

Meanwhile, away in the back quarters, sat the small informal South Sea club, talking of another world and surely of a different century. Old schooner captains they were, old South Sea traders, cooks, and mates: fine creatures, softened by residence among a softer race: full men besides, though not by reading, but by strange experience; and for days together I could hear their yarns with an unfading pleasure. All had indeed some touch of the poetic; for the beach-comber, when not a mere ruffian, is the poor relation of the artist. Even through Johnson's inarticulate speech, his "O yes, there ain't no harm in them Kanakas," or "O yes, that's a son of a gun of a fine island, mountainious right down; I didn't never ought to have left that island," there pierced a certain gusto of appreciation: and some of the rest were master-talkers. From their long tales, their traits of character and unpremeditated landscape, there began to piece itself together in my head some image of the islands and the island life: precipitous shores, spired mountain tops, the deep shade of hanging forests, the unresting surf upon the reef, and the unending peace of the lagoon; sun, moon, and stars of an imperial brightness; man moving in these scenes scarce fallen, and woman lovelier than Eve; the primal curse abrogated, the bed made ready for the stranger, life set to perpetual music, and the guest welcomed, the boat urged, and the long night beguiled, with poetry and choral song. A man must have been an unsuccessful artist; he must have starved on the streets of Paris; he must have been yoked to a commercial force like Pinkerton, before he can conceive the longings that at times assailed me. The draughty, rowdy city of San Francisco, the bustling office where my friend Jim paced like a caged lion daily between ten and four, even (at times) the retrospect of Paris, faded in comparison. Many a man less tempted would have thrown up all to realise his visions; but I was by nature unadventurous and uninitiative: to divert me from all former paths and send me cruising through the isles of paradise, some force external to myself must be exerted; Destiny herself must use the fitting wedge; and little as I deemed it, that tool was already in her hand of brass.

I sat, one afternoon, in the corner of a great, glassy, silvered saloon, a free lunch at my one elbow, at the other a "conscientious nude" from the brush of local talent; when, with the tramp of feet and a sudden buzz of voices, the swing-doors were flung broadly open and the place carried as by storm. The crowd which thus entered (mostly seafaring men, and all prodigiously excited) contained a sort of kernel or general centre of interest, which the rest merely surrounded and advertised, as children in the Old World surround and escort the Punch-and-Judy man; the word went round the bar like wildfire that these were Captain Trent and the survivors of the British brig Flying Scud, picked up by a British war-ship on Midway Island, arrived that morning in San Francisco Bay, and now fresh from making the necessary declarations. Presently I had a good sight of them: four brown, seamanlike fellows, standing by the counter, glass in hand, the centre of a score of questioners. One was a Kanaka—the cook, I was informed; one carried a cage with a canary, which occasionally trilled into thin song; one had his left arm in a sling and looked gentlemanlike, and somewhat sickly, as though the injury had been severe and he was scarce recovered; and the captain himself—a red-faced, blue-eyed, thickset man of five and forty—wore a bandage on his right hand. The incident struck me; I was struck particularly to see captain, cook, and foremost hands walking the street and visiting saloons in company; and, as when anything impressed me, I got my sketch-book out, and began to steal a sketch of the four castaways. The crowd, sympathising with my design, made a clear lane across the room; and I was thus enabled, all unobserved myself, to observe with a still-growing closeness the face and the demeanour of Captain Trent.

Warmed by whiskey and encouraged by the eagerness of the bystanders, that gentleman was now rehearsing the history of his misfortune. It was but scraps that reached me: how he "filled her on the starboard tack," and how "it came up sudden out of the nor'nor'west," and "there she was, high and dry." Sometimes he would appeal to one of the men—"That was how it was, Jack?"—and the man would reply, "That was the way of it, Captain Trent." Lastly, he started a fresh tide of popular sympathy by enunciating the sentiment, "Damn all these Admirality Charts, and that's what I say!" From the nodding of heads and the murmurs of assent that followed, I could see that Captain Trent had established himself in the public mind as a gentleman and a thorough navigator: about which period, my sketch of the four men and the canary-bird being finished, and all (especially the canary-bird) excellent likenesses, I buckled up my book, and slipped from the saloon.

Little did I suppose that I was leaving Act I, Scene I, of the drama of my life; and yet the scene, or rather the captain's face, lingered for some time in my memory. I was no prophet, as I say; but I was something else: I was an observer; and one thing I knew, I knew when a man was terrified. Captain Trent, of the British brig Flying Scud, had been glib; he had been ready; he had been loud; but in his blue eyes I could detect the chill, and in the lines of his countenance spy the agitation of perpetual terror. Was he trembling for his certificate? In my judgment, it was some livelier kind of fear that thrilled in the man's marrow as he turned to drink. Was it the result of recent shock, and had he not yet recovered the disaster to his brig? I remembered how a friend of mine had been in a railway accident, and shook and started for a month; and although Captain Trent of the Flying Scud had none of the appearance of a nervous man, I told myself, with incomplete conviction, that his must be a similar case.

CHAPTER IX. THE WRECK OF THE "FLYING SCUD."

The next morning I found Pinkerton, who had risen before me, seated at our usual table, and deep in the perusal of what I will call the Daily Occidental. This was a paper (I know not if it be so still) that stood out alone among its brethren in the West; the others, down to their smallest item, were defaced with capitals, head-lines, alliterations, swaggering misquotations, and the shoddy picturesque and unpathetic pathos of the Harry Millers: the Occidental alone appeared to be written by a dull, sane, Christian gentleman, singly desirous of communicating knowledge. It had not only this merit, which endeared it to me, but was admittedly the best informed on business matters, which attracted Pinkerton.

"Loudon," said he, looking up from the journal, "you sometimes think I have too many irons in the fire. My notion, on the other hand, is, when you see a dollar lying, pick it up! Well, here I've tumbled over a whole pile of 'em on a reef in the middle of the Pacific."

"Why, Jim, you miserable fellow!" I exclaimed; "haven't we Depew City, one of God's green centres for this State? haven't we——"

"Just listen to this," interrupted Jim. "It's miserable copy; these Occidental reporter fellows have no fire; but the facts are right enough, I guess." And he began to read:—

"WRECK OF THE BRITISH BRIG, 'FLYING SCUD.'

"H.B.M.S. Tempest, which arrived yesterday at this port, brings Captain Trent and four men of the British brig Flying Scud, cast away February 12th on Midway Island, and most providentially rescued the next day. The Flying Scud was of 200 tons burthen, owned in London, and has been out nearly two years tramping. Captain Trent left Hong Kong December 8th, bound for this port in rice and a small mixed cargo of silks, teas, and China notions, the whole valued at $10,000, fully covered by insurance. The log shows plenty of fine weather, with light airs, calms, and squalls. In lat. 28 N., long. 177 W., his water going rotten, and misled by Hoyt's North Pacific Directory, which informed him there was a coaling station on the island, Captain Trent put in to Midway Island. He found it a literal sandbank, surrounded by a coral reef mostly submerged. Birds were very plenty, there was good fish in the lagoon, but no firewood; and the water, which could be obtained by digging, brackish. He found good holding-ground off the north end of the larger bank in fifteen fathoms water; bottom sandy, with coral patches. Here he was detained seven days by a calm, the crew suffering severely from the water, which was gone quite bad; and it was only on the evening of the 12th, that a little wind sprang up, coming puffy out of N.N.E. Late as it was, Captain Trent immediately weighed anchor and attempted to get out. While the vessel was beating up to the passage, the wind took a sudden lull, and then veered squally into N. and even N.N.W., driving the brig ashore on the sand at about twenty minutes before six o'clock. John Wallen, a native of Finland, and Charles Holdorsen, a native of Sweden, were drowned alongside, in attempting to lower a boat, neither being able to swim, the squall very dark, and the noise of the breakers drowning everything. At the same time John Brown, another of the crew, had his arm broken by the falls. Captain Trent further informed the OCCIDENTAL reporter, that the brig struck heavily at first bows on, he supposes upon coral; that she then drove over the obstacle, and now lies in sand, much down by the head and with a list to starboard. In the first collision she must have sustained some damage, as she was making water forward. The rice will probably be all destroyed: but the more valuable part of the cargo is fortunately in the afterhold. Captain Trent was preparing his long-boat for sea, when the providential arrival of the Tempest, pursuant to Admiralty orders to call at islands in her course for castaways, saved the gallant captain from all further danger. It is scarcely necessary to add that both the officers and men of the unfortunate vessel speak in high terms of the kindness they received on board the man-of-war. We print a list of the survivors: Jacob Trent, master, of Hull, England; Elias Goddedaal, mate, native of Christiansand, Sweden; Ah Wing, cook, native of Sana, China; John Brown, native of Glasgow, Scotland; John Hardy, native of London, England. The Flying Scud is ten years old, and this morning will be sold as she stands, by order of Lloyd's agent, at public auction for the benefit of the underwriters. The auction will take place in the Merchants' Exchange at ten o'clock.

"Farther Particulars.—Later in the afternoon the OCCIDENTAL reporter found Lieutenant Sebright, first officer of H.B.M.S. Tempest, at the Palace Hotel. The gallant officer was somewhat pressed for time, but confirmed the account given by Captain Trent in all particulars. He added that the Flying Scud is in an excellent berth, and except in the highly improbable event of a heavy N.W. gale, might last until next winter."

"You will never know anything of literature," said I, when Jim had finished. "That is a good, honest, plain piece of work, and tells the story clearly. I see only one mistake: the cook is not a Chinaman; he is a Kanaka, and I think a Hawaiian."

"Why, how do you know that?" asked Jim.

"I saw the whole gang yesterday in a saloon," said I. "I even heard the tale, or might have heard it, from Captain Trent himself, who struck me as thirsty and nervous."

"Well, that's neither here nor there," cried Pinkerton. "The point is, how about these dollars lying on a reef?"

"Will it pay?" I asked.

"Pay like a sugar trust!" exclaimed Pinkerton. "Don't you see what this British officer says about the safety? Don't you see the cargo's valued at ten thousand? Schooners are begging just now; I can get my pick of them at two hundred and fifty a month; and how does that foot up? It looks like three hundred per cent. to me."

"You forget," I objected, "the captain himself declares the rice is damaged."

"That's a point, I know," admitted Jim. "But the rice is the sluggish article, anyway; it's little more account than ballast; it's the tea and silks that I look to: all we have to find is the proportion, and one look at the manifest will settle that. I've rung up Lloyd's on purpose; the captain is to meet me there in an hour, and then I'll be as posted on that brig as if I built her. Besides, you've no idea what pickings there are about a wreck—copper, lead, rigging, anchors, chains, even the crockery, Loudon!"

"You seem to me to forget one trifle," said I. "Before you pick that wreck, you've got to buy her, and how much will she cost?"

"One hundred dollars," replied Jim, with the promptitude of an automaton.

"How on earth do you guess that?" I cried.

"I don't guess; I know it," answered the Commercial Force. "My dear boy, I may be a galoot about literature, but you'll always be an outsider in business. How do you suppose I bought the James L. Moody for two hundred and fifty, her boats alone worth four times the money? Because my name stood first in the list. Well it stands there again; I have the naming of the figure, and I name a small one because of the distance: but it wouldn't matter what I named; that would be the price."

"It sounds mysterious enough," said I. "Is this public auction conducted in a subterranean vault? Could a plain citizen—myself, for instance—come and see?"

"O, everything's open and above board!" he cried indignantly. "Anybody can come, only nobody bids against us; and if he did, he would get frozen out. It's been tried before now, and once was enough. We hold the plant; we've got the connection; we can afford to go higher than any outsider; there's two million dollars in the ring; and we stick at nothing. Or suppose anybody did buy over our head—I tell you, Loudon, he would think this town gone crazy; he could no more get business through on the city front than I can dance; schooners, divers, men—all he wanted—the prices would fly right up and strike him."

"But how did you get in?" I asked. "You were once an outsider like your neighbours, I suppose?"

"I took hold of that thing, Loudon, and just studied it up," he replied. "It took my fancy; it was so romantic, and then I saw there was boodle in the thing; and I figured on the business till no man alive could give me points. Nobody knew I had an eye on wrecks till one fine morning I dropped in upon Douglas B. Longhurst in his den, gave him all the facts and figures, and put it to him straight: 'Do you want me in this ring? or shall I start another?' He took half an hour, and when I came back, 'Pink,' says he, 'I've put your name on.' The first time I came to the top, it was that Moody racket; now it's the Flying Scud."

Whereupon Pinkerton, looking at his watch, uttered an exclamation, made a hasty appointment with myself for the doors of the Merchants' Exchange, and fled to examine manifests and interview the skipper. I finished my cigarette with the deliberation of a man at the end of many picnics; reflecting to myself that of all forms of the dollar hunt, this wrecking had by far the most address to my imagination. Even as I went down town, in the brisk bustle and chill of the familiar San Francisco thoroughfares, I was haunted by a vision of the wreck, baking so far away in the strong sun, under a cloud of sea-birds; and even then, and for no better reason, my heart inclined towards the adventure. If not myself, something that was mine, some one at least in my employment, should voyage to that ocean-bounded pin-point and descend to that deserted cabin.

Pinkerton met me at the appointed moment, pinched of lip and more than usually erect of bearing, like one conscious of great resolves.

"Well?" I asked.

"Well," said he, "it might be better, and it might be worse. This Captain Trent is a remarkably honest fellow—one out of a thousand. As soon as he knew I was in the market, he owned up about the rice in so many words. By his calculation, if there's thirty mats of it saved, it's an outside figure. However, the manifest was cheerier. There's about five thousand dollars of the whole value in silks and teas and nut-oils and that, all in the lazarette, and as safe as if it was in Kearney Street. The brig was new coppered a year ago. There's upwards of a hundred and fifty fathom away-up chain. It's not a bonanza, but there's boodle in it; and we'll try it on."

It was by that time hard on ten o'clock, and we turned at once into the place of sale. The Flying Scud, although so important to ourselves, appeared to attract a very humble share of popular attention. The auctioneer was surrounded by perhaps a score of lookers-on, big fellows, for the most part, of the true Western build, long in the leg, broad in the shoulder, and adorned (to a plain man's taste) with needless finery. A jaunty, ostentatious comradeship prevailed. Bets were flying, and nicknames. "The boys" (as they would have called themselves) were very boyish; and it was plain they were here in mirth, and not on business. Behind, and certainly in strong contrast to these gentlemen, I could detect the figure of my friend Captain Trent, come (as I could very well imagine that a captain would) to hear the last of his old vessel. Since yesterday, he had rigged himself anew in ready-made black clothes, not very aptly fitted; the upper left-hand pocket showing a corner of silk handkerchief, the lower, on the other side, bulging with papers. Pinkerton had just given this man a high character. Certainly he seemed to have been very frank, and I looked at him again to trace (if possible) that virtue in his face. It was red and broad and flustered and (I thought) false. The whole man looked sick with some unknown anxiety; and as he stood there, unconscious of my observation, he tore at his nails, scowled on the floor, or glanced suddenly, sharply, and fearfully at passers-by. I was still gazing at the man in a kind of fascination, when the sale began.

Some preliminaries were rattled through, to the irreverent, uninterrupted gambolling of the boys; and then, amid a trifle more attention, the auctioneer sounded for some two or three minutes the pipe of the charmer. Fine brig—new copper—valuable fittings—three fine boats—remarkably choice cargo—what the auctioneer would call a perfectly safe investment; nay, gentlemen, he would go further, he would put a figure on it: he had no hesitation (had that bold auctioneer) in putting it in figures; and in his view, what with this and that, and one thing and another, the purchaser might expect to clear a sum equal to the entire estimated value of the cargo; or, gentlemen, in other words, a sum of ten thousand dollars. At this modest computation the roof immediately above the speaker's head (I suppose, through the intervention of a spectator of ventriloquial tastes) uttered a clear "Cock-a-doodle-doo!"—whereat all laughed, the auctioneer himself obligingly joining.

"Now, gentlemen, what shall we say?" resumed that gentleman, plainly ogling Pinkerton,—"what shall we say for this remarkable opportunity?"

"One hundred dollars," said Pinkerton.

"One hundred dollars from Mr. Pinkerton," went the auctioneer, "one hundred dollars. No other gentleman inclined to make any advance? One hundred dollars, only one hundred dollars——"

The auctioneer was droning on to some such tune as this, and I, on my part, was watching with something between sympathy and amazement the undisguised emotion of Captain Trent, when we were all startled by the interjection of a bid.

"And fifty," said a sharp voice.

Pinkerton, the auctioneer, and the boys, who were all equally in the open secret of the ring, were now all equally and simultaneously taken aback.

"I beg your pardon," said the auctioneer. "Anybody bid?"

"And fifty," reiterated the voice, which I was now able to trace to its origin, on the lips of a small, unseemly rag of human-kind. The speaker's skin was gray and blotched; he spoke in a kind of broken song, with much variety of key; his gestures seemed (as in the disease called Saint Vitus's dance) to be imperfectly under control; he was badly dressed; he carried himself with an air of shrinking assumption, as though he were proud to be where he was and to do what he was doing, and yet half expected to be called in question and kicked out. I think I never saw a man more of a piece; and the type was new to me; I had never before set eyes upon his parallel, and I thought instinctively of Balzac and the lower regions of the Comedie Humaine.

Pinkerton stared a moment on the intruder with no friendly eye, tore a leaf from his note-book, and scribbled a line in pencil, turned, beckoned a messenger boy, and whispered, "To Longhurst." Next moment the boy had sped upon his errand, and Pinkerton was again facing the auctioneer.

"Two hundred dollars," said Jim.

"And fifty," said the enemy.

"This looks lively," whispered I to Pinkerton.

"Yes; the little beast means cold drawn biz," returned my friend. "Well, he'll have to have a lesson. Wait till I see Longhurst. Three hundred," he added aloud.

"And fifty," came the echo.

It was about this moment when my eye fell again on Captain Trent. A deeper shade had mounted to his crimson face: the new coat was unbuttoned and all flying open; the new silk handkerchief in busy requisition; and the man's eye, of a clear sailor blue, shone glassy with excitement. He was anxious still, but now (if I could read a face) there was hope in his anxiety.

"Jim," I whispered, "look at Trent. Bet you what you please he was expecting this."

"Yes," was the reply, "there's some blame' thing going on here." And he renewed his bid.

The figure had run up into the neighbourhood of a thousand when I was aware of a sensation in the faces opposite, and looking over my shoulder, saw a very large, bland, handsome man come strolling forth and make a little signal to the auctioneer.

"One word, Mr. Borden," said he; and then to Jim, "Well, Pink, where are we up to now?"

Pinkerton gave him the figure. "I ran up to that on my own responsibility, Mr. Longhurst," he added, with a flush. "I thought it the square thing."

"And so it was," said Mr. Longhurst, patting him kindly on the shoulder, like a gratified uncle. "Well, you can drop out now; we take hold ourselves. You can run it up to five thousand; and if he likes to go beyond that, he's welcome to the bargain."

"By the by, who is he?" asked Pinkerton. "He looks away down."

"I've sent Billy to find out." And at the very moment Mr. Longhurst received from the hands of one of the expensive young gentlemen a folded paper. It was passed round from one to another till it came to me, and I read: "Harry D. Bellairs, Attorney-at-Law; defended Clara Varden; twice nearly disbarred."

"Well, that gets me!" observed Mr. Longhurst. "Who can have put up a shyster [1] like that? Nobody with money, that's a sure thing. Suppose you tried a big bluff? I think I would, Pink. Well, ta-ta! Your partner, Mr. Dodd? Happy to have the pleasure of your acquaintance, sir." And the great man withdrew.

[1] A low lawyer.

"Well, what do you think of Douglas B.?" whispered Pinkerton, looking reverently after him as he departed. "Six foot of perfect gentleman and culture to his boots."

During this interview the auction had stood transparently arrested, the auctioneer, the spectators, and even Bellairs, all well aware that Mr. Longhurst was the principal, and Jim but a speaking-trumpet. But now that the Olympian Jupiter was gone, Mr. Borden thought proper to affect severity.

"Come, come, Mr. Pinkerton. Any advance?" he snapped.

And Pinkerton, resolved on the big bluff, replied, "Two thousand dollars."

Bellairs preserved his composure. "And fifty," said he. But there was a stir among the onlookers, and what was of more importance, Captain Trent had turned pale and visibly gulped.

"Pitch it in again, Jim," said I. "Trent is weakening."

"Three thousand," said Jim.

"And fifty," said Bellairs.

And then the bidding returned to its original movement by hundreds and fifties; but I had been able in the meanwhile to draw two conclusions. In the first place, Bellairs had made his last advance with a smile of gratified vanity; and I could see the creature was glorying in the kudos of an unusual position and secure of ultimate success. In the second, Trent had once more changed colour at the thousand leap, and his relief, when he heard the answering fifty was manifest and unaffected. Here then was a problem: both were presumably in the same interest, yet the one was not in the confidence of the other. Nor was this all. A few bids later it chanced that my eye encountered that of Captain Trent, and his, which glittered with excitement, was instantly, and I thought guiltily, withdrawn. He wished, then, to conceal his interest? As Jim had said, there was some blamed thing going on. And for certain, here were these two men, so strangely united, so strangely divided, both sharp-set to keep the wreck from us, and that at an exorbitant figure.

Was the wreck worth more than we supposed? A sudden heat was kindled in my brain; the bids were nearing Longhurst's limit of five thousand; another minute, and all would be too late. Tearing a leaf from my sketch-book, and inspired (I suppose) by vanity in my own powers of inference and observation, I took the one mad decision of my life. "If you care to go ahead," I wrote, "I'm in for all I'm worth."

Jim read and looked round at me like one bewildered; then his eyes lightened, and turning again to the auctioneer, he bid, "Five thousand one hundred dollars."

"And fifty," said monotonous Bellairs.

Presently Pinkerton scribbled, "What can it be?" and I answered, still on paper: "I can't imagine; but there's something. Watch Bellairs; he'll go up to the ten thousand, see if he don't."

And he did, and we followed. Long before this, word had gone abroad that there was battle royal: we were surrounded by a crowd that looked on wondering; and when Pinkerton had offered ten thousand dollars (the outside value of the cargo, even were it safe in San Francisco Bay) and Bellairs, smirking from ear to ear to be the centre of so much attention, had jerked out his answering, "And fifty," wonder deepened to excitement.

"Ten thousand one hundred," said Jim; and even as he spoke he made a sudden gesture with his hand, his face changed, and I could see that he had guessed, or thought that he had guessed, the mystery. As he scrawled another memorandum in his note-book, his hand shook like a telegraph-operator's.

"Chinese ship," ran the legend; and then, in big, tremulous half-text, and with a flourish that overran the margin, "Opium!"

To be sure! thought I: this must be the secret. I knew that scarce a ship came in from any Chinese port, but she carried somewhere, behind a bulkhead, or in some cunning hollow of the beams, a nest of the valuable poison. Doubtless there was some such treasure on the Flying

Scud. How much was it worth? We knew not, we were gambling in the dark; but Trent knew, and Bellairs; and we could only watch and judge.

By this time neither Pinkerton nor I were of sound mind. Pinkerton was beside himself, his eyes like lamps. I shook in every member. To any stranger entering (say) in the course of the fifteenth thousand, we should probably have cut a poorer figure than Bellairs himself. But we did not pause; and the crowd watched us, now in silence, now with a buzz of whispers.

Seventeen thousand had been reached, when Douglas B. Longhurst, forcing his way into the opposite row of faces, conspicuously and repeatedly shook his head at Jim. Jim's answer was a note of two words: "My racket!" which, when the great man had perused, he shook his finger warningly and departed, I thought, with a sorrowful countenance.

Although Mr. Longhurst knew nothing of Bellairs, the shady lawyer knew all about the Wrecker Boss. He had seen him enter the ring with manifest expectation; he saw him depart, and the bids continue, with manifest surprise and disappointment. "Hullo," he plainly thought, "this is not the ring I'm fighting, then?" And he determined to put on a spurt.

"Eighteen thousand," said he.

"And fifty," said Jim, taking a leaf out of his adversary's book.

"Twenty thousand," from Bellairs.

"And fifty," from Jim, with a little nervous titter.

And with one consent they returned to the old pace, only now it was Bellairs who took the hundreds, and Jim who did the fifty business. But by this time our idea had gone abroad. I could hear the word "opium" pass from mouth to mouth; and by the looks directed at us, I could see we were supposed to have some private information. And here an incident occurred highly typical of San Francisco. Close at my back there had stood for some time a stout, middle-aged gentleman, with pleasant eyes, hair pleasantly grizzled, and a ruddy, pleasing face. All of a sudden he appeared as a third competitor, skied the Flying Scud with four fat bids of a thousand dollars each, and then as suddenly fled the field, remaining thenceforth (as before) a silent, interested spectator.

Ever since Mr. Longhurst's useless intervention, Bellairs had seemed uneasy; and at this new attack, he began (in his turn) to scribble a note between the bids. I imagined naturally enough that it would go to Captain Trent; but when it was done, and the writer turned and looked behind him in the crowd, to my unspeakable amazement, he did not seem to remark the captain's presence.

"Messenger boy, messenger boy!" I heard him say. "Somebody call me a messenger boy."

At last somebody did, but it was not the captain.

"He's sending for instructions," I wrote to Pinkerton.

"For money," he wrote back. "Shall I strike out? I think this is the time."

I nodded.

"Thirty thousand," said Pinkerton, making a leap of close upon three thousand dollars.

I could see doubt in Bellairs's eye; then, sudden resolution. "Thirty-five thousand," said he.

"Forty thousand," said Pinkerton.

There was a long pause, during which Bellairs's countenance was as a book; and then, not much too soon for the impending hammer, "Forty thousand and five dollars," said he.

Pinkerton and I exchanged eloquent glances. We were of one mind. Bellairs had tried a bluff; now he perceived his mistake, and was bidding against time; he was trying to spin out the sale until the messenger boy returned.

"Forty-five thousand dollars," said Pinkerton: his voice was like a ghost's and tottered with emotion.

"Forty-five thousand and five dollars," said Bellairs.

"Fifty thousand," said Pinkerton.

"I beg your pardon, Mr. Pinkerton. Did I hear you make an advance, sir?" asked the auctioneer.

"I—I have a difficulty in speaking," gasped Jim. "It's fifty thousand, Mr. Borden."

Bellairs was on his feet in a moment. "Auctioneer," he said, "I have to beg the favour of three moments at the telephone. In this matter, I am acting on behalf of a certain party to whom I have just written——"

"I have nothing to do with any of this," said the auctioneer, brutally. "I am here to sell this wreck. Do you make any advance on fifty thousand?"

"I have the honour to explain to you, sir," returned Bellairs, with a miserable assumption of dignity. "Fifty thousand was the figure named by my principal; but if you will give me the small favour of two moments at the telephone—"

"O, nonsense!" said the auctioneer. "If you make no advance, I'll knock it down to Mr. Pinkerton."

"I warn you," cried the attorney, with sudden shrillness. "Have a care what you're about. You are here to sell for the underwriters, let me tell you—not to act for Mr. Douglas Longhurst. This sale has been already disgracefully interrupted to allow that person to hold a consultation with his minions. It has been much commented on."

"There was no complaint at the time," said the auctioneer, manifestly discountenanced. "You should have complained at the time."

"I am not here to conduct this sale," replied Bellairs; "I am not paid for that."

"Well, I am, you see," retorted the auctioneer, his impudence quite restored; and he resumed his sing-song. "Any advance on fifty thousand dollars? No advance on fifty thousand? No advance, gentlemen? Going at fifty thousand, the wreck of the brig Flying Scud—going—going—gone!"

"My God, Jim, can we pay the money?" I cried, as the stroke of the hammer seemed to recall me from a dream.

"It's got to be raised," said he, white as a sheet. "It'll be a hell of a strain, Loudon. The credit's good for it, I think; but I shall have to get around. Write me a cheque for your stuff. Meet me at the Occidental in an hour."

I wrote my cheque at a desk, and I declare I could never have recognised my signature. Jim was gone in a moment; Trent had vanished even earlier; only Bellairs remained exchanging insults with the auctioneer; and, behold! as I pushed my way out of the exchange, who should run full tilt into my arms, but the messenger boy?

It was by so near a margin that we became the owners of the Flying Scud.

CHAPTER X. IN WHICH THE CREW VANISH.

At the door of the exchange I found myself along-side of the short, middle-aged gentleman who had made an appearance, so vigorous and so brief, in the great battle.

"Congratulate you, Mr. Dodd," he said. "You and your friend stuck to your guns nobly."

"No thanks to you, sir," I replied, "running us up a thousand at a time, and tempting all the speculators in San Francisco to come and have a try."

"O, that was temporary insanity," said he; "and I thank the higher powers I am still a free man. Walking this way, Mr. Dodd? I'll walk along with you. It's pleasant for an old fogy like myself to see the young bloods in the ring; I've done some pretty wild gambles in my time in this very city, when it was a smaller place and I was a younger man. Yes, I know you, Mr. Dodd. By sight, I may say I know you extremely well, you and your followers, the fellows in the kilts, eh? Pardon me. But I have the misfortune to own a little box on the Saucelito shore. I'll be glad to see you there any Sunday—without the fellows in kilts, you know; and I can give you a bottle of wine, and show you the best collection of Arctic voyages in the States. Morgan is my name—Judge Morgan—a Welshman and a forty-niner."

"O, if you're a pioneer," cried I, "come to me and I'll provide you with an axe."

"You'll want your axes for yourself, I fancy," he returned, with one of his quick looks. "Unless you have private knowledge, there will be a good deal of rather violent wrecking to do before you find that—opium, do you call it?"

"Well, it's either opium, or we are stark, staring mad," I replied. "But I assure you we have no private information. We went in (as I suppose you did yourself) on observation."

"An observer, sir?" inquired the judge.

"I may say it is my trade—or, rather, was," said I.

"Well now, and what did you think of Bellairs?" he asked.

"Very little indeed," said I.

"I may tell you," continued the judge, "that to me, the employment of a fellow like that appears inexplicable. I knew him; he knows me, too; he has often heard from me in court; and I assure you the man is utterly blown upon; it is not safe to trust him with a dollar; and here we find him dealing up to fifty thousand. I can't think who can have so trusted him, but I am very sure it was a stranger in San Francisco."

"Some one for the owners, I suppose," said I.

"Surely not!" exclaimed the judge. "Owners in London can have nothing to say to opium smuggled between Hong Kong and San Francisco. I should rather fancy they would be the last to hear of it—until the ship was seized. No; I was thinking of the captain. But where would he get the money? above all, after having laid out so much to buy the stuff in China? Unless, indeed, he were acting for some one in 'Frisco; and in that case—here we go round again in the vicious circle—Bellairs would not have been employed."

"I think I can assure you it was not the captain," said I; "for he and Bellairs are not acquainted."

"Wasn't that the captain with the red face and coloured handkerchief? He seemed to me to follow Bellairs's game with the most thrilling interest," objected Mr. Morgan.

"Perfectly true," said I; "Trent is deeply interested; he very likely knew Bellairs, and he certainly knew what he was there for; but I can put my hand in the fire that Bellairs didn't know Trent."

"Another singularity," observed the judge. "Well, we have had a capital forenoon. But you take an old lawyer's advice, and get to Midway Island as fast as you can. There's a pot of money on the table, and Bellairs and Co. are not the men to stick at trifles."

With this parting counsel Judge Morgan shook hands and made off along Montgomery Street, while I entered the Occidental Hotel, on the steps of which we had finished our conversation. I was well known to the clerks, and as soon as it was understood that I was there to wait for Pinkerton and lunch, I was invited to a seat inside the counter. Here, then, in a retired corner, I was beginning to come a little to myself after these so violent experiences, when who should come hurrying in, and (after a moment with a clerk) fly to one of the telephone boxes but Mr. Henry D. Bellairs in person? Call it what you will, but the impulse was irresistible, and I rose and took a place immediately at the man's back. It may be some excuse that I had often practised this very innocent form of eavesdropping upon strangers, and for fun. Indeed, I scarce know anything that gives a lower view of man's intelligence than to overhear (as you thus do) one side of a communication.

"Central," said the attorney, "2241 and 584 B" (or some such numbers)—"Who's that?—All right—Mr. Bellairs—Occidental; the wires are fouled in the other place—Yes, about three minutes—Yes—Yes—Your figure, I am sorry to say—No—I had no authority—Neither more nor less—I have every reason to suppose so—O, Pinkerton, Montana Block—Yes—Yes—Very good, sir—As you will, sir—Disconnect 584 B."

Bellairs turned to leave; at sight of me behind him, up flew his hands, and he winced and cringed, as though in fear of bodily attack. "O, it's you!" he cried; and then, somewhat recovered, "Mr. Pinkerton's partner, I believe? I am pleased to see you, sir—to congratulate you on your late success." And with that he was gone, obsequiously bowing as he passed.

And now a madcap humour came upon me. It was plain Bellairs had been communicating with his principal; I knew the number, if not the name; should I ring up at once, it was more than likely he would return in person to the telephone; why should not I dash (vocally) into the presence of this mysterious person, and have some fun for my money. I pressed the bell.

"Central," said I, "connect again 2241 and 584 B."

A phantom central repeated the numbers; there was a pause, and then "Two two four one," came in a tiny voice into my ear—a voice with the English sing-song—the voice plainly of a gentleman. "Is that you again, Mr. Bellairs?" it trilled. "I tell you it's no use. Is that you, Mr. Bellairs? Who is that?"

"I only want to put a single question," said I, civilly. "Why do you want to buy the Flying Scud?"

No answer came. The telephone vibrated and hummed in miniature with all the numerous talk of a great city; but the voice of 2241 was silent. Once and twice I put my question; but the tiny, sing-song English voice, I heard no more. The man, then, had fled? fled from an impertinent question? It scarce seemed natural to me; unless on the principle that the wicked fleeth when no man pursueth. I took the telephone list and turned the number up: "2241, Mrs. Keane, res. 942 Mission Street." And that, short of driving to the house and renewing my impertinence in person, was all that I could do.

Yet, as I resumed my seat in the corner of the office, I was conscious of a new element of the uncertain, the underhand, perhaps even the dangerous, in our adventure; and there was now a new picture in my mental gallery, to hang beside that of the wreck under its canopy of sea-birds and of Captain Trent mopping his red brow—the picture of a man with a telephone dice-box to his ear, and at the small voice of a single question, struck suddenly as white as ashes.

From these considerations I was awakened by the striking of the clock. An hour and nearly twenty minutes had elapsed since Pinkerton departed for the money: he was twenty minutes behind time; and to me who knew so well his gluttonous despatch of business and had so frequently admired his iron punctuality, the fact spoke volumes. The twenty minutes slowly stretched into an hour; the hour had nearly extended to a second; and I still sat in my corner of the office, or paced the marble pavement of the hall, a prey to the most wretched anxiety and penitence. The hour for lunch was nearly over before I remembered that I had not eaten. Heaven knows I had no appetite; but there might still be much to do—it was needful I should keep myself in proper trim, if it were only to digest the now too probable bad news; and leaving word at the office for Pinkerton, I sat down to table and called for soup, oysters, and a pint of champagne.

I was not long set, before my friend returned. He looked pale and rather old, refused to hear of food, and called for tea.

"I suppose all's up?" said I, with an incredible sinking.

"No," he replied; "I've pulled it through, Loudon; just pulled it through. I couldn't have raised another cent in all 'Frisco. People don't like it; Longhurst even went back on me; said he wasn't a three-card-monte man."

"Well, what's the odds?" said I. "That's all we wanted, isn't it?"

"Loudon, I tell you I've had to pay blood for that money," cried my friend, with almost savage energy and gloom. "It's all on ninety days, too; I couldn't get another day—not another day. If we go ahead with this affair, Loudon, you'll have to go yourself and make the fur fly. I'll stay of course—I've got to stay and face the trouble in this city; though, I tell you, I just long to go. I would show these fat brutes of sailors what work was; I would be all through that wreck and out at the other end, before they had boosted themselves upon the deck! But you'll do your level best, Loudon; I depend on you for that. You must be all fire and grit and dash from the word 'go.' That schooner and the boodle on board of her are bound to be here before three months, or it's B. U. S. T.—bust."

"I'll swear I'll do my best, Jim; I'll work double tides," said I. "It is my fault that you are in this thing, and I'll get you out again or kill myself. But what is that you say? 'If we go ahead?' Have we any choice, then?"

"I'm coming to that," said Jim. "It isn't that I doubt the investment. Don't blame yourself for that; you showed a fine, sound business instinct: I always knew it was in you, but then it ripped right out. I guess that little beast of an attorney knew what he was doing; and he wanted nothing better than to go beyond. No, there's profit in the deal; it's not that; it's these ninety-day bills, and the strain I've given the credit, for I've been up and down, borrowing, and begging and bribing to borrow. I don't believe there's another man but me in 'Frisco," he cried, with a sudden fervor of self admiration, "who could have raised that last ten thousand!—Then there's another thing. I had hoped you might have peddled that opium through the islands, which is safer and more profitable. But with this three-month limit, you must make tracks for Honolulu straight, and communicate by steamer. I'll try to put up something for you there; I'll have a man spoken to who's posted on that line of biz. Keep a bright lookout for him as soon's you make the islands; for it's on the cards he might pick you up at sea in a whaleboat or a steam-launch, and bring the dollars right on board."

It shows how much I had suffered morally during my sojourn in San Francisco, that even now when our fortunes trembled in the balance, I should have consented to become a smuggler and (of all things) a smuggler of opium. Yet I did, and that in silence; without a protest, not without a twinge.

"And suppose," said I, "suppose the opium is so securely hidden that I can't get hands on it?"

"Then you will stay there till that brig is kindling-wood, and stay and split that kindling-wood with your penknife," cried Pinkerton. "The stuff is there; we know that; and it must be found. But all this is only the one string to our bow—though I tell you I've gone into it head-first, as if it was our bottom dollar. Why, the first thing I did before I'd raised a cent, and with this other notion in my head already—the first thing I did was to secure the schooner. The Nora Creina, she is, sixty-four tons, quite big enough for our purpose since the rice is spoiled, and the fastest thing of her tonnage out of San Francisco. For a bonus of two hundred, and a monthly charter of three, I have her for my own time; wages and provisions, say four hundred more: a drop in the bucket. They began firing the cargo out of her (she was part loaded) near two hours ago; and about the same time John Smith got the order for the stores. That's what I call business."

"No doubt of that," said I. "But the other notion?"

"Well, here it is," said Jim. "You agree with me that Bellairs was ready to go higher?"

I saw where he was coming. "Yes—and why shouldn't he?" said I. "Is that the line?"

"That's the line, Loudon Dodd," assented Jim. "If Bellairs and his principal have any desire to go me better, I'm their man."

A sudden thought, a sudden fear, shot into my mind. What if I had been right? What if my childish pleasantry had frightened the principal away, and thus destroyed our chance? Shame closed my mouth; I began instinctively a long course of reticence; and it was without a word of my meeting with Bellairs, or my discovery of the address in Mission Street, that I continued the discussion.

"Doubtless fifty thousand was originally mentioned as a round sum," said I, "or at least, so Bellairs supposed. But at the same time it may be an outside sum; and to cover the expenses we have already incurred for the money and the schooner—I am far from blaming you; I see how needful it was to be ready for either event—but to cover them we shall want a rather large advance."

"Bellairs will go to sixty thousand; it's my belief, if he were properly handled, he would take the hundred," replied Pinkerton. "Look back on the way the sale ran at the end."

"That is my own impression as regards Bellairs," I admitted. "The point I am trying to make is that Bellairs himself may be mistaken; that what he supposed to be a round sum was really an outside figure."

"Well, Loudon, if that is so," said Jim, with extraordinary gravity of face and voice, "if that is so, let him take the Flying Scud at fifty thousand, and joy go with her! I prefer the loss."

"Is that so, Jim? Are we dipped as bad as that?" I cried.

"We've put our hand farther out than we can pull it in again, Loudon," he replied. "Why, man, that fifty thousand dollars, before we get clear again, will cost us nearer seventy. Yes, it figures up overhead to more than ten per cent a month; and I could do no better, and there isn't the man breathing could have done as well. It was a miracle, Loudon. I couldn't but admire myself. O, if we had just the four months! And you know, Loudon, it may still be done. With your energy and charm, if the worst comes to the worst, you can run that schooner as you ran one of your picnics; and we may have luck. And, O, man! if we do pull it through, what a dashing operation it will be! What an advertisement! what a thing to talk of, and remember all our lives! However," he broke off suddenly, "we must try the safe thing first. Here's for the shyster!"

There was another struggle in my mind, whether I should even now admit my knowledge of the Mission Street address. But I had let the favourable moment slip. I had now, which made it the more awkward, not merely the original discovery, but my late suppression to confess. I could not help reasoning, besides, that the more natural course was to approach the principal by the road of his agent's office; and there weighed upon my spirits a conviction that we were already too late, and that the man was gone two hours ago. Once more, then, I held my peace; and after an exchange of words at the telephone to assure ourselves he was at home, we set out for the attorney's office.

The endless streets of any American city pass, from one end to another, through strange degrees and vicissitudes of splendour and distress, running under the same name between monumental warehouses, the dens and taverns of thieves, and the sward and shrubbery of villas. In San Francisco, the sharp inequalities of the ground, and the sea bordering on so many sides, greatly exaggerate these contrasts. The street for which we were now bound took its rise among blowing sands, somewhere in view of the Lone Mountain Cemetery; ran for a term across that rather windy Olympus of Nob Hill, or perhaps just skirted its frontier; passed almost immediately after through a stage of little houses, rather impudently painted, and offering to the eye of the observer this diagnostic peculiarity, that the huge brass plates upon the small and highly coloured doors bore only the first names of ladies—Norah or Lily or Florence; traversed China Town, where it was doubtless undermined with opium cellars, and its blocks pierced, after the similitude of rabbit-warrens, with a hundred doors and passages and galleries; enjoyed a glimpse of high publicity at the corner of Kearney; and proceeded, among dives and warehouses, towards the City Front and the region of the water-rats. In this last stage of its career, where it was both grimy and solitary, and alternately quiet and roaring to the wheels of drays, we found a certain house of some pretension to neatness, and furnished with a rustic outside stair. On the pillar of the stair a black plate bore in gilded lettering this device: "Harry D. Bellairs, Attorney-at-law. Consultations, 9 to 6." On ascending the stairs, a door was found to stand open on the balcony, with this further inscription, "Mr. Bellairs In."

"I wonder what we do next," said I.

"Guess we sail right in," returned Jim, and suited the action to the word.

The room in which we found ourselves was clean, but extremely bare. A rather old-fashioned secretaire stood by the wall, with a chair drawn to the desk; in one corner was a shelf with half-a-dozen law books; and I can remember literally not another stick of furniture. One inference imposed itself: Mr. Bellairs was in the habit of sitting down himself and suffering his clients to stand. At the far end, and veiled by a curtain of red baize, a second door communicated with the interior of the house. Hence, after some coughing and stamping, we elicited the shyster, who came timorously forth, for all the world like a man in fear of bodily assault, and then, recognising his guests, suffered from what I can only call a nervous paroxysm of courtesy.

"Mr. Pinkerton and partner!" said he. "I will go and fetch you seats."

"Not the least," said Jim. "No time. Much rather stand. This is business, Mr. Bellairs. This morning, as you know, I bought the wreck, Flying Scud."

The lawyer nodded.

"And bought her," pursued my friend, "at a figure out of all proportion to the cargo and the circumstances, as they appeared?"

"And now you think better of it, and would like to be off with your bargain? I have been figuring upon this," returned the lawyer. "My client, I will not hide from you, was displeased with me for putting her so high. I think we were both too heated, Mr. Pinkerton: rivalry—the spirit of competition. But I will be quite frank—I know when I am dealing with gentlemen—and I am almost certain, if you leave the matter in my hands, my client would relieve you of the bargain, so as you would lose"—he consulted our faces with gimlet-eyed calculation—"nothing," he added shrilly.

And here Pinkerton amazed me.

"That's a little too thin," said he. "I have the wreck. I know there's boodle in her, and I mean to keep her. What I want is some points which may save me needless expense, and which I'm prepared to pay for, money down. The thing for you to consider is just this: am I to deal with you or direct with your principal? If you are prepared to give me the facts right off, why, name your figure. Only one thing!" added Jim, holding a finger up, "when I say 'money down,' I mean bills payable when the ship returns, and if the information proves reliable. I don't buy pigs in pokes."

I had seen the lawyer's face light up for a moment, and then, at the sound of Jim's proviso, miserably fade. "I guess you know more about this wreck than I do, Mr. Pinkerton," said he. "I only know that I was told to buy the thing, and tried, and couldn't."

"What I like about you, Mr. Bellairs, is that you waste no time," said Jim. "Now then, your client's name and address."

"On consideration," replied the lawyer, with indescribable furtivity, "I cannot see that I am entitled to communicate my client's name. I will sound him for you with pleasure, if you care to instruct me; but I cannot see that I can give you his address."

"Very well," said Jim, and put his hat on. "Rather a strong step, isn't it?" (Between every sentence was a clear pause.) "Not think better of it? Well, come—call it a dollar?"

"Mr. Pinkerton, sir!" exclaimed the offended attorney; and, indeed, I myself was almost afraid that Jim had mistaken his man and gone too far.

"No present use for a dollar?" says Jim. "Well, look here, Mr. Bellairs: we're both busy men, and I'll go to my outside figure with you right away—"

"Stop this, Pinkerton," I broke in. "I know the address: 924 Mission Street."

I do not know whether Pinkerton or Bellairs was the more taken aback.

"Why in snakes didn't you say so, Loudon?" cried my friend.

"You didn't ask for it before," said I, colouring to my temples under his troubled eyes.

It was Bellairs who broke silence, kindly supplying me with all that I had yet to learn. "Since you know Mr. Dickson's address," said he, plainly burning to be rid of us, "I suppose I need detain you no longer."

I do not know how Pinkerton felt, but I had death in my soul as we came down the outside stair, from the den of this blotched spider. My whole being was strung, waiting for Jim's first question, and prepared to blurt out, I believe, almost with tears, a full avowal. But my friend asked nothing.

"We must hack it," said he, tearing off in the direction of the nearest stand. "No time to be lost. You saw how I changed ground. No use in paying the shyster's commission."

Again I expected a reference to my suppression; again I was disappointed. It was plain Jim feared the subject, and I felt I almost hated him for that fear. At last, when we were already in the hack and driving towards Mission Street, I could bear my suspense no longer.

"You do not ask me about that address," said I.

"No," said he, quickly and timidly. "What was it? I would like to know."

The note of timidity offended me like a buffet; my temper rose as hot as mustard. "I must request you do not ask me," said I. "It is a matter I cannot explain."

The moment the foolish words were said, that moment I would have given worlds to recall them: how much more, when Pinkerton, patting my hand, replied: "All right, dear boy; not another word; that's all done. I'm convinced it's perfectly right." To return upon the subject was beyond my courage; but I vowed inwardly that I should do my utmost in the future for this mad speculation, and that I would cut myself in pieces before Jim should lose one dollar.

We had no sooner arrived at the address than I had other things to think of.

"Mr. Dickson? He's gone," said the landlady.

Where had he gone?

"I'm sure I can't tell you," she answered. "He was quite a stranger to me."

"Did he express his baggage, ma'am?" asked Pinkerton.

"Hadn't any," was the reply. "He came last night and left again to-day with a satchel."

"When did he leave?" I inquired.

"It was about noon," replied the landlady. "Some one rang up the telephone, and asked for him; and I reckon he got some news, for he left right away, although his rooms were taken by the week. He seemed considerable put out: I reckon it was a death."

My heart sank; perhaps my idiotic jest had indeed driven him away; and again I asked myself, Why? and whirled for a moment in a vortex of untenable hypotheses.

"What was he like, ma'am?" Pinkerton was asking, when I returned to consciousness of my surroundings.

"A clean shaved man," said the woman, and could be led or driven into no more significant description.

"Pull up at the nearest drug-store," said Pinkerton to the driver; and when there, the telephone was put in operation, and the message sped to the Pacific Mail Steamship Company's office—this was in the days before Spreckels had arisen—"When does the next China steamer touch at Honolulu?"

"The City of Pekin; she cast off the dock to-day, at half-past one," came the reply.

"It's a clear case of bolt," said Jim. "He's skipped, or my name's not Pinkerton. He's gone to head us off at Midway Island."

Somehow I was not so sure; there were elements in the case, not known to Pinkerton—the fears of the captain, for example—that inclined me otherwise; and the idea that I had terrified Mr. Dickson into flight, though resting on so slender a foundation, clung obstinately in my mind. "Shouldn't we see the list of passengers?" I asked.

"Dickson is such a blamed common name," returned Jim; "and then, as like as not, he would change it."

At this I had another intuition. A negative of a street scene, taken unconsciously when I was absorbed in other thought, rose in my memory with not a feature blurred: a view, from Bellairs's door as we were coming down, of muddy roadway, passing drays, matted telegraph wires, a Chinaboy with a basket on his head, and (almost opposite) a corner grocery with the name of Dickson in great gilt letters.

"Yes," said I, "you are right; he would change it. And anyway, I don't believe it was his name at all; I believe he took it from a corner grocery beside Bellairs's."

"As like as not," said Jim, still standing on the sidewalk with contracted brows.

"Well, what shall we do next?" I asked.

"The natural thing would be to rush the schooner," he replied. "But I don't know. I telephoned the captain to go at it head down and heels in air; he answered like a little man; and I guess he's getting around. I believe, Loudon, we'll give Trent a chance. Trent was in it; he was in it up to the neck; even if he couldn't buy, he could give us the straight tip."

"I think so, too," said I. "Where shall we find him?"

"British consulate, of course," said Jim. "And that's another reason for taking him first. We can hustle that schooner up all evening; but when the consulate's shut, it's shut."

At the consulate, we learned that Captain Trent had alighted (such is I believe the classic phrase) at the What Cheer House. To that large and unaristocratic hostelry we drove, and addressed ourselves to a large clerk, who was chewing a toothpick and looking straight before him.

"Captain Jacob Trent?"

"Gone," said the clerk.

"Where has he gone?" asked Pinkerton.

"Cain't say," said the clerk.

"When did he go?" I asked.

"Don't know," said the clerk, and with the simplicity of a monarch offered us the spectacle of his broad back.

What might have happened next I dread to picture, for Pinkerton's excitement had been growing steadily, and now burned dangerously high; but we were spared extremities by the intervention of a second clerk.

"Why! Mr. Dodd!" he exclaimed, running forward to the counter. "Glad to see you, sir! Can I do anything in your way?"

How virtuous actions blossom! Here was a young man to whose pleased ears I had rehearsed Just before the battle, mother, at some weekly picnic; and now, in that tense moment of my life, he came (from the machine) to be my helper.

"Captain Trent, of the wreck? O yes, Mr. Dodd; he left about twelve; he and another of the men. The Kanaka went earlier by the City of Pekin; I know that; I remember expressing his chest. Captain Trent? I'll inquire, Mr. Dodd. Yes, they were all here. Here are the names on the register; perhaps you would care to look at them while I go and see about the baggage?"

I drew the book toward me, and stood looking at the four names all written in the same hand, rather a big and rather a bad one: Trent, Brown, Hardy, and (instead of Ah Sing) Jos. Amalu.

"Pinkerton," said I, suddenly, "have you that Occidental in your pocket?"

"Never left me," said Pinkerton, producing the paper.

I turned to the account of the wreck. "Here," said I; "here's the name. 'Elias Goddedaal, mate.' Why do we never come across Elias Goddedaal?"

"That's so," said Jim. "Was he with the rest in that saloon when you saw them?"

"I don't believe it," said I. "They were only four, and there was none that behaved like a mate."

At this moment the clerk returned with his report.

"The captain," it appeared, "came with some kind of an express waggon, and he and the man took off three chests and a big satchel. Our porter helped to put them on, but they drove the cart themselves. The porter thinks they went down town. It was about one."

"Still in time for the City of Pekin," observed Jim.

"How many of them were here?" I inquired.

"Three, sir, and the Kanaka," replied the clerk. "I can't somehow fin out about the third, but he's gone too."

"Mr. Goddedaal, the mate, wasn't here then?" I asked.

"No, Mr. Dodd, none but what you see," says the clerk.

"Nor you never heard where he was?"

"No. Any particular reason for finding these men, Mr. Dodd?" inquired the clerk.

"This gentleman and I have bought the wreck," I explained; "we wished to get some information, and it is very annoying to find the men all gone."

A certain group had gradually formed about us, for the wreck was still a matter of interest; and at this, one of the bystanders, a rough seafaring man, spoke suddenly.

"I guess the mate won't be gone," said he. "He's main sick; never left the sick-bay aboard the Tempest; so they tell ME."

Jim took me by the sleeve. "Back to the consulate," said he.

But even at the consulate nothing was known of Mr. Goddedaal. The doctor of the Tempest had certified him very sick; he had sent his papers in, but never appeared in person before the authorities.

"Have you a telephone laid on to the Tempest?" asked Pinkerton.

"Laid on yesterday," said the clerk.

"Do you mind asking, or letting me ask? We are very anxious to get hold of Mr. Goddedaal."

"All right," said the clerk, and turned to the telephone. "I'm sorry," he said presently, "Mr. Goddedaal has left the ship, and no one knows where he is."

"Do you pay the men's passage home?" I inquired, a sudden thought striking me.

"If they want it," said the clerk; "sometimes they don't. But we paid the Kanaka's passage to Honolulu this morning; and by what Captain Trent was saying, I understand the rest are going home together."

"Then you haven't paid them?" said I.

"Not yet," said the clerk.

"And you would be a good deal surprised, if I were to tell you they were gone already?" I asked.

"O, I should think you were mistaken," said he.

"Such is the fact, however," said I.

"I am sure you must be mistaken," he repeated.

"May I use your telephone one moment?" asked Pinkerton; and as soon as permission had been granted, I heard him ring up the printing-office where our advertisements were usually handled. More I did not hear; for suddenly recalling the big, bad hand in the register of the What Cheer House, I asked the consulate clerk if he had a specimen of Captain Trent's writing. Whereupon I learned that the captain could not write, having cut his hand open a little before the loss of the brig; that the latter part of the log even had been written up by Mr. Goddedaal; and that Trent had always signed with his left hand. By the time I had gleaned this information, Pinkerton was ready.

"That's all that we can do. Now for the schooner," said he; "and by to-morrow evening I lay hands on Goddedaal, or my name's not Pinkerton."

"How have you managed?" I inquired.

"You'll see before you get to bed," said Pinkerton. "And now, after all this backwarding and forwarding, and that hotel clerk, and that bug Bellairs, it'll be a change and a kind of consolation to see the schooner. I guess things are humming there."

But on the wharf, when we reached it, there was no sign of bustle, and, but for the galley smoke, no mark of life on the Norah Creina. Pinkerton's face grew pale, and his mouth straightened, as he leaped on board.

"Where's the captain of this———?" and he left the phrase unfinished, finding no epithet sufficiently energetic for his thoughts.

It did not appear whom or what he was addressing; but a head, presumably the cook's, appeared in answer at the galley door.

"In the cabin, at dinner," said the cook deliberately, chewing as he spoke.

"Is that cargo out?"

"No, sir."

"None of it?"

"O, there's some of it out. We'll get at the rest of it livelier to-morrow, I guess."

"I guess there'll be something broken first," said Pinkerton, and strode to the cabin.

Here we found a man, fat, dark, and quiet, seated gravely at what seemed a liberal meal. He looked up upon our entrance; and seeing Pinkerton continue to stand facing him in silence, hat on head, arms folded, and lips compressed, an expression of mingled wonder and annoyance began to dawn upon his placid face.

"Well!" said Jim; "and so this is what you call rushing around?"

"Who are you?" cries the captain.

"Me! I'm Pinkerton!" retorted Jim, as though the name had been a talisman.

"You're not very civil, whoever you are," was the reply. But still a certain effect had been produced, for he scrambled to his feet, and added hastily, "A man must have a bit of dinner, you know, Mr. Pinkerton."

"Where's your mate?" snapped Jim.

"He's up town," returned the other.

"Up town!" sneered Pinkerton. "Now, I'll tell you what you are: you're a Fraud; and if I wasn't afraid of dirtying my boot, I would kick you and your dinner into that dock."

"I'll tell you something, too," retorted the captain, duskily flushing. "I wouldn't sail this ship for the man you are, if you went upon your knees. I've dealt with gentlemen up to now."

"I can tell you the names of a number of gentlemen you'll never deal with any more, and that's the whole of Longhurst's gang," said Jim. "I'll put your pipe out in that quarter, my friend. Here, rout out your traps as quick as look at it, and take your vermin along with you. I'll have a captain in, this very night, that's a sailor, and some sailors to work for him."

"I'll go when I please, and that's to-morrow morning," cried the captain after us, as we departed for the shore.

"There's something gone wrong with the world to-day; it must have come bottom up!" wailed Pinkerton. "Bellairs, and then the hotel clerk, and now This Fraud! And what am I to do for a captain, Loudon, with Longhurst gone home an hour ago, and the boys all scattered?"

"I know," said I. "Jump in!" And then to the driver: "Do you know Black Tom's?"

Thither then we rattled; passed through the bar, and found (as I had hoped) Johnson in the enjoyment of club life. The table had been thrust upon one side; a South Sea merchant was discoursing music from a mouth-organ in one corner; and in the middle of the floor Johnson and a fellow-seaman, their arms clasped about each other's bodies, somewhat heavily danced. The room was both cold and close; a jet of gas, which continually menaced the heads of the performers, shed a coarse illumination; the mouth-organ sounded shrill and dismal; and the faces of all concerned were church-like in their gravity. It were, of course, indelicate to interrupt these solemn frolics; so we edged ourselves to chairs, for all the world like belated comers in a concert-room, and patiently waited for the end. At length the organist, having exhausted his supply of breath, ceased abruptly in the middle of a bar. With the cessation of the strain, the dancers likewise came to a full stop, swayed a moment, still embracing, and then separated and looked about the circle for applause.

"Very well danced!" said one; but it appears the compliment was not strong enough for the performers, who (forgetful of the proverb) took up the tale in person.

"Well," said Johnson. "I mayn't be no sailor, but I can dance!"

And his late partner, with an almost pathetic conviction, added, "My foot is as light as a feather."

Seeing how the wind set, you may be sure I added a few words of praise before I carried Johnson alone into the passage: to whom, thus mollified, I told so much as I judged needful of our situation, and begged him, if he would not take the job himself, to find me a smart man.

"Me!" he cried. "I couldn't no more do it than I could try to go to hell!"

"I thought you were a mate?" said I.

"So I am a mate," giggled Johnson, "and you don't catch me shipping noways else. But I'll tell you what, I believe I can get you Arty Nares: you seen Arty; first-rate navigator and a son of a gun for style." And he proceeded to explain to me that Mr. Nares, who had the promise of a fine barque in six months, after things had quieted down, was in the meantime living very private, and would be pleased to have a change of air.

I called out Pinkerton and told him. "Nares!" he cried, as soon as I had come to the name. "I would jump at the chance of a man that had had Nares's trousers on! Why, Loudon, he's the smartest deep-water mate out of San Francisco, and draws his dividends regular in service and out." This hearty indorsation clinched the proposal; Johnson agreed to produce Nares before six the following morning; and Black Tom, being called into the consultation, promised us four smart hands for the same hour, and even (what appeared to all of us excessive) promised them sober.

The streets were fully lighted when we left Black Tom's: street after street sparkling with gas or electricity, line after line of distant luminaries climbing the steep sides of hills towards the overvaulting darkness; and on the other hand, where the waters of the bay invisibly trembled, a hundred riding lanterns marked the position of a hundred ships. The sea-fog flew high in heaven; and at the level of man's life and business it was clear and chill. By silent consent, we paid the hack off, and proceeded arm in arm towards the Poodle Dog for dinner.

At one of the first hoardings, I was aware of a bill-sticker at work: it was a late hour for this employment, and I checked Pinkerton until the sheet should be unfolded. This is what I read:—

TWO HUNDRED DOLLARS REWARD.

OFFICERS AND MEN OF THE

WRECKED BRIG FLYING SCUD

APPLYING,

PERSONALLY OR BY LETTER,

AT THE OFFICE OF JAMES PINKERTON, MONTANA BLOCK,

BEFORE NOON TO-MORROW, TUESDAY, 12TH,

WILL RECEIVE

TWO HUNDRED DOLLARS REWARD.

"This is your idea, Pinkerton!" I cried.

"Yes. They've lost no time; I'll say that for them—not like the Fraud," said he. "But mind you, Loudon, that's not half of it. The cream of the idea's here: we know our man's sick; well, a copy of that has been mailed to every hospital, every doctor, and every drug-store in San Francisco."

Of course, from the nature of our business, Pinkerton could do a thing of the kind at a figure extremely reduced; for all that, I was appalled at the extravagance, and said so.

"What matter a few dollars now?" he replied sadly. "It's in three months that the pull comes, Loudon."

We walked on again in silence, not without a shiver. Even at the Poodle Dog, we took our food with small appetite and less speech; and it was not until he was warmed with a third glass of champagne that Pinkerton cleared his throat and looked upon me with a deprecating eye.

"Loudon," said he, "there was a subject you didn't wish to be referred to. I only want to do so indirectly. It wasn't"—he faltered—"it wasn't because you were dissatisfied with me?" he concluded, with a quaver.

"Pinkerton!" cried I.

"No, no, not a word just now," he hastened to proceed. "Let me speak first. I appreciate, though

I can't imitate, the delicacy of your nature; and I can well understand you would rather die than speak of it, and yet might feel disappointed. I did think I could have done better myself. But when I found how tight money was in this city, and a man like Douglas B. Longhurst—a forty-niner, the man that stood at bay in a corn patch for five hours against the San Diablo squatters—weakening on the operation, I tell you, Loudon, I began to despair; and—I may have made mistakes, no doubt there are thousands who could have done better—but I give you a loyal hand on it, I did my best."

"My poor Jim," said I, "as if I ever doubted you! as if I didn't know you had done wonders! All day I've been admiring your energy and resource. And as for that affair——"

"No, Loudon, no more, not a word more! I don't want to hear," cried Jim.

"Well, to tell you the truth, I don't want to tell you," said I; "for it's a thing I'm ashamed of."

"Ashamed, Loudon? O, don't say that; don't use such an expression even in jest!" protested Pinkerton.

"Do you never do anything you're ashamed of?" I inquired.

"No," says he, rolling his eyes. "Why? I'm sometimes sorry afterwards, when it pans out different from what I figured. But I can't see what I would want to be ashamed for."

I sat a while considering with admiration the simplicity of my friend's character. Then I sighed. "Do you know, Jim, what I'm sorriest for?" said I. "At this rate, I can't be best man at your marriage."

"My marriage!" he repeated, echoing the sigh. "No marriage for me now. I'm going right down to-night to break it to her. I think that's what's shaken me all day. I feel as if I had had no right (after I was engaged) to operate so widely."

"Well, you know, Jim, it was my doing, and you must lay the blame on me," said I.

"Not a cent of it!" he cried. "I was as eager as yourself, only not so bright at the beginning. No; I've myself to thank for it; but it's a wrench."

While Jim departed on his dolorous mission, I returned alone to the office, lit the gas, and sat down to reflect on the events of that momentous day: on the strange features of the tale that had been so far unfolded, the disappearances, the terrors, the great sums of money; and on the dangerous and ungrateful task that awaited me in the immediate future.

It is difficult, in the retrospect of such affairs, to avoid attributing to ourselves in the past a measure of the knowledge we possess to-day. But I may say, and yet be well within the mark, that I was consumed that night with a fever of suspicion and curiosity; exhausted my fancy in solutions, which I still dismissed as incommensurable with the facts; and in the mystery by which I saw myself surrounded, found a precious stimulus for my courage and a convenient soothing draught for conscience. Even had all been plain sailing, I do not hint that I should have drawn back. Smuggling is one of the meanest of crimes, for by that we rob a whole country pro rata, and are therefore certain to impoverish the poor: to smuggle opium is an offence particularly dark, since it stands related not so much to murder, as to massacre. Upon all these points I was quite clear; my sympathy was all in arms against my interest; and had not Jim been involved, I could have dwelt almost with satisfaction on the idea of my failure. But Jim, his whole fortune, and his marriage, depended upon my success; and I preferred the interests of my friend before those of all the islanders in the South Seas. This is a poor, private morality, if you like; but it is mine, and the best I have; and I am not half so much ashamed of having embarked at all on this adventure, as I am proud that (while I was in it, and for the sake of my friend) I was up early and down late, set my own hand to everything, took dangers as they came, and for once in my life played the man throughout. At the same time, I could have desired another field of energy; and I was the more grateful for the redeeming element of mystery. Without that, though I might have gone ahead and done as well, it would scarce have been with ardour; and what inspired me that night with an impatient greed of the sea, the island, and the wreck, was the hope that I might stumble there upon the answer to a hundred questions, and learn why Captain Trent fanned his red face in the exchange, and why Mr. Dickson fled from the telephone in the Mission Street lodging-house.

CHAPTER XI. IN WHICH JIM AND I TAKE DIFFERENT WAYS.

I was unhappy when I closed my eyes; and it was to unhappiness that I opened them again next morning, to a confused sense of some calamity still inarticulate, and to the consciousness of jaded limbs and of a swimming head. I must have lain for some time inert and stupidly miserable, before I became aware of a reiterated knocking at the door; with which discovery all my wits flowed back in their accustomed channels, and I remembered the sale, and the wreck, and Goddedaal, and Nares, and Johnson, and Black Tom, and the troubles of yesterday, and the manifold engagements of the day that was to come. The thought thrilled me like a trumpet in the hour of battle. In a moment, I had leaped from bed, crossed the office where Pinkerton lay in a deep trance of sleep on the convertible sofa, and stood in the doorway, in my night gear, to receive our visitors.

Johnson was first, by way of usher, smiling. From a little behind, with his Sunday hat tilted forward over his brow, and a cigar glowing between his lips, Captain Nares acknowledged our previous acquaintance with a succinct nod. Behind him again, in the top of the stairway, a knot of sailors, the new crew of the Norah Creina, stood polishing the wall with back and elbow. These I left without to their reflections. But our two officers I carried at once into the office, where (taking Jim by the shoulder) I shook him slowly into consciousness. He sat up, all abroad for the moment, and stared on the new captain.

"Jim," said I, "this is Captain Nares. Captain, Mr. Pinkerton."

Nares repeated his curt nod, still without speech; and I thought he held us both under a watchful scrutiny.

"O!" says Jim, "this is Captain Nares, is it? Good morning, Captain Nares. Happy to have the pleasure of your acquaintance, sir. I know you well by reputation."

Perhaps, under the circumstances of the moment, this was scarce a welcome speech. At least, Nares received it with a grunt.

"Well, Captain," Jim continued, "you know about the size of the business? You're to take the Nora Creina to Midway Island, break up a wreck, call at Honolulu, and back to this port? I suppose that's understood?"

"Well," returned Nares, with the same unamiable reserve, "for a reason, which I guess you know, the cruise may suit me; but there's a point or two to settle. We shall have to talk, Mr. Pinkerton. But whether I go or not, somebody will; there's no sense in losing time; and you might give Mr. Johnson a note, let him take the hands right down, and set to to overhaul the rigging. The beasts look sober," he added, with an air of great disgust, "and need putting to work to keep them so."

This being agreed upon, Nares watched his subordinate depart and drew a visible breath.

"And now we're alone and can talk," said he. "What's this thing about? It's been advertised like Barnum's museum; that poster of yours has set the Front talking; that's an objection in itself, for I'm laying a little dark just now; and anyway, before I take the ship, I require to know what I'm going after."

Thereupon Pinkerton gave him the whole tale, beginning with a businesslike precision, and working himself up, as he went on, to the boiling-point of narrative enthusiasm. Nares sat and smoked, hat still on head, and acknowledged each fresh feature of the story with a frowning nod. But his pale blue eyes betrayed him, and lighted visibly.

"Now you see for yourself," Pinkerton concluded: "there's every last chance that Trent has skipped to Honolulu, and it won't take much of that fifty thousand dollars to charter a smart schooner down to Midway. Here's where I want a man!" cried Jim, with contagious energy. "That wreck's mine; I've paid for it, money down; and if it's got to be fought for, I want to see it fought for lively. If you're not back in ninety days, I tell you plainly, I'll make one of the biggest busts ever seen upon this coast; it's life or death for Mr. Dodd and me. As like as not, it'll come to grapples on the island; and when I heard your name last night—and a blame' sight more this morning when I saw the eye you've got in your head—I said, 'Nares is good enough for me!'"

"I guess," observed Nares, studying the ash of his cigar, "the sooner I get that schooner outside the Farallones, the better you'll be pleased."

"You're the man I dreamed of!" cried Jim, bouncing on the bed. "There's not five per cent of fraud in all your carcase."

"Just hold on," said Nares. "There's another point. I heard some talk about a supercargo."

"That's Mr. Dodd, here, my partner," said Jim.

"I don't see it," returned the captain drily. "One captain's enough for any ship that ever I was aboard."

"Now don't you start disappointing me," said Pinkerton; "for you're talking without thought. I'm not going to give you the run of the books of this firm, am I? I guess not. Well, this is not only a cruise; it's a business operation; and that's in the hands of my partner. You sail that ship, you see to breaking up that wreck and keeping the men upon the jump, and you'll find your hands about full. Only, no mistake about one thing: it has to be done to Mr. Dodd's satisfaction; for it's Mr. Dodd that's paying."

"I'm accustomed to give satisfaction," said Mr. Nares, with a dark flush.

"And so you will here!" cried Pinkerton. "I understand you. You're prickly to handle, but you're straight all through."

"The position's got to be understood, though," returned Nares, perhaps a trifle mollified. "My position, I mean. I'm not going to ship sailing-master; it's enough out of my way already, to set a foot on this mosquito schooner."

"Well, I'll tell you," retorted Jim, with an indescribable twinkle: "you just meet me on the ballast, and we'll make it a barquentine."

Nares laughed a little; tactless Pinkerton had once more gained a victory in tact. "Then there's another point," resumed the captain, tacitly relinquishing the last. "How about the owners?"

"O, you leave that to me; I'm one of Longhurst's crowd, you know," said Jim, with sudden bristling vanity. "Any man that's good enough for me, is good enough for them."

"Who are they?" asked Nares.

"M'Intyre and Spittal," said Jim.

"O, well, give me a card of yours," said the captain: "you needn't bother to write; I keep M'Intyre and Spittal in my vest-pocket."

Boast for boast; it was always thus with Nares and Pinkerton—the two vainest men of my acquaintance. And having thus reinstated himself in his own opinion, the captain rose, and, with a couple of his stiff nods, departed.

"Jim," I cried, as the door closed behind him, "I don't like that man."

"You've just got to, Loudon," returned Jim. "He's a typical American seaman—brave as a lion, full of resource, and stands high with his owners. He's a man with a record."

"For brutality at sea," said I.

"Say what you like," exclaimed Pinkerton, "it was a good hour we got him in: I'd trust Mamie's life to him to-morrow."

"Well, and talking of Mamie?" says I.

Jim paused with his trousers half on. "She's the gallantest little soul God ever made!" he cried. "Loudon, I'd meant to knock you up last night, and I hope you won't take it unfriendly that I didn't. I went in and looked at you asleep; and I saw you were all broken up, and let you be. The news would keep, anyway; and even you, Loudon, couldn't feel it the same way as I did."

"What news?" I asked.

"It's this way," says Jim. "I told her how we stood, and that I backed down from marrying. 'Are you tired of me?' says she: God bless her! Well, I explained the whole thing over again, the chance of smash, your absence unavoidable, the point I made of having you for the best man, and that. 'If you're not tired of me, I think I see one way to manage,' says she. 'Let's get married to-morrow, and Mr. Loudon can be best man before he goes to sea.' That's how she said it, crisp and bright, like one of Dickens's characters. It was no good for me to talk about the smash. 'You'll want me all the more,' she said. Loudon, I only pray I can make it up to her; I prayed for it last night beside your bed, while you lay sleeping—for you, and Mamie and myself; and—I don't know if you quite believe in prayer, I'm a bit Ingersollian myself—but a kind of sweetness came over me, and I couldn't help but think it was an answer. Never was a man so lucky! You and me and Mamie; it's a triple cord, Loudon. If either of you were to die! And she likes you so much, and thinks you so accomplished and distingue-looking, and was just as set as I was to have you for best man. 'Mr. Loudon,' she calls you; seems to me so friendly! And she sat up till three in the morning fixing up a costume for the marriage; it did me good to see her, Loudon, and to see that needle going, going, and to say 'All this hurry, Jim, is just to marry you!' I couldn't believe it; it was so like some blame' fairy story. To think of those old tin-type times about turned my head; I was so unrefined then, and so illiterate, and so lonesome; and here I am in clover, and I'm blamed if I can see what I've done to deserve it."

So he poured forth with innocent volubility the fulness of his heart; and I, from these irregular communications, must pick out, here a little and there a little, the particulars of his new plan. They were to be married, sure enough, that day; the wedding breakfast was to be at Frank's; the evening to be passed in a visit of God-speed aboard the Norah Creina; and then we were to part, Jim and I, he to his married life, I on my sea-enterprise. If ever I cherished an ill-feeling for Miss Mamie, I forgave her now; so brave and kind, so pretty and venturesome, was her decision. The weather frowned overhead with a leaden sky, and San Francisco had never (in all my experience) looked so bleak and gaunt, and shoddy, and crazy, like a city prematurely old; but through all my wanderings and errands to and fro, by the dock side or in the jostling street, among rude sounds and ugly sights, there ran in my mind, like a tiny strain of music, the thought of my friend's happiness.

For that was indeed a day of many and incongruous occupations. Breakfast was scarce swallowed before Jim must run to the City Hall and Frank's about the cares of marriage, and I hurry to John Smith's upon the account of stores, and thence, on a visit of certification, to the Norah Creina. Methought she looked smaller than ever, sundry great ships overspiring her from close without. She was already a nightmare of disorder; and the wharf alongside was piled with a world of casks, and cases, and tins, and tools, and coils of rope, and miniature barrels of giant powder, such as it seemed no human ingenuity could stuff on board of her. Johnson was in the waist, in a red shirt and dungaree trousers, his eye kindled with activity. With him I exchanged a word or two; thence stepped aft along the narrow alleyway between the house and the rail, and down the companion to the main cabin, where the captain sat with the commissioner at wine.

I gazed with disaffection at the little box which for many a day I was to call home. On the starboard was a stateroom for the captain; on the port, a pair of frowsy berths, one over the other, and abutting astern upon the side of an unsavoury cupboard. The walls were yellow and damp, the floor black and greasy; there was a prodigious litter of straw, old newspapers, and broken packing-cases; and by way of ornament, only a glass-rack, a thermometer presented "with compliments" of some advertising whiskey-dealer, and a swinging lamp. It was hard to foresee that, before a week was up, I should regard that cabin as cheerful, lightsome, airy, and even spacious.

I was presented to the commissioner, and to a young friend of his whom he had brought with him for the purpose (apparently) of smoking cigars; and after we had pledged one another in a glass of California port, a trifle sweet and sticky for a morning beverage, the functionary spread his papers on the table, and the hands were summoned. Down they trooped, accordingly, into the cabin; and stood eyeing the ceiling or the floor, the picture of sheepish embarrassment, and with a common air of wanting to expectorate and not quite daring. In admirable contrast, stood the Chinese cook, easy, dignified, set apart by spotless raiment, the hidalgo of the seas.

I daresay you never had occasion to assist at the farce which followed. Our shipping laws in the United States (thanks to the inimitable Dana) are conceived in a spirit of paternal stringency, and proceed throughout on the hypothesis that poor Jack is an imbecile, and the other parties to the contract, rogues and ruffians. A long and wordy paper of precautions, a fo'c's'le bill of rights, must be read separately to each man. I had now the benefit of hearing it five times in brisk succession; and you would suppose I was acquainted with its contents. But the commissioner (worthy man) spends his days in doing little else; and when we bear in mind the parallel case of the irreverent curate, we need not be surprised that he took the passage tempo prestissimo, in one roulade of gabble—that I, with the trained attention of an educated man, could gather but a fraction of its import—and the sailors nothing. No profanity in giving orders, no sheath-knives, Midway Island and any other port the master may direct, not to exceed six calendar months, and to this port to be paid off: so it seemed to run, with surprising verbiage; so ended. And with the end, the commissioner, in each case, fetched a deep breath, resumed his natural voice, and proceeded to business. "Now, my man," he would say, "you ship A. B. at so many dollars, American gold coin. Sign your name here, if you have one, and can write." Whereupon, and the name (with infinite hard breathing) being signed, the commissioner would proceed to fill in the man's appearance, height, etc., on the official form. In this task of literary portraiture he seemed to rely wholly upon temperament; for I could not perceive him to cast one glance on any of his models. He was assisted, however, by a running commentary from the captain: "Hair blue and eyes red, nose five foot seven, and stature broken"—jests as old, presumably, as the American marine; and, like the similar pleasantries of the billiard board, perennially relished. The highest note of humour was reached in the case of the Chinese cook, who was shipped under the name of "One Lung," to the sound of his own protests and the self-approving chuckles of the functionary.

"Now, captain," said the latter, when the men were gone, and he had bundled up his papers, "the law requires you to carry a slop-chest and a chest of medicines."

"I guess I know that," said Nares.

"I guess you do," returned the commissioner, and helped himself to port.

But when he was gone, I appealed to Nares on the same subject, for I was well aware we carried none of these provisions.

"Well," drawled Nares, "there's sixty pounds of niggerhead on the quay, isn't there? and twenty pounds of salts; and I never travel without some painkiller in my gripsack."

As a matter of fact, we were richer. The captain had the usual sailor's provision of quack medicines, with which, in the usual sailor fashion, he would daily drug himself, displaying an extreme inconstancy, and flitting from Kennedy's Red Discovery to Kennedy's White, and from Hood's Sarsaparilla to Mother Seigel's Syrup. And there were, besides, some mildewed and half-empty bottles, the labels obliterated, over which Nares would sometimes sniff and speculate. "Seems to smell like diarrhoea stuff," he would remark. "I wish't I knew, and I would try it." But the slop-chest was indeed represented by the plugs of niggerhead, and nothing else. Thus paternal laws are made, thus they are evaded; and the schooner put to sea, like plenty of her neighbours, liable to a fine of six hundred dollars.

This characteristic scene, which has delayed me overlong, was but a moment in that day of exercise and agitation. To fit out a schooner for sea, and improvise a marriage between dawn and dusk, involves heroic effort. All day Jim and I ran, and tramped, and laughed, and came near crying, and fell in sudden anxious consultations, and were sped (with a prepared sarcasm on our lips) to some fallacious milliner, and made dashes to the schooner and John Smith's, and at every second corner were reminded (by our own huge posters) of our desperate estate. Between whiles, I had found the time to hover at some half-a-dozen jewellers' windows; and my present, thus intemperately chosen, was graciously accepted. I believe, indeed, that was the last (though not the least) of my concerns, before the old minister, shabby and benign, was routed from his house and led to the office like a performing poodle; and there, in the growing dusk, under the cold glitter of Thirteen Star, two hundred strong, and beside the garish glories of the agricultural engine, Mamie and Jim were made one. The scene was incongruous, but the business pretty, whimsical, and affecting: the typewriters with such kindly faces and fine posies, Mamie so demure, and Jim—how shall I describe that poor, transfigured Jim? He began by taking the minister aside to the far end of the office. I knew not what he said, but I have reason to believe he was protesting his unfitness; for he wept as he said it: and the old minister, himself genuinely moved, was heard to console and encourage him, and at one time to use this expression: "I assure you, Mr. Pinkerton, there are not many who can say so much"—from which I gathered that my friend had tempered his self-accusations with at least one legitimate boast. From this ghostly counselling, Jim turned to me; and though he never got beyond the explosive utterance of my name and one fierce handgrip, communicated some of his own emotion, like a charge of electricity, to his best man. We stood up to the ceremony at last, in a general and kindly discomposure. Jim was all abroad; and the divine himself betrayed his sympathy in voice and demeanour, and concluded with a fatherly allocution, in which he congratulated Mamie (calling her "my dear") upon the fortune of an excellent husband, and protested he had rarely married a more interesting couple. At this stage, like a glory descending, there was handed in, ex machina, the card of Douglas B. Longhurst, with congratulations and four dozen Perrier-Jouet. A bottle was opened; and the minister pledged the bride, and the bridesmaids simpered and tasted, and

I made a speech with airy bacchanalianism, glass in hand. But poor Jim must leave the wine untasted. "Don't touch it," I had found the opportunity to whisper; "in your state it will make you as drunk as a fiddler." And Jim had wrung my hand with a "God bless you, Loudon!—saved me again!"

Hard following upon this, the supper passed off at Frank's with somewhat tremulous gaiety. And thence, with one half of the Perrier-Jouet—I would accept no more—we voyaged in a hack to the Norah Creina.

"What a dear little ship!" cried Mamie, as our miniature craft was pointed out to her. And then, on second thought, she turned to the best man. "And how brave you must be, Mr. Dodd," she cried, "to go in that tiny thing so far upon the ocean!" And I perceived I had risen in the lady's estimation.

The dear little ship presented a horrid picture of confusion, and its occupants of weariness and ill-humour. From the cabin the cook was storing tins into the lazarette, and the four hands, sweaty and sullen, were passing them from one to another from the waist. Johnson was three parts asleep over the table; and in his bunk, in his own cabin, the captain sourly chewed and puffed at a cigar.

"See here," he said, rising; "you'll be sorry you came. We can't stop work if we're to get away to-morrow. A ship getting ready for sea is no place for people, anyway. You'll only interrupt my men."

I was on the point of answering something tart; but Jim, who was acquainted with the breed, as he was with most things that had a bearing on affairs, made haste to pour in oil.

"Captain," he said, "I know we're a nuisance here, and that you've had a rough time. But all we want is that you should drink one glass of wine with us, Perrier-Jouet, from Longhurst, on the occasion of my marriage, and Loudon's—Mr. Dodd's—departure."

"Well, it's your lookout," said Nares. "I don't mind half an hour. Spell, O!" he added to the men; "go and kick your heels for half an hour, and then you can turn to again a trifle livelier. Johnson, see if you can't wipe off a chair for the lady."

His tone was no more gracious than his language; but when Mamie had turned upon him the soft fire of her eyes, and informed him that he was the first sea-captain she had ever met, "except captains of steamers, of course"—she so qualified the statement—and had expressed a lively sense of his courage, and perhaps implied (for I suppose the arts of ladies are the same as those of men) a modest consciousness of his good looks, our bear began insensibly to soften; and it was already part as an apology, though still with unaffected heat of temper, that he volunteered some sketch of his annoyances.

"A pretty mess we've had!" said he. "Half the stores were wrong; I'll wring John Smith's neck for him some of these days. Then two newspaper beasts came down, and tried to raise copy out of me, till I threatened them with the first thing handy; and then some kind of missionary bug, wanting to work his passage to Raiatea or somewhere. I told him I would take him off the wharf with the butt end of my boot, and he went away cursing. This vessel's been depreciated by the look of him."

While the captain spoke, with his strange, humorous, arrogant abruptness, I observed Jim to be sizing him up, like a thing at once quaint and familiar, and with a scrutiny that was both curious and knowing.

"One word, dear boy," he said, turning suddenly to me. And when he had drawn me on deck, "That man," says he, "will carry sail till your hair grows white; but never you let on, never breathe a word. I know his line: he'll die before he'll take advice; and if you get his back up, he'll run you right under. I don't often jam in my advice, Loudon; and when I do, it means I'm thoroughly posted."

The little party in the cabin, so disastrously begun, finished, under the mellowing influence of wine and woman, in excellent feeling and with some hilarity. Mamie, in a plush Gainsborough hat and a gown of wine-coloured silk, sat, an apparent queen, among her rude surroundings and companions. The dusky litter of the cabin set off her radiant trimness: tarry Johnson was a foil to her fair beauty; she glowed in that poor place, fair as a star; until even I, who was not usually of her admirers, caught a spark of admiration; and even the captain, who was in no courtly humour, proposed that the scene should be commemorated by my pencil. It was the last act of the evening. Hurriedly as I went about my task, the half-hour had lengthened out to more than three before it was completed: Mamie in full value, the rest of the party figuring in outline only, and the artist himself introduced in a back view, which was pronounced a likeness. But it was to Mamie that I devoted the best of my attention; and it was with her I made my chief success.

"O!" she cried, "am I really like that? No wonder Jim ..." She paused. "Why it's just as lovely as he's good!" she cried: an epigram which was appreciated, and repeated as we made our salutations, and called out after the retreating couple as they passed away under the lamplight on the wharf.

Thus it was that our farewells were smuggled through under an ambuscade of laughter, and the parting over ere I knew it was begun. The figures vanished, the steps died away along the silent city front; on board, the men had returned to their labours, the captain to his solitary cigar; and after that long and complex day of business and emotion, I was at last alone and free. It was, perhaps, chiefly fatigue that made my heart so heavy. I leaned at least upon the house, and stared at the foggy heaven, or over the rail at the wavering reflection of the lamps, like a man that was quite done with hope and would have welcomed the asylum of the grave. And all at once, as I thus stood, the City of Pekin flashed into my mind, racing her thirteen knots for Honolulu, with the hated Trent—perhaps with the mysterious Goddedaal—on board; and with the thought, the blood leaped and careered through all my body. It seemed no chase at all; it seemed we had no chance, as we lay there bound to iron pillars, and fooling away the precious moments over tins of beans. "Let them get there first!" I thought. "Let them! We can't be long behind." And from that moment, I date myself a man of a rounded experience: nothing had lacked but this, that I should entertain and welcome the grim thought of bloodshed.

It was long before the toil remitted in the cabin, and it was worth my while to get to bed; long after that, before sleep favoured me; and scarce a moment later (or so it seemed) when I was recalled to consciousness by bawling men and the jar of straining hawsers.

The schooner was cast off before I got on deck. In the misty obscurity of the first dawn, I saw the tug heading us with glowing fires and blowing smoke, and heard her beat the roughened waters of the bay. Beside us, on her flock of hills, the lighted city towered up and stood swollen in the raw fog. It was strange to see her burn on thus wastefully, with half-quenched luminaries, when the dawn was already grown strong enough to show me, and to suffer me to recognise, a solitary figure standing by the piles.

Or was it really the eye, and not rather the heart, that identified that shadow in the dusk, among the shoreside lamps? I know not. It was Jim, at least; Jim, come for a last look; and we had but time to wave a valedictory gesture and exchange a wordless cry. This was our second parting, and our capacities were now reversed. It was mine to play the Argonaut, to speed affairs, to plan and to accomplish—if need were, at the price of life; it was his to sit at home, to study the calendar, and to wait. I knew besides another thing that gave me joy. I knew that my friend had succeeded in my education; that the romance of business, if our fantastic purchase merited the name, had at last stirred my dilletante nature; and, as we swept under cloudy Tamalpais and through the roaring narrows of the bay, the Yankee blood sang in my veins with suspense and exultation.

Outside the heads, as if to meet my desire, we found it blowing fresh from the northeast. No time had been lost. The sun was not yet up before the tug cast off the hawser, gave us a salute of three whistles, and turned homeward toward the coast, which now began to gleam along its margin with the earliest rays of day. There was no other ship in view when the Norah Creina, lying over under all plain sail, began her long and lonely voyage to the wreck.

CHAPTER XII. THE "NORAH CREINA."

I love to recall the glad monotony of a Pacific voyage, when the trades are not stinted, and the ship, day after day, goes free. The mountain scenery of trade-wind clouds, watched (and in my case painted) under every vicissitude of light—blotting stars, withering in the moon's glory, barring the scarlet eve, lying across the dawn collapsed into the unfeatured morning bank, or at noon raising their snowy summits between the blue roof of heaven and the blue floor of sea; the small, busy, and deliberate world of the schooner, with its unfamiliar scenes, the spearing of dolphin from the bowsprit end, the holy war on sharks, the cook making bread on the main hatch; reefing down before a violent squall, with the men hanging out on the foot-ropes; the squall itself, the catch at the heart, the opened sluices of the sky; and the relief, the renewed loveliness of life, when all is over, the sun forth again, and our out-fought enemy only a blot upon the leeward sea. I love to recall, and would that I could reproduce that life, the unforgettable, the unrememberable. The memory, which shows so wise a backwardness in registering pain, is besides an imperfect recorder of extended pleasures; and a long-continued well-being escapes (as it were, by its mass) our petty methods of commemoration. On a part of our life's map there lies a roseate, undecipherable haze, and that is all.

Of one thing, if I am at all to trust my own annals, I was delightedly conscious. Day after day, in the sun-gilded cabin, the whiskey-dealer's thermometer stood at 84. Day after day, the air had the same indescribable liveliness and sweetness, soft and nimble, and cool as the cheek of health. Day after day the sun flamed; night after night the moon beaconed, or the stars paraded their lustrous regiment. I was aware of a spiritual change, or, perhaps, rather a molecular reconstitution. My bones were sweeter to me. I had come home to my own climate, and looked back with pity on those damp and wintry zones, miscalled the temperate.

"Two years of this, and comfortable quarters to live in, kind of shake the grit out of a man," the captain remarked; "can't make out to be happy anywhere else. A townie of mine was lost down this way, in a coalship that took fire at sea. He struck the beach somewhere in the Navigators; and he wrote to me that when he left the place, it would be feet first. He's well off, too, and his father owns some coasting craft Down East; but Billy prefers the beach, and hot rolls off the bread-fruit trees."

A voice told me I was on the same track as Billy. But when was this? Our outward track in the Norah Creina lay well to the northward; and perhaps it is but the impression of a few pet days which I have unconsciously spread longer, or perhaps the feeling grew upon me later, in the run to Honolulu. One thing I am sure: it was before I had ever seen an island worthy of the name that I must date my loyalty to the South Seas. The blank sea itself grew desirable under such skies; and wherever the trade-wind blows, I know no better country than a schooner's deck.

But for the tugging anxiety as to the journey's end, the journey itself must thus have counted for the best of holidays. My physical well-being was over-proof; effects of sea and sky kept me for ever busy with my pencil; and I had no lack of intellectual exercise of a different order in the study of my inconsistent friend, the captain. I call him friend, here on the threshold; but that is to look well ahead. At first, I was too much horrified by what I considered his barbarities, too much puzzled by his shifting humours, and too frequently annoyed by his small vanities, to regard him otherwise than as the cross of my existence. It was only by degrees, in his rare hours of pleasantness, when he forgot (and made me forget) the weaknesses to which he was so prone, that he won me to a kind of unconsenting fondness. Lastly, the faults were all embraced in a more generous view: I saw them in their place, like discords in a musical progression; and accepted them and found them picturesque, as we accept and admire, in the habitable face of nature, the smoky head of the volcano or the pernicious thicket of the swamp.

He was come of good people Down East, and had the beginnings of a thorough education. His temper had been ungovernable from the first; and it is likely the defect was inherited, and the blame of the rupture not entirely his. He ran away at least to sea; suffered horrible maltreatment, which seemed to have rather hardened than enlightened him; ran away again to shore in a South American port; proved his capacity and made money, although still a child; fell among thieves and was robbed; worked back a passage to the States, and knocked one morning at the door of an old lady whose orchard he had often robbed. The introduction appears insufficient; but Nares knew what he was doing. The sight of her old neighbourly depredator shivering at the door in tatters, the very oddity of his appeal, touched a soft spot in the spinster's heart. "I always had a fancy for the old lady," Nares said, "even when she used to stampede me out of the orchard, and shake her thimble and her old curls at me out of the window as I was going by; I always thought she was a kind of pleasant old girl. Well, when she came to the door that morning, I told her so, and that I was stone-broke; and she took me right in, and fetched out the pie." She clothed him, taught him, and had him to sea again in better shape, welcomed him to her hearth on his return from every cruise, and when she died bequeathed him her possessions. "She was a good old girl," he would say. "I tell you, Mr. Dodd, it was a queer thing to see me and the old lady talking a pasear in the garden, and the old man scowling at us over the pickets. She lived right next door to the old man, and I guess that's just what took me there. I wanted him to know that I was badly beat, you see, and would rather go to the devil than to him. What made the dig harder, he had quarrelled with the old lady about me and the orchard: I guess that made him rage. Yes, I was a beast when I was young. But I was always pretty good to the old lady." Since then he had prospered, not uneventfully, in his profession; the old lady's money had fallen in during the voyage of the Gleaner, and he was now, as soon as the smoke of that engagement cleared away, secure of his ship. I suppose he was about thirty: a powerful, active man, with a blue eye, a thick head of hair, about the colour of oakum and growing low over the brow; clean-shaved and lean about the jaw; a good singer; a good performer on that sea-instrument, the accordion; a quick observer, a close reasoner; when he pleased, of a really elegant address; and when he chose, the greatest brute upon the seas.

His usage of the men, his hazing, his bullying, his perpetual fault-finding for no cause, his perpetual and brutal sarcasm, might have raised a mutiny in a slave galley. Suppose the steersman's eye to have wandered: "You ——, ——, little, mutton-faced Dutchman," Nares would bawl; "you want a booting to keep you on your course! I know a little city-front slush when I see one. Just you glue your eye to that compass, or I'll show you round the vessel at the butt-end of my boot." Or suppose a hand to linger aft, whither he had perhaps been summoned not a minute before. "Mr. Daniells, will you oblige me by stepping clear of that main-sheet?" the captain might begin, with truculent courtesy. "Thank you. And perhaps you'll be so kind as to tell me what the hell you're doing on my quarter-deck? I want no dirt of your sort here. Is there nothing for you to do? Where's the mate? Don't you set ME to find work for you, or I'll find you some that will keep you on your back a fortnight." Such allocutions, conceived with a perfect knowledge of his audience, so that every insult carried home, were delivered with a mien so menacing, and an eye so fiercely cruel, that his unhappy subordinates shrank and quailed. Too often violence followed; too often I have heard and seen and boiled at the cowardly aggression; and the victim, his hands bound by law, has risen again from deck and crawled forward stupefied—I know not what passion of revenge in his wronged heart.

It seems strange I should have grown to like this tyrant. It may even seem strange that I should have stood by and suffered his excesses to proceed. But I was not quite such a chicken as to interfere in public; for I would rather have a man or two mishandled than one half of us butchered in a mutiny and the rest suffer on the gallows. And in private, I was unceasing in my protests.

"Captain," I once said to him, appealing to his patriotism, which was of a hardy quality, "this is no way to treat American seamen. You don't call it American to treat men like dogs?"

"Americans?" he said grimly. "Do you call these Dutchmen and Scattermouches [1] Americans? I've been fourteen years to sea, all but one trip under American colours, and I've never laid eye on an American foremast hand. There used to be such things in the old days, when thirty-five dollars were the wages out of Boston; and then you could see ships handled and run the way they want to be. But that's all past and gone; and nowadays the only thing that flies in an American ship is a belaying-pin. You don't know; you haven't a guess. How would you like to go on deck for your middle watch, fourteen months on end, with all your duty to do and every one's life depending on you, and expect to get a knife ripped into you as you come out of your stateroom, or be sand-bagged as you pass the boat, or get tripped into the hold, if the hatches are off in fine weather? That kind of shakes the starch out of the brotherly love and New Jerusalem business. You go through the mill, and you'll have a bigger grudge against every old shellback that dirties his plate in the three oceans, than the Bank of California could settle up. No; it has an ugly look to it, but the only way to run a ship is to make yourself a terror."

[1] In sea-lingo (Pacific) DUTCHMAN includes all Teutons and folk from the basin of the Baltic; SCATTERMOUCH, all Latins and Levantines.

"Come, Captain," said I, "there are degrees in everything. You know American ships have a bad name; you know perfectly well if it wasn't for the high wage and the good food, there's not a man would ship in one if he could help; and even as it is, some prefer a British ship, beastly food and all."

"O, the lime-juicers?" said he. "There's plenty booting in lime-juicers, I guess; though I don't deny but what some of them are soft." And with that he smiled like a man recalling something. "Look here, that brings a yarn in my head," he resumed; "and for the sake of the joke, I'll give myself away. It was in 1874, I shipped mate in the British ship Maria, from 'Frisco for Melbourne. She was the queerest craft in some ways that ever I was aboard of. The food was a caution; there was nothing fit to put your lips to—but the lime-juice, which was from the end bin no doubt: it used to make me sick to see the men's dinners, and sorry to see my own. The old man was good enough, I guess; Green was his name; a mild, fatherly old galoot. But the hands were the lowest gang I ever handled; and whenever I tried to knock a little spirit into them, the old man took their part! It was Gilbert and Sullivan on the high seas; but you bet I wouldn't let any man dictate to me. 'You give me your orders, Captain Green,' I said, 'and you'll find I'll carry them out; that's all you've got to say. You'll find I do my duty,' I said; 'how I do it is my lookout; and there's no man born that's going to give me lessons.' Well, there was plenty dirt on board that Maria first and last. Of course, the old man put my back up, and, of course, he put up the crew's; and I had to regular fight my way through every watch. The men got to hate me, so's I would hear them grit their teeth when I came up. At last, one day, I saw a big hulking beast of a Dutchman booting the ship's boy. I made one shoot of it off the house and laid that Dutchman out. Up he came, and I laid him out again. 'Now,' I said, 'if there's a kick left in you, just mention it, and I'll stamp your ribs in like a packing-case.' He thought better of it, and never let on; lay there as mild as a deacon at a funeral; and they took him below to reflect on his native Dutchland. One night we got caught in rather a dirty thing about 25 south. I guess we were all asleep; for the first thing I knew there was the fore-royal gone. I ran forward, bawling blue hell; and just as I came by the foremast, something struck me right through the forearm and stuck there. I put my other hand up, and by George! it was the grain; the beasts had speared me like a porpoise. 'Cap'n!' I cried.—'What's wrong?' says he.—'They've grained me,' says I.—'Grained you?' says he. 'Well, I've been looking for that.'——'And by God,' I cried, 'I want to have some of these beasts murdered for it!'—'Now, Mr. Nares,' says he, 'you better go below. If I had been one of the men, you'd have got more than this. And I want no more of your language on deck. You've cost me my fore-royal already,' says he; 'and if you carry on, you'll have the three sticks out of her.' That was old man Green's idea of supporting officers. But you wait a bit; the cream's coming. We made Melbourne right enough, and the old man said: 'Mr. Nares, you and me don't draw together. You're a first-rate seaman, no mistake of that; but you're the most disagreeable man I ever sailed with; and your language and your conduct to the crew I cannot stomach. I guess we'll separate.' I didn't care about the berth, you may be sure; but I felt kind of mean; and if he made one kind of stink, I thought I could make another. So I said I would go ashore and see how things stood; went, found I was all right, and came aboard again on the top rail.—'Are you getting your traps together, Mr. Nares?' says the old man.—'No,' says I, 'I don't know as we'll separate much before 'Frisco; at least,' I said, 'it's a point for your consideration. I'm very willing to say good-by to the Maria, but I don't know whether you'll care to start me out with three months' wages.' He got his money-box right away. 'My son,' says he, 'I think it cheap at the money.' He had me there."

It was a singular tale for a man to tell of himself; above all, in the midst of our discussion; but it was quite in character for Nares. I never made a good hit in our disputes, I never justly resented any act or speech of his, but what I found it long after carefully posted in his day-book and reckoned (here was the man's oddity) to my credit. It was the same with his father, whom he had hated; he would give a sketch of the old fellow, frank and credible, and yet so honestly touched that it was charming. I have never met a man so strangely constituted: to possess a reason of the most equal justice, to have his nerves at the same time quivering with petty spite, and to act upon the nerves and not the reason.

A kindred wonder in my eyes was the nature of his courage. There was never a braver man: he went out to welcome danger; an emergency (came it never so sudden) strung him like a tonic. And yet, upon the other hand, I have known none so nervous, so oppressed with possibilities, looking upon the world at large, and the life of a sailor in particular, with so constant and haggard a consideration of the ugly chances. All his courage was in blood, not merely cold, but icy with reasoned apprehension. He would lay our little craft rail under, and "hang on" in a squall, until I gave myself up for lost, and the men were rushing to their stations of their own accord. "There," he would say, "I guess there's not a man on board would have hung on as long as I did that time; they'll have to give up thinking me no schooner sailor. I guess I can shave just as near capsizing as any other captain of this vessel, drunk or sober." And then he would fall to repining and wishing himself well out of the enterprise, and dilate on the peril of the seas, the particular dangers of the schooner rig, which he abhorred, the various ways in which we might go to the bottom, and the prodigious fleet of ships that have sailed out in the course of history, dwindled from the eyes of watchers, and returned no more. "Well," he would wind up, "I guess it don't much matter. I can't see what any one wants to live for, anyway. If I could get into some one else's apple-tree, and be about twelve years old, and just stick the way I was, eating stolen apples, I won't say. But there's no sense in this grown-up business—sailorising, politics, the piety mill, and all the rest of it. Good clean drowning is good enough for me." It is hard to imagine any more depressing talk for a poor landsman on a dirty night; it is hard to imagine anything less sailor-like (as sailors are supposed to be, and generally are) than this persistent harping on the minor.

But I was to see more of the man's gloomy constancy ere the cruise was at an end.

On the morning of the seventeenth day I came on deck, to find the schooner under double reefs, and flying rather wild before a heavy run of sea. Snoring trades and humming sails had been our portion hitherto. We were already nearing the island. My restrained excitement had begun again to overmaster me; and for some time my only book had been the patent log that trailed over the taffrail, and my chief interest the daily observation and our caterpillar progress across the chart. My first glance, which was at the compass, and my second, which was at the log, were all that I could wish. We lay our course; we had been doing over eight since nine the night before; and

I drew a heavy breath of satisfaction. And then I know not what odd and wintry appearance of the sea and sky knocked suddenly at my heart. I observed the schooner to look more than usually small, the men silent and studious of the weather. Nares, in one of his rusty humours, afforded me no shadow of a morning salutation. He, too, seemed to observe the behaviour of the ship with an intent and anxious scrutiny. What I liked still less, Johnson himself was at the wheel, which he span busily, often with a visible effort; and as the seas ranged up behind us, black and imminent, he kept casting behind him eyes of animal swiftness, and drawing in his neck between his shoulders, like a man dodging a blow. From these signs, I gathered that all was not exactly for the best; and I would have given a good handful of dollars for a plain answer to the questions which I dared not put. Had I dared, with the present danger signal in the captain's face, I should only have been reminded of my position as supercargo—an office never touched upon in kindness—and advised, in a very indigestible manner, to go below. There was nothing for it, therefore, but to entertain my vague apprehensions as best I should be able, until it pleased the captain to enlighten me of his own accord. This he did sooner than I had expected; as soon, indeed, as the Chinaman had summoned us to breakfast, and we sat face to face across the narrow board.

"See here, Mr. Dodd," he began, looking at me rather queerly, "here is a business point arisen. This sea's been running up for the last two days, and now it's too high for comfort. The glass is falling, the wind is breezing up, and I won't say but what there's dirt in it. If I lay her to, we may have to ride out a gale of wind and drift God knows where—on these French Frigate Shoals, for instance. If I keep her as she goes, we'll make that island to-morrow afternoon, and have the lee of it to lie under, if we can't make out to run in. The point you have to figure on, is whether you'll take the big chances of that Captain Trent making the place before you, or take the risk of something happening. I'm to run this ship to your satisfaction," he added, with an ugly sneer. "Well, here's a point for the supercargo."

"Captain," I returned, with my heart in my mouth, "risk is better than certain failure."

"Life is all risk, Mr. Dodd," he remarked. "But there's one thing: it's now or never; in half an hour, Archdeacon Gabriel couldn't lay her to, if he came down stairs on purpose."

"All right," said I. "Let's run."

"Run goes," said he; and with that he fell to breakfast, and passed half an hour in stowing away pie and devoutly wishing himself back in San Francisco.

When we came on deck again, he took the wheel from Johnson—it appears they could trust none among the hands—and I stood close beside him, feeling safe in this proximity, and tasting a fearful joy from our surroundings and the consciousness of my decision. The breeze had already risen, and as it tore over our heads, it uttered at times a long hooting note that sent my heart into my boots. The sea pursued us without remission, leaping to the assault of the low rail. The quarter-deck was all awash, and we must close the companion doors.

"And all this, if you please, for Mr. Pinkerton's dollars!" the captain suddenly exclaimed. "There's many a fine fellow gone under, Mr. Dodd, because of drivers like your friend. What do they care for a ship or two? Insured, I guess. What do they care for sailors' lives alongside of a few thousand dollars? What they want is speed between ports, and a damned fool of a captain that'll drive a ship under as I'm doing this one. You can put in the morning, asking why I do it."

I sheered off to another part of the vessel as fast as civility permitted. This was not at all the talk that I desired, nor was the train of reflection which it started anyway welcome. Here I was, running some hazard of my life, and perilling the lives of seven others; exactly for what end, I was now at liberty to ask myself. For a very large amount of a very deadly poison, was the obvious answer; and I thought if all tales were true, and I were soon to be subjected to cross-examination at the bar of Eternal Justice, it was one which would not increase my popularity with the court. "Well, never mind, Jim," thought I. "I'm doing it for you."

Before eleven, a third reef was taken in the mainsail; and Johnson filled the cabin with a storm-sail of No. 1 duck and sat cross-legged on the streaming floor, vigorously putting it to rights with a couple of the hands. By dinner I had fled the deck, and sat in the bench corner, giddy, dumb, and stupefied with terror. The frightened leaps of the poor Norah Creina, spanking like a stag for bare existence, bruised me between the table and the berths. Overhead, the wild huntsman of the storm passed continuously in one blare of mingled noises; screaming wind, straining timber, lashing rope's end, pounding block and bursting sea contributed; and I could have thought there was at times another, a more piercing, a more human note, that dominated all, like the wailing of an angel; I could have thought I knew the angel's name, and that his wings were black. It seemed incredible that any creature of man's art could long endure the barbarous mishandling of the seas, kicked as the schooner was from mountain side to mountain side, beaten and blown upon and wrenched in every joint and sinew, like a child upon the rack. There was not a plank of her that did not cry aloud for mercy; and as she continued to hold together, I became conscious of a growing sympathy with her endeavours, a growing admiration for her gallant staunchness, that amused and at times obliterated my terrors for myself. God bless every man that swung a mallet on that tiny and strong hull! It was not for wages only that he laboured, but to save men's lives.

All the rest of the day, and all the following night, I sat in the corner or lay wakeful in my bunk; and it was only with the return of morning that a new phase of my alarms drove me once more on deck. A gloomier interval I never passed. Johnson and Nares steadily relieved each other at the wheel and came below. The first glance of each was at the glass, which he repeatedly knuckled and frowned upon; for it was sagging lower all the time. Then, if Johnson were the visitor, he would pick a snack out of the cupboard, and stand, braced against the table, eating it, and perhaps obliging me with a word or two of his hee-haw conversation: how it was "a son of a gun of a cold night on deck, Mr. Dodd" (with a grin); how "it wasn't no night for panjammers, he could tell me": having transacted all which, he would throw himself down in his bunk and sleep his two hours with compunction. But the captain neither ate nor slept. "You there, Mr. Dodd?" he would say, after the obligatory visit to the glass. "Well, my son, we're one hundred and four miles" (or whatever it was) "off the island, and scudding for all we're worth. We'll make it to-morrow about four, or not, as the case may be. That's the news. And now, Mr. Dodd, I've stretched a point for you; you can see I'm dead tired; so just you stretch away back to your bunk again." And with this attempt at geniality, his teeth would settle hard down on his cigar, and he would pass his spell below staring and blinking at the cabin lamp through a cloud of tobacco smoke. He has told me since that he was happy, which I should never have divined. "You see," he said, "the wind we had was never anything out of the way; but the sea was really nasty, the schooner wanted a lot of humouring, and it was clear from the glass that we were close to some dirt. We might be running out of it, or we might be running right crack into it. Well, there's always something sublime about a big deal like that; and it kind of raises a man in his own liking. We're a queer kind of beasts, Mr. Dodd."

The morning broke with sinister brightness; the air alarmingly transparent, the sky pure, the rim of the horizon clear and strong against the heavens. The wind and the wild seas, now vastly swollen, indefatigably hunted us. I stood on deck, choking with fear; I seemed to lose all power upon my limbs; my knees were as paper when she plunged into the murderous valleys; my heart collapsed when some black mountain fell in avalanche beside her counter, and the water, that was more than spray, swept round my ankles like a torrent. I was conscious of but one strong desire, to bear myself decently in my terrors, and whatever should happen to my life, preserve my character: as the captain said, we are a queer kind of beasts. Breakfast time came, and I made shift to swallow some hot tea. Then I must stagger below to take the time, reading the chronometer with dizzy eyes, and marvelling the while what value there could be in observations taken in a ship launched (as ours then was) like a missile among flying seas. The forenoon dragged on in a grinding monotony of peril; every spoke of the wheel a rash, but an obliged experiment—rash as a forlorn hope, needful as the leap that lands a fireman from a burning staircase. Noon was made; the captain dined on his day's work, and I on watching him; and our place was entered on the chart with a meticulous precision which seemed to me half pitiful and half absurd, since the next eye to behold that sheet of paper might be the eye of an exploring fish. One o'clock came, then two; the captain gloomed and chafed, as he held to the coaming of the house, and if ever I saw dormant murder in man's eye, it was in his. God help the hand that should have disobeyed him.

Of a sudden, he turned towards the mate, who was doing his trick at the wheel.

"Two points on the port bow," I heard him say. And he took the wheel himself.

Johnson nodded, wiped his eyes with the back of his wet hand, watched a chance as the vessel lunged up hill, and got to the main rigging, where he swarmed aloft. Up and up, I watched him go, hanging on at every ugly plunge, gaining with every lull of the schooner's movement, until, clambering into the cross-trees and clinging with one arm around the masts, I could see him take one comprehensive sweep of the southwesterly horizon. The next moment, he had slid down the backstay and stood on deck, with a grin, a nod, and a gesture of the finger that said "yes"; the next again, and he was back sweating and squirming at the wheel, his tired face streaming and smiling, and his hair and the rags and corners of his clothes lashing round him in the wind.

Nares went below, fetched up his binocular, and fell into a silent perusal of the sea-line; I also, with my unaided eyesight. Little by little, in that white waste of water, I began to make out a quarter where the whiteness appeared more condensed: the sky above was whitish likewise, and misty like a squall; and little by little there thrilled upon my ears a note deeper and more terrible than the yelling of the gale—the long, thundering roll of breakers. Nares wiped his night glass on his sleeve and passed it to me, motioning, as he did so, with his hand. An endless wilderness of raging billows came and went and danced in the circle of the glass; now and then a pale corner of sky, or the strong line of the horizon rugged with the heads of waves; and then of a sudden—come and gone ere I could fix it, with a swallow's swiftness—one glimpse of what we had come so far and paid so dear to see: the masts and rigging of a brig pencilled on heaven, with an ensign streaming at the main, and the ragged ribbons of a topsail thrashing from the yard. Again and again, with toilful searching, I recalled that apparition. There was no sign of any land; the wreck stood between sea and sky, a thing the most isolated I had ever viewed; but as we drew nearer, I perceived her to be defended by a line of breakers which drew off on either hand, and marked, indeed, the nearest segment of the reef. Heavy spray hung over them like a smoke, some hundred feet into the air; and the sound of their consecutive explosions rolled like a cannonade.

In half an hour we were close in; for perhaps as long again, we skirted that formidable barrier toward its farther side; and presently the sea began insensibly to moderate and the ship to go more sweetly. We had gained the lee of the island as (for form's sake) I may call that ring of foam and haze and thunder; and shaking out a reef, wore ship and headed for the passage.

CHAPTER XIII. THE ISLAND AND THE WRECK.

All hands were filled with joy. It was betrayed in their alacrity and easy faces: Johnson smiling broadly at the wheel, Nares studying the sketch chart of the island with an eye at peace, and the hands clustered forward, eagerly talking and pointing: so manifest was our escape, so wonderful the attraction of a single foot of earth after so many suns had set and risen on an empty sea. To add to the relief, besides, by one of those malicious coincidences which suggest for fate the image of an underbred and grinning schoolboy, we had no sooner worn ship than the wind began to abate.

For myself, however, I did but exchange anxieties. I was no sooner out of one fear than I fell upon another; no sooner secure that I should myself make the intended haven, than I began to be convinced that Trent was there before me. I climbed into the rigging, stood on the board, and eagerly scanned that ring of coral reef and bursting breaker, and the blue lagoon which they enclosed. The two islets within began to show plainly—Middle Brooks and Lower Brooks Island, the Directory named them: two low, bush-covered, rolling strips of sand, each with glittering beaches, each perhaps a mile or a mile and a half in length, running east and west, and divided by a narrow channel. Over these, innumerable as maggots, there hovered, chattered, screamed and clanged, millions of twinkling sea-birds: white and black; the black by far the largest. With singular scintillations, this vortex of winged life swayed to and fro in the strong sunshine, whirled continually through itself, and would now and again burst asunder and scatter as wide as the lagoon: so that I was irresistibly reminded of what I had read of nebular convulsions. A thin cloud overspread the area of the reef and the adjacent sea—the dust, as I could not but fancy, of earlier explosions. And a little apart, there was yet another focus of centrifugal and centripetal flight, where, hard by the deafening line of breakers, her sails (all but the tattered topsail) snugly furled down, and the red rag that marks Old England on the seas beating, union down, at the main—the Flying Scud, the fruit of so many toilers, a recollection in so many lives of men, whose tall spars had been mirrored in the remotest corners of the sea—lay stationary at last and forever, in the first stage of naval dissolution. Towards her, the taut Norah Creina, vulture-wise, wriggled to windward: come from so far to pick her bones. And, look as I pleased, there was no other presence of man or of man's handiwork; no Honolulu schooner lay there crowded with armed rivals, no smoke rose from the fire at which I fancied Trent cooking a meal of sea-birds. It seemed, after all, we were in time, and I drew a mighty breath.

I had not arrived at this reviving certainty before the breakers were already close aboard, the leadsman at his station, and the captain posted in the fore cross-trees to con us through the coral lumps of the lagoon. All circumstances were in our favour, the light behind, the sun low, the wind still fresh and steady, and the tide about the turn. A moment later we shot at racing speed betwixt two pier heads of broken water; the lead began to be cast, the captain to bawl down his anxious directions, the schooner to tack and dodge among the scattered dangers of the lagoon; and at one bell in the first dog watch, we had come to our anchor off the north-east end of Middle Brooks Island, in five fathoms water. The sails were gasketted and covered, the boats emptied of the miscellaneous stores and odds and ends of sea-furniture, that accumulate in the course of a voyage, the kedge sent ashore, and the decks tidied down: a good three-quarters of an hour's work, during which I raged about the deck like a man with a strong toothache. The transition from the wild sea to the comparative immobility of the lagoon had wrought strange distress among my nerves: I could not hold still whether in hand or foot; the slowness of the men, tired as dogs after our rough experience outside, irritated me like something personal; and the irrational screaming of the sea-birds saddened me like a dirge. It was a relief when, with Nares, and a couple of hands, I might drop into the boat and move off at last for the Flying Scud.

"She looks kind of pitiful, don't she?" observed the captain, nodding towards the wreck, from which we were separated by some half a mile. "Looks as if she didn't like her berth, and Captain Trent had used her badly. Give her ginger, boys!" he added to the hands, "and you can all have shore liberty to-night to see the birds and paint the town red."

We all laughed at the pleasantry, and the boat skimmed the faster over the rippling face of the lagoon. The Flying Scud would have seemed small enough beside the wharves of San Francisco, but she was some thrice the size of the Norah Creina, which had been so long our continent; and as we craned up at her wall-sides, she impressed us with a mountain magnitude. She lay head to the reef, where the huge blue wall of the rollers was for ever ranging up and crumbling down; and to gain her starboard side, we must pass below the stern. The rudder was hard aport, and we could read the legend:

FLYING SCUD

HULL

On the other side, about the break of the poop, some half a fathom of rope ladder trailed over the rail, and by this we made our entrance.

She was a roomy ship inside, with a raised poop standing some three feet higher than the deck, and a small forward house, for the men's bunks and the galley, just abaft the foremast. There was one boat on the house, and another and larger one, in beds on deck, on either hand of it. She had been painted white, with tropical economy, outside and in; and we found, later on, that the stanchions of the rail, hoops of the scuttle but, etc., were picked out with green. At that time, however, when we first stepped aboard, all was hidden under the droppings of innumerable sea-birds.

The birds themselves gyrated and screamed meanwhile among the rigging; and when we looked into the galley, their outrush drove us back. Savage-looking fowl they were, savagely beaked, and some of the black ones great as eagles. Half-buried in the slush, we were aware of a litter of kegs in the waist; and these, on being somewhat cleaned, proved to be water beakers and quarter casks of mess beef with some colonial brand, doubtless collected there before the Tempest hove in sight, and while Trent and his men had no better expectation than to strike for Honolulu in the boats. Nothing else was notable on deck, save where the loose topsail had played some havoc with the rigging, and there hung, and swayed, and sang in the declining wind, a raffle of intorted cordage.

With a shyness that was almost awe, Nares and I descended the companion. The stair turned upon itself and landed us just forward of a thwart-ship bulkhead that cut the poop in two. The fore part formed a kind of miscellaneous store-room, with a double-bunked division for the cook (as Nares supposed) and second mate. The after part contained, in the midst, the main cabin, running in a kind of bow into the curvature of the stern; on the port side, a pantry opening forward and a stateroom for the mate; and on the starboard, the captain's berth and water-closet. Into these we did but glance: the main cabin holding us. It was dark, for the sea-birds had obscured the skylight with their droppings; it smelt rank and fusty; and it was beset with a loud swarm of flies that beat continually in our faces. Supposing them close attendants upon man and his broken meat, I marvelled how they had found their way to Midway reef; it was sure at least some vessel must have brought them, and that long ago, for they had multiplied exceedingly. Part of the floor was strewn with a confusion of clothes, books, nautical instruments, odds and ends of finery, and such trash as might be expected from the turning out of several seamen's chests, upon a sudden emergency and after a long cruise. It was strange in that dim cabin, quivering with the near thunder of the breakers and pierced with the screaming of the fowls, to turn over so many things that other men had coveted, and prized, and worn on their warm bodies—frayed old underclothing, pyjamas of strange design, duck suits in every stage of rustiness, oil skins, pilot coats, bottles of scent, embroidered shirts, jackets of Ponjee silk—clothes for the night watch at sea or the day ashore in the hotel verandah; and mingled among these, books, cigars, fancy pipes, quantities of tobacco, many keys, a rusty pistol, and a sprinkling of cheap curiosities—Benares brass, Chinese jars and pictures, and bottles of odd shells in cotton, each designed no doubt for somebody at home—perhaps in Hull, of which Trent had been a native and his ship a citizen.

Thence we turned our attention to the table, which stood spread, as if for a meal, with stout ship's crockery and the remains of food—a pot of marmalade, dregs of coffee in the mugs, unrecognisable remains of foods, bread, some toast, and a tin of condensed milk. The table-cloth, originally of a red colour, was stained a dark brown at the captain's end, apparently with coffee; at the other end, it had been folded back, and a pen and ink-pot stood on the bare table. Stools were here and there about the table, irregularly placed, as though the meal had been finished and the men smoking and chatting; and one of the stools lay on the floor, broken.

"See! they were writing up the log," said Nares, pointing to the ink-bottle. "Caught napping, as usual. I wonder if there ever was a captain yet, that lost a ship with his log-book up to date? He generally has about a month to fill up on a clean break, like Charles Dickens and his serial novels.—What a regular, lime-juicer spread!" he added contemptuously. "Marmalade—and toast for the old man! Nasty, slovenly pigs!"

There was something in this criticism of the absent that jarred upon my feelings. I had no love indeed for Captain Trent or any of his vanished gang; but the desertion and decay of this once habitable cabin struck me hard: the death of man's handiwork is melancholy like the death of man himself; and I was impressed with an involuntary and irrational sense of tragedy in my surroundings.

"This sickens me," I said. "Let's go on deck and breathe."

The captain nodded. "It IS kind of lonely, isn't it?" he said. "But I can't go up till I get the code signals. I want to run up 'Got Left' or something, just to brighten up this island home. Captain Trent hasn't been here yet, but he'll drop in before long; and it'll cheer him up to see a signal on the brig."

"Isn't there some official expression we could use?" I asked, vastly taken by the fancy. "'Sold for the benefit of the underwriters: for further particulars, apply to J. Pinkerton, Montana Block, S.F.'"

"Well," returned Nares, "I won't say but what an old navy quartermaster might telegraph all that, if you gave him a day to do it in and a pound of tobacco for himself. But it's above my register. I must try something short and sweet: KB, urgent signal, 'Heave all aback'; or LM, urgent, 'The berth you're now in is not safe'; or what do you say to PQH?—'Tell my owners the ship answers remarkably well.'"

"It's premature," I replied; "but it seems calculated to give pain to Trent. PQH for me."

The flags were found in Trent's cabin, neatly stored behind a lettered grating; Nares chose what he required and (I following) returned on deck, where the sun had already dipped, and the dusk was coming.

"Here! don't touch that, you fool!" shouted the captain to one of the hands, who was drinking from the scuttle but. "That water's rotten!"

"Beg pardon, sir," replied the man. "Tastes quite sweet."

"Let me see," returned Nares, and he took the dipper and held it to his lips. "Yes, it's all right," he said. "Must have rotted and come sweet again. Queer, isn't it, Mr. Dodd? Though I've known the same on a Cape Horner."

There was something in his intonation that made me look him in the face; he stood a little on tiptoe to look right and left about the ship, like a man filled with curiosity, and his whole expression and bearing testified to some suppressed excitement.

"You don't believe what you're saying!" I broke out.

"O, I don't know but what I do!" he replied, laying a hand upon me soothingly. "The thing's very possible. Only, I'm bothered about something else."

And with that he called a hand, gave him the code flags, and stepped himself to the main signal halliards, which vibrated under the weight of the ensign overhead. A minute later, the American colours, which we had brought in the boat, replaced the English red, and PQH was fluttering at the fore.

"Now, then," said Nares, who had watched the breaking out of his signal with the old-maidish particularity of an American sailor, "out with those handspikes, and let's see what water there is in the lagoon."

The bars were shoved home; the barbarous cacophony of the clanking pump rose in the waist; and streams of ill-smelling water gushed on deck and made valleys in the slab guano. Nares leaned on the rail, watching the steady stream of bilge as though he found some interest in it.

"What is it that bothers you?" I asked.

"Well, I'll tell you one thing shortly," he replied. "But here's another. Do you see those boats there, one on the house and two on the beds? Well, where is the boat Trent lowered when he lost the hands?"

"Got it aboard again, I suppose," said I.

"Well, if you'll tell me why!" returned the captain.

"Then it must have been another," I suggested.

"She might have carried another on the main hatch, I won't deny," admitted Nares; "but I can't see what she wanted with it, unless it was for the old man to go out and play the accordion in, on moonlight nights."

"It can't much matter, anyway," I reflected.

"O, I don't suppose it does," said he, glancing over his shoulder at the spouting of the scuppers.

"And how long are we to keep up this racket?" I asked. "We're simply pumping up the lagoon. Captain Trent himself said she had settled down and was full forward."

"Did he?" said Nares, with a significant dryness. And almost as he spoke the pumps sucked, and sucked again, and the men threw down their bars. "There, what do you make of that?" he asked. "Now, I'll tell, Mr. Dodd," he went on, lowering his voice, but not shifting from his easy attitude against the rail, "this ship is as sound as the Norah Creina. I had a guess of it before we came aboard, and now I know."

"It's not possible!" I cried. "What do you make of Trent?"

"I don't make anything of Trent; I don't know whether he's a liar or only an old wife; I simply tell you what's the fact," said Nares. "And I'll tell you something more," he added: "I've taken the ground myself in deep-water vessels; I know what I'm saying; and I say that, when she first struck and before she bedded down, seven or eight hours' work would have got this hooker off, and there's no man that ever went two years to sea but must have known it."

I could only utter an exclamation.

Nares raised his finger warningly. "Don't let THEM get hold of it," said he. "Think what you like, but say nothing."

I glanced round; the dusk was melting into early night; the twinkle of a lantern marked the schooner's position in the distance; and our men, free from further labour, stood grouped together in the waist, their faces illuminated by their glowing pipes.

"Why didn't Trent get her off?" inquired the captain. "Why did he want to buy her back in 'Frisco for these fabulous sums, when he might have sailed her into the bay himself?"

"Perhaps he never knew her value until then," I suggested.

"I wish we knew her value now," exclaimed Nares. "However, I don't want to depress you; I'm sorry for you, Mr. Dodd; I know how bothering it must be to you; and the best I can say's this: I haven't taken much time getting down, and now I'm here I mean to work this thing in proper style. I just want to put your mind at rest: you shall have no trouble with me."

There was something trusty and friendly in his voice; and I found myself gripping hands with him, in that hard, short shake that means so much with English-speaking people.

"We'll do, old fellow," said he. "We've shaken down into pretty good friends, you and me; and you won't find me working the business any the less hard for that. And now let's scoot for supper."

After supper, with the idle curiosity of the seafarer, we pulled ashore in a fine moonlight, and landed on Middle Brook's Island. A flat beach surrounded it upon all sides; and the midst was occupied by a thicket of bushes, the highest of them scarcely five feet high, in which the seafowl lived. Through this we tried at first to strike; but it were easier to cross Trafalgar Square on a day of demonstration than to invade these haunts of sleeping sea-birds. The nests sank, and the eggs burst under footing; wings beat in our faces, beaks menaced our eyes, our minds were confounded with the screeching, and the coil spread over the island and mounted high into the air.

"I guess we'll saunter round the beach," said Nares, when we had made good our retreat.

The hands were all busy after sea-birds' eggs, so there were none to follow us. Our way lay on the crisp sand by the margin of the water: on one side, the thicket from which we had been dislodged; on the other, the face of the lagoon, barred with a broad path of moonlight, and beyond that, the line, alternately dark and shining, alternately hove high and fallen prone, of the external breakers. The beach was strewn with bits of wreck and drift: some redwood and spruce logs, no less than two lower masts of junks, and the stern-post of a European ship; all of which we looked on with a shade of serious concern, speaking of the dangers of the sea and the hard case of castaways. In this sober vein we made the greater part of the circuit of the island; had a near view of its neighbour from the southern end; walked the whole length of the westerly side in the shadow of the thicket; and came forth again into the moonlight at the opposite extremity.

On our right, at the distance of about half a mile, the schooner lay faintly heaving at her anchors. About half a mile down the beach, at a spot still hidden from us by the thicket, an upboiling of the birds showed where the men were still (with sailor-like insatiability) collecting eggs. And right before us, in a small indentation of the sand, we were aware of a boat lying high and dry, and right side up.

Nares crouched back into the shadow of the bushes.

"What the devil's this?" he whispered.

"Trent," I suggested, with a beating heart.

"We were damned fools to come ashore unarmed," said he. "But I've got to know where I stand." In the shadow, his face looked conspicuously white, and his voice betrayed a strong excitement. He took his boat's whistle from his pocket. "In case I might want to play a tune," said he, grimly, and thrusting it between his teeth, advanced into the moonlit open; which we crossed with rapid steps, looking guiltily about us as we went. Not a leaf stirred; and the boat, when we came up to it, offered convincing proof of long desertion. She was an eighteen-foot whaleboat of the ordinary type, equipped with oars and thole-pins. Two or three quarter-casks lay on the bilge amidships, one of which must have been broached, and now stank horribly; and these, upon examination, proved to bear the same New Zealand brand as the beef on board the wreck.

"Well, here's the boat," said I; "here's one of your difficulties cleared away."

"H'm," said he. There was a little water in the bilge, and here he stooped and tasted it.

"Fresh," he said. "Only rain-water."

"You don't object to that?" I asked.

"No," said he.

"Well, then, what ails you?" I cried.

"In plain United States, Mr. Dodd," he returned, "a whaleboat, five ash sweeps, and a barrel of stinking pork."

"Or, in other words, the whole thing?" I commented.

"Well, it's this way," he condescended to explain. "I've no use for a fourth boat at all; but a boat of this model tops the business. I don't say the type's not common in these waters; it's as common as dirt; the traders carry them for surf-boats. But the Flying Scud? a deep-water tramp, who was lime-juicing around between big ports, Calcutta and Rangoon and 'Frisco and the Canton River? No, I don't see it."

We were leaning over the gunwale of the boat as we spoke. The captain stood nearest the bow, and he was idly playing with the trailing painter, when a thought arrested him. He hauled the line in hand over hand, and stared, and remained staring, at the end.

"Anything wrong with it?" I asked.

"Do you know, Mr. Dodd," said he, in a queer voice, "this painter's been cut? A sailor always seizes a rope's end, but this is sliced short off with the cold steel. This won't do at all for the men," he added. "Just stand by till I fix it up more natural."

"Any guess what it all means?" I asked.

"Well, it means one thing," said he. "It means Trent was a liar. I guess the story of the Flying Scud was a sight more picturesque than he gave out."

Half an hour later, the whaleboat was lying astern of the Norah Creina; and Nares and I sought our bunks, silent and half-bewildered by our late discoveries.

CHAPTER XIV. THE CABIN OF THE "FLYING SCUD."

The sun of the morrow had not cleared the morning bank: the lake of the lagoon, the islets, and the wall of breakers now beginning to subside, still lay clearly pictured in the flushed obscurity of early day, when we stepped again upon the deck of the Flying Scud: Nares, myself, the mate, two of the hands, and one dozen bright, virgin axes, in war against that massive structure. I think we all drew pleasurable breath; so profound in man is the instinct of destruction, so engaging is the interest of the chase. For we were now about to taste, in a supreme degree, the double joys of demolishing a toy and playing "Hide the handkerchief": sports from which we had all perhaps desisted since the days of infancy. And the toy we were to burst in pieces was a deep-sea ship; and the hidden good for which we were to hunt was a prodigious fortune.

The decks were washed down, the main hatch removed, and a gun-tackle purchase rigged before the boat arrived with breakfast. I had grown so suspicious of the wreck, that it was a positive relief to me to look down into the hold, and see it full, or nearly full, of undeniable rice packed in the Chinese fashion in boluses of matting. Breakfast over, Johnson and the hands turned to upon the cargo; while Nares and I, having smashed open the skylight and rigged up a windsail on deck, began the work of rummaging the cabins.

I must not be expected to describe our first day's work, or (for that matter) any of the rest, in order and detail as it occurred. Such particularity might have been possible for several officers and a draft of men from a ship of war, accompanied by an experienced secretary with a knowledge of shorthand. For two plain human beings, unaccustomed to the use of the broad-axe and consumed with an impatient greed of the result, the whole business melts, in the retrospect, into a nightmare of exertion, heat, hurry, and bewilderment; sweat pouring from the face like rain, the scurry of rats, the choking exhalations of the bilge, and the throbs and splinterings of the toiling axes. I shall content myself with giving the cream of our discoveries in a logical rather than a temporal order; though the two indeed practically coincided, and we had finished our exploration of the cabin, before we could be certain of the nature of the cargo.

Nares and I began operations by tossing up pell-mell through the companion, and piling in a squalid heap about the wheel, all clothes, personal effects, the crockery, the carpet, stale victuals, tins of meat, and in a word, all movables from the main cabin. Thence, we transferred our attention to the captain's quarters on the starboard side. Using the blankets for a basket, we sent up the books, instruments, and clothes to swell our growing midden on the deck; and then Nares, going on hands and knees, began to forage underneath the bed. Box after box of Manilla cigars rewarded his search. I took occasion to smash some of these boxes open, and even to guillotine the bundles of cigars; but quite in vain—no secret cache of opium encouraged me to continue.

"I guess I've got hold of the dicky now!" exclaimed Nares, and turning round from my perquisitions, I found he had drawn forth a heavy iron box, secured to the bulkhead by chain and padlock. On this he was now gazing, not with the triumph that instantly inflamed my own bosom, but with a somewhat foolish appearance of surprise.

"By George, we have it now!" I cried, and would have shaken hands with my companion; but he did not see, or would not accept, the salutation.

"Let's see what's in it first," he remarked dryly. And he adjusted the box upon its side, and with some blows of an axe burst the lock open. I threw myself beside him, as he replaced the box on its bottom and removed the lid. I cannot tell what I expected; a million's worth of diamonds might perhaps have pleased me; my cheeks burned, my heart throbbed to bursting; and lo! there was disclosed but a trayful of papers, neatly taped, and a cheque-book of the customary pattern. I made a snatch at the tray to see what was beneath; but the captain's hand fell on mine, heavy and hard.

"Now, boss!" he cried, not unkindly, "is this to be run shipshape? or is it a Dutch grab-racket?"

And he proceeded to untie and run over the contents of the papers, with a serious face and what seemed an ostentation of delay. Me and my impatience it would appear he had forgotten; for when he was quite done, he sat a while thinking, whistled a bar or two, refolded the papers, tied them up again; and then, and not before, deliberately raised the tray.

I saw a cigar-box, tied with a piece of fishing-line, and four fat canvas-bags. Nares whipped out his knife, cut the line, and opened the box. It was about half full of sovereigns.

"And the bags?" I whispered.

The captain ripped them open one by one, and a flood of mixed silver coin burst forth and rattled in the rusty bottom of the box. Without a word, he set to work to count the gold.

"What is this?" I asked.

"It's the ship's money," he returned, doggedly continuing his work.

"The ship's money?" I repeated. "That's the money Trent tramped and traded with? And there's his cheque-book to draw upon his owners? And he has left it?"

"I guess he has," said Nares, austerely, jotting down a note of the gold; and I was abashed into silence till his task should be completed.

It came, I think, to three hundred and seventy-eight pounds sterling; some nineteen pounds of it in silver: all of which we turned again into the chest.

"And what do you think of that?" I asked.

"Mr. Dodd," he replied, "you see something of the rumness of this job, but not the whole. The specie bothers you, but what gets me is the papers. Are you aware that the master of a ship has charge of all the cash in hand, pays the men advances, receives freight and passage money, and runs up bills in every port? All this he does as the owner's confidential agent, and his integrity is proved by his receipted bills. I tell you, the captain of a ship is more likely to forget his pants than these bills which guarantee his character. I've known men drown to save them: bad men, too; but this is the shipmaster's honour. And here this Captain Trent—not hurried, not threatened with anything but a free passage in a British man-of-war—has left them all behind! I don't want to express myself too strongly, because the facts appear against me, but the thing is impossible."

Dinner came to us not long after, and we ate it on deck, in a grim silence, each privately racking his brain for some solution of the mysteries. I was indeed so swallowed up in these considerations, that the wreck, the lagoon, the islets, and the strident sea-fowl, the strong sun then beating on my head, and even the gloomy countenance of the captain at my elbow, all vanished from the field of consciousness. My mind was a blackboard, on which I scrawled and blotted out hypotheses; comparing each with the pictorial records in my memory: cyphering with pictures. In the course of this tense mental exercise I recalled and studied the faces of one memorial masterpiece, the scene of the saloon; and here I found myself, on a sudden, looking in the eyes of the Kanaka.

"There's one thing I can put beyond doubt, at all events," I cried, relinquishing my dinner and getting briskly afoot. "There was that Kanaka I saw in the bar with Captain Trent, the fellow the newspapers and ship's articles made out to be a Chinaman. I mean to rout his quarters out and settle that."

"All right," said Nares. "I'll lazy off a bit longer, Mr. Dodd; I feel pretty rocky and mean."

We had thoroughly cleared out the three after-compartments of the ship: all the stuff from the main cabin and the mate's and captain's quarters lay piled about the wheel; but in the forward stateroom with the two bunks, where Nares had said the mate and cook most likely berthed, we had as yet done nothing. Thither I went. It was very bare; a few photographs were tacked on the bulkhead, one of them indecent; a single chest stood open, and, like all we had yet found, it had been partly rifled. An armful of two-shilling novels proved to me beyond a doubt it was a European's; no Chinaman would have possessed any, and the most literate Kanaka conceivable in a ship's galley was not likely to have gone beyond one. It was plain, then, that the cook had not berthed aft, and I must look elsewhere.

The men had stamped down the nests and driven the birds from the galley, so that I could now enter without contest. One door had been already blocked with rice; the place was in part darkness, full of a foul stale smell, and a cloud of nasty flies; it had been left, besides, in some disorder, or else the birds, during their time of tenancy, had knocked the things about; and the floor, like the deck before we washed it, was spread with pasty filth. Against the wall, in the far corner, I found a handsome chest of camphor-wood bound with brass, such as Chinamen and sailors love, and indeed all of mankind that plies in the Pacific. From its outside view I could thus make no deduction; and, strange to say, the interior was concealed. All the other chests, as I have said already, we had found gaping open, and their contents scattered abroad; the same remark we found to apply afterwards in the quarters of the seamen; only this camphor-wood chest, a singular exception, was both closed and locked.

I took an axe to it, readily forced the paltry Chinese fastening, and, like a Custom-House officer, plunged my hands among the contents. For some while I groped among linen and cotton. Then my teeth were set on edge with silk, of which I drew forth several strips covered with mysterious characters. And these settled the business, for I recognised them as a kind of bed-hanging popular with the commoner class of the Chinese. Nor were further evidences wanting, such as night-clothes of an extraordinary design, a three-stringed Chinese fiddle, a silk handkerchief full of roots and herbs, and a neat apparatus for smoking opium, with a liberal provision of the drug. Plainly, then, the cook had been a Chinaman; and, if so, who was Jos. Amalu? Or had Jos. stolen the chest before he proceeded to ship under a false name and domicile? It was possible, as anything was possible in such a welter; but, regarded as a solution, it only led and left me deeper in the bog. For why should this chest have been deserted and neglected, when the others were rummaged or removed? and where had Jos. come by that second chest, with which (according to the clerk at the What Cheer) he had started for Honolulu?

"And how have YOU fared?" inquired the captain, whom I found luxuriously reclining in our mound of litter. And the accent on the pronoun, the heightened colour of the speaker's face, and the contained excitement in his tones, advertised me at once that I had not been alone to make discoveries.

"I have found a Chinaman's chest in the galley," said I, "and John (if there was any John) was not so much as at the pains to take his opium."

Nares seemed to take it mighty quietly. "That so?" said he. "Now, cast your eyes on that and own you're beaten!" And with a formidable clap of his open hand he flattened out before me, on the deck, a pair of newspapers.

I gazed upon them dully, being in no mood for fresh discoveries.

"Look at them, Mr. Dodd," cried the captain sharply. "Can't you look at them?" And he ran a dirty thumb along the title. "'Sydney Morning Herald, November 26th,' can't you make that out?" he cried, with rising energy. "And don't you know, sir, that not thirteen days after this paper appeared in New South Pole, this ship we're standing in heaved her blessed anchors out of China? How did the Sydney Morning Herald get to Hong Kong in thirteen days? Trent made no land, he spoke no ship, till he got here. Then he either got it here or in Hong Kong. I give you your choice, my son!" he cried, and fell back among the clothes like a man weary of life.

"Where did you find them?" I asked. "In that black bag?"

"Guess so," he said. "You needn't fool with it. There's nothing else but a lead-pencil and a kind of worked-out knife."

I looked in the bag, however, and was well rewarded.

"Every man to his trade, captain," said I. "You're a sailor, and you've given me plenty of points; but I am an artist, and allow me to inform you this is quite as strange as all the rest. The knife is a palette-knife; the pencil a Winsor and Newton, and a B B B at that. A palette-knife and a B B B on a tramp brig! It's against the laws of nature."

"It would sicken a dog, wouldn't it?" said Nares.

"Yes," I continued, "it's been used by an artist, too: see how it's sharpened—not for writing—no man could write with that. An artist, and straight from Sydney? How can he come in?"

"O, that's natural enough," sneered Nares. "They cabled him to come up and illustrate this dime novel."

We fell a while silent.

"Captain," I said at last, "there is something deuced underhand about this brig. You tell me you've been to sea a good part of your life. You must have seen shady things done on ships, and heard of more. Well, what is this? is it insurance? is it piracy? what is it ABOUT? what can it be for?"

"Mr. Dodd," returned Nares, "you're right about me having been to sea the bigger part of my life. And you're right again when you think I know a good many ways in which a dishonest captain mayn't be on the square, nor do exactly the right thing by his owners, and altogether be just a little too smart by ninety-nine and three-quarters. There's a good many ways, but not so many as you'd think; and not one that has any mortal thing to do with Trent. Trent and his whole racket has got to do with nothing—that's the bed-rock fact; there's no sense to it, and no use in it, and no story to it: it's a beastly dream. And don't you run away with that notion that landsmen take about ships. A society actress don't go around more publicly than what a ship does, nor is more interviewed, nor more humbugged, nor more run after by all sorts of little fussinesses in brass buttons. And more than an actress, a ship has a deal to lose; she's capital, and the actress only character—if she's that. The ports of the world are thick with people ready to kick a captain into the penitentiary if he's not as bright as a dollar and as honest as the morning star; and what with Lloyd keeping watch and watch in every corner of the three oceans, and the insurance leeches, and the consuls, and the customs bugs, and the medicos, you can only get the idea by thinking of a landsman watched by a hundred and fifty detectives, or a stranger in a village Down East."

"Well, but at sea?" I said.

"You make me tired," retorted the captain. "What's the use—at sea? Everything's got to come to bearings at some port, hasn't it? You can't stop at sea for ever, can you?—No; the Flying Scud is rubbish; if it meant anything, it would have to mean something so almighty intricate that James G. Blaine hasn't got the brains to engineer it; and I vote for more axeing, pioneering, and opening up the resources of this phenomenal brig, and less general fuss," he added, arising. "The dime-museum symptoms will drop in of themselves, I guess, to keep us cheery."

But it appeared we were at the end of discoveries for the day; and we left the brig about sundown, without being further puzzled or further enlightened. The best of the cabin spoils—books, instruments, papers, silks, and curiosities—we carried along with us in a blanket, however, to divert the evening hours; and when supper was over, and the table cleared, and Johnson set down to a dreary game of cribbage between his right hand and his left, the captain and I turned out our blanket on the floor, and sat side by side to examine and appraise the spoils.

The books were the first to engage our notice. These were rather numerous (as Nares contemptuously put it) "for a lime-juicer." Scorn of the British mercantile marine glows in the breast of every Yankee merchant captain; as the scorn is not reciprocated, I can only suppose it justified in fact; and certainly the old country mariner appears of a less studious disposition. The more credit to the officers of the Flying Scud, who had quite a library, both literary and professional. There were Findlay's five directories of the world—all broken-backed, as is usual with Findlay, and all marked and scribbled over with corrections and additions—several books of navigation, a signal code, and an Admiralty book of a sort of orange hue, called Islands of the Eastern Pacific Ocean, Vol. III., which appeared from its imprint to be the latest authority, and showed marks of frequent consultation in the passages about the French Frigate Shoals, the Harman, Cure, Pearl, and Hermes reefs, Lisiansky Island, Ocean Island, and the place where we then lay—Brooks or Midway. A volume of Macaulay's Essays and a shilling Shakespeare led the van of the belles lettres; the rest were novels: several Miss Braddons—of course, Aurora Floyd, which has penetrated to every isle of the Pacific, a good many cheap detective books, Rob Roy, Auerbach's Auf der Hohe in the German, and a prize temperance story, pillaged (to judge by the stamp) from an Anglo-Indian circulating library.

"The Admiralty man gives a fine picture of our island," remarked Nares, who had turned up Midway Island. "He draws the dreariness rather mild, but you can make out he knows the place."

"Captain," I cried, "you've struck another point in this mad business. See here," I went on eagerly, drawing from my pocket a crumpled fragment of the Daily Occidental which I had inherited from Jim: "'misled by Hoyt's Pacific Directory'? Where's Hoyt?"

"Let's look into that," said Nares. "I got that book on purpose for this cruise." Therewith he fetched it from the shelf in his berth, turned to Midway Island, and read the account aloud. It stated with precision that the Pacific Mail Company were about to form a depot there, in preference to Honolulu, and that they had already a station on the island.

"I wonder who gives these Directory men their information," Nares reflected. "Nobody can blame Trent after that. I never got in company with squarer lying; it reminds a man of a presidential campaign."

"All very well," said I. "That's your Hoyt, and a fine, tall copy. But what I want to know is, where is Trent's Hoyt?"

"Took it with him," chuckled Nares. "He had left everything else, bills and money and all the rest; he was bound to take something, or it would have aroused attention on the Tempest:

'Happy thought,' says he, 'let's take Hoyt.'"

"And has it not occurred to you," I went on, "that all the Hoyts in creation couldn't have misled Trent, since he had in his hand that red admiralty book, an official publication, later in date, and particularly full on Midway Island?"

"That's a fact!" cried Nares; "and I bet the first Hoyt he ever saw was out of the mercantile library of San Francisco. Looks as if he had brought her here on purpose, don't it? But then that's inconsistent with the steam-crusher of the sale. That's the trouble with this brig racket; any one can make half a dozen theories for sixty or seventy per cent of it; but when they're made, there's always a fathom or two of slack hanging out of the other end."

I believe our attention fell next on the papers, of which we had altogether a considerable bulk. I had hoped to find among these matter for a full-length character of Captain Trent; but here I was doomed, on the whole, to disappointment. We could make out he was an orderly man, for all his bills were docketed and preserved. That he was convivial, and inclined to be frugal even in conviviality, several documents proclaimed. Such letters as we found were, with one exception, arid notes from tradesmen. The exception, signed Hannah Trent, was a somewhat fervid appeal for a loan. "You know what misfortunes I have had to bear," wrote Hannah, "and how much I am disappointed in George. The landlady appeared a true friend when I first came here, and I thought her a perfect lady. But she has come out since then in her true colours; and if you will not be softened by this last appeal, I can't think what is to become of your affectionate——" and then the signature. This document was without place or date, and a voice told me that it had gone likewise without answer. On the whole, there were few letters anywhere in the ship; but we found one before we were finished, in a seaman's chest, of which I must transcribe some sentences. It was dated from some place on the Clyde. "My dearest son," it ran, "this is to tell you your dearest father passed away, Jan twelft, in the peace of the Lord. He had your photo and dear David's lade upon his bed, made me sit by him. Let's be a' thegither, he said, and gave you all his blessing. O my dear laddie, why were nae you and Davie here? He would have had a happier passage. He spok of both of ye all night most beautiful, and how ye used to stravaig on the Saturday afternoons, and of auld Kelvinside. Sooth the tune to me, he said, though it was the Sabbath, and I had to sooth him Kelvin Grove, and he looked at his fiddle, the dear man. I cannae bear the sight of it, he'll never play it mair. O my lamb, come home to me, I'm all by my lane now." The rest was in a religious vein and quite conventional. I have never seen any one more put out than Nares, when I handed him this letter; he had read but a few words, before he cast it down; it was perhaps a minute ere he picked it up again, and the performance was repeated the third time before he reached the end.

"It's touching, isn't it?" said I.

For all answer, Nares exploded in a brutal oath; and it was some half an hour later that he vouchsafed an explanation. "I'll tell you what broke me up about that letter," said he. "My old man played the fiddle, played it all out of tune: one of the things he played was Martyrdom, I remember—it was all martyrdom to me. He was a pig of a father, and I was a pig of a son; but it sort of came over me I would like to hear that fiddle squeak again. Natural," he added; "I guess we're all beasts."

"All sons are, I guess," said I. "I have the same trouble on my conscience: we can shake hands on that." Which (oddly enough, perhaps) we did.

Amongst the papers we found a considerable sprinkling of photographs; for the most part either of very debonair-looking young ladies or old women of the lodging-house persuasion. But one among them was the means of our crowning discovery.

"They're not pretty, are they, Mr. Dodd?" said Nares, as he passed it over.

"Who?" I asked, mechanically taking the card (it was a quarter-plate) in hand, and smothering a yawn; for the hour was late, the day had been laborious, and I was wearying for bed.

"Trent and Company," said he. "That's a historic picture of the gang."

I held it to the light, my curiosity at a low ebb: I had seen Captain Trent once, and had no delight in viewing him again. It was a photograph of the deck of the brig, taken from forward: all in apple-pie order; the hands gathered in the waist, the officers on the poop. At the foot of the card was written "Brig Flying Scud, Rangoon," and a date; and above or below each individual figure the name had been carefully noted.

As I continued to gaze, a shock went through me; the dimness of sleep and fatigue lifted from my eyes, as fog lifts in the channel; and I beheld with startled clearness the photographic presentment of a crowd of strangers. "J. Trent, Master" at the top of the card directed me to a smallish, weazened man, with bushy eyebrows and full white beard, dressed in a frock coat and white trousers; a flower stuck in his button-hole, his bearded chin set forward, his mouth clenched with habitual determination. There was not much of the sailor in his looks, but plenty of the martinet: a dry, precise man, who might pass for a preacher in some rigid sect; and whatever he was, not the Captain Trent of San Francisco. The men, too, were all new to me: the cook, an unmistakable Chinaman, in his characteristic dress, standing apart on the poop steps. But perhaps I turned on the whole with the greatest curiosity to the figure labelled "E. Goddedaal, 1st off." He whom I had never seen, he might be the identical; he might be the clue and spring of all this mystery; and I scanned his features with the eye of a detective. He was of great stature, seemingly blonde as a viking, his hair clustering round his head in frowsy curls, and two enormous whiskers, like the tusks of some strange animal, jutting from his cheeks. With these virile appendages and the defiant attitude in which he stood, the expression of his face only imperfectly harmonised. It was wild, heroic, and womanish looking; and I felt I was prepared to hear he was a sentimentalist, and to see him weep.

For some while I digested my discovery in private, reflecting how best, and how with most of drama, I might share it with the captain. Then my sketch-book came in my head; and I fished it out from where it lay, with other miscellaneous possessions, at the foot of my bunk and turned to my sketch of Captain Trent and the survivors of the British brig Flying Scud in the San Francisco bar-room.

"Nares," said I, "I've told you how I first saw Captain Trent in that saloon in 'Frisco? how he came with his men, one of them a Kanaka with a canary-bird in a cage? and how I saw him afterwards at the auction, frightened to death, and as much surprised at how the figures skipped up as anybody there? Well," said I, "there's the man I saw"—and I laid the sketch before him—"there's Trent of 'Frisco and there are his three hands. Find one of them in the photograph, and I'll be obliged."

Nares compared the two in silence. "Well," he said at last, "I call this rather a relief: seems to clear the horizon. We might have guessed at something of the kind from the double ration of chests that figured."

"Does it explain anything?" I asked.

"It would explain everything," Nares replied, "but for the steam-crusher. It'll all tally as neat as a patent puzzle, if you leave out the way these people bid the wreck up. And there we come to a stone wall. But whatever it is, Mr. Dodd, it's on the crook."

"And looks like piracy," I added.

"Looks like blind hookey!" cried the captain. "No, don't you deceive yourself; neither your head nor mine is big enough to put a name on this business."

CHAPTER XV. THE CARGO OF THE "FLYING SCUD."

In my early days I was a man, the most wedded to his idols of my generation. I was a dweller under roofs: the gull of that which we call civilisation; a superstitious votary of the plastic arts; a cit; and a prop of restaurants. I had a comrade in those days, somewhat of an outsider, though he moved in the company of artists, and a man famous in our small world for gallantry, knee breeches, and dry and pregnant sayings. He, looking on the long meals and waxing bellies of the French, whom I confess I somewhat imitated, branded me as "a cultivator of restaurant fat." And I believe he had his finger on the dangerous spot; I believe, if things had gone smooth with me, I should be now swollen like a prize-ox in body, and fallen in mind to a thing perhaps as low as many types of bourgeois—the implicit or exclusive artist. That was a home word of Pinkerton's, deserving to be writ in letters of gold on the portico of every school of art: "What I can't see is why you should want to do nothing else." The dull man is made, not by the nature, but by the degree of his immersion in a single business. And all the more if that be sedentary, uneventful, and ingloriously safe. More than one half of him will then remain unexercised and undeveloped; the rest will be distended and deformed by over-nutrition, over-cerebration, and the heat of rooms. And I have often marvelled at the impudence of gentlemen, who describe and pass judgment on the life of man, in almost perfect ignorance of all its necessary elements and natural careers. Those who dwell in clubs and studios may paint excellent pictures or write enchanting novels. There is one thing that they should not do: they should pass no judgment on man's destiny, for it is a thing with which they are unacquainted. Their own life is an excrescence of the moment, doomed, in the vicissitude of history, to pass and disappear: the eternal life of man, spent under sun and rain and in rude physical effort, lies upon one side, scarce changed since the beginning.

I would I could have carried along with me to Midway Island all the writers and the prating artists of my time. Day after day of hope deferred, of heat, of unremitting toil; night after night of aching limbs, bruised hands, and a mind obscured with the grateful vacancy of physical fatigue: the scene, the nature of my employment; the rugged speech and faces of my fellow-toilers, the glare of the day on deck, the stinking twilight in the bilge, the shrill myriads of the ocean-fowl: above all, the sense of our immitigable isolation from the world and from the current epoch;—keeping another time, some eras old; the new day heralded by no daily paper, only by the rising sun; and the State, the churches, the peopled empires, war, and the rumours of war, and the voices of the arts, all gone silent as in the days ere they were yet invented. Such were the conditions of my new experience in life, of which (if I had been able) I would have had all my confreres and contemporaries to partake: forgetting, for that while, the orthodoxies of the moment, and devoted to a single and material purpose under the eye of heaven.

Of the nature of our task, I must continue to give some summary idea. The forecastle was lumbered with ship's chandlery, the hold nigh full of rice, the lazarette crowded with the teas and silks. These must all be dug out; and that made but a fraction of our task. The hold was ceiled throughout; a part, where perhaps some delicate cargo was once stored, had been lined, in addition, with inch boards; and between every beam there was a movable panel into the bilge. Any of these, the bulkheads of the cabins, the very timbers of the hull itself, might be the place of hiding. It was therefore necessary to demolish, as we proceeded, a great part of the ship's inner skin and fittings, and to auscultate what remained, like a doctor sounding for a lung disease. Upon the return, from any beam or bulkhead, of a flat or doubtful sound, we must up axe and hew into the timber: a violent and—from the amount of dry rot in the wreck—a mortifying exercise. Every night saw a deeper inroad into the bones of the Flying Scud—more beams tapped and hewn in splinters, more planking peeled away and tossed aside—and every night saw us as far as ever from the end and object of our arduous devastation. In this perpetual disappointment, my courage did not fail me, but my spirits dwindled; and Nares himself grew silent and morose. At night, when supper was done, we passed an hour in the cabin, mostly without speech: I, sometimes dozing over a book; Nares, sullenly but busily drilling sea-shells with the instrument called a Yankee Fiddle. A stranger might have supposed we were estranged; as a matter of fact, in this silent comradeship of labour, our intimacy grew.

I had been struck, at the first beginning of our enterprise upon the wreck, to find the men so ready at the captain's lightest word. I dare not say they liked, but I can never deny that they admired him thoroughly. A mild word from his mouth was more valued than flattery and half a dollar from myself; if he relaxed at all from his habitual attitude of censure, smiling alacrity surrounded him; and I was led to think his theory of captainship, even if pushed to excess, reposed upon some ground of reason. But even terror and admiration of the captain failed us before the end. The men wearied of the hopeless, unremunerative quest and the long strain of labour. They began to shirk and grumble. Retribution fell on them at once, and retribution multiplied the grumblings. With every day it took harder driving to keep them to the daily drudge; and we, in our narrow boundaries, were kept conscious every moment of the ill-will of our assistants.

In spite of the best care, the object of our search was perfectly well known to all on board; and there had leaked out besides some knowledge of those inconsistencies that had so greatly amazed the captain and myself. I could overhear the men debate the character of Captain Trent, and set forth competing theories of where the opium was stowed; and as they seemed to have been eavesdropping on ourselves, I thought little shame to prick up my ears when I had the return chance of spying upon them, in this way. I could diagnose their temper and judge how far they were informed upon the mystery of the Flying Scud. It was after having thus overheard some almost mutinous speeches that a fortunate idea crossed my mind. At night, I matured it in my bed, and the first thing the next morning, broached it to the captain.

"Suppose I spirit up the hands a bit," I asked, "by the offer of a reward?"

"If you think you're getting your month's wages out of them the way it is, I don't," was his reply. "However, they are all the men you've got, and you're the supercargo."

This, from a person of the captain's character, might be regarded as complete adhesion; and the crew were accordingly called aft. Never had the captain worn a front more menacing. It was supposed by all that some misdeed had been discovered, and some surprising punishment was to be announced.

"See here, you!" he threw at them over his shoulder as he walked the deck, "Mr. Dodd here is going to offer a reward to the first man who strikes the opium in that wreck. There's two ways of making a donkey go; both good, I guess: the one's kicks and the other's carrots. Mr. Dodd's going to try the carrots. Well, my sons,"—and here he faced the men for the first time with his hands behind him—"if that opium's not found in five days, you can come to me for the kicks."

He nodded to the present narrator, who took up the tale. "Here is what I propose, men," said I: "I put up one hundred and fifty dollars. If any man can lay hands on the stuff right away, and off his own club, he shall have the hundred and fifty down. If any one can put us on the scent of where to look, he shall have a hundred and twenty-five, and the balance shall be for the lucky one who actually picks it up. We'll call it the Pinkerton Stakes, captain," I added, with a smile.

"Call it the Grand Combination Sweep, then," cries he. "For I go you better.—Look here, men, I make up this jack-pot to two hundred and fifty dollars, American gold coin."

"Thank you, Captain Nares," said I; "that was handsomely done."

"It was kindly meant," he returned.

The offer was not made in vain; the hands had scarce yet realised the magnitude of the reward, they had scarce begun to buzz aloud in the extremity of hope and wonder, ere the Chinese cook stepped forward with gracious gestures and explanatory smiles.

"Captain," he began, "I serv-um two year Melican navy; serv-um six year mail-boat steward. Savvy plenty."

"Oho!" cried Nares, "you savvy plenty, do you? (Beggar's seen this trick in the mail-boats, I guess.) Well, why you no savvy a little sooner, sonny?"

"I think bimeby make-um reward," replied the cook, with smiling dignity.

"Well, you can't say fairer than that," the captain admitted, "and now the reward's offered, you'll talk? Speak up, then. Suppose you speak true, you get reward. See?"

"I think long time," replied the Chinaman. "See plenty litty mat lice; too-muchy plenty litty mat lice; sixty ton, litty mat lice. I think all-e-time: perhaps plenty opium plenty litty mat lice."

"Well, Mr. Dodd, how does that strike you?" asked the captain. "He may be right, he may be wrong. He's likely to be right: for if he isn't, where can the stuff be? On the other hand, if he's wrong, we destroy a hundred and fifty tons of good rice for nothing. It's a point to be considered."

"I don't hesitate," said I. "Let's get to the bottom of the thing. The rice is nothing; the rice will neither make nor break us."

"That's how I expected you to see it," returned Nares.

And we called the boat away and set forth on our new quest.

The hold was now almost entirely emptied; the mats (of which there went forty to the short ton) had been stacked on deck, and now crowded the ship's waist and forecastle. It was our task to disembowel and explore six thousand individual mats, and incidentally to destroy a hundred and fifty tons of valuable food. Nor were the circumstances of the day's business less strange than its essential nature. Each man of us, armed with a great knife, attacked the pile from his own quarter, slashed into the nearest mat, burrowed in it with his hands, and shed forth the rice upon the deck, where it heaped up, overflowed, and was trodden down, poured at last into the scuppers, and occasionally spouted from the vents. About the wreck, thus transformed into an overflowing granary, the sea-fowl swarmed in myriads and with surprising insolence. The sight of so much food confounded them; they deafened us with their shrill tongues, swooped in our midst, dashed in our faces, and snatched the grain from between our fingers. The men—their hands bleeding from these assaults—turned savagely on the offensive, drove their knives into the birds, drew them out crimsoned, and turned again to dig among the rice, unmindful of the gawking creatures that struggled and died among their feet. We made a singular picture: the hovering and diving birds; the bodies of the dead discolouring the rice with blood; the scuppers vomiting breadstuff; the men, frenzied by the gold hunt, toiling, slaying, and shouting aloud: over all, the lofty intricacy of rigging and the radiant heaven of the Pacific. Every man there toiled in the immediate hope of fifty dollars; and I, of fifty thousand. Small wonder if we waded callously in blood and food.

It was perhaps about ten in the forenoon when the scene was interrupted. Nares, who had just ripped open a fresh mat, drew forth, and slung at his feet, among the rice, a papered tin box.

"How's that?" he shouted.

A cry broke from all hands: the next moment, forgetting their own disappointment, in that contagious sentiment of success, they gave three cheers that scared the sea-birds; and the next, they had crowded round the captain, and were jostling together and groping with emulous hands in the new-opened mat. Box after box rewarded them, six in all; wrapped, as I have said, in a paper envelope, and the paper printed on, in Chinese characters.

Nares turned to me and shook my hand. "I began to think we should never see this day," said he. "I congratulate you, Mr. Dodd, on having pulled it through."

The captain's tones affected me profoundly; and when Johnson and the men pressed round me in turn with congratulations, the tears came in my eyes.

"These are five-tael boxes, more than two pounds," said Nares, weighing one in his hand. "Say two hundred and fifty dollars to the mat. Lay into it, boys! We'll make Mr. Dodd a millionnaire before dark."

It was strange to see with what a fury we fell to. The men had now nothing to expect; the mere idea of great sums inspired them with disinterested ardour. Mats were slashed and disembowelled, the rice flowed to our knees in the ship's waist, the sweat ran in our eyes and blinded us, our arms ached to agony; and yet our fire abated not. Dinner came; we were too weary to eat, too hoarse for conversation; and yet dinner was scarce done, before we were afoot again and delving in the rice. Before nightfall not a mat was unexplored, and we were face to face with the astonishing result.

For of all the inexplicable things in the story of the Flying Scud, here was the most inexplicable. Out of the six thousand mats, only twenty were found to have been sugared; in each we found the same amount, about twelve pounds of drug; making a grand total of two hundred and forty pounds. By the last San Francisco quotation, opium was selling for a fraction over twenty dollars a pound; but it had been known not long before to bring as much as forty in Honolulu, where it was contraband.

Taking, then, this high Honolulu figure, the value of the opium on board the Flying Scud fell considerably short of ten thousand dollars, while at the San Francisco rate it lacked a trifle of five thousand. And fifty thousand was the price that Jim and I had paid for it. And Bellairs had been eager to go higher! There is no language to express the stupor with which I contemplated this result.

It may be argued we were not yet sure; there might be yet another cache; and you may be certain in that hour of my distress the argument was not forgotten. There was never a ship more ardently perquested; no stone was left unturned, and no expedient untried; day after day of growing despair, we punched and dug in the brig's vitals, exciting the men with promises and presents; evening after evening Nares and I sat face to face in the narrow cabin, racking our minds for some neglected possibility of search. I could stake my salvation on the certainty of the result: in all that ship there was nothing left of value but the timber and the copper nails. So that our case was lamentably plain; we had paid fifty thousand dollars, borne the charges of the schooner, and paid fancy interest on money; and if things went well with us, we might realise fifteen per cent of the first outlay. We were not merely bankrupt, we were comic bankrupts: a fair butt for jeering in the streets. I hope I bore the blow with a good countenance; indeed, my mind had long been quite made up, and since the day we found the opium I had known the result. But the thought of Jim and Mamie ached in me like a physical pain, and I shrank from speech and companionship.

I was in this frame of mind when the captain proposed that we should land upon the island. I saw he had something to say, and only feared it might be consolation; for I could just bear my grief, not bungling sympathy; and yet I had no choice but to accede to his proposal.

We walked awhile along the beach in silence. The sun overhead reverberated rays of heat; the staring sand, the glaring lagoon, tortured our eyes; and the birds and the boom of the far-away breakers made a savage symphony.

"I don't require to tell you the game's up?" Nares asked.

"No," said I.

"I was thinking of getting to sea to-morrow," he pursued.

"The best thing you can do," said I.

"Shall we say Honolulu?" he inquired.

"O, yes; let's stick to the programme," I cried. "Honolulu be it!"

There was another silence, and then Nares cleared his throat.

"We've been pretty good friends, you and me, Mr. Dodd," he resumed. "We've been going through the kind of thing that tries a man. We've had the hardest kind of work, we've been badly backed, and now we're badly beaten. And we've fetched through without a word of disagreement. I don't say this to praise myself: it's my trade; it's what I'm paid for, and trained for, and brought up to. But it was another thing for you; it was all new to you; and it did me good to see you stand right up to it and swing right into it, day in, day out. And then see how you've taken this disappointment, when everybody knows you must have been tautened up to shying-point! I wish you'd let me tell you, Mr. Dodd, that you've stood out mighty manly and handsomely in all this business, and made every one like you and admire you. And I wish you'd let me tell you, besides, that I've taken this wreck business as much to heart as you have; something kind of rises in my throat when I think we're beaten; and if I thought waiting would do it, I would stick on this reef until we starved."

I tried in vain to thank him for these generous words, but he was beforehand with me in a moment.

"I didn't bring you ashore to sound my praises," he interrupted. "We understand one another now, that's all; and I guess you can trust me. What I wished to speak about is more important, and it's got to be faced. What are we to do about the Flying Scud and the dime novel?"

"I really have thought nothing about that," I replied. "But I expect I mean to get at the bottom of it; and if the bogus Captain Trent is to be found on the earth's surface, I guess I mean to find him."

"All you've got to do is talk," said Nares; "you can make the biggest kind of boom; it isn't often the reporters have a chance at such a yarn as this; and I can tell you how it will go. It will go by telegraph, Mr. Dodd; it'll be telegraphed by the column, and head-lined, and frothed up, and denied by authority, and it'll hit bogus Captain Trent in a Mexican bar-room, and knock over bogus Goddedaal in a slum somewhere up the Baltic, and bowl down Hardy and Brown in sailors' music halls round Greenock. O, there's no doubt you can have a regular domestic Judgment Day. The only point is whether you deliberately want to."

"Well," said I, "I deliberately don't want one thing: I deliberately don't want to make a public exhibition of myself and Pinkerton: so moral—smuggling opium; such damned fools—paying fifty thousand for a 'dead horse'!"

"No doubt it might damage you in a business sense," the captain agreed. "And I'm pleased you take that view; for I've turned kind of soft upon the job. There's been some crookedness about, no doubt of it; but, Law bless you! if we dropped upon the troupe, all the premier artists would slip right out with the boodle in their grip-sacks, and you'd only collar a lot of old mutton-headed shell-backs that didn't know the back of the business from the front. I don't take much stock in Mercantile Jack, you know that; but, poor devil, he's got to go where he's told; and if you make trouble, ten to one it'll make you sick to see the innocents who have to stand the racket. It would be different if we understood the operation; but we don't, you see: there's a lot of queer corners in life; and my vote is to let the blame' thing lie."

"You speak as if we had that in our power," I objected.

"And so we have," said he.

"What about the men?" I asked. "They know too much by half; and you can't keep them from talking."

"Can't I?" returned Nares. "I bet a boarding-master can! They can be all half-seas-over, when they get ashore, blind drunk by dark, and cruising out of the Golden Gate in different deep-sea ships by the next morning. Can't keep them from talking, can't I? Well, I can make 'em talk separate, leastways. If a whole crew came talking, parties would listen; but if it's only one lone old shell-back, it's the usual yarn. And at least, they needn't talk before six months, or—if we have luck, and there's a whaler handy—three years. And by that time, Mr. Dodd, it's ancient history."

"That's what they call Shanghaiing, isn't it?" I asked. "I thought it belonged to the dime novel."

"O, dime novels are right enough," returned the captain. "Nothing wrong with the dime novel, only that things happen thicker than they do in life, and the practical seamanship is off-colour."

"So we can keep the business to ourselves," I mused.

"There's one other person that might blab," said the captain. "Though I don't believe she has anything left to tell."

"And who is SHE?" I asked.

"The old girl there," he answered, pointing to the wreck. "I know there's nothing in her; but somehow I'm afraid of some one else—it's the last thing you'd expect, so it's just the first that'll happen—some one dropping into this God-forgotten island where nobody drops in, waltzing into that wreck that we've grown old with searching, stooping straight down, and picking right up the very thing that tells the story. What's that to me? you may ask, and why am I gone Soft Tommy on this Museum of Crooks? They've smashed up you and Mr. Pinkerton; they've turned my hair grey with conundrums; they've been up to larks, no doubt; and that's all I know of them—you say. Well, and that's just where it is. I don't know enough; I don't know what's uppermost; it's just such a lot of miscellaneous eventualities as I don't care to go stirring up; and I ask you to let me deal with the old girl after a patent of my own."

"Certainly—what you please," said I, scarce with attention, for a new thought now occupied my brain. "Captain," I broke out, "you are wrong: we cannot hush this up. There is one thing you have forgotten."

"What is that?" he asked.

"A bogus Captain Trent, a bogus Goddedaal, a whole bogus crew, have all started home," said I. "If we are right, not one of them will reach his journey's end. And do you mean to say that such a circumstance as that can pass without remark?"

"Sailors," said the captain, "only sailors! If they were all bound for one place, in a body, I don't say so; but they're all going separate—to Hull, to Sweden, to the Clyde, to the Thames. Well, at each place, what is it? Nothing new. Only one sailor man missing: got drunk, or got drowned, or got left: the proper sailor's end."

Something bitter in the thought and in the speaker's tones struck me hard. "Here is one that has got left!" I cried, getting sharply to my feet; for we had been some time seated. "I wish it were the other. I don't—don't relish going home to Jim with this!"

"See here," said Nares, with ready tact, "I must be getting aboard. Johnson's in the brig annexing chandlery and canvas, and there's some things in the Norah that want fixing against we go to sea. Would you like to be left here in the chicken-ranch? I'll send for you to supper."

I embraced the proposal with delight. Solitude, in my frame of mind, was not too dearly purchased at the risk of sunstroke or sand-blindness; and soon I was alone on the ill-omened islet. I should find it hard to tell of what I thought—of Jim, of Mamie, of our lost fortune, of my lost hopes, of the doom before me: to turn to at some mechanical occupation in some subaltern rank, and to toil there, unremarked and unamused, until the hour of the last deliverance. I was, at least, so sunk in sadness that I scarce remarked where I was going; and chance (or some finer sense that lives in us, and only guides us when the mind is in abeyance) conducted my steps into a quarter of the island where the birds were few. By some devious route, which I was unable to retrace for my return, I was thus able to mount, without interruption, to the highest point of land. And here I was recalled to consciousness by a last discovery.

The spot on which I stood was level, and commanded a wide view of the lagoon, the bounding reef, the round horizon. Nearer hand I saw the sister islet, the wreck, the Norah Creina, and the Norah's boat already moving shoreward. For the sun was now low, flaming on the sea's verge; and the galley chimney smoked on board the schooner.

It thus befell that though my discovery was both affecting and suggestive, I had no leisure to examine further. What I saw was the blackened embers of fire of wreck. By all the signs, it must have blazed to a good height and burned for days; from the scantling of a spar that lay upon the margin only half consumed, it must have been the work of more than one; and I received at once the image of a forlorn troop of castaways, houseless in that lost corner of the earth, and feeding there their fire of signal. The next moment a hail reached me from the boat; and bursting through the bushes and the rising sea-fowl, I said farewell (I trust for ever) to that desert isle.

CHAPTER XVI. IN WHICH I TURN SMUGGLER, AND THE CAPTAIN CASUIST

The last night at Midway, I had little sleep; the next morning, after the sun was risen, and the clatter of departure had begun to reign on deck, I lay a long while dozing; and when at last I stepped from the companion, the schooner was already leaping through the pass into the open sea. Close on her board, the huge scroll of a breaker unfurled itself along the reef with a prodigious clamour; and behind I saw the wreck vomiting into the morning air a coil of smoke. The wreaths already blew out far to leeward, flames already glittered in the cabin skylight; and the sea-fowl were scattered in surprise as wide as the lagoon. As we drew farther off, the conflagration of the Flying Scud flamed higher; and long after we had dropped all signs of Midway Island, the smoke still hung in the horizon like that of a distant steamer. With the fading out of that last vestige, the Norah Creina, passed again into the empty world of cloud and water by which she had approached; and the next features that appeared, eleven days later, to break the line of sky, were the arid mountains of Oahu.

It has often since been a comfortable thought to me that we had thus destroyed the tell-tale remnants of the Flying Scud; and often a strange one that my last sight and reminiscence of that fatal ship should be a pillar of smoke on the horizon. To so many others besides myself the same appearance had played a part in the various stages of that business: luring some to what they little imagined, filling some with unimaginable terrors. But ours was the last smoke raised in the story; and with its dying away the secret of the Flying Scud became a private property.

It was by the first light of dawn that we saw, close on board, the metropolitan island of Hawaii. We held along the coast, as near as we could venture, with a fresh breeze and under an unclouded heaven; beholding, as we went, the arid mountain sides and scrubby cocoa-palms of that somewhat melancholy archipelago. About four of the afternoon we turned Waimanolo Point, the westerly headland of the great bight of Honolulu; showed ourselves for twenty minutes in full view; and then fell again to leeward, and put in the rest of daylight, plying under shortened sail under the lee of Waimanolo.

A little after dark we beat once more about the point, and crept cautiously toward the mouth of the Pearl Lochs, where Jim and I had arranged I was to meet the smugglers. The night was happily obscure, the water smooth. We showed, according to instructions, no light on deck: only a red lantern dropped from either cathead to within a couple of feet of the water. A lookout was stationed on the bowsprit end, another in the crosstrees; and the whole ship's company crowded forward, scouting for enemies or friends. It was now the crucial moment of our enterprise; we were now risking liberty and credit; and that for a sum so small to a man in my bankrupt situation, that I could have laughed aloud in bitterness. But the piece had been arranged, and we must play it to the finish.

For some while, we saw nothing but the dark mountain outline of the island, the torches of native fishermen glittering here and there along the foreshore, and right in the midst that cluster of brave lights with which the town of Honolulu advertises itself to the seaward. Presently a ruddy star appeared inshore of us, and seemed to draw near unsteadily. This was the anticipated signal; and we made haste to show the countersign, lowering a white light from the quarter, extinguishing the two others, and laying the schooner incontinently to. The star approached slowly; the sounds of oars and of men's speech came to us across the water; and then a voice hailed us.

"Is that Mr. Dodd?"

"Yes," I returned. "Is Jim Pinkerton there?"

"No, sir," replied the voice. "But there's one of his crowd here; name of Speedy."

"I'm here, Mr. Dodd," added Speedy himself. "I have letters for you."

"All right," I replied. "Come aboard, gentlemen, and let me see my mail."

A whaleboat accordingly ranged alongside, and three men boarded us: my old San Francisco friend, the stock-gambler Speedy, a little wizened person of the name of Sharpe, and a big, flourishing, dissipated-looking man called Fowler. The two last (I learned afterward) were frequent partners; Sharpe supplied the capital, and Fowler, who was quite a character in the islands and occupied a considerable station, brought activity, daring, and a private influence, highly necessary in the case. Both seemed to approach the business with a keen sense of romance; and I believe this was the chief attraction, at least with Fowler—for whom I early conceived a sentiment of liking. But in that first moment I had something else to think of than to judge my new acquaintances; and before Speedy had fished out the letters, the full extent of our misfortune was revealed.

"We've rather bad news for you, Mr. Dodd," said Fowler. "Your firm's gone up."

"Already!" I exclaimed.

"Well, it was thought rather a wonder Pinkerton held on as long as he did," was the reply. "The wreck deal was too big for your credit; you were doing a big business, no doubt, but you were doing it on precious little capital; and when the strain came, you were bound to go. Pinkerton's through all right: seven cents dividend; some remarks made, but nothing to hurt; the press let you down easy—I guess Jim had relations there. The only trouble is, that all this Flying Scud affair got in the papers with the rest; everybody's wide awake in Honolulu, and the sooner we get the stuff in and the dollars out, the better for all concerned."

"Gentlemen," said I, "you must excuse me. My friend, the captain here, will drink a glass of champagne with you to give you patience; but as for myself, I am unfit even for ordinary conversation till I have read these letters."

They demurred a little: and indeed the danger of delay seemed obvious; but the sight of my distress, which I was unable entirely to control, appealed strongly to their good-nature; and I was suffered at last to get by myself on deck, where, by the light of a lantern smuggled under shelter of the low rail, I read the following wretched correspondence.

"My dear Loudon," ran the first, "this will be handed you by your friend Speedy of the Catamount. His sterling character and loyal devotion to yourself pointed him out as the best man for our purposes in Honolulu—the parties on the spot being difficult to manipulate. A man called Billy Fowler (you must have heard of Billy) is the boss; he is in politics some, and squares the officers. I have hard times before me in the city, but I feel as bright as a dollar and as strong as John L. Sullivan. What with Mamie here, and my partner speeding over the seas, and the bonanza in the wreck, I feel like I could juggle with the Pyramids of Egypt, same as conjurers do with aluminium balls. My earnest prayers follow you, Loudon, that you may feel the way I do—just inspired! My feet don't touch the ground; I kind of swim. Mamie is like Moses and Aaron that held up the other individual's arms. She carries me along like a horse and buggy. I am beating the record.

"Your true partner,

"J. PINKERTON."

Number two was in a different style:—

"My dearest Loudon, how am I to prepare you for this dire intelligence? O dear me, it will strike you to the earth. The Fiat has gone forth; our firm went bust at a quarter before twelve. It was a bill of Bradley's (for $200) that brought these vast operations to a close, and evolved liabilities of upwards of two hundred and fifty thousand. O, the shame and pity of it! and you but three weeks gone! Loudon, don't blame your partner: if human hands and brains could have sufficed, I would have held the thing together. But it just slowly crumbled; Bradley was the last kick, but the blamed business just MELTED. I give the liabilities; it's supposed they're all in; for the cowards were waiting, and the claims were filed like taking tickets to hear Patti. I don't quite have the hang of the assets yet, our interests were so extended; but I am at it day and night, and I guess will make a creditable dividend. If the wreck pans out only half the way it ought, we'll turn the laugh still. I am as full of grit and work as ever, and just tower above our troubles. Mamie is a host in herself. Somehow I feel like it was only me that had gone bust, and you and she soared clear of it. Hurry up. That's all you have to do.

"Yours ever,

"J. PINKERTON."

The third was yet more altered:—

"My poor Loudon," it began, "I labour far into the night getting our affairs in order; you could not believe their vastness and complexity. Douglas B. Longhurst said humorously that the receiver's work would be cut out for him. I cannot deny that some of them have a speculative look. God forbid a sensitive, refined spirit like yours should ever come face to face with a Commissioner in Bankruptcy; these men get all the sweetness knocked right out of them. But I could bear up better if it weren't for press comments. Often and often, Loudon, I recall to mind your most legitimate critiques of the press system. They published an interview with me, not the least like what I said, and with JEERING comments; it would make your blood boil, it was literally INHUMANE; I wouldn't have written it about a yellow dog that was in trouble like what I am. Mamie just winced, the first time she has turned a hair right through the whole catastrophe. How wonderfully true was what you said long ago in Paris, about touching on people's personal appearance! The fellow said—" And then these words had been scored through; and my distressed friend turned to another subject. "I cannot bear to dwell upon our assets. They simply don't show up. Even Thirteen Star, as sound a line as can be produced upon this coast, goes begging. The wreck has thrown a blight on all we ever touched. And where's the use? God never made a wreck big enough to fill our deficit. I am haunted by the thought that you may blame me; I know how I despised your remonstrances. O, Loudon, don't be hard on your miserable partner. The funny-dog business is what kills. I fear your stern rectitude of mind like the eye of God. I cannot think but what some of my books seem mixed up; otherwise, I don't seem to see my way as plain as I could wish to. Or else my brain is gone soft. Loudon, if there should be any unpleasantness, you can trust me to do the right thing and keep you clear. I've been telling them already, how you had no business grip and never saw the books. O, I trust I have done right in this! I knew it was a liberty; I know you may justly complain; but it was some things that were said. And mind you, all legitimate business! Not even your shrinking sensitiveness could find fault with the first look of one of them, if they had panned out right. And you know, the Flying Scud was the biggest gamble of the crowd, and that was your own idea. Mamie says she never could bear to look you in the face, if that idea had been mine, she is SO conscientious!

"Your broken-hearted

"JIM."

The last began without formality:—

"This is the end of me commercially. I give up; my nerve is gone. I suppose I ought to be glad; for we're through the court. I don't know as ever I knew how, and I'm sure I don't remember. If it pans out—the wreck, I mean—we'll go to Europe, and live on the interest of our money. No more work for me. I shake when people speak to me. I have gone on, hoping and hoping, and working and working, and the lead has pinched right out. I want to lie on my back in a garden and read Shakespeare and E. P. Roe. Don't suppose it's cowardice, Loudon. I'm a sick man. Rest is what I must have. I've worked hard all my life; I never spared myself; every dollar I ever made, I've coined my brains for it. I've never done a mean thing; I've lived respectable, and given to the poor. Who has a better right to a holiday than I have? And I mean to have a year of it straight out; and if I don't, I shall lie right down here in my tracks, and die of worry and brain trouble. Don't mistake. That's so. If there are any pickings at all, TRUST SPEEDY; don't let the creditors get wind of what there is. I helped you when you were down; help me now. Don't deceive yourself; you've got to help me right now, or never. I am clerking, and NOT FIT TO CYPHER. Mamie's typewriting at the Phoenix Guano Exchange, down town. The light is right out of my life. I know you'll not like to do what I propose. Think only of this; that it's life or death for

"JIM PINKERTON.

"P.S. Our figure was seven per cent. O, what a fall was there! Well, well, it's past mending; I don't want to whine. But, Loudon, I do want to live. No more ambition; all I ask is life. I have so much to make it sweet to me! I am clerking, and USELESS AT THAT. I know I would have fired such a clerk inside of forty minutes, in MY time. But my time's over. I can only cling on to you. Don't fail

"JIM PINKERTON."

There was yet one more postscript, yet one more outburst of self-pity and pathetic adjuration; and a doctor's opinion, unpromising enough, was besides enclosed. I pass them both in silence. I think shame to have shown, at so great length, the half-baked virtues of my friend dissolving in the crucible of sickness and distress; and the effect upon my spirits can be judged already. I got to my feet when I had done, drew a deep breath, and stared hard at Honolulu. One moment the world seemed at an end; the next, I was conscious of a rush of independent energy. On Jim I could rely no longer; I must now take hold myself. I must decide and act on my own better thoughts.

The word was easy to say; the thing, at the first blush, was undiscoverable. I was overwhelmed with miserable, womanish pity for my broken friend; his outcries grieved my spirit; I saw him then and now—then, so invincible; now, brought so low—and knew neither how to refuse, nor how to consent to his proposal. The remembrance of my father, who had fallen in the same field unstained, the image of his monument incongruously rising, a fear of the law, a chill air that seemed to blow upon my fancy from the doors of prisons, and the imaginary clank of fetters, recalled me to a different resolve. And then again, the wails of my sick partner intervened. So I stood hesitating, and yet with a strong sense of capacity behind: sure, if I could but choose my path, that I should walk in it with resolution.

Then I remembered that I had a friend on board, and stepped to the companion.

"Gentlemen," said I, "only a few moments more: but these, I regret to say, I must make more tedious still by removing your companion. It is indispensable that I should have a word or two with Captain Nares."

Both the smugglers were afoot at once, protesting. The business, they declared, must be despatched at once; they had run risk enough, with a conscience; and they must either finish now, or go.

"The choice is yours, gentlemen," said I, "and, I believe, the eagerness. I am not yet sure that I have anything in your way; even if I have, there are a hundred things to be considered; and I assure you it is not at all my habit to do business with a pistol to my head."

"That is all very proper, Mr. Dodd; there is no wish to coerce you, believe me," said Fowler; "only, please consider our position. It is really dangerous; we were not the only people to see your schooner off Waimanolo."

"Mr. Fowler," I replied, "I was not born yesterday. Will you allow me to express an opinion, in which I may be quite wrong, but to which I am entirely wedded? If the custom-house officers had been coming, they would have been here now. In other words, somebody is working the oracle, and (for a good guess) his name is Fowler."

Both men laughed loud and long; and being supplied with another bottle of Longhurst's champagne, suffered the captain and myself to leave them without further word.

I gave Nares the correspondence, and he skimmed it through.

"Now, captain," said I, "I want a fresh mind on this. What does it mean?"

"It's large enough text," replied the captain. "It means you're to stake your pile on Speedy, hand him over all you can, and hold your tongue. I almost wish you hadn't shown it me," he added wearily. "What with the specie from the wreck and the opium money, it comes to a biggish deal."

"That's supposing that I do it?" said I.

"Exactly," said he, "supposing you do it."

"And there are pros and cons to that," I observed.

"There's San Quentin, to start in with," said the captain; "and suppose you clear the penitentiary, there's the nasty taste in the mouth. The figure's big enough to make bad trouble, but it's not big enough to be picturesque; and I should guess a man always feels kind of small who has sold himself under six cyphers. That would be my way, at least; there's an excitement about a million that might carry me on; but the other way, I should feel kind of lonely when I woke in bed. Then there's Speedy. Do you know him well?"

"No, I do not," said I.

"Well, of course he can vamoose with the entire speculation, if he chooses," pursued the captain, "and if he don't I can't see but what you've got to support and bed and board with him to the end of time. I guess it would weary me. Then there's Mr. Pinkerton, of course. He's been a good friend to you, hasn't he? Stood by you, and all that? and pulled you through for all he was worth?"

"That he has," I cried; "I could never begin telling you my debt to him!"

"Well, and that's a consideration," said the captain. "As a matter of principle, I wouldn't look at this business at the money. 'Not good enough,' would be my word. But even principle goes under when it comes to friends—the right sort, I mean. This Pinkerton is frightened, and he seems sick; the medico don't seem to care a cent about his state of health; and you've got to figure how you would like it if he came to die. Remember, the risk of this little swindle is all yours; it's no sort of risk to Mr. Pinkerton. Well, you've got to put it that way plainly, and see how you like the sound of it: my friend Pinkerton is in danger of the New Jerusalem, I am in danger of San Quentin; which risk do I propose to run?"

"That's an ugly way to put it," I objected, "and perhaps hardly fair. There's right and wrong to be considered."

"Don't know the parties," replied Nares; "and I'm coming to them, anyway. For it strikes me, when it came to smuggling opium, you walked right up?"

"So I did," I said; "sick I am to have to say it!"

"All the same," continued Nares, "you went into the opium-smuggling with your head down; and a good deal of fussing I've listened to, that you hadn't more of it to smuggle. Now, maybe your partner's not quite fixed the same as you are; maybe he sees precious little difference between the one thing and the other."

"You could not say truer: he sees none, I do believe," cried I; "and though I see one, I could never tell you how."

"We never can," said the oracular Nares; "taste is all a matter of opinion. But the point is, how will your friend take it? You refuse a favour, and you take the high horse at the same time; you disappoint him, and you rap him over the knuckles. It won't do, Mr. Dodd; no friendship can stand that. You must be as good as your friend, or as bad as your friend, or start on a fresh deal without him."

"I don't see it!" said I. "You don't know Jim!"

"Well, you WILL see," said Nares. "And now, here's another point. This bit of money looks mighty big to Mr. Pinkerton; it may spell life or health to him; but among all your creditors, I don't see that it amounts to a hill of beans—I don't believe it'll pay their car-fares all round. And don't you think you'll ever get thanked. You were known to pay a long price for the chance of rummaging that wreck; you do the rummaging, you come home, and you hand over ten thousand—or twenty, if you like—a part of which you'll have to own up you made by smuggling; and, mind! you'll never get Billy Fowler to stick his name to a receipt. Now just glance at the transaction from the outside, and see what a clear case it makes. Your ten thousand is a sop; and people will only wonder you were so damned impudent as to offer such a small one! Whichever way you take it, Mr. Dodd, the bottom's out of your character; so there's one thing less to be considered."

"I daresay you'll scarce believe me," said I, "but I feel that a positive relief."

"You must be made some way different from me, then," returned Nares. "And, talking about me, I might just mention how I stand. You'll have no trouble from me—you've trouble enough of your own; and I'm friend enough, when a friend's in need, to shut my eyes and go right where he tells me. All the same, I'm rather queerly fixed. My owners'll have to rank with the rest on their charter-party. Here am I, their representative! and I have to look over the ship's side while the bankrupt walks his assets ashore in Mr. Speedy's hat-box. It's a thing I wouldn't do for James G. Blaine; but I'll do it for you, Mr. Dodd, and only sorry I can't do more."

"Thank you, captain; my mind is made up," said I. "I'll go straight, RUAT COELUM! I never understood that old tag before to-night."

"I hope it isn't my business that decides you?" asked the captain.

"I'll never deny it was an element," said I. "I hope, I hope I'm not cowardly; I hope I could steal for Jim myself; but when it comes to dragging in you and Speedy, and this one and the other, why, Jim has got to die, and there's an end. I'll try and work for him when I get to 'Frisco, I suppose; and I suppose I'll fail, and look on at his death, and kick myself: it can't be helped—I'll fight it on this line."

"I don't say as you're wrong," replied Nares, "and I'll be hanged if I know if you're right. It suits me anyway. And look here—hadn't you better just show our friends over the side?" he added; "no good of being at the risk and worry of smuggling for the benefit of creditors."

"I don't think of the creditors," said I. "But I've kept this pair so long, I haven't got the brass to fire them now."

Indeed, I believe that was my only reason for entering upon a transaction which was now outside my interest, but which (as it chanced) repaid me fifty-fold in entertainment. Fowler and Sharpe were both preternaturally sharp; they did me the honour in the beginning to attribute to myself their proper vices; and before we were done had grown to regard me with an esteem akin to worship. This proud position I attained by no more recondite arts, than telling the mere truth and unaffectedly displaying my indifference to the result. I have doubtless stated the essentials of all good diplomacy, which may be rather regarded, therefore, as a grace of state, than the effect of management. For to tell the truth is not in itself diplomatic, and to have no care for the result a thing involuntary. When I mentioned, for instance, that I had but two hundred and forty pounds of drug, my smugglers exchanged meaning glances, as who should say, "Here is a foeman worthy of our steel!" But when I carelessly proposed thirty-five dollars a pound, as an amendment to their offered twenty, and wound up with the remark: "The whole thing is a matter of moonshine to me, gentlemen. Take it or want it, and fill your glasses"—I had the indescribable gratification to see Sharpe nudge Fowler warningly, and Fowler choke down the jovial acceptance that stood ready on his lips, and lamely substitute a "No—no more wine, please, Mr. Dodd!" Nor was this all: for when the affair was settled at fifty dollars a pound—a shrewd stroke of business for my creditors—and our friends had got on board their whaleboat and shoved off, it appeared they were imperfectly acquainted with the conveyance of sound upon still water, and I had the joy to overhear the following testimonial.

"Deep man, that Dodd," said Sharpe.

And the bass-toned Fowler echoed, "Damned if I understand his game."

Thus we were left once more alone upon the Norah Creina; and the news of the night, and the lamentations of Pinkerton, and the thought of my own harsh decision, returned and besieged me in the dark. According to all the rubbish I had read, I should have been sustained by the warm consciousness of virtue. Alas, I had but the one feeling: that I had sacrificed my sick friend to the fear of prison-cells and stupid starers. And no moralist has yet advanced so far as to number cowardice amongst the things that are their own reward.

CHAPTER XVII. LIGHT FROM THE MAN OF WAR.

In the early sunlight of the next day, we tossed close off the buoy and saw the city sparkle in its groves about the foot of the Punch-bowl, and the masts clustering thick in the small harbour. A good breeze, which had risen with the sea, carried us triumphantly through the intricacies of the passage; and we had soon brought up not far from the landing-stairs. I remember to have remarked an ugly horned reptile of a modern warship in the usual moorings across the port, but my mind was so profoundly plunged in melancholy that I paid no heed.

Indeed, I had little time at my disposal. Messieurs Sharpe and Fowler had left the night before in the persuasion that I was a liar of the first magnitude; the genial belief brought them aboard again with the earliest opportunity, proffering help to one who had proved how little he required it, and hospitality to so respectable a character. I had business to mind, I had some need both of assistance and diversion; I liked Fowler—I don't know why; and in short, I let them do with me as they desired. No creditor intervening, I spent the first half of the day inquiring into the conditions of the tea and silk market under the auspices of Sharpe; lunched with him in a private apartment at the Hawaiian Hotel—for Sharpe was a teetotaler in public; and about four in the afternoon was delivered into the hands of Fowler. This gentleman owned a bungalow on the Waikiki beach; and there in company with certain young bloods of Honolulu, I was entertained to a sea-bathe, indiscriminate cocktails, a dinner, a hula-hula, and (to round off the night), poker and assorted liquors. To lose money in the small hours to pale, intoxicated youth, has always appeared to me a pleasure overrated. In my then frame of mind, I confess I found it even delightful; put up my money (or rather my creditors'), and put down Fowler's champagne with equal avidity and success; and awoke the next morning to a mild headache and the rather agreeable lees of the last night's excitement. The young bloods, many of whom were still far from sober, had taken the kitchen into their own hands, vice the Chinaman deposed; and since each was engaged upon a dish of his own, and none had the least scruple in demolishing his neighbour's handiwork, I became early convinced that many eggs would be broken and few omelets made. The discovery of a jug of milk and a crust of bread enabled me to stay my appetite; and since it was Sunday, when no business could be done, and the festivities were to be renewed that night in the abode of Fowler, it occurred to me to slip silently away and enjoy some air and solitude.

I turned seaward under the dead crater known as Diamond Head. My way was for some time under the shade of certain thickets of green, thorny trees, dotted with houses. Here I enjoyed some pictures of the native life: wide-eyed, naked children, mingled with pigs; a youth asleep under a tree; an old gentleman spelling through glasses his Hawaiian Bible; the somewhat embarrassing spectacle of a lady at her bath in a spring; and the glimpse of gaudy-coloured gowns in the deep shade of the houses. Thence I found a road along the beach itself, wading in sand, opposed and buffeted by the whole weight of the Trade: on one hand, the glittering and sounding surf, and the bay lively with many sails; on the other, precipitous, arid gullies and sheer cliffs, mounting towards the crater and the blue sky. For all the companionship of skimming vessels, the place struck me with a sense of solitude. There came in my head what I had been told the day before at dinner, of a cavern above in the bowels of the volcano, a place only to be visited with the light of torches, a treasure-house of the bones of priests and warriors, and clamorous with the voice of an unseen river pouring seaward through the crannies of the mountain. At the thought, it was revealed to me suddenly, how the bungalows, and the Fowlers, and the bright busy town and crowding ships, were all children of yesterday; and for centuries before, the obscure life of the natives, with its glories and ambitions, its joys and crimes and agonies, had rolled unseen, like the mountain river, in that sea-girt place. Not Chaldea appeared more ancient, nor the Pyramids of Egypt more abstruse; and I heard time measured by "the drums and tramplings" of immemorial conquests, and saw myself the creature of an hour. Over the bankruptcy of Pinkerton and Dodd, of Montana Block, S. F., and the conscientious troubles of the junior partner, the spirit of eternity was seen to smile.

To this mood of philosophic sadness, my excesses of the night before no doubt contributed; for more things than virtue are at times their own reward: but I was greatly healed at least of my distresses. And while I was yet enjoying my abstracted humour, a turn of the beach brought me in view of the signal-station, with its watch-house and flag-staff, perched on the immediate margin of a cliff. The house was new and clean and bald, and stood naked to the Trades. The wind beat about it in loud squalls; the seaward windows rattled without mercy; the breach of the surf below contributed its increment of noise; and the fall of my foot in the narrow verandah passed unheard by those within.

There were two on whom I thus entered unexpectedly: the look-out man, with grizzled beard, keen seaman's eyes, and that brand on his countenance that comes of solitary living; and a visitor, an oldish, oratorical fellow, in the smart tropical array of the British man-o'-war's man, perched on a table, and smoking a cigar. I was made pleasantly welcome, and was soon listening with amusement to the sea-lawyer.

"No, if I hadn't have been born an Englishman," was one of his sentiments, "damn me! I'd rather 'a been born a Frenchy! I'd like to see another nation fit to black their boots." Presently after, he developed his views on home politics with similar trenchancy. "I'd rather be a brute beast than what I'd be a liberal," he said. "Carrying banners and that! a pig's got more sense. Why, look at our chief engineer—they do say he carried a banner with his own 'ands: 'Hooroar for Gladstone!' I suppose, or 'Down with the Aristocracy!' What 'arm does the aristocracy do? Show me a country any good without one! Not the States; why, it's the 'ome of corruption! I knew a man—he was a good man, 'ome born—who was signal quartermaster in the Wyandotte. He told me he could never have got there if he hadn't have 'run with the boys'—told it me as I'm telling you. Now, we're all British subjects here——" he was going on.

"I am afraid I am an American," I said apologetically.

He seemed the least bit taken aback, but recovered himself; and with the ready tact of his betters, paid me the usual British compliment on the riposte. "You don't say so!" he exclaimed. "Well, I give you my word of honour, I'd never have guessed it. Nobody could tell it on you," said he, as though it were some form of liquor.

I thanked him, as I always do, at this particular stage, with his compatriots: not so much perhaps for the compliment to myself and my poor country, as for the revelation (which is ever fresh to me) of Britannic self-sufficiency and taste. And he was so far softened by my gratitude as to add a word of praise on the American method of lacing sails. "You're ahead of us in lacing sails," he said. "You can say that with a clear conscience."

"Thank you," I replied. "I shall certainly do so."

At this rate, we got along swimmingly; and when I rose to retrace my steps to the Fowlery, he at once started to his feet and offered me the welcome solace of his company for the return. I believe I discovered much alacrity at the idea, for the creature (who seemed to be unique, or to represent a type like that of the dodo) entertained me hugely. But when he had produced his hat, I found I was in the way of more than entertainment; for on the ribbon I could read the legend: "H.M.S. Tempest."

"I say," I began, when our adieus were paid, and we were scrambling down the path from the look-out, "it was your ship that picked up the men on board the Flying Scud, wasn't it?"

"You may say so," said he. "And a blessed good job for the Flying-Scuds. It's a God-forsaken spot, that Midway Island."

"I've just come from there," said I. "It was I who bought the wreck."

"Beg your pardon, sir," cried the sailor: "gen'lem'n in the white schooner?"

"The same," said I.

My friend saluted, as though we were now, for the first time, formally introduced.

"Of course," I continued, "I am rather taken up with the whole story; and I wish you would tell me what you can of how the men were saved."

"It was like this," said he. "We had orders to call at Midway after castaways, and had our distance pretty nigh run down the day before. We steamed half-speed all night, looking to make it about noon; for old Tootles—beg your pardon, sir—the captain—was precious scared of the place at night. Well, there's nasty, filthy currents round that Midway; YOU know, as has been there; and one on 'em must have set us down. Leastways, about six bells, when we had ought to been miles away, some one sees a sail, and lo and be'old, there was the spars of a full-rigged brig! We raised her pretty fast, and the island after her; and made out she was hard aground, canted on her bilge, and had her ens'n flying, union down. It was breaking 'igh on the reef, and we laid well out, and sent a couple of boats. I didn't go in neither; only stood and looked on; but it seems they was all badly scared and muddled, and didn't know which end was uppermost. One on 'em kep' snivelling and wringing of his 'ands; he come on board all of a sop like a monthly nurse. That Trent, he come first, with his 'and in a bloody rag. I was near 'em as I am to you; and I could make out he was all to bits—'eard his breath rattle in his blooming lungs as he come down the ladder. Yes, they was a scared lot, small blame to 'em, I say! The next after Trent, come him as was mate."

"Goddedaal!" I exclaimed.

"And a good name for him too," chuckled the man-o'-war's man, who probably confounded the word with a familiar oath. "A good name too; only it weren't his. He was a gen'lem'n born, sir, as had gone maskewerading. One of our officers knowed him at 'ome, reckonises him, steps up, 'olds out his 'and right off, and says he: ''Ullo, Norrie, old chappie!' he says. The other was coming up, as bold as look at it; didn't seem put out—that's where blood tells, sir! Well, no sooner does he 'ear his born name given him, than he turns as white as the Day of Judgment, stares at Mr. Sebright like he was looking at a ghost, and then (I give you my word of honour) turned to, and doubled up in a dead faint. 'Take him down to my berth,' says Mr. Sebright. ''Tis poor old Norrie Carthew,' he says."

"And what—what sort of a gentleman was this Mr. Carthew?" I gasped.

"The ward-room steward told me he was come of the best blood in England," was my friend's reply: "Eton and 'Arrow bred;—and might have been a bar'net!"

"No, but to look at?" I corrected him.

"The same as you or me," was the uncompromising answer: "not much to look at. I didn't know he was a gen'lem'n; but then, I never see him cleaned up."

"How was that?" I cried. "O yes, I remember: he was sick all the way to 'Frisco, was he not?"

"Sick, or sorry, or something," returned my informant. "My belief, he didn't hanker after showing up. He kep' close; the ward-room steward, what took his meals in, told me he ate nex' to nothing; and he was fetched ashore at 'Frisco on the quiet. Here was how it was. It seems his brother had took and died, him as had the estate. This one had gone in for his beer, by what I could make out; the old folks at 'ome had turned rusty; no one knew where he had gone to. Here he was, slaving in a merchant brig, shipwrecked on Midway, and packing up his duds for a long voyage in a open boat. He comes on board our ship, and by God, here he is a landed proprietor, and may be in Parliament to-morrow! It's no less than natural he should keep dark: so would you and me in the same box."

"I daresay," said I. "But you saw more of the others?"

"To be sure," says he: "no 'arm in them from what I see. There was one 'Ardy there: colonial born he was, and had been through a power of money. There was no nonsense about 'Ardy; he had been up, and he had come down, and took it so. His 'eart was in the right place; and he was well-informed, and knew French; and Latin, I believe, like a native! I liked that 'Ardy; he was a good-looking boy, too."

"Did they say much about the wreck?" I asked.

"There wasn't much to say, I reckon," replied the man-o'-war's man. "It was all in the papers. 'Ardy used to yarn most about the coins he had gone through; he had lived with book-makers, and jockeys, and pugs, and actors, and all that: a precious low lot!" added this judicious person. "But it's about here my 'orse is moored, and by your leave I'll be getting ahead."

"One moment," said I. "Is Mr. Sebright on board?"

"No, sir, he's ashore to-day," said the sailor. "I took up a bag for him to the 'otel."

With that we parted. Presently after my friend overtook and passed me on a hired steed which seemed to scorn its cavalier; and I was left in the dust of his passage, a prey to whirling thoughts. For I now stood, or seemed to stand, on the immediate threshold of these mysteries. I knew the name of the man Dickson—his name was Carthew; I knew where the money came from that opposed us at the sale—it was part of Carthew's inheritance; and in my gallery of illustrations to the history of the wreck, one more picture hung; perhaps the most dramatic of the series. It showed me the deck of a warship in that distant part of the great ocean, the officers and seamen looking curiously on; and a man of birth and education, who had been sailing under an alias on a trading brig, and was now rescued from desperate peril, felled like an ox by the bare sound of his own name. I could not fail to be reminded of my own experience at the Occidental telephone. The hero of three styles, Dickson, Goddedaal, or Carthew, must be the owner of a lively—or a loaded—conscience, and the reflection recalled to me the photograph found on board the Flying Scud; just such a man, I reasoned, would be capable of just such starts and crises, and I inclined to think that Goddedaal (or Carthew) was the mainspring of the mystery.

One thing was plain: as long as the Tempest was in reach, I must make the acquaintance of both Sebright and the doctor. To this end, I excused myself with Mr. Fowler, returned to Honolulu, and passed the remainder of the day hanging vainly round the cool verandahs of the hotel. It was near nine o'clock at night before I was rewarded.

"That is the gentleman you were asking for," said the clerk.

I beheld a man in tweeds, of an incomparable languor of demeanour, and carrying a cane with genteel effort. From the name, I had looked to find a sort of Viking and young ruler of the battle and the tempest; and I was the more disappointed, and not a little alarmed, to come face to face with this impracticable type.

"I believe I have the pleasure of addressing Lieutenant Sebright," said I, stepping forward.

"Aw, yes," replied the hero; "but, aw! I dawn't knaw you, do I?" (He spoke for all the world like Lord Foppington in the old play—a proof of the perennial nature of man's affectations. But his limping dialect, I scorn to continue to reproduce.)

"It was with the intention of making myself known, that I have taken this step," said I, entirely unabashed (for impudence begets in me its like—perhaps my only martial attribute). "We have a common subject of interest, to me very lively; and I believe I may be in a position to be of some service to a friend of yours—to give him, at least, some very welcome information."

The last clause was a sop to my conscience: I could not pretend, even to myself, either the power or the will to serve Mr. Carthew; but I felt sure he would like to hear the Flying Scud was burned.

"I don't know—I—I don't understand you," stammered my victim. "I don't have any friends in Honolulu, don't you know?"

"The friend to whom I refer is English," I replied. "It is Mr. Carthew, whom you picked up at Midway. My firm has bought the wreck; I am just returned from breaking her up; and—to make my business quite clear to you—I have a communication it is necessary I should make; and have to trouble you for Mr. Carthew's address."

It will be seen how rapidly I had dropped all hope of interesting the frigid British bear. He, on his side, was plainly on thorns at my insistence; I judged he was suffering torments of alarm lest I should prove an undesirable acquaintance; diagnosed him for a shy, dull, vain, unamiable animal, without adequate defence—a sort of dishoused snail; and concluded, rightly enough, that he would consent to anything to bring our interview to a conclusion. A moment later, he had fled, leaving me with a sheet of paper, thus inscribed:—

Norris Carthew,

Stallbridge-le-Carthew,

Dorset.

I might have cried victory, the field of battle and some of the enemy's baggage remaining in my occupation. As a matter of fact, my moral sufferings during the engagement had rivalled those of Mr. Sebright; I was left incapable of fresh hostilities; I owned that the navy of old England was (for me) invincible as of yore; and giving up all thought of the doctor, inclined to salute her veteran flag, in the future, from a prudent distance. Such was my inclination, when I retired to rest; and my first experience the next morning strengthened it to certainty. For I had the pleasure of encountering my fair antagonist on his way on board; and he honoured me with a recognition so disgustingly dry, that my impatience overflowed, and (recalling the tactics of Nelson) I neglected to perceive or to return it.

Judge of my astonishment, some half-hour later, to receive a note of invitation from the Tempest.

"Dear Sir," it began, "we are all naturally very much interested in the wreck of the Flying Scud, and as soon as I mentioned that I had the pleasure of making your acquaintance, a very general wish was expressed that you would come and dine on board. It will give us all the greatest pleasure to see you to-night, or in case you should be otherwise engaged, to luncheon either to-morrow or to-day." A note of the hours followed, and the document wound up with the name of "J. Lascelles Sebright," under an undeniable statement that he was sincerely mine.

"No, Mr. Lascelles Sebright," I reflected, "you are not, but I begin to suspect that (like the lady in the song) you are another's. You have mentioned your adventure, my friend; you have been blown up; you have got your orders; this note has been dictated; and I am asked on board (in spite of your melancholy protests) not to meet the men, and not to talk about the Flying Scud, but to undergo the scrutiny of some one interested in Carthew: the doctor, for a wager. And for a second wager, all this springs from your facility in giving the address." I lost no time in answering the billet, electing for the earliest occasion; and at the appointed hour, a somewhat blackguard-looking boat's crew from the Norah Creina conveyed me under the guns of the Tempest.

The ward-room appeared pleased to see me; Sebright's brother officers, in contrast to himself, took a boyish interest in my cruise; and much was talked of the Flying Scud; of how she had been lost, of how I had found her, and of the weather, the anchorage, and the currents about Midway Island. Carthew was referred to more than once without embarrassment; the parallel case of a late Earl of Aberdeen, who died mate on board a Yankee schooner, was adduced. If they told me little of the man, it was because they had not much to tell, and only felt an interest in his recognition and pity for his prolonged ill-health. I could never think the subject was avoided; and it was clear that the officers, far from practising concealment, had nothing to conceal.

So far, then, all seemed natural, and yet the doctor troubled me. This was a tall, rugged, plain man, on the wrong side of fifty, already gray, and with a restless mouth and bushy eyebrows: he spoke seldom, but then with gaiety; and his great, quaking, silent laughter was infectious. I could make out that he was at once the quiz of the ward-room and perfectly respected; and I made sure that he observed me covertly. It is certain I returned the compliment. If Carthew had feigned sickness—and all seemed to point in that direction—here was the man who knew all—or certainly knew much. His strong, sterling face progressively and silently persuaded of his full knowledge. That was not the mouth, these were not the eyes, of one who would act in ignorance, or could be led at random. Nor again was it the face of a man squeamish in the case of malefactors; there was even a touch of Brutus there, and something of the hanging judge. In short, he seemed the last character for the part assigned him in my theories; and wonder and curiosity contended in my mind.

Luncheon was over, and an adjournment to the smoking-room proposed, when (upon a sudden impulse) I burned my ships, and pleading indisposition, requested to consult the doctor.

"There is nothing the matter with my body, Dr. Urquart," said I, as soon as we were alone.

He hummed, his mouth worked, he regarded me steadily with his gray eyes, but resolutely held his peace.

"I want to talk to you about the Flying Scud and Mr. Carthew," I resumed. "Come: you must have expected this. I am sure you know all; you are shrewd, and must have a guess that I know much. How are we to stand to one another? and how am I to stand to Mr. Carthew?"

"I do not fully understand you," he replied, after a pause; and then, after another: "It is the spirit I refer to, Mr. Dodd."

"The spirit of my inquiries?" I asked.

He nodded.

"I think we are at cross-purposes," said I. "The spirit is precisely what I came in quest of. I bought the Flying Scud at a ruinous figure, run up by Mr. Carthew through an agent; and I am, in consequence, a bankrupt. But if I have found no fortune in the wreck, I have found unmistakable evidences of foul play. Conceive my position: I am ruined through this man, whom I never saw; I might very well desire revenge or compensation; and I think you will admit I have the means to extort either."

He made no sign in answer to this challenge.

"Can you not understand, then," I resumed, "the spirit in which I come to one who is surely in the secret, and ask him, honestly and plainly: How do I stand to Mr. Carthew?"

"I must ask you to be more explicit," said he.

"You do not help me much," I retorted. "But see if you can understand: my conscience is not very fine-spun; still, I have one. Now, there are degrees of foul play, to some of which I have no particular objection. I am sure with Mr. Carthew, I am not at all the person to forgo an advantage; and I have much curiosity. But on the other hand, I have no taste for persecution; and I ask you to believe that I am not the man to make bad worse, or heap trouble on the unfortunate."

"Yes; I think I understand," said he. "Suppose I pass you my word that, whatever may have occurred, there were excuses—great excuses—I may say, very great?"

"It would have weight with me, doctor," I replied.

"I may go further," he pursued. "Suppose I had been there, or you had been there: after a certain event had taken place, it's a grave question what we might have done—it's even a question what we could have done—ourselves. Or take me. I will be plain with you, and own that I am in possession of the facts. You have a shrewd guess how I have acted in that knowledge. May I ask you to judge from the character of my action, something of the nature of that knowledge, which I have no call, nor yet no title, to share with you?"

I cannot convey a sense of the rugged conviction and judicial emphasis of Dr. Urquart's speech. To those who did not hear him, it may appear as if he fed me on enigmas; to myself, who heard, I seemed to have received a lesson and a compliment.

"I thank you," I said. "I feel you have said as much as possible, and more than I had any right to ask. I take that as a mark of confidence, which I will try to deserve. I hope, sir, you will let me regard you as a friend."

He evaded my proffered friendship with a blunt proposal to rejoin the mess; and yet a moment later, contrived to alleviate the snub. For, as we entered the smoking-room, he laid his hand on my shoulder with a kind familiarity.

"I have just prescribed for Mr. Dodd," says he, "a glass of our Madeira."

I have never again met Dr. Urquart: but he wrote himself so clear upon my memory that I think I see him still. And indeed I had cause to remember the man for the sake of his communication. It was hard enough to make a theory fit the circumstances of the Flying Scud; but one in which the chief actor should stand the least excused, and might retain the esteem or at least the pity of a man like Dr. Urquart, failed me utterly. Here at least was the end of my discoveries; I learned no more, till I learned all; and my reader has the evidence complete. Is he more astute than I was? or, like me, does he give it up?

CHAPTER XVIII. CROSS-QUESTIONS AND CROOKED ANSWERS.

I have said hard words of San Francisco; they must scarce be literally understood (one cannot suppose the Israelites did justice to the land of Pharaoh); and the city took a fine revenge of me on my return. She had never worn a more becoming guise; the sun shone, the air was lively, the people had flowers in their button-holes and smiles upon their faces; and as I made my way towards Jim's place of employment, with some very black anxieties at heart, I seemed to myself a blot on the surrounding gaiety.

My destination was in a by-street in a mean, rickety building; "The Franklin H. Dodge Steam Printing Company" appeared upon its front, and in characters of greater freshness, so as to suggest recent conversion, the watch-cry, "White Labour Only." In the office, in a dusty pen, Jim sat alone before a table. A wretched change had overtaken him in clothes, body, and bearing; he looked sick and shabby; he who had once rejoiced in his day's employment, like a horse among pastures, now sat staring on a column of accounts, idly chewing a pen, at times heavily sighing, the picture of inefficiency and inattention. He was sunk deep in a painful reverie; he neither saw nor heard me; and I stood and watched him unobserved. I had a sudden vain relenting. Repentance bludgeoned me. As I had predicted to Nares, I stood and kicked myself. Here was I come home again, my honour saved; there was my friend in want of rest, nursing, and a generous diet; and I asked myself with Falstaff, "What is in that word honour? what is that honour?" and, like Falstaff, I told myself that it was air.

"Jim!" said I.

"Loudon!" he gasped, and jumped from his chair and stood shaking.

The next moment I was over the barrier, and we were hand in hand.

"My poor old man!" I cried.

"Thank God, you're home at last!" he gulped, and kept patting my shoulder with his hand.

"I've no good news for you, Jim!" said I.

"You've come—that's the good news that I want," he replied. "O, how I've longed for you, Loudon!"

"I couldn't do what you wrote me," I said, lowering my voice. "The creditors have it all. I couldn't do it."

"Ssh!" returned Jim. "I was crazy when wrote. I could never have looked Mamie in the face if we had done it. O, Loudon, what a gift that woman is! You think you know something of life: you just don't know anything. It's the GOODNESS of the woman, it's a revelation!"

"That's all right," said I. "That's how I hoped to hear you, Jim."

"And so the Flying Scud was a fraud," he resumed. "I didn't quite understand your letter, but I made out that."

"Fraud is a mild term for it," said I. "The creditors will never believe what fools we were. And that reminds me," I continued, rejoicing in the transition, "how about the bankruptcy?"

"You were lucky to be out of that," answered Jim, shaking his head; "you were lucky not to see the papers. The Occidental called me a fifth-rate Kerbstone broker with water on the brain; another said I was a tree-frog that had got into the same meadow with Longhurst, and had blown myself out till I went pop. It was rough on a man in his honeymoon; so was what they said about my looks, and what I had on, and the way I perspired. But I braced myself up with the Flying Scud. How did it exactly figure out anyway? I don't seem to catch on to that story, Loudon."

"The devil you don't!" thinks I to myself; and then aloud: "You see we had neither one of us good luck. I didn't do much more than cover current expenses; and you got floored immediately. How did we come to go so soon?"

"Well, we'll have to have a talk over all this," said Jim with a sudden start. "I should be getting to my books; and I guess you had better go up right away to Mamie. She's at Speedy's. She expects you with impatience. She regards you in the light of a favourite brother, Loudon."

Any scheme was welcome which allowed me to postpone the hour of explanation, and avoid (were it only for a breathing space) the topic of the Flying Scud. I hastened accordingly to Bush Street. Mrs. Speedy, already rejoicing in the return of a spouse, hailed me with acclamation. "And it's beautiful you're looking, Mr. Dodd, my dear," she was kind enough to say. "And a miracle they naygur waheenies let ye lave the oilands. I have my suspicions of Shpeedy," she added, roguishly. "Did ye see him after the naygresses now?"

I gave Speedy an unblemished character.

"The one of ye will niver bethray the other," said the playful dame, and ushered me into a bare room, where Mamie sat working a type-writer.

I was touched by the cordiality of her greeting. With the prettiest gesture in the world she gave me both her hands; wheeled forth a chair; and produced, from a cupboard, a tin of my favourite tobacco, and a book of my exclusive cigarette papers.

"There!" she cried; "you see, Mr. Loudon, we were all prepared for you; the things were bought the very day you sailed."

I imagined she had always intended me a pleasant welcome; but the certain fervour of sincerity, which I could not help remarking, flowed from an unexpected source. Captain Nares, with a kindness for which I can never be sufficiently grateful, had stolen a moment from his occupations, driven to call on Mamie, and drawn her a generous picture of my prowess at the wreck. She was careful not to breathe a word of this interview, till she had led me on to tell my adventures for myself.

"Ah! Captain Nares was better," she cried, when I had done. "From your account, I have only learned one new thing, that you are modest as well as brave."

I cannot tell with what sort of disclamation I sought to reply.

"It is of no use," said Mamie. "I know a hero. And when I heard of you working all day like a common labourer, with your hands bleeding and your nails broken—and how you told the captain to 'crack on' (I think he said) in the storm, when he was terrified himself—and the danger of that horrid mutiny"—(Nares had been obligingly dipping his brush in earthquake and eclipse)—"and how it was all done, in part at least, for Jim and me—I felt we could never say how we admired and thanked you."

"Mamie," I cried, "don't talk of thanks; it is not a word to be used between friends. Jim and

I have been prosperous together; now we shall be poor together. We've done our best, and that's all that need be said. The next thing is for me to find a situation, and send you and Jim up country for a long holiday in the redwoods—for a holiday Jim has got to have."

"Jim can't take your money, Mr. Loudon," said Mamie.

"Jim?" cried I. "He's got to. Didn't I take his?"

Presently after, Jim himself arrived, and before he had yet done mopping his brow, he was at me with the accursed subject. "Now, Loudon," said he, "here we are all together, the day's work done and the evening before us; just start in with the whole story."

"One word on business first," said I, speaking from the lips outward, and meanwhile (in the private apartments of my brain) trying for the thousandth time to find some plausible arrangement of my story. "I want to have a notion how we stand about the bankruptcy."

"O, that's ancient history," cried Jim. "We paid seven cents, and a wonder we did as well. The receiver——" (methought a spasm seized him at the name of this official, and he broke off). "But it's all past and done with anyway; and what I want to get at is the facts about the wreck. I don't seem to understand it; appears to me like as there was something underneath."

"There was nothing IN it, anyway," I said, with a forced laugh.

"That's what I want to judge of," returned Jim.

"How the mischief is it I can never keep you to that bankruptcy? It looks as if you avoided it," said I—for a man in my situation, with unpardonable folly.

"Don't it look a little as if you were trying to avoid the wreck?" asked Jim.

It was my own doing; there was no retreat. "My dear fellow, if you make a point of it, here goes!" said I, and launched with spurious gaiety into the current of my tale. I told it with point and spirit; described the island and the wreck, mimicked Anderson and the Chinese, maintained the suspense.... My pen has stumbled on the fatal word. I maintained the suspense so well that it was never relieved; and when I stopped—I dare not say concluded, where there was no conclusion—I found Jim and Mamie regarding me with surprise.

"Well?" said Jim.

"Well, that's all," said I.

"But how do you explain it?" he asked.

"I can't explain it," said I.

Mamie wagged her head ominously.

"But, great Caesar's ghost! the money was offered!" cried Jim. "It won't do, Loudon; it's nonsense, on the face of it! I don't say but what you and Nares did your best; I'm sure, of course, you did; but I do say, you got fooled. I say the stuff is in that ship to-day, and I say I mean to get it."

"There is nothing in the ship, I tell you, but old wood and iron!" said I.

"You'll see," said Jim. "Next time I go myself. I'll take Mamie for the trip; Longhurst won't refuse me the expense of a schooner. You wait till I get the searching of her."

"But you can't search her!" cried I. "She's burned."

"Burned!" cried Mamie, starting a little from the attitude of quiescent capacity in which she had hitherto sat to hear me, her hands folded in her lap.

There was an appreciable pause.

"I beg your pardon, Loudon," began Jim at last, "but why in snakes did you burn her?"

"It was an idea of Nares's," said I.

"This is certainly the strangest circumstance of all," observed Mamie.

"I must say, Loudon, it does seem kind of unexpected," added Jim. "It seems kind of crazy even. What did you—what did Nares expect to gain by burning her?"

"I don't know; it didn't seem to matter; we had got all there was to get," said I.

"That's the very point," cried Jim. "It was quite plain you hadn't."

"What made you so sure?" asked Mamie.

"How can I tell you?" I cried. "We had been all through her. We WERE sure; that's all that I can say."

"I begin to think you were," she returned, with a significant emphasis.

Jim hurriedly intervened. "What I don't quite make out, Loudon, is that you don't seem to appreciate the peculiarities of the thing," said he. "It doesn't seem to have struck you same as it does me."

"Pshaw! why go on with this?" cried Mamie, suddenly rising. "Mr. Dodd is not telling us either what he thinks or what he knows."

"Mamie!" cried Jim.

"You need not be concerned for his feelings, James; he is not concerned for yours," returned the lady. "He dare not deny it, besides. And this is not the first time he has practised reticence. Have you forgotten that he knew the address, and did not tell it you until that man had escaped?"

Jim turned to me pleadingly—we were all on our feet. "Loudon," he said, "you see Mamie has some fancy; and I must say there's just a sort of a shadow of an excuse; for it IS bewildering—even to me, Loudon, with my trained business intelligence. For God's sake, clear it up."

"This serves me right," said I. "I should not have tried to keep you in the dark; I should have told you at first that I was pledged to secrecy; I should have asked you to trust me in the beginning. It is all I can do now. There is more of the story, but it concerns none of us, and my tongue is tied. I have given my word of honour. You must trust me and try to forgive me."

"I daresay I am very stupid, Mr. Dodd," began Mamie, with an alarming sweetness, "but I thought you went upon this trip as my husband's representative and with my husband's money? You tell us now that you are pledged, but I should have thought you were pledged first of all to James. You say it does not concern us; we are poor people, and my husband is sick, and it concerns us a great deal to understand how we come to have lost our money, and why our representative comes back to us with nothing. You ask that we should trust you; you do not seem to understand; the question we are asking ourselves is whether we have not trusted you too much."

"I do not ask you to trust me," I replied. "I ask Jim. He knows me."

"You think you can do what you please with James; you trust to his affection, do you not? And me, I suppose, you do not consider," said Mamie. "But it was perhaps an unfortunate day for you when we were married, for I at least am not blind. The crew run away, the ship is sold for a great deal of money, you know that man's address and you conceal it, you do not find what you were sent to look for, and yet you burn the ship; and now, when we ask explanations, you are pledged to secrecy! But I am pledged to no such thing; I will not stand by in silence and see my sick and ruined husband betrayed by his condescending friend. I will give you the truth for once. Mr. Dodd, you have been bought and sold."

"Mamie," cried Jim, "no more of this! It's me you're striking; it's only me you hurt. You don't know, you cannot understand these things. Why, to-day, if it hadn't been for Loudon, I couldn't have looked you in the face. He saved my honesty."

"I have heard plenty of this talk before," she replied. "You are a sweet-hearted fool, and I love you for it. But I am a clear-headed woman; my eyes are open, and I understand this man's hypocrisy. Did he not come here to-day and pretend he would take a situation—pretend he would share his hard-earned wages with us until you were well? Pretend! It makes me furious! His wages! a share of his wages! That would have been your pittance, that would have been your share of the Flying Scud—you who worked and toiled for him when he was a beggar in the streets of Paris. But we do not want your charity; thank God, I can work for my own husband! See what it is to have obliged a gentleman. He would let you pick him up when he was begging; he would stand and look on, and let you black his shoes, and sneer at you. For you were always sneering at my James; you always looked down upon him in your heart, you know it!" She turned back to Jim. "And now when he is rich," she began, and then swooped again on me. "For you are rich, I dare you to deny it; I defy you to look me in the face and try to deny that you are rich—rich with our money—my husband's money——"

Heaven knows to what a height she might have risen, being, by this time, bodily whirled away in her own hurricane of words. Heart-sickness, a black depression, a treacherous sympathy with my assailant, pity unutterable for poor Jim, already filled, divided, and abashed my spirit. Flight seemed the only remedy; and making a private sign to Jim, as if to ask permission, I slunk from the unequal field.

I was but a little way down the street, when I was arrested by the sound of some one running, and Jim's voice calling me by name. He had followed me with a letter which had been long awaiting my return.

I took it in a dream. "This has been a devil of a business," said I.

"Don't think hard of Mamie," he pleaded. "It's the way she's made; it's her high-toned loyalty. And of course I know it's all right. I know your sterling character; but you didn't, somehow, make out to give us the thing straight, Loudon. Anybody might have—I mean it—I mean——"

"Never mind what you mean, my poor Jim," said I. "She's a gallant little woman and a loyal wife: and I thought her splendid. My story was as fishy as the devil. I'll never think the less of either her or you."

"It'll blow over; it must blow over," said he.

"It never can," I returned, sighing: "and don't you try to make it! Don't name me, unless it's with an oath. And get home to her right away. Good by, my best of friends. Good by, and God bless you. We shall never meet again."

"O Loudon, that we should live to say such words!" he cried.

I had no views on life, beyond an occasional impulse to commit suicide, or to get drunk, and drifted down the street, semi-conscious, walking apparently on air, in the light-headedness of grief. I had money in my pocket, whether mine or my creditors' I had no means of guessing; and, the Poodle Dog lying in my path, I went mechanically in and took a table. A waiter attended me, and I suppose I gave my orders; for presently I found myself, with a sudden return of consciousness, beginning dinner. On the white cloth at my elbow lay the letter, addressed in a clerk's hand, and bearing an English stamp and the Edinburgh postmark. A bowl of bouillon and a glass of wine awakened in one corner of my brain (where all the rest was in mourning, the blinds down as for a funeral) a faint stir of curiosity; and while I waited the next course, wondering the while what I had ordered, I opened and began to read the epoch-making document.

"DEAR SIR: I am charged with the melancholy duty of announcing to you the death of your excellent grandfather, Mr. Alexander Loudon, on the 17th ult. On Sunday the 13th, he went to church as usual in the forenoon, and stopped on his way home, at the corner of Princes Street, in one of our seasonable east winds, to talk with an old friend. The same evening acute bronchitis declared itself; from the first, Dr. M'Combie anticipated a fatal result, and the old gentleman appeared to have no illusion as to his own state. He repeatedly assured me it was 'by' with him now; 'and high time, too,' he once added with characteristic asperity. He was not in the least changed on the approach of death: only (what I am sure must be very grateful to your feelings) he seemed to think and speak even more kindly than usual of yourself: referring to you as 'Jeannie's yin,' with strong expressions of regard. 'He was the only one I ever liket of the hale jing-bang,' was one of his expressions; and you will be glad to know that he dwelt particularly on the dutiful respect you had always displayed in your relations. The small codicil, by which he bequeaths you his Molesworth and other professional works, was added (you will observe) on the day before his death; so that you were in his thoughts until the end. I should say that, though rather a trying patient, he was most tenderly nursed by your uncle, and your cousin, Miss Euphemia. I enclose a copy of the testament, by which you will see that you share equally with Mr. Adam, and that I hold at your disposal a sum nearly approaching seventeen thousand pounds. I beg to congratulate you on this considerable acquisition, and expect your orders, to which I shall hasten to give my best attention. Thinking that you might desire to return at once to this country, and not knowing how you may be placed, I enclose a credit for six hundred pounds. Please sign the accompanying slip, and let me have it at your earliest convenience.

"I am, dear sir, yours truly,

"W. RUTHERFORD GREGG."

"God bless the old gentleman!" I thought; "and for that matter God bless Uncle Adam! and my cousin Euphemia! and Mr. Gregg!" I had a vision of that grey old life now brought to an end—"and high time too"—a vision of those Sabbath streets alternately vacant and filled with silent people; of the babel of the bells, the long-drawn psalmody, the shrewd sting of the east wind, the hollow, echoing, dreary house to which "Ecky" had returned with the hand of death already on his shoulder; a vision, too, of the long, rough country lad, perhaps a serious courtier of the lasses in the hawthorn den, perhaps a rustic dancer on the green, who had first earned and answered to that harsh diminutive. And I asked myself if, on the whole, poor Ecky had succeeded in life; if the last state of that man were not on the whole worse than the first; and the house in Randolph Crescent a less admirable dwelling than the hamlet where he saw the day and grew to manhood. Here was a consolatory thought for one who was himself a failure.

Yes, I declare the word came in my mind; and all the while, in another partition of the brain, I was glowing and singing for my new-found opulence. The pile of gold—four thousand two hundred and fifty double eagles, seventeen thousand ugly sovereigns, twenty-one thousand two hundred and fifty Napoleons—danced, and rang and ran molten, and lit up life with their effulgence, in the eye of fancy. Here were all things made plain to me: Paradise—Paris, I mean—Regained, Carthew protected, Jim restored, the creditors...

"The creditors!" I repeated, and sank back benumbed. It was all theirs to the last farthing: my grandfather had died too soon to save me.

I must have somewhere a rare vein of decision. In that revolutionary moment, I found myself prepared for all extremes except the one: ready to do anything, or to go anywhere, so long as I might save my money. At the worst, there was flight, flight to some of those blest countries where the serpent, extradition, has not yet entered in.

On no condition is extradition

Allowed in Callao!

—the old lawless words haunted me; and I saw myself hugging my gold in the company of such men as had once made and sung them, in the rude and bloody wharfside drinking-shops of Chili and Peru. The run of my ill-luck, the breach of my old friendship, this bubble fortune flaunted for a moment in my eyes and snatched again, had made me desperate and (in the expressive vulgarism) ugly. To drink vile spirits among vile companions by the flare of a pine-torch; to go burthened with my furtive treasure in a belt; to fight for it knife in hand, rolling on a clay floor; to flee perpetually in fresh ships and to be chased through the sea from isle to isle, seemed, in my then frame of mind, a welcome series of events.

That was for the worst; but it began to dawn slowly on my mind that there was yet a possible better. Once escaped, once safe in Callao, I might approach my creditors with a good grace; and properly handled by a cunning agent, it was just possible they might accept some easy composition. The hope recalled me to the bankruptcy. It was strange, I reflected: often as I had questioned Jim, he had never obliged me with an answer. In his haste for news about the wreck, my own no less legitimate curiosity had gone disappointed. Hateful as the thought was to me, I must return at once and find out where I stood.

I left my dinner still unfinished, paying for the whole, of course, and tossing the waiter a gold piece. I was reckless; I knew not what was mine and cared not: I must take what I could get and give as I was able; to rob and to squander seemed the complementary parts of my new destiny. I walked up Bush Street, whistling, brazening myself to confront Mamie in the first place, and the world at large and a certain visionary judge upon a bench in the second. Just outside, I stopped and lighted a cigar to give me greater countenance; and puffing this and wearing what (I am sure) was a wretched assumption of braggadocio, I reappeared on the scene of my disgrace.

My friend and his wife were finishing a poor meal—rags of old mutton, the remainder cakes from breakfast eaten cold, and a starveling pot of coffee.

"I beg your pardon, Mrs. Pinkerton," said I. "Sorry to inflict my presence where it cannot be desired; but there is a piece of business necessary to be discussed."

"Pray do not consider me," said Mamie, rising, and she sailed into the adjoining bedroom.

Jim watched her go and shook his head; he looked miserably old and ill.

"What is it, now?" he asked.

"Perhaps you remember you answered none of my questions," said I.

"Your questions?" faltered Jim.

"Even so, Jim. My questions," I repeated. "I put questions as well as yourself; and however little I may have satisfied Mamie with my answers, I beg to remind you that you gave me none at all."

"You mean about the bankruptcy?" asked Jim.

I nodded.

He writhed in his chair. "The straight truth is, I was ashamed," he said. "I was trying to dodge you. I've been playing fast and loose with you, Loudon; I've deceived you from the first, I blush to own it. And here you came home and put the very question I was fearing. Why did we bust so soon? Your keen business eye had not deceived you. That's the point, that's my shame; that's what killed me this afternoon when Mamie was treating you so, and my conscience was telling me all the time, Thou art the man."

"What was it, Jim?" I asked.

"What I had been at all the time, Loudon," he wailed; "and I don't know how I'm to look you in the face and say it, after my duplicity. It was stocks," he added in a whisper.

"And you were afraid to tell me that!" I cried. "You poor, old, cheerless dreamer! what would it matter what you did or didn't? Can't you see we're doomed? And anyway, that's not my point. It's how I stand that I want to know. There is a particular reason. Am I clear? Have I a certificate, or what have I to do to get one? And when will it be dated? You can't think what hangs by it!"

"That's the worst of all," said Jim, like a man in a dream, "I can't see how to tell him!"

"What do you mean?" I cried, a small pang of terror at my heart.

"I'm afraid I sacrificed you, Loudon," he said, looking at me pitifully.

"Sacrificed me?" I repeated. "How? What do you mean by sacrifice?"

"I know it'll shock your delicate self-respect," he said; "but what was I to do? Things looked so bad. The receiver——" (as usual, the name stuck in his throat, and he began afresh). "There was a lot of talk; the reporters were after me already; there was the trouble and all about the Mexican business; and I got scared right out, and I guess I lost my head. You weren't there, you see, and that was my temptation."

I did not know how long he might thus beat about the bush with dreadful hintings, and I was already beside myself with terror. What had he done? I saw he had been tempted; I knew from his letters that he was in no condition to resist. How had he sacrificed the absent?

"Jim," I said, "you must speak right out. I've got all that I can carry."

"Well," he said—"I know it was a liberty—I made it out you were no business man, only a stone-broke painter; that half the time you didn't know anything anyway, particularly money and accounts. I said you never could be got to understand whose was whose. I had to say that because of some entries in the books——"

"For God's sake," I cried, "put me out of this agony! What did you accuse me of?"

"Accuse you of?" repeated Jim. "Of what I'm telling you. And there being no deed of partnership, I made out you were only a kind of clerk that I called a partner just to give you taffy; and so I got you ranked a creditor on the estate for your wages and the money you had lent. And——"

I believe I reeled. "A creditor!" I roared; "a creditor! I'm not in the bankruptcy at all?"

"No," said Jim. "I know it was a liberty——"

"O, damn your liberty! read that," I cried, dashing the letter before him on the table, "and call in your wife, and be done with eating this truck "—as I spoke, I slung the cold mutton in the empty grate—"and let's all go and have a champagne supper. I've dined—I'm sure I don't remember what I had; I'd dine again ten scores of times upon a night like this. Read it, you blaying ass! I'm not insane. Here, Mamie," I continued, opening the bedroom door, "come out and make it up with me, and go and kiss your husband; and I'll tell you what, after the supper, let's go to some place where there's a band, and I'll waltz with you till sunrise."

"What does it all mean?" cried Jim.

"It means we have a champagne supper to-night, and all go to Napa Valley or to Monterey to-morrow," said I. "Mamie, go and get your things on; and you, Jim, sit down right where you are, take a sheet of paper, and tell Franklin Dodge to go to Texas. Mamie, you were right, my dear; I was rich all the time, and didn't know it."

CHAPTER XIX. TRAVELS WITH A SHYSTER.

The absorbing and disastrous adventure of the Flying Scud was now quite ended; we had dashed into these deep waters and we had escaped again to starve, we had been ruined and were saved, had quarrelled and made up; there remained nothing but to sing Te Deum, draw a line, and begin on a fresh page of my unwritten diary. I do not pretend that I recovered all I had lost with Mamie; it would have been more than I had merited; and I had certainly been more uncommunicative than became either the partner or the friend. But she accepted the position handsomely; and during the week that I now passed with them, both she and Jim had the grace to spare me questions. It was to Calistoga that we went; there was some rumour of a Napa land-boom at the moment, the possibility of stir attracted Jim, and he informed me he would find a certain joy in looking on, much as Napoleon on St. Helena took a pleasure to read military works. The field of his ambition was quite closed; he was done with action; and looked forward to a ranch in a mountain dingle, a patch of corn, a pair of kine, a leisurely and contemplative age in the green shade of forests. "Just let me get down on my back in a hayfield," said he, "and you'll find there's no more snap to me than that much putty."

And for two days the perfervid being actually rested. The third, he was observed in consultation with the local editor, and owned he was in two minds about purchasing the press and paper. "It's a kind of a hold for an idle man," he said, pleadingly; "and if the section was to open up the way it ought to, there might be dollars in the thing." On the fourth day he was gone till dinner-time alone; on the fifth we made a long picnic drive to the fresh field of enterprise; and the sixth was passed entirely in the preparation of prospectuses. The pioneer of McBride City was already upright and self-reliant as of yore; the fire rekindled in his eye, the ring restored to his voice; a charger sniffing battle and saying ha-ha, among the spears. On the seventh morning we signed a deed of partnership, for Jim would not accept a dollar of my money otherwise; and having once more engaged myself—or that mortal part of me, my purse—among the wheels of his machinery, I returned alone to San Francisco and took quarters in the Palace Hotel.

The same night I had Nares to dinner. His sunburnt face, his queer and personal strain of talk, recalled days that were scarce over and that seemed already distant. Through the music of the band outside, and the chink and clatter of the dining-room, it seemed to me as if I heard the foaming of the surf and the voices of the sea-birds about Midway Island. The bruises on our hands were not yet healed; and there we sat, waited on by elaborate darkies, eating pompano and drinking iced champagne.

"Think of our dinners on the Norah, captain, and then oblige me by looking round the room for contrast."

He took the scene in slowly. "Yes, it is like a dream," he said: "like as if the darkies were really about as big as dimes; and a great big scuttle might open up there, and Johnson stick in a great big head and shoulders, and cry, 'Eight bells!'—and the whole thing vanish."

"Well, it's the other thing that has done that," I replied. "It's all bygone now, all dead and buried. Amen! say I."

"I don't know that, Mr. Dodd; and to tell you the fact, I don't believe it," said Nares. "There's more Flying Scud in the oven; and the baker's name, I take it, is Bellairs. He tackled me the day we came in: sort of a razee of poor old humanity—jury clothes—full new suit of pimples: knew him at once from your description. I let him pump me till I saw his game. He knows a good deal that we don't know, a good deal that we do, and suspects the balance. There's trouble brewing for somebody."

I was surprised I had not thought of this before. Bellairs had been behind the scenes; he had known Dickson; he knew the flight of the crew; it was hardly possible but what he should suspect; it was certain if he suspected, that he would seek to trade on the suspicion. And sure enough, I was not yet dressed the next morning ere the lawyer was knocking at my door. I let him in, for I was curious; and he, after some ambiguous prolegomena, roundly proposed I should go shares with him.

"Shares in what?" I inquired.

"If you will allow me to clothe my idea in a somewhat vulgar form," said he, "I might ask you, did you go to Midway for your health?"

"I don't know that I did," I replied.

"Similarly, Mr. Dodd, you may be sure I would never have taken the present step without influential grounds," pursued the lawyer. "Intrusion is foreign to my character. But you and I, sir, are engaged on the same ends. If we can continue to work the thing in company, I place at your disposal my knowledge of the law and a considerable practice in delicate negotiations similar to this. Should you refuse to consent, you might find in me a formidable and"—he hesitated—"and to my own regret, perhaps a dangerous competitor."

"Did you get this by heart?" I asked, genially.

"I advise YOU to!" he said, with a sudden sparkle of temper and menace, instantly gone, instantly succeeded by fresh cringing. "I assure you, sir, I arrive in the character of a friend; and I believe you underestimate my information. If I may instance an example, I am acquainted to the last dime with what you made (or rather lost), and I know you have since cashed a considerable draft on London."

"What do you infer?" I asked.

"I know where that draft came from," he cried, wincing back like one who has greatly dared, and instantly regrets the venture.

"So?" said I.

"You forget I was Mr. Dickson's confidential agent," he explained. "You had his address, Mr. Dodd. We were the only two that he communicated with in San Francisco. You see my deductions are quite obvious: you see how open and frank I deal with you, as I should wish to do with any gentleman with whom I was conjoined in business. You see how much I know; and it can scarcely escape your strong common-sense, how much better it would be if I knew all. You cannot hope to get rid of me at this time of day, I have my place in the affair, I cannot be shaken off; I am, if you will excuse a rather technical pleasantry, an encumbrance on the estate. The actual harm I can do, I leave you to valuate for yourself. But without going so far, Mr. Dodd, and without in any way inconveniencing myself, I could make things very uncomfortable. For instance, Mr. Pinkerton's liquidation. You and I know, sir—and you better than I—on what a large fund you draw. Is Mr. Pinkerton in the thing at all? It was you only who knew the address, and you were concealing it. Suppose I should communicate with Mr. Pinkerton——"

"Look here!" I interrupted, "communicate with him (if you will permit me to clothe my idea in a vulgar shape) till you are blue in the face. There is only one person with whom I refuse to allow you to communicate further, and that is myself. Good morning."

He could not conceal his rage, disappointment, and surprise; and in the passage (I have no doubt) was shaken by St. Vitus.

I was disgusted by this interview; it struck me hard to be suspected on all hands, and to hear again from this trafficker what I had heard already from Jim's wife; and yet my strongest impression was different and might rather be described as an impersonal fear. There was something against nature in the man's craven impudence; it was as though a lamb had butted me; such daring at the hands of such a dastard, implied unchangeable resolve, a great pressure of necessity, and powerful means. I thought of the unknown Carthew, and it sickened me to see this ferret on his trail.

Upon inquiry I found the lawyer was but just disbarred for some malpractice; and the discovery added excessively to my disquiet. Here was a rascal without money or the means of making it, thrust out of the doors of his own trade, publicly shamed, and doubtless in a deuce of a bad temper with the universe. Here, on the other hand, was a man with a secret; rich, terrified, practically in hiding; who had been willing to pay ten thousand pounds for the bones of the Flying Scud. I slipped insensibly into a mental alliance with the victim; the business weighed on me; all day long, I was wondering how much the lawyer knew, how much he guessed, and when he would open his attack.

Some of these problems are unsolved to this day; others were soon made clear. Where he got Carthew's name is still a mystery; perhaps some sailor on the Tempest, perhaps my own sea-lawyer served him for a tool; but I was actually at his elbow when he learned the address. It fell so. One evening, when I had an engagement and was killing time until the hour, I chanced to walk in the court of the hotel while the band played. The place was bright as day with the electric light; and I recognised, at some distance among the loiterers, the person of Bellairs in talk with a gentleman whose face appeared familiar. It was certainly some one I had seen, and seen recently; but who or where, I knew not. A porter standing hard by, gave me the necessary hint. The stranger was an English navy man, invalided home from Honolulu, where he had left his ship; indeed, it was only from the change of clothes and the effects of sickness, that I had not immediately recognised my friend and correspondent, Lieutenant Sebright.

The conjunction of these planets seeming ominous, I drew near; but it seemed Bellairs had done his business; he vanished in the crowd, and I found my officer alone.

"Do you know whom you have been talking to, Mr. Sebright?" I began.

"No," said he; "I don't know him from Adam. Anything wrong?"

"He is a disreputable lawyer, recently disbarred," said I. "I wish I had seen you in time. I trust you told him nothing about Carthew?"

He flushed to his ears. "I'm awfully sorry," he said. "He seemed civil, and I wanted to get rid of him. It was only the address he asked."

"And you gave it?" I cried.

"I'm really awfully sorry," said Sebright. "I'm afraid I did."

"God forgive you!" was my only comment, and I turned my back upon the blunderer.

The fat was in the fire now: Bellairs had the address, and I was the more deceived or Carthew would have news of him. So strong was this impression, and so painful, that the next morning I had the curiosity to pay the lawyer's den a visit. An old woman was scrubbing the stair, and the board was down.

"Lawyer Bellairs?" said the old woman. "Gone East this morning. There's Lawyer Dean next block up."

I did not trouble Lawyer Dean, but walked slowly back to my hotel, ruminating as I went. The image of the old woman washing that desecrated stair had struck my fancy; it seemed that all the water-supply of the city and all the soap in the State would scarce suffice to cleanse it, it had been so long a clearing-house of dingy secrets and a factory of sordid fraud. And now the corner was untenanted; some judge, like a careful housewife, had knocked down the web, and the bloated spider was scuttling elsewhere after new victims. I had of late (as I have said) insensibly taken sides with Carthew; now when his enemy was at his heels, my interest grew more warm; and I began to wonder if I could not help. The drama of the Flying Scud was entering on a new phase. It had been singular from the first: it promised an extraordinary conclusion; and I, who had paid so much to learn the beginning, might pay a little more and see the end. I lingered in San Francisco, indemnifying myself after the hardships of the cruise, spending money, regretting it, continually promising departure for the morrow. Why not go indeed, and keep a watch upon Bellairs? If I missed him, there was no harm done, I was the nearer Paris. If I found and kept his trail, it was hard if I could not put some stick in his machinery, and at the worst I could promise myself interesting scenes and revelations.

In such a mixed humour, I made up what it pleases me to call my mind, and once more involved myself in the story of Carthew and the Flying Scud. The same night I wrote a letter of farewell to Jim, and one of anxious warning to Dr. Urquart begging him to set Carthew on his guard; the morrow saw me in the ferry-boat; and ten days later, I was walking the hurricane deck on the City of Denver. By that time my mind was pretty much made down again, its natural condition: I told myself that I was bound for Paris or Fontainebleau to resume the study of the arts; and I thought no more of Carthew or Bellairs, or only to smile at my own fondness. The one I could not serve, even if I wanted; the other I had no means of finding, even if I could have at all influenced him after he was found.

And for all that, I was close on the heels of an absurd adventure. My neighbour at table that evening was a 'Frisco man whom I knew slightly. I found he had crossed the plains two days in front of me, and this was the first steamer that had left New York for Europe since his arrival. Two days before me meant a day before Bellairs; and dinner was scarce done before I was closeted with the purser.

"Bellairs?" he repeated. "Not in the saloon, I am sure. He may be in the second class. The lists are not made out, but—Hullo! 'Harry D. Bellairs?' That the name? He's there right enough."

And the next morning I saw him on the forward deck, sitting in a chair, a book in his hand, a shabby puma skin rug about his knees: the picture of respectable decay. Off and on, I kept him in my eye. He read a good deal, he stood and looked upon the sea, he talked occasionally with his neighbours, and once when a child fell he picked it up and soothed it. I damned him in my heart; the book, which I was sure he did not read—the sea, to which I was ready to take oath he was indifferent—the child, whom I was certain he would as lieve have tossed overboard—all seemed to me elements in a theatrical performance; and I made no doubt he was already nosing after the secrets of his fellow-passengers. I took no pains to conceal myself, my scorn for the creature being as strong as my disgust. But he never looked my way, and it was night before I learned he had observed me.

I was smoking by the engine-room door, for the air was a little sharp, when a voice rose close beside me in the darkness.

"I beg your pardon, Mr. Dodd," it said.

"That you, Bellairs?" I replied.

"A single word, sir. Your presence on this ship has no connection with our interview?" he asked. "You have no idea, Mr. Dodd, of returning upon your determination?"

"None," said I; and then, seeing he still lingered, I was polite enough to add "Good evening;" at which he sighed and went away.

The next day, he was there again with the chair and the puma skin; read his book and looked at the sea with the same constancy; and though there was no child to be picked up, I observed him to attend repeatedly on a sick woman. Nothing fosters suspicion like the act of watching; a man spied upon can hardly blow his nose but we accuse him of designs; and I took an early opportunity to go forward and see the woman for myself. She was poor, elderly, and painfully plain; I stood abashed at the sight, felt I owed Bellairs amends for the injustice of my thoughts, and seeing him standing by the rail in his usual attitude of contemplation, walked up and addressed him by name.

"You seem very fond of the sea," said I.

"I may really call it a passion, Mr. Dodd," he replied. "And the tall cataract haunted me like a passion," he quoted. "I never weary of the sea, sir. This is my first ocean voyage. I find it a glorious experience." And once more my disbarred lawyer dropped into poetry: "Roll on, thou deep and dark blue ocean, roll!"

Though I had learned the piece in my reading-book at school, I came into the world a little too late on the one hand—and I daresay a little too early on the other—to think much of Byron; and the sonorous verse, prodigiously well delivered, struck me with surprise.

"You are fond of poetry, too?" I asked.

"I am a great reader," he replied. "At one time I had begun to amass quite a small but well selected library; and when that was scattered, I still managed to preserve a few volumes—chiefly of pieces designed for recitation—which have been my travelling companions."

"Is that one of them?" I asked, pointing to the volume in his hand.

"No, sir," he replied, showing me a translation of the Sorrows of Werther, "that is a novel I picked up some time ago. It has afforded me great pleasure, though immoral."

"O, immoral!" cried I, indignant as usual at any complication of art and ethics.

"Surely you cannot deny that, sir—if you know the book," he said. "The passion is illicit, although certainly drawn with a good deal of pathos. It is not a work one could possibly put into the hands of a lady; which is to be regretted on all accounts, for I do not know how it may strike you; but it seems to me—as a depiction, if I make myself clear—to rise high above its compeers—even famous compeers. Even in Scott, Dickens, Thackeray, or Hawthorne, the sentiment of love appears to me to be frequently done less justice to."

"You are expressing a very general opinion," said I.

"Is that so, indeed, sir?" he exclaimed, with unmistakable excitement. "Is the book well known? and who was GO-EATH? I am interested in that, because upon the title-page the usual initials are omitted, and it runs simply 'by GO-EATH.' Was he an author of distinction? Has he written other works?"

Such was our first interview, the first of many; and in all he showed the same attractive qualities and defects. His taste for literature was native and unaffected; his sentimentality, although extreme and a thought ridiculous, was plainly genuine. I wondered at my own innocent wonder.

I knew that Homer nodded, that Caesar had compiled a jest-book, that Turner lived by preference the life of Puggy Booth, that Shelley made paper boats, and Wordsworth wore green spectacles! and with all this mass of evidence before me, I had expected Bellairs to be entirely of one piece, subdued to what he worked in, a spy all through. As I abominated the man's trade, so I had expected to detest the man himself; and behold, I liked him. Poor devil! he was essentially a man on wires, all sensibility and tremor, brimful of a cheap poetry, not without parts, quite without courage. His boldness was despair; the gulf behind him thrust him on; he was one of those who might commit a murder rather than confess the theft of a postage-stamp. I was sure that his coming interview with Carthew rode his imagination like a nightmare; when the thought crossed his mind, I used to think I knew of it, and that the qualm appeared in his face visibly. Yet he would never flinch: necessity stalking at his back, famine (his old pursuer) talking in his ear; and I used to wonder whether I most admired, or most despised, this quivering heroism for evil. The image that occurred to me after his visit was just; I had been butted by a lamb; and the phase of life that I was now studying might be called the Revolt of a Sheep.

It could be said of him that he had learned in sorrow what he taught in song—or wrong; and his life was that of one of his victims. He was born in the back parts of the State of New York; his father a farmer, who became subsequently bankrupt and went West. The lawyer and money-lender who had ruined this poor family seems to have conceived in the end a feeling of remorse; he turned the father out indeed, but he offered, in compensation, to charge himself with one of the sons: and Harry, the fifth child and already sickly, was chosen to be left behind. He made himself useful in the office; picked up the scattered rudiments of an education; read right and left; attended and debated at the Young Men's Christian Association; and in all his early years, was the model for a good story-book. His landlady's daughter was his bane. He showed me her photograph; she was a big, handsome, dashing, dressy, vulgar hussy, without character, without tenderness, without mind, and (as the result proved) without virtue. The sickly and timid boy was in the house; he was handy; when she was otherwise unoccupied, she used and played with him: Romeo and Cressida; till in that dreary life of a poor boy in a country town, she grew to be the light of his days and the subject of his dreams. He worked hard, like Jacob, for a wife; he surpassed his patron in sharp practice; he was made head clerk; and the same night, encouraged by a hundred freedoms, depressed by the sense of his youth and his infirmities, he offered marriage and was received with laughter. Not a year had passed, before his master, conscious of growing infirmities, took him for a partner; he proposed again; he was accepted; led two years of troubled married life; and awoke one morning to find his wife had run away with a dashing drummer, and had left him heavily in debt. The debt, and not the drummer, was supposed to be the cause of the hegira; she had concealed her liabilities, they were on the point of bursting forth, she was weary of Bellairs; and she took the drummer as she might have taken a cab. The blow disabled her husband, his partner was dead; he was now alone in the business, for which he was no longer fit; the debts hampered him; bankruptcy followed; and he fled from city to city, falling daily into lower practice. It is to be considered that he had been taught, and had learned as a delightful duty, a kind of business whose highest merit is to escape the commentaries of the bench: that of the usurious lawyer in a county town. With this training, he was now shot, a penniless stranger, into the deeper gulfs of cities; and the result is scarce a thing to be surprised at.

"Have you heard of your wife again?" I asked.

He displayed a pitiful agitation. "I am afraid you will think ill of me," he said.

"Have you taken her back?" I asked.

"No, sir. I trust I have too much self-respect," he answered, "and, at least, I was never tempted. She won't come, she dislikes, she seems to have conceived a positive distaste for me, and yet I was considered an indulgent husband."

"You are still in relations, then?" I asked.

"I place myself in your hands, Mr. Dodd," he replied. "The world is very hard; I have found it bitter hard myself—bitter hard to live. How much worse for a woman, and one who has placed herself (by her own misconduct, I am far from denying that) in so unfortunate a position!"

"In short, you support her?" I suggested.

"I cannot deny it. I practically do," he admitted. "It has been a mill-stone round my neck. But I think she is grateful. You can see for yourself."

He handed me a letter in a sprawling, ignorant hand, but written with violet ink on fine, pink paper with a monogram. It was very foolishly expressed, and I thought (except for a few obvious cajoleries) very heartless and greedy in meaning. The writer said she had been sick, which I disbelieved; declared the last remittance was all gone in doctor's bills, for which I took the liberty of substituting dress, drink, and monograms; and prayed for an increase, which I could only hope had been denied her.

"I think she is really grateful?" he asked, with some eagerness, as I returned it.

"I daresay," said I. "Has she any claim on you?"

"O no, sir. I divorced her," he replied. "I have a very strong sense of self-respect in such matters, and I divorced her immediately."

"What sort of life is she leading now?" I asked.

"I will not deceive you, Mr. Dodd. I do not know, I make a point of not knowing; it appears more dignified. I have been very harshly criticised," he added, sighing.

It will be seen that I had fallen into an ignominious intimacy with the man I had gone out to thwart. My pity for the creature, his admiration for myself, his pleasure in my society, which was clearly unassumed, were the bonds with which I was fettered; perhaps I should add, in honesty, my own ill-regulated interest in the phases of life and human character. The fact is (at least) that we spent hours together daily, and that I was nearly as much on the forward deck as in the saloon. Yet all the while I could never forget he was a shabby trickster, embarked that very moment in a dirty enterprise. I used to tell myself at first that our acquaintance was a stroke of art, and that I was somehow fortifying Carthew. I told myself, I say; but I was no such fool as to believe it, even then. In these circumstances I displayed the two chief qualities of my character on the largest scale—my helplessness and my instinctive love of procrastination—and fell upon a course of action so ridiculous that I blush when I recall it.

We reached Liverpool one forenoon, the rain falling thickly and insidiously on the filthy town. I had no plans, beyond a sensible unwillingness to let my rascal escape; and I ended by going to the same inn with him, dining with him, walking with him in the wet streets, and hearing with him in a penny gaff that venerable piece, The Ticket-of-Leave Man. It was one of his first visits to a theatre, against which places of entertainment he had a strong prejudice; and his innocent, pompous talk, innocent old quotations, and innocent reverence for the character of Hawkshaw delighted me beyond relief. In charity to myself, I dwell upon and perhaps exaggerate my pleasures. I have need of all conceivable excuses, when I confess that I went to bed without one word upon the matter of Carthew, but not without having covenanted with my rascal for a visit to Chester the next day. At Chester we did the Cathedral, walked on the walls, discussed

Shakespeare and the musical glasses—and made a fresh engagement for the morrow. I do not know, and I am glad to have forgotten, how long these travels were continued. We visited at least, by singular zigzags, Stratford, Warwick, Coventry, Gloucester, Bristol, Bath, and Wells. At each stage we spoke dutifully of the scene and its associations; I sketched, the Shyster spouted poetry and copied epitaphs. Who could doubt we were the usual Americans, travelling with a design of self-improvement? Who was to guess that one was a blackmailer, trembling to approach the scene of action—the other a helpless, amateur detective, waiting on events?

It is unnecessary to remark that none occurred, or none the least suitable with my design of protecting Carthew. Two trifles, indeed, completed though they scarcely changed my conception of the Shyster. The first was observed in Gloucester, where we spent Sunday, and I proposed we should hear service in the cathedral. To my surprise, the creature had an ISM of his own, to which he was loyal; and he left me to go alone to the cathedral—or perhaps not to go at all—and stole off down a deserted alley to some Bethel or Ebenezer of the proper shade. When we met again at lunch, I rallied him, and he grew restive.

"You need employ no circumlocutions with me, Mr. Dodd," he said suddenly. "You regard my behaviour from an unfavourable point of view: you regard me, I much fear, as hypocritical."

I was somewhat confused by the attack. "You know what I think of your trade," I replied, lamely and coarsely.

"Excuse me, if I seem to press the subject," he continued, "but if you think my life erroneous, would you have me neglect the means of grace? Because you consider me in the wrong on one point, would you have me place myself on the wrong in all? Surely, sir, the church is for the sinner."

"Did you ask a blessing on your present enterprise?" I sneered.

He had a bad attack of St. Vitus, his face was changed, and his eyes flashed. "I will tell you what I did!" he cried. "I prayed for an unfortunate man and a wretched woman whom he tries to support."

I cannot pretend that I found any repartee.

The second incident was at Bristol, where I lost sight of my gentleman some hours. From this eclipse, he returned to me with thick speech, wandering footsteps, and a back all whitened with plaster. I had half expected, yet I could have wept to see it. All disabilities were piled on that weak back—domestic misfortune, nervous disease, a displeasing exterior, empty pockets, and the slavery of vice.

I will never deny that our prolonged conjunction was the result of double cowardice. Each was afraid to leave the other, each was afraid to speak, or knew not what to say. Save for my ill-judged allusion at Gloucester, the subject uppermost in both our minds was buried. Carthew, Stallbridge-le-Carthew, Stallbridge-Minster—which we had long since (and severally) identified to be the nearest station—even the name of Dorsetshire was studiously avoided. And yet we were making progress all the time, tacking across broad England like an unweatherly vessel on a wind; approaching our destination, not openly, but by a sort of flying sap. And at length, I can scarce tell how, we were set down by a dilatory butt-end of local train on the untenanted platform of Stallbridge-Minster.

The town was ancient and compact: a domino of tiled houses and walled gardens, dwarfed by the disproportionate bigness of the church. From the midst of the thoroughfare which divided it in half, fields and trees were visible at either end; and through the sally-port of every street, there flowed in from the country a silent invasion of green grass. Bees and birds appeared to make the majority of the inhabitants; every garden had its row of hives, the eaves of every house were plastered with the nests of swallows, and the pinnacles of the church were flickered about all day long by a multitude of wings. The town was of Roman foundation; and as I looked out that afternoon from the low windows of the inn, I should scarce have been surprised to see a centurion coming up the street with a fatigue draft of legionaries. In short, Stallbridge-Minster was one of those towns which appear to be maintained by England for the instruction and delight of the American rambler; to which he seems guided by an instinct not less surprising than the setter's; and which he visits and quits with equal enthusiasm.

I was not at all in the humour of the tourist. I had wasted weeks of time and accomplished nothing; we were on the eve of the engagement, and I had neither plans nor allies. I had thrust myself into the trade of private providence and amateur detective; I was spending money and I was reaping disgrace. All the time, I kept telling myself that I must at least speak; that this ignominious silence should have been broken long ago, and must be broken now. I should have broken it when he first proposed to come to Stallbridge-Minster; I should have broken it in the train; I should break it there and then, on the inn doorstep, as the omnibus rolled off. I turned toward him at the thought; he seemed to wince, the words died on my lips, and I proposed instead that we should visit the Minster.

While we were engaged upon this duty, it came on to rain in a manner worthy of the tropics. The vault reverberated; every gargoyle instantly poured its full discharge; we waded back to the inn, ankle-deep in impromptu brooks; and the rest of the afternoon sat weatherbound, hearkening to the sonorous deluge. For two hours I talked of indifferent matters, laboriously feeding the conversation; for two hours my mind was quite made up to do my duty instantly—and at each particular instant I postponed it till the next. To screw up my faltering courage, I called at dinner for some sparkling wine. It proved when it came to be detestable; I could not put it to my lips; and Bellairs, who had as much palate as a weevil, was left to finish it himself. Doubtless the wine flushed him; doubtless he may have observed my embarrassment of the afternoon; doubtless he was conscious that we were approaching a crisis, and that that evening, if I did not join with him, I must declare myself an open enemy. At least he fled. Dinner was done; this was the time when I had bound myself to break my silence; no more delays were to be allowed, no more excuses received. I went upstairs after some tobacco; which I felt to be a mere necessity in the circumstances; and when I returned, the man was gone. The waiter told me he had left the house.

The rain still plumped, like a vast shower-bath, over the deserted town. The night was dark and windless: the street lit glimmeringly from end to end, lamps, house windows, and the reflections in the rain-pools all contributing. From a public-house on the other side of the way, I heard a harp twang and a doleful voice upraised in the "Larboard Watch," "The Anchor's Weighed," and other naval ditties. Where had my Shyster wandered? In all likelihood to that lyrical tavern; there was no choice of diversion; in comparison with Stallbridge-Minster on a rainy night, a sheepfold would seem gay.

Again I passed in review the points of my interview, on which I was always constantly resolved so long as my adversary was absent from the scene: and again they struck me as inadequate. From this dispiriting exercise I turned to the native amusements of the inn coffee-room, and studied for some time the mezzotints that frowned upon the wall. The railway guide, after showing me how soon I could leave Stallbridge and how quickly I could reach Paris, failed to hold my attention. An illustrated advertisement book of hotels brought me very low indeed; and when it came to the local paper, I could have wept. At this point, I found a passing solace in a copy of Whittaker's Almanac, and obtained in fifty minutes more information than I have yet been able to use.

Then a fresh apprehension assailed me. Suppose Bellairs had given me the slip? suppose he was now rolling on the road to Stallbridge-le-Carthew? or perhaps there already and laying before a very white-faced auditor his threats and propositions? A hasty person might have instantly pursued. Whatever I am, I am not hasty, and I was aware of three grave objections. In the first place, I could not be certain that Bellairs was gone. In the second, I had no taste whatever for a long drive at that hour of the night and in so merciless a rain. In the third, I had no idea how I was to get admitted if I went, and no idea what I should say if I got admitted. "In short," I concluded, "the whole situation is the merest farce. You have thrust yourself in where you had no business and have no power. You would be quite as useful in San Francisco; far happier in Paris; and being (by the wrath of God) at Stallbridge-Minster, the wisest thing is to go quietly to bed." On the way to my room, I saw (in a flash) that which I ought to have done long ago, and which it was now too late to think of—written to Carthew, I mean, detailing the facts and describing Bellairs, letting him defend himself if he were able, and giving him time to flee if he were not. It was the last blow to my self-respect; and I flung myself into my bed with contumely.

I have no guess what hour it was, when I was wakened by the entrance of Bellairs carrying a candle. He had been drunk, for he was bedaubed with mire from head to foot; but he was now sober and under the empire of some violent emotion which he controlled with difficulty. He trembled visibly; and more than once, during the interview which followed, tears suddenly and silently overflowed his cheeks.

"I have to ask your pardon, sir, for this untimely visit," he said. "I make no defence, I have no excuse, I have disgraced myself, I am properly punished; I appear before you to appeal to you in mercy for the most trifling aid or, God help me! I fear I may go mad."

"What on earth is wrong?" I asked.

"I have been robbed," he said. "I have no defence to offer; it was of my own fault, I am properly punished."

"But, gracious goodness me!" I cried, "who is there to rob you in a place like this?"

"I can form no opinion," he replied. "I have no idea. I was lying in a ditch inanimate. This is a degrading confession, sir; I can only say in self-defence that perhaps (in your good nature) you have made yourself partly responsible for my shame. I am not used to these rich wines."

"In what form was your money? Perhaps it may be traced," I suggested.

"It was in English sovereigns. I changed it in New York; I got very good exchange," he said, and then, with a momentary outbreak, "God in heaven, how I toiled for it!" he cried.

"That doesn't sound encouraging," said I. "It may be worth while to apply to the police, but it doesn't sound a hopeful case."

"And I have no hope in that direction," said Bellairs. "My hopes, Mr. Dodd, are all fixed upon yourself. I could easily convince you that a small, a very small advance, would be in the nature of an excellent investment; but I prefer to rely on your humanity. Our acquaintance began on an unusual footing; but you have now known me for some time, we have been some time—I was going to say we had been almost intimate. Under the impulse of instinctive sympathy, I have bared my heart to you, Mr. Dodd, as I have done to few; and I believe—I trust—I may say that I feel sure—you heard me with a kindly sentiment. This is what brings me to your side at this most inexcusable hour. But put yourself in my place—how could I sleep—how could I dream of sleeping, in this blackness of remorse and despair? There was a friend at hand—so I ventured to think of you; it was instinctive; I fled to your side, as the drowning man clutches at a straw. These expressions are not exaggerated, they scarcely serve to express the agitation of my mind. And think, sir, how easily you can restore me to hope and, I may say, to reason. A small loan, which shall be faithfully repaid. Five hundred dollars would be ample." He watched me with burning eyes. "Four hundred would do. I believe, Mr. Dodd, that I could manage with economy on two."

"And then you will repay me out of Carthew's pocket?" I said. "I am much obliged. But I will tell you what I will do: I will see you on board a steamer, pay your fare through to San Francisco, and place fifty dollars in the purser's hands, to be given you in New York."

He drank in my words; his face represented an ecstasy of cunning thought. I could read there, plain as print, that he but thought to overreach me.

"And what am I to do in 'Frisco?" he asked. "I am disbarred, I have no trade, I cannot dig, to beg——" he paused in the citation. "And you know that I am not alone," he added, "others depend upon me."

"I will write to Pinkerton," I returned. "I feel sure he can help you to some employment, and in the meantime, and for three months after your arrival, he shall pay to yourself personally, on the first and the fifteenth, twenty-five dollars."

"Mr. Dodd, I scarce believe you can be serious in this offer," he replied. "Have you forgotten the circumstances of the case? Do you know these people are the magnates of the section? They were spoken of to-night in the saloon; their wealth must amount to many millions of dollars in real estate alone; their house is one of the sights of the locality, and you offer me a bribe of a few hundred!"

"I offer you no bribe, Mr. Bellairs, I give you alms," I returned. "I will do nothing to forward you in your hateful business; yet I would not willingly have you starve."

"Give me a hundred dollars then, and be done with it," he cried.

"I will do what I have said, and neither more nor less," said I.

"Take care," he cried. "You are playing a fool's game; you are making an enemy for nothing; you will gain nothing by this, I warn you of it!" And then with one of his changes, "Seventy dollars—only seventy—in mercy, Mr. Dodd, in common charity. Don't dash the bowl from my lips! You have a kindly heart. Think of my position, remember my unhappy wife."

"You should have thought of her before," said I. "I have made my offer, and I wish to sleep."

"Is that your last word, sir? Pray consider; pray weigh both sides: my misery, your own danger. I warn you—I beseech you; measure it well before you answer," so he half pleaded, half threatened me, with clasped hands.

"My first word, and my last," said I.

The change upon the man was shocking. In the storm of anger that now shook him, the lees of his intoxication rose again to the surface; his face was deformed, his words insane with fury; his pantomime excessive in itself, was distorted by an access of St. Vitus.

"You will perhaps allow me to inform you of my cold opinion," he began, apparently self-possessed, truly bursting with rage: "when I am a glorified saint, I shall see you howling for a drop of water and exult to see you. That your last word! Take it in your face, you spy, you false friend, you fat hypocrite! I defy, I defy and despise and spit upon you! I'm on the trail, his trail or yours, I smell blood, I'll follow it on my hands and knees, I'll starve to follow it! I'll hunt you down, hunt you, hunt you down! If I were strong, I'd tear your vitals out, here in this room—tear them out—I'd tear them out! Damn, damn, damn! You think me weak! I can bite, bite to the blood, bite you, hurt you, disgrace you ..."

He was thus incoherently raging, when the scene was interrupted by the arrival of the landlord and inn servants in various degrees of deshabille, and to them I gave my temporary lunatic in charge.

"Take him to his room," I said, "he's only drunk."

These were my words; but I knew better. After all my study of Mr. Bellairs, one discovery had been reserved for the last moment: that of his latent and essential madness.

CHAPTER XX. STALLBRIDGE-LE-CARTHEW.

Long before I was awake, the shyster had disappeared, leaving his bill unpaid. I did not need to inquire where he was gone, I knew too well, I knew there was nothing left me but to follow; and about ten in the morning, set forth in a gig for Stallbridge-le-Carthew.

The road, for the first quarter of the way, deserts the valley of the river, and crosses the summit of a chalk-down, grazed over by flocks of sheep and haunted by innumerable larks. It was a pleasant but a vacant scene, arousing but not holding the attention; and my mind returned to the violent passage of the night before. My thought of the man I was pursuing had been greatly changed. I conceived of him, somewhere in front of me, upon his dangerous errand, not to be turned aside, not to be stopped, by either fear or reason. I had called him a ferret; I conceived him now as a mad dog. Methought he would run, not walk; methought, as he ran, that he would bark and froth at the lips; methought, if the great wall of China were to rise across his path, he would attack it with his nails.

Presently the road left the down, returned by a precipitous descent into the valley of the Stall, and ran thenceforward among enclosed fields and under the continuous shade of trees. I was told we had now entered on the Carthew property. By and by, a battlemented wall appeared on the left hand, and a little after I had my first glimpse of the mansion. It stood in a hollow of a bosky park, crowded to a degree that surprised and even displeased me, with huge timber and dense shrubberies of laurel and rhododendron. Even from this low station and the thronging neighbourhood of the trees, the pile rose conspicuous like a cathedral. Behind, as we continued to skirt the park wall, I began to make out a straggling town of offices which became conjoined to the rear with those of the home farm. On the left was an ornamental water sailed in by many swans. On the right extended a flower garden, laid in the old manner, and at this season of the year, as brilliant as stained glass. The front of the house presented a facade of more than sixty windows, surmounted by a formal pediment and raised upon a terrace. A wide avenue, part in gravel, part in turf, and bordered by triple alleys, ran to the great double gateways. It was impossible to look without surprise on a place that had been prepared through so many generations, had cost so many tons of minted gold, and was maintained in order by so great a company of emulous servants. And yet of these there was no sign but the perfection of their work. The whole domain was drawn to the line and weeded like the front plot of some suburban amateur; and I looked in vain for any belated gardener, and listened in vain for any sounds of labour. Some lowing of cattle and much calling of birds alone disturbed the stillness, and even the little hamlet, which clustered at the gates, appeared to hold its breath in awe of its great neighbour, like a troop of children who should have strayed into a king's anteroom.

The Carthew Arms, the small but very comfortable inn, was a mere appendage and outpost of the family whose name it bore. Engraved portraits of by-gone Carthews adorned the walls; Fielding Carthew, Recorder of the city of London; Major-General John Carthew in uniform, commanding some military operations; the Right Honourable Bailley Carthew, Member of Parliament for Stallbridge, standing by a table and brandishing a document; Singleton Carthew, Esquire, represented in the foreground of a herd of cattle—doubtless at the desire of his tenantry, who had made him a compliment of this work of art; and the Venerable Archdeacon Carthew, D.D., LL.D., A.M., laying his hand on the head of a little child in a manner highly frigid and ridiculous. So far as my memory serves me, there were no other pictures in this exclusive hostelry; and I was not surprised to learn that the landlord was an ex-butler, the landlady an ex-lady's-maid, from the great house; and that the bar-parlour was a sort of perquisite of former servants.

To an American, the sense of the domination of this family over so considerable a tract of earth was even oppressive; and as I considered their simple annals, gathered from the legends of the engravings, surprise began to mingle with my disgust. "Mr. Recorder" doubtless occupies an honourable post; but I thought that, in the course of so many generations, one Carthew might have clambered higher. The soldier had stuck at Major-General; the churchman bloomed unremarked in an archidiaconate; and though the Right Honourable Bailley seemed to have sneaked into the privy council, I have still to learn what he did when he had got there. Such vast means, so long a start, and such a modest standard of achievement, struck in me a strong sense of the dulness of that race.

I found that to come to the hamlet and not visit the Hall, would be regarded as a slight. To feed the swans, to see the peacocks and the Raphaels—for these commonplace people actually possessed two Raphaels—to risk life and limb among a famous breed of cattle called the Carthew Chillinghams, and to do homage to the sire (still living) of Donibristle, a renowned winner of the oaks: these, it seemed, were the inevitable stations of the pilgrimage. I was not so foolish as to resist, for I might have need before I was done of general good-will; and two pieces of news fell in which changed my resignation to alacrity. It appeared in the first place, that Mr. Norris was from home "travelling"; in the second, that a visitor had been before me and already made the tour of the Carthew curiosities. I thought I knew who this must be; I was anxious to learn what he had done and seen; and fortune so far favoured me that the under-gardener singled out to be my guide had already performed the same function for my predecessor.

"Yes, sir," he said, "an American gentleman right enough. At least, I don't think he was quite a gentleman, but a very civil person."

The person, it seems, had been civil enough to be delighted with the Carthew Chillinghams, to perform the whole pilgrimage with rising admiration, and to have almost prostrated himself before the shrine of Donibristle's sire.

"He told me, sir," continued the gratified under-gardener, "that he had often read of the 'stately 'omes of England,' but ours was the first he had the chance to see. When he came to the 'ead of the long alley, he fetched his breath. 'This is indeed a lordly domain!' he cries. And it was natural he should be interested in the place, for it seems Mr. Carthew had been kind to him in the States. In fact, he seemed a grateful kind of person, and wonderful taken up with flowers."

I heard this story with amazement. The phrases quoted told their own tale; they were plainly from the shyster's mint. A few hours back I had seen him a mere bedlamite and fit for a strait-waistcoat; he was penniless in a strange country; it was highly probable he had gone without breakfast; the absence of Norris must have been a crushing blow; the man (by all reason) should have been despairing. And now I heard of him, clothed and in his right mind, deliberate, insinuating, admiring vistas, smelling flowers, and talking like a book. The strength of character implied amazed and daunted me.

"This is curious," I said to the under-gardener. "I have had the pleasure of some acquaintance with Mr. Carthew myself; and I believe none of our western friends ever were in England. Who can this person be? He couldn't—no, that's impossible, he could never have had the impudence. His name was not Bellairs?"

"I didn't 'ear the name, sir. Do you know anything against him?" cried my guide.

"Well," said I, "he is certainly not the person Carthew would like to have here in his absence."

"Good gracious me!" exclaimed the gardener. "He was so pleasant spoken, too; I thought he was some form of a schoolmaster. Perhaps, sir, you wouldn't mind going right up to Mr. Denman? I recommended him to Mr. Denman, when he had done the grounds. Mr. Denman is our butler, sir," he added.

The proposal was welcome, particularly as affording me a graceful retreat from the neighbourhood of the Carthew Chillinghams; and, giving up our projected circuit, we took a short cut through the shrubbery and across the bowling green to the back quarters of the Hall.

The bowling green was surrounded by a great hedge of yew, and entered by an archway in the quick. As we were issuing from this passage, my conductor arrested me.

"The Honourable Lady Ann Carthew," he said, in an august whisper. And looking over his shoulder, I was aware of an old lady with a stick, hobbling somewhat briskly along the garden path. She must have been extremely handsome in her youth; and even the limp with which she walked could not deprive her of an unusual and almost menacing dignity of bearing. Melancholy was impressed besides on every feature, and her eyes, as she looked straight before her, seemed to contemplate misfortune.

"She seems sad," said I, when she had hobbled past and we had resumed our walk.

"She enjoy rather poor spirits, sir," responded the under-gardener. "Mr. Carthew—the old gentleman, I mean—died less than a year ago; Lord Tillibody, her ladyship's brother, two months after; and then there was the sad business about the young gentleman. Killed in the 'unting-field, sir; and her ladyship's favourite. The present Mr. Norris has never been so equally."

"So I have understood," said I, persistently, and (I think) gracefully pursuing my inquiries and fortifying my position as a family friend. "Dear, dear, how sad! And has this change—poor Carthew's return, and all—has this not mended matters?"

"Well, no, sir, not a sign of it," was the reply. "Worse, we think, than ever."

"Dear, dear!" said I again.

"When Mr. Norris arrived, she DID seem glad to see him," he pursued; "and we were all pleased, I'm sure; for no one knows the young gentleman but what likes him. Ah, sir, it didn't last long! That very night they had a talk, and fell out or something; her ladyship took on most painful; it was like old days, but worse. And the next morning Mr. Norris was off again upon his travels. 'Denman,' he said to Mr. Denman, 'Denman, I'll never come back,' he said, and shook him by the 'and. I wouldn't be saying all this to a stranger, sir," added my informant, overcome with a sudden fear lest he had gone too far.

He had indeed told me much, and much that was unsuspected by himself. On that stormy night of his return, Carthew had told his story; the old lady had more upon her mind than mere bereavements; and among the mental pictures on which she looked, as she walked staring down the path, was one of Midway Island and the Flying Scud.

Mr. Denman heard my inquiries with discomposure, but informed me the shyster was already gone.

"Gone?" cried I. "Then what can he have come for? One thing I can tell you, it was not to see the house."

"I don't see it could have been anything else," replied the butler.

"You may depend upon it it was," said I. "And whatever it was, he has got it. By the way, where is Mr. Carthew at present? I was sorry to find he was from home."

"He is engaged in travelling, sir," replied the butler, dryly.

"Ah, bravo!" cried I. "I laid a trap for you there, Mr. Denman. Now I need not ask you; I am sure you did not tell this prying stranger."

"To be sure not, sir," said the butler.

I went through the form of "shaking him by the 'and"—like Mr. Norris—not, however, with genuine enthusiasm. For I had failed ingloriously to get the address for myself; and I felt a sure conviction that Bellairs had done better, or he had still been here and still cultivating Mr. Denman.

I had escaped the grounds and the cattle; I could not escape the house. A lady with silver hair, a slender silver voice, and a stream of insignificant information not to be diverted, led me through the picture gallery, the music-room, the great dining-room, the long drawing-room, the Indian room, the theatre, and every corner (as I thought) of that interminable mansion. There was but one place reserved; the garden-room, whither Lady Ann had now retired. I paused a moment on the outside of the door, and smiled to myself. The situation was indeed strange, and these thin boards divided the secret of the Flying Scud.

All the while, as I went to and fro, I was considering the visit and departure of Bellairs. That he had got the address, I was quite certain: that he had not got it by direct questioning, I was convinced; some ingenuity, some lucky accident, had served him. A similar chance, an equal ingenuity, was required; or I was left helpless, the ferret must run down his prey, the great oaks fall, the Raphaels be scattered, the house let to some stockbroker suddenly made rich, and the name which now filled the mouths of five or six parishes dwindle to a memory. Strange that such great matters, so old a mansion, a family so ancient and so dull, should come to depend for perpetuity upon the intelligence, the discretion, and the cunning of a Latin-Quarter student! What Bellairs had done, I must do likewise. Chance or ingenuity, ingenuity or chance—so I continued to ring the changes as I walked down the avenue, casting back occasional glances at the red brick facade and the twinkling windows of the house. How was I to command chance? where was I to find the ingenuity?

These reflections brought me to the door of the inn. And here, pursuant to my policy of keeping well with all men, I immediately smoothed my brow, and accepted (being the only guest in the house) an invitation to dine with the family in the bar-parlour. I sat down accordingly with Mr. Higgs the ex-butler, Mrs. Higgs the ex-lady's-maid, and Miss Agnes Higgs their frowsy-headed little girl, the least promising and (as the event showed) the most useful of the lot. The talk ran endlessly on the great house and the great family; the roast beef, the Yorkshire pudding, the jam-roll, and the cheddar cheese came and went, and still the stream flowed on; near four generations of Carthews were touched upon without eliciting one point of interest; and we had killed Mr. Henry in "the 'unting-field," with a vast elaboration of painful circumstance, and buried him in the midst of a whole sorrowing county, before I could so much as manage to bring upon the stage my intimate friend, Mr. Norris. At the name, the ex-butler grew diplomatic, and the ex-lady's-maid tender. He was the only person of the whole featureless series who seemed to have accomplished anything worth mention; and his achievements, poor dog, seemed to have been confined to going to the devil and leaving some regrets. He had been the image of the Right Honourable Bailley, one of the lights of that dim house, and a career of distinction had been predicted of him in consequence almost from the cradle. But before he was out of long clothes, the cloven foot began to show; he proved to be no Carthew, developed a taste for low pleasures and bad company, went birdnesting with a stable-boy before he was eleven, and when he was near twenty, and might have been expected to display at least some rudiments of the family gravity, rambled the country over with a knapsack, making sketches and keeping company in wayside inns. He had no pride about him, I was told; he would sit down with any man; and it was somewhat woundingly implied that I was indebted to this peculiarity for my own acquaintance with the hero. Unhappily, Mr. Norris was not only eccentric, he was fast. His debts were still remembered at the University; still more, it appeared, the highly humorous circumstances attending his expulsion. "He was always fond of his jest," commented Mrs. Higgs.

"That he were!" observed her lord.

But it was after he went into the diplomatic service that the real trouble began.

"It seems, sir, that he went the pace extraordinary," said the ex-butler, with a solemn gusto.

"His debts were somethink awful," said the lady's-maid. "And as nice a young gentleman all the time as you would wish to see!"

"When word came to Mr. Carthew's ears, the turn up was 'orrible," continued Mr. Higgs. "I remember it as if it was yesterday. The bell was rung after her la'ship was gone, which I answered it myself, supposing it were the coffee. There was Mr. Carthew on his feet. ''Iggs,' he says, pointing with his stick, for he had a turn of the gout, 'order the dog-cart instantly for this son of mine which has disgraced hisself.' Mr. Norris say nothink: he sit there with his 'ead down, making belief to be looking at a walnut. You might have bowled me over with a straw," said Mr. Higgs.

"Had he done anything very bad?" I asked.

"Not he, Mr. Dodsley!" cried the lady—it was so she had conceived my name. "He never did anythink to all really wrong in his poor life. The 'ole affair was a disgrace. It was all rank favouritising."

"Mrs. 'Iggs! Mrs. 'Iggs!" cried the butler warningly.

"Well, what do I care?" retorted the lady, shaking her ringlets. "You know it was yourself, Mr. 'Iggs, and so did every member of the staff."

While I was getting these facts and opinions, I by no means neglected the child. She was not attractive; but fortunately she had reached the corrupt age of seven, when half a crown appears about as large as a saucer and is fully as rare as the dodo. For a shilling down, sixpence in her money-box, and an American gold dollar which I happened to find in my pocket, I bought the creature soul and body. She declared her intention to accompany me to the ends of the earth; and had to be chidden by her sire for drawing comparisons between myself and her uncle William, highly damaging to the latter.

Dinner was scarce done, the cloth was not yet removed, when Miss Agnes must needs climb into my lap with her stamp album, a relic of the generosity of Uncle William. There are few things I despise more than old stamps, unless perhaps it be crests; for cattle (from the Carthew Chillinghams down to the old gate-keeper's milk-cow in the lane) contempt is far from being my first sentiment. But it seemed I was doomed to pass that day in viewing curiosities, and smothering a yawn, I devoted myself once more to tread the well-known round. I fancy Uncle William must have begun the collection himself and tired of it, for the book (to my surprise) was quite respectably filled. There were the varying shades of the English penny, Russians with the coloured heart, old undecipherable Thurn-und-Taxis, obsolete triangular Cape of Good Hopes, Swan Rivers with the Swan, and Guianas with the sailing ship. Upon all these I looked with the eyes of a fish and the spirit of a sheep; I think indeed I was at times asleep; and it was probably in one of these moments that I capsized the album, and there fell from the end of it, upon the floor, a considerable number of what I believe to be called "exchanges."

Here, against all probability, my chance had come to me; for as I gallantly picked them up, I was struck with the disproportionate amount of five-sous French stamps. Some one, I reasoned, must write very regularly from France to the neighbourhood of Stallbridge-le-Carthew. Could it be Norris? On one stamp I made out an initial C; upon a second I got as far as CH; beyond which point, the postmark used was in every instance undecipherable. CH, when you consider that about a quarter of the towns in France begin with "chateau," was an insufficient clue; and I promptly annexed the plainest of the collection in order to consult the post-office.

The wretched infant took me in the fact. "Naughty man, to 'teal my 'tamp!" she cried; and when I would have brazened it off with a denial, recovered and displayed the stolen article.

My position was now highly false; and I believe it was in mere pity that Mrs. Higgs came to my rescue with a welcome proposition. If the gentleman was really interested in stamps, she said, probably supposing me a monomaniac on the point, he should see Mr. Denman's album. Mr. Denman had been collecting forty years, and his collection was said to be worth a mint of money. "Agnes," she went on, "if you were a kind little girl, you would run over to the 'All, tell Mr. Denman there's a connaiseer in the 'ouse, and ask him if one of the young gentlemen might bring the album down."

"I should like to see his exchanges too," I cried, rising to the occasion. "I may have some of mine in my pocket-book and we might trade."

Half an hour later Mr. Denman arrived himself with a most unconscionable volume under his arm. "Ah, sir," he cried, "when I 'eard you was a collector, I dropped all. It's a saying of mine, Mr. Dodsley, that collecting stamps makes all collectors kin. It's a bond, sir; it creates a bond."

Upon the truth of this, I cannot say; but there is no doubt that the attempt to pass yourself off for a collector falsely creates a precarious situation.

"Ah, here's the second issue!" I would say, after consulting the legend at the side. "The pink— no, I mean the mauve—yes, that's the beauty of this lot. Though of course, as you say," I would hasten to add, "this yellow on the thin paper is more rare."

Indeed I must certainly have been detected, had I not plied Mr. Denman in self-defence with his favourite liquor—a port so excellent that it could never have ripened in the cellar of the Carthew Arms, but must have been transported, under cloud of night, from the neighbouring vaults of the great house. At each threat of exposure, and in particular whenever I was directly challenged for an opinion, I made haste to fill the butler's glass, and by the time we had got to the exchanges, he was in a condition in which no stamp collector need be seriously feared. God forbid I should hint that he was drunk; he seemed incapable of the necessary liveliness; but the man's eyes were set, and so long as he was suffered to talk without interruption, he seemed careless of my heeding him.

In Mr. Denman's exchanges, as in those of little Agnes, the same peculiarity was to be remarked, an undue preponderance of that despicably common stamp, the French twenty-five centimes. And here joining them in stealthy review, I found the C and the CH; then something of an A just following; and then a terminal Y. Here was also the whole name spelt out to me; it seemed familiar, too; and yet for some time I could not bridge the imperfection. Then I came upon another stamp, in which an L was legible before the Y, and in a moment the word leaped up complete. Chailly, that was the name; Chailly-en-Biere, the post town of Barbizon—ah, there was the very place for any man to hide himself—there was the very place for Mr. Norris, who had rambled over England making sketches—the very place for Goddedaal, who had left a palette-knife on board the Flying Scud. Singular, indeed, that while I was drifting over England with the shyster, the man we were in quest of awaited me at my own ultimate destination.

Whether Mr. Denman had shown his album to Bellairs, whether, indeed, Bellairs could have caught (as I did) this hint from an obliterated postmark, I shall never know, and it mattered not. We were equal now; my task at Stallbridge-le-Carthew was accomplished; my interest in postage-stamps died shamelessly away; the astonished Denman was bowed out; and ordering the horse to be put in, I plunged into the study of the time-table.

CHAPTER XXI. FACE TO FACE.

I fell from the skies on Barbizon about two o'clock of a September afternoon. It is the dead hour of the day; all the workers have gone painting, all the idlers strolling, in the forest or the plain; the winding causewayed street is solitary, and the inn deserted. I was the more pleased to find one of my old companions in the dining-room; his town clothes marked him for a man in the act of departure; and indeed his portmanteau lay beside him on the floor.

"Why, Stennis," I cried, "you're the last man I expected to find here."

"You won't find me here long," he replied. "King Pandion he is dead; all his friends are lapped in lead. For men of our antiquity, the poor old shop is played out."

"I have had playmates, I have had companions," I quoted in return. We were both moved, I think, to meet again in this scene of our old pleasure parties so unexpectedly, after so long an interval, and both already so much altered.

"That is the sentiment," he replied. "All, all are gone, the old familiar faces. I have been here a week, and the only living creature who seemed to recollect me was the Pharaon. Bar the Sirons, of course, and the perennial Bodmer."

"Is there no survivor?" I inquired.

"Of our geological epoch? not one," he replied. "This is the city of Petra in Edom."

"And what sort of Bedouins encamp among the ruins?" I asked.

"Youth, Dodd, youth; blooming, conscious youth," he returned. "Such a gang, such reptiles! to think we were like that! I wonder Siron didn't sweep us from his premises."

"Perhaps we weren't so bad," I suggested.

"Don't let me depress you," said he. "We were both Anglo-Saxons, anyway, and the only redeeming feature to-day is another."

The thought of my quest, a moment driven out by this rencounter, revived in my mind. "Who is he?" I cried. "Tell me about him."

"What, the Redeeming Feature?" said he. "Well, he's a very pleasing creature, rather dim, and dull, and genteel, but really pleasing. He is very British, though, the artless Briton! Perhaps you'll find him too much so for the transatlantic nerves. Come to think of it, on the other hand, you ought to get on famously. He is an admirer of your great republic in one of its (excuse me) shoddiest features; he takes in and sedulously reads a lot of American papers. I warned you he was artless."

"What papers are they?" cried I.

"San Francisco papers," said he. "He gets a bale of them about twice a week, and studies them like the Bible. That's one of his weaknesses; another is to be incalculably rich. He has taken Masson's old studio—you remember?—at the corner of the road; he has furnished it regardless of expense, and lives there surrounded with vins fins and works of art. When the youth of to-day goes up to the Caverne des Brigands to make punch—they do all that we did, like some nauseous form of ape (I never appreciated before what a creature of tradition mankind is)—this

Madden follows with a basket of champagne. I told him he was wrong, and the punch tasted better; but he thought the boys liked the style of the thing, and I suppose they do. He is a very good-natured soul, and a very melancholy, and rather a helpless. O, and he has a third weakness which I came near forgetting. He paints. He has never been taught, and he's past thirty, and he paints."

"How?" I asked.

"Rather well, I think," was the reply. "That's the annoying part of it. See for yourself. That panel is his."

I stepped toward the window. It was the old familiar room, with the tables set like a Greek P, and the sideboard, and the aphasiac piano, and the panels on the wall. There were Romeo and Juliet, Antwerp from the river, Enfield's ships among the ice, and the huge huntsman winding a huge horn; mingled with them a few new ones, the thin crop of a succeeding generation, not better and not worse. It was to one of these I was directed; a thing coarsely and wittily handled, mostly with the palette-knife, the colour in some parts excellent, the canvas in others loaded with mere clay. But it was the scene, and not the art or want of it, that riveted my notice. The foreground was of sand and scrub and wreckwood; in the middle distance the many-hued and smooth expanse of a lagoon, enclosed by a wall of breakers; beyond, a blue strip of ocean. The sky was cloudless, and I could hear the surf break. For the place was Midway Island; the point of view the very spot at which I had landed with the captain for the first time, and from which I had re-embarked the day before we sailed. I had already been gazing for some seconds, before my attention was arrested by a blur on the sea-line; and stooping to look, I recognised the smoke of a steamer.

"Yes," said I, turning toward Stennis, "it has merit. What is it?"

"A fancy piece," he returned. "That's what pleased me. So few of the fellows in our time had the imagination of a garden snail."

"Madden, you say his name is?" I pursued.

"Madden," he repeated.

"Has he travelled much?" I inquired.

"I haven't an idea. He is one of the least autobiographical of men. He sits, and smokes, and giggles, and sometimes he makes small jests; but his contributions to the art of pleasing are generally confined to looking like a gentleman and being one. No," added Stennis, "he'll never suit you, Dodd; you like more head on your liquor. You'll find him as dull as ditch water."

"Has he big blonde side-whiskers like tusks?" I asked, mindful of the photograph of Goddedaal.

"Certainly not: why should he?" was the reply.

"Does he write many letters?" I continued.

"God knows," said Stennis. "What is wrong with you? I never saw you taken this way before."

"The fact is, I think I know the man," said I. "I think I'm looking for him. I rather think he is my long-lost brother."

"Not twins, anyway," returned Stennis.

And about the same time, a carriage driving up to the inn, he took his departure.

I walked till dinner-time in the plain, keeping to the fields; for I instinctively shunned observation, and was racked by many incongruous and impatient feelings. Here was a man whose voice I had once heard, whose doings had filled so many days of my life with interest and distress, whom I had lain awake to dream of like a lover; and now his hand was on the door; now we were to meet; now I was to learn at last the mystery of the substituted crew. The sun went down over the plain of the Angelus, and as the hour approached, my courage lessened. I let the laggard peasants pass me on the homeward way. The lamps were lit, the soup was served, the company were all at table, and the room sounded already with multitudinous talk before I entered. I took my place and found I was opposite to Madden. Over six feet high and well set up, the hair dark and streaked with silver, the eyes dark and kindly, the mouth very good-natured, the teeth admirable; linen and hands exquisite; English clothes, an English voice, an English bearing: the man stood out conspicuous from the company. Yet he had made himself at home, and seemed to enjoy a certain quiet popularity among the noisy boys of the table d'hote. He had an odd, silver giggle of a laugh, that sounded nervous even when he was really amused, and accorded ill with his big stature and manly, melancholy face. This laugh fell in continually all through dinner like the note of the triangle in a piece of modern French music; and he had at times a kind of pleasantry, rather of manner than of words, with which he started or maintained the merriment. He took his share in these diversions, not so much like a man in high spirits, but like one of an approved good nature, habitually self-forgetful, accustomed to please and to follow others. I have remarked in old soldiers much the same smiling sadness and sociable self-effacement.

I feared to look at him, lest my glances should betray my deep excitement, and chance served me so well that the soup was scarce removed before we were naturally introduced. My first sip of Chateau Siron, a vintage from which I had been long estranged, startled me into speech.

"O, this'll never do!" I cried, in English.

"Dreadful stuff, isn't it?" said Madden, in the same language. "Do let me ask you to share my bottle. They call it Chambertin, which it isn't; but it's fairly palatable, and there's nothing in this house that a man can drink at all."

I accepted; anything would do that paved the way to better knowledge.

"Your name is Madden, I think," said I. "My old friend Stennis told me about you when I came."

"Yes, I am sorry he went; I feel such a Grandfather William, alone among all these lads," he replied.

"My name is Dodd," I resumed.

"Yes," said he, "so Madame Siron told me."

"Dodd, of San Francisco," I continued. "Late of Pinkerton and Dodd."

"Montana Block, I think?" said he.

"The same," said I.

Neither of us looked at each other; but I could see his hand deliberately making bread pills.

"That's a nice thing of yours," I pursued, "that panel. The foreground is a little clayey, perhaps, but the lagoon is excellent."

"You ought to know," said he.

"Yes," returned I, "I'm rather a good judge of—that panel."

There was a considerable pause.

"You know a man by the name of Bellairs, don't you?" he resumed.

"Ah!" cried I, "you have heard from Doctor Urquart?"

"This very morning," he replied.

"Well, there is no hurry about Bellairs," said I. "It's rather a long story and rather a silly one. But I think we have a good deal to tell each other, and perhaps we had better wait till we are more alone."

"I think so," said he. "Not that any of these fellows know English, but we'll be more comfortable over at my place. Your health, Dodd."

And we took wine together across the table.

Thus had this singular introduction passed unperceived in the midst of more than thirty persons, art students, ladies in dressing-gowns and covered with rice powder, six foot of Siron whisking dishes over our head, and his noisy sons clattering in and out with fresh relays.

"One question more," said I: "Did you recognise my voice?"

"Your voice?" he repeated. "How should I? I had never heard it—we have never met."

"And yet, we have been in conversation before now," said I, "and I asked you a question which you never answered, and which I have since had many thousand better reasons for putting to myself."

He turned suddenly white. "Good God!" he cried, "are you the man in the telephone?"

I nodded.

"Well, well!" said he. "It would take a good deal of magnanimity to forgive you that. What nights I have passed! That little whisper has whistled in my ear ever since, like the wind in a keyhole. Who could it be? What could it mean? I suppose I have had more real, solid misery out of that ..." He paused, and looked troubled. "Though I had more to bother me, or ought to have," he added, and slowly emptied his glass.

"It seems we were born to drive each other crazy with conundrums," said I. "I have often thought my head would split."

Carthew burst into his foolish laugh. "And yet neither you nor I had the worst of the puzzle," he cried. "There were others deeper in."

"And who were they?" I asked.

"The underwriters," said he.

"Why, to be sure!" cried I, "I never thought of that. What could they make of it?"

"Nothing," replied Carthew. "It couldn't be explained. They were a crowd of small dealers at

Lloyd's who took it up in syndicate; one of them has a carriage now; and people say he is a deuce of a deep fellow, and has the makings of a great financier. Another furnished a small villa on the profits. But they're all hopelessly muddled; and when they meet each other, they don't know where to look, like the Augurs."

Dinner was no sooner at an end than he carried me across the road to Masson's old studio. It was strangely changed. On the walls were tapestry, a few good etchings, and some amazing pictures—a Rousseau, a Corot, a really superb old Crome, a Whistler, and a piece which my host claimed (and I believe) to be a Titian. The room was furnished with comfortable English smoking-room chairs, some American rockers, and an elaborate business table; spirits and soda-water (with the mark of Schweppe, no less) stood ready on a butler's tray, and in one corner, behind a half-drawn curtain, I spied a camp-bed and a capacious tub. Such a room in Barbizon astonished the beholder, like the glories of the cave of Monte Cristo.

"Now," said he, "we are quiet. Sit down, if you don't mind, and tell me your story all through."

I did as he asked, beginning with the day when Jim showed me the passage in the Daily Occidental, and winding up with the stamp album and the Chailly postmark. It was a long business; and Carthew made it longer, for he was insatiable of details; and it had struck midnight on the old eight-day clock in the corner, before I had made an end.

"And now," said he, "turn about: I must tell you my side, much as I hate it. Mine is a beastly story. You'll wonder how I can sleep. I've told it once before, Mr. Dodd."

"To Lady Ann?" I asked.

"As you suppose," he answered; "and to say the truth, I had sworn never to tell it again. Only, you seem somehow entitled to the thing; you have paid dear enough, God knows; and God knows I hope you may like it, now you've got it!"

With that he began his yarn. A new day had dawned, the cocks crew in the village and the early woodmen were afoot, when he concluded.

CHAPTER XXII. THE REMITTANCE MAN.

Singleton Carthew, the father of Norris, was heavily built and feebly vitalised, sensitive as a musician, dull as a sheep, and conscientious as a dog. He took his position with seriousness, even with pomp; the long rooms, the silent servants, seemed in his eyes like the observances of some religion of which he was the mortal god. He had the stupid man's intolerance of stupidity in others; the vain man's exquisite alarm lest it should be detected in himself. And on both sides Norris irritated and offended him. He thought his son a fool, and he suspected that his son returned the compliment with interest. The history of their relation was simple; they met seldom, they quarrelled often. To his mother, a fiery, pungent, practical woman, already disappointed in her husband and her elder son, Norris was only a fresh disappointment.

Yet the lad's faults were no great matter; he was diffident, placable, passive, unambitious, unenterprising; life did not much attract him; he watched it like a curious and dull exhibition, not much amused, and not tempted in the least to take a part. He beheld his father ponderously grinding sand, his mother fiercely breaking butterflies, his brother labouring at the pleasures of the Hawbuck with the ardour of a soldier in a doubtful battle; and the vital sceptic looked on wondering. They were careful and troubled about many things; for him there seemed not even one thing needful. He was born disenchanted, the world's promises awoke no echo in his bosom, the world's activities and the world's distinctions seemed to him equally without a base in fact. He liked the open air; he liked comradeship, it mattered not with whom, his comrades were only a remedy for solitude. And he had a taste for painted art. An array of fine pictures looked upon his childhood, and from these roods of jewelled canvas he received an indelible impression. The gallery at Stallbridge betokened generations of picture lovers; Norris was perhaps the first of his race to hold the pencil. The taste was genuine, it grew and strengthened with his growth; and yet he suffered it to be suppressed with scarce a struggle. Time came for him to go to Oxford, and he resisted faintly. He was stupid, he said; it was no good to put him through the mill; he wished to be a painter. The words fell on his father like a thunderbolt, and Norris made haste to give way. "It didn't really matter, don't you know?" said he. "And it seemed an awful shame to vex the old boy."

To Oxford he went obediently, hopelessly; and at Oxford became the hero of a certain circle. He was active and adroit; when he was in the humour, he excelled in many sports; and his singular melancholy detachment gave him a place apart. He set a fashion in his clique. Envious undergraduates sought to parody his unaffected lack of zeal and fear; it was a kind of new Byronism more composed and dignified. "Nothing really mattered"; among other things, this formula embraced the dons; and though he always meant to be civil, the effect on the college authorities was one of startling rudeness. His indifference cut like insolence; and in some outbreak of his constitutional levity (the complement of his melancholy) he was "sent down" in the middle of the second year.

The event was new in the annals of the Carthews, and Singleton was prepared to make the most of it. It had been long his practice to prophesy for his second son a career of ruin and disgrace. There is an advantage in this artless parental habit. Doubtless the father is interested in his son; but doubtless also the prophet grows to be interested in his prophecies. If the one goes wrong, the others come true. Old Carthew drew from this source esoteric consolations; he dwelt at length on his own foresight; he produced variations hitherto unheard from the old theme "I told you so," coupled his son's name with the gallows and the hulks, and spoke of his small handful of college debts as though he must raise money on a mortgage to discharge them.

"I don't think that is fair, sir," said Norris. "I lived at college exactly as you told me. I am sorry I was sent down, and you have a perfect right to blame me for that; but you have no right to pitch into me about these debts."

The effect upon a stupid man not unjustly incensed need scarcely be described. For a while Singleton raved.

"I'll tell you what, father," said Norris at last, "I don't think this is going to do. I think you had better let me take to painting. It's the only thing I take a spark of interest in. I shall never be steady as long as I'm at anything else."

"When you stand here, sir, to the neck in disgrace," said the father, "I should have hoped you would have had more good taste than to repeat this levity."

The hint was taken; the levity was never more obtruded on the father's notice, and Norris was inexorably launched upon a backward voyage. He went abroad to study foreign languages, which he learned, at a very expensive rate; and a fresh crop of debts fell soon to be paid, with similar lamentations, which were in this case perfectly justified, and to which Norris paid no regard. He had been unfairly treated over the Oxford affair; and with a spice of malice very surprising in one so placable, and an obstinacy remarkable in one so weak, refused from that day forward to exercise the least captaincy on his expenses. He wasted what he would; he allowed his servants to despoil him at their pleasure; he sowed insolvency; and when the crop was ripe, notified his father with exasperating calm. His own capital was put in his hands, he was planted in the diplomatic service and told he must depend upon himself.

He did so till he was twenty-five; by which time he had spent his money, laid in a handsome choice of debts, and acquired (like so many other melancholic and uninterested persons) a habit of gambling. An Austrian colonel—the same who afterwards hanged himself at Monte Carlo—gave him a lesson which lasted two-and-twenty hours, and left him wrecked and helpless. Old Singleton once more repurchased the honour of his name, this time at a fancy figure; and Norris was set afloat again on stern conditions. An allowance of three hundred pounds in the year was to be paid to him quarterly by a lawyer in Sydney, New South Wales. He was not to write. Should he fail on any quarter-day to be in Sydney, he was to be held for dead, and the allowance tacitly withdrawn. Should he return to Europe, an advertisement publicly disowning him was to appear in every paper of repute.

It was one of his most annoying features as a son, that he was always polite, always just, and in whatever whirlwind of domestic anger, always calm. He expected trouble; when trouble came, he was unmoved: he might have said with Singleton, "I told you so"; he was content with thinking, "just as I expected." On the fall of these last thunderbolts, he bore himself like a person only distantly interested in the event; pocketed the money and the reproaches, obeyed orders punctually; took ship and came to Sydney. Some men are still lads at twenty-five; and so it was with Norris. Eighteen days after he landed, his quarter's allowance was all gone, and with the light-hearted hopefulness of strangers in what is called a new country, he began to besiege offices and apply for all manner of incongruous situations. Everywhere, and last of all from his lodgings, he was bowed out; and found himself reduced, in a very elegant suit of summer tweeds, to herd and camp with the degraded outcasts of the city.

In this strait, he had recourse to the lawyer who paid him his allowance.

"Try to remember that my time is valuable, Mr. Carthew," said the lawyer. "It is quite unnecessary you should enlarge on the peculiar position in which you stand. Remittance men, as we call them here, are not so rare in my experience; and in such cases I act upon a system. I make you a present of a sovereign; here it is. Every day you choose to call, my clerk will advance you a shilling; on Saturday, since my office is closed on Sunday, he will advance you half a crown. My conditions are these: that you do not come to me, but to my clerk; that you do not come here the worse of liquor; and you go away the moment you are paid and have signed a receipt. I wish you a good-morning."

"I have to thank you, I suppose," said Carthew. "My position is so wretched that I cannot even refuse this starvation allowance."

"Starvation!" said the lawyer, smiling. "No man will starve here on a shilling a day. I had on my hands another young gentleman, who remained continuously intoxicated for six years on the same allowance." And he once more busied himself with his papers.

In the time that followed, the image of the smiling lawyer haunted Carthew's memory. "That three minutes' talk was all the education I ever had worth talking of," says he. "It was all life in a nut-shell. Confound it! I thought, have I got to the point of envying that ancient fossil?"

Every morning for the next two or three weeks, the stroke of ten found Norris, unkempt and haggard, at the lawyer's door. The long day and longer night he spent in the Domain, now on a bench, now on the grass under a Norfolk Island pine, the companion of perhaps the lowest class on earth, the Larrikins of Sydney. Morning after morning, the dawn behind the lighthouse recalled him from slumber; and he would stand and gaze upon the changing east, the fading lenses, the smokeless city, and the many-armed and many-masted harbour growing slowly clear under his eyes. His bed-fellows (so to call them) were less active; they lay sprawled upon the grass and benches, the dingy men, the frowsy women, prolonging their late repose; and Carthew wandered among the sleeping bodies alone, and cursed the incurable stupidity of his behaviour. Day brought a new society of nursery-maids and children, and fresh-dressed and (I am sorry to say) tight-laced maidens, and gay people in rich traps; upon the skirts of which Carthew and "the other blackguards"—his own bitter phrase—skulked, and chewed grass, and looked on. Day passed, the light died, the green and leafy precinct sparkled with lamps or lay in shadow, and the round of the night began again, the loitering women, the lurking men, the sudden outburst of screams, the sound of flying feet. "You mayn't believe it," says Carthew, "but I got to that pitch that I didn't care a hang. I have been wakened out of my sleep to hear a woman screaming, and I have only turned upon my other side. Yes, it's a queer place, where the dowagers and the kids walk all day, and at night you can hear people bawling for help as if it was the Forest of Bondy, with the lights of a great town all round, and parties spinning through in cabs from Government House and dinner with my lord!"

It was Norris's diversion, having none other, to scrape acquaintance, where, how, and with whom he could. Many a long dull talk he held upon the benches or the grass; many a strange waif he came to know; many strange things he heard, and saw some that were abominable. It was to one of these last that he owed his deliverance from the Domain. For some time the rain had been merciless; one night after another he had been obliged to squander fourpence on a bed and reduce his board to the remaining eightpence: and he sat one morning near the Macquarrie Street entrance, hungry, for he had gone without breakfast, and wet, as he had already been for several days, when the cries of an animal in distress attracted his attention. Some fifty yards away, in the extreme angle of the grass, a party of the chronically unemployed had got hold of a dog, whom they were torturing in a manner not to be described. The heart of Norris, which had grown indifferent to the cries of human anger or distress, woke at the appeal of the dumb creature. He ran amongst the Larrikins, scattered them, rescued the dog, and stood at bay. They were six in number, shambling gallowsbirds; but for once the proverb was right, cruelty was coupled with cowardice, and the wretches cursed him and made off. It chanced that this act of prowess had not passed unwitnessed. On a bench near by there was seated a shopkeeper's assistant out of employ, a diminutive, cheerful, red-headed creature by the name of Hemstead. He was the last man to have interfered himself, for his discretion more than equalled his valour; but he made haste to congratulate Carthew, and to warn him he might not always be so fortunate.

"They're a dyngerous lot of people about this park. My word! it doesn't do to ply with them!" he observed, in that RYCY AUSTRYLIAN English, which (as it has received the imprimatur of Mr. Froude) we should all make haste to imitate.

"Why, I'm one of that lot myself," returned Carthew.

Hemstead laughed and remarked that he knew a gentleman when he saw one.

"For all that, I am simply one of the unemployed," said Carthew, seating himself beside his new acquaintance, as he had sat (since this experience began) beside so many dozen others.

"I'm out of a plyce myself," said Hemstead.

"You beat me all the way and back," says Carthew. "My trouble is that I have never been in one."

"I suppose you've no tryde?" asked Hemstead.

"I know how to spend money," replied Carthew, "and I really do know something of horses and something of the sea. But the unions head me off; if it weren't for them, I might have had a dozen berths."

"My word!" cried the sympathetic listener. "Ever try the mounted police?" he inquired.

"I did, and was bowled out," was the reply; "couldn't pass the doctors."

"Well, what do you think of the ryleways, then?" asked Hemstead.

"What do YOU think of them, if you come to that?" asked Carthew.

"O, I don't think of them; I don't go in for manual labour," said the little man proudly. "But if a man don't mind that, he's pretty sure of a job there."

"By George, you tell me where to go!" cried Carthew, rising.

The heavy rains continued, the country was already overrun with floods; the railway system daily required more hands, daily the superintendent advertised; but "the unemployed" preferred the resources of charity and rapine, and a navvy, even an amateur navvy, commanded money in the market. The same night, after a tedious journey, and a change of trains to pass a landslip, Norris found himself in a muddy cutting behind South Clifton, attacking his first shift of manual labour.

For weeks the rain scarce relented. The whole front of the mountain slipped seaward from above, avalanches of clay, rock, and uprooted forest spewed over the cliffs and fell upon the beach or in the breakers. Houses were carried bodily away and smashed like nuts; others were menaced and deserted, the door locked, the chimney cold, the dwellers fled elsewhere for safety. Night and day the fire blazed in the encampment; night and day hot coffee was served to the overdriven toilers in the shift; night and day the engineer of the section made his rounds with words of encouragement, hearty and rough and well suited to his men. Night and day, too, the telegraph clicked with disastrous news and anxious inquiry. Along the terraced line of rail, rare trains came creeping and signalling; and paused at the threatened corner, like living things conscious of peril. The commandant of the post would hastily review his labours, make (with a dry throat) the signal to advance; and the whole squad line the way and look on in a choking silence, or burst into a brief cheer as the train cleared the point of danger and shot on, perhaps through the thin sunshine between squalls, perhaps with blinking lamps into the gathering, rainy twilight.

One such scene Carthew will remember till he dies. It blew great guns from the seaward; a huge surf bombarded, five hundred feet below him, the steep mountain's foot; close in was a vessel in distress, firing shots from a fowling-piece, if any help might come. So he saw and heard her the moment before the train appeared and paused, throwing up a Babylonian tower of smoke into the rain, and oppressing men's hearts with the scream of her whistle. The engineer was there himself; he paled as he made the signal: the engine came at a foot's pace; but the whole bulk of mountain shook and seemed to nod seaward, and the watching navvies instinctively clutched at shrubs and trees: vain precautions, vain as the shots from the poor sailors. Once again fear was disappointed; the train passed unscathed; and Norris, drawing a long breath, remembered the labouring ship and glanced below. She was gone.

So the days and the nights passed: Homeric labour in Homeric circumstance. Carthew was sick with sleeplessness and coffee; his hands, softened by the wet, were cut to ribbons; yet he enjoyed a peace of mind and health of body hitherto unknown. Plenty of open air, plenty of physical exertion, a continual instancy of toil; here was what had been hitherto lacking in that misdirected life, and the true cure of vital scepticism. To get the train through: there was the recurrent problem; no time remained to ask if it were necessary. Carthew, the idler, the spendthrift, the drifting dilettant, was soon remarked, praised, and advanced. The engineer swore by him and pointed him out for an example. "I've a new chum, up here," Norris overheard him saying, "a young swell. He's worth any two in the squad." The words fell on the ears of the discarded son like music; and from that moment, he not only found an interest, he took a pride, in his plebeian tasks.

The press of work was still at its highest when quarter-day approached. Norris was now raised to a position of some trust; at his discretion, trains were stopped or forwarded at the dangerous cornice near North Clifton; and he found in this responsibility both terror and delight. The thought of the seventy-five pounds that would soon await him at the lawyer's, and of his own obligation to be present every quarter-day in Sydney, filled him for a little with divided councils. Then he made up his mind, walked in a slack moment to the inn at Clifton, ordered a sheet of paper and a bottle of beer, and wrote, explaining that he held a good appointment which he would lose if he came to Sydney, and asking the lawyer to accept this letter as an evidence of his presence in the colony, and retain the money till next quarter-day. The answer came in course of post, and was not merely favourable but cordial. "Although what you propose is contrary to the terms of my instructions," it ran, "I willingly accept the responsibility of granting your request. I should say I am agreeably disappointed in your behaviour. My experience has not led me to found much expectations on gentlemen in your position."

The rains abated, and the temporary labour was discharged; not Norris, to whom the engineer clung as to found money; not Norris, who found himself a ganger on the line in the regular staff of navvies. His camp was pitched in a grey wilderness of rock and forest, far from any house; as he sat with his mates about the evening fire, the trains passing on the track were their next and indeed their only neighbours, except the wild things of the wood. Lovely weather, light and monotonous employment, long hours of somnolent camp-fire talk, long sleepless nights, when he reviewed his foolish and fruitless career as he rose and walked in the moonlit forest, an occasional paper of which he would read all, the advertisements with as much relish as the text: such was the tenor of an existence which soon began to weary and harass him. He lacked and regretted the fatigue, the furious hurry, the suspense, the fires, the midnight coffee, the rude and mud-bespattered poetry of the first toilful weeks. In the quietness of his new surroundings, a voice summoned him from this exorbital part of life, and about the middle of October he threw up his situation and bade farewell to the camp of tents and the shoulder of Bald Mountain.

Clad in his rough clothes, with a bundle on his shoulder and his accumulated wages in his pocket, he entered Sydney for the second time, and walked with pleasure and some bewilderment in the cheerful streets, like a man landed from a voyage. The sight of the people led him on. He forgot his necessary errands, he forgot to eat. He wandered in moving multitudes like a stick upon a river. Last he came to the Domain and strolled there, and remembered his shame and sufferings, and looked with poignant curiosity at his successors. Hemstead, not much shabbier and no less cheerful than before, he recognised and addressed like an old family friend.

"That was a good turn you did me," said he. "That railway was the making of me. I hope you've had luck yourself."

"My word, no!" replied the little man. "I just sit here and read the Dead Bird. It's the depression in tryde, you see. There's no positions goin' that a man like me would care to look at." And he showed Norris his certificates and written characters, one from a grocer in Wooloomooloo, one from an ironmonger, and a third from a billiard saloon. "Yes," he said, "I tried bein' a billiard marker. It's no account; these lyte hours are no use for a man's health. I won't be no man's slyve," he added firmly.

On the principle that he who is too proud to be a slave is usually not too modest to become a pensioner, Carthew gave him half a sovereign, and departed, being suddenly struck with hunger, in the direction of the Paris House. When he came to that quarter of the city, the barristers were trotting in the streets in wig and gown, and he stood to observe them with his bundle on his shoulder, and his mind full of curious recollections of the past.

"By George!" cried a voice, "it's Mr. Carthew!"

And turning about he found himself face to face with a handsome sunburnt youth, somewhat fatted, arrayed in the finest of fine raiment, and sporting about a sovereign's worth of flowers in his buttonhole. Norris had met him during his first days in Sydney at a farewell supper; had even escorted him on board a schooner full of cockroaches and black-boy sailors, in which he was bound for six months among the islands; and had kept him ever since in entertained remembrance. Tom Hadden (known to the bulk of Sydney folk as Tommy) was heir to a considerable property, which a prophetic father had placed in the hands of rigorous trustees. The income supported Mr. Hadden in splendour for about three months out of twelve; the rest of the year he passed in retreat among the islands. He was now about a week returned from his eclipse, pervading Sydney in hansom cabs and airing the first bloom of six new suits of clothes; and yet the unaffected creature hailed Carthew in his working jeans and with the damning bundle on his shoulder, as he might have claimed acquaintance with a duke.

"Come and have a drink!" was his cheerful cry.

"I'm just going to have lunch at the Paris House," returned Carthew. "It's a long time since I have had a decent meal."

"Splendid scheme!" said Hadden. "I've only had breakfast half an hour ago; but we'll have a private room, and I'll manage to pick something. It'll brace me up. I was on an awful tear last night, and I've met no end of fellows this morning." To meet a fellow, and to stand and share a drink, were with Tom synonymous terms.

They were soon at table in the corner room up-stairs, and paying due attention to the best fare in Sydney. The odd similarity of their positions drew them together, and they began soon to exchange confidences. Carthew related his privations in the Domain and his toils as a navvy; Hadden gave his experience as an amateur copra merchant in the South Seas, and drew a humorous picture of life in a coral island. Of the two plans of retirement, Carthew gathered that his own had been vastly the more lucrative; but Hadden's trading outfit had consisted largely of bottled stout and brown sherry for his own consumption.

"I had champagne too," said Hadden, "but I kept that in case of sickness, until I didn't seem to be going to be sick, and then I opened a pint every Sunday. Used to sleep all morning, then breakfast with my pint of fizz, and lie in a hammock and read Hallam's Middle Ages. Have you read that? I always take something solid to the islands. There's no doubt I did the thing in rather a fine style; but if it was gone about a little cheaper, or there were two of us to bear the expense, it ought to pay hand over fist. I've got the influence, you see. I'm a chief now, and sit in the speak-house under my own strip of roof. I'd like to see them taboo ME! They daren't try it; I've a strong party, I can tell you. Why, I've had upwards of thirty cowtops sitting in my front verandah eating tins of salmon."

"Cowtops?" asked Carthew, "what are they?"

"That's what Hallam would call feudal retainers," explained Hadden, not without vainglory. "They're My Followers. They belong to My Family. I tell you, they come expensive, though; you can't fill up all these retainers on tinned salmon for nothing; but whenever I could get it, I would give 'em squid. Squid's good for natives, but I don't care for it, do you?—or shark either. It's like the working classes at home. With copra at the price it is, they ought to be willing to bear their share of the loss; and so I've told them again and again. I think it's a man's duty to open their minds, and I try to, but you can't get political economy into them; it doesn't seem to reach their intelligence."

There was an expression still sticking in Carthew's memory, and he returned upon it with a smile. "Talking of political economy," said he, "you said if there were two of us to bear the expense, the profits would increase. How do you make out that?"

"I'll show you! I'll figure it out for you!" cried Hadden, and with a pencil on the back of the bill of fare proceeded to perform miracles. He was a man, or let us rather say a lad, of unusual projective power. Give him the faintest hint of any speculation, and the figures flowed from him by the page. A lively imagination and a ready though inaccurate memory supplied his data; he delivered himself with an inimitable heat that made him seem the picture of pugnacity; lavished contradiction; had a form of words, with or without significance, for every form of criticism; and the looker-on alternately smiled at his simplicity and fervour, or was amazed by his unexpected shrewdness. He was a kind of Pinkerton in play. I have called Jim's the romance of business; this was its Arabian tale.

"Have you any idea what this would cost?" he asked, pausing at an item.

"Not I," said Carthew.

"Ten pounds ought to be ample," concluded the projector.

"O, nonsense!" cried Carthew. "Fifty at the very least."

"You told me yourself this moment you knew nothing about it!" cried Tommy. "How can I make a calculation, if you blow hot and cold? You don't seem able to be serious!"

But he consented to raise his estimate to twenty; and a little after, the calculation coming out with a deficit, cut it down again to five pounds ten, with the remark, "I told you it was nonsense. This sort of thing has to be done strictly, or where's the use?"

Some of these processes struck Carthew as unsound; and he was at times altogether thrown out by the capricious startings of the prophet's mind. These plunges seemed to be gone into for exercise and by the way, like the curvets of a willing horse. Gradually the thing took shape; the glittering if baseless edifice arose; and the hare still ran on the mountains, but the soup was already served in silver plate. Carthew in a few days could command a hundred and fifty pounds; Hadden was ready with five hundred; why should they not recruit a fellow or two more, charter an old ship, and go cruising on their own account? Carthew was an experienced yachtsman; Hadden professed himself able to "work an approximate sight." Money was undoubtedly to be made, or why should so many vessels cruise about the islands? they, who worked their own ship, were sure of a still higher profit.

"And whatever else comes of it, you see," cried Hadden, "we get our keep for nothing. Come, buy some togs, that's the first thing you have to do of course; and then we'll take a hansom and go to the Currency Lass."

"I'm going to stick to the togs I have," said Norris.

"Are you?" cried Hadden. "Well, I must say I admire you. You're a regular sage. It's what you call Pythagoreanism, isn't it? if I haven't forgotten my philosophy."

"Well, I call it economy," returned Carthew. "If we are going to try this thing on, I shall want every sixpence."

"You'll see if we're going to try it!" cried Tommy, rising radiant from table. "Only, mark you, Carthew, it must be all in your name. I have capital, you see; but you're all right. You can play vacuus viator, if the thing goes wrong."

"I thought we had just proved it was quite safe," said Carthew.

"There's nothing safe in business, my boy," replied the sage; "not even bookmaking."

The public house and tea garden called the Currency Lass represented a moderate fortune gained by its proprietor, Captain Bostock, during a long, active, and occasionally historic career among the islands. Anywhere from Tonga to the Admiralty Isles, he knew the ropes and could lie in the native dialect. He had seen the end of sandal wood, the end of oil, and the beginning of copra; and he was himself a commercial pioneer, the first that ever carried human teeth into the Gilberts. He was tried for his life in Fiji in Sir Arthur Gordon's time; and if ever he prayed at all, the name of Sir Arthur was certainly not forgotten. He was speared in seven places in New Ireland—the same time his mate was killed—the famous "outrage on the brig Jolly Roger"; but the treacherous savages made little by their wickedness, and Bostock, in spite of their teeth, got seventy-five head of volunteer labour on board, of whom not more than a dozen died of injuries. He had a hand, besides, in the amiable pleasantry which cost the life of Patteson; and when the sham bishop landed, prayed, and gave his benediction to the natives, Bostock, arrayed in a female chemise out of the traderoom, had stood at his right hand and boomed amens. This, when he was sure he was among good fellows, was his favourite yarn. "Two hundred head of labour for a hatful of amens," he used to name the tale; and its sequel, the death of the real bishop, struck him as a circumstance of extraordinary humour.

Many of these details were communicated in the hansom, to the surprise of Carthew.

"Why do we want to visit this old ruffian?" he asked.

"You wait till you hear him," replied Tommy. "That man knows everything."

On descending from the hansom at the Currency Lass, Hadden was struck with the appearance of the cabman, a gross, salt-looking man, red-faced, blue-eyed, short-handed and short-winded, perhaps nearing forty.

"Surely I know you?" said he. "Have you driven me before?"

"Many's the time, Mr. Hadden," returned the driver. "The last time you was back from the islands, it was me that drove you to the races, sir."

"All right: jump down and have a drink then," said Tom, and he turned and led the way into the garden.

Captain Bostock met the party: he was a slow, sour old man, with fishy eyes; greeted Tommy offhand, and (as was afterwards remembered) exchanged winks with the driver.

"A bottle of beer for the cabman there at that table," said Tom. "Whatever you please from shandygaff to champagne at this one here; and you sit down with us. Let me make you acquainted with my friend, Mr. Carthew. I've come on business, Billy; I want to consult you as a friend; I'm going into the island trade upon my own account."

Doubtless the captain was a mine of counsel, but opportunity was denied him. He could not venture on a statement, he was scarce allowed to finish a phrase, before Hadden swept him from the field with a volley of protest and correction. That projector, his face blazing with inspiration, first laid before him at inordinate length a question, and as soon as he attempted to reply, leaped at his throat, called his facts in question, derided his policy, and at times thundered on him from the heights of moral indignation.

"I beg your pardon," he said once. "I am a gentleman, Mr. Carthew here is a gentleman, and we don't mean to do that class of business. Can't you see who you are talking to? Can't you talk sense? Can't you give us 'a dead bird' for a good traderoom?"

"No, I don't suppose I can," returned old Bostock; "not when I can't hear my own voice for two seconds together. It was gin and guns I did it with."

"Take your gin and guns to Putney!" cried Hadden. "It was the thing in your times, that's right enough; but you're old now, and the game's up. I'll tell you what's wanted now-a-days, Bill Bostock," said he; and did, and took ten minutes to it.

Carthew could not refrain from smiling. He began to think less seriously of the scheme, Hadden appearing too irresponsible a guide; but on the other hand, he enjoyed himself amazingly. It was far from being the same with Captain Bostock.

"You know a sight, don't you?" remarked that gentleman, bitterly, when Tommy paused.

"I know a sight more than you, if that's what you mean," retorted Tom. "It stands to reason I do. You're not a man of any education; you've been all your life at sea or in the islands; you don't suppose you can give points to a man like me?"

"Here's your health, Tommy," returned Bostock. "You'll make an A-one bake in the New Hebrides."

"That's what I call talking," cried Tom, not perhaps grasping the spirit of this doubtful compliment. "Now you give me your attention. We have the money and the enterprise, and I have the experience: what we want is a cheap, smart boat, a good captain, and an introduction to some house that will give us credit for the trade."

"Well, I'll tell you," said Captain Bostock. "I have seen men like you baked and eaten, and complained of afterwards. Some was tough, and some hadn't no flaviour," he added grimly.

"What do you mean by that?" cried Tom.

"I mean I don't care," cried Bostock. "It ain't any of my interests. I haven't underwrote your life. Only I'm blest if I'm not sorry for the cannibal as tries to eat your head. And what I recommend is a cheap, smart coffin and a good undertaker. See if you can find a house to give you credit for a coffin! Look at your friend there; HE'S got some sense; he's laughing at you so as he can't stand."

The exact degree of ill-feeling in Mr. Bostock's mind was difficult to gauge; perhaps there was not much, perhaps he regarded his remarks as a form of courtly badinage. But there is little doubt that Hadden resented them. He had even risen from his place, and the conference was on the point of breaking up, when a new voice joined suddenly in the conversation.

The cabman sat with his back turned upon the party, smoking a meerschaum pipe. Not a word of Tommy's eloquence had missed him, and he now faced suddenly about with these amazing words:—

"Excuse me, gentlemen; if you'll buy me the ship I want, I'll get you the trade on credit."

There was a pause.

"Well, what do YOU, mean?" gasped Tommy.

"Better tell 'em who I am, Billy," said the cabman.

"Think it safe, Joe?" inquired Mr. Bostock.

"I'll take my risk of it," returned the cabman.

"Gentlemen," said Bostock, rising solemnly, "let me make you acquainted with Captain Wicks of the Grace Darling."

"Yes, gentlemen, that is what I am," said the cabman. "You know I've been in trouble; and I don't deny but what I struck the blow, and where was I to get evidence of my provocation? So I turned to and took a cab, and I've driven one for three year now and nobody the wiser."

"I beg your pardon," said Carthew, joining almost for the first time; "I'm a new chum. What was the charge?"

"Murder," said Captain Wicks, "and I don't deny but what I struck the blow. And there's no sense in my trying to deny I was afraid to go to trial, or why would I be here? But it's a fact it was flat mutiny. Ask Billy here. He knows how it was."

Carthew breathed long; he had a strange, half-pleasurable sense of wading deeper in the tide of life. "Well," said he, "you were going on to say?"

"I was going on to say this," said the captain sturdily. "I've overheard what Mr. Hadden has been saying, and I think he talks good sense. I like some of his ideas first chop. He's sound on traderooms; he's all there on the traderoom, and I see that he and I would pull together. Then you're both gentlemen, and I like that," observed Captain Wicks. "And then I'll tell you I'm tired of this cabbing cruise, and I want to get to work again. Now, here's my offer. I've a little money I can stake up,—all of a hundred anyway. Then my old firm will give me trade, and jump at the chance; they never lost by me; they know what I'm worth as supercargo. And, last of all, you want a good captain to sail your ship for you. Well, here I am. I've sailed schooners for ten years. Ask Billy if I can handle a schooner."

"No man better," said Billy.

"And as for my character as a shipmate," concluded Wicks, "go and ask my old firm."

"But look here!" cried Hadden, "how do you mean to manage? You can whisk round in a hansom, and no questions asked. But if you try to come on a quarter-deck, my boy, you'll get nabbed."

"I'll have to keep back till the last," replied Wicks, "and take another name."

"But how about clearing? what other name?" asked Tommy, a little bewildered.

"I don't know yet," returned the captain, with a grin. "I'll see what the name is on my new certificate, and that'll be good enough for me. If I can't get one to buy, though I never heard of such a thing, there's old Kirkup, he's turned some sort of farmer down Bondi way; he'll hire me his."

"You seemed to speak as if you had a ship in view," said Carthew.

"So I have, too," said Captain Wicks, "and a beauty. Schooner yacht Dream; got lines you never saw the beat of; and a witch to go. She passed me once off Thursday Island, doing two knots to my one and laying a point and a half better; and the Grace Darling was a ship that I was proud of. I took and tore my hair. The Dream's been MY dream ever since. That was in her old days, when she carried a blue ens'n. Grant Sanderson was the party as owned her; he was rich and mad, and got a fever at last somewhere about the Fly River, and took and died. The captain brought the body back to Sydney, and paid off. Well, it turned out Grant Sanderson had left any quantity of wills and any quantity of widows, and no fellow could make out which was the genuine article. All the widows brought lawsuits against all the rest, and every will had a firm of lawyers on the quarterdeck as long as your arm. They tell me it was one of the biggest turns-to that ever was seen, bar Tichborne; the Lord Chamberlain himself was floored, and so was the Lord Chancellor; and all that time the Dream lay rotting up by Glebe Point. Well, it's done now; they've picked out a widow and a will; tossed up for it, as like as not; and the Dream's for sale. She'll go cheap; she's had a long turn-to at rotting."

"What size is she?"

"Well, big enough. We don't want her bigger. A hundred and ninety, going two hundred," replied the captain. "She's fully big for us three; it would be all the better if we had another hand, though it's a pity too, when you can pick up natives for half nothing. Then we must have a cook. I can fix raw sailor-men, but there's no going to sea with a new-chum cook. I can lay hands on the man we want for that: a Highway boy, an old shipmate of mine, of the name of Amalu. Cooks first rate, and it's always better to have a native; he aint fly, you can turn him to as you please, and he don't know enough to stand out for his rights."

From the moment that Captain Wicks joined in the conversation, Carthew recovered interest and confidence; the man (whatever he might have done) was plainly good-natured, and plainly capable; if he thought well of the enterprise, offered to contribute money, brought experience, and could thus solve at a word the problem of the trade, Carthew was content to go ahead. As for Hadden, his cup was full; he and Bostock forgave each other in champagne; toast followed toast; it was proposed and carried amid acclamation to change the name of the schooner (when she should be bought) to the Currency Lass; and the Currency Lass Island Trading Company was practically founded before dusk.

Three days later, Carthew stood before the lawyer, still in his jean suit, received his hundred and fifty pounds, and proceeded rather timidly to ask for more indulgence.

"I have a chance to get on in the world," he said. "By to-morrow evening I expect to be part owner of a ship."

"Dangerous property, Mr. Carthew," said the lawyer.

"Not if the partners work her themselves and stand to go down along with her," was the reply.

"I conceive it possible you might make something of it in that way," returned the other. "But are you a seaman? I thought you had been in the diplomatic service."

"I am an old yachtsman," said Norris. "And I must do the best I can. A fellow can't live in New South Wales upon diplomacy. But the point I wish to prepare you for is this. It will be impossible I should present myself here next quarter-day; we expect to make a six months' cruise of it among the islands."

"Sorry, Mr. Carthew: I can't hear of that," replied the lawyer.

"I mean upon the same conditions as the last," said Carthew.

"The conditions are exactly opposite," said the lawyer. "Last time I had reason to know you were in the colony; and even then I stretched a point. This time, by your own confession, you are contemplating a breach of the agreement; and I give you warning if you carry it out and I receive proof of it (for I will agree to regard this conversation as confidential) I shall have no choice but to do my duty. Be here on quarter-day, or your allowance ceases."

"This is very hard and, I think, rather silly," returned Carthew.

"It is not of my doing. I have my instructions," said the lawyer.

"And you so read these instructions, that I am to be prohibited from making an honest livelihood?" asked Carthew.

"Let us be frank," said the lawyer. "I find nothing in these instructions about an honest livelihood. I have no reason to suppose my clients care anything about that. I have reason to suppose only one thing,—that they mean you shall stay in this colony, and to guess another, Mr. Carthew. And to guess another."

"What do you mean by that?" asked Norris.

"I mean that I imagine, on very strong grounds, that your family desire to see no more of you," said the lawyer. "O, they may be very wrong; but that is the impression conveyed, that is what I suppose I am paid to bring about, and I have no choice but to try and earn my hire."

"I would scorn to deceive you," said Norris, with a strong flush, "you have guessed rightly. My family refuse to see me; but I am not going to England, I am going to the islands. How does that affect the islands?"

"Ah, but I don't know that you are going to the islands," said the lawyer, looking down, and spearing the blotting-paper with a pencil.

"I beg your pardon. I have the pleasure of informing you," said Norris.

"I am afraid, Mr. Carthew, that I cannot regard that communication as official," was the slow reply.

"I am not accustomed to have my word doubted!" cried Norris.

"Hush! I allow no one to raise his voice in my office," said the lawyer. "And for that matter—you seem to be a young gentleman of sense—consider what I know of you. You are a discarded son; your family pays money to be shut of you. What have you done? I don't know. But do you not see how foolish I should be, if I exposed my business reputation on the safeguard of the honour of a gentleman of whom I know just so much and no more? This interview is very disagreeable. Why prolong it? Write home, get my instructions changed, and I will change my behaviour. Not otherwise."

"I am very fond of three hundred a year," said Norris, "but I cannot pay the price required. I shall not have the pleasure of seeing you again."

"You must please yourself," said the lawyer. "Fail to be here next quarter-day, and the thing stops. But I warn you, and I mean the warning in a friendly spirit. Three months later you will be here begging, and I shall have no choice but to show you in the street."

"I wish you a good-evening," said Norris.

"The same to you, Mr. Carthew," retorted the lawyer, and rang for his clerk.

So it befell that Norris during what remained to him of arduous days in Sydney, saw not again the face of his legal adviser; and he was already at sea, and land was out of sight, when Hadden brought him a Sydney paper, over which he had been dozing in the shadow of the galley, and showed him an advertisement.

"Mr. Norris Carthew is earnestly entreated to call without delay at the office of Mr. ——, where important intelligence awaits him."

"It must manage to wait for me six months," said Norris, lightly enough, but yet conscious of a pang of curiosity.

CHAPTER XXIII. THE BUDGET OF THE "CURRENCY LASS."

Before noon on the 26th November, there cleared from the port of Sydney the schooner, Currency Lass. The owner, Norris Carthew, was on board in the somewhat unusual position of mate; the master's name purported to be William Kirkup; the cook was a Hawaiian boy, Joseph Amalu; and there were two hands before the mast, Thomas Hadden and Richard Hemstead, the latter chosen partly because of his humble character, partly because he had an odd-job-man's handiness with tools. The Currency Lass was bound for the South Sea Islands, and first of all for Butaritari in the Gilberts, on a register; but it was understood about the harbour that her cruise was more than half a pleasure trip. A friend of the late Grant Sanderson (of Auchentroon and Kilclarty) might have recognised in that tall-masted ship, the transformed and rechristened Dream; and the Lloyd's surveyor, had the services of such a one been called in requisition, must have found abundant subject of remark.

For time, during her three years' inaction, had eaten deep into the Dream and her fittings; she had sold in consequence a shade above her value as old junk; and the three adventurers had scarce been able to afford even the most vital repairs. The rigging, indeed, had been partly renewed, and the rest set up; all Grant Sanderson's old canvas had been patched together into one decently serviceable suit of sails; Grant Sanderson's masts still stood, and might have wondered at themselves. "I haven't the heart to tap them," Captain Wicks used to observe, as he squinted up their height or patted their rotundity; and "as rotten as our foremast" was an accepted metaphor in the ship's company. The sequel rather suggests it may have been sounder than was thought; but no one knew for certain, just as no one except the captain appreciated the dangers of the cruise. The captain, indeed, saw with clear eyes and spoke his mind aloud; and though a man of an astonishing hot-blooded courage, following life and taking its dangers in the spirit of a hound upon the slot, he had made a point of a big whaleboat. "Take your choice," he had said; "either new masts and rigging or that boat. I simply ain't going to sea without the one or the other. Chicken coops are good enough, no doubt, and so is a dinghy; but they ain't for Joe." And his partners had been forced to consent, and saw six and thirty pounds of their small capital vanish in the turn of a hand.

All four had toiled the best part of six weeks getting ready; and though Captain Wicks was of course not seen or heard of, a fifth was there to help them, a fellow in a bushy red beard, which he would sometimes lay aside when he was below, and who strikingly resembled Captain Wicks in voice and character. As for Captain Kirkup, he did not appear till the last moment, when he proved to be a burly mariner, bearded like Abou Ben Adhem. All the way down the harbour and through the Heads, his milk-white whiskers blew in the wind and were conspicuous from shore; but the Currency Lass had no sooner turned her back upon the lighthouse, than he went below for the inside of five seconds and reappeared clean shaven. So many doublings and devices were required to get to sea with an unseaworthy ship and a captain that was "wanted." Nor might even these have sufficed, but for the fact that Hadden was a public character, and the whole cruise regarded with an eye of indulgence as one of Tom's engaging eccentricities. The ship, besides, had been a yacht before; and it came the more natural to allow her still some of the dangerous liberties of her old employment.

A strange ship they had made of it, her lofty spars disfigured with patched canvas, her panelled cabin fitted for a traderoom with rude shelves. And the life they led in that anomalous schooner was no less curious than herself. Amalu alone berthed forward; the rest occupied staterooms, camped upon the satin divans, and sat down in Grant Sanderson's parquetry smoking-room to meals of junk and potatoes, bad of their kind and often scant in quantity. Hemstead grumbled;

Tommy had occasional moments of revolt and increased the ordinary by a few haphazard tins or a bottle of his own brown sherry. But Hemstead grumbled from habit, Tommy revolted only for the moment, and there was underneath a real and general acquiescence in these hardships. For besides onions and potatoes, the Currency Lass may be said to have gone to sea without stores. She carried two thousand pounds' worth of assorted trade, advanced on credit, their whole hope and fortune. It was upon this that they subsisted—mice in their own granary. They dined upon their future profits; and every scanty meal was so much in the savings bank.

Republican as were their manners, there was no practical, at least no dangerous, lack of discipline. Wicks was the only sailor on board, there was none to criticise; and besides, he was so easy-going, and so merry-minded, that none could bear to disappoint him. Carthew did his best, partly for the love of doing it, partly for love of the captain; Amalu was a willing drudge, and even Hemstead and Hadden turned to upon occasion with a will. Tommy's department was the trade and traderoom; he would work down in the hold or over the shelves of the cabin, till the Sydney dandy was unrecognizable; come up at last, draw a bucket of sea-water, bathe, change, and lie down on deck over a big sheaf of Sydney Heralds and Dead Birds, or perhaps with a volume of Buckle's History of Civilisation, the standard work selected for that cruise. In the latter case, a smile went round the ship, for Buckle almost invariably laid his student out, and when Tom awoke again he was almost always in the humour for brown sherry. The connection was so well established that "a glass of Buckle" or "a bottle of civilisation" became current pleasantries on board the Currency Lass.

Hemstead's province was that of the repairs, and he had his hands full. Nothing on board but was decayed in a proportion; the lamps leaked; so did the decks; door-knobs came off in the hand, mouldings parted company with the panels, the pump declined to suck, and the defective bathroom came near to swamp the ship. Wicks insisted that all the nails were long ago consumed, and that she was only glued together by the rust. "You shouldn't make me laugh so much, Tommy," he would say. "I'm afraid I'll shake the sternpost out of her." And, as Hemstead went to and fro with his tool basket on an endless round of tinkering, Wicks lost no opportunity of chaffing him upon his duties. "If you'd turn to at sailoring or washing paint or something useful, now," he would say, "I could see the fun of it. But to be mending things that haven't no insides to them appears to me the height of foolishness." And doubtless these continual pleasantries helped to reassure the landsmen, who went to and fro unmoved, under circumstances that might have daunted Nelson.

The weather was from the outset splendid, and the wind fair and steady. The ship sailed like a witch. "This Currency Lass is a powerful old girl, and has more complaints than I would care to put a name on," the captain would say, as he pricked the chart; "but she could show her blooming heels to anything of her size in the Western Pacific." To wash decks, relieve the wheel, do the day's work after dinner on the smoking-room table, and take in kites at night,— such was the easy routine of their life. In the evening—above all, if Tommy had produced some of his civilisation—yarns and music were the rule. Amalu had a sweet Hawaiian voice; and Hemstead, a great hand upon the banjo, accompanied his own quavering tenor with effect. There was a sense in which the little man could sing. It was great to hear him deliver My Boy Tammie in Austrylian; and the words (some of the worst of the ruffian Macneil's) were hailed in his version with inextinguishable mirth.

Where hye ye been a' dye?

he would ask, and answer himself:—

I've been by burn and flowery brye,

Meadow green an' mountain grye,

Courtin' o' this young thing,

Just come frye her mammie.

It was the accepted jest for all hands to greet the conclusion of this song with the simultaneous cry: "My word!" thus winging the arrow of ridicule with a feather from the singer's wing. But he had his revenge with Home, Sweet Home, and Where is my Wandering Boy To-night?—ditties into which he threw the most intolerable pathos. It appeared he had no home, nor had ever had one, nor yet any vestige of a family, except a truculent uncle, a baker in Newcastle, N.S.W. His domestic sentiment was therefore wholly in the air, and expressed an unrealised ideal. Or perhaps, of all his experiences, this of the Currency Lass, with its kindly, playful, and tolerant society, approached it the most nearly.

It is perhaps because I know the sequel, but I can never think upon this voyage without a profound sense of pity and mystery; of the ship (once the whim of a rich blackguard) faring with her battered fineries and upon her homely errand, across the plains of ocean, and past the gorgeous scenery of dawn and sunset; and the ship's company, so strangely assembled, so Britishly chuckle-headed, filling their days with chaff in place of conversation; no human book on board with them except Hadden's Buckle, and not a creature fit either to read or to understand it; and the one mark of any civilised interest, being when Carthew filled in his spare hours with the pencil and the brush: the whole unconscious crew of them posting in the meanwhile towards so tragic a disaster.

Twenty-eight days out of Sydney, on Christmas eve, they fetched up to the entrance of the lagoon, and plied all that night outside, keeping their position by the lights of fishers on the reef and the outlines of the palms against the cloudy sky. With the break of day, the schooner was hove to, and the signal for a pilot shown. But it was plain her lights must have been observed in the darkness by the native fishermen, and word carried to the settlement, for a boat was already under weigh. She came towards them across the lagoon under a great press of sail, lying dangerously down, so that at times, in the heavier puffs, they thought she would turn turtle; covered the distance in fine style, luffed up smartly alongside, and emitted a haggard looking white man in pyjamas.

"Good-mornin', Cap'n," said he, when he had made good his entrance. "I was taking you for a Fiji man-of-war, what with your flush decks and them spars. Well, gen'lemen all, here's wishing you a Merry Christmas and a Happy New Year," he added, and lurched against a stay.

"Why, you're never the pilot?" exclaimed Wicks, studying him with a profound disfavour. "You've never taken a ship in—don't tell me!"

"Well, I should guess I have," returned the pilot. "I'm Captain Dobbs, I am; and when I take charge, the captain of that ship can go below and shave."

"But, man alive! you're drunk, man!" cried the captain.

"Drunk!" repeated Dobbs. "You can't have seen much life if you call me drunk. I'm only just beginning. Come night, I won't say; I guess I'll be properly full by then. But now I'm the soberest man in all Big Muggin."

"It won't do," retorted Wicks. "Not for Joseph, sir. I can't have you piling up my schooner."

"All right," said Dobbs, "lay and rot where you are, or take and go in and pile her up for yourself like the captain of the Leslie. That's business, I guess; grudged me twenty dollars' pilotage, and lost twenty thousand in trade and a brand new schooner; ripped the keel right off of her, and she went down in the inside of four minutes, and lies in twenty fathom, trade and all."

"What's all this?" cried Wicks. "Trade? What vessel was this Leslie, anyhow?"

"Consigned to Cohen and Co., from 'Frisco,'" returned the pilot, "and badly wanted. There's a barque inside filling up for Hamburg—you see her spars over there; and there's two more ships due, all the way from Germany, one in two months, they say, and one in three; Cohen and Co.'s agent (that's Mr. Topelius) has taken and lain down with the jaundice on the strength of it. I guess most people would, in his shoes; no trade, no copra, and twenty hundred ton of shipping due. If you've any copra on board, cap'n, here's your chance. Topelius will buy, gold down, and give three cents. It's all found money to him, the way it is, whatever he pays for it. And that's what come of going back on the pilot."

"Excuse me one moment, Captain Dobbs. I wish to speak with my mate," said the captain, whose face had begun to shine and his eyes to sparkle.

"Please yourself," replied the pilot. "You couldn't think of offering a man a nip, could you? just to brace him up. This kind of thing looks damned inhospitable, and gives a schooner a bad name."

"I'll talk about that after the anchor's down," returned Wicks, and he drew Carthew forward. "I say," he whispered, "here's a fortune."

"How much do you call that?" asked Carthew.

"I can't put a figure on it yet—I daren't!" said the captain. "We might cruise twenty years and not find the match of it. And suppose another ship came in to-night? Everything's possible! And the difficulty is this Dobbs. He's as drunk as a marine. How can we trust him? We ain't insured—worse luck!"

"Suppose you took him aloft and got him to point out the channel?" suggested Carthew. "If he tallied at all with the chart, and didn't fall out of the rigging, perhaps we might risk it."

"Well, all's risk here," returned the captain. "Take the wheel yourself, and stand by. Mind, if there's two orders, follow mine, not his. Set the cook for'ard with the heads'ls, and the two others at the main sheet, and see they don't sit on it." With that he called the pilot; they swarmed aloft in the fore rigging, and presently after there was bawled down the welcome order to ease sheets and fill away.

At a quarter before nine o'clock on Christmas morning the anchor was let go.

The first cruise of the Currency Lass had thus ended in a stroke of fortune almost beyond hope. She had brought two thousand pounds' worth of trade, straight as a homing pigeon, to the place where it was most required. And Captain Wicks (or, rather, Captain Kirkup) showed himself the man to make the best of his advantage. For hard upon two days he walked a verandah with Topelius, for hard upon two days his partners watched from the neighbouring public house the field of battle; and the lamps were not yet lighted on the evening of the second before the enemy surrendered. Wicks came across to the Sans Souci, as the saloon was called, his face nigh black, his eyes almost closed and all bloodshot, and yet bright as lighted matches.

"Come out here, boys," he said; and when they were some way off among the palms, "I hold twenty-four," he added in a voice scarcely recognizable, and doubtless referring to the venerable game of cribbage.

"What do you mean?" asked Tommy.

"I've sold the trade," answered Wicks; "or, rather, I've sold only some of it, for I've kept back all the mess beef and half the flour and biscuit; and, by God, we're still provisioned for four months! By God, it's as good as stolen!"

"My word!" cried Hemstead.

"But what have you sold it for?" gasped Carthew, the captain's almost insane excitement shaking his nerve.

"Let me tell it my own way," cried Wicks, loosening his neck. "Let me get at it gradual, or I'll explode. I've not only sold it, boys, I've wrung out a charter on my own terms to 'Frisco and back; on my own terms. I made a point of it. I fooled him first by making believe I wanted copra, which of course I knew he wouldn't hear of—couldn't, in fact; and whenever he showed fight, I trotted out the copra, and that man dived! I would take nothing but copra, you see; and so I've got the blooming lot in specie—all but two short bills on 'Frisco. And the sum? Well, this whole adventure, including two thousand pounds of credit, cost us two thousand seven hundred and some odd. That's all paid back; in thirty days' cruise we've paid for the schooner and the trade. Heard ever any man the match of that? And it's not all! For besides that," said the captain, hammering his words, "we've got Thirteen Blooming Hundred Pounds of profit to divide. I bled him in four Thou.!" he cried, in a voice that broke like a schoolboy's.

For a moment the partners looked upon their chief with stupefaction, incredulous surprise their only feeling. Tommy was the first to grasp the consequences.

"Here," he said, in a hard, business tone. "Come back to that saloon. I've got to get drunk."

"You must please excuse me, boys," said the captain, earnestly. "I daren't taste nothing. If I was to drink one glass of beer, it's my belief I'd have the apoplexy. The last scrimmage, and the blooming triumph, pretty nigh hand done me."

"Well, then, three cheers for the captain," proposed Tommy.

But Wicks held up a shaking hand. "Not that either, boys," he pleaded. "Think of the other buffer, and let him down easy. If I'm like this, just fancy what Topelius is! If he heard us singing out, he'd have the staggers."

As a matter of fact, Topelius accepted his defeat with a good grace; but the crew of the wrecked Leslie, who were in the same employment and loyal to their firm, took the thing more bitterly. Rough words and ugly looks were common. Once even they hooted Captain Wicks from the saloon verandah; the Currency Lasses drew out on the other side; for some minutes there had like to have been a battle in Butaritari; and though the occasion passed off without blows, it left on either side an increase of ill-feeling.

No such small matter could affect the happiness of the successful traders. Five days more the ship lay in the lagoon, with little employment for any one but Tommy and the captain, for Topelius's natives discharged cargo and brought ballast; the time passed like a pleasant dream; the adventurers sat up half the night debating and praising their good fortune, or strayed by day in the narrow isle, gaping like Cockney tourists; and on the first of the new year, the Currency Lass weighed anchor for the second time and set sail for 'Frisco, attended by the same fine weather and good luck. She crossed the doldrums with but small delay; on a wind and in ballast of broken coral, she outdid expectations; and, what added to the happiness of the ship's company, the small amount of work that fell on them to do, was now lessened by the presence of another hand. This was the boatswain of the Leslie; he had been on bad terms with his own captain, had already spent his wages in the saloons of Butaritari, had wearied of the place, and while all his shipmates coldly refused to set foot on board the Currency Lass, he had offered to work his passage to the coast. He was a north of Ireland man, between Scotch and Irish, rough, loud, humorous, and emotional, not without sterling qualities, and an expert and careful sailor. His frame of mind was different indeed from that of his new shipmates; instead of making an unexpected fortune, he had lost a berth; and he was besides disgusted with the rations, and really appalled at the condition of the schooner. A stateroom door had stuck, the first day at sea, and Mac (as they called him) laid his strength to it and plucked it from the hinges.

"Glory!" said he, "this ship's rotten."

"I believe you, my boy," said Captain Wicks.

The next day the sailor was observed with his nose aloft.

"Don't you get looking at these sticks," the captain said, "or you'll have a fit and fall overboard."

Mac turned towards the speaker with rather a wild eye. "Why, I see what looks like a patch of dry rot up yonder, that I bet I could stick my fist into," said he.

"Looks as if a fellow could stick his head into it, don't it?" returned Wicks. "But there's no good prying into things that can't be mended."

"I think I was a Currency Ass to come on board of her!" reflected Mac.

"Well, I never said she was seaworthy," replied the captain: "I only said she could show her blooming heels to anything afloat. And besides, I don't know that it's dry rot; I kind of sometimes hope it isn't. Here; turn to and heave the log; that'll cheer you up."

"Well, there's no denying it, you're a holy captain," said Mac.

And from that day on, he made but the one reference to the ship's condition; and that was whenever Tommy drew upon his cellar. "Here's to the junk trade!" he would say, as he held out his can of sherry.

"Why do you always say that?" asked Tommy.

"I had an uncle in the business," replied Mac, and launched at once into a yarn, in which an incredible number of the characters were "laid out as nice as you would want to see," and the oaths made up about two-fifths of every conversation.

Only once he gave them a taste of his violence; he talked of it, indeed, often; "I'm rather a voilent man," he would say, not without pride; but this was the only specimen. Of a sudden, he turned on Hemstead in the ship's waist, knocked him against the foresail boom, then knocked him under it, and had set him up and knocked him down once more, before any one had drawn a breath.

"Here! Belay that!" roared Wicks, leaping to his feet. "I won't have none of this."

Mac turned to the captain with ready civility. "I only want to learn him manners," said he. "He took and called me Irishman."

"Did he?" said Wicks. "O, that's a different story! What made you do it, you tomfool? You ain't big enough to call any man that."

"I didn't call him it," spluttered Hemstead, through his blood and tears. "I only mentioned-like he was."

"Well, let's have no more of it," said Wicks.

"But you ARE Irish, ain't you?" Carthew asked of his new shipmate shortly after.

"I may be," replied Mac, "but I'll allow no Sydney duck to call me so. No," he added, with a sudden heated countenance, "nor any Britisher that walks! Why, look here," he went on, "you're a young swell, aren't you? Suppose I called you that! 'I'll show you,' you would say, and turn to and take it out of me straight."

On the 28th of January, when in lat. 27 degrees 20' N., long. 177 degrees W., the wind chopped suddenly into the west, not very strong, but puffy and with flaws of rain. The captain, eager for easting, made a fair wind of it and guyed the booms out wing and wing. It was Tommy's trick at the wheel, and as it was within half an hour of the relief (seven thirty in the morning), the captain judged it not worth while to change him.

The puffs were heavy but short; there was nothing to be called a squall, no danger to the ship, and scarce more than usual to the doubtful spars. All hands were on deck in their oilskins, expecting breakfast; the galley smoked, the ship smelt of coffee, all were in good humour to be speeding eastward a full nine; when the rotten foresail tore suddenly between two cloths and then split to either hand. It was for all the world as though some archangel with a huge sword had slashed it with the figure of a cross; all hands ran to secure the slatting canvas; and in the sudden uproar and alert, Tommy Hadden lost his head. Many of his days have been passed since then in explaining how the thing happened; of these explanations it will be sufficient to say that they were all different and none satisfactory; and the gross fact remains that the main boom gybed, carried away the tackle, broke the mainmast some three feet above the deck and whipped it overboard. For near a minute the suspected foremast gallantly resisted; then followed its companion; and by the time the wreck was cleared, of the whole beautiful fabric that enabled them to skim the seas, two ragged stumps remained.

In these vast and solitary waters, to be dismasted is perhaps the worst calamity. Let the ship turn turtle and go down, and at least the pang is over. But men chained on a hulk may pass months scanning the empty sea line and counting the steps of death's invisible approach. There is no help but in the boats, and what a help is that! There heaved the Currency Lass, for instance, a wingless lump, and the nearest human coast (that of Kauai in the Sandwiches) lay about a thousand miles to south and east of her. Over the way there, to men contemplating that passage in an open boat, all kinds of misery, and the fear of death and of madness, brooded.

A serious company sat down to breakfast; but the captain helped his neighbours with a smile.

"Now, boys," he said, after a pull at the hot coffee, "we're done with this Currency Lass, and no mistake. One good job: we made her pay while she lasted, and she paid first rate; and if we were to try our hand again, we can try in style. Another good job: we have a fine, stiff, roomy boat, and you know who you have to thank for that. We've got six lives to save, and a pot of money; and the point is, where are we to take 'em?"

"It's all two thousand miles to the nearest of the Sandwiches, I fancy," observed Mac.

"No, not so bad as that," returned the captain. "But it's bad enough: rather better'n a thousand."

"I know a man who once did twelve hundred in a boat," said Mac, "and he had all he wanted. He fetched ashore in the Marquesas, and never set a foot on anything floating from that day to this. He said he would rather put a pistol to his head and knock his brains out."

"Ay, ay!" said Wicks. "Well I remember a boat's crew that made this very island of Kauai, and from just about where we lie, or a bit further. When they got up with the land, they were clean crazy. There was an iron-bound coast and an Old Bob Ridley of a surf on. The natives hailed 'em from fishing-boats, and sung out it couldn't be done at the money. Much they cared! there was the land, that was all they knew; and they turned to and drove the boat slap ashore in the thick of it, and was all drowned but one. No; boat trips are my eye," concluded the captain, gloomily.

The tone was surprising in a man of his indomitable temper. "Come, Captain," said Carthew, "you have something else up your sleeve; out with it!"

"It's a fact," admitted Wicks. "You see there's a raft of little bally reefs about here, kind of chicken-pox on the chart. Well, I looked 'em all up, and there's one—Midway or Brooks they call it, not forty mile from our assigned position—that I got news of. It turns out it's a coaling station of the Pacific Mail," he said, simply.

"Well, and I know it ain't no such a thing," said Mac. "I been quartermaster in that line myself."

"All right," returned Wicks. "There's the book. Read what Hoyt says—read it aloud and let the others hear."

Hoyt's falsehood (as readers know) was explicit; incredulity was impossible, and the news itself delightful beyond hope. Each saw in his mind's eye the boat draw in to a trim island with a wharf, coal-sheds, gardens, the Stars and Stripes and the white cottage of the keeper; saw themselves idle a few weeks in tolerable quarters, and then step on board the China mail, romantic waifs, and yet with pocketsful of money, calling for champagne, and waited on by troops of stewards. Breakfast, that had begun so dully, ended amid sober jubilation, and all hands turned immediately to prepare the boat.

Now that all spars were gone, it was no easy job to get her launched. Some of the necessary cargo was first stowed on board; the specie, in particular, being packed in a strong chest and secured with lashings to the afterthwart in case of a capsize. Then a piece of the bulwark was razed to the level of the deck, and the boat swung thwart-ship, made fast with a slack line to either stump, and successfully run out. For a voyage of forty miles to hospitable quarters, not much food or water was required; but they took both in superfluity. Amalu and Mac, both ingrained sailor-men, had chests which were the headquarters of their lives; two more chests with handbags, oilskins, and blankets supplied the others; Hadden, amid general applause, added the last case of the brown sherry; the captain brought the log, instruments, and chronometer; nor did Hemstead forget the banjo or a pinned handkerchief of Butaritari shells.

It was about three P.M. when they pushed off, and (the wind being still westerly) fell to the oars. "Well, we've got the guts out of YOU!" was the captain's nodded farewell to the hulk of the Currency Lass, which presently shrank and faded in the sea. A little after a calm succeeded, with much rain; and the first meal was eaten, and the watch below lay down to their uneasy slumber on the bilge under a roaring shower-bath. The twenty-ninth dawned overhead from out of ragged clouds; there is no moment when a boat at sea appears so trenchantly black and so conspicuously little; and the crew looked about them at the sky and water with a thrill of loneliness and fear. With sunrise the trade set in, lusty and true to the point; sail was made; the boat flew; and by about four in the afternoon, they were well up with the closed part of the reef, and the captain standing on the thwart, and holding by the mast, was studying the island through the binoculars.

"Well, and where's your station?" cried Mac.

"I don't someway pick it up," replied the captain.

"No, nor never will!" retorted Mac, with a clang of despair and triumph in his tones.

The truth was soon plain to all. No buoys, no beacons, no lights, no coal, no station; the castaways pulled through a lagoon and landed on an isle, where was no mark of man but wreckwood, and no sound but of the sea. For the seafowl that harboured and lived there at the epoch of my visit were then scattered into the uttermost parts of the ocean, and had left no traces of their sojourn besides dropped feathers and addled eggs. It was to this they had been sent, for this they had stooped all night over the dripping oars, hourly moving further from relief. The boat, for as small as it was, was yet eloquent of the hands of men, a thing alone indeed upon the sea but yet in itself all human; and the isle, for which they had exchanged it, was ingloriously savage, a place of distress, solitude, and hunger unrelieved. There was a strong glare and shadow of the evening over all; in which they sat or lay, not speaking, careless even to eat, men swindled out of life and riches by a lying book. In the great good nature of the whole party, no word of reproach had been addressed to Hadden, the author of these disasters. But the new blow was less magnanimously borne, and many angry glances rested on the captain.

Yet it was himself who roused them from their lethargy. Grudgingly they obeyed, drew the boat beyond tidemark, and followed him to the top of the miserable islet, whence a view was commanded of the whole wheel of the horizon, then part darkened under the coming night, part dyed with the hues of the sunset and populous with the sunset clouds. Here the camp was pitched and a tent run up with the oars, sails, and mast. And here Amalu, at no man's bidding, from the mere instinct of habitual service, built a fire and cooked a meal. Night was come, and the stars and the silver sickle of new moon beamed overhead, before the meal was ready. The cold sea shone about them, and the fire glowed in their faces, as they ate. Tommy had opened his case, and the brown sherry went the round; but it was long before they came to conversation.

"Well, is it to be Kauai after all?" asked Mac suddenly.

"This is bad enough for me," said Tommy. "Let's stick it out where we are."

"Well, I can tell ye one thing," said Mac, "if ye care to hear it. When I was in the China mail, we once made this island. It's in the course from Honolulu."

"Deuce it is!" cried Carthew. "That settles it, then. Let's stay. We must keep good fires going; and there's plenty wreck."

"Lashings of wreck!" said the Irishman. "There's nothing here but wreck and coffin boards."

"But we'll have to make a proper blyze," objected Hemstead. "You can't see a fire like this, not any wye awye, I mean."

"Can't you?" said Carthew. "Look round."

They did, and saw the hollow of the night, the bare, bright face of the sea, and the stars regarding them; and the voices died in their bosoms at the spectacle. In that huge isolation, it seemed they must be visible from China on the one hand and California on the other.

"My God, it's dreary!" whispered Hemstead.

"Dreary?" cried Mac, and fell suddenly silent.

"It's better than a boat, anyway," said Hadden. "I've had my bellyful of boat."

"What kills me is that specie!" the captain broke out. "Think of all that riches,—four thousand in gold, bad silver, and short bills—all found money, too!—and no more use than that much dung!"

"I'll tell you one thing," said Tommy. "I don't like it being in the boat—I don't care to have it so far away."

"Why, who's to take it?" cried Mac, with a guffaw of evil laughter.

But this was not at all the feeling of the partners, who rose, clambered down the isle, brought back the inestimable treasure-chest slung upon two oars, and set it conspicuous in the shining of the fire.

"There's my beauty!" cried Wicks, viewing it with a cocked head. "That's better than a bonfire. What! we have a chest here, and bills for close upon two thousand pounds; there's no show to that,—it would go in your vest-pocket,—but the rest! upwards of forty pounds avoirdupois of coined gold, and close on two hundredweight of Chile silver! What! ain't that good enough to fetch a fleet? Do you mean to say that won't affect a ship's compass? Do you mean to tell me that the lookout won't turn to and SMELL it?" he cried.

Mac, who had no part nor lot in the bills, the forty pounds of gold, or the two hundredweight of silver, heard this with impatience, and fell into a bitter, choking laughter. "You'll see!" he said harshly. "You'll be glad to feed them bills into the fire before you're through with ut!" And he turned, passed by himself out of the ring of the firelight, and stood gazing seaward.

His speech and his departure extinguished instantly those sparks of better humour kindled by the dinner and the chest. The group fell again to an ill-favoured silence, and Hemstead began to touch the banjo, as was his habit of an evening. His repertory was small: the chords of Home, Sweet Home fell under his fingers; and when he had played the symphony, he instinctively raised up his voice. "Be it never so 'umble, there's no plyce like 'ome," he sang. The last word was still upon his lips, when the instrument was snatched from him and dashed into the fire; and he turned with a cry to look into the furious countenance of Mac.

"I'll be damned if I stand this!" cried the captain, leaping up belligerent.

"I told ye I was a voilent man," said Mac, with a movement of deprecation very surprising in one of his character. "Why don't he give me a chance then? Haven't we enough to bear the way we are?" And to the wonder and dismay of all, the man choked upon a sob. "It's ashamed of meself I am," he said presently, his Irish accent twenty-fold increased. "I ask all your pardons for me voilence; and especially the little man's, who is a harmless crayture, and here's me hand to'm, if he'll condescind to take me by 't."

So this scene of barbarity and sentimentalism passed off, leaving behind strange and incongruous impressions. True, every one was perhaps glad when silence succeeded that all too appropriate music; true, Mac's apology and subsequent behaviour rather raised him in the opinion of his fellow-castaways. But the discordant note had been struck, and its harmonics tingled in the brain. In that savage, houseless isle, the passions of man had sounded, if only for the moment, and all men trembled at the possibilities of horror.

It was determined to stand watch and watch in case of passing vessels; and Tommy, on fire with an idea, volunteered to stand the first. The rest crawled under the tent, and were soon enjoying that comfortable gift of sleep, which comes everywhere and to all men, quenching anxieties and speeding time. And no sooner were all settled, no sooner had the drone of many snorers begun to mingle with and overcome the surf, than Tommy stole from his post with the case of sherry, and dropped it in a quiet cove in a fathom of water. But the stormy inconstancy of Mac's behaviour had no connection with a gill or two of wine; his passions, angry and otherwise, were on a different sail plan from his neighbours'; and there were possibilities of good and evil in that hybrid Celt beyond their prophecy.

About two in the morning, the starry sky—or so it seemed, for the drowsy watchman had not observed the approach of any cloud—brimmed over in a deluge; and for three days it rained without remission. The islet was a sponge, the castaways sops; the view all gone, even the reef concealed behind the curtain of the falling water. The fire was soon drowned out; after a couple of boxes of matches had been scratched in vain, it was decided to wait for better weather; and the party lived in wretchedness on raw tins and a ration of hard bread.

By the 2nd February, in the dark hours of the morning watch, the clouds were all blown by; the sun rose glorious; and once more the castaways sat by a quick fire, and drank hot coffee with the greed of brutes and sufferers. Thenceforward their affairs moved in a routine. A fire was constantly maintained; and this occupied one hand continuously, and the others for an hour or so in the day. Twice a day, all hands bathed in the lagoon, their chief, almost their only pleasure. Often they fished in the lagoon with good success. And the rest was passed in lolling, strolling, yarns, and disputation. The time of the China steamers was calculated to a nicety; which done, the thought was rejected and ignored. It was one that would not bear consideration. The boat voyage having been tacitly set aside, the desperate part chosen to wait there for the coming of help or of starvation, no man had courage left to look his bargain in the face, far less to discuss it with his neighbours. But the unuttered terror haunted them; in every hour of idleness, at every moment of silence, it returned, and breathed a chill about the circle, and carried men's eyes to the horizon. Then, in a panic of self-defence, they would rally to some other subject. And, in that lone spot, what else was to be found to speak of but the treasure?

That was indeed the chief singularity, the one thing conspicuous in their island life; the presence of that chest of bills and specie dominated the mind like a cathedral; and there were besides connected with it, certain irking problems well fitted to occupy the idle. Two thousand pounds were due to the Sydney firm: two thousand pounds were clear profit, and fell to be divided in varying proportions among six. It had been agreed how the partners were to range; every pound of capital subscribed, every pound that fell due in wages, was to count for one "lay." Of these, Tommy could claim five hundred and ten, Carthew one hundred and seventy, Wicks one hundred and forty, and Hemstead and Amalu ten apiece: eight hundred and forty "lays" in all. What was the value of a lay? This was at first debated in the air and chiefly by the strength of Tommy's lungs. Then followed a series of incorrect calculations; from which they issued, arithmetically foiled, but agreed from weariness upon an approximate value of 2 pounds, 7 shillings 7 1/4 pence. The figures were admittedly incorrect; the sum of the shares came not to 2000 pounds, but to 1996 pounds, 6 shillings: 3 pounds, 14 shillings being thus left unclaimed. But it was the nearest they had yet found, and the highest as well, so that the partners were made the less critical by the contemplation of their splendid dividends. Wicks put in 100 pounds and stood to draw captain's wages for two months; his taking was 333 pounds 3 shillings 6 1/2 pence. Carthew had put in 150 pounds: he was to take out 401 pounds, 18 shillings 6 1/2 pence. Tommy's 500 pounds had grown to be 1213 pounds 12 shillings 9 3/4 pence; and Amalu and Hemstead, ranking for wages only, had 22 pounds, 16 shillings 1/2 pence, each.

From talking and brooding on these figures, it was but a step to opening the chest; and once the chest open, the glamour of the cash was irresistible. Each felt that he must see his treasure separate with the eye of flesh, handle it in the hard coin, mark it for his own, and stand forth to himself the approved owner. And here an insurmountable difficulty barred the way. There were some seventeen shillings in English silver: the rest was Chile; and the Chile dollar, which had been taken at the rate of six to the pound sterling, was practically their smallest coin. It was decided, therefore, to divide the pounds only, and to throw the shillings, pence, and fractions in a common fund. This, with the three pound fourteen already in the heel, made a total of seven pounds one shilling.

"I'll tell you," said Wicks. "Let Carthew and Tommy and me take one pound apiece, and

Hemstead and Amalu split the other four, and toss up for the odd bob."

"O, rot!" said Carthew. "Tommy and I are bursting already. We can take half a sov' each, and let the other three have forty shillings."

"I'll tell you now—it's not worth splitting," broke in Mac. "I've cards in my chest. Why don't you play for the slump sum?"

In that idle place, the proposal was accepted with delight. Mac, as the owner of the cards, was given a stake; the sum was played for in five games of cribbage; and when Amalu, the last survivor in the tournament, was beaten by Mac, it was found the dinner hour was past. After a hasty meal, they fell again immediately to cards, this time (on Carthew's proposal) to Van John. It was then probably two P.M. of the 9th February; and they played with varying chances for twelve hours, slept heavily, and rose late on the morrow to resume the game. All day of the 10th, with grudging intervals for food, and with one long absence on the part of Tommy from which he returned dripping with the case of sherry, they continued to deal and stake. Night fell: they drew the closer to the fire. It was maybe two in the morning, and Tommy was selling his deal by auction, as usual with that timid player; when Carthew, who didn't intend to bid, had a moment of leisure and looked round him. He beheld the moonlight on the sea, the money piled and scattered in that incongruous place, the perturbed faces of the players; he felt in his own breast the familiar tumult; and it seemed as if there rose in his ears a sound of music, and the moon seemed still to shine upon a sea, but the sea was changed, and the Casino towered from among lamplit gardens, and the money clinked on the green board. "Good God!" he thought, "am I gambling again?" He looked the more curiously about the sandy table. He and Mac had played and won like gamblers; the mingled gold and silver lay by their places in the heap. Amalu and Hemstead had each more than held their own, but Tommy was cruel far to leeward, and the captain was reduced to perhaps fifty pounds.

"I say, let's knock off," said Carthew.

"Give that man a glass of Buckle," said some one, and a fresh bottle was opened, and the game went inexorably on.

Carthew was himself too heavy a winner to withdraw or to say more; and all the rest of the night he must look on at the progress of this folly, and make gallant attempts to lose with the not uncommon consequence of winning more. The first dawn of the 11th February found him well-nigh desperate. It chanced he was then dealer, and still winning. He had just dealt a round of many tens; every one had staked heavily; the captain had put up all that remained to him, twelve pounds in gold and a few dollars; and Carthew, looking privately at his cards before he showed them, found he held a natural.

"See here, you fellows," he broke out, "this is a sickening business, and I'm done with it for one." So saying, he showed his cards, tore them across, and rose from the ground.

The company stared and murmured in mere amazement; but Mac stepped gallantly to his support.

"We've had enough of it, I do believe," said he. "But of course it was all fun, and here's my counters back. All counters in, boys!" and he began to pour his winnings into the chest, which stood fortunately near him.

Carthew stepped across and wrung him by the hand. "I'll never forget this," he said.

"And what are ye going to do with the Highway boy and the plumber?" inquired Mac, in a low tone of voice. "They've both wan, ye see."

"That's true!" said Carthew aloud. "Amalu and Hemstead, count your winnings; Tommy and I pay that."

It was carried without speech: the pair glad enough to receive their winnings, it mattered not from whence; and Tommy, who had lost about five hundred pounds, delighted with the compromise.

"And how about Mac?" asked Hemstead. "Is he to lose all?"

"I beg your pardon, plumber. I'm sure ye mean well," returned the Irishman, "but you'd better shut your face, for I'm not that kind of a man. If I t'ought I had wan that money fair, there's never a soul here could get it from me. But I t'ought it was in fun; that was my mistake, ye see; and there's no man big enough upon this island to give a present to my mother's son. So there's my opinion to ye, plumber, and you can put it in your pockut till required."

"Well, I will say, Mac, you're a gentleman," said Carthew, as he helped him to shovel back his winnings into the treasure chest.

"Divil a fear of it, sir! a drunken sailor-man," said Mac.

The captain had sat somewhile with his face in his hands: now he rose mechanically, shaking and stumbling like a drunkard after a debauch. But as he rose, his face was altered, and his voice rang out over the isle, "Sail, ho!"

All turned at the cry, and there, in the wild light of the morning, heading straight for Midway Reef, was the brig Flying Scud of Hull.

CHAPTER XXIV. A HARD BARGAIN.

The ship which thus appeared before the castaways had long "tramped" the ocean, wandering from one port to another as freights offered. She was two years out from London, by the Cape of Good Hope, India, and the Archipelago; and was now bound for San Francisco in the hope of working homeward round the Horn. Her captain was one Jacob Trent. He had retired some five years before to a suburban cottage, a patch of cabbages, a gig, and the conduct of what he called a Bank. The name appears to have been misleading. Borrowers were accustomed to choose works of art and utility in the front shop; loaves of sugar and bolts of broadcloth were deposited in pledge; and it was a part of the manager's duty to dash in his gig on Saturday evenings from one small retailer's to another, and to annex in each the bulk of the week's takings. His was thus an active life, and to a man of the type of a rat, filled with recondite joys. An unexpected loss, a law suit, and the unintelligent commentary of the judge upon the bench, combined to disgust him of the business. I was so extraordinarily fortunate as to find, in an old newspaper, a report of the proceedings in Lyall v. The Cardiff Mutual Accommodation Banking Co. "I confess I fail entirely to understand the nature of the business," the judge had remarked, while Trent was being examined in chief; a little after, on fuller information—"They call it a bank," he had opined, "but it seems to me to be an unlicensed pawnshop"; and he wound up with this appalling allocution: "Mr. Trent, I must put you on your guard; you must be very careful, or we shall see you here again." In the inside of a week the captain disposed of the bank, the cottage, and the gig and horse; and to sea again in the Flying Scud, where he did well and gave high satisfaction to his owners. But the glory clung to him; he was a plain sailor-man, he said, but he could never long allow you to forget that he had been a banker.

His mate, Elias Goddedaal, was a huge viking of a man, six feet three and of proportionate mass, strong, sober, industrious, musical, and sentimental. He ran continually over into Swedish melodies, chiefly in the minor. He had paid nine dollars to hear Patti; to hear Nilsson, he had deserted a ship and two months' wages; and he was ready at any time to walk ten miles for a good concert, or seven to a reasonable play. On board he had three treasures: a canary bird, a concertina, and a blinding copy of the works of Shakespeare. He had a gift, peculiarly Scandinavian, of making friends at sight: an elemental innocence commended him; he was without fear, without reproach, and without money or the hope of making it.

Holdorsen was second mate, and berthed aft, but messed usually with the hands.

Of one more of the crew, some image lives. This was a foremast hand out of the Clyde, of the name of Brown. A small, dark, thickset creature, with dog's eyes, of a disposition incomparably mild and harmless, he knocked about seas and cities, the uncomplaining whiptop of one vice. "The drink is my trouble, ye see," he said to Carthew shyly; "and it's the more shame to me because I'm come of very good people at Bowling, down the wa'er." The letter that so much affected Nares, in case the reader should remember it, was addressed to this man Brown.

Such was the ship that now carried joy into the bosoms of the castaways. After the fatigue and the bestial emotions of their night of play, the approach of salvation shook them from all self-control. Their hands trembled, their eyes shone, they laughed and shouted like children as they cleared their camp: and some one beginning to whistle Marching Through Georgia, the remainder of the packing was conducted, amidst a thousand interruptions, to these martial strains. But the strong head of Wicks was only partly turned.

"Boys," he said, "easy all! We're going aboard of a ship of which we don't know nothing; we've got a chest of specie, and seeing the weight, we can't turn to and deny it. Now, suppose she was fishy; suppose it was some kind of a Bully Hayes business! It's my opinion we'd better be on hand with the pistols."

Every man of the party but Hemstead had some kind of a revolver; these were accordingly loaded and disposed about the persons of the castaways, and the packing was resumed and finished in the same rapturous spirit as it was begun. The sun was not yet ten degrees above the eastern sea, but the brig was already close in and hove to, before they had launched the boat and sped, shouting at the oars, towards the passage.

It was blowing fresh outside, with a strong send of sea. The spray flew in the oarsmen's faces. They saw the Union Jack blow abroad from the Flying Scud, the men clustered at the rail, the cook in the galley door, the captain on the quarter-deck with a pith helmet and binoculars. And the whole familiar business, the comfort, company, and safety of a ship, heaving nearer at each stroke, maddened them with joy.

Wicks was the first to catch the line, and swarm on board, helping hands grabbing him as he came and hauling him across the rail.

"Captain, sir, I suppose?" he said, turning to the hard old man in the pith helmet.

"Captain Trent, sir," returned the old gentleman.

"Well, I'm Captain Kirkup, and this is the crew of the Sydney schooner Currency Lass, dismasted at sea January 28th."

"Ay, ay," said Trent. "Well, you're all right now. Lucky for you I saw your signal. I didn't know I was so near this beastly island, there must be a drift to the south'ard here; and when I came on deck this morning at eight bells, I thought it was a ship afire."

It had been agreed that, while Wicks was to board the ship and do the civil, the rest were to remain in the whaleboat and see the treasure safe. A tackle was passed down to them; to this they made fast the invaluable chest, and gave the word to heave. But the unexpected weight brought the hand at the tackle to a stand; two others ran to tail on and help him, and the thing caught the eye of Trent.

"'Vast heaving!" he cried sharply; and then to Wicks: "What's that? I don't ever remember to have seen a chest weigh like that."

"It's money," said Wicks.

"It's what?" cried Trent.

"Specie," said Wicks; "saved from the wreck."

Trent looked at him sharply. "Here, let go that chest again, Mr. Goddedaal," he commanded, "shove the boat off, and stream her with a line astern."

"Ay, ay, sir!" from Goddedaal.

"What the devil's wrong?" asked Wicks.

"Nothing, I daresay," returned Trent. "But you'll allow it's a queer thing when a boat turns up in mid-ocean with half a ton of specie,—and everybody armed," he added, pointing to Wicks's pocket. "Your boat will lay comfortably astern, while you come below and make yourself satisfactory."

"O, if that's all!" said Wicks. "My log and papers are as right as the mail; nothing fishy about us." And he hailed his friends in the boat, bidding them have patience, and turned to follow Captain Trent.

"This way, Captain Kirkup," said the latter. "And don't blame a man for too much caution; no offence intended; and these China rivers shake a fellow's nerve. All I want is just to see you're what you say you are; it's only my duty, sir, and what you would do yourself in the circumstances. I've not always been a ship-captain: I was a banker once, and I tell you that's the trade to learn caution in. You have to keep your weather-eye lifting Saturday nights." And with a dry, business-like cordiality, he produced a bottle of gin.

The captains pledged each other; the papers were overhauled; the tale of Topelius and the trade was told in appreciative ears and cemented their acquaintance. Trent's suspicions, thus finally disposed of, were succeeded by a fit of profound thought, during which he sat lethargic and stern, looking at and drumming on the table.

"Anything more?" asked Wicks.

"What sort of a place is it inside?" inquired Trent, sudden as though Wicks had touched a spring.

"It's a good enough lagoon—a few horses' heads, but nothing to mention," answered Wicks.

"I've a good mind to go in," said Trent. "I was new rigged in China; it's given very bad, and I'm getting frightened for my sticks. We could set it up as good as new in a day. For I daresay your lot would turn to and give us a hand?"

"You see if we don't!" said Wicks.

"So be it, then," concluded Trent. "A stitch in time saves nine."

They returned on deck; Wicks cried the news to the Currency Lasses; the foretopsail was filled again, and the brig ran into the lagoon lively, the whaleboat dancing in her wake, and came to single anchor off Middle Brooks Island before eight. She was boarded by the castaways, breakfast was served, the baggage slung on board and piled in the waist, and all hands turned to upon the rigging. All day the work continued, the two crews rivalling each other in expense of strength. Dinner was served on deck, the officers messing aft under the slack of the spanker, the men fraternising forward. Trent appeared in excellent spirits, served out grog to all hands, opened a bottle of Cape wine for the after-table, and obliged his guests with many details of the life of a financier in Cardiff. He had been forty years at sea, had five times suffered shipwreck, was once nine months the prisoner of a pepper rajah, and had seen service under fire in Chinese rivers; but the only thing he cared to talk of, the only thing of which he was vain, or with which he thought it possible to interest a stranger, was his career as a money-lender in the slums of a seaport town.

The afternoon spell told cruelly on the Currency Lasses. Already exhausted as they were with sleeplessness and excitement, they did the last hours of this violent employment on bare nerves; and when Trent was at last satisfied with the condition of his rigging, expected eagerly the word to put to sea. But the captain seemed in no hurry. He went and walked by himself softly, like a man in thought. Presently he hailed Wicks.

"You're a kind of company, ain't you, Captain Kirkup?" he inquired.

"Yes, we're all on board on lays," was the reply.

"Well, then, you won't mind if I ask the lot of you down to tea in the cabin?" asked Trent.

Wicks was amazed, but he naturally ventured no remark; and a little after, the six Currency Lasses sat down with Trent and Goddedaal to a spread of marmalade, butter, toast, sardines, tinned tongue, and steaming tea. The food was not very good, and I have no doubt Nares would have reviled it, but it was manna to the castaways. Goddedaal waited on them with a kindness far before courtesy, a kindness like that of some old, honest countrywoman in her farm. It was remembered afterwards that Trent took little share in these attentions, but sat much absorbed in thought, and seemed to remember and forget the presence of his guests alternately.

Presently he addressed the Chinaman.

"Clear out!" said he, and watched him till he had disappeared in the stair. "Now, gentlemen," he went on, "I understand you're a joint-stock sort of crew, and that's why I've had you all down; for there's a point I want made clear. You see what sort of a ship this is—a good ship, though I say it, and you see what the rations are—good enough for sailor-men."

There was a hurried murmur of approval, but curiosity for what was coming next prevented an articulate reply.

"Well," continued Trent, making bread pills and looking hard at the middle of the table, "I'm glad of course to be able to give you a passage to 'Frisco; one sailor-man should help another, that's my motto. But when you want a thing in this world, you generally always have to pay for it." He laughed a brief, joyless laugh. "I have no idea of losing by my kindness."

"We have no idea you should, captain," said Wicks.

"We are ready to pay anything in reason," added Carthew.

At the words, Goddedaal, who sat next to him, touched him with his elbow, and the two mates exchanged a significant look. The character of Captain Trent was given and taken in that silent second.

"In reason?" repeated the captain of the brig. "I was waiting for that. Reason's between two people, and there's only one here. I'm the judge; I'm reason. If you want an advance you have to pay for it"—he hastily corrected himself—"If you want a passage in my ship, you have to pay my price," he substituted. "That's business, I believe. I don't want you; you want me."

"Well, sir," said Carthew, "and what IS your price?"

The captain made bread pills. "If I were like you," he said, "when you got hold of that merchant in the Gilberts, I might surprise you. You had your chance then; seems to me it's mine now. Turn about's fair play. What kind of mercy did you have on that Gilbert merchant?" he cried, with a sudden stridency. "Not that I blame you. All's fair in love and business," and he laughed again, a little frosty giggle.

"Well, sir?" said Carthew, gravely.

"Well, this ship's mine, I think?" he asked sharply.

"Well, I'm of that way of thinking meself," observed Mac.

"I say it's mine, sir!" reiterated Trent, like a man trying to be angry. "And I tell you all, if I was a driver like what you are, I would take the lot. But there's two thousand pounds there that don't belong to you, and I'm an honest man. Give me the two thousand that's yours, and I'll give you a passage to the coast, and land every man-jack of you in 'Frisco with fifteen pounds in his pocket, and the captain here with twenty-five."

Goddedaal laid down his head on the table like a man ashamed.

"You're joking," said Wicks, purple in the face.

"Am I?" said Trent. "Please yourselves. You're under no compulsion. This ship's mine, but there's that Brooks Island don't belong to me, and you can lay there till you die for what I care."

"It's more than your blooming brig's worth!" cried Wicks.

"It's my price anyway," returned Trent.

"And do you mean to say you would land us there to starve?" cried Tommy.

Captain Trent laughed the third time. "Starve? I defy you to," said he. "I'll sell you all the provisions you want at a fair profit."

"I beg your pardon, sir," said Mac, "but my case is by itself I'm working me passage; I got no share in that two thousand pounds nor nothing in my pockut; and I'll be glad to know what you have to say to me?"

"I ain't a hard man," said Trent. "That shall make no difference. I'll take you with the rest, only of course you get no fifteen pound."

The impudence was so extreme and startling, that all breathed deep, and Goddedaal raised up his face and looked his superior sternly in the eye.

But Mac was more articulate. "And you're what ye call a British sayman, I suppose? the sorrow in your guts!" he cried.

"One more such word, and I clap you in irons!" said Trent, rising gleefully at the face of opposition.

"And where would I be the while you were doin' ut?" asked Mac. "After you and your rigging, too! Ye ould puggy, ye haven't the civility of a bug, and I'll learn ye some."

His voice did not even rise as he uttered the threat; no man present, Trent least of all, expected that which followed. The Irishman's hand rose suddenly from below the table, an open clasp-knife balanced on the palm; there was a movement swift as conjuring; Trent started half to his feet, turning a little as he rose so as to escape the table, and the movement was his bane. The missile struck him in the jugular; he fell forward, and his blood flowed among the dishes on the cloth.

The suddenness of the attack and the catastrophe, the instant change from peace to war and from life to death, held all men spellbound. Yet a moment they sat about the table staring open-mouthed upon the prostrate captain and the flowing blood. The next, Goddedaal had leaped to his feet, caught up the stool on which he had been sitting, and swung it high in air, a man transfigured, roaring (as he stood) so that men's ears were stunned with it. There was no thought of battle in the Currency Lasses; none drew his weapon; all huddled helplessly from before the face of the baresark Scandinavian. His first blow sent Mac to ground with a broken arm. His second bashed out the brains of Hemstead. He turned from one to another, menacing and trumpeting like a wounded elephant, exulting in his rage. But there was no counsel, no light of reason, in that ecstasy of battle; and he shied from the pursuit of victory to hail fresh blows upon the supine Hemstead, so that the stool was shattered and the cabin rang with their violence. The sight of that post-mortem cruelty recalled Carthew to the life of instinct, and his revolver was in hand and he had aimed and fired before he knew. The ear-bursting sound of the report was accompanied by a yell of pain; the colossus paused, swayed, tottered, and fell headlong on the body of his victim.

In the instant silence that succeeded, the sound of feet pounding on the deck and in the companion leaped into hearing; and a face, that of the sailor Holdorsen, appeared below the bulkheads in the cabin doorway. Carthew shattered it with a second shot, for he was a marksman.

"Pistols!" he cried, and charged at the companion, Wicks at his heels, Tommy and Amalu following. They trod the body of Holdorsen underfoot, and flew up-stairs and forth into the dusky blaze of a sunset red as blood. The numbers were still equal, but the Flying Scuds dreamed not of defence, and fled with one accord for the forecastle scuttle. Brown was first in flight; he disappeared below unscathed; the Chinaman followed head-foremost with a ball in his side; and the others shinned into the rigging.

A fierce composure settled upon Wicks and Carthew, their fighting second wind. They posted Tommy at the fore and Amalu at the main to guard the masts and shrouds, and going themselves into the waist, poured out a box of cartridges on deck and filled the chambers. The poor devils aloft bleated aloud for mercy. But the hour of any mercy was gone by; the cup was brewed and must be drunken to the dregs; since so many had fallen all must fall. The light was bad, the cheap revolvers fouled and carried wild, the screaming wretches were swift to flatten themselves against the masts and yards or find a momentary refuge in the hanging sails. The fell business took long, but it was done at last. Hardy the Londoner was shot on the foreroyal yard, and hung horribly suspended in the brails. Wallen, the other, had his jaw broken on the maintop-gallant crosstrees, and exposed himself, shrieking, till a second shot dropped him on the deck.

This had been bad enough, but worse remained behind. There was still Brown in the forepeak. Tommy, with a sudden clamour of weeping, begged for his life. "One man can't hurt us," he sobbed. "We can't go on with this. I spoke to him at dinner. He's an awful decent little cad. It can't be done. Nobody can go into that place and murder him. It's too damned wicked."

The sound of his supplications was perhaps audible to the unfortunate below.

"One left, and we all hang," said Wicks. "Brown must go the same road." The big man was deadly white and trembled like an aspen; and he had no sooner finished speaking, than he went to the ship's side and vomited.

"We can never do it if we wait," said Carthew. "Now or never," and he marched towards the scuttle.

"No, no, no!" wailed Tommy, clutching at his jacket.

But Carthew flung him off, and stepped down the ladder, his heart rising with disgust and shame. The Chinaman lay on the floor, still groaning; the place was pitch dark.

"Brown!" cried Carthew, "Brown, where are you?"

His heart smote him for the treacherous apostrophe, but no answer came.

He groped in the bunks: they were all empty. Then he moved towards the forepeak, which was hampered with coils of rope and spare chandlery in general.

"Brown!" he said again.

"Here, sir," answered a shaking voice; and the poor invisible caitiff called on him by name, and poured forth out of the darkness an endless, garrulous appeal for mercy. A sense of danger, of daring, had alone nerved Carthew to enter the forecastle; and here was the enemy crying and pleading like a frightened child. His obsequious "Here, sir," his horrid fluency of obtestation, made the murder tenfold more revolting. Twice Carthew raised the pistol, once he pressed the trigger (or thought he did) with all his might, but no explosion followed; and with that the lees of his courage ran quite out, and he turned and fled from before his victim.

Wicks sat on the fore hatch, raised the face of a man of seventy, and looked a wordless question. Carthew shook his head. With such composure as a man displays marching towards the gallows, Wicks arose, walked to the scuttle, and went down. Brown thought it was Carthew returning, and discovered himself, half crawling from his shelter, with another incoherent burst of pleading. Wicks emptied his revolver at the voice, which broke into mouse-like whimperings and groans. Silence succeeded, and the murderer ran on deck like one possessed.

The other three were now all gathered on the fore hatch, and Wicks took his place beside them without question asked or answered. They sat close, like children in the dark, and shook each other with their shaking. The dusk continued to fall; and there was no sound but the beating of the surf and the occasional hiccup of a sob from Tommy Hadden.

"God, if there was another ship!" cried Carthew of a sudden.

Wicks started and looked aloft with the trick of all seamen, and shuddered as he saw the hanging figure on the royal yard.

"If I went aloft, I'd fall," he said simply. "I'm done up."

It was Amalu who volunteered, climbed to the very truck, swept the fading horizon, and announced nothing within sight.

"No odds," said Wicks. "We can't sleep ..."

"Sleep!" echoed Carthew; and it seemed as if the whole of Shakespeare's Macbeth thundered at the gallop through his mind.

"Well, then, we can't sit and chitter here," said Wicks, "till we've cleaned ship; and I can't turn to till I've had gin, and the gin's in the cabin, and who's to fetch it?"

"I will," said Carthew, "if any one has matches."

Amalu passed him a box, and he went aft and down the companion and into the cabin, stumbling upon bodies. Then he struck a match, and his looks fell upon two living eyes.

"Well?" asked Mac, for it was he who still survived in that shambles of a cabin.

"It's done; they're all dead," answered Carthew.

"Christ!" said the Irishman, and fainted.

The gin was found in the dead captain's cabin; it was brought on deck, and all hands had a dram, and attacked their farther task. The night was come, the moon would not be up for hours; a lamp was set on the main hatch to light Amalu as he washed down decks; and the galley lantern was taken to guide the others in their graveyard business. Holdorsen, Hemstead, Trent, and Goddedaal were first disposed of, the last still breathing as he went over the side; Wallen followed; and then Wicks, steadied by the gin, went aloft with a boathook and succeeded in dislodging Hardy. The Chinaman was their last task; he seemed to be light-headed, talked aloud in his unknown language as they brought him up, and it was only with the splash of his sinking body that the gibberish ceased. Brown, by common consent, was left alone. Flesh and blood could go no further.

All this time they had been drinking undiluted gin like water; three bottles stood broached in different quarters; and none passed without a gulp. Tommy collapsed against the mainmast; Wicks fell on his face on the poop ladder and moved no more; Amalu had vanished unobserved. Carthew was the last afoot: he stood swaying at the break of the poop, and the lantern, which he still carried, swung with his movement. His head hummed; it swarmed with broken thoughts; memory of that day's abominations flared up and died down within him like the light of a lamp in a strong draught. And then he had a drunkard's inspiration.

"There must be no more of this," he thought, and stumbled once more below.

The absence of Holdorsen's body brought him to a stand. He stood and stared at the empty floor, and then remembered and smiled. From the captain's room he took the open case with one dozen and three bottles of gin, put the lantern inside, and walked precariously forth. Mac was once more conscious, his eyes haggard, his face drawn with pain and flushed with fever; and Carthew remembered he had never been seen to, had lain there helpless, and was so to lie all night, injured, perhaps dying. But it was now too late; reason had now fled from that silent ship. If Carthew could get on deck again, it was as much as he could hope; and casting on the unfortunate a glance of pity, the tragic drunkard shouldered his way up the companion, dropped the case overboard, and fell in the scuppers helpless.

CHAPTER XXV. A BAD BARGAIN.

With the first colour in the east, Carthew awoke and sat up. A while he gazed at the scroll of the morning bank and the spars and hanging canvas of the brig, like a man who wakes in a strange bed, with a child's simplicity of wonder. He wondered above all what ailed him, what he had lost, what disfavour had been done him, which he knew he should resent, yet had forgotten. And then, like a river bursting through a dam, the truth rolled on him its instantaneous volume: his memory teemed with speech and pictures that he should never again forget; and he sprang to his feet, stood a moment hand to brow, and began to walk violently to and fro by the companion. As he walked, he wrung his hands. "God—God—God," he kept saying, with no thought of prayer, uttering a mere voice of agony.

The time may have been long or short, it was perhaps minutes, perhaps only seconds, ere he awoke to find himself observed, and saw the captain sitting up and watching him over the break of the poop, a strange blindness as of fever in his eyes, a haggard knot of corrugations on his brow. Cain saw himself in a mirror. For a flash they looked upon each other, and then glanced guiltily aside; and Carthew fled from the eye of his accomplice, and stood leaning on the taffrail.

An hour went by, while the day came brighter, and the sun rose and drank up the clouds: an hour of silence in the ship, an hour of agony beyond narration for the sufferers. Brown's gabbling prayers, the cries of the sailors in the rigging, strains of the dead Hemstead's minstrelsy, ran together in Carthew's mind, with sickening iteration. He neither acquitted nor condemned himself: he did not think, he suffered. In the bright water into which he stared, the pictures changed and were repeated: the baresark rage of Goddedaal; the blood-red light of the sunset into which they had run forth; the face of the babbling Chinaman as they cast him over; the face of the captain, seen a moment since, as he awoke from drunkenness into remorse. And time passed, and the sun swam higher, and his torment was not abated.

Then were fulfilled many sayings, and the weakest of these condemned brought relief and healing to the others. Amalu the drudge awoke (like the rest) to sickness of body and distress of mind; but the habit of obedience ruled in that simple spirit, and appalled to be so late, he went direct into the galley, kindled the fire, and began to get breakfast. At the rattle of dishes, the snapping of the fire, and the thin smoke that went up straight into the air, the spell was lifted. The condemned felt once more the good dry land of habit under foot; they touched again the familiar guide-ropes of sanity; they were restored to a sense of the blessed revolution and return of all things earthly. The captain drew a bucket of water and began to bathe. Tommy sat up, watched him awhile, and slowly followed his example; and Carthew, remembering his last thoughts of the night before, hastened to the cabin.

Mac was awake; perhaps had not slept. Over his head Goddedaal's canary twittered shrilly from its cage.

"How are you?" asked Carthew.

"Me arrum's broke," returned Mac; "but I can stand that. It's this place I can't abide. I was coming on deck anyway."

"Stay where you are, though," said Carthew. "It's deadly hot above, and there's no wind. I'll wash out this——" and he paused, seeking a word and not finding one for the grisly foulness of the cabin.

"Faith, I'll be obliged to ye, then," replied the Irishman. He spoke mild and meek, like a sick child with its mother. There was now no violence in the violent man; and as Carthew fetched a bucket and swab and the steward's sponge, and began to cleanse the field of battle, he alternately watched him or shut his eyes and sighed like a man near fainting. "I have to ask all your pardons," he began again presently, "and the more shame to me as I got ye into trouble and couldn't do nothing when it came. Ye saved me life, sir; ye're a clane shot."

"For God's sake, don't talk of it!" cried Carthew. "It can't be talked of; you don't know what it was. It was nothing down here; they fought. On deck—O, my God!" And Carthew, with the bloody sponge pressed to his face, struggled a moment with hysteria.

"Kape cool, Mr. Cart'ew. It's done now," said Mac; "and ye may bless God ye're not in pain and helpless in the bargain."

There was no more said by one or other, and the cabin was pretty well cleansed when a stroke on the ship's bell summoned Carthew to breakfast. Tommy had been busy in the meanwhile; he had hauled the whaleboat close aboard, and already lowered into it a small keg of beef that he found ready broached beside the galley door; it was plain he had but the one idea—to escape.

"We have a shipful of stores to draw upon," he said. "Well, what are we staying for? Let's get off at once for Hawaii. I've begun preparing already."

"Mac has his arm broken," observed Carthew; "how would he stand the voyage?"

"A broken arm?" repeated the captain. "That all? I'll set it after breakfast. I thought he was dead like the rest. That madman hit out like——" and there, at the evocation of the battle, his voice ceased and the talk died with it.

After breakfast, the three white men went down into the cabin.

"I've come to set your arm," said the captain.

"I beg your pardon, captain," replied Mac; "but the firrst thing ye got to do is to get this ship to sea. We'll talk of me arrum after that."

"O, there's no such blooming hurry," returned Wicks.

"When the next ship sails in, ye'll tell me stories!" retorted Mac.

"But there's nothing so unlikely in the world," objected Carthew.

"Don't be deceivin' yourself," said Mac. "If ye want a ship, divil a one'll look near ye in six year; but if ye don't, ye may take my word for ut, we'll have a squadron layin' here."

"That's what I say," cried Tommy; "that's what I call sense! Let's stock that whaleboat and be off."

"And what will Captain Wicks be thinking of the whaleboat?" asked the Irishman.

"I don't think of it at all," said Wicks. "We've a smart-looking brig under foot; that's all the whaleboat I want."

"Excuse me!" cried Tommy. "That's childish talk. You've got a brig, to be sure, and what use is she? You daren't go anywhere in her. What port are you to sail for?"

"For the port of Davy Jones's Locker, my son," replied the captain. "This brig's going to be lost at sea. I'll tell you where, too, and that's about forty miles to windward of Kauai. We're going to stay by her till she's down; and once the masts are under, she's the Flying Scud no more, and we never heard of such a brig; and it's the crew of the schooner Currency Lass that comes ashore in the boat, and takes the first chance to Sydney."

"Captain dear, that's the first Christian word I've heard of ut!" cried Mac. "And now, just let me arrum be, jewel, and get the brig outside."

"I'm as anxious as yourself, Mac," returned Wicks; "but there's not wind enough to swear by. So let's see your arm, and no more talk."

The arm was set and splinted; the body of Brown fetched from the forepeak, where it lay still and cold, and committed to the waters of the lagoon; and the washing of the cabin rudely finished. All these were done ere midday; and it was past three when the first cat's-paw ruffled the lagoon, and the wind came in a dry squall, which presently sobered to a steady breeze.

The interval was passed by all in feverish impatience, and by one of the party in secret and extreme concern of mind. Captain Wicks was a fore-and-aft sailor; he could take a schooner through a Scotch reel, felt her mouth and divined her temper like a rider with a horse; she, on her side, recognising her master and following his wishes like a dog. But by a not very unusual train of circumstance, the man's dexterity was partial and circumscribed. On a schooner's deck he was Rembrandt or (at the least) Mr. Whistler; on board a brig he was Pierre Grassou. Again and again in the course of the morning, he had reasoned out his policy and rehearsed his orders; and ever with the same depression and weariness. It was guess-work; it was chance; the ship might behave as he expected, and might not; suppose she failed him, he stood there helpless, beggared of all the proved resources of experience. Had not all hands been so weary, had he not feared to communicate his own misgivings, he could have towed her out. But these reasons sufficed, and the most he could do was to take all possible precautions. Accordingly he had Carthew aft, explained what was to be done with anxious patience, and visited along with him the various sheets and braces.

"I hope I'll remember," said Carthew. "It seems awfully muddled."

"It's the rottenest kind of rig," the captain admitted: "all blooming pocket handkerchiefs! And not one sailor-man on deck! Ah, if she'd only been a brigantine, now! But it's lucky the passage is so plain; there's no manoeuvring to mention. We get under way before the wind, and run right so till we begin to get foul of the island; then we haul our wind and lie as near south-east as may be till we're on that line; 'bout ship there and stand straight out on the port tack. Catch the idea?"

"Yes, I see the idea," replied Carthew, rather dismally, and the two incompetents studied for a long time in silence the complicated gear above their heads.

But the time came when these rehearsals must be put in practice. The sails were lowered, and all hands heaved the anchor short. The whaleboat was then cut adrift, the upper topsails and the spanker set, the yards braced up, and the spanker sheet hauled out to starboard.

"Heave away on your anchor, Mr. Carthew."

"Anchor's gone, sir."

"Set jibs."

It was done, and the brig still hung enchanted. Wicks, his head full of a schooner's mainsail, turned his mind to the spanker. First he hauled in the sheet, and then he hauled it out, with no result.

"Brail the damned thing up!" he bawled at last, with a red face. "There ain't no sense in it."

It was the last stroke of bewilderment for the poor captain, that he had no sooner brailed up the spanker than the vessel came before the wind. The laws of nature seemed to him to be suspended; he was like a man in a world of pantomime tricks; the cause of any result, and the probable result of any action, equally concealed from him. He was the more careful not to shake the nerve of his amateur assistants. He stood there with a face like a torch; but he gave his orders with aplomb; and indeed, now the ship was under weigh, supposed his difficulties over.

The lower topsails and courses were then set, and the brig began to walk the water like a thing of life, her forefoot discoursing music, the birds flying and crying over her spars. Bit by bit the passage began to open and the blue sea to show between the flanking breakers on the reef; bit by bit, on the starboard bow, the low land of the islet began to heave closer aboard. The yards were braced up, the spanker sheet hauled aft again; the brig was close hauled, lay down to her work like a thing in earnest, and had soon drawn near to the point of advantage, where she might stay and lie out of the lagoon in a single tack.

Wicks took the wheel himself, swelling with success. He kept the brig full to give her heels, and began to bark his orders: "Ready about. Helm's a-lee. Tacks and sheets. Mainsail haul." And then the fatal words: "That'll do your mainsail; jump forrard and haul round your foreyards."

To stay a square-rigged ship is an affair of knowledge and swift sight; and a man used to the succinct evolutions of a schooner will always tend to be too hasty with a brig. It was so now. The order came too soon; the topsails set flat aback; the ship was in irons. Even yet, had the helm been reversed, they might have saved her. But to think of a stern-board at all, far more to think of profiting by one, were foreign to the schooner-sailor's mind. Wicks made haste instead to wear ship, a manoeuvre for which room was wanting, and the Flying Scud took ground on a bank of sand and coral about twenty minutes before five.

Wicks was no hand with a square-rigger, and he had shown it. But he was a sailor and a born captain of men for all homely purposes, where intellect is not required and an eye in a man's head and a heart under his jacket will suffice. Before the others had time to understand the misfortune, he was bawling fresh orders, and had the sails clewed up, and took soundings round the ship.

"She lies lovely," he remarked, and ordered out a boat with the starboard anchor.

"Here! steady!" cried Tommy. "You ain't going to turn us to, to warp her off?"

"I am though," replied Wicks.

"I won't set a hand to such tomfoolery for one," replied Tommy. "I'm dead beat." He went and sat down doggedly on the main hatch. "You got us on; get us off again," he added.

Carthew and Wicks turned to each other.

"Perhaps you don't know how tired we are," said Carthew.

"The tide's flowing!" cried the captain. "You wouldn't have me miss a rising tide?"

"O, gammon! there's tides to-morrow!" retorted Tommy.

"And I'll tell you what," added Carthew, "the breeze is failing fast, and the sun will soon be down. We may get into all kinds of fresh mess in the dark and with nothing but light airs."

"I don't deny it," answered Wicks, and stood awhile as if in thought. "But what I can't make out," he began again, with agitation, "what I can't make out is what you're made of! To stay in this place is beyond me. There's the bloody sun going down—and to stay here is beyond me!"

The others looked upon him with horrified surprise. This fall of their chief pillar—this irrational passion in the practical man, suddenly barred out of his true sphere, the sphere of action—shocked and daunted them. But it gave to another and unseen hearer the chance for which he had been waiting. Mac, on the striking of the brig, had crawled up the companion, and he now showed himself and spoke up.

"Captain Wicks," said he, "it's me that brought this trouble on the lot of ye. I'm sorry for ut, I ask all your pardons, and if there's any one can say 'I forgive ye,' it'll make my soul the lighter."

Wicks stared upon the man in amaze; then his self-control returned to him. "We're all in glass houses here," he said; "we ain't going to turn to and throw stones. I forgive you, sure enough; and much good may it do you!"

The others spoke to the same purpose.

"I thank ye for ut, and 'tis done like gentlemen," said Mac. "But there's another thing I have upon my mind. I hope we're all Prodestan's here?"

It appeared they were; it seemed a small thing for the Protestant religion to rejoice in!

"Well, that's as it should be," continued Mac. "And why shouldn't we say the Lord's Prayer? There can't be no hurt in ut."

He had the same quiet, pleading, childlike way with him as in the morning; and the others accepted his proposal, and knelt down without a word.

"Knale if ye like!" said he. "I'll stand." And he covered his eyes.

So the prayer was said to the accompaniment of the surf and seabirds, and all rose refreshed and felt lightened of a load. Up to then, they had cherished their guilty memories in private, or only referred to them in the heat of a moment and fallen immediately silent. Now they had faced their remorse in company, and the worst seemed over. Nor was it only that. But the petition "Forgive us our trespasses," falling in so apposite after they had themselves forgiven the immediate author of their miseries, sounded like an absolution.

Tea was taken on deck in the time of the sunset, and not long after the five castaways—castaways once more—lay down to sleep.

Day dawned windless and hot. Their slumbers had been too profound to be refreshing, and they woke listless, and sat up, and stared about them with dull eyes. Only Wicks, smelling a hard day's work ahead, was more alert. He went first to the well, sounded it once and then a second time, and stood awhile with a grim look, so that all could see he was dissatisfied. Then he shook himself, stripped to the buff, clambered on the rail, drew himself up and raised his arms to plunge. The dive was never taken. He stood instead transfixed, his eyes on the horizon.

"Hand up that glass," he said.

In a trice they were all swarming aloft, the nude captain leading with the glass.

On the northern horizon was a finger of grey smoke, straight in the windless air like a point of admiration.

"What do you make it?" they asked of Wicks.

"She's truck down," he replied; "no telling yet. By the way the smoke builds, she must be heading right here."

"What can she be?"

"She might be a China mail," returned Wicks, "and she might be a blooming man-of-war, come to look for castaways. Here! This ain't the time to stand staring. On deck, boys!"

He was the first on deck, as he had been the first aloft, handed down the ensign, bent it again to the signal halliards, and ran it up union down.

"Now hear me," he said, jumping into his trousers, "and everything I say you grip on to. If that's a man-of-war, she'll be in a tearing hurry; all these ships are what don't do nothing and have their expenses paid. That's our chance; for we'll go with them, and they won't take the time to look twice or to ask a question. I'm Captain Trent; Carthew, you're Goddedaal; Tommy, you're Hardy; Mac's Brown; Amalu—Hold hard! we can't make a Chinaman of him! Ah Wing must have deserted; Amalu stowed away; and I turned him to as cook, and was never at the bother to sign him. Catch the idea? Say your names."

And that pale company recited their lesson earnestly.

"What were the names of the other two?" he asked. "Him Carthew shot in the companion, and the one I caught in the jaw on the main top-gallant?"

"Holdorsen and Wallen," said some one.

"Well, they're drowned," continued Wicks; "drowned alongside trying to lower a boat. We had a bit of a squall last night: that's how we got ashore." He ran and squinted at the compass. "Squall out of nor'-nor'-west-half-west; blew hard; every one in a mess, falls jammed, and Holdorsen and Wallen spilt overboard. See? Clear your blooming heads!" He was in his jacket now, and spoke with a feverish impatience and contention that rang like anger.

"But is it safe?" asked Tommy.

"Safe?" bellowed the captain. "We're standing on the drop, you moon-calf! If that ship's bound for China (which she don't look to be), we're lost as soon as we arrive; if she's bound the other way, she comes from China, don't she? Well, if there's a man on board of her that ever clapped eyes on Trent or any blooming hand out of this brig, we'll all be in irons in two hours. Safe! no, it ain't safe; it's a beggarly last chance to shave the gallows, and that's what it is."

At this convincing picture, fear took hold on all.

"Hadn't we a hundred times better stay by the brig?" cried Carthew. "They would give us a hand to float her off."

"You'll make me waste this holy day in chattering!" cried Wicks. "Look here, when I sounded the well this morning, there was two foot of water there against eight inches last night. What's wrong? I don't know; might be nothing; might be the worst kind of smash. And then, there we are in for a thousand miles in an open boat, if that's your taste!"

"But it may be nothing, and anyway their carpenters are bound to help us repair her," argued Carthew.

"Moses Murphy!" cried the captain. "How did she strike? Bows on, I believe. And she's down by the head now. If any carpenter comes tinkering here, where'll he go first? Down in the forepeak, I suppose! And then, how about all that blood among the chandlery? You would think you were a lot of members of Parliament discussing Plimsoll; and you're just a pack of murderers with the halter round your neck. Any other ass got any time to waste? No? Thank God for that! Now, all hands! I'm going below, and I leave you here on deck. You get the boat cover off that boat; then you turn to and open the specie chest. There are five of us; get five chests, and divide the specie equal among the five—put it at the bottom—and go at it like tigers. Get blankets, or canvas, or clothes, so it won't rattle. It'll make five pretty heavy chests, but we can't help that. You, Carthew—dash me!—You, Mr. Goddedaal, come below. We've our share before us."

And he cast another glance at the smoke, and hurried below with Carthew at his heels.

The logs were found in the main cabin behind the canary's cage; two of them, one kept by Trent, one by Goddedaal. Wicks looked first at one, then at the other, and his lip stuck out.

"Can you forge hand of write?" he asked.

"No," said Carthew.

"There's luck for you—no more can I!" cried the captain. "Hullo! here's worse yet, here's this Goddedaal up to date; he must have filled it in before supper. See for yourself: 'Smoke observed.—Captain Kirkup and five hands of the schooner Currency Lass.' Ah! this is better," he added, turning to the other log. "The old man ain't written anything for a clear fortnight. We'll dispose of your log altogether, Mr. Goddedaal, and stick to the old man's—to mine, I mean; only I ain't going to write it up, for reasons of my own. You are. You're going to sit down right here and fill it in the way I tell you."

"How to explain the loss of mine?" asked Carthew.

"You never kept one," replied the captain. "Gross neglect of duty. You'll catch it."

"And the change of writing?" resumed Carthew. "You began; why do you stop and why do I come in? And you'll have to sign anyway."

"O! I've met with an accident and can't write," replied Wicks.

"An accident?" repeated Carthew. "It don't sound natural. What kind of an accident?"

Wicks spread his hand face-up on the table, and drove a knife through his palm.

"That kind of an accident," said he. "There's a way to draw to windward of most difficulties, if you've a head on your shoulders." He began to bind up his hand with a handkerchief, glancing the while over Goddedaal's log. "Hullo!" he said, "this'll never do for us—this is an impossible kind of a yarn. Here, to begin with, is this Captain Trent trying some fancy course, leastways he's a thousand miles to south'ard of the great circle. And here, it seems, he was close up with this island on the sixth, sails all these days, and is close up with it again by daylight on the eleventh."

"Goddedaal said they had the deuce's luck," said Carthew.

"Well, it don't look like real life—that's all I can say," returned Wicks.

"It's the way it was, though," argued Carthew.

"So it is; and what the better are we for that, if it don't look so?" cried the captain, sounding unwonted depths of art criticism. "Here! try and see if you can't tie this bandage; I'm bleeding like a pig."

As Carthew sought to adjust the handkerchief, his patient seemed sunk in a deep muse, his eye veiled, his mouth partly open. The job was yet scarce done, when he sprang to his feet.

"I have it," he broke out, and ran on deck. "Here, boys!" he cried, "we didn't come here on the eleventh; we came in here on the evening of the sixth, and lay here ever since becalmed. As soon as you've done with these chests," he added, "you can turn to and roll out beef and water breakers; it'll look more shipshape—like as if we were getting ready for the boat voyage."

And he was back again in a moment, cooking the new log. Goddedaal's was then carefully destroyed, and a hunt began for the ship's papers. Of all the agonies of that breathless morning, this was perhaps the most poignant. Here and there the two men searched, cursing, cannoning together, streaming with heat, freezing with terror. News was bawled down to them that the ship was indeed a man-of-war, that she was close up, that she was lowering a boat; and still they sought in vain. By what accident they missed the iron box with the money and accounts, is hard to fancy; but they did. And the vital documents were found at last in the pocket of Trent's shore-going coat, where he had left them when last he came on board.

Wicks smiled for the first time that morning. "None too soon," said he. "And now for it! Take these others for me; I'm afraid I'll get them mixed if I keep both."

"What are they?" Carthew asked.

"They're the Kirkup and Currency Lass papers," he replied. "Pray God we need 'em again!"

"Boat's inside the lagoon, sir," hailed down Mac, who sat by the skylight doing sentry while the others worked.

"Time we were on deck, then, Mr. Goddedaal," said Wicks.

As they turned to leave the cabin, the canary burst into piercing song.

"My God!" cried Carthew, with a gulp, "we can't leave that wretched bird to starve. It was poor Goddedaal's."

"Bring the bally thing along!" cried the captain.

And they went on deck.

An ugly brute of a modern man-of-war lay just without the reef, now quite inert, now giving a flap or two with her propeller. Nearer hand, and just within, a big white boat came skimming to the stroke of many oars, her ensign blowing at the stern.

"One word more," said Wicks, after he had taken in the scene. "Mac, you've been in China ports? All right; then you can speak for yourself. The rest of you I kept on board all the time we were in Hongkong, hoping you would desert; but you fooled me and stuck to the brig. That'll make your lying come easier."

The boat was now close at hand; a boy in the stern sheets was the only officer, and a poor one plainly, for the men were talking as they pulled.

"Thank God, they've only sent a kind of a middy!" ejaculated Wicks. "Here you, Hardy, stand for'ard! I'll have no deck hands on my quarter-deck," he cried, and the reproof braced the whole crew like a cold douche.

The boat came alongside with perfect neatness, and the boy officer stepped on board, where he was respectfully greeted by Wicks.

"You the master of this ship?" he asked.

"Yes, sir," said Wicks. "Trent is my name, and this is the Flying Scud of Hull."

"You seem to have got into a mess," said the officer.

"If you'll step aft with me here, I'll tell you all there is of it," said Wicks.

"Why, man, you're shaking!" cried the officer.

"So would you, perhaps, if you had been in the same berth," returned Wicks; and he told the whole story of the rotten water, the long calm, the squall, the seamen drowned; glibly and hotly; talking, with his head in the lion's mouth, like one pleading in the dock. I heard the same tale from the same narrator in the saloon in San Francisco; and even then his bearing filled me with suspicion. But the officer was no observer.

"Well, the captain is in no end of a hurry," said he; "but I was instructed to give you all the assistance in my power, and signal back for another boat if more hands were necessary. What can I do for you?"

"O, we won't keep you no time," replied Wicks cheerily. "We're all ready, bless you—men's chests, chronometer, papers and all."

"Do you mean to leave her?" cried the officer. "She seems to me to lie nicely; can't we get your ship off?"

"So we could, and no mistake; but how we're to keep her afloat's another question. Her bows is stove in," replied Wicks.

The officer coloured to the eyes. He was incompetent and knew he was; thought he was already detected, and feared to expose himself again. There was nothing further from his mind than that the captain should deceive him; if the captain was pleased, why, so was he. "All right," he said. "Tell your men to get their chests aboard."

"Mr. Goddedaal, turn the hands to to get the chests aboard," said Wicks.

The four Currency Lasses had waited the while on tenter-hooks. This welcome news broke upon them like the sun at midnight; and Hadden burst into a storm of tears, sobbing aloud as he heaved upon the tackle. But the work went none the less briskly forward; chests, men, and bundles were got over the side with alacrity; the boat was shoved off; it moved out of the long shadow of the Flying Scud, and its bows were pointed at the passage.

So much, then, was accomplished. The sham wreck had passed muster; they were clear of her, they were safe away; and the water widened between them and her damning evidences. On the other hand, they were drawing nearer to the ship of war, which might very well prove to be their prison and a hangman's cart to bear them to the gallows—of which they had not yet learned either whence she came or whither she was bound; and the doubt weighed upon their heart like mountains.

It was Wicks who did the talking. The sound was small in Carthew's ears, like the voices of men miles away, but the meaning of each word struck home to him like a bullet. "What did you say your ship was?" inquired Wicks.

"Tempest, don't you know?" returned the officer.

Don't you know? What could that mean? Perhaps nothing: perhaps that the ships had met already. Wicks took his courage in both hands. "Where is she bound?" he asked.

"O, we're just looking in at all these miserable islands here," said the officer. "Then we bear up for San Francisco."

"O, yes, you're from China ways, like us?" pursued Wicks.

"Hong Kong," said the officer, and spat over the side.

Hong Kong. Then the game was up; as soon as they set foot on board, they would be seized; the wreck would be examined, the blood found, the lagoon perhaps dredged, and the bodies of the dead would reappear to testify. An impulse almost incontrollable bade Carthew rise from the thwart, shriek out aloud, and leap overboard; it seemed so vain a thing to dissemble longer, to dally with the inevitable, to spin out some hundred seconds more of agonised suspense, with shame and death thus visibly approaching. But the indomitable Wicks persevered. His face was like a skull, his voice scarce recognisable; the dullest of men and officers (it seemed) must have remarked that telltale countenance and broken utterance. And still he persevered, bent upon certitude.

"Nice place, Hong Kong?" he said.

"I'm sure I don't know," said the officer. "Only a day and a half there; called for orders and came straight on here. Never heard of such a beastly cruise." And he went on describing and lamenting the untoward fortunes of the Tempest.

But Wicks and Carthew heeded him no longer. They lay back on the gunnel, breathing deep, sunk in a stupor of the body: the mind within still nimbly and agreeably at work, measuring the past danger, exulting in the present relief, numbering with ecstasy their ultimate chances of escape. For the voyage in the man-of-war they were now safe; yet a few more days of peril, activity, and presence of mind in San Francisco, and the whole horrid tale was blotted out; and Wicks again became Kirkup, and Goddedaal became Carthew—men beyond all shot of possible suspicion, men who had never heard of the Flying Scud, who had never been in sight of Midway Reef.

So they came alongside, under many craning heads of seamen and projecting mouths of guns; so they climbed on board somnambulous, and looked blindly about them at the tall spars, the white decks, and the crowding ship's company, and heard men as from far away, and answered them at random.

And then a hand fell softly on Carthew's shoulder.

"Why, Norrie, old chappie, where have you dropped from? All the world's been looking for you. Don't you know you've come into your kingdom?"

He turned, beheld the face of his old schoolmate Sebright, and fell unconscious at his feet.

The doctor was attending him, a while later, in Lieutenant Sebright's cabin, when he came to himself. He opened his eyes, looked hard in the strange face, and spoke with a kind of solemn vigour.

"Brown must go the same road," he said; "now or never." And then paused, and his reason coming to him with more clearness, spoke again: "What was I saying? Where am I? Who are you?"

"I am the doctor of the Tempest," was the reply. "You are in Lieutenant Sebright's berth, and you may dismiss all concern from your mind. Your troubles are over, Mr. Carthew."

"Why do you call me that?" he asked. "Ah, I remember—Sebright knew me! O!" and he groaned and shook. "Send down Wicks to me; I must see Wicks at once!" he cried, and seized the doctor's wrist with unconscious violence.

"All right," said the doctor. "Let's make a bargain. You swallow down this draught, and I'll go and fetch Wicks."

And he gave the wretched man an opiate that laid him out within ten minutes and in all likelihood preserved his reason.

It was the doctor's next business to attend to Mac; and he found occasion, while engaged upon his arm, to make the man repeat the names of the rescued crew. It was now the turn of the captain, and there is no doubt he was no longer the man that we have seen; sudden relief, the sense of perfect safety, a square meal and a good glass of grog, had all combined to relax his vigilance and depress his energy.

"When was this done?" asked the doctor, looking at the wound.

"More than a week ago," replied Wicks, thinking singly of his log.

"Hey?" cried the doctor, and he raised his hand and looked the captain in the eyes.

"I don't remember exactly," faltered Wicks.

And at this remarkable falsehood, the suspicions of the doctor were at once quadrupled.

"By the way, which of you is called Wicks?" he asked easily.

"What's that?" snapped the captain, falling white as paper.

"Wicks," repeated the doctor; "which of you is he? that's surely a plain question."

Wicks stared upon his questioner in silence.

"Which is Brown, then?" pursued the doctor.

"What are you talking of? what do you mean by this?" cried Wicks, snatching his half-bandaged hand away, so that the blood sprinkled in the surgeon's face.

He did not trouble to remove it. Looking straight at his victim, he pursued his questions. "Why must Brown go the same way?" he asked.

Wicks fell trembling on a locker. "Carthew's told you," he cried.

"No," replied the doctor, "he has not. But he and you between you have set me thinking, and I think there's something wrong."

"Give me some grog," said Wicks. "I'd rather tell than have you find out. I'm damned if it's half as bad as what any one would think."

And with the help of a couple of strong grogs, the tragedy of the Flying Scud was told for the first time.

It was a fortunate series of accidents that brought the story to the doctor. He understood and pitied the position of these wretched men, and came whole-heartedly to their assistance. He and Wicks and Carthew (so soon as he was recovered) held a hundred councils and prepared a policy for San Francisco. It was he who certified "Goddedaal" unfit to be moved and smuggled Carthew ashore under cloud of night; it was he who kept Wicks's wound open that he might sign with his left hand; he who took all their Chile silver and (in the course of the first day) got it converted for them into portable gold. He used his influence in the wardroom to keep the tongues of the young officers in order, so that Carthew's identification was kept out of the papers. And he rendered another service yet more important. He had a friend in San Francisco, a millionaire; to this man he privately presented Carthew as a young gentleman come newly into a huge estate, but troubled with Jew debts which he was trying to settle on the quiet. The millionaire came readily to help; and it was with his money that the wrecker gang was to be fought. What was his name, out of a thousand guesses? It was Douglas Longhurst.

As long as the Currency Lasses could all disappear under fresh names, it did not greatly matter if the brig were bought, or any small discrepancies should be discovered in the wrecking. The identification of one of their number had changed all that. The smallest scandal must now direct attention to the movements of Norris. It would be asked how he who had sailed in a schooner from Sydney, had turned up so shortly after in a brig out of Hong Kong; and from one question to another all his original shipmates were pretty sure to be involved. Hence arose naturally the idea of preventing danger, profiting by Carthew's new-found wealth, and buying the brig under an alias; and it was put in hand with equal energy and caution. Carthew took lodgings alone under a false name, picked up Bellairs at random, and commissioned him to buy the wreck.

"What figure, if you please?" the lawyer asked.

"I want it bought," replied Carthew. "I don't mind about the price."

"Any price is no price," said Bellairs. "Put a name upon it."

"Call it ten thousand pounds then, if you like!" said Carthew.

In the meanwhile, the captain had to walk the streets, appear in the consulate, be cross-examined by Lloyd's agent, be badgered about his lost accounts, sign papers with his left hand, and repeat his lies to every skipper in San Francisco: not knowing at what moment he might run into the arms of some old friend who should hail him by the name of Wicks, or some new enemy who should be in a position to deny him that of Trent. And the latter incident did actually befall him, but was transformed by his stout countenance into an element of strength. It was in the consulate (of all untoward places) that he suddenly heard a big voice inquiring for Captain Trent. He turned with the customary sinking at his heart.

"YOU ain't Captain Trent!" said the stranger, falling back. "Why, what's all this? They tell me you're passing off as Captain Trent—Captain Jacob Trent—a man I knew since I was that high."

"O, you're thinking of my uncle as had the bank in Cardiff," replied Wicks, with desperate aplomb.

"I declare I never knew he had a nevvy!" said the stranger.

"Well, you see he has!" says Wicks.

"And how is the old man?" asked the other.

"Fit as a fiddle," answered Wicks, and was opportunely summoned by the clerk.

This alert was the only one until the morning of the sale, when he was once more alarmed by his interview with Jim; and it was with some anxiety that he attended the sale, knowing only that Carthew was to be represented, but neither who was to represent him nor what were the instructions given. I suppose Captain Wicks is a good life. In spite of his personal appearance and his own known uneasiness, I suppose he is secure from apoplexy, or it must have struck him there and then, as he looked on at the stages of that insane sale and saw the old brig and her not very valuable cargo knocked down at last to a total stranger for ten thousand pounds.

It had been agreed that he was to avoid Carthew, and above all Carthew's lodging, so that no connexion might be traced between the crew and the pseudonymous purchaser. But the hour for caution was gone by, and he caught a tram and made all speed to Mission Street.

Carthew met him in the door.

"Come away, come away from here," said Carthew; and when they were clear of the house, "All's up!" he added.

"O, you've heard of the sale, then?" said Wicks.

"The sale!" cried Carthew. "I declare I had forgotten it." And he told of the voice in the telephone, and the maddening question: "Why did you want to buy the Flying Scud?"

This circumstance, coming on the back of the monstrous improbabilities of the sale, was enough to have shaken the reason of Immanuel Kant. The earth seemed banded together to defeat them; the stones and the boys on the street appeared to be in possession of their guilty secret. Flight was their one thought. The treasure of the Currency Lass they packed in waist-belts, expressed their chests to an imaginary address in British Columbia, and left San Francisco the same afternoon, booked for Los Angeles.

The next day they pursued their retreat by the Southern Pacific route, which Carthew followed on his way to England; but the other three branched off for Mexico.

EPILOGUE:
TO WILL H. LOW.

DEAR LOW: The other day (at Manihiki of all places) I had the pleasure to meet Dodd. We sat some two hours in the neat, little, toy-like church, set with pews after the manner of Europe, and inlaid with mother-of-pearl in the style (I suppose) of the New Jerusalem. The natives, who are decidedly the most attractive inhabitants of this planet, crowded round us in the pew, and fawned upon and patted us; and here it was I put my questions, and Dodd answered me.

I first carried him back to the night in Barbizon when Carthew told his story, and asked him what was done about Bellairs. It seemed he had put the matter to his friend at once, and that Carthew took it with an inimitable lightness. "He's poor, and I'm rich," he had said. "I can afford to smile at him. I go somewhere else, that's all—somewhere that's far away and dear to get to. Persia would be found to answer, I fancy. No end of a place, Persia. Why not come with me?" And they had left the next afternoon for Constantinople, on their way to Teheran. Of the shyster, it is only known (by a newspaper paragraph) that he returned somehow to San Francisco and died in the hospital.

"Now there's another point," said I. "There you are off to Persia with a millionaire, and rich yourself. How come you here in the South Seas, running a trader?"

He said, with a smile, that I had not yet heard of Jim's last bankruptcy. "I was about cleaned out once more," he said; "and then it was that Carthew had this schooner built, and put me in as supercargo. It's his yacht and it's my trader; and as nearly all the expenses go to the yacht, I do pretty well. As for Jim, he's right again: one of the best businesses, they say, in the West, fruit, cereals, and real estate; and he has a Tartar of a partner now—Nares, no less. Nares will keep him straight, Nares has a big head. They have their country-places next door at Saucelito, and I stayed with them time about, the last time I was on the coast. Jim had a paper of his own—I think he has a notion of being senator one of these days—and he wanted me to throw up the schooner and come and write his editorials. He holds strong views on the State Constitution, and so does Mamie."

"And what became of the other three Currency Lasses after they left Carthew?" I inquired.

"Well, it seems they had a huge spree in the city of Mexico," said Dodd; "and then Hadden and the Irishman took a turn at the gold fields in Venezuela, and Wicks went on alone to Valparaiso. There's a Kirkup in the Chilean navy to this day, I saw the name in the papers about the Balmaceda war. Hadden soon wearied of the mines, and I met him the other day in Sydney. The last news he had from Venezuela, Mac had been knocked over in an attack on the gold train. So there's only the three of them left, for Amalu scarcely counts. He lives on his own land in Maui, at the side of Hale-a-ka-la, where he keeps Goddedaal's canary; and they say he sticks to his dollars, which is a wonder in a Kanaka. He had a considerable pile to start with, for not only Hemstead's share but Carthew's was divided equally among the other four—Mac being counted."

"What did that make for him altogether?" I could not help asking, for I had been diverted by the number of calculations in his narrative.

"One hundred and twenty-eight pounds nineteen shillings and eleven pence halfpenny," he replied with composure. "That's leaving out what little he won at Van John. It's something for a Kanaka, you know."

And about that time we were at last obliged to yield to the solicitations of our native admirers, and go to the pastor's house to drink green cocoanuts. The ship I was in was sailing the same night, for Dodd had been beforehand and got all the shell in the island; and though he pressed me to desert and return with him to Auckland (whither he was now bound to pick up Carthew) I was firm in my refusal.

The truth is, since I have been mixed up with Havens and Dodd in the design to publish the latter's narrative, I seem to feel no want for Carthew's society. Of course I am wholly modern in sentiment, and think nothing more noble than to publish people's private affairs at so much a line. They like it, and if they don't, they ought to. But a still small voice keeps telling me they will not like it always, and perhaps not always stand it. Memory besides supplies me with the face of a pressman (in the sacred phrase) who proved altogether too modern for one of his neighbours, and

    Qui nunc it per iter tenebricosum

as it were, marshalling us our way. I am in no haste to

    —nos proecedens—

be that man's successor. Carthew has a record as "a clane shot," and for some years Samoa will be good enough for me.

We agreed to separate, accordingly; but he took me on board in his own boat with the hardwood fittings, and entertained me on the way with an account of his late visit to Butaritari, whither he had gone on an errand for Carthew, to see how Topelius was getting along, and, if necessary, to give him a helping hand. But Topelius was in great force, and had patronised and—well—out-manoeuvred him.

"Carthew will be pleased," said Dodd; "for there's no doubt they oppressed the man abominably when they were in the Currency Lass. It's diamond cut diamond now."

This, I think, was the most of the news I got from my friend Loudon; and I hope I was well inspired, and have put all the questions to which you would be curious to hear an answer.

But there is one more that I daresay you are burning to put to myself; and that is, what your own name is doing in this place, cropping up (as it were uncalled-for) on the stern of our poor ship? If you were not born in Arcadia, you linger in fancy on its margin; your thoughts are busied with the flutes of antiquity, with daffodils, and the classic poplar, and the footsteps of the nymphs, and the elegant and moving aridity of ancient art. Why dedicate to you a tale of a caste so modern;—full of details of our barbaric manners and unstable morals;—full of the need and the lust of money, so that there is scarce a page in which the dollars do not jingle;—full of the unrest and movement of our century, so that the reader is hurried from place to place and sea to sea, and the book is less a romance than a panorama—in the end, as blood-bespattered as an epic?

Well, you are a man interested in all problems of art, even the most vulgar; and it may amuse you to hear the genesis and growth of The Wrecker. On board the schooner Equator, almost within sight of the Johnstone Islands (if anybody knows where these are) and on a moonlit night when it was a joy to be alive, the authors were amused with several stories of the sale of wrecks. The subject tempted them; and they sat apart in the alley-way to discuss its possibilities. "What a tangle it would make," suggested one, "if the wrong crew were aboard. But how to get the wrong crew there?"—"I have it!" cried the other; "the so-and-so affair!" For not so many months before, and not so many hundred miles from where we were then sailing, a proposition almost tantamount to that of Captain Trent had been made by a British skipper to some British castaways.

Before we turned in, the scaffolding of the tale had been put together. But the question of treatment was as usual more obscure. We had long been at once attracted and repelled by that very modern form of the police novel or mystery story, which consists in beginning your yarn anywhere but at the beginning, and finishing it anywhere but at the end; attracted by its peculiar interest when done, and the peculiar difficulties that attend its execution; repelled by that appearance of insincerity and shallowness of tone, which seems its inevitable drawback. For the mind of the reader, always bent to pick up clews, receives no impression of reality or life, rather of an airless, elaborate mechanism; and the book remains enthralling, but insignificant, like a game of chess, not a work of human art. It seemed the cause might lie partly in the abrupt attack; and that if the tale were gradually approached, some of the characters introduced (as it were) beforehand, and the book started in the tone of a novel of manners and experience briefly treated, this defect might be lessened and our mystery seem to inhere in life. The tone of the age, its movement, the mingling of races and classes in the dollar hunt, the fiery and not quite unromantic struggle for existence with its changing trades and scenery, and two types in particular, that of the American handy-man of business and that of the Yankee merchant sailor—we agreed to dwell upon at some length, and make the woof to our not very precious warp. Hence Dodd's father, and Pinkerton, and Nares, and the Dromedary picnics, and the railway work in New South Wales—the last an unsolicited testimonial from the powers that be, for the tale was half written before I saw Carthew's squad toil in the rainy cutting at South Clifton, or heard from the engineer of his "young swell." After we had invented at some expense of time this method of approaching and fortifying our police novel, it occurred to us it had been invented previously by some one else, and was in fact—however painfully different the results may seem—the method of Charles Dickens in his later work.

I see you staring. Here, you will say, is a prodigious quantity of theory to our halfpenny worth of police novel; and withal not a shadow of an answer to your question.

Well, some of us like theory. After so long a piece of practice, these may be indulged for a few pages. And the answer is at hand. It was plainly desirable, from every point of view of convenience and contrast, that our hero and narrator should partly stand aside from those with whom he mingles, and be but a pressed-man in the dollar hunt. Thus it was that Loudon Dodd became a student of the plastic arts, and that our globe-trotting story came to visit Paris and look in at Barbizon. And thus it is, dear Low, that your name appears in the address of this epilogue.

For sure, if any person can here appreciate and read between the lines, it must be you—and one other, our friend. All the dominos will be transparent to your better knowledge; the statuary contract will be to you a piece of ancient history; and you will not have now heard for the first time of the dangers of Roussillon. Dead leaves from the Bas Breau, echoes from Lavenue's and the Rue Racine, memories of a common past, let these be your bookmarkers as you read. And if you care for naught else in the story, be a little pleased to breathe once more for a moment the airs of our youth.

The End.

THE MASTER OF BALLANTRAE
A WINTER'S TALE

CHAPTER I.
SUMMARY OF EVENTS DURING
THIS MASTER'S WANDERINGS.

The full truth of this odd matter is what the world has long been looking for, and public curiosity is sure to welcome. It so befell that I was intimately mingled with the last years and history of the house; and there does not live one man so able as myself to make these matters plain, or so desirous to narrate them faithfully. I knew the Master; on many secret steps of his career I have an authentic memoir in my hand; I sailed with him on his last voyage almost alone; I made one upon that winter's journey of which so many tales have gone abroad; and I was there at the man's death. As for my late Lord Durrisdeer, I served him and loved him near twenty years; and thought more of him the more I knew of him. Altogether, I think it not fit that so much evidence should perish; the truth is a debt I owe my lord's memory; and I think my old years will flow more smoothly, and my white hair lie quieter on the pillow, when the debt is paid.

The Duries of Durrisdeer and Ballantrae were a strong family in the south-west from the days of David First. A rhyme still current in the countryside—

Kittle folk are the Durrisdeers,
They ride wi' over mony spears—

bears the mark of its antiquity; and the name appears in another, which common report attributes to Thomas of Ercildoune himself—I cannot say how truly, and which some have applied—I dare not say with how much justice—to the events of this narration:

Twa Duries in Durrisdeer,
   Ane to tie and ane to ride,
An ill day for the groom
   And a waur day for the bride.

Authentic history besides is filled with their exploits which (to our modern eyes) seem not very commendable: and the family suffered its full share of those ups and downs to which the great houses of Scotland have been ever liable. But all these I pass over, to come to that memorable year 1745, when the foundations of this tragedy were laid.

At that time there dwelt a family of four persons in the house of Durrisdeer, near St. Bride's, on the Solway shore; a chief hold of their race since the Reformation. My old lord, eighth of the name, was not old in years, but he suffered prematurely from the disabilities of age; his place was at the chimney side; there he sat reading, in a lined gown, with few words for any man, and wry words for none: the model of an old retired housekeeper; and yet his mind very well nourished with study, and reputed in the country to be more cunning than he seemed. The master of Ballantrae, James in baptism, took from his father the love of serious reading; some of his tact perhaps as well, but that which was only policy in the father became black dissimulation in the son. The face of his behaviour was merely popular and wild: he sat late at wine, later at the cards; had the name in the country of "an unco man for the lasses;" and was ever in the front of broils. But for all he was the first to go in, yet it was observed he was invariably the best to come off; and his partners in mischief were usually alone to pay the piper. This luck or dexterity got him several ill-wishers, but with the rest of the country, enhanced his reputation; so that great things were looked for in his future, when he should have gained more gravity. One very black mark he had to his name; but the matter was hushed up at the time, and so defaced by legends before I came into those parts, that I scruple to set it down. If it was true, it was a horrid fact in one so young; and if false, it was a horrid calumny. I think it notable that he had always vaunted himself quite implacable, and was taken at his word; so that he had the addition among his neighbours of "an ill man to cross." Here was altogether a young nobleman (not yet twenty-four in the year '45) who had made a figure in the country beyond his time of life. The less marvel if there were little heard of the second son, Mr. Henry (my late Lord Durrisdeer), who was neither very bad nor yet very able, but an honest, solid sort of lad like many of his neighbours. Little heard, I say; but indeed it was a case of little spoken. He was known among the salmon fishers in the firth, for that was a sport that he assiduously followed; he was an excellent good horse-doctor besides; and took a chief hand, almost from a boy, in the management of the estates. How hard a part that was, in the situation of that family, none knows better than myself; nor yet with how little colour of justice a man may there acquire the reputation of a tyrant and a miser. The fourth person in the house was Miss Alison Graeme, a near kinswoman, an orphan, and the heir to a considerable fortune which her father had acquired in trade. This money was loudly called for by my lord's necessities; indeed the land was deeply mortgaged; and Miss Alison was designed accordingly to be the Master's wife, gladly enough on her side; with how much good-will on his, is another matter. She was a comely girl, and in those days very spirited and self-willed; for the old lord having no daughter of his own, and my lady being long dead, she had grown up as best she might.

To these four came the news of Prince Charlie's landing, and set them presently by the ears. My lord, like the chimney-keeper that he was, was all for temporising. Miss Alison held the other side, because it appeared romantical; and the Master (though I have heard they did not agree often) was for this once of her opinion. The adventure tempted him, as I conceive; he was tempted by the opportunity to raise the fortunes of the house, and not less by the hope of paying off his private liabilities, which were heavy beyond all opinion. As for Mr. Henry, it appears he said little enough at first; his part came later on. It took the three a whole day's disputation, before they agreed to steer a middle course, one son going forth to strike a blow for King James, my lord and the other staying at home to keep in favour with King George. Doubtless this was my lord's decision; and, as is well known, it was the part played by many considerable families. But the one dispute settled, another opened. For my lord, Miss Alison, and Mr. Henry all held the one view: that it was the cadet's part to go out; and the Master, what with restlessness and vanity, would at no rate consent to stay at home. My lord pleaded, Miss Alison wept, Mr. Henry was very plain spoken: all was of no avail.

"It is the direct heir of Durrisdeer that should ride by his King's bridle," says the Master.

"If we were playing a manly part," says Mr. Henry, "there might be sense in such talk. But what are we doing? Cheating at cards!"

"We are saving the house of Durrisdeer, Henry," his father said.

"And see, James," said Mr. Henry, "if I go, and the Prince has the upper hand, it will be easy to make your peace with King James. But if you go, and the expedition fails, we divide the right and the title. And what shall I be then?"

"You will be Lord Durrisdeer," said the Master. "I put all I have upon the table."

"I play at no such game," cries Mr. Henry. "I shall be left in such a situation as no man of sense and honour could endure. I shall be neither fish nor flesh!" he cried. And a little after he had another expression, plainer perhaps than he intended. "It is your duty to be here with my father," said he. "You know well enough you are the favourite."

"Ay?" said the Master. "And there spoke Envy! Would you trip up my heels—Jacob?" said he, and dwelled upon the name maliciously.

Mr. Henry went and walked at the low end of the hall without reply; for he had an excellent gift of silence. Presently he came back.

"I am the cadet and I should go," said he. "And my lord here is the master, and he says I shall go. What say ye to that, my brother?"

"I say this, Harry," returned the Master, "that when very obstinate folk are met, there are only two ways out: Blows—and I think none of us could care to go so far; or the arbitrament of chance—and here is a guinea piece. Will you stand by the toss of the coin?"

"I will stand and fall by it," said Mr. Henry. "Heads, I go; shield, I stay."

The coin was spun, and it fell shield. "So there is a lesson for Jacob," says the Master.

"We shall live to repent of this," says Mr. Henry, and flung out of the hall.

As for Miss Alison, she caught up that piece of gold which had just sent her lover to the wars, and flung it clean through the family shield in the great painted window.

"If you loved me as well as I love you, you would have stayed," cried she.

"'I could not love you, dear, so well, loved I not honour more,'" sang the Master.

"Oh!" she cried, "you have no heart—I hope you may be killed!" and she ran from the room, and in tears, to her own chamber.

It seems the Master turned to my lord with his most comical manner, and says he, "This looks like a devil of a wife."

"I think you are a devil of a son to me," cried his father, "you that have always been the favourite, to my shame be it spoken. Never a good hour have I gotten of you, since you were born; no, never one good hour," and repeated it again the third time. Whether it was the Master's levity, or his insubordination, or Mr. Henry's word about the favourite son, that had so much disturbed my lord, I do not know; but I incline to think it was the last, for I have it by all accounts that Mr. Henry was more made up to from that hour.

Altogether it was in pretty ill blood with his family that the Master rode to the North; which was the more sorrowful for others to remember when it seemed too late. By fear and favour he had scraped together near upon a dozen men, principally tenants' sons; they were all pretty full when they set forth, and rode up the hill by the old abbey, roaring and singing, the white cockade in every hat. It was a desperate venture for so small a company to cross the most of Scotland unsupported; and (what made folk think so the more) even as that poor dozen was clattering up the hill, a great ship of the king's navy, that could have brought them under with a single boat, lay with her broad ensign streaming in the bay. The next afternoon, having given the Master a fair start, it was Mr. Henry's turn; and he rode off, all by himself, to offer his sword and carry letters from his father to King George's Government. Miss Alison was shut in her room, and did little but weep, till both were gone; only she stitched the cockade upon the Master's hat, and (as John Paul told me) it was wetted with tears when he carried it down to him.

In all that followed, Mr. Henry and my old lord were true to their bargain. That ever they accomplished anything is more than I could learn; and that they were anyway strong on the king's side, more than believe. But they kept the letter of loyalty, corresponded with my Lord President, sat still at home, and had little or no commerce with the Master while that business lasted. Nor was he, on his side, more communicative. Miss Alison, indeed, was always sending him expresses, but I do not know if she had many answers. Macconochie rode for her once, and found the highlanders before Carlisle, and the Master riding by the Prince's side in high favour; he took the letter (so Macconochie tells), opened it, glanced it through with a mouth like a man whistling, and stuck it in his belt, whence, on his horse passageing, it fell unregarded to the ground. It was Macconochie who picked it up; and he still kept it, and indeed I have seen it in his hands. News came to Durrisdeer of course, by the common report, as it goes travelling through a country, a thing always wonderful to me. By that means the family learned more of the Master's favour with the Prince, and the ground it was said to stand on: for by a strange condescension in a man so proud—only that he was a man still more ambitious—he was said to have crept into notability by truckling to the Irish. Sir Thomas Sullivan, Colonel Burke and the rest, were his daily comrades, by which course he withdrew himself from his own country-folk. All the small intrigues he had a hand in fomenting; thwarted my Lord George upon a thousand points; was always for the advice that seemed palatable to the Prince, no matter if it was good or bad; and seems upon the whole (like the gambler he was all through life) to have had less regard to the chances of the campaign than to the greatness of favour he might aspire to, if, by any luck, it should succeed. For the rest, he did very well in the field; no one questioned that; for he was no coward.

The next was the news of Culloden, which was brought to Durrisdeer by one of the tenants' sons—the only survivor, he declared, of all those that had gone singing up the hill. By an unfortunate chance John Paul and Macconochie had that very morning found the guinea piece—which was the root of all the evil—sticking in a holly bush; they had been "up the gait," as the servants say at Durrisdeer, to the change-house; and if they had little left of the guinea, they had less of their wits. What must John Paul do but burst into the hall where the family sat at dinner, and cry the news to them that "Tam Macmorland was but new lichtit at the door, and—wirra, wirra—there were nane to come behind him"?

They took the word in silence like folk condemned; only Mr. Henry carrying his palm to his face, and Miss Alison laying her head outright upon her hands. As for my lord, he was like ashes.

"I have still one son," says he. "And, Henry, I will do you this justice—it is the kinder that is left."

It was a strange thing to say in such a moment; but my lord had never forgotten Mr. Henry's speech, and he had years of injustice on his conscience. Still it was a strange thing, and more than Miss Alison could let pass. She broke out and blamed my lord for his unnatural words, and Mr. Henry because he was sitting there in safety when his brother lay dead, and herself because she had given her sweetheart ill words at his departure, calling him the flower of the flock, wringing her hands, protesting her love, and crying on him by his name—so that the servants stood astonished.

Mr. Henry got to his feet, and stood holding his chair. It was he that was like ashes now.

"Oh!" he burst out suddenly, "I know you loved him."

"The world knows that, glory be to God!" cries she; and then to Mr. Henry: "There is none but me to know one thing—that you were a traitor to him in your heart."

"God knows," groans he, "it was lost love on both sides."

Time went by in the house after that without much change; only they were now three instead of four, which was a perpetual reminder of their loss. Miss Alison's money, you are to bear in mind, was highly needful for the estates; and the one brother being dead, my old lord soon set his heart upon her marrying the other. Day in, day out, he would work upon her, sitting by the chimney-side with his finger in his Latin book, and his eyes set upon her face with a kind of pleasant intentness that became the old gentleman very well. If she wept, he would condole with her like an ancient man that has seen worse times and begins to think lightly even of sorrow; if she raged, he would fall to reading again in his Latin book, but always with some civil excuse; if she offered, as she often did, to let them have her money in a gift, he would show her how little it consisted with his honour, and remind her, even if he should consent, that Mr. Henry would certainly refuse. Non vi sed sæpe cadendo was a favourite word of his; and no doubt this quiet persecution wore away much of her resolve; no doubt, besides, he had a great influence on the girl, having stood in the place of both her parents; and, for that matter, she was herself filled with the spirit of the Duries, and would have gone a great way for the glory of Durrisdeer; but not so far, I think, as to marry my poor patron, had it not been—strangely enough—for the circumstance of his extreme unpopularity.

This was the work of Tam Macmorland. There was not much harm in Tam; but he had that grievous weakness, a long tongue; and as the only man in that country who had been out—or, rather, who had come in again—he was sure of listeners. Those that have the underhand in any fighting, I have observed, are ever anxious to persuade themselves they were betrayed. By Tam's account of it, the rebels had been betrayed at every turn and by every officer they had; they had been betrayed at Derby, and betrayed at Falkirk; the night march was a step of treachery of my Lord George's; and Culloden was lost by the treachery of the Macdonalds. This habit of imputing treason grew upon the fool, till at last he must have in Mr. Henry also. Mr. Henry (by his account) had betrayed the lads of Durrisdeer; he had promised to follow with more men, and instead of that he had ridden to King George. "Ay, and the next day!" Tam would cry. "The puir bonnie Master, and the puir, kind lads that rade wi' him, were hardly ower the scaur, or he was aff—the Judis! Ay, weel—he has his way o't: he's to be my lord, nae less, and there's mony a cold corp amang the Hieland heather!" And at this, if Tam had been drinking, he would begin to weep.

Let anyone speak long enough, he will get believers. This view of Mr. Henry's behaviour crept about the country by little and little; it was talked upon by folk that knew the contrary, but were short of topics; and it was heard and believed and given out for gospel by the ignorant and the ill-willing. Mr. Henry began to be shunned; yet awhile, and the commons began to murmur as he went by, and the women (who are always the most bold because they are the most safe) to cry out their reproaches to his face. The Master was cried up for a saint. It was remembered how he had never any hand in pressing the tenants; as, indeed, no more he had, except to spend the money. He was a little wild perhaps, the folk said; but how much better was a natural, wild lad that would soon have settled down, than a skinflint and a sneckdraw, sitting, with his nose in an account book, to persecute poor tenants! One trollop, who had had a child to the Master, and by all accounts been very badly used, yet made herself a kind of champion of his memory. She flung a stone one day at Mr. Henry.

"Whaur's the bonnie lad that trustit ye?" she cried.

Mr. Henry reined in his horse and looked upon her, the blood flowing from his lip. "Ay, Jess?" says he. "You too? And yet ye should ken me better." For it was he who had helped her with money.

The woman had another stone ready, which she made as if she would cast; and he, to ward himself, threw up the hand that held his riding-rod.

"What, would ye beat a lassie, ye ugly—?" cries she, and ran away screaming as though he had struck her.

Next day word went about the country like wildfire that Mr. Henry had beaten Jessie Broun within an inch of her life. I give it as one instance of how this snowball grew, and one calumny brought another; until my poor patron was so perished in reputation that he began to keep the house like my lord. All this while, you may be very sure, he uttered no complaints at home; the very ground of the scandal was too sore a matter to be handled; and Mr. Henry was very proud and strangely obstinate in silence. My old lord must have heard of it, by John Paul, if by no one else; and he must at least have remarked the altered habits of his son. Yet even he, it is probable, knew not how high the feeling ran; and as for Miss Alison, she was ever the last person to hear news, and the least interested when she heard them.

In the height of the ill-feeling (for it died away as it came, no man could say why) there was an election forward in the town of St. Bride's, which is the next to Durrisdeer, standing on the Water of Swift; some grievance was fermenting, I forget what, if ever I heard; and it was currently said there would be broken heads ere night, and that the sheriff had sent as far as Dumfries for soldiers. My lord moved that Mr. Henry should be present, assuring him it was necessary to appear, for the credit of the house. "It will soon be reported," said he, "that we do not take the lead in our own country."

"It is a strange lead that I can take," said Mr. Henry; and when they had pushed him further, "I tell you the plain truth," he said, "I dare not show my face."

"You are the first of the house that ever said so," cries Miss Alison.

"We will go all three," said my lord; and sure enough he got into his boots (the first time in four years—a sore business John Paul had to get them on), and Miss Alison into her riding-coat, and all three rode together to St. Bride's.

The streets were full of the riff-raff of all the countryside, who had no sooner clapped eyes on Mr. Henry than the hissing began, and the hooting, and the cries of "Judas!" and "Where was the Master?" and "Where were the poor lads that rode with him?" Even a stone was cast; but the more part cried shame at that, for my old lord's sake, and Miss Alison's. It took not ten minutes to persuade my lord that Mr. Henry had been right. He said never a word, but turned his horse about, and home again, with his chin upon his bosom. Never a word said Miss Alison; no doubt she thought the more; no doubt her pride was stung, for she was a bone-bred Durie; and no doubt her heart was touched to see her cousin so unjustly used. That night she was never in bed; I have often blamed my lady—when I call to mind that night, I readily forgive her all; and the first thing in the morning she came to the old lord in his usual seat.

"If Henry still wants me," said she, "he can have me now." To himself she had a different speech: "I bring you no love, Henry; but God knows, all the pity in the world."

June the 1st, 1748, was the day of their marriage. It was December of the same year that first saw me alighting at the doors of the great house; and from there I take up the history of events as they befell under my own observation, like a witness in a court.

CHAPTER II.
SUMMARY OF EVENTS (continued)

I made the last of my journey in the cold end of December, in a mighty dry day of frost, and who should be my guide but Patey Macmorland, brother of Tam! For a tow-headed, bare-legged brat of ten, he had more ill tales upon his tongue than ever I heard the match of; having drunken betimes in his brother's cup. I was still not so old myself; pride had not yet the upper hand of curiosity; and indeed it would have taken any man, that cold morning, to hear all the old clashes of the country, and be shown all the places by the way where strange things had fallen out. I had tales of Claverhouse as we came through the bogs, and tales of the devil, as we came over the top of the scaur. As we came in by the abbey I heard somewhat of the old monks, and more of the freetraders, who use its ruins for a magazine, landing for that cause within a cannon-shot of Durrisdeer; and along all the road the Duries and poor Mr. Henry were in the first rank of slander. My mind was thus highly prejudiced against the family I was about to serve, so that I was half surprised when I beheld Durrisdeer itself, lying in a pretty, sheltered bay, under the Abbey Hill; the house most commodiously built in the French fashion, or perhaps Italianate, for I have no skill in these arts; and the place the most beautified with gardens, lawns, shrubberies, and trees I had ever seen. The money sunk here unproductively would have quite restored the family; but as it was, it cost a revenue to keep it up.

Mr. Henry came himself to the door to welcome me: a tall dark young gentleman (the Duries are all black men) of a plain and not cheerful face, very strong in body, but not so strong in health: taking me by the hand without any pride, and putting me at home with plain kind speeches. He led me into the hall, booted as I was, to present me to my lord. It was still daylight; and the first thing I observed was a lozenge of clear glass in the midst of the shield in the painted window, which I remember thinking a blemish on a room otherwise so handsome, with its family portraits, and the pargeted ceiling with pendants, and the carved chimney, in one corner of which my old lord sat reading in his Livy. He was like Mr. Henry, with much the same plain countenance, only more subtle and pleasant, and his talk a thousand times more entertaining. He had many questions to ask me, I remember, of Edinburgh College, where I had just received my mastership of arts, and of the various professors, with whom and their proficiency he seemed well acquainted; and thus, talking of things that I knew, I soon got liberty of speech in my new home.

In the midst of this came Mrs. Henry into the room; she was very far gone, Miss Katharine being due in about six weeks, which made me think less of her beauty at the first sight; and she used me with more of condescension than the rest; so that, upon all accounts, I kept her in the third place of my esteem.

It did not take long before all Patey Macmorland's tales were blotted out of my belief, and I was become, what I have ever since remained, a loving servant of the house of Durrisdeer. Mr. Henry had the chief part of my affection. It was with him I worked; and I found him an exacting master, keeping all his kindness for those hours in which we were unemployed, and in the steward's office not only loading me with work, but viewing me with a shrewd supervision. At length one day he looked up from his paper with a kind of timidness, and says he, "Mr. Mackellar, I think I ought to tell you that you do very well." That was my first word of commendation; and from that day his jealousy of my performance was relaxed; soon it was "Mr. Mackellar" here, and "Mr. Mackellar" there, with the whole family; and for much of my service at Durrisdeer, I have transacted everything at my own time, and to my own fancy, and never a farthing challenged. Even while he was driving me, I had begun to find my heart go out to Mr. Henry; no doubt, partly in pity, he was a man so palpably unhappy. He would fall into a deep muse over our accounts, staring at the page or out of the window; and at those times the look of his face, and the sigh that would break from him, awoke in me strong feelings of curiosity and commiseration. One day, I remember, we were late upon some business in the steward's room.

This room is in the top of the house, and has a view upon the bay, and over a little wooded cape, on the long sands; and there, right over against the sun, which was then dipping, we saw the freetraders, with a great force of men and horses, scouring on the beach. Mr. Henry had been staring straight west, so that I marvelled he was not blinded by the sun; suddenly he frowns, rubs his hand upon his brow, and turns to me with a smile.

"You would not guess what I was thinking," says he. "I was thinking I would be a happier man if I could ride and run the danger of my life, with these lawless companions."

I told him I had observed he did not enjoy good spirits; and that it was a common fancy to envy others and think we should be the better of some change; quoting Horace to the point, like a young man fresh from college.

"Why, just so," said he. "And with that we may get back to our accounts."

It was not long before I began to get wind of the causes that so much depressed him. Indeed a blind man must have soon discovered there was a shadow on that house, the shadow of the Master of Ballantrae. Dead or alive (and he was then supposed to be dead) that man was his brother's rival: his rival abroad, where there was never a good word for Mr. Henry, and nothing but regret and praise for the Master; and his rival at home, not only with his father and his wife, but with the very servants.

They were two old serving-men that were the leaders. John Paul, a little, bald, solemn, stomachy man, a great professor of piety and (take him for all in all) a pretty faithful servant, was the chief of the Master's faction. None durst go so far as John. He took a pleasure in disregarding Mr. Henry publicly, often with a slighting comparison. My lord and Mrs. Henry took him up, to be sure, but never so resolutely as they should; and he had only to pull his weeping face and begin his lamentations for the Master—"his laddie," as he called him—to have the whole condoned. As for Henry, he let these things pass in silence, sometimes with a sad and sometimes with a black look. There was no rivalling the dead, he knew that; and how to censure an old serving-man for a fault of loyalty, was more than he could see. His was not the tongue to do it.

Macconochie was chief upon the other side; an old, ill-spoken, swearing, ranting, drunken dog; and I have often thought it an odd circumstance in human nature that these two serving-men should each have been the champion of his contrary, and blackened their own faults and made light of their own virtues when they beheld them in a master. Macconochie had soon smelled out my secret inclination, took me much into his confidence, and would rant against the Master by the hour, so that even my work suffered. "They're a' daft here," he would cry, "and be damned to them! The Master—the deil's in their thrapples that should call him sae! it's Mr. Henry should be master now! They were nane sae fond o' the Master when they had him, I'll can tell ye that. Sorrow on his name! Never a guid word did I hear on his lips, nor naebody else, but just fleering and flyting and profane cursing—deil hae him! There's nane kent his wickedness: him a gentleman! Did ever ye hear tell, Mr. Mackellar, o' Wully White the wabster? No? Aweel, Wully was an unco praying kind o' man; a dreigh body, nane o' my kind, I never could abide the sight o' him; onyway he was a great hand by his way of it, and he up and rebukit the Master for some of his on-goings. It was a grand thing for the Master o' Ball'ntrae to tak up a feud wi' a' wabster, wasnae't?" Macconochie would sneer; indeed, he never took the full name upon his lips but with a sort of a whine of hatred. "But he did! A fine employ it was: chapping at the man's door, and crying 'boo' in his lum, and puttin' poother in his fire, and pee-oys [1] in his window; till the man thocht it was auld Hornie was come seekin' him. Weel, to mak a lang story short, Wully gaed gyte. At the hinder end, they couldnae get him frae his knees, but he just roared and prayed and grat straucht on, till he got his release. It was fair murder, a'body said that. Ask John Paul—he was brawly ashamed o' that game, him that's sic a Christian man! Grand doin's for the Master o' Ball'ntrae!" I asked him what the Master had thought of it himself. "How would I ken?" says he. "He never said naething." And on again in his usual manner of banning and swearing, with every now and again a "Master of Ballantrae" sneered through his nose. It was in one of these confidences that he showed me the Carlisle letter, the print of the horse-shoe still stamped in the paper. Indeed, that was our last confidence; for he then expressed himself so ill-naturedly of Mrs. Henry that I had to reprimand him sharply, and must thenceforth hold him at a distance.

My old lord was uniformly kind to Mr. Henry; he had even pretty ways of gratitude, and would sometimes clap him on the shoulder and say, as if to the world at large: "This is a very good son to me." And grateful he was, no doubt, being a man of sense and justice. But I think that was all, and I am sure Mr. Henry thought so. The love was all for the dead son. Not that this was often given breath to; indeed, with me but once. My lord had asked me one day how I got on with Mr. Henry, and I had told him the truth.

"Ay," said he, looking sideways on the burning fire, "Henry is a good lad, a very good lad," said he. "You have heard, Mr. Mackellar, that I had another son? I am afraid he was not so virtuous a lad as Mr. Henry; but dear me, he's dead, Mr. Mackellar! and while he lived we were all very proud of him, all very proud. If he was not all he should have been in some ways, well, perhaps we loved him better!" This last he said looking musingly in the fire; and then to me, with a great deal of briskness, "But I am rejoiced you do so well with Mr. Henry. You will find him a good master." And with that he opened his book, which was the customary signal of dismission. But it would be little that he read, and less that he understood; Culloden field and the Master, these would be the burthen of his thought; and the burthen of mine was an unnatural jealousy of the dead man for Mr. Henry's sake, that had even then begun to grow on me.

I am keeping Mrs. Henry for the last, so that this expression of my sentiment may seem unwarrantably strong: the reader shall judge for himself when I have done. But I must first tell of another matter, which was the means of bringing me more intimate. I had not yet been six months at Durrisdeer when it chanced that John Paul fell sick and must keep his bed; drink was the root of his malady, in my poor thought; but he was tended, and indeed carried himself, like an afflicted saint; and the very minister, who came to visit him, professed himself edified when he went away. The third morning of his sickness, Mr. Henry comes to me with something of a hang-dog look.

"Mackellar," says he, "I wish I could trouble you upon a little service. There is a pension we pay; it is John's part to carry it, and now that he is sick I know not to whom I should look unless it was yourself. The matter is very delicate; I could not carry it with my own hand for a sufficient reason; I dare not send Macconochie, who is a talker, and I am—I have—I am desirous this should not come to Mrs. Henry's ears," says he, and flushed to his neck as he said it.

To say truth, when I found I was to carry money to one Jessie Broun, who was no better than she should be, I supposed it was some trip of his own that Mr. Henry was dissembling. I was the more impressed when the truth came out.

It was up a wynd off a side street in St. Bride's that Jessie had her lodging. The place was very ill inhabited, mostly by the freetrading sort. There was a man with a broken head at the entry; half-way up, in a tavern, fellows were roaring and singing, though it was not yet nine in the day. Altogether, I had never seen a worse neighbourhood, even in the great city of Edinburgh, and

I was in two minds to go back. Jessie's room was of a piece with her surroundings, and herself no better. She would not give me the receipt (which Mr. Henry had told me to demand, for he was very methodical) until she had sent out for spirits, and I had pledged her in a glass; and all the time she carried on in a light-headed, reckless way—now aping the manners of a lady, now breaking into unseemly mirth, now making coquettish advances that oppressed me to the ground. Of the money she spoke more tragically.

"It's blood money!" said she; "I take it for that: blood money for the betrayed! See what I'm brought down to! Ah, if the bonnie lad were back again, it would be changed days. But he's deid—he's lyin' deid amang the Hieland hills—the bonnie lad, the bonnie lad!"

She had a rapt manner of crying on the bonnie lad, clasping her hands and casting up her eyes, that I think she must have learned of strolling players; and I thought her sorrow very much of an affectation, and that she dwelled upon the business because her shame was now all she had to be proud of. I will not say I did not pity her, but it was a loathing pity at the best; and her last change of manner wiped it out. This was when she had had enough of me for an audience, and had set her name at last to the receipt. "There!" says she, and taking the most unwomanly oaths upon her tongue, bade me begone and carry it to the Judas who had sent me. It was the first time I had heard the name applied to Mr. Henry; I was staggered besides at her sudden vehemence of word and manner, and got forth from the room, under this shower of curses, like a beaten dog. But even then I was not quit, for the vixen threw up her window, and, leaning forth, continued to revile me as I went up the wynd; the freetraders, coming to the tavern door, joined in the mockery, and one had even the inhumanity to set upon me a very savage small dog, which bit me in the ankle. This was a strong lesson, had I required one, to avoid ill company; and I rode home in much pain from the bite and considerable indignation of mind.

Mr. Henry was in the steward's room, affecting employment, but I could see he was only impatient to hear of my errand.

"Well?" says he, as soon as I came in; and when I had told him something of what passed, and that Jessie seemed an undeserving woman and far from grateful: "She is no friend to me," said he; "but, indeed, Mackellar, I have few friends to boast of, and Jessie has some cause to be unjust. I need not dissemble what all the country knows: she was not very well used by one of our family." This was the first time I had heard him refer to the Master even distantly; and I think he found his tongue rebellious even for that much, but presently he resumed—"This is why I would have nothing said. It would give pain to Mrs. Henry . . . and to my father," he added, with another flush.

"Mr. Henry," said I, "if you will take a freedom at my hands, I would tell you to let that woman be. What service is your money to the like of her? She has no sobriety and no economy—as for gratitude, you will as soon get milk from a whinstone; and if you will pretermit your bounty, it will make no change at all but just to save the ankles of your messengers."

Mr. Henry smiled. "But I am grieved about your ankle," said he, the next moment, with a proper gravity.

"And observe," I continued, "I give you this advice upon consideration; and yet my heart was touched for the woman in the beginning."

"Why, there it is, you see!" said Mr. Henry. "And you are to remember that I knew her once a very decent lass. Besides which, although I speak little of my family, I think much of its repute."

And with that he broke up the talk, which was the first we had together in such confidence. But the same afternoon I had the proof that his father was perfectly acquainted with the business, and that it was only from his wife that Mr. Henry kept it secret.

"I fear you had a painful errand to-day," says my lord to me, "for which, as it enters in no way among your duties, I wish to thank you, and to remind you at the same time (in case Mr. Henry should have neglected) how very desirable it is that no word of it should reach my daughter. Reflections on the dead, Mr. Mackellar, are doubly painful."

Anger glowed in my heart; and I could have told my lord to his face how little he had to do, bolstering up the image of the dead in Mrs. Henry's heart, and how much better he were employed to shatter that false idol; for by this time I saw very well how the land lay between my patron and his wife.

My pen is clear enough to tell a plain tale; but to render the effect of an infinity of small things, not one great enough in itself to be narrated; and to translate the story of looks, and the message of voices when they are saying no great matter; and to put in half a page the essence of near eighteen months—this is what I despair to accomplish. The fault, to be very blunt, lay all in Mrs. Henry. She felt it a merit to have consented to the marriage, and she took it like a martyrdom; in which my old lord, whether he knew it or not, fomented her. She made a merit, besides, of her constancy to the dead, though its name, to a nicer conscience, should have seemed rather disloyalty to the living; and here also my lord gave her his countenance. I suppose he was glad to talk of his loss, and ashamed to dwell on it with Mr. Henry. Certainly, at least, he made a little coterie apart in that family of three, and it was the husband who was shut out. It seems it was an old custom when the family were alone in Durrisdeer, that my lord should take his wine to the chimney-side, and Miss Alison, instead of withdrawing, should bring a stool to his knee, and chatter to him privately; and after she had become my patron's wife the same manner of doing was continued. It should have been pleasant to behold this ancient gentleman so loving with his daughter, but I was too much a partisan of Mr. Henry's to be anything but wroth at his exclusion. Many's the time I have seen him make an obvious resolve, quit the table, and go and join himself to his wife and my Lord Durrisdeer; and on their part, they were never backward to make him welcome, turned to him smilingly as to an intruding child, and took him into their talk with an effort so ill-concealed that he was soon back again beside me at the table, whence (so great is the hall of Durrisdeer) we could but hear the murmur of voices at the chimney. There he would sit and watch, and I along with him; and sometimes by my lord's head sorrowfully shaken, or his hand laid on Mrs. Henry's head, or hers upon his knee as if in consolation, or sometimes by an exchange of tearful looks, we would draw our conclusion that the talk had gone to the old subject and the shadow of the dead was in the hall.

I have hours when I blame Mr. Henry for taking all too patiently; yet we are to remember he was married in pity, and accepted his wife upon that term. And, indeed, he had small encouragement to make a stand. Once, I remember, he announced he had found a man to replace the pane of the stained window, which, as it was he that managed all the business, was a thing clearly within his attributions. But to the Master's fancies, that pane was like a relic; and on the first word of any change, the blood flew to Mrs. Henry's face.

"I wonder at you!" she cried.

"I wonder at myself," says Mr. Henry, with more of bitterness than I had ever heard him to express.

Thereupon my old lord stepped in with his smooth talk, so that before the meal was at an end all seemed forgotten; only that, after dinner, when the pair had withdrawn as usual to the chimney-side, we could see her weeping with her head upon his knee. Mr. Henry kept up the talk with me upon some topic of the estates—he could speak of little else but business, and was never the best of company; but he kept it up that day with more continuity, his eye straying ever and again to the chimney, and his voice changing to another key, but without check of delivery. The pane, however, was not replaced; and I believe he counted it a great defeat.

Whether he was stout enough or no, God knows he was kind enough. Mrs. Henry had a manner of condescension with him, such as (in a wife) would have pricked my vanity into an ulcer; he took it like a favour. She held him at the staff's end; forgot and then remembered and unbent to him, as we do to children; burthened him with cold kindness; reproved him with a change of colour and a bitten lip, like one shamed by his disgrace: ordered him with a look of the eye, when she was off her guard; when she was on the watch, pleaded with him for the most natural attentions, as though they were unheard-of favours. And to all this he replied with the most unwearied service, loving, as folk say, the very ground she trod on, and carrying that love in his eyes as bright as a lamp. When Miss Katharine was to be born, nothing would serve but he must stay in the room behind the head of the bed. There he sat, as white (they tell me) as a sheet, and the sweat dropping from his brow; and the handkerchief he had in his hand was crushed into a little ball no bigger than a musket-bullet. Nor could he bear the sight of Miss Katharine for many a day; indeed, I doubt if he was ever what he should have been to my young lady; for the which want of natural feeling he was loudly blamed.

Such was the state of this family down to the 7th April, 1749, when there befell the first of that series of events which were to break so many hearts and lose so many lives.

On that day I was sitting in my room a little before supper, when John Paul burst open the door with no civility of knocking, and told me there was one below that wished to speak with the steward; sneering at the name of my office.

I asked what manner of man, and what his name was; and this disclosed the cause of John's ill-humour; for it appeared the visitor refused to name himself except to me, a sore affront to the major-domo's consequence.

"Well," said I, smiling a little, "I will see what he wants."

I found in the entrance hall a big man, very plainly habited, and wrapped in a sea-cloak, like one new landed, as indeed he was. Not far off Macconochie was standing, with his tongue out of his mouth and his hand upon his chin, like a dull fellow thinking hard; and the stranger, who had brought his cloak about his face, appeared uneasy. He had no sooner seen me coming than he went to meet me with an effusive manner.

"My dear man," said he, "a thousand apologies for disturbing you, but I'm in the most awkward position. And there's a son of a ramrod there that I should know the looks of, and more betoken I believe that he knows mine. Being in this family, sir, and in a place of some responsibility (which was the cause I took the liberty to send for you), you are doubtless of the honest party?"

"You may be sure at least," says I, "that all of that party are quite safe in Durrisdeer."

"My dear man, it is my very thought," says he. "You see, I have just been set on shore here by a very honest man, whose name I cannot remember, and who is to stand off and on for me till morning, at some danger to himself; and, to be clear with you, I am a little concerned lest it should be at some to me. I have saved my life so often, Mr. —, I forget your name, which is a very good one—that, faith, I would be very loath to lose it after all. And the son of a ramrod, whom I believe I saw before Carlisle . . . "

"Oh, sir," said I, "you can trust Macconochie until to-morrow."

"Well, and it's a delight to hear you say so," says the stranger. "The truth is that my name is not a very suitable one in this country of Scotland. With a gentleman like you, my dear man, I would have no concealments of course; and by your leave I'll just breathe it in your ear. They call me Francis Burke—Colonel Francis Burke; and I am here, at a most damnable risk to myself, to see your masters—if you'll excuse me, my good man, for giving them the name, for I'm sure it's a circumstance I would never have guessed from your appearance. And if you would just be so very obliging as to take my name to them, you might say that I come bearing letters which I am sure they will be very rejoiced to have the reading of."

Colonel Francis Burke was one of the Prince's Irishmen, that did his cause such an infinity of hurt, and were so much distasted of the Scots at the time of the rebellion; and it came at once into my mind, how the Master of Ballantrae had astonished all men by going with that party. In the same moment a strong foreboding of the truth possessed my soul.

"If you will step in here," said I, opening a chamber door, "I will let my lord know."

"And I am sure it's very good of you, Mr. What-is-your-name," says the Colonel.

Up to the hall I went, slow-footed. There they were, all three—my old lord in his place, Mrs. Henry at work by the window, Mr. Henry (as was much his custom) pacing the low end. In the midst was the table laid for supper. I told them briefly what I had to say. My old lord lay back in his seat. Mrs. Henry sprang up standing with a mechanical motion, and she and her husband stared at each other's eyes across the room; it was the strangest, challenging look these two exchanged, and as they looked, the colour faded in their faces. Then Mr. Henry turned to me; not to speak, only to sign with his finger; but that was enough, and I went down again for the Colonel.

When we returned, these three were in much the same position I same left them in; I believe no word had passed.

"My Lord Durrisdeer, no doubt?" says the Colonel, bowing, and my lord bowed in answer. "And this," continues the Colonel, "should be the Master of Ballantrae?"

"I have never taken that name," said Mr. Henry; "but I am Henry Durie, at your service."

Then the Colonel turns to Mrs. Henry, bowing with his hat upon his heart and the most killing airs of gallantry. "There can be no mistake about so fine a figure of a lady," says he. "I address the seductive Miss Alison, of whom I have so often heard?"

Once more husband and wife exchanged a look.

"I am Mrs. Henry Durie," said she; "but before my marriage my name was Alison Graeme."

Then my lord spoke up. "I am an old man, Colonel Burke," said he, "and a frail one. It will be mercy on your part to be expeditious. Do you bring me news of—" he hesitated, and then the words broke from him with a singular change of voice—"my son?"

"My dear lord, I will be round with you like a soldier," said the Colonel. "I do."

My lord held out a wavering hand; he seemed to wave a signal, but whether it was to give him time or to speak on, was more than we could guess. At length he got out the one word, "Good?"

"Why, the very best in the creation!" cries the Colonel. "For my good friend and admired comrade is at this hour in the fine city of Paris, and as like as not, if I know anything of his habits, he will be drawing in his chair to a piece of dinner.—Bedad, I believe the lady's fainting."

Mrs. Henry was indeed the colour of death, and drooped against the window-frame. But when Mr. Henry made a movement as if to run to her, she straightened with a sort of shiver. "I am well," she said, with her white lips.

Mr. Henry stopped, and his face had a strong twitch of anger. The next moment he had turned to the Colonel. "You must not blame yourself," says he, "for this effect on Mrs. Durie. It is only natural; we were all brought up like brother and sister."

Mrs. Henry looked at her husband with something like relief or even gratitude. In my way of thinking, that speech was the first step he made in her good graces.

"You must try to forgive me, Mrs. Durie, for indeed and I am just an Irish savage," said the Colonel; "and I deserve to be shot for not breaking the matter more artistically to a lady. But here are the Master's own letters; one for each of the three of you; and to be sure (if I know anything of my friend's genius) he will tell his own story with a better grace."

He brought the three letters forth as he spoke, arranged them by their superscriptions, presented the first to my lord, who took it greedily, and advanced towards Mrs. Henry holding out the second.

But the lady waved it back. "To my husband," says she, with a choked voice.

The Colonel was a quick man, but at this he was somewhat nonplussed. "To be sure!" says he; "how very dull of me! To be sure!" But he still held the letter.

At last Mr. Henry reached forth his hand, and there was nothing to be done but give it up. Mr. Henry took the letters (both hers and his own), and looked upon their outside, with his brows knit hard, as if he were thinking. He had surprised me all through by his excellent behaviour; but he was to excel himself now.

"Let me give you a hand to your room," said he to his wife. "This has come something of the suddenest; and, at any rate, you will wish to read your letter by yourself."

Again she looked upon him with the same thought of wonder; but he gave her no time, coming straight to where she stood. "It will be better so, believe me," said he; "and Colonel Burke is too considerate not to excuse you." And with that he took her hand by the fingers, and led her from the hall.

Mrs. Henry returned no more that night; and when Mr. Henry went to visit her next morning, as I heard long afterwards, she gave him the letter again, still unopened.

"Oh, read it and be done!" he had cried.

"Spare me that," said she.

And by these two speeches, to my way of thinking, each undid a great part of what they had previously done well. But the letter, sure enough, came into my hands, and by me was burned, unopened.

To be very exact as to the adventures of the Master after Culloden, I wrote not long ago to Colonel Burke, now a Chevalier of the Order of St. Louis, begging him for some notes in writing, since I could scarce depend upon my memory at so great an interval. To confess the truth, I have been somewhat embarrassed by his response; for he sent me the complete memoirs of his life, touching only in places on the Master; running to a much greater length than my whole story, and not everywhere (as it seems to me) designed for edification. He begged in his letter, dated from Ettenheim, that I would find a publisher for the whole, after I had made what use of it I required; and I think I shall best answer my own purpose and fulfil his wishes by printing certain parts of it in full. In this way my readers will have a detailed, and, I believe, a very genuine account of some essential matters; and if any publisher should take a fancy to the Chevalier's manner of narration, he knows where to apply for the rest, of which there is plenty at his service. I put in my first extract here, so that it may stand in the place of what the Chevalier told us over our wine in the hall of Durrisdeer; but you are to suppose it was not the brutal fact, but a very varnished version that he offered to my lord.

CHAPTER III.
THE MASTER'S WANDERINGS.

From the Memoirs of the Chevalier de Burke.

. . . I left Ruthven (it's hardly necessary to remark) with much greater satisfaction than I had come to it; but whether I missed my way in the deserts, or whether my companions failed me, I soon found myself alone. This was a predicament very disagreeable; for I never understood this horrid country or savage people, and the last stroke of the Prince's withdrawal had made us of the Irish more unpopular than ever. I was reflecting on my poor chances, when I saw another horseman on the hill, whom I supposed at first to have been a phantom, the news of his death in the very front at Culloden being current in the army generally. This was the Master of Ballantrae, my Lord Durrisdeer's son, a young nobleman of the rarest gallantry and parts, and equally designed by nature to adorn a Court and to reap laurels in the field. Our meeting was the more welcome to both, as he was one of the few Scots who had used the Irish with consideration, and as he might now be of very high utility in aiding my escape. Yet what founded our particular friendship was a circumstance, by itself as romantic as any fable of King Arthur.

This was on the second day of our flight, after we had slept one night in the rain upon the inclination of a mountain. There was an Appin man, Alan Black Stewart (or some such name, [2] but I have seen him since in France) who chanced to be passing the same way, and had a jealousy of my companion. Very uncivil expressions were exchanged; and Stewart calls upon the Master to alight and have it out.

"Why, Mr. Stewart," says the Master, "I think at the present time I would prefer to run a race with you." And with the word claps spurs to his horse.

Stewart ran after us, a childish thing to do, for more than a mile; and I could not help laughing, as I looked back at last and saw him on a hill, holding his hand to his side, and nearly burst with running.

"But, all the same," I could not help saying to my companion, "I would let no man run after me for any such proper purpose, and not give him his desire. It was a good jest, but it smells a trifle cowardly."

He bent his brows at me. "I do pretty well," says he, "when I saddle myself with the most unpopular man in Scotland, and let that suffice for courage."

"O, bedad," says I, "I could show you a more unpopular with the naked eye. And if you like not my company, you can 'saddle' yourself on some one else."

"Colonel Burke," says he, "do not let us quarrel; and, to that effect, let me assure you I am the least patient man in the world."

"I am as little patient as yourself," said I. "I care not who knows that."

"At this rate," says he, reining in, "we shall not go very far. And I propose we do one of two things upon the instant: either quarrel and be done; or make a sure bargain to bear everything at each other's hands."

"Like a pair of brothers?" said I.

"I said no such foolishness," he replied. "I have a brother of my own, and I think no more of him than of a colewort. But if we are to have our noses rubbed together in this course of flight, let us each dare to be ourselves like savages, and each swear that he will neither resent nor deprecate the other. I am a pretty bad fellow at bottom, and I find the pretence of virtues very irksome."

"O, I am as bad as yourself," said I. "There is no skim milk in Francis Burke. But which is it to be? Fight or make friends?"

"Why," says he, "I think it will be the best manner to spin a coin for it."

This proposition was too highly chivalrous not to take my fancy; and, strange as it may seem of two well-born gentlemen of to-day, we span a half-crown (like a pair of ancient paladins) whether we were to cut each other's throats or be sworn friends. A more romantic circumstance can rarely have occurred; and it is one of those points in my memoirs, by which we may see the old tales of Homer and the poets are equally true to-day—at least, of the noble and genteel. The coin fell for peace, and we shook hands upon our bargain. And then it was that my companion explained to me his thought in running away from Mr. Stewart, which was certainly worthy of his political intellect. The report of his death, he said, was a great guard to him; Mr. Stewart having recognised him, had become a danger; and he had taken the briefest road to that gentleman's silence. "For," says he, "Alan Black is too vain a man to narrate any such story of himself."

Towards afternoon we came down to the shores of that loch for which we were heading; and there was the ship, but newly come to anchor. She was the Sainte-Marie-des-Anges, out of the port of Havre-de-Grace. The Master, after we had signalled for a boat, asked me if I knew the captain. I told him he was a countryman of mine, of the most unblemished integrity, but, I was afraid, a rather timorous man.

"No matter," says he. "For all that, he should certainly hear the truth."

I asked him if he meant about the battle? for if the captain once knew the standard was down, he would certainly put to sea again at once.

"And even then!" said he; "the arms are now of no sort of utility."

"My dear man," said I, "who thinks of the arms? But, to be sure, we must remember our friends. They will be close upon our heels, perhaps the Prince himself, and if the ship be gone, a great number of valuable lives may be imperilled."

"The captain and the crew have lives also, if you come to that," says Ballantrae.

This I declared was but a quibble, and that I would not hear of the captain being told; and then it was that Ballantrae made me a witty answer, for the sake of which (and also because I have been blamed myself in this business of the Sainte-Marie-des-Anges) I have related the whole conversation as it passed.

"Frank," says he, "remember our bargain. I must not object to your holding your tongue, which I hereby even encourage you to do; but, by the same terms, you are not to resent my telling."

I could not help laughing at this; though I still forewarned him what would come of it.

"The devil may come of it for what I care," says the reckless fellow. "I have always done exactly as I felt inclined."

As is well known, my prediction came true. The captain had no sooner heard the news than he cut his cable and to sea again; and before morning broke, we were in the Great Minch.

The ship was very old; and the skipper, although the most honest of men (and Irish too), was one of the least capable. The wind blew very boisterous, and the sea raged extremely. All that day we had little heart whether to eat or drink; went early to rest in some concern of mind; and (as if to give us a lesson) in the night the wind chopped suddenly into the north-east, and blew a hurricane. We were awaked by the dreadful thunder of the tempest and the stamping of the mariners on deck; so that I supposed our last hour was certainly come; and the terror of my mind was increased out of all measure by Ballantrae, who mocked at my devotions. It is in hours like these that a man of any piety appears in his true light, and we find (what we are taught as babes) the small trust that can be set in worldly friends. I would be unworthy of my religion if I let this pass without particular remark. For three days we lay in the dark in the cabin, and had but a biscuit to nibble. On the fourth the wind fell, leaving the ship dismasted and heaving on vast billows. The captain had not a guess of whither we were blown; he was stark ignorant of his trade, and could do naught but bless the Holy Virgin; a very good thing, too, but scarce the whole of seamanship. It seemed, our one hope was to be picked up by another vessel; and if that should prove to be an English ship, it might be no great blessing to the Master and myself.

The fifth and sixth days we tossed there helpless. The seventh some sail was got on her, but she was an unwieldy vessel at the best, and we made little but leeway. All the time, indeed, we had been drifting to the south and west, and during the tempest must have driven in that direction with unheard-of violence. The ninth dawn was cold and black, with a great sea running, and every mark of foul weather. In this situation we were overjoyed to sight a small ship on the horizon, and to perceive her go about and head for the Sainte-Marie. But our gratification did not very long endure; for when she had laid to and lowered a boat, it was immediately filled with disorderly fellows, who sang and shouted as they pulled across to us, and swarmed in on our deck with bare cutlasses, cursing loudly. Their leader was a horrible villain, with his face blacked and his whiskers curled in ringlets; Teach, his name; a most notorious pirate. He stamped about the deck, raving and crying out that his name was Satan, and his ship was called Hell. There was something about him like a wicked child or a half-witted person, that daunted me beyond expression. I whispered in the ear of Ballantrae that I would not be the last to volunteer, and only prayed God they might be short of hands; he approved my purpose with a nod.

"Bedad," said I to Master Teach, "if you are Satan, here is a devil for ye."

The word pleased him; and (not to dwell upon these shocking incidents) Ballantrae and I and two others were taken for recruits, while the skipper and all the rest were cast into the sea by the method of walking the plank. It was the first time I had seen this done; my heart died within me at the spectacle; and Master Teach or one of his acolytes (for my head was too much lost to be precise) remarked upon my pale face in a very alarming manner. I had the strength to cut a step or two of a jig, and cry out some ribaldry, which saved me for that time; but my legs were like water when I must get down into the skiff among these miscreants; and what with my horror of my company and fear of the monstrous billows, it was all I could do to keep an Irish tongue and break a jest or two as we were pulled aboard. By the blessing of God, there was a fiddle in the pirate ship, which I had no sooner seen than I fell upon; and in my quality of crowder I had the heavenly good luck to get favour in their eyes. Crowding Pat was the name they dubbed me with; and it was little I cared for a name so long as my skin was whole.

What kind of a pandemonium that vessel was, I cannot describe, but she was commanded by a lunatic, and might be called a floating Bedlam. Drinking, roaring, singing, quarrelling, dancing, they were never all sober at one time; and there were days together when, if a squall had supervened, it must have sent us to the bottom; or if a king's ship had come along, it would have found us quite helpless for defence. Once or twice we sighted a sail, and, if we were sober enough, overhauled it, God forgive us! and if we were all too drunk, she got away, and I would bless the saints under my breath. Teach ruled, if you can call that rule which brought no order, by the terror he created; and I observed the man was very vain of his position. I have known marshals of France—ay, and even Highland chieftains—that were less openly puffed up; which throws a singular light on the pursuit of honour and glory. Indeed, the longer we live, the more we perceive the sagacity of Aristotle and the other old philosophers; and though I have all my life been eager for legitimate distinctions, I can lay my hand upon my heart, at the end of my career, and declare there is not one—no, nor yet life itself—which is worth acquiring or preserving at the slightest cost of dignity.

It was long before I got private speech of Ballantrae; but at length one night we crept out upon the boltsprit, when the rest were better employed, and commiserated our position.

"None can deliver us but the saints," said I.

"My mind is very different," said Ballantrae; "for I am going to deliver myself. This Teach is the poorest creature possible; we make no profit of him, and lie continually open to capture; and," says he, "I am not going to be a tarry pirate for nothing, nor yet to hang in chains if I can help it." And he told me what was in his mind to better the state of the ship in the way of discipline, which would give us safety for the present, and a sooner hope of deliverance when they should have gained enough and should break up their company.

I confessed to him ingenuously that my nerve was quite shook amid these horrible surroundings, and I durst scarce tell him to count upon me.

"I am not very easy frightened," said he, "nor very easy beat."

A few days after, there befell an accident which had nearly hanged us all; and offers the most extraordinary picture of the folly that ruled in our concerns. We were all pretty drunk: and some bedlamite spying a sail, Teach put the ship about in chase without a glance, and we began to bustle up the arms and boast of the horrors that should follow. I observed Ballantrae stood quiet in the bows, looking under the shade of his hand; but for my part, true to my policy among these savages, I was at work with the busiest and passing Irish jests for their diversion.

"Run up the colours," cries Teach. "Show the —s the Jolly Roger!"

It was the merest drunken braggadocio at such a stage, and might have lost us a valuable prize; but I thought it no part of mine to reason, and I ran up the black flag with my own hand.

Ballantrae steps presently aft with a smile upon his face.

"You may perhaps like to know, you drunken dog," says he, "that you are chasing a king's ship."

Teach roared him the lie; but he ran at the same time to the bulwarks, and so did they all. I have never seen so many drunken men struck suddenly sober. The cruiser had gone about, upon our impudent display of colours; she was just then filling on the new tack; her ensign blew out quite plain to see; and even as we stared, there came a puff of smoke, and then a report, and a shot plunged in the waves a good way short of us. Some ran to the ropes, and got the Sarah round with an incredible swiftness. One fellow fell on the rum barrel, which stood broached upon the deck, and rolled it promptly overboard. On my part, I made for the Jolly Roger, struck it, tossed it in the sea; and could have flung myself after, so vexed was I with our mismanagement. As for Teach, he grew as pale as death, and incontinently went down to his cabin. Only twice he came on deck that afternoon; went to the taffrail; took a long look at the king's ship, which was still on the horizon heading after us; and then, without speech, back to his cabin. You may say he deserted us; and if it had not been for one very capable sailor we had on board, and for the lightness of the airs that blew all day, we must certainly have gone to the yard-arm.

It is to be supposed Teach was humiliated, and perhaps alarmed for his position with the crew; and the way in which he set about regaining what he had lost, was highly characteristic of the man. Early next day we smelled him burning sulphur in his cabin and crying out of "Hell, hell!" which was well understood among the crew, and filled their minds with apprehension. Presently he comes on deck, a perfect figure of fun, his face blacked, his hair and whiskers curled, his belt stuck full of pistols; chewing bits of glass so that the blood ran down his chin, and brandishing a dirk. I do not know if he had taken these manners from the Indians of America, where he was a native; but such was his way, and he would always thus announce that he was wound up to horrid deeds. The first that came near him was the fellow who had sent the rum overboard the day before; him he stabbed to the heart, damning him for a mutineer; and then capered about the body, raving and swearing and daring us to come on. It was the silliest exhibition; and yet dangerous too, for the cowardly fellow was plainly working himself up to another murder.

All of a sudden Ballantrae stepped forth. "Have done with this play-acting," says he. "Do you think to frighten us with making faces? We saw nothing of you yesterday, when you were wanted; and we did well without you, let me tell you that."

There was a murmur and a movement in the crew, of pleasure and alarm, I thought, in nearly equal parts. As for Teach, he gave a barbarous howl, and swung his dirk to fling it, an art in which (like many seamen) he was very expert.

"Knock that out of his hand!" says Ballantrae, so sudden and sharp that my arm obeyed him before my mind had understood.

Teach stood like one stupid, never thinking on his pistols.

"Go down to your cabin," cries Ballantrae, "and come on deck again when you are sober. Do you think we are going to hang for you, you black-faced, half-witted, drunken brute and butcher? Go down!" And he stamped his foot at him with such a sudden smartness that Teach fairly ran for it to the companion.

"And now, mates," says Ballantrae, "a word with you. I don't know if you are gentlemen of fortune for the fun of the thing, but I am not. I want to make money, and get ashore again, and spend it like a man. And on one thing my mind is made up: I will not hang if I can help it. Come: give me a hint; I'm only a beginner! Is there no way to get a little discipline and common sense about this business?"

One of the men spoke up: he said by rights they should have a quartermaster; and no sooner was the word out of his mouth than they were all of that opinion. The thing went by acclamation, Ballantrae was made quartermaster, the rum was put in his charge, laws were passed in imitation of those of a pirate by the name of Roberts, and the last proposal was to make an end of Teach. But Ballantrae was afraid of a more efficient captain, who might be a counterweight to himself, and he opposed this stoutly. Teach, he said, was good enough to board ships and frighten fools with his blacked face and swearing; we could scarce get a better man than Teach for that; and besides, as the man was now disconsidered and as good as deposed, we might reduce his proportion of the plunder. This carried it; Teach's share was cut down to a mere derision, being actually less than mine; and there remained only two points: whether he would consent, and who was to announce to him this resolution.

"Do not let that stick you," says Ballantrae, "I will do that."

And he stepped to the companion and down alone into the cabin to face that drunken savage.

"This is the man for us," cries one of the hands. "Three cheers for the quartermaster!" which were given with a will, my own voice among the loudest, and I dare say these plaudits had their effect on Master Teach in the cabin, as we have seen of late days how shouting in the streets may trouble even the minds of legislators.

What passed precisely was never known, though some of the heads of it came to the surface later on; and we were all amazed, as well as gratified, when Ballantrae came on deck with Teach upon his arm, and announced that all had been consented.

I pass swiftly over those twelve or fifteen months in which we continued to keep the sea in the North Atlantic, getting our food and water from the ships we over-hauled, and doing on the whole a pretty fortunate business. Sure, no one could wish to read anything so ungenteel as the memoirs of a pirate, even an unwilling one like me! Things went extremely better with our designs, and Ballantrae kept his lead, to my admiration, from that day forth. I would be tempted to suppose that a gentleman must everywhere be first, even aboard a rover: but my birth is every whit as good as any Scottish lord's, and I am not ashamed to confess that I stayed Crowding Pat until the end, and was not much better than the crew's buffoon. Indeed, it was no scene to bring out my merits. My health suffered from a variety of reasons; I was more at home to the last on a horse's back than a ship's deck; and, to be ingenuous, the fear of the sea was constantly in my mind, battling with the fear of my companions. I need not cry myself up for courage; I have done well on many fields under the eyes of famous generals, and earned my late advancement by an act of the most distinguished valour before many witnesses. But when we must proceed on one of our abordages, the heart of Francis Burke was in his boots; the little eggshell skiff in which we must set forth, the horrible heaving of the vast billows, the height of the ship that we must scale, the thought of how many might be there in garrison upon their legitimate defence, the scowling heavens which (in that climate) so often looked darkly down upon our exploits, and the mere crying of the wind in my ears, were all considerations most unpalatable to my valour. Besides which, as I was always a creature of the nicest sensibility, the scenes that must follow on our success tempted me as little as the chances of defeat. Twice we found women on board; and though I have seen towns sacked, and of late days in France some very horrid public tumults, there was something in the smallness of the numbers engaged, and the bleak dangerous sea-surroundings, that made these acts of piracy far the most revolting. I confess ingenuously I could never proceed unless I was three parts drunk; it was the same even with the crew; Teach himself was fit for no enterprise till he was full of rum; and it was one of the most difficult parts of Ballantrae's performance, to serve us with liquor in the proper quantities. Even this he did to admiration; being upon the whole the most capable man I ever met with, and the one of the most natural genius. He did not even scrape favour with the crew, as I did, by continual buffoonery made upon a very anxious heart; but preserved on most occasions a great deal of gravity and distance; so that he was like a parent among a family of young children, or a schoolmaster with his boys. What made his part the harder to perform, the men were most inveterate grumblers; Ballantrae's discipline, little as it was, was yet irksome to their love of licence; and what was worse, being kept sober they had time to think. Some of them accordingly would fall to repenting their abominable crimes; one in particular, who was a good Catholic, and with whom I would sometimes steal apart for prayer; above all in bad weather, fogs, lashing rain and the like, when we would be the less observed; and I am sure no two criminals in the cart have ever performed their devotions with more anxious sincerity. But the rest, having no such grounds of hope, fell to another pastime, that of computation. All day long they would be telling up their shares or grooming over the result. I have said we were pretty fortunate. But an observation fails to be made: that in this world, in no business that I have tried, do the profits rise to a man's expectations. We found many ships and took many; yet few of them contained much money, their goods were usually nothing to our purpose—what did we want with a cargo of ploughs, or even of tobacco?—and it is quite a painful reflection how many whole crews we have made to walk the plank for no more than a stock of biscuit or an anker or two of spirit.

In the meanwhile our ship was growing very foul, and it was high time we should make for our port de carrénage, which was in the estuary of a river among swamps. It was openly understood that we should then break up and go and squander our proportions of the spoil; and this made every man greedy of a little more, so that our decision was delayed from day to day. What finally decided matters, was a trifling accident, such as an ignorant person might suppose incidental to our way of life. But here I must explain: on only one of all the ships we boarded, the first on which we found women, did we meet with any genuine resistance. On that occasion we had two men killed and several injured, and if it had not been for the gallantry of Ballantrae we had surely been beat back at last. Everywhere else the defence (where there was any at all) was what the worst troops in Europe would have laughed at; so that the most dangerous part of our employment was to clamber up the side of the ship; and I have even known the poor souls on board to cast us a line, so eager were they to volunteer instead of walking the plank. This constant immunity had made our fellows very soft, so that I understood how Teach had made so deep a mark upon their minds; for indeed the company of that lunatic was the chief danger in our way of life. The accident to which I have referred was this:—We had sighted a little full-rigged ship very close under our board in a haze; she sailed near as well as we did—I should be nearer truth if I said, near as ill; and we cleared the bow-chaser to see if we could bring a spar or two about their ears. The swell was exceeding great; the motion of the ship beyond description; it was little wonder if our gunners should fire thrice and be still quite broad of what they aimed at. But in the meanwhile the chase had cleared a stern gun, the thickness of the air concealing them; and being better marksmen, their first shot struck us in the bows, knocked our two gunners into mince-meat, so that we were all sprinkled with the blood, and plunged through the deck into the forecastle, where we slept. Ballantrae would have held on; indeed, there was nothing in this contretemps to affect the mind of any soldier; but he had a quick perception of the men's wishes, and it was plain this lucky shot had given them a sickener of their trade. In a moment they were all of one mind: the chase was drawing away from us, it was needless to hold on, the Sarah was too foul to overhaul a bottle, it was mere foolery to keep the sea with her; and on these pretended grounds her head was incontinently put about and the course laid for the river. It was strange to see what merriment fell on that ship's company, and how they stamped about the deck jesting, and each computing what increase had come to his share by the death of the two gunners.

We were nine days making our port, so light were the airs we had to sail on, so foul the ship's bottom; but early on the tenth, before dawn, and in a light lifting haze, we passed the head. A little after, the haze lifted, and fell again, showing us a cruiser very close. This was a sore blow, happening so near our refuge. There was a great debate of whether she had seen us, and if so whether it was likely they had recognised the Sarah. We were very careful, by destroying every member of those crews we overhauled, to leave no evidence as to our own persons; but the appearance of the Sarah herself we could not keep so private; and above all of late, since she had been foul, and we had pursued many ships without success, it was plain that her description had been often published. I supposed this alert would have made us separate upon the instant. But here again that original genius of Ballantrae's had a surprise in store for me. He and Teach (and it was the most remarkable step of his success) had gone hand in hand since the first day of his appointment. I often questioned him upon the fact, and never got an answer but once, when he told me he and Teach had an understanding "which would very much surprise the crew if they should hear of it, and would surprise himself a good deal if it was carried out." Well, here again he and Teach were of a mind; and by their joint procurement the anchor was no sooner down than the whole crew went off upon a scene of drunkenness indescribable. By afternoon we were a mere shipful of lunatical persons, throwing of things overboard, howling of different songs at the same time, quarrelling and falling together, and then forgetting our quarrels to embrace. Ballantrae had bidden me drink nothing, and feign drunkenness, as I valued my life; and I have never passed a day so wearisomely, lying the best part of the time upon the forecastle and watching the swamps and thickets by which our little basin was entirely surrounded for the eye. A little after dusk Ballantrae stumbled up to my side, feigned to fall, with a drunken laugh, and before he got his feet again, whispered me to "reel down into the cabin and seem to fall asleep upon a locker, for there would be need of me soon." I did as I was told, and coming into the cabin, where it was quite dark, let myself fall on the first locker. There was a man there already; by the way he stirred and threw me off, I could not think he was much in liquor; and yet when I had found another place, he seemed to continue to sleep on. My heart now beat very hard, for I saw some desperate matter was in act. Presently down came Ballantrae, lit the lamp, looked about the cabin, nodded as if pleased, and on deck again without a word. I peered out from between my fingers, and saw there were three of us slumbering, or feigning to slumber, on the lockers: myself, one Dutton and one Grady, both resolute men. On deck the rest were got to a pitch of revelry quite beyond the bounds of what is human; so that no reasonable name can describe the sounds they were now making. I have heard many a drunken bout in my time, many on board that very Sarah, but never anything the least like this, which made me early suppose the liquor had been tampered with. It was a long while before these yells and howls died out into a sort of miserable moaning, and then to silence; and it seemed a long while after that before Ballantrae came down again, this time with Teach upon his heels. The latter cursed at the sight of us three upon the lockers.

"Tut," says Ballantrae, "you might fire a pistol at their ears. You know what stuff they have been swallowing."

There was a hatch in the cabin floor, and under that the richest part of the booty was stored against the day of division. It fastened with a ring and three padlocks, the keys (for greater security) being divided; one to Teach, one to Ballantrae, and one to the mate, a man called Hammond. Yet I was amazed to see they were now all in the one hand; and yet more amazed (still looking through my fingers) to observe Ballantrae and Teach bring up several packets, four of them in all, very carefully made up and with a loop for carriage.

"And now," says Teach, "let us be going."

"One word," says Ballantrae. "I have discovered there is another man besides yourself who knows a private path across the swamp; and it seems it is shorter than yours."

Teach cried out, in that case, they were undone.

"I do not know for that," says Ballantrae. "For there are several other circumstances with which I must acquaint you. First of all, there is no bullet in your pistols, which (if you remember) I was kind enough to load for both of us this morning. Secondly, as there is someone else who knows a passage, you must think it highly improbable I should saddle myself with a lunatic like you. Thirdly, these gentlemen (who need no longer pretend to be asleep) are those of my party, and will now proceed to gag and bind you to the mast; and when your men awaken (if they ever do awake after the drugs we have mingled in their liquor), I am sure they will be so obliging as to deliver you, and you will have no difficulty, I daresay, to explain the business of the keys."

Not a word said Teach, but looked at us like a frightened baby as we gagged and bound him.

"Now you see, you moon-calf," says Ballantrae, "why we made four packets. Heretofore you have been called Captain Teach, but I think you are now rather Captain Learn."

That was our last word on board the Sarah. We four, with our four packets, lowered ourselves softly into a skiff, and left that ship behind us as silent as the grave, only for the moaning of some of the drunkards. There was a fog about breast-high on the waters; so that Dutton, who knew the passage, must stand on his feet to direct our rowing; and this, as it forced us to row gently, was the means of our deliverance. We were yet but a little way from the ship, when it began to come grey, and the birds to fly abroad upon the water. All of a sudden Dutton clapped down upon his hams, and whispered us to be silent for our lives, and hearken. Sure enough, we heard a little faint creak of oars upon one hand, and then again, and further off, a creak of oars upon the other. It was clear we had been sighted yesterday in the morning; here were the cruiser's boats to cut us out; here were we defenceless in their very midst. Sure, never were poor souls more perilously placed; and as we lay there on our oars, praying God the mist might hold, the sweat poured from my brow. Presently we heard one of the boats where we might have thrown a biscuit in her. "Softly, men," we heard an officer whisper; and I marvelled they could not hear the drumming of my heart.

"Never mind the path," says Ballantrae; "we must get shelter anyhow; let us pull straight ahead for the sides of the basin."

This we did with the most anxious precaution, rowing, as best we could, upon our hands, and steering at a venture in the fog, which was (for all that) our only safety. But Heaven guided us; we touched ground at a thicket; scrambled ashore with our treasure; and having no other way of concealment, and the mist beginning already to lighten, hove down the skiff and let her sink. We were still but new under cover when the sun rose; and at the same time, from the midst of the basin, a great shouting of seamen sprang up, and we knew the Sarah was being boarded. I heard afterwards the officer that took her got great honour; and it's true the approach was creditably managed, but I think he had an easy capture when he came to board. [3]

I was still blessing the saints for my escape, when I became aware we were in trouble of another kind. We were here landed at random in a vast and dangerous swamp; and how to come at the path was a concern of doubt, fatigue, and peril. Dutton, indeed, was of opinion we should wait until the ship was gone, and fish up the skiff; for any delay would be more wise than to go blindly ahead in that morass. One went back accordingly to the basin-side and (peering through the thicket) saw the fog already quite drunk up, and English colours flying on the Sarah, but no movement made to get her under way. Our situation was now very doubtful. The swamp was an unhealthful place to linger in; we had been so greedy to bring treasures that we had brought but little food; it was highly desirable, besides, that we should get clear of the neighbourhood and into the settlements before the news of the capture went abroad; and against all these considerations, there was only the peril of the passage on the other side. I think it not wonderful we decided on the active part.

It was already blistering hot when we set forth to pass the marsh, or rather to strike the path, by compass. Dutton took the compass, and one or other of us three carried his proportion of the treasure. I promise you he kept a sharp eye to his rear, for it was like the man's soul that he must trust us with. The thicket was as close as a bush; the ground very treacherous, so that we often sank in the most terrifying manner, and must go round about; the heat, besides, was stifling, the air singularly heavy, and the stinging insects abounded in such myriads that each of us walked under his own cloud. It has often been commented on, how much better gentlemen of birth endure fatigue than persons of the rabble; so that walking officers who must tramp in the dirt beside their men, shame them by their constancy. This was well to be observed in the present instance; for here were Ballantrae and I, two gentlemen of the highest breeding, on the one hand; and on the other, Grady, a common mariner, and a man nearly a giant in physical strength. The case of Dutton is not in point, for I confess he did as well as any of us. [4] But as for Grady, he began early to lament his case, tailed in the rear, refused to carry Dutton's packet when it came his turn, clamoured continually for rum (of which we had too little), and at last even threatened us from behind with a cocked pistol, unless we should allow him rest.

Ballantrae would have fought it out, I believe; but I prevailed with him the other way; and we made a stop and ate a meal. It seemed to benefit Grady little; he was in the rear again at once, growling and bemoaning his lot; and at last, by some carelessness, not having followed properly in our tracks, stumbled into a deep part of the slough where it was mostly water, gave some very dreadful screams, and before we could come to his aid had sunk along with his booty. His fate, and above all these screams of his, appalled us to the soul; yet it was on the whole a fortunate circumstance and the means of our deliverance, for it moved Dutton to mount into a tree, whence he was able to perceive and to show me, who had climbed after him, a high piece of the wood, which was a landmark for the path. He went forward the more carelessly, I must suppose; for presently we saw him sink a little down, draw up his feet and sink again, and so twice. Then he turned his face to us, pretty white.

"Lend a hand," said he, "I am in a bad place."

"I don't know about that," says Ballantrae, standing still.

Dutton broke out into the most violent oaths, sinking a little lower as he did, so that the mud was nearly to his waist, and plucking a pistol from his belt, "Help me," he cries, "or die and be damned to you!"

"Nay," says Ballantrae, "I did but jest. I am coming." And he set down his own packet and Dutton's, which he was then carrying. "Do not venture near till we see if you are needed," said he to me, and went forward alone to where the man was bogged. He was quiet now, though he still held the pistol; and the marks of terror in his countenance were very moving to behold.

"For the Lord's sake," says he, "look sharp."

Ballantrae was now got close up. "Keep still," says he, and seemed to consider; and then, "Reach out both your hands!"

Dutton laid down his pistol, and so watery was the top surface that it went clear out of sight; with an oath he stooped to snatch it; and as he did so, Ballantrae leaned forth and stabbed him between the shoulders. Up went his hands over his head—I know not whether with the pain or to ward himself; and the next moment he doubled forward in the mud.

Ballantrae was already over the ankles; but he plucked himself out, and came back to me, where I stood with my knees smiting one another. "The devil take you, Francis!" says he. "I believe you are a half-hearted fellow, after all. I have only done justice on a pirate. And here we are quite clear of the Sarah! Who shall now say that we have dipped our hands in any irregularities?"

I assured him he did me injustice; but my sense of humanity was so much affected by the horridness of the fact that I could scarce find breath to answer with.

"Come," said he, "you must be more resolved. The need for this fellow ceased when he had shown you where the path ran; and you cannot deny I would have been daft to let slip so fair an opportunity."

I could not deny but he was right in principle; nor yet could I refrain from shedding tears, of which I think no man of valour need have been ashamed; and it was not until I had a share of the rum that I was able to proceed. I repeat, I am far from ashamed of my generous emotion; mercy is honourable in the warrior; and yet I cannot altogether censure Ballantrae, whose step was really fortunate, as we struck the path without further misadventure, and the same night, about sundown, came to the edge of the morass.

We were too weary to seek far; on some dry sands, still warm with the day's sun, and close under a wood of pines, we lay down and were instantly plunged in sleep.

We awaked the next morning very early, and began with a sullen spirit a conversation that came near to end in blows. We were now cast on shore in the southern provinces, thousands of miles from any French settlement; a dreadful journey and a thousand perils lay in front of us; and sure, if there was ever need for amity, it was in such an hour. I must suppose that Ballantrae had suffered in his sense of what is truly polite; indeed, and there is nothing strange in the idea, after the sea-wolves we had consorted with so long; and as for myself, he fubbed me off unhandsomely, and any gentleman would have resented his behaviour.

I told him in what light I saw his conduct; he walked a little off, I following to upbraid him; and at last he stopped me with his hand.

"Frank," says he, "you know what we swore; and yet there is no oath invented would induce me to swallow such expressions, if I did not regard you with sincere affection. It is impossible you should doubt me there: I have given proofs. Dutton I had to take, because he knew the pass, and Grady because Dutton would not move without him; but what call was there to carry you along? You are a perpetual danger to me with your cursed Irish tongue. By rights you should now be in irons in the cruiser. And you quarrel with me like a baby for some trinkets!"

I considered this one of the most unhandsome speeches ever made; and indeed to this day I can scarce reconcile it to my notion of a gentleman that was my friend. I retorted upon him with his Scotch accent, of which he had not so much as some, but enough to be very barbarous and disgusting, as I told him plainly; and the affair would have gone to a great length, but for an alarming intervention.

We had got some way off upon the sand. The place where we had slept, with the packets lying undone and the money scattered openly, was now between us and the pines; and it was out of these the stranger must have come. There he was at least, a great hulking fellow of the country, with a broad axe on his shoulder, looking open-mouthed, now at the treasure, which was just at his feet, and now at our disputation, in which we had gone far enough to have weapons in our hands. We had no sooner observed him than he found his legs and made off again among the pines.

This was no scene to put our minds at rest: a couple of armed men in sea-clothes found quarrelling over a treasure, not many miles from where a pirate had been captured—here was enough to bring the whole country about our ears. The quarrel was not even made up; it was blotted from our minds; and we got our packets together in the twinkling of an eye, and made off, running with the best will in the world. But the trouble was, we did not know in what direction, and must continually return upon our steps. Ballantrae had indeed collected what he could from Dutton; but it's hard to travel upon hearsay; and the estuary, which spreads into a vast irregular harbour, turned us off upon every side with a new stretch of water.

We were near beside ourselves, and already quite spent with running, when, coming to the top of a dune, we saw we were again cut off by another ramification of the bay. This was a creek, however, very different from those that had arrested us before; being set in rocks, and so precipitously deep that a small vessel was able to lie alongside, made fast with a hawser; and her crew had laid a plank to the shore. Here they had lighted a fire, and were sitting at their meal. As for the vessel herself, she was one of those they build in the Bermudas.

The love of gold and the great hatred that everybody has to pirates were motives of the most influential, and would certainly raise the country in our pursuit. Besides, it was now plain we were on some sort of straggling peninsula, like the fingers of a hand; and the wrist, or passage to the mainland, which we should have taken at the first, was by this time not improbably secured. These considerations put us on a bolder counsel. For as long as we dared, looking every moment to hear sounds of the chase, we lay among some bushes on the top of the dune; and having by this means secured a little breath and recomposed our appearance, we strolled down at last, with a great affectation of carelessness, to the party by the fire.

It was a trader and his negroes, belonging to Albany, in the province of New York, and now on the way home from the Indies with a cargo; his name I cannot recall. We were amazed to learn he had put in here from terror of the Sarah; for we had no thought our exploits had been so notorious. As soon as the Albanian heard she had been taken the day before, he jumped to his feet, gave us a cup of spirits for our good news, and sent big negroes to get sail on the Bermudan. On our side, we profited by the dram to become more confidential, and at last offered ourselves as passengers. He looked askance at our tarry clothes and pistols, and replied civilly enough that he had scarce accommodation for himself; nor could either our prayers or our offers of money, in which we advanced pretty far, avail to shake him.

"I see, you think ill of us," says Ballantrae, "but I will show you how well we think of you by telling you the truth. We are Jacobite fugitives, and there is a price upon our heads."

At this, the Albanian was plainly moved a little. He asked us many questions as to the Scotch war, which Ballantrae very patiently answered. And then, with a wink, in a vulgar manner, "I guess you and your Prince Charlie got more than you cared about," said he.

"Bedad, and that we did," said I. "And, my dear man, I wish you would set a new example and give us just that much."

This I said in the Irish way, about which there is allowed to be something very engaging. It's a remarkable thing, and a testimony to the love with which our nation is regarded, that this address scarce ever fails in a handsome fellow. I cannot tell how often I have seen a private soldier escape the horse, or a beggar wheedle out a good alms by a touch of the brogue. And, indeed, as soon as the Albanian had laughed at me I was pretty much at rest. Even then, however, he made many conditions, and—for one thing—took away our arms, before he suffered us aboard; which was the signal to cast off; so that in a moment after, we were gliding down the bay with a good breeze, and blessing the name of God for our deliverance. Almost in the mouth of the estuary, we passed the cruiser, and a little after the poor Sarah with her prize crew; and these were both sights to make us tremble. The Bermudan seemed a very safe place to be in, and our bold stroke to have been fortunately played, when we were thus reminded of the case of our companions. For all that, we had only exchanged traps, jumped out of the frying-pan into the fire, ran from the yard-arm to the block, and escaped the open hostility of the man-of-war to lie at the mercy of the doubtful faith of our Albanian merchant.

From many circumstances, it chanced we were safer than we could have dared to hope. The town of Albany was at that time much concerned in contraband trade across the desert with the Indians and the French. This, as it was highly illegal, relaxed their loyalty, and as it brought them in relation with the politest people on the earth, divided even their sympathies. In short, they were like all the smugglers in the world, spies and agents ready-made for either party. Our Albanian, besides, was a very honest man indeed, and very greedy; and, to crown our luck, he conceived a great delight in our society. Before we had reached the town of New York we had come to a full agreement, that he should carry us as far as Albany upon his ship, and thence put us on a way to pass the boundaries and join the French. For all this we were to pay at a high rate; but beggars cannot be choosers, nor outlaws bargainers.

We sailed, then, up the Hudson River, which, I protest, is a very fine stream, and put up at the "King's Arms" in Albany. The town was full of the militia of the province, breathing slaughter against the French. Governor Clinton was there himself, a very busy man, and, by what I could learn, very near distracted by the factiousness of his Assembly. The Indians on both sides were on the war-path; we saw parties of them bringing in prisoners and (what was much worse) scalps, both male and female, for which they were paid at a fixed rate; and I assure you the sight was not encouraging. Altogether, we could scarce have come at a period more unsuitable for our designs; our position in the chief inn was dreadfully conspicuous; our Albanian fubbed us off with a thousand delays, and seemed upon the point of a retreat from his engagements; nothing but peril appeared to environ the poor fugitives, and for some time we drowned our concern in a very irregular course of living.

This, too, proved to be fortunate; and it's one of the remarks that fall to be made upon our escape, how providentially our steps were conducted to the very end. What a humiliation to the dignity of man! My philosophy, the extraordinary genius of Ballantrae, our valour, in which I grant that we were equal—all these might have proved insufficient without the Divine blessing on our efforts. And how true it is, as the Church tells us, that the Truths of Religion are, after all, quite applicable even to daily affairs! At least, it was in the course of our revelry that we made the acquaintance of a spirited youth by the name of Chew. He was one of the most daring of the Indian traders, very well acquainted with the secret paths of the wilderness, needy, dissolute, and, by a last good fortune, in some disgrace with his family. Him we persuaded to come to our relief; he privately provided what was needful for our flight, and one day we slipped out of Albany, without a word to our former friend, and embarked, a little above, in a canoe.

To the toils and perils of this journey, it would require a pen more elegant than mine to do full justice. The reader must conceive for himself the dreadful wilderness which we had now to thread; its thickets, swamps, precipitous rocks, impetuous rivers, and amazing waterfalls. Among these barbarous scenes we must toil all day, now paddling, now carrying our canoe upon our shoulders; and at night we slept about a fire, surrounded by the howling of wolves and other savage animals. It was our design to mount the headwaters of the Hudson, to the neighbourhood of Crown Point, where the French had a strong place in the woods, upon Lake Champlain. But to have done this directly were too perilous; and it was accordingly gone upon by such a labyrinth of rivers, lakes, and portages as makes my head giddy to remember. These paths were in ordinary times entirely desert; but the country was now up, the tribes on the war-path, the woods full of Indian scouts. Again and again we came upon these parties when we least expected them; and one day, in particular, I shall never forget, how, as dawn was coming in, we were suddenly surrounded by five or six of these painted devils, uttering a very dreary sort of cry, and brandishing their hatchets. It passed off harmlessly, indeed, as did the rest of our encounters; for Chew was well known and highly valued among the different tribes. Indeed, he was a very gallant, respectable young man; but even with the advantage of his companionship, you must not think these meetings were without sensible peril. To prove friendship on our part, it was needful to draw upon our stock of rum—indeed, under whatever disguise, that is the true business of the Indian trader, to keep a travelling public-house in the forest; and when once the braves had got their bottle of scaura (as they call this beastly liquor), it behoved us to set forth and paddle for our scalps. Once they were a little drunk, goodbye to any sense or decency; they had but the one thought, to get more scaura. They might easily take it in their heads to give us chase, and had we been overtaken, I had never written these memoirs.

We were come to the most critical portion of our course, where we might equally expect to fall into the hands of French or English, when a terrible calamity befell us. Chew was taken suddenly sick with symptoms like those of poison, and in the course of a few hours expired in the bottom of the canoe. We thus lost at once our guide, our interpreter, our boatman, and our passport, for he was all these in one; and found ourselves reduced, at a blow, to the most desperate and irremediable distress. Chew, who took a great pride in his knowledge, had indeed often lectured us on the geography; and Ballantrae, I believe, would listen. But for my part I have always found such information highly tedious; and beyond the fact that we were now in the country of the Adirondack Indians, and not so distant from our destination, could we but have found the way, I was entirely ignorant. The wisdom of my course was soon the more apparent; for with all his pains, Ballantrae was no further advanced than myself. He knew we must continue to go up one stream; then, by way of a portage, down another; and then up a third. But you are to consider, in a mountain country, how many streams come rolling in from every hand. And how is a gentleman, who is a perfect stranger in that part of the world, to tell any one of them from any other? Nor was this our only trouble. We were great novices, besides, in handling a canoe; the portages were almost beyond our strength, so that I have seen us sit down in despair for half an hour at a time without one word; and the appearance of a single Indian, since we had now no means of speaking to them, would have been in all probability the means of our destruction. There is altogether some excuse if Ballantrae showed something of a grooming disposition; his habit of imputing blame to others, quite as capable as himself, was less tolerable, and his language it was not always easy to accept. Indeed, he had contracted on board the pirate ship a manner of address which was in a high degree unusual between gentlemen; and now, when you might say he was in a fever, it increased upon him hugely.

The third day of these wanderings, as we were carrying the canoe upon a rocky portage, she fell, and was entirely bilged. The portage was between two lakes, both pretty extensive; the track, such as it was, opened at both ends upon the water, and on both hands was enclosed by the unbroken woods; and the sides of the lakes were quite impassable with bog: so that we beheld ourselves not only condemned to go without our boat and the greater part of our provisions, but to plunge at once into impenetrable thickets and to desert what little guidance we still had—the course of the river. Each stuck his pistols in his belt, shouldered an axe, made a pack of his treasure and as much food as he could stagger under; and deserting the rest of our possessions, even to our swords, which would have much embarrassed us among the woods, we set forth on this deplorable adventure. The labours of Hercules, so finely described by Homer, were a trifle to what we now underwent. Some parts of the forest were perfectly dense down to the ground, so that we must cut our way like mites in a cheese. In some the bottom was full of deep swamp, and the whole wood entirely rotten. I have leaped on a great fallen log and sunk to the knees in touchwood; I have sought to stay myself, in falling, against what looked to be a solid trunk, and the whole thing has whiffed away at my touch like a sheet of paper. Stumbling, falling, bogging to the knees, hewing our way, our eyes almost put out with twigs and branches, our clothes plucked from our bodies, we laboured all day, and it is doubtful if we made two miles. What was worse, as we could rarely get a view of the country, and were perpetually justled from our path by obstacles, it was impossible even to have a guess in what direction we were moving.

A little before sundown, in an open place with a stream, and set about with barbarous mountains, Ballantrae threw down his pack. "I will go no further," said he, and bade me light the fire, damning my blood in terms not proper for a chairman.

I told him to try to forget he had ever been a pirate, and to remember he had been a gentleman.

"Are you mad?" he cried. "Don't cross me here!" And then, shaking his fist at the hills, "To think," cries he, "that I must leave my bones in this miserable wilderness! Would God I had died upon the scaffold like a gentleman!" This he said ranting like an actor; and then sat biting his fingers and staring on the ground, a most unchristian object.

I took a certain horror of the man, for I thought a soldier and a gentleman should confront his end with more philosophy. I made him no reply, therefore, in words; and presently the evening fell so chill that I was glad, for my own sake, to kindle a fire. And yet God knows, in such an open spot, and the country alive with savages, the act was little short of lunacy. Ballantrae seemed never to observe me; but at last, as I was about parching a little corn, he looked up.

"Have you ever a brother?" said be.

"By the blessing of Heaven," said I, "not less than five."

"I have the one," said he, with a strange voice; and then presently, "He shall pay me for all this," he added. And when I asked him what was his brother's part in our distress, "What!" he cried, "he sits in my place, he bears my name, he courts my wife; and I am here alone with a damned Irishman in this tooth-chattering desert! Oh, I have been a common gull!" he cried.

The explosion was in all ways so foreign to my friend's nature that I was daunted out of all my just susceptibility. Sure, an offensive expression, however vivacious, appears a wonderfully small affair in circumstances so extreme! But here there is a strange thing to be noted. He had only once before referred to the lady with whom he was contracted. That was when we came in view of the town of New York, when he had told me, if all had their rights, he was now in sight of his own property, for Miss Graeme enjoyed a large estate in the province. And this was certainly a natural occasion; but now here she was named a second time; and what is surely fit to be observed, in this very month, which was November, '47, and I believe upon that very day as we sat among these barbarous mountains, his brother and Miss Graeme were married. I am the least superstitious of men; but the hand of Providence is here displayed too openly not to be remarked. [5]

The next day, and the next, were passed in similar labours; Ballantrae often deciding on our course by the spinning of a coin; and once, when I expostulated on this childishness, he had an odd remark that I have never forgotten. "I know no better way," said he, "to express my scorn of human reason." I think it was the third day that we found the body of a Christian, scalped and most abominably mangled, and lying in a pudder of his blood; the birds of the desert screaming over him, as thick as flies. I cannot describe how dreadfully this sight affected us; but it robbed me of all strength and all hope for this world. The same day, and only a little after, we were scrambling over a part of the forest that had been burned, when Ballantrae, who was a little ahead, ducked suddenly behind a fallen trunk. I joined him in this shelter, whence we could look abroad without being seen ourselves; and in the bottom of the next vale, beheld a large war party of the savages going by across our line. There might be the value of a weak battalion present; all naked to the waist, blacked with grease and soot, and painted with white lead and vermilion, according to their beastly habits. They went one behind another like a string of geese, and at a quickish trot; so that they took but a little while to rattle by, and disappear again among the woods. Yet I suppose we endured a greater agony of hesitation and suspense in these few minutes than goes usually to a man's whole life. Whether they were French or English Indians, whether they desired scalps or prisoners, whether we should declare ourselves upon the chance, or lie quiet and continue the heart-breaking business of our journey: sure, I think these were questions to have puzzled the brains of Aristotle himself. Ballantrae turned to me with a face all wrinkled up and his teeth showing in his mouth, like what I have read of people starving; he said no word, but his whole appearance was a kind of dreadful question.

"They may be of the English side," I whispered; "and think! the best we could then hope, is to begin this over again."

"I know—I know," he said. "Yet it must come to a plunge at last." And he suddenly plucked out his coin, shook it in his closed hands, looked at it, and then lay down with his face in the dust.

Addition by Mr. Mackellar.—I drop the Chevalier's narration at this point because the couple quarrelled and separated the same day; and the Chevalier's account of the quarrel seems to me (I must confess) quite incompatible with the nature of either of the men. Henceforth they wandered alone, undergoing extraordinary sufferings; until first one and then the other was picked up by a party from Fort St. Frederick. Only two things are to be noted. And first (as most important for my purpose) that the Master, in the course of his miseries buried his treasure, at a point never since discovered, but of which he took a drawing in his own blood on the lining of his hat. And second, that on his coming thus penniless to the Fort, he was welcomed like a brother by the Chevalier, who thence paid his way to France. The simplicity of Mr. Burke's character leads him at this point to praise the Master exceedingly; to an eye more worldly wise, it would seem it was the Chevalier alone that was to be commended. I have the more pleasure in pointing to this really very noble trait of my esteemed correspondent, as I fear I may have wounded him immediately before. I have refrained from comments on any of his extraordinary and (in my eyes) immoral opinions, for I know him to be jealous of respect. But his version of the quarrel is really more than I can reproduce; for I knew the Master myself, and a man more insusceptible of fear is not conceivable. I regret this oversight of the Chevalier's, and all the more because the tenor of his narrative (set aside a few flourishes) strikes me as highly ingenuous.

CHAPTER IV.
PERSECUTIONS ENDURED BY MR. HENRY.

You can guess on what part of his adventures the Colonel principally dwelled. Indeed, if we had heard it all, it is to be thought the current of this business had been wholly altered; but the pirate ship was very gently touched upon. Nor did I hear the Colonel to an end even of that which he was willing to disclose; for Mr. Henry, having for some while been plunged in a brown study, rose at last from his seat and (reminding the Colonel there were matters that he must attend to) bade me follow him immediately to the office.

Once there, he sought no longer to dissemble his concern, walking to and fro in the room with a contorted face, and passing his hand repeatedly upon his brow.

"We have some business," he began at last; and there broke off, declared we must have wine, and sent for a magnum of the best. This was extremely foreign to his habits; and what was still more so, when the wine had come, he gulped down one glass upon another like a man careless of appearances. But the drink steadied him.

"You will scarce be surprised, Mackellar," says he, "when I tell you that my brother—whose safety we are all rejoiced to learn—stands in some need of money."

I told him I had misdoubted as much; but the time was not very fortunate, as the stock was low.

"Not mine," said he. "There is the money for the mortgage."

I reminded him it was Mrs. Henry's.

"I will be answerable to my wife," he cried violently.

"And then," said I, "there is the mortgage."

"I know," said he; "it is on that I would consult you."

I showed him how unfortunate a time it was to divert this money from its destination; and how, by so doing, we must lose the profit of our past economies, and plunge back the estate into the mire. I even took the liberty to plead with him; and when he still opposed me with a shake of the head and a bitter dogged smile, my zeal quite carried me beyond my place. "This is midsummer madness," cried I; "and I for one will be no party to it."

"You speak as though I did it for my pleasure," says he. "But I have a child now; and, besides, I love order; and to say the honest truth, Mackellar, I had begun to take a pride in the estates." He gloomed for a moment. "But what would you have?" he went on. "Nothing is mine, nothing. This day's news has knocked the bottom out of my life. I have only the name and the shadow of things—only the shadow; there is no substance in my rights."

"They will prove substantial enough before a court," said I.

He looked at me with a burning eye, and seemed to repress the word upon his lips; and I repented what I had said, for I saw that while he spoke of the estate he had still a side-thought to his marriage. And then, of a sudden, he twitched the letter from his pocket, where it lay all crumpled, smoothed it violently on the table, and read these words to me with a trembling tongue: "'My dear Jacob'—This is how he begins!" cries he—"'My dear Jacob, I once called you so, you may remember; and you have now done the business, and flung my heels as high as Criffel.' What do you think of that, Mackellar," says he, "from an only brother? I declare to God I liked him very well; I was always staunch to him; and this is how he writes! But I will not sit down under the imputation"—walking to and fro—"I am as good as he; I am a better man than he, I call on God to prove it! I cannot give him all the monstrous sum he asks; he knows the estate to be incompetent; but I will give him what I have, and it is more than he expects. I have borne all this too long. See what he writes further on; read it for yourself: 'I know you are a niggardly dog.' A niggardly dog! I niggardly? Is that true, Mackellar? You think it is?" I really thought he would have struck me at that. "Oh, you all think so! Well, you shall see, and he shall see, and God shall see. If I ruin the estate and go barefoot, I shall stuff this bloodsucker. Let him ask all—all, and he shall have it! It is all his by rights. Ah!" he cried, "and I foresaw all this, and worse, when he would not let me go." He poured out another glass of wine, and was about to carry it to his lips, when I made so bold as to lay a finger on his arm. He stopped a moment. "You are right," said he, and flung glass and all in the fireplace. "Come, let us count the money."

I durst no longer oppose him; indeed, I was very much affected by the sight of so much disorder in a man usually so controlled; and we sat down together, counted the money, and made it up in packets for the greater ease of Colonel Burke, who was to be the bearer. This done, Mr. Henry returned to the hall, where he and my old lord sat all night through with their guest.

A little before dawn I was called and set out with the Colonel. He would scarce have liked a less responsible convoy, for he was a man who valued himself; nor could we afford him one more dignified, for Mr. Henry must not appear with the freetraders. It was a very bitter morning of wind, and as we went down through the long shrubbery the Colonel held himself muffled in his cloak.

"Sir," said I, "this is a great sum of money that your friend requires. I must suppose his necessities to be very great."

"We must suppose so," says he, I thought drily; but perhaps it was the cloak about his mouth.

"I am only a servant of the family," said I. "You may deal openly with me. I think we are likely to get little good by him?"

"My dear man," said the Colonel, "Ballantrae is a gentleman of the most eminent natural abilities, and a man that I admire, and that I revere, to the very ground he treads on." And then he seemed to me to pause like one in a difficulty.

"But for all that," said I, "we are likely to get little good by him?"

"Sure, and you can have it your own way, my dear man," says the Colonel.

By this time we had come to the side of the creek, where the boat awaited him. "Well," said he, "I am sure I am very much your debtor for all your civility, Mr. Whatever-your-name-is; and just as a last word, and since you show so much intelligent interest, I will mention a small circumstance that may be of use to the family. For I believe my friend omitted to mention that he has the largest pension on the Scots Fund of any refugee in Paris; and it's the more disgraceful, sir," cries the Colonel, warming, "because there's not one dirty penny for myself."

He cocked his hat at me, as if I had been to blame for this partiality; then changed again into his usual swaggering civility, shook me by the hand, and set off down to the boat, with the money under his arms, and whistling as he went the pathetic air of Shule Aroon. It was the first time I had heard that tune; I was to hear it again, words and all, as you shall learn, but I remember how that little stave of it ran in my head after the freetraders had bade him "Wheesht, in the deil's name," and the grating of the oars had taken its place, and I stood and watched the dawn creeping on the sea, and the boat drawing away, and the lugger lying with her foresail backed awaiting it.

The gap made in our money was a sore embarrassment, and, among other consequences, it had this: that I must ride to Edinburgh, and there raise a new loan on very questionable terms to keep the old afloat; and was thus, for close upon three weeks, absent from the house of Durrisdeer.

What passed in the interval I had none to tell me, but I found Mrs. Henry, upon my return, much changed in her demeanour. The old talks with my lord for the most part pretermitted; a certain deprecation visible towards her husband, to whom I thought she addressed herself more often; and, for one thing, she was now greatly wrapped up in Miss Katharine. You would think the change was agreeable to Mr. Henry; no such matter! To the contrary, every circumstance of alteration was a stab to him; he read in each the avowal of her truant fancies. That constancy to the Master of which she was proud while she supposed him dead, she had to blush for now she knew he was alive, and these blushes were the hated spring of her new conduct. I am to conceal no truth; and I will here say plainly, I think this was the period in which Mr. Henry showed the worst. He contained himself, indeed, in public; but there was a deep-seated irritation visible underneath. With me, from whom he had less concealment, he was often grossly unjust, and even for his wife he would sometimes have a sharp retort: perhaps when she had ruffled him with some unwonted kindness; perhaps upon no tangible occasion, the mere habitual tenor of the man's annoyance bursting spontaneously forth. When he would thus forget himself (a thing so strangely out of keeping with the terms of their relation), there went a shook through the whole company, and the pair would look upon each other in a kind of pained amazement.

All the time, too, while he was injuring himself by this defect of temper, he was hurting his position by a silence, of which I scarce know whether to say it was the child of generosity or pride. The freetraders came again and again, bringing messengers from the Master, and none departed empty-handed. I never durst reason with Mr. Henry; he gave what was asked of him in a kind of noble rage. Perhaps because he knew he was by nature inclining to the parsimonious, he took a backforemost pleasure in the recklessness with which he supplied his brother's exigence. Perhaps the falsity of the position would have spurred a humbler man into the same excess. But the estate (if I may say so) groaned under it; our daily expenses were shorn lower and lower; the stables were emptied, all but four roadsters; servants were discharged, which raised a dreadful murmuring in the country, and heated up the old disfavour upon Mr. Henry; and at last the yearly visit to Edinburgh must be discontinued.

This was in 1756. You are to suppose that for seven years this bloodsucker had been drawing the life's blood from Durrisdeer, and that all this time my patron had held his peace. It was an effect of devilish malice in the Master that he addressed Mr. Henry alone upon the matter of his demands, and there was never a word to my lord. The family had looked on, wondering at our economies. They had lamented, I have no doubt, that my patron had become so great a miser—a fault always despicable, but in the young abhorrent, and Mr. Henry was not yet thirty years of age. Still, he had managed the business of Durrisdeer almost from a boy; and they bore with these changes in a silence as proud and bitter as his own, until the coping-stone of the Edinburgh visit.

At this time I believe my patron and his wife were rarely together, save at meals. Immediately on the back of Colonel Burke's announcement Mrs. Henry made palpable advances; you might say she had laid a sort of timid court to her husband, different, indeed, from her former manner of unconcern and distance. I never had the heart to blame Mr. Henry because he recoiled from these advances; nor yet to censure the wife, when she was cut to the quick by their rejection. But the result was an entire estrangement, so that (as I say) they rarely spoke, except at meals. Even the matter of the Edinburgh visit was first broached at table, and it chanced that Mrs. Henry was that day ailing and querulous. She had no sooner understood her husband's meaning than the red flew in her face.

"At last," she cried, "this is too much! Heaven knows what pleasure I have in my life, that I should be denied my only consolation. These shameful proclivities must be trod down; we are already a mark and an eyesore in the neighbourhood. I will not endure this fresh insanity."

"I cannot afford it," says Mr. Henry.

"Afford?" she cried. "For shame! But I have money of my own."

"That is all mine, madam, by marriage," he snarled, and instantly left the room.

My old lord threw up his hands to Heaven, and he and his daughter, withdrawing to the chimney, gave me a broad hint to be gone. I found Mr. Henry in his usual retreat, the steward's room, perched on the end of the table, and plunging his penknife in it with a very ugly countenance.

"Mr. Henry," said I, "you do yourself too much injustice, and it is time this should cease."

"Oh!" cries he, "nobody minds here. They think it only natural. I have shameful proclivities. I am a niggardly dog," and he drove his knife up to the hilt. "But I will show that fellow," he cried with an oath, "I will show him which is the more generous."

"This is no generosity," said I; "this is only pride."

"Do you think I want morality?" he asked.

I thought he wanted help, and I should give it him, willy-nilly; and no sooner was Mrs. Henry gone to her room than I presented myself at her door and sought admittance.

She openly showed her wonder. "What do you want with me, Mr. Mackellar?" said she.

"The Lord knows, madam," says I, "I have never troubled you before with any freedoms; but this thing lies too hard upon my conscience, and it will out. Is it possible that two people can be so blind as you and my lord? and have lived all these years with a noble gentleman like Mr. Henry, and understand so little of his nature?"

"What does this mean?" she cried.

"Do you not know where his money goes to? his—and yours—and the money for the very wine he does not drink at table?" I went on. "To Paris—to that man! Eight thousand pounds has he had of us in seven years, and my patron fool enough to keep it secret!"

"Eight thousand pounds!" she repeated. "It in impossible; the estate is not sufficient."

"God knows how we have sweated farthings to produce it," said I. "But eight thousand and sixty is the sum, beside odd shillings. And if you can think my patron miserly after that, this shall be my last interference."

"You need say no more, Mr. Mackellar," said she. "You have done most properly in what you too modestly call your interference. I am much to blame; you must think me indeed a very unobservant wife" (looking upon me with a strange smile), "but I shall put this right at once. The Master was always of a very thoughtless nature; but his heart is excellent; he is the soul of generosity. I shall write to him myself. You cannot think how you have pained me by this communication."

"Indeed, madam, I had hoped to have pleased you," said I, for I raged to see her still thinking of the Master.

"And pleased," said she, "and pleased me of course."

That same day (I will not say but what I watched) I had the satisfaction to see Mr. Henry come from his wife's room in a state most unlike himself; for his face was all bloated with weeping, and yet he seemed to me to walk upon the air. By this, I was sure his wife had made him full amends for once. "Ah," thought I to myself, "I have done a brave stroke this day."

On the morrow, as I was seated at my books, Mr. Henry came in softly behind me, took me by the shoulders, and shook me in a manner of playfulness. "I find you are a faithless fellow after all," says he, which was his only reference to my part; but the tone he spoke in was more to me than any eloquence of protestation. Nor was this all I had effected; for when the next messenger came (as he did not long afterwards) from the Master, he got nothing away with him but a letter. For some while back it had been I myself who had conducted these affairs; Mr. Henry not setting pen to paper, and I only in the dryest and most formal terms. But this letter I did not even see; it would scarce be pleasant reading, for Mr. Henry felt he had his wife behind him for once, and I observed, on the day it was despatched, he had a very gratified expression.

Things went better now in the family, though it could scarce be pretended they went well. There was now at least no misconception; there was kindness upon all sides; and I believe my patron and his wife might again have drawn together if he could but have pocketed his pride, and she forgot (what was the ground of all) her brooding on another man. It is wonderful how a private thought leaks out; it is wonderful to me now how we should all have followed the current of her sentiments; and though she bore herself quietly, and had a very even disposition, yet we should have known whenever her fancy ran to Paris. And would not any one have thought that my disclosure must have rooted up that idol? I think there is the devil in women: all these years passed, never a sight of the man, little enough kindness to remember (by all accounts) even while she had him, the notion of his death intervening, his heartless rapacity laid bare to her; that all should not do, and she must still keep the best place in her heart for this accursed fellow, is a thing to make a plain man rage. I had never much natural sympathy for the passion of love; but this unreason in my patron's wife disgusted me outright with the whole matter. I remember checking a maid because she sang some bairnly kickshaw while my mind was thus engaged; and my asperity brought about my ears the enmity of all the petticoats about the house; of which I reeked very little, but it amused Mr. Henry, who rallied me much upon our joint unpopularity. It is strange enough (for my own mother was certainly one of the salt of the earth, and my Aunt Dickson, who paid my fees at the University, a very notable woman), but I have never had much toleration for the female sex, possibly not much understanding; and being far from a bold man, I have ever shunned their company. Not only do I see no cause to regret this diffidence in myself, but have invariably remarked the most unhappy consequences follow those who were less wise. So much I thought proper to set down, lest I show myself unjust to Mrs. Henry. And, besides, the remark arose naturally, on a re-perusal of the letter which was the next step in these affairs, and reached me, to my sincere astonishment, by a private hand, some week or so after the departure of the last messenger.

Letter from Colonel Burke (afterwards Chevalier) to Mr. Mackellar.
Troyes in Champagne,
July 12, 1756

My Dear Sir,—You will doubtless be surprised to receive a communication from one so little known to you; but on the occasion I had the good fortune to rencounter you at Durrisdeer, I remarked you for a young man of a solid gravity of character: a qualification which I profess

I admire and revere next to natural genius or the bold chivalrous spirit of the soldier. I was, besides, interested in the noble family which you have the honour to serve, or (to speak more by the book) to be the humble and respected friend of; and a conversation I had the pleasure to have with you very early in the morning has remained much upon my mind.

Being the other day in Paris, on a visit from this famous city, where I am in garrison, I took occasion to inquire your name (which I profess I had forgot) at my friend, the Master of B.; and a fair opportunity occurring, I write to inform you of what's new.

The Master of B. (when we had last some talk of him together) was in receipt, as I think I then told you, of a highly advantageous pension on the Scots Fund. He next received a company, and was soon after advanced to a regiment of his own. My dear sir, I do not offer to explain this circumstance; any more than why I myself, who have rid at the right hand of Princes, should be fubbed off with a pair of colours and sent to rot in a hole at the bottom of the province. Accustomed as I am to Courts, I cannot but feel it is no atmosphere for a plain soldier; and I could never hope to advance by similar means, even could I stoop to the endeavour. But our friend has a particular aptitude to succeed by the means of ladies; and if all be true that I have heard, he enjoyed a remarkable protection. It is like this turned against him; for when I had the honour to shake him by the hand, he was but newly released from the Bastille, where he had been cast on a sealed letter; and, though now released, has both lost his regiment and his pension. My dear sir, the loyalty of a plain Irishman will ultimately succeed in the place of craft; as I am sure a gentleman of your probity will agree.

Now, sir, the Master is a man whose genius I admire beyond expression, and, besides, he is my friend; but I thought a little word of this revolution in his fortunes would not come amiss, for, in my opinion, the man's desperate. He spoke, when I saw him, of a trip to India (whither I am myself in some hope of accompanying my illustrious countryman, Mr. Lally); but for this he would require (as I understood) more money than was readily at his command. You may have heard a military proverb: that it is a good thing to make a bridge of gold to a flying enemy? I trust you will take my meaning and I subscribe myself, with proper respects to my Lord Durrisdeer, to his son, and to the beauteous Mrs. Durie,

My dear Sir,
Your obedient humble servant,
Francis Burke.

This missive I carried at once to Mr. Henry; and I think there was but the one thought between the two of us: that it had come a week too late. I made haste to send an answer to Colonel Burke, in which I begged him, if he should see the Master, to assure him his next messenger would be attended to. But with all my haste I was not in time to avert what was impending; the arrow had been drawn, it must now fly. I could almost doubt the power of Providence (and certainly His will) to stay the issue of events; and it is a strange thought, how many of us had been storing up the elements of this catastrophe, for how long a time, and with how blind an ignorance of what we did.

From the coming of the Colonel's letter, I had a spyglass in my room, began to drop questions to the tenant folk, and as there was no great secrecy observed, and the freetrade (in our part) went by force as much as stealth, I had soon got together a knowledge of the signals in use, and knew pretty well to an hour when any messenger might be expected. I say, I questioned the tenants; for with the traders themselves, desperate blades that went habitually armed, I could never bring myself to meddle willingly. Indeed, by what proved in the sequel an unhappy chance, I was an object of scorn to some of these braggadocios; who had not only gratified me with a nickname, but catching me one night upon a by-path, and being all (as they would have said) somewhat merry, had caused me to dance for their diversion. The method employed was that of cruelly chipping at my toes with naked cutlasses, shouting at the same time "Square-Toes"; and though they did me no bodily mischief, I was none the less deplorably affected, and was indeed for several days confined to my bed: a scandal on the state of Scotland on which no comment is required.

It happened on the afternoon of November 7th, in this same unfortunate year, that I espied, during my walk, the smoke of a beacon fire upon the Muckleross. It was drawing near time for my return; but the uneasiness upon my spirits was that day so great that I must burst through the thickets to the edge of what they call the Craig Head. The sun was already down, but there was still a broad light in the west, which showed me some of the smugglers treading out their signal fire upon the Ross, and in the bay the lugger lying with her sails brailed up. She was plainly but new come to anchor, and yet the skiff was already lowered and pulling for the landing-place at the end of the long shrubbery. And this I knew could signify but one thing, the coming of a messenger for Durrisdeer.

I laid aside the remainder of my terrors, clambered down the brae—a place I had never ventured through before, and was hid among the shore-side thickets in time to see the boat touch. Captain Crail himself was steering, a thing not usual; by his side there sat a passenger; and the men gave way with difficulty, being hampered with near upon half a dozen portmanteaus, great and small. But the business of landing was briskly carried through; and presently the baggage was all tumbled on shore, the boat on its return voyage to the lugger, and the passenger standing alone upon the point of rock, a tall slender figure of a gentleman, habited in black, with a sword by his side and a walking-cane upon his wrist. As he so stood, he waved the cane to Captain Crail by way of salutation, with something both of grace and mockery that wrote the gesture deeply on my mind.

No sooner was the boat away with my sworn enemies than I took a sort of half courage, came forth to the margin of the thicket, and there halted again, my mind being greatly pulled about between natural diffidence and a dark foreboding of the truth. Indeed, I might have stood there swithering all night, had not the stranger turned, spied me through the mists, which were beginning to fall, and waved and cried on me to draw near. I did so with a heart like lead.

"Here, my good man," said he, in the English accent, "there are some things for Durrisdeer."

I was now near enough to see him, a very handsome figure and countenance, swarthy, lean, long, with a quick, alert, black look, as of one who was a fighter, and accustomed to command; upon one cheek he had a mole, not unbecoming; a large diamond sparkled on his hand; his clothes, although of the one hue, were of a French and foppish design; his ruffles, which he wore longer than common, of exquisite lace; and I wondered the more to see him in such a guise when he was but newly landed from a dirty smuggling lugger. At the same time he had a better look at me, toised me a second time sharply, and then smiled.

"I wager, my friend," says he, "that I know both your name and your nickname. I divined these very clothes upon your hand of writing, Mr. Mackellar."

At these words I fell to shaking.

"Oh," says he, "you need not be afraid of me. I bear no malice for your tedious letters; and it is my purpose to employ you a good deal. You may call me Mr. Bally: it is the name I have assumed; or rather (since I am addressing so great a precision) it is so I have curtailed my own. Come now, pick up that and that"—indicating two of the portmanteaus. "That will be as much as you are fit to bear, and the rest can very well wait. Come, lose no more time, if you please."

His tone was so cutting that I managed to do as he bid by a sort of instinct, my mind being all the time quite lost. No sooner had I picked up the portmanteaus than he turned his back and marched off through the long shrubbery, where it began already to be dusk, for the wood is thick and evergreen. I followed behind, loaded almost to the dust, though I profess I was not conscious of the burthen; being swallowed up in the monstrosity of this return, and my mind flying like a weaver's shuttle.

On a sudden I set the portmanteaus to the ground and halted. He turned and looked back at me.

"Well?" said he.

"You are the Master of Ballantrae?"

"You will do me the justice to observe," says he, "I have made no secret with the astute Mackellar."

"And in the name of God," cries I, "what brings you here? Go back, while it is yet time."

"I thank you," said he. "Your master has chosen this way, and not I; but since he has made the choice, he (and you also) must abide by the result. And now pick up these things of mine, which you have set down in a very boggy place, and attend to that which I have made your business."

But I had no thought now of obedience; I came straight up to him. "If nothing will move you to go back," said I; "though, sure, under all the circumstances, any Christian or even any gentleman would scruple to go forward . . . "

"These are gratifying expressions," he threw in.

"If nothing will move you to go back," I continued, "there are still some decencies to be observed. Wait here with your baggage, and I will go forward and prepare your family. Your father is an old man; and . . . " I stumbled . . . "there are decencies to be observed."

"Truly," said he, "this Mackellar improves upon acquaintance. But look you here, my man, and understand it once for all—you waste your breath upon me, and I go my own way with inevitable motion."

"Ah!" says I. "Is that so? We shall see then!"

And I turned and took to my heels for Durrisdeer. He clutched at me and cried out angrily, and then I believe I heard him laugh, and then I am certain he pursued me for a step or two, and (I suppose) desisted. One thing at least is sure, that I came but a few minutes later to the door of the great house, nearly strangled for the lack of breath, but quite alone. Straight up the stair I ran, and burst into the hall, and stopped before the family without the power of speech; but I must have carried my story in my looks, for they rose out of their places and stared on me like changelings.

"He has come," I panted out at last.

"He?" said Mr. Henry.

"Himself," said I.

"My son?" cried my lord. "Imprudent, imprudent boy! Oh, could he not stay where he was safe!"

Never a word says Mrs. Henry; nor did I look at her, I scarce knew why.

"Well," said Mr. Henry, with a very deep breath, "and where is he?"

"I left him in the long shrubbery," said I.

"Take me to him," said he.

So we went out together, he and I, without another word from any one; and in the midst of the gravelled plot encountered the Master strolling up, whistling as he came, and beating the air with his cane. There was still light enough overhead to recognise, though not to read, a countenance.

"Ah! Jacob," says the Master. "So here is Esau back."

"James," says Mr. Henry, "for God's sake, call me by my name. I will not pretend that I am glad to see you; but I would fain make you as welcome as I can in the house of our fathers."

"Or in my house? or yours?" says the Master. "Which were you about to say? But this is an old sore, and we need not rub it. If you would not share with me in Paris, I hope you will yet scarce deny your elder brother a corner of the fire at Durrisdeer?"

"That is very idle speech," replied Mr. Henry. "And you understand the power of your position excellently well."

"Why, I believe I do," said the other with a little laugh. And this, though they had never touched hands, was (as we may say) the end of the brothers' meeting; for at this the Master turned to me and bade me fetch his baggage.

I, on my side, turned to Mr. Henry for a confirmation; perhaps with some defiance.

"As long as the Master is here, Mr. Mackellar, you will very much oblige me by regarding his wishes as you would my own," says Mr. Henry. "We are constantly troubling you: will you be so good as send one of the servants?"—with an accent on the word.

If this speech were anything at all, it was surely a well-deserved reproof upon the stranger; and yet, so devilish was his impudence, he twisted it the other way.

"And shall we be common enough to say 'Sneck up'?" inquires he softly, looking upon me sideways.

Had a kingdom depended on the act, I could not have trusted myself in words; even to call a servant was beyond me; I had rather serve the man myself than speak; and I turned away in silence and went into the long shrubbery, with a heart full of anger and despair. It was dark under the trees, and I walked before me and forgot what business I was come upon, till I near broke my shin on the portmanteaus. Then it was that I remarked a strange particular; for whereas I had before carried both and scarce observed it, it was now as much as I could do to manage one. And this, as it forced me to make two journeys, kept me the longer from the hall.

When I got there, the business of welcome was over long ago; the company was already at supper; and by an oversight that cut me to the quick, my place had been forgotten. I had seen one side of the Master's return; now I was to see the other. It was he who first remarked my coming in and standing back (as I did) in some annoyance. He jumped from his seat.

"And if I have not got the good Mackellar's place!" cries he. "John, lay another for Mr. Bally;

I protest he will disturb no one, and your table is big enough for all."

I could scarce credit my ears, nor yet my senses, when he took me by the shoulders and thrust me, laughing, into my own place—such an affectionate playfulness was in his voice. And while John laid the fresh place for him (a thing on which he still insisted), he went and leaned on his father's chair and looked down upon him, and the old man turned about and looked upwards on his son, with such a pleasant mutual tenderness that I could have carried my hand to my head in mere amazement.

Yet all was of a piece. Never a harsh word fell from him, never a sneer showed upon his lip. He had laid aside even his cutting English accent, and spoke with the kindly Scots' tongue, that set a value on affectionate words; and though his manners had a graceful elegance mighty foreign to our ways in Durrisdeer, it was still a homely courtliness, that did not shame but flattered us. All that, he did throughout the meal, indeed, drinking wine with me with a notable respect, turning about for a pleasant word with John, fondling his father's hand, breaking into little merry tales of his adventures, calling up the past with happy reference—all he did was so becoming, and himself so handsome, that I could scarce wonder if my lord and Mrs. Henry sat about the board with radiant faces, or if John waited behind with dropping tears.

As soon as supper was over, Mrs. Henry rose to withdraw.

"This was never your way, Alison," said he.

"It is my way now," she replied: which was notoriously false, "and I will give you a good-night, James, and a welcome—from the dead," said she, and her voice dropped and trembled.

Poor Mr. Henry, who had made rather a heavy figure through the meal, was more concerned than ever; pleased to see his wife withdraw, and yet half displeased, as he thought upon the cause of it; and the next moment altogether dashed by the fervour of her speech.

On my part, I thought I was now one too many; and was stealing after Mrs. Henry, when the Master saw me.

"Now, Mr. Mackellar," says he, "I take this near on an unfriendliness. I cannot have you go: this is to make a stranger of the prodigal son; and let me remind you where—in his own father's house! Come, sit ye down, and drink another glass with Mr. Bally."

"Ay, ay, Mr. Mackellar," says my lord, "we must not make a stranger either of him or you. I have been telling my son," he added, his voice brightening as usual on the word, "how much we valued all your friendly service."

So I sat there, silent, till my usual hour; and might have been almost deceived in the man's nature but for one passage, in which his perfidy appeared too plain. Here was the passage; of which, after what he knows of the brothers' meeting, the reader shall consider for himself. Mr. Henry sitting somewhat dully, in spite of his best endeavours to carry things before my lord, up jumps the Master, passes about the board, and claps his brother on the shoulder.

"Come, come, Hairry lad," says he, with a broad accent such as they must have used together when they were boys, "you must not be downcast because your brother has come home. All's yours, that's sure enough, and little I grudge it you. Neither must you grudge me my place beside my father's fire."

"And that is too true, Henry," says my old lord with a little frown, a thing rare with him. "You have been the elder brother of the parable in the good sense; you must be careful of the other."

"I am easily put in the wrong," said Mr. Henry.

"Who puts you in the wrong?" cried my lord, I thought very tartly for so mild a man. "You have earned my gratitude and your brother's many thousand times: you may count on its endurance; and let that suffice."

"Ay, Harry, that you may," said the Master; and I thought Mr. Henry looked at him with a kind of wildness in his eye.

On all the miserable business that now followed, I have four questions that I asked myself often at the time and ask myself still:—Was the man moved by a particular sentiment against Mr. Henry? or by what he thought to be his interest? or by a mere delight in cruelty such as cats display and theologians tell us of the devil? or by what he would have called love? My common opinion halts among the three first; but perhaps there lay at the spring of his behaviour an element of all. As thus:—Animosity to Mr. Henry would explain his hateful usage of him when they were alone; the interests he came to serve would explain his very different attitude before my lord; that and some spice of a design of gallantry, his care to stand well with Mrs. Henry; and the pleasure of malice for itself, the pains he was continually at to mingle and oppose these lines of conduct.

Partly because I was a very open friend to my patron, partly because in my letters to Paris I had often given myself some freedom of remonstrance, I was included in his diabolical amusement. When I was alone with him, he pursued me with sneers; before the family he used me with the extreme of friendly condescension. This was not only painful in itself; not only did it put me continually in the wrong; but there was in it an element of insult indescribable. That he should thus leave me out in his dissimulation, as though even my testimony were too despicable to be considered, galled me to the blood. But what it was to me is not worth notice. I make but memorandum of it here; and chiefly for this reason, that it had one good result, and gave me the quicker sense of Mr. Henry's martyrdom.

It was on him the burthen fell. How was he to respond to the public advances of one who never lost a chance of gibing him in private? How was he to smile back on the deceiver and the insulter? He was condemned to seem ungracious. He was condemned to silence. Had he been less proud, had he spoken, who would have credited the truth? The acted calumny had done its work; my lord and Mrs. Henry were the daily witnesses of what went on; they could have sworn in court that the Master was a model of long-suffering good-nature, and Mr. Henry a pattern of jealousy and thanklessness. And ugly enough as these must have appeared in any one, they seemed tenfold uglier in Mr. Henry; for who could forget that the Master lay in peril of his life, and that he had already lost his mistress, his title, and his fortune?

"Henry, will you ride with me?" asks the Master one day.

And Mr. Henry, who had been goaded by the man all morning, raps out: "I will not."

"I sometimes wish you would be kinder, Henry," says the other, wistfully.

I give this for a specimen; but such scenes befell continually. Small wonder if Mr. Henry was blamed; small wonder if I fretted myself into something near upon a bilious fever; nay, and at the mere recollection feel a bitterness in my blood.

Sure, never in this world was a more diabolical contrivance: so perfidious, so simple, so impossible to combat. And yet I think again, and I think always, Mrs. Henry might have read between the lines; she might have had more knowledge of her husband's nature; after all these years of marriage she might have commanded or captured his confidence. And my old lord, too—that very watchful gentleman—where was all his observation? But, for one thing, the deceit was practised by a master hand, and might have gulled an angel. For another (in the case of Mrs. Henry), I have observed there are no persons so far away as those who are both married and estranged, so that they seem out of ear-shot or to have no common tongue. For a third (in the case of both of these spectators), they were blinded by old ingrained predilection. And for a fourth, the risk the Master was supposed to stand in (supposed, I say—you will soon hear why) made it seem the more ungenerous to criticise; and, keeping them in a perpetual tender solicitude about his life, blinded them the more effectually to his faults.

It was during this time that I perceived most clearly the effect of manner, and was led to lament most deeply the plainness of my own. Mr. Henry had the essence of a gentleman; when he was moved, when there was any call of circumstance, he could play his part with dignity and spirit; but in the day's commerce (it is idle to deny it) he fell short of the ornamental. The Master (on the other hand) had never a movement but it commanded him. So it befell that when the one appeared gracious and the other ungracious, every trick of their bodies seemed to call out confirmation. Not that alone: but the more deeply Mr. Henry floundered in his brother's toils, the more clownish he grew; and the more the Master enjoyed his spiteful entertainment, the more engagingly, the more smilingly, he went! So that the plot, by its own scope and progress, furthered and confirmed itself.

It was one of the man's arts to use the peril in which (as I say) he was supposed to stand. He spoke of it to those who loved him with a gentle pleasantry, which made it the more touching. To Mr. Henry he used it as a cruel weapon of offence. I remember his laying his finger on the clean lozenge of the painted window one day when we three were alone together in the hall. "Here went your lucky guinea, Jacob," said he. And when Mr. Henry only looked upon him darkly, "Oh!" he added, "you need not look such impotent malice, my good fly. You can be rid of your spider when you please. How long, O Lord? When are you to be wrought to the point of a denunciation, scrupulous brother? It is one of my interests in this dreary hole. I ever loved experiment." Still Mr. Henry only stared upon him with a grooming brow, and a changed colour; and at last the Master broke out in a laugh and clapped him on the shoulder, calling him a sulky dog. At this my patron leaped back with a gesture I thought very dangerous; and I must suppose the Master thought so too, for he looked the least in the world discountenance, and I do not remember him again to have laid hands on Mr. Henry.

But though he had his peril always on his lips in the one way or the other, I thought his conduct strangely incautious, and began to fancy the Government—who had set a price upon his head—was gone sound asleep. I will not deny I was tempted with the wish to denounce him; but two thoughts withheld me: one, that if he were thus to end his life upon an honourable scaffold, the man would be canonised for good in the minds of his father and my patron's wife; the other, that if I was anyway mingled in the matter, Mr. Henry himself would scarce escape some glancings of suspicion. And in the meanwhile our enemy went in and out more than I could have thought possible, the fact that he was home again was buzzed about all the country-side, and yet he was never stirred. Of all these so-many and so-different persons who were acquainted with his presence, none had the least greed—as I used to say in my annoyance—or the least loyalty; and the man rode here and there—fully more welcome, considering the lees of old unpopularity, than Mr. Henry—and considering the freetraders, far safer than myself.

Not but what he had a trouble of his own; and this, as it brought about the gravest consequences, I must now relate. The reader will scarce have forgotten Jessie Broun; her way of life was much among the smuggling party; Captain Crail himself was of her intimates; and she had early word of Mr. Bally's presence at the house. In my opinion, she had long ceased to care two straws for the Master's person; but it was become her habit to connect herself continually with the Master's name; that was the ground of all her play-acting; and so now, when he was back, she thought she owed it to herself to grow a haunter of the neighbourhood of Durrisdeer. The Master could scarce go abroad but she was there in wait for him; a scandalous figure of a woman, not often sober; hailing him wildly as "her bonny laddie," quoting pedlar's poetry, and, as I receive the story, even seeking to weep upon his neck. I own I rubbed my hands over this persecution; but the Master, who laid so much upon others, was himself the least patient of men. There were strange scenes enacted in the policies. Some say he took his cane to her, and Jessie fell back upon her former weapons—stones. It is certain at least that he made a motion to Captain Crail to have the woman trepanned, and that the Captain refused the proposition with uncommon vehemence. And the end of the matter was victory for Jessie. Money was got together; an interview took place, in which my proud gentleman must consent to be kissed and wept upon; and the woman was set up in a public of her own, somewhere on Solway side (but I forget where), and, by the only news I ever had of it, extremely ill-frequented.

This is to look forward. After Jessie had been but a little while upon his heels, the Master comes to me one day in the steward's office, and with more civility than usual, "Mackellar," says he, "there is a damned crazy wench comes about here. I cannot well move in the matter myself, which brings me to you. Be so good as to see to it: the men must have a strict injunction to drive the wench away."

"Sir," said I, trembling a little, "you can do your own dirty errands for yourself."

He said not a word to that, and left the room.

Presently came Mr. Henry. "Here is news!" cried he. "It seems all is not enough, and you must add to my wretchedness. It seems you have insulted Mr. Bally."

"Under your kind favour, Mr. Henry," said I, "it was he that insulted me, and, as I think, grossly. But I may have been careless of your position when I spoke; and if you think so when you know all, my dear patron, you have but to say the word. For you I would obey in any point whatever, even to sin, God pardon me!" And thereupon I told him what had passed.

Mr. Henry smiled to himself; a grimmer smile I never witnessed. "You did exactly well," said he. "He shall drink his Jessie Broun to the dregs." And then, spying the Master outside, he opened the window, and crying to him by the name of Mr. Bally, asked him to step up and have a word.

"James," said he, when our persecutor had come in and closed the door behind him, looking at me with a smile, as if he thought I was to be humbled, "you brought me a complaint against Mr. Mackellar, into which I have inquired. I need not tell you I would always take his word against yours; for we are alone, and I am going to use something of your own freedom. Mr. Mackellar is a gentleman I value; and you must contrive, so long as you are under this roof, to bring yourself into no more collisions with one whom I will support at any possible cost to me or mine. As for the errand upon which you came to him, you must deliver yourself from the consequences of your own cruelty, and, none of my servants shall be at all employed in such a case."

"My father's servants, I believe," says the Master.

"Go to him with this tale," said Mr. Henry.

The Master grew very white. He pointed at me with his finger. "I want that man discharged," he said.

"He shall not be," said Mr. Henry.

"You shall pay pretty dear for this," says the Master.

"I have paid so dear already for a wicked brother," said Mr. Henry, "that I am bankrupt even of fears. You have no place left where you can strike me."

"I will show you about that," says the Master, and went softly away.

"What will he do next, Mackellar?" cries Mr. Henry.

"Let me go away," said I. "My dear patron, let me go away; I am but the beginning of fresh sorrows."

"Would you leave me quite alone?" said he.

We were not long in suspense as to the nature of the new assault. Up to that hour the Master had played a very close game with Mrs. Henry; avoiding pointedly to be alone with her, which I took at the time for an effect of decency, but now think to be a most insidious art; meeting her, you may say, at meal-time only; and behaving, when he did so, like an affectionate brother. Up to that hour, you may say he had scarce directly interfered between Mr. Henry and his wife; except in so far as he had manoeuvred the one quite forth from the good graces of the other. Now all that was to be changed; but whether really in revenge, or because he was wearying of Durrisdeer and looked about for some diversion, who but the devil shall decide?

From that hour, at least, began the siege of Mrs. Henry; a thing so deftly carried on that I scarce know if she was aware of it herself, and that her husband must look on in silence. The first parallel was opened (as was made to appear) by accident. The talk fell, as it did often, on the exiles in France; so it glided to the matter of their songs.

"There is one," says the Master, "if you are curious in these matters, that has always seemed to me very moving. The poetry is harsh; and yet, perhaps because of my situation, it has always found the way to my heart. It is supposed to be sung, I should tell you, by an exile's sweetheart; and represents perhaps, not so much the truth of what she is thinking, as the truth of what he hopes of her, poor soul! in these far lands." And here the Master sighed, "I protest it is a pathetic sight when a score of rough Irish, all common sentinels, get to this song; and you may see, by their falling tears, how it strikes home to them. It goes thus, father," says he, very adroitly taking my lord for his listener, "and if I cannot get to the end of it, you must think it is a common case with us exiles." And thereupon he struck up the same air as I had heard the Colonel whistle; but now to words, rustic indeed, yet most pathetically setting forth a poor girl's aspirations for an exiled lover; of which one verse indeed (or something like it) still sticks by me:—

O, I will dye my petticoat red,
With my dear boy I'll beg my bread,
Though all my friends should wish me dead,
    For Willie among the rushes, O!

He sang it well, even as a song; but he did better yet a performer. I have heard famous actors, when there was not a dry eye in the Edinburgh theatre; a great wonder to behold; but no more wonderful than how the Master played upon that little ballad, and on those who heard him, like an instrument, and seemed now upon the point of failing, and now to conquer his distress, so that words and music seemed to pour out of his own heart and his own past, and to be aimed directly at Mrs. Henry. And his art went further yet; for all was so delicately touched, it seemed impossible to suspect him of the least design; and so far from making a parade of emotion, you would have sworn he was striving to be calm. When it came to an end, we all sat silent for a time; he had chosen the dusk of the afternoon, so that none could see his neighbour's face; but it seemed as if we held our breathing; only my old lord cleared his throat. The first to move was the singer, who got to his feet suddenly and softly, and went and walked softly to and fro in the low end of the hall, Mr. Henry's customary place. We were to suppose that he there struggled down the last of his emotion; for he presently returned and launched into a disquisition on the nature of the Irish (always so much miscalled, and whom he defended) in his natural voice; so that, before the lights were brought, we were in the usual course of talk. But even then, methought Mrs. Henry's face was a shade pale; and, for another thing, she withdrew almost at once.

The next sign was a friendship this insidious devil struck up with innocent Miss Katharine; so that they were always together, hand in hand, or she climbing on his knee, like a pair of children. Like all his diabolical acts, this cut in several ways. It was the last stroke to Mr. Henry, to see his own babe debauched against him; it made him harsh with the poor innocent, which brought him still a peg lower in his wife's esteem; and (to conclude) it was a bond of union between the lady and the Master. Under this influence, their old reserve melted by daily stages. Presently there came walks in the long shrubbery, talks in the Belvedere, and I know not what tender familiarity. I am sure Mrs. Henry was like many a good woman; she had a whole conscience but perhaps by the means of a little winking. For even to so dull an observer as myself, it was plain her kindness was of a more moving nature than the sisterly. The tones of her voice appeared more numerous; she had a light and softness in her eye; she was more gentle with all of us, even with Mr. Henry, even with myself; methought she breathed of some quiet melancholy happiness.

To look on at this, what a torment it was for Mr. Henry! And yet it brought our ultimate deliverance, as I am soon to tell.

The purport of the Master's stay was no more noble (gild it as they might) than to wring money out. He had some design of a fortune in the French Indies, as the Chevalier wrote me; and it was the sum required for this that he came seeking. For the rest of the family it spelled ruin; but my lord, in his incredible partiality, pushed ever for the granting. The family was now so narrowed down (indeed, there were no more of them than just the father and the two sons) that it was possible to break the entail and alienate a piece of land. And to this, at first by hints, and then by open pressure, Mr. Henry was brought to consent. He never would have done so, I am very well assured, but for the weight of the distress under which he laboured. But for his passionate eagerness to see his brother gone, he would not thus have broken with his own sentiment and the traditions of his house. And even so, he sold them his consent at a dear rate, speaking for once openly, and holding the business up in its own shameful colours.

"You will observe," he said, "this is an injustice to my son, if ever I have one."

"But that you are not likely to have," said my lord.

"God knows!" says Mr. Henry. "And considering the cruel falseness of the position in which I stand to my brother, and that you, my lord, are my father, and have the right to command me, I set my hand to this paper. But one thing I will say first: I have been ungenerously pushed, and when next, my lord, you are tempted to compare your sons, I call on you to remember what I have done and what he has done. Acts are the fair test."

My lord was the most uneasy man I ever saw; even in his old face the blood came up. "I think this is not a very wisely chosen moment, Henry, for complaints," said he. "This takes away from the merit of your generosity."

"Do not deceive yourself, my lord," said Mr. Henry. "This injustice is not done from generosity to him, but in obedience to yourself."

"Before strangers . . ." begins my lord, still more unhappily affected.

"There is no one but Mackellar here," said Mr. Henry; "he is my friend. And, my lord, as you make him no stranger to your frequent blame, it were hard if I must keep him one to a thing so rare as my defence."

Almost I believe my lord would have rescinded his decision; but the Master was on the watch.

"Ah! Henry, Henry," says he, "you are the best of us still. Rugged and true! Ah! man, I wish I was as good."

And at that instance of his favourite's generosity my lord desisted from his hesitation, and the deed was signed.

As soon as it could he brought about, the land of Ochterhall was sold for much below its value, and the money paid over to our leech and sent by some private carriage into France. Or so he said; though I have suspected since it did not go so far. And now here was all the man's business brought to a successful head, and his pockets once more bulging with our gold; and yet the point for which we had consented to this sacrifice was still denied us, and the visitor still lingered on at Durrisdeer. Whether in malice, or because the time was not yet come for his adventure to the Indies, or because he had hopes of his design on Mrs. Henry, or from the orders of the Government, who shall say? but linger he did, and that for weeks.

You will observe I say: from the orders of Government; for about this time the man's disreputable secret trickled out.

The first hint I had was from a tenant, who commented on the Master's stay, and yet more on his security; for this tenant was a Jacobitish sympathiser, and had lost a son at Culloden, which gave him the more critical eye. "There is one thing," said he, "that I cannot but think strange; and that is how he got to Cockermouth."

"To Cockermouth?" said I, with a sudden memory of my first wonder on beholding the man disembark so point-de-vice after so long a voyage.

"Why, yes," says the tenant, "it was there he was picked up by Captain Crail. You thought he had come from France by sea? And so we all did."

I turned this news a little in my head, and then carried it to Mr. Henry. "Here is an odd circumstance," said I, and told him.

"What matters how he came, Mackellar, so long as he is here?" groans Mr. Henry.

"No, sir," said I, "but think again! Does not this smack a little of some Government connivance? You know how much we have wondered already at the man's security."

"Stop," said Mr. Henry. "Let me think of this." And as he thought, there came that grim smile upon his face that was a little like the Master's. "Give me paper," said he. And he sat without another word and wrote to a gentleman of his acquaintance—I will name no unnecessary names, but he was one in a high place. This letter I despatched by the only hand I could depend upon in such a case—Macconochie's; and the old man rode hard, for he was back with the reply before even my eagerness had ventured to expect him. Again, as he read it, Mr. Henry had the same grim smile.

"This is the best you have done for me yet, Mackellar," says he. "With this in my hand I will give him a shog. Watch for us at dinner."

At dinner accordingly Mr. Henry proposed some very public appearance for the Master; and my lord, as he had hoped, objected to the danger of the course.

"Oh!" says Mr. Henry, very easily, "you need no longer keep this up with me. I am as much in the secret as yourself."

"In the secret?" says my lord. "What do you mean, Henry? I give you my word, I am in no secret from which you are excluded."

The Master had changed countenance, and I saw he was struck in a joint of his harness.

"How?" says Mr. Henry, turning to him with a huge appearance of surprise. "I see you serve your masters very faithfully; but I had thought you would have been humane enough to set your father's mind at rest."

"What are you talking of? I refuse to have my business publicly discussed. I order this to cease," cries the Master very foolishly and passionately, and indeed more like a child than a man.

"So much discretion was not looked for at your hands, I can assure you," continued Mr. Henry. "For see what my correspondent writes"—unfolding the paper—"'It is, of course, in the interests both of the Government and the gentleman whom we may perhaps best continue to call Mr. Bally, to keep this understanding secret; but it was never meant his own family should continue to endure the suspense you paint so feelingly; and I am pleased mine should be the hand to set these fears at rest. Mr. Bally is as safe in Great Britain as yourself.'"

"Is this possible?" cries my lord, looking at his son, with a great deal of wonder and still more of suspicion in his face.

"My dear father," says the Master, already much recovered. "I am overjoyed that this may be disclosed. My own instructions, direct from London, bore a very contrary sense, and I was charged to keep the indulgence secret from every one, yourself not excepted, and indeed yourself expressly named—as I can show in black and white unless I have destroyed the letter. They must have changed their mind very swiftly, for the whole matter is still quite fresh; or rather, Henry's correspondent must have misconceived that part, as he seems to have misconceived the rest. To tell you the truth, sir," he continued, getting visibly more easy, "I had supposed this unexplained favour to a rebel was the effect of some application from yourself; and the injunction to secrecy among my family the result of a desire on your part to conceal your kindness. Hence I was the more careful to obey orders. It remains now to guess by what other channel indulgence can have flowed on so notorious an offender as myself; for I do not think your son need defend himself from what seems hinted at in Henry's letter. I have never yet heard of a Durrisdeer who was a turncoat or a spy," says he, proudly.

And so it seemed he had swum out of this danger unharmed; but this was to reckon without a blunder he had made, and without the pertinacity of Mr. Henry, who was now to show he had something of his brother's spirit.

"You say the matter is still fresh," says Mr. Henry.

"It is recent," says the Master, with a fair show of stoutness and yet not without a quaver.

"Is it so recent as that?" asks Mr. Henry, like a man a little puzzled, and spreading his letter forth again.

In all the letter there was no word as to the date; but how was the Master to know that?

"It seemed to come late enough for me," says he, with a laugh. And at the sound of that laugh, which rang false, like a cracked bell, my lord looked at him again across the table, and I saw his old lips draw together close.

"No," said Mr. Henry, still glancing on his letter, "but I remember your expression. You said it was very fresh."

And here we had a proof of our victory, and the strongest instance yet of my lord's incredible indulgence; for what must he do but interfere to save his favourite from exposure!

"I think, Henry," says he, with a kind of pitiful eagerness, "I think we need dispute no more. We are all rejoiced at last to find your brother safe; we are all at one on that; and, as grateful subjects, we can do no less than drink to the king's health and bounty."

Thus was the Master extricated; but at least he had been put to his defence, he had come lamely out, and the attraction of his personal danger was now publicly plucked away from him. My lord, in his heart of hearts, now knew his favourite to be a Government spy; and Mrs. Henry (however she explained the tale) was notably cold in her behaviour to the discredited hero of romance. Thus in the best fabric of duplicity, there is some weak point, if you can strike it, which will loosen all; and if, by this fortunate stroke, we had not shaken the idol, who can say how it might have gone with us at the catastrophe?

And yet at the time we seemed to have accomplished nothing. Before a day or two he had wiped off the ill-results of his discomfiture, and, to all appearance, stood as high as ever. As for my Lord Durrisdeer, he was sunk in parental partiality; it was not so much love, which should be an active quality, as an apathy and torpor of his other powers; and forgiveness (so to mis-apply a noble word) flowed from him in sheer weakness, like the tears of senility. Mrs. Henry's was a different case; and Heaven alone knows what he found to say to her, or how he persuaded her from her contempt. It is one of the worst things of sentiment, that the voice grows to be more important than the words, and the speaker than that which is spoken. But some excuse the Master must have found, or perhaps he had even struck upon some art to wrest this exposure to his own advantage; for after a time of coldness, it seemed as if things went worse than ever between him and Mrs. Henry. They were then constantly together. I would not be thought to cut one shadow of blame, beyond what is due to a half-wilful blindness, on that unfortunate lady; but I do think, in these last days, she was playing very near the fire; and whether I be wrong or not in that, one thing is sure and quite sufficient: Mr. Henry thought so. The poor gentleman sat for days in my room, so great a picture of distress that I could never venture to address him; yet it is to be thought he found some comfort even in my presence and the knowledge of my sympathy. There were times, too, when we talked, and a strange manner of talk it was; there was never a person named, nor an individual circumstance referred to; yet we had the same matter in our minds, and we were each aware of it. It is a strange art that can thus be practised; to talk for hours of a thing, and never name nor yet so much as hint at it. And I remember I wondered if it was by some such natural skill that the Master made love to Mrs. Henry all day long (as he manifestly did), yet never startled her into reserve.

To show how far affairs had gone with Mr. Henry, I will give some words of his, uttered (as I have cause not to forget) upon the 26th of February, 1757. It was unseasonable weather, a cast back into Winter: windless, bitter cold, the world all white with rime, the sky low and gray: the sea black and silent like a quarry-hole. Mr. Henry sat close by the fire, and debated (as was now common with him) whether "a man" should "do things," whether "interference was wise," and the like general propositions, which each of us particularly applied. I was by the window, looking out, when there passed below me the Master, Mrs. Henry, and Miss Katharine, that now constant trio. The child was running to and fro, delighted with the frost; the Master spoke close in the lady's ear with what seemed (even from so far) a devilish grace of insinuation; and she on her part looked on the ground like a person lost in listening. I broke out of my reserve.

"If I were you, Mr. Henry," said I, "I would deal openly with my lord."

"Mackellar, Mackellar," said he, "you do not see the weakness of my ground. I can carry no such base thoughts to any one—to my father least of all; that would be to fall into the bottom of his scorn. The weakness of my ground," he continued, "lies in myself, that I am not one who engages love. I have their gratitude, they all tell me that; I have a rich estate of it! But I am not present in their minds; they are moved neither to think with me nor to think for me. There is my loss!" He got to his feet, and trod down the fire. "But some method must be found, Mackellar," said he, looking at me suddenly over his shoulder; "some way must be found. I am a man of a great deal of patience—far too much—far too much. I begin to despise myself. And yet, sure, never was a man involved in such a toil!" He fell back to his brooding.

"Cheer up," said I. "It will burst of itself."

"I am far past anger now," says he, which had so little coherency with my own observation that I let both fall.

CHAPTER V.
ACCOUNT OF ALL THAT PASSED
ON THE NIGHT ON FEBRUARY 27TH, 1757.

On the evening of the interview referred to, the Master went abroad; he was abroad a great deal of the next day also, that fatal 27th; but where he went, or what he did, we never concerned ourselves to ask until next day. If we had done so, and by any chance found out, it might have changed all. But as all we did was done in ignorance, and should be so judged, I shall so narrate these passages as they appeared to us in the moment of their birth, and reserve all that I since discovered for the time of its discovery. For I have now come to one of the dark parts of my narrative, and must engage the reader's indulgence for my patron.

All the 27th that rigorous weather endured: a stifling cold; the folk passing about like smoking chimneys; the wide hearth in the hall piled high with fuel; some of the spring birds that had already blundered north into our neighbourhood, besieging the windows of the house or trotting on the frozen turf like things distracted. About noon there came a blink of sunshine, showing a very pretty, wintry, frosty landscape of white hills and woods, with Crail's lugger waiting for a wind under the Craig Head, and the smoke mounting straight into the air from every farm and cottage. With the coming of night, the haze closed in overhead; it fell dark and still and starless, and exceeding cold: a night the most unseasonable, fit for strange events.

Mrs. Henry withdrew, as was now her custom, very early. We had set ourselves of late to pass the evening with a game of cards; another mark that our visitor was wearying mightily of the life at Durrisdeer; and we had not been long at this when my old lord slipped from his place beside the fire, and was off without a word to seek the warmth of bed. The three thus left together had neither love nor courtesy to share; not one of us would have sat up one instant to oblige another; yet from the influence of custom, and as the cards had just been dealt, we continued the form of playing out the round. I should say we were late sitters; and though my lord had departed earlier than was his custom, twelve was already gone some time upon the clock, and the servants long ago in bed. Another thing I should say, that although I never saw the Master anyway affected with liquor, he had been drinking freely, and was perhaps (although he showed it not) a trifle heated.

Anyway, he now practised one of his transitions; and so soon as the door closed behind my lord, and without the smallest change of voice, shifted from ordinary civil talk into a stream of insult.

"My dear Henry, it is yours to play," he had been saying, and now continued: "It is a very strange thing how, even in so small a matter as a game of cards, you display your rusticity. You play, Jacob, like a bonnet laird, or a sailor in a tavern. The same dulness, the same petty greed, cette lenteur d'hebété qui me fait rager; it is strange I should have such a brother. Even Square-toes has a certain vivacity when his stake is imperilled; but the dreariness of a game with you I positively lack language to depict."

Mr. Henry continued to look at his cards, as though very maturely considering some play; but his mind was elsewhere.

"Dear God, will this never be done?" cries the Master. "Quel lourdeau! But why do I trouble you with French expressions, which are lost on such an ignoramus? A lourdeau, my dear brother, is as we might say a bumpkin, a clown, a clodpole: a fellow without grace, lightness, quickness; any gift of pleasing, any natural brilliancy: such a one as you shall see, when you desire, by looking in the mirror. I tell you these things for your good, I assure you; and besides, Square-toes" (looking at me and stifling a yawn), "it is one of my diversions in this very dreary spot to toast you and your master at the fire like chestnuts. I have great pleasure in your case, for I observe the nickname (rustic as it is) has always the power to make you writhe. But sometimes I have more trouble with this dear fellow here, who seems to have gone to sleep upon his cards. Do you not see the applicability of the epithet I have just explained, dear Henry? Let me show you. For instance, with all those solid qualities which I delight to recognise in you, I never knew a woman who did not prefer me—nor, I think," he continued, with the most silken deliberation, "I think—who did not continue to prefer me."

Mr. Henry laid down his cards. He rose to his feet very softly, and seemed all the while like a person in deep thought. "You coward!" he said gently, as if to himself. And then, with neither hurry nor any particular violence, he struck the Master in the mouth.

The Master sprang to his feet like one transfigured; I had never seen the man so beautiful. "A blow!" he cried. "I would not take a blow from God Almighty!"

"Lower your voice," said Mr. Henry. "Do you wish my father to interfere for you again?"

"Gentlemen, gentlemen," I cried, and sought to come between them.

The Master caught me by the shoulder, held me at arm's length, and still addressing his brother: "Do you know what this means?" said he.

"It was the most deliberate act of my life," says Mr. Henry.

"I must have blood, I must have blood for this," says the Master.

"Please God it shall be yours," said Mr. Henry; and he went to the wall and took down a pair of swords that hung there with others, naked. These he presented to the Master by the points. "Mackellar shall see us play fair," said Mr. Henry. "I think it very needful."

"You need insult me no more," said the Master, taking one of the swords at random. "I have hated you all my life."

"My father is but newly gone to bed," said Mr. Henry. "We must go somewhere forth of the house."

"There is an excellent place in the long shrubbery," said the Master.

"Gentlemen," said I, "shame upon you both! Sons of the same mother, would you turn against the life she gave you?"

"Even so, Mackellar," said Mr. Henry, with the same perfect quietude of manner he had shown throughout.

"It is what I will prevent," said I.

And now here is a blot upon my life. At these words of mine the Master turned his blade against my bosom; I saw the light run along the steel; and I threw up my arms and fell to my knees before him on the floor. "No, no," I cried, like a baby.

"We shall have no more trouble with him," said the Master. "It is a good thing to have a coward in the house."

"We must have light," said Mr. Henry, as though there had been no interruption.

"This trembler can bring a pair of candles," said the Master.

To my shame be it said, I was still so blinded with the flashing of that bare sword that I volunteered to bring a lantern.

"We do not need a l-l-lantern," says the Master, mocking me. "There is no breath of air. Come, get to your feet, take a pair of lights, and go before. I am close behind with this—" making the blade glitter as he spoke.

I took up the candlesticks and went before them, steps that I would give my hand to recall; but a coward is a slave at the best; and even as I went, my teeth smote each other in my mouth. It was as he had said: there was no breath stirring; a windless stricture of frost had bound the air; and as we went forth in the shine of the candles, the blackness was like a roof over our heads. Never a word was said; there was never a sound but the creaking of our steps along the frozen path. The cold of the night fell about me like a bucket of water; I shook as I went with more than terror; but my companions, bare-headed like myself, and fresh from the warm ball, appeared not even conscious of the change.

"Here is the place," said the Master. "Set down the candles."

I did as he bid me, and presently the flames went up, as steady as in a chamber, in the midst of the frosted trees, and I beheld these two brothers take their places.

"The light is something in my eyes," said the Master.

"I will give you every advantage," replied Mr. Henry, shifting his ground, "for I think you are about to die." He spoke rather sadly than otherwise, yet there was a ring in his voice.

"Henry Durie," said the Master, "two words before I begin. You are a fencer, you can hold a foil; you little know what a change it makes to hold a sword! And by that I know you are to fall. But see how strong is my situation! If you fall, I shift out of this country to where my money is before me. If I fall, where are you? My father, your wife—who is in love with me, as you very well know—your child even, who prefers me to yourself:—how will these avenge me! Had you thought of that, dear Henry?" He looked at his brother with a smile; then made a fencing-room salute.

Never a word said Mr. Henry, but saluted too, and the swords rang together.

I am no judge of the play; my head, besides, was gone with cold and fear and horror; but it seems that Mr. Henry took and kept the upper hand from the engagement, crowding in upon his foe with a contained and glowing fury. Nearer and nearer he crept upon the man, till of a sudden the Master leaped back with a little sobbing oath; and I believe the movement brought the light once more against his eyes. To it they went again, on the fresh ground; but now methought closer, Mr. Henry pressing more outrageously, the Master beyond doubt with shaken confidence. For it is beyond doubt he now recognised himself for lost, and had some taste of the cold agony of fear; or he had never attempted the foul stroke. I cannot say I followed it, my untrained eye was never quick enough to seize details, but it appears he caught his brother's blade with his left hand, a practice not permitted. Certainly Mr. Henry only saved himself by leaping on one side; as certainly the Master, lunging in the air, stumbled on his knee, and before he could move the sword was through his body.

I cried out with a stifled scream, and ran in; but the body was already fallen to the ground, where it writhed a moment like a trodden worm, and then lay motionless.

"Look at his left hand," said Mr. Henry.

"It is all bloody," said I.

"On the inside?" said he.

"It is cut on the inside," said I.

"I thought so," said he, and turned his back.

I opened the man's clothes; the heart was quite still, it gave not a flutter.

"God forgive us, Mr. Henry!" said I. "He is dead."

"Dead?" he repeated, a little stupidly; and then with a rising tone, "Dead? dead?" says he, and suddenly cast his bloody sword upon the ground.

"What must we do?" said I. "Be yourself, sir. It is too late now: you must be yourself."

He turned and stared at me. "Oh, Mackellar!" says he, and put his face in his hands.

I plucked him by the coat. "For God's sake, for all our sakes, be more courageous!" said I. "What must we do?"

He showed me his face with the same stupid stare.

"Do?" says he. And with that his eye fell on the body, and "Oh!" he cries out, with his hand to his brow, as if he had never remembered; and, turning from me, made off towards the house of Durrisdeer at a strange stumbling run.

I stood a moment mused; then it seemed to me my duty lay most plain on the side of the living; and I ran after him, leaving the candles on the frosty ground and the body lying in their light under the trees. But run as I pleased, he had the start of me, and was got into the house, and up to the hall, where I found him standing before the fire with his face once more in his hands, and as he so stood he visibly shuddered.

"Mr. Henry, Mr. Henry," I said, "this will be the ruin of us all."

"What is this that I have done?" cries he, and then looking upon me with a countenance that I shall never forget, "Who is to tell the old man?" he said.

The word knocked at my heart; but it was no time for weakness. I went and poured him out a glass of brandy. "Drink that," said I, "drink it down." I forced him to swallow it like a child; and, being still perished with the cold of the night, I followed his example.

"It has to be told, Mackellar," said he. "It must be told." And he fell suddenly in a seat—my old lord's seat by the chimney-side—and was shaken with dry sobs.

Dismay came upon my soul; it was plain there was no help in Mr. Henry. "Well," said I, "sit there, and leave all to me." And taking a candle in my hand, I set forth out of the room in the dark house. There was no movement; I must suppose that all had gone unobserved; and I was now to consider how to smuggle through the rest with the like secrecy. It was no hour for scruples; and I opened my lady's door without so much as a knock, and passed boldly in.

"There is some calamity happened," she cried, sitting up in bed.

"Madam," said I, "I will go forth again into the passage; and do you get as quickly as you can into your clothes. There is much to be done."

She troubled me with no questions, nor did she keep me waiting. Ere I had time to prepare a word of that which I must say to her, she was on the threshold signing me to enter.

"Madam," said I, "if you cannot be very brave, I must go elsewhere; for if no one helps me to-night, there is an end of the house of Durrisdeer."

"I am very courageous," said she; and she looked at me with a sort of smile, very painful to see, but very brave too.

"It has come to a duel," said I.

"A duel?" she repeated. "A duel! Henry and—"

"And the Master," said I. "Things have been borne so long, things of which you know nothing, which you would not believe if I should tell. But to-night it went too far, and when he insulted you—"

"Stop," said she. "He? Who?"

"Oh! madam," cried I, my bitterness breaking forth, "do you ask me such a question? Indeed, then, I may go elsewhere for help; there is none here!"

"I do not know in what I have offended you," said she. "Forgive me; put me out of this suspense."

But I dared not tell her yet; I felt not sure of her; and at the doubt, and under the sense of impotence it brought with it, I turned on the poor woman with something near to anger.

"Madam," said I, "we are speaking of two men: one of them insulted you, and you ask me which. I will help you to the answer. With one of these men you have spent all your hours: has the other reproached you? To one you have been always kind; to the other, as God sees me and judges between us two, I think not always: has his love ever failed you? To-night one of these two men told the other, in my hearing—the hearing of a hired stranger,—that you were in love with him. Before I say one word, you shall answer your own question: Which was it? Nay, madam, you shall answer me another: If it has come to this dreadful end, whose fault is it?"

She stared at me like one dazzled. "Good God!" she said once, in a kind of bursting exclamation; and then a second time in a whisper to herself: "Great God!—In the name of mercy, Mackellar, what is wrong?" she cried. "I am made up; I can hear all."

"You are not fit to hear," said I. "Whatever it was, you shall say first it was your fault."

"Oh!" she cried, with a gesture of wringing her hands, "this man will drive me mad! Can you not put me out of your thoughts?"

"I think not once of you," I cried. "I think of none but my dear unhappy master."

"Ah!" she cried, with her hand to her heart, "is Henry dead?"

"Lower your voice," said I. "The other."

I saw her sway like something stricken by the wind; and I know not whether in cowardice or misery, turned aside and looked upon the floor. "These are dreadful tidings," said I at length, when her silence began to put me in some fear; "and you and I behove to be the more bold if the house is to be saved." Still she answered nothing. "There is Miss Katharine, besides," I added: "unless we bring this matter through, her inheritance is like to be of shame."

I do not know if it was the thought of her child or the naked word shame, that gave her deliverance; at least, I had no sooner spoken than a sound passed her lips, the like of it I never heard; it was as though she had lain buried under a hill and sought to move that burthen. And the next moment she had found a sort of voice.

"It was a fight," she whispered. "It was not—" and she paused upon the word.

"It was a fair fight on my dear master's part," said I. "As for the other, he was slain in the very act of a foul stroke."

"Not now!" she cried.

"Madam," said I, "hatred of that man glows in my bosom like a burning fire; ay, even now he is dead. God knows, I would have stopped the fighting, had I dared. It is my shame I did not. But when I saw him fall, if I could have spared one thought from pitying of my master, it had been to exult in that deliverance."

I do not know if she marked; but her next words were, "My lord?"

"That shall be my part," said I.

"You will not speak to him as you have to me?" she asked.

"Madam," said I, "have you not some one else to think of? Leave my lord to me."

"Some one else?" she repeated.

"Your husband," said I. She looked at me with a countenance illegible. "Are you going to turn your back on him?" I asked.

Still she looked at me; then her hand went to her heart again. "No," said she.

"God bless you for that word!" I said. "Go to him now, where he sits in the hall; speak to him—it matters not what you say; give him your hand; say, 'I know all;'—if God gives you grace enough, say, 'Forgive me.'"

"God strengthen you, and make you merciful," said she. "I will go to my husband."

"Let me light you there," said I, taking up the candle.

"I will find my way in the dark," she said, with a shudder, and I think the shudder was at me.

So we separated—she down stairs to where a little light glimmered in the hall-door, I along the passage to my lord's room. It seems hard to say why, but I could not burst in on the old man as I could on the young woman; with whatever reluctance, I must knock. But his old slumbers were light, or perhaps he slept not; and at the first summons I was bidden enter.

He, too, sat up in bed; very aged and bloodless he looked; and whereas he had a certain largeness of appearance when dressed for daylight, he now seemed frail and little, and his face (the wig being laid aside) not bigger than a child's. This daunted me; nor less, the haggard surmise of misfortune in his eye. Yet his voice was even peaceful as he inquired my errand. I set my candle down upon a chair, leaned on the bed-foot, and looked at him.

"Lord Durrisdeer," said I, "it is very well known to you that I am a partisan in your family."

"I hope we are none of us partisans," said he. "That you love my son sincerely, I have always been glad to recognise."

"Oh! my lord, we are past the hour of these civilities," I replied. "If we are to save anything out of the fire, we must look the fact in its bare countenance. A partisan I am; partisans we have all been; it is as a partisan that I am here in the middle of the night to plead before you. Hear me; before I go, I will tell you why."

"I would always hear you, Mr. Mackellar," said he, "and that at any hour, whether of the day or night, for I would be always sure you had a reason. You spoke once before to very proper purpose; I have not forgotten that."

"I am here to plead the cause of my master," I said. "I need not tell you how he acts. You know how he is placed. You know with what generosity, he has always met your other—met your wishes," I corrected myself, stumbling at that name of son. "You know—you must know—what he has suffered—what he has suffered about his wife."

"Mr. Mackellar!" cried my lord, rising in bed like a bearded lion.

"You said you would hear me," I continued. "What you do not know, what you should know, one of the things I am here to speak of, is the persecution he must bear in private. Your back is not turned before one whom I dare not name to you falls upon him with the most unfeeling taunts; twits him—pardon me, my lord—twits him with your partiality, calls him Jacob, calls him clown, pursues him with ungenerous raillery, not to be borne by man. And let but one of you appear, instantly he changes; and my master must smile and courtesy to the man who has been feeding him with insults; I know, for I have shared in some of it, and I tell you the life is insupportable. All these months it has endured; it began with the man's landing; it was by the name of Jacob that my master was greeted the first night."

My lord made a movement as if to throw aside the clothes and rise. "If there be any truth in this—" said he.

"Do I look like a man lying?" I interrupted, checking him with my hand.

"You should have told me at first," he odd.

"Ah, my lord! indeed I should, and you may well hate the face of this unfaithful servant!" I cried.

"I will take order," said he, "at once." And again made the movement to rise.

Again I checked him. "I have not done," said I. "Would God I had! All this my dear, unfortunate patron has endured without help or countenance. Your own best word, my lord, was only gratitude. Oh, but he was your son, too! He had no other father. He was hated in the country, God knows how unjustly. He had a loveless marriage. He stood on all hands without affection or support—dear, generous, ill-fated, noble heart!"

"Your tears do you much honour and me much shame," says my lord, with a palsied trembling. "But you do me some injustice. Henry has been ever dear to me, very dear. James (I do not deny it, Mr. Mackellar), James is perhaps dearer; you have not seen my James in quite a favourable light; he has suffered under his misfortunes; and we can only remember how great and how unmerited these were. And even now his is the more affectionate nature. But I will not speak of him. All that you say of Henry is most true; I do not wonder, I know him to be very magnanimous; you will say I trade upon the knowledge? It is possible; there are dangerous virtues: virtues that tempt the encroacher. Mr. Mackellar, I will make it up to him; I will take order with all this. I have been weak; and, what is worse, I have been dull!"

"I must not hear you blame yourself, my lord, with that which I have yet to tell upon my conscience," I replied. "You have not been weak; you have been abused by a devilish dissembler. You saw yourself how he had deceived you in the matter of his danger; he has deceived you throughout in every step of his career. I wish to pluck him from your heart; I wish to force your eyes upon your other son; ah, you have a son there!"

"No, no," said he, "two sons—I have two sons."

I made some gesture of despair that struck him; he looked at me with a changed face. "There is much worse behind?" he asked, his voice dying as it rose upon the question.

"Much worse," I answered. "This night he said these words to Mr. Henry: 'I have never known a woman who did not prefer me to you, and I think who did not continue to prefer me.'"

"I will hear nothing against my daughter," he cried; and from his readiness to stop me in this direction, I conclude his eyes were not so dull as I had fancied, and he had looked not without anxiety upon the siege of Mrs. Henry.

"I think not of blaming her," cried I. "It is not that. These words were said in my hearing to Mr. Henry; and if you find them not yet plain enough, these others but a little after: Your wife, who is in love with me!'"

"They have quarrelled?" he said.

I nodded.

"I must fly to them," he said, beginning once again to leave his bed.

"No, no!" I cried, holding forth my hands.

"You do not know," said he. "These are dangerous words."

"Will nothing make you understand, my lord?" said I.

His eyes besought me for the truth.

I flung myself on my knees by the bedside. "Oh, my lord," cried I, "think on him you have left; think of this poor sinner whom you begot, whom your wife bore to you, whom we have none of us strengthened as we could; think of him, not of yourself; he is the other sufferer—think of him! That is the door for sorrow—Christ's door, God's door: oh! it stands open. Think of him, even as he thought of you. 'Who is to tell the old man?'—these were his words. It was for that I came; that is why I am here pleading at your feet."

"Let me get up," he cried, thrusting me aside, and was on his feet before myself. His voice shook like a sail in the wind, yet he spoke with a good loudness; his face was like the snow, but his eyes were steady and dry.

"Here is too much speech," said he. "Where was it?"

"In the shrubbery," said I.

"And Mr. Henry?" he asked. And when I had told him he knotted his old face in thought.

"And Mr. James?" says he.

"I have left him lying," said I, "beside the candles."

"Candles?" he cried. And with that he ran to the window, opened it, and looked abroad. "It might be spied from the road."

"Where none goes by at such an hour," I objected.

"It makes no matter," he said. "One might. Hark!" cries he. "What is that?"

It was the sound of men very guardedly rowing in the bay; and I told him so.

"The freetraders," said my lord. "Run at once, Mackellar; put these candles out. I will dress in the meanwhile; and when you return we can debate on what is wisest."

I groped my way downstairs, and out at the door. From quite a far way off a sheen was visible, making points of brightness in the shrubbery; in so black a night it might have been remarked for miles; and I blamed myself bitterly for my incaution. How much more sharply when I reached the place! One of the candlesticks was overthrown, and that taper quenched. The other burned steadily by itself, and made a broad space of light upon the frosted ground. All within that circle seemed, by the force of contrast and the overhanging blackness, brighter than by day. And there was the bloodstain in the midst; and a little farther off Mr. Henry's sword, the pommel of which was of silver; but of the body, not a trace. My heart thumped upon my ribs, the hair stirred upon my scalp, as I stood there staring—so strange was the sight, so dire the fears it wakened. I looked right and left; the ground was so hard, it told no story. I stood and listened till my ears ached, but the night was hollow about me like an empty church; not even a ripple stirred upon the shore; it seemed you might have heard a pin drop in the county.

I put the candle out, and the blackness fell about me groping dark; it was like a crowd surrounding me; and I went back to the house of Durrisdeer, with my chin upon my shoulder, startling, as I went, with craven suppositions. In the door a figure moved to meet me, and I had near screamed with terror ere I recognised Mrs. Henry.

"Have you told him?" says she.

"It was he who sent me," said I. "It is gone. But why are you here?"

"It is gone!" she repeated. "What is gone?"

"The body," said I. "Why are you not with your husband?"

"Gone!" said she. "You cannot have looked. Come back."

"There is no light now," said I. "I dare not."

"I can see in the dark. I have been standing here so long—so long," said she. "Come, give me your hand."

We returned to the shrubbery hand in hand, and to the fatal place.

"Take care of the blood," said I.

"Blood?" she cried, and started violently back.

"I suppose it will be," said I. "I am like a blind man."

"No!" said she, "nothing! Have you not dreamed?"

"Ah, would to God we had!" cried I.

She spied the sword, picked it up, and seeing the blood, let it fall again with her hands thrown wide. "Ah!" she cried. And then, with an instant courage, handled it the second time, and thrust it to the hilt into the frozen ground. "I will take it back and clean it properly," says she, and again looked about her on all sides. "It cannot be that he was dead?" she added.

"There was no flutter of his heart," said I, and then remembering: "Why are you not with your husband?"

"It is no use," said she; "he will not speak to me."

"Not speak to you?" I repeated. "Oh! you have not tried."

"You have a right to doubt me," she replied, with a gentle dignity.

At this, for the first time, I was seized with sorrow for her. "God knows, madam," I cried, "God knows I am not so hard as I appear; on this dreadful night who can veneer his words? But I am a friend to all who are not Henry Durie's enemies."

"It is hard, then, you should hesitate about his wife," said she.

I saw all at once, like the rending of a veil, how nobly she had borne this unnatural calamity, and how generously my reproaches.

"We must go back and tell this to my lord," said I.

"Him I cannot face," she cried.

"You will find him the least moved of all of us," said I.

"And yet I cannot face him," said she.

"Well," said I, "you can return to Mr. Henry; I will see my lord."

As we walked back, I bearing the candlesticks, she the sword—a strange burthen for that woman—she had another thought. "Should we tell Henry?" she asked.

"Let my lord decide," said I.

My lord was nearly dressed when I came to his chamber. He heard me with a frown. "The freetraders," said he. "But whether dead or alive?"

"I thought him—" said I, and paused, ashamed of the word.

"I know; but you may very well have been in error. Why should they remove him if not living?" he asked. "Oh! here is a great door of hope. It must be given out that he departed—as he came—without any note of preparation. We must save all scandal."

I saw he had fallen, like the rest of us, to think mainly of the house. Now that all the living members of the family were plunged in irremediable sorrow, it was strange how we turned to that conjoint abstraction of the family itself, and sought to bolster up the airy nothing of its reputation: not the Duries only, but the hired steward himself.

"Are we to tell Mr. Henry?" I asked him.

"I will see," said he. "I am going first to visit him; then I go forth with you to view the shrubbery and consider."

We went downstairs into the hall. Mr. Henry sat by the table with his head upon his hand, like a man of stone. His wife stood a little back from him, her hand at her mouth; it was plain she could not move him. My old lord walked very steadily to where his son was sitting; he had a steady countenance, too, but methought a little cold. When he was come quite up, he held out both his hands and said, "My son!"

With a broken, strangled cry, Mr. Henry leaped up and fell on his father's neck, crying and weeping, the most pitiful sight that ever a man witnessed. "Oh! father," he cried, "you know I loved him; you know I loved him in the beginning; I could have died for him—you know that! I would have given my life for him and you. Oh! say you know that. Oh! say you can forgive me. O father, father, what have I done—what have I done? And we used to be bairns together!" and wept and sobbed, and fondled the old man, and clutched him about the neck, with the passion of a child in terror.

And then he caught sight of his wife (you would have thought for the first time), where she stood weeping to hear him, and in a moment had fallen at her knees. "And O my lass," he cried, "you must forgive me, too! Not your husband—I have only been the ruin of your life. But you knew me when I was a lad; there was no harm in Henry Durie then; he meant aye to be a friend to you. It's him—it's the old bairn that played with you—oh, can ye never, never forgive him?"

Throughout all this my lord was like a cold, kind spectator with his wits about him. At the first cry, which was indeed enough to call the house about us, he had said to me over his shoulder, "Close the door." And now he nodded to himself.

"We may leave him to his wife now," says he. "Bring a light, Mr. Mackellar."

Upon my going forth again with my lord, I was aware of a strange phenomenon; for though it was quite dark, and the night not yet old, methought I smelt the morning. At the same time there went a tossing through the branches of the evergreens, so that they sounded like a quiet sea, and the air pulled at times against our faces, and the flame of the candle shook. We made the more speed, I believe, being surrounded by this bustle; visited the scene of the duel, where my lord looked upon the blood with stoicism; and passing farther on toward the landing-place, came at last upon some evidences of the truth. For, first of all, where there was a pool across the path, the ice had been trodden in, plainly by more than one man's weight; next, and but a little farther, a young tree was broken, and down by the landing-place, where the traders' boats were usually beached, another stain of blood marked where the body must have been infallibly set down to rest the bearers.

This stain we set ourselves to wash away with the sea-water, carrying it in my lord's hat; and as we were thus engaged there came up a sudden moaning gust and left us instantly benighted.

"It will come to snow," says my lord; "and the best thing that we could hope. Let us go back now; we can do nothing in the dark."

As we went houseward, the wind being again subsided, we were aware of a strong pattering noise about us in the night; and when we issued from the shelter of the trees, we found it raining smartly.

Throughout the whole of this, my lord's clearness of mind, no less than his activity of body, had not ceased to minister to my amazement. He set the crown upon it in the council we held on our return. The freetraders had certainly secured the Master, though whether dead or alive we were still left to our conjectures; the rain would, long before day, wipe out all marks of the transaction; by this we must profit. The Master had unexpectedly come after the fall of night; it must now be given out he had as suddenly departed before the break of day; and, to make all this plausible, it now only remained for me to mount into the man's chamber, and pack and conceal his baggage. True, we still lay at the discretion of the traders; but that was the incurable weakness of our guilt.

I heard him, as I said, with wonder, and hastened to obey. Mr. and Mrs. Henry were gone from the hall; my lord, for warmth's sake, hurried to his bed; there was still no sign of stir among the servants, and as I went up the tower stair, and entered the dead man's room, a horror of solitude weighed upon my mind. To my extreme surprise, it was all in the disorder of departure. Of his three portmanteaux, two were already locked; the third lay open and near full. At once there flashed upon me some suspicion of the truth. The man had been going, after all; he had but waited upon Crail, as Crail waited upon the wind; early in the night the seamen had perceived the weather changing; the boat had come to give notice of the change and call the passenger aboard, and the boat's crew had stumbled on him dying in his blood. Nay, and there was more behind. This pre-arranged departure shed some light upon his inconceivable insult of the night before; it was a parting shot, hatred being no longer checked by policy. And, for another thing, the nature of that insult, and the conduct of Mrs. Henry, pointed to one conclusion, which I have never verified, and can now never verify until the great assize—the conclusion that he had at last forgotten himself, had gone too far in his advances, and had been rebuffed. It can never be verified, as I say; but as I thought of it that morning among his baggage, the thought was sweet to me like honey.

Into the open portmanteau I dipped a little ere I closed it. The most beautiful lace and linen, many suits of those fine plain clothes in which he loved to appear; a book or two, and those of the best, Cæsar's "Commentaries," a volume of Mr. Hobbes, the "Henriade" of M. de Voltaire, a book upon the Indies, one on the mathematics, far beyond where I have studied: these were what I observed with very mingled feelings. But in the open portmanteau, no papers of any description. This set me musing. It was possible the man was dead; but, since the traders had carried him away, not likely. It was possible he might still die of his wound; but it was also possible he might not. And in this latter case I was determined to have the means of some defence.

One after another I carried his portmanteaux to a loft in the top of the house which we kept locked; went to my own room for my keys, and, returning to the loft, had the gratification to find two that fitted pretty well. In one of the portmanteaux there was a shagreen letter-case, which I cut open with my knife; and thenceforth (so far as any credit went) the man was at my mercy. Here was a vast deal of gallant correspondence, chiefly of his Paris days; and, what was more to the purpose, here were the copies of his own reports to the English Secretary, and the originals of the Secretary's answers: a most damning series: such as to publish would be to wreck the Master's honour and to set a price upon his life. I chuckled to myself as I ran through the documents; I rubbed my hands, I sang aloud in my glee. Day found me at the pleasing task; nor did I then remit my diligence, except in so far as I went to the window—looked out for a moment, to see the frost quite gone, the world turned black again, and the rain and the wind driving in the bay—and to assure myself that the lugger was gone from its anchorage, and the Master (whether dead or alive) now tumbling on the Irish Sea.

It is proper I should add in this place the very little I have subsequently angled out upon the doings of that night. It took me a long while to gather it; for we dared not openly ask, and the freetraders regarded me with enmity, if not with scorn. It was near six months before we even knew for certain that the man survived; and it was years before I learned from one of Crail's men, turned publican on his ill-gotten gain, some particulars which smack to me of truth. It seems the traders found the Master struggled on one elbow, and now staring round him, and now gazing at the candle or at his hand which was all bloodied, like a man stupid. Upon their coming, he would seem to have found his mind, bade them carry him aboard, and hold their tongues; and on the captain asking how he had come in such a pickle, replied with a burst of passionate swearing, and incontinently fainted. They held some debate, but they were momently looking for a wind, they were highly paid to smuggle him to France, and did not care to delay. Besides which, he was well enough liked by these abominable wretches: they supposed him under capital sentence, knew not in what mischief he might have got his wound, and judged it a piece of good nature to remove him out of the way of danger. So he was taken aboard, recovered on the passage over, and was set ashore a convalescent at the Havre de Grace. What is truly notable: he said not a word to anyone of the duel, and not a trader knows to this day in what quarrel, or by the hand of what adversary, he fell. With any other man I should have set this down to natural decency; with him, to pride. He could not bear to avow, perhaps even to himself, that he had been vanquished by one whom he had so much insulted whom he so cruelly despised.

CHAPTER VI.
SUMMARY OF EVENTS DURING THE MASTER'S SECOND ABSENCE.

Of the heavy sickness which declared itself next morning I can think with equanimity, as of the last unmingled trouble that befell my master; and even that was perhaps a mercy in disguise; for what pains of the body could equal the miseries of his mind? Mrs. Henry and I had the watching by the bed. My old lord called from time to time to take the news, but would not usually pass the door. Once, I remember, when hope was nigh gone, he stepped to the bedside, looked awhile in his son's face, and turned away with a gesture of the head and hand thrown up, that remains upon my mind as something tragic; such grief and such a scorn of sublunary things were there expressed. But the most of the time Mrs. Henry and I had the room to ourselves, taking turns by night, and bearing each other company by day, for it was dreary watching. Mr. Henry, his shaven head bound in a napkin, tossed fro without remission, beating the bed with his hands. His tongue never lay; his voice ran continuously like a river, so that my heart was weary with the sound of it. It was notable, and to me inexpressibly mortifying, that he spoke all the while on matters of no import: comings and goings, horses—which he was ever calling to have saddled, thinking perhaps (the poor soul!) that he might ride away from his discomfort—matters of the garden, the salmon nets, and (what I particularly raged to hear) continually of his affairs, cyphering figures and holding disputation with the tenantry. Never a word of his father or his wife, nor of the Master, save only for a day or two, when his mind dwelled entirely in the past, and he supposed himself a boy again and upon some innocent child's play with his brother. What made this the more affecting: it appeared the Master had then run some peril of his life, for there was a cry—"Oh! Jamie will be drowned—Oh, save Jamie!" which he came over and over with a great deal of passion.

This, I say, was affecting, both to Mrs. Henry and myself; but the balance of my master's wanderings did him little justice. It seemed he had set out to justify his brother's calumnies; as though he was bent to prove himself a man of a dry nature, immersed in money-getting. Had I been there alone, I would not have troubled my thumb; but all the while, as I listened, I was estimating the effect on the man's wife, and telling myself that he fell lower every day. I was the one person on the surface of the globe that comprehended him, and I was bound there should be yet another. Whether he was to die there and his virtues perish: or whether he should save his days and come back to that inheritance of sorrows, his right memory: I was bound he should be heartily lamented in the one case, and unaffectedly welcomed in the other, by the person he loved the most, his wife.

Finding no occasion of free speech, I bethought me at last of a kind of documentary disclosure; and for some nights, when I was off duty and should have been asleep, I gave my time to the preparation of that which I may call my budget. But this I found to be the easiest portion of my task, and that which remained—namely, the presentation to my lady—almost more than I had fortitude to overtake. Several days I went about with my papers under my arm, spying for some juncture of talk to serve as introduction. I will not deny but that some offered; only when they did my tongue clove to the roof of my mouth; and I think I might have been carrying about my packet till this day, had not a fortunate accident delivered me from all my hesitations. This was at night, when I was once more leaving the room, the thing not yet done, and myself in despair at my own cowardice.

"What do you carry about with you, Mr. Mackellar?" she asked. "These last days, I see you always coming in and out with the same armful."

I returned upon my steps without a word, laid the papers before her on the table, and left her to her reading. Of what that was, I am now to give you some idea; and the best will be to reproduce a letter of my own which came first in the budget and of which (according to an excellent habitude) I have preserved the scroll. It will show, too, the moderation of my part in these affairs, a thing which some have called recklessly in question.

"Durrisdeer.
"1757.

"Honoured Madam,

"I trust I would not step out of my place without occasion; but I see how much evil has flowed in the past to all of your noble house from that unhappy and secretive fault of reticency, and the papers on which I venture to call your attention are family papers, and all highly worthy your acquaintance.

"I append a schedule with some necessary observations,

"And am,
"Honoured Madam,
"Your ladyship's obliged, obedient servant,
"Ephraim Mackellar.

"Schedule of Papers.

"A. Scroll of ten letters from Ephraim Mackellar to the Hon. James Durie, Esq., by courtesy Master of Ballantrae during the latter's residence in Paris: under dates . . . " (follow the dates) . . . "Nota: to be read in connection with B. and C.

"B. Seven original letters from the said Mr of Ballantrae to the said E. Mackellar, under dates . . . " (follow the dates.)

"C. Three original letters from the Mr of Ballantrae to the Hon. Henry Durie, Esq., under dates . . . " (follow the dates) . . . "Nota: given me by Mr. Henry to answer: copies of my answers A 4, A 5, and A 9 of these productions. The purport of Mr. Henry's communications, of which I can find no scroll, may be gathered from those of his unnatural brother.

"D. A correspondence, original and scroll, extending over a period of three years till January of the current year, between the said Mr of Ballantrae and —— ——, Under Secretary of State; twenty-seven in all. Nota: found among the Master's papers."

Weary as I was with watching and distress of mind, it was impossible for me to sleep. All night long I walked in my chamber, revolving what should be the issue, and sometimes repenting the temerity of my immixture in affairs so private; and with the first peep of the morning I was at the sick-room door. Mrs. Henry had thrown open the shutters and even the window, for the temperature was mild. She looked steadfastly before her; where was nothing to see, or only the blue of the morning creeping among woods. Upon the stir of my entrance she did not so much as turn about her face: a circumstance from which I augured very ill.

"Madam," I began; and then again, "Madam;" but could make no more of it. Nor yet did Mrs. Henry come to my assistance with a word. In this pass I began gathering up the papers where they lay scattered on the table; and the first thing that struck me, their bulk appeared to have diminished. Once I ran them through, and twice; but the correspondence with the Secretary of State, on which I had reckoned so much against the future, was nowhere to be found. I looked in the chimney; amid the smouldering embers, black ashes of paper fluttered in the draught; and at that my timidity vanished.

"Good God, madam," cried I, in a voice not fitting for a sick-room, "Good God, madam, what have you done with my papers?"

"I have burned them," said Mrs. Henry, turning about. "It is enough, it is too much, that you and I have seen them."

"This is a fine night's work that you have done!" cried I. "And all to save the reputation of a man that ate bread by the shedding of his comrades' blood, as I do by the shedding of ink."

"To save the reputation of that family in which you are a servant, Mr. Mackellar," she returned, "and for which you have already done so much."

"It is a family I will not serve much longer," I cried, "for I am driven desperate. You have stricken the sword out of my hands; you have left us all defenceless. I had always these letters I could shake over his head; and now—What is to do? We are so falsely situate we dare not show the man the door; the country would fly on fire against us; and I had this one hold upon him— and now it is gone—now he may come back to-morrow, and we must all sit down with him to dinner, go for a stroll with him on the terrace, or take a hand at cards, of all things, to divert his leisure! No, madam! God forgive you, if He can find it in His heart; for I cannot find it in mine."

"I wonder to find you so simple, Mr. Mackellar," said Mrs. Henry. "What does this man value reputation? But he knows how high we prize it; he knows we would rather die than make these letters public; and do you suppose he would not trade upon the knowledge? What you call your sword, Mr. Mackellar, and which had been one indeed against a man of any remnant of propriety, would have been but a sword of paper against him. He would smile in your face at such a threat. He stands upon his degradation, he makes that his strength; it is in vain to struggle with such characters." She cried out this last a little desperately, and then with more quiet: "No, Mr. Mackellar; I have thought upon this matter all night, and there is no way out of it. Papers or no papers, the door of this house stands open for him; he is the rightful heir, forsooth! If we sought to exclude him, all would redound against poor Henry, and I should see him stoned again upon the streets. Ah! if Henry dies, it is a different matter! They have broke the entail for their own good purposes; the estate goes to my daughter; and I shall see who sets a foot upon it. But if Henry lives, my poor Mr. Mackellar, and that man returns, we must suffer: only this time it will be together."

On the whole I was well pleased with Mrs. Henry's attitude of mind; nor could I even deny there was some cogency in that which she advanced about the papers.

"Let us say no more about it," said I. "I can only be sorry I trusted a lady with the originals, which was an unbusinesslike proceeding at the best. As for what I said of leaving the service of the family, it was spoken with the tongue only; and you may set your mind at rest. I belong to Durrisdeer, Mrs. Henry, as if I had been born there."

I must do her the justice to say she seemed perfectly relieved; so that we began this morning, as we were to continue for so many years, on a proper ground of mutual indulgence and respect.

The same day, which was certainly prededicate to joy, we observed the first signal of recovery in Mr. Henry; and about three of the following afternoon he found his mind again, recognising me by name with the strongest evidences of affection. Mrs. Henry was also in the room, at the bedfoot; but it did not appear that he observed her. And indeed (the fever being gone) he was so weak that he made but the one effort and sank again into lethargy. The course of his restoration was now slow but equal; every day his appetite improved; every week we were able to remark an increase both of strength and flesh; and before the end of the month he was out of bed and had even begun to be carried in his chair upon the terrace.

It was perhaps at this time that Mrs. Henry and I were the most uneasy in mind. Apprehension for his days was at an end; and a worse fear succeeded. Every day we drew consciously nearer to a day of reckoning; and the days passed on, and still there was nothing. Mr. Henry bettered in strength, he held long talks with us on a great diversity of subjects, his father came and sat with him and went again; and still there was no reference to the late tragedy or to the former troubles which had brought it on. Did he remember, and conceal his dreadful knowledge? or was the whole blotted from his mind? This was the problem that kept us watching and trembling all day when we were in his company and held us awake at night when we were in our lonely beds. We knew not even which alternative to hope for, both appearing so unnatural and pointing so directly to an unsound brain. Once this fear offered, I observed his conduct with sedulous particularity. Something of the child he exhibited: a cheerfulness quite foreign to his previous character, an interest readily aroused, and then very tenacious, in small matters which he had heretofore despised. When he was stricken down, I was his only confidant, and I may say his only friend, and he was on terms of division with his wife; upon his recovery, all was changed, the past forgotten, the wife first and even single in his thoughts. He turned to her with all his emotions, like a child to its mother, and seemed secure of sympathy; called her in all his needs with something of that querulous familiarity that marks a certainty of indulgence; and I must say, in justice to the woman, he was never disappointed. To her, indeed, this changed behaviour was inexpressibly affecting; and I think she felt it secretly as a reproach; so that I have seen her, in early days, escape out of the room that she might indulge herself in weeping. But to me the change appeared not natural; and viewing it along with all the rest, I began to wonder, with many head-shakings, whether his reason were perfectly erect.

As this doubt stretched over many years, endured indeed until my master's death, and clouded all our subsequent relations, I may well consider of it more at large. When he was able to resume some charge of his affairs, I had many opportunities to try him with precision. There was no lack of understanding, nor yet of authority; but the old continuous interest had quite departed; he grew readily fatigued, and fell to yawning; and he carried into money relations, where it is certainly out of place, a facility that bordered upon slackness. True, since we had no longer the exactions of the Master to contend against, there was the less occasion to raise strictness into principle or do battle for a farthing. True, again, there was nothing excessive in these relaxations, or I would have been no party to them. But the whole thing marked a change, very slight yet very perceptible; and though no man could say my master had gone at all out of his mind, no man could deny that he had drifted from his character. It was the same to the end, with his manner and appearance. Some of the heat of the fever lingered in his veins: his movements a little hurried, his speech notably more voluble, yet neither truly amiss. His whole mind stood open to happy impressions, welcoming these and making much of them; but the smallest suggestion of trouble or sorrow he received with visible impatience and dismissed again with immediate relief. It was to this temper that he owed the felicity of his later days; and yet here it was, if anywhere, that you could call the man insane. A great part of this life consists in contemplating what we cannot cure; but Mr. Henry, if he could not dismiss solicitude by an effort of the mind, must instantly and at whatever cost annihilate the cause of it; so that he played alternately the ostrich and the bull. It is to this strenuous cowardice of pain that I have to set down all the unfortunate and excessive steps of his subsequent career. Certainly this was the reason of his beating McManus, the groom, a thing so much out of all his former practice, and which awakened so much comment at the time. It is to this, again, that I must lay the total loss of near upon two hundred pounds, more than the half of which I could have saved if his impatience would have suffered me. But he preferred loss or any desperate extreme to a continuance of mental suffering.

All this has led me far from our immediate trouble: whether he remembered or had forgotten his late dreadful act; and if he remembered, in what light he viewed it. The truth burst upon us suddenly, and was indeed one of the chief surprises of my life. He had been several times abroad, and was now beginning to walk a little with an arm, when it chanced I should be left alone with him upon the terrace. He turned to me with a singular furtive smile, such as schoolboys use when in fault; and says he, in a private whisper and without the least preface: "Where have you buried him?"

I could not make one sound in answer.

"Where have you buried him?" he repeated. "I want to see his grave."

I conceived I had best take the bull by the horns. "Mr. Henry," said I, "I have news to give that will rejoice you exceedingly. In all human likelihood, your hands are clear of blood. I reason from certain indices; and by these it should appear your brother was not dead, but was carried in a swound on board the lugger. But now he may be perfectly recovered."

What there was in his countenance I could not read. "James?" he asked.

"Your brother James," I answered. "I would not raise a hope that may be found deceptive, but in my heart I think it very probable he is alive."

"Ah!" says Mr. Henry; and suddenly rising from his seat with more alacrity than he had yet discovered, set one finger on my breast, and cried at me in a kind of screaming whisper, "Mackellar"—these were his words—"nothing can kill that man. He is not mortal. He is bound upon my back to all eternity—to all eternity!" says he, and, sitting down again, fell upon a stubborn silence.

A day or two after, with the same secret smile, and first looking about as if to be sure we were alone, "Mackellar," said he, "when you have any intelligence, be sure and let me know. We must keep an eye upon him, or he will take us when we least expect."

"He will not show face here again," said I.

"Oh yes he will," said Mr. Henry. "Wherever I am, there will he be." And again he looked all about him.

"You must not dwell upon this thought, Mr. Henry," said I.

"No," said he, "that is a very good advice. We will never think of it, except when you have news. And we do not know yet," he added; "he may be dead."

The manner of his saying this convinced me thoroughly of what I had scarce ventured to suspect: that, so far from suffering any penitence for the attempt, he did but lament his failure. This was a discovery I kept to myself, fearing it might do him a prejudice with his wife. But I might have saved myself the trouble; she had divined it for herself, and found the sentiment quite natural. Indeed, I could not but say that there were three of us, all of the same mind; nor could any news have reached Durrisdeer more generally welcome than tidings of the Master's death.

This brings me to speak of the exception, my old lord. As soon as my anxiety for my own master began to be relaxed, I was aware of a change in the old gentleman, his father, that seemed to threaten mortal consequences.

His face was pale and swollen; as he sat in the chimney-side with his Latin, he would drop off sleeping and the book roll in the ashes; some days he would drag his foot, others stumble in speaking. The amenity of his behaviour appeared more extreme; full of excuses for the least trouble, very thoughtful for all; to myself, of a most flattering civility. One day, that he had sent for his lawyer and remained a long while private, he met me as he was crossing the hall with painful footsteps, and took me kindly by the hand. "Mr. Mackellar," said he, "I have had many occasions to set a proper value on your services; and to-day, when I re-cast my will, I have taken the freedom to name you for one of my executors. I believe you bear love enough to our house to render me this service." At that very time he passed the greater portion of his days in slumber, from which it was often difficult to rouse him; seemed to have lost all count of years, and had several times (particularly on waking) called for his wife and for an old servant whose very gravestone was now green with moss. If I had been put to my oath, I must have declared he was incapable of testing; and yet there was never a will drawn more sensible in every trait, or showing a more excellent judgment both of persons and affairs.

His dissolution, though it took not very long, proceeded by infinitesimal gradations. His faculties decayed together steadily; the power of his limbs was almost gone, he was extremely deaf, his speech had sunk into mere mumblings; and yet to the end he managed to discover something of his former courtesy and kindness, pressing the hand of any that helped him, presenting me with one of his Latin books, in which he had laboriously traced my name, and in a thousand ways reminding us of the greatness of that loss which it might almost be said we had already suffered. To the end, the power of articulation returned to him in flashes; it seemed he had only forgotten the art of speech as a child forgets his lesson, and at times he would call some part of it to mind. On the last night of his life he suddenly broke silence with these words from Virgil: "Gnatique patrisque, alma, precor, miserere," perfectly uttered, and with a fitting accent. At the sudden clear sound of it we started from our several occupations; but it was in vain we turned to him; he sat there silent, and, to all appearance, fatuous. A little later he was had to bed with more difficulty than ever before; and some time in the night, without any more violence, his spirit fled.

At a far later period I chanced to speak of these particulars with a doctor of medicine, a man of so high a reputation that I scruple to adduce his name. By his view of it father and son both suffered from the affection: the father from the strain of his unnatural sorrows—the son perhaps in the excitation of the fever; each had ruptured a vessel on the brain, and there was probably (my doctor added) some predisposition in the family to accidents of that description. The father sank, the son recovered all the externals of a healthy man; but it is like there was some destruction in those delicate tissues where the soul resides and does her earthly business; her heavenly, I would fain hope, cannot be thus obstructed by material accidents. And yet, upon a more mature opinion, it matters not one jot; for He who shall pass judgment on the records of our life is the same that formed us in frailty.

The death of my old lord was the occasion of a fresh surprise to us who watched the behaviour of his successor. To any considering mind, the two sons had between them slain their father, and he who took the sword might be even said to have slain him with his hand, but no such thought appeared to trouble my new lord. He was becomingly grave; I could scarce say sorrowful, or only with a pleasant sorrow; talking of the dead with a regretful cheerfulness, relating old examples of his character, smiling at them with a good conscience; and when the day of the funeral came round, doing the honours with exact propriety. I could perceive, besides, that he found a solid gratification in his accession to the title; the which he was punctilious in exacting.

And now there came upon the scene a new character, and one that played his part, too, in the story; I mean the present lord, Alexander, whose birth (17th July, 1757) filled the cup of my poor master's happiness. There was nothing then left him to wish for; nor yet leisure to wish for it. Indeed, there never was a parent so fond and doting as he showed himself. He was continually uneasy in his son's absence. Was the child abroad? the father would be watching the clouds in case it rained. Was it night? he would rise out of his bed to observe its slumbers. His conversation grew even wearyful to strangers, since he talked of little but his son. In matters relating to the estate, all was designed with a particular eye to Alexander; and it would be:—

"Let us put it in hand at once, that the wood may be grown against Alexander's majority;" or, "This will fall in again handsomely for Alexander's marriage." Every day this absorption of the man's nature became more observable, with many touching and some very blameworthy particulars. Soon the child could walk abroad with him, at first on the terrace, hand in hand, and afterward at large about the policies; and this grew to be my lord's chief occupation. The sound of their two voices (audible a great way off, for they spoke loud) became familiar in the neighbourhood; and for my part I found it more agreeable than the sound of birds. It was pretty to see the pair returning, full of briars, and the father as flushed and sometimes as bemuddied as the child, for they were equal sharers in all sorts of boyish entertainment, digging in the beach, damming of streams, and what not; and I have seen them gaze through a fence at cattle with the same childish contemplation.

The mention of these rambles brings me to a strange scene of which I was a witness. There was one walk I never followed myself without emotion, so often had I gone there upon miserable errands, so much had there befallen against the house of Durrisdeer. But the path lay handy from all points beyond the Muckle Ross; and I was driven, although much against my will, to take my use of it perhaps once in the two months. It befell when Mr. Alexander was of the age of seven or eight, I had some business on the far side in the morning, and entered the shrubbery, on my homeward way, about nine of a bright forenoon. It was that time of year when the woods are all in their spring colours, the thorns all in flower, and the birds in the high season of their singing. In contrast to this merriment, the shrubbery was only the more sad, and I the more oppressed by its associations. In this situation of spirit it struck me disagreeably to hear voices a little way in front, and to recognise the tones of my lord and Mr. Alexander. I pushed ahead, and came presently into their view. They stood together in the open space where the duel was, my lord with his hand on his son's shoulder, and speaking with some gravity. At least, as he raised his head upon my coming, I thought I could perceive his countenance to lighten.

"Ah!" says he, "here comes the good Mackellar. I have just been telling Sandie the story of this place, and how there was a man whom the devil tried to kill, and how near he came to kill the devil instead."

I had thought it strange enough he should bring the child into that scene; that he should actually be discoursing of his act, passed measure. But the worst was yet to come; for he added, turning to his son—"You can ask Mackellar; he was here and saw it."

"Is it true, Mr. Mackellar?" asked the child. "And did you really see the devil?"

"I have not heard the tale," I replied; "and I am in a press of business." So far I said a little sourly, fencing with the embarrassment of the position; and suddenly the bitterness of the past, and the terror of that scene by candle-light, rushed in upon my mind. I bethought me that, for a difference of a second's quickness in parade, the child before me might have never seen the day; and the emotion that always fluttered round my heart in that dark shrubbery burst forth in words. "But so much is true," I cried, "that I have met the devil in these woods, and seen him foiled here. Blessed be God that we escaped with life—blessed be God that one stone yet stands upon another in the walls of Durrisdeer! And, oh! Mr. Alexander, if ever you come by this spot, though it was a hundred years hence, and you came with the gayest and the highest in the land, I would step aside and remember a bit prayer."

My lord bowed his head gravely. "Ah!" says he, "Mackellar is always in the right. Come, Alexander, take your bonnet off." And with that he uncovered, and held out his hand. "O Lord," said he, "I thank Thee, and my son thanks Thee, for Thy manifold great mercies. Let us have peace for a little; defend us from the evil man. Smite him, O Lord, upon the lying mouth!" The last broke out of him like a cry; and at that, whether remembered anger choked his utterance, or whether he perceived this was a singular sort of prayer, at least he suddenly came to a full stop; and, after a moment, set back his hat upon his head.

"I think you have forgot a word, my lord," said I. "'Forgive us our trespasses, as we forgive them that trespass against us. For Thine is the kingdom, and the power, and the glory, for ever and ever. Amen.'"

"Ah! that is easy saying," said my lord. "That is very easy saying, Mackellar. But for me to forgive!—I think I would cut a very silly figure if I had the affectation to pretend it."

"The bairn, my lord!" said I, with some severity, for I thought his expressions little fitted for the care of children.

"Why, very true," said he. "This is dull work for a bairn. Let's go nesting."

I forget if it was the same day, but it was soon after, my lord, finding me alone, opened himself a little more on the same head.

"Mackellar," he said, "I am now a very happy man."

"I think so indeed, my lord," said I, "and the sight of it gives me a light heart."

"There is an obligation in happiness—do you not think so?" says he, musingly.

"I think so indeed," says I, "and one in sorrow, too. If we are not here to try to do the best, in my humble opinion the sooner we are away the better for all parties."

"Ay, but if you were in my shoes, would you forgive him?" asks my lord.

The suddenness of the attack a little gravelled me.

"It is a duty laid upon us strictly," said I.

"Hut!" said he. "These are expressions! Do you forgive the man yourself?"

"Well—no!" said I. "God forgive me, I do not."

"Shake hands upon that!" cries my lord, with a kind of joviality.

"It is an ill sentiment to shake hands upon," said I, "for Christian people. I think I will give you mine on some more evangelical occasion."

This I said, smiling a little; but as for my lord, he went from the room laughing aloud.

For my lord's slavery to the child, I can find no expression adequate. He lost himself in that continual thought: business, friends, and wife being all alike forgotten, or only remembered with a painful effort, like that of one struggling with a posset. It was most notable in the matter of his wife. Since I had known Durrisdeer, she had been the burthen of his thought and the loadstone of his eyes; and now she was quite cast out. I have seen him come to the door of a room, look round, and pass my lady over as though she were a dog before the fire. It would be Alexander he was seeking, and my lady knew it well. I have heard him speak to her so ruggedly that I nearly found it in my heart to intervene: the cause would still be the same, that she had in some way thwarted Alexander. Without doubt this was in the nature of a judgment on my lady. Without doubt she had the tables turned upon her, as only Providence can do it; she who had been cold so many years to every mark of tenderness, it was her part now to be neglected: the more praise to her that she played it well.

An odd situation resulted: that we had once more two parties in the house, and that now I was of my lady's. Not that ever I lost the love I bore my master. But, for one thing, he had the less use for my society. For another, I could not but compare the case of Mr. Alexander with that of Miss Katharine; for whom my lord had never found the least attention. And for a third, I was wounded by the change he discovered to his wife, which struck me in the nature of an infidelity. I could not but admire, besides, the constancy and kindness she displayed. Perhaps her sentiment to my lord, as it had been founded from the first in pity, was that rather of a mother than a wife; perhaps it pleased her—if I may so say—to behold her two children so happy in each other; the more as one had suffered so unjustly in the past. But, for all that, and though I could never trace in her one spark of jealousy, she must fall back for society on poor neglected Miss Katharine; and I, on my part, came to pass my spare hours more and more with the mother and daughter. It would be easy to make too much of this division, for it was a pleasant family, as families go; still the thing existed; whether my lord knew it or not, I am in doubt. I do not think he did; he was bound up so entirely in his son; but the rest of us knew it, and in a manner suffered from the knowledge.

What troubled us most, however, was the great and growing danger to the child. My lord was his father over again; it was to be feared the son would prove a second Master. Time has proved these fears to have been quite exaggerate. Certainly there is no more worthy gentleman to-day in Scotland than the seventh Lord Durrisdeer. Of my own exodus from his employment it does not become me to speak, above all in a memorandum written only to justify his father. . . .

[Editor's Note. Five pages of Mr. Mackellar's MS. are here omitted. I have gathered from their perusal an impression that Mr. Mackellar, in his old age, was rather an exacting servant. Against the seventh Lord Durrisdeer (with whom, at any rate, we have no concern) nothing material is alleged.—R. L. S.]

. . . But our fear at the time was lest he should turn out, in the person of his son, a second edition of his brother. My lady had tried to interject some wholesome discipline; she had been glad to give that up, and now looked on with secret dismay; sometimes she even spoke of it by hints; and sometimes, when there was brought to her knowledge some monstrous instance of my lord's indulgence, she would betray herself in a gesture or perhaps an exclamation. As for myself, I was haunted by the thought both day and night: not so much for the child's sake as for the father's. The man had gone to sleep, he was dreaming a dream, and any rough wakening must infallibly prove mortal. That he should survive its death was inconceivable; and the fear of its dishonour made me cover my face.

It was this continual preoccupation that screwed me up at last to a remonstrance: a matter worthy to be narrated in detail. My lord and I sat one day at the same table upon some tedious business of detail; I have said that he had lost his former interest in such occupations; he was plainly itching to be gone, and he looked fretful, weary, and methought older than I had ever previously observed. I suppose it was the haggard face that put me suddenly upon my enterprise.

"My lord," said I, with my head down, and feigning to continue my occupation—"or, rather, let me call you again by the name of Mr. Henry, for I fear your anger and want you to think upon old times—"

"My good Mackellar!" said he; and that in tones so kindly that I had near forsook my purpose. But I called to mind that I was speaking for his good, and stuck to my colours.

"Has it never come in upon your mind what you are doing?" I asked.

"What I am doing?" he repeated; "I was never good at guessing riddles."

"What you are doing with your son?" said I.

"Well," said he, with some defiance in his tone, "and what am I doing with my son?"

"Your father was a very good man," says I, straying from the direct path. "But do you think he was a wise father?"

There was a pause before he spoke, and then: "I say nothing against him," he replied. "I had the most cause perhaps; but I say nothing."

"Why, there it is," said I. "You had the cause at least. And yet your father was a good man; I never knew a better, save on the one point, nor yet a wiser. Where he stumbled, it is highly possible another man should fail. He had the two sons—"

My lord rapped suddenly and violently on the table.

"What is this?" cried he. "Speak out!"

"I will, then," said I, my voice almost strangled with the thumping of my heart. "If you continue to indulge Mr. Alexander, you are following in your father's footsteps. Beware, my lord, lest (when he grows up) your son should follow in the Master's."

I had never meant to put the thing so crudely; but in the extreme of fear, there comes a brutal kind of courage, the most brutal indeed of all; and I burnt my ships with that plain word. I never had the answer. When I lifted my head, my lord had risen to his feet, and the next moment he fell heavily on the floor. The fit or seizure endured not very long; he came to himself vacantly, put his hand to his head, which I was then supporting, and says he, in a broken voice: "I have been ill," and a little after: "Help me." I got him to his feet, and he stood pretty well, though he kept hold of the table. "I have been ill, Mackellar," he said again. "Something broke, Mackellar—or was going to break, and then all swam away. I think I was very angry. Never you mind, Mackellar; never you mind, my man. I wouldnae hurt a hair upon your head. Too much has come and gone. It's a certain thing between us two. But I think, Mackellar, I will go to Mrs. Henry—I think I will go to Mrs. Henry," said he, and got pretty steadily from the room, leaving me overcome with penitence.

Presently the door flew open, and my lady swept in with flashing eyes. "What is all this?" she cried. "What have you done to my husband? Will nothing teach you your position in this house? Will you never cease from making and meddling?"

"My lady," said I, "since I have been in this house I have had plenty of hard words. For a while they were my daily diet, and I swallowed them all. As for to-day, you may call me what you please; you will never find the name hard enough for such a blunder. And yet I meant it for the best."

I told her all with ingenuity, even as it is written here; and when she had heard me out, she pondered, and I could see her animosity fall. "Yes," she said, "you meant well indeed. I have had the same thought myself, or the same temptation rather, which makes me pardon you. But, dear God, can you not understand that he can bear no more? He can bear no more!" she cried. "The cord is stretched to snapping. What matters the future if he have one or two good days?"

"Amen," said I. "I will meddle no more. I am pleased enough that you should recognise the kindness of my meaning."

"Yes," said my lady; "but when it came to the point, I have to suppose your courage failed you; for what you said was said cruelly." She paused, looking at me; then suddenly smiled a little, and said a singular thing: "Do you know what you are, Mr. Mackellar? You are an old maid."

No more incident of any note occurred in the family until the return of that ill-starred man the Master. But I have to place here a second extract from the memoirs of Chevalier Burke, interesting in itself, and highly necessary for my purpose. It is our only sight of the Master on his Indian travels; and the first word in these pages of Secundra Dass. One fact, it is to observe, appears here very clearly, which if we had known some twenty years ago, how many calamities and sorrows had been spared!—that Secundra Dass spoke English.

CHAPTER VII.
ADVENTURE OF CHEVALIER BURKE IN INDIA.

Extracted from his Memoirs.

. . . Here was I, therefore, on the streets of that city, the name of which I cannot call to mind, while even then I was so ill-acquainted with its situation that I knew not whether to go south or north. The alert being sudden, I had run forth without shoes or stockings; my hat had been struck from my head in the mellay; my kit was in the hands of the English; I had no companion but the cipaye, no weapon but my sword, and the devil a coin in my pocket. In short, I was for all the world like one of those calendars with whom Mr. Galland has made us acquainted in his elegant tales. These gentlemen, you will remember, were for ever falling in with extraordinary incidents; and I was myself upon the brink of one so astonishing that I protest I cannot explain it to this day.

The cipaye was a very honest man; he had served many years with the French colours, and would have let himself be cut to pieces for any of the brave countrymen of Mr. Lally. It is the same fellow (his name has quite escaped me) of whom I have narrated already a surprising instance of generosity of mind—when he found Mr. de Fessac and myself upon the ramparts, entirely overcome with liquor, and covered us with straw while the commandant was passing by. I consulted him, therefore, with perfect freedom. It was a fine question what to do; but we decided at last to escalade a garden wall, where we could certainly sleep in the shadow of the trees, and might perhaps find an occasion to get hold of a pair of slippers and a turban. In that part of the city we had only the difficulty of the choice, for it was a quarter consisting entirely of walled gardens, and the lanes which divided them were at that hour of the night deserted. I gave the cipaye a back, and we had soon dropped into a large enclosure full of trees. The place was soaking with the dew, which, in that country, is exceedingly unwholesome, above all to whites; yet my fatigue was so extreme that I was already half asleep, when the cipaye recalled me to my senses. In the far end of the enclosure a bright light had suddenly shone out, and continued to burn steadily among the leaves. It was a circumstance highly unusual in such a place and hour; and, in our situation, it behoved us to proceed with some timidity. The cipaye was sent to reconnoitre, and pretty soon returned with the intelligence that we had fallen extremely amiss, for the house belonged to a white man, who was in all likelihood English.

"Faith," says I, "if there is a white man to be seen, I will have a look at him; for, the Lord be praised! there are more sorts than the one!"

The cipaye led me forward accordingly to a place from which I had a clear view upon the house. It was surrounded with a wide verandah; a lamp, very well trimmed, stood upon the floor of it, and on either side of the lamp there sat a man, cross-legged, after the Oriental manner. Both, besides, were bundled up in muslin like two natives; and yet one of them was not only a white man, but a man very well known to me and the reader, being indeed that very Master of Ballantrae of whose gallantry and genius I have had to speak so often. Word had reached me that he was come to the Indies, though we had never met at least, and I heard little of his occupations. But, sure, I had no sooner recognised him, and found myself in the arms of so old a comrade, than I supposed my tribulations were quite done. I stepped plainly forth into the light of the moon, which shone exceeding strong, and hailing Ballantrae by name, made him in a few words master of my grievous situation. He turned, started the least thing in the world, looked me fair in the face while I was speaking, and when I had done addressed himself to his companion in the barbarous native dialect. The second person, who was of an extraordinary delicate appearance, with legs like walking canes and fingers like the stalk of a tobacco pipe, [6] now rose to his feet.

"The Sahib," says he, "understands no English language. I understand it myself, and I see you make some small mistake—oh! which may happen very often. But the Sahib would be glad to know how you come in a garden."

"Ballantrae!" I cried, "have you the damned impudence to deny me to my face?"

Ballantrae never moved a muscle, staring at me like an image in a pagoda.

"The Sahib understands no English language," says the native, as glib as before. "He be glad to know how you come in a garden."

"Oh! the divil fetch him," says I. "He would be glad to know how I come in a garden, would he? Well, now, my dear man, just have the civility to tell the Sahib, with my kind love, that we are two soldiers here whom he never met and never heard of, but the cipaye is a broth of a boy, and I am a broth of a boy myself; and if we don't get a full meal of meat, and a turban, and slippers, and the value of a gold mohur in small change as a matter of convenience, bedad, my friend, I could lay my finger on a garden where there is going to be trouble."

They carried their comedy so far as to converse awhile in Hindustanee; and then says the Hindu, with the same smile, but sighing as if he were tired of the repetition, "The Sahib would be glad to know how you come in a garden."

"Is that the way of it?" says I, and laying my hand on my sword-hilt I bade the cipaye draw.

Ballantrae's Hindu, still smiling, pulled out a pistol from his bosom, and though Ballantrae himself never moved a muscle I knew him well enough to be sure he was prepared.

"The Sahib thinks you better go away," says the Hindu.

Well, to be plain, it was what I was thinking myself; for the report of a pistol would have been, under Providence, the means of hanging the pair of us.

"Tell the Sahib I consider him no gentleman," says I, and turned away with a gesture of contempt.

I was not gone three steps when the voice of the Hindu called me back. "The Sahib would be glad to know if you are a dam low Irishman," says he; and at the words Ballantrae smiled and bowed very low.

"What is that?" says I.

"The Sahib say you ask your friend Mackellar," says the Hindu. "The Sahib he cry quits."

"Tell the Sahib I will give him a cure for the Scots fiddle when next we meet," cried I.

The pair were still smiling as I left.

There is little doubt some flaws may be picked in my own behaviour; and when a man, however gallant, appeals to posterity with an account of his exploits, he must almost certainly expect to share the fate of Cæsar and Alexander, and to meet with some detractors. But there is one thing that can never be laid at the door of Francis Burke: he never turned his back on a friend....

(Here follows a passage which the Chevalier Burke has been at the pains to delete before sending me his manuscript. Doubtless it was some very natural complaint of what he supposed to be an indiscretion on my part; though, indeed, I can call none to mind. Perhaps Mr. Henry was less guarded; or it is just possible the Master found the means to examine my correspondence, and himself read the letter from Troyes: in revenge for which this cruel jest was perpetrated on Mr. Burke in his extreme necessity. The Master, for all his wickedness, was not without some natural affection; I believe he was sincerely attached to Mr. Burke in the beginning; but the thought of treachery dried up the springs of his very shallow friendship, and his detestable nature appeared naked.—E. McK.)

CHAPTER VIII.
THE ENEMY IN THE HOUSE.

It is a strange thing that I should be at a stick for a date—the date, besides, of an incident that changed the very nature of my life, and sent us all into foreign lands. But the truth is, I was stricken out of all my habitudes, and find my journals very ill redd-up, [7] the day not indicated sometimes for a week or two together, and the whole fashion of the thing like that of a man near desperate. It was late in March at least, or early in April, 1764. I had slept heavily, and wakened with a premonition of some evil to befall. So strong was this upon my spirit that I hurried downstairs in my shirt and breeches, and my hand (I remember) shook upon the rail. It was a cold, sunny morning, with a thick white frost; the blackbirds sang exceeding sweet and loud about the house of Durrisdeer, and there was a noise of the sea in all the chambers. As I came by the doors of the hall, another sound arrested me—of voices talking. I drew nearer, and stood like a man dreaming. Here was certainly a human voice, and that in my own master's house, and yet I knew it not; certainly human speech, and that in my native land; and yet, listen as I pleased, I could not catch one syllable. An old tale started up in my mind of a fairy wife (or perhaps only a wandering stranger), that came to the place of my fathers some generations back, and stayed the matter of a week, talking often in a tongue that signified nothing to the hearers; and went again, as she had come, under cloud of night, leaving not so much as a name behind her. A little fear I had, but more curiosity; and I opened the hall-door, and entered.

The supper-things still lay upon the table; the shutters were still closed, although day peeped in the divisions; and the great room was lighted only with a single taper and some lurching reverberation of the fire. Close in the chimney sat two men. The one that was wrapped in a cloak and wore boots, I knew at once: it was the bird of ill omen back again. Of the other, who was set close to the red embers, and made up into a bundle like a mummy, I could but see that he was an alien, of a darker hue than any man of Europe, very frailly built, with a singular tall forehead, and a secret eye. Several bundles and a small valise were on the floor; and to judge by the smallness of this luggage, and by the condition of the Master's boots, grossly patched by some unscrupulous country cobbler, evil had not prospered.

He rose upon my entrance; our eyes crossed; and I know not why it should have been, but my courage rose like a lark on a May morning.

"Ha!" said I, "is this you?"—and I was pleased with the unconcern of my own voice.

"It is even myself, worthy Mackellar," says the Master.

"This time you have brought the black dog visibly upon your back," I continued.

"Referring to Secundra Dass?" asked the Master. "Let me present you. He is a native gentleman of India."

"Hum!" said I. "I am no great lover either of you or your friends, Mr. Bally. But I will let a little daylight in, and have a look at you." And so saying, I undid the shutters of the eastern window.

By the light of the morning I could perceive the man was changed. Later, when we were all together, I was more struck to see how lightly time had dealt with him; but the first glance was otherwise.

"You are getting an old man," said I.

A shade came upon his face. "If you could see yourself," said he, "you would perhaps not dwell upon the topic."

"Hut!" I returned, "old age is nothing to me. I think I have been always old; and I am now, I thank God, better known and more respected. It is not every one that can say that, Mr. Bally! The lines in your brow are calamities; your life begins to close in upon you like a prison; death will soon be rapping at the door; and I see not from what source you are to draw your consolations."

Here the Master addressed himself to Secundra Dass in Hindustanee, from which I gathered (I freely confess, with a high degree of pleasure) that my remarks annoyed him. All this while, you may be sure, my mind had been busy upon other matters, even while I rallied my enemy; and chiefly as to how I should communicate secretly and quickly with my lord. To this, in the breathing-space now given me, I turned all the forces of my mind; when, suddenly shifting my eyes, I was aware of the man himself standing in the doorway, and, to all appearance, quite composed. He had no sooner met my looks than he stepped across the threshold. The Master heard him coming, and advanced upon the other side; about four feet apart, these brothers came to a full pause, and stood exchanging steady looks, and then my lord smiled, bowed a little forward, and turned briskly away.

"Mackellar," says he, "we must see to breakfast for these travellers."

It was plain the Master was a trifle disconcerted; but he assumed the more impudence of speech and manner. "I am as hungry as a hawk," says he. "Let it be something good, Henry."

My lord turned to him with the same hard smile.

"Lord Durrisdeer," says he.

"Oh! never in the family," returned the Master.

"Every one in this house renders me my proper title," says my lord. "If it please you to make an exception, I will leave you to consider what appearance it will bear to strangers, and whether it may not be translated as an effect of impotent jealousy."

I could have clapped my hands together with delight: the more so as my lord left no time for any answer, but, bidding me with a sign to follow him, went straight out of the hall.

"Come quick," says he; "we have to sweep vermin from the house." And he sped through the passages, with so swift a step that I could scarce keep up with him, straight to the door of John Paul, the which he opened without summons and walked in. John was, to all appearance, sound asleep, but my lord made no pretence of waking him.

"John Paul," said he, speaking as quietly as ever I heard him, "you served my father long, or I would pack you from the house like a dog. If in half an hour's time I find you gone, you shall continue to receive your wages in Edinburgh. If you linger here or in St. Bride's—old man, old servant, and altogether—I shall find some very astonishing way to make you smart for your disloyalty. Up and begone. The door you let them in by will serve for your departure. I do not choose my son shall see your face again."

"I am rejoiced to find you bear the thing so quietly," said I, when we were forth again by ourselves.

"Quietly!" cries he, and put my hand suddenly against his heart, which struck upon his bosom like a sledge.

At this revelation I was filled with wonder and fear. There was no constitution could bear so violent a strain—his least of all, that was unhinged already; and I decided in my mind that we must bring this monstrous situation to an end.

"It would be well, I think, if I took word to my lady," said I. Indeed, he should have gone himself, but I counted—not in vain—on his indifference.

"Aye," says he, "do. I will hurry breakfast: we must all appear at the table, even Alexander; it must appear we are untroubled."

I ran to my lady's room, and with no preparatory cruelty, disclosed my news.

"My mind was long ago made up," said she. "We must make our packets secretly to-day, and leave secretly to-night. Thank Heaven, we have another house! The first ship that sails shall bear us to New York."

"And what of him?" I asked.

"We leave him Durrisdeer," she cried. "Let him work his pleasure upon that."

"Not so, by your leave," said I. "There shall be a dog at his heels that can hold fast. Bed he shall have, and board, and a horse to ride upon, if he behave himself; but the keys—if you think well of it, my lady—shall be left in the hands of one Mackellar. There will be good care taken; trust him for that."

"Mr. Mackellar," she cried, "I thank you for that thought. All shall be left in your hands. If we must go into a savage country, I bequeath it to you to take our vengeance. Send Macconochie to St. Bride's, to arrange privately for horses and to call the lawyer. My lord must leave procuration."

At that moment my lord came to the door, and we opened our plan to him.

"I will never hear of it," he cried; "he would think I feared him. I will stay in my own house, please God, until I die. There lives not the man can beard me out of it. Once and for all, here I am, and here I stay in spite of all the devils in hell." I can give no idea of the vehemency of his words and utterance; but we both stood aghast, and I in particular, who had been a witness of his former self-restraint.

My lady looked at me with an appeal that went to my heart and recalled me to my wits. I made her a private sign to go, and when my lord and I were alone, went up to him where he was racing to and fro in one end of the room like a half-lunatic, and set my hand firmly on his shoulder.

"My lord," says I, "I am going to be the plain-dealer once more; if for the last time, so much the better, for I am grown weary of the part."

"Nothing will change me," he answered. "God forbid I should refuse to hear you; but nothing will change me." This he said firmly, with no signal of the former violence, which already raised my hopes.

"Very well," said I "I can afford to waste my breath." I pointed to a chair, and he sat down and looked at me. "I can remember a time when my lady very much neglected you," said I.

"I never spoke of it while it lasted," returned my lord, with a high flush of colour; "and it is all changed now."

"Do you know how much?" I said. "Do you know how much it is all changed? The tables are turned, my lord! It is my lady that now courts you for a word, a look—ay, and courts you in vain. Do you know with whom she passes her days while you are out gallivanting in the policies? My lord, she is glad to pass them with a certain dry old grieve [8] of the name of Ephraim Mackellar; and I think you may be able to remember what that means, for I am the more in a mistake or you were once driven to the same company yourself."

"Mackellar!" cries my lord, getting to his feet. "O my God, Mackellar!"

"It is neither the name of Mackellar nor the name of God that can change the truth," said I; "and I am telling you the fact. Now for you, that suffered so much, to deal out the same suffering to another, is that the part of any Christian? But you are so swallowed up in your new friend that the old are all forgotten. They are all clean vanished from your memory. And yet they stood by you at the darkest; my lady not the least. And does my lady ever cross your mind? Does it ever cross your mind what she went through that night?—or what manner of a wife she has been to you thenceforward?—or in what kind of a position she finds herself to-day? Never. It is your pride to stay and face him out, and she must stay along with you. Oh! my lord's pride—that's the great affair! And yet she is the woman, and you are a great hulking man! She is the woman that you swore to protect; and, more betoken, the own mother of that son of yours!"

"You are speaking very bitterly, Mackellar," said he; "but, the Lord knows, I fear you are speaking very true. I have not proved worthy of my happiness. Bring my lady back."

My lady was waiting near at hand to learn the issue. When I brought her in, my lord took a hand of each of us, and laid them both upon his bosom. "I have had two friends in my life," said he. "All the comfort ever I had, it came from one or other. When you two are in a mind, I think I would be an ungrateful dog—" He shut his mouth very hard, and looked on us with swimming eyes. "Do what ye like with me," says he, "only don't think—" He stopped again. "Do what ye please with me: God knows I love and honour you." And dropping our two hands, he turned his back and went and gazed out of the window. But my lady ran after, calling his name, and threw herself upon his neck in a passion of weeping.

I went out and shut the door behind me, and stood and thanked God from the bottom of my heart.

At the breakfast board, according to my lord's design, we were all met. The Master had by that time plucked off his patched boots and made a toilet suitable to the hour; Secundra Dass was no longer bundled up in wrappers, but wore a decent plain black suit, which misbecame him strangely; and the pair were at the great window, looking forth, when the family entered. They turned; and the black man (as they had already named him in the house) bowed almost to his knees, but the Master was for running forward like one of the family. My lady stopped him, curtseying low from the far end of the hall, and keeping her children at her back. My lord was a little in front: so there were the three cousins of Durrisdeer face to face. The hand of time was very legible on all; I seemed to read in their changed faces a memento mori; and what affected me still more, it was the wicked man that bore his years the handsomest. My lady was quite transfigured into the matron, a becoming woman for the head of a great tableful of children and dependents. My lord was grown slack in his limbs; he stooped; he walked with a running motion, as though he had learned again from Mr. Alexander; his face was drawn; it seemed a trifle longer than of old; and it wore at times a smile very singularly mingled, and which (in my eyes) appeared both bitter and pathetic. But the Master still bore himself erect, although perhaps with effort; his brow barred about the centre with imperious lines, his mouth set as for command. He had all the gravity and something of the splendour of Satan in the "Paradise Lost." I could not help but see the man with admiration, and was only surprised that I saw him with so little fear.

But indeed (as long as we were at the table) it seemed as if his authority were quite vanished and his teeth all drawn. We had known him a magician that controlled the elements; and here he was, transformed into an ordinary gentleman, chatting like his neighbours at the breakfast-board. For now the father was dead, and my lord and lady reconciled, in what ear was he to pour his calumnies? It came upon me in a kind of vision how hugely I had overrated the man's subtlety. He had his malice still; he was false as ever; and, the occasion being gone that made his strength, he sat there impotent; he was still the viper, but now spent his venom on a file. Two more thoughts occurred to me while yet we sat at breakfast: the first, that he was abashed—I had almost said, distressed—to find his wickedness quite unavailing; the second, that perhaps my lord was in the right, and we did amiss to fly from our dismasted enemy. But my poor man's leaping heart came in my mind, and I remembered it was for his life we played the coward.

When the meal was over, the Master followed me to my room, and, taking a chair (which I had never offered him), asked me what was to be done with him.

"Why, Mr. Bally," said I, "the house will still be open to you for a time."

"For a time?" says he. "I do not know if I quite take your meaning."

"It is plain enough," said I. "We keep you for our reputation; as soon as you shall have publicly disgraced yourself by some of your misconduct, we shall pack you forth again."

"You are become an impudent rogue," said the Master, bending his brows at me dangerously.

"I learned in a good school," I returned. "And you must have perceived yourself that with my old lord's death your power is quite departed. I do not fear you now, Mr. Bally; I think even—God forgive me—that I take a certain pleasure in your company."

He broke out in a burst of laughter, which I clearly saw to be assumed.

"I have come with empty pockets," says he, after a pause.

"I do not think there will be any money going," I replied. "I would advise you not to build on that."

"I shall have something to say on the point," he returned.

"Indeed?" said I. "I have not a guess what it will be, then."

"Oh! you affect confidence," said the Master. "I have still one strong position—that you people fear a scandal, and I enjoy it."

"Pardon me, Mr. Bally," says I. "We do not in the least fear a scandal against you."

He laughed again. "You have been studying repartee," he said. "But speech is very easy, and sometimes very deceptive. I warn you fairly: you will find me vitriol in the house. You would do wiser to pay money down and see my back." And with that he waved his hand to me and left the room.

A little after, my lord came with the lawyer, Mr. Carlyle; a bottle of old wine was brought, and we all had a glass before we fell to business. The necessary deeds were then prepared and executed, and the Scotch estates made over in trust to Mr. Carlyle and myself.

"There is one point, Mr. Carlyle," said my lord, when these affairs had been adjusted, "on which I wish that you would do us justice. This sudden departure coinciding with my brother's return will be certainly commented on. I wish you would discourage any conjunction of the two."

"I will make a point of it, my lord," said Mr. Carlyle. "The Mas— Bally does not, then, accompany you?"

"It is a point I must approach," said my lord. "Mr. Bally remains at Durrisdeer, under the care of Mr. Mackellar; and I do not mean that he shall even know our destination."

"Common report, however—" began the lawyer.

"Ah! but, Mr. Carlyle, this is to be a secret quite among ourselves," interrupted my lord. "None but you and Mackellar are to be made acquainted with my movements."

"And Mr. Bally stays here? Quite so," said Mr. Carlyle. "The powers you leave—" Then he broke off again. "Mr. Mackellar, we have a rather heavy weight upon us."

"No doubt," said I.

"No doubt," said he. "Mr. Bally will have no voice?"

"He will have no voice," said my lord; "and, I hope, no influence. Mr. Bally is not a good adviser."

"I see," said the lawyer. "By the way, has Mr. Bally means?"

"I understand him to have nothing," replied my lord. "I give him table, fire, and candle in this house."

"And in the matter of an allowance? If I am to share the responsibility, you will see how highly desirable it is that I should understand your views," said the lawyer. "On the question of an allowance?"

"There will be no allowance," said my lord. "I wish Mr. Bally to live very private. We have not always been gratified with his behaviour."

"And in the matter of money," I added, "he has shown himself an infamous bad husband. Glance your eye upon that docket, Mr. Carlyle, where I have brought together the different sums the man has drawn from the estate in the last fifteen or twenty years. The total is pretty."

Mr. Carlyle made the motion of whistling. "I had no guess of this," said he. "Excuse me once more, my lord, if I appear to push you; but it is really desirable I should penetrate your intentions. Mr. Mackellar might die, when I should find myself alone upon this trust. Would it not be rather your lordship's preference that Mr. Bally should—ahem—should leave the country?"

My lord looked at Mr. Carlyle. "Why do you ask that?" said he.

"I gather, my lord, that Mr. Bally is not a comfort to his family," says the lawyer with a smile.

My lord's face became suddenly knotted. "I wish he was in hell!" cried he, and filled himself a glass of wine, but with a hand so tottering that he spilled the half into his bosom. This was the second time that, in the midst of the most regular and wise behaviour, his animosity had spirted out. It startled Mr. Carlyle, who observed my lord thenceforth with covert curiosity; and to me it restored the certainty that we were acting for the best in view of my lord's health and reason.

Except for this explosion the interview was very successfully conducted. No doubt Mr. Carlyle would talk, as lawyers do, little by little. We could thus feel we had laid the foundations of a better feeling in the country, and the man's own misconduct would certainly complete what we had begun. Indeed, before his departure, the lawyer showed us there had already gone abroad some glimmerings of the truth.

"I should perhaps explain to you, my lord," said he, pausing, with his hat in his hand, "that I have not been altogether surprised with your lordship's dispositions in the case of Mr. Bally. Something of this nature oozed out when he was last in Durrisdeer. There was some talk of a woman at St. Bride's, to whom you had behaved extremely handsome, and Mr. Bally with no small degree of cruelty. There was the entail, again, which was much controverted. In short, there was no want of talk, back and forward; and some of our wise-acres took up a strong opinion. I remained in suspense, as became one of my cloth; but Mr. Mackellar's docket here has finally opened my eyes. I do not think, Mr. Mackellar, that you and I will give him that much rope."

The rest of that important day passed prosperously through. It was our policy to keep the enemy in view, and I took my turn to be his watchman with the rest. I think his spirits rose as he perceived us to be so attentive, and I know that mine insensibly declined. What chiefly daunted me was the man's singular dexterity to worm himself into our troubles. You may have felt (after a horse accident) the hand of a bone-setter artfully divide and interrogate the muscles, and settle strongly on the injured place? It was so with the Master's tongue, that was so cunning to question; and his eyes, that were so quick to observe. I seemed to have said nothing, and yet to have let all out. Before I knew where I was the man was condoling with me on my lord's neglect of my lady and myself, and his hurtful indulgence to his son. On this last point I perceived him (with panic fear) to return repeatedly. The boy had displayed a certain shrinking from his uncle; it was strong in my mind his father had been fool enough to indoctrinate the same, which was no wise beginning: and when I looked upon the man before me, still so handsome, so apt a speaker, with so great a variety of fortunes to relate, I saw he was the very personage to captivate a boyish fancy. John Paul had left only that morning; it was not to be supposed he had been altogether dumb upon his favourite subject: so that here would be Mr. Alexander in the part of Dido, with a curiosity inflamed to hear; and there would be the Master, like a diabolical Æneas, full of matter the most pleasing in the world to any youthful ear, such as battles, sea-disasters, flights, the forests of the West, and (since his later voyage) the ancient cities of the Indies. How cunningly these baits might be employed, and what an empire might be so founded, little by little, in the mind of any boy, stood obviously clear to me. There was no inhibition, so long as the man was in the house, that would be strong enough to hold these two apart; for if it be hard to charm serpents, it is no very difficult thing to cast a glamour on a little chip of manhood not very long in breeches. I recalled an ancient sailor-man who dwelt in a lone house beyond the Figgate Whins (I believe, he called it after Portobello), and how the boys would troop out of Leith on a Saturday, and sit and listen to his swearing tales, as thick as crows about a carrion: a thing I often remarked as I went by, a young student, on my own more meditative holiday diversion. Many of these boys went, no doubt, in the face of an express command; many feared and even hated the old brute of whom they made their hero; and I have seen them flee from him when he was tipsy, and stone him when he was drunk. And yet there they came each Saturday! How much more easily would a boy like Mr. Alexander fall under the influence of a high-looking, high-spoken gentleman-adventurer, who should conceive the fancy to entrap him; and, the influence gained, how easy to employ it for the child's perversion!

I doubt if our enemy had named Mr. Alexander three times before I perceived which way his mind was aiming—all this train of thought and memory passed in one pulsation through my own—and you may say I started back as though an open hole had gaped across a pathway. Mr. Alexander: there was the weak point, there was the Eve in our perishable paradise; and the serpent was already hissing on the trail.

I promise you, I went the more heartily about the preparations; my last scruple gone, the danger of delay written before me in huge characters. From that moment forth I seem not to have sat down or breathed. Now I would be at my post with the Master and his Indian; now in the garret, buckling a valise; now sending forth Macconochie by the side postern and the wood-path to bear it to the trysting-place; and, again, snatching some words of counsel with my lady. This was the verso of our life in Durrisdeer that day; but on the recto all appeared quite settled, as of a family at home in its paternal seat; and what perturbation may have been observable, the Master would set down to the blow of his unlooked-for coming, and the fear he was accustomed to inspire.

Supper went creditably off, cold salutations passed and the company trooped to their respective chambers. I attended the Master to the last. We had put him next door to his Indian, in the north wing; because that was the most distant and could be severed from the body of the house with doors. I saw he was a kind friend or a good master (whichever it was) to his Secundra Dass—seeing to his comfort; mending the fire with his own hand, for the Indian complained of cold; inquiring as to the rice on which the stranger made his diet; talking with him pleasantly in the Hindustanee, while I stood by, my candle in my hand, and affected to be overcome with slumber. At length the Master observed my signals of distress. "I perceive," says he, "that you have all your ancient habits: early to bed and early to rise. Yawn yourself away!"

Once in my own room, I made the customary motions of undressing, so that I might time myself; and when the cycle was complete, set my tinder-box ready, and blew out my taper. The matter of an hour afterward I made a light again, put on my shoes of list that I had worn by my lord's sick-bed, and set forth into the house to call the voyagers. All were dressed and waiting—my lord, my lady, Miss Katharine, Mr. Alexander, my lady's woman Christie; and I observed the effect of secrecy even upon quite innocent persons, that one after another showed in the chink of the door a face as white as paper. We slipped out of the side postern into a night of darkness, scarce broken by a star or two; so that at first we groped and stumbled and fell among the bushes. A few hundred yards up the wood-path Macconochie was waiting us with a great lantern; so the rest of the way we went easy enough, but still in a kind of guilty silence. A little beyond the abbey the path debauched on the main road and some quarter of a mile farther, at the place called Eagles, where the moors begin, we saw the lights of the two carriages stand shining by the wayside. Scarce a word or two was uttered at our parting, and these regarded business: a silent grasping of hands, a turning of faces aside, and the thing was over; the horses broke into a trot, the lamplight sped like Will-o'-the-Wisp upon the broken moorland, it dipped beyond Stony Brae; and there were Macconochie and I alone with our lantern on the road. There was one thing more to wait for, and that was the reappearance of the coach upon Cartmore. It seems they must have pulled up upon the summit, looked back for a last time, and seen our lantern not yet moved away from the place of separation. For a lamp was taken from a carriage, and waved three times up and down by way of a farewell. And then they were gone indeed, having looked their last on the kind roof of Durrisdeer, their faces toward a barbarous country. I never knew before, the greatness of that vault of night in which we two poor serving-men—the one old, and the one elderly—stood for the first time deserted; I had never felt before my own dependency upon the countenance of others. The sense of isolation burned in my bowels like a fire. It seemed that we who remained at home were the true exiles, and that Durrisdeer and Solwayside, and all that made my country native, its air good to me, and its language welcome, had gone forth and was far over the sea with my old masters.

The remainder of that night I paced to and fro on the smooth highway, reflecting on the future and the past. My thoughts, which at first dwelled tenderly on those who were just gone, took a more manly temper as I considered what remained for me to do. Day came upon the inland mountain-tops, and the fowls began to cry, and the smoke of homesteads to arise in the brown bosom of the moors, before I turned my face homeward, and went down the path to where the roof of Durrisdeer shone in the morning by the sea.

At the customary hour I had the Master called, and awaited his coming in the hall with a quiet mind. He looked about him at the empty room and the three covers set.

"We are a small party," said he. "How comes?"

"This is the party to which we must grow accustomed," I replied.

He looked at me with a sudden sharpness. "What is all this?" said he.

"You and I and your friend Mr. Dass are now all the company," I replied. "My lord, my lady, and the children, are gone upon a voyage."

"Upon my word!" said he. "Can this be possible? I have indeed fluttered your Volscians in Corioli! But this is no reason why our breakfast should go cold. Sit down, Mr. Mackellar, if you please"—taking, as he spoke, the head of the table, which I had designed to occupy myself—"and as we eat, you can give me the details of this evasion."

I could see he was more affected than his language carried, and I determined to equal him in coolness. "I was about to ask you to take the head of the table," said I; "for though I am now thrust into the position of your host, I could never forget that you were, after all, a member of the family."

For a while he played the part of entertainer, giving directions to Macconochie, who received them with an evil grace, and attending specially upon Secundra. "And where has my good family withdrawn to?" he asked carelessly.

"Ah! Mr. Bally, that is another point," said I. "I have no orders to communicate their destination."

"To me," he corrected.

"To any one," said I.

"It is the less pointed," said the master; "c'est de bon ton: my brother improves as he continues. And I, dear Mr. Mackellar?"

"You will have bed and board, Mr. Bally," said I. "I am permitted to give you the run of the cellar, which is pretty reasonably stocked. You have only to keep well with me, which is no very difficult matter, and you shall want neither for wine nor a saddle-horse."

He made an excuse to send Macconochie from the room.

"And for money?" he inquired. "Have I to keep well with my good friend Mackellar for my pocket-money also? This is a pleasing return to the principles of boyhood."

"There was no allowance made," said I; "but I will take it on myself to see you are supplied in moderation."

"In moderation?" he repeated. "And you will take it on yourself?" He drew himself up, and looked about the hall at the dark rows of portraits. "In the name of my ancestors, I thank you," says he; and then, with a return to irony, "But there must certainly be an allowance for Secundra Dass?" he said. "It in not possible they have omitted that?"

"I will make a note of it, and ask instructions when I write," said I.

And he, with a sudden change of manner, and leaning forward with an elbow on the table—"Do you think this entirely wise?"

"I execute my orders, Mr. Bally," said I.

"Profoundly modest," said the Master; "perhaps not equally ingenuous. You told me yesterday my power was fallen with my father's death. How comes it, then, that a peer of the realm flees under cloud of night out of a house in which his fathers have stood several sieges? that he conceals his address, which must be a matter of concern to his Gracious Majesty and to the whole republic? and that he should leave me in possession, and under the paternal charge of his invaluable Mackellar? This smacks to me of a very considerable and genuine apprehension."

I sought to interrupt him with some not very truthful denegation; but he waved me down, and pursued his speech.

"I say, it smacks of it," he said; "but I will go beyond that, for I think the apprehension grounded. I came to this house with some reluctance. In view of the manner of my last departure, nothing but necessity could have induced me to return. Money, however, is that which I must have. You will not give with a good grace; well, I have the power to force it from you. Inside of a week, without leaving Durrisdeer, I will find out where these fools are fled to. I will follow; and when I have run my quarry down, I will drive a wedge into that family that shall once more burst it into shivers. I shall see then whether my Lord Durrisdeer" (said with indescribable scorn and rage) "will choose to buy my absence; and you will all see whether, by that time, I decide for profit or revenge."

I was amazed to hear the man so open. The truth is, he was consumed with anger at my lord's successful flight, felt himself to figure as a dupe, and was in no humour to weigh language.

"Do you consider this entirely wise?" said I, copying his words.

"These twenty years I have lived by my poor wisdom," he answered with a smile that seemed almost foolish in its vanity.

"And come out a beggar in the end," said I, "if beggar be a strong enough word for it."

"I would have you to observe, Mr. Mackellar," cried he, with a sudden imperious heat, in which I could not but admire him, "that I am scrupulously civil: copy me in that, and we shall be the better friends."

Throughout this dialogue I had been incommoded by the observation of Secundra Dass. Not one of us, since the first word, had made a feint of eating: our eyes were in each other's faces—you might say, in each other's bosoms; and those of the Indian troubled me with a certain changing brightness, as of comprehension. But I brushed the fancy aside, telling myself once more he understood no English; only, from the gravity of both voices, and the occasional scorn and anger in the Master's, smelled out there was something of import in the wind.

For the matter of three weeks we continued to live together in the house of Durrisdeer: the beginning of that most singular chapter of my life—what I must call my intimacy with the Master. At first he was somewhat changeable in his behaviour: now civil, now returning to his old manner of flouting me to my face; and in both I met him half-way. Thanks be to Providence, I had now no measure to keep with the man; and I was never afraid of black brows, only of naked swords. So that I found a certain entertainment in these bouts of incivility, and was not always ill-inspired in my rejoinders. At last (it was at supper) I had a droll expression that entirely vanquished him. He laughed again and again; and "Who would have guessed," he cried, "that this old wife had any wit under his petticoats?"

"It is no wit, Mr. Bally," said I: "a dry Scot's humour, and something of the driest." And, indeed, I never had the least pretension to be thought a wit.

From that hour he was never rude with me, but all passed between us in a manner of pleasantry. One of our chief times of daffing [9] was when he required a horse, another bottle, or some money. He would approach me then after the manner of a schoolboy, and I would carry it on by way of being his father: on both sides, with an infinity of mirth. I could not but perceive that he thought more of me, which tickled that poor part of mankind, the vanity. He dropped, besides (I must suppose unconsciously), into a manner that was not only familiar, but even friendly; and this, on the part of one who had so long detested me, I found the more insidious. He went little abroad; sometimes even refusing invitations. "No," he would say, "what do I care for these thick-headed bonnet-lairds? I will stay at home, Mackellar; and we shall share a bottle quietly, and have one of our good talks." And, indeed, meal-time at Durrisdeer must have been a delight to any one, by reason of the brilliancy of the discourse. He would often express wonder at his former indifference to my society. "But, you see," he would add, "we were upon opposite sides. And so we are to-day; but let us never speak of that. I would think much less of you if you were not staunch to your employer." You are to consider he seemed to me quite impotent for any evil; and how it is a most engaging form of flattery when (after many years) tardy justice is done to a man's character and parts. But I have no thought to excuse myself. I was to blame; I let him cajole me, and, in short, I think the watch-dog was going sound asleep, when he was suddenly aroused.

I should say the Indian was continually travelling to and fro in the house. He never spoke, save in his own dialect and with the Master; walked without sound; and was always turning up where you would least expect him, fallen into a deep abstraction, from which he would start (upon your coming) to mock you with one of his grovelling obeisances. He seemed so quiet, so frail, and so wrapped in his own fancies, that I came to pass him over without much regard, or even to pity him for a harmless exile from his country. And yet without doubt the creature was still eavesdropping; and without doubt it was through his stealth and my security that our secret reached the Master.

It was one very wild night, after supper, and when we had been making more than usually merry, that the blow fell on me.

"This is all very fine," says the Master, "but we should do better to be buckling our valise."

"Why so?" I cried. "Are you leaving?"

"We are all leaving to-morrow in the morning," said he. "For the port of Glascow first, thence for the province of New York."

I suppose I must have groaned aloud.

"Yes," he continued, "I boasted; I said a week, and it has taken me near twenty days. But never mind; I shall make it up; I will go the faster."

"Have you the money for this voyage?" I asked.

"Dear and ingenuous personage, I have," said he. "Blame me, if you choose, for my duplicity; but while I have been wringing shillings from my daddy, I had a stock of my own put by against a rainy day. You will pay for your own passage, if you choose to accompany us on our flank march; I have enough for Secundra and myself, but not more—enough to be dangerous, not enough to be generous. There is, however, an outside seat upon the chaise which I will let you have upon a moderate commutation; so that the whole menagerie can go together—the house-dog, the monkey, and the tiger."

"I go with you," said I.

"I count upon it," said the Master. "You have seen me foiled; I mean you shall see me victorious. To gain that I will risk wetting you like a sop in this wild weather."

"And at least," I added, "you know very well you could not throw me off."

"Not easily," said he. "You put your finger on the point with your usual excellent good sense. I never fight with the inevitable."

"I suppose it is useless to appeal to you?" said I.

"Believe me, perfectly," said he.

"And yet, if you would give me time, I could write—" I began.

"And what would be my Lord Durrisdeer's answer?" asks he.

"Aye," said I, "that is the rub."

"And, at any rate, how much more expeditious that I should go myself!" says he. "But all this is quite a waste of breath. At seven to-morrow the chaise will be at the door. For I start from the door, Mackellar; I do not skulk through woods and take my chaise upon the wayside—shall we say, at Eagles?"

My mind was now thoroughly made up. "Can you spare me quarter of an hour at St. Bride's?" said I. "I have a little necessary business with Carlyle."

"An hour, if you prefer," said he. "I do not seek to deny that the money for your seat is an object to me; and you could always get the first to Glasgow with saddle-horses."

"Well," said I, "I never thought to leave old Scotland."

"It will brisken you up," says he.

"This will be an ill journey for some one," I said. "I think, sir, for you. Something speaks in my bosom; and so much it says plain—that this is an ill-omened journey."

"If you take to prophecy," says he, "listen to that."

There came up a violent squall off the open Solway, and the rain was dashed on the great windows.

"Do ye ken what that bodes, warlock?" said he, in a broad accent: "that there'll be a man Mackellar unco' sick at sea."

When I got to my chamber, I sat there under a painful excitation, hearkening to the turmoil of the gale, which struck full upon that gable of the house. What with the pressure on my spirits, the eldritch cries of the wind among the turret-tops, and the perpetual trepidation of the masoned house, sleep fled my eyelids utterly. I sat by my taper, looking on the black panes of the window, where the storm appeared continually on the point of bursting in its entrance; and upon that empty field I beheld a perspective of consequences that made the hair to rise upon my scalp. The child corrupted, the home broken up, my master dead or worse than dead, my mistress plunged in desolation—all these I saw before me painted brightly on the darkness; and the outcry of the wind appeared to mock at my inaction.

CHAPTER IX.
MR. MACKELLAR'S JOURNEY WITH THE MASTER.

The chaise came to the door in a strong drenching mist. We took our leave in silence: the house of Durrisdeer standing with dropping gutters and windows closed, like a place dedicate to melancholy. I observed the Master kept his head out, looking back on these splashed walls and glimmering roofs, till they were suddenly swallowed in the mist; and I must suppose some natural sadness fell upon the man at this departure; or was it some provision of the end? At least, upon our mounting the long brae from Durrisdeer, as we walked side by side in the wet, he began first to whistle and then to sing the saddest of our country tunes, which sets folk weeping in a tavern, Wandering Willie. The set of words he used with it I have not heard elsewhere, and could never come by any copy; but some of them which were the most appropriate to our departure linger in my memory. One verse began—

Home was home then, my dear, full of kindly faces,
Home was home then, my dear, happy for the child.

And ended somewhat thus—

Now, when day dawns on the brow of the moorland,
  Lone stands the house, and the chimney-stone is cold.
Lone let it stand, now the folks are all departed,
  The kind hearts, the true hearts, that loved the place of old.

I could never be a judge of the merit of these verses; they were so hallowed by the melancholy of the air, and were sung (or rather "soothed") to me by a master-singer at a time so fitting. He looked in my face when he had done, and saw that my eyes watered.

"Ah! Mackellar," said he, "do you think I have never a regret?"

"I do not think you could be so bad a man," said I, "if you had not all the machinery to be a good one."

"No, not all," says he: "not all. You are there in error. The malady of not wanting, my evangelist." But methought he sighed as he mounted again into the chaise.

All day long we journeyed in the same miserable weather: the mist besetting us closely, the heavens incessantly weeping on my head. The road lay over moorish hills, where was no sound but the crying of moor-fowl in the wet heather and the pouring of the swollen burns. Sometimes I would doze off in slumber, when I would find myself plunged at once in some foul and ominous nightmare, from the which I would awake strangling. Sometimes, if the way was steep and the wheels turning slowly, I would overhear the voices from within, talking in that tropical tongue which was to me as inarticulate as the piping of the fowls. Sometimes, at a longer ascent, the Master would set foot to ground and walk by my side, mostly without speech. And all the time, sleeping or waking, I beheld the same black perspective of approaching ruin; and the same pictures rose in my view, only they were now painted upon hillside mist. One, I remember, stood before me with the colours of a true illusion. It showed me my lord seated at a table in a small room; his head, which was at first buried in his hands, he slowly raised, and turned upon me a countenance from which hope had fled. I saw it first on the black window-panes, my last night in Durrisdeer; it haunted and returned upon me half the voyage through; and yet it was no effect of lunacy, for I have come to a ripe old age with no decay of my intelligence; nor yet (as I was then tempted to suppose) a heaven-sent warning of the future, for all manner of calamities befell, not that calamity—and I saw many pitiful sights, but never that one.

It was decided we should travel on all night; and it was singular, once the dusk had fallen, my spirits somewhat rose. The bright lamps, shining forth into the mist and on the smoking horses and the hodding post-boy, gave me perhaps an outlook intrinsically more cheerful than what day had shown; or perhaps my mind had become wearied of its melancholy. At least, I spent some waking hours, not without satisfaction in my thoughts, although wet and weary in my body; and fell at last into a natural slumber without dreams. Yet I must have been at work even in the deepest of my sleep; and at work with at least a measure of intelligence. For I started broad awake, in the very act of crying out to myself

Home was home then, my dear, happy for the child,

stricken to find in it an appropriateness, which I had not yesterday observed, to the Master's detestable purpose in the present journey.

We were then close upon the city of Glascow, where we were soon breakfasting together at an inn, and where (as the devil would have it) we found a ship in the very article of sailing. We took our places in the cabin; and, two days after, carried our effects on board. Her name was the Nonesuch, a very ancient ship and very happily named. By all accounts this should be her last voyage; people shook their heads upon the quays, and I had several warnings offered me by strangers in the street to the effect that she was rotten as a cheese, too deeply loaden, and must infallibly founder if we met a gale. From this it fell out we were the only passengers; the Captain, McMurtrie, was a silent, absorbed man, with the Glasgow or Gaelic accent; the mates ignorant rough seafarers, come in through the hawsehole; and the Master and I were cast upon each other's company.

The Nonesuch carried a fair wind out of the Clyde, and for near upon a week we enjoyed bright weather and a sense of progress. I found myself (to my wonder) a born seaman, in so far at least as I was never sick; yet I was far from tasting the usual serenity of my health. Whether it was the motion of the ship on the billows, the confinement, the salted food, or all of these together, I suffered from a blackness of spirit and a painful strain upon my temper. The nature of my errand on that ship perhaps contributed; I think it did no more; the malady (whatever it was) sprang from my environment; and if the ship were not to blame, then it was the Master. Hatred and fear are ill bedfellows; but (to my shame be it spoken) I have tasted those in other places, lain down and got up with them, and eaten and drunk with them, and yet never before, nor after, have I been so poisoned through and through, in soul and body, as I was on board the Nonesuch. I freely confess my enemy set me a fair example of forbearance; in our worst days displayed the most patient geniality, holding me in conversation as long as I would suffer, and when I had rebuffed his civility, stretching himself on deck to read. The book he had on board with him was Mr. Richardson's famous Clarissa! and among other small attentions he would read me passages aloud; nor could any elocutionist have given with greater potency the pathetic portions of that work. I would retort upon him with passages out of the Bible, which was all my library—and very fresh to me, my religious duties (I grieve to say it) being always and even to this day extremely neglected. He tasted the merits of the word like the connoisseur he was; and would sometimes take it from my hand, turn the leaves over like a man that knew his way, and give me, with his fine declamation, a Roland for my Oliver. But it was singular how little he applied his reading to himself; it passed high above his head like summer thunder: Lovelace and Clarissa, the tales of David's generosity, the psalms of his penitence, the solemn questions of the book of Job, the touching poetry of Isaiah—they were to him a source of entertainment only, like the scraping of a fiddle in a change-house. This outer sensibility and inner toughness set me against him; it seemed of a piece with that impudent grossness which I knew to underlie the veneer of his fine manners; and sometimes my gorge rose against him as though he were deformed—and sometimes I would draw away as though from something partly spectral. I had moments when I thought of him as of a man of pasteboard—as though, if one should strike smartly through the buckram of his countenance, there would be found a mere vacuity within. This horror (not merely fanciful, I think) vastly increased my detestation of his neighbourhood; I began to feel something shiver within me on his drawing near; I had at times a longing to cry out; there were days when I thought I could have struck him. This frame of mind was doubtless helped by shame, because I had dropped during our last days at Durrisdeer into a certain toleration of the man; and if any one had then told me I should drop into it again, I must have laughed in his face. It is possible he remained unconscious of this extreme fever of my resentment; yet I think he was too quick; and rather that he had fallen, in a long life of idleness, into a positive need of company, which obliged him to confront and tolerate my unconcealed aversion. Certain, at least, that he loved the note of his own tongue, as, indeed, he entirely loved all the parts and properties of himself; a sort of imbecility which almost necessarily attends on wickedness. I have seen him driven, when I proved recalcitrant, to long discourses with the skipper; and this, although the man plainly testified his weariness, fiddling miserably with both hand and foot, and replying only with a grunt.

After the first week out we fell in with foul winds and heavy weather. The sea was high. The Nonesuch, being an old-fashioned ship and badly loaden, rolled beyond belief; so that the skipper trembled for his masts, and I for my life. We made no progress on our course. An unbearable ill-humour settled on the ship: men, mates, and master, girding at one another all day long. A saucy word on the one hand, and a blow on the other, made a daily incident. There were times when the whole crew refused their duty; and we of the afterguard were twice got under arms—being the first time that ever I bore weapons—in the fear of mutiny.

In the midst of our evil season sprang up a hurricane of wind; so that all supposed she must go down. I was shut in the cabin from noon of one day till sundown of the next; the Master was somewhere lashed on deck. Secundra had eaten of some drug and lay insensible; so you may say I passed these hours in an unbroken solitude. At first I was terrified beyond motion, and almost beyond thought, my mind appearing to be frozen. Presently there stole in on me a ray of comfort. If the Nonesuch foundered, she would carry down with her into the deeps of that unsounded sea the creature whom we all so feared and hated; there would be no more Master of Ballantrae, the fish would sport among his ribs; his schemes all brought to nothing, his harmless enemies at peace. At first, I have said, it was but a ray of comfort; but it had soon grown to be broad sunshine. The thought of the man's death, of his deletion from this world, which he embittered for so many, took possession of my mind. I hugged it, I found it sweet in my belly. I conceived the ship's last plunge, the sea bursting upon all sides into the cabin, the brief mortal conflict there, all by myself, in that closed place; I numbered the horrors, I had almost said with satisfaction; I felt I could bear all and more, if the Nonesuch carried down with her, overtook by the same ruin, the enemy of my poor master's house. Towards noon of the second day the screaming of the wind abated; the ship lay not so perilously over, and it began to be clear to me that we were past the height of the tempest. As I hope for mercy, I was singly disappointed. In the selfishness of that vile, absorbing passion of hatred, I forgot the case of our innocent shipmates, and thought but of myself and my enemy. For myself, I was already old; I had never been young, I was not formed for the world's pleasures, I had few affections; it mattered not the toss of a silver tester whether I was drowned there and then in the Atlantic, or dribbled out a few more years, to die, perhaps no less terribly, in a deserted sick-bed. Down I went upon my knees—holding on by the locker, or else I had been instantly dashed across the tossing cabin—and, lifting up my voice in the midst of that clamour of the abating hurricane, impiously prayed for my own death. "O God!" I cried, "I would be liker a man if I rose and struck this creature down; but Thou madest me a coward from my mother's womb. O Lord, Thou madest me so, Thou knowest my weakness, Thou knowest that any face of death will set me shaking in my shoes. But, lo! here is Thy servant ready, his mortal weakness laid aside. Let me give my life for this creature's; take the two of them, Lord! take the two, and have mercy on the innocent!" In some such words as these, only yet more irreverent and with more sacred adjurations, I continued to pour forth my spirit. God heard me not, I must suppose in mercy; and I was still absorbed in my agony of supplication when some one, removing the tarpaulin cover, let the light of the sunset pour into the cabin. I stumbled to my feet ashamed, and was seized with surprise to find myself totter and ache like one that had been stretched upon the rack. Secundra Dass, who had slept off the effects of his drug, stood in a corner not far off, gazing at me with wild eyes; and from the open skylight the captain thanked me for my supplications.

"It's you that saved the ship, Mr. Mackellar," says he. "There is no craft of seamanship that could have kept her floating: well may we say, 'Except the Lord the city keep, the watchmen watch in vain!'"

I was abashed by the captain's error; abashed, also, by the surprise and fear with which the Indian regarded me at first, and the obsequious civilities with which he soon began to cumber me. I know now that he must have overheard and comprehended the peculiar nature of my prayers. It is certain, of course, that he at once disclosed the matter to his patron; and looking back with greater knowledge, I can now understand what so much puzzled me at the moment, those singular and (so to speak) approving smiles with which the Master honoured me. Similarly, I can understand a word that I remember to have fallen from him in conversation that same night; when, holding up his hand and smiling, "Ah! Mackellar," said he, "not every man is so great a coward as he thinks he is—nor yet so good a Christian." He did not guess how true he spoke! For the fact is, the thoughts which had come to me in the violence of the storm retained their hold upon my spirit; and the words that rose to my lips unbidden in the instancy of prayer continued to sound in my ears: with what shameful consequences, it is fitting I should honestly relate; for I could not support a part of such disloyalty as to describe the sins of others and conceal my own.

The wind fell, but the sea hove ever the higher. All night the Nonesuch rolled outrageously; the next day dawned, and the next, and brought no change. To cross the cabin was scarce possible; old experienced seamen were cast down upon the deck, and one cruelly mauled in the concussion; every board and block in the old ship cried out aloud; and the great bell by the anchor-bitts continually and dolefully rang. One of these days the Master and I sate alone together at the break of the poop. I should say the Nonesuch carried a high, raised poop. About the top of it ran considerable bulwarks, which made the ship unweatherly; and these, as they approached the front on each side, ran down in a fine, old-fashioned, carven scroll to join the bulwarks of the waist. From this disposition, which seems designed rather for ornament than use, it followed there was a discontinuance of protection: and that, besides, at the very margin of the elevated part where (in certain movements of the ship) it might be the most needful. It was here we were sitting: our feet hanging down, the Master betwixt me and the side, and I holding on with both hands to the grating of the cabin skylight; for it struck me it was a dangerous position, the more so as I had continually before my eyes a measure of our evolutions in the person of the Master, which stood out in the break of the bulwarks against the sun. Now his head would be in the zenith and his shadow fall quite beyond the Nonesuch on the farther side; and now he would swing down till he was underneath my feet, and the line of the sea leaped high above him like the ceiling of a room. I looked on upon this with a growing fascination, as birds are said to look on snakes. My mind, besides, was troubled with an astonishing diversity of noises; for now that we had all sails spread in the vain hope to bring her to the sea, the ship sounded like a factory with their reverberations. We spoke first of the mutiny with which we had been threatened; this led us on to the topic of assassination; and that offered a temptation to the Master more strong than he was able to resist. He must tell me a tale, and show me at the same time how clever he was and how wicked. It was a thing he did always with affectation and display; generally with a good effect. But this tale, told in a high key in the midst of so great a tumult, and by a narrator who was one moment looking down at me from the skies and the next up from under the soles of my feet—this particular tale, I say, took hold upon me in a degree quite singular.

"My friend the count," it was thus that he began his story, "had for an enemy a certain German baron, a stranger in Rome. It matters not what was the ground of the count's enmity; but as he had a firm design to be revenged, and that with safety to himself, he kept it secret even from the baron. Indeed, that is the first principle of vengeance; and hatred betrayed is hatred impotent. The count was a man of a curious, searching mind; he had something of the artist; if anything fell for him to do, it must always be done with an exact perfection, not only as to the result, but in the very means and instruments, or he thought the thing miscarried. It chanced he was one day riding in the outer suburbs, when he came to a disused by-road branching off into the moor which lies about Rome. On the one hand was an ancient Roman tomb; on the other a deserted house in a garden of evergreen trees. This road brought him presently into a field of ruins, in the midst of which, in the side of a hill, he saw an open door, and, not far off, a single stunted pine no greater than a currant-bush. The place was desert and very secret; a voice spoke in the count's bosom that there was something here to his advantage. He tied his horse to the pine-tree, took his flint and steel in his hand to make a light, and entered into the hill. The doorway opened on a passage of old Roman masonry, which shortly after branched in two. The count took the turning to the right, and followed it, groping forward in the dark, till he was brought up by a kind of fence, about elbow-high, which extended quite across the passage. Sounding forward with his foot, he found an edge of polished stone, and then vacancy. All his curiosity was now awakened, and, getting some rotten sticks that lay about the floor, he made a fire. In front of him was a profound well; doubtless some neighbouring peasant had once used it for his water, and it was he that had set up the fence. A long while the count stood leaning on the rail and looking down into the pit. It was of Roman foundation, and, like all that nation set their hands to, built as for eternity; the sides were still straight, and the joints smooth; to a man who should fall in, no escape was possible. 'Now,' the count was thinking, 'a strong impulsion brought me to this place. What for? what have I gained? why should I be sent to gaze into this well?' when the rail of the fence gave suddenly under his weight, and he came within an ace of falling headlong in. Leaping back to save himself, he trod out the last flicker of his fire, which gave him thenceforward no more light, only an incommoding smoke. 'Was I sent here to my death?' says he, and shook from head to foot. And then a thought flashed in his mind. He crept forth on hands and knees to the brink of the pit, and felt above him in the air. The rail had been fast to a pair of uprights; it had only broken from the one, and still depended from the other. The count set it back again as he had found it, so that the place meant death to the first comer, and groped out of the catacomb like a sick man. The next day, riding in the Corso with the baron, he purposely betrayed a strong preoccupation. The other (as he had designed) inquired into the cause; and he, after some fencing, admitted that his spirits had been dashed by an unusual dream. This was calculated to draw on the baron—a superstitious man, who affected the scorn of superstition. Some rallying followed, and then the count, as if suddenly carried away, called on his friend to beware, for it was of him that he had dreamed. You know enough of human nature, my excellent Mackellar, to be certain of one thing: I mean that the baron did not rest till he had heard the dream. The count, sure that he would never desist, kept him in play till his curiosity was highly inflamed, and then suffered himself, with seeming reluctance, to be overborne. 'I warn you,' says he, 'evil will come of it; something tells me so. But since there is to be no peace either for you or me except on this condition, the blame be on your own head! This was the dream:—I beheld you riding, I know not where, yet I think it must have been near Rome, for on your one hand was an ancient tomb, and on the other a garden of evergreen trees. Methought I cried and cried upon you to come back in a very agony of terror; whether you heard me I know not, but you went doggedly on. The road brought you to a desert place among ruins, where was a door in a hillside, and hard by the door a misbegotten pine. Here you dismounted (I still crying on you to beware), tied your horse to the pine-tree, and entered resolutely in by the door. Within, it was dark; but in my dream I could still see you, and still besought you to hold back. You felt your way along the right-hand wall, took a branching passage to the right, and came to a little chamber, where was a well with a railing. At this—I know not why—my alarm for you increased a thousandfold, so that I seemed to scream myself hoarse with warnings, crying it was still time, and bidding you begone at once from that vestibule. Such was the word I used in my dream, and it seemed then to have a clear significancy; but to-day, and awake, I profess I know not what it means. To all my outcry you rendered not the least attention, leaning the while upon the rail and looking down intently in the water. And then there was made to you a communication; I do not think I even gathered what it was, but the fear of it plucked me clean out of my slumber, and I awoke shaking and sobbing. And now,' continues the count, 'I thank you from my heart for your insistency. This dream lay on me like a load; and now I have told it in plain words and in the broad daylight, it seems no great matter.'—'I do not know,' says the baron. 'It is in some points strange. A communication, did you say? Oh! it is an odd dream. It will make a story to amuse our friends.'—'I am not so sure,' says the count. 'I am sensible of some reluctance. Let us rather forget it.'—'By all means,' says the baron. And (in fact) the dream was not again referred to. Some days after, the count proposed a ride in the fields, which the baron (since they were daily growing faster friends) very readily accepted. On the way back to Rome, the count led them insensibly by a particular route. Presently he reined in his horse, clapped his hand before his eyes, and cried out aloud. Then he showed his face again (which was now quite white, for he was a consummate actor), and stared upon the baron. 'What ails you?' cries the baron. 'What is wrong with you?'—'Nothing,' cries the count. 'It is nothing. A seizure, I know not what. Let us hurry back to Rome.' But in the meanwhile the baron had looked about him; and there, on the left-hand side of the way as they went back to Rome, he saw a dusty by-road with a tomb upon the one hand and a garden of evergreen trees upon the other.—'Yes,' says he, with a changed voice. 'Let us by all means hurry back to Rome. I fear you are not well in health.'—'Oh, for God's sake!' cries the count, shuddering, 'back to Rome and let me get to bed.' They made their return with scarce a word; and the count, who should by rights have gone into society, took to his bed and gave out he had a touch of country fever. The next day the baron's horse was found tied to the pine, but himself was never heard of from that hour.—And, now, was that a murder?" says the Master, breaking sharply off.

"Are you sure he was a count?" I asked.

"I am not certain of the title," said he, "but he was a gentleman of family: and the Lord deliver you, Mackellar, from an enemy so subtile!"

These last words he spoke down at me, smiling, from high above; the next, he was under my feet. I continued to follow his evolutions with a childish fixity; they made me giddy and vacant, and I spoke as in a dream.

"He hated the baron with a great hatred?" I asked.

"His belly moved when the man came near him," said the Master.

"I have felt that same," said I.

"Verily!" cries the Master. "Here is news indeed! I wonder—do I flatter myself? or am I the cause of these ventral perturbations?"

He was quite capable of choosing out a graceful posture, even with no one to behold him but myself, and all the more if there were any element of peril. He sat now with one knee flung across the other, his arms on his bosom, fitting the swing of the ship with an exquisite balance, such as a featherweight might overthrow. All at once I had the vision of my lord at the table, with his head upon his hands; only now, when he showed me his countenance, it was heavy with reproach. The words of my own prayer—I were liker a man if I struck this creature down—shot at the same time into my memory. I called my energies together, and (the ship then heeling downward toward my enemy) thrust at him swiftly with my foot. It was written I should have the guilt of this attempt without the profit. Whether from my own uncertainty or his incredible quickness, he escaped the thrust, leaping to his feet and catching hold at the same moment of a stay.

I do not know how long a time passed by. I lying where I was upon the deck, overcome with terror and remorse and shame: he standing with the stay in his hand, backed against the bulwarks, and regarding me with an expression singularly mingled. At last he spoke.

"Mackellar," said he, "I make no reproaches, but I offer you a bargain. On your side, I do not suppose you desire to have this exploit made public; on mine, I own to you freely I do not care to draw my breath in a perpetual terror of assassination by the man I sit at meat with. Promise me—but no," says he, breaking off, "you are not yet in the quiet possession of your mind; you might think I had extorted the promise from your weakness; and I would leave no door open for casuistry to come in—that dishonesty of the conscientious. Take time to meditate."

With that he made off up the sliding deck like a squirrel, and plunged into the cabin. About half an hour later he returned—I still lying as he had left me.

"Now," says he, "will you give me your troth as a Christian, and a faithful servant of my brother's, that I shall have no more to fear from your attempts?"

"I give it you," said I.

"I shall require your hand upon it," says he.

"You have the right to make conditions," I replied, and we shook hands.

He sat down at once in the same place and the old perilous attitude.

"Hold on!" cried I, covering my eyes. "I cannot bear to see you in that posture. The least irregularity of the sea might plunge you overboard."

"You are highly inconsistent," he replied, smiling, but doing as I asked. "For all that, Mackellar, I would have you to know you have risen forty feet in my esteem. You think I cannot set a price upon fidelity? But why do you suppose I carry that Secundra Dass about the world with me? Because he would die or do murder for me to-morrow; and I love him for it. Well, you may think it odd, but I like you the better for this afternoon's performance. I thought you were magnetised with the Ten Commandments; but no—God damn my soul!"—he cries, "the old wife has blood in his body after all! Which does not change the fact," he continued, smiling again, "that you have done well to give your promise; for I doubt if you would ever shine in your new trade."

"I suppose," said I, "I should ask your pardon and God's for my attempt. At any rate, I have passed my word, which I will keep faithfully. But when I think of those you persecute—" I paused.

"Life is a singular thing," said he, "and mankind a very singular people. You suppose yourself to love my brother. I assure you, it is merely custom. Interrogate your memory; and when first you came to Durrisdeer, you will find you considered him a dull, ordinary youth. He is as dull and ordinary now, though not so young. Had you instead fallen in with me, you would to-day be as strong upon my side."

"I would never say you were ordinary, Mr. Bally," I returned; "but here you prove yourself dull. You have just shown your reliance on my word. In other terms, that is my conscience—the same which starts instinctively back from you, like the eye from a strong light."

"Ah!" says he, "but I mean otherwise. I mean, had I met you in my youth. You are to consider I was not always as I am to-day; nor (had I met in with a friend of your description) should I have ever been so."

"Hut, Mr. Bally," says I, "you would have made a mock of me; you would never have spent ten civil words on such a Square-toes."

But he was now fairly started on his new course of justification, with which he wearied me throughout the remainder of the passage. No doubt in the past he had taken pleasure to paint himself unnecessarily black, and made a vaunt of his wickedness, bearing it for a coat-of-arms. Nor was he so illogical as to abate one item of his old confessions. "But now that I know you are a human being," he would say, "I can take the trouble to explain myself. For I assure you I am human, too, and have my virtues, like my neighbours." I say, he wearied me, for I had only the one word to say in answer: twenty times I must have said it: "Give up your present purpose and return with me to Durrisdeer; then I will believe you."

Thereupon he would shake his head at me. "Ah! Mackellar, you might live a thousand years and never understand my nature," he would say. "This battle is now committed, the hour of reflection quite past, the hour for mercy not yet come. It began between us when we span a coin in the hall of Durrisdeer, now twenty years ago; we have had our ups and downs, but never either of us dreamed of giving in; and as for me, when my glove is cast, life and honour go with it."

"A fig for your honour!" I would say. "And by your leave, these warlike similitudes are something too high-sounding for the matter in hand. You want some dirty money; there is the bottom of your contention; and as for your means, what are they? to stir up sorrow in a family that never harmed you, to debauch (if you can) your own nephew, and to wring the heart of your born brother! A footpad that kills an old granny in a woollen mutch with a dirty bludgeon, and that for a shilling-piece and a paper of snuff—there is all the warrior that you are."

When I would attack him thus (or somewhat thus) he would smile, and sigh like a man misunderstood. Once, I remember, he defended himself more at large, and had some curious sophistries, worth repeating, for a light upon his character.

"You are very like a civilian to think war consists in drums and banners," said he. "War (as the ancients said very wisely) is ultima ratio. When we take our advantage unrelentingly, then we make war. Ah! Mackellar, you are a devil of a soldier in the steward's room at Durrisdeer, or the tenants do you sad injustice!"

"I think little of what war is or is not," I replied. "But you weary me with claiming my respect. Your brother is a good man, and you are a bad one—neither more nor less."

"Had I been Alexander—" he began.

"It is so we all dupe ourselves," I cried. "Had I been St. Paul, it would have been all one; I would have made the same hash of that career that you now see me making of my own."

"I tell you," he cried, bearing down my interruption, "had I been the least petty chieftain in the Highlands, had I been the least king of naked negroes in the African desert, my people would have adored me. A bad man, am I? Ah! but I was born for a good tyrant! Ask Secundra Dass; he will tell you I treat him like a son. Cast in your lot with me to-morrow, become my slave, my chattel, a thing I can command as I command the powers of my own limbs and spirit—you will see no more that dark side that I turn upon the world in anger. I must have all or none. But where all is given, I give it back with usury. I have a kingly nature: there is my loss!"

"It has been hitherto rather the loss of others," I remarked, "which seems a little on the hither side of royalty."

"Tilly-vally!" cried he. "Even now, I tell you, I would spare that family in which you take so great an interest: yes, even now—to-morrow I would leave them to their petty welfare, and disappear in that forest of cut-throats and thimble-riggers that we call the world. I would do it to-morrow!" says he. "Only—only—"

"Only what?" I asked.

"Only they must beg it on their bended knees. I think in public, too," he added, smiling. "Indeed, Mackellar, I doubt if there be a hall big enough to serve my purpose for that act of reparation."

"Vanity, vanity!" I moralised. "To think that this great force for evil should be swayed by the same sentiment that sets a lassie mincing to her glass!"

"Oh! there are double words for everything: the word that swells, the word that belittles; you cannot fight me with a word!" said he. "You said the other day that I relied on your conscience: were I in your humour of detraction, I might say I built upon your vanity. It is your pretension to be un homme de parole; 'tis mine not to accept defeat. Call it vanity, call it virtue, call it greatness of soul—what signifies the expression? But recognise in each of us a common strain: that we both live for an idea."

It will be gathered from so much familiar talk, and so much patience on both sides, that we now lived together upon excellent terms. Such was again the fact, and this time more seriously than before. Apart from disputations such as that which I have tried to reproduce, not only consideration reigned, but, I am tempted to say, even kindness. When I fell sick (as I did shortly after our great storm), he sat by my berth to entertain me with his conversation, and treated me with excellent remedies, which I accepted with security. Himself commented on the circumstance. "You see," says he, "you begin to know me better. A very little while ago, upon this lonely ship, where no one but myself has any smattering of science, you would have made sure I had designs upon your life. And, observe, it is since I found you had designs upon my own, that I have shown you most respect. You will tell me if this speaks of a small mind." I found little to reply. In so far as regarded myself, I believed him to mean well; I am, perhaps, the more a dupe of his dissimulation, but I believed (and I still believe) that he regarded me with genuine kindness. Singular and sad fact! so soon as this change began, my animosity abated, and these haunting visions of my master passed utterly away. So that, perhaps, there was truth in the man's last vaunting word to me, uttered on the second day of July, when our long voyage was at last brought almost to an end, and we lay becalmed at the sea end of the vast harbour of New York, in a gasping heat, which was presently exchanged for a surprising waterfall of rain. I stood on the poop, regarding the green shores near at hand, and now and then the light smoke of the little town, our destination. And as I was even then devising how to steal a march on my familiar enemy, I was conscious of a shade of embarrassment when he approached me with his hand extended.

"I am now to bid you farewell," said he, "and that for ever. For now you go among my enemies, where all your former prejudices will revive. I never yet failed to charm a person when I wanted; even you, my good friend—to call you so for once—even you have now a very different portrait of me in your memory, and one that you will never quite forget. The voyage has not lasted long enough, or I should have wrote the impression deeper. But now all is at an end, and we are again at war. Judge by this little interlude how dangerous I am; and tell those fools"—pointing with his finger to the town—"to think twice and thrice before they set me at defiance."

CHAPTER X.
PASSAGES AT NEW YORK.

I have mentioned I was resolved to steal a march upon the Master; and this, with the complicity of Captain McMurtrie, was mighty easily effected: a boat being partly loaded on the one side of our ship and the Master placed on board of it, the while a skiff put off from the other, carrying me alone. I had no more trouble in finding a direction to my lord's house, whither I went at top speed, and which I found to be on the outskirts of the place, a very suitable mansion, in a fine garden, with an extraordinary large barn, byre, and stable, all in one. It was here my lord was walking when I arrived; indeed, it had become his chief place of frequentation, and his mind was now filled with farming. I burst in upon him breathless, and gave him my news: which was indeed no news at all, several ships having outsailed the Nonesuch in the interval.

"We have been expecting you long," said my lord; "and indeed, of late days, ceased to expect you any more. I am glad to take your hand again, Mackellar. I thought you had been at the bottom of the sea."

"Ah! my lord, would God I had!" cried I. "Things would have been better for yourself."

"Not in the least," says he, grimly. "I could not ask better. There is a long score to pay, and now—at last—I can begin to pay it."

I cried out against his security.

"Oh!" says he, "this is not Durrisdeer, and I have taken my precautions. His reputation awaits him; I have prepared a welcome for my brother. Indeed, fortune has served me; for I found here a merchant of Albany who knew him after the '45 and had mighty convenient suspicions of a murder: some one of the name of Chew it was, another Albanian. No one here will be surprised if I deny him my door; he will not be suffered to address my children, nor even to salute my wife: as for myself, I make so much exception for a brother that he may speak to me. I should lose my pleasure else," says my lord, rubbing his palms.

Presently he bethought himself, and set men off running, with billets, to summon the magnates of the province. I cannot recall what pretext he employed; at least, it was successful; and when our ancient enemy appeared upon the scene, he found my lord pacing in front of his house under some trees of shade, with the Governor upon one hand and various notables upon the other. My lady, who was seated in the verandah, rose with a very pinched expression and carried her children into the house.

The Master, well dressed and with an elegant walking-sword, bowed to the company in a handsome manner and nodded to my lord with familiarity. My lord did not accept the salutation, but looked upon his brother with bended brows.

"Well, sir," says he, at last, "what ill wind brings you hither of all places, where (to our common disgrace) your reputation has preceded you?"

"Your lordship is pleased to be civil," said the Master, with a fine start.

"I am pleased to be very plain," returned my lord; "because it is needful you should clearly understand your situation. At home, where you were so little known, it was still possible to keep appearances; that would be quite vain in this province; and I have to tell you that I am quite resolved to wash my hands of you. You have already ruined me almost to the door, as you ruined my father before me;—whose heart you also broke. Your crimes escape the law; but my friend the Governor has promised protection to my family. Have a care, sir!" cries my lord, shaking his cane at him: "if you are observed to utter two words to any of my innocent household, the law shall be stretched to make you smart for it."

"Ah!" says the Master, very slowly. "And so this is the advantage of a foreign land! These gentlemen are unacquainted with our story, I perceive. They do not know that I am the Lord Durrisdeer; they do not know you are my younger brother, sitting in my place under a sworn family compact; they do not know (or they would not be seen with you in familiar correspondence) that every acre is mine before God Almighty—and every doit of the money you withhold from me, you do it as a thief, a perjurer, and a disloyal brother!"

"General Clinton," I cried, "do not listen to his lies. I am the steward of the estate, and there is not one word of truth in it. The man is a forfeited rebel turned into a hired spy: there is his story in two words."

It was thus that (in the heat of the moment) I let slip his infamy.

"Fellow," said the Governor, turning his face sternly on the Master, "I know more of you than you think for. We have some broken ends of your adventures in the provinces, which you will do very well not to drive me to investigate. There is the disappearance of Mr. Jacob Chew with all his merchandise; there is the matter of where you came ashore from with so much money and jewels, when you were picked up by a Bermudan out of Albany. Believe me, if I let these matters lie, it is in commiseration for your family and out of respect for my valued friend, Lord Durrisdeer."

There was a murmur of applause from the provincials.

"I should have remembered how a title would shine out in such a hole as this," says the Master, white as a sheet: "no matter how unjustly come by. It remains for me, then, to die at my lord's door, where my dead body will form a very cheerful ornament."

"Away with your affectations!" cries my lord. "You know very well I have no such meaning; only to protect myself from calumny, and my home from your intrusion. I offer you a choice. Either I shall pay your passage home on the first ship, when you may perhaps be able to resume your occupations under Government, although God knows I would rather see you on the highway! Or, if that likes you not, stay here and welcome! I have inquired the least sum on which body and soul can be decently kept together in New York; so much you shall have, paid weekly; and if you cannot labour with your hands to better it, high time you should betake yourself to learn. The condition is—that you speak with no member of my family except myself," he added.

I do not think I have ever seen any man so pale as was the Master; but he was erect and his mouth firm.

"I have been met here with some very unmerited insults," said he, "from which I have certainly no idea to take refuge by flight. Give me your pittance; I take it without shame, for it is mine already—like the shirt upon your back; and I choose to stay until these gentlemen shall understand me better. Already they must spy the cloven hoof, since with all your pretended eagerness for the family honour, you take a pleasure to degrade it in my person."

"This is all very fine," says my lord; "but to us who know you of old, you must be sure it signifies nothing. You take that alternative out of which you think that you can make the most. Take it, if you can, in silence; it will serve you better in the long run, you may believe me, than this ostentation of ingratitude."

"Oh, gratitude, my lord!" cries the Master, with a mounting intonation and his forefinger very conspicuously lifted up. "Be at rest: it will not fail you. It now remains that I should salute these gentlemen whom we have wearied with our family affairs."

And he bowed to each in succession, settled his walking-sword, and took himself off, leaving every one amazed at his behaviour, and me not less so at my lord's.

We were now to enter on a changed phase of this family division. The Master was by no manner of means so helpless as my lord supposed, having at his hand, and entirely devoted to his service, an excellent artist in all sorts of goldsmith work. With my lord's allowance, which was not so scanty as he had described it, the pair could support life; and all the earnings of Secundra Dass might be laid upon one side for any future purpose. That this was done, I have no doubt. It was in all likelihood the Master's design to gather a sufficiency, and then proceed in quest of that treasure which he had buried long before among the mountains; to which, if he had confined himself, he would have been more happily inspired. But unfortunately for himself and all of us, he took counsel of his anger. The public disgrace of his arrival—which I sometimes wonder he could manage to survive—rankled in his bones; he was in that humour when a man—in the words of the old adage—will cut off his nose to spite his face; and he must make himself a public spectacle in the hopes that some of the disgrace might spatter on my lord.

He chose, in a poor quarter of the town, a lonely, small house of boards, overhung with some acacias. It was furnished in front with a sort of hutch opening, like that of a dog's kennel, but about as high as a table from the ground, in which the poor man that built it had formerly displayed some wares; and it was this which took the Master's fancy and possibly suggested his proceedings. It appears, on board the pirate ship he had acquired some quickness with the needle—enough, at least, to play the part of tailor in the public eye; which was all that was required by the nature of his vengeance. A placard was hung above the hutch, bearing these words in something of the following disposition:

James Durie,
formerly MASTER of BALLANTRAE.
Clothes Neatly Clouted.

SECUNDRA DASS,
Decayed Gentleman of India.
Fine Goldsmith Work.

Underneath this, when he had a job, my gentleman sat withinside tailor-wise and busily stitching. I say, when he had a job; but such customers as came were rather for Secundra, and the Master's sewing would be more in the manner of Penelope's. He could never have designed to gain even butter to his bread by such a means of livelihood: enough for him that there was the name of Durie dragged in the dirt on the placard, and the sometime heir of that proud family set up cross-legged in public for a reproach upon his brother's meanness. And in so far his device succeeded that there was murmuring in the town and a party formed highly inimical to my lord. My lord's favour with the Governor laid him more open on the other side; my lady (who was never so well received in the colony) met with painful innuendoes; in a party of women, where it would be the topic most natural to introduce, she was almost debarred from the naming of needle-work; and I have seen her return with a flushed countenance and vow that she would go abroad no more.

In the meanwhile my lord dwelled in his decent mansion, immersed in farming; a popular man with his intimates, and careless or unconscious of the rest. He laid on flesh; had a bright, busy face; even the heat seemed to prosper with him; and my lady—in despite of her own annoyances—daily blessed Heaven her father should have left her such a paradise. She had looked on from a window upon the Master's humiliation; and from that hour appeared to feel at ease. I was not so sure myself; as time went on, there seemed to me a something not quite wholesome in my lord's condition. Happy he was, beyond a doubt, but the grounds of this felicity were wont; even in the bosom of his family he brooded with manifest delight upon some private thought; and I conceived at last the suspicion (quite unworthy of us both) that he kept a mistress somewhere in the town. Yet he went little abroad, and his day was very fully occupied; indeed, there was but a single period, and that pretty early in the morning, while Mr. Alexander was at his lesson-book, of which I was not certain of the disposition. It should be borne in mind, in the defence of that which I now did, that I was always in some fear my lord was not quite justly in his reason; and with our enemy sitting so still in the same town with us, I did well to be upon my guard. Accordingly I made a pretext, had the hour changed at which I taught Mr. Alexander the foundation of cyphering and the mathematic, and set myself instead to dog my master's footsteps.

Every morning, fair or foul, he took his gold-headed cane, set his hat on the back of his head—a recent habitude, which I thought to indicate a burning brow—and betook himself to make a certain circuit. At the first his way was among pleasant trees and beside a graveyard, where he would sit awhile, if the day were fine, in meditation. Presently the path turned down to the waterside, and came back along the harbour-front and past the Master's booth. As he approached this second part of his circuit, my Lord Durrisdeer began to pace more leisurely, like a man delighted with the air and scene; and before the booth, half-way between that and the water's edge, would pause a little, leaning on his staff. It was the hour when the Master sate within upon his board and plied his needle. So these two brothers would gaze upon each other with hard faces; and then my lord move on again, smiling to himself.

It was but twice that I must stoop to that ungrateful necessity of playing spy. I was then certain of my lord's purpose in his rambles and of the secret source of his delight. Here was his mistress: it was hatred and not love that gave him healthful colours. Some moralists might have been relieved by the discovery; I confess that I was dismayed. I found this situation of two brethren not only odious in itself, but big with possibilities of further evil; and I made it my practice, in so far as many occupations would allow, to go by a shorter path and be secretly present at their meeting. Coming down one day a little late, after I had been near a week prevented, I was struck with surprise to find a new development. I should say there was a bench against the Master's house, where customers might sit to parley with the shopman; and here I found my lord seated, nursing his cane and looking pleasantly forth upon the bay. Not three feet from him sate the Master, stitching. Neither spoke; nor (in this new situation) did my lord so much as cut a glance upon his enemy. He tasted his neighbourhood, I must suppose, less indirectly in the bare proximity of person; and, without doubt, drank deep of hateful pleasures.

He had no sooner come away than I openly joined him. "My lord, my lord," said I, "this is no manner of behaviour."

"I grow fat upon it," he replied; and not merely the words, which were strange enough, but the whole character of his expression, shocked me.

"I warn you, my lord, against this indulgency of evil feeling," said I. "I know not to which it is more perilous, the soul or the reason; but you go the way to murder both."

"You cannot understand," said he. "You had never such mountains of bitterness upon your heart."

"And if it were no more," I added, "you will surely goad the man to some extremity."

"To the contrary; I am breaking his spirit," says my lord.

Every morning for hard upon a week my lord took his same place upon the bench. It was a pleasant place, under the green acacias, with a sight upon the bay and shipping, and a sound (from some way off) of marines singing at their employ. Here the two sate without speech or any external movement, beyond that of the needle or the Master biting off a thread, for he still clung to his pretence of industry; and here I made a point to join them, wondering at myself and my companions. If any of my lord's friends went by, he would hail them cheerfully, and cry out he was there to give some good advice to his brother, who was now (to his delight) grown quite industrious. And even this the Master accepted with a steady countenance; what was in his mind, God knows, or perhaps Satan only.

All of a sudden, on a still day of what they call the Indian Summer, when the woods were changed into gold and pink and scarlet, the Master laid down his needle and burst into a fit of merriment. I think he must have been preparing it a long while in silence, for the note in itself was pretty naturally pitched; but breaking suddenly from so extreme a silence, and in circumstances so averse from mirth, it sounded ominously on my ear.

"Henry," said he, "I have for once made a false step, and for once you have had the wit to profit by it. The farce of the cobbler ends to-day; and I confess to you (with my compliments) that you have had the best of it. Blood will out; and you have certainly a choice idea of how to make yourself unpleasant."

Never a word said my lord; it was just as though the Master had not broken silence.

"Come," resumed the Master, "do not be sulky; it will spoil your attitude. You can now afford (believe me) to be a little gracious; for I have not merely a defeat to accept. I had meant to continue this performance till I had gathered enough money for a certain purpose; I confess ingenuously, I have not the courage. You naturally desire my absence from this town; I have come round by another way to the same idea. And I have a proposition to make; or, if your lordship prefers, a favour to ask."

"Ask it," says my lord.

"You may have heard that I had once in this country a considerable treasure," returned the Master; "it matters not whether or no—such is the fact; and I was obliged to bury it in a spot of which I have sufficient indications. To the recovery of this, has my ambition now come down; and, as it is my own, you will not grudge it me."

"Go and get it," says my lord. "I make no opposition."

"Yes," said the Master; "but to do so, I must find men and carriage. The way is long and rough, and the country infested with wild Indians. Advance me only so much as shall be needful: either as a lump sum, in lieu of my allowance; or, if you prefer it, as a loan, which I shall repay on my return. And then, if you so decide, you may have seen the last of me."

My lord stared him steadily in the eyes; there was a hard smile upon his face, but he uttered nothing.

"Henry," said the Master, with a formidable quietness, and drawing at the same time somewhat back—"Henry, I had the honour to address you."

"Let us be stepping homeward," says my lord to me, who was plucking at his sleeve; and with that he rose, stretched himself, settled his hat, and still without a syllable of response, began to walk steadily along the shore.

I hesitated awhile between the two brothers, so serious a climax did we seem to have reached. But the Master had resumed his occupation, his eyes lowered, his hand seemingly as deft as ever; and I decided to pursue my lord.

"Are you mad?" I cried, so soon as I had overtook him. "Would you cast away so fair an opportunity?"

"Is it possible you should still believe in him?" inquired my lord, almost with a sneer.

"I wish him forth of this town!" I cried. "I wish him anywhere and anyhow but as he is."

"I have said my say," returned my lord, "and you have said yours. There let it rest."

But I was bent on dislodging the Master. That sight of him patiently returning to his needlework was more than my imagination could digest. There was never a man made, and the Master the least of any, that could accept so long a series of insults. The air smelt blood to me. And I vowed there should be no neglect of mine if, through any chink of possibility, crime could be yet turned aside. That same day, therefore, I came to my lord in his business room, where he sat upon some trivial occupation.

"My lord," said I, "I have found a suitable investment for my small economies. But these are unhappily in Scotland; it will take some time to lift them, and the affair presses. Could your lordship see his way to advance me the amount against my note?"

He read me awhile with keen eyes. "I have never inquired into the state of your affairs, Mackellar," says he. "Beyond the amount of your caution, you may not be worth a farthing, for what I know."

"I have been a long while in your service, and never told a lie, nor yet asked a favour for myself," said I, "until to-day."

"A favour for the Master," he returned, quietly. "Do you take me for a fool, Mackellar? Understand it once and for all, I treat this beast in my own way; fear nor favour shall not move me; and before I am hoodwinked, it will require a trickster less transparent than yourself. I ask service, loyal service; not that you should make and mar behind my back, and steal my own money to defeat me."

"My lord," said I, "these are very unpardonable expressions."

"Think once more, Mackellar," he replied; "and you will see they fit the fact. It is your own subterfuge that is unpardonable. Deny (if you can) that you designed this money to evade my orders with, and I will ask your pardon freely. If you cannot, you must have the resolution to hear your conduct go by its own name."

"If you think I had any design but to save you—" I began.

"Oh! my old friend," said he, "you know very well what I think! Here is my hand to you with all my heart; but of money, not one rap."

Defeated upon this side, I went straight to my room, wrote a letter, ran with it to the harbour, for I knew a ship was on the point of sailing; and came to the Master's door a little before dusk. Entering without the form of any knock, I found him sitting with his Indian at a simple meal of maize porridge with some milk. The house within was clean and poor; only a few books upon a shelf distinguished it, and (in one corner) Secundra's little bench.

"Mr. Bally," said I, "I have near five hundred pounds laid by in Scotland, the economies of a hard life. A letter goes by yon ship to have it lifted. Have so much patience till the return ship comes in, and it is all yours, upon the same condition you offered to my lord this morning."

He rose from the table, came forward, took me by the shoulders, and looked me in the face, smiling.

"And yet you are very fond of money!" said he. "And yet you love money beyond all things else, except my brother!"

"I fear old age and poverty," said I, "which is another matter."

"I will never quarrel for a name. Call it so," he replied. "Ah! Mackellar, Mackellar, if this were done from any love to me, how gladly would I close upon your offer!"

"And yet," I eagerly answered—"I say it to my shame, but I cannot see you in this poor place without compunction. It is not my single thought, nor my first; and yet it's there! I would gladly see you delivered. I do not offer it in love, and far from that; but, as God judges me—and I wonder at it too!—quite without enmity."

"Ah!" says he, still holding my shoulders, and now gently shaking me, "you think of me more than you suppose. 'And I wonder at it too,'" he added, repeating my expression and, I suppose, something of my voice. "You are an honest man, and for that cause I spare you."

"Spare me?" I cried.

"Spare you," he repeated, letting me go and turning away. And then, fronting me once more. "You little know what I would do with it, Mackellar! Did you think I had swallowed my defeat indeed? Listen: my life has been a series of unmerited cast-backs. That fool, Prince Charlie, mismanaged a most promising affair: there fell my first fortune. In Paris I had my foot once more high upon the ladder: that time it was an accident; a letter came to the wrong hand, and I was bare again. A third time, I found my opportunity; I built up a place for myself in India with an infinite patience; and then Clive came, my rajah was swallowed up, and I escaped out of the convulsion, like another Æneas, with Secundra Dass upon my back. Three times I have had my hand upon the highest station: and I am not yet three-and-forty. I know the world as few men know it when they come to die—Court and camp, the East and the West; I know where to go, I see a thousand openings. I am now at the height of my resources, sound of health, of inordinate ambition. Well, all this I resign; I care not if I die, and the world never hear of me; I care only for one thing, and that I will have. Mind yourself; lest, when the roof falls, you, too, should be crushed under the ruins."

As I came out of his house, all hope of intervention quite destroyed, I was aware of a stir on the harbour-side, and, raising my eyes, there was a great ship newly come to anchor. It seems strange I could have looked upon her with so much indifference, for she brought death to the brothers of Durrisdeer. After all the desperate episodes of this contention, the insults, the opposing interests, the fraternal duel in the shrubbery, it was reserved for some poor devil in Grub Street, scribbling for his dinner, and not caring what he scribbled, to cast a spell across four thousand miles of the salt sea, and send forth both these brothers into savage and wintry deserts, there to die. But such a thought was distant from my mind; and while all the provincials were fluttered about me by the unusual animation of their port, I passed throughout their midst on my return homeward, quite absorbed in the recollection of my visit and the Master's speech.

The same night there was brought to us from the ship a little packet of pamphlets. The next day my lord was under engagement to go with the Governor upon some party of pleasure; the time was nearly due, and I left him for a moment alone in his room and skimming through the pamphlets. When I returned, his head had fallen upon the table, his arms lying abroad amongst the crumpled papers.

"My lord, my lord!" I cried as I ran forward, for I supposed he was in some fit.

He sprang up like a figure upon wires, his countenance deformed with fury, so that in a strange place I should scarce have known him. His hand at the same time flew above his head, as though to strike me down. "Leave me alone!" he screeched, and I fled, as fast as my shaking legs would bear me, for my lady. She, too, lost no time; but when we returned, he had the door locked within, and only cried to us from the other side to leave him be. We looked in each other's faces, very white—each supposing the blow had come at last.

"I will write to the Governor to excuse him," says she. "We must keep our strong friends." But when she took up the pen, it flew out of her fingers. "I cannot write," said she. "Can you?"

"I will make a shift, my lady," said I.

She looked over me as I wrote. "That will do," she said, when I had done. "Thank God, Mackellar, I have you to lean upon! But what can it be now? What, what can it be?"

In my own mind, I believed there was no explanation possible, and none required; it was my fear that the man's madness had now simply burst forth its way, like the long-smothered flames of a volcano; but to this (in mere mercy to my lady) I durst not give expression.

"It is more to the purpose to consider our own behaviour," said I. "Must we leave him there alone?"

"I do not dare disturb him," she replied. "Nature may know best; it may be Nature that cries to be alone; and we grope in the dark. Oh yes, I would leave him as he is."

"I will, then, despatch this letter, my lady, and return here, if you please, to sit with you," said I.

"Pray do," cries my lady.

All afternoon we sat together, mostly in silence, watching my lord's door. My own mind was busy with the scene that had just passed, and its singular resemblance to my vision. I must say a word upon this, for the story has gone abroad with great exaggeration, and I have even seen it printed, and my own name referred to for particulars. So much was the same: here was my lord in a room, with his head upon the table, and when he raised his face, it wore such an expression as distressed me to the soul. But the room was different, my lord's attitude at the table not at all the same, and his face, when he disclosed it, expressed a painful degree of fury instead of that haunting despair which had always (except once, already referred to) characterised it in the vision. There is the whole truth at last before the public; and if the differences be great, the coincidence was yet enough to fill me with uneasiness. All afternoon, as I say, I sat and pondered upon this quite to myself; for my lady had trouble of her own, and it was my last thought to vex her with fancies. About the midst of our time of waiting, she conceived an ingenious scheme, had Mr. Alexander fetched, and bid him knock at his father's door. My lord sent the boy about his business, but without the least violence, whether of manner or expression; so that I began to entertain a hope the fit was over.

At last, as the night fell and I was lighting a lamp that stood there trimmed, the door opened and my lord stood within upon the threshold. The light was not so strong that we could read his countenance; when he spoke, methought his voice a little altered but yet perfectly steady.

"Mackellar," said he, "carry this note to its destination with your own hand. It is highly private. Find the person alone when you deliver it."

"Henry," says my lady, "you are not ill?"

"No, no," says he, querulously, "I am occupied. Not at all; I am only occupied. It is a singular thing a man must be supposed to be ill when he has any business! Send me supper to this room, and a basket of wine: I expect the visit of a friend. Otherwise I am not to be disturbed."

And with that he once more shut himself in.

The note was addressed to one Captain Harris, at a tavern on the portside. I knew Harris (by reputation) for a dangerous adventurer, highly suspected of piracy in the past, and now following the rude business of an Indian trader. What my lord should have to say to him, or he to my lord, it passed my imagination to conceive: or yet how my lord had heard of him, unless by a disgraceful trial from which the man was recently escaped. Altogether I went upon the errand with reluctance, and from the little I saw of the captain, returned from it with sorrow. I found him in a foul-smelling chamber, sitting by a guttering candle and an empty bottle; he had the remains of a military carriage, or rather perhaps it was an affectation, for his manners were low.

"Tell my lord, with my service, that I will wait upon his lordship in the inside of half an hour," says he, when he had read the note; and then had the servility, pointing to his empty bottle, to propose that I should buy him liquor.

Although I returned with my best speed, the Captain followed close upon my heels, and he stayed late into the night. The cock was crowing a second time when I saw (from my chamber window) my lord lighting him to the gate, both men very much affected with their potations, and sometimes leaning one upon the other to confabulate. Yet the next morning my lord was abroad again early with a hundred pounds of money in his pocket. I never supposed that he returned with it; and yet I was quite sure it did not find its way to the Master, for I lingered all morning within view of the booth. That was the last time my Lord Durrisdeer passed his own enclosure till we left New York; he walked in his barn, or sat and talked with his family, all much as usual; but the town saw nothing of him, and his daily visits to the Master seemed forgotten. Nor yet did Harris reappear; or not until the end.

I was now much oppressed with a sense of the mysteries in which we had begun to move. It was plain, if only from his change of habitude, my lord had something on his mind of a grave nature; but what it was, whence it sprang, or why he should now keep the house and garden, I could make no guess at. It was clear, even to probation, the pamphlets had some share in this revolution; I read all I could find, and they were all extremely insignificant, and of the usual kind of party scurrility; even to a high politician, I could spy out no particular matter of offence, and my lord was a man rather indifferent on public questions. The truth is, the pamphlet which was the spring of this affair, lay all the time on my lord's bosom. There it was that I found it at last, after he was dead, in the midst of the north wilderness: in such a place, in such dismal circumstances, I was to read for the first time these idle, lying words of a Whig pamphleteer declaiming against indulgency to Jacobites:—"Another notorious Rebel, the M—r of B—e, is to have his Title restored," the passage ran. "This Business has been long in hand, since he rendered some very disgraceful Services in Scotland and France. His Brother, L—d D—r, is known to be no better than himself in Inclination; and the supposed Heir, who is now to be set aside, was bred up in the most detestable Principles. In the old Phrase, it is six of the one and half a dozen of the other; but the Favour of such a Reposition is too extreme to be passed over." A man in his right wits could not have cared two straws for a tale so manifestly false; that Government should ever entertain the notion, was inconceivable to any reasoning creature, unless possibly the fool that penned it; and my lord, though never brilliant, was ever remarkable for sense. That he should credit such a rodomontade, and carry the pamphlet on his bosom and the words in his heart, is the clear proof of the man's lunacy. Doubtless the mere mention of Mr. Alexander, and the threat directly held out against the child's succession, precipitated that which had so long impended. Or else my master had been truly mad for a long time, and we were too dull or too much used to him, and did not perceive the extent of his infirmity.

About a week after the day of the pamphlets I was late upon the harbour-side, and took a turn towards the Master's, as I often did. The door opened, a flood of light came forth upon the road, and I beheld a man taking his departure with friendly salutations. I cannot say how singularly I was shaken to recognise the adventurer Harris. I could not but conclude it was the hand of my lord that had brought him there; and prolonged my walk in very serious and apprehensive thought. It was late when I came home, and there was my lord making up his portmanteau for a voyage.

"Why do you come so late?" he cried. "We leave to-morrow for Albany, you and I together; and it is high time you were about your preparations."

"For Albany, my lord?" I cried. "And for what earthly purpose?"

"Change of scene," said he.

And my lady, who appeared to have been weeping, gave me the signal to obey without more parley. She told me a little later (when we found occasion to exchange some words) that he had suddenly announced his intention after a visit from Captain Harris, and her best endeavours, whether to dissuade him from the journey, or to elicit some explanation of its purpose, had alike proved unavailing.

CHAPTER XI.
THE JOURNEY IN THE WILDERNESS.

We made a prosperous voyage up that fine river of the Hudson, the weather grateful, the hills singularly beautified with the colours of the autumn. At Albany we had our residence at an inn, where I was not so blind and my lord not so cunning but what I could see he had some design to hold me prisoner. The work he found for me to do was not so pressing that we should transact it apart from necessary papers in the chamber of an inn; nor was it of such importance that I should be set upon as many as four or five scrolls of the same document. I submitted in appearance; but I took private measures on my own side, and had the news of the town communicated to me daily by the politeness of our host. In this way I received at last a piece of intelligence for which, I may say, I had been waiting. Captain Harris (I was told) with "Mr. Mountain, the trader," had gone by up the river in a boat. I would have feared the landlord's eye, so strong the sense of some complicity upon my master's part oppressed me. But I made out to say I had some knowledge of the Captain, although none of Mr. Mountain, and to inquire who else was of the party. My informant knew not; Mr. Mountain had come ashore upon some needful purchases; had gone round the town buying, drinking, and prating; and it seemed the party went upon some likely venture, for he had spoken much of great things he would do when he returned. No more was known, for none of the rest had come ashore, and it seemed they were pressed for time to reach a certain spot before the snow should fall.

And sure enough, the next day, there fell a sprinkle even in Albany; but it passed as it came, and was but a reminder of what lay before us. I thought of it lightly then, knowing so little as I did of that inclement province: the retrospect is different; and I wonder at times if some of the horror of these events which I must now rehearse flowed not from the foul skies and savage winds to which we were exposed, and the agony of cold that we must suffer.

The boat having passed by, I thought at first we should have left the town. But no such matter. My lord continued his stay in Albany where he had no ostensible affairs, and kept me by him, far from my due employment, and making a pretence of occupation. It is upon this passage I expect, and perhaps deserve, censure. I was not so dull but what I had my own thoughts. I could not see the Master entrust himself into the hands of Harris, and not suspect some underhand contrivance. Harris bore a villainous reputation, and he had been tampered with in private by my lord; Mountain, the trader, proved, upon inquiry, to be another of the same kidney; the errand they were all gone upon being the recovery of ill-gotten treasures, offered in itself a very strong incentive to foul play; and the character of the country where they journeyed promised impunity to deeds of blood. Well: it is true I had all these thoughts and fears, and guesses of the Master's fate. But you are to consider I was the same man that sought to dash him from the bulwarks of a ship in the mid-sea; the same that, a little before, very impiously but sincerely offered God a bargain, seeking to hire God to be my bravo. It is true again that I had a good deal melted towards our enemy. But this I always thought of as a weakness of the flesh and even culpable; my mind remaining steady and quite bent against him. True, yet again, that it was one thing to assume on my own shoulders the guilt and danger of a criminal attempt, and another to stand by and see my lord imperil and besmirch himself. But this was the very ground of my inaction. For (should I anyway stir in the business) I might fail indeed to save the Master, but I could not miss to make a byword of my lord.

Thus it was that I did nothing; and upon the same reasons, I am still strong to justify my course. We lived meanwhile in Albany, but though alone together in a strange place, had little traffic beyond formal salutations. My lord had carried with him several introductions to chief people of the town and neighbourhood; others he had before encountered in New York: with this consequence, that he went much abroad, and I am sorry to say was altogether too convivial in his habits. I was often in bed, but never asleep, when he returned; and there was scarce a night when he did not betray the influence of liquor. By day he would still lay upon me endless tasks, which he showed considerable ingenuity to fish up and renew, in the manner of Penelope's web. I never refused, as I say, for I was hired to do his bidding; but I took no pains to keep my penetration under a bushel, and would sometimes smile in his face.

"I think I must be the devil and you Michael Scott," I said to him one day. "I have bridged Tweed and split the Eildons; and now you set me to the rope of sand."

He looked at me with shining eyes, and looked away again, his jaw chewing, but without words.

"Well, well, my lord," said I, "your will is my pleasure. I will do this thing for the fourth time; but I would beg of you to invent another task against to-morrow, for by my troth, I am weary of this one."

"You do not know what you are saying," returned my lord, putting on his hat and turning his back to me. "It is a strange thing you should take a pleasure to annoy me. A friend—but that is a different affair. It is a strange thing. I am a man that has had ill-fortune all my life through. I am still surrounded by contrivances. I am always treading in plots," he burst out. "The whole world is banded against me."

"I would not talk wicked nonsense if I were you," said I; "but I will tell you what I would do—I would put my head in cold water, for you had more last night than you could carry."

"Do ye think that?" said he, with a manner of interest highly awakened. "Would that be good for me? It's a thing I never tried."

"I mind the days when you had no call to try, and I wish, my lord, that they were back again," said I. "But the plain truth is, if you continue to exceed, you will do yourself a mischief."

"I don't appear to carry drink the way I used to," said my lord. "I get overtaken, Mackellar. But I will be more upon my guard."

"That is what I would ask of you," I replied. "You are to bear in mind that you are Mr. Alexander's father: give the bairn a chance to carry his name with some responsibility."

"Ay, ay," said he. "Ye're a very sensible man, Mackellar, and have been long in my employ. But I think, if you have nothing more to say to me I will be stepping. If you have nothing more to say?" he added, with that burning, childish eagerness that was now so common with the man.

"No, my lord, I have nothing more," said I, dryly enough.

"Then I think I will be stepping," says my lord, and stood and looked at me fidgeting with his hat, which he had taken off again. "I suppose you will have no errands? No? I am to meet Sir William Johnson, but I will be more upon my guard." He was silent for a time, and then, smiling: "Do you call to mind a place, Mackellar—it's a little below Engles—where the burn runs very deep under a wood of rowans. I mind being there when I was a lad—dear, it comes over me like an old song!—I was after the fishing, and I made a bonny cast. Eh, but I was happy. I wonder, Mackellar, why I am never happy now?"

"My lord," said I, "if you would drink with more moderation you would have the better chance. It is an old byword that the bottle is a false consoler."

"No doubt," said he, "no doubt. Well, I think I will be going."

"Good-morning, my lord," said I.

"Good-morning, good-morning," said he, and so got himself at last from the apartment.

I give that for a fair specimen of my lord in the morning; and I must have described my patron very ill if the reader does not perceive a notable falling off. To behold the man thus fallen: to know him accepted among his companions for a poor, muddled toper, welcome (if he were welcome at all) for the bare consideration of his title; and to recall the virtues he had once displayed against such odds of fortune; was not this a thing at once to rage and to be humbled at?

In his cups, he was more excessive. I will give but the one scene, close upon the end, which is strongly marked upon my memory to this day, and at the time affected me almost with horror.

I was in bed, lying there awake, when I heard him stumbling on the stair and singing. My lord had no gift of music, his brother had all the graces of the family, so that when I say singing, you are to understand a manner of high, carolling utterance, which was truly neither speech nor song. Something not unlike is to be heard upon the lips of children, ere they learn shame; from those of a man grown elderly, it had a strange effect. He opened the door with noisy precaution; peered in, shading his candle; conceived me to slumber; entered, set his light upon the table, and took off his hat. I saw him very plain; a high, feverish exultation appeared to boil in his veins, and he stood and smiled and smirked upon the candle. Presently he lifted up his arm, snapped his fingers, and fell to undress. As he did so, having once more forgot my presence, he took back to his singing; and now I could hear the words, which were those from the old song of the Twa Corbies endlessly repeated:

"And over his banes when they are bare
The wind sall blaw for evermair!"

I have said there was no music in the man. His strains had no logical succession except in so far as they inclined a little to the minor mode; but they exercised a rude potency upon the feelings, and followed the words, and signified the feelings of the singer with barbaric fitness. He took it first in the time and manner of a rant; presently this ill-favoured gleefulness abated, he began to dwell upon the notes more feelingly, and sank at last into a degree of maudlin pathos that was to me scarce bearable. By equal steps, the original briskness of his acts declined; and when he was stripped to his breeches, he sat on the bedside and fell to whimpering. I know nothing less respectable than the tears of drunkenness, and turned my back impatiently on this poor sight.

But he had started himself (I am to suppose) on that slippery descent of self-pity; on the which, to a man unstrung by old sorrows and recent potations there is no arrest except exhaustion. His tears continued to flow, and the man to sit there, three parts naked, in the cold air of the chamber. I twitted myself alternately with inhumanity and sentimental weakness, now half rising in my bed to interfere, now reading myself lessons of indifference and courting slumber, until, upon a sudden, the quantum mutatus ab illo shot into my mind; and calling to remembrance his old wisdom, constancy, and patience, I was overborne with a pity almost approaching the passionate, not for my master alone but for the sons of man.

At this I leaped from my place, went over to his side and laid a hand on his bare shoulder, which was cold as stone. He uncovered his face and showed it me all swollen and begrutten [10] like a child's; and at the sight my impatience partially revived.

"Think shame to yourself," said I. "This is bairnly conduct. I might have been snivelling myself, if I had cared to swill my belly with wine. But I went to my bed sober like a man. Come: get into yours, and have done with this pitiable exhibition."

"Oh, Mackellar," said he, "my heart is wae!"

"Wae?" cried I. "For a good cause, I think. What words were these you sang as you came in? Show pity to others, we then can talk of pity to yourself. You can be the one thing or the other, but I will be no party to half-way houses. If you're a striker, strike, and if you're a bleater, bleat!"

"Cry!" cries he, with a burst, "that's it—strike! that's talking! Man, I've stood it all too long. But when they laid a hand upon the child, when the child's threatened"—his momentary vigour whimpering off—"my child, my Alexander!"—and he was at his tears again.

I took him by the shoulders and shook him. "Alexander!" said I. "Do you even think of him? Not you! Look yourself in the face like a brave man, and you'll find you're but a self-deceiver. The wife, the friend, the child, they're all equally forgot, and you sunk in a mere log of selfishness."

"Mackellar," said he, with a wonderful return to his old manner and appearance, "you may say what you will of me, but one thing I never was—I was never selfish."

"I will open your eyes in your despite," said I. "How long have we been here? and how often have you written to your family? I think this is the first time you were ever separate: have you written at all? Do they know if you are dead or living?"

I had caught him here too openly; it braced his better nature; there was no more weeping, he thanked me very penitently, got to bed and was soon fast asleep; and the first thing he did the next morning was to sit down and begin a letter to my lady: a very tender letter it was too, though it was never finished. Indeed all communication with New York was transacted by myself; and it will be judged I had a thankless task of it. What to tell my lady and in what words, and how far to be false and how far cruel, was a thing that kept me often from my slumber.

All this while, no doubt, my lord waited with growing impatiency for news of his accomplices. Harris, it is to be thought, had promised a high degree of expedition; the time was already overpast when word was to be looked for; and suspense was a very evil counsellor to a man of an impaired intelligence. My lord's mind throughout this interval dwelled almost wholly in the Wilderness, following that party with whose deeds he had so much concern. He continually conjured up their camps and progresses, the fashion of the country, the perpetration in a thousand different manners of the same horrid fact, and that consequent spectacle of the Master's bones lying scattered in the wind. These private, guilty considerations I would continually observe to peep forth in the man's talk, like rabbits from a hill. And it is the less wonder if the scene of his meditations began to draw him bodily.

It is well known what pretext he took. Sir William Johnson had a diplomatic errand in these parts; and my lord and I (from curiosity, as was given out) went in his company. Sir William was well attended and liberally supplied. Hunters brought us venison, fish was taken for us daily in the streams, and brandy ran like water. We proceeded by day and encamped by night in the military style; sentinels were set and changed; every man had his named duty; and Sir William was the spring of all. There was much in this that might at times have entertained me; but for our misfortune, the weather was extremely harsh, the days were in the beginning open, but the nights frosty from the first. A painful keen wind blew most of the time, so that we sat in the boat with blue fingers, and at night, as we scorched our faces at the fire, the clothes upon our back appeared to be of paper. A dreadful solitude surrounded our steps; the land was quite dispeopled, there was no smoke of fires, and save for a single boat of merchants on the second day, we met no travellers. The season was indeed late, but this desertion of the waterways impressed Sir William himself; and I have heard him more than once express a sense of intimidation. "I have come too late, I fear; they must have dug up the hatchet;" he said; and the future proved how justly he had reasoned.

I could never depict the blackness of my soul upon this journey. I have none of those minds that are in love with the unusual: to see the winter coming and to lie in the field so far from any house, oppressed me like a nightmare; it seemed, indeed, a kind of awful braving of God's power; and this thought, which I daresay only writes me down a coward, was greatly exaggerated by my private knowledge of the errand we were come upon. I was besides encumbered by my duties to Sir William, whom it fell upon me to entertain; for my lord was quite sunk into a state bordering on pervigilium, watching the woods with a rapt eye, sleeping scarce at all, and speaking sometimes not twenty words in a whole day. That which he said was still coherent; but it turned almost invariably upon the party for whom he kept his crazy lookout. He would tell Sir William often, and always as if it were a new communication, that he had "a brother somewhere in the woods," and beg that the sentinels should be directed "to inquire for him." "I am anxious for news of my brother," he would say. And sometimes, when we were under way, he would fancy he spied a canoe far off upon the water or a camp on the shore, and exhibit painful agitation. It was impossible but Sir William should be struck with these singularities; and at last he led me aside, and hinted his uneasiness. I touched my head and shook it; quite rejoiced to prepare a little testimony against possible disclosures.

"But in that case," cries Sir William, "is it wise to let him go at large?"

"Those that know him best," said I, "are persuaded that he should be humoured."

"Well, well," replied Sir William, "it is none of my affairs. But if I had understood, you would never have been here."

Our advance into this savage country had thus uneventfully proceeded for about a week, when we encamped for a night at a place where the river ran among considerable mountains clothed in wood. The fires were lighted on a level space at the water's edge; and we supped and lay down to sleep in the customary fashion. It chanced the night fell murderously cold; the stringency of the frost seized and bit me through my coverings so that pain kept me wakeful; and I was afoot again before the peep of day, crouching by the fires or trotting to and fro at the stream's edge, to combat the aching of my limbs. At last dawn began to break upon hoar woods and mountains, the sleepers rolled in their robes, and the boisterous river dashing among spears of ice. I stood looking about me, swaddled in my stiff coat of a bull's fur, and the breath smoking from my scorched nostrils, when, upon a sudden, a singular, eager cry rang from the borders of the wood. The sentries answered it, the sleepers sprang to their feet; one pointed, the rest followed his direction with their eyes, and there, upon the edge of the forest and betwixt two trees, we beheld the figure of a man reaching forth his hands like one in ecstasy. The next moment he ran forward, fell on his knees at the side of the camp, and burst in tears.

This was John Mountain, the trader, escaped from the most horrid perils; and his first word, when he got speech, was to ask if we had seen Secundra Dass.

"Seen what?" cries Sir William.

"No," said I, "we have seen nothing of him. Why?"

"Nothing?" says Mountain. "Then I was right after all." With that he struck his palm upon his brow. "But what takes him back?" he cried. "What takes the man back among dead bodies. There is some damned mystery here."

This was a word which highly aroused our curiosity, but I shall be more perspicacious, if I narrate these incidents in their true order. Here follows a narrative which I have compiled out of three sources, not very consistent in all points:

First, a written statement by Mountain, in which everything criminal is cleverly smuggled out of view;

Second, two conversations with Secundra Dass; and

Third, many conversations with Mountain himself, in which he was pleased to be entirely plain; for the truth is he regarded me as an accomplice.

NARRATIVE OF THE TRADER, MOUNTAIN.

The crew that went up the river under the joint command of Captain Harris and the Master numbered in all nine persons, of whom (if I except Secundra Dass) there was not one that had not merited the gallows. From Harris downward the voyagers were notorious in that colony for desperate, bloody-minded miscreants; some were reputed pirates, the most hawkers of rum; all ranters and drinkers; all fit associates, embarking together without remorse, upon this treacherous and murderous design. I could not hear there was much discipline or any set captain in the gang; but Harris and four others, Mountain himself, two Scotchmen—Pinkerton and Hastie—and a man of the name of Hicks, a drunken shoemaker, put their heads together and agreed upon the course. In a material sense, they were well enough provided; and the Master in particular brought with him a tent where he might enjoy some privacy and shelter.

Even this small indulgence told against him in the minds of his companions. But indeed he was in a position so entirely false (and even ridiculous) that all his habit of command and arts of pleasing were here thrown away. In the eyes of all, except Secundra Dass, he figured as a common gull and designated victim; going unconsciously to death; yet he could not but suppose himself the contriver and the leader of the expedition; he could scarce help but so conduct himself and at the least hint of authority or condescension, his deceivers would be laughing in their sleeves. I was so used to see and to conceive him in a high, authoritative attitude, that when I had conceived his position on this journey, I was pained and could have blushed. How soon he may have entertained a first surmise, we cannot know; but it was long, and the party had advanced into the Wilderness beyond the reach of any help, ere he was fully awakened to the truth.

It fell thus. Harris and some others had drawn apart into the woods for consultation, when they were startled by a rustling in the brush. They were all accustomed to the arts of Indian warfare, and Mountain had not only lived and hunted, but fought and earned some reputation, with the savages. He could move in the woods without noise, and follow a trail like a hound; and upon the emergence of this alert, he was deputed by the rest to plunge into the thicket for intelligence. He was soon convinced there was a man in his close neighbourhood, moving with precaution but without art among the leaves and branches; and coming shortly to a place of advantage, he was able to observe Secundra Dass crawling briskly off with many backward glances. At this he knew not whether to laugh or cry; and his accomplices, when he had returned and reported, were in much the same dubiety. There was now no danger of an Indian onslaught; but on the other hand, since Secundra Dass was at the pains to spy upon them, it was highly probable he knew English, and if he knew English it was certain the whole of their design was in the Master's knowledge. There was one singularity in the position. If Secundra Dass knew and concealed his knowledge of English, Harris was a proficient in several of the tongues of India, and as his career in that part of the world had been a great deal worse than profligate, he had not thought proper to remark upon the circumstance. Each side had thus a spy-hole on the counsels of the other. The plotters, so soon as this advantage was explained, returned to camp; Harris, hearing the Hindustani was once more closeted with his master, crept to the side of the tent; and the rest, sitting about the fire with their tobacco, awaited his report with impatience. When he came at last, his face was very black. He had overheard enough to confirm the worst of his suspicions. Secundra Dass was a good English scholar; he had been some days creeping and listening, the Master was now fully informed of the conspiracy, and the pair proposed on the morrow to fall out of line at a carrying place and plunge at a venture in the woods: preferring the full risk of famine, savage beasts, and savage men to their position in the midst of traitors.

What, then, was to be done? Some were for killing the Master on the spot; but Harris assured them that would be a crime without profit, since the secret of the treasure must die along with him that buried it. Others were for desisting at once from the whole enterprise and making for New York; but the appetising name of treasure, and the thought of the long way they had already travelled dissuaded the majority. I imagine they were dull fellows for the most part. Harris, indeed, had some acquirements, Mountain was no fool, Hastie was an educated man; but even these had manifestly failed in life, and the rest were the dregs of colonial rascality. The conclusion they reached, at least, was more the offspring of greed and hope, than reason. It was to temporise, to be wary and watch the Master, to be silent and supply no further aliment to his suspicions, and to depend entirely (as well as I make out) on the chance that their victim was as greedy, hopeful, and irrational as themselves, and might, after all, betray his life and treasure.

Twice in the course of the next day Secundra and the Master must have appeared to themselves to have escaped; and twice they were circumvented. The Master, save that the second time he grew a little pale, displayed no sign of disappointment, apologised for the stupidity with which he had fallen aside, thanked his recapturers as for a service, and rejoined the caravan with all his usual gallantry and cheerfulness of mien and bearing. But it is certain he had smelled a rat; for from thenceforth he and Secundra spoke only in each other's ear, and Harris listened and shivered by the tent in vain. The same night it was announced they were to leave the boats and proceed by foot, a circumstance which (as it put an end to the confusion of the portages) greatly lessened the chances of escape.

And now there began between the two sides a silent contest, for life on the one hand, for riches on the other. They were now near that quarter of the desert in which the Master himself must begin to play the part of guide; and using this for a pretext of persecution, Harris and his men sat with him every night about the fire, and laboured to entrap him into some admission. If he let slip his secret, he knew well it was the warrant for his death; on the other hand, he durst not refuse their questions, and must appear to help them to the best of his capacity, or he practically published his mistrust. And yet Mountain assures me the man's brow was never ruffled. He sat in the midst of these jackals, his life depending by a thread, like some easy, witty householder at home by his own fire; an answer he had for everything—as often as not, a jesting answer; avoided threats, evaded insults; talked, laughed, and listened with an open countenance; and, in short, conducted himself in such a manner as must have disarmed suspicion, and went near to stagger knowledge. Indeed, Mountain confessed to me they would soon have disbelieved the Captain's story, and supposed their designated victim still quite innocent of their designs; but for the fact that he continued (however ingeniously) to give the slip to questions, and the yet stronger confirmation of his repeated efforts to escape. The last of these, which brought things to a head, I am now to relate. And first I should say that by this time the temper of Harris's companions was utterly worn out; civility was scarce pretended; and for one very significant circumstance, the Master and Secundra had been (on some pretext) deprived of weapons. On their side, however, the threatened pair kept up the parade of friendship handsomely; Secundra was all bows, the Master all smiles; and on the last night of the truce he had even gone so far as to sing for the diversion of the company. It was observed that he had also eaten with unusual heartiness, and drank deep, doubtless from design.

At least, about three in the morning, he came out of the tent into the open air, audibly mourning and complaining, with all the manner of a sufferer from surfeit. For some while, Secundra publicly attended on his patron, who at last became more easy, and fell asleep on the frosty ground behind the tent, the Indian returning within. Some time after, the sentry was changed; had the Master pointed out to him, where he lay in what is called a robe of buffalo: and thenceforth kept an eye upon him (he declared) without remission. With the first of the dawn, a draught of wind came suddenly and blew open one side the corner of the robe; and with the same puff, the Master's hat whirled in the air and fell some yards away. The sentry thinking it remarkable the sleeper should not awaken, thereupon drew near; and the next moment, with a great shout, informed the camp their prisoner was escaped. He had left behind his Indian, who (in the first vivacity of the surprise) came near to pay the forfeit of his life, and was, in fact, inhumanly mishandled; but Secundra, in the midst of threats and cruelties, stuck to it with extraordinary loyalty, that he was quite ignorant of his master's plans, which might indeed be true, and of the manner of his escape, which was demonstrably false. Nothing was therefore left to the conspirators but to rely entirely on the skill of Mountain. The night had been frosty, the ground quite hard; and the sun was no sooner up than a strong thaw set in. It was Mountain's boast that few men could have followed that trail, and still fewer (even of the native Indians) found it. The Master had thus a long start before his pursuers had the scent, and he must have travelled with surprising energy for a pedestrian so unused, since it was near noon before Mountain had a view of him. At this conjuncture the trader was alone, all his companions following, at his own request, several hundred yards in the rear; he knew the Master was unarmed; his heart was besides heated with the exercise and lust of hunting; and seeing the quarry so close, so defenceless, and seeming so fatigued, he vain-gloriously determined to effect the capture with his single hand. A step or two farther brought him to one margin of a little clearing; on the other, with his arms folded and his back to a huge stone, the Master sat. It is possible Mountain may have made a rustle, it is certain, at least, the Master raised his head and gazed directly at that quarter of the thicket where his hunter lay; "I could not be sure he saw me," Mountain said; "he just looked my way like a man with his mind made up, and all the courage ran out of me like rum out of a bottle." And presently, when the Master looked away again, and appeared to resume those meditations in which he had sat immersed before the trader's coming, Mountain slunk stealthily back and returned to seek the help of his companions.

And now began the chapter of surprises, for the scout had scarce informed the others of his discovery, and they were yet preparing their weapons for a rush upon the fugitive, when the man himself appeared in their midst, walking openly and quietly, with his hands behind his back.

"Ah, men!" says he, on his beholding them. "Here is a fortunate encounter. Let us get back to camp."

Mountain had not mentioned his own weakness or the Master's disconcerting gaze upon the thicket, so that (with all the rest) his return appeared spontaneous. For all that, a hubbub arose; oaths flew, fists were shaken, and guns pointed.

"Let us get back to camp," said the Master. "I have an explanation to make, but it must be laid before you all. And in the meanwhile I would put up these weapons, one of which might very easily go off and blow away your hopes of treasure. I would not kill," says he, smiling, "the goose with the golden eggs."

The charm of his superiority once more triumphed; and the party, in no particular order, set off on their return. By the way, he found occasion to get a word or two apart with Mountain.

"You are a clever fellow and a bold," says he, "but I am not so sure that you are doing yourself justice. I would have you to consider whether you would not do better, ay, and safer, to serve me instead of serving so commonplace a rascal as Mr. Harris. Consider of it," he concluded, dealing the man a gentle tap upon the shoulder, "and don't be in haste. Dead or alive, you will find me an ill man to quarrel with."

When they were come back to the camp, where Harris and Pinkerton stood guard over Secundra, these two ran upon the Master like viragoes, and were amazed out of measure when they were bidden by their comrades to "stand back and hear what the gentleman had to say." The Master had not flinched before their onslaught; nor, at this proof of the ground he had gained, did he betray the least sufficiency.

"Do not let us be in haste," says he. "Meat first and public speaking after."

With that they made a hasty meal: and as soon as it was done, the Master, leaning on one elbow, began his speech. He spoke long, addressing himself to each except Harris, finding for each (with the same exception) some particular flattery. He called them "bold, honest blades," declared he had never seen a more jovial company, work better done, or pains more merrily supported. "Well, then," says he, "some one asks me, Why the devil I ran away? But that is scarce worth answer, for I think you all know pretty well. But you know only pretty well: that is a point I shall arrive at presently, and be you ready to remark it when it comes. There is a traitor here: a double traitor: I will give you his name before I am done; and let that suffice for now. But here comes some other gentleman and asks me, 'Why, in the devil, I came back?' Well, before I answer that question, I have one to put to you. It was this cur here, this Harris, that speaks Hindustani?" cries he, rising on one knee and pointing fair at the man's face, with a gesture indescribably menacing; and when he had been answered in the affirmative, "Ah!" says he, "then are all my suspicions verified, and I did rightly to come back. Now, men, hear the truth for the first time." Thereupon he launched forth in a long story, told with extraordinary skill, how he had all along suspected Harris, how he had found the confirmation of his fears, and how Harris must have misrepresented what passed between Secundra and himself. At this point he made a bold stroke with excellent effect. "I suppose," says he, "you think you are going shares with Harris; I suppose you think you will see to that yourselves; you would naturally not think so flat a rogue could cozen you. But have a care! These half idiots have a sort of cunning, as the skunk has its stench; and it may be news to you that Harris has taken care of himself already. Yes, for him the treasure is all money in the bargain. You must find it or go starve. But he has been paid beforehand; my brother paid him to destroy me; look at him, if you doubt—look at him, grinning and gulping, a detected thief!" Thence, having made this happy impression, he explained how he had escaped, and thought better of it, and at last concluded to come back, lay the truth before the company, and take his chance with them once more: persuaded as he was, they would instantly depose Harris and elect some other leader. "There is the whole truth," said he: "and with one exception, I put myself entirely in your hands. What is the exception? There he sits," he cried, pointing once more to Harris; "a man that has to die! Weapons and conditions are all one to me; put me face to face with him, and if you give me nothing but a stick, in five minutes I will show you a sop of broken carrion, fit for dogs to roll in."

It was dark night when he made an end; they had listened in almost perfect silence; but the firelight scarce permitted any one to judge, from the look of his neighbours, with what result of persuasion or conviction. Indeed, the Master had set himself in the brightest place, and kept his face there, to be the centre of men's eyes: doubtless on a profound calculation. Silence followed for awhile, and presently the whole party became involved in disputation: the Master lying on his back, with his hands knit under his head and one knee flung across the other, like a person unconcerned in the result. And here, I daresay, his bravado carried him too far and prejudiced his case. At least, after a cast or two back and forward, opinion settled finally against him. It's possible he hoped to repeat the business of the pirate ship, and be himself, perhaps, on hard enough conditions, elected leader; and things went so far that way, that Mountain actually threw out the proposition. But the rock he split upon was Hastie. This fellow was not well liked, being sour and slow, with an ugly, glowering disposition, but he had studied some time for the church at Edinburgh College, before ill conduct had destroyed his prospects, and he now remembered and applied what he had learned. Indeed he had not proceeded very far, when the Master rolled carelessly upon one side, which was done (in Mountain's opinion) to conceal the beginnings of despair upon his countenance. Hastie dismissed the most of what they had heard as nothing to the matter: what they wanted was the treasure. All that was said of Harris might be true, and they would have to see to that in time. But what had that to do with the treasure? They had heard a vast of words; but the truth was just this, that Mr. Durie was damnably frightened and had several times run off. Here he was—whether caught or come back was all one to Hastie:

the point was to make an end of the business. As for the talk of deposing and electing captains, he hoped they were all free men and could attend their own affairs. That was dust flung in their eyes, and so was the proposal to fight Harris. "He shall fight no one in this camp, I can tell him that," said Hastie. "We had trouble enough to get his arms away from him, and we should look pretty fools to give them back again. But if it's excitement the gentleman is after, I can supply him with more than perhaps he cares about. For I have no intention to spend the remainder of my life in these mountains; already I have been too long; and I propose that he should immediately tell us where that treasure is, or else immediately be shot. And there," says he, producing his weapon, "there is the pistol that I mean to use."

"Come, I call you a man," cries the Master, sitting up and looking at the speaker with an air of admiration.

"I didn't ask you to call me anything," returned Hastie; "which is it to be?"

"That's an idle question," said the Master. "Needs must when the devil drives. The truth is we are within easy walk of the place, and I will show it you to-morrow."

With that, as if all were quite settled, and settled exactly to his mind, he walked off to his tent, whither Secundra had preceded him.

I cannot think of these last turns and wriggles of my old enemy except with admiration; scarce even pity is mingled with the sentiment, so strongly the man supported, so boldly resisted his misfortunes. Even at that hour, when he perceived himself quite lost, when he saw he had but effected an exchange of enemies, and overthrown Harris to set Hastie up, no sign of weakness appeared in his behaviour, and he withdrew to his tent, already determined (I must suppose) upon affronting the incredible hazard of his last expedient, with the same easy, assured, genteel expression and demeanour as he might have left a theatre withal to join a supper of the wits. But doubtless within, if we could see there, his soul trembled.

Early in the night, word went about the camp that he was sick; and the first thing the next morning he called Hastie to his side, and inquired most anxiously if he had any skill in medicine. As a matter of fact, this was a vanity of that fallen divinity student's, to which he had cunningly addressed himself. Hastie examined him; and being flattered, ignorant, and highly auspicious, knew not in the least whether the man was sick or malingering. In this state he went forth again to his companions; and (as the thing which would give himself most consequence either way) announced that the patient was in a fair way to die.

"For all that," he added with an oath, "and if he bursts by the wayside, he must bring us this morning to the treasure."

But there were several in the camp (Mountain among the number) whom this brutality revolted. They would have seen the Master pistolled, or pistolled him themselves, without the smallest sentiment of pity; but they seemed to have been touched by his gallant fight and unequivocal defeat the night before; perhaps, too, they were even already beginning to oppose themselves to their new leader: at least, they now declared that (if the man was sick) he should have a day's rest in spite of Hastie's teeth.

The next morning he was manifestly worse, and Hastie himself began to display something of humane concern, so easily does even the pretence of doctoring awaken sympathy. The third the Master called Mountain and Hastie to the tent, announced himself to be dying, gave them full particulars as to the position of the cache, and begged them to set out incontinently on the quest, so that they might see if he deceived them, and (if they were at first unsuccessful) he should be able to correct their error.

But here arose a difficulty on which he doubtless counted. None of these men would trust another, none would consent to stay behind. On the other hand, although the Master seemed extremely low, spoke scarce above a whisper, and lay much of the time insensible, it was still possible it was a fraudulent sickness; and if all went treasure-hunting, it might prove they had gone upon a wild-goose chase, and return to find their prisoner flown. They concluded, therefore, to hang idling round the camp, alleging sympathy to their reason; and certainly, so mingled are our dispositions, several were sincerely (if not very deeply) affected by the natural peril of the man whom they callously designed to murder. In the afternoon, Hastie was called to the bedside to pray: the which (incredible as it must appear) he did with unction; about eight at night, the wailing of Secundra announced that all was over; and before ten, the Indian, with a link stuck in the ground, was toiling at the grave. Sunrise of next day beheld the Master's burial, all hands attending with great decency of demeanour; and the body was laid in the earth, wrapped in a fur robe, with only the face uncovered; which last was of a waxy whiteness, and had the nostrils plugged according to some Oriental habit of Secundra's. No sooner was the grave filled than the lamentations of the Indian once more struck concern to every heart; and it appears this gang of murderers, so far from resenting his outcries, although both distressful and (in such a country) perilous to their own safety, roughly but kindly endeavoured to console him.

But if human nature is even in the worst of men occasionally kind, it is still, and before all things, greedy; and they soon turned from the mourner to their own concerns. The cache of the treasure being hard by, although yet unidentified, it was concluded not to break camp; and the day passed, on the part of the voyagers, in unavailing exploration of the woods, Secundra the while lying on his master's grave. That night they placed no sentinel, but lay altogether about the fire, in the customary woodman fashion, the heads outward, like the spokes of a wheel. Morning found them in the same disposition; only Pinkerton, who lay on Mountain's right, between him and Hastie, had (in the hours of darkness) been secretly butchered, and there lay, still wrapped as to his body in his mantle, but offering above that ungodly and horrific spectacle of the scalped head. The gang were that morning as pale as a company of phantoms, for the pertinacity of Indian war (or to speak more correctly, Indian murder) was well known to all. But they laid the chief blame on their unsentinelled posture; and fired with the neighbourhood of the treasure, determined to continue where they were. Pinkerton was buried hard by the Master; the survivors again passed the day in exploration, and returned in a mingled humour of anxiety and hope, being partly certain they were now close on the discovery of what they sought, and on the other hand (with the return of darkness) were infected with the fear of Indians. Mountain was the first sentry; he declares he neither slept nor yet sat down, but kept his watch with a perpetual and straining vigilance, and it was even with unconcern that (when he saw by the stars his time was up) he drew near the fire to awaken his successor. This man (it was Hicks the shoemaker) slept on the lee side of the circle, something farther off in consequence than those to windward, and in a place darkened by the blowing smoke. Mountain stooped and took him by the shoulder; his hand was at once smeared by some adhesive wetness; and (the wind at the moment veering) the firelight shone upon the sleeper, and showed him, like Pinkerton, dead and scalped.

It was clear they had fallen in the hands of one of those matchless Indian bravos, that will sometimes follow a party for days, and in spite of indefatigable travel, and unsleeping watch, continue to keep up with their advance, and steal a scalp at every resting-place. Upon this discovery, the treasure-seekers, already reduced to a poor half dozen, fell into mere dismay, seized a few necessaries, and deserting the remainder of their goods, fled outright into the forest. Their fire they left still burning, and their dead comrade unburied. All day they ceased not to flee, eating by the way, from hand to mouth; and since they feared to sleep, continued to advance at random even in the hours of darkness. But the limit of man's endurance is soon reached; when they rested at last it was to sleep profoundly; and when they woke, it was to find that the enemy was still upon their heels, and death and mutilation had once more lessened and deformed their company.

By this they had become light-headed, they had quite missed their path in the wilderness, their stores were already running low. With the further horrors, it is superfluous that I should swell this narrative, already too prolonged. Suffice it to say that when at length a night passed by innocuous, and they might breathe again in the hope that the murderer had at last desisted from pursuit, Mountain and Secundra were alone. The trader is firmly persuaded their unseen enemy was some warrior of his own acquaintance, and that he himself was spared by favour. The mercy extended to Secundra he explains on the ground that the East Indian was thought to be insane; partly from the fact that, through all the horrors of the flight and while others were casting away their very food and weapons, Secundra continued to stagger forward with a mattock on his shoulder, and partly because, in the last days and with a great degree of heat and fluency, he perpetually spoke with himself in his own language. But he was sane enough when it came to English.

"You think he will be gone quite away?" he asked, upon their blest awakening in safety.

"I pray God so, I believe so, I dare to believe so," Mountain had replied almost with incoherence, as he described the scene to me.

And indeed he was so much distempered that until he met us, the next morning, he could scarce be certain whether he had dreamed, or whether it was a fact, that Secundra had thereupon turned directly about and returned without a word upon their footprints, setting his face for these wintry and hungry solitudes, along a path whose every stage was mile-stoned with a mutilated corpse.

CHAPTER XII.
THE JOURNEY IN THE WILDERNESS (continued).

Mountain's story, as it was laid before Sir William Johnson and my lord, was shorn, of course, of all the earlier particulars, and the expedition described to have proceeded uneventfully, until the Master sickened. But the latter part was very forcibly related, the speaker visibly thrilling to his recollections; and our then situation, on the fringe of the same desert, and the private interests of each, gave him an audience prepared to share in his emotions. For Mountain's intelligence not only changed the world for my Lord Durrisdeer, but materially affected the designs of Sir William Johnson.

These I find I must lay more at length before the reader. Word had reached Albany of dubious import; it had been rumoured some hostility was to be put in act; and the Indian diplomatist had, thereupon, sped into the wilderness, even at the approach of winter, to nip that mischief in the bud. Here, on the borders, he learned that he was come too late; and a difficult choice was thus presented to a man (upon the whole) not any more bold than prudent. His standing with the painted braves may be compared to that of my Lord President Culloden among the chiefs of our own Highlanders at the 'forty-five; that is as much as to say, he was, to these men, reason's only speaking trumpet, and counsels of peace and moderation, if they were to prevail at all, must prevail singly through his influence. If, then, he should return, the province must lie open to all the abominable tragedies of Indian war—the houses blaze, the wayfarer be cut off, and the men of the woods collect their usual disgusting spoil of human scalps. On the other side, to go farther forth, to risk so small a party deeper in the desert, to carry words of peace among warlike savages already rejoicing to return to war: here was an extremity from which it was easy to perceive his mind revolted.

"I have come too late," he said more than once, and would fall into a deep consideration, his head bowed in his hands, his foot patting the ground.

At length he raised his face and looked upon us, that is to say upon my lord, Mountain, and myself, sitting close round a small fire, which had been made for privacy in one corner of the camp.

"My lord, to be quite frank with you, I find myself in two minds," said he. "I think it very needful I should go on, but not at all proper I should any longer enjoy the pleasure of your company. We are here still upon the water side; and I think the risk to southward no great matter. Will not yourself and Mr. Mackellar take a single boat's crew and return to Albany?"

My lord, I should say, had listened to Mountain's narrative, regarding him throughout with a painful intensity of gaze; and since the tale concluded, had sat as in a dream. There was something very daunting in his look; something to my eyes not rightly human; the face, lean, and dark, and aged, the mouth painful, the teeth disclosed in a perpetual rictus; the eyeball swimming clear of the lids upon a field of blood-shot white. I could not behold him myself without a jarring irritation, such as, I believe, is too frequently the uppermost feeling on the sickness of those dear to us. Others, I could not but remark, were scarce able to support his neighbourhood—Sir William eviting to be near him, Mountain dodging his eye, and, when he met it, blenching and halting in his story. At this appeal, however, my lord appeared to recover his command upon himself.

"To Albany?" said he, with a good voice.

"Not short of it, at least," replied Sir William. "There is no safety nearer hand."

"I would be very sweir [11] to return," says my lord. "I am not afraid—of Indians," he added, with a jerk.

"I wish that I could say so much," returned Sir William, smiling; "although, if any man durst say it, it should be myself. But you are to keep in view my responsibility, and that as the voyage has now become highly dangerous, and your business—if you ever had any," says he, "brought quite to a conclusion by the distressing family intelligence you have received, I should be hardly justified if I even suffered you to proceed, and run the risk of some obloquy if anything regrettable should follow."

My lord turned to Mountain. "What did he pretend he died of?" he asked.

"I don't think I understand your honour," said the trader, pausing like a man very much affected, in the dressing of some cruel frost-bites.

For a moment my lord seemed at a full stop; and then, with some irritation, "I ask you what he died of. Surely that's a plain question," said he.

"Oh! I don't know," said Mountain. "Hastie even never knew. He seemed to sicken natural, and just pass away."

"There it is, you see!" concluded my lord, turning to Sir William.

"Your lordship is too deep for me," replied Sir William.

"Why," says my lord, "this in a matter of succession; my son's title may be called in doubt; and the man being supposed to be dead of nobody can tell what, a great deal of suspicion would be naturally roused."

"But, God damn me, the man's buried!" cried Sir William.

"I will never believe that," returned my lord, painfully trembling. "I'll never believe it!" he cried again, and jumped to his feet. "Did he look dead?" he asked of Mountain.

"Look dead?" repeated the trader. "He looked white. Why, what would he be at? I tell you, I put the sods upon him."

My lord caught Sir William by the coat with a hooked hand. "This man has the name of my brother," says he, "but it's well understood that he was never canny."

"Canny?" says Sir William. "What is that?"

"He's not of this world," whispered my lord, "neither him nor the black deil that serves him. I have struck my sword throughout his vitals," he cried; "I have felt the hilt dirl [12] on his breastbone, and the hot blood spirt in my very face, time and again, time and again!" he repeated, with a gesture indescribable. "But he was never dead for that," said he, and I sighed aloud. "Why should I think he was dead now? No, not till I see him rotting," says he.

Sir William looked across at me with a long face. Mountain forgot his wounds, staring and gaping.

"My lord," said I, "I wish you would collect your spirits." But my throat was so dry, and my own wits so scattered, I could add no more.

"No," says my lord, "it's not to be supposed that he would understand me. Mackellar does, for he kens all, and has seen him buried before now. This is a very good servant to me, Sir William, this man Mackellar; he buried him with his own hands—he and my father—by the light of two siller candlesticks. The other man is a familiar spirit; he brought him from Coromandel. I would have told ye this long syne, Sir William, only it was in the family." These last remarks he made with a kind of a melancholy composure, and his time of aberration seemed to pass away. "You can ask yourself what it all means," he proceeded. "My brother falls sick, and dies, and is buried, as so they say; and all seems very plain. But why did the familiar go back? I think ye must see for yourself it's a point that wants some clearing."

"I will be at your service, my lord, in half a minute," said Sir William, rising. "Mr. Mackellar, two words with you;" and he led me without the camp, the frost crunching in our steps, the trees standing at our elbow, hoar with frost, even as on that night in the Long Shrubbery. "Of course, this is midsummer madness," said Sir William, as soon as we were gotten out of bearing.

"Why, certainly," said I. "The man is mad. I think that manifest."

"Shall I seize and bind him?" asked Sir William. "I will upon your authority. If these are all ravings, that should certainly be done."

I looked down upon the ground, back at the camp, with its bright fires and the folk watching us, and about me on the woods and mountains; there was just the one way that I could not look, and that was in Sir William's face.

"Sir William," said I at last, "I think my lord not sane, and have long thought him so. But there are degrees in madness; and whether he should be brought under restraint—Sir William, I am no fit judge," I concluded.

"I will be the judge," said he. "I ask for facts. Was there, in all that jargon, any word of truth or sanity? Do you hesitate?" he asked. "Am I to understand you have buried this gentleman before?"

"Not buried," said I; and then, taking up courage at last, "Sir William," said I, "unless I were to tell you a long story, which much concerns a noble family (and myself not in the least), it would be impossible to make this matter clear to you. Say the word, and I will do it, right or wrong. And, at any rate, I will say so much, that my lord is not so crazy as he seems. This is a strange matter, into the tail of which you are unhappily drifted."

"I desire none of your secrets," replied Sir William; "but I will be plain, at the risk of incivility, and confess that I take little pleasure in my present company."

"I would be the last to blame you," said I, "for that."

"I have not asked either for your censure or your praise, sir," returned Sir William. "I desire simply to be quit of you; and to that effect, I put a boat and complement of men at your disposal."

"This is fairly offered," said I, after reflection. "But you must suffer me to say a word upon the other side. We have a natural curiosity to learn the truth of this affair; I have some of it myself; my lord (it is very plain) has but too much. The matter of the Indian's return is enigmatical."

"I think so myself," Sir William interrupted, "and I propose (since I go in that direction) to probe it to the bottom. Whether or not the man has gone like a dog to die upon his master's grave, his life, at least, is in great danger, and I propose, if I can, to save it. There is nothing against his character?"

"Nothing, Sir William," I replied.

"And the other?" he said. "I have heard my lord, of course; but, from the circumstances of his servant's loyalty, I must suppose he had some noble qualities."

"You must not ask me that!" I cried. "Hell may have noble flames. I have known him a score of years, and always hated, and always admired, and always slavishly feared him."

"I appear to intrude again upon your secrets," said Sir William, "believe me, inadvertently. Enough that I will see the grave, and (if possible) rescue the Indian. Upon these terms, can you persuade your master to return to Albany?"

"Sir William," said I, "I will tell you how it is. You do not see my lord to advantage; it will seem even strange to you that I should love him; but I do, and I am not alone. If he goes back to Albany, it must be by force, and it will be the death-warrant of his reason, and perhaps his life. That is my sincere belief; but I am in your hands, and ready to obey, if you will assume so much responsibility as to command."

"I will have no shred of responsibility; it is my single endeavour to avoid the same," cried Sir William. "You insist upon following this journey up; and be it so! I wash my hands of the whole matter."

With which word, he turned upon his heel and gave the order to break camp; and my lord, who had been hovering near by, came instantly to my side.

"Which is it to be?" said he.

"You are to have your way," I answered. "You shall see the grave."

The situation of the Master's grave was, between guides, easily described; it lay, indeed, beside a chief landmark of the wilderness, a certain range of peaks, conspicuous by their design and altitude, and the source of many brawling tributaries to that inland sea, Lake Champlain. It was therefore possible to strike for it direct, instead of following back the blood-stained trail of the fugitives, and to cover, in some sixteen hours of march, a distance which their perturbed wanderings had extended over more than sixty. Our boats we left under a guard upon the river; it was, indeed, probable we should return to find them frozen fast; and the small equipment with which we set forth upon the expedition, included not only an infinity of furs to protect us from the cold, but an arsenal of snow-shoes to render travel possible, when the inevitable snow should fall. Considerable alarm was manifested at our departure; the march was conducted with soldierly precaution, the camp at night sedulously chosen and patrolled; and it was a consideration of this sort that arrested us, the second day, within not many hundred yards of our destination—the night being already imminent, the spot in which we stood well qualified to be a strong camp for a party of our numbers; and Sir William, therefore, on a sudden thought, arresting our advance.

Before us was the high range of mountains toward which we had been all day deviously drawing near. From the first light of the dawn, their silver peaks had been the goal of our advance across a tumbled lowland forest, thrid with rough streams, and strewn with monstrous boulders; the peaks (as I say) silver, for already at the higher altitudes the snow fell nightly; but the woods and the low ground only breathed upon with frost. All day heaven had been charged with ugly vapours, in the which the sun swam and glimmered like a shilling piece; all day the wind blew on our left cheek barbarous cold, but very pure to breathe. With the end of the afternoon, however, the wind fell; the clouds, being no longer reinforced, were scattered or drunk up; the sun set behind us with some wintry splendour, and the white brow of the mountains shared its dying glow.

It was dark ere we had supper; we ate in silence, and the meal was scarce despatched before my lord slunk from the fireside to the margin of the camp; whither I made haste to follow him. The camp was on high ground, overlooking a frozen lake, perhaps a mile in its longest measurement; all about us, the forest lay in heights and hollows; above rose the white mountains; and higher yet, the moon rode in a fair sky. There was no breath of air; nowhere a twig creaked; and the sounds of our own camp were hushed and swallowed up in the surrounding stillness. Now that the sun and the wind were both gone down, it appeared almost warm, like a night of July: a singular illusion of the sense, when earth, air, and water were strained to bursting with the extremity of frost.

My lord (or what I still continued to call by his loved name) stood with his elbow in one hand, and his chin sunk in the other, gazing before him on the surface of the wood. My eyes followed his, and rested almost pleasantly upon the frosted contexture of the pines, rising in moonlit hillocks, or sinking in the shadow of small glens. Hard by, I told myself, was the grave of our enemy, now gone where the wicked cease from troubling, the earth heaped for ever on his once so active limbs. I could not but think of him as somehow fortunate to be thus done with man's anxiety and weariness, the daily expense of spirit, and that daily river of circumstance to be swum through, at any hazard, under the penalty of shame or death. I could not but think how good was the end of that long travel; and with that, my mind swung at a tangent to my lord. For was not my lord dead also? a maimed soldier, looking vainly for discharge, lingering derided in the line of battle? A kind man, I remembered him; wise, with a decent pride, a son perhaps too dutiful, a husband only too loving, one that could suffer and be silent, one whose hand I loved to press. Of a sudden, pity caught in my windpipe with a sob; I could have wept aloud to remember and behold him; and standing thus by his elbow, under the broad moon, I prayed fervently either that he should be released, or I strengthened to persist in my affection.

"Oh God," said I, "this was the best man to me and to himself, and now I shrink from him. He did no wrong, or not till he was broke with sorrows; these are but his honourable wounds that we begin to shrink from. Oh, cover them up, oh, take him away, before we hate him!"

I was still so engaged in my own bosom, when a sound broke suddenly upon the night. It was neither very loud, nor very near; yet, bursting as it did from so profound and so prolonged a silence, it startled the camp like an alarm of trumpets. Ere I had taken breath, Sir William was beside me, the main part of the voyagers clustered at his back, intently giving ear. Methought, as I glanced at them across my shoulder, there was a whiteness, other than moonlight, on their cheeks; and the rays of the moon reflected with a sparkle on the eyes of some, and the shadows lying black under the brows of others (according as they raised or bowed the head to listen) gave to the group a strange air of animation and anxiety. My lord was to the front, crouching a little forth, his hand raised as for silence: a man turned to stone. And still the sounds continued, breathlessly renewed with a precipitate rhythm.

Suddenly Mountain spoke in a loud, broken whisper, as of a man relieved. "I have it now," he said; and, as we all turned to hear him, "the Indian must have known the cache," he added. "That is he—he is digging out the treasure."

"Why, to be sure!" exclaimed Sir William. "We were geese not to have supposed so much."

"The only thing is," Mountain resumed, "the sound is very close to our old camp. And, again, I do not see how he is there before us, unless the man had wings!"

"Greed and fear are wings," remarked Sir William. "But this rogue has given us an alert, and I have a notion to return the compliment. What say you, gentlemen, shall we have a moonlight hunt?"

It was so agreed; dispositions were made to surround Secundra at his task; some of Sir William's Indians hastened in advance; and a strong guard being left at our headquarters, we set forth along the uneven bottom of the forest; frost crackling, ice sometimes loudly splitting under foot; and overhead the blackness of pine-woods, and the broken brightness of the moon. Our way led down into a hollow of the land; and as we descended, the sounds diminished and had almost died away. Upon the other slope it was more open, only dotted with a few pines, and several vast and scattered rocks that made inky shadows in the moonlight. Here the sounds began to reach us more distinctly; we could now perceive the ring of iron, and more exactly estimate the furious degree of haste with which the digger plied his instrument. As we neared the top of the ascent, a bird or two winged aloft and hovered darkly in the moonlight; and the next moment we were gazing through a fringe of trees upon a singular picture.

A narrow plateau, overlooked by the white mountains, and encompassed nearer hand by woods, lay bare to the strong radiance of the moon. Rough goods, such as make the wealth of foresters, were sprinkled here and there upon the ground in meaningless disarray. About the midst, a tent stood, silvered with frost: the door open, gaping on the black interior. At the one end of this small stage lay what seemed the tattered remnants of a man. Without doubt we had arrived upon the scene of Harris's encampment; there were the goods scattered in the panic of flight; it was in yon tent the Master breathed his last; and the frozen carrion that lay before us was the body of the drunken shoemaker. It was always moving to come upon the theatre of any tragic incident; to come upon it after so many days, and to find it (in the seclusion of a desert) still unchanged, must have impressed the mind of the most careless. And yet it was not that which struck us into pillars of stone; but the sight (which yet we had been half expecting) of Secundra ankle deep in the grave of his late master. He had cast the main part of his raiment by, yet his frail arms and shoulders glistered in the moonlight with a copious sweat; his face was contracted with anxiety and expectation; his blows resounded on the grave, as thick as sobs; and behind him, strangely deformed and ink-black upon the frosty ground, the creature's shadow repeated and parodied his swift gesticulations. Some night birds arose from the boughs upon our coming, and then settled back; but Secundra, absorbed in his toil; heard or heeded not at all.

I heard Mountain whisper to Sir William, "Good God! it's the grave! He's digging him up!" It was what we had all guessed, and yet to hear it put in language thrilled me. Sir William violently started.

"You damned sacrilegious hound!" he cried. "What's this?"

Secundra leaped in the air, a little breathless cry escaped him, the tool flew from his grasp, and he stood one instant staring at the speaker. The next, swift as an arrow, he sped for the woods upon the farther side; and the next again, throwing up his hands with a violent gesture of resolution, he had begun already to retrace his steps.

"Well, then, you come, you help—" he was saying. But by now my lord had stepped beside Sir William; the moon shone fair upon his face, and the words were still upon Secundra's lips, when he beheld and recognised his master's enemy. "Him!" he screamed, clasping his hands, and shrinking on himself.

"Come, come!" said Sir William. "There is none here to do you harm, if you be innocent; and if you be guilty, your escape is quite cut off. Speak, what do you here among the graves of the dead and the remains of the unburied?"

"You no murderer?" inquired Secundra. "You true man? you see me safe?"

"I will see you safe, if you be innocent," returned Sir William. "I have said the thing, and I see not wherefore you should doubt it."

"There all murderers," cried Secundra, "that is why! He kill—murderer," pointing to Mountain; "there two hire-murderers," pointing to my lord and myself—"all gallows—murderers! Ah! I see you all swing in a rope. Now I go save the sahib; he see you swing in a rope. The sahib," he continued, pointing to the grave, "he not dead. He bury, he not dead."

My lord uttered a little noise, moved nearer to the grave, and stood and stared in it.

"Buried and not dead?" exclaimed Sir William. "What kind of rant is this?"

"See, sahib," said Secundra. "The sahib and I alone with murderers; try all way to escape, no way good. Then try this way: good way in warm climate, good way in India; here, in this dam cold place, who can tell? I tell you pretty good hurry: you help, you light a fire, help rub."

"What is the creature talking of?" cried Sir William. "My head goes round."

"I tell you I bury him alive," said Secundra. "I teach him swallow his tongue. Now dig him up pretty good hurry, and he not much worse. You light a fire."

Sir William turned to the nearest of his men. "Light a fire," said he. "My lot seems to be cast with the insane."

"You good man," returned Secundra. "Now I go dig the sahib up."

He returned as he spoke to the grave, and resumed his former toil. My lord stood rooted, and I at my lord's side, fearing I knew not what.

The frost was not yet very deep, and presently the Indian threw aside his tool, and began to scoop the dirt by handfuls. Then he disengaged a corner of a buffalo robe; and then I saw hair catch among his fingers: yet, a moment more, and the moon shone on something white. Awhile Secundra crouched upon his knees, scraping with delicate fingers, breathing with puffed lips; and when he moved aside, I beheld the face of the Master wholly disengaged. It was deadly white, the eyes closed, the ears and nostrils plugged, the cheeks fallen, the nose sharp as if in death; but for all he had lain so many days under the sod, corruption had not approached him, and (what strangely affected all of us) his lips and chin were mantled with a swarthy beard.

"My God!" cried Mountain, "he was as smooth as a baby when we laid him there!"

"They say hair grows upon the dead," observed Sir William; but his voice was thick and weak.

Secundra paid no heed to our remarks, digging swift as a terrier in the loose earth. Every moment the form of the Master, swathed in his buffalo robe, grew more distinct in the bottom of that shallow trough; the moon shining strong, and the shadows of the standers-by, as they drew forward and back, falling and flitting over his emergent countenance. The sight held us with a horror not before experienced. I dared not look my lord in the face; but for as long as it lasted, I never observed him to draw breath; and a little in the background one of the men (I know not whom) burst into a kind of sobbing.

"Now," said Secundra, "you help me lift him out."

Of the flight of time, I have no idea; it may have been three hours, and it may have been five, that the Indian laboured to reanimate his master's body. One thing only I know, that it was still night, and the moon was not yet set, although it had sunk low, and now barred the plateau with long shadows, when Secundra uttered a small cry of satisfaction; and, leaning swiftly forth, I thought I could myself perceive a change upon that icy countenance of the unburied. The next moment I beheld his eyelids flutter; the next they rose entirely, and the week-old corpse looked me for a moment in the face.

So much display of life I can myself swear to. I have heard from others that he visibly strove to speak, that his teeth showed in his beard, and that his brow was contorted as with an agony of pain and effort. And this may have been; I know not, I was otherwise engaged. For at that first disclosure of the dead man's eyes, my Lord Durrisdeer fell to the ground, and when I raised him up, he was a corpse.

Day came, and still Secundra could not be persuaded to desist from his unavailing efforts. Sir William, leaving a small party under my command, proceeded on his embassy with the first light; and still the Indian rubbed the limbs and breathed in the mouth of the dead body. You would think such labours might have vitalised a stone; but, except for that one moment (which was my lord's death), the black spirit of the Master held aloof from its discarded clay; and by about the hour of noon, even the faithful servant was at length convinced. He took it with unshaken quietude.

"Too cold," said he, "good way in India, no good here." And, asking for some food, which he ravenously devoured as soon as it was set before him, he drew near to the fire and took his place at my elbow. In the same spot, as soon as he had eaten, he stretched himself out, and fell into a childlike slumber, from which I must arouse him, some hours afterwards, to take his part as one of the mourners at the double funeral. It was the same throughout; he seemed to have outlived at once and with the same effort, his grief for his master and his terror of myself and Mountain.

One of the men left with me was skilled in stone-cutting; and before Sir William returned to pick us up, I had chiselled on a boulder this inscription, with a copy of which I may fitly bring my narrative to a close:##

CATRIONA

PART I.
THE LORD ADVOCATE

CHAPTER I.
A BEGGAR ON HORSEBACK

The 25th day of August, 1751, about two in the afternoon, I, David Balfour, came forth of the British Linen Company, a porter attending me with a bag of money, and some of the chief of these merchants bowing me from their doors. Two days before, and even so late as yestermorning, I was like a beggar-man by the wayside, clad in rags, brought down to my last shillings, my companion a condemned traitor, a price set on my own head for a crime with the news of which the country rang. To-day I was served heir to my position in life, a landed laird, a bank porter by me carrying my gold, recommendations in my pocket, and (in the words of the saying) the ball directly at my foot.

There were two circumstances that served me as ballast to so much sail. The first was the very difficult and deadly business I had still to handle; the second, the place that I was in. The tall, black city, and the numbers and movement and noise of so many folk, made a new world for me, after the moorland braes, the sea-sands and the still country-sides that I had frequented up to then. The throng of the citizens in particular abashed me. Rankeillor's son was short and small in the girth; his clothes scarce held on me; and it was plain I was ill qualified to strut in the front of a bank-porter. It was plain, if I did so, I should but set folk laughing, and (what was worse in my case) set them asking questions. So that I behooved to come by some clothes of my own, and in the meanwhile to walk by the porter's side, and put my hand on his arm as though we were a pair of friends.

At a merchant's in the Luckenbooths I had myself fitted out: none too fine, for I had no idea to appear like a beggar on horseback; but comely and responsible, so that servants should respect me. Thence to an armourer's, where I got a plain sword, to suit with my degree in life. I felt safer with the weapon, though (for one so ignorant of defence) it might be called an added danger. The porter, who was naturally a man of some experience, judged my accoutrement to be well chosen.

"Naething kenspeckle,"[1] said he; "plain, dacent claes. As for the rapier, nae doubt it sits wi' your degree; but an I had been you, I would has waired my siller better-gates than that." And he proposed I should buy winter-hosen from a wife in the Cowgate-back, that was a cousin of his own, and made them "extraordinar endurable."

But I had other matters on my hand more pressing. Here I was in this old, black city, which was for all the world like a rabbit-warren, not only by the number of its indwellers, but the complication of its passages and holes. It was, indeed, a place where no stranger had a chance to find a friend, let be another stranger. Suppose him even to hit on the right close, people dwelt so thronged in these tall houses, he might very well seek a day before he chanced on the right door. The ordinary course was to hire a lad they called a caddie, who was like a guide or pilot, led you where you had occasion, and (your errands being done) brought you again where you were lodging. But these caddies, being always employed in the same sort of services, and having it for obligation to be well informed of every house and person in the city, had grown to form a brotherhood of spies; and I knew from tales of Mr. Campbell's how they communicated one with another, what a rage of curiosity they conceived as to their employer's business, and how they were like eyes and fingers to the police. It would be a piece of little wisdom, the way I was now placed, to take such a ferret to my tails. I had three visits to make, all immediately needful: to my kinsman Mr. Balfour of Pilrig, to Stewart the Writer that was Appin's agent, and to William Grant Esquire of Prestongrange, Lord Advocate of Scotland. Mr. Balfour's was a non-committal visit; and besides (Pilrig being in the country) I made bold to find the way to it myself, with the help of my two legs and a Scots tongue. But the rest were in a different case. Not only was the visit to Appin's agent, in the midst of the cry about the Appin murder, dangerous in itself, but it was highly inconsistent with the other. I was like to have a bad enough time of it with my Lord Advocate Grant, the best of ways; but to go to him hot-foot from Appin's agent, was little likely to mend my own affairs, and might prove the mere ruin of friend Alan's. The whole thing, besides, gave me a look of running with the hare and hunting with the hounds that was little to my fancy. I determined, therefore, to be done at once with Mr. Stewart and the whole Jacobitical side of my business, and to profit for that purpose by the guidance of the porter at my side. But it chanced I had scarce given him the address, when there came a sprinkle of rain—nothing to hurt, only for my new clothes—and we took shelter under a pend at the head of a close or alley.

Being strange to what I saw, I stepped a little farther in. The narrow paved way descended swiftly. Prodigious tall houses sprang upon each side and bulged out, one storey beyond another, as they rose. At the top only a ribbon of sky showed in. By what I could spy in the windows, and by the respectable persons that passed out and in, I saw the houses to be very well occupied; and the whole appearance of the place interested me like a tale.

I was still gazing, when there came a sudden brisk tramp of feet in time and clash of steel behind me. Turning quickly, I was aware of a party of armed soldiers, and, in their midst, a tall man in a great coat. He walked with a stoop that was like a piece of courtesy, genteel and insinuating: he waved his hands plausibly as he went, and his face was sly and handsome. I thought his eye took me in, but could not meet it. This procession went by to a door in the close, which a serving-man in a fine livery set open; and two of the soldier-lads carried the prisoner within, the rest lingering with their firelocks by the door.

There can nothing pass in the streets of a city without some following of idle folk and children. It was so now; but the more part melted away incontinent until but three were left. One was a girl; she was dressed like a lady, and had a screen of the Drummond colours on her head; but her comrades or (I should say) followers were ragged gillies, such as I had seen the matches of by the dozen in my Highland journey. They all spoke together earnestly in Gaelic, the sound of which was pleasant in my ears for the sake of Alan; and, though the rain was by again, and my porter plucked at me to be going, I even drew nearer where they were, to listen. The lady scolded sharply, the others making apologies and cringeing before her, so that I made sure she was come of a chief's house. All the while the three of them sought in their pockets, and by what I could make out, they had the matter of half a farthing among the party; which made me smile a little to see all Highland folk alike for fine obeisances and empty sporrans.

It chanced the girl turned suddenly about, so that I saw her face for the first time. There is no greater wonder than the way the face of a young woman fits in a man's mind, and stays there, and he could never tell you why; it just seems it was the thing he wanted. She had wonderful bright eyes like stars, and I daresay the eyes had a part in it; but what I remember the most clearly was the way her lips were a trifle open as she turned. And, whatever was the cause, I stood there staring like a fool. On her side, as she had not known there was anyone so near, she looked at me a little longer, and perhaps with more surprise, than was entirely civil.

It went through my country head she might be wondering at my new clothes; with that, I blushed to my hair, and at the sight of my colouring it is to be supposed she drew her own conclusions, for she moved her gillies farther down the close, and they fell again to this dispute, where I could hear no more of it.

I had often admired a lassie before then, if scarce so sudden and strong; and it was rather my disposition to withdraw than to come forward, for I was much in fear of mockery from the womenkind. You would have thought I had now all the more reason to pursue my common practice, since I had met this young lady in the city street, seemingly following a prisoner, and accompanied with two very ragged indecent-like Highlandmen. But there was here a different ingredient; it was plain the girl thought I had been prying in her secrets; and with my new clothes and sword, and at the top of my new fortunes, this was more than I could swallow. The beggar on horseback could not bear to be thrust down so low, or, at least of it, not by this young lady.

I followed, accordingly, and took off my new hat to her the best that I was able.

"Madam," said I, "I think it only fair to myself to let you understand I have no Gaelic. It is true I was listening, for I have friends of my own across the Highland line, and the sound of that tongue comes friendly; but for your private affairs, if you had spoken Greek, I might have had more guess at them."

She made me a little, distant curtsey. "There is no harm done," said she, with a pretty accent, most like the English (but more agreeable). "A cat may look at a king."

"I do not mean to offend," said I. "I have no skill of city manners; I never before this day set foot inside the doors of Edinburgh. Take me for a country lad—it's what I am; and I would rather I told you than you found it out."

"Indeed, it will be a very unusual thing for strangers to be speaking to each other on the causeway," she replied. "But if you are landward [2] bred it will be different. I am as landward as yourself; I am Highland, as you see, and think myself the farther from my home."

"It is not yet a week since I passed the line," said I. "Less than a week ago I was on the braes of Balwhidder."

"Balwhither?" she cries. "Come ye from Balwhither! The name of it makes all there is of me rejoice. You will not have been long there, and not known some of our friends or family?"

"I lived with a very honest, kind man called Duncan Dhu Maclaren," I replied.

"Well, I know Duncan, and you give him the true name!" she said; "and if he is an honest man, his wife is honest indeed."

"Ay," said I, "they are fine people, and the place is a bonny place."

"Where in the great world is such another!" she cries; "I am loving the smell of that place and the roots that grow there."

I was infinitely taken with the spirit of the maid. "I could be wishing I had brought you a spray of that heather," says I. "And, though I did ill to speak with you at the first, now it seems we have common acquaintance, I make it my petition you will not forget me. David Balfour is the name I am known by. This is my lucky day, when I have just come into a landed estate, and am not very long out of a deadly peril. I wish you would keep my name in mind for the sake of Balwhidder," said I, "and I will yours for the sake of my lucky day."

"My name is not spoken," she replied, with a great deal of haughtiness. "More than a hundred years it has not gone upon men's tongues, save for a blink. I am nameless, like the Folk of Peace. [3] Catriona Drummond is the one I use."

Now indeed I knew where I was standing. In all broad Scotland there was but the one name proscribed, and that was the name of the Macgregors. Yet so far from fleeing this undesirable acquaintancy, I plunged the deeper in.

"I have been sitting with one who was in the same case with yourself," said I, "and I think he will be one of your friends. They called him Robin Oig."

"Did ye so?" cries she. "Ye met Rob?"

"I passed the night with him," said I.

"He is a fowl of the night," said she.

"There was a set of pipes there," I went on, "so you may judge if the time passed."

"You should be no enemy, at all events," said she. "That was his brother there a moment since, with the red soldiers round him. It is him that I call father."

"Is it so?" cried I. "Are you a daughter of James More's?"

"All the daughter that he has," says she: "the daughter of a prisoner; that I should forget it so, even for one hour, to talk with strangers!"

Here one of the gillies addressed her in what he had of English, to know what "she" (meaning by that himself) was to do about "ta sneeshin." I took some note of him for a short, bandy-legged, red-haired, big-headed man, that I was to know more of to my cost.

"There can be none the day, Neil," she replied. "How will you get 'sneeshin,' wanting siller! It will teach you another time to be more careful; and I think James More will not be very well pleased with Neil of the Tom."

"Miss Drummond," I said, "I told you I was in my lucky day. Here I am, and a bank-porter at my tail. And remember I have had the hospitality of your own country of Balwhidder."

"It was not one of my people gave it," said she.

"Ah, well," said I, "but I am owing your uncle at least for some springs upon the pipes. Besides which, I have offered myself to be your friend, and you have been so forgetful that you did not refuse me in the proper time."

"If it had been a great sum, it might have done you honour," said she; "but I will tell you what this is. James More lies shackled in prison; but this time past they will be bringing him down here daily to the Advocate's. . . ."

"The Advocate's!" I cried. "Is that . . . ?"

"It is the house of the Lord Advocate Grant of Prestongrange," said she. "There they bring my father one time and another, for what purpose I have no thought in my mind; but it seems there is some hope dawned for him. All this same time they will not let me be seeing him, nor yet him write; and we wait upon the King's street to catch him; and now we give him his snuff as he goes by, and now something else. And here is this son of trouble, Neil, son of Duncan, has lost my four-penny piece that was to buy that snuff, and James More must go wanting, and will think his daughter has forgotten him."

I took sixpence from my pocket, gave it to Neil, and bade him go about his errand. Then to her, "That sixpence came with me by Balwhidder," said I.

"Ah!" she said, "you are a friend to the Gregara!"

"I would not like to deceive you, either," said I. "I know very little of the Gregara and less of James More and his doings, but since the while I have been standing in this close, I seem to know something of yourself; and if you will just say 'a friend to Miss Catriona' I will see you are the less cheated."

"The one cannot be without the other," said she.

"I will even try," said I.

"And what will you be thinking of myself!" she cried, "to be holding my hand to the first stranger!"

"I am thinking nothing but that you are a good daughter," said I.

"I must not be without repaying it," she said; "where is it you stop!"

"To tell the truth, I am stopping nowhere yet," said I, "being not full three hours in the city; but if you will give me your direction, I will be so bold as come seeking my sixpence for myself."

"Will I can trust you for that?" she asked.

"You need have little fear," said I.

"James More could not bear it else," said she. "I stop beyond the village of Dean, on the north side of the water, with Mrs. Drummond-Ogilvy of Allardyce, who is my near friend and will be glad to thank you."

"You are to see me, then, so soon as what I have to do permits," said I; and, the remembrance of Alan rolling in again upon my mind, I made haste to say farewell.

I could not but think, even as I did so, that we had made extraordinary free upon short acquaintance, and that a really wise young lady would have shown herself more backward. I think it was the bank-porter that put me from this ungallant train of thought.

"I thoucht ye had been a lad of some kind o' sense," he began, shooting out his lips. "Ye're no likely to gang far this gate. A fule and his siller's shune parted. Eh, but ye're a green callant!" he cried, "an' a veecious, tae! Cleikin' up wi' baubeejoes!"

"If you dare to speak of the young lady. . . " I began.

"Leddy!" he cried. "Haud us and safe us, whatten leddy? Ca' thon a leddy? The toun's fu' o' them. Leddies! Man, its weel seen ye're no very acquant in Embro!"

A clap of anger took me.

"Here," said I, "lead me where I told you, and keep your foul mouth shut!"

He did not wholly obey me, for, though he no more addressed me directly, he very impudent sang at me as he went in a manner of innuendo, and with an exceedingly ill voice and ear—

"As Mally Lee cam doun the street, her capuchin did flee,
She cuist a look ahint her to see her negligee.
And we're a' gaun east and wast, we're a' gann ajee,
We're a' gaun east and wast courtin' Mally Lee."

CHAPTER II.
THE HIGHLAND WRITER

Mr. Charles Stewart the Writer dwelt at the top of the longest stair ever mason set a hand to; fifteen flights of it, no less; and when I had come to his door, and a clerk had opened it, and told me his master was within, I had scarce breath enough to send my porter packing.

"Awa' east and west wi' ye!" said I, took the money bag out of his hands, and followed the clerk in.

The outer room was an office with the clerk's chair at a table spread with law papers. In the inner chamber, which opened from it, a little brisk man sat poring on a deed, from which he scarce raised his eyes on my entrance; indeed, he still kept his finger in the place, as though prepared to show me out and fall again to his studies. This pleased me little enough; and what pleased me less, I thought the clerk was in a good posture to overhear what should pass between us.

I asked if he was Mr. Charles Stewart the Writer.

"The same," says he; "and, if the question is equally fair, who may you be yourself?"

"You never heard tell of my name nor of me either," said I, "but I bring you a token from a friend that you know well. That you know well," I repeated, lowering my voice, "but maybe are not just so keen to hear from at this present being. And the bits of business that I have to propone to you are rather in the nature of being confidential. In short, I would like to think we were quite private."

He rose without more words, casting down his paper like a man ill-pleased, sent forth his clerk of an errand, and shut to the house-door behind him.

"Now, sir," said he, returning, "speak out your mind and fear nothing; though before you begin," he cries out, "I tell you mine misgives me! I tell you beforehand, ye're either a Stewart or a Stewart sent ye. A good name it is, and one it would ill-become my father's son to lightly. But I begin to grue at the sound of it."

"My name is called Balfour," said I, "David Balfour of Shaws. As for him that sent me, I will let his token speak." And I showed the silver button.

"Put it in your pocket, sir!" cries he. "Ye need name no names. The deevil's buckie, I ken the button of him! And de'il hae't! Where is he now!"

I told him I knew not where Alan was, but he had some sure place (or thought he had) about the north side, where he was to lie until a ship was found for him; and how and where he had appointed to be spoken with.

"It's been always my opinion that I would hang in a tow for this family of mine," he cried, "and, dod! I believe the day's come now! Get a ship for him, quot' he! And who's to pay for it? The man's daft!"

"That is my part of the affair, Mr. Stewart," said I. "Here is a bag of good money, and if more be wanted, more is to be had where it came from."

"I needn't ask your politics," said he.

"Ye need not," said I, smiling, "for I'm as big a Whig as grows."

"Stop a bit, stop a bit," says Mr. Stewart. "What's all this? A Whig? Then why are you here with Alan's button? and what kind of a black-foot traffic is this that I find ye out in, Mr. Whig? Here is a forfeited rebel and an accused murderer, with two hundred pounds on his life, and ye ask me to meddle in his business, and then tell me ye're a Whig! I have no mind of any such Whigs before, though I've kent plenty of them."

"He's a forfeited rebel, the more's the pity," said I, "for the man's my friend. I can only wish he had been better guided. And an accused murderer, that he is too, for his misfortune; but wrongfully accused."

"I hear you say so," said Stewart.

"More than you are to hear me say so, before long," said I. "Alan Breck is innocent, and so is James."

"Oh!" says he, "the two cases hang together. If Alan is out, James can never be in."

Hereupon I told him briefly of my acquaintance with Alan, of the accident that brought me present at the Appin murder, and the various passages of our escape among the heather, and my recovery of my estate. "So, sir, you have now the whole train of these events," I went on, "and can see for yourself how I come to be so much mingled up with the affairs of your family and friends, which (for all of our sakes) I wish had been plainer and less bloody. You can see for yourself, too, that I have certain pieces of business depending, which were scarcely fit to lay before a lawyer chosen at random. No more remains, but to ask if you will undertake my service?"

"I have no great mind to it; but coming as you do with Alan's button, the choice is scarcely left me," said he. "What are your instructions?" he added, and took up his pen.

"The first point is to smuggle Alan forth of this country," said I, "but I need not be repeating that."

"I am little likely to forget it," said Stewart.

"The next thing is the bit money I am owing to Cluny," I went on. "It would be ill for me to find a conveyance, but that should be no stick to you. It was two pounds five shillings and three-halfpence farthing sterling."

He noted it.

"Then," said I, "there's a Mr. Henderland, a licensed preacher and missionary in Ardgour, that I would like well to get some snuff into the hands of; and, as I daresay you keep touch with your friends in Appin (so near by), it's a job you could doubtless overtake with the other."

"How much snuff are we to say?" he asked.

"I was thinking of two pounds," said I.

"Two," said he.

"Then there's the lass Alison Hastie, in Lime Kilns," said I. "Her that helped Alan and me across the Forth. I was thinking if I could get her a good Sunday gown, such as she could wear with decency in her degree, it would be an ease to my conscience; for the mere truth is, we owe her our two lives."

"I am glad so see you are thrifty, Mr. Balfour," says he, making his notes.

"I would think shame to be otherwise the first day of my fortune," said I. "And now, if you will compute the outlay and your own proper charges, I would be glad to know if I could get some spending-money back. It's not that I grudge the whole of it to get Alan safe; it's not that I lack more; but having drawn so much the one day, I think it would have a very ill appearance if I was back again seeking, the next. Only be sure you have enough," I added, "for I am very undesirous to meet with you again."

"Well, and I'm pleased to see you're cautious, too," said the Writer. "But I think ye take a risk to lay so considerable a sum at my discretion."

He said this with a plain sneer.

"I'll have to run the hazard," I replied. "O, and there's another service I would ask, and that's to direct me to a lodging, for I have no roof to my head. But it must be a lodging I may seem to have hit upon by accident, for it would never do if the Lord Advocate were to get any jealousy of our acquaintance."

"Ye may set your weary spirit at rest," said he. "I will never name your name, sir; and it's my belief the Advocate is still so much to be sympathised with that he doesnae ken of your existence."

I saw I had got to the wrong side of the man.

"There's a braw day coming for him, then," said I, "for he'll have to learn of it on the deaf side of his head no later than to-morrow, when I call on him."

"When ye call on him!" repeated Mr. Stewart. "Am I daft, or are you! What takes ye near the Advocate!"

"O, just to give myself up," said I.

"Mr. Balfour," he cried, "are ye making a mock of me?"

"No, sir," said I, "though I think you have allowed yourself some such freedom with myself. But I give you to understand once and for all that I am in no jesting spirit."

"Nor yet me," says Stewart. "And I give yon to understand (if that's to be the word) that I like the looks of your behaviour less and less. You come here to me with all sorts of propositions, which will put me in a train of very doubtful acts and bring me among very undesirable persons this many a day to come. And then you tell me you're going straight out of my office to make your peace with the Advocate! Alan's button here or Alan's button there, the four quarters of Alan wouldnae bribe me further in."

"I would take it with a little more temper," said I, "and perhaps we can avoid what you object to. I can see no way for it but to give myself up, but perhaps you can see another; and if you could, I could never deny but what I would be rather relieved. For I think my traffic with his lordship is little likely to agree with my health. There's just the one thing clear, that I have to give my evidence; for I hope it'll save Alan's character (what's left of it), and James's neck, which is the more immediate."

He was silent for a breathing-space, and then, "My man," said he, "you'll never be allowed to give such evidence."

"We'll have to see about that," said I; "I'm stiff-necked when I like."

"Ye muckle ass!" cried Stewart, "it's James they want; James has got to hang—Alan, too, if they could catch him—but James whatever! Go near the Advocate with any such business, and you'll see! he'll find a way to muzzle, ye."

"I think better of the Advocate than that," said I.

"The Advocate be dammed!" cries he. "It's the Campbells, man! You'll have the whole clanjamfry of them on your back; and so will the Advocate too, poor body! It's extraordinar ye cannot see where ye stand! If there's no fair way to stop your gab, there's a foul one gaping. They can put ye in the dock, do ye no see that?" he cried, and stabbed me with one finger in the leg.

"Ay," said I, "I was told that same no further back than this morning by another lawyer."

"And who was he?" asked Stewart, "He spoke sense at least."

I told I must be excused from naming him, for he was a decent stout old Whig, and had little mind to be mixed up in such affairs.

"I think all the world seems to be mixed up in it!" cries Stewart. "But what said you?"

I told him what had passed between Rankeillor and myself before the house of Shaws.

"Well, and so ye will hang!" said he. "Ye'll hang beside James Stewart. There's your fortune told."

"I hope better of it yet than that," said I; "but I could never deny there was a risk."

"Risk!" says he, and then sat silent again. "I ought to thank you for your staunchness to my friends, to whom you show a very good spirit," he says, "if you have the strength to stand by it. But I warn you that you're wading deep. I wouldn't put myself in your place (me that's a Stewart born!) for all the Stewarts that ever there were since Noah. Risk? ay, I take over-many; but to be tried in court before a Campbell jury and a Campbell judge, and that in a Campbell country and upon a Campbell quarrel—think what you like of me, Balfour, it's beyond me."

"It's a different way of thinking, I suppose," said I; "I was brought up to this one by my father before me."

"Glory to his bones! he has left a decent son to his name," says he. "Yet I would not have you judge me over-sorely. My case is dooms hard. See, sir, ye tell me ye're a Whig: I wonder what I am. No Whig to be sure; I couldnae be just that. But—laigh in your ear, man—I'm maybe no very keen on the other side."

"Is that a fact?" cried I. "It's what I would think of a man of your intelligence."

"Hut! none of your whillywhas!" [4] cries he. "There's intelligence upon both sides. But for my private part I have no particular desire to harm King George; and as for King James, God bless him! he does very well for me across the water. I'm a lawyer, ye see: fond of my books and my bottle, a good plea, a well-drawn deed, a crack in the Parliament House with other lawyer bodies, and perhaps a turn at the golf on a Saturday at e'en. Where do ye come in with your Hieland plaids and claymores?"

"Well," said I, "it's a fact ye have little of the wild Highlandman."

"Little?" quoth he. "Nothing, man! And yet I'm Hieland born, and when the clan pipes, who but me has to dance! The clan and the name, that goes by all. It's just what you said yourself; my father learned it to me, and a bonny trade I have of it. Treason and traitors, and the smuggling of them out and in; and the French recruiting, weary fall it! and the smuggling through of the recruits; and their pleas—a sorrow of their pleas! Here have I been moving one for young Ardsheil, my cousin; claimed the estate under the marriage contract—a forfeited estate! I told them it was nonsense: muckle they cared! And there was I cocking behind a yadvocate that liked the business as little as myself, for it was fair ruin to the pair of us—a black mark, disaffected, branded on our hurdies, like folk's names upon their kye! And what can I do? I'm a Stewart, ye see, and must fend for my clan and family. Then no later by than yesterday there was one of our Stewart lads carried to the Castle. What for? I ken fine: Act of 1736: recruiting for King Lewie. And you'll see, he'll whistle me in to be his lawyer, and there'll be another black mark on my chara'ter! I tell you fair: if I but kent the heid of a Hebrew word from the hurdies of it, be dammed but I would fling the whole thing up and turn minister!"

"It's rather a hard position," said I.

"Dooms hard!" cries he. "And that's what makes me think so much of ye—you that's no Stewart—to stick your head so deep in Stewart business. And for what, I do not know: unless it was the sense of duty."

"I hope it will be that," said I.

"Well," says he, "it's a grand quality. But here is my clerk back; and, by your leave, we'll pick a bit of dinner, all the three of us. When that's done, I'll give you the direction of a very decent man, that'll be very fain to have you for a lodger. And I'll fill your pockets to ye, forbye, out of your ain bag. For this business'll not be near as dear as ye suppose—not even the ship part of it."

I made him a sign that his clerk was within hearing.

"Hoot, ye neednae mind for Robbie," cries he. "A Stewart, too, puir deevil! and has smuggled out more French recruits and trafficking Papists than what he has hairs upon his face. Why, it's Robin that manages that branch of my affairs. Who will we have now, Rob, for across the water!"

"There'll be Andie Scougal, in the Thristle," replied Rob. "I saw Hoseason the other day, but it seems he's wanting the ship. Then there'll be Tam Stobo; but I'm none so sure of Tam. I've seen him colloguing with some gey queer acquaintances; and if was anybody important, I would give Tam the go-by."

"The head's worth two hundred pounds, Robin," said Stewart.

"Gosh, that'll no be Alan Breck!" cried the clerk.

"Just Alan," said his master.

"Weary winds! that's sayrious," cried Robin. "I'll try Andie, then; Andie'll be the best."

"It seems it's quite a big business," I observed.

"Mr. Balfour, there's no end to it," said Stewart.

"There was a name your clerk mentioned," I went on: "Hoseason. That must be my man, I think: Hoseason, of the brig Covenant. Would you set your trust on him?"

"He didnae behave very well to you and Alan," said Mr. Stewart; "but my mind of the man in general is rather otherwise. If he had taken Alan on board his ship on an agreement, it's my notion he would have proved a just dealer. How say ye, Rob?"

"No more honest skipper in the trade than Eli," said the clerk. "I would lippen to [5] Eli's word—ay, if it was the Chevalier, or Appin himsel'," he added.

"And it was him that brought the doctor, wasnae't?" asked the master.

"He was the very man," said the clerk.

"And I think he took the doctor back?" says Stewart.

"Ay, with his sporran full!" cried Robin. "And Eli kent of that!" [6]

"Well, it seems it's hard to ken folk rightly," said I.

"That was just what I forgot when ye came in, Mr. Balfour!" says the Writer.

CHAPTER III.
I GO TO PILRIG

The next morning, I was no sooner awake in my new lodging than I was up and into my new clothes; and no sooner the breakfast swallowed, than I was forth on my adventurers. Alan, I could hope, was fended for; James was like to be a more difficult affair, and I could not but think that enterprise might cost me dear, even as everybody said to whom I had opened my opinion. It seemed I was come to the top of the mountain only to cast myself down; that I had clambered up, through so many and hard trials, to be rich, to be recognised, to wear city clothes and a sword to my side, all to commit mere suicide at the last end of it, and the worst kind of suicide, besides, which is to get hanged at the King's charges.

What was I doing it for? I asked, as I went down the high Street and out north by Leith Wynd. First I said it was to save James Stewart; and no doubt the memory of his distress, and his wife's cries, and a word or so I had let drop on that occasion worked upon me strongly. At the same time I reflected that it was (or ought to be) the most indifferent matter to my father's son, whether James died in his bed or from a scaffold. He was Alan's cousin, to be sure; but so far as regarded Alan, the best thing would be to lie low, and let the King, and his Grace of Argyll, and the corbie crows, pick the bones of his kinsman their own way. Nor could I forget that, while we were all in the pot together, James had shown no such particular anxiety whether for Alan or me.

Next it came upon me I was acting for the sake of justice: and I thought that a fine word, and reasoned it out that (since we dwelt in polities, at some discomfort to each one of us) the main thing of all must still be justice, and the death of any innocent man a wound upon the whole community. Next, again, it was the Accuser of the Brethren that gave me a turn of his argument; bade me think shame for pretending myself concerned in these high matters, and told me I was but a prating vain child, who had spoken big words to Rankeillor and to Stewart, and held myself bound upon my vanity to make good that boastfulness. Nay, and he hit me with the other end of the stick; for he accused me of a kind of artful cowardice, going about at the expense of a little risk to purchase greater safety. No doubt, until I had declared and cleared myself, I might any day encounter Mungo Campbell or the sheriff's officer, and be recognised, and dragged into the Appin murder by the heels; and, no doubt, in case I could manage my declaration with success, I should breathe more free for ever after. But when I looked this argument full in the face I could see nothing to be ashamed of. As for the rest, "Here are the two roads," I thought, "and both go to the same place. It's unjust that James should hang if I can save him; and it would be ridiculous in me to have talked so much and then do nothing. It's lucky for James of the Glens that I have boasted beforehand; and none so unlucky for myself, because now I'm committed to do right. I have the name of a gentleman and the means of one; it would be a poor duty that I was wanting in the essence." And then I thought this was a Pagan spirit, and said a prayer in to myself, asking for what courage I might lack, and that I might go straight to my duty like a soldier to battle, and come off again scatheless, as so many do.

This train of reasoning brought me to a more resolved complexion; though it was far from closing up my sense of the dangers that surrounded me, nor of how very apt I was (if I went on) to stumble on the ladder of the gallows. It was a plain, fair morning, but the wind in the east. The little chill of it sang in my blood, and gave me a feeling of the autumn, and the dead leaves, and dead folks' bodies in their graves. It seemed the devil was in it, if I was to die in that tide of my fortunes and for other folks' affairs. On the top of the Calton Hill, though it was not the customary time of year for that diversion, some children were crying and running with their kites. These toys appeared very plain against the sky; I remarked a great one soar on the wind to a high altitude and then plump among the whins; and I thought to myself at sight of it,

"There goes Davie."

My way lay over Mouter's Hill, and through an end of a clachan on the braeside among fields. There was a whirr of looms in it went from house to house; bees bummed in the gardens; the neighbours that I saw at the doorsteps talked in a strange tongue; and I found out later that this was Picardy, a village where the French weavers wrought for the Linen Company. Here I got a fresh direction for Pilrig, my destination; and a little beyond, on the wayside, came by a gibbet and two men hanged in chains. They were dipped in tar, as the manner is; the wind span them, the chains clattered, and the birds hung about the uncanny jumping-jacks and cried. The sight coming on me suddenly, like an illustration of my fears, I could scarce be done with examining it and drinking in discomfort. And, as I thus turned and turned about the gibbet, what should I strike on, but a weird old wife, that sat behind a leg of it, and nodded, and talked aloud to herself with becks and courtesies.

"Who are these two, mother?" I asked, and pointed to the corpses.

"A blessing on your precious face!" she cried. "Twa joes [7] o'mine: just two o' my old joes, my hinny dear."

"What did they suffer for?" I asked.

"Ou, just for the guid cause," said she. "Aften I spaed to them the way that it would end. Twa shillin' Scots: no pickle mair; and there are twa bonny callants hingin' for 't! They took it frae a wean [8] belanged to Brouchton."

"Ay!" said I to myself, and not to the daft limmer, "and did they come to such a figure for so poor a business? This is to lose all indeed."

"Gie's your loof, [9] hinny," says she, "and let me spae your weird to ye."

"No, mother," said I, "I see far enough the way I am. It's an unco thing to see too far in front."

"I read it in your bree," she said. "There's a bonnie lassie that has bricht een, and there's a wee man in a braw coat, and a big man in a pouthered wig, and there's the shadow of the wuddy, [10] joe, that lies braid across your path. Gie's your loof, hinny, and let Auld Merren spae it to ye bonny."

The two chance shots that seemed to point at Alan and the daughter of James More struck me hard; and I fled from the eldritch creature, casting her a baubee, which she continued to sit and play with under the moving shadows of the hanged.

My way down the causeway of Leith Walk would have been more pleasant to me but for this encounter. The old rampart ran among fields, the like of them I had never seen for artfulness of agriculture; I was pleased, besides, to be so far in the still countryside; but the shackles of the gibbet clattered in my head; and the mope and mows of the old witch, and the thought of the dead men, hag-rode my spirits. To hang on a gallows, that seemed a hard case; and whether a man came to hang there for two shillings Scots, or (as Mr. Stewart had it) from the sense of duty, once he was tarred and shackled and hung up, the difference seemed small. There might David Balfour hang, and other lads pass on their errands and think light of him; and old daft limmers sit at a leg-foot and spae their fortunes; and the clean genty maids go by, and look to the other aide, and hold a nose. I saw them plain, and they had grey eyes, and their screens upon their heads were of the Drummed colours.

I was thus in the poorest of spirits, though still pretty resolved, when I came in view of Pilrig, a pleasant gabled house set by the walkside among some brave young woods. The laird's horse was standing saddled at the door as I came up, but himself was in the study, where he received me in the midst of learned works and musical instruments, for he was not only a deep philosopher but much of a musician. He greeted me at first pretty well, and when he had read Rankeillor's letter, placed himself obligingly at my disposal.

"And what is it, cousin David!" said he—"since it appears that we are cousins—what is this that I can do for you! A word to Prestongrange! Doubtless that is easily given. But what should be the word?"

"Mr. Balfour," said I, "if I were to tell you my whole story the way it fell out, it's my opinion (and it was Rankeillor's before me) that you would be very little made up with it."

"I am sorry to hear this of you, kinsman," says he.

"I must not take that at your hands, Mr. Balfour," said I; "I have nothing to my charge to make me sorry, or you for me, but just the common infirmities of mankind. 'The guilt of Adam's first sin, the want of original righteousness, and the corruption of my whole nature,' so much I must answer for, and I hope I have been taught where to look for help," I said; for I judged from the look of the man he would think the better of me if I knew my questions. [11] "But in the way of worldly honour I have no great stumble to reproach myself with; and my difficulties have befallen me very much against my will and (by all that I can see) without my fault. My trouble is to have become dipped in a political complication, which it is judged you would be blythe to avoid a knowledge of."

"Why, very well, Mr. David," he replied, "I am pleased to see you are all that Rankeillor represented. And for what you say of political complications, you do me no more than justice. It is my study to be beyond suspicion, and indeed outside the field of it. The question is," says he, "how, if I am to know nothing of the matter, I can very well assist you?"

"Why sir," said I, "I propose you should write to his lordship, that I am a young man of reasonable good family and of good means: both of which I believe to be the case."

"I have Rankeillor's word for it," said Mr. Balfour, "and I count that a warran-dice against all deadly."

"To which you might add (if you will take my word for so much) that I am a good churchman, loyal to King George, and so brought up," I went on.

"None of which will do you any harm," said Mr. Balfour.

"Then you might go on to say that I sought his lordship on a matter of great moment, connected with His Majesty's service and the administration of justice," I suggested.

"As I am not to hear the matter," says the laird, "I will not take upon myself to qualify its weight. 'Great moment' therefore falls, and 'moment' along with it. For the rest I might express myself much as you propose."

"And then, sir," said I, and rubbed my neck a little with my thumb, "then I would be very desirous if you could slip in a word that might perhaps tell for my protection."

"Protection?" says he, "for your protection! Here is a phrase that somewhat dampens me. If the matter be so dangerous, I own I would be a little loath to move in it blindfold."

"I believe I could indicate in two words where the thing sticks," said I.

"Perhaps that would be the best," said he.

"Well, it's the Appin murder," said I.

He held up both his hands. "Sirs! sirs!" cried he.

I thought by the expression of his face and voice that I had lost my helper.

"Let me explain. . ." I began.

"I thank you kindly, I will hear no more of it," says he. "I decline in toto to hear more of it. For your name's sake and Rankeillor's, and perhaps a little for your own, I will do what I can to help you; but I will hear no more upon the facts. And it is my first clear duty to warn you. These are deep waters, Mr. David, and you are a young man. Be cautious and think twice."

"It is to be supposed I will have thought oftener than that, Mr. Balfour," said I, "and I will direct your attention again to Rankeillor's letter, where (I hope and believe) he has registered his approval of that which I design."

"Well, well," said he; and then again, "Well, well! I will do what I can for you." There with he took a pen and paper, sat a while in thought, and began to write with much consideration. "I understand that Rankeillor approved of what you have in mind?" he asked presently.

"After some discussion, sir, he bade me to go forward in God's name," said I.

"That is the name to go in," said Mr. Balfour, and resumed his writing. Presently, he signed, re-read what he had written, and addressed me again. "Now here, Mr. David," said he, "is a letter of introduction, which I will seal without closing, and give into your hands open, as the form requires. But, since I am acting in the dark, I will just read it to you, so that you may see if it will secure your end—

"Pilrig, August 26th, 1751.

"My Lord,—This is to bring to your notice my namesake and cousin, David Balfour Esquire of Shaws, a young gentleman of unblemished descent and good estate. He has enjoyed, besides, the more valuable advantages of a godly training, and his political principles are all that your lordship can desire. I am not in Mr. Balfour's confidence, but I understand him to have a matter to declare, touching His Majesty's service and the administration of justice; purposes for which your Lordship's zeal is known. I should add that the young gentleman's intention is known to and approved by some of his friends, who will watch with hopeful anxiety the event of his success or failure.

"Whereupon," continued Mr. Balfour, "I have subscribed myself with the usual compliments. You observe I have said 'some of your friends'; I hope you can justify my plural?"

"Perfectly, sir; my purpose is known and approved by more than one," said I. "And your letter, which I take a pleasure to thank you for, is all I could have hoped."

"It was all I could squeeze out," said he; "and from what I know of the matter you design to meddle in, I can only pray God that it may prove sufficient."

CHAPTER IV.
LORD ADVOCATE PRESTONGRANGE

My kinsman kept me to a meal, "for the honour of the roof," he said; and I believe I made the better speed on my return. I had no thought but to be done with the next stage, and have myself fully committed; to a person circumstanced as I was, the appearance of closing a door on hesitation and temptation was itself extremely tempting; and I was the more disappointed, when I came to Prestongrange's house, to be informed he was abroad. I believe it was true at the moment, and for some hours after; and then I have no doubt the Advocate came home again, and enjoyed himself in a neighbouring chamber among friends, while perhaps the very fact of my arrival was forgotten. I would have gone away a dozen times, only for this strong drawing to have done with my declaration out of hand and be able to lay me down to sleep with a free conscience. At first I read, for the little cabinet where I was left contained a variety of books. But I fear I read with little profit; and the weather falling cloudy, the dusk coming up earlier than usual, and my cabinet being lighted with but a loophole of a window, I was at last obliged to desist from this diversion (such as it was), and pass the rest of my time of waiting in a very burthensome vacuity. The sound of people talking in a near chamber, the pleasant note of a harpsichord, and once the voice of a lady singing, bore me a kind of company.

I do not know the hour, but the darkness was long come, when the door of the cabinet opened, and I was aware, by the light behind him, of a tall figure of a man upon the threshold. I rose at once.

"Is anybody there?" he asked. "Who in that?"

"I am bearer of a letter from the laird of Pilrig to the Lord Advocate," said I.

"Have you been here long?" he asked.

"I would not like to hazard an estimate of how many hours," said I.

"It is the first I hear of it," he replied, with a chuckle. "The lads must have forgotten you. But you are in the bit at last, for I am Prestongrange."

So saying, he passed before me into the next room, whither (upon his sign) I followed him, and where he lit a candle and took his place before a business-table. It was a long room, of a good proportion, wholly lined with books. That small spark of light in a corner struck out the man's handsome person and strong face. He was flushed, his eye watered and sparkled, and before he sat down I observed him to sway back and forth. No doubt, he had been supping liberally; but his mind and tongue were under full control.

"Well, sir, sit ye down," said he, "and let us see Pilrig's letter."

He glanced it through in the beginning carelessly, looking up and bowing when he came to my name; but at the last words I thought I observed his attention to redouble, and I made sure he read them twice. All this while you are to suppose my heart was beating, for I had now crossed my Rubicon and was come fairly on the field of battle.

"I am pleased to make your acquaintance, Mr. Balfour," he said, when he had done. "Let me offer you a glass of claret."

"Under your favour, my lord, I think it would scarce be fair on me," said I. "I have come here, as the letter will have mentioned, on a business of some gravity to myself; and, as I am little used with wine, I might be the sooner affected."

"You shall be the judge," said he. "But if you will permit, I believe I will even have the bottle in myself."

He touched a bell, and a footman came, as at a signal, bringing wine and glasses.

"You are sure you will not join me?" asked the Advocate. "Well, here is to our better acquaintance! In what way can I serve you?"

"I should, perhaps, begin by telling you, my lord, that I am here at your own pressing invitation," said I.

"You have the advantage of me somewhere," said he, "for I profess I think I never heard of you before this evening."

"Right, my lord; the name is, indeed, new to you," said I. "And yet you have been for some time extremely wishful to make my acquaintance, and have declared the same in public."

"I wish you would afford me a clue," says he. "I am no Daniel."

"It will perhaps serve for such," said I, "that if I was in a jesting humour—which is far from the case—I believe I might lay a claim on your lordship for two hundred pounds."

"In what sense?" he inquired.

"In the sense of rewards offered for my person," said I.

He thrust away his glass once and for all, and sat straight up in the chair where he had been previously lolling. "What am I to understand?" said he.

"A tall strong lad of about eighteen," I quoted, "speaks like a Lowlander and has no beard."

"I recognise those words," said he, "which, if you have come here with any ill-judged intention of amusing yourself, are like to prove extremely prejudicial to your safety."

"My purpose in this," I replied, "is just entirely as serious as life and death, and you have understood me perfectly. I am the boy who was speaking with Glenure when he was shot."

"I can only suppose (seeing you here) that you claim to be innocent," said he.

"The inference is clear," I said. "I am a very loyal subject to King George, but if I had anything to reproach myself with, I would have had more discretion than to walk into your den."

"I am glad of that," said he. "This horrid crime, Mr. Balfour, is of a dye which cannot permit any clemency. Blood has been barbarously shed. It has been shed in direct opposition to his Majesty and our whole frame of laws, by those who are their known and public oppugnants. I take a very high sense of this. I will not deny that I consider the crime as directly personal to his Majesty."

"And unfortunately, my lord," I added, a little drily, "directly personal to another great personage who may be nameless."

"If you mean anything by those words, I must tell you I consider them unfit for a good subject; and were they spoke publicly I should make it my business to take note of them," said he. "You do not appear to me to recognise the gravity of your situation, or you would be more careful not to pejorate the same by words which glance upon the purity of justice. Justice, in this country, and in my poor hands, is no respecter of persons."

"You give me too great a share in my own speech, my lord," said I. "I did but repeat the common talk of the country, which I have heard everywhere, and from men of all opinions as I came along."

"When you are come to more discretion you will understand such talk in not to be listened to, how much less repeated," says the Advocate. "But I acquit you of an ill intention. That nobleman, whom we all honour, and who has indeed been wounded in a near place by the late barbarity, sits too high to be reached by these aspersions. The Duke of Argyle—you see that I deal plainly with you—takes it to heart as I do, and as we are both bound to do by our judicial functions and the service of his Majesty; and I could wish that all hands, in this ill age, were equally clean of family rancour. But from the accident that this is a Campbell who has fallen martyr to his duty—as who else but the Campbells have ever put themselves foremost on that path?—I may say it, who am no Campbell—and that the chief of that great house happens (for all our advantages) to be the present head of the College of Justice, small minds and disaffected tongues are set agog in every changehouse in the country; and I find a young gentleman like Mr. Balfour so ill-advised as to make himself their echo." So much he spoke with a very oratorical delivery, as if in court, and then declined again upon the manner of a gentleman. "All this apart," said he. "It now remains that I should learn what I am to do with you."

"I had thought it was rather I that should learn the same from your lordship," said I.

"Ay, true," says the Advocate. "But, you see, you come to me well recommended. There is a good honest Whig name to this letter," says he, picking it up a moment from the table. "And— extra-judicially, Mr. Balfour—there is always the possibility of some arrangement, I tell you, and I tell you beforehand that you may be the more upon your guard, your fate lies with me singly. In such a matter (be it said with reverence) I am more powerful than the King's Majesty; and should you please me—and of course satisfy my conscience—in what remains to be held of our interview, I tell you it may remain between ourselves."

"Meaning how?" I asked.

"Why, I mean it thus, Mr. Balfour," said he, "that if you give satisfaction, no soul need know so much as that you visited my house; and you may observe that I do not even call my clerk."

I saw what way he was driving. "I suppose it is needless anyone should be informed upon my visit," said I, "though the precise nature of my gains by that I cannot see. I am not at all ashamed of coming here."

"And have no cause to be," says he, encouragingly. "Nor yet (if you are careful) to fear the consequences."

"My lord," said I, "speaking under your correction, I am not very easy to be frightened."

"And I am sure I do not seek to frighten you," says he. "But to the interrogation; and let me warn you to volunteer nothing beyond the questions I shall ask you. It may consist very immediately with your safety. I have a great discretion, it is true, but there are bounds to it."

"I shall try to follow your lordship's advice," said I.

He spread a sheet of paper on the table and wrote a heading. "It appears you were present, by the way, in the wood of Lettermore at the moment of the fatal shot," he began. "Was this by accident?"

"By accident," said I.

"How came you in speech with Colin Campbell?" he asked.

"I was inquiring my way of him to Aucharn," I replied.

I observed he did not write this answer down.

"H'm, true," said he, "I had forgotten that. And do you know, Mr. Balfour, I would dwell, if I were you, as little as might be on your relations with these Stewarts. It might be found to complicate our business. I am not yet inclined to regard these matters as essential."

"I had thought, my lord, that all points of fact were equally material in such a case," said I.

"You forget we are now trying these Stewarts," he replied, with great significance. "If we should ever come to be trying you, it will be very different; and I shall press these very questions that I am now willing to glide upon. But to resume: I have it here in Mr. Mungo Campbell's precognition that you ran immediately up the brae. How came that?"

"Not immediately, my lord, and the cause was my seeing of the murderer."

"You saw him, then?"

"As plain as I see your lordship, though not so near hand."

"You know him?"

"I should know him again."

"In your pursuit you were not so fortunate, then, as to overtake him?"

"I was not."

"Was he alone?"

"He was alone."

"There was no one else in that neighbourhood?"

"Alan Breck Stewart was not far off, in a piece of a wood."

The Advocate laid his pen down. "I think we are playing at cross purposes," said he, "which you will find to prove a very ill amusement for yourself."

"I content myself with following your lordship's advice, and answering what I am asked," said I.

"Be so wise as to bethink yourself in time," said he, "I use you with the most anxious tenderness, which you scarce seem to appreciate, and which (unless you be more careful) may prove to be in vain."

"I do appreciate your tenderness, but conceive it to be mistaken," I replied, with something of a falter, for I saw we were come to grips at last. "I am here to lay before you certain information, by which I shall convince you Alan had no hand whatever in the killing of Glenure."

The Advocate appeared for a moment at a stick, sitting with pursed lips, and blinking his eyes upon me like an angry cat. "Mr. Balfour," he said at last, "I tell you pointedly you go an ill way for your own interests."

"My lord," I said, "I am as free of the charge of considering my own interests in this matter as your lordship. As God judges me, I have but the one design, and that is to see justice executed and the innocent go clear. If in pursuit of that I come to fall under your lordship's displeasure, I must bear it as I may."

At this he rose from his chair, lit a second candle, and for a while gazed upon me steadily. I was surprised to see a great change of gravity fallen upon his face, and I could have almost thought he was a little pale.

"You are either very simple, or extremely the reverse, and I see that I must deal with you more confidentially," says he. "This is a political case—ah, yes, Mr. Balfour! whether we like it or no, the case is political—and I tremble when I think what issues may depend from it. To a political case, I need scarce tell a young man of your education, we approach with very different thoughts from one which is criminal only. Salus populi suprema lex is a maxim susceptible of great abuse, but it has that force which we find elsewhere only in the laws of nature: I mean it has the force of necessity. I will open this out to you, if you will allow me, at more length. You would have me believe—"

"Under your pardon, my lord, I would have you to believe nothing but that which I can prove," said I.

"Tut! tut; young gentleman," says he, "be not so pragmatical, and suffer a man who might be your father (if it was nothing more) to employ his own imperfect language, and express his own poor thoughts, even when they have the misfortune not to coincide with Mr. Balfour's. You would have me to believe Breck innocent. I would think this of little account, the more so as we cannot catch our man. But the matter of Breck's innocence shoots beyond itself. Once admitted, it would destroy the whole presumptions of our case against another and a very different criminal; a man grown old in treason, already twice in arms against his king and already twice forgiven; a fomentor of discontent, and (whoever may have fired the shot) the unmistakable original of the deed in question. I need not tell you that I mean James Stewart."

"And I can just say plainly that the innocence of Alan and of James is what I am here to declare in private to your lordship, and what I am prepared to establish at the trial by my testimony," said I.

"To which I can only answer by an equal plainness, Mr. Balfour," said he, "that (in that case) your testimony will not be called by me, and I desire you to withhold it altogether."

"You are at the head of Justice in this country," I cried, "and you propose to me a crime!"

"I am a man nursing with both hands the interests of this country," he replied, "and I press on you a political necessity. Patriotism is not always moral in the formal sense. You might be glad of it, I think: it is your own protection; the facts are heavy against you; and if I am still trying to except you from a very dangerous place, it is in part of course because I am not insensible to your honesty in coming here; in part because of Pilrig's letter; but in part, and in chief part, because I regard in this matter my political duty first and my judicial duty only second. For the same reason—I repeat it to you in the same frank words—I do not want your testimony."

"I desire not to be thought to make a repartee, when I express only the plain sense of our position," said I. "But if your lordship has no need of my testimony, I believe the other side would be extremely blythe to get it."

Prestongrange arose and began to pace to and fro in the room. "You are not so young," he said, "but what you must remember very clearly the year '45 and the shock that went about the country. I read in Pilrig's letter that you are sound in Kirk and State. Who saved them in that fatal year? I do not refer to His Royal Highness and his ramrods, which were extremely useful in their day; but the country had been saved and the field won before ever Cumberland came upon Drummossie. Who saved it? I repeat; who saved the Protestant religion and the whole frame of our civil institutions? The late Lord President Culloden, for one; he played a man's part, and small thanks he got for it—even as I, whom you see before you, straining every nerve in the same service, look for no reward beyond the conscience of my duties done. After the President, who else? You know the answer as well as I do; 'tis partly a scandal, and you glanced at it yourself, and I reproved you for it, when you first came in. It was the Duke and the great clan of Campbell. Now here is a Campbell foully murdered, and that in the King's service. The Duke and I are Highlanders. But we are Highlanders civilised, and it is not so with the great mass of our clans and families. They have still savage virtues and defects. They are still barbarians, like these Stewarts; only the Campbells were barbarians on the right side, and the Stewarts were barbarians on the wrong. Now be you the judge. The Campbells expect vengeance. If they do not get it—if this man James escape—there will be trouble with the Campbells. That means disturbance in the Highlands, which are uneasy and very far from being disarmed: the disarming is a farce. . ."

"I can bear you out in that," said I.

"Disturbance in the Highlands makes the hour of our old watchful enemy," pursued his lordship, holding out a finger as he paced; "and I give you my word we may have a '45 again with the Campbells on the other side. To protect the life of this man Stewart—which is forfeit already on half-a-dozen different counts if not on this—do you propose to plunge your country in war, to jeopardise the faith of your fathers, and to expose the lives and fortunes of how many thousand innocent persons? . . . These are considerations that weigh with me, and that I hope will weigh no less with yourself, Mr. Balfour, as a lover of your country, good government, and religious truth."

"You deal with me very frankly, and I thank you for it," said I. "I will try on my side to be no less honest. I believe your policy to be sound. I believe these deep duties may lie upon your lordship; I believe you may have laid them on your conscience when you took the oath of the high office which you hold. But for me, who am just a plain man—or scarce a man yet—the plain duties must suffice. I can think but of two things, of a poor soul in the immediate and unjust danger of a shameful death, and of the cries and tears of his wife that still tingle in my head. I cannot see beyond, my lord. It's the way that I am made. If the country has to fall, it has to fall. And I pray God, if this be wilful blindness, that He may enlighten me before too late."

He had heard me motionless, and stood so a while longer.

"This is an unexpected obstacle," says he, aloud, but to himself.

"And how is your lordship to dispose of me?" I asked.

"If I wished," said he, "you know that you might sleep in gaol?"

"My lord," said I, "I have slept in worse places."

"Well, my boy," said he, "there is one thing appears very plainly from our interview, that I may rely on your pledged word. Give me your honour that you will be wholly secret, not only on what has passed to-night, but in the matter of the Appin case, and I let you go free."

"I will give it till to-morrow or any other near day that you may please to set," said I. "I would not be thought too wily; but if I gave the promise without qualification your lordship would have attained his end."

"I had no thought to entrap you," said he.

"I am sure of that," said I.

"Let me see," he continued. "To-morrow is the Sabbath. Come to me on Monday by eight in the morning, and give me your promise until then."

"Freely given, my lord," said I. "And with regard to what has fallen from yourself, I will give it for an long as it shall please God to spare your days."

"You will observe," he said next, "that I have made no employment of menaces."

"It was like your lordship's nobility," said I. "Yet I am not altogether so dull but what I can perceive the nature of those you have not uttered."

"Well," said he, "good-night to you. May you sleep well, for I think it is more than I am like to do."

With that he sighed, took up a candle, and gave me his conveyance as far as the street door.

CHAPTER V.
IN THE ADVOCATE'S HOUSE

The next day, Sabbath, August 27th, I had the occasion I had long looked forward to, to hear some of the famous Edinburgh preachers, all well known to me already by the report of Mr Campbell. Alas! and I might just as well have been at Essendean, and sitting under Mr. Campbell's worthy self! the turmoil of my thoughts, which dwelt continually on the interview with Prestongrange, inhibiting me from all attention. I was indeed much less impressed by the reasoning of the divines than by the spectacle of the thronged congregation in the churches, like what I imagined of a theatre or (in my then disposition) of an assize of trial; above all at the West Kirk, with its three tiers of galleries, where I went in the vain hope that I might see Miss Drummond.

On the Monday I betook me for the first time to a barber's, and was very well pleased with the result. Thence to the Advocate's, where the red coats of the soldiers showed again about his door, making a bright place in the close. I looked about for the young lady and her gillies: there was never a sign of them. But I was no sooner shown into the cabinet or antechamber where I had spent so wearyful a time upon the Saturday, than I was aware of the tall figure of James More in a corner. He seemed a prey to a painful uneasiness, reaching forth his feet and hands, and his eyes speeding here and there without rest about the walls of the small chamber, which recalled to me with a sense of pity the man's wretched situation. I suppose it was partly this, and partly my strong continuing interest in his daughter, that moved me to accost him.

"Give you a good-morning, sir," said I.

"And a good-morning to you, sir," said he.

"You bide tryst with Prestongrange?" I asked.

"I do, sir, and I pray your business with that gentleman be more agreeable than mine," was his reply.

"I hope at least that yours will be brief, for I suppose you pass before me," said I.

"All pass before me," he said, with a shrug and a gesture upward of the open hands. "It was not always so, sir, but times change. It was not so when the sword was in the scale, young gentleman, and the virtues of the soldier might sustain themselves."

There came a kind of Highland snuffle out of the man that raised my dander strangely.

"Well, Mr. Macgregor," said I, "I understand the main thing for a soldier is to be silent, and the first of his virtues never to complain."

"You have my name, I perceive"—he bowed to me with his arms crossed—"though it's one I must not use myself. Well, there is a publicity—I have shown my face and told my name too often in the beards of my enemies. I must not wonder if both should be known to many that I know not."

"That you know not in the least, sir," said I, "nor yet anybody else; but the name I am called, if you care to hear it, is Balfour."

"It is a good name," he replied, civilly; "there are many decent folk that use it. And now that I call to mind, there was a young gentleman, your namesake, that marched surgeon in the year

'45 with my battalion."

"I believe that would be a brother to Balfour of Baith," said I, for I was ready for the surgeon now.

"The same, sir," said James More. "And since I have been fellow-soldier with your kinsman, you must suffer me to grasp your hand."

He shook hands with me long and tenderly, beaming on me the while as though he had found a brother.

"Ah!" says he, "these are changed days since your cousin and I heard the balls whistle in our lugs."

"I think he was a very far-away cousin," said I, drily, "and I ought to tell you that I never clapped eyes upon the man."

"Well, well," said he, "it makes no change. And you—I do not think you were out yourself, sir—I have no clear mind of your face, which is one not probable to be forgotten."

"In the year you refer to, Mr. Macgregor, I was getting skelped in the parish school," said I.

"So young!" cries he. "Ah, then, you will never be able to think what this meeting is to me. In the hour of my adversity, and here in the house of my enemy, to meet in with the blood of an old brother-in-arms—it heartens me, Mr. Balfour, like the skirling of the highland pipes! Sir, this is a sad look back that many of us have to make: some with falling tears. I have lived in my own country like a king; my sword, my mountains, and the faith of my friends and kinsmen sufficed for me. Now I lie in a stinking dungeon; and do you know, Mr. Balfour," he went on, taking my arm and beginning to lead me about, "do you know, sir, that I lack mere necessaries? The malice of my foes has quite sequestered my resources. I lie, as you know, sir, on a trumped-up charge, of which I am as innocent as yourself. They dare not bring me to my trial, and in the meanwhile I am held naked in my prison. I could have wished it was your cousin I had met, or his brother Baith himself. Either would, I know, have been rejoiced to help me; while a comparative stranger like yourself—"

I would be ashamed to set down all he poured out to me in this beggarly vein, or the very short and grudging answers that I made to him. There were times when I was tempted to stop his mouth with some small change; but whether it was from shame or pride—whether it was for my own sake or Catriona's—whether it was because I thought him no fit father for his daughter, or because I resented that grossness of immediate falsity that clung about the man himself—the thing was clean beyond me. And I was still being wheedled and preached to, and still being marched to and fro, three steps and a turn, in that small chamber, and had already, by some very short replies, highly incensed, although not finally discouraged, my beggar, when Prestongrange appeared in the doorway and bade me eagerly into his big chamber.

"I have a moment's engagements," said he; "and that you may not sit empty-handed I am going to present you to my three braw daughters, of whom perhaps you may have heard, for I think they are more famous than papa. This way."

He led me into another long room above, where a dry old lady sat at a frame of embroidery, and the three handsomest young women (I suppose) in Scotland stood together by a window.

"This is my new friend, Mr Balfour," said he, presenting me by the arm, "David, here is my sister, Miss Grant, who is so good as keep my house for me, and will be very pleased if she can help you. And here," says he, turning to the three younger ladies, "here are my three braw dauchters. A fair question to ye, Mr. Davie: which of the three is the best favoured? And I wager he will never have the impudence to propound honest Alan Ramsay's answer!"

Hereupon all three, and the old Miss Grant as well, cried out against this sally, which (as I was acquainted with the verses he referred to) brought shame into my own check. It seemed to me a citation unpardonable in a father, and I was amazed that these ladies could laugh even while they reproved, or made believe to.

Under cover of this mirth, Prestongrange got forth of the chamber, and I was left, like a fish upon dry land, in that very unsuitable society. I could never deny, in looking back upon what followed, that I was eminently stockish; and I must say the ladies were well drilled to have so long a patience with me. The aunt indeed sat close at her embroidery, only looking now and again and smiling; but the misses, and especially the eldest, who was besides the most handsome, paid me a score of attentions which I was very ill able to repay. It was all in vain to tell myself I was a young follow of some worth as well as a good estate, and had no call to feel abashed before these lasses, the eldest not so much older than myself, and no one of them by any probability half as learned. Reasoning would not change the fact; and there were times when the colour came into my face to think I was shaved that day for the first time.

The talk going, with all their endeavours, very heavily, the eldest took pity on my awkwardness, sat down to her instrument, of which she was a passed mistress, and entertained me for a while with playing and singing, both in the Scots and in the Italian manners; this put me more at my ease, and being reminded of Alan's air that he had taught me in the hole near Carriden, I made so bold as to whistle a bar or two, and ask if she knew that.

She shook her head. "I never heard a note of it," said she. "Whistle it all through. And now once again," she added, after I had done so.

Then she picked it out upon the keyboard, and (to my surprise) instantly enriched the same with well-sounding chords, and sang, as she played, with a very droll expression and broad accent—

"Haenae I got just the lilt of it?
Isnae this the tune that ye whustled?"

"You see," she says, "I can do the poetry too, only it won't rhyme. And then again:

"I am Miss Grant, sib to the Advocate:
You, I believe, are Dauvit Balfour."

I told her how much astonished I was by her genius.

"And what do you call the name of it?" she asked.

"I do not know the real name," said I. "I just call it Alan's air."

She looked at me directly in the face. "I shall call it David's air," said she; "though if it's the least like what your namesake of Israel played to Saul I would never wonder that the king got little good by it, for it's but melancholy music. Your other name I do not like; so if you was ever wishing to hear your tune again you are to ask for it by mine."

This was said with a significance that gave my heart a jog. "Why that, Miss Grant?" I asked.

"Why," says she, "if ever you should come to get hanged, I will set your last dying speech and confession to that tune and sing it."

This put it beyond a doubt that she was partly informed of my story and peril. How, or just how much, it was more difficult to guess. It was plain she knew there was something of danger in the name of Alan, and thus warned me to leave it out of reference; and plain she knew that I stood under some criminal suspicion. I judged besides that the harshness of her last speech (which besides she had followed up immediately with a very noisy piece of music) was to put an end to the present conversation. I stood beside her, affecting to listen and admire, but truly whirled away by my own thoughts. I have always found this young lady to be a lover of the mysterious; and certainly this first interview made a mystery that was beyond my plummet. One thing I learned long after, the hours of the Sunday had been well employed, the bank porter had been found and examined, my visit to Charles Stewart was discovered, and the deduction made that I was pretty deep with James and Alan, and most likely in a continued correspondence with the last. Hence this broad hint that was given me across the harpsichord.

In the midst of the piece of music, one of the younger misses, who was at a window over the close, cried on her sisters to come quick, for there was "Grey eyes again." The whole family trooped there at once, and crowded one another for a look. The window whither they ran was in an odd corner of that room, gave above the entrance door, and flanked up the close.

"Come, Mr. Balfour," they cried, "come and see. She is the most beautiful creature! She hangs round the close-head these last days, always with some wretched-like gillies, and yet seems quite a lady."

I had no need to look; neither did I look twice, or long. I was afraid she might have seen me there, looking down upon her from that chamber of music, and she without, and her father in the same house, perhaps begging for his life with tears, and myself come but newly from rejecting his petitions. But even that glance set me in a better conceit of myself and much less awe of the young ladies. They were beautiful, that was beyond question, but Catriona was beautiful too, and had a kind of brightness in her like a coal of fire. As much as the others cast me down, she lifted me up. I remembered I had talked easily with her. If I could make no hand of it with these fine maids, it was perhaps something their own fault. My embarrassment began to be a little mingled and lightened with a sense of fun; and when the aunt smiled at me from her embroidery, and the three daughters unbent to me like a baby, all with "papa's orders" written on their faces, there were times when I could have found it in my heart to smile myself.

Presently papa returned, the same kind, happy-like, pleasant-spoken man.

"Now, girls," said he, "I must take Mr. Balfour away again; but I hope you have been able to persuade him to return where I shall be always gratified to find him."

So they each made me a little farthing compliment, and I was led away.

If this visit to the family had been meant to soften my resistance, it was the worst of failures. I was no such ass but what I understood how poor a figure I had made, and that the girls would be yawning their jaws off as soon as my stiff back was turned. I felt I had shown how little I had in me of what was soft and graceful; and I longed for a chance to prove that I had something of the other stuff, the stern and dangerous.

Well, I was to be served to my desire, for the scene to which he was conducting me was of a different character.

CHAPTER VI.
UMQUILE THE MASTER OF LOVAT

There was a man waiting us in Prestongrange's study, whom I distasted at the first look, as we distaste a ferret or an earwig. He was bitter ugly, but seemed very much of a gentleman; had still manners, but capable of sudden leaps and violences; and a small voice, which could ring out shrill and dangerous when he so desired.

The Advocate presented us in a familiar, friendly way.

"Here, Fraser," said he, "here is Mr. Balfour whom we talked about. Mr. David, this is Mr. Simon Fraser, whom we used to call by another title, but that is an old song. Mr. Fraser has an errand to you."

With that he stepped aside to his book-shelves, and made believe to consult a quarto volume in the far end.

I was thus left (in a sense) alone with perhaps the last person in the world I had expected. There was no doubt upon the terms of introduction; this could be no other than the forfeited Master of Lovat and chief of the great clan Fraser. I knew he had led his men in the Rebellion; I knew his father's head—my old lord's, that grey fox of the mountains—to have fallen on the block for that offence, the lands of the family to have been seized, and their nobility attainted. I could not conceive what he should be doing in Grant's house; I could not conceive that he had been called to the bar, had eaten all his principles, and was now currying favour with the Government even to the extent of acting Advocate-Depute in the Appin murder.

"Well, Mr. Balfour," said he, "what is all this I hear of ye?"

"It would not become me to prejudge," said I, "but if the Advocate was your authority he is fully possessed of my opinions."

"I may tell you I am engaged in the Appin case," he went on; "I am to appear under Prestongrange; and from my study of the precognitions I can assure you your opinions are erroneous. The guilt of Breck is manifest; and your testimony, in which you admit you saw him on the hill at the very moment, will certify his hanging."

"It will be rather ill to hang him till you catch him," I observed. "And for other matters I very willingly leave you to your own impressions."

"The Duke has been informed," he went on. "I have just come from his Grace, and he expressed himself before me with an honest freedom like the great nobleman he is. He spoke of you by name, Mr. Balfour, and declared his gratitude beforehand in case you would be led by those who understand your own interests and those of the country so much better than yourself. Gratitude is no empty expression in that mouth: experto-crede. I daresay you know something of my name and clan, and the damnable example and lamented end of my late father, to say nothing of my own errata. Well, I have made my peace with that good Duke; he has intervened for me with our friend Prestongrange; and here I am with my foot in the stirrup again and some of the responsibility shared into my hand of prosecuting King George's enemies and avenging the late daring and barefaced insult to his Majesty."

"Doubtless a proud position for your father's son," says I.

He wagged his bald eyebrows at me. "You are pleased to make experiments in the ironical, I think," said he. "But I am here upon duty, I am here to discharge my errand in good faith, it is in vain you think to divert me. And let me tell you, for a young fellow of spirit and ambition like yourself, a good shove in the beginning will do more than ten years' drudgery. The shove is now at your command; choose what you will to be advanced in, the Duke will watch upon you with the affectionate disposition of a father."

"I am thinking that I lack the docility of the son," says I.

"And do you really suppose, sir, that the whole policy of this country is to be suffered to trip up and tumble down for an ill-mannered colt of a boy?" he cried. "This has been made a test case, all who would prosper in the future must put a shoulder to the wheel. Look at me! Do you suppose it is for my pleasure that I put myself in the highly invidious position of persecuting a man that I have drawn the sword alongside of? The choice is not left me."

"But I think, sir, that you forfeited your choice when you mixed in with that unnatural rebellion," I remarked. "My case is happily otherwise; I am a true man, and can look either the Duke or King George in the face without concern."

"Is it so the wind sits?" says he. "I protest you are fallen in the worst sort of error. Prestongrange has been hitherto so civil (he tells me) as not to combat your allegations; but you must not think they are not looked upon with strong suspicion. You say you are innocent. My dear sir, the facts declare you guilty."

"I was waiting for you there," said I.

"The evidence of Mungo Campbell; your flight after the completion of the murder; your long course of secresy—my good young man!" said Mr. Simon, "here is enough evidence to hang a bullock, let be a David Balfour! I shall be upon that trial; my voice shall be raised; I shall then speak much otherwise from what I do to-day, and far less to your gratification, little as you like it now! Ah, you look white!" cries he. "I have found the key of your impudent heart. You look pale, your eyes waver, Mr. David! You see the grave and the gallows nearer by than you had fancied."

"I own to a natural weakness," said I. "I think no shame for that. Shame. . ." I was going on.

"Shame waits for you on the gibbet," he broke in.

"Where I shall but be even'd with my lord your father," said I.

"Aha, but not so!" he cried, "and you do not yet see to the bottom of this business. My father suffered in a great cause, and for dealing in the affairs of kings. You are to hang for a dirty murder about boddle-pieces. Your personal part in it, the treacherous one of holding the poor wretch in talk, your accomplices a pack of ragged Highland gillies. And it can be shown, my great Mr. Balfour—it can be shown, and it will be shown, trust me that has a finger in the pie—it can be shown, and shall be shown, that you were paid to do it. I think I can see the looks go round the court when I adduce my evidence, and it shall appear that you, a young man of education, let yourself be corrupted to this shocking act for a suit of cast clothes, a bottle of Highland spirits, and three-and-fivepence-halfpenny in copper money."

There was a touch of the truth in these words that knocked me like a blow: clothes, a bottle of usquebaugh, and three-and-fivepence-halfpenny in change made up, indeed, the most of what Alan and I had carried from Auchurn; and I saw that some of James's people had been blabbing in their dungeons.

"You see I know more than you fancied," he resumed in triumph. "And as for giving it this turn, great Mr. David, you must not suppose the Government of Great Britain and Ireland will ever be stuck for want of evidence. We have men here in prison who will swear out their lives as we direct them; as I direct, if you prefer the phrase. So now you are to guess your part of glory if you choose to die. On the one hand, life, wine, women, and a duke to be your handgun: on the other, a rope to your craig, and a gibbet to clatter your bones on, and the lousiest, lowest story to hand down to your namesakes in the future that was ever told about a hired assassin. And see here!" he cried, with a formidable shrill voice, "see this paper that I pull out of my pocket. Look at the name there: it is the name of the great David, I believe, the ink scarce dry yet. Can you guess its nature? It is the warrant for your arrest, which I have but to touch this bell beside me to have executed on the spot. Once in the Tolbooth upon this paper, may God help you, for the die is cast!"

I must never deny that I was greatly horrified by so much baseness, and much unmanned by the immediacy and ugliness of my danger. Mr. Simon had already gloried in the changes of my hue; I make no doubt I was now no ruddier than my shirt; my speech besides trembled.

"There is a gentleman in this room," cried I. "I appeal to him. I put my life and credit in his hands."

Prestongrange shut his book with a snap. "I told you so, Simon," said he; "you have played your hand for all it was worth, and you have lost. Mr. David," he went on, "I wish you to believe it was by no choice of mine you were subjected to this proof. I wish you could understand how glad I am you should come forth from it with so much credit. You may not quite see how, but it is a little of a service to myself. For had our friend here been more successful than I was last night, it might have appeared that he was a better judge of men than I; it might have appeared we were altogether in the wrong situations, Mr. Simon and myself. And I know our friend Simon to be ambitious," says he, striking lightly on Fraser's shoulder. "As for this stage play, it is over; my sentiments are very much engaged in your behalf; and whatever issue we can find to this unfortunate affair, I shall make it my business to see it is adopted with tenderness to you."

These were very good words, and I could see besides that there was little love, and perhaps a spice of genuine ill-will, between these two who were opposed to me. For all that, it was unmistakable this interview had been designed, perhaps rehearsed, with the consent of both; it was plain my adversaries were in earnest to try me by all methods; and now (persuasion, flattery, and menaces having been tried in vain) I could not but wonder what would be their next expedient. My eyes besides were still troubled, and my knees loose under me, with the distress of the late ordeal; and I could do no more than stammer the same form of words: "I put my life and credit in your hands."

"Well, well," said he, "we must try to save them. And in the meanwhile let us return to gentler methods. You must not bear any grudge upon my friend, Mr. Simon, who did but speak by his brief. And even if you did conceive some malice against myself, who stood by and seemed rather to hold a candle, I must not let that extend to innocent members of my family. These are greatly engaged to see more of you, and I cannot consent to have my young womenfolk disappointed. To-morrow they will be going to Hope Park, where I think it very proper you should make your bow. Call for me first, when I may possibly have something for your private hearing; then you shall be turned abroad again under the conduct of my misses; and until that time repeat to me your promise of secrecy."

I had done better to have instantly refused, but in truth I was beside the power of reasoning; did as I was bid; took my leave I know not how; and when I was forth again in the close, and the door had shut behind me, was glad to lean on a house wall and wipe my face. That horrid apparition (as I may call it) of Mr. Simon rang in my memory, as a sudden noise rings after it is over in the ear. Tales of the man's father, of his falseness, of his manifold perpetual treacheries, rose before me from all that I had heard and read, and joined on with what I had just experienced of himself. Each time it occurred to me, the ingenious foulness of that calumny he had proposed to nail upon my character startled me afresh. The case of the man upon the gibbet by Leith Walk appeared scarce distinguishable from that I was now to consider as my own. To rob a child of so little more than nothing was certainly a paltry enterprise for two grown men; but my own tale, as it was to be represented in a court by Simon Fraser, appeared a fair second in every possible point of view of sordidness and cowardice.

The voices of two of Prestongrange's liveried men upon his doorstep recalled me to myself.

"Ha'e," said the one, "this billet as fast as ye can link to the captain."

"Is that for the cateran back again?" asked the other.

"It would seem sae," returned the first. "Him and Simon are seeking him."

"I think Prestongrange is gane gyte," says the second. "He'll have James More in bed with him next."

"Weel, it's neither your affair nor mine's," said the first.

And they parted, the one upon his errand, and the other back into the house.

This looked as ill as possible. I was scarce gone and they were sending already for James More, to whom I thought Mr. Simon must have pointed when he spoke of men in prison and ready to redeem their lives by all extremities. My scalp curdled among my hair, and the next moment the blood leaped in me to remember Catriona. Poor lass! her father stood to be hanged for pretty indefensible misconduct. What was yet more unpalatable, it now seemed he was prepared to save his four quarters by the worst of shame and the most foul of cowardly murders—murder by the false oath; and to complete our misfortunes, it seemed myself was picked out to be the victim.

I began to walk swiftly and at random, conscious only of a desire for movement, air, and the open country.

CHAPTER VII.
I MAKE A FAULT IN HONOUR

I came forth, I vow I know not how, on the Lang Dykes [12]. This is a rural road which runs on the north side over against the city. Thence I could see the whole black length of it tail down, from where the castle stands upon its crags above the loch in a long line of spires and gable ends, and smoking chimneys, and at the sight my heart swelled in my bosom. My youth, as I have told, was already inured to dangers; but such danger as I had seen the face of but that morning, in the midst of what they call the safety of a town, shook me beyond experience. Peril of slavery, peril of shipwreck, peril of sword and shot, I had stood all of these without discredit; but the peril there was in the sharp voice and the fat face of Simon, properly Lord Lovat, daunted me wholly.

I sat by the lake side in a place where the rushes went down into the water, and there steeped my wrists and laved my temples. If I could have done so with any remains of self-esteem, I would now have fled from my foolhardy enterprise. But (call it courage or cowardice, and I believe it was both the one and the other) I decided I was ventured out beyond the possibility of a retreat. I had out-faced these men, I would continue to out-face them; come what might, I would stand by the word spoken.

The sense of my own constancy somewhat uplifted my spirits, but not much. At the best of it there was an icy place about my heart, and life seemed a black business to be at all engaged in. For two souls in particular my pity flowed. The one was myself, to be so friendless and lost among dangers. The other was the girl, the daughter of James More. I had seen but little of her; yet my view was taken and my judgment made. I thought her a lass of a clean honour, like a man's; I thought her one to die of a disgrace; and now I believed her father to be at that moment bargaining his vile life for mine. It made a bond in my thoughts betwixt the girl and me. I had seen her before only as a wayside appearance, though one that pleased me strangely; I saw her now in a sudden nearness of relation, as the daughter of my blood foe, and I might say, my murderer. I reflected it was hard I should be so plagued and persecuted all my days for other folks' affairs, and have no manner of pleasure myself. I got meals and a bed to sleep in when my concerns would suffer it; beyond that my wealth was of no help to me. If I was to hang, my days were like to be short; if I was not to hang but to escape out of this trouble, they might yet seem long to me ere I was done with them. Of a sudden her face appeared in my memory, the way I had first seen it, with the parted lips; at that, weakness came in my bosom and strength into my legs; and I set resolutely forward on the way to Dean. If I was to hang to-morrow, and it was sure enough I might very likely sleep that night in a dungeon, I determined I should hear and speak once more with Catriona.

The exercise of walking and the thought of my destination braced me yet more, so that I began to pluck up a kind of spirit. In the village of Dean, where it sits in the bottom of a glen beside the river, I inquired my way of a miller's man, who sent me up the hill upon the farther side by a plain path, and so to a decent-like small house in a garden of lawns and apple-trees. My heart beat high as I stepped inside the garden hedge, but it fell low indeed when I came face to face with a grim and fierce old lady, walking there in a white mutch with a man's hat strapped upon the top of it.

"What do ye come seeking here?" she asked.

I told her I was after Miss Drummond.

"And what may be your business with Miss Drummond?" says she.

I told her I had met her on Saturday last, had been so fortunate as to render her a trifling service, and was come now on the young lady's invitation.

"O, so you're Saxpence!" she cried, with a very sneering manner. "A braw gift, a bonny gentleman. And hae ye ony ither name and designation, or were ye bapteesed Saxpence?" she asked.

I told my name.

"Preserve me!" she cried. "Has Ebenezer gotten a son?"

"No, ma'am," said I. "I am a son of Alexander's. It's I that am the Laird of Shaws."

"Ye'll find your work cut out for ye to establish that," quoth she.

"I perceive you know my uncle," said I; "and I daresay you may be the better pleased to hear that business is arranged."

"And what brings ye here after Miss Drummond?" she pursued.

"I'm come after my saxpence, mem," said I. "It's to be thought, being my uncle's nephew, I would be found a careful lad."

"So ye have a spark of sleeness in ye?" observed the old lady, with some approval. "I thought ye had just been a cuif—you and your saxpence, and your lucky day and your sake of Balwhidder"— from which I was gratified to learn that Catriona had not forgotten some of our talk. "But all this is by the purpose," she resumed. "Am I to understand that ye come here keeping company?"

"This is surely rather an early question," said I. "The maid is young, so am I, worse fortune. I have but seen her the once. I'll not deny," I added, making up my mind to try her with some frankness, "I'll not deny but she has run in my head a good deal since I met in with her. That is one thing; but it would be quite another, and I think I would look very like a fool, to commit myself."

"You can speak out of your mouth, I see," said the old lady. "Praise God, and so can I! I was fool enough to take charge of this rogue's daughter: a fine charge I have gotten; but it's mine, and I'll carry it the way I want to. Do ye mean to tell me, Mr. Balfour of Shaws, that you would marry James More's daughter, and him hanged! Well, then, where there's no possible marriage there shall be no manner of carryings on, and take that for said. Lasses are bruckle things," she added, with a nod; "and though ye would never think it by my wrunkled chafts, I was a lassie mysel', and a bonny one."

"Lady Allardyce," said I, "for that I suppose to be your name, you seem to do the two sides of the talking, which is a very poor manner to come to an agreement. You give me rather a home thrust when you ask if I would marry, at the gallow's foot, a young lady whom I have seen but once. I have told you already I would never be so untenty as to commit myself. And yet I'll go some way with you. If I continue to like the lass as well as I have reason to expect, it will be something more than her father, or the gallows either, that keeps the two of us apart. As for my family, I found it by the wayside like a lost bawbee! I owe less than nothing to my uncle and if ever I marry, it will be to please one person: that's myself."

"I have heard this kind of talk before ye were born," said Mrs. Ogilvy, "which is perhaps the reason that I think of it so little. There's much to be considered. This James More is a kinsman of mine, to my shame be it spoken. But the better the family, the mair men hanged or headed, that's always been poor Scotland's story. And if it was just the hanging! For my part I think I would be best pleased with James upon the gallows, which would be at least an end to him. Catrine's a good lass enough, and a good-hearted, and lets herself be deaved all day with a runt of an auld wife like me. But, ye see, there's the weak bit. She's daft about that long, false, fleeching beggar of a father of hers, and red-mad about the Gregara, and proscribed names, and King James, and a wheen blethers. And you might think ye could guide her, ye would find yourself sore mista'en. Ye say ye've seen her but the once. . ."

"Spoke with her but the once, I should have said," I interrupted. "I saw her again this morning from a window at Prestongrange's."

This I daresay I put in because it sounded well; but I was properly paid for my ostentation on the return.

"What's this of it?" cries the old lady, with a sudden pucker of her face. "I think it was at the Advocate's door-cheek that ye met her first."

I told her that was so.

"H'm," she said; and then suddenly, upon rather a scolding tone, "I have your bare word for it," she cries, "as to who and what you are. By your way of it, you're Balfour of the Shaws; but for what I ken you may be Balfour of the Deevil's oxter. It's possible ye may come here for what ye say, and it's equally possible ye may come here for deil care what! I'm good enough Whig to sit quiet, and to have keepit all my men-folk's heads upon their shoulders. But I'm not just a good enough Whig to be made a fool of neither. And I tell you fairly, there's too much Advocate's door and Advocate's window here for a man that comes taigling after a Macgregor's daughter. Ye can tell that to the Advocate that sent ye, with my fond love. And I kiss my loof to ye, Mr. Balfour," says she, suiting the action to the word; "and a braw journey to ye back to where ye cam frae."

"If you think me a spy," I broke out, and speech stuck in my throat. I stood and looked murder at the old lady for a space, then bowed and turned away.

"Here! Hoots! The callant's in a creel!" she cried. "Think ye a spy? what else would I think ye—me that kens naething by ye? But I see that I was wrong; and as I cannot fight, I'll have to apologise. A bonny figure I would be with a broadsword. Ay! ay!" she went on, "you're none such a bad lad in your way; I think ye'll have some redeeming vices. But, O! Davit Balfour, ye're damned countryfeed. Ye'll have to win over that, lad; ye'll have to soople your back-bone, and think a wee pickle less of your dainty self; and ye'll have to try to find out that women-folk are nae grenadiers. But that can never be. To your last day you'll ken no more of women-folk than what I do of sow-gelding."

I had never been used with such expressions from a lady's tongue, the only two ladies I had known, Mrs. Campbell and my mother, being most devout and most particular women; and I suppose my amazement must have been depicted in my countenance, for Mrs. Ogilvy burst forth suddenly in a fit of laughter.

"Keep me!" she cried, struggling with her mirth, "you have the finest timber face—and you to marry the daughter of a Hieland cateran! Davie, my dear, I think we'll have to make a match of it—if it was just to see the weans. And now," she went on, "there's no manner of service in your daidling here, for the young woman is from home, and it's my fear that the old woman is no suitable companion for your father's son. Forbye that I have nobody but myself to look after my reputation, and have been long enough alone with a sedooctive youth. And come back another day for your saxpence!" she cried after me as I left.

My skirmish with this disconcerting lady gave my thoughts a boldness they had otherwise wanted. For two days the image of Catriona had mixed in all my meditations; she made their background, so that I scarce enjoyed my own company without a glint of her in a corner of my mind. But now she came immediately near; I seemed to touch her, whom I had never touched but the once; I let myself flow out to her in a happy weakness, and looking all about, and before and behind, saw the world like an undesirable desert, where men go as soldiers on a march, following their duty with what constancy they have, and Catriona alone there to offer me some pleasure of my days. I wondered at myself that I could dwell on such considerations in that time of my peril and disgrace; and when I remembered my youth I was ashamed. I had my studies to complete: I had to be called into some useful business; I had yet to take my part of service in a place where all must serve; I had yet to learn, and know, and prove myself a man; and I had so much sense as blush that I should be already tempted with these further-on and holier delights and duties. My education spoke home to me sharply; I was never brought up on sugar biscuits but on the hard food of the truth. I knew that he was quite unfit to be a husband who was not prepared to be a father also; and for a boy like me to play the father was a mere derision.

When I was in the midst of these thoughts and about half-way back to town I saw a figure coming to meet me, and the trouble of my heart was heightened. It seemed I had everything in the world to say to her, but nothing to say first; and remembering how tongue-tied I had been that morning at the Advocate's I made sure that I would find myself struck dumb. But when she came up my fears fled away; not even the consciousness of what I had been privately thinking disconcerted me the least; and I found I could talk with her as easily and rationally as I might with Alan.

"O!" she cried, "you have been seeking your sixpence; did you get it?"

I told her no; but now I had met with her my walk was not in vain. "Though I have seen you to-day already," said I, and told her where and when.

"I did not see you," she said. "My eyes are big, but there are better than mine at seeing far. Only I heard singing in the house."

"That was Miss Grant," said I, "the eldest and the bonniest."

"They say they are all beautiful," said she.

"They think the same of you, Miss Drummond," I replied, "and were all crowding to the window to observe you."

"It is a pity about my being so blind," said she, "or I might have seen them too. And you were in the house? You must have been having the fine time with the fine music and the pretty ladies."

"There is just where you are wrong," said I; "for I was as uncouth as a sea-fish upon the brae of a mountain. The truth is that I am better fitted to go about with rudas men than pretty ladies."

"Well, I would think so too, at all events!" said she, at which we both of us laughed.

"It is a strange thing, now," said I. "I am not the least afraid with you, yet I could have run from the Miss Grants. And I was afraid of your cousin too."

"O, I think any man will be afraid of her," she cried. "My father is afraid of her himself."

The name of her father brought me to a stop. I looked at her as she walked by my side; I recalled the man, and the little I knew and the much I guessed of him; and comparing the one with the other, felt like a traitor to be silent.

"Speaking of which," said I, "I met your father no later than this morning."

"Did you?" she cried, with a voice of joy that seemed to mock at me. "You saw James More? You will have spoken with him then?"

"I did even that," said I.

Then I think things went the worst way for me that was humanly possible. She gave me a look of mere gratitude. "Ah, thank you for that!" says she.

"You thank me for very little," said I, and then stopped. But it seemed when I was holding back so much, something at least had to come out. "I spoke rather ill to him," said I; "I did no like him very much; I spoke him rather ill, and he was angry."

"I think you had little to do then, and less to tell it to his daughter!" she cried out. "But those that do not love and cherish him I will not know."

"I will take the freedom of a word yet," said I, beginning to tremble. "Perhaps neither your father nor I are in the best of spirits at Prestongrange's. I daresay we both have anxious business there, for it's a dangerous house. I was sorry for him too, and spoke to him the first, if I could but have spoken the wiser. And for one thing, in my opinion, you will soon find that his affairs are mending."

"It will not be through your friendship, I am thinking," said she; "and he is much made up to you for your sorrow."

"Miss Drummond," cried I, "I am alone in this world."

"And I am not wondering at that," said she.

"O, let me speak!" said I. "I will speak but the once, and then leave you, if you will, for ever. I came this day in the hopes of a kind word that I am sore in want of. I know that what I said must hurt you, and I knew it then. It would have been easy to have spoken smooth, easy to lie to you; can you not think how I was tempted to the same? Cannot you see the truth of my heart shine out?"

"I think here is a great deal of work, Mr. Balfour," said she. "I think we will have met but the once, and will can part like gentle folk."

"O, let me have one to believe in me!" I pleaded, "I cannae bear it else. The whole world is clanned against me. How am I to go through with my dreadful fate? If there's to be none to believe in me I cannot do it. The man must just die, for I cannot do it."

She had still looked straight in front of her, head in air; but at my words or the tone of my voice she came to a stop. "What is this you say?" she asked. "What are you talking of?"

"It is my testimony which may save an innocent life," said I, "and they will not suffer me to bear it. What would you do yourself? You know what this is, whose father lies in danger. Would you desert the poor soul? They have tried all ways with me. They have sought to bribe me; they offered me hills and valleys. And to-day that sleuth-hound told me how I stood, and to what a length he would go to butcher and disgrace me. I am to be brought in a party to the murder; I am to have held Glenure in talk for money and old clothes; I am to be killed and shamed. If this is the way I am to fall, and me scarce a man—if this is the story to be told of me in all Scotland—if you are to believe it too, and my name is to be nothing but a by-word—Catriona, how can I go through with it? The thing's not possible; it's more than a man has in his heart."

I poured my words out in a whirl, one upon the other; and when I stopped I found her gazing on me with a startled face.

"Glenure! It is the Appin murder," she said softly, but with a very deep surprise.

I had turned back to bear her company, and we were now come near the head of the brae above Dean village. At this word I stepped in front of her like one suddenly distracted.

"For God's sake!" I cried, "for God's sake, what is this that I have done?" and carried my fists to my temples. "What made me do it? Sure, I am bewitched to say these things!"

"In the name of heaven, what ails you now!" she cried.

"I gave my honour," I groaned, "I gave my honour and now I have broke it. O, Catriona!"

"I am asking you what it is," she said; "was it these things you should not have spoken? And do you think I have no honour, then? or that I am one that would betray a friend? I hold up my right hand to you and swear."

"O, I knew you would be true!" said I. "It's me—it's here. I that stood but this morning and out-faced them, that risked rather to die disgraced upon the gallows than do wrong—and a few hours after I throw my honour away by the roadside in common talk! 'There is one thing clear upon our interview,' says he, 'that I can rely on your pledged word.' Where is my word now? Who could believe me now? You could not believe me. I am clean fallen down; I had best die!" All this I said with a weeping voice, but I had no tears in my body.

"My heart is sore for you," said she, "but be sure you are too nice. I would not believe you, do you say? I would trust you with anything. And these men? I would not be thinking of them! Men who go about to entrap and to destroy you! Fy! this is no time to crouch. Look up! Do you not think I will be admiring you like a great hero of the good—and you a boy not much older than myself? And because you said a word too much in a friend's ear, that would die ere she betrayed you—to make such a matter! It is one thing that we must both forget."

"Catriona," said I, looking at her, hang-dog, "is this true of it? Would ye trust me yet?"

"Will you not believe the tears upon my face?" she cried. "It is the world I am thinking of you, Mr. David Balfour. Let them hang you; I will never forget, I will grow old and still remember you. I think it is great to die so: I will envy you that gallows."

"And maybe all this while I am but a child frighted with bogles," said I. "Maybe they but make a mock of me."

"It is what I must know," she said. "I must hear the whole. The harm is done at all events, and I must hear the whole."

I had sat down on the wayside, where she took a place beside me, and I told her all that matter much as I have written it, my thoughts about her father's dealings being alone omitted.

"Well," she said, when I had finished, "you are a hero, surely, and I never would have thought that same! And I think you are in peril, too. O, Simon Fraser! to think upon that man! For his life and the dirty money, to be dealing in such traffic!" And just then she called out aloud with a queer word that was common with her, and belongs, I believe, to her own language. "My torture!" says she, "look at the sun!"

Indeed, it was already dipping towards the mountains.

She bid me come again soon, gave me her hand, and left me in a turmoil of glad spirits. I delayed to go home to my lodging, for I had a terror of immediate arrest; but got some supper at a change house, and the better part of that night walked by myself in the barley-fields, and had such a sense of Catriona's presence that I seemed to bear her in my arms.

CHAPTER VIII.
THE BRAVO

The next day, August 29th, I kept my appointment at the Advocate's in a coat that I had made to my own measure, and was but newly ready.

"Aha," says Prestongrange, "you are very fine to-day; my misses are to have a fine cavalier. Come, I take that kind of you. I take that kind of you, Mr. David. O, we shall do very well yet, and I believe your troubles are nearly at an end."

"You have news for me?" cried I.

"Beyond anticipation," he replied. "Your testimony is after all to be received; and you may go, if you will, in my company to the trial, which in to be held at Inverary, Thursday, 21st proximo."

I was too much amazed to find words.

"In the meanwhile," he continued, "though I will not ask you to renew your pledge, I must caution you strictly to be reticent. To-morrow your precognition must be taken; and outside of that, do you know, I think least said will be soonest mended."

"I shall try to go discreetly," said I. "I believe it is yourself that I must thank for this crowning mercy, and I do thank you gratefully. After yesterday, my lord, this is like the doors of Heaven. I cannot find it in my heart to get the thing believed."

"Ah, but you must try and manage, you must try and manage to believe it," says he, soothing-like, "and I am very glad to hear your acknowledgment of obligation, for I think you may be able to repay me very shortly"—he coughed—"or even now. The matter is much changed. Your testimony, which I shall not trouble you for to-day, will doubtless alter the complexion of the case for all concerned, and this makes it less delicate for me to enter with you on a side issue."

"My Lord," I interrupted, "excuse me for interrupting you, but how has this been brought about? The obstacles you told me of on Saturday appeared even to me to be quite insurmountable; how has it been contrived?"

"My dear Mr. David," said he, "it would never do for me to divulge (even to you, as you say) the councils of the Government; and you must content yourself, if you please, with the gross fact."

He smiled upon me like a father as he spoke, playing the while with a new pen; methought it was impossible there could be any shadow of deception in the man: yet when he drew to him a sheet of paper, dipped his pen among the ink, and began again to address me, I was somehow not so certain, and fell instinctively into an attitude of guard.

"There is a point I wish to touch upon," he began. "I purposely left it before upon one side, which need be now no longer necessary. This is not, of course, a part of your examination, which is to follow by another hand; this is a private interest of my own. You say you encountered Alan Breck upon the hill?"

"I did, my lord," said I.

"This was immediately after the murder?"

"It was."

"Did you speak to him?"

"I did."

"You had known him before, I think?" says my lord, carelessly.

"I cannot guess your reason for so thinking, my lord," I replied, "but such in the fact."

"And when did you part with him again?" said he.

"I reserve my answer," said I. "The question will be put to me at the assize."

"Mr. Balfour," said he, "will you not understand that all this is without prejudice to yourself? I have promised you life and honour; and, believe me, I can keep my word. You are therefore clear of all anxiety. Alan, it appears, you suppose you can protect; and you talk to me of your gratitude, which I think (if you push me) is not ill-deserved. There are a great many different considerations all pointing the same way; and I will never be persuaded that you could not help us (if you chose) to put salt on Alan's tail."

"My lord," said I, "I give you my word I do not so much as guess where Alan is."

He paused a breath. "Nor how he might be found?" he asked.

I sat before him like a log of wood.

"And so much for your gratitude, Mr. David!" he observed. Again there was a piece of silence. "Well," said he, rising, "I am not fortunate, and we are a couple at cross purposes. Let us speak of it no more; you will receive notice when, where, and by whom, we are to take your precognition. And in the meantime, my misses must be waiting you. They will never forgive me if I detain their cavalier."

Into the hands of these Graces I was accordingly offered up, and found them dressed beyond what I had thought possible, and looking fair as a posy.

As we went forth from the doors a small circumstance occurred which came afterwards to look extremely big. I heard a whistle sound loud and brief like a signal, and looking all about, spied for one moment the red head of Neil of the Tom, the son of Duncan. The next moment he was gone again, nor could I see so much as the skirt-tail of Catriona, upon whom I naturally supposed him to be then attending.

My three keepers led me out by Bristo and the Bruntsfield Links; whence a path carried us to Hope Park, a beautiful pleasance, laid with gravel-walks, furnished with seats and summer-sheds, and warded by a keeper. The way there was a little longsome; the two younger misses affected an air of genteel weariness that damped me cruelly, the eldest considered me with something that at times appeared like mirth; and though I thought I did myself more justice than the day before, it was not without some effort. Upon our reaching the park I was launched on a bevy of eight or ten young gentlemen (some of them cockaded officers, the rest chiefly advocates) who crowded to attend upon these beauties; and though I was presented to all of them in very good words, it seemed I was by all immediately forgotten. Young folk in a company are like to savage animals: they fall upon or scorn a stranger without civility, or I may say, humanity; and I am sure, if I had been among baboons, they would have shown me quite as much of both. Some of the advocates set up to be wits, and some of the soldiers to be rattles; and I could not tell which of these extremes annoyed me most. All had a manner of handling their swords and coat-skirts, for the which (in mere black envy) I could have kicked them from the park. I daresay, upon their side, they grudged me extremely the fine company in which I had arrived; and altogether I had soon fallen behind, and stepped stiffly in the rear of all that merriment with my own thoughts.

From these I was recalled by one of the officers, Lieutenant Hector Duncansby, a gawky, leering Highland boy, asking if my name was not "Palfour."

I told him it was, not very kindly, for his manner was scant civil.

"Ha, Palfour," says he, and then, repeating it, "Palfour, Palfour!"

"I am afraid you do not like my name, sir," says I, annoyed with myself to be annoyed with such a rustical fellow.

"No," says he, "but I wass thinking."

"I would not advise you to make a practice of that, sir," says I. "I feel sure you would not find it to agree with you."

"Tit you effer hear where Alan Grigor fand the tangs?" said he.

I asked him what he could possibly mean, and he answered, with a heckling laugh, that he thought I must have found the poker in the same place and swallowed it.

There could be no mistake about this, and my cheek burned.

"Before I went about to put affronts on gentlemen," said I, "I think I would learn the English language first."

He took me by the sleeve with a nod and a wink and led me quietly outside Hope Park. But no sooner were we beyond the view of the promenaders, than the fashion of his countenance changed. "You tam lowland scoon'rel!" cries he, and hit me a buffet on the jaw with his closed fist.

I paid him as good or better on the return; whereupon he stepped a little back and took off his hat to me decorously.

"Enough plows I think," says he. "I will be the offended shentleman, for who effer heard of such suffeeciency as tell a shentlemans that is the king's officer he cannae speak Cot's English? We have swords at our hurdles, and here is the King's Park at hand. Will ye walk first, or let me show ye the way?"

I returned his bow, told him to go first, and followed him. As he went I heard him grumble to himself about Cot's English and the King's coat, so that I might have supposed him to be seriously offended. But his manner at the beginning of our interview was there to belie him. It was manifest he had come prepared to fasten a quarrel on me, right or wrong; manifest that I was taken in a fresh contrivance of my enemies; and to me (conscious as I was of my deficiencies) manifest enough that I should be the one to fall in our encounter.

As we came into that rough rocky desert of the King's Park I was tempted half-a-dozen times to take to my heels and run for it, so loath was I to show my ignorance in fencing, and so much averse to die or even to be wounded. But I considered if their malice went as far as this, it would likely stick at nothing; and that to fall by the sword, however ungracefully, was still an improvement on the gallows. I considered besides that by the unguarded pertness of my words and the quickness of my blow I had put myself quite out of court; and that even if I ran, my adversary would probably pursue and catch me, which would add disgrace to my misfortune.

So that, taking all in all, I continued marching behind him, much as a man follows the hangman, and certainly with no more hope.

We went about the end of the long craigs, and came into the Hunter's Bog. Here, on a piece of fair turf, my adversary drew. There was nobody there to see us but some birds; and no resource for me but to follow his example, and stand on guard with the best face I could display. It seems it was not good enough for Mr. Dancansby, who spied some flaw in my manœuvres, paused, looked upon me sharply, and came off and on, and menaced me with his blade in the air. As I had seen no such proceedings from Alan, and was besides a good deal affected with the proximity of death, I grew quite bewildered, stood helpless, and could have longed to run away.

"Fat deil ails her?" cries the lieutenant.

And suddenly engaging, he twitched the sword out of my grasp and sent it flying far among the rushes.

Twice was this manœuvre repeated; and the third time when I brought back my humiliated weapon, I found he had returned his own to the scabbard, and stood awaiting me with a face of some anger, and his hands clasped under his skirt.

"Pe tamned if I touch you!" he cried, and asked me bitterly what right I had to stand up before "shentlemans" when I did not know the back of a sword from the front of it.

I answered that was the fault of my upbringing; and would he do me the justice to say I had given him all the satisfaction it was unfortunately in my power to offer, and had stood up like a man?

"And that is the truth," said he. "I am fery prave myself, and pold as a lions. But to stand up there—and you ken naething of fence!—the way that you did, I declare it was peyond me. And I am sorry for the plow; though I declare I pelief your own was the elder brother, and my heid still sings with it. And I declare if I had kent what way it wass, I would not put a hand to such a piece of pusiness."

"That is handsomely said," I replied, "and I am sure you will not stand up a second time to be the actor for my private enemies."

"Indeed, no, Palfour," said he; "and I think I was used extremely suffeeciently myself to be set up to fecht with an auld wife, or all the same as a bairn whateffer! And I will tell the Master so, and fecht him, by Cot, himself!"

"And if you knew the nature of Mr. Simon's quarrel with me," said I, "you would be yet the more affronted to be mingled up with such affairs."

He swore he could well believe it; that all the Lovats were made of the same meal and the devil was the miller that ground that; then suddenly shaking me by the hand, he vowed I was a pretty enough fellow after all, that it was a thousand pities I had been neglected, and that if he could find the time, he would give an eye himself to have me educated.

"You can do me a better service than even what you propose," said I; and when he had asked its nature—"Come with me to the house of one of my enemies, and testify how I have carried myself this day," I told him. "That will be the true service. For though he has sent me a gallant adversary for the first, the thought in Mr. Simon's mind is merely murder. There will be a second and then a third; and by what you have seen of my cleverness with the cold steel, you can judge for yourself what is like to be the upshot."

"And I would not like it myself, if I was no more of a man than what you wass!" he cried. "But I will do you right, Palfour. Lead on!"

If I had walked slowly on the way into that accursed park my heels were light enough on the way out. They kept time to a very good old air, that is as ancient as the Bible, and the words of it are: "Surely the bitterness of death is passed." I mind that I was extremely thirsty, and had a drink at Saint Margaret's well on the road down, and the sweetness of that water passed belief. We went through the sanctuary, up the Canongate, in by the Netherbow, and straight to Prestongrange's door, talking as we came and arranging the details of our affair. The footman owned his master was at home, but declared him engaged with other gentlemen on very private business, and his door forbidden.

"My business is but for three minutes, and it cannot wait," said I. "You may say it is by no means private, and I shall be even glad to have some witnesses."

As the man departed unwillingly enough upon this errand, we made so bold as to follow him to the ante-chamber, whence I could hear for a while the murmuring of several voices in the room within. The truth is, they were three at the one table—Prestongrange, Simon Fraser, and Mr. Erskine, Sheriff of Perth; and as they were met in consultation on the very business of the Appin murder, they were a little disturbed at my appearance, but decided to receive me.

"Well, well, Mr. Balfour, and what brings you here again? and who is this you bring with you?" says Prestongrange.

As for Fraser, he looked before him on the table.

"He is here to bear a little testimony in my favour, my lord, which I think it very needful you should hear," said I, and turned to Duncansby.

"I have only to say this," said the lieutenant, "that I stood up this day with Palfour in the Hunter's Pog, which I am now fery sorry for, and he behaved himself as pretty as a shentlemans could ask it. And I have creat respects for Palfour," he added.

"I thank you for your honest expressions," said I.

Whereupon Duncansby made his bow to the company, and left the chamber, as we had agreed upon before.

"What have I to do with this?" says Prestongrange.

"I will tell your lordship in two words," said I. "I have brought this gentleman, a King's officer, to do me so much justice. Now I think my character is covered, and until a certain date, which your lordship can very well supply, it will be quite in vain to despatch against me any more officers. I will not consent to fight my way through the garrison of the castle."

The veins swelled on Prestongrange's brow, and he regarded me with fury.

"I think the devil uncoupled this dog of a lad between my legs!" he cried; and then, turning fiercely on his neighbour, "This is some of your work, Simon," he said. "I spy your hand in the business, and, let me tell you, I resent it. It is disloyal, when we are agreed upon one expedient, to follow another in the dark. You are disloyal to me. What! you let me send this lad to the place with my very daughters! And because I let drop a word to you..... Fy, sir, keep your dishonours to yourself!"

Simon was deadly pale. "I will be a kick-ball between you and the Duke no longer," he exclaimed. "Either come to an agreement, or come to a differ, and have it out among yourselves. But I will no longer fetch and carry, and get your contrary instructions, and be blamed by both. For if I were to tell you what I think of all your Hanover business it would make your head sing."

But Sheriff Erskine had preserved his temper, and now intervened smoothly. "And in the meantime," says he, "I think we should tell Mr. Balfour that his character for valour is quite established. He may sleep in peace. Until the date he was so good as to refer to it shall be put to the proof no more."

His coolness brought the others to their prudence; and they made haste, with a somewhat distracted civility, to pack me from the house.

CHAPTER IX.
THE HEATHER ON FIRE

When I left Prestongrange that afternoon I was for the first time angry. The Advocate had made a mock of me. He had pretended my testimony was to be received and myself respected; and in that very hour, not only was Simon practising against my life by the hands of the Highland soldier, but (as appeared from his own language) Prestongrange himself had some design in operation. I counted my enemies; Prestongrange with all the King's authority behind him; and the Duke with the power of the West Highlands; and the Lovat interest by their side to help them with so great a force in the north, and the whole clan of old Jacobite spies and traffickers. And when I remembered James More, and the red head of Neil the son of Duncan, I thought there was perhaps a fourth in the confederacy, and what remained of Rob Roy's old desperate sept of caterans would be banded against me with the others. One thing was requisite—some strong friend or wise adviser. The country must be full of such, both able and eager to support me, or Lovat and the Duke and Prestongrange had not been nosing for expedients; and it made me rage to think that I might brush against my champions in the street and be no wiser.

And just then (like an answer) a gentleman brushed against me going by, gave me a meaning look, and turned into a close. I knew him with the tail of my eye—it was Stewart the Writer; and, blessing my good fortune, turned in to follow him. As soon as I had entered the close I saw him standing in the mouth of a stair, where he made me a signal and immediately vanished. Seven storeys up, there he was again in a house door, the which he looked behind us after we had entered. The house was quite dismantled, with not a stick of furniture; indeed, it was one of which Stewart had the letting in his hands.

"We'll have to sit upon the floor," said he; "but we're safe here for the time being, and I've been wearying to see ye, Mr. Balfour."

"How's it with Alan?" I asked.

"Brawly," said he. "Andie picks him up at Gillane sands to-morrow, Wednesday. He was keen to say good-bye to ye, but the way that things were going, I was feared the pair of ye was maybe best apart. And that brings me to the essential: how does your business speed?"

"Why," said I, "I was told only this morning that my testimony was accepted, and I was to travel to Inverary with the Advocate, no less."

"Hout awa!" cried Stewart. "I'll never believe that."

"I have maybe a suspicion of my own," says I, "but I would like fine to hear your reasons."

"Well, I tell ye fairly, I'm horn-mad," cries Stewart. "If my one hand could pull their Government down I would pluck it like a rotten apple. I'm doer for Appin and for James of the Glens; and, of course, it's my duty to defend my kinsman for his life. Hear how it goes with me, and I'll leave the judgment of it to yourself. The first thing they have to do is to get rid of Alan. They cannae bring in James as art and part until they've brought in Alan first as principal; that's sound law: they could never put the cart before the horse."

"And how are they to bring in Alan till they can catch him?" says I.

"Ah, but there is a way to evite that arrestment," said he. "Sound law, too. It would be a bonny thing if, by the escape of one ill-doer another was to go scatheless, and the remeid is to summon the principal and put him to outlawry for the non-compearance. Now there's four places where a person can be summoned: at his dwelling-house; at a place where he has resided forty days; at the head burgh of the shire where he ordinarily resorts; or lastly (if there be ground to think him forth of Scotland) at the cross of Edinburgh, and the pier and shore of Leith, for sixty days. The purpose of which last provision is evident upon its face: being that outgoing ships may have time to carry news of the transaction, and the summonsing be something other than a form. Now take the case of Alan. He has no dwelling-house that ever I could hear of; I would be obliged if anyone would show me where he has lived forty days together since the '45; there is no shire where he resorts whether ordinarily or extraordinarily; if he has a domicile at all, which I misdoubt, it must be with his regiment in France; and if he is not yet forth of Scotland (as we happen to know and they happen to guess) it must be evident to the most dull it's what he's aiming for. Where, then, and what way should he be summoned? I ask it at yourself, a layman."

"You have given the very words," said I. "Here at the cross, and at the pier and shore of Leith, for sixty days."

"Ye're a sounder Scots lawyer than Prestongrange, then!" cries the Writer. "He has had Alan summoned once; that was on the twenty-fifth, the day that we first met. Once, and done with it. And where? Where, but at the cross of Inverary, the head burgh of the Campbells? A word in your ear, Mr. Balfour—they're not seeking Alan."

"What do you mean?" I cried. "Not seeking him?"

"By the best that I can make of it," said he. "Not wanting to find him, in my poor thought. They think perhaps he might set up a fair defence, upon the back of which James, the man they're really after, might climb out. This is not a case, ye see, it's a conspiracy."

"Yet I can tell you Prestongrange asked after Alan keenly," said I; "though, when I come to think of it, he was something of the easiest put by."

"See that!" says he. "But there! I may be right or wrong, that's guesswork at the best, and let me get to my facts again. It comes to my ears that James and the witnesses—the witnesses, Mr. Balfour!—lay in close dungeons, and shackled forbye, in the military prison at Fort William; none allowed in to them, nor they to write. The witnesses, Mr. Balfour; heard ye ever the match of that? I assure ye, no old, crooked Stewart of the gang ever out-faced the law more impudently. It's clean in the two eyes of the Act of Parliament of 1700, anent wrongous imprisonment. No sooner did I get the news than I petitioned the Lord Justice Clerk. I have his word to-day. There's law for ye! here's justice!"

He put a paper in my hand, that same mealy-mouthed, false-faced paper that was printed since in the pamphlet "by a bystander," for behoof (as the title says) of James's "poor widow and five children."

"See," said Stewart, "he couldn't dare to refuse me access to my client, so he recommends the commanding officer to let me in. Recommends!—the Lord Justice Clerk of Scotland recommends. Is not the purpose of such language plain? They hope the officer may be so dull, or so very much the reverse, as to refuse the recommendation. I would have to make the journey back again betwixt here and Fort William. Then would follow a fresh delay till I got fresh authority, and they had disavowed the officer—military man, notoriously ignorant of the law, and that—I ken the cant of it. Then the journey a third time; and there we should be on the immediate heels of the trial before I had received my first instruction. Am I not right to call this a conspiracy?"

"It will bear that colour," said I.

"And I'll go on to prove it you outright," said he. "They have the right to hold James in prison, yet they cannot deny me to visit him. They have no right to hold the witnesses; but am I to get a sight of them, that should be as free as the Lord Justice Clerk himself! See—read: For the rest, refuses to give any orders to keepers of prisons who are not accused as having done anything contrary to the duties of their office. Anything contrary! Sirs! And the Act of seventeen hunner? Mr. Balfour, this makes my heart to burst; the heather is on fire inside my wame."

"And the plain English of that phrase," said I, "is that the witnesses are still to lie in prison and you are not to see them?"

"And I am not to see them until Inverary, when the court is set!" cries he, "and then to hear Prestongrange upon the anxious responsibilities of his office and the great facilities afforded the defence! But I'll begowk them there, Mr. David. I have a plan to waylay the witnesses upon the road, and see if I cannae get I a little harle of justice out of the military man notoriously ignorant of the law that shall command the party."

It was actually so—it was actually on the wayside near Tynedrum, and by the connivance of a soldier officer, that Mr. Stewart first saw the witnesses upon the case.

"There is nothing that would surprise me in this business," I remarked.

"I'll surprise you ere I'm done!" cries he. "Do ye see this?"—producing a print still wet from the press. "This is the libel: see, there's Prestongrange's name to the list of witnesses, and I find no word of any Balfour. But here is not the question. Who do ye think paid for the printing of this paper?"

"I suppose it would likely be King George," said I.

"But it happens it was me!" he cried. "Not but it was printed by and for themselves, for the Grants and the Erskines, and yon thief of the black midnight, Simon Fraser. But could I win to get a copy! No! I was to go blindfold to my defence; I was to hear the charges for the first time in court alongst the jury."

"Is not this against the law?" I asked.

"I cannot say so much," he replied. "It was a favour so natural and so constantly rendered (till this nonesuch business) that the law has never looked to it. And now admire the hand of Providence! A stranger is in Fleming's printing house, spies a proof on the floor, picks it up, and carries it to me. Of all things, it was just this libel. Whereupon I had it set again—printed at the expense of the defence: sumptibus moesti rei; heard ever man the like of it?—and here it is for anybody, the muckle secret out—all may see it now. But how do you think I would enjoy this, that has the life of my kinsman on my conscience?"

"Troth, I think you would enjoy it ill," said I.

"And now you see how it is," he concluded, "and why, when you tell me your evidence is to be let in, I laugh aloud in your face."

It was now my turn. I laid before him in brief Mr. Simon's threats and offers, and the whole incident of the bravo, with the subsequent scene at Prestongrange's. Of my first talk, according to promise, I said nothing, nor indeed was it necessary. All the time I was talking Stewart nodded his head like a mechanical figure; and no sooner had my voice ceased, than he opened his mouth and gave me his opinion in two words, dwelling strong on both of them.

"Disappear yourself," said he.

"I do not take you," said I.

"Then I'll carry you there," said he. "By my view of it you're to disappear whatever. O, that's outside debate. The Advocate, who is not without some spunks of a remainder decency, has wrung your life-safe out of Simon and the Duke. He has refused to put you on your trial, and refused to have you killed; and there is the clue to their ill words together, for Simon and the Duke can keep faith with neither friend nor enemy. Ye're not to be tried then, and ye're not to be murdered; but I'm in bitter error if ye're not to be kidnapped and carried away like the Lady Grange. Bet me what ye please—there was their expedient!"

"You make me think," said I, and told him of the whistle and the red-headed retainer, Neil.

"Wherever James More is there's one big rogue, never be deceived on that," said he. "His father was none so ill a man, though a kenning on the wrong side of the law, and no friend to my family, that I should waste my breath to be defending him! But as for James he's a brock and a blagyard. I like the appearance of this red-headed Neil as little as yourself. It looks uncanny: fiegh! it smells bad. It was old Lovat that managed the Lady Grange affair; if young Lovat is to handle yours, it'll be all in the family. What's James More in prison for? The same offence: abduction. His men have had practice in the business. He'll be to lend them to be Simon's instruments; and the next thing we'll be hearing, James will have made his peace, or else he'll have escaped; and you'll be in Benbecula or Applecross."

"Ye make a strong case," I admitted.

"And what I want," he resumed, "is that you should disappear yourself ere they can get their hands upon ye. Lie quiet until just before the trial, and spring upon them at the last of it when they'll be looking for you least. This is always supposing Mr. Balfour, that your evidence is worth so very great a measure of both risk and fash."

"I will tell you one thing," said I. "I saw the murderer and it was not Alan."

"Then, by God, my cousin's saved!" cried Stewart. "You have his life upon your tongue; and there's neither time, risk, nor money to be spared to bring you to the trial." He emptied his pockets on the floor. "Here is all that I have by me," he went on, "Take it, ye'll want it ere ye're through. Go straight down this close, there's a way out by there to the Lang Dykes, and by my will of it! see no more of Edinburgh till the clash is over."

"Where am I to go, then?" I inquired.

"And I wish that I could tell ye!" says he, "but all the places that I could send ye to, would be just the places they would seek. No, ye must fend for yourself, and God be your guiding! Five days before the trial, September the sixteen, get word to me at the King's Arms in Stirling; and if ye've managed for yourself as long as that, I'll see that ye reach Inverary."

"One thing more," said I. "Can I no see Alan?"

He seemed boggled. "Hech, I would rather you wouldnae," said he. "But I can never deny that Alan is extremely keen of it, and is to lie this night by Silvermills on purpose. If you're sure that you're not followed, Mr. Balfour—but make sure of that—lie in a good place and watch your road for a clear hour before ye risk it. It would be a dreadful business if both you and him was to miscarry!"

CHAPTER X.
THE RED-HEADED MAN

It was about half-past three when I came forth on the Lang Dykes. Dean was where I wanted to go. Since Catriona dwelled there, and her kinsfolk the Glengyle Macgregors appeared almost certainly to be employed against me, it was just one of the few places I should have kept away from; and being a very young man, and beginning to be very much in love, I turned my face in that direction without pause. As a slave to my conscience and common sense, however, I took a measure of precaution. Coming over the crown of a bit of a rise in the road, I clapped down suddenly among the barley and lay waiting. After a while, a man went by that looked to be a Highlandman, but I had never seen him till that hour. Presently after came Neil of the red head. The next to go past was a miller's cart, and after that nothing but manifest country people. Here was enough to have turned the most foolhardy from his purpose, but my inclination ran too strong the other way. I argued it out that if Neil was on that road, it was the right road to find him in, leading direct to his chief's daughter; as for the other Highlandman, if I was to be startled off by every Highlandman I saw, I would scarce reach anywhere. And having quite satisfied myself with this disingenuous debate, I made the better speed of it, and came a little after four to Mrs. Drumond-Ogilvy's.

Both ladies were within the house; and upon my perceiving them together by the open door, I plucked off my hat and said, "Here was a lad come seeking saxpence," which I thought might please the dowager.

Catriona ran out to greet me heartily, and, to my surprise, the old lady seemed scarce less forward than herself. I learned long afterwards that she had despatched a horseman by daylight to Rankeillor at the Queensferry, whom she knew to be the doer for Shaws, and had then in her pocket a letter from that good friend of mine, presenting, in the most favourable view, my character and prospects. But had I read it I could scarce have seen more clear in her designs. Maybe I was countryfeed; at least, I was not so much so as she thought; and it was even to my homespun wits, that she was bent to hammer up a match between her cousin and a beardless boy that was something of a laird in Lothian.

"Saxpence had better take his broth with us, Catrine," says she. "Run and tell the lasses."

And for the little while we were alone was at a good deal of pains to flatter me; always cleverly, always with the appearance of a banter, still calling me Saxpence, but with such a turn that should rather uplift me in my own opinion. When Catriona returned, the design became if possible more obvious; and she showed off the girl's advantages like a horse-couper with a horse. My face flamed that she should think me so obtuse. Now I would fancy the girl was being innocently made a show of, and then I could have beaten the old carline wife with a cudgel; and now, that perhaps these two had set their heads together to entrap me, and at that I sat and gloomed betwixt them like the very image of ill-will. At last the matchmaker had a better device, which was to leave the pair of us alone. When my suspicions are anyway roused it is sometimes a little the wrong side of easy to allay them. But though I knew what breed she was of, and that was a breed of thieves, I could never look in Catriona's face and disbelieve her.

"I must not ask?" says she, eagerly, the same moment we were left alone.

"Ah, but to-day I can talk with a free conscience," I replied. "I am lightened of my pledge, and indeed (after what has come and gone since morning) I would not have renewed it were it asked."

"Tell me," she said. "My cousin will not be so long."

So I told her the tale of the lieutenant from the first step to the last of it, making it as mirthful as I could, and, indeed, there was matter of mirth in that absurdity.

"And I think you will be as little fitted for the rudas men as for the pretty ladies, after all!" says she, when I had done. "But what was your father that he could not learn you to draw the sword! It is most ungentle; I have not heard the match of that in anyone."

"It is most misconvenient at least," said I; "and I think my father (honest man!) must have been wool-gathering to learn me Latin in the place of it. But you see I do the best I can, and just stand up like Lot's wife and let them hammer at me."

"Do you know what makes me smile?" said she. "Well, it is this. I am made this way, that I should have been a man child. In my own thoughts it is so I am always; and I go on telling myself about this thing that is to befall and that. Then it comes to the place of the fighting, and it comes over me that I am only a girl at all events, and cannot hold a sword or give one good blow; and then I have to twist my story round about, so that the fighting is to stop, and yet me have the best of it, just like you and the lieutenant; and I am the boy that makes the fine speeches all through, like Mr. David Balfour."

"You are a bloodthirsty maid," said I.

"Well, I know it is good to sew and spin, and to make samplers," she said, "but if you were to do nothing else in the great world, I think you will say yourself it is a driech business; and it is not that I want to kill, I think. Did ever you kill anyone?"

"That I have, as it chances. Two, no less, and me still a lad that should be at the college," said I. "But yet, in the look-back, I take no shame for it."

"But how did you feel, then—after it?" she asked.

"'Deed, I sat down and grat like a bairn," said I.

"I know that, too," she cried. "I feel where these tears should come from. And at any rate, I would not wish to kill, only to be Catherine Douglas that put her arm through the staples of the bolt, where it was broken. That is my chief hero. Would you not love to die so—for your king?" she asked.

"Troth," said I, "my affection for my king, God bless the puggy face of him, is under more control; and I thought I saw death so near to me this day already, that I am rather taken up with the notion of living."

"Right," she said, "the right mind of a man! Only you must learn arms; I would not like to have a friend that cannot strike. But it will not have been with the sword that you killed these two?"

"Indeed, no," said I, "but with a pair of pistols. And a fortunate thing it was the men were so near-hand to me, for I am about as clever with the pistols as I am with the sword."

So then she drew from me the story of our battle in the brig, which I had omitted in my first account of my affairs.

"Yes," said she, "you are brave. And your friend, I admire and love him."

"Well, and I think anyone would!" said I. "He has his faults like other folk; but he is brave and staunch and kind, God bless him! That will be a strange day when I forget Alan." And the thought of him, and that it was within my choice to speak with him that night, had almost overcome me.

"And where will my head be gone that I have not told my news!" she cried, and spoke of a letter from her father, bearing that she might visit him to-morrow in the castle whither he was now transferred, and that his affairs were mending. "You do not like to hear it," said she. "Will you judge my father and not know him?"

"I am a thousand miles from judging," I replied. "And I give you my word I do rejoice to know your heart is lightened. If my face fell at all, as I suppose it must, you will allow this is rather an ill day for compositions, and the people in power extremely ill persons to be compounding with. I have Simon Fraser extremely heavy on my stomach still."

"Ah!" she cried, "you will not be evening these two; and you should bear in mind that Prestongrange and James More, my father, are of the one blood."

"I never heard tell of that," said I.

"It is rather singular how little you are acquainted with," said she. "One part may call themselves Grant, and one Macgregor, but they are still of the same clan. They are all the sons of Alpin, from whom, I think, our country has its name."

"What country is that?" I asked.

"My country and yours," said she.

"This is my day for discovering I think," said I, "for I always thought the name of it was Scotland."

"Scotland is the name of what you call Ireland," she replied. "But the old ancient true name of this place that we have our foot-soles on, and that our bones are made of, will be Alban. It was Alban they called it when our forefathers will be fighting for it against Rome and Alexander; and it is called so still in your own tongue that you forget."

"Troth," said I, "and that I never learned!" For I lacked heart to take her up about the Macedonian.

"But your fathers and mothers talked it, one generation with another," said she. "And it was sung about the cradles before you or me were ever dreamed of; and your name remembers it still. Ah, if you could talk that language you would find me another girl. The heart speaks in that tongue."

I had a meal with the two ladies, all very good, served in fine old plate, and the wine excellent, for it seems that Mrs. Ogilvy was rich. Our talk, too, was pleasant enough; but as soon as I saw the sun decline sharply and the shadows to run out long, I rose to take my leave. For my mind was now made up to say farewell to Alan; and it was needful I should see the trysting wood, and reconnoitre it, by daylight. Catriona came with me as far as to the garden gate.

"It is long till I see you now?" she asked.

"It is beyond my judging," I replied. "It will be long, it may be never."

"It may be so," said she. "And you are sorry?"

I bowed my head, looking upon her.

"So am I, at all events," said she. "I have seen you but a small time, but I put you very high. You are true, you are brave; in time I think you will be more of a man yet. I will be proud to hear of that. If you should speed worse, if it will come to fall as we are afraid—O well! think you have the one friend. Long after you are dead and me an old wife, I will be telling the bairns about David Balfour, and my tears running. I will be telling how we parted, and what I said to you, and did to you. God go with you and guide you, prays your little friend: so I said—I will be telling them—and here is what I did."

She took up my hand and kissed it. This so surprised my spirits that I cried out like one hurt. The colour came strong in her face, and she looked at me and nodded.

"O yes, Mr. David," said she, "that is what I think of you. The head goes with the lips."

I could read in her face high spirit, and a chivalry like a brave child's; not anything besides. She kissed my hand, as she had kissed Prince Charlie's, with a higher passion than the common kind of clay has any sense of. Nothing before had taught me how deep I was her lover, nor how far I had yet to climb to make her think of me in such a character. Yet I could tell myself I had advanced some way, and that her heart had beat and her blood flowed at thoughts of me.

After that honour she had done me I could offer no more trivial civility. It was even hard for me to speak; a certain lifting in her voice had knocked directly at the door of my own tears.

"I praise God for your kindness, dear," said I. "Farewell, my little friend!" giving her that name which she had given to herself; with which I bowed and left her.

My way was down the glen of the Leith River, towards Stockbridge and Silvermills. A path led in the foot of it, the water bickered and sang in the midst; the sunbeams overhead struck out of the west among long shadows and (as the valley turned) made like a new scene and a new world of it at every corner. With Catriona behind and Alan before me, I was like one lifted up. The place besides, and the hour, and the talking of the water, infinitely pleased me; and I lingered in my steps and looked before and behind me as I went. This was the cause, under Providence, that I spied a little in my rear a red head among some bushes.

Anger sprang in my heart, and I turned straight about and walked at a stiff pace to where I came from. The path lay close by the bushes where I had remarked the head. The cover came to the wayside, and as I passed I was all strung up to meet and to resist an onfall. No such thing befell, I went by unmeddled with; and at that fear increased upon me. It was still day indeed, but the place exceeding solitary. If my haunters had let slip that fair occasion I could but judge they aimed at something more than David Balfour. The lives of Alan and James weighed upon my spirit with the weight of two grown bullocks.

Catriona was yet in the garden walking by herself.

"Catriona," said I, "you see me back again."

"With a changed face," said she.

"I carry two men's lives besides my own," said I. "It would be a sin and shame not to walk carefully. I was doubtful whether I did right to come here. I would like it ill, if it was by that means we were brought to harm."

"I could tell you one that would be liking it less, and will like little enough to hear you talking at this very same time," she cried. "What have I done, at all events?"

"O, you I you are not alone," I replied. "But since I went off I have been dogged again, and I can give you the name of him that follows me. It is Neil, son of Duncan, your man or your father's."

"To be sure you are mistaken there," she said, with a white face. "Neil is in Edinburgh on errands from my father."

"It is what I fear," said I, "the last of it. But for his being in Edinburgh I think I can show you another of that. For sure you have some signal, a signal of need, such as would bring him to your help, if he was anywhere within the reach of ears and legs?"

"Why, how will you know that?" says she.

"By means of a magical talisman God gave to me when I was born, and the name they call it by is Common-sense," said I. "Oblige me so far as make your signal, and I will show you the red head of Neil."

No doubt but I spoke bitter and sharp. My heart was bitter. I blamed myself and the girl and hated both of us: her for the vile crew that she was come of, myself for my wanton folly to have stuck my head in such a byke of wasps.

Catriona set her fingers to her lips and whistled once, with an exceeding clear, strong, mounting note, as full as a ploughman's. A while we stood silent; and I was about to ask her to repeat the same, when I heard the sound of some one bursting through the bushes below on the braeside. I pointed in that direction with a smile, and presently Neil leaped into the garden. His eyes burned, and he had a black knife (as they call it on the Highland side) naked in his hand; but, seeing me beside his mistress, stood like a man struck.

"He has come to your call," said I; "judge how near he was to Edinburgh, or what was the nature of your father's errands. Ask himself. If I am to lose my life, or the lives of those that hang by me, through the means of your clan, let me go where I have to go with my eyes open."

She addressed him tremulously in the Gaelic. Remembering Alan's anxious civility in that particular, I could have laughed out loud for bitterness; here, sure, in the midst of these suspicions, was the hour she should have stuck by English.

Twice or thrice they spoke together, and I could make out that Neil (for all his obsequiousness) was an angry man.

Then she turned to me. "He swears it is not," she said.

"Catriona," said I, "do you believe the man yourself?"

She made a gesture like wringing the hands.

"How will I can know?" she cried.

"But I must find some means to know," said I. "I cannot continue to go dovering round in the black night with two men's lives at my girdle! Catriona, try to put yourself in my place, as I vow to God I try hard to put myself in yours. This is no kind of talk that should ever have fallen between me and you; no kind of talk; my heart is sick with it. See, keep him here till two of the morning, and I care not. Try him with that."

They spoke together once more in the Gaelic.

"He says he has James More my father's errand," said she. She was whiter than ever, and her voice faltered as she said it.

"It is pretty plain now," said I, "and may God forgive the wicked!"

She said never anything to that, but continued gazing at me with the same white face.

"This is a fine business," said I again. "Am I to fall, then, and those two along with me?"

"O, what am I to do?" she cried. "Could I go against my father's orders, him in prison, in the danger of his life!"

"But perhaps we go too fast," said I. "This may be a lie too. He may have no right orders; all may be contrived by Simon, and your father knowing nothing."

She burst out weeping between the pair of us; and my heart smote me hard, for I thought this girl was in a dreadful situation.

"Here," said I, "keep him but the one hour; and I'll chance it, and may God bless you."

She put out her hand to me, "I will he needing one good word," she sobbed.

"The full hour, then?" said I, keeping her hand in mine. "Three lives of it, my lass!"

"The full hour!" she said, and cried aloud on her Redeemer to forgive her.

I thought it no fit place for me, and fled.

CHAPTER XI.
THE WOOD BY SILVERMILLS

I lost no time, but down through the valley and by Stockbridge and Silvermills as hard as I could stave. It was Alan's tryst to be every night between twelve and two "in a bit scrog of wood by east of Silvermills and by south the south mill-lade." This I found easy enough, where it grew on a steep brae, with the mill-lade flowing swift and deep along the foot of it; and here I began to walk slower and to reflect more reasonably on my employment. I saw I had made but a fool's bargain with Catriona. It was not to be supposed that Neil was sent alone upon his errand, but perhaps he was the only man belonging to James More; in which case I should have done all I could to hang Catriona's father, and nothing the least material to help myself. To tell the truth, I fancied neither one of these ideas. Suppose by holding back Neil, the girl should have helped to hang her father, I thought she would never forgive herself this side of time. And suppose there were others pursuing me that moment, what kind of a gift was I come bringing to Alan? and how would I like that?

I was up with the west end of that wood when these two considerations struck me like a cudgel. My feet stopped of themselves and my heart along with them. "What wild game is this that I have been playing?" thought I; and turned instantly upon my heels to go elsewhere.

This brought my face to Silvermills; the path came past the village with a crook, but all plainly visible; and, Highland or Lowland, there was nobody stirring. Here was my advantage, here was just such a conjuncture as Stewart had counselled me to profit by, and I ran by the side of the mill-lade, fetched about beyond the east corner of the wood, threaded through the midst of it, and returned to the west selvage, whence I could again command the path, and yet be myself unseen. Again it was all empty, and my heart began to rise.

For more than an hour I sat close in the border of the trees, and no hare or eagle could have kept a more particular watch. When that hour began the sun was already set, but the sky still all golden and the daylight clear; before the hour was done it had fallen to be half mirk, the images and distances of things were mingled, and observation began to be difficult. All that time not a foot of man had come east from Silvermills, and the few that had gone west were honest countryfolk and their wives upon the road to bed. If I were tracked by the most cunning spies in Europe, I judged it was beyond the course of nature they could have any jealousy of where I was: and going a little further home into the wood I lay down to wait for Alan.

The strain of my attention had been great, for I had watched not the path only, but every bush and field within my vision. That was now at an end. The moon, which was in her first quarter, glinted a little in the wood; all round there was a stillness of the country; and as I lay there on my back, the next three or four hours, I had a fine occasion to review my conduct.

Two things became plain to me first: that I had no right to go that day to Dean, and (having gone there) had now no right to be lying where I was. This (where Alan was to come) was just the one wood in all broad Scotland that was, by every proper feeling, closed against me; I admitted that, and yet stayed on, wondering at myself. I thought of the measure with which I had meted to Catriona that same night; how I had prated of the two lives I carried, and had thus forced her to enjeopardy her father's; and how I was here exposing them again, it seemed in wantonness. A good conscience is eight parts of courage. No sooner had I lost conceit of my behaviour, than I seemed to stand disarmed amidst a throng of terrors. Of a sudden I sat up. How if I went now to Prestongrange, caught him (as I still easily might) before he slept, and made a full submission? Who could blame me? Not Stewart the Writer; I had but to say that I was followed, despaired of getting clear, and so gave in. Not Catriona: here, too, I had my answer ready; that I could not bear she should expose her father. So, in a moment, I could lay all these troubles by, which were after all and truly none of mine; swim clear of the Appin Murder; get forth out of hand-stroke of all the Stewarts and Campbells, all the Whigs and Tories, in the land; and live henceforth to my own mind, and be able to enjoy and to improve my fortunes, and devote some hours of my youth to courting Catriona, which would be surely a more suitable occupation than to hide and run and be followed like a hunted thief, and begin over again the dreadful miseries of my escape with Alan.

At first I thought no shame of this capitulation; I was only amazed I had not thought upon the thing and done it earlier; and began to inquire into the causes of the change. These I traced to my lowness of spirits, that back to my late recklessness, and that again to the common, old, public, disconsidered sin of self-indulgence. Instantly the text came in my head, "How can Satan cast out Satan?" What? (I thought) I had, by self-indulgence; and the following of pleasant paths, and the lure of a young maid, cast myself wholly out of conceit with my own character, and jeopardised the lives of James and Alan? And I was to seek the way out by the same road as I had entered in? No; the hurt that had been caused by self-indulgence must be cured by self-denial; the flesh I had pampered must be crucified. I looked about me for that course which I least liked to follow: this was to leave the wood without waiting to see Alan, and go forth again alone, in the dark and in the midst of my perplexed and dangerous fortunes.

I have been the more careful to narrate this passage of my reflections, because I think it is of some utility, and may serve as an example to young men. But there is reason (they say) in planting kale, and even in ethic and religion, room for common sense. It was already close on Alan's hour, and the moon was down. If I left (as I could not very decently whistle to my spies to follow me) they might miss me in the dark and tack themselves to Alan by mistake. If I stayed, I could at the least of it set my friend upon his guard which might prove his mere salvation. I had adventured other peoples' safety in a course of self-indulgence; to have endangered them again, and now on a mere design of penance, would have been scarce rational. Accordingly, I had scarce risen from my place ere I sat down again, but already in a different frame of spirits, and equally marvelling at my past weakness and rejoicing in my present composure.

Presently after came a crackling in the thicket. Putting my mouth near down to the ground, I whistled a note or two, of Alan's air; an answer came in the like guarded tone, and soon we had knocked together in the dark.

"Is this you at last, Davie?" he whispered.

"Just myself," said I.

"God, man, but I've been wearying to see ye!" says he. "I've had the longest kind of a time. A' day, I've had my dwelling into the inside of a stack of hay, where I couldnae see the nebs of my ten fingers; and then two hours of it waiting here for you, and you never coming! Dod, and ye're none too soon the way it is, with me to sail the morn! The morn? what am I saying?—the day, I mean."

"Ay, Alan, man, the day, sure enough," said I. "It's past twelve now, surely, and ye sail the day. This'll be a long road you have before you."

"We'll have a long crack of it first," said he.

"Well, indeed, and I have a good deal it will be telling you to hear," said I.

And I told him what behooved, making rather a jumble of it, but clear enough when done. He heard me out with very few questions, laughing here and there like a man delighted: and the sound of his laughing (above all there, in the dark, where neither one of us could see the other) was extraordinary friendly to my heart.

"Ay, Davie, ye're a queer character," says he, when I had done: "a queer bitch after a', and I have no mind of meeting with the like of ye. As for your story, Prestongrange is a Whig like yoursel', so I'll say the less of him; and, dod! I believe he was the best friend ye had, if ye could only trust him. But Simon Fraser and James More are my ain kind of cattle, and I'll give them the name that they deserve. The muckle black deil was father to the Frasers, a'body kens that; and as for the Gregara, I never could abye the reek of them since I could stotter on two feet. I bloodied the nose of one, I mind, when I was still so wambly on my legs that I cowped upon the top of him. A proud man was my father that day, God rest him! and I think he had the cause. I'll never can deny but what Robin was something of a piper," he added; "but as for James More, the deil guide him for me!"

"One thing we have to consider," said I. "Was Charles Stewart right or wrong? Is it only me they're after, or the pair of us?"

"And what's your ain opinion, you that's a man of so much experience?" said he.

"It passes me," said I.

"And me too," says Alan. "Do ye think this lass would keep her word to ye?" he asked.

"I do that," said I.

"Well, there's nae telling," said he. "And anyway, that's over and done: he'll be joined to the rest of them lang syne."

"How many would ye think there would be of them?" I asked.

"That depends," said Alan. "If it was only you, they would likely send two-three lively, brisk young birkies, and if they thought that I was to appear in the employ, I daresay ten or twelve," said he.

It was no use, I gave a little crack of laughter.

"And I think your own two eyes will have seen me drive that number, or the double of it, nearer hand!" cries he.

"It matters the less," said I, "because I am well rid of them for this time."

"Nae doubt that's your opinion," said he; "but I wouldnae be the least surprised if they were hunkering this wood. Ye see, David man; they'll be Hieland folk. There'll be some Frasers, I'm thinking, and some of the Gregara; and I would never deny but what the both of them, and the Gregara in especial, were clever experienced persons. A man kens little till he's driven a spreagh of neat cattle (say) ten miles through a throng lowland country and the black soldiers maybe at his tail. It's there that I learned a great part of my penetration. And ye need nae tell me: it's better than war; which is the next best, however, though generally rather a bauchle of a business. Now the Gregara have had grand practice."

"No doubt that's a branch of education that was left out with me," said I.

"And I can see the marks of it upon ye constantly," said Alan. "But that's the strange thing about you folk of the college learning: ye're ignorat, and ye cannae see 't. Wae's me for my Greek and Hebrew; but, man, I ken that I dinnae ken them—there's the differ of it. Now, here's you. Ye lie on your wame a bittie in the bield of this wood, and ye tell me that ye've cuist off these Frasers and Macgregors. Why? Because I couldnae see them, says you. Ye blockhead, that's their livelihood."

"Take the worst of it," said I, "and what are we to do?"

"I am thinking of that same," said he. "We might twine. It wouldnae be greatly to my taste; and forbye that, I see reasons against it. First, it's now unco dark, and it's just humanly possible we might give them the clean slip. If we keep together, we make but the ae line of it; if we gang separate, we make twae of them: the more likelihood to stave in upon some of these gentry of yours. And then, second, if they keep the track of us, it may come to a fecht for it yet, Davie; and then, I'll confess I would be blythe to have you at my oxter, and I think you would be none the worse of having me at yours. So, by my way of it, we should creep out of this wood no further gone than just the inside of next minute, and hold away east for Gillane, where I'm to find my ship. It'll be like old days while it lasts, Davie; and (come the time) we'll have to think what you should be doing. I'm wae to leave ye here, wanting me."

"Have with ye, then!" says I. "Do ye gang back where you were stopping?"

"Deil a fear!" said Alan. "They were good folks to me, but I think they would be a good deal disappointed if they saw my bonny face again. For (the way times go) I am nae just what ye could call a Walcome Guest. Which makes me the keener for your company, Mr. David Balfour of the Shaws, and set ye up! For, leave aside twa cracks here in the wood with Charlie Stewart, I have scarce said black or white since the day we parted at Corstorphine."

With which he rose from his place, and we began to move quietly eastward through the wood.

CHAPTER XII.
ON THE MARCH AGAIN WITH ALAN

It was likely between one and two; the moon (as I have said) was down; a strongish wind, carrying a heavy wrack of cloud, had set in suddenly from the west; and we began our movement in as black a night as ever a fugitive or a murderer wanted. The whiteness of the path guided us into the sleeping town of Broughton, thence through Picardy, and beside my old acquaintance the gibbet of the two thieves. A little beyond we made a useful beacon, which was a light in an upper window of Lochend. Steering by this, but a good deal at random, and with some trampling of the harvest, and stumbling and falling down upon the banks, we made our way across country, and won forth at last upon the linky, boggy muirland that they call the Figgate Whins. Here, under a bush of whin, we lay down the remainder of that night and slumbered.

The day called us about five. A beautiful morning it was, the high westerly wind still blowing strong, but the clouds all blown away to Europe. Alan was already sitting up and smiling to himself. It was my first sight of my friend since we were parted, and I looked upon him with enjoyment. He had still the same big great-coat on his back; but (what was new) he had now a pair of knitted boot-hose drawn above the knee. Doubtless these were intended for disguise; but, as the day promised to be warm, he made a most unseasonable figure.

"Well, Davie," said he, "is this no a bonny morning? Here is a day that looks the way that a day ought to. This is a great change of it from the belly of my haystack; and while you were there sottering and sleeping I have done a thing that maybe I do very seldom."

"And what was that?" said I.

"O, just said my prayers," said he.

"And where are my gentry, as ye call them?" I asked.

"Gude kens," says he; "and the short and the long of it is that we must take our chance of them. Up with your foot-soles, Davie! Forth, Fortune, once again of it! And a bonny walk we are like to have."

So we went east by the beach of the sea, towards where the salt-pans were smoking in by the Esk mouth. No doubt there was a by-ordinary bonny blink of morning sun on Arthur's Seat and the green Pentlands; and the pleasantness of the day appeared to set Alan among nettles.

"I feel like a gomeral," says he, "to be leaving Scotland on a day like this. It sticks in my head; I would maybe like it better to stay here and hing."

"Ay, but ye wouldnae, Alan," said I.

"No, but what France is a good place too," he explained; "but it's some way no the same. It's brawer I believe, but it's no Scotland. I like it fine when I'm there, man; yet I kind of weary for Scots divots and the Scots peat-reek."

"If that's all you have to complain of, Alan, it's no such great affair," said I.

"And it sets me ill to be complaining, whatever," said he, "and me but new out of yon deil's haystack."

"And so you were unco weary of your haystack?" I asked.

"Weary's nae word for it," said he. "I'm not just precisely a man that's easily cast down; but I do better with caller air and the lift above my head. I'm like the auld Black Douglas (wasnae't?) that likit better to hear the laverock sing than the mouse cheep. And yon place, ye see, Davie—whilk was a very suitable place to hide in, as I'm free to own—was pit mirk from dawn to gloaming. There were days (or nights, for how would I tell one from other?) that seemed to me as long as a long winter."

"How did you know the hour to bide your tryst?" I asked.

"The goodman brought me my meat and a drop brandy, and a candle-dowp to eat it by, about eleeven," said he. "So, when I had swallowed a bit, it would he time to be getting to the wood. There I lay and wearied for ye sore, Davie," says he, laying his hand on my shoulder "and guessed when the two hours would be about by—unless Charlie Stewart would come and tell me on his watch—and then back to the dooms haystack. Na, it was a driech employ, and praise the Lord that I have warstled through with it!"

"What did you do with yourself?" I asked.

"Faith," said he, "the best I could! Whiles I played at the knucklebones. I'm an extraordinar good hand at the knucklebones, but it's a poor piece of business playing with naebody to admire ye. And whiles I would make songs."

"What were they about?" says I.

"O, about the deer and the heather," says he, "and about the ancient old chiefs that are all by with it lang syne, and just about what songs are about in general. And then whiles I would make believe I had a set of pipes and I was playing. I played some grand springs, and I thought I played them awful bonny; I vow whiles that I could hear the squeal of them! But the great affair is that it's done with."

With that he carried me again to my adventures, which he heard all over again with more particularity, and extraordinary approval, swearing at intervals that I was "a queer character of a callant."

"So ye were frich'ened of Sim Fraser?" he asked once.

"In troth was I!" cried I.

"So would I have been, Davie," said he. "And that is indeed a driedful man. But it is only proper to give the deil his due: and I can tell you he is a most respectable person on the field of war."

"Is he so brave?" I asked.

"Brave!" said he. "He is as brave as my steel sword."

The story of my duel set him beside himself.

"To think of that!" he cried. "I showed ye the trick in Corrynakiegh too. And three times—three times disarmed! It's a disgrace upon my character that learned ye! Here, stand up, out with your airn; ye shall walk no step beyond this place upon the road till ye can do yoursel' and me mair credit."

"Alan," said I, "this is midsummer madness. Here is no time for fencing lessons."

"I cannae well say no to that," he admitted. "But three times, man! And you standing there like a straw bogle and rinning to fetch your ain sword like a doggie with a pocket-napkin! David, this man Duncansby must be something altogether by-ordinar! He maun be extraordinar skilly. If I had the time, I would gang straight back and try a turn at him mysel'. The man must be a provost."

"You silly fellow," said I, "you forget it was just me."

"Na," said he, "but three times!"

"When ye ken yourself that I am fair incompetent," I cried.

"Well, I never heard tell the equal of it," said he.

"I promise you the one thing, Alan," said I. "The next time that we forgather, I'll be better learned. You shall not continue to bear the disgrace of a friend that cannot strike."

"Ay, the next time!" says he. "And when will that be, I would like to ken?"

"Well, Alan, I have had some thoughts of that, too," said I; "and my plan is this. It's my opinion to be called an advocate."

"That's but a weary trade, Davie," says Alan, "and rather a blagyard one forby. Ye would be better in a king's coat than that."

"And no doubt that would be the way to have us meet," cried I. "But as you'll be in King Lewie's coat, and I'll be in King Geordie's, we'll have a dainty meeting of it."

"There's some sense in that," he admitted.

"An advocate, then, it'll have to be," I continued, "and I think it a more suitable trade for a gentleman that was three times disarmed. But the beauty of the thing is this: that one of the best colleges for that kind of learning—and the one where my kinsman, Pilrig, made his studies—is the college of Leyden in Holland. Now, what say you, Alan? Could not a cadet of Royal Ecossais get a furlough, slip over the marches, and call in upon a Leyden student?"

"Well, and I would think he could!" cried he. "Ye see, I stand well in with my colonel, Count Drummond-Melfort; and, what's mair to the purpose I have a cousin of mine lieutenant-colonel in a regiment of the Scots-Dutch. Naething could be mair proper than what I would get a leave to see Lieutenant-Colonel Stewart of Halkett's. And Lord Melfort, who is a very scienteefic kind of a man, and writes books like Cæsar, would be doubtless very pleased to have the advantage of my observes."

"Is Lord Meloort an author, then?" I asked, for much as Alan thought of soldiers, I thought more of the gentry that write books.

"The very same, Davie," said he. "One would think a colonel would have something better to attend to. But what can I say that make songs?"

"Well, then," said I, "it only remains you should give me an address to write you at in France; and as soon as I am got to Leyden I will send you mine."

"The best will be to write me in the care of my chieftain," said he, "Charles Stewart, of Ardsheil, Esquire, at the town of Melons, in the Isle of France. It might take long, or it might take short, but it would aye get to my hands at the last of it."

We had a haddock to our breakfast in Musselburgh, where it amused me vastly to hear Alan. His great-coat and boot-hose were extremely remarkable this warm morning, and perhaps some hint of an explanation had been wise; but Alan went into that matter like a business, or I should rather say, like a diversion. He engaged the goodwife of the house with some compliments upon the rizzoring of our haddocks; and the whole of the rest of our stay held her in talk about a cold he had taken on his stomach, gravely relating all manner of symptoms and sufferings, and hearing with a vast show of interest all the old wives' remedies she could supply him with in return.

We left Musselburgh before the first ninepenny coach was due from Edinburgh for (as Alan said) that was a rencounter we might very well avoid. The wind although still high, was very mild, the sun shone strong, and Alan began to suffer in proportion. From Prestonpans he had me aside to the field of Gladsmuir, where he exerted himself a great deal more than needful to describe the stages of the battle. Thence, at his old round pace, we travelled to Cockenzie. Though they were building herring-busses there at Mrs. Cadell's, it seemed a desert-like, back-going town, about half full of ruined houses; but the ale-house was clean, and Alan, who was now in a glowing heat, must indulge himself with a bottle of ale, and carry on to the new luckie with the old story of the cold upon his stomach, only now the symptoms were all different.

I sat listening; and it came in my mind that I had scarce ever heard him address three serious words to any woman, but he was always drolling and fleering and making a private mock of them, and yet brought to that business a remarkable degree of energy and interest. Something to this effect I remarked to him, when the good-wife (as chanced) was called away.

"What do ye want?" says he. "A man should aye put his best foot forrit with the womankind; he should aye give them a bit of a story to divert them, the poor lambs! It's what ye should learn to attend to, David; ye should get the principles, it's like a trade. Now, if this had been a young lassie, or onyways bonnie, she would never have heard tell of my stomach, Davie. But aince they're too old to be seeking joes, they a' set up to be apotecaries. Why? What do I ken? They'll be just the way God made them, I suppose. But I think a man would be a gomeral that didnae give his attention to the same."

And here, the luckie coming back, he turned from me as if with impatience to renew their former conversation. The lady had branched some while before from Alan's stomach to the case of a goodbrother of her own in Aberlady, whose last sickness and demise she was describing at extraordinary length. Sometimes it was merely dull, sometimes both dull and awful, for she talked with unction. The upshot was that I fell in a deep muse, looking forth of the window on the road, and scarce marking what I saw. Presently had any been looking they might have seen me to start.

"We pit a fomentation to his feet," the good-wife was saying, "and a het stane to his wame, and we gied him hyssop and water of pennyroyal, and fine, clean balsam of sulphur for the hoast. . ."

"Sir," says I, cutting very quietly in, "there's a friend of mine gone by the house."

"Is that e'en sae?" replies Alan, as though it were a thing of small account. And then, "Ye were saying, mem?" says he; and the wearyful wife went on.

Presently, however, he paid her with a half-crown piece, and she must go forth after the change.

"Was it him with the red head?" asked Alan.

"Ye have it," said I.

"What did I tell you in the wood?" he cried. "And yet it's strange he should be here too! Was he his lane?"

"His lee-lane for what I could see," said I.

"Did he gang by?" he asked.

"Straight by," said I, "and looked neither to the right nor left."

"And that's queerer yet," said Alan. "It sticks in my mind, Davie, that we should be stirring. But where to?—deil hae't! This is like old days fairly," cries he.

"There is one big differ, though," said I, "that now we have money in our pockets."

"And another big differ, Mr. Balfour," says he, "that now we have dogs at our tail. They're on the scent; they're in full cry, David. It's a bad business and be damned to it." And he sat thinking hard with a look of his that I knew well.

"I'm saying, Luckie," says he, when the goodwife returned, "have ye a back road out of this change house?"

She told him there was and where it led to.

"Then, sir," says he to me, "I think that will be the shortest road for us. And here's good-bye to ye, my braw woman; and I'll no forget thon of the cinnamon water."

We went out by way of the woman's kale yard, and up a lane among fields. Alan looked sharply to all sides, and seeing we were in a little hollow place of the country, out of view of men, sat down.

"Now for a council of war, Davie," said he. "But first of all, a bit lesson to ye. Suppose that I had been like you, what would yon old wife have minded of the pair of us! Just that we had gone out by the back gate. And what does she mind now? A fine, canty, friendly, cracky man, that suffered with the stomach, poor body! and was real ta'en up about the goodbrother. O man, David, try and learn to have some kind of intelligence!"

"I'll try, Alan," said I.

"And now for him of the red head," says he; "was he gaun fast or slow?"

"Betwixt and between," said I.

"No kind of a hurry about the man?" he asked.

"Never a sign of it," said I.

"Nhm!" said Alan, "it looks queer. We saw nothing of them this morning on the Whins; he's passed us by, he doesnae seem to be looking, and yet here he is on our road! Dod, Davie, I begin to take a notion. I think it's no you they're seeking, I think it's me; and I think they ken fine where they're gaun."

"They ken?" I asked.

"I think Andie Scougal's sold me—him or his mate wha kent some part of the affair—or else Charlie's clerk callant, which would be a pity too," says Alan; "and if you askit me for just my inward private conviction, I think there'll be heads cracked on Gillane sands."

"Alan," I cried, "if you're at all right there'll be folk there and to spare. It'll be small service to crack heads."

"It would aye be a satisfaction though," says Alan. "But bide a bit; bide a bit; I'm thinking—and thanks to this bonny westland wind, I believe I've still a chance of it. It's this way, Davie. I'm no trysted with this man Scougal till the gloaming comes. But," says he, "if I can get a bit of a wind out of the west I'll be there long or that," he says, "and lie-to for ye behind the Isle of Fidra. Now if your gentry kens the place, they ken the time forbye. Do ye see me coming, Davie? Thanks to Johnnie Cope and other red-coat gomerals, I should ken this country like the back of my hand; and if ye're ready for another bit run with Alan Breck, we'll can cast back inshore, and come to the seaside again by Dirleton. If the ship's there, we'll try and get on board of her. If she's no there, I'll just have to get back to my weary haystack. But either way of it, I think we will leave your gentry whistling on their thumbs."

"I believe there's some chance in it," said I. "Have on with ye, Alan!"

CHAPTER XIII.
GILLANE SANDS

I did not profit by Alan's pilotage as he had done by his marchings under General Cope; for I can scarce tell what way we went. It is my excuse that we travelled exceeding fast. Some part we ran, some trotted, and the rest walked at a vengeance of a pace. Twice, while we were at top speed, we ran against country-folk; but though we plumped into the first from round a corner, Alan was as ready as a loaded musket.

"Has ye seen my horse?" he gasped.

"Na, man, I haenae seen nae horse the day," replied the countryman.

And Alan spared the time to explain to him that we were travelling "ride and tie"; that our charger had escaped, and it was feared he had gone home to Linton. Not only that, but he expended some breath (of which he had not very much left) to curse his own misfortune and my stupidity which was said to be its cause.

"Them that cannae tell the truth," he observed to myself as we went on again, "should be aye mindful to leave an honest, handy lee behind them. If folk dinnae ken what ye're doing, Davie, they're terrible taken up with it; but if they think they ken, they care nae mair for it than what I do for pease porridge."

As we had first made inland, so our road came in the end to lie very near due north; the old Kirk of Aberlady for a landmark on the left; on the right, the top of the Berwick Law; and it was thus we struck the shore again, not far from Dirleton. From north Berwick west to Gillane Ness there runs a string of four small islets, Craigleith, the Lamb, Fidra, and Eyebrough, notable by their diversity of size and shape. Fidra is the most particular, being a strange grey islet of two humps, made the more conspicuous by a piece of ruin; and I mind that (as we drew closer to it) by some door or window of these ruins the sea peeped through like a man's eye. Under the lee of Fidra there is a good anchorage in westerly winds, and there, from a far way off, we could see the Thistle riding.

The shore in face of these islets is altogether waste. Here is no dwelling of man, and scarce any passage, or at most of vagabond children running at their play. Gillane is a small place on the far side of the Ness, the folk of Dirleton go to their business in the inland fields, and those of North Berwick straight to the sea-fishing from their haven; so that few parts of the coast are lonelier. But I mind, as we crawled upon our bellies into that multiplicity of heights and hollows, keeping a bright eye upon all sides, and our hearts hammering at our ribs, there was such a shining of the sun and the sea, such a stir of the wind in the bent grass, and such a bustle of down-popping rabbits and up-flying gulls, that the desert seemed to me, like a place alive. No doubt it was in all ways well chosen for a secret embarcation, if the secret had been kept; and even now that it was out, and the place watched, we were able to creep unperceived to the front of the sandhills, where they look down immediately on the beach and sea.

But here Alan came to a full stop.

"Davie," said he, "this is a kittle passage! As long as we lie here we're safe; but I'm nane sae muckle nearer to my ship or the coast of France. And as soon as we stand up and signal the brig, it's another matter. For where will your gentry be, think ye?"

"Maybe they're no come yet," said I. "And even if they are, there's one clear matter in our favour. They'll be all arranged to take us, that's true. But they'll have arranged for our coming from the east and here we are upon their west."

"Ay," says Alan, "I wish we were in some force, and this was a battle, we would have bonnily out-manœuvred them! But it isnae, Davit; and the way it is, is a wee thing less inspiring to Alan Breck. I swither, Davie."

"Time flies, Alan," said I.

"I ken that," said Alan. "I ken naething else, as the French folk say. But this is a dreidful case of heids or tails. O! if I could but ken where your gentry were!"

"Alan," said I, "this is no like you. It's got to be now or never."

"This is no me, quo' he,"

sang Alan, with a queer face betwixt shame and drollery.

"Neither you nor me, quo' he, neither you nor me.
Wow, na, Johnnie man! neither you nor me."

And then of a sudden he stood straight up where he was, and with a handkerchief flying in his right hand, marched down upon the beach. I stood up myself, but lingered behind him, scanning the sand-hills to the east. His appearance was at first unremarked: Scougal not expecting him so early, and my gentry watching on the other side. Then they awoke on board the Thistle, and it seemed they had all in readiness, for there was scarce a second's bustle on the deck before we saw a skiff put round her stern and begin to pull lively for the coast. Almost at the same moment of time, and perhaps half a mile away towards Gillane Ness, the figure of a man appeared for a blink upon a sandhill, waving with his arms; and though he was gone again in the same flash, the gulls in that part continued a little longer to fly wild.

Alan had not seen this, looking straight to seaward at the ship and skiff.

"It maun be as it will!" said he, when I had told him, "Weel may yon boatie row, or my craig'll have to thole a raxing."

That part of the beach was long and flat, and excellent walking when the tide was down; a little cressy burn flowed over it in one place to the sea; and the sandhills ran along the head of it like the rampart of a town. No eye of ours could spy what was passing behind there in the bents, no hurry of ours could mend the speed of the boat's coming: time stood still with us through that uncanny period of waiting.

"There is one thing I would like to ken," say Alan. "I would like to ken these gentry's orders. We're worth four hunner pound the pair of us: how if they took the guns to us, Davie! They would get a bonny shot from the top of that lang sandy bank."

"Morally impossible," said I. "The point is that they can have no guns. This thing has been gone about too secret; pistols they may have, but never guns."

"I believe ye'll be in the right," says Alan. "For all which I am wearing a good deal for yon boat."

And he snapped his fingers and whistled to it like a dog.

It was now perhaps a third of the way in, and we ourselves already hard on the margin of the sea, so that the soft sand rose over my shoes. There was no more to do whatever but to wait, to look as much as we were able at the creeping nearer of the boat, and as little as we could manage at the long impenetrable front of the sandhills, over which the gulls twinkled and behind which our enemies were doubtless marshalling.

"This is a fine, bright, caller place to get shot in," says Alan suddenly; "and, man, I wish that I had your courage!"

"Alan!" I cried, "what kind of talk is this of it! You're just made of courage; it's the character of the man, as I could prove myself if there was nobody else."

"And you would be the more mistaken," said he. "What makes the differ with me is just my great penetration and knowledge of affairs. But for auld, cauld, dour, deadly courage, I am not fit to hold a candle to yourself. Look at us two here upon the sands. Here am I, fair hotching to be off; here's you (for all that I ken) in two minds of it whether you'll no stop. Do you think that I could do that, or would? No me! Firstly, because I havenae got the courage and wouldnae daur; and secondly, because I am a man of so much penetration and would see ye damned first."

"It's there ye're coming, is it?" I cried. "Ah, man Alan, you can wile your old wives, but you never can wile me."

Remembrance of my temptation in the wood made me strong as iron.

"I have a tryst to keep," I continued. "I am trysted with your cousin Charlie; I have passed my word."

"Braw trysts that you'll can keep," said Alan. "Ye'll just mistryst aince and for a' with the gentry in the bents. And what for?" he went on with an extreme threatening gravity. "Just tell me that, my mannie! Are ye to be speerited away like Lady Grange? Are they to drive a dirk in your inside and bury ye in the bents? Or is it to be the other way, and are they to bring ye in with James? Are they folk to be trustit? Would ye stick your head in the mouth of Sim Fraser and the ither Whigs?" he added with extraordinary bitterness.

"Alan," cried I, "they're all rogues and liars, and I'm with ye there. The more reason there should be one decent man in such a land of thieves! My word is passed, and I'll stick to it. I said long syne to your kinswoman that I would stumble at no risk. Do ye mind of that?—the night Red Colin fell, it was. No more I will, then. Here I stop. Prestongrange promised me my life: if he's to be mansworn, here I'll have to die."

"Aweel aweel," said Alan.

All this time we had seen or heard no more of our pursuers. In truth we had caught them unawares; their whole party (as I was to learn afterwards) had not yet reached the scene; what there was of them was spread among the bents towards Gillane. It was quite an affair to call them in and bring them over, and the boat was making speed. They were besides but cowardly fellows: a mere leash of Highland cattle-thieves, of several clans, no gentleman there to be the captain and the more they looked at Alan and me upon the beach, the less (I must suppose) they liked the look of us.

Whoever had betrayed Alan it was not the captain: he was in the skiff himself, steering and stirring up his oarsmen, like a man with his heart in his employ. Already he was near in, and the boat securing—already Alan's face had flamed crimson with the excitement of his deliverance, when our friends in the bents, either in their despair to see their prey escape them or with some hope of scaring Andie, raised suddenly a shrill cry of several voices.

This sound, arising from what appeared to be a quite deserted coast, was really very daunting, and the men in the boat held water instantly.

"What's this of it?" sings out the captain, for he was come within an easy hail.

"Freens o'mine," says Alan, and began immediately to wade forth in the shallow water towards the boat. "Davie," he said, pausing, "Davie, are ye no coming? I am swier to leave ye."

"Not a hair of me," said I.

"He stood part of a second where he was to his knees in the salt water, hesitating.

"He that will to Cupar, maun to Cupar," said he, and swashing in deeper than his waist, was hauled into the skiff, which was immediately directed for the ship.

I stood where he had left me, with my hands behind my back; Alan sat with his head turned watching me; and the boat drew smoothly away. Of a sudden I came the nearest hand to shedding tears, and seemed to myself the most deserted solitary lad in Scotland. With that I turned my back upon the sea and faced the sandhills. There was no sight or sound of man; the sun shone on the wet sand and the dry, the wind blew in the bents, the gulls made a dreary piping. As I passed higher up the beach, the sand-lice were hopping nimbly about the stranded tangles. The devil any other sight or sound in that unchancy place. And yet I knew there were folk there, observing me, upon some secret purpose. They were no soldiers, or they would have fallen on and taken us ere now; doubtless they were some common rogues hired for my undoing, perhaps to kidnap, perhaps to murder me outright. From the position of those engaged, the first was the more likely; from what I knew of their character and ardency in this business, I thought the second very possible; and the blood ran cold about my heart.

I had a mad idea to loosen my sword in the scabbard; for though I was very unfit to stand up like a gentleman blade to blade, I thought I could do some scathe in a random combat. But I perceived in time the folly of resistance. This was no doubt the joint "expedient" on which Prestongrange and Fraser were agreed. The first, I was very sure, had done something to secure my life; the second was pretty likely to have slipped in some contrary hints into the ears of Neil and his companions; and if I were to show bare steel I might play straight into the hands of my worst enemy and seal my own doom.

These thoughts brought me to the head of the beach. I cast a look behind, the boat was nearing the brig, and Alan flew his handkerchief for a farewell, which I replied to with the waving of my hand. But Alan himself was shrunk to a small thing in my view, alongside of this pass that lay in front of me. I set my hat hard on my head, clenched my teeth, and went right before me up the face of the sand-wreath. It made a hard climb, being steep, and the sand like water underfoot. But I caught hold at last by the long bent-grass on the brae-top, and pulled myself to a good footing. The same moment men stirred and stood up here and there, six or seven of them, ragged-like knaves, each with a dagger in his hand. The fair truth is, I shut my eyes and prayed. When I opened them again, the rogues were crept the least thing nearer without speech or hurry. Every eye was upon mine, which struck me with a strange sensation of their brightness, and of the fear with which they continued to approach me. I held out my hands empty; whereupon one asked, with a strong Highland brogue, if I surrendered.

"Under protest," said I, "if ye ken what that means, which I misdoubt."

At that word, they came all in upon me like a flight of birds upon a carrion, seized me, took my sword, and all the money from my pockets, bound me hand and foot with some strong line, and cast me on a tussock of bent. There they sat about their captive in a part of a circle and gazed upon him silently like something dangerous, perhaps a lion or a tiger on the spring. Presently this attention was relaxed. They drew nearer together, fell to speech in the Gaelic, and very cynically divided my property before my eyes. It was my diversion in this time that I could watch from my place the progress of my friend's escape. I saw the boat come to the brig and be hoisted in, the sails fill, and the ship pass out seaward behind the isles and by North Berwick.

In the course of two hours or so, more and more ragged Highlandmen kept collecting. Neil among the first, until the party must have numbered near a score. With each new arrival there was a fresh bout of talk, that sounded like complaints and explanations; but I observed one thing, none of those who came late had any share in the division of my spoils. The last discussion was very violent and eager, so that once I thought they would have quarrelled; on the heels of which their company parted, the bulk of them returning westward in a troop, and only three, Neil and two others, remaining sentries on the prisoner.

"I could name one who would be very ill pleased with your day's work, Neil Duncanson," said I, when the rest had moved away.

He assured me in answer I should be tenderly used, for he knew he was "acquent wi' the leddy."

This was all our talk, nor did any other son of man appear upon that portion of the coast until the sun had gone down among the Highland mountains, and the gloaming was beginning to grow dark. At which hour I was aware of a long, lean, bony-like Lothian man of a very swarthy countenance, that came towards us among the bents on a farm horse.

"Lads," cried he, "has ye a paper like this?" and held up one in his hand. Neil produced a second, which the newcomer studied through a pair of horn spectacles, and saying all was right and we were the folk he was seeking, immediately dismounted. I was then set in his place, my feet tied under the horse's belly, and we set forth under the guidance of the Lowlander. His path must have been very well chosen, for we met but one pair—a pair of lovers—the whole way, and these, perhaps taking us to be free-traders, fled on our approach. We were at one time close at the foot of Berwick Law on the south side; at another, as we passed over some open hills, I spied the lights of a clachan and the old tower of a church among some trees not far off, but too far to cry for help, if I had dreamed of it. At last we came again within sound of the sea. There was moonlight, though not much; and by this I could see the three huge towers and broken battlements of Tantallon, that old chief place of the Red Douglases. The horse was picketed in the bottom of the ditch to graze, and I was led within, and forth into the court, and thence into the tumble-down stone hall. Here my conductors built a brisk fire in the midst of the pavement, for there was a chill in the night. My hands were loosed, I was set by the wall in the inner end, and (the Lowlander having produced provisions) I was given oatmeal bread and a pitcher of French brandy. This done, I was left once more alone with my three Highlandmen. They sat close by the fire drinking and talking; the wind blew in by the breaches, cast about the smoke and flames, and sang in the tops of the towers; I could hear the sea under the cliffs, and, my mind being reassured as to my life, and my body and spirits wearied with the day's employment, I turned upon one side and slumbered.

I had no means of guessing at what hour I was wakened, only the moon was down and the fire was low. My feet were now loosed, and I was carried through the ruins and down the cliff-side by a precipitous path to where I found a fisher's boat in a haven of the rocks. This I was had on board of, and we began to put forth from the shore in a fine starlight.

CHAPTER XIV.
THE BASS

I had no thought where they were taking me; only looked here and there for the appearance of a ship; and there ran the while in my head a word of Ransome's—the twenty-pounders. If I were to be exposed a second time to that same former danger of the plantations, I judged it must turn ill with me; there was no second Alan; and no second shipwreck and spare yard to be expected now; and I saw myself hoe tobacco under the whip's lash. The thought chilled me; the air was sharp upon the water, the stretchers of the boat drenched with a cold dew: and I shivered in my place beside the steersman. This was the dark man whom I have called hitherto the Lowlander; his name was Dale, ordinarily called Black Andie. Feeling the thrill of my shiver, he very kindly handed me a rough jacket full of fish-scales, with which I was glad to cover myself.

"I thank you for this kindness," said I, "and will make so free as to repay it with a warning. You take a high responsibility in this affair. You are not like these ignorant, barbarous Highlanders, but know what the law is and the risks of those that break it."

"I am no just exactly what ye would ca' an extremist for the law," says he, "at the best of times; but in this business I act with a good warranty."

"What are you going to do with me?" I asked.

"Nae harm," said he, "nae harm ava'. Ye'll have strong freens, I'm thinking. Ye'll be richt eneuch yet."

There began to fall a greyness on the face of the sea; little dabs of pink and red, like coals of slow fire, came in the east; and at the same time the geese awakened, and began crying about the top of the Bass. It is just the one crag of rock, as everybody knows, but great enough to carve a city from. The sea was extremely little, but there went a hollow plowter round the base of it. With the growing of the dawn I could see it clearer and clearer; the straight crags painted with sea-birds' droppings like a morning frost, the sloping top of it green with grass, the clan of white geese that cried about the sides, and the black, broken buildings of the prison sitting close on the sea's edge.

At the sight the truth came in upon me in a clap.

"It's there you're taking me!" I cried.

"Just to the Bass, mannie," said he: "Whaur the auld saints were afore ye, and I misdoubt if ye have come so fairly by your preeson."

"But none dwells there now," I cried; "the place is long a ruin."

"It'll be the mair pleisand a change for the solan geese, then," quoth Andie dryly.

The day coming slowly brighter I observed on the bilge, among the big stones with which fisherfolk ballast their boats, several kegs and baskets, and a provision of fuel. All these were discharged upon the crag. Andie, myself, and my three Highlanders (I call them mine, although it was the other way about), landed along with them. The sun was not yet up when the boat moved away again, the noise of the oars on the thole-pins echoing from the cliffs, and left us in our singular reclusion:

Andie Dale was the Prefect (as I would jocularly call him) of the Bass, being at once the shepherd and the gamekeeper of that small and rich estate. He had to mind the dozen or so of sheep that fed and fattened on the grass of the sloping part of it, like beasts grazing the roof of a cathedral. He had charge besides of the solan geese that roosted in the crags; and from these an extraordinary income is derived. The young are dainty eating, as much as two shillings a-piece being a common price, and paid willingly by epicures; even the grown birds are valuable for their oil and feathers; and a part of the minister's stipend of North Berwick is paid to this day in solan geese, which makes it (in some folks' eyes) a parish to be coveted. To perform these several businesses, as well as to protect the geese from poachers, Andie had frequent occasion to sleep and pass days together on the crag; and we found the man at home there like a farmer in his steading. Bidding us all shoulder some of the packages, a matter in which I made haste to bear a hand, he led us in by a locked gate, which was the only admission to the island, and through the ruins of the fortress, to the governor's house. There we saw by the ashes in the chimney and a standing bed-place in one corner, that he made his usual occupation.

This bed he now offered me to use, saying he supposed I would set up to be gentry.

"My gentrice has nothing to do with where I lie," said I. "I bless God I have lain hard ere now, and can do the same again with thankfulness. While I am here, Mr. Andie, if that be your name, I will do my part and take my place beside the rest of you; and I ask you on the other hand to spare me your mockery, which I own I like ill."

He grumbled a little at this speech, but seemed upon reflection to approve it. Indeed, he was a long-headed, sensible man, and a good Whig and Presbyterian; read daily in a pocket Bible, and was both able and eager to converse seriously on religion, leaning more than a little towards the Cameronian extremes. His morals were of a more doubtful colour. I found he was deep in the free trade, and used the ruins of Tantallon for a magazine of smuggled merchandise. As for a gauger, I do not believe he valued the life of one at half-a-farthing. But that part of the coast of Lothian is to this day as wild a place, and the commons there as rough a crew, as any in Scotland.

One incident of my imprisonment is made memorable by a consequence it had long after. There was a warship at this time stationed in the Firth, the Seahorse, Captain Palliser. It chanced she was cruising in the month of September, plying between Fife and Lothian, and sounding for sunk dangers. Early one fine morning she was seen about two miles to east of us, where she lowered a boat, and seemed to examine the Wildfire Rocks and Satan's Bush, famous dangers of that coast. And presently after having got her boat again, she came before the wind and was headed directly for the Bass. This was very troublesome to Andie and the Highlanders; the whole business of my sequestration was designed for privacy, and here, with a navy captain perhaps blundering ashore, it looked to become public enough, if it were nothing worse. I was in a minority of one, I am no Alan to fall upon so many, and I was far from sure that a warship was the least likely to improve my condition. All which considered, I gave Andie my parole of good behaviour and obedience, and was had briskly to the summit of the rock, where we all lay down, at the cliff's edge, in different places of observation and concealment. The Seahorse came straight on till I thought she would have struck, and we (looking giddily down) could see the ship's company at their quarters and hear the leadsman singing at the lead. Then she suddenly wore and let fly a volley of I know not how many great guns. The rock was shaken with the thunder of the sound, the smoke flowed over our heads, and the geese rose in number beyond computation or belief. To hear their screaming and to see the twinkling of their wings, made a most inimitable curiosity; and I suppose it was after this somewhat childish pleasure that Captain Palliser had come so near the Bass. He was to pay dear for it in time. During his approach I had the opportunity to make a remark upon the rigging of that ship by which I ever after knew it miles away; and this was a means (under Providence) of my averting from a friend a great calamity, and inflicting on Captain Palliser himself a sensible disappointment.

All the time of my stay on the rock we lived well. We had small ale and brandy, and oatmeal, of which we made our porridge night and morning. At times a boat came from the Castleton and brought us a quarter of mutton, for the sheep upon the rock we must not touch, these being specially fed to market. The geese were unfortunately out of season, and we let them be. We fished ourselves, and yet more often made the geese to fish for us: observing one when he had made a capture and scaring him from his prey ere he had swallowed it.

The strange nature of this place, and the curiosities with which it abounded, held me busy and amused. Escape being impossible, I was allowed my entire liberty, and continually explored the surface of the isle wherever it might support the foot of man. The old garden of the prison was still to be observed, with flowers and pot-herbs running wild, and some ripe cherries on a bush. A little lower stood a chapel or a hermit's cell; who built or dwelt in it, none may know, and the thought of its age made a ground of many meditations. The prison, too, where I now bivouacked with Highland cattle-thieves, was a place full of history, both human and divine. I thought it strange so many saints and martyrs should have gone by there so recently, and left not so much as a leaf out of their Bibles, or a name carved upon the wall, while the rough soldier lads that mounted guard upon the battlements had filled the neighbourhood with their mementoes— broken tobacco-pipes for the most part, and that in a surprising plenty, but also metal buttons from their coats. There were times when I thought I could have heard the pious sound of psalms out of the martyr's dungeons, and seen the soldiers tramp the ramparts with their glinting pipes, and the dawn rising behind them out of the North Sea.

No doubt it was a good deal Andie and his tales that put these fancies in my head. He was extraordinarily well acquainted with the story of the rock in all particulars, down to the names of private soldiers, his father having served there in that same capacity. He was gifted besides with a natural genius for narration, so that the people seemed to speak and the things to be done before your face. This gift of his and my assiduity to listen brought us the more close together. I could not honestly deny but what I liked him; I soon saw that he liked me; and indeed, from the first I had set myself out to capture his good-will. An odd circumstance (to be told presently) effected this beyond my expectation; but even in early days we made a friendly pair to be a prisoner and his gaoler.

I should trifle with my conscience if I pretended my stay upon the Bass was wholly disagreeable. It seemed to me a safe place, as though I was escaped there out of my troubles. No harm was to be offered me; a material impossibility, rock and the deep sea, prevented me from fresh attempts; I felt I had my life safe and my honour safe, and there were times when I allowed myself to gloat on them like stolen waters. At other times my thoughts were very different, I recalled how strong I had expressed myself both to Rankeillor and to Stewart; I reflected that my captivity upon the Bass, in view of a great part of the coasts of Fife and Lothian, was a thing I should be thought more likely to have invented than endured; and in the eyes of these two gentlemen, at least, I must pass for a boaster and a coward. Now I would take this lightly enough; tell myself that so long as I stood well with Catriona Drummond, the opinion of the rest of man was but moonshine and spilled water; and thence pass off into those meditations of a lover which are so delightful to himself and must always appear so surprisingly idle to a reader. But anon the fear would take me otherwise; I would be shaken with a perfect panic of self-esteem, and these supposed hard judgments appear an injustice impossible to be supported. With that another train of thought would be presented, and I had scarce begun to be concerned about men's judgments of myself, than I was haunted with the remembrance of James Stewart in his dungeon and the lamentations of his wife. Then, indeed, passion began to work in me; I could not forgive myself to sit there idle: it seemed (if I were a man at all) that I could fly or swim out of my place of safety; and it was in such humours and to amuse my self-reproaches that I would set the more particularly to win the good side of Andie Dale.

At last, when we two were alone on the summit of the rock on a bright morning, I put in some hint about a bribe. He looked at me, cast back his head, and laughed out loud.

"Ay, you're funny, Mr. Dale," said I, "but perhaps if you'll glance an eye upon that paper you may change your note."

The stupid Highlanders had taken from me at the time of my seizure nothing but hard money, and the paper I now showed Andie was an acknowledgment from the British Linen Company for a considerable sum.

He read it. "Troth, and ye're nane sae ill aff," said he.

"I thought that would maybe vary your opinions," said I.

"Hout!" said he. "It shows me ye can bribe; but I'm no to be bribit."

"We'll see about that yet a while," says I. "And first, I'll show you that I know what I am talking. You have orders to detain me here till after Thursday, 21st September."

"Ye're no a'thegether wrong either," says Andie. "I'm to let you gang, bar orders contrair, on Saturday, the 23rd."

I could not but feel there was something extremely insidious in this arrangement. That I was to re-appear precisely in time to be too late would cast the more discredit on my tale, if I were minded to tell one; and this screwed me to fighting point.

"Now then, Andie, you that kens the world, listen to me, and think while ye listen," said I. "I know there are great folks in the business, and I make no doubt you have their names to go upon. I have seen some of them myself since this affair began, and said my say into their faces too. But what kind of a crime would this be that I had committed? or what kind of a process is this that I am fallen under? To be apprehended by some ragged John-Hielandman on August 30th, carried to a rickle of old stones that is now neither fort nor gaol (whatever it once was) but just the gamekeeper's lodge of the Bass Rock, and set free again, September 23rd, as secretly as I was first arrested—does that sound like law to you? or does it sound like justice? or does it not sound honestly like a piece of some low dirty intrigue, of which the very folk that meddle with it are ashamed?"

"I canna gainsay ye, Shaws. It looks unco underhand," says Andie. "And werenae the folk guid sound Whigs and true-blue Presbyterians I would has seen them ayont Jordan and Jeroozlem or I would have set hand to it."

"The Master of Lovat'll be a braw Whig," says I, "and a grand Presbyterian."

"I ken naething by him," said he. "I hae nae trokings wi' Lovats."

"No, it'll be Prestongrange that you'll be dealing with," said I.

"Ah, but I'll no tell ye that," said Andie.

"Little need when I ken," was my retort.

"There's just the ae thing ye can be fairly sure of, Shaws," says Andie. "And that is that (try as ye please) I'm no dealing wi' yoursel'; nor yet I amnae goin' to," he added.

"Well, Andie, I see I'll have to be speak out plain with you," I replied. And told him so much as I thought needful of the facts.

He heard me out with some serious interest, and when I had done, seemed to consider a little with himself.

"Shaws," said he at last, "I'll deal with the naked hand. It's a queer tale, and no very creditable, the way you tell it; and I'm far frae minting that is other than the way that ye believe it. As for yoursel', ye seem to me rather a dacent-like young man. But me, that's aulder and mair judeecious, see perhaps a wee bit further forrit in the job than what ye can dae. And here the maitter clear and plain to ye. There'll be nae skaith to yoursel' if I keep ye here; far free that, I think ye'll be a hantle better by it. There'll be nae skaith to the kintry—just ae mair Hielantman hangit—Gude kens, a guid riddance! On the ither hand, it would be considerable skaith to me if I would let you free. Sae, speakin' as a guid Whig, an honest freen' to you, and an anxious freen' to my ainsel', the plain fact is that I think ye'll just have to bide here wi' Andie an' the solans."

"Andie," said I, laying my hand upon his knee, "this Hielantman's innocent."

"Ay, it's a peety about that," said he. "But ye see, in this warld, the way God made it, we cannae just get a'thing that we want."

CHAPTER XV.
BLACK ANDIE'S TALE OF TOD LAPRAIK

I have yet said little of the Highlanders. They were all three of the followers of James More, which bound the accusation very tight about their master's neck. All understood a word or two of English, but Neil was the only one who judged he had enough of it for general converse, in which (when once he got embarked) his company was often tempted to the contrary opinion. They were tractable, simple creatures; showed much more courtesy than might have been expected from their raggedness and their uncouth appearance, and fell spontaneously to be like three servants for Andie and myself.

Dwelling in that isolated place, in the old falling ruins of a prison, and among endless strange sounds of the sea and the sea-birds, I thought I perceived in them early the effects of superstitious fear. When there was nothing doing they would either lie and sleep, for which their appetite appeared insatiable, or Neil would entertain the others with stories which seemed always of a terrifying strain. If neither of these delights were within reach—if perhaps two were sleeping and the third could find no means to follow their example—I would see him sit and listen and look about him in a progression of uneasiness, starting, his face blenching, his hands clutched, a man strung like a bow. The nature of these fears I had never an occasion to find out, but the sight of them was catching, and the nature of the place that we were in favourable to alarms. I can find no word for it in the English, but Andie had an expression for it in the Scots from which he never varied.

"Ay," he would say, "it's an unco place, the Bass."

It is so I always think of it. It was an unco place by night, unco by day; and these were unco sounds, of the calling of the solans, and the plash of the sea and the rock echoes, that hung continually in our ears. It was chiefly so in moderate weather. When the waves were anyway great they roared about the rock like thunder and the drums of armies, dreadful but merry to hear; and it was in the calm days that a man could daunt himself with listening—not a Highlandman only, as I several times experimented on myself, so many still, hollow noises haunted and reverberated in the porches of the rock.

This brings me to a story I heard, and a scene I took part in, which quite changed our terms of living, and had a great effect on my departure. It chanced one night I fell in a muse beside the fire and (that little air of Alan's coming back to my memory) began to whistle. A hand was laid upon my arm, and the voice of Neil bade me to stop, for it was not "canny musics."

"Not canny?" I asked. "How can that be?"

"Na," said he; "it will be made by a bogle and her wanting ta heid upon his body." [13]

"Well," said I, "there can be no bogles here, Neil; for it's not likely they would fash themselves to frighten geese."

"Ay?" says Andie, "is that what ye think of it! But I'll can tell ye there's been waur nor bogles here."

"What's waur than bogles, Andie?" said I.

"Warlocks," said he. "Or a warlock at the least of it. And that's a queer tale, too," he added. "And if ye would like, I'll tell it ye."

To be sure we were all of the one mind, and even the Highlander that had the least English of the three set himself to listen with all his might.

THE TALE OF TOD LAPRAIK

My faither, Tam Dale, peace to his banes, was a wild, sploring lad in his young days, wi' little wisdom and little grace. He was fond of a lass and fond of a glass, and fond of a ran-dan; but I could never hear tell that he was muckle use for honest employment. Frae ae thing to anither, he listed at last for a sodger and was in the garrison of this fort, which was the first way that ony of the Dales cam to set foot upon the Bass. Sorrow upon that service! The governor brewed his ain ale; it seems it was the warst conceivable. The rock was proveesioned free the shore with vivers, the thing was ill-guided, and there were whiles when they but to fish and shoot solans for their diet. To crown a', thir was the Days of the Persecution. The perishin' cauld chalmers were all occupeed wi' sants and martyrs, the saut of the yearth, of which it wasnae worthy. And though Tam Dale carried a firelock there, a single sodger, and liked a lass and a glass, as I was sayin,' the mind of the man was mair just than set with his position. He had glints of the glory of the kirk; there were whiles when his dander rase to see the Lord's sants misguided, and shame covered him that he should be haulding a can'le (or carrying a firelock) in so black a business. There were nights of it when he was here on sentry, the place a' wheesht, the frosts o' winter maybe riving in the wa's, and he would hear ane o' the prisoners strike up a psalm, and the rest join in, and the blessed sounds rising from the different chalmers—or dungeons, I would rather say—so that this auld craig in the sea was like a pairt of Heev'n. Black shame was on his saul; his sins hove up before him muckle as the Bass, and above a', that chief sin, that he should have a hand in hagging and hashing at Christ's Kirk. But the truth is that he resisted the spirit. Day cam, there were the rousing compainions, and his guid resolves depairtit.

In thir days, dwalled upon the Bass a man of God, Peden the Prophet was his name. Ye'll have heard tell of Prophet Peden. There was never the wale of him sinsyne, and it's a question wi' mony if there ever was his like afore. He was wild's a peat-hag, fearsome to look at, fearsome to hear, his face like the day of judgment. The voice of him was like a solan's and dinnle'd in folks' lugs, and the words of him like coals of fire.

Now there was a lass on the rock, and I think she had little to do, for it was nae place far decent weemen; but it seems she was bonny, and her and Tam Dale were very well agreed. It befell that Peden was in the gairden his lane at the praying when Tam and the lass cam by; and what should the lassie do but mock with laughter at the sant's devotions? He rose and lookit at the twa o' them, and Tam's knees knoitered thegether at the look of him. But whan he spak, it was mair in sorrow than in anger. "Poor thing, poor thing!" says he, and it was the lass he lookit at, "I hear you skirl and laugh," he says, "but the Lord has a deid shot prepared for you, and at that surprising judgment ye shall skirl but the ae time!" Shortly thereafter she was daundering on the craigs wi' twa-three sodgers, and it was a blawy day. There cam a gowst of wind, claught her by the coats, and awa' wi' her bag and baggage. And it was remarked by the sodgers that she gied but the ae skirl.

Nae doubt this judgment had some weicht upon Tam Dale; but it passed again and him none the better. Ae day he was flyting wi' anither sodger-lad. "Deil hae me!" quo' Tam, for he was a profane swearer. And there was Peden glowering at him, gash an' waefu'; Peden wi' his lang chafts an' luntin' een, the maud happed about his kist, and the hand of him held out wi' the black nails upon the finger-nebs—for he had nae care of the body. "Fy, fy, poor man!" cries he, "the poor fool man! Deil hae me, quo' he; an' I see the deil at his oxter." The conviction of guilt and grace cam in on Tam like the deep sea; he flang doun the pike that was in his hands—"I will nae mair lift arms against the cause o' Christ!" says he, and was as gude's word. There was a sair fyke in the beginning, but the governor, seeing him resolved, gied him his discharge, and he went and dwallt and merried in North Berwick, and had aye a gude name with honest folk free that day on.

It was in the year seeventeen hunner and sax that the Bass cam in the hands o' the Da'rymples, and there was twa men soucht the chairge of it. Baith were weel qualified, for they had baith been sodgers in the garrison, and kent the gate to handle solans, and the seasons and values of them. Forby that they were baith—or they baith seemed—earnest professors and men of comely conversation. The first of them was just Tam Dale, my faither. The second was ane Lapraik, whom the folk ca'd Tod Lapraik maistly, but whether for his name or his nature I could never hear tell. Weel, Tam gaed to see Lapraik upon this business, and took me, that was a toddlin' laddie, by the hand. Tod had his dwallin' in the lang loan benorth the kirkyaird. It's a dark uncanny loan, forby that the kirk has aye had an ill name since the days o' James the Saxt and the deevil's cantrips played therein when the Queen was on the seas; and as for Tod's house, it was in the mirkest end, and was little liked by some that kenned the best. The door was on the sneck that day, and me and my faither gaed straucht in. Tod was a wabster to his trade; his loom stood in the but. There he sat, a muckle fat, white hash of a man like creish, wi' a kind of a holy smile that gart me scunner. The hand of him aye cawed the shuttle, but his een was steeked. We cried to him by his name, we skirled in the deid lug of him, we shook him by the shou'ther. Nae mainner o' service! There he sat on his dowp, an' cawed the shuttle and smiled like creish.

"God be guid to us," says Tam Dale, "this is no canny?"

He had jimp said the word, when Tod Lapraik cam to himsel'.

"Is this you, Tam?" says he. "Haith, man! I'm blythe to see ye. I whiles fa' into a bit dwam like this," he says; "its frae the stamach."

Weel, they began to crack about the Bass and which of them twa was to get the warding o't, and little by little cam to very ill words, and twined in anger. I mind weel that as my faither and me gaed hame again, he cam ower and ower the same expression, how little he likit Tod Lapraik and his dwams.

"Dwam!" says he. "I think folk hae brunt for dwams like yon."

Aweel, my faither got the Bass and Tod had to go wantin'. It was remembered sinsyne what way he had ta'en the thing. "Tam," says he, "ye hae gotten the better o' me aince mair, and I hope," says he, "ye'll find at least a' that ye expeckit at the Bass." Which have since been thought remarkable expressions. At last the time came for Tam Dale to take young solans. This was a business he was weel used wi', he had been a craigsman frae a laddie, and trustit nane but himsel'. So there was he hingin' by a line an' speldering on the craig face, whaur its hieest and steighest. Fower tenty lads were on the tap, hauldin' the line and mindin' for his signals. But whaur Tam hung there was naething but the craig, and the sea belaw, and the solans skirlin and flying. It was a braw spring morn, and Tam whustled as he claught in the young geese. Mony's the time I've heard him tell of this experience, and aye the swat ran upon the man.

It chanced, ye see, that Tam keeked up, and he was awaur of a muckle solan, and the solan pyking at the line. He thocht this by-ordinar and outside the creature's habits. He minded that ropes was unco saft things, and the solan's neb and the Bass Rock unco hard, and that twa hunner feet were raither mair than he would care to fa'.

"Shoo!" says Tam. "Awa', bird! Shoo, awa' wi' ye!" says he.

The solan keekit doon into Tam's face, and there was something unco in the creature's ee. Just the ae keek it gied, and back to the rope. But now it wroucht and warstl't like a thing dementit.

There never was the solan made that wroucht as that solan wroucht; and it seemed to understand its employ brawly, birzing the saft rope between the neb of it and a crunkled jag o' stane.

There gaed a cauld stend o' fear into Tam's heart. "This thing is nae bird," thinks he. His een turnt backward in his heid and the day gaed black aboot him. "If I get a dwam here," he toucht, "it's by wi' Tam Dale." And he signalled for the lads to pu' him up.

And it seemed the solan understood about signals. For nae sooner was the signal made than he let be the rope, spried his wings, squawked out loud, took a turn flying, and dashed straucht at Tam Dale's een. Tam had a knife, he gart the cauld steel glitter. And it seemed the solan understood about knives, for nae suner did the steel glint in the sun than he gied the ae squawk, but laighter, like a body disappointit, and flegged aff about the roundness of the craig, and Tam saw him nae mair. And as sune as that thing was gane, Tam's heid drapt upon his shouther, and they pu'd him up like a deid corp, dadding on the craig.

A dram of brandy (which he went never without) broucht him to his mind, or what was left of it. Up he sat.

"Rin, Geordie, rin to the boat, mak' sure of the boat, man—rin!" he cries, "or yon solan'll have it awa'," says he.

The fower lads stared at ither, an' tried to whilly-wha him to be quiet. But naething would satisfy Tam Dale, till ane o' them had startit on aheid to stand sentry on the boat. The ithers askit if he was for down again.

"Na," says he, "and niether you nor me," says he, "and as sune as I can win to stand on my twa feet we'll be aff frae this craig o' Sawtan."

Sure eneuch, nae time was lost, and that was ower muckle; for before they won to North Berwick Tam was in a crying fever. He lay a' the simmer; and wha was sae kind as come speiring for him, but Tod Lapraik! Folk thocht afterwards that ilka time Tod cam near the house the fever had worsened. I kenna for that; but what I ken the best, that was the end of it.

It was about this time o' the year; my grandfaither was out at the white fishing; and like a bairn, I but to gang wi' him. We had a grand take, I mind, and the way that the fish lay broucht us near in by the Bass, whaur we foregaithered wi' anither boat that belanged to a man Sandie Fletcher in Castleton. He's no lang deid neither, or ye could speir at himsel'. Weel, Sandie hailed.

"What's yon on the Bass?" says he.

"On the Bass?" says grandfaither.

"Ay," says Sandie, "on the green side o't."

"Whatten kind of a thing?" says grandfaither. "There cannae be naething on the Bass but just the sheep."

"It looks unco like a body," quo' Sandie, who was nearer in.

"A body!" says we, and we none of us likit that. For there was nae boat that could have brought a man, and the key o' the prison yett hung ower my faither's at hame in the press bed.

We keepit the twa boats close for company, and crap in nearer hand. Grandfaither had a gless, for he had been a sailor, and the captain of a smack, and had lost her on the sands of Tay. And when we took the glass to it, sure eneuch there was a man. He was in a crunkle o' green brae, a wee below the chaipel, a' by his lee lane, and lowped and flang and danced like a daft quean at a waddin'.

"It's Tod," says grandfather, and passed the gless to Sandie.

"Ay, it's him," says Sandie.

"Or ane in the likeness o' him," says grandfaither.

"Sma' is the differ," quo' Sandie. "De'il or warlock, I'll try the gun at him," quo' he, and broucht up a fowling-piece that he aye carried, for Sandie was a notable famous shot in all that country.

"Haud your hand, Sandie," says grandfaither; "we maun see clearer first," says he, "or this may be a dear day's wark to the baith of us."

"Hout!" says Sandie, "this is the Lord's judgment surely, and be damned to it," says he.

"Maybe ay, and maybe no," says my grandfaither, worthy man! "But have you a mind of the Procurator Fiscal, that I think ye'll have foregaithered wi' before," says he.

This was ower true, and Sandie was a wee thing set ajee. "Aweel, Edie," says he, "and what would be your way of it?"

"Ou, just this," says grandfaither. "Let me that has the fastest boat gang back to North Berwick, and let you bide here and keep an eye on Thon. If I cannae find Lapraik, I'll join ye and the twa of us'll have a crack wi' him. But if Lapraik's at hame, I'll rin up the flag at the harbour, and ye can try Thon Thing wi' the gun."

Aweel, so it was agreed between them twa. I was just a bairn, an' clum in Sandie's boat, whaur I thought I would see the best of the employ. My grandsire gied Sandie a siller tester to pit in his gun wi' the leid draps, bein mair deidly again bogles. And then the as boat set aff for North Berwick, an' the tither lay whaur it was and watched the wanchancy thing on the brae-side.

A' the time we lay there it lowped and flang and capered and span like a teetotum, and whiles we could hear it skelloch as it span. I hae seen lassies, the daft queans, that would lowp and dance a winter's nicht, and still be lowping and dancing when the winter's day cam in. But there would be fowk there to hauld them company, and the lads to egg them on; and this thing was its lee-lane. And there would be a fiddler diddling his elbock in the chimney-side; and this thing had nae music but the skirling of the solans. And the lassies were bits o' young things wi' the reid life dinnling and stending in their members; and this was a muckle, fat, creishy man, and him fa'n in the vale o' years. Say what ye like, I maun say what I believe. It was joy was in the creature's heart, the joy o' hell, I daursay: joy whatever. Mony a time I have askit mysel' why witches and warlocks should sell their sauls (whilk are their maist dear possessions) and be auld, duddy, wrunkl't wives or auld, feckless, doddered men; and then I mind upon Tod Lapraik dancing a' the hours by his lane in the black glory of his heart. Nae doubt they burn for it muckle in hell, but they have a grand time here of it, whatever!—and the Lord forgie us!

Weel, at the hinder end, we saw the wee flag yirk up to the mast-heid upon the harbour rocks. That was a' Sandie waited for. He up wi' the gun, took a deleeberate aim, an' pu'd the trigger. There cam' a bang and then ae waefu' skirl frae the Bass. And there were we rubbin' our een and lookin' at ither like daft folk. For wi' the bang and the skirl the thing had clean disappeared. The sun glintit, the wund blew, and there was the bare yaird whaur the Wonder had been lowping and flinging but ae second syne.

The hale way hame I roared and grat wi' the terror o' that dispensation. The grawn folk were nane sae muckle better; there was little said in Sandie's boat but just the name of God; and when we won in by the pier, the harbour rocks were fair black wi' the folk waitin' us. It seems they had fund Lapraik in ane of his dwams, cawing the shuttle and smiling. Ae lad they sent to hoist the flag, and the rest abode there in the wabster's house. You may be sure they liked it little; but it was a means of grace to severals that stood there praying in to themsel's (for nane cared to pray out loud) and looking on thon awesome thing as it cawed the shuttle. Syne, upon a suddenty, and wi' the ae dreidfu' skelloch, Tod sprang up frae his hinderlands and fell forrit on the wab, a bluidy corp.

When the corp was examined the leid draps hadnae played buff upon the warlock's body; sorrow a leid drap was to be fund! but there was grandfaither's siller tester in the puddock's heart of him.

Andie had scarce done when there befell a mighty silly affair that had its consequence. Neil, as I have said, was himself a great narrator. I have heard since that he knew all the stories in the Highlands; and thought much of himself, and was thought much of by others on the strength of it. Now Andie's tale reminded him of one he had already heard.

"She would ken that story afore," he said. "She was the story of Uistean More M'Gillie Phadrig and the Gavar Vore."

"It is no sic a thing," cried Andie. "It is the story of my faither (now wi' God) and Tod Lapraik. And the same in your beard," says he; "and keep the tongue of ye inside your Hielant chafts!"

In dealing with Highlanders it will be found, and has been shown in history, how well it goes with Lowland gentlefolk; but the thing appears scarce feasible for Lowland commons. I had already remarked that Andie was continually on the point of quarrelling with our three MacGregors, and now, sure enough, it was to come.

"Thir will be no words to use to shentlemans," says Neil.

"Shentlemans!" cries Andie. "Shentlemans, ye hielant stot! If God would give ye the grace to see yoursel' the way that ithers see ye, ye would throw your denner up."

There came some kind of a Gaelic oath from Neil, and the black knife was in his hand that moment.

There was no time to think; and I caught the Highlander by the leg, and had him down, and his armed hand pinned out, before I knew what I was doing. His comrades sprang to rescue him, Andie and I were without weapons, the Gregara three to two. It seemed we were beyond salvation, when Neil screamed in his own tongue, ordering the others back, and made his submission to myself in a manner the most abject, even giving me up his knife which (upon a repetition of his promises) I returned to him on the morrow.

Two things I saw plain: the first, that I must not build too high on Andie, who had shrunk against the wall and stood there, as pale as death, till the affair was over; the second, the strength of my own position with the Highlanders, who must have received extraordinary charges to be tender of my safety. But if I thought Andie came not very well out in courage, I had no fault to find with him upon the account of gratitude. It was not so much that he troubled me with thanks, as that his whole mind and manner appeared changed; and as he preserved ever after a great timidity of our companions, he and I were yet more constantly together.

CHAPTER XVI.
THE MISSING WITNESS

On the seventeenth, the day I was trysted with the Writer, I had much rebellion against fate. The thought of him waiting in the King's Arms, and of what he would think, and what he would say when next we met, tormented and oppressed me. The truth was unbelievable, so much I had to grant, and it seemed cruel hard I should be posted as a liar and a coward, and have never consciously omitted what it was possible that I should do. I repeated this form of words with a kind of bitter relish, and re-examined in that light the steps of my behaviour. It seemed I had behaved to James Stewart as a brother might; all the past was a picture that I could be proud of, and there was only the present to consider. I could not swim the sea, nor yet fly in the air, but there was always Andie. I had done him a service, he liked me; I had a lever there to work on; if it were just for decency, I must try once more with Andie.

It was late afternoon; there was no sound in all the Bass but the lap and bubble of a very quiet sea; and my four companions were all crept apart, the three Macgregors higher on the rock, and Andie with his Bible to a sunny place among the ruins; there I found him in deep sleep, and, as soon as he was awake, appealed to him with some fervour of manner and a good show of argument.

"If I thoucht it was to do guid to ye, Shaws!" said he, staring at me over his spectacles.

"It's to save another," said I, "and to redeem my word. What would be more good than that? Do ye no mind the scripture, Andie? And you with the Book upon your lap! What shall it profit a man if he gain the whole world?"

"Ay," said he, "that's grand for you. But where do I come in! I have my word to redeem the same's yoursel'. And what are ye asking me to do, but just to sell it ye for siller?"

"Andie! have I named the name of siller?" cried I.

"Ou, the name's naething", said he; "the thing is there, whatever. It just comes to this; if I am to service ye the way that you propose, I'll lose my lifelihood. Then it's clear ye'll have to make it up to me, and a pickle mair, for your ain credit like. And what's that but just a bribe? And if even I was certain of the bribe! But by a' that I can learn, it's far frae that; and if you were to hang, where would I be? Na: the thing's no possible. And just awa' wi' ye like a bonny lad! and let Andie read his chapter."

I remember I was at bottom a good deal gratified with this result; and the next humour I fell into was one (I had near said) of gratitude to Prestongrange, who had saved me, in this violent, illegal manner, out of the midst of my dangers, temptations, and perplexities. But this was both too flimsy and too cowardly to last me long, and the remembrance of James began to succeed to the possession of my spirits. The 21st, the day set for the trial, I passed in such misery of mind as I can scarce recall to have endured, save perhaps upon Isle Earraid only. Much of the time I lay on a brae-side betwixt sleep and waking, my body motionless, my mind full of violent thoughts. Sometimes I slept indeed; but the court-house of Inverary and the prisoner glancing on all sides to find his missing witness, followed me in slumber; and I would wake again with a start to darkness of spirit and distress of body. I thought Andie seemed to observe me, but I paid him little heed. Verily, my bread was bitter to me, and my days a burthen.

Early the next morning (Friday, 22nd) a boat came with provisions, and Andie placed a packet in my hand. The cover was without address but sealed with a Government seal. It enclosed two notes. "Mr. Balfour can now see for himself it is too late to meddle. His conduct will be observed and his discretion rewarded." So ran the first, which seemed to be laboriously writ with the left hand. There was certainly nothing in these expressions to compromise the writer, even if that person could be found; the seal, which formidably served instead of signature, was affixed to a separate sheet on which there was no scratch of writing; and I had to confess that (so far) my adversaries knew what they were doing, and to digest as well as I was able the threat that peeped under the promise.

But the second enclosure was by far the more surprising. It was in a lady's hand of writ. "Maister Dauvit Balfour is informed a friend was speiring for him and her eyes were of the grey," it ran—and seemed so extraordinary a piece to come to my hands at such a moment and under cover of a Government seal, that I stood stupid. Catriona's grey eyes shone in my remembrance. I thought, with a bound of pleasure, she must be the friend. But who should the writer be, to have her billet thus enclosed with Prestongrange's? And of all wonders, why was it thought needful to give me this pleasing but most inconsequent intelligence upon the Bass? For the writer, I could hit upon none possible except Miss Grant. Her family, I remembered, had remarked on Catriona's eyes and even named her for their colour; and she herself had been much in the habit to address me with a broad pronunciation, by way of a sniff, I supposed, at my rusticity. No doubt, besides, but she lived in the same house as this letter came from. So there remained but one step to be accounted for; and that was how Prestongrange should have permitted her at all in an affair so secret, or let her daft-like billet go in the same cover with his own. But even here I had a glimmering. For, first of all, there was something rather alarming about the young lady, and papa might be more under her domination than I knew. And, second, there was the man's continual policy to be remembered, how his conduct had been continually mingled with caresses, and he had scarce ever, in the midst of so much contention, laid aside a mask of friendship. He must conceive that my imprisonment had incensed me. Perhaps this little jesting, friendly message was intended to disarm my rancour?

I will be honest—and I think it did. I felt a sudden warmth towards that beautiful Miss Grant, that she should stoop to so much interest in my affairs. The summoning up of Catriona moved me of itself to milder and more cowardly counsels. If the Advocate knew of her and our acquaintance—if I should please him by some of that "discretion" at which his letter pointed— to what might not this lead! In vain is the net prepared in the sight of any fowl, the Scripture says. Well, fowls must be wiser than folk! For I thought I perceived the policy, and yet fell in with it.

I was in this frame, my heart beating, the grey eyes plain before me like two stars, when Andie broke in upon my musing.

"I see ye has gotten guid news," said he.

I found him looking curiously in my face; with that there came before me like a vision of James Stewart and the court of Inverary; and my mind turned at once like a door upon its hinges. Trials, I reflected, sometimes draw out longer than is looked for. Even if I came to Inverary just too late, something might yet be attempted in the interests of James—and in those of my own character, the best would be accomplished. In a moment, it seemed without thought, I had a plan devised.

"Andie," said I, "is it still to be to-morrow?"

He told me nothing was changed.

"Was anything said about the hour?" I asked.

He told me it was to be two o'clock afternoon.

"And about the place?" I pursued.

"Whatten place?" says Andie.

"The place I am to be landed at?" said I.

He owned there was nothing as to that.

"Very well, then," I said, "this shall be mine to arrange. The wind is in the east, my road lies westward: keep your boat, I hire it; let us work up the Forth all day; and land me at two o'clock to-morrow at the westmost we'll can have reached."

"Ye daft callant!" he cried; "ye would try for Inverary after a'!"

"Just that, Andie," says I.

"Weel, ye're ill to beat!" says he. "And I was a kind o' sorry for ye a' day yesterday," he added. "Ye see, I was never entirely sure till then, which way of it ye really wantit."

Here was a spur to a lame horse!

"A word in your ear, Andie," said I. "This plan of mine has another advantage yet. We can leave these Hielandman behind us on the rock, and one of your boats from the Castleton can bring them off to-morrow. Yon Neil has a queer eye when he regards you; maybe, if I was once out of the gate there might be knives again; these red-shanks are unco grudgeful. And if there should come to be any question, here is your excuse. Our lives were in danger by these savages; being answerable for my safety, you chose the part to bring me from their neighbourhood and detain me the rest of the time on board your boat: and do you know, Andie?" says I, with a smile, "I think it was very wisely chosen."

"The truth is I have nae goo for Neil," says Andie, "nor he for me, I'm thinking; and I would like ill to come to my hands wi' the man. Tam Anster will make a better hand of it with the cattle onyway." (For this man, Anster, came from Fife, where the Gaelic is still spoken.) "Ay, ay!" says Andie, "Tam'll can deal with them the best. And troth! the mair I think of it, the less I see we would be required. The place—ay, feggs! they had forgot the place. Eh, Shaws, ye're a lang-heided child when ye like! Forby that I'm awing ye my life," he added, with more solemnity, and offered me his hand upon the bargain.

Whereupon, with scarce more words, we stepped suddenly on board the boat, cast off, and set the lug. The Gregara were then busy upon breakfast, for the cookery was their usual part; but, one of them stepping to the battlements, our flight was observed before we were twenty fathoms from the rock; and the three of them ran about the ruins and the landing-shelf, for all the world like ants about a broken nest, hailing and crying on us to return. We were still in both the lee and the shadow of the rock, which last lay broad upon the waters, but presently came forth in almost the same moment into the wind and sunshine; the sail filled, the boat heeled to the gunwale, and we swept immediately beyond sound of the men's voices. To what terrors they endured upon the rock, where they were now deserted without the countenance of any civilised person or so much as the protection of a Bible, no limit can be set; nor had they any brandy left to be their consolation, for even in the haste and secrecy of our departure Andie had managed to remove it.

It was our first care to set Anster ashore in a cove by the Glenteithy Rocks, so that the deliverance of our maroons might be duly seen to the next day. Thence we kept away up Firth. The breeze, which was then so spirited, swiftly declined, but never wholly failed us. All day we kept moving, though often not much more; and it was after dark ere we were up with the Queensferry. To keep the letter of Andie's engagement (or what was left of it) I must remain on board, but I thought no harm to communicate with the shore in writing. On Prestongrange's cover, where the Government seal must have a good deal surprised my correspondent, I writ, by the boat's lantern, a few necessary words, aboard and Andie carried them to Rankeillor. In about an hour he came again, with a purse of money and the assurance that a good horse should be standing saddled for me by two to-morrow at Clackmannan Pool. This done, and the boat riding by her stone anchor, we lay down to sleep under the sail.

We were in the Pool the next day long ere two; and there was nothing left for me but to sit and wait. I felt little alacrity upon my errand. I would have been glad of any passable excuse to lay it down; but none being to be found, my uneasiness was no less great than if I had been running to some desired pleasure. By shortly after one the horse was at the waterside, and I could see a man walking it to and fro till I should land, which vastly swelled my impatience. Andie ran the moment of my liberation very fine, showing himself a man of his bare word, but scarce serving his employers with a heaped measure; and by about fifty seconds after two I was in the saddle and on the full stretch for Stirling. In a little more than an hour I had passed that town, and was already mounting Alan Water side, when the weather broke in a small tempest. The rain blinded me, the wind had nearly beat me from the saddle, and the first darkness of the night surprised me in a wilderness still some way east of Balwhidder, not very sure of my direction and mounted on a horse that began already to be weary.

In the press of my hurry, and to be spared the delay and annoyance of a guide, I had followed (so far as it was possible for any horseman) the line of my journey with Alan. This I did with open eyes, foreseeing a great risk in it, which the tempest had now brought to a reality. The last that I knew of where I was, I think it must have been about Uam Var; the hour perhaps six at night. I must still think it great good fortune that I got about eleven to my destination, the house of Duncan Dhu. Where I had wandered in the interval perhaps the horse could tell. I know we were twice down, and once over the saddle and for a moment carried away in a roaring burn. Steed and rider were bemired up to the eyes.

From Duncan I had news of the trial. It was followed in all these Highland regions with religious interest; news of it spread from Inverary as swift as men could travel; and I was rejoiced to learn that, up to a late hour that Saturday it was not yet concluded; and all men began to suppose it must spread over the Monday. Under the spur of this intelligence I would not sit to eat; but, Duncan having agreed to be my guide, took the road again on foot, with the piece in my hand and munching as I went. Duncan brought with him a flask of usquebaugh and a hand-lantern; which last enlightened us just so long as we could find houses where to rekindle it, for the thing leaked outrageously and blew out with every gust. The more part of the night we walked blindfold among sheets of rain, and day found us aimless on the mountains. Hard by we struck a hut on a burn-side, where we got bite and a direction; and, a little before the end of the sermon, came to the kirk doors of Inverary.

The rain had somewhat washed the upper parts of me, but I was still bogged as high as to the knees; I streamed water; I was so weary I could hardly limp, and my face was like a ghost's. I stood certainly more in need of a change of raiment and a bed to lie on, than of all the benefits in Christianity. For all which (being persuaded the chief point for me was to make myself immediately public) I set the door of the church with the dirty Duncan at my tails, and finding a vacant place sat down.

"Thirteently, my brethren, and in parenthesis, the law itself must be regarded as a means of grace," the minister was saying, in the voice of one delighting to pursue an argument.

The sermon was in English on account of the assize. The judges were present with their armed attendants, the halberts glittered in a corner by the door, and the seats were thronged beyond custom with the array of lawyers. The text was in Romans 5th and 13th—the minister a skilled hand; and the whole of that able churchful—from Argyle, and my Lords Elchies and Kilkerran, down to the halbertmen that came in their attendance—was sunk with gathered brows in a profound critical attention. The minister himself and a sprinkling of those about the door observed our entrance at the moment and immediately forgot the same; the rest either did not hear or would not hear or would not be heard; and I sat amongst my friends and enemies unremarked.

The first that I singled out was Prestongrange. He sat well forward, like an eager horseman in the saddle, his lips moving with relish, his eyes glued on the minister; the doctrine was clearly to his mind. Charles Stewart, on the other hand, was half asleep, and looked harassed and pale. As for Simon Fraser, he appeared like a blot, and almost a scandal, in the midst of that attentive congregation, digging his hands in his pockets, shifting his legs, clearing his throat, and rolling up his bald eyebrows and shooting out his eyes to right and left, now with a yawn, now with a secret smile. At times, too, he would take the Bible in front of him, run it through, seem to read a bit, run it through again, and stop and yawn prodigiously: the whole as if for exercise.

In the course of this restlessness his eye alighted on myself. He sat a second stupefied, then tore a half-leaf out of the Bible, scrawled upon it with a pencil, and passed it with a whispered word to his next neighbour. The note came to Prestongrange, who gave me but the one look; thence it voyaged to the hands of Mr. Erskine; thence again to Argyle, where he sat between the other two lords of session, and his Grace turned and fixed me with an arrogant eye. The last of those interested in my presence was Charlie Stewart, and he too began to pencil and hand about dispatches, none of which I was able to trace to their destination in the crowd.

But the passage of these notes had aroused notice; all who were in the secret (or supposed themselves to be so) were whispering information—the rest questions; and the minister himself seemed quite discountenanced by the flutter in the church and sudden stir and whispering. His voice changed, he plainly faltered, nor did he again recover the easy conviction and full tones of his delivery. It would be a puzzle to him till his dying day, why a sermon that had gone with triumph through four parts, should thus miscarry in the fifth.

As for me, I continued to sit there, very wet and weary, and a good deal anxious as to what should happen next, but greatly exulting in my success.

CHAPTER XVII.
THE MEMORIAL

The last word of the blessing was scarce out of the minister's mouth before Stewart had me by the arm. We were the first to be forth of the church, and he made such extraordinary expedition that we were safe within the four walls of a house before the street had begun to be thronged with the home-going congregation.

"Am I yet in time?" I asked.

"Ay and no," said he. "The case is over; the jury is enclosed, and will so kind as let us ken their view of it to-morrow in the morning, the same as I could have told it my own self three days ago before the play began. The thing has been public from the start. The panel kent it, 'Ye may do what ye will for me,' whispers he two days ago. 'Ye ken my fate by what the Duke of Argyle has just said to Mr. Macintosh.' O, it's been a scandal!

"The great Agyle he gaed before,
He gart the cannons and guns to roar,"

and the very macer cried 'Cruachan!' But now that I have got you again I'll never despair. The oak shall go over the myrtle yet; we'll ding the Campbells yet in their own town. Praise God that I should see the day!"

He was leaping with excitement, emptied out his mails upon the floor that I might have a change of clothes, and incommoded me with his assistance as I changed. What remained to be done, or how I was to do it, was what he never told me nor, I believe, so much as thought of. "We'll ding the Campbells yet!" that was still his overcome. And it was forced home upon my mind how this, that had the externals of a sober process of law, was in its essence a clan battle between savage clans. I thought my friend the Writer none of the least savage. Who that had only seen him at a counsel's back before the Lord Ordinary or following a golf ball and laying down his clubs on Bruntsfield links, could have recognised for the same person this voluble and violent clansman?

James Stewart's counsel were four in number—Sheriffs Brown of Colstoun and Miller, Mr. Robert Macintosh, and Mr. Stewart younger of Stewart Hall. These were covenanted to dine with the Writer after sermon, and I was very obligingly included of the party. No sooner the cloth lifted, and the first bowl very artfully compounded by Sheriff Miller, than we fell to the subject in hand. I made a short narration of my seizure and captivity, and was then examined and re-examined upon the circumstances of the murder. It will be remembered this was the first time I had had my say out, or the matter at all handled, among lawyers; and the consequence was very dispiriting to the others and (I must own) disappointing to myself.

"To sum up," said Colstoun, "you prove that Alan was on the spot; you have heard him proffer menaces against Glenure; and though you assure us he was not the man who fired, you leave a strong impression that he was in league with him, and consenting, perhaps immediately assisting, in the act. You show him besides, at the risk of his own liberty, actively furthering the criminal's escape. And the rest of your testimony (so far as the least material) depends on the bare word of Alan or of James, the two accused. In short, you do not at all break, but only lengthen by one personage, the chain that binds our client to the murderer; and I need scarcely say that the introduction of a third accomplice rather aggravates that appearance of a conspiracy which has been our stumbling block from the beginning."

"I am of the same opinion," said Sheriff Miller. "I think we may all be very much obliged to Prestongrange for taking a most uncomfortable witness out of our way. And chiefly, I think, Mr. Balfour himself might be obliged. For you talk of a third accomplice, but Mr. Balfour (in my view) has very much the appearance of a fourth."

"Allow me, sirs!" interposed Stewart the Writer. "There is another view. Here we have a witness—never fash whether material or not—a witness in this cause, kidnapped by that old, lawless, bandit crew of the Glengyle Macgregors, and sequestered for near upon a month in a bourock of old ruins on the Bass. Move that and see what dirt you fling on the proceedings! Sirs, this is a tale to make the world ring with! It would be strange, with such a grip as this, if we couldnae squeeze out a pardon for my client."

"And suppose we took up Mr. Balfour's cause to-morrow?" said Stewart Hall. "I am much deceived or we should find so many impediments thrown in our path, as that James should have been hanged before we had found a court to hear us. This is a great scandal, but I suppose we have none of us forgot a greater still, I mean the matter of the Lady Grange. The woman was still in durance; my friend Mr. Hope of Rankeillor did what was humanly possible; and how did he speed? He never got a warrant! Well, it'll be the same now; the same weapons will be used. This is a scene, gentleman, of clan animosity. The hatred of the name which I have the honour to bear, rages in high quarters. There is nothing here to be viewed but naked Campbell spite and scurvy Campbell intrigue."

You may be sure this was to touch a welcome topic, and I sat for some time in the midst of my learned counsel, almost deaved with their talk but extremely little the wiser for its purport. The Writer was led into some hot expressions; Colstoun must take him up and set him right; the rest joined in on different sides, but all pretty noisy; the Duke of Argyle was beaten like a blanket; King George came in for a few digs in the by-going and a great deal of rather elaborate defence; and there was only one person that seemed to be forgotten, and that was James of the Glens.

Through all this Mr. Miller sat quiet. He was a slip of an oldish gentleman, ruddy and twinkling; he spoke in a smooth rich voice, with an infinite effect of pawkiness, dealing out each word the way an actor does, to give the most expression possible; and even now, when he was silent, and sat there with his wig laid aside, his glass in both hands, his mouth funnily pursed, and his chin out, he seemed the mere picture of a merry slyness. It was plain he had a word to say, and waited for the fit occasion.

It came presently. Colstoun had wound up one of his speeches with some expression of their duty to their client. His brother sheriff was pleased, I suppose, with the transition. He took the table in his confidence with a gesture and a look.

"That suggests to me a consideration which seems overlooked," said he. "The interest of our client goes certainly before all, but the world does not come to an end with James Stewart." Whereat he cocked his eye. "I might condescend, exempli gratia, upon a Mr. George Brown, a Mr. Thomas Miller, and a Mr. David Balfour. Mr. David Balfour has a very good ground of complaint, and I think, gentlemen—if his story was properly redd out—I think there would be a number of wigs on the green."

The whole table turned to him with a common movement.

"Properly handled and carefully redd out, his is a story that could scarcely fail to have some consequence," he continued. "The whole administration of justice, from its highest officer downward, would be totally discredited; and it looks to me as if they would need to be replaced." He seemed to shine with cunning as he said it. "And I need not point out to ye that this of Mr. Balfour's would be a remarkable bonny cause to appear in," he added.

Well, there they all were started on another hare; Mr. Balfour's cause, and what kind of speeches could be there delivered, and what officials could be thus turned out, and who would succeed to their positions. I shall give but the two specimens. It was proposed to approach Simon Fraser, whose testimony, if it could be obtained, would prove certainly fatal to Argyle and to Prestongrange. Miller highly approved of the attempt. "We have here before us a dreeping roast," said he, "here is cut-and-come-again for all." And methought all licked their lips. The other was already near the end. Stewart the Writer was out of the body with delight, smelling vengeance on his chief enemy, the Duke.

"Gentlemen," cried he, charging his glass, "here is to Sheriff Miller. His legal abilities are known to all. His culinary, this bowl in front of us is here to speak for. But when it comes to the poleetical!"—cries he, and drains the glass.

"Ay, but it will hardly prove politics in your meaning, my friend," said the gratified Miller. "A revolution, if you like, and I think I can promise you that historical writers shall date from Mr. Balfour's cause. But properly guided, Mr. Stewart, tenderly guided, it shall prove a peaceful revolution."

"And if the damned Campbells get their ears rubbed, what care I?" cries Stewart, smiting down his fist.

It will be thought I was not very well pleased with all this, though I could scarce forbear smiling at a kind of innocency in these old intriguers. But it was not my view to have undergone so many sorrows for the advancement of Sheriff Miller or to make a revolution in the Parliament House: and I interposed accordingly with as much simplicity of manner as I could assume.

"I have to thank you, gentlemen, for your advice," said I. "And now I would like, by your leave, to set you two or three questions. There is one thing that has fallen rather on one aide, for instance: Will this cause do any good to our friend James of the Glens?"

They seemed all a hair set back, and gave various answers, but concurring practically in one point, that James had now no hope but in the King's mercy.

"To proceed, then," said I, "will it do any good to Scotland? We have a saying that it is an ill bird that fouls his own nest. I remember hearing we had a riot in Edinburgh when I was an infant child, which gave occasion to the late Queen to call this country barbarous; and I always understood that we had rather lost than gained by that. Then came the year 'Forty-five, which made Scotland to be talked of everywhere; but I never heard it said we had anyway gained by the 'Forty-five. And now we come to this cause of Mr. Balfour's, as you call it. Sheriff Miller tells us historical writers are to date from it, and I would not wonder. It is only my fear they would date from it as a period of calamity and public reproach."

The nimble-witted Miller had already smelt where I was travelling to, and made haste to get on the same road. "Forcibly put, Mr. Balfour," says he. "A weighty observe, sir."

"We have next to ask ourselves if it will be good for King George," I pursued. "Sheriff Miller appears pretty easy upon this; but I doubt you will scarce be able to pull down the house from under him, without his Majesty coming by a knock or two, one of which might easily prove fatal."

I gave them a chance to answer, but none volunteered.

"Of those for whom the case was to be profitable," I went on, "Sheriff Miller gave us the names of several, among the which he was good enough to mention mine. I hope he will pardon me if I think otherwise. I believe I hung not the least back in this affair while there was life to be saved; but I own I thought myself extremely hazarded, and I own I think it would be a pity for a young man, with some idea of coming to the Bar, to ingrain upon himself the character of a turbulent, factious fellow before he was yet twenty. As for James, it seems—at this date of the proceedings, with the sentence as good as pronounced—he has no hope but in the King's mercy. May not his Majesty, then, be more pointedly addressed, the characters of these high officers sheltered from the public, and myself kept out of a position which I think spells ruin for me?"

They all sat and gazed into their glasses, and I could see they found my attitude on the affair unpalatable. But Miller was ready at all events.

"If I may be allowed to put my young friend's notion in more formal shape," says he, "I understand him to propose that we should embody the fact of his sequestration, and perhaps some heads of the testimony he was prepared to offer, in a memorial to the Crown. This plan has elements of success. It is as likely as any other (and perhaps likelier) to help our client. Perhaps his Majesty would have the goodness to feel a certain gratitude to all concerned in such a memorial, which might be construed into an expression of a very delicate loyalty; and I think, in the drafting of the same, this view might be brought forward."

They all nodded to each other, not without sighs, for the former alternative was doubtless more after their inclination.

"Paper, then, Mr. Stewart, if you please," pursued Miller; "and I think it might very fittingly be signed by the five of us here present, as procurators for the condemned man.'"

"It can do none of us any harm, at least," says Colstoun, heaving another sigh, for he had seen himself Lord Advocate the last ten minutes.

Thereupon they set themselves, not very enthusiastically, to draft the memorial—a process in the course of which they soon caught fire; and I had no more ado but to sit looking on and answer an occasional question. The paper was very well expressed; beginning with a recitation of the facts about myself, the reward offered for my apprehension, my surrender, the pressure brought to bear upon me; my sequestration; and my arrival at Inverary in time to be too late; going on to explain the reasons of loyalty and public interest for which it was agreed to waive any right of action; and winding up with a forcible appeal to the King's mercy on behalf of James.

Methought I was a good deal sacrificed, and rather represented in the light of a firebrand of a fellow whom my cloud of lawyers had restrained with difficulty from extremes. But I let it pass, and made but the one suggestion, that I should be described as ready to deliver my own evidence and adduce that of others before any commission of inquiry—and the one demand, that I should be immediately furnished with a copy.

Colstoun hummed and hawed. "This is a very confidential document," said he.

"And my position towards Prestongrange is highly peculiar," I replied. "No question but I must have touched his heart at our first interview, so that he has since stood my friend consistently. But for him, gentlemen, I must now be lying dead or awaiting my sentence alongside poor James. For which reason I choose to communicate to him the fact of this memorial as soon as it is copied. You are to consider also that this step will make for my protection. I have enemies here accustomed to drive hard; his Grace is in his own country, Lovat by his side; and if there should hang any ambiguity over our proceedings I think I might very well awake in gaol."

Not finding any very ready answer to these considerations, my company of advisers were at the last persuaded to consent, and made only this condition that I was to lay the paper before Prestongrange with the express compliments of all concerned.

The Advocate was at the castle dining with his Grace. By the hand of one of Colstoun's servants I sent him a billet asking for an interview, and received a summons to meet him at once in a private house of the town. Here I found him alone in a chamber; from his face there was nothing to be gleaned; yet I was not so unobservant but what I spied some halberts in the hall, and not so stupid but what I could gather he was prepared to arrest me there and then, should it appear advisable.

"So, Mr. David, this is you?" said he.

"Where I fear I am not overly welcome, my lord," said I. "And I would like before I go further to express my sense of your lordship's good offices, even should they now cease."

"I have heard of your gratitude before," he replied drily, "and I think this can scarce be the matter you called me from my wine to listen to. I would remember also, if I were you, that you still stand on a very boggy foundation."

"Not now, my lord, I think," said I; "and if your lordship will but glance an eye along this, you will perhaps think as I do."

He read it sedulously through, frowning heavily; then turned back to one part and another which he seemed to weigh and compare the effect of. His face a little lightened.

"This is not so bad but what it might be worse," said he; "though I am still likely to pay dear for my acquaintance with Mr. David Balfour."

"Rather for your indulgence to that unlucky young man, my lord," said I.

He still skimmed the paper, and all the while his spirits seemed to mend.

"And to whom am I indebted for this?" he asked presently. "Other counsels must have been discussed, I think. Who was it proposed this private method? Was it Miller?"

"My lord, it was myself," said I. "These gentlemen have shown me no such consideration, as that I should deny myself any credit I can fairly claim, or spare them any responsibility they should properly bear. And the mere truth is, that they were all in favour of a process which should have remarkable consequences in the Parliament House, and prove for them (in one of their own expressions) a dripping roast. Before I intervened, I think they were on the point of sharing out the different law appointments. Our friend Mr. Simon was to be taken in upon some composition."

Prestongrange smiled. "These are our friends," said he. "And what were your reasons for dissenting, Mr. David?"

I told them without concealment, expressing, however, with more force and volume those which regarded Prestongrange himself.

"You do me no more than justice," said he. "I have fought as hard in your interest as you have fought against mine. And how came you here to-day?" he asked. "As the case drew out, I began to grow uneasy that I had clipped the period so fine, and I was even expecting you to-morrow. But to-day—I never dreamed of it."

I was not of course, going to betray Andie.

"I suspect there is some very weary cattle by the road," said I.

"If I had known you were such a mosstrooper you should have tasted longer of the Bass," says he.

"Speaking of which, my lord, I return your letter." And I gave him the enclosure in the counterfeit hand.

"There was the cover also with the seal," said he.

"I have it not," said I. "It bore not even an address, and could not compromise a cat. The second enclosure I have, and with your permission, I desire to keep it."

I thought he winced a little, but he said nothing to the point. "To-morrow," he resumed, "our business here is to be finished, and I proceed by Glasgow. I would be very glad to have you of my party, Mr David."

"My lord . . ." I began.

"I do not deny it will be of service to me," he interrupted. "I desire even that, when we shall come to Edinburgh, you should alight at my house. You have very warm friends in the Miss Grants, who will be overjoyed to have you to themselves. If you think I have been of use to you, you can thus easily repay me, and so far from losing, may reap some advantage by the way. It is not every strange young man who is presented in society by the King's Advocate."

Often enough already (in our brief relations) this gentleman had caused my head to spin; no doubt but what for a moment he did so again now. Here was the old fiction still maintained of my particular favour with his daughters, one of whom had been so good as to laugh at me, while the other two had scarce deigned to remark the fact of my existence. And now I was to ride with my lord to Glasgow; I was to dwell with him in Edinburgh; I was to be brought into society under his protection! That he should have so much good-nature as to forgive me was surprising enough; that he could wish to take me up and serve me seemed impossible; and I began to seek some ulterior meaning. One was plain. If I became his guest, repentance was excluded; I could never think better of my present design and bring any action. And besides, would not my presence in his house draw out the whole pungency of the memorial? For that complaint could not be very seriously regarded, if the person chiefly injured was the guest of the official most incriminated. As I thought upon this I could not quite refrain from smiling.

"This is in the nature of a countercheck to the memorial?" said I.

"You are cunning, Mr. David," said he, "and you do not wholly guess wrong the fact will be of use to me in my defence. Perhaps, however, you underrate friendly sentiments, which are perfectly genuine. I have a respect for you, David, mingled with awe," says he, smiling.

"I am more than willing, I am earnestly desirous to meet your wishes," said I. "It is my design to be called to the Bar, where your lordship's countenance would be invaluable; and I am besides sincerely grateful to yourself and family for different marks of interest and of indulgence. The difficulty is here. There is one point in which we pull two ways. You are trying to hang James Stewart, I am trying to save him. In so far as my riding with you would better your lordship's defence, I am at your lordships orders; but in so far as it would help to hang James Stewart, you see me at a stick."

I thought he swore to himself. "You should certainly be called; the Bar is the true scene for your talents," says he, bitterly, and then fell a while silent. "I will tell you," he presently resumed, "there is no question of James Stewart, for or against, James is a dead man; his life is given and taken—bought (if you like it better) and sold; no memorial can help—no defalcation of a faithful Mr. David hurt him. Blow high, blow low, there will be no pardon for James Stewart: and take that for said! The question is now of myself: am I to stand or fall? and I do not deny to you that I am in some danger. But will Mr. David Balfour consider why? It is not because I pushed the case unduly against James; for that, I am sure of condonation. And it is not because I have sequestered Mr. David on a rock, though it will pass under that colour; but because I did not take the ready and plain path, to which I was pressed repeatedly, and send Mr. David to his grave or to the gallows. Hence the scandal—hence this damned memorial," striking the paper on his leg. "My tenderness for you has brought me in this difficulty. I wish to know if your tenderness to your own conscience is too great to let you help me out of it."

No doubt but there was much of the truth in what he said; if James was past helping, whom was it more natural that I should turn to help than just the man before me, who had helped myself so often, and was even now setting me a pattern of patience? I was besides not only weary, but beginning to be ashamed, of my perpetual attitude of suspicion and refusal.

"If you will name the time and place, I will be punctually ready to attend your lordship," said I.

He shook hands with me. "And I think my misses have some news for you," says he, dismissing me.

I came away, vastly pleased to have my peace made, yet a little concerned in conscience; nor could I help wondering, as I went back, whether, perhaps, I had not been a scruple too good-natured. But there was the fact, that this was a man that might have been my father, an able man, a great dignitary, and one that, in the hour of my need, had reached a hand to my assistance. I was in the better humour to enjoy the remainder of that evening, which I passed with the advocates, in excellent company no doubt, but perhaps with rather more than a sufficiency of punch: for though I went early to bed I have no clear mind of how I got there.

CHAPTER XVIII.
THE TEE'D BALL

On the morrow, from the justices' private room, where none could see me, I heard the verdict given in and judgment rendered upon James. The Duke's words I am quite sure I have correctly; and since that famous passage has been made a subject of dispute, I may as well commemorate my version. Having referred to the year '45, the chief of the Campbells, sitting as Justice-General upon the bench, thus addressed the unfortunate Stewart before him: "If you had been successful in that rebellion, you might have been giving the law where you have now received the judgment of it; we, who are this day your judges, might have been tried before one of your mock courts of judicature; and then you might have been satiated with the blood of any name or clan to which you had an aversion."

"This is to let the cat out of the bag, indeed," thought I. And that was the general impression. It was extraordinary how the young advocate lads took hold and made a mock of this speech, and how scarce a meal passed but what someone would get in the words: "And then you might have been satiated." Many songs were made in time for the hour's diversion, and are near all forgot. I remember one began:

"What do ye want the bluid of, bluid of?
Is it a name, or is it a clan,
Or is it an aefauld Hielandman,
That ye want the bluid of, bluid of?"

Another went to my old favourite air, The House of Airlie, and began thus:

"It fell on a day when Argyle was on the bench,
That they served him a Stewart for his denner."

And one of the verses ran:

"Then up and spak' the Duke, and flyted on his cook,
I regard it as a sensible aspersion,
That I would sup ava', an' satiate my maw,
With the bluid of ony clan of my aversion."

James was as fairly murdered as though the Duke had got a fowling-piece and stalked him. So much of course I knew: but others knew not so much, and were more affected by the items of scandal that came to light in the progress of the cause. One of the chief was certainly this sally of the justice's. It was run hard by another of a juryman, who had struck into the midst of Coulston's speech for the defence with a "Pray, sir, cut it short, we are quite weary," which seemed the very excess of impudence and simplicity. But some of my new lawyer friends were still more staggered with an innovation that had disgraced and even vitiated the proceedings. One witness was never called. His name, indeed, was printed, where it may still be seen on the fourth page of the list:

"James Drummond, alias Macgregor, alias James More, late tenant in Inveronachile"; and his precognition had been taken, as the manner is, in writing. He had remembered or invented (God help him) matter which was lead in James Stewart's shoes, and I saw was like to prove wings to his own. This testimony it was highly desirable to bring to the notice of the jury, without exposing the man himself to the perils of cross-examination; and the way it was brought about was a matter of surprise to all. For the paper was handed round (like a curiosity) in court; passed through the jury-box, where it did its work; and disappeared again (as though by accident) before it reached the counsel for the prisoner. This was counted a most insidious device; and that the name of James More should be mingled up with it filled me with shame for Catriona and concern for myself.

The following day, Prestongrange and I, with a considerable company, set out for Glasgow, where (to my impatience) we continued to linger some time in a mixture of pleasure and affairs. I lodged with my lord, with whom I was encouraged to familiarity; had my place at entertainments; was presented to the chief guests; and altogether made more of than I thought accorded either with my parts or station; so that, on strangers being present, I would often blush for Prestongrange. It must be owned the view I had taken of the world in these last months was fit to cast a gloom upon my character. I had met many men, some of them leaders in Israel whether by their birth or talents; and who among them all had shown clean hands? As for the Browns and Millers, I had seen their self-seeking, I could never again respect them. Prestongrange was the best yet; he had saved me, spared me rather, when others had it in their minds to murder me outright; but the blood of James lay at his door; and I thought his present dissimulation with myself a thing below pardon. That he should affect to find pleasure in my discourse almost surprised me out of my patience. I would sit and watch him with a kind of a slow fire of anger in my bowels. "Ah, friend, friend," I would think to myself, "if you were but through with this affair of the memorial, would you not kick me in the streets?" Here I did him, as events have proved, the most grave injustice; and I think he was at once far more sincere, and a far more artful performer, than I supposed.

But I had some warrant for my incredulity in the behaviour of that court of young advocates that hung about in the hope of patronage. The sudden favour of a lad not previously heard of troubled them at first out of measure; but two days were not gone by before I found myself surrounded with flattery and attention. I was the same young man, and neither better nor bonnier, that they had rejected a month before; and now there was no civility too fine for me! The same, do I say? It was not so; and the by-name by which I went behind my back confirmed it. Seeing me so firm with the Advocate, and persuaded that I was to fly high and far, they had taken a word from the golfing green, and called me the Tee'd Ball. [14] I was told I was now "one of themselves"; I was to taste of their soft lining, who had already made my own experience of the roughness of the outer husk; and one, to whom I had been presented in Hope Park, was so aspired as even to remind me of that meeting. I told him I had not the pleasure of remembering it.

"Why" says he, "it was Miss Grant herself presented me! My name is so-and-so."

"It may very well be, sir," said I; "but I have kept no mind of it."

At which he desisted; and in the midst of the disgust that commonly overflowed my spirits I had a glisk of pleasure.

But I have not patience to dwell upon that time at length. When I was in company with these young politics I was borne down with shame for myself and my own plain ways, and scorn for them and their duplicity. Of the two evils, I thought Prestongrange to be the least; and while I was always as stiff as buckram to the young bloods, I made rather a dissimulation of my hard feelings towards the Advocate, and was (in old Mr. Campbell's word) "soople to the laird." Himself commented on the difference, and bid me be more of my age, and make friends with my young comrades.

I told him I was slow of making friends.

"I will take the word back," said he. "But there is such a thing as Fair gude s'en and fair gude day, Mr. David. These are the same young men with whom you are to pass your days and get through life: your backwardness has a look of arrogance; and unless you can assume a little more lightness of manner, I fear you will meet difficulties in the path."

"It will be an ill job to make a silk purse of a sow's ear," said I.

On the morning of October 1st I was awakened by the clattering in of an express; and getting to my window almost before he had dismounted, I saw the messenger had ridden hard. Somewhile after I was called to Prestongrange, where he was sitting in his bedgown and nightcap, with his letters round him.

"Mr. David," add he, "I have a piece of news for you. It concerns some friends of yours, of whom I sometimes think you are a little ashamed, for you have never referred to their existence."

I suppose I blushed.

"See you understand, since you make the answering signal," said he. "And I must compliment you on your excellent taste in beauty. But do you know, Mr. David? this seems to me a very enterprising lass. She crops up from every side. The Government of Scotland appears unable to proceed for Mistress Katrine Drummond, which was somewhat the case (no great while back) with a certain Mr. David Balfour. Should not these make a good match? Her first intromission in politics—but I must not tell you that story, the authorities have decided you are to hear it otherwise and from a livelier narrator. This new example is more serious, however; and I am afraid I must alarm you with the intelligence that she is now in prison."

I cried out.

"Yes," said he, "the little lady is in prison. But I would not have you to despair. Unless you (with your friends and memorials) shall procure my downfall, she is to suffer nothing."

"But what has she done? What is her offence?" I cried.

"It might be almost construed a high treason," he returned, "for she has broke the king's Castle of Edinburgh."

"The lady is much my friend," I said. "I know you would not mock me if the thing were serious."

"And yet it is serious in a sense," said he; "for this rogue of a Katrine—or Cateran, as we may call her—has set adrift again upon the world that very doubtful character, her papa."

Here was one of my previsions justified: James More was once again at liberty. He had lent his men to keep me a prisoner; he had volunteered his testimony in the Appin case, and the same (no matter by what subterfuge) had been employed to influence the jury. Now came his reward, and he was free. It might please the authorities to give to it the colour of an escape; but I knew better—I knew it must be the fulfilment of a bargain. The same course of thought relieved me of the least alarm for Catriona. She might be thought to have broke prison for her father; she might have believed so herself. But the chief hand in the whole business was that of Prestongrange; and I was sure, so far from letting her come to punishment, he would not suffer her to be even tried. Whereupon thus came out of me the not very politic ejaculation:

"Ah! I was expecting that!"

"You have at times a great deal of discretion, too!" says Prestongrange.

"And what is my lord pleased to mean by that?" I asked.

"I was just marvelling", he replied, "that being so clever as to draw these inferences, you should not be clever enough to keep them to yourself. But I think you would like to hear the details of the affair. I have received two versions: and the least official is the more full and far the more entertaining, being from the lively pen of my eldest daughter. 'Here is all the town bizzing with a fine piece of work,' she writes, 'and what would make the thing more noted (if it were only known) the malefactor is a protégée of his lordship my papa. I am sure your heart is too much in your duty (if it were nothing else) to have forgotten Grey Eyes. What does she do, but get a broad hat with the flaps open, a long hairy-like man's greatcoat, and a big gravatt; kilt her coats up to Gude kens whaur, clap two pair of boot-hose upon her legs, take a pair of clouted brogues [15] in her hand, and off to the Castle! Here she gives herself out to be a soutar [16] in the employ of James More, and gets admitted to his cell, the lieutenant (who seems to have been full of pleasantry) making sport among his soldiers of the soutar's greatcoat. Presently they hear disputation and the sound of blows inside. Out flies the cobbler, his coat flying, the flaps of his hat beat about his face, and the lieutenant and his soldiers mock at him as he runs off. They laughed no so hearty the next time they had occasion to visit the cell and found nobody but a tall, pretty, grey-eyed lass in the female habit! As for the cobbler, he was 'over the hills ayout Dumblane,' and it's thought that poor Scotland will have to console herself without him. I drank Catriona's health this night in public. Indeed, the whole town admires her; and I think the beaux would wear bits of her garters in their button-holes if they could only get them. I would have gone to visit her in prison too, only I remembered in time I was papa's daughter; so I wrote her a billet instead, which I entrusted to the faithful Doig, and I hope you will admit I can be political when I please. The same faithful gomeral is to despatch this letter by the express along with those of the wiseacres, so that you may hear Tom Fool in company with Solomon. Talking of gomerals, do tell Dauvit Balfour. I would I could see the face of him at the thought of a long-legged lass in such a predicament; to say nothing of the levities of your affectionate daughter, and his respectful friend.' So my rascal signs herself!" continued Prestongrange. "And you see, Mr. David, it is quite true what I tell you, that my daughters regard you with the most affectionate playfulness."

"The gomeral is much obliged," said I.

"And was not this prettily done!" he went on. "Is not this Highland maid a piece of a heroine?"

"I was always sure she had a great heart," said I. "And I wager she guessed nothing . . . But I beg your pardon, this is to tread upon forbidden subjects."

"I will go bail she did not," he returned, quite openly. "I will go bail she thought she was flying straight into King George's face."

Remembrance of Catriona and the thought of her lying in captivity, moved me strangely. I could see that even Prestongrange admired, and could not withhold his lips from smiling when he considered her behaviour. As for Miss Grant, for all her ill habit of mockery, her admiration shone out plain. A kind of a heat came on me.

"I am not your lordship's daughter. . . " I began.

"That I know of!" he put in, smiling.

"I speak like a fool," said I; "or rather I began wrong. It would doubtless be unwise in Mistress Grant to go to her in prison; but for me, I think I would look like a half-hearted friend if I did not fly there instantly."

"So-ho, Mr. David," says he; "I thought that you and I were in a bargain?"

"My lord," I said, "when I made that bargain I was a good deal affected by your goodness, but

I'll never can deny that I was moved besides by my own interest. There was self-seeking in my heart, and I think shame of it now. It may be for your lordship's safety to say this fashious Davie Balfour is your friend and housemate. Say it then; I'll never contradict you. But as for your patronage, I give it all back. I ask but the one thing—let me go, and give me a pass to see her in her prison."

He looked at me with a hard eye. "You put the cart before the horse, I think," says he. "That which I had given was a portion of my liking, which your thankless nature does not seem to have remarked. But for my patronage, it is not given, nor (to be exact) is it yet offered." He paused a bit. "And I warn you, you do not know yourself," he added. "Youth is a hasty season; you will think better of all this before a year."

"Well, and I would like to be that kind of youth!" I cried. "I have seen too much of the other party in these young advocates that fawn upon your lordship and are even at the pains to fawn on me. And I have seen it in the old ones also. They are all for by-ends, the whole clan of them! It's this that makes me seem to misdoubt your lordship's liking. Why would I think that you would like me? But ye told me yourself ye had an interest!"

I stopped at this, confounded that I had run so far; he was observing me with an unfathomable face.

"My lord, I ask your pardon," I resumed. "I have nothing in my chafts but a rough country tongue. I think it would be only decent-like if I would go to see my friend in her captivity; but I'm owing you my life—I'll never forget that; and if it's for your lordship's good, here I'll stay. That's barely gratitude."

"This might have been reached in fewer words," says Prestongrange grimly. "It is easy, and it is at times gracious, to say a plain Scots 'ay'."

"Ah, but, my lord, I think ye take me not yet entirely!" cried I. "For your sake, for my life-safe, and the kindness that ye say ye bear to me—for these, I'll consent; but not for any good that might be coming to myself. If I stand aside when this young maid is in her trial, it's a thing I will be noways advantaged by; I will lose by it, I will never gain. I would rather make a shipwreck wholly than to build on that foundation."

He was a minute serious, then smiled. "You mind me of the man with the long nose," said he; "was you to see the moon by a telescope you would see David Balfour there! But you shall have your way of it. I will ask at you one service, and then set you free: My clerks are overdriven; be so good as copy me these few pages, and when that is done, I shall bid you God speed! I would never charge myself with Mr. David's conscience; and if you could cast some part of it (as you went by) in a moss hag, you would find yourself to ride much easier without it."

"Perhaps not just entirely in the same direction though, my lord!" says I.

"And you shall have the last word, too!" cries he gaily.

Indeed, he had some cause for gaiety, having now found the means to gain his purpose. To lessen the weight of the memorial, or to have a readier answer at his hand, he desired I should appear publicly in the character of his intimate. But if I were to appear with the same publicity as a visitor to Catriona in her prison the world would scarce stint to draw conclusions, and the true nature of James More's escape must become evident to all. This was the little problem I had to set him of a sudden, and to which he had so briskly found an answer. I was to be tethered in Glasgow by that job of copying, which in mere outward decency I could not well refuse; and during these hours of employment Catriona was privately got rid of. I think shame to write of this man that loaded me with so many goodnesses. He was kind to me as any father, yet I ever thought him as false as a cracked bell.

CHAPTER XIX.
I AM MUCH IN THE HANDS OF THE LADIES

The copying was a weary business, the more so as I perceived very early there was no sort of urgency in the matters treated, and began very early to consider my employment a pretext. I had no sooner finished than I got to horse, used what remained of daylight to the best purpose, and being at last fairly benighted, slept in a house by Almond-Water side. I was in the saddle again before the day, and the Edinburgh booths were just opening when I clattered in by the West Bow and drew up a smoking horse at my lord Advocate's door. I had a written word for Doig, my lord's private hand that was thought to be in all his secrets—a worthy little plain man, all fat and snuff and self-sufficiency. Him I found already at his desk and already bedabbled with maccabaw, in the same anteroom where I rencountered with James More. He read the note scrupulously through like a chapter in his Bible.

"H'm," says he; "ye come a wee thing ahint-hand, Mr. Balfour. The bird's flaen—we hae letten her out."

"Miss Drummond is set free?" I cried.

"Achy!" said he. "What would we keep her for, ye ken? To hae made a steer about the bairn would has pleased naebody."

"And where'll she be now?" says I.

"Gude kens!" says Doig, with a shrug.

"She'll have gone home to Lady Allardyce, I'm thinking," said I.

"That'll be it," said he.

"Then I'll gang there straight," says I.

"But ye'll be for a bite or ye go?" said he.

"Neither bite nor sup," said I. "I had a good wauch of milk in by Ratho."

"Aweel, aweel," says Doig. "But ye'll can leave your horse here and your bags, for it seems we're to have your up-put."

"Na, na", said I. "Tamson's mear [17] would never be the thing for me this day of all days."

Doig speaking somewhat broad, I had been led by imitation into an accent much more countrified than I was usually careful to affect a good deal broader, indeed, than I have written it down; and I was the more ashamed when another voice joined in behind me with a scrap of a ballad:

"Gae saddle me the bonny black,
Gae saddle sune and mak' him ready
For I will down the Gatehope-slack,
And a' to see my bonny leddy."

The young lady, when I turned to her, stood in a morning gown, and her hands muffled in the same, as if to hold me at a distance. Yet I could not but think there was kindness in the eye with which she saw me.

"My best respects to you, Mistress Grant," said I, bowing.

"The like to yourself, Mr. David," she replied with a deep courtesy. "And I beg to remind you of an old musty saw, that meat and mass never hindered man. The mass I cannot afford you, for we are all good Protestants. But the meat I press on your attention. And I would not wonder but I could find something for your private ear that would be worth the stopping for."

"Mistress Grant," said I, "I believe I am already your debtor for some merry words—and I think they were kind too—on a piece of unsigned paper."

"Unsigned paper?" says she, and made a droll face, which was likewise wondrous beautiful, as of one trying to remember.

"Or else I am the more deceived," I went on. "But to be sure, we shall have the time to speak of these, since your father is so good as to make me for a while your inmate; and the gomeral begs you at this time only for the favour of his liberty."

"You give yourself hard names," said she.

"Mr. Doig and I would be blythe to take harder at your clever pen," says I.

"Once more I have to admire the discretion of all men-folk," she replied. "But if you will not eat, off with you at once; you will be back the sooner, for you go on a fool's errand. Off with you, Mr. David," she continued, opening the door.

"He has lowpen on his bonny grey,
He rade the richt gate and the ready
I trow he would neither stint nor stay,
For he was seeking his bonny leddy."

I did not wait to be twice bidden, and did justice to Miss Grant's citation on the way to Dean.

Old Lady Allardyce walked there alone in the garden, in her hat and mutch, and having a silver-mounted staff of some black wood to lean upon. As I alighted from my horse, and drew near to her with congees, I could see the blood come in her face, and her head fling into the air like what I had conceived of empresses.

"What brings you to my poor door?" she cried, speaking high through her nose. "I cannot bar it. The males of my house are dead and buried; I have neither son nor husband to stand in the gate for me; any beggar can pluck me by the baird [18]—and a baird there is, and that's the worst of it yet!" she added partly to herself.

I was extremely put out at this reception, and the last remark, which seemed like a daft wife's, left me near hand speechless.

"I see I have fallen under your displeasure, ma'am," said I. "Yet I will still be so bold as ask after Mistress Drummond."

She considered me with a burning eye, her lips pressed close together into twenty creases, her hand shaking on her staff. "This cows all!" she cried. "Ye come to me to speir for her? Would God I knew!"

"She is not here?" I cried.

She threw up her chin and made a step and a cry at me, so that I fell back incontinent.

"Out upon your leeing throat!" she cried. "What! ye come and speir at me! She's in jyle, whaur ye took her to—that's all there is to it. And of a' the beings ever I beheld in breeks, to think it should be to you! Ye timmer scoun'rel, if I had a male left to my name I would have your jaicket dustit till ye raired."

I thought it not good to delay longer in that place, because I remarked her passion to be rising. As I turned to the horse-post she even followed me; and I make no shame to confess that I rode away with the one stirrup on and scrambling for the other.

As I knew no other quarter where I could push my inquiries, there was nothing left me but to return to the Advocate's. I was well received by the four ladies, who were now in company together, and must give the news of Prestongrange and what word went in the west country, at the most inordinate length and with great weariness to myself; while all the time that young lady, with whom I so much desired to be alone again, observed me quizzically and seemed to find pleasure in the sight of my impatience. At last, after I had endured a meal with them, and was come very near the point of appealing for an interview before her aunt, she went and stood by the music-case, and picking out a tune, sang to it on a high key—"He that will not when he may, When he will he shall have nay." But this was the end of her rigours, and presently, after making some excuse of which I have no mind, she carried me away in private to her father's library. I should not fail to say she was dressed to the nines, and appeared extraordinary handsome.

"Now, Mr. David, sit ye down here and let us have a two-handed crack," said she. "For I have much to tell you, and it appears besides that I have been grossly unjust to your good taste."

"In what manner, Mistress Grant?" I asked. "I trust I have never seemed to fail in due respect."

"I will be your surety, Mr. David," said she. "Your respect, whether to yourself or your poor neighbours, has been always and most fortunately beyond imitation. But that is by the question. You got a note from me?" she asked.

"I was so bold as to suppose so upon inference," said I, "and it was kindly thought upon."

"It must have prodigiously surprised you," said she. "But let us begin with the beginning. You have not perhaps forgot a day when you were so kind as to escort three very tedious misses to Hope Park? I have the less cause to forget it myself, because you was so particular obliging as to introduce me to some of the principles of the Latin grammar, a thing which wrote itself profoundly on my gratitude."

"I fear I was sadly pedantical," said I, overcome with confusion at the memory. "You are only to consider I am quite unused with the society of ladies."

"I will say the less about the grammar then," she replied. "But how came you to desert your charge? 'He has thrown her out, overboard, his ain dear Annie!'" she hummed; "and his ain dear Annie and her two sisters had to taigle home by theirselves like a string of green geese! It seems you returned to my papa's, where you showed yourself excessively martial, and then on to realms unknown, with an eye (it appears) to the Bass Rock; solan geese being perhaps more to your mind than bonny lasses."

Through all this raillery there was something indulgent in the lady's eye which made me suppose there might be better coming.

"You take a pleasure to torment me," said I, "and I make a very feckless plaything; but let me ask you to be more merciful. At this time there is but the one thing that I care to hear of, and that will be news of Catriona."

"Do you call her by that name to her face, Mr. Balfour?" she asked.

"In troth, and I am not very sure," I stammered.

"I would not do so in any case to strangers," said Miss Grant. "And why are you so much immersed in the affairs of this young lady?"

"I heard she was in prison," said I.

"Well, and now you hear that she is out of it," she replied, "and what more would you have? She has no need of any further champion."

"I may have the greater need of her, ma'am," said I.

"Come, this is better!" says Miss Grant. "But look me fairly in the face; am I not bonnier than she?"

"I would be the last to be denying it," said I. "There is not your marrow in all Scotland."

"Well, here you have the pick of the two at your hand, and must needs speak of the other," said she. "This is never the way to please the ladies, Mr. Balfour."

"But, mistress," said I, "there are surely other things besides mere beauty."

"By which I am to understand that I am no better than I should be, perhaps?" she asked.

"By which you will please understand that I am like the cock in the midden in the fable book," said I. "I see the braw jewel—and I like fine to see it too—but I have more need of the pickle corn."

"Bravissimo!" she cried. "There is a word well said at last, and I will reward you for it with my story. That same night of your desertion I came late from a friend's house—where I was excessively admired, whatever you may think of it—and what should I hear but that a lass in a tartan screen desired to speak with me? She had been there an hour or better, said the servant-lass, and she grat in to herself as she sat waiting. I went to her direct; she rose as I came in, and I knew her at a look. 'Grey Eyes!' says I to myself, but was more wise than to let on. You will be Miss Grant at last? she says, rising and looking at me hard and pitiful. Ay, it was true he said, you are bonny at all events.—The way God made me, my dear, I said, but I would be gey and obliged if you could tell me what brought you here at such a time of the night.—Lady, she said, we are kinsfolk, we are both come of the blood of the sons of Alpin.—My dear, I replied, I think no more of Alpin or his sons than what I do of a kalestock. You have a better argument in these tears upon your bonny face. And at that I was so weak-minded as to kiss her, which is what you would like to do dearly, and I wager will never find the courage of. I say it was weak-minded of me, for I knew no more of her than the outside; but it was the wisest stroke I could have hit upon. She is a very staunch, brave nature, but I think she has been little used with tenderness; and at that caress (though to say the truth, it was but lightly given) her heart went out to me. I will never betray the secrets of my sex, Mr. Davie; I will never tell you the way she turned me round her thumb, because it is the same she will use to twist yourself. Ay, it is a fine lass! She is as clean as hill well water."

"She is e'en't!" I cried.

"Well, then, she told me her concerns," pursued Miss Grant, "and in what a swither she was in about her papa, and what a taking about yourself, with very little cause, and in what a perplexity she had found herself after you was gone away. And then I minded at long last, says she, that we were kinswomen, and that Mr. David should have given you the name of the bonniest of the bonny, and I was thinking to myself 'If she is so bonny she will be good at all events'; and I took up my foot soles out of that. That was when I forgave yourself, Mr. Davie. When you was in my society, you seemed upon hot iron: by all marks, if ever I saw a young man that wanted to be gone, it was yourself, and I and my two sisters were the ladies you were so desirous to be gone from; and now it appeared you had given me some notice in the by-going, and was so kind as to comment on my attractions! From that hour you may date our friendship, and I began to think with tenderness upon the Latin grammar."

"You will have many hours to rally me in," said I; "and I think besides you do yourself injustice. I think it was Catriona turned your heart in my direction. She is too simple to perceive as you do the stiffness of her friend."

"I would not like to wager upon that, Mr. David," said she. "The lasses have clear eyes. But at least she is your friend entirely, as I was to see. I carried her in to his lordship my papa; and his Advocacy being in a favourable stage of claret, was so good as to receive the pair of us. Here is Grey Eyes that you have been deaved with these days past, said I, she is come to prove that we spoke true, and I lay the prettiest lass in the three Lothians at your feet—making a papistical reservation of myself. She suited her action to my words: down she went upon her knees to him—I would not like to swear but he saw two of her, which doubtless made her appeal the more irresistible, for you are all a pack of Mahomedans—told him what had passed that night, and how she had withheld her father's man from following of you, and what a case she was in about her father, and what a flutter for yourself; and begged with weeping for the lives of both of you (neither of which was in the slightest danger), till I vow I was proud of my sex because it was done so pretty, and ashamed for it because of the smallness of the occasion. She had not gone far, I assure you, before the Advocate was wholly sober, to see his inmost politics ravelled out by a young lass and discovered to the most unruly of his daughters. But we took him in hand, the pair of us, and brought that matter straight. Properly managed—and that means managed by me—there is no one to compare with my papa."

"He has been a good man to me," said I.

"Well, he was a good man to Katrine, and I was there to see to it," said she.

"And she pled for me?" say I.

"She did that, and very movingly," said Miss Grant. "I would not like to tell you what she said—I find you vain enough already."

"God reward her for it!" cried I.

"With Mr. David Balfour, I suppose?" says she.

"You do me too much injustice at the last!" I cried. "I would tremble to think of her in such hard hands. Do you think I would presume, because she begged my life? She would do that for a new whelped puppy! I have had more than that to set me up, if you but ken'd. She kissed that hand of mine. Ay, but she did. And why? because she thought I was playing a brave part and might be going to my death. It was not for my sake—but I need not be telling that to you, that cannot look at me without laughter. It was for the love of what she thought was bravery. I believe there is none but me and poor Prince Charlie had that honour done them. Was this not to make a god of me? and do you not think my heart would quake when I remember it?"

"I do laugh at you a good deal, and a good deal more than is quite civil," said she; "but I will tell you one thing: if you speak to her like that, you have some glimmerings of a chance."

"Me?" I cried, "I would never dare. I can speak to you, Miss Grant, because it's a matter of indifference what ye think of me. But her? no fear!" said I.

"I think you have the largest feet in all broad Scotland," says she.

"Troth they are no very small," said I, looking down.

"Ah, poor Catriona!" cries Miss Grant.

And I could but stare upon her; for though I now see very well what she was driving at (and perhaps some justification for the same), I was never swift at the uptake in such flimsy talk.

"Ah well, Mr. David," she said, "it goes sore against my conscience, but I see I shall have to be your speaking board. She shall know you came to her straight upon the news of her imprisonment; she shall know you would not pause to eat; and of our conversation she shall hear just so much as I think convenient for a maid of her age and inexperience. Believe me, you will be in that way much better served than you could serve yourself, for I will keep the big feet out of the platter."

"You know where she is, then?" I exclaimed.

"That I do, Mr. David, and will never tell," said she.

"Why that?" I asked.

"Well," she said, "I am a good friend, as you will soon discover; and the chief of those that I am friend to is my papa. I assure you, you will never heat nor melt me out of that, so you may spare me your sheep's eyes; and adieu to your David-Balfourship for the now."

"But there is yet one thing more," I cried. "There is one thing that must be stopped, being mere ruin to herself, and to me too."

"Well," she said, "be brief; I have spent half the day on you already."

"My Lady Allardyce believes," I began—"she supposes—she thinks that I abducted her."

The colour came into Miss Grant's face, so that at first I was quite abashed to find her ear so delicate, till I bethought me she was struggling rather with mirth, a notion in which I was altogether confirmed by the shaking of her voice as she replied—

"I will take up the defence of your reputation," she said. "You may leave it in my hands."

And with that she withdrew out of the library.

CHAPTER XX.
I CONTINUE TO MOVE IN GOOD SOCIETY

For about exactly two months I remained a guest in Prestongrange's family, where I bettered my acquaintance with the bench, the bar, and the flower of Edinburgh company. You are not to suppose my education was neglected; on the contrary, I was kept extremely busy. I studied the French, so as to be more prepared to go to Leyden; I set myself to the fencing, and wrought hard, sometimes three hours in the day, with notable advancement; at the suggestion of my cousin, Pilrig, who was an apt musician, I was put to a singing class; and by the orders of my Miss Grant, to one for the dancing, at which I must say I proved far from ornamental. However, all were good enough to say it gave me an address a little more genteel; and there is no question but I learned to manage my coat skirts and sword with more dexterity, and to stand in a room as though the same belonged to me. My clothes themselves were all earnestly re-ordered; and the most trifling circumstance, such as where I should tie my hair, or the colour of my ribbon, debated among the three misses like a thing of weight. One way with another, no doubt I was a good deal improved to look at, and acquired a bit of modest air that would have surprised the good folks at Essendean.

The two younger misses were very willing to discuss a point of my habiliment, because that was in the line of their chief thoughts. I cannot say that they appeared any other way conscious of my presence; and though always more than civil, with a kind of heartless cordiality, could not hide how much I wearied them. As for the aunt, she was a wonderful still woman; and I think she gave me much the same attention as she gave the rest of the family, which was little enough. The eldest daughter and the Advocate himself were thus my principal friends, and our familiarity was much increased by a pleasure that we took in common. Before the court met we spent a day or two at the house of Grange, living very nobly with an open table, and here it was that we three began to ride out together in the fields, a practice afterwards maintained in Edinburgh, so far as the Advocate's continual affairs permitted. When we were put in a good frame by the briskness of the exercise, the difficulties of the way, or the accidents of bad weather, my shyness wore entirely off; we forgot that we were strangers, and speech not being required, it flowed the more naturally on. Then it was that they had my story from me, bit by bit, from the time that I left Essendean, with my voyage and battle in the Covenant, wanderings in the heather, etc.; and from the interest they found in my adventures sprung the circumstance of a jaunt we made a little later on, on a day when the courts were not sitting, and of which I will tell a trifle more at length.

We took horse early, and passed first by the house of Shaws, where it stood smokeless in a great field of white frost, for it was yet early in the day. Here Prestongrange alighted down, gave me his horse, an proceeded alone to visit my uncle. My heart, I remember, swelled up bitter within me at the sight of that bare house and the thought of the old miser sitting chittering within in the cold kitchen!

"There is my home," said I; "and my family."

"Poor David Balfour!" said Miss Grant.

What passed during the visit I have never heard; but it would doubtless not be very agreeable to Ebenezer, for when the Advocate came forth again his face was dark.

"I think you will soon be the laird indeed, Mr. Davie," says he, turning half about with the one foot in the stirrup.

"I will never pretend sorrow," said I; and, to say the truth, during his absence Miss Grant and I had been embellishing the place in fancy with plantations, parterres, and a terrace—much as I have since carried out in fact.

Thence we pushed to the Queensferry, where Rankeillor gave us a good welcome, being indeed out of the body to receive so great a visitor. Here the Advocate was so unaffectedly good as to go quite fully over my affairs, sitting perhaps two hours with the Writer in his study, and expressing (I was told) a great esteem for myself and concern for my fortunes. To while this time, Miss Grant and I and young Rankeillor took boat and passed the Hope to Limekilns. Rankeillor made himself very ridiculous (and, I thought, offensive) with his admiration for the young lady, and to my wonder (only it is so common a weakness of her sex) she seemed, if anything, to be a little gratified. One use it had: for when we were come to the other side, she laid her commands on him to mind the boat, while she and I passed a little further to the alehouse. This was her own thought, for she had been taken with my account of Alison Hastie, and desired to see the lass herself. We found her once more alone—indeed, I believe her father wrought all day in the fields—and she curtsied dutifully to the gentry-folk and the beautiful young lady in the riding-coat.

"Is this all the welcome I am to get?" said I, holding out my hand. "And have you no more memory of old friends?"

"Keep me! wha's this of it?" she cried, and then, "God's truth, it's the tautit [19] laddie!"

"The very same," says I.

"Mony's the time I've thocht upon you and your freen, and blythe am I to see in your braws," [20] she cried. "Though I kent ye were come to your ain folk by the grand present that ye sent me and that I thank ye for with a' my heart."

"There," said Miss Grant to me, "run out by with ye, like a guid bairn. I didnae come here to stand and haud a candle; it's her and me that are to crack."

I suppose she stayed ten minutes in the house, but when she came forth I observed two things—that her eyes were reddened, and a silver brooch was gone out of her bosom. This very much affected me.

"I never saw you so well adorned," said I.

"O Davie man, dinna be a pompous gowk!" said she, and was more than usually sharp to me the remainder of the day.

About candlelight we came home from this excursion.

For a good while I heard nothing further of Catriona—my Miss Grant remaining quite impenetrable, and stopping my mouth with pleasantries. At last, one day that she returned from walking and found me alone in the parlour over my French, I thought there was something unusual in her looks; the colour heightened, the eyes sparkling high, and a bit of a smile continually bitten in as she regarded me. She seemed indeed like the very spirit of mischief, and, walking briskly in the room, had soon involved me in a kind of quarrel over nothing and (at the least) with nothing intended on my side. I was like Christian in the slough—the more I tried to clamber out upon the side, the deeper I became involved; until at last I heard her declare, with a great deal of passion, that she would take that answer from the hands of none, and I must down upon my knees for pardon.

The causelessness of all this fuff stirred my own bile. "I have said nothing you can properly object to," said I, "and as for my knees, that is an attitude I keep for God."

"And as a goddess I am to be served!" she cried, shaking her brown locks at me and with a bright colour. "Every man that comes within waft of my petticoats shall use me so!"

"I will go so far as ask your pardon for the fashion's sake, although I vow I know not why," I replied. "But for these play-acting postures, you can go to others."

"O Davie!" she said. "Not if I was to beg you?"

I bethought me I was fighting with a woman, which is the same as to say a child, and that upon a point entirely formal.

"I think it a bairnly thing," I said, "not worthy in you to ask, or me to render. Yet I will not refuse you, neither," said I; "and the stain, if there be any, rests with yourself." And at that I kneeled fairly down.

"There!" she cried. "There is the proper station, there is where I have been manoeuvring to bring you." And then, suddenly, "Kep," [21] said she, flung me a folded billet, and ran from the apartment laughing.

The billet had neither place nor date. "Dear Mr. David," it began, "I get your news continually by my cousin, Miss Grant, and it is a pleisand hearing. I am very well, in a good place, among good folk, but necessitated to be quite private, though I am hoping that at long last we may meet again. All your friendships have been told me by my loving cousin, who loves us both. She bids me to send you this writing, and oversees the same. I will be asking you to do all her commands, and rest your affectionate friend, Catriona Macgregor-Drummond. P.S.—Will you not see my cousin, Allardyce?"

I think it not the least brave of my campaigns (as the soldiers say) that I should have done as I was here bidden and gone forthright to the house by Dean. But the old lady was now entirely changed and supple as a glove. By what means Miss Grant had brought this round I could never guess; I am sure, at least, she dared not to appear openly in the affair, for her papa was compromised in it pretty deep. It was he, indeed, who had persuaded Catriona to leave, or rather, not to return, to her cousin's, placing her instead with a family of Gregorys—decent people, quite at the Advocate's disposition, and in whom she might have the more confidence because they were of his own clan and family. These kept her private till all was ripe, heated and helped her to attempt her father's rescue, and after she was discharged from prison received her again into the same secrecy. Thus Prestongrange obtained and used his instrument; nor did there leak out the smallest word of his acquaintance with the daughter of James More. There was some whispering, of course, upon the escape of that discredited person; but the Government replied by a show of rigour, one of the cell porters was flogged, the lieutenant of the guard (my poor friend, Duncansby) was broken of his rank, and as for Catriona, all men were well enough pleased that her fault should be passed by in silence.

I could never induce Miss Grant to carry back an answer. "No," she would say, when I persisted, "I am going to keep the big feet out of the platter." This was the more hard to bear, as I was aware she saw my little friend many times in the week, and carried her my news whenever (as she said) I "had behaved myself." At last she treated me to what she called an indulgence, and I thought rather more of a banter. She was certainly a strong, almost a violent, friend to all she liked, chief among whom was a certain frail old gentlewoman, very blind and very witty, who dwelt on the top of a tall land on a strait close, with a nest of linnets in a cage, and thronged all day with visitors. Miss Grant was very fond to carry me there and put me to entertain her friend with the narrative of my misfortunes: and Miss Tibbie Ramsay (that was her name) was particular kind, and told me a great deal that was worth knowledge of old folks and past affairs in Scotland. I should say that from her chamber window, and not three feet away, such is the straitness of that close, it was possible to look into a barred loophole lighting the stairway of the opposite house.

Here, upon some pretext, Miss Grant left me one day alone with Miss Ramsay. I mind I thought that lady inattentive and like one preoccupied. I was besides very uncomfortable, for the window, contrary to custom, was left open and the day was cold. All at once the voice of Miss Grant sounded in my ears as from a distance.

"Here, Shaws!" she cried, "keek out of the window and see what I have broughten you."

I think it was the prettiest sight that ever I beheld. The well of the close was all in clear shadow where a man could see distinctly, the walls very black and dingy; and there from the barred loophole I saw two faces smiling across at me—Miss Grant's and Catriona's.

"There!" says Miss Grant, "I wanted her to see you in your braws like the lass of Limekilns. I wanted her to see what I could make of you, when I buckled to the job in earnest!"

It came in my mind that she had been more than common particular that day upon my dress; and I think that some of the same care had been bestowed upon Catriona. For so merry and sensible a lady, Miss Grant was certainly wonderful taken up with duds.

"Catriona!" was all I could get out.

As for her, she said nothing in the world, but only waved her hand and smiled to me, and was suddenly carried away again from before the loophole.

That vision was no sooner lost than I ran to the house door, where I found I was locked in; thence back to Miss Ramsay, crying for the key, but might as well have cried upon the castle rock. She had passed her word, she said, and I must be a good lad. It was impossible to burst the door, even if it had been mannerly; it was impossible I should leap from the window, being seven storeys above ground. All I could do was to crane over the close and watch for their reappearance from the stair. It was little to see, being no more than the tops of their two heads each on a ridiculous bobbin of skirts, like to a pair of pincushions. Nor did Catriona so much as look up for a farewell; being prevented (as I heard afterwards) by Miss Grant, who told her folk were never seen to less advantage than from above downward.

On the way home, as soon as I was set free, I upbraided Miss Grant with her cruelty.

"I am sorry you was disappointed," says she demurely. "For my part I was very pleased. You looked better than I dreaded; you looked—if it will not make you vain—a mighty pretty young man when you appeared in the window. You are to remember that she could not see your feet," says she, with the manner of one reassuring me.

"O!" cried I, "leave my feet be—they are no bigger than my neighbours'."

"They are even smaller than some," said she, "but I speak in parables like a Hebrew prophet."

"I marvel little they were sometimes stoned!" says I. "But, you miserable girl, how could you do it? Why should you care to tantalise me with a moment?"

"Love is like folk," says she; "it needs some kind of vivers." [22]

"Oh, Barbara, let me see her properly!" I pleaded. "You can—you see her when you please; let me have half an hour."

"Who is it that is managing this love affair! You! Or me?" she asked, and as I continued to press her with my instances, fell back upon a deadly expedient: that of imitating the tones of my voice when I called on Catriona by name; with which, indeed, she held me in subjection for some days to follow.

There was never the least word heard of the memorial, or none by me. Prestongrange and his grace the Lord President may have heard of it (for what I know) on the deafest sides of their heads; they kept it to themselves, at least—the public was none the wiser; and in course of time, on November 8th, and in the midst of a prodigious storm of wind and rain, poor James of the Glens was duly hanged at Lettermore by Ballachulish.

So there was the final upshot of my politics! Innocent men have perished before James, and are like to keep on perishing (in spite of all our wisdom) till the end of time. And till the end of time young folk (who are not yet used with the duplicity of life and men) will struggle as I did, and make heroical resolves, and take long risks; and the course of events will push them upon the one side and go on like a marching army. James was hanged; and here was I dwelling in the house of Prestongrange, and grateful to him for his fatherly attention. He was hanged; and behold! when I met Mr. Simon in the causeway, I was fain to pull off my beaver to him like a good little boy before his dominie. He had been hanged by fraud and violence, and the world wagged along, and there was not a pennyweight of difference; and the villains of that horrid plot were decent, kind, respectable fathers of families, who went to kirk and took the sacrament!

But I had had my view of that detestable business they call politics—I had seen it from behind, when it is all bones and blackness; and I was cured for life of any temptations to take part in it again. A plain, quiet, private path was that which I was ambitious to walk in, when I might keep my head out of the way of dangers and my conscience out of the road of temptation. For, upon a retrospect, it appeared I had not done so grandly, after all; but with the greatest possible amount of big speech and preparation, had accomplished nothing.

The 25th of the same month a ship was advertised to sail from Leith; and I was suddenly recommended to make up my mails for Leyden. To Prestongrange I could, of course, say nothing; for I had already been a long while sorning on his house and table. But with his daughter I was more open, bewailing my fate that I should be sent out of the country, and assuring her, unless she should bring me to farewell with Catriona, I would refuse at the last hour.

"Have I not given you my advice?" she asked.

"I know you have," said I, "and I know how much I am beholden to you already, and that I am bidden to obey your orders. But you must confess you are something too merry a lass at times to lippen [23] to entirely."

"I will tell you, then," said she. "Be you on board by nine o'clock forenoon; the ship does not sail before one; keep your boat alongside; and if you are not pleased with my farewells when I shall send them, you can come ashore again and seek Katrine for yourself."

Since I could make no more of her, I was fain to be content with this.

The day came round at last when she and I were to separate. We had been extremely intimate and familiar; I was much in her debt; and what way we were to part was a thing that put me from my sleep, like the vails I was to give to the domestic servants. I knew she considered me too backward, and rather desired to rise in her opinion on that head. Besides which, after so much affection shown and (I believe) felt upon both sides, it would have looked cold-like to be anyways stiff. Accordingly, I got my courage up and my words ready, and the last chance we were like to be alone, asked pretty boldly to be allowed to salute her in farewell.

"You forget yourself strangely, Mr. Balfour," said she. "I cannot call to mind that I have given you any right to presume on our acquaintancy."

I stood before her like a stopped clock, and knew not what to think, far less to say, when of a sudden she cast her arms about my neck and kissed me with the best will in the world.

"You inimitable bairn!" she cried. "Did you think that I would let us part like strangers? Because I can never keep my gravity at you five minutes on end, you must not dream I do not love you very well: I am all love and laughter, every time I cast an eye on you! And now I will give you an advice to conclude your education, which you will have need of before it's very long. Never ask womenfolk. They're bound to answer 'No'; God never made the lass that could resist the temptation. It's supposed by divines to be the curse of Eve: because she did not say it when the devil offered her the apple, her daughters can say nothing else."

"Since I am so soon to lose my bonny professor," I began.

"This is gallant, indeed," says she curtseying.

"I would put the one question," I went on. "May I ask a lass to marry to me?"

"You think you could not marry her without!" she asked. "Or else get her to offer?"

"You see you cannot be serious," said I.

"I shall be very serious in one thing, David," said she: "I shall always be your friend."

As I got to my horse the next morning, the four ladies were all at that same window whence we had once looked down on Catriona, and all cried farewell and waved their pocket napkins as I rode away. One out of the four I knew was truly sorry; and at the thought of that, and how I had come to the door three months ago for the first time, sorrow and gratitude made a confusion in my mind.

PART II.
FATHER AND DAUGHTER

CHAPTER XXI.
THE VOYAGE INTO HOLLAND

The ship lay at a single anchor, well outside the pier of Leith, so that all we passengers must come to it by the means of skiffs. This was very little troublesome, for the reason that the day was a flat calm, very frosty and cloudy, and with a low shifting fog upon the water. The body of the vessel was thus quite hid as I drew near, but the tall spars of her stood high and bright in a sunshine like the flickering of a fire. She proved to be a very roomy, commodious merchant, but somewhat blunt in the bows, and loaden extraordinary deep with salt, salted salmon, and fine white linen stockings for the Dutch. Upon my coming on board, the captain welcomed me—one Sang (out of Lesmahago, I believe), a very hearty, friendly tarpaulin of a man, but at the moment in rather of a bustle. There had no other of the passengers yet appeared, so that I was left to walk about upon the deck, viewing the prospect and wondering a good deal what these farewells should be which I was promised.

All Edinburgh and the Pentland Hills glinted above me in a kind of smuisty brightness, now and again overcome with blots of cloud; of Leith there was no more than the tops of chimneys visible, and on the face of the water, where the haar [24] lay, nothing at all. Out of this I was presently aware of a sound of oars pulling, and a little after (as if out of the smoke of a fire) a boat issued. There sat a grave man in the stern sheets, well muffled from the cold, and by his side a tall, pretty, tender figure of a maid that brought my heart to a stand. I had scarce the time to catch my breath in, and be ready to meet her, as she stepped upon the deck, smiling, and making my best bow, which was now vastly finer than some months before, when first I made it to her ladyship. No doubt we were both a good deal changed: she seemed to have shot up like a young, comely tree. She had now a kind of pretty backwardness that became her well as of one that regarded herself more highly and was fairly woman; and for another thing, the hand of the same magician had been at work upon the pair of us, and Miss Grant had made us both braw, if she could make but the one bonny.

The same cry, in words not very different, came from both of us, that the other was come in compliment to say farewell, and then we perceived in a flash we were to ship together.

"O, why will not Baby have been telling me!" she cried; and then remembered a letter she had been given, on the condition of not opening it till she was well on board. Within was an enclosure for myself, and ran thus:

"Dear Davie,—What do you think of my farewell? and what do you say to your fellow passenger? Did you kiss, or did you ask? I was about to have signed here, but that would leave the purport of my question doubtful, and in my own case I ken the answer. So fill up here with good advice. Do not be too blate, [25] and for God's sake do not try to be too forward; nothing acts you worse. I am

"Your affectionate friend and governess,
"Barbara Grant."

I wrote a word of answer and compliment on a leaf out of my pocketbook, put it in with another scratch from Catriona, sealed the whole with my new signet of the Balfour arms, and despatched it by the hand of Prestongrange's servant that still waited in my boat.

Then we had time to look upon each other more at leisure, which we had not done for a piece of a minute before (upon a common impulse) we shook hands again.

"Catriona?" said I. It seemed that was the first and last word of my eloquence.

"You will be glad to see me again?" says she.

"And I think that is an idle word," said I. "We are too deep friends to make speech upon such trifles."

"Is she not the girl of all the world?" she cried again. "I was never knowing such a girl so honest and so beautiful."

"And yet she cared no more for Alpin than what she did for a kale-stock," said I.

"Ah, she will say so indeed!" cries Catriona. "Yet it was for the name and the gentle kind blood that she took me up and was so good to me."

"Well, I will tell you why it was," said I. "There are all sorts of people's faces in this world. There is Barbara's face, that everyone must look at and admire, and think her a fine, brave, merry girl. And then there is your face, which is quite different—I never knew how different till to-day. You cannot see yourself, and that is why you do not understand; but it was for the love of your face that she took you up and was so good to you. And everybody in the world would do the same."

"Everybody?" says she.

"Every living soul!" said I.

"Ah, then, that will be why the soldiers at the castle took me up!" she cried.

"Barbara has been teaching you to catch me," said I.

"She will have taught me more than that at all events. She will have taught me a great deal about Mr. David—all the ill of him, and a little that was not so ill either, now and then," she said, smiling. "She will have told me all there was of Mr. David, only just that he would sail upon this very same ship. And why it is you go?"

I told her.

"Ah, well," said she, "we will be some days in company and then (I suppose) good-bye for altogether! I go to meet my father at a place of the name of Helvoetsluys, and from there to France, to be exiles by the side of our chieftain."

I could say no more than just "O!" the name of James More always drying up my very voice.

She was quick to perceive it, and to guess some portion of my thought.

"There is one thing I must be saying first of all, Mr. David," said she. "I think two of my kinsfolk have not behaved to you altogether very well. And the one of them two is James More, my father, and the other is the Laird of Prestongrange. Prestongrange will have spoken by himself, or his daughter in the place of him. But for James More, my father, I have this much to say: he lay shackled in a prison; he is a plain honest soldier and a plain Highland gentleman;

what they would be after he would never be guessing; but if he had understood it was to be some prejudice to a young gentleman like yourself, he would have died first. And for the sake of all your friendships, I will be asking you to pardon my father and family for that same mistake."

"Catriona," said I, "what that mistake was I do not care to know. I know but the one thing—that you went to Prestongrange and begged my life upon your knees. O, I ken well enough it was for your father that you went, but when you were there you pleaded for me also. It is a thing I cannot speak of. There are two things I cannot think of into myself: and the one is your good words when you called yourself my little friend, and the other that you pleaded for my life. Let us never speak more, we two, of pardon or offence."

We stood after that silent, Catriona looking on the deck and I on her; and before there was more speech, a little wind having sprung up in the nor'-west, they began to shake out the sails and heave in upon the anchor.

There were six passengers besides our two selves, which made of it a full cabin. Three were solid merchants out of Leith, Kirkcaldy, and Dundee, all engaged in the same adventure into High Germany. One was a Hollander returning; the rest worthy merchants' wives, to the charge of one of whom Catriona was recommended. Mrs. Gebbie (for that was her name) was by great good fortune heavily incommoded by the sea, and lay day and night on the broad of her back. We were besides the only creatures at all young on board the Rose, except a white-faced boy that did my old duty to attend upon the table; and it came about that Catriona and I were left almost entirely to ourselves. We had the next seats together at the table, where I waited on her with extraordinary pleasure. On deck, I made her a soft place with my cloak; and the weather being singularly fine for that season, with bright frosty days and nights, a steady, gentle wind, and scarce a sheet started all the way through the North Sea, we sat there (only now and again walking to and fro for warmth) from the first blink of the sun till eight or nine at night under the clear stars. The merchants or Captain Sang would sometimes glance and smile upon us, or pass a merry word or two and give us the go-by again; but the most part of the time they were deep in herring and chintzes and linen, or in computations of the slowness of the passage, and left us to our own concerns, which were very little important to any but ourselves.

At the first, we had a great deal to say, and thought ourselves pretty witty; and I was at a little pains to be the beau, and she (I believe) to play the young lady of experience. But soon we grew plainer with each other. I laid aside my high, clipped English (what little there was left of it) and forgot to make my Edinburgh bows and scrapes; she, upon her side, fell into a sort of kind familiarity; and we dwelt together like those of the same household, only (upon my side) with a more deep emotion. About the same time the bottom seemed to fall out of our conversation, and neither one of us the less pleased. Whiles she would tell me old wives' tales, of which she had a wonderful variety, many of them from my friend red-headed Niel. She told them very pretty, and they were pretty enough childish tales; but the pleasure to myself was in the sound of her voice, and the thought that she was telling and I listening. Whiles, again, we would sit entirely silent, not communicating even with a look, and tasting pleasure enough in the sweetness of that neighbourhood. I speak here only for myself. Of what was in the maid's mind, I am not very sure that ever I asked myself; and what was in my own, I was afraid to consider. I need make no secret of it now, either to myself or to the reader; I was fallen totally in love. She came between me and the sun. She had grown suddenly taller, as I say, but with a wholesome growth; she seemed all health, and lightness, and brave spirits; and I thought she walked like a young deer, and stood like a birch upon the mountains. It was enough for me to sit near by her on the deck; and I declare I scarce spent two thoughts upon the future, and was so well content with what I then enjoyed that I was never at the pains to imagine any further step; unless perhaps that I would be sometimes tempted to take her hand in mine and hold it there. But I was too like a miser of what joys I had, and would venture nothing on a hazard.

What we spoke was usually of ourselves or of each other, so that if anyone had been at so much pains as overhear us, he must have supposed us the most egotistical persons in the world. It befell one day when we were at this practice, that we came on a discourse of friends and friendship, and I think now that we were sailing near the wind. We said what a fine thing friendship was, and how little we had guessed of it, and how it made life a new thing, and a thousand covered things of the same kind that will have been said, since the foundation of the world, by young folk in the same predicament. Then we remarked upon the strangeness of that circumstance, that friends came together in the beginning as if they were there for the first time, and yet each had been alive a good while, losing time with other people.

"It is not much that I have done," said she, "and I could be telling you the five-fifths of it in two-three words. It is only a girl I am, and what can befall a girl, at all events? But I went with the clan in the year '45. The men marched with swords and fire-locks, and some of them in brigades in the same set of tartan; they were not backward at the marching, I can tell you. And there were gentlemen from the Low Country, with their tenants mounted and trumpets to sound, and there was a grand skirling of war-pipes. I rode on a little Highland horse on the right hand of my father, James More, and of Glengyle himself. And here is one fine thing that I remember, that Glengyle kissed me in the face, because (says he) 'my kinswoman, you are the only lady of the clan that has come out,' and me a little maid of maybe twelve years old! I saw Prince Charlie too, and the blue eyes of him; he was pretty indeed! I had his hand to kiss in front of the army. O, well, these were the good days, but it is all like a dream that I have seen and then awakened. It went what way you very well know; and these were the worst days of all, when the red-coat soldiers were out, and my father and uncles lay in the hill, and I was to be carrying them their meat in the middle night, or at the short sight of day when the cocks crow. Yes, I have walked in the night, many's the time, and my heart great in me for terror of the darkness. It is a strange thing I will never have been meddled with by a bogle; but they say a maid goes safe. Next there was my uncle's marriage, and that was a dreadful affair beyond all. Jean Kay was that woman's name; and she had me in the room with her that night at Inversnaid, the night we took her from her friends in the old, ancient manner. She would and she wouldn't; she was for marrying Rob the one minute, and the next she would be for none of him. I will never have seen such a feckless creature of a woman; surely all there was of her would tell her ay or no. Well, she was a widow; and I can never be thinking a widow a good woman."

"Catriona!" says I, "how do you make out that?"

"I do not know," said she; "I am only telling you the seeming in my heart. And then to marry a new man! Fy! But that was her; and she was married again upon my Uncle Robin, and went with him awhile to kirk and market; and then wearied, or else her friends got claught of her and talked her round, or maybe she turned ashamed; at the least of it, she ran away, and went back to her own folk, and said we had held her in the lake, and I will never tell you all what. I have never thought much of any females since that day. And so in the end my father, James More, came to be cast in prison, and you know the rest of it an well as me."

"And through all you had no friends?" said I.

"No," said she; "I have been pretty chief with two-three lasses on the braes, but not to call it friends."

"Well, mine is a plain tale," said I. "I never had a friend to my name till I met in with you."

"And that brave Mr. Stewart?" she asked.

"O, yes, I was forgetting him," I said. "But he is a man, and that is very different."

"I would think so," said she. "O, yes, it is quite different."

"And then there was one other," said I. "I once thought I had a friend, but it proved a disappointment."

She asked me who she was?

"It was a he, then," said I. "We were the two best lads at my father's school, and we thought we loved each other dearly. Well, the time came when he went to Glasgow to a merchant's house, that was his second cousin once removed; and wrote me two-three times by the carrier; and then he found new friends, and I might write till I was tired, he took no notice. Eh, Catriona, it took me a long while to forgive the world. There is not anything more bitter than to lose a fancied friend."

Then she began to question me close upon his looks and character, for we were each a great deal concerned in all that touched the other; till at last, in a very evil hour, I minded of his letters and went and fetched the bundle from the cabin.

"Here are his letters," said I, "and all the letters that ever I got. That will be the last I'll can tell of myself; ye know the lave [26] as well as I do."

"Will you let me read them, then?" says she.

I told her, if she would be at the pains; and she bade me go away and she would read them from the one end to the other. Now, in this bundle that I gave her, there were packed together not only all the letters of my false friend, but one or two of Mr. Campbell's when he was in town at the Assembly, and to make a complete roll of all that ever was written to me, Catriona's little word, and the two I had received from Miss Grant, one when I was on the Bass and one on board that ship. But of these last I had no particular mind at the moment.

I was in that state of subjection to the thought of my friend that it mattered not what I did, nor scarce whether I was in her presence or out of it; I had caught her like some kind of a noble fever that lived continually in my bosom, by night and by day, and whether I was waking or asleep. So it befell that after I was come into the fore-part of the ship where the broad bows splashed into the billows, I was in no such hurry to return as you might fancy; rather prolonged my absence like a variety in pleasure. I do not think I am by nature much of an Epicurean: and there had come till then so small a share of pleasure in my way that I might be excused perhaps to dwell on it unduly.

When I returned to her again, I had a faint, painful impression as of a buckle slipped, so coldly she returned the packet.

"You have read them?" said I; and I thought my voice sounded not wholly natural, for I was turning in my mind for what could ail her.

"Did you mean me to read all?" she asked.

I told her "Yes," with a drooping voice.

"The last of them as well?" said she.

I knew where we were now; yet I would not lie to her either. "I gave them all without afterthought," I said, "as I supposed that you would read them. I see no harm in any."

"I will be differently made," said she. "I thank God I am differently made. It was not a fit letter to be shown me. It was not fit to be written."

"I think you are speaking of your own friend, Barbara Grant?" said I.

"There will not be anything as bitter as to lose a fancied friend," said she, quoting my own expression.

"I think it is sometimes the friendship that was fancied!" I cried. "What kind of justice do you call this, to blame me for some words that a tomfool of a madcap lass has written down upon a piece of paper? You know yourself with what respect I have behaved—and would do always."

"Yet you would show me that same letter!" says she. "I want no such friends. I can be doing very well, Mr. Balfour, without her—or you."

"This is your fine gratitude!" says I.

"I am very much obliged to you," said she. "I will be asking you to take away your—letters." She seemed to choke upon the word, so that it sounded like an oath.

"You shall never ask twice," said I; picked up that bundle, walked a little way forward and cast them as far as possible into the sea. For a very little more I could have cast myself after them.

The rest of the day I walked up and down raging. There were few names so ill but what I gave her them in my own mind before the sun went down. All that I had ever heard of Highland pride seemed quite outdone; that a girl (scarce grown) should resent so trifling an allusion, and that from her next friend, that she had near wearied me with praising of! I had bitter, sharp, hard thoughts of her, like an angry boy's. If I had kissed her indeed (I thought), perhaps she would have taken it pretty well; and only because it had been written down, and with a spice of jocularity, up she must fuff in this ridiculous passion. It seemed to me there was a want of penetration in the female sex, to make angels weep over the case of the poor men.

We were side by side again at supper, and what a change was there! She was like curdled milk to me; her face was like a wooden doll's; I could have indifferently smitten her or grovelled at her feet, but she gave me not the least occasion to do either. No sooner the meal done than she betook herself to attend on Mrs. Gebbie, which I think she had a little neglected heretofore. But she was to make up for lost time, and in what remained of the passage was extraordinary assiduous with the old lady, and on deck began to make a great deal more than I thought wise of Captain Sang. Not but what the Captain seemed a worthy, fatherly man; but I hated to behold her in the least familiarity with anyone except myself.

Altogether, she was so quick to avoid me, and so constant to keep herself surrounded with others, that I must watch a long while before I could find my opportunity; and after it was found, I made not much of it, as you are now to hear.

"I have no guess how I have offended," said I; "it should scarce be beyond pardon, then. O, try if you can pardon me."

"I have no pardon to give," said she; and the words seemed to come out of her throat like marbles. "I will be very much obliged for all your friendships." And she made me an eighth part of a curtsey.

But I had schooled myself beforehand to say more, and I was going to say it too.

"There is one thing," said I. "If I have shocked your particularity by the showing of that letter, it cannot touch Miss Grant. She wrote not to you, but to a poor, common, ordinary lad, who might have had more sense than show it. If you are to blame me—"

"I will advise you to say no more about that girl, at all events!" said Catriona. "It is her I will never look the road of, not if she lay dying." She turned away from me, and suddenly back. "Will you swear you will have no more to deal with her?" she cried.

"Indeed, and I will never be so unjust then," said I; "nor yet so ungrateful."

And now it was I that turned away.

CHAPTER XXII.
HELVOETSLUYS

The weather in the end considerably worsened; the wind sang in the shrouds, the sea swelled higher, and the ship began to labour and cry out among the billows. The song of the leadsman in the chains was now scarce ceasing, for we thrid all the way among shoals. About nine in the morning, in a burst of wintry sun between two squalls of hail, I had my first look of Holland—a line of windmills birling in the breeze. It was besides my first knowledge of these daft-like contrivances, which gave me a near sense of foreign travel and a new world and life. We came to an anchor about half-past eleven, outside the harbour of Helvoetsluys, in a place where the sea sometimes broke and the ship pitched outrageously. You may be sure we were all on deck save Mrs. Gebbie, some of us in cloaks, others mantled in the ship's tarpaulins, all clinging on by ropes, and jesting the most like old sailor-folk that we could imitate.

Presently a boat, that was backed like a partancrab, came gingerly alongside, and the skipper of it hailed our master in the Dutch. Thence Captain Sang turned, very troubled-like, to Catriona; and the rest of us crowding about, the nature of the difficulty was made plain to all. The Rose was bound to the port of Rotterdam, whither the other passengers were in a great impatience to arrive, in view of a conveyance due to leave that very evening in the direction of the Upper Germany. This, with the present half-gale of wind, the captain (if no time were lost) declared himself still capable to save. Now James More had trysted in Helvoet with his daughter, and the captain had engaged to call before the port and place her (according to the custom) in a shore boat. There was the boat, to be sure, and here was Catriona ready: but both our master and the patroon of the boat scrupled at the risk, and the first was in no humour to delay.

"Your father," said he, "would be gey an little pleased if we was to break a leg to ye, Miss Drummond, let-a-be drowning of you. Take my way of it," says he, "and come on-by with the rest of us here to Rotterdam. Ye can get a passage down the Maes in a sailing scoot as far as to the Brill, and thence on again, by a place in a rattel-waggon, back to Helvoet."

But Catriona would hear of no change. She looked white-like as she beheld the bursting of the sprays, the green seas that sometimes poured upon the fore-castle, and the perpetual bounding and swooping of the boat among the billows; but she stood firmly by her father's orders. "My father, James More, will have arranged it so," was her first word and her last. I thought it very idle and indeed wanton in the girl to be so literal and stand opposite to so much kind advice; but the fact is she had a very good reason, if she would have told us. Sailing scoots and rattel-waggons are excellent things; only the use of them must first be paid for, and all she was possessed of in the world was just two shillings and a penny halfpenny sterling. So it fell out that captain and passengers, not knowing of her destitution—and she being too proud to tell them—spoke in vain.

"But you ken nae French and nae Dutch neither," said one.

"It is very true," says she, "but since the year '46 there are so many of the honest Scotch abroad that I will be doing very well. I thank you."

There was a pretty country simplicity in this that made some laugh, others looked the more sorry, and Mr. Gebbie fall outright in a passion. I believe he knew it was his duty (his wife having accepted charge of the girl) to have gone ashore with her and seen her safe: nothing would have induced him to have done so, since it must have involved the lose of his conveyance; and I think he made it up to his conscience by the loudness of his voice. At least he broke out upon Captain

Sang, raging and saying the thing was a disgrace; that it was mere death to try to leave the ship, and at any event we could not cast down an innocent maid in a boatful of nasty Holland fishers, and leave her to her fate. I was thinking something of the same; took the mate upon one side, arranged with him to send on my chests by track-scoot to an address I had in Leyden, and stood up and signalled to the fishers.

"I will go ashore with the young lady, Captain Sang," said I. "It is all one what way I go to Leyden;" and leaped at the same time into the boat, which I managed not so elegantly but what I fell with two of the fishers in the bilge.

From the boat the business appeared yet more precarious than from the ship, she stood so high over us, swung down so swift, and menaced us so perpetually with her plunging and passaging upon the anchor cable. I began to think I had made a fool's bargain, that it was merely impossible Catriona should be got on board to me, and that I stood to be set ashore at Helvoet all by myself and with no hope of any reward but the pleasure of embracing James More, if I should want to. But this was to reckon without the lass's courage. She had seen me leap with very little appearance (however much reality) of hesitation; to be sure, she was not to be beat by her discarded friend. Up she stood on the bulwarks and held by a stay, the wind blowing in her petticoats, which made the enterprise more dangerous, and gave us rather more of a view of her stockings than would be thought genteel in cities. There was no minute lost, and scarce time given for any to interfere if they had wished the same. I stood up on the other side and spread my arms; the ship swung down on us, the patroon humoured his boat nearer in than was perhaps wholly safe, and Catriona leaped into the air. I was so happy as to catch her, and the fishers readily supporting us, escaped a fall. She held to me a moment very tight, breathing quick and deep; thence (she still clinging to me with both hands) we were passed aft to our places by the steersman; and Captain Sang and all the crew and passengers cheering and crying farewell, the boat was put about for shore.

As soon as Catriona came a little to herself she unhanded me suddenly, but said no word. No more did I; and indeed the whistling of the wind and the breaching of the sprays made it no time for speech; and our crew not only toiled excessively but made extremely little way, so that the Rose had got her anchor and was off again before we had approached the harbour mouth.

We were no sooner in smooth water than the patroon, according to their beastly Hollands custom, stopped his boat and required of us our fares. Two guilders was the man's demand—between three and four shillings English money—for each passenger. But at this Catriona began to cry out with a vast deal of agitation. She had asked of Captain Sang, she said, and the fare was but an English shilling. "Do you think I will have come on board and not ask first?" cries she. The patroon scolded back upon her in a lingo where the oaths were English and the rest right Hollands; till at last (seeing her near tears) I privately slipped in the rogue's hand six shillings, whereupon he was obliging enough to receive from her the other shilling without more complaint. No doubt I was a good deal nettled and ashamed. I like to see folk thrifty, but not with so much passion; and I daresay it would be rather coldly that I asked her, as the boat moved on again for shore, where it was that she was trysted with her father.

"He is to be inquired of at the house of one Sprott, an honest Scotch merchant," says she; and then with the same breath, "I am wishing to thank you very much—you are a brave friend to me."

"It will be time enough when I get you to your father," said I, little thinking that I spoke so true. "I can tell him a fine tale of a loyal daughter."

"O, I do not think I will be a loyal girl, at all events," she cried, with a great deal of painfulness in the expression. "I do not think my heart is true."

"Yet there are very few that would have made that leap, and all to obey a father's orders," I observed.

"I cannot have you to be thinking of me so," she cried again. "When you had done that same, how would I stop behind? And at all events that was not all the reasons." Whereupon, with a burning face, she told me the plain truth upon her poverty.

"Good guide us!" cried I, "what kind of daft-like proceeding is this, to let yourself be launched on the continent of Europe with an empty purse—I count it hardly decent—scant decent!" I cried.

"You forget James More, my father, is a poor gentleman," said she. "He is a hunted exile."

"But I think not all your friends are hunted exiles," I exclaimed. "And was this fair to them that care for you? Was it fair to me? was it fair to Miss Grant that counselled you to go, and would be driven fair horn-mad if she could hear of it? Was it even fair to these Gregory folk that you were living with, and used you lovingly? It's a blessing you have fallen in my hands! Suppose your father hindered by an accident, what would become of you here, and you your lee-lone in a strange place? The thought of the thing frightens me," I said.

"I will have lied to all of them," she replied. "I will have told them all that I had plenty. I told her too. I could not be lowering James More to them."

I found out later on that she must have lowered him in the very dust, for the lie was originally the father's, not the daughter's, and she thus obliged to persevere in it for the man's reputation. But at the time I was ignorant of this, and the mere thought of her destitution and the perils in which see must have fallen, had ruffled me almost beyond reason.

"Well, well, well," said I, "you will have to learn more sense."

I left her mails for the moment in an inn upon the shore, where I got a direction for Sprott's house in my new French, and we walked there—it was some little way—beholding the place with wonder as we went. Indeed, there was much for Scots folk to admire: canals and trees being intermingled with the houses; the houses, each within itself, of a brave red brick, the colour of a rose, with steps and benches of blue marble at the cheek of every door, and the whole town so clean you might have dined upon the causeway. Sprott was within, upon his ledgers, in a low parlour, very neat and clean, and set out with china and pictures, and a globe of the earth in a brass frame. He was a big-chafted, ruddy, lusty man, with a crooked hard look to him; and he made us not that much civility as offer us a seat.

"Is James More Macgregor now in Helvoet, sir?" says I.

"I ken nobody by such a name," says he, impatient-like.

"Since you are so particular," says I, "I will amend my question, and ask you where we are to find in Helvoet one James Drummond, alias Macgregor, alias James More, late tenant in Inveronachile?"

"Sir," says he, "he may be in Hell for what I ken, and for my part I wish he was."

"The young lady is that gentleman's daughter, sir," said I, "before whom, I think you will agree with me, it is not very becoming to discuss his character."

"I have nothing to make either with him, or her, or you!" cries he in his gross voice.

"Under your favour, Mr. Sprott," said I, "this young lady is come from Scotland seeking him, and by whatever mistake, was given the name of your house for a direction. An error it seems to have been, but I think this places both you and me—who am but her fellow-traveller by accident—under a strong obligation to help our countrywoman."

"Will you ding me daft?" he cries. "I tell ye I ken naething and care less either for him or his breed. I tell ye the man owes me money."

"That may very well be, sir," said I, who was now rather more angry than himself. "At least, I owe you nothing; the young lady is under my protection; and I am neither at all used with these manners, nor in the least content with them."

As I said this, and without particularly thinking what I did, I drew a step or two nearer to his table; thus striking, by mere good fortune, on the only argument that could at all affect the man. The blood left his lusty countenance.

"For the Lord's sake dinna be hasty, sir!" he cried. "I am truly wishfu' no to be offensive. But ye ken, sir, I'm like a wheen guid-natured, honest, canty auld fellows—my bark is waur nor my bite. To hear me, ye micht whiles fancy I was a wee thing dour; but na, na! it's a kind auld fallow at heart, Sandie Sprott! And ye could never imagine the fyke and fash this man has been to me."

"Very good, sir," said I. "Then I will make that much freedom with your kindness as trouble you for your last news of Mr. Drummond."

"You're welcome, sir!" said he. "As for the young leddy (my respects to her!), he'll just have clean forgotten her. I ken the man, ye see; I have lost siller by him ere now. He thinks of naebody but just himsel'; clan, king, or dauchter, if he can get his wameful, he would give them a' the go-by! ay, or his correspondent either. For there is a sense in whilk I may be nearly almost said to be his correspondent. The fact is, we are employed thegether in a business affair, and I think it's like to turn out a dear affair for Sandie Sprott. The man's as guid's my pairtner, and I give ye my mere word I ken naething by where he is. He micht be coming here to Helvoet; he micht come here the morn, he michtnae come for a twalmouth; I would wonder at naething—or just at the ae thing, and that's if he was to pay me my siller. Ye see what way I stand with it; and it's clear I'm no very likely to meddle up with the young leddy, as ye ca' her. She cannae stop here, that's ae thing certain sure. Dod, sir, I'm a lone man! If I was to tak her in, its highly possible the hellicat would try and gar me marry her when he turned up."

"Enough of this talk," said I. "I will take the young leddy among better friends. Give me, pen, ink, and paper, and I will leave here for James More the address of my correspondent in Leyden. He can inquire from me where he is to seek his daughter."

This word I wrote and sealed; which while I was doing, Sprott of his own motion made a welcome offer, to charge himself with Miss Drummond's mails, and even send a porter for them to the inn. I advanced him to that effect a dollar or two to be a cover, and he gave me an acknowledgment in writing of the sum.

Whereupon (I giving my arm to Catriona) we left the house of this unpalatable rascal. She had said no word throughout, leaving me to judge and speak in her place; I, upon my side, had been careful not to embarrass her by a glance; and even now, although my heart still glowed inside of me with shame and anger, I made it my affair to seem quite easy.

"Now," said I, "let us get back to yon same inn where they can speak the French, have a piece of dinner, and inquire for conveyances to Rotterdam. I will never be easy till I have you safe again in the hands of Mrs. Gebbie."

"I suppose it will have to be," said Catriona, "though whoever will be pleased, I do not think it will be her. And I will remind you this once again that I have but one shilling, and three baubees."

"And just this once again," said I, "I will remind you it was a blessing that I came alongst with you."

"What else would I be thinking all this time?" says she, and I thought weighed a little on my arm. "It is you that are the good friend to me."

CHAPTER XXIII.
TRAVELS IN HOLLAND

The rattel-waggon, which is a kind of a long waggon set with benches, carried us in four hours of travel to the great city of Rotterdam. It was long past dark by then, but the streets were pretty brightly lighted and thronged with wild-like, outlandish characters—bearded Hebrews, black men, and the hordes of courtesans, most indecently adorned with finery and stopping seamen by their very sleeves; the clash of talk about us made our heads to whirl; and what was the most unexpected of all, we appeared to be no more struck with all these foreigners than they with us. I made the best face I could, for the lass's sake and my own credit; but the truth is I felt like a lost sheep, and my heart beat in my bosom with anxiety. Once or twice I inquired after the harbour or the berth of the ship Rose: but either fell on some who spoke only Hollands, or my own French failed me. Trying a street at a venture, I came upon a lane of lighted houses, the doors and windows thronged with wauf-like painted women; these jostled and mocked upon us as we passed, and I was thankful we had nothing of their language. A little after we issued forth upon an open place along the harbour.

"We shall be doing now," cries I, as soon as I spied masts. "Let us walk here by the harbour. We are sure to meet some that has the English, and at the best of it we may light upon that very ship."

We did the next best, as happened; for, about nine of the evening, whom should we walk into the arms of but Captain Sang? He told us they had made their run in the most incredible brief time, the wind holding strong till they reached port; by which means his passengers were all gone already on their further travels. It was impossible to chase after the Gebbies into the High Germany, and we had no other acquaintance to fall back upon but Captain Sang himself. It was the more gratifying to find the man friendly and wishful to assist. He made it a small affair to find some good plain family of merchants, where Catriona might harbour till the Rose was loaden; declared he would then blithely carry her back to Leith for nothing and see her safe in the hands of Mr. Gregory; and in the meanwhile carried us to a late ordinary for the meal we stood in need of. He seemed extremely friendly, as I say, but what surprised me a good deal, rather boisterous in the bargain; and the cause of this was soon to appear. For at the ordinary, calling for Rhenish wine and drinking of it deep, he soon became unutterably tipsy. In this case, as too common with all men, but especially with those of his rough trade, what little sense or manners he possessed deserted him; and he behaved himself so scandalous to the young lady, jesting most ill-favouredly at the figure she had made on the ship's rail, that I had no resource but carry her suddenly away.

She came out of the ordinary clinging to me close. "Take me away, David," she said. "You keep me. I am not afraid with you."

"And have no cause, my little friend!" cried I, and could have found it in my heart to weep.

"Where will you be taking me?" she said again. "Don't leave me at all events—never leave me."

"Where am I taking you to?" says I stopping, for I had been staving on ahead in mere blindness. "I must stop and think. But I'll not leave you, Catriona; the Lord do so to me, and more also, if I should fail or fash you."

She crept close into me by way of a reply.

"Here," I said, "is the stillest place we have hit on yet in this busy byke of a city. Let us sit down here under yon tree and consider of our course."

That tree (which I am little like to forget) stood hard by the harbour side. It was like a black night, but lights were in the houses, and nearer hand in the quiet ships; there was a shining of the city on the one hand, and a buzz hung over it of many thousands walking and talking; on the other, it was dark and the water bubbled on the sides. I spread my cloak upon a builder's stone, and made her sit there; she would have kept her hold upon me, for she still shook with the late affronts; but I wanted to think clear, disengaged myself, and paced to and fro before her, in the manner of what we call a smuggler's walk, belabouring my brains for any remedy. By the course of these scattering thoughts I was brought suddenly face to face with a remembrance that, in the heat and haste of our departure, I had left Captain Sang to pay the ordinary. At this I began to laugh out loud, for I thought the man well served; and at the same time, by an instinctive movement, carried my hand to the pocket where my money was. I suppose it was in the lane where the women jostled us; but there is only the one thing certain, that my purse was gone.

"You will have thought of something good," said she, observing me to pause.

At the pinch we were in, my mind became suddenly clear as a perspective glass, and I saw there was no choice of methods. I had not one doit of coin, but in my pocket-book I had still my letter on the Leyden merchant; and there was now but the one way to get to Leyden, and that was to walk on our two feet.

"Catriona," said I, "I know you're brave and I believe you're strong—do you think you could walk thirty miles on a plain road?" We found it, I believe, scarce the two-thirds of that, but such was my notion of the distance.

"David," she said, "if you will just keep near, I will go anywhere and do anything. The courage of my heart, it is all broken. Do not be leaving me in this horrible country by myself, and I will do all else."

"Can you start now and march all night?" said I.

"I will do all that you can ask of me," she said, "and never ask you why. I have been a bad ungrateful girl to you; and do what you please with me now! And I think Miss Barbara Grant is the best lady in the world," she added, "and I do not see what she would deny you for at all events."

This was Greek and Hebrew to me; but I had other matters to consider, and the first of these was to get clear of that city on the Leyden road. It proved a cruel problem; and it may have been one or two at night ere we had solved it. Once beyond the houses, there was neither moon nor stars to guide us; only the whiteness of the way in the midst and a blackness of an alley on both hands. The walking was besides made most extraordinary difficult by a plain black frost that fell suddenly in the small hours and turned that highway into one long slide.

"Well, Catriona," said I, "here we are like the king's sons and the old wives' daughters in your daft-like Highland tales. Soon we'll be going over the 'seven Bens, the seven glens and the seven mountain moors'." Which was a common byword or overcome in those tales of hers that had stuck in my memory.

"Ah," says she, "but here are no glens or mountains! Though I will never be denying but what the trees and some of the plain places hereabouts are very pretty. But our country is the best yet."

"I wish we could say as much for our own folk," says I, recalling Sprott and Sang, and perhaps James More himself.

"I will never complain of the country of my friend," said she, and spoke it out with an accent so particular that I seemed to see the look upon her face.

I caught in my breath sharp and came near falling (for my pains) on the black ice.

"I do not know what you think, Catriona," said I, when I was a little recovered, "but this has been the best day yet! I think shame to say it, when you have met in with such misfortunes and disfavours; but for me, it has been the best day yet."

"It was a good day when you showed me so much love," said she.

"And yet I think shame to be happy too," I went on, "and you here on the road in the black night."

"Where in the great world would I be else?" she cried. "I am thinking I am safest where I am with you."

"I am quite forgiven, then?" I asked.

"Will you not forgive me that time so much as not to take it in your mouth again?" she cried. "There is nothing in this heart to you but thanks. But I will be honest too," she added, with a kind of suddenness, "and I'll never can forgive that girl."

"Is this Miss Grant again?" said I. "You said yourself she was the best lady in the world."

"So she will be, indeed!" says Catriona. "But I will never forgive her for all that. I will never, never forgive her, and let me hear tell of her no more."

"Well," said I, "this beats all that ever came to my knowledge; and I wonder that you can indulge yourself in such bairnly whims. Here is a young lady that was the best friend in the world to the both of us, that learned us how to dress ourselves, and in a great manner how to behave, as anyone can see that knew us both before and after."

But Catriona stopped square in the midst of the highway.

"It is this way of it," said she. "Either you will go on to speak of her, and I will go back to yon town, and let come of it what God pleases! Or else you will do me that politeness to talk of other things."

I was the most nonplussed person in this world; but I bethought me that she depended altogether on my help, that she was of the frail sex and not so much beyond a child, and it was for me to be wise for the pair of us.

"My dear girl," said I, "I can make neither head nor tails of this; but God forbid that I should do anything to set you on the jee. As for talking of Miss Grant, I have no such a mind to it, and I believe it was yourself began it. My only design (if I took you up at all) was for your own improvement, for I hate the very look of injustice. Not that I do not wish you to have a good pride and a nice female delicacy; they become you well; but here you show them to excess."

"Well, then, have you done?" said she.

"I have done," said I.

"A very good thing," said she, and we went on again, but now in silence.

It was an eerie employment to walk in the gross night, beholding only shadows and hearing nought but our own steps. At first, I believe our hearts burned against each other with a deal of enmity; but the darkness and the cold, and the silence, which only the cocks sometimes interrupted, or sometimes the farmyard dogs, had pretty soon brought down our pride to the dust; and for my own particular, I would have jumped at any decent opening for speech.

Before the day peeped, came on a warmish rain, and the frost was all wiped away from among our feet. I took my cloak to her and sought to hap her in the same; she bade me, rather impatiently, to keep it.

"Indeed and I will do no such thing," said I. "Here am I, a great, ugly lad that has seen all kinds of weather, and here are you a tender, pretty maid! My dear, you would not put me to a shame?"

Without more words she let me cover her; which as I was doing in the darkness, I let my hand rest a moment on her shoulder, almost like an embrace.

"You must try to be more patient of your friend," said I.

I thought she seemed to lean the least thing in the world against my bosom, or perhaps it was but fancy.

"There will be no end to your goodness," said she.

And we went on again in silence; but now all was changed; and the happiness that was in my heart was like a fire in a great chimney.

The rain passed ere day; it was but a sloppy morning as we came into the town of Delft. The red gabled houses made a handsome show on either hand of a canal; the servant lassies were out slestering and scrubbing at the very stones upon the public highway; smoke rose from a hundred kitchens; and it came in upon me strongly it was time to break our fasts.

"Catriona," said I, "I believe you have yet a shilling and three baubees?"

"Are you wanting it?" said she, and passed me her purse. "I am wishing it was five pounds! What will you want it for?"

"And what have we been walking for all night, like a pair of waif Egyptians!" says I. "Just because I was robbed of my purse and all I possessed in that unchancy town of Rotterdam. I will tell you of it now, because I think the worst is over, but we have still a good tramp before us till we get to where my money is, and if you would not buy me a piece of bread, I were like to go fasting."

She looked at me with open eyes. By the light of the new day she was all black and pale for weariness, so that my heart smote me for her. But as for her, she broke out laughing.

"My torture! are we beggars then!" she cried. "You too? O, I could have wished for this same thing! And I am glad to buy your breakfast to you. But it would be pleisand if I would have had to dance to get a meal to you! For I believe they are not very well acquainted with our manner of dancing over here, and might be paying for the curiosity of that sight."

I could have kissed her for that word, not with a lover's mind, but in a heat of admiration. For it always warms a man to see a woman brave.

We got a drink of milk from a country wife but new come to the town, and in a baker's, a piece of excellent, hot, sweet-smelling bread, which we ate upon the road as we went on. That road from Delft to the Hague is just five miles of a fine avenue shaded with trees, a canal on the one hand, on the other excellent pastures of cattle. It was pleasant here indeed.

"And now, Davie," said she, "what will you do with me at all events?"

"It is what we have to speak of," said I, "and the sooner yet the better. I can come by money in Leyden; that will be all well. But the trouble is how to dispose of you until your father come. I thought last night you seemed a little sweir to part from me?"

"It will be more than seeming then," said she.

"You are a very young maid," said I, "and I am but a very young callant. This is a great piece of difficulty. What way are we to manage? Unless indeed, you could pass to be my sister?"

"And what for no?" said she, "if you would let me!"

"I wish you were so, indeed," I cried. "I would be a fine man if I had such a sister. But the rub is that you are Catriona Drummond."

"And now I will be Catriona Balfour," she said. "And who is to ken? They are all strange folk here."

"If you think that it would do," says I. "I own it troubles me. I would like it very ill, if I advised you at all wrong."

"David, I have no friend here but you," she said.

"The mere truth is, I am too young to be your friend," said I. "I am too young to advise you, or you to be advised. I see not what else we are to do, and yet I ought to warn you."

"I will have no choice left," said she. "My father James More has not used me very well, and it is not the first time, I am cast upon your hands like a sack of barley meal, and have nothing else to think of but your pleasure. If you will have me, good and well. If you will not"—she turned and touched her hand upon my arm—"David, I am afraid," said she.

"No, but I ought to warn you," I began; and then bethought me I was the bearer of the purse, and it would never do to seem too churlish. "Catriona," said I, "don't misunderstand me: I am just trying to do my duty by you, girl! Here am I going alone to this strange city, to be a solitary student there; and here is this chance arisen that you might dwell with me a bit, and be like my sister; you can surely understand this much, my dear, that I would just love to have you?"

"Well, and here I am," said she. "So that's soon settled."

I know I was in duty bounden to have spoke more plain. I know this was a great blot on my character, for which I was lucky that I did not pay more dear. But I minded how easy her delicacy had been startled with a word of kissing her in Barbara's letter; now that she depended on me, how was I to be more bold? Besides, the truth is, I could see no other feasible method to dispose of her. And I daresay inclination pulled me very strong.

A little beyond the Hague she fell very lame and made the rest of the distance heavily enough. Twice she must rest by the wayside, which she did with pretty apologies, calling herself a shame to the Highlands and the race she came of, and nothing but a hindrance to myself. It was her excuse, she said, that she was not much used with walking shod. I would have had her strip off her shoes and stockings and go barefoot. But she pointed out to me that the women of that country, even in the landward roads, appeared to be all shod.

"I must not be disgracing my brother," said she, and was very merry with it all, although her face told tales of her.

There is a garden in that city we were bound to, sanded below with clean sand, the trees meeting overhead, some of them trimmed, some preached, and the whole place beautified with alleys and arbours. Here I left Catriona, and went forward by myself to find my correspondent. There I drew on my credit, and asked to be recommended to some decent, retired lodging. My baggage being not yet arrived, I told him I supposed I should require his caution with the people of the house; and explained that, my sister being come for a while to keep house with me, I should be wanting two chambers. This was all very well; but the trouble was that Mr. Balfour in his letter of recommendation had condescended on a great deal of particulars, and never a word of any sister in the case. I could see my Dutchman was extremely suspicious; and viewing me over the rims of a great pair of spectacles—he was a poor, frail body, and reminded me of an infirm rabbit—he began to question me close.

Here I fell in a panic. Suppose he accept my tale (thinks I), suppose he invite my sister to his house, and that I bring her. I shall have a fine ravelled pirn to unwind, and may end by disgracing both the lassie and myself. Thereupon I began hastily to expound to him my sister's character. She was of a bashful disposition, it appeared, and be extremely fearful of meeting strangers that I had left her at that moment sitting in a public place alone. And then, being launched upon the stream of falsehood, I must do like all the rest of the world in the same circumstance, and plunge in deeper than was any service; adding some altogether needless particulars of Miss Balfour's ill-health and retirement during childhood. In the midst of which I awoke to a sense of my behaviour, and was turned to one blush.

The old gentleman was not so much deceived but what he discovered a willingness to be quit of me. But he was first of all a man of business; and knowing that my money was good enough, however it might be with my conduct, he was so far obliging as to send his son to be my guide and caution in the matter of a lodging. This implied my presenting of the young man to Catriona. The poor, pretty child was much recovered with resting, looked and behaved to perfection, and took my arm and gave me the name of brother more easily than I could answer her. But there was one misfortune: thinking to help, she was rather towardly than otherwise to my Dutchman. And I could not but reflect that Miss Balfour had rather suddenly outgrown her bashfulness. And there was another thing, the difference of our speech. I had the Low Country tongue and dwelled upon my words; she had a hill voice, spoke with something of an English accent, only far more delightful, and was scarce quite fit to be called a deacon in the craft of talking English grammar; so that, for a brother and sister, we made a most uneven pair. But the young Hollander was a heavy dog, without so much spirit in his belly as to remark her prettiness, for which I scorned him. And as soon as he had found a cover to our heads, he left us alone, which was the greater service of the two.

CHAPTER XXIV.
FULL STORY OF A COPY OF HEINECCIUS

The place found was in the upper part of a house backed on a canal. We had two rooms, the second entering from the first; each had a chimney built out into the floor in the Dutch manner; and being alongside, each had the same prospect from the window of the top of a tree below us in a little court, of a piece of the canal, and of houses in the Hollands architecture and a church spire upon the further side. A full set of bells hung in that spire and made delightful music; and when there was any sun at all, it shone direct in our two chambers. From a tavern hard by we had good meals sent in.

The first night we were both pretty weary, and she extremely so. There was little talk between us, and I packed her off to her bed as soon as she had eaten. The first thing in the morning I wrote word to Sprott to have her mails sent on, together with a line to Alan at his chief's; and had the same despatched, and her breakfast ready, ere I waked her. I was a little abashed when she came forth in her one habit, and the mud of the way upon her stockings. By what inquiries I had made, it seemed a good few days must pass before her mails could come to hand in Leyden, and it was plainly needful she must have a shift of things. She was unwilling at first that I should go to that expense; but I reminded her she was now a rich man's sister and must appear suitably in the part, and we had not got to the second merchant's before she was entirely charmed into the spirit of the thing, and her eyes shining. It pleased me to see her so innocent and thorough in this pleasure. What was more extraordinary was the passion into which I fell on it myself; being never satisfied that I had bought her enough or fine enough, and never weary of beholding her in different attires. Indeed, I began to understand some little of Miss Grant's immersion in the interest of clothes; for the truth is, when you have the ground of a beautiful person to adorn, the whole business becomes beautiful. The Dutch chintzes I should say were extraordinary cheap and fine; but I would be ashamed to set down what I paid for stockings to her. Altogether I spent so great a sum upon this pleasuring (as I may call it) that I was ashamed for a great while to spend more; and by way of a set-off, I left our chambers pretty bare. If we had beds, if Catriona was a little braw, and I had light to see her by, we were richly enough lodged for me.

By the end of this merchandising I was glad to leave her at the door with all our purchases, and go for a long walk alone in which to read myself a lecture. Here had I taken under my roof, and as good as to my bosom, a young lass extremely beautiful, and whose innocence was her peril. My talk with the old Dutchman, and the lies to which I was constrained, had already given me a sense of how my conduct must appear to others; and now, after the strong admiration I had just experienced and the immoderacy with which I had continued my vain purchases, I began to think of it myself as very hazarded. I bethought me, if I had a sister indeed, whether I would so expose her; then, judging the case too problematical, I varied my question into this, whether I would so trust Catriona in the hands of any other Christian being; the answer to which made my face to burn. The more cause, since I had been entrapped and had entrapped the girl into an undue situation, that I should behave in it with scrupulous nicety. She depended on me wholly for her bread and shelter; in case I should alarm her delicacy, she had no retreat. Besides I was her host and her protector; and the more irregularly I had fallen in these positions, the less excuse for me if I should profit by the same to forward even the most honest suit; for with the opportunities that I enjoyed, and which no wise parent would have suffered for a moment, even the most honest suit would be unfair. I saw I must be extremely hold-off in my relations; and yet not too much so neither; for if I had no right to appear at all in the character of a suitor, I must yet appear continually, and if possible agreeably, in that of host. It was plain I should require a great deal of tact and conduct, perhaps more than my years afforded. But I had rushed in where angels might have feared to tread, and there was no way out of that position save by behaving right while I was in it. I made a set of rules for my guidance; prayed for strength to be enabled to observe them, and as a more human aid to the same end purchased a study-book in law. This being all that I could think of, I relaxed from these grave considerations; whereupon my mind bubbled at once into an effervescency of pleasing spirits, and it was like one treading on air that I turned homeward. As I thought that name of home, and recalled the image of that figure awaiting me between four walls, my heart beat upon my bosom.

My troubles began with my return. She ran to greet me with an obvious and affecting pleasure. She was clad, besides, entirely in the new clothes that I had bought for her; looked in them beyond expression well; and must walk about and drop me curtseys to display them and to be admired. I am sure I did it with an ill grace, for I thought to have choked upon the words.

"Well," she said, "if you will not be caring for my pretty clothes, see what I have done with our two chambers." And she showed me the place all very finely swept, and the fires glowing in the two chimneys.

I was glad of a chance to seem a little more severe than I quite felt. "Catriona," said I, "I am very much displeased with you, and you must never again lay a hand upon my room. One of us two must have the rule while we are here together; it is most fit it should be I who am both the man and the elder; and I give you that for my command."

She dropped me one of her curtseys; which were extraordinary taking. "If you will be cross," said she, "I must be making pretty manners at you, Davie. I will be very obedient, as I should be when every stitch upon all there is of me belongs to you. But you will not be very cross either, because now I have not anyone else."

This struck me hard, and I made haste, in a kind of penitence, to blot out all the good effect of my last speech. In this direction progress was more easy, being down hill; she led me forward, smiling; at the sight of her, in the brightness of the fire and with her pretty becks and looks, my heart was altogether melted. We made our meal with infinite mirth and tenderness; and the two seemed to be commingled into one, so that our very laughter sounded like a kindness.

In the midst of which I awoke to better recollections, made a lame word of excuse, and set myself boorishly to my studies. It was a substantial, instructive book that I had bought, by the late Dr. Heineccius, in which I was to do a great deal reading these next few days, and often very glad that I had no one to question me of what I read. Methought she bit her lip at me a little, and that cut me. Indeed it left her wholly solitary, the more as she was very little of a reader, and had never a book. But what was I to do?

So the rest of the evening flowed by almost without speech.

I could have beat myself. I could not lie in my bed that night for rage and repentance, but walked to and fro on my bare feet till I was nearly perished, for the chimney was gone out and the frost keen. The thought of her in the next room, the thought that she might even hear me as I walked, the remembrance of my churlishness and that I must continue to practise the same ungrateful course or be dishonoured, put me beside my reason. I stood like a man between Scylla and Charybdis: What must she think of me? was my one thought that softened me continually into weakness. What is to become of us? the other which steeled me again to resolution. This was my first night of wakefulness and divided counsels, of which I was now to pass many, pacing like a madman, sometimes weeping like a childish boy, sometimes praying (I fain would hope) like a Christian.

But prayer is not very difficult, and the hitch comes in practice. In her presence, and above all if I allowed any beginning of familiarity, I found I had very little command of what should follow. But to sit all day in the same room with her, and feign to be engaged upon Heineccius, surpassed my strength. So that I fell instead upon the expedient of absenting myself so much as I was able; taking out classes and sitting there regularly, often with small attention, the test of which I found the other day in a note-book of that period, where I had left off to follow an edifying lecture and actually scribbled in my book some very ill verses, though the Latinity is rather better than I thought that I could ever have compassed. The evil of this course was unhappily near as great as its advantage. I had the less time of trial, but I believe, while the time lasted, I was tried the more extremely. For she being so much left to solitude, she came to greet my return with an increasing fervour that came nigh to overmaster me. These friendly offers I must barbarously cast back; and my rejection sometimes wounded her so cruelly that I must unbend and seek to make it up to her in kindness. So that our time passed in ups and downs, tiffs and disappointments, upon the which I could almost say (if it may be said with reverence) that I was crucified.

The base of my trouble was Catriona's extraordinary innocence, at which I was not so much surprised as filled with pity and admiration. She seemed to have no thought of our position, no sense of my struggles; welcomed any mark of my weakness with responsive joy; and when I was drove again to my retrenchments, did not always dissemble her chagrin. There were times when I have thought to myself, "If she were over head in love, and set her cap to catch me, she would scarce behave much otherwise;" and then I would fall again into wonder at the simplicity of woman, from whom I felt (in these moments) that I was not worthy to be descended.

There was one point in particular on which our warfare turned, and of all things, this was the question of her clothes. My baggage had soon followed me from Rotterdam, and hers from Helvoet. She had now, as it were, two wardrobes; and it grew to be understood between us (I could never tell how) that when she was friendly she would wear my clothes, and when otherwise her own. It was meant for a buffet, and (as it were) the renunciation of her gratitude; and I felt it so in my bosom, but was generally more wise than to appear to have observed the circumstance.

Once, indeed, I was betrayed into a childishness greater than her own; it fell in this way. On my return from classes, thinking upon her devoutly with a great deal of love and a good deal of annoyance in the bargain, the annoyance began to fade away out of my mind; and spying in a window one of those forced flowers, of which the Hollanders are so skilled in the artifice, I gave way to an impulse and bought it for Catriona. I do not know the name of that flower, but it was of the pink colour, and I thought she would admire the same, and carried it home to her with a wonderful soft heart. I had left her in my clothes, and when I returned to find her all changed and a face to match, I cast but the one look at her from head to foot, ground my teeth together, flung the window open, and my flower into the court, and then (between rage and prudence) myself out of that room again, of which I slammed she door as I went out.

On the steep stair I came near falling, and this brought me to myself, so that I began at once to see the folly of my conduct. I went, not into the street as I had purposed, but to the house court, which was always a solitary place, and where I saw my flower (that had cost me vastly more than it was worth) hanging in the leafless tree. I stood by the side of the canal, and looked upon the ice. Country people went by on their skates, and I envied them. I could see no way out of the pickle I was in no way so much as to return to the room I had just left. No doubt was in my mind but I had now betrayed the secret of my feelings; and to make things worse, I had shown at the same time (and that with wretched boyishness) incivility to my helpless guest.

I suppose she must have seen me from the open window. It did not seem to me that I had stood there very long before I heard the crunching of footsteps on the frozen snow, and turning somewhat angrily (for I was in no spirit to be interrupted) saw Catriona drawing near. She was all changed again, to the clocked stockings.

"Are we not to have our walk to-day?" said she.

I was looking at her in a maze. "Where is your brooch?" says I.

She carried her hand to her bosom and coloured high. "I will have forgotten it," said she. "I will run upstairs for it quick, and then surely we'll can have our walk?"

There was a note of pleading in that last that staggered me; I had neither words nor voice to utter them; I could do no more than nod by way of answer; and the moment she had left me, climbed into the tree and recovered my flower, which on her return I offered her.

"I bought it for you, Catriona," said I.

She fixed it in the midst of her bosom with the brooch, I could have thought tenderly.

"It is none the better of my handling," said I again, and blushed.

"I will be liking it none the worse, you may be sure of that," said she.

We did not speak so much that day; she seemed a thought on the reserve, though not unkindly. As for me, all the time of our walking, and after we came home, and I had seen her put my flower into a pot of water, I was thinking to myself what puzzles women were. I was thinking, the one moment, it was the most stupid thing on earth she should not have perceived my love; and the next, that she had certainly perceived it long ago, and (being a wise girl with the fine female instinct of propriety) concealed her knowledge.

We had our walk daily. Out in the streets I felt more safe; I relaxed a little in my guardedness; and for one thing, there was no Heineccius. This made these periods not only a relief to myself, but a particular pleasure to my poor child. When I came back about the hour appointed, I would generally find her ready dressed, and glowing with anticipation. She would prolong their duration to the extreme, seeming to dread (as I did myself) the hour of the return; and there is scarce a field or waterside near Leyden, scarce a street or lane there, where we have not lingered. Outside of these, I bade her confine herself entirely to our lodgings; this in the fear of her encountering any acquaintance, which would have rendered our position very difficult. From the same apprehension I would never suffer her to attend church, nor even go myself; but made some kind of shift to hold worship privately in our own chamber—I hope with an honest, but I am quite sure with a very much divided mind. Indeed, there was scarce anything that more affected me, than thus to kneel down alone with her before God like man and wife.

One day it was snowing downright hard. I had thought it not possible that we should venture forth, and was surprised to find her waiting for me ready dressed.

"I will not be doing without my walk," she cried. "You are never a good boy, Davie, in the house; I will never be caring for you only in the open air. I think we two will better turn Egyptian and dwell by the roadside."

That was the best walk yet of all of them; she clung near to me in the falling snow; it beat about and melted on us, and the drops stood upon her bright cheeks like tears and ran into her smiling mouth. Strength seemed to come upon me with the sight like a giant's; I thought I could have caught her up and run with her into the uttermost places in the earth; and we spoke together all that time beyond belief for freedom and sweetness.

It was the dark night when we came to the house door. She pressed my arm upon her bosom.

"Thank you kindly for these same good hours," said she, on a deep note of her voice.

The concern in which I fell instantly on this address, put me with the same swiftness on my guard; and we were no sooner in the chamber, and the light made, than she beheld the old, dour, stubborn countenance of the student of Heineccius. Doubtless she was more than usually hurt; and I know for myself, I found it more than usually difficult to maintain any strangeness. Even at the meal, I durst scarce unbuckle and scarce lift my eyes to her; and it was no sooner over than I fell again to my civilian, with more seeming abstraction and less understanding than before. Methought, as I read, I could hear my heart strike like an eight-day clock. Hard as I feigned to study, there was still some of my eyesight that spilled beyond the book upon Catriona. She sat on the floor by the side of my great mail, and the chimney lighted her up, and shone and blinked upon her, and made her glow and darken through a wonder of fine hues. Now she would be gazing in the fire, and then again at me; and at that I would be plunged in a terror of myself, and turn the pages of Heineccius like a man looking for the text in church.

Suddenly she called out aloud. "O, why does not my father come?" she cried, and fell at once into a storm of tears.

I leaped up, flung Heineccius fairly in the fire, ran to her side, and cast an arm around her sobbing body.

She put me from her sharply, "You do not love your friend," says she. "I could be so happy too, if you would let me!" And then, "O, what will I have done that you should hate me so?"

"Hate you!" cries I, and held her firm. "You blind lass, can you not see a little in my wretched heart? Do you not think when I sit there, reading in that fool-book that I have just burned and be damned to it, I take ever the least thought of any stricken thing but just yourself? Night after night I could have grat to see you sitting there your lone. And what was I to do? You are here under my honour; would you punish me for that? Is it for that that you would spurn a loving servant?"

At the word, with a small, sudden motion, she clung near to me. I raised her face to mine, I kissed it, and she bowed her brow upon my bosom, clasping me tight. I saw in a mere whirl like a man drunken. Then I heard her voice sound very small and muffled in my clothes.

"Did you kiss her truly?" she asked.

There went through me so great a heave of surprise that I was all shook with it.

"Miss Grant?" I cried, all in a disorder. "Yes, I asked her to kiss me good-bye, the which she did."

"Ah, well!" said she, "you have kissed me too, at all events."

At the strangeness and sweetness of that word, I saw where we had fallen; rose, and set her on her feet.

"This will never do," said I. "This will never, never do. O Catrine, Catrine!" Then there came a pause in which I was debarred from any speaking. And then, "Go away to your bed," said I. "Go away to your bed and leave me."

She turned to obey me like a child, and the next I knew of it, had stopped in the very doorway.

"Good night, Davie!" said she.

"And O, good night, my love!" I cried, with a great outbreak of my soul, and caught her to me again, so that it seemed I must have broken her. The next moment I had thrust her from the room, shut to the door even with violence, and stood alone.

The milk was spilt now, the word was out and the truth told. I had crept like an untrusty man into the poor maid's affections; she was in my hand like any frail, innocent thing to make or mar; and what weapon of defence was left me? It seemed like a symbol that Heineccius, my old protection, was now burned. I repented, yet could not find it in my heart to blame myself for that great failure. It seemed not possible to have resisted the boldness of her innocence or that last temptation of her weeping. And all that I had to excuse me did but make my sin appear the greater—it was upon a nature so defenceless, and with such advantages of the position, that I seemed to have practised.

What was to become of us now? It seemed we could no longer dwell in the one place. But where was I to go? or where she? Without either choice or fault of ours, life had conspired to wall us together in that narrow place. I had a wild thought of marrying out of hand; and the next moment put it from me with revolt. She was a child, she could not tell her own heart; I had surprised her weakness, I must never go on to build on that surprisal; I must keep her not only clear of reproach, but free as she had come to me.

Down I sat before the fire, and reflected, and repented, and beat my brains in vain for any means of escape. About two of the morning, there were three red embers left and the house and all the city was asleep, when I was aware of a small sound of weeping in the next room. She thought that I slept, the poor soul; she regretted her weakness—and what perhaps (God help her!) she called her forwardness—and in the dead of the night solaced herself with tears. Tender and bitter feelings, love and penitence and pity, struggled in my soul; it seemed I was under bond to heal that weeping.

"O, try to forgive me!" I cried out, "try, try to forgive me. Let us forget it all, let us try if we'll no can forget it!"

There came no answer, but the sobbing ceased. I stood a long while with my hands still clasped as I had spoken; then the cold of the night laid hold upon me with a shudder, and I think my reason reawakened.

"You can make no hand of this, Davie," thinks I. "To bed with you like a wise lad, and try if you can sleep. To-morrow you may see your way."

CHAPTER XXV.
THE RETURN OF JAMES MORE

I was called on the morrow out of a late and troubled slumber by a knocking on my door, ran to open it, and had almost swooned with the contrariety of my feelings, mostly painful; for on the threshold, in a rough wraprascal and an extraordinary big laced hat, there stood James More.

I ought to have been glad perhaps without admixture, for there was a sense in which the man came like an answer to prayer. I had been saying till my head was weary that Catriona and I must separate, and looking till my head ached for any possible means of separation. Here were the means come to me upon two legs, and joy was the hindmost of my thoughts. It is to be considered, however, that even if the weight of the future were lifted off me by the man's arrival, the present heaved up the more black and menacing; so that, as I first stood before him in my shirt and breeches, I believe I took a leaping step backward like a person shot.

"Ah," said he, "I have found you, Mr. Balfour." And offered me his large, fine hand, the which (recovering at the same time my post in the doorway, as if with some thought of resistance) I took him by doubtfully. "It is a remarkable circumstance how our affairs appear to intermingle," he continued. "I am owing you an apology for an unfortunate intrusion upon yours, which I suffered myself to be entrapped into by my confidence in that false-face, Prestongrange; I think shame to own to you that I was ever trusting to a lawyer." He shrugged his shoulders with a very French air. "But indeed the man is very plausible," says he. "And now it seems that you have busied yourself handsomely in the matter of my daughter, for whose direction I was remitted to yourself."

"I think, sir," said I, with a very painful air, "that it will be necessary we two should have an explanation."

"There is nothing amiss?" he asked. "My agent, Mr. Sprott—"

"For God's sake moderate your voice!" I cried. "She must not hear till we have had an explanation."

"She is in this place?" cries he.

"That is her chamber door," said I.

"You are here with her alone?" he asked.

"And who else would I have got to stay with us?" cries I.

I will do him the justice to admit that he turned pale.

"This is very unusual," said he. "This is a very unusual circumstance. You are right, we must hold an explanation."

So saying he passed me by, and I must own the tall old rogue appeared at that moment extraordinary dignified. He had now, for the first time, the view of my chamber, which I scanned (I may say) with his eyes. A bit of morning sun glinted in by the window pane, and showed it off; my bed, my mails, and washing dish, with some disorder of my clothes, and the unlighted chimney, made the only plenishing; no mistake but it looked bare and cold, and the most unsuitable, beggarly place conceivable to harbour a young lady. At the same time came in on my mind the recollection of the clothes that I had bought for her; and I thought this contrast of poverty and prodigality bore an ill appearance.

He looked all about the chamber for a seat, and finding nothing else to his purpose except my bed, took a place upon the side of it; where, after I had closed the door, I could not very well avoid joining him. For however this extraordinary interview might end, it must pass if possible without waking Catriona; and the one thing needful was that we should sit close and talk low. But I can scarce picture what a pair we made; he in his great coat which the coldness of my chamber made extremely suitable; I shivering in my shirt and breeks; he with very much the air of a judge; and I (whatever I looked) with very much the feelings of a man who has heard the last trumpet.

"Well?" says he.

And "Well," I began, but found myself unable to go further.

"You tell me she is here?" said he again, but now with a spice of impatience that seemed to brace me up.

"She is in this house," said I, "and I knew the circumstance would be called unusual. But you are to consider how very unusual the whole business was from the beginning. Here is a young lady landed on the coast of Europe with two shillings and a penny halfpenny. She is directed to yon man Sprott in Helvoet. I hear you call him your agent. All I can say is he could do nothing but damn and swear at the mere mention of your name, and I must fee him out of my own pocket even to receive the custody of her effects. You speak of unusual circumstances, Mr. Drummond, if that be the name you prefer. Here was a circumstance, if you like, to which it was barbarity to have exposed her."

"But this is what I cannot understand the least," said James. "My daughter was placed into the charge of some responsible persons, whose names I have forgot."

"Gebbie was the name," said I; "and there is no doubt that Mr. Gebbie should have gone ashore with her at Helvoet. But he did not, Mr. Drummond; and I think you might praise God that I was there to offer in his place."

"I shall have a word to say to Mr. Gebbie before long," said he. "As for yourself, I think it might have occurred that you were somewhat young for such a post."

"But the choice was not between me and somebody else, it was between me and nobody," cried I. "Nobody offered in my place, and I must say I think you show a very small degree of gratitude to me that did."

"I shall wait until I understand my obligation a little more in the particular," says he.

"Indeed, and I think it stares you in the face, then," said I. "Your child was deserted, she was clean flung away in the midst of Europe, with scarce two shillings, and not two words of any language spoken there: I must say, a bonny business! I brought her to this place. I gave her the name and the tenderness due to a sister. All this has not gone without expense, but that I scarce need to hint at. They were services due to the young lady's character which I respect; and I think it would be a bonny business too, if I was to be singing her praises to her father."

"You are a young man," he began.

"So I hear you tell me," said I, with a good deal of heat.

"You are a very young man," he repeated, "or you would have understood the significance of the step."

"I think you speak very much at your ease," cried I. "What else was I to do? It is a fact I might have hired some decent, poor woman to be a third to us, and I declare I never thought of it until this moment! But where was I to find her, that am a foreigner myself? And let me point out to your observation, Mr. Drummond, that it would have cost me money out of my pocket. For here is just what it comes to, that I had to pay through the nose for your neglect; and there is only the one story to it, just that you were so unloving and so careless as to have lost your daughter."

"He that lives in a glass house should not be casting stones," says he; "and we will finish inquiring into the behaviour of Miss Drummond before we go on to sit in judgment on her father."

"But I will be entrapped into no such attitude," said I. "The character of Miss Drummond is far above inquiry, as her father ought to know. So is mine, and I am telling you that. There are but the two ways of it open. The one is to express your thanks to me as one gentleman to another, and to say no more. The other (if you are so difficult as to be still dissatisfied) is to pay me, that which I have expended and be done."

He seemed to soothe me with a hand in the air. "There, there," said he. "You go too fast, you go too fast, Mr. Balfour. It is a good thing that I have learned to be more patient. And I believe you forget that I have yet to see my daughter."

I began to be a little relieved upon this speech and a change in the man's manner that I spied in him as soon as the name of money fell between us.

"I was thinking it would be more fit—if you will excuse the plainness of my dressing in your presence—that I should go forth and leave you to encounter her alone?" said I.

"What I would have looked for at your hands!" says he; and there was no mistake but what he said it civilly.

I thought this better and better still, and as I began to pull on my hose, recalling the man's impudent mendicancy at Prestongrange's, I determined to pursue what seemed to be my victory.

"If you have any mind to stay some while in Leyden," said I, "this room is very much at your disposal, and I can easy find another for myself: in which way we shall have the least amount of flitting possible, there being only one to change."

"Why, sir," said he, making his bosom big, "I think no shame of a poverty I have come by in the service of my king; I make no secret that my affairs are quite involved; and for the moment, it would be even impossible for me to undertake a journey."

"Until you have occasion to communicate with your friends," said I, "perhaps it might be convenient for you (as of course it would be honourable to myself) if you were to regard yourself in the light of my guest?"

"Sir," said he, "when an offer is frankly made, I think I honour myself most to imitate that frankness. Your hand, Mr. David; you have the character that I respect the most; you are one of those from whom a gentleman can take a favour and no more words about it. I am an old soldier," he went on, looking rather disgusted-like around my chamber, "and you need not fear I shall prove burthensome. I have ate too often at a dyke-side, drank of the ditch, and had no roof but the rain."

"I should be telling you," said I, "that our breakfasts are sent customarily in about this time of morning. I propose I should go now to the tavern, and bid them add a cover for yourself and delay the meal the matter of an hour, which will give you an interval to meet your daughter in."

Methought his nostrils wagged at this. "O, an hour?" says he. "That is perhaps superfluous. Half an hour, Mr. David, or say twenty minutes; I shall do very well in that. And by the way," he adds, detaining me by the coat, "what is it you drink in the morning, whether ale or wine?"

"To be frank with you, sir," says I, "I drink nothing else but spare, cold water."

"Tut-tut," says he, "that is fair destruction to the stomach, take an old campaigner's word for it. Our country spirit at home is perhaps the most entirely wholesome; but as that is not come-at-able, Rhenish or a white wine of Burgundy will be next best."

"I shall make it my business to see you are supplied," said I.

"Why, very good," said he, "and we shall make a man of you yet, Mr. David."

By this time, I can hardly say that I was minding him at all, beyond an odd thought of the kind of father-in-law that he was like to prove; and all my cares centred about the lass his daughter, to whom I determined to convey some warning of her visitor. I stepped to the door accordingly, and cried through the panels, knocking thereon at the same time: "Miss Drummond, here is your father come at last."

With that I went forth upon my errand, having (by two words) extraordinarily damaged my affairs.

CHAPTER XXVI.
THE THREESOME

Whether or not I was to be so much blamed, or rather perhaps pitied, I must leave others to judge. My shrewdness (of which I have a good deal, too) seems not so great with the ladies. No doubt, at the moment when I awaked her, I was thinking a good deal of the effect upon James More; and similarly when I returned and we were all sat down to breakfast, I continued to behave to the young lady with deference and distance; as I still think to have been most wise. Her father had cast doubts upon the innocence of my friendship; and these, it was my first business to allay. But there is a kind of an excuse for Catriona also. We had shared in a scene of some tenderness and passion, and given and received caresses: I had thrust her from me with violence; I had called aloud upon her in the night from the one room to the other; she had passed hours of wakefulness and weeping; and it is not to be supposed I had been absent from her pillow thoughts. Upon the back of this, to be awaked, with unaccustomed formality, under the name of Miss Drummond, and to be thenceforth used with a great deal of distance and respect, led her entirely in error on my private sentiments; and she was indeed so incredibly abused as to imagine me repentant and trying to draw off!

The trouble betwixt us seems to have been this: that whereas I (since I had first set eyes on his great hat) thought singly of James More, his return and suspicions, she made so little of these that I may say she scarce remarked them, and all her troubles and doings regarded what had passed between us in the night before. This is partly to be explained by the innocence and boldness of her character; and partly because James More, having sped so ill in his interview with me, or had his mouth closed by my invitation, said no word to her upon the subject. At the breakfast, accordingly, it soon appeared we were at cross purposes. I had looked to find her in clothes of her own: I found her (as if her father were forgotten) wearing some of the best that I had bought for her, and which she knew (or thought) that I admired her in. I had looked to find her imitate my affectation of distance, and be most precise and formal; instead I found her flushed and wild-like, with eyes extraordinary bright, and a painful and varying expression, calling me by name with a sort of appeal of tenderness, and referring and deferring to my thoughts and wishes like an anxious or a suspected wife.

But this was not for long. As I behold her so regardless of her own interests, which I had jeopardised and was now endeavouring to recover, I redoubled my own coldness in the manner of a lesson to the girl. The more she came forward, the farther I drew back; the more she betrayed the closeness of our intimacy, the more pointedly civil I became, until even her father (if he had not been so engrossed with eating) might have observed the opposition. In the midst of which, of a sudden, she became wholly changed, and I told myself, with a good deal of relief, that she had took the hint at last.

All day I was at my classes or in quest of my new lodging; and though the hour of our customary walk hung miserably on my hands, I cannot say but I was happy on the whole to find my way cleared, the girl again in proper keeping, the father satisfied or at least acquiescent, and myself free to prosecute my love with honour. At supper, as at all our meals, it was James More that did the talking. No doubt but he talked well if anyone could have believed him. But I will speak of him presently more at large. The meal at an end, he rose, got his great coat, and looking (as I thought) at me, observed he had affairs abroad. I took this for a hint that I was to be going also, and got up; whereupon the girl, who had scarce given me greeting at my entrance, turned her eyes upon me wide open with a look that bade me stay. I stood between them like a fish out of water, turning from one to the other; neither seemed to observe me, she gazing on the floor, he buttoning his coat: which vastly swelled my embarrassment. This appearance of indifference argued, upon her side, a good deal of anger very near to burst out. Upon his, I thought it horribly alarming; I made sure there was a tempest brewing there; and considering that to be the chief peril, turned towards him and put myself (so to speak) in the man's hands.

"Can I do anything for you, Mr. Drummond?" says I.

He stifled a yawn, which again I thought to be duplicity. "Why, Mr. David," said he, "since you are so obliging as to propose it, you might show me the way to a certain tavern" (of which he gave the name) "where I hope to fall in with some old companions in arms."

There was no more to say, and I got my hat and cloak to bear him company.

"And as for you," say he to his daughter, "you had best go to your bed. I shall be late home, and Early to bed and early to rise, gars bonny lasses have bright eyes."

Whereupon he kissed her with a good deal of tenderness, and ushered me before him from the door. This was so done (I thought on purpose) that it was scarce possible there should be any parting salutation; but I observed she did not look at me, and set it down to terror of James More.

It was some distance to that tavern. He talked all the way of matters which did not interest me the smallest, and at the door dismissed me with empty manners. Thence I walked to my new lodging, where I had not so much as a chimney to hold me warm, and no society but my own thoughts. These were still bright enough; I did not so much as dream that Catriona was turned against me; I thought we were like folk pledged; I thought we had been too near and spoke too warmly to be severed, least of all by what were only steps in a most needful policy. And the chief of my concern was only the kind of father-in-law that I was getting, which was not at all the kind I would have chosen: and the matter of how soon I ought to speak to him, which was a delicate point on several sides. In the first place, when I thought how young I was I blushed all over, and could almost have found it in my heart to have desisted; only that if once I let them go from Leyden without explanation, I might lose her altogether. And in the second place, there was our very irregular situation to be kept in view, and the rather scant measure of satisfaction I had given James More that morning. I concluded, on the whole, that delay would not hurt anything, yet I would not delay too long neither; and got to my cold bed with a full heart.

The next day, as James More seemed a little on the complaining hand in the matter of my chamber, I offered to have in more furniture; and coming in the afternoon, with porters bringing chairs and tables, found the girl once more left to herself. She greeted me on my admission civilly, but withdrew at once to her own room, of which she shut the door. I made my disposition, and paid and dismissed the men so that she might hear them go, when I supposed she would at once come forth again to speak to me. I waited yet awhile, then knocked upon her door.

"Catriona!" said I.

The door was opened so quickly, even before I had the word out, that I thought she must have stood behind it listening. She remained there in the interval quite still; but she had a look that I cannot put a name on, as of one in a bitter trouble.

"Are we not to have our walk to-day either?" so I faltered.

"I am thanking you," said she. "I will not be caring much to walk, now that my father is come home."

"But I think he has gone out himself and left you here alone," said I.

"And do you think that was very kindly said?" she asked.

"It was not unkindly meant," I replied. "What ails you, Catriona? What have I done to you that you should turn from me like this?"

"I do not turn from you at all," she said, speaking very carefully. "I will ever be grateful to my friend that was good to me; I will ever be his friend in all that I am able. But now that my father James More is come again, there is a difference to be made, and I think there are some things said and done that would be better to be forgotten. But I will ever be your friend in all that I am able, and if that is not all that . . . . if it is not so much . . . . Not that you will be caring! But I would not have you think of me too hard. It was true what you said to me, that I was too young to be advised, and I am hoping you will remember I was just a child. I would not like to lose your friendship, at all events."

She began this very pale; but before she was done, the blood was in her face like scarlet, so that not her words only, but her face and the trembling of her very hands, besought me to be gentle. I saw, for the first time, how very wrong I had done to place the child in that position, where she had been entrapped into a moment's weakness, and now stood before me like a person shamed.

"Miss Drummond," I said, and stuck, and made the same beginning once again, "I wish you could see into my heart," I cried. "You would read there that my respect is undiminished. If that were possible, I should say it was increased. This is but the result of the mistake we made; and had to come; and the less said of it now the better. Of all of our life here, I promise you it shall never pass my lips; I would like to promise you too that I would never think of it, but it's a memory that will be always dear to me. And as for a friend, you have one here that would die for you."

"I am thanking you," said she.

We stood awhile silent, and my sorrow for myself began to get the upper hand; for here were all my dreams come to a sad tumble, and my love lost, and myself alone again in the world as at the beginning.

"Well," said I, "we shall be friends always, that's a certain thing. But this is a kind of farewell, too: it's a kind of a farewell after all; I shall always ken Miss Drummond, but this is a farewell to my Catriona."

I looked at her; I could hardly say I saw her, but she seemed to grow great and brighten in my eyes; and with that I suppose I must have lost my head, for I called out her name again and made a step at her with my hands reached forth.

She shrank back like a person struck, her face flamed; but the blood sprang no faster up into her cheeks, than what it flowed back upon my own heart, at sight of it, with penitence and concern. I found no words to excuse myself, but bowed before her very deep, and went my ways out of the house with death in my bosom.

I think it was about five days that followed without any change. I saw her scarce ever but at meals, and then of course in the company of James More. If we were alone even for a moment, I made it my devoir to behave the more distantly and to multiply respectful attentions, having always in my mind's eye that picture of the girl shrinking and flaming in a blush, and in my heart more pity for her than I could depict in words. I was sorry enough for myself, I need not dwell on that, having fallen all my length and more than all my height in a few seconds; but, indeed, I was near as sorry for the girl, and sorry enough to be scarce angry with her save by fits and starts. Her plea was good; she had been placed in an unfair position; if she had deceived herself and me, it was no more than was to have been looked for.

And for another thing she was now very much alone. Her father, when he was by, was rather a caressing parent; but he was very easy led away by his affairs and pleasures, neglected her without compunction or remark, spent his nights in taverns when he had the money, which was more often than I could at all account for; and even in the course of these few days, failed once to come to a meal, which Catriona and I were at last compelled to partake of without him. It was the evening meal, and I left immediately that I had eaten, observing I supposed she would prefer to be alone; to which she agreed and (strange as it may seem) I quite believed her. Indeed, I thought myself but an eyesore to the girl, and a reminder of a moment's weakness that she now abhorred to think of. So she must sit alone in that room where she and I had been so merry, and in the blink of that chimney whose light had shone upon our many difficult and tender moments. There she must sit alone, and think of herself as of a maid who had most unmaidenly proffered her affections and had the same rejected. And in the meanwhile I would be alone some other place, and reading myself (whenever I was tempted to be angry) lessons upon human frailty and female delicacy. And altogether I suppose there were never two poor fools made themselves more unhappy in a greater misconception.

As for James, he paid not so much heed to us, or to anything in nature but his pocket, and his belly, and his own prating talk. Before twelve hours were gone he had raised a small loan of me; before thirty, he had asked for a second and been refused. Money and refusal he took with the same kind of high good nature. Indeed, he had an outside air of magnanimity that was very well fitted to impose upon a daughter; and the light in which he was constantly presented in his talk, and the man's fine presence and great ways went together pretty harmoniously. So that a man that had no business with him, and either very little penetration or a furious deal of prejudice, might almost have been taken in. To me, after my first two interviews, he was as plain as print; I saw him to be perfectly selfish, with a perfect innocency in the same; and I would hearken to his swaggering talk (of arms, and "an old soldier," and "a poor Highland gentleman," and "the strength of my country and my friends") as I might to the babbling of a parrot.

The odd thing was that I fancy he believed some part of it himself, or did at times; I think he was so false all through that he scarce knew when he was lying; and for one thing, his moments of dejection must have been wholly genuine. There were times when he would be the most silent, affectionate, clinging creature possible, holding Catriona's hand like a big baby, and begging of me not to leave if I had any love to him; of which, indeed, I had none, but all the more to his daughter. He would press and indeed beseech us to entertain him with our talk, a thing very difficult in the state of our relations; and again break forth in pitiable regrets for his own land and friends, or into Gaelic singing.

"This is one of the melancholy airs of my native land," he would say. "You may think it strange to see a soldier weep, and indeed it is to make a near friend of you," says he. "But the notes of this singing are in my blood, and the words come out of my heart. And when I mind upon my red mountains and the wild birds calling there, and the brave streams of water running down, I would scarce think shame to weep before my enemies." Then he would sing again, and translate to me pieces of the song, with a great deal of boggling and much expressed contempt against the English language. "It says here," he would say, "that the sun is gone down, and the battle is at an end, and the brave chiefs are defeated. And it tells here how the stars see them fleeing into strange countries or lying dead on the red mountain; and they will never more shout the call of battle or wash their feet in the streams of the valley. But if you had only some of this language, you would weep also because the words of it are beyond all expression, and it is mere mockery to tell you it in English."

Well, I thought there was a good deal of mockery in the business, one way and another; and yet, there was some feeling too, for which I hated him, I think, the worst of all. And it used to cut me to the quick to see Catriona so much concerned for the old rogue, and weeping herself to see him weep, when I was sure one half of his distress flowed from his last night's drinking in some tavern. There were times when I was tempted to lend him a round sum, and see the last of him for good; but this would have been to see the last of Catriona as well, for which I was scarcely so prepared; and besides, it went against my conscience to squander my good money on one who was so little of a husband.

CHAPTER XXVII.
A TWOSOME

I believe it was about the fifth day, and I know at least that James was in one of his fits of gloom, when I received three letters. The first was from Alan, offering to visit me in Leyden; the other two were out of Scotland and prompted by the same affair, which was the death of my uncle and my own complete accession to my rights. Rankeillor's was, of course, wholly in the business view; Miss Grant's was like herself, a little more witty than wise, full of blame to me for not having written (though how was I to write with such intelligence?) and of rallying talk about Catriona, which it cut me to the quick to read in her very presence.

For it was of course in my own rooms that I found them, when I came to dinner, so that I was surprised out of my news in the very first moment of reading it. This made a welcome diversion for all three of us, nor could any have foreseen the ill consequences that ensued. It was accident that brought the three letters the same day, and that gave them into my hand in the same room with James More; and of all the events that flowed from that accident, and which I might have prevented if I had held my tongue, the truth is that they were preordained before Agricola came into Scotland or Abraham set out upon his travels.

The first that I opened was naturally Alan's; and what more natural than that I should comment on his design to visit me? but I observed James to sit up with an air of immediate attention.

"Is that not Alan Breck that was suspected of the Appin accident?" he inquired.

I told him, "Ay," it was the same; and he withheld me some time from my other letters, asking of our acquaintance, of Alan's manner of life in France, of which I knew very little, and further of his visit as now proposed.

"All we forfeited folk hang a little together," he explained, "and besides I know the gentleman: and though his descent is not the thing, and indeed he has no true right to use the name of Stewart, he was very much admired in the day of Drummossie. He did there like a soldier; if some that need not be named had done as well, the upshot need not have been so melancholy to remember. There were two that did their best that day, and it makes a bond between the pair of us," says he.

I could scarce refrain from shooting out my tongue at him, and could almost have wished that Alan had been there to have inquired a little further into that mention of his birth. Though, they tell me, the same was indeed not wholly regular.

Meanwhile, I had opened Miss Grant's, and could not withhold an exclamation.

"Catriona," I cried, forgetting, the first time since her father was arrived, to address her by a handle, "I am come into my kingdom fairly, I am the laird of Shaws indeed—my uncle is dead at last."

She clapped her hands together leaping from her seat. The next moment it must have come over both of us at once what little cause of joy was left to either, and we stood opposite, staring on each other sadly.

But James showed himself a ready hypocrite. "My daughter," says he, "is this how my cousin learned you to behave? Mr. David has lost a new friend, and we should first condole with him on his bereavement."

"Troth, sir," said I, turning to him in a kind of anger, "I can make no such great faces. His death is as blithe news as ever I got."

"It's a good soldier's philosophy," says James. "'Tis the way of flesh, we must all go, all go. And if the gentleman was so far from your favour, why, very well! But we may at least congratulate you on your accession to your estates."

"Nor can I say that either," I replied, with the same heat. "It is a good estate; what matters that to a lone man that has enough already? I had a good revenue before in my frugality; and but for the man's death—which gratifies me, shame to me that must confess it!—I see not how anyone is to be bettered by this change."

"Come, come," said he, "you are more affected than you let on, or you would never make yourself out so lonely. Here are three letters; that means three that wish you well; and I could name two more, here in this very chamber. I have known you not so very long, but Catriona, when we are alone, is never done with the singing of your praises."

She looked up at him, a little wild at that; and he slid off at once into another matter, the extent of my estate, which (during the most of the dinner time) he continued to dwell upon with interest. But it was to no purpose he dissembled; he had touched the matter with too gross a hand: and I knew what to expect. Dinner was scarce ate when he plainly discovered his designs. He reminded Catriona of an errand, and bid her attend to it. "I do not see you should be one beyond the hour," he added, "and friend David will be good enough to bear me company till you return." She made haste to obey him without words. I do not know if she understood, I believe not; but I was completely satisfied, and sat strengthening my mind for what should follow.

The door had scarce closed behind her departure, when the man leaned back in his chair and addressed me with a good affectation of easiness. Only the one thing betrayed him, and that was his face; which suddenly shone all over with fine points of sweat.

"I am rather glad to have a word alone with you," says he, "because in our first interview there were some expressions you misapprehended and I have long meant to set you right upon. My daughter stands beyond doubt. So do you, and I would make that good with my sword against all gainsayers. But, my dear David, this world is a censorious place—as who should know it better than myself, who have lived ever since the days of my late departed father, God sain him! in a perfect spate of calumnies? We have to face to that; you and me have to consider of that; we have to consider of that." And he wagged his head like a minister in a pulpit.

"To what effect, Mr. Drummond?" said I. "I would be obliged to you if you would approach your point."

"Ay, ay," said he, laughing, "like your character, indeed! and what I most admire in it. But the point, my worthy fellow, is sometimes in a kittle bit." He filled a glass of wine. "Though between you and me, that are such fast friends, it need not bother us long. The point, I need scarcely tell you, is my daughter. And the first thing is that I have no thought in my mind of blaming you. In the unfortunate circumstances, what could you do else? 'Deed, and I cannot tell."

"I thank you for that," said I, pretty close upon my guard.

"I have besides studied your character," he went on; "your talents are fair; you seem to have a moderate competence, which does no harm; and one thing with another, I am very happy to have to announce to you that I have decided on the latter of the two ways open."

"I am afraid I am dull," said I. "What ways are these?"

He bent his brows upon me formidably and uncrossed his legs. "Why, sir," says he, "I think I need scarce describe them to a gentleman of your condition; either that I should cut your throat or that you should marry my daughter."

"You are pleased to be quite plain at last," said I.

"And I believe I have been plain from the beginning!" cries he robustiously. "I am a careful parent, Mr. Balfour; but I thank God, a patient and deleeborate man. There is many a father, sir, that would have hirsled you at once either to the altar or the field. My esteem for your character—"

"Mr. Drummond," I interrupted, "if you have any esteem for me at all, I will beg of you to moderate your voice. It is quite needless to rowt at a gentleman in the same chamber with yourself and lending you his best attention."

"Why, very true," says he, with an immediate change. "And you must excuse the agitations of a parent."

"I understand you then," I continued—"for I will take no note of your other alternative, which perhaps it was a pity you let fall—I understand you rather to offer me encouragement in case I should desire to apply for your daughter's hand?"

"It is not possible to express my meaning better," said he, "and I see we shall do well together."

"That remains to be yet seen," said I. "But so much I need make no secret of, that I bear the lady you refer to the most tender affection, and I could not fancy, even in a dream, a better fortune than to get her."

"I was sure of it, I felt certain of you, David," he cried, and reached out his hand to me.

I put it by. "You go too fast, Mr. Drummond," said I. "There are conditions to be made; and there is a difficulty in the path, which I see not entirely how we shall come over. I have told you that, upon my side, there is no objection to the marriage, but I have good reason to believe there will be much on the young lady's."

"This is all beside the mark," says he. "I will engage for her acceptance."

"I think you forget, Mr. Drummond," said I, "that, even in dealing with myself, you have been betrayed into two-three unpalatable expressions. I will have none such employed to the young lady. I am here to speak and think for the two of us; and I give you to understand that I would no more let a wife be forced upon myself, than what I would let a husband be forced on the young lady."

He sat and glowered at me like one in doubt and a good deal of temper.

"So that is to be the way of it," I concluded. "I will marry Miss Drummond, and that blithely, if she is entirely willing. But if there be the least unwillingness, as I have reason to fear—marry her will I never."

"Well well," said he, "this is a small affair. As soon as she returns I will sound her a bit, and hope to reassure you—"

But I cut in again. "Not a finger of you, Mr. Drummond, or I cry off, and you can seek a husband to your daughter somewhere else," said I. "It is I that am to be the only dealer and the only judge. I shall satisfy myself exactly; and none else shall anyways meddle—you the least of all."

"Upon my word, sir!" he exclaimed, "and who are you to be the judge?"

"The bridegroom, I believe," said I.

"This is to quibble," he cried. "You turn your back upon the fact. The girl, my daughter, has no choice left to exercise. Her character is gone."

"And I ask your pardon," said I, "but while this matter lies between her and you and me, that is not so."

"What security have I!" he cried. "Am I to let my daughter's reputation depend upon a chance?"

"You should have thought of all this long ago," said I, "before you were so misguided as to lose her; and not afterwards when it is quite too late. I refuse to regard myself as any way accountable for your neglect, and I will be browbeat by no man living. My mind is quite made up, and come what may, I will not depart from it a hair's breadth. You and me are to sit here in company till her return: upon which, without either word or look from you, she and I are to go forth again to hold our talk. If she can satisfy me that she is willing to this step, I will then make it; and if she cannot, I will not."

He leaped out of his chair like a man stung. "I can spy your manœuvre," he cried; "you would work upon her to refuse!"

"Maybe ay, and maybe no," said I. "That is the way it is to be, whatever."

"And if I refuse?" cries he.

"Then, Mr. Drummond, it will have to come to the throat-cutting," said I.

What with the size of the man, his great length of arm in which he came near rivalling his father, and his reputed skill at weapons, I did not use this word without trepidation, to say nothing at all of the circumstance that he was Catriona's father. But I might have spared myself alarms. From the poorness of my lodging—he does not seem to have remarked his daughter's dresses, which were indeed all equally new to him—and from the fact that I had shown myself averse to lend, he had embraced a strong idea of my poverty. The sudden news of my estate convinced him of his error, and he had made but the one bound of it on this fresh venture, to which he was now so wedded, that I believe he would have suffered anything rather than fall to the alternative of fighting.

A little while longer he continued to dispute with me, until I hit upon a word that silenced him.

"If I find you so averse to let me see the lady by herself," said I, "I must suppose you have very good grounds to think me in the right about her unwillingness."

He gabbled some kind of an excuse.

"But all this is very exhausting to both of our tempers," I added, "and I think we would do better to preserve a judicious silence."

The which we did until the girl returned, and I must suppose would have cut a very ridiculous figure had there been any there to view us.

CHAPTER XXVIII.
IN WHICH I AM LEFT ALONE

I opened the door to Catriona and stopped her on the threshold.

"Your father wishes us to take our walk," said I.

She looked to James More, who nodded, and at that, like a trained soldier, she turned to go with me.

We took one of our old ways, where we had gone often together, and been more happy than I can tell of in the past. I came a half a step behind, so that I could watch her unobserved. The knocking of her little shoes upon the way sounded extraordinary pretty and sad; and I thought it a strange moment that I should be so near both ends of it at once, and walk in the midst between two destinies, and could not tell whether I was hearing these steps for the last time, or whether the sound of them was to go in and out with me till death should part us.

She avoided even to look at me, only walked before her, like one who had a guess of what was coming. I saw I must speak soon before my courage was run out, but where to begin I knew not. In this painful situation, when the girl was as good as forced into my arms and had already besought my forbearance, any excess of pressure must have seemed indecent; yet to avoid it wholly would have a very cold-like appearance. Between these extremes I stood helpless, and could have bit my fingers; so that, when at last I managed to speak at all, it may be said I spoke at random.

"Catriona," said I, "I am in a very painful situation; or rather, so we are both; and I would be a good deal obliged to you if you would promise to let me speak through first of all, and not to interrupt me till I have done."

She promised me that simply.

"Well," said I, "this that I have got to say is very difficult, and I know very well I have no right to be saying it. After what passed between the two of us last Friday, I have no manner of right. We have got so ravelled up (and all by my fault) that I know very well the least I could do is just to hold my tongue, which was what I intended fully, and there was nothing further from my thoughts than to have troubled you again. But, my dear, it has become merely necessary, and no way by it. You see, this estate of mine has fallen in, which makes of me rather a better match; and the—the business would not have quite the same ridiculous-like appearance that it would before. Besides which, it's supposed that our affairs have got so much ravelled up (as I was saying) that it would be better to let them be the way they are. In my view, this part of the thing is vastly exagerate, and if I were you I would not wear two thoughts on it. Only it's right I should mention the same, because there's no doubt it has some influence on James More. Then I think we were none so unhappy when we dwelt together in this town before. I think we did pretty well together. If you would look back, my dear—"

"I will look neither back nor forward," she interrupted. "Tell me the one thing: this is my father's doing?"

"He approves of it," said I. "He approved I that I should ask your hand in marriage," and was going on again with somewhat more of an appeal upon her feelings; but she marked me not, and struck into the midst.

"He told you to!" she cried. "It is no sense denying it, you said yourself that there was nothing farther from your thoughts. He told you to."

"He spoke of it the first, if that is what you mean," I began.

She was walking ever the faster, and looking fain in front of her; but at this she made a little noise in her head, and I thought she would have run.

"Without which," I went on, "after what you said last Friday, I would never have been so troublesome as make the offer. But when he as good as asked me, what was I to do?"

She stopped and turned round upon me.

"Well, it is refused at all events," she cried, "and there will be an end of that."

And she began again to walk forward.

"I suppose I could expect no better," said I, "but I think you might try to be a little kind to me for the last end of it. I see not why you should be harsh. I have loved you very well, Catriona—no harm that I should call you so for the last time. I have done the best that I could manage, I am trying the same still, and only vexed that I can do no better. It is a strange thing to me that you can take any pleasure to be hard to me."

"I am not thinking of you," she said, "I am thinking of that man, my father."

"Well, and that way, too!" said I. "I can be of use to you that way, too; I will have to be. It is very needful, my dear, that we should consult about your father; for the way this talk has gone, an angry man will be James More."

She stopped again. "It is because I am disgraced?" she asked.

"That is what he is thinking," I replied, "but I have told you already to make nought of it."

"It will be all one to me," she cried. "I prefer to be disgraced!"

I did not know very well what to answer, and stood silent.

There seemed to be something working in her bosom after that last cry; presently she broke out, "And what is the meaning of all this? Why is all this shame loundered on my head? How could you dare it, David Balfour?"

"My dear," said I, "what else was I to do?"

"I am not your dear," she said, "and I defy you to be calling me these words."

"I am not thinking of my words," said I. "My heart bleeds for you, Miss Drummond. Whatever I may say, be sure you have my pity in your difficult position. But there is just the one thing that I wish you would bear in view, if it was only long enough to discuss it quietly; for there is going to be a collieshangie when we two get home. Take my word for it, it will need the two of us to make this matter end in peace."

"Ay," said she. There sprang a patch of red in either of her cheeks. "Was he for fighting you?" said she.

"Well, he was that," said I.

She gave a dreadful kind of laugh. "At all events, it is complete!" she cried. And then turning on me. "My father and I are a fine pair," said she, "but I am thanking the good God there will be somebody worse than what we are. I am thanking the good God that he has let me see you so. There will never be the girl made that will not scorn you."

I had borne a good deal pretty patiently, but this was over the mark.

"You have no right to speak to me like that," said I. "What have I done but to be good to you, or try to be? And here is my repayment! O, it is too much."

She kept looking at me with a hateful smile. "Coward!" said she.

"The word in your throat and in your father's!" I cried. "I have dared him this day already in your interest. I will dare him again, the nasty pole-cat; little I care which of us should fall! Come," said I, "back to the house with us; let us be done with it, let me be done with the whole Hieland crew of you! You will see what you think when I am dead."

She shook her head at me with that same smile I could have struck her for.

"O, smile away!" I cried. "I have seen your bonny father smile on the wrong side this day. Not that I mean he was afraid, of course," I added hastily, "but he preferred the other way of it."

"What is this?" she asked.

"When I offered to draw with him," said I.

"You offered to draw upon James More!" she cried.

"And I did so," said I, "and found him backward enough, or how would we be here?"

"There is a meaning upon this," said she. "What is it you are meaning?"

"He was to make you take me," I replied, "and I would not have it. I said you should be free, and I must speak with you alone; little I supposed it would be such a speaking! 'And what if I refuse?' said he.—'Then it must come to the throat-cutting,' says I, 'for I will no more have a husband forced on that young lady, than what I would have a wife forced upon myself.' These were my words, they were a friend's words; bonnily have I paid for them! Now you have refused me of your own clear free will, and there lives no father in the Highlands, or out of them, that can force on this marriage. I will see that your wishes are respected; I will make the same my business, as I have all through. But I think you might have that decency as to affect some gratitude. 'Deed, and I thought you knew me better! I have not behaved quite well to you, but that was weakness. And to think me a coward, and such a coward as that—O, my lass, there was a stab for the last of it!"

"Davie, how would I guess?" she cried. "O, this is a dreadful business! Me and mine,"—she gave a kind of a wretched cry at the word—"me and mine are not fit to speak to you. O, I could be kneeling down to you in the street, I could be kissing your hands for forgiveness!"

"I will keep the kisses I have got from you already," cried I. "I will keep the ones I wanted and that were something worth; I will not be kissed in penitence."

"What can you be thinking of this miserable girl?" says she.

"What I am trying to tell you all this while!" said I, "that you had best leave me alone, whom you can make no more unhappy if you tried, and turn your attention to James More, your father, with whom you are like to have a queer pirn to wind."

"O, that I must be going out into the world alone with such a man!" she cried, and seemed to catch herself in with a great effort. "But trouble yourself no more for that," said she. "He does not know what kind of nature is in my heart. He will pay me dear for this day of it; dear, dear, will he pay."

She turned, and began to go home and I to accompany her. At which she stopped.

"I will be going alone," she said. "It is alone I must be seeing him."

Some little time I raged about the streets, and told myself I was the worst used lad in Christendom. Anger choked me; it was all very well for me to breathe deep; it seemed there was not air enough about Leyden to supply me, and I thought I would have burst like a man at the bottom of the sea. I stopped and laughed at myself at a street corner a minute together, laughing out loud, so that a passenger looked at me, which brought me to myself.

"Well," I thought, "I have been a gull and a ninny and a soft Tommy long enough. Time it was done. Here is a good lesson to have nothing to do with that accursed sex, that was the ruin of the man in the beginning and will be so to the end. God knows I was happy enough before ever I saw her; God knows I can be happy enough again when I have seen the last of her."

That seemed to me the chief affair: to see them go. I dwelled upon the idea fiercely; and presently slipped on, in a kind of malevolence, to consider how very poorly they were likely to fare when Davie Balfour was no longer by to be their milk-cow; at which, to my very own great surprise, the disposition of my mind turned bottom up. I was still angry; I still hated her; and yet I thought I owed it to myself that she should suffer nothing.

This carried me home again at once, where I found the mails drawn out and ready fastened by the door, and the father and daughter with every mark upon them of a recent disagreement. Catriona was like a wooden doll; James More breathed hard, his face was dotted with white spots, and his nose upon one side. As soon as I came in, the girl looked at him with a steady, clear, dark look that might have been followed by a blow. It was a hint that was more contemptuous than a command, and I was surprised to see James More accept it. It was plain he had had a master talking-to; and I could see there must be more of the devil in the girl than I had guessed, and more good humour about the man than I had given him the credit of.

He began, at least, calling me Mr. Balfour, and plainly speaking from a lesson; but he got not very far, for at the first pompous swell of his voice, Catriona cut in.

"I will tell you what James More is meaning," said she. "He means we have come to you, beggar-folk, and have not behaved to you very well, and we are ashamed of our ingratitude and ill-behaviour. Now we are wanting to go away and be forgotten; and my father will have guided his gear so ill, that we cannot even do that unless you will give us some more alms. For that is what we are, at an events, beggar-folk and sorners."

"By your leave, Miss Drummond," said I, "I must speak to your father by myself."

She went into her own room and shut the door, without a word or a look.

"You must excuse her, Mr. Balfour," says James More. "She has no delicacy."

"I am not here to discuss that with you," said I, "but to be quit of you. And to that end I must talk of your position. Now, Mr. Drummond, I have kept the run of your affairs more closely than you bargained for. I know you had money of your own when you were borrowing mine.

I know you have had more since you were here in Leyden, though you concealed it even from your daughter."

"I bid you beware. I will stand no more baiting," he broke out. "I am sick of her and you. What kind of a damned trade is this to be a parent! I have had expressions used to me—" There he broke off. "Sir, this is the heart of a soldier and a parent," he went on again, laying his hand on his bosom, "outraged in both characters—and I bid you beware."

"If you would have let me finish," says I, "you would have found I spoke for your advantage."

"My dear friend," he cried, "I know I might have relied upon the generosity of your character."

"Man! will you let me speak?" said I. "The fact is that I cannot win to find out if you are rich or poor. But it is my idea that your means, as they are mysterious in their source, so they are something insufficient in amount; and I do not choose your daughter to be lacking. If I durst speak to herself, you may be certain I would never dream of trusting it to you; because I know you like the back of my hand, and all your blustering talk is that much wind to me. However, I believe in your way you do still care something for your daughter after all; and I must just be doing with that ground of confidence, such as it is."

Whereupon, I arranged with him that he was to communicate with me, as to his whereabouts and Catriona's welfare, in consideration of which I was to serve him a small stipend.

He heard the business out with a great deal of eagerness; and when it was done, "My dear fellow, my dear son," he cried out, "this is more like yourself than any of it yet! I will serve you with a soldier's faithfulness—"

"Let me hear no more of it!" says I. "You have got me to that pitch that the bare name of soldier rises on my stomach. Our traffic is settled; I am now going forth and will return in one half-hour, when I expect to find my chambers purged of you."

I gave them good measure of time; it was my one fear that I might see Catriona again, because tears and weakness were ready in my heart, and I cherished my anger like a piece of dignity. Perhaps an hour went by; the sun had gone down, a little wisp of a new moon was following it across a scarlet sunset; already there were stars in the east, and in my chambers, when at last I entered them, the night lay blue. I lit a taper and reviewed the rooms; in the first there remained nothing so much as to awake a memory of those who were gone; but in the second, in a corner of the floor, I spied a little heap that brought my heart into my mouth. She had left behind at her departure all that she had ever had of me. It was the blow that I felt sorest, perhaps because it was the last; and I fell upon that pile of clothing and behaved myself more foolish than I care to tell of.

Late in the night, in a strict frost, and my teeth chattering, I came again by some portion of my manhood and considered with myself. The sight of these poor frocks and ribbons, and her shifts, and the clocked stockings, was not to be endured; and if I were to recover any constancy of mind, I saw I must be rid of them ere the morning. It was my first thought to have made a fire and burned them; but my disposition has always been opposed to wastery, for one thing; and for another, to have burned these things that she had worn so close upon her body seemed in the nature of a cruelty. There was a corner cupboard in that chamber; there I determined to bestow them. The which I did and made it a long business, folding them with very little skill indeed but the more care; and sometimes dropping them with my tears. All the heart was gone out of me, I was weary as though I had run miles, and sore like one beaten; when, as I was folding a kerchief that she wore often at her neck, I observed there was a corner neatly cut from it. It was a kerchief of a very pretty hue, on which I had frequently remarked; and once that she had it on, I remembered telling her (by way of a banter) that she wore my colours. There came a glow of hope and like a tide of sweetness in my bosom; and the next moment I was plunged back in a fresh despair. For there was the corner crumpled in a knot and cast down by itself in another part of the floor.

But when I argued with myself, I grew more hopeful. She had cut that corner off in some childish freak that was manifestly tender; that she had cast it away again was little to be wondered at; and I was inclined to dwell more upon the first than upon the second, and to be more pleased that she had ever conceived the idea of that keepsake, than concerned because she had flung it from her in an hour of natural resentment.

CHAPTER XXIX.
WE MEET IN DUNKIRK

Altogether, then, I was scare so miserable the next days but what I had many hopeful and happy snatches; threw myself with a good deal of constancy upon my studies; and made out to endure the time till Alan should arrive, or I might hear word of Catriona by the means of James More. I had altogether three letters in the time of our separation. One was to announce their arrival in the town of Dunkirk in France, from which place James shortly after started alone upon a private mission. This was to England and to see Lord Holderness; and it has always been a bitter thought that my good money helped to pay the charges of the same. But he has need of a long spoon who soups with the de'il, or James More either. During this absence, the time was to fall due for another letter; and as the letter was the condition of his stipend, he had been so careful as to prepare it beforehand and leave it with Catriona to be despatched. The fact of our correspondence aroused her suspicions, and he was no sooner gone than she had burst the seal. What I received began accordingly in the writing of James More:

"My dear Sir,—Your esteemed favour came to hand duly, and I have to acknowledge the inclosure according to agreement. It shall be all faithfully expended on my daughter, who is well, and desires to be remembered to her dear friend. I find her in rather a melancholy disposition, but trust in the mercy of God to see her re-established. Our manner of life is very much alone, but we solace ourselves with the melancholy tunes of our native mountains, and by walking up the margin of the sea that lies next to Scotland. It was better days with me when I lay with five wounds upon my body on the field of Gladsmuir. I have found employment here in the haras of a French nobleman, where my experience is valued. But, my dear Sir, the wages are so exceedingly unsuitable that I would be ashamed to mention them, which makes your remittances the more necessary to my daughter's comfort, though I daresay the sight of old friends would be still better.

"My dear Sir,
"Your affectionate, obedient servant,
"James Macgregor Drummond."

Below it began again in the hand of Catriona:—

"Do not be believing him, it is all lies together,—C. M. D."

Not only did she add this postscript, but I think she must have come near suppressing the letter; for it came long after date, and was closely followed by the third. In the time betwixt them, Alan had arrived, and made another life to me with his merry conversation; I had been presented to his cousin of the Scots-Dutch, a man that drank more than I could have thought possible and was not otherwise of interest; I had been entertained to many jovial dinners and given some myself, all with no great change upon my sorrow; and we two (by which I mean Alan and myself, and not at all the cousin) had discussed a good deal the nature of my relations with James More and his daughter. I was naturally diffident to give particulars; and this disposition was not anyway lessened by the nature of Alan's commentary upon those I gave.

"I cannae make heed nor tail of it," he would say, "but it sticks in my mind ye've made a gowk of yourself. There's few people that has had more experience than Alan Breck: and I can never call to mind to have heard tell of a lassie like this one of yours. The way that you tell it, the thing's fair impossible. Ye must have made a terrible hash of the business, David."

"There are whiles that I am of the same mind," said I.

"The strange thing is that ye seem to have a kind of fancy for her too!" said Alan.

"The biggest kind, Alan," said I, "and I think I'll take it to my grave with me."

"Well, ye beat me, whatever!" he would conclude.

I showed him the letter with Catriona's postscript. "And here again!" he cried. "Impossible to deny a kind of decency to this Catriona, and sense forby! As for James More, the man's as boss as a drum; he's just a wame and a wheen words; though I'll can never deny that he fought reasonably well at Gladsmuir, and it's true what he says here about the five wounds. But the loss of him is that the man's boss."

"Ye see, Alan," said I, "it goes against the grain with me to leave the maid in such poor hands."

"Ye couldnae weel find poorer," he admitted. "But what are ye to do with it? It's this way about a man and a woman, ye see, Davie: The weemenfolk have got no kind of reason to them. Either they like the man, and then a' goes fine; or else they just detest him, and ye may spare your breath—ye can do naething. There's just the two sets of them—them that would sell their coats for ye, and them that never look the road ye're on. That's a' that there is to women; and you seem to be such a gomeral that ye cannae tell the tane frae the tither."

"Well, and I'm afraid that's true for me," said I.

"And yet there's naething easier!" cried Alan. "I could easy learn ye the science of the thing; but ye seem to me to be born blind, and there's where the deefficulty comes in."

"And can you no help me?" I asked, "you that are so clever at the trade?"

"Ye see, David, I wasnae here," said he. "I'm like a field officer that has naebody but blind men for scouts and éclaireurs; and what would he ken? But it sticks in my mind that ye'll have made some kind of bauchle; and if I was you I would have a try at her again."

"Would ye so, man Alan?" said I.

"I would e'en't," says he.

The third letter came to my hand while we were deep in some such talk: and it will be seen how pat it fell to the occasion. James professed to be in some concern upon his daughter's health, which I believe was never better; abounded in kind expressions to myself; and finally proposed that I should visit them at Dunkirk.

"You will now be enjoying the society of my old comrade Mr. Stewart," he wrote. "Why not accompany him so far in his return to France? I have something very particular for Mr. Stewart's ear; and, at any rate, I would be pleased to meet in with an old fellow-soldier and one so mettle as himself. As for you, my dear sir, my daughter and I would be proud to receive our benefactor, whom we regard as a brother and a son. The French nobleman has proved a person of the most filthy avarice of character, and I have been necessitate to leave the haras. You will find us in consequence a little poorly lodged in the auberge of a man Bazin on the dunes; but the situation is caller, and I make no doubt but we might spend some very pleasant days, when Mr. Stewart and I could recall our services, and you and my daughter divert yourselves in a manner more befitting your age. I beg at least that Mr. Stewart would come here; my business with him opens a very wide door."

"What does the man want with me?" cried Alan, when he had read. "What he wants with you is clear enough—it's siller. But what can he want with Alan Breck?"

"O, it'll be just an excuse," said I. "He is still after this marriage, which I wish from my heart that we could bring about. And he asks you because he thinks I would be less likely to come wanting you."

"Well, I wish that I kent," says Alan. "Him and me were never onyways pack; we used to girn at ither like a pair of pipers. 'Something for my ear,' quo' he! I'll maybe have something for his hinder-end, before we're through with it. Dod, I'm thinking it would be a kind of divertisement to gang and see what he'll be after! Forby that I could see your lassie then. What say ye, Davie? Will ye ride with Alan?"

You may be sure I was not backward, and Alan's furlough running towards an end, we set forth presently upon this joint adventure.

It was near dark of a January day when we rode at last into the town of Dunkirk. We left our horses at the post, and found a guide to Bazin's Inn, which lay beyond the walls. Night was quite fallen, so that we were the last to leave that fortress, and heard the doors of it close behind us as we passed the bridge. On the other side there lay a lighted suburb, which we thridded for a while, then turned into a dark lane, and presently found ourselves wading in the night among deep sand where we could hear a bullering of the sea. We travelled in this fashion for some while, following our conductor mostly by the sound of his voice; and I had begun to think he was perhaps misleading us, when we came to the top of a small brae, and there appeared out of the darkness a dim light in a window.

"Voilà l'auberge à Bazin," says the guide.

Alan smacked his lips. "An unco lonely bit," said he, and I thought by his tone he was not wholly pleased.

A little after, and we stood in the lower storey of that house, which was all in the one apartment, with a stairs leading to the chambers at the side, benches and tables by the wall, the cooking fire at the one end of it, and shelves of bottles and the cellar-trap at the other. Here Bazin, who was an ill-looking, big man, told us the Scottish gentleman was gone abroad he knew not where, but the young lady was above, and he would call her down to us.

I took from my breast that kerchief wanting the corner, and knotted it about my throat. I could hear my heart go; and Alan patting me on the shoulder with some of his laughable expressions, I could scarce refrain from a sharp word. But the time was not long to wait. I heard her step pass overhead, and saw her on the stair. This she descended very quietly, and greeted me with a pale face and a certain seeming of earnestness, or uneasiness, in her manner that extremely dashed me.

"My father, James More, will be here soon. He will be very pleased to see you," she said. And then of a sudden her face flamed, her eyes lightened, the speech stopped upon her lips; and I made sure she had observed the kerchief. It was only for a breath that she was discomposed; but methought it was with a new animation that she turned to welcome Alan. "And you will be his friend, Alan Breck?" she cried. "Many is the dozen times I will have heard him tell of you; and I love you already for all your bravery and goodness."

"Well, well," says Alan, holding her hand in his and viewing her, "and so this is the young lady at the last of it! David, ye're an awful poor hand of a description."

I do not know that ever I heard him speak so straight to people's hearts; the sound of his voice was like song.

"What? will he have been describing me?" she cried.

"Little else of it since I ever came out of France!" says he, "forby a bit of a speciment one night in Scotland in a shaw of wood by Silvermills. But cheer up, my dear! ye're bonnier than what he said. And now there's one thing sure; you and me are to be a pair of friends. I'm a kind of a henchman to Davie here; I'm like a tyke at his heels; and whatever he cares for, I've got to care for too—and by the holy airn! they've got to care for me! So now you can see what way you stand with Alan Breck, and ye'll find ye'll hardly lose on the transaction. He's no very bonnie, my dear, but he's leal to them he loves."

"I thank you from my heart for your good words," said she. "I have that honour for a brave, honest man that I cannot find any to be answering with."

Using travellers' freedom, we spared to wait for James More, and sat down to meat, we threesome. Alan had Catriona sit by him and wait upon his wants: he made her drink first out of his glass, he surrounded her with continual kind gallantries, and yet never gave me the most small occasion to be jealous; and he kept the talk so much in his own hand, and that in so merry a note, that neither she nor I remembered to be embarrassed. If any had seen us there, it must have been supposed that Alan was the old friend and I the stranger. Indeed, I had often cause to love and to admire the man, but I never loved or admired him better than that night; and I could not help remarking to myself (what I was sometimes rather in danger of forgetting) that he had not only much experience of life, but in his own way a great deal of natural ability besides. As for Catriona, she seemed quite carried away; her laugh was like a peal of bells, her face gay as a May morning; and I own, although I was well pleased, yet I was a little sad also, and thought myself a dull, stockish character in comparison of my friend, and very unfit to come into a young maid's life, and perhaps ding down her gaiety.

But if that was like to be my part, I found that at least I was not alone in it; for, James More returning suddenly, the girl was changed into a piece of stone. Through the rest of that evening, until she made an excuse and slipped to bed, I kept an eye upon her without cease; and I can bear testimony that she never smiled, scarce spoke, and looked mostly on the board in front of her. So that I really marvelled to see so much devotion (as it used to be) changed into the very sickness of hate.

Of James More it is unnecessary to say much; you know the man already, what there was to know of him; and I am weary of writing out his lies. Enough that he drank a great deal, and told us very little that was to any possible purpose. As for the business with Alan, that was to be reserved for the morrow and his private hearing.

It was the more easy to be put off, because Alan and I were pretty weary with four day's ride, and sat not very late after Catriona.

We were soon alone in a chamber where we were to make-shift with a single bed. Alan looked on me with a queer smile.

"Ye muckle ass!" said he.

"What do ye mean by that?" I cried.

"Mean? What do I mean! It's extraordinar, David man," say he, "that you should be so mortal stupit."

Again I begged him to speak out.

"Well, it's this of it," said he. "I told ye there were the two kinds of women—them that would sell their shifts for ye, and the others. Just you try for yoursel, my bonny man! But what's that neepkin at your craig?"

I told him.

"I thocht it was something thereabout," said he.

Nor would he say another word though I besieged him long with importunities.

CHAPTER XXX.
THE LETTER FROM THE SHIP

Daylight showed us how solitary the inn stood. It was plainly hard upon the sea, yet out of all view of it, and beset on every side with scabbit hills of sand. There was, indeed, only one thing in the nature of a prospect, where there stood out over a brae the two sails of a windmill, like an ass's ears, but with the ass quite hidden. It was strange (after the wind rose, for at first it was dead calm) to see the turning and following of each other of these great sails behind the hillock. Scarce any road came by there; but a number of footways travelled among the bents in all directions up to Mr. Bazin's door. The truth is, he was a man of many trades, not any one of them honest, and the position of his inn was the best of his livelihood. Smugglers frequented it; political agents and forfeited persons bound across the water came there to await their passages; and I daresay there was worse behind, for a whole family might have been butchered in that house and nobody the wiser.

I slept little and ill. Long ere it was day, I had slipped from beside my bedfellow, and was warming myself at the fire or walking to and fro before the door. Dawn broke mighty sullen; but a little after, sprang up a wind out of the west, which burst the clouds, let through the sun, and set the mill to the turning. There was something of spring in the sunshine, or else it was in my heart; and the appearing of the great sails one after another from behind the hill, diverted me extremely. At times I could hear a creak of the machinery; and by half-past eight of the day, and I thought this dreary, desert place was like a paradise.

For all which, as the day drew on and nobody came near, I began to be aware of an uneasiness that I could scarce explain. It seemed there was trouble afoot; the sails of the windmill, as they came up and went down over the hill, were like persons spying; and outside of all fancy, it was surely a strange neighbourhood and house for a young lady to be brought to dwell in.

At breakfast, which we took late, it was manifest that James More was in some danger or perplexity; manifest that Alan was alive to the same, and watched him close; and this appearance of duplicity upon the one side, and vigilance upon the other, held me on live coals. The meal was no sooner over than James seemed to come began to make apologies. He had an appointment of a private nature in the town (it was with the French nobleman, he told me), and we would please excuse him till about noon. Meanwhile he carried his daughter aside to the far end of the room, where he seemed to speak rather earnestly and she to listen with much inclination.

"I am caring less and less about this man James," said Alan. "There's something no right with the man James, and I shouldnae wonder but what Alan Breck would give an eye to him this day. I would like fine to see yon French nobleman, Davie; and I daresay you could find an employ to yoursel, and that would be to speir at the lassie for some news o' your affair. Just tell it to her plainly—tell her ye're a muckle ass at the off-set; and then, if I were you, and ye could do it naitural, I would just mint to her I was in some kind of a danger; a' weemenfolk likes that."

"I cannae lee, Alan, I cannae do it naitural," says I, mocking him.

"The more fool you!" says he. "Then ye'll can tell her that I recommended it; that'll set her to the laughing; and I wouldnae wonder but what that was the next best. But see to the pair of them! If I didnae feel just sure of the lassie, and that she was awful pleased and chief with Alan, I would think there was some kind of hocus-pocus about you."

"And is she so pleased with ye, then, Alan?" I asked.

"She thinks a heap of me," says he. "And I'm no like you: I'm one that can tell. That she does—she thinks a heap of Alan. And troth! I'm thinking a good deal of him mysel; and with your permission, Shaws, I'll be getting a wee yont amang the bents, so that I can see what way James goes."

One after another went, till I was left alone beside the breakfast table; James to Dunkirk, Alan dogging him, Catriona up the stairs to her own chamber. I could very well understand how she should avoid to be alone with me; yet was none the better pleased with it for that, and bent my mind to entrap her to an interview before the men returned. Upon the whole, the best appeared to me to do like Alan. If I was out of view among the sandhills, the fine morning would decoy her forth; and once I had her in the open, I could please myself.

No sooner said than done; nor was I long under the bield of a hillock before she appeared at the inn door, looked here and there, and (seeing nobody) set out by a path that led directly seaward, and by which I followed her. I was in no haste to make my presence known; the further she went I made sure of the longer hearing to my suit; and the ground being all sandy it was easy to follow her unheard. The path rose and came at last to the head of a knowe. Thence I had a picture for the first time of what a desolate wilderness that inn stood hidden in; where was no man to be seen, nor any house of man, except just Bazin's and the windmill. Only a little further on, the sea appeared and two or three ships upon it, pretty as a drawing. One of these was extremely close in to be so great a vessel; and I was aware of a shock of new suspicion, when I recognised the trim of the Seahorse. What should an English ship be doing so near in to France? Why was Alan brought into her neighbourhood, and that in a place so far from any hope of rescue? and was it by accident, or by design, that the daughter of James More should walk that day to the seaside?

Presently I came forth behind her in the front of the sandhills and above the beach. It was here long and solitary; with a man-o'-war's boat drawn up about the middle of the prospect, and an officer in charge and pacing the sands like one who waited. I sat down where the rough grass a good deal covered me, and looked for what should follow. Catriona went straight to the boat; the officer met her with civilities; they had ten words together; I saw a letter changing hands; and there was Catriona returning. At the same time, as if this were all her business on the Continent, the boat shoved off and was headed for the Seahorse. But I observed the officer to remain behind and disappear among the bents.

I liked the business little; and the more I considered of it, liked it less. Was it Alan the officer was seeking? or Catriona? She drew near with her head down, looking constantly on the sand, and made so tender a picture that I could not bear to doubt her innocence. The next, she raised her face and recognised me; seemed to hesitate, and then came on again, but more slowly, and I thought with a changed colour. And at that thought, all else that was upon my bosom—fears, suspicions, the care of my friend's life—was clean swallowed up; and I rose to my feet and stood waiting her in a drunkenness of hope.

I gave her "good morning" as she came up, which she returned with a good deal of composure.

"Will you forgive my having followed you?" said I.

"I know you are always meaning kindly," she replied; and then, with a little outburst, "but why will you be sending money to that man! It must not be."

"I never sent it for him," said I, "but for you, as you know well."

"And you have no right to be sending it to either one of us," she said. "David, it is not right."

"It is not, it is all wrong," said I, "and I pray God he will help this dull fellow (if it be at all possible) to make it better. Catriona, this is no kind of life for you to lead; and I ask your pardon for the word, but yon man is no fit father to take care of you."

"Do not be speaking of him, even!" was her cry.

"And I need speak of him no more; it is not of him that I am thinking, O, be sure of that!" says I. "I think of the one thing. I have been alone now this long time in Leyden; and when I was by way of at my studies, still I was thinking of that. Next Alan came, and I went among soldier-men to their big dinners; and still I had the same thought. And it was the same before, when I had her there beside me. Catriona, do you see this napkin at my throat! You cut a corner from it once and then cast it from you. They're your colours now; I wear them in my heart. My dear, I cannot be wanting you. O, try to put up with me!"

I stepped before her so as to intercept her walking on.

"Try to put up with me," I was saying, "try and bear me with a little."

Still she had never the word, and a fear began to rise in me like a fear of death.

"Catriona," I cried, gazing on her hard, "is it a mistake again? Am I quite lost?"

She raised her face to me, breathless.

"Do you want me, Davie, truly?" said she, and I scarce could hear her say it.

"I do that," said I. "O, sure you know it—I do that."

"I have nothing left to give or to keep back," said she. "I was all yours from the first day, if you would have had a gift of me!" she said.

This was on the summit of a brae; the place was windy and conspicuous, we were to be seen there even from the English ship; but I kneeled down before her in the sand, and embraced her knees, and burst into that storm of weeping that I thought it must have broken me. All thought was wholly beaten from my mind by the vehemency of my discomposure. I knew not where I was. I had forgot why I was happy; only I knew she stooped, and I felt her cherish me to her face and bosom, and heard her words out of a whirl.

"Davie," she was saying, "O, Davie, is this what you think of me! Is it so that you were caring for poor me! O, Davie, Davie!"

With that she wept also, and our tears were commingled in a perfect gladness.

It might have been ten in the day before I came to a clear sense of what a mercy had befallen me; and sitting over against her, with her hands in mine, gazed in her face, and laughed out loud for pleasure like a child, and called her foolish and kind names. I have never seen the place that looked so pretty as those bents by Dunkirk; and the windmill sails, as they bobbed over the knowe, were like a tune of music.

I know not how much longer we might have continued to forget all else besides ourselves, had I not chanced upon a reference to her father, which brought us to reality.

"My little friend," I was calling her again and again, rejoicing to summon up the past by the sound of it, and to gaze across on her, and to be a little distant—"My little friend, now you are mine altogether; mine for good, my little friend and that man's no longer at all."

There came a sudden whiteness in her face, she plucked her hands from mine.

"Davie, take me away from him!" she cried. "There's something wrong; he's not true. There will be something wrong; I have a dreadful terror here at my heart. What will he be wanting at all events with that King's ship? What will this word be saying?" And she held the letter forth. "My mind misgives me, it will be some ill to Alan. Open it, Davie—open it and see."

I took it, and looked at it, and shook my head.

"No," said I, "it goes against me, I cannot open a man's letter."

"Not to save your friend?" she cried.

"I cannae tell," said I. "I think not. If I was only sure!"

"And you have but to break the seal!" said she.

"I know it," said I, "but the thing goes against me."

"Give it here," said she, "and I will open it myself."

"Nor you neither," said I. "You least of all. It concerns your father, and his honour, dear, which we are both misdoubting. No question but the place is dangerous-like, and the English ship being here, and your father having word from it, and yon officer that stayed ashore. He would not be alone either; there must be more along with him; I daresay we are spied upon this minute. Ay, no doubt, the letter should be opened; but somehow, not by you nor me."

I was about thus far with it, and my spirit very much overcome with a sense of danger and hidden enemies, when I spied Alan, come back again from following James and walking by himself among the sand-hills. He was in his soldier's coat, of course, and mighty fine; but I could not avoid to shudder when I thought how little that jacket would avail him, if he were once caught and flung in a skiff, and carried on board of the Seahorse, a deserter, a rebel, and now a condemned murderer.

"There," said I, "there is the man that has the best right to open it: or not, as he thinks fit."

With which I called upon his name, and we both stood up to be a mark for him.

"If it is so—if it be more disgrace—will you can bear it?" she asked, looking upon me with a burning eye.

"I was asked something of the same question when I had seen you but the once," said I. "What do you think I answered? That if I liked you as I thought I did—and O, but I like you better!—I would marry you at his gallows' foot."

The blood rose in her face; she came close up and pressed upon me, holding my hand: and it was so that we awaited Alan.

He came with one of his queer smiles. "What was I telling ye, David?" says he.

"There is a time for all things, Alan," said I, "and this time is serious. How have you sped? You can speak out plain before this friend of ours."

"I have been upon a fool's errand," said he.

"I doubt we have done better than you, then," said I; "and, at least, here is a great deal of matter that you must judge of. Do you see that?" I went on, pointing to the ship. "That is the Seahorse, Captain Palliser."

"I should ken her, too," says Alan. "I had fyke enough with her when she was stationed in the Forth. But what ails the man to come so close?"

"I will tell you why he came there first," said I. "It was to bring this letter to James More. Why he stops here now that it's delivered, what it's likely to be about, why there's an officer hiding in the bents, and whether or not it's probable that he's alone—I would rather you considered for yourself."

"A letter to James More?" said he.

"The same," said I.

"Well, and I can tell ye more than that," said Alan. "For the last night, when you were fast asleep, I heard the man colloguing with some one in the French, and then the door of that inn to be opened and shut."

"Alan!" cried I, "you slept all night, and I am here to prove it."

"Ay, but I would never trust Alan whether he was asleep or waking!" says he. "But the business looks bad. Let's see the letter."

I gave it him.

"Catriona," said he, "you have to excuse me, my dear; but there's nothing less than my fine bones upon the cast of it, and I'll have to break this seal."

"It is my wish," said Catriona.

He opened it, glanced it through, and flung his hand in the air.

"The stinking brock!" says he, and crammed the paper in his pocket. "Here, let's get our things together. This place is fair death to me." And he began to walk towards the inn.

It was Catriona that spoke the first. "He has sold you?" she asked.

"Sold me, my dear," said Alan. "But thanks to you and Davie, I'll can jink him yet. Just let me win upon my horse," he added.

"Catriona must come with us," said I. "She can have no more traffic with that man. She and I are to be married." At which she pressed my hand to her side.

"Are ye there with it?" says Alan, looking back. "The best day's work that ever either of you did yet! And I'm bound to say, my dawtie, ye make a real, bonny couple."

The way that he was following brought us close in by the windmill, where I was aware of a man in seaman's trousers, who seemed to be spying from behind it. Only, of course, we took him in the rear.

"See, Alan!"

"Wheesht!" said, he, "this is my affairs."

The man was, no doubt, a little deafened by the clattering of the mill, and we got up close before he noticed. Then he turned, and we saw he was a big fellow with a mahogany face.

"I think, sir," says Alan, "that you speak the English?"

"Non, monsieur," says he, with an incredible bad accent.

"Non, monsieur," cries Alan, mocking him. "Is that how they learn you French on the Seahorse? Ye muckle, gutsey hash, here's a Scots boot to your English hurdies!"

And bounding on him before he could escape, he dealt the man a kick that laid him on his nose. Then he stood, with a savage smile, and watched him scramble to his feet and scamper off into the sand-hills.

"But it's high time I was clear of these empty bents!" said Alan; and continued his way at top speed, and we still following, to the backdoor of Bazin's inn.

It chanced that as we entered by the one door we came face to face with James More entering by the other.

"Here!" said I to Catriona, "quick! upstairs with you and make your packets; this is no fit scene for you."

In the meanwhile James and Alan had met in the midst of the long room. She passed them close by to reach the stairs; and after she was some way up I saw her turn and glance at them again, though without pausing. Indeed, they were worth looking at. Alan wore as they met one of his best appearances of courtesy and friendliness, yet with something eminently warlike, so that James smelled danger off the man, as folk smell fire in a house, and stood prepared for accidents.

Time pressed. Alan's situation in that solitary place, and his enemies about him, might have daunted Cæsar. It made no change in him; and it was in his old spirit of mockery and daffing that he began the interview.

"A braw good day to ye again, Mr. Drummond," said he. "What'll yon business of yours be just about?"

"Why, the thing being private, and rather of a long story," says James, "I think it will keep very well till we have eaten."

"I'm none so sure of that," said Alan. "It sticks in my mind it's either now or never; for the fact is me and Mr. Balfour here have gotten a line, and we're thinking of the road."

I saw a little surprise in James's eye; but he held himself stoutly.

"I have but the one word to say to cure you of that," said he, "and that is the name of my business."

"Say it then," says Alan. "Hout! wha minds for Davie?"

"It is a matter that would make us both rich men," said James.

"Do you tell me that?" cries Alan.

"I do, sir," said James. "The plain fact is that it is Cluny's Treasure."

"No!" cried Alan. "Have ye got word of it?"

"I ken the place, Mr. Stewart, and can take you there," said James.

"This crowns all!" says Alan. "Well, and I'm glad I came to Dunkirk. And so this was your business, was it? Halvers, I'm thinking?"

"That is the business, sir," said James.

"Well, well," said Alan; and then in the same tone of childlike interest, "it has naething to do with the Seahorse, then?" he asked.

"With what?" says James.

"Or the lad that I have just kicked the bottom of behind yon windmill?" pursued Alan. "Hut, man! have done with your lees! I have Palliser's letter here in my pouch. You're by with it, James More. You can never show your face again with dacent folk."

James was taken all aback with it. He stood a second, motionless and white, then swelled with the living anger.

"Do you talk to me, you bastard?" he roared out.

"Ye glee'd swine!" cried Alan, and hit him a sounding buffet on the mouth, and the next wink of time their blades clashed together.

At the first sound of the bare steel I instinctively leaped back from the collision. The next I saw, James parried a thrust so nearly that I thought him killed; and it lowed up in my mind that this was the girl's father, and in a manner almost my own, and I drew and ran in to sever them.

"Keep back, Davie! Are ye daft! Damn ye, keep back!" roared Alan. "Your blood be on your ain heid then!"

I beat their blades down twice. I was knocked reeling against the wall; I was back again betwixt them. They took no heed of me, thrusting at each other like two furies. I can never think how I avoided being stabbed myself or stabbing one of these two Rodomonts, and the whole business turned about me like a piece of a dream; in the midst of which I heard a great cry from the stair, and Catriona sprang before her father. In the same moment the point of my sword encountered some thing yielding. It came back to me reddened. I saw the blood flow on the girl's kerchief, and stood sick.

"Will you be killing him before my eyes, and me his daughter after all!" she cried.

"My dear, I have done with him," said Alan, and went, and sat on a table, with his arms crossed and the sword naked in his hand.

Awhile she stood before the man, panting, with big eyes, then swung suddenly about and faced him.

"Begone!" was her word, "take your shame out of my sight; leave me with clean folk. I am a daughter of Alpin! Shame of the sons of Alpin, begone!"

It was said with so much passion as awoke me from the horror of my own bloodied sword. The two stood facing, she with the red stain on her kerchief, he white as a rag. I knew him well enough—I knew it must have pierced him in the quick place of his soul; but he betook himself to a bravado air.

"Why," says he, sheathing his sword, though still with a bright eye on Alan, "if this brawl is over I will but get my portmanteau—"

"There goes no pockmantie out of this place except with me," says Alan.

"Sir!" cries James.

"James More," says Alan, "this lady daughter of yours is to marry my friend Davie, upon the which account I let you pack with a hale carcase. But take you my advice of it and get that carcase out of harm's way or ower late. Little as you suppose it, there are leemits to my temper."

"Be damned, sir, but my money's there!" said James.

"I'm vexed about that, too," says Alan, with his funny face, "but now, ye see, it's mines." And then with more gravity, "Be you advised, James More, you leave this house."

James seemed to cast about for a moment in his mind; but it's to be thought he had enough of Alan's swordsmanship, for he suddenly put off his hat to us and (with a face like one of the damned) bade us farewell in a series. With which he was gone.

At the same time a spell was lifted from me.

"Catriona," I cried, "it was me—it was my sword. O, are you much hurt?"

"I know it, Davie, I am loving you for the pain of it; it was done defending that bad man, my father. See!" she said, and showed me a bleeding scratch, "see, you have made a man of me now. I will carry a wound like an old soldier."

Joy that she should be so little hurt, and the love of her brave nature, supported me. I embraced her, I kissed the wound.

"And am I to be out of the kissing, me that never lost a chance?" says Alan; and putting me aside and taking Catriona by either shoulder, "My dear," he said, "you're a true daughter of Alpin. By all accounts, he was a very fine man, and he may weel be proud of you. If ever I was to get married, it's the marrow of you I would be seeking for a mother to my sons. And I bear's a king's name and speak the truth."

He said it with a serious heat of admiration that was honey to the girl, and through her, to me. It seemed to wipe us clean of all James More's disgraces. And the next moment he was just himself again.

"And now by your leave, my dawties," said he, "this is a' very bonny; but Alan Breck'll be a wee thing nearer to the gallows than he's caring for; and Dod! I think this is a grand place to be leaving."

The word recalled us to some wisdom. Alan ran upstairs and returned with our saddle-bags and James More's portmanteau; I picked up Catriona's bundle where she had dropped it on the stair; and we were setting forth out of that dangerous house, when Bazin stopped the way with cries and gesticulations. He had whipped under a table when the swords were drawn, but now he was as bold as a lion. There was his bill to be settled, there was a chair broken, Alan had sat among his dinner things, James More had fled.

"Here," I cried, "pay yourself," and flung him down some Lewie d'ors; for I thought it was no time to be accounting.

He sprang upon that money, and we passed him by, and ran forth into the open. Upon three sides of the house were seamen hasting and closing in; a little nearer to us James More waved his hat as if to hurry them; and right behind him, like some foolish person holding up his hands, were the sails of the windmill turning.

Alan gave but one glance, and laid himself down to run. He carried a great weight in James More's portmanteau; but I think he would as soon have lost his life as cast away that booty which was his revenge; and he ran so that I was distressed to follow him, and marvelled and exulted to see the girl bounding at my side.

As soon as we appeared, they cast off all disguise upon the other side; and the seamen pursued us with shouts and view-hullohs. We had a start of some two hundred yards, and they were but bandy-legged tarpaulins after all, that could not hope to better us at such an exercise. I suppose they were armed, but did not care to use their pistols on French ground. And as soon as I perceived that we not only held our advantage but drew a little away, I began to feel quite easy of the issue. For all which, it was a hot, brisk bit of work, so long as it lasted; Dunkirk was still far off; and when we popped over a knowe, and found a company of the garrison marching on the other side on some manœuvre, I could very well understand the word that Alan had.

He stopped running at once; and mopping at his brow, "They're a real bonny folk, the French nation," says he.

CONCLUSION

No sooner were we safe within the walls of Dunkirk than we held a very necessary council-of-war on our position. We had taken a daughter from her father at the sword's point; any judge would give her back to him at once, and by all likelihood clap me and Alan into jail; and though we had an argument upon our side in Captain Palliser's letter, neither Catriona nor I were very keen to be using it in public. Upon all accounts it seemed the most prudent to carry the girl to Paris to the hands of her own chieftain, Macgregor of Bohaldie, who would be very willing to help his kinswoman, on the one hand, and not at all anxious to dishonour James upon other.

We made but a slow journey of it up, for Catriona was not so good at the riding as the running, and had scarce sat in the saddle since the 'Forty-five. But we made it out at last, reached Paris early of a Sabbath morning, and made all speed, under Alan's guidance, to find Bohaldie. He was finely lodged, and lived in a good style, having a pension on the Scots Fund, as well as private means; greeted Catriona like one of his own house, and seemed altogether very civil and discreet, but not particularly open. We asked of the news of James More. "Poor James!" said he, and shook his head and smiled, so that I thought he knew further than he meant to tell. Then we showed him Palliser's letter, and he drew a long face at that.

"Poor James!" said he again. "Well, there are worse folk than James More, too. But this is dreadful bad. Tut, tut, he must have forgot himself entirely! This is a most undesirable letter. But, for all that, gentlemen, I cannot see what we would want to make it public for. It's an ill bird that fouls his own nest, and we are all Scots folk and all Hieland."

Upon this we all agreed, save perhaps Alan; and still more upon the question of our marriage, which Bohaldie took in his own hands, as though there had been no such person as James More, and gave Catriona away with very pretty manners and agreeable compliments in French. It was not till all was over, and our healths drunk, that he told us James was in that city, whither he had preceded us some days, and where he now lay sick, and like to die. I thought I saw by my wife's face what way her inclination pointed.

"And let us go see him, then," said I.

"If it is your pleasure," said Catriona. These were early days.

He was lodged in the same quarter of the city with his chief, in a great house upon a corner; and we were guided up to the garret where he lay by the sound of Highland piping. It seemed he had just borrowed a set of them from Bohaldie to amuse his sickness; though he was no such hand as was his brother Rob, he made good music of the kind; and it was strange to observe the French folk crowding on the stairs, and some of them laughing. He lay propped in a pallet. The first look of him I saw he was upon his last business; and, doubtless, this was a strange place for him to die in. But even now I find I can scarce dwell upon his end with patience. Doubtless, Bohaldie had prepared him; he seemed to know we were married, complimented us on the event, and gave us a benediction like a patriarch.

"I have been never understood," said he. "I forgive you both without an afterthought;" after which he spoke for all the world in his old manner, was so obliging as to play us a tune or two upon his pipes, and borrowed a small sum before I left.

I could not trace even a hint of shame in any part of his behaviour; but he was great upon forgiveness; it seemed always fresh to him. I think he forgave me every time we met; and when after some four days he passed away in a kind of odour of affectionate sanctity, I could have torn my hair out for exasperation. I had him buried; but what to put upon his tomb was quite beyond me, till at last I considered the date would look best alone.

I thought it wiser to resign all thoughts of Leyden, where we had appeared once as brother and sister, and it would certainly look strange to return in a new character. Scotland would be doing for us; and thither, after I had recovered that which I had left behind, we sailed in a Low Country ship.

And now, Miss Barbara Balfour (to set the ladies first), and Mr. Alan Balfour younger of Shaws, here is the story brought fairly to an end. A great many of the folk that took a part in it, you will find (if you think well) that you have seen and spoken with. Alison Hastie in Limekilns was the lass that rocked your cradle when you were too small to know of it, and walked abroad with you in the policy when you were bigger. That very fine great lady that is Miss Barbara's name-mamma is no other than the same Miss Grant that made so much a fool of David Balfour in the house of the Lord Advocate. And I wonder whether you remember a little, lean, lively gentleman in a scratch-wig and a wraprascal, that came to Shaws very late of a dark night, and whom you were awakened out of your beds and brought down to the dining-hall to be presented to, by the name of Mr. Jamieson? Or has Alan forgotten what he did at Mr. Jamieson's request—a most disloyal act—for which, by the letter of the law, he might be hanged—no less than drinking the king's health across the water? These were strange doings in a good Whig house! But Mr. Jamieson is a man privileged, and might set fire to my corn-barn; and the name they know him by now in France is the Chevalier Stewart.

As for Davie and Catriona, I shall watch you pretty close in the next days, and see if you are so bold as to be laughing at papa and mamma. It is true we were not so wise as we might have been, and made a great deal of sorrow out of nothing; but you will find as you grow up that even the artful Miss Barbara, and even the valiant Mr. Alan, will be not so very much wiser than their parents. For the life of man upon this world of ours is a funny business. They talk of the angels weeping; but I think they must more often be holding their sides as they look on; and there was one thing I determined to do when I began this long story, and that was to tell out everything as it befell.

THE MERRY MEN

CHAPTER I.
EILEAN AROS.

It was a beautiful morning in the late July when I set forth on foot for the last time for Aros. A boat had put me ashore the night before at Grisapol; I had such breakfast as the little inn afforded, and, leaving all my baggage till I had an occasion to come round for it by sea, struck right across the promontory with a cheerful heart.

I was far from being a native of these parts, springing, as I did, from an unmixed lowland stock. But an uncle of mine, Gordon Darnaway, after a poor, rough youth, and some years at sea, had married a young wife in the islands; Mary Maclean she was called, the last of her family; and when she died in giving birth to a daughter, Aros, the sea-girt farm, had remained in his possession. It brought him in nothing but the means of life, as I was well aware; but he was a man whom ill-fortune had pursued; he feared, cumbered as he was with the young child, to make a fresh adventure upon life; and remained in Aros, biting his nails at destiny. Years passed over his head in that isolation, and brought neither help nor contentment. Meantime our family was dying out in the lowlands; there is little luck for any of that race; and perhaps my father was the luckiest of all, for not only was he one of the last to die, but he left a son to his name and a little money to support it. I was a student of Edinburgh University, living well enough at my own charges, but without kith or kin; when some news of me found its way to Uncle Gordon on the Ross of Grisapol; and he, as he was a man who held blood thicker than water, wrote to me the day he heard of my existence, and taught me to count Aros as my home. Thus it was that I came to spend my vacations in that part of the country, so far from all society and comfort, between the codfish and the moorcocks; and thus it was that now, when I had done with my classes, I was returning thither with so light a heart that July day.

The Ross, as we call it, is a promontory neither wide nor high, but as rough as God made it to this day; the deep sea on either hand of it, full of rugged isles and reefs most perilous to seamen—all overlooked from the eastward by some very high cliffs and the great peals of Ben Kyaw. The Mountain of the Mist, they say the words signify in the Gaelic tongue; and it is well named. For that hill-top, which is more than three thousand feet in height, catches all the clouds that come blowing from the seaward; and, indeed, I used often to think that it must make them for itself; since when all heaven was clear to the sea level, there would ever be a streamer on Ben Kyaw. It brought water, too, and was mossy[5] to the top in consequence. I have seen us sitting in broad sunshine on the Ross, and the rain falling black like crape upon the mountain. But the wetness of it made it often appear more beautiful to my eyes; for when the sun struck upon the hill sides, there were many wet rocks and watercourses that shone like jewels even as far as Aros, fifteen miles away.

The road that I followed was a cattle-track. It twisted so as nearly to double the length of my journey; it went over rough boulders so that a man had to leap from one to another, and through soft bottoms where the moss came nearly to the knee. There was no cultivation anywhere, and not one house in the ten miles from Grisapol to Aros. Houses of course there were—three at least; but they lay so far on the one side or the other that no stranger could have found them from the track. A large part of the Ross is covered with big granite rocks, some of them larger than a two-roomed house, one beside another, with fern and deep heather in between them where the vipers breed. Anyway the wind was, it was always sea air, as salt as on a ship; the gulls were as free as moorfowl over all the Ross; and whenever the way rose a little, your eye would kindle with the brightness of the sea. From the very midst of the land, on a day of wind and a high spring, I have heard the Roost roaring, like a battle where it runs by Aros, and the great and fearful voices of the breakers that we call the Merry Men.

Aros itself—Aros Jay, I have heard the natives call it, and they say it means the House of God—Aros itself was not properly a piece of the Ross, nor was it quite an islet. It formed the south-west corner of the land, fitted close to it, and was in one place only separated from the coast by a little gut of the sea, not forty feet across the narrowest. When the tide was full, this was clear and still, like a pool on a land river; only there was a difference in the weeds and fishes, and the water itself was green instead of brown; but when the tide went out, in the bottom of the ebb, there was a day or two in every month when you could pass dryshod from Aros to the mainland. There was some good pasture, where my uncle fed the sheep he lived on; perhaps the feed was better because the ground rose higher on the islet than the main level of the Ross, but this I am not skilled enough to settle. The house was a good one for that country, two storeys high. It looked westward over a bay, with a pier hard by for a boat, and from the door you could watch the vapours blowing on Ben Kyaw.

On all this part of the coast, and especially near Aros, these great granite rocks that I have spoken of go down together in troops into the sea, like cattle on a summer's day. There they stand, for all the world like their neighbours ashore; only the salt water sobbing between them instead of the quiet earth, and clots of sea-pink blooming on their sides instead of heather; and the great sea conger to wreathe about the base of them instead of the poisonous viper of the land. On calm days you can go wandering between them in a boat for hours, echoes following you about the labyrinth; but when the sea is up, Heaven help the man that hears that cauldron boiling.

Off the south-west end of Aros these blocks are very many, and much greater in size. Indeed, they must grow monstrously bigger out to sea, for there must be ten sea miles of open water sown with them as thick as a country place with houses, some standing thirty feet above the tides, some covered, but all perilous to ships; so that on a clear, westerly blowing day, I have counted, from the top of Aros, the great rollers breaking white and heavy over as many as six-and-forty buried reefs. But it is nearer in shore that the danger is worst; for the tide, here running like a mill race, makes a long belt of broken water—a Roost we call it—at the tail of the land. I have often been out there in a dead calm at the slack of the tide; and a strange place it is, with the sea swirling and combing up and boiling like the cauldrons of a linn, and now and again a little dancing mutter of sound as though the Roost were talking to itself. But when the tide begins to run again, and above all in heavy weather, there is no man could take a boat within half a mile of it, nor a ship afloat that could either steer or live in such a place. You can hear the roaring of it six miles away. At the seaward end there comes the strongest of the bubble; and it's here that these big breakers dance together—the dance of death, it may be called—that have got the name, in these parts, of the Merry Men. I have heard it said that they run fifty feet high; but that must be the green water only, for the spray runs twice as high as that. Whether they got the name from their movements, which are swift and antic, or from the shouting they make about the turn of the tide, so that all Aros shakes with it, is more than I can tell.

The truth is, that in a south-westerly wind, that part of our archipelago is no better than a trap. If a ship got through the reefs, and weathered the Merry Men, it would be to come ashore on the south coast of Aros, in Sandag Bay, where so many dismal things befell our family, as I propose to tell. The thought of all these dangers, in the place I knew so long, makes me particularly welcome the works now going forward to set lights upon the headlands and buoys along the channels of our iron-bound, inhospitable islands.

The country people had many a story about Aros, as I used to hear from my uncle's man, Rorie, an old servant of the Macleans, who had transferred his services without afterthought on the occasion of the marriage. There was some tale of an unlucky creature, a sea-kelpie, that dwelt and did business in some fearful manner of his own among the boiling breakers of the Roost. A mermaid had once met a piper on Sandag beach, and there sang to him a long, bright midsummer's night, so that in the morning he was found stricken crazy, and from thenceforward, till the day he died, said only one form of words; what they were in the original Gaelic I cannot tell, but they were thus translated: "Ah, the sweet singing out of the sea." Seals that haunted on that coast have been known to speak to man in his own tongue, presaging great disasters. It was here that a certain saint first landed on his voyage out of Ireland to convert the Hebrideans. And, indeed, I think he had some claim to be called saint; for, with the boats of that past age, to make so rough a passage, and land on such a ticklish coast, was surely not far short of the miraculous. It was to him, or to some of his monkish underlings who had a cell there, that the islet owes its holy and beautiful name, the House of God.

Among these old wives' stories there was one which I was inclined to hear with more credulity. As I was told, in that tempest which scattered the ships of the Invincible Armada over all the north and west of Scotland, one great vessel came ashore on Aros, and before the eyes of some solitary people on a hill-top, went down in a moment with all hands, her colours flying even as she sank. There was some likelihood in this tale; for another of that fleet lay sunk on the north side, twenty miles from Grisapol. It was told, I thought, with more detail and gravity than its companion stories, and there was one particularity which went far to convince me of its truth: the name, that is, of the ship was still remembered, and sounded, in my ears, Spanishly. The Espirito Santo they called it, a great ship of many decks of guns, laden with treasure and grandees of Spain, and fierce soldadoes, that now lay fathom deep to all eternity, done with her wars and voyages, in Sandag bay, upon the west of Aros. No more salvos of ordnance for that tall ship, the "Holy Spirit," no more fair winds or happy ventures; only to rot there deep in the sea-tangle and hear the shoutings of the Merry Men as the tide ran high about the island. It was a strange thought to me first and last, and only grew stranger as I learned the more of Spain, from which she had set sail with so proud a company, and King Philip, the wealthy king, that sent her on that voyage.

And now I must tell you, as I walked from Grisapol that day, the Espirito Santo was very much in my reflections. I had been favourably remarked by our then Principal in Edinburgh College, that famous writer, Dr. Robertson, and by him had been set to work on some papers of an ancient date to rearrange and sift of what was worthless; and in one of these, to my great wonder, I found a note of this very ship, the Espirito Santo, with her captain's name, and how she carried a great part of the Spaniard's treasure, and had been lost upon the Ross of Grisapol; but in what particular spot, the wild tribes of that place and period would give no information to the king's inquiries. Putting one thing with another, and taking our island tradition together with this note of old King Jamie's perquisitions after wealth, it had come strongly on my mind that the spot for which he sought in vain could be no other than the small bay of Sandag on my uncle's land; and being a fellow of a mechanical turn, I had ever since been plotting how to weigh that good ship up again with all her ingots, ounces, and doubloons, and bring back our house of Darnaway to its long-forgotten dignity and wealth.

This was a design of which I soon had reason to repent. My mind was sharply turned on different reflections; and since I became the witness of a strange judgment of God's, the thought of dead men's treasures has been intolerable to my conscience. But even at that time I must acquit myself of sordid greed; for if I desired riches, it was not for their own sake, but for the sake of a person who was dear to my heart—my uncle's daughter, Mary Ellen. She had been educated well, and had been a time to school upon the mainland; which, poor girl, she would have been happier without. For Aros was no place for her, with old Rorie the servant, and her father, who was one of the unhappiest men in Scotland, plainly bred up in a country place among Cameronians, long a skipper sailing out of the Clyde about the islands, and now, with infinite discontent, managing his sheep and a little "long shore fishing for the necessary bread. If it was sometimes weariful to me, who was there but a month or two, you may fancy what it was to her who dwelt in that same desert all the year round, with the sheep and flying sea-gulls, and the Merry Men singing and dancing in the Roost!

CHAPTER II.
WHAT THE WRECK HAD BROUGHT TO AROS.

It was half-flood when I got the length of Aros; and there was nothing for it but to stand on the far shore and whistle for Rorie with the boat. I had no need to repeat the signal. At the first sound, Mary was at the door flying a handkerchief by way of answer, and the old long-legged serving-man was shambling down the gravel to the pier. For all his hurry, it took him a long while to pull across the bay; and I observed him several times to pause, go into the stern, and look over curiously into the wake. As he came nearer, he seemed to me aged and haggard, and I thought he avoided my eye. The coble had been repaired, with two new thwarts and several patches of some rare and beautiful foreign wood, the name of it unknown to me.

"Why, Rorie," said I, as we began the return voyage, "this is fine wood. How came you by that?"

"It will be hard to cheesel," Rorie opined reluctantly; and just then, dropping the oars, he made another of those dives into the stern which I had remarked as he came across to fetch me, and, leaning his hand on my shoulder, stared with an awful look into the waters of the bay.

"What is wrong?" I asked, a good deal startled.

"It will be a great feesh," said the old man, returning to his oars; and nothing more could I get out of him, but strange glances and an ominous nodding of the head. In spite of myself, I was infected with a measure of uneasiness; I turned also, and studied the wake. The water was still and transparent, but, out here in the middle of the bay, exceeding deep. For some time I could see naught; but at last it did seem to me as if something dark—a great fish, or perhaps only a shadow—followed studiously in the track of the moving coble. And then I remembered one of Rorie's superstitions: how in a ferry in Morven, in some great, exterminating feud among the clans; a fish, the like of it unknown in all our waters, followed for some years the passage of the ferry-boat, until no man dared to make the crossing.

"He will be waiting for the right man," said Rorie.

Mary met me on the beach, and led me up the brae and into the house of Aros. Outside and inside there were many changes. The garden was fenced with the same wood that I had noted in the boat; there were chairs in the kitchen covered with strange brocade; curtains of brocade hung from the window; a clock stood silent on the dresser; a lamp of brass was swinging from the roof; the table was set for dinner with the finest of linen and silver; and all these new riches were displayed in the plain old kitchen that I knew so well, with the high-backed settle, and the stools, and the closet bed for Rorie; with the wide chimney the sun shone into, and the clear-smouldering peats; with the pipes on the mantelshelf and the three-cornered spittoons, filled with sea-shells instead of sand, on the floor; with the bare stone walls and the bare wooden floor, and the three patchwork rugs that were of yore its sole adornment—poor man's patchwork, the like of it unknown in cities, woven with homespun, and Sunday black, and sea-cloth polished on the bench of rowing. The room, like the house, had been a sort of wonder in that country-side, it was so neat and habitable; and to see it now, shamed by these incongruous additions, filled me with indignation and a kind of anger. In view of the errand I had come upon to Aros, the feeling was baseless and unjust; but it burned high, at the first moment, in my heart.

"Mary, girl," said I, "this is the place I had learned to call my home, and I do not know it."

"It is my home by nature, not by the learning," she replied; "the place I was born and the place

I'm like to die in; and I neither like these changes, nor the way they came, nor that which came with them. I would have liked better, under God's pleasure, they had gone down into the sea, and the Merry Men were dancing on them now."

Mary was always serious; it was perhaps the only trait that she shared with her father; but the tone with which she uttered these words was even graver than of custom.

"Ay," said I, "I feared it came by wreck, and that's by death; yet when my father died, I took his goods without remorse."

"Your father died a clean strae death, as the folk say," said Mary.

"True," I returned; "and a wreck is like a judgment. What was she called?"

"They ca'd her the Christ-Anna," said a voice behind me; and, turning round, I saw my uncle standing in the doorway.

He was a sour, small, bilious man, with a long face and very dark eyes; fifty-six years old, sound and active in body, and with an air somewhat between that of a shepherd and that of a man following the sea. He never laughed, that I heard; read long at the Bible; prayed much, like the Cameronians he had been brought up among; and indeed, in many ways, used to remind me of one of the hill-preachers in the killing times before the Revolution. But he never got much comfort, nor even, as I used to think, much guidance, by his piety. He had his black fits when he was afraid of hell; but he had led a rough life, to which he would look back with envy, and was still a rough, cold, gloomy man.

As he came in at the door out of the sunlight, with his bonnet on his head and a pipe hanging in his button-hole, he seemed, like Rorie, to have grown older and paler, the lines were deeplier ploughed upon his face, and the whites of his eyes were yellow, like old stained ivory, or the bones of the dead.

"Ay" he repeated, dwelling upon the first part of the word, "the Christ-Anna. It's an awfu' name."

I made him my salutations, and complimented him upon his look of health; for I feared he had perhaps been ill.

"I'm in the body," he replied, ungraciously enough; "aye in the body and the sins of the body, like yoursel'. Denner," he said abruptly to Mary, and then ran on to me: "They're grand braws, thir that we hae gotten, are they no? Yon's a bonny knock[15], but it'll no gang; and the napery's by ordnar. Bonny, bairnly braws; it's for the like o' them folk sells the peace of God that passeth understanding; it's for the like o' them, an' maybe no even sae muckle worth, folk daunton God to His face and burn in muckle hell; and it's for that reason the Scripture ca's them, as I read the passage, the accursed thing. Mary, ye girzie," he interrupted himself to cry with some asperity, "what for hae ye no put out the twa candlesticks?"

"Why should we need them at high noon?" she asked.

But my uncle was not to be turned from his idea. "We'll bruik[16] them while we may," he said; and so two massive candlesticks of wrought silver were added to the table equipage, already so unsuited to that rough sea-side farm.

"She cam' ashore Februar' 10, about ten at nicht," he went on to me. "There was nae wind, and a sair run o' sea; and she was in the sook o' the Roost, as I jaloose. We had seen her a' day, Rorie and me, beating to the wind. She wasnae a handy craft, I'm thinking, that Christ-Anna; for she would neither steer nor stey wi' them. A sair day they had of it; their hands was never aff the sheets, and it perishin' cauld—ower cauld to snaw; and aye they would get a bit nip o' wind, and awa' again, to pit the emp'y hope into them. Eh, man! but they had a sair day for the last o't! He would have had a prood, prood heart that won ashore upon the back o' that."

"And were all lost?" I cried. "God held them!"

"Wheesht!" he said sternly. "Nane shall pray for the deid on my hearth-stane."

I disclaimed a Popish sense for my ejaculation; and he seemed to accept my disclaimer with unusual facility, and ran on once more upon what had evidently become a favourite subject.

"We fand her in Sandag Bay, Rorie an' me, and a' thae braws in the inside of her. There's a kittle bit, ye see, about Sandag; whiles the sook rins strong for the Merry Men; an' whiles again, when the tide's makin' hard an' ye can hear the Roost blawin' at the far-end of Aros, there comes a back-spang of current straucht into Sandag Bay. Weel, there's the thing that got the grip on the Christ-Anna. She but to have come in ram-stam an' stern forrit; for the bows of her are aften under, and the back-side of her is clear at hie-water o' neaps. But, man! the dunt that she cam doon wi' when she struck! Lord save us a'! but it's an unco life to be a sailor—a cauld, wanchancy life. Mony's the gliff I got mysel' in the great deep; and why the Lord should hae made yon unco water is mair than ever I could win to understand. He made the vales and the pastures, the bonny green yaird, the halesome, canty land—

And now they shout and sing to Thee,
For Thou hast made them glad,

as the Psalms say in the metrical version. No that I would preen my faith to that clink neither; but it's bonny, and easier to mind. 'Who go to sea in ships,' they hae't again—

And in
Great waters trading be,
Within the deep these men God's works
And His great wonders see.

Weel, it's easy sayin' sae. Maybe Dauvit wasnae very weel acquant wi' the sea. But, troth, if it wasnae prentit in the Bible, I wad whiles be temp'it to think it wasnae the Lord, but the muckle, black deil that made the sea. There's naething good comes oot o't but the fish; an' the spectacle o' God riding on the tempest, to be shure, whilk would be what Dauvit was likely ettling at. But, man, they were sair wonders that God showed to the Christ-Anna—wonders, do I ca' them? Judgments, rather: judgments in the mirk nicht among the draygons o' the deep. And their souls—to think o' that—their souls, man, maybe no prepared! The sea—a muckle yett to hell!"

I observed, as my uncle spoke, that his voice was unnaturally moved and his manner unwontedly demonstrative. He leaned forward at these last words, for example, and touched me on the knee with his spread fingers, looking up into my face with a certain pallor, and I could see that his eyes shone with a deep-seated fire, and that the lines about his mouth were drawn and tremulous.

Even the entrance of Rorie, and the beginning of our meal, did not detach him from his train of thought beyond a moment. He condescended, indeed, to ask me some questions as to my success at college, but I thought it was with half his mind; and even in his extempore grace, which was, as usual, long and wandering, I could find the trace of his preoccupation, praying, as he did, that God would "remember in mercy fower puir, feckless, fiddling, sinful creatures here by their lee-lane beside the great and dowie waters."

Soon there came an interchange of speeches between him and Rorie.

"Was it there?" asked my uncle.

"Ou, ay!" said Rorie.

I observed that they both spoke in a manner of aside, and with some show of embarrassment, and that Mary herself appeared to colour, and looked down on her plate. Partly to show my knowledge, and so relieve the party from an awkward strain, partly because I was curious, I pursued the subject.

"You mean the fish?" I asked.

"Whatten fish?" cried my uncle. "Fish, quo' he! Fish! Your een are fu' o' fatness, man; your heid dozened wi' carnal leir. Fish! it's a bogle!"

He spoke with great vehemence, as though angry; and perhaps I was not very willing to be put down so shortly, for young men are disputatious. At least I remember I retorted hotly, crying out upon childish superstitions.

"And ye come frae the College!" sneered Uncle Gordon. "Gude kens what they learn folk there; it's no muckle service onyway. Do ye think, man, that there's naething in a' yon saut wilderness o' a world oot wast there, wi' the sea grasses growin', an' the sea beasts fechtin', an' the sun glintin' down into it, day by day? Na; the sea's like the land, but fearsomer. If there's folk ashore, there's folk in the sea—deid they may be, but they're folk whatever; and as for deils, there's nane that's like the sea deils. There's no sae muckle harm in the land deils, when a's said and done. Lang syne, when I was a callant in the south country, I mind there was an auld, bald bogle in the Peewie Moss. I got a glisk o' him mysel', sittin' on his hunkers in a hag, as gray's a tombstane. An', troth, he was a fearsome-like taed. But he steered naebody. Nae doobt, if ane that was a reprobate, ane the Lord hated, had gane by there wi' his sin still upon his stamach, nae doobt the creature would hae lowped upo' the likes o' him. But there's deils in the deep sea would yoke on a communicant! Eh, sirs, if ye had gane doon wi' the puir lads in the Christ-Anna, ye would ken by now the mercy o' the seas. If ye had sailed it for as lang as me, ye would hate the thocht of it as I do. If ye had but used the een God gave ye, ye would hae learned the wickedness o' that fause, saut, cauld, bullering creature, and of a' that's in it by the Lord's permission: labsters an' partans, an' sic like, howking in the deid; muckle, gutsy, blawing whales; an' fish—the hale clan o' them—cauld-wamed, blind-eed uncanny ferlies. O, sirs," he cried, "the horror—the horror o' the sea!"

We were all somewhat staggered by this outburst; and the speaker himself, after that last hoarse apostrophe, appeared to sink gloomily into his own thoughts. But Rorie, who was greedy of superstitious lore, recalled him to the subject by a question.

"You will not ever have seen a teevil of the sea?" he asked.

"No clearly," replied the other. "I misdoobt if a mere man could see ane clearly and conteenue in the body. I hae sailed wi' a lad—they ca'd him Sandy Gabart; he saw ane, shure eneueh, an' shure eneueh it was the end of him. We were seeven days oot frae the Clyde—a sair wark we had had—gaun north wi' seeds an' braws an' things for the Macleod. We had got in ower near under the Cutchull'ns, an' had just gane about by soa, an' were off on a lang tack, we thocht would maybe hauld as far's Copnahow. I mind the nicht weel; a mune smoored wi' mist; a fine gaun breeze upon the water, but no steedy; an'—what nane o' us likit to hear—anither wund gurlin' owerheid, amang thae fearsome, auld stane craigs o' the Cutchull'ns. Weel, Sandy was forrit wi' the jib sheet; we couldnae see him for the mains'l, that had just begude to draw, when a' at ance he gied a skirl. I luffed for my life, for I thocht we were ower near Soa; but na, it wasnae that, it was puir Sandy Gabart's deid skreigh, or near hand, for he was deid in half an hour. A't he could tell was that a sea deil, or sea bogle, or sea spenster, or sic-like, had clum up by the bowsprit, an' gi'en him ae cauld, uncanny look. An', or the life was oot o' Sandy's body, we kent weel what the thing betokened, and why the wund gurled in the taps o' the Cutchull'ns; for doon it cam'—a wund do I ca' it! it was the wund o' the Lord's anger—an' a' that nicht we foucht like men dementit, and the niest that we kenned we were ashore in Loch Uskevagh, an' the cocks were crawin' in Benbecula."

"It will have been a merman," Rorie said.

"A merman!" screamed my uncle with immeasurable scorn. "Auld wives' clavers! There's nae sic things as mermen."

"But what was the creature like?" I asked.

"What like was it? Gude forbid that we suld ken what like it was! It had a kind of a heid upon it—man could say nae mair."

Then Rorie, smarting under the affront, told several tales of mermen, mermaids, and sea-horses that had come ashore upon the islands and attacked the crews of boats upon the sea; and my uncle, in spite of his incredulity, listened with uneasy interest.

"Aweel, aweel," he said, "it may be sae; I may be wrang; but I find nae word o' mermen in the Scriptures."

"And you will find nae word of Aros Roost, maybe," objected Rorie, and his argument appeared to carry weight.

When dinner was over, my uncle carried me forth with him to a bank behind the house. It was a very hot and quiet afternoon; scarce a ripple anywhere upon the sea, nor any voice but the familiar voice of sheep and gulls; and perhaps in consequence of this repose in nature, my kinsman showed himself more rational and tranquil than before. He spoke evenly and almost cheerfully of my career, with every now and then a reference to the lost ship or the treasures it had brought to Aros. For my part, I listened to him in a sort of trance, gazing with all my heart on that remembered scene, and drinking gladly the sea-air and the smoke of peats that had been lit by Mary.

Perhaps an hour had passed when my uncle, who had all the while been covertly gazing on the surface of the little bay, rose to his feet and bade me follow his example. Now I should say that the great run of tide at the south-west end of Aros exercises a perturbing influence round all the coast. In Sandag Bay, to the south, a strong current runs at certain periods of the flood and ebb respectively; but in this northern bay—Aros Bay, as it is called—where the house stands and on which my uncle was now gazing, the only sign of disturbance is towards the end of the ebb, and even then it is too slight to be remarkable. When there is any swell, nothing can be seen at all; but when it is calm, as it often is, there appear certain strange, undecipherable marks—sea-runes, as we may name them—on the glassy surface of the bay. The like is common in a thousand places on the coast; and many a boy must have amused himself as I did, seeking to read in them some reference to himself or those he loved. It was to these marks that my uncle now directed my attention, struggling, as he did so, with an evident reluctance.

"Do ye see yon scart upo' the water?" he inquired; "yon ane wast the gray stane? Ay? Weel, it'll no be like a letter, wull it?"

"Certainly it is," I replied. "I have often remarked it. It is like a C."

He heaved a sigh as if heavily disappointed with my answer, and then added below his breath: "Ay, for the Christ-Anna."

"I used to suppose, sir, it was for myself," said I; "for my name is Charles."

"And so ye saw't afore?", he ran on, not heeding my remark. "Weel, weel, but that's unco strange. Maybe, it's been there waitin', as a man wad say, through a' the weary ages. Man, but that's awfu'." And then, breaking off: "Ye'll no see anither, will ye?" he asked.

"Yes," said I. "I see another very plainly, near the Ross side, where the road comes down—an M."

"An M," he repeated very low; and then, again after another pause: "An' what wad ye make o' that?" he inquired.

"I had always thought it to mean Mary, sir," I answered, growing somewhat red, convinced as I was in my own mind that I was on the threshold of a decisive explanation.

But we were each following his own train of thought to the exclusion of the other's. My uncle once more paid no attention to my words; only hung his head and held his peace; and I might have been led to fancy that he had not heard me, if his next speech had not contained a kind of echo from my own.

"I would say naething o' thae clavers to Mary," he observed, and began to walk forward.

There is a belt of turf along the side of Aros Bay, where walking is easy; and it was along this that I silently followed my silent kinsman. I was perhaps a little disappointed at having lost so good an opportunity to declare my love; but I was at the same time far more deeply exercised at the change that had befallen my uncle. He was never an ordinary, never, in the strict sense, an amiable, man; but there was nothing in even the worst that I had known of him before, to prepare me for so strange a transformation. It was impossible to close the eyes against one fact; that he had, as the saying goes, something on his mind; and as I mentally ran over the different words which might be represented by the letter M—misery, mercy, marriage, money, and the like—I was arrested with a sort of start by the word murder. I was still considering the ugly sound and fatal meaning of the word, when the direction of our walk brought us to a point from which a view was to be had to either side, back towards Aros Bay and homestead, and forward on the ocean, dotted to the north with isles, and lying to the southward blue and open to the sky. There my guide came to a halt, and stood staring for awhile on that expanse. Then he turned to me and laid a hand on my arm.

"Ye think there's naething there?" he said, pointing with his pipe; and then cried out aloud, with a kind of exultation: "I'll tell ye, man! The deid are down there—thick like rattons!"

He turned at once, and, without another word, we retraced our steps to the house of Aros.

I was eager to be alone with Mary; yet it was not till after supper, and then but for a short while, that I could have a word with her. I lost no time beating about the bush, but spoke out plainly what was on my mind.

"Mary," I said, "I have not come to Aros without a hope. If that should prove well founded, we may all leave and go somewhere else, secure of daily bread and comfort; secure, perhaps, of something far beyond that, which it would seem extravagant in me to promise. But there's a hope that lies nearer to my heart than money." And at that I paused. "You can guess fine what that is, Mary," I said. She looked away from me in silence, and that was small encouragement, but I was not to be put off. "All my days I have thought the world of you," I continued; "the time goes on and I think always the more of you; I could not think to be happy or hearty in my life without you: you are the apple of my eye." Still she looked away, and said never a word; but I thought I saw that her hands shook. "Mary," I cried in fear, "do ye no like me?"

"O, Charlie man," she said, "is this a time to speak of it? Let me be, a while; let me be the way I am; it'll not be you that loses by the waiting!"

I made out by her voice that she was nearly weeping, and this put me out of any thought but to compose her. "Mary Ellen," I said, "say no more; I did not come to trouble you: your way shall be mine, and your time too; and you have told me all I wanted. Only just this one thing more: what ails you?"

She owned it was her father, but would enter into no particulars, only shook her head, and said he was not well and not like himself, and it was a great pity. She knew nothing of the wreck. "I havenae been near it," said she. "What for would I go near it, Charlie lad? The poor souls are gone to their account long syne; and I would just have wished they had ta'en their gear with them—poor souls!"

This was scarcely any great encouragement for me to tell her of the Espirito Santo; yet I did so, and at the very first word she cried out in surprise. "There was a man at Grisapol," she said, "in the month of May—a little, yellow, black-avised body, they tell me, with gold rings upon his fingers, and a beard; and he was speiring high and low for that same ship."

It was towards the end of April that I had been given these papers to sort out by Dr. Robertson: and it came suddenly back upon my mind that they were thus prepared for a Spanish historian, or a man calling himself such, who had come with high recommendations to the Principal, on a mission of inquiry as to the dispersion of the great Armada. Putting one thing with another, I fancied that the visitor "with the gold rings upon his fingers" might be the same with Dr. Robertson's historian from Madrid. If that were so, he would be more likely after treasure for himself than information for a learned society. I made up my mind, I should lose no time over my undertaking; and if the ship lay sunk in Sandag Bay, as perhaps both he and I supposed, it should not be for the advantage of this ringed adventurer, but for Mary and myself, and for the good, old, honest, kindly family of the Darnaways.

CHAPTER III.
LAND AND SEA IN SANDAG BAY.

I was early afoot next morning; and as soon as I had a bite to eat, set forth upon a tour of exploration. Something in my heart distinctly told me that I should find the ship of the Armada; and although I did not give way entirely to such hopeful thoughts, I was still very light in spirits and walked upon air. Aros is a very rough islet, its surface strewn with great rocks and shaggy with fernland heather; and my way lay almost north and south across the highest knoll; and though the whole distance was inside of two miles it took more time and exertion than four upon a level road. Upon the summit, I paused. Although not very high—not three hundred feet, as I think—it yet outtops all the neighbouring lowlands of the Ross, and commands a great view of sea and islands. The sun, which had been up some time, was already hot upon my neck; the air was listless and thundery, although purely clear; away over the north-west, where the isles lie thickliest congregated, some half-a-dozen small and ragged clouds hung together in a covey; and the head of Ben Kyaw wore, not merely a few streamers, but a solid hood of vapour. There was a threat in the weather. The sea, it is true, was smooth like glass: even the Roost was but a seam on that wide mirror, and the Merry Men no more than caps of foam; but to my eye and ear, so long familiar with these places, the sea also seemed to lie uneasily; a sound of it, like a long sigh, mounted to me where I stood; and, quiet as it was, the Roost itself appeared to be revolving mischief. For I ought to say that all we dwellers in these parts attributed, if not prescience, at least a quality of warning, to that strange and dangerous creature of the tides.

I hurried on, then, with the greater speed, and had soon descended the slope of Aros to the part that we call Sandag Bay. It is a pretty large piece of water compared with the size of the isle; well sheltered from all but the prevailing wind; sandy and shoal and bounded by low sand-hills to the west, but to the eastward lying several fathoms deep along a ledge of rocks. It is upon that side that, at a certain time each flood, the current mentioned by my uncle sets so strong into the bay; a little later, when the Roost begins to work higher, an undertow runs still more strongly in the reverse direction; and it is the action of this last, as I suppose, that has scoured that part so deep. Nothing is to be seen out of Sandag Bay, but one small segment of the horizon and, in heavy weather, the breakers flying high over a deep sea reef.

From half-way down the hill, I had perceived the wreck of February last, a brig of considerable tonnage, lying, with her back broken, high and dry on the east corner of the sands; and I was making directly towards it, and already almost on the margin of the turf, when my eyes were suddenly arrested by a spot, cleared of fern and heather, and marked by one of those long, low, and almost human-looking mounds that we see so commonly in graveyards. I stopped like a man shot. Nothing had been said to me of any dead man or interment on the island; Rorie, Mary, and my uncle had all equally held their peace; of her at least, I was certain that she must be ignorant; and yet here, before my eyes, was proof indubitable of the fact. Here was a grave; and I had to ask myself, with a chill, what manner of man lay there in his last sleep, awaiting the signal of the Lord in that solitary, sea-beat resting-place? My mind supplied no answer but what I feared to entertain. Shipwrecked, at least, he must have been; perhaps, like the old Armada mariners, from some far and rich land over-sea; or perhaps one of my own race, perishing within eyesight of the smoke of home. I stood awhile uncovered by his side, and I could have desired that it had lain in our religion to put up some prayer for that unhappy stranger, or, in the old classic way, outwardly to honour his misfortune. I knew, although his bones lay there, a part of Aros, till the trumpet sounded, his imperishable soul was forth and far away, among the raptures of the everlasting Sabbath or the pangs of hell; and yet my mind misgave me even with a fear, that perhaps he was near me where I stood, guarding his sepulchre, and lingering on the scene of his unhappy fate.

Certainly it was with a spirit somewhat over-shadowed that I turned away from the grave to the hardly less melancholy spectacle of the wreck. Her stem was above the first arc of the flood; she was broken in two a little abaft the foremast—though indeed she had none, both masts having broken short in her disaster; and as the pitch of the beach was very sharp and sudden, and the bows lay many feet below the stern, the fracture gaped widely open, and you could see right through her poor hull upon the farther side. Her name was much defaced, and I could not make out clearly whether she was called Christiania, after the Norwegian city, or Christiana, after the good woman, Christian's wife, in that old book the "Pilgrim's Progress." By her build she was a foreign ship, but I was not certain of her nationality. She had been painted green, but the colour was faded and weathered, and the paint peeling off in strips. The wreck of the mainmast lay alongside, half buried in sand. She was a forlorn sight, indeed, and I could not look without emotion at the bits of rope that still hung about her, so often handled of yore by shouting seamen; or the little scuttle where they had passed up and down to their affairs; or that poor noseless angel of a figure-head that had dipped into so many running billows.

I do not know whether it came most from the ship or from the grave, but I fell into some melancholy scruples, as I stood there, leaning with one hand against the battered timbers. The homelessness of men and even of inanimate vessels, cast away upon strange shores, came strongly in upon my mind. To make a profit of such pitiful misadventures seemed an unmanly and a sordid act; and I began to think of my then quest as of something sacrilegious in its nature. But when I remembered Mary, I took heart again. My uncle would never consent to an imprudent marriage, nor would she, as I was persuaded, wed without his full approval. It behoved me, then, to be up and doing for my wife; and I thought with a laugh how long it was since that great sea-castle, the Espirito Santo, had left her bones in Sandag Bay, and how weak it would be to consider rights so long extinguished and misfortunes so long forgotten in the process of time.

I had my theory of where to seek for her remains. The set of the current and the soundings both pointed to the east side of the bay under the ledge of rocks. If she had been lost in Sandag Bay, and if, after these centuries, any portion of her held together, it was there that I should find it. The water deepens, as I have said, with great rapidity, and even close along-side the rocks several fathoms may be found. As I walked upon the edge I could see far and wide over the sandy bottom of the bay; the sun shone clear and green and steady in the deeps; the bay seemed rather like a great transparent crystal, as one sees them in a lapidary's shop; there was naught to show that it was water but an internal trembling, a hovering within of sun-glints and netted shadows, and now and then a faint lap and a dying bubble round the edge. The shadows of the rocks lay out for some distance at their feet, so that my own shadow, moving, pausing, and stooping on the top of that, reached sometimes half across the bay. It was above all in this belt of shadows that I hunted for the Espirito Santo; since it was there the undertow ran strongest, whether in or out. Cool as the whole water seemed this broiling day, it looked, in that part, yet cooler, and had a mysterious invitation for the eyes. Peer as I pleased, however, I could see nothing but a few fishes or a bush of sea-tangle, and here and there a lump of rock that had fallen from above and now lay separate on the sandy floor. Twice did I pass from one end to the other of the rocks, and in the whole distance I could see nothing of the wreck, nor any place but one where it was possible for it to be. This was a large terrace in five fathoms of water, raised off the surface of the sand to a considerable height, and looking from above like a mere outgrowth of the rocks on which I walked. It was one mass of great sea-tangles like a grove, which prevented me judging of its nature, but in shape and size it bore some likeness to a vessel's hull. At least it was my best chance. If the Espirito Santo lay not there under the tangles, it lay nowhere at all in Sandag Bay; and I prepared to put the question to the proof, once and for all, and either go back to Aros a rich man or cured for ever of my dreams of wealth.

I stripped to the skin, and stood on the extreme margin with my hands clasped, irresolute. The bay at that time was utterly quiet; there was no sound but from a school of porpoises somewhere out of sight behind the point; yet a certain fear withheld me on the threshold of my venture. Sad sea-feelings, scraps of my uncle's superstitions, thoughts of the dead, of the grave, of the old broken ships, drifted through my mind. But the strong sun upon my shoulders warmed me to the heart, and I stooped forward and plunged into the sea.

It was all that I could do to catch a trail of the sea-tangle that grew so thickly on the terrace; but once so far anchored I secured myself by grasping a whole armful of these thick and slimy stalks, and, planting my feet against the edge, I looked around me. On all sides the clear sand stretched forth unbroken; it came to the foot of the rocks, scoured into the likeness of an alley in a garden by the action of the tides; and before me, for as far as I could see, nothing was visible but the same many-folded sand upon the sun-bright bottom of the bay. Yet the terrace to which I was then holding was as thick with strong sea-growths as a tuft of heather, and the cliff from which it bulged hung draped below the water-line with brown lianas. In this complexity of forms, all swaying together in the current, things were hard to be distinguished; and I was still uncertain whether my feet were pressed upon the natural rock or upon the timbers of the Armada treasure-ship, when the whole tuft of tangle came away in my hand, and in an instant I was on the surface, and the shores of the bay and the bright water swam before my eyes in a glory of crimson.

I clambered back upon the rocks, and threw the plant of tangle at my feet. Something at the same moment rang sharply, like a falling coin. I stooped, and there, sure enough, crusted with the red rust, there lay an iron shoe-buckle. The sight of this poor human relic thrilled me to the heart, but not with hope nor fear, only with a desolate melancholy. I held it in my hand, and the thought of its owner appeared before me like the presence of an actual man. His weather-beaten face, his sailor's hands, his sea-voice hoarse with singing at the capstan, the very foot that had once worn that buckle and trod so much along the swerving decks—the whole human fact of him, as a creature like myself, with hair and blood and seeing eyes, haunted me in that sunny, solitary place, not like a spectre, but like some friend whom I had basely injured. Was the great treasure ship indeed below there, with her guns and chain and treasure, as she had sailed from Spain; her decks a garden for the seaweed, her cabin a breeding place for fish, soundless but for the dredging water, motionless but for the waving of the tangle upon her battlements—that old, populous, sea-riding castle, now a reef in Sandag Bay? Or, as I thought it likelier, was this a waif from the disaster of the foreign brig—was this shoe-buckle bought but the other day and worn by a man of my own period in the world's history, hearing the same news from day to day, thinking the same thoughts, praying, perhaps, in the same temple with myself? However it was, I was assailed with dreary thoughts; my uncle's words, "the dead are down there," echoed in my ears; and though I determined to dive once more, it was with a strong repugnance that I stepped forward to the margin of the rocks.

A great change passed at that moment over the appearance of the bay. It was no more that clear, visible interior, like a house roofed with glass, where the green, submarine sunshine slept so stilly. A breeze, I suppose, had flawed the surface, and a sort of trouble and blackness filled its bosom, where flashes of light and clouds of shadow tossed confusedly together. Even the terrace below obscurely rocked and quivered. It seemed a graver thing to venture on this place of ambushes; and when I leaped into the sea the second time it was with a quaking in my soul.

I secured myself as at first, and groped among the waving tangle. All that met my touch was cold and soft and gluey. The thicket was alive with crabs and lobsters, trundling to and fro lopsidedly, and I had to harden my heart against the horror of their carrion neighbourhood. On all sides I could feel the grain and the clefts of hard, living stone; no planks, no iron, not a sign of any wreck; the Espirito Santo was not there. I remember I had almost a sense of relief in my disappointment, and I was about ready to leave go, when something happened that sent me to the surface with my heart in my mouth. I had already stayed somewhat late over my explorations; the current was freshening with the change of the tide, and Sandag Bay was no longer a safe place for a single swimmer. Well, just at the last moment there came a sudden flush of current, dredging through the tangles like a wave. I lost one hold, was flung sprawling on my side, and, instinctively grasping for a fresh support, my fingers closed on something hard and cold. I think I knew at that moment what it was. At least I instantly left hold of the tangle, leaped for the surface, and clambered out next moment on the friendly rocks with the bone of a man's leg in my grasp.

Mankind is a material creature, slow to think and dull to perceive connections. The grave, the wreck of the brig, and the rusty shoe-buckle were surely plain advertisements. A child might have read their dismal story, and yet it was not until I touched that actual piece of mankind that the full horror of the charnel ocean burst upon my spirit. I laid the bone beside the buckle, picked up my clothes, and ran as I was along the rocks towards the human shore. I could not be far enough from the spot; no fortune was vast enough to tempt me back again. The bones of the drowned dead should henceforth roll undisturbed by me, whether on tangle or minted gold. But as soon as I trod the good earth again, and had covered my nakedness against the sun, I knelt down over against the ruins of the brig, and out of the fulness of my heart prayed long and passionately for all poor souls upon the sea. A generous prayer is never presented in vain; the petition may be refused, but the petitioner is always, I believe, rewarded by some gracious visitation. The horror, at least, was lifted from my mind; I could look with calm of spirit on that great bright creature, God's ocean; and as I set off homeward up the rough sides of Aros, nothing remained of my concern beyond a deep determination to meddle no more with the spoils of wrecked vessels or the treasures of the dead.

I was already some way up the hill before I paused to breathe and look behind me. The sight that met my eyes was doubly strange.

For, first, the storm that I had foreseen was now advancing with almost tropical rapidity. The whole surface of the sea had been dulled from its conspicuous brightness to an ugly hue of corrugated lead; already in the distance the white waves, the "skipper's daughters," had begun to flee before a breeze that was still insensible on Aros; and already along the curve of Sandag Bay there was a splashing run of sea that I could hear from where I stood. The change upon the sky was even more remarkable. There had begun to arise out of the south-west a huge and solid continent of scowling cloud; here and there, through rents in its contexture, the sun still poured a sheaf of spreading rays; and here and there, from all its edges, vast inky streamers lay forth along the yet unclouded sky. The menace was express and imminent. Even as I gazed, the sun was blotted out. At any moment the tempest might fall upon Aros in its might.

The suddenness of this change of weather so fixed my eyes on heaven that it was some seconds before they alighted on the bay, mapped out below my feet, and robbed a moment later of the sun. The knoll which I had just surmounted overflanked a little amphitheatre of lower hillocks sloping towards the sea, and beyond that the yellow arc of beach and the whole extent of Sandag Bay. It was a scene on which I had often looked down, but where I had never before beheld a human figure. I had but just turned my back upon it and left it empty, and my wonder may be fancied when I saw a boat and several men in that deserted spot. The boat was lying by the rocks. A pair of fellows, bareheaded, with their sleeves rolled up, and one with a boathook, kept her with difficulty to her moorings for the current was growing brisker every moment. A little way off upon the ledge two men in black clothes, whom I judged to be superior in rank, laid their heads together over some task which at first I did not understand, but a second after I had made it out—they were taking bearings with the compass; and just then I saw one of them unroll a sheet of paper and lay his finger down, as though identifying features in a map. Meanwhile a third was walking to and fro, polling among the rocks and peering over the edge into the water. While I was still watching them with the stupefaction of surprise, my mind hardly yet able to work on what my eyes reported, this third person suddenly stooped and summoned his companions with a cry so loud that it reached my ears upon the hill. The others ran to him, even dropping the compass in their hurry, and I could see the bone and the shoe-buckle going from hand to hand, causing the most unusual gesticulations of surprise and interest. Just then I could hear the seamen crying from the boat, and saw them point westward to that cloud continent which was ever the more rapidly unfurling its blackness over heaven. The others seemed to consult; but the danger was too pressing to be braved, and they bundled into the boat carrying my relics with them, and set forth out of the bay with all speed of oars.

I made no more ado about the matter, but turned and ran for the house. Whoever these men were, it was fit my uncle should be instantly informed. It was not then altogether too late in the day for a descent of the Jacobites; and may be Prince Charlie, whom I knew my uncle to detest, was one of the three superiors whom I had seen upon the rock. Yet as I ran, leaping from rock to rock, and turned the matter loosely in my mind, this theory grew ever the longer the less welcome to my reason. The compass, the map, the interest awakened by the buckle, and the conduct of that one among the strangers who had looked so often below him in the water, all seemed to point to a different explanation of their presence on that outlying, obscure islet of the western sea. The Madrid historian, the search instituted by Dr. Robertson, the bearded stranger with the rings, my own fruitless search that very morning in the deep water of Sandag Bay, ran together, piece by piece, in my memory, and I made sure that these strangers must be Spaniards in quest of ancient treasure and the lost ship of the Armada. But the people living in outlying islands, such as Aros, are answerable for their own security; there is none near by to protect or even to help them; and the presence in such a spot of a crew of foreign adventurers—poor, greedy, and most likely lawless—filled me with apprehensions for my uncle's money, and even for the safety of his daughter. I was still wondering how we were to get rid of them when I came, all breathless, to the top of Aros. The whole world was shadowed over; only in the extreme east, on a hill of the mainland, one last gleam of sunshine lingered like a jewel; rain had begun to fall, not heavily, but in great drops; the sea was rising with each moment, and already a band of white encircled Aros and the nearer coasts of Grisapol. The boat was still pulling seaward, but I now became aware of what had been hidden from me lower down—a large, heavily sparred, handsome schooner, lying to at the south end of Aros. Since I had not seen her in the morning when I had looked around so closely at the signs of the weather, and upon these lone waters where a sail was rarely visible, it was clear she must have lain last night behind the uninhabited Eilean Gour, and this proved conclusively that she was manned by strangers to our coast, for that anchorage, though good enough to look at, is little better than a trap for ships. With such ignorant sailors upon so wild a coast, the coming gale was not unlikely to bring death upon its wings.

CHAPTER IV.
THE GALE.

I found my uncle at the gable end, watching the signs of the weather, with a pipe in his fingers.

"Uncle," said I, "there were men ashore at Sandag Bay—"

I had no time to go further; indeed, I not only forgot my words, but even my weariness, so strange was the effect on Uncle Gordon. He dropped his pipe and fell back against the end of the house with his jaw fallen, his eyes staring, and his long face as white as paper. We must have looked at one another silently for a quarter of a minute, before he made answer in this extraordinary fashion: "Had he a hair kep on?"

I knew as well as if I had been there that the man who now lay buried at Sandag had worn a hairy cap, and that he had come ashore alive. For the first and only time I lost toleration for the man who was my benefactor and the father of the woman I hoped to call my wife.

"These were living men," said I, "perhaps Jacobites, perhaps the French, perhaps pirates, perhaps adventurers come here to seek the Spanish treasure ship; but, whatever they may be, dangerous at least to your daughter and my cousin. As for your own guilty terrors, man, the dead sleeps well where you have laid him. I stood this morning by his grave; he will not wake before the trump of doom."

My kinsman looked upon me, blinking, while I spoke; then he fixed his eyes for a little on the ground, and pulled his fingers foolishly; but it was plain that he was past the power of speech.

"Come," said I. "You must think for others. You must come up the hill with me, and see this ship."

He obeyed without a word or a look, following slowly after my impatient strides. The spring seemed to have gone out of his body, and he scrambled heavily up and down the rocks, instead of leaping, as he was wont, from one to another. Nor could I, for all my cries, induce him to make better haste. Only once he replied to me complainingly, and like one in bodily pain: "Ay, ay, man, I'm coming." Long before we had reached the top, I had no other thought for him but pity. If the crime had been monstrous the punishment was in proportion.

At last we emerged above the sky-line of the hill, and could see around us. All was black and stormy to the eye; the last gleam of sun had vanished; a wind had sprung up, not yet high, but gusty and unsteady to the point; the rain, on the other hand, had ceased. Short as was the interval, the sea already ran vastly higher than when I had stood there last; already it had begun to break over some of the outward reefs, and already it moaned aloud in the sea-caves of Aros. I looked, at first, in vain for the schooner.

"There she is," I said at last. But her new position, and the course she was now lying, puzzled me. "They cannot mean to beat to sea," I cried.

"That's what they mean," said my uncle, with something like joy; and just then the schooner went about and stood upon another tack, which put the question beyond the reach of doubt. These strangers, seeing a gale on hand, had thought first of sea-room. With the wind that threatened, in these reef-sown waters and contending against so violent a stream of tide, their course was certain death.

"Good God!" said I, "they are all lost."

"Ay," returned my uncle, "a'—a' lost. They hadnae a chance but to rin for Kyle Dona. The gate they're gaun the noo, they couldnae win through an the muckle deil were there to pilot them. Eh, man," he continued, touching me on the sleeve, "it's a braw nicht for a shipwreck! Twa in ae twalmonth! Eh, but the Merry Men'll dance bonny!"

I looked at him, and it was then that I began to fancy him no longer in his right mind. He was peering up to me, as if for sympathy, a timid joy in his eyes. All that had passed between us was already forgotten in the prospect of this fresh disaster.

"If it were not too late," I cried with indignation, "I would take the coble and go out to warn them."

"Na, na," he protested, "ye maunnae interfere; ye maunnae meddle wi' the like o' that. It's His"—doffing his bonnet—"His wull. And, eh, man! but it's a braw nicht for't!"

Something like fear began to creep into my soul and, reminding him that I had not yet dined, I proposed we should return to the house. But no; nothing would tear him from his place of outlook.

"I maun see the hail thing, man, Cherlie," he explained—and then as the schooner went about a second time, "Eh, but they han'le her bonny!" he cried. "The Christ-Anna was naething to this."

Already the men on board the schooner must have begun to realise some part, but not yet the twentieth, of the dangers that environed their doomed ship. At every lull of the capricious wind they must have seen how fast the current swept them back. Each tack was made shorter, as they saw how little it prevailed. Every moment the rising swell began to boom and foam upon another sunken reef; and ever and again a breaker would fall in sounding ruin under the very bows of her, and the brown reef and streaming tangle appear in the hollow of the wave. I tell you, they had to stand to their tackle: there was no idle men aboard that ship, God knows. It was upon the progress of a scene so horrible to any human-hearted man that my misguided uncle now pored and gloated like a connoisseur. As I turned to go down the hill, he was lying on his belly on the summit, with his hands stretched forth and clutching in the heather. He seemed rejuvenated, mind and body.

When I got back to the house already dismally affected, I was still more sadly downcast at the sight of Mary. She had her sleeves rolled up over her strong arms, and was quietly making bread. I got a bannock from the dresser and sat down to eat it in silence.

"Are ye wearied, lad?" she asked after a while.

"I am not so much wearied, Mary," I replied, getting on my feet, "as I am weary of delay, and perhaps of Aros too. You know me well enough to judge me fairly, say what I like. Well, Mary, you may be sure of this: you had better be anywhere but here."

"I'll be sure of one thing," she returned: "I'll be where my duty is."

"You forget, you have a duty to yourself," I said.

"Ay, man?" she replied, pounding at the dough; "will you have found that in the Bible, now?"

"Mary," I said solemnly, "you must not laugh at me just now. God knows I am in no heart for laughing. If we could get your father with us, it would be best; but with him or without him, I want you far away from here, my girl; for your own sake, and for mine, ay, and for your father's too, I want you far—far away from here. I came with other thoughts; I came here as a man comes home; now it is all changed, and I have no desire nor hope but to flee—for that's the word—flee, like a bird out of the fowler's snare, from this accursed island."

She had stopped her work by this time.

"And do you think, now," said she, "do you think, now, I have neither eyes nor ears? Do ye think I havenae broken my heart to have these braws (as he calls them, God forgive him!) thrown into the sea? Do ye think I have lived with him, day in, day out, and not seen what you saw in an hour or two? No," she said, "I know there's wrong in it; what wrong, I neither know nor want to know. There was never an ill thing made better by meddling, that I could hear of. But, my lad, you must never ask me to leave my father. While the breath is in his body, I'll be with him. And he's not long for here, either: that I can tell you, Charlie—he's not long for here. The mark is on his brow; and better so—maybe better so."

I was a while silent, not knowing what to say; and when I roused my head at last to speak, she got before me.

"Charlie," she said, "what's right for me, neednae be right for you. There's sin upon this house and trouble; you are a stranger; take your things upon your back and go your ways to better places and to better folk, and if you were ever minded to come back, though it were twenty years syne, you would find me aye waiting."

"Mary Ellen," I said, "I asked you to be my wife, and you said as good as yes. That's done for good. Wherever you are, I am; as I shall answer to my God."

As I said the words, the wind suddenly burst out raving, and then seemed to stand still and shudder round the house of Aros. It was the first squall, or prologue, of the coming tempest, and as we started and looked about us, we found that a gloom, like the approach of evening, had settled round the house.

"God pity all poor folks at sea!" she said. "We'll see no more of my father till the morrow's morning."

And then she told me, as we sat by the fire and hearkened to the rising gusts, of how this change had fallen upon my uncle. All last winter he had been dark and fitful in his mind. Whenever the Roost ran high, or, as Mary said, whenever the Merry Men were dancing, he would lie out for hours together on the Head, if it were at night, or on the top of Aros by day, watching the tumult of the sea, and sweeping the horizon for a sail. After February the tenth, when the wealth-bringing wreck was cast ashore at Sandag, he had been at first unnaturally gay, and his excitement had never fallen in degree, but only changed in kind from dark to darker. He neglected his work, and kept Rorie idle. They two would speak together by the hour at the gable end, in guarded tones and with an air of secrecy and almost of guilt; and if she questioned either, as at first she sometimes did, her inquiries were put aside with confusion. Since Rorie had first remarked the fish that hung about the ferry, his master had never set foot but once upon the mainland of the Ross. That once—it was in the height of the springs—he had passed dryshod while the tide was out; but, having lingered overlong on the far side, found himself cut off from Aros by the returning waters. It was with a shriek of agony that he had leaped across the gut, and he had reached home thereafter in a fever-fit of fear. A fear of the sea, a constant haunting thought of the sea, appeared in his talk and devotions, and even in his looks when he was silent.

Rorie alone came in to supper; but a little later my uncle appeared, took a bottle under his arm, put some bread in his pocket, and set forth again to his outlook, followed this time by Rorie. I heard that the schooner was losing ground, but the crew were still fighting every inch with hopeless ingenuity and course; and the news filled my mind with blackness.

A little after sundown the full fury of the gale broke forth, such a gale as I have never seen in summer, nor, seeing how swiftly it had come, even in winter. Mary and I sat in silence, the house quaking overhead, the tempest howling without, the fire between us sputtering with raindrops. Our thoughts were far away with the poor fellows on the schooner, or my not less unhappy uncle, houseless on the promontory; and yet ever and again we were startled back to ourselves, when the wind would rise and strike the gable like a solid body, or suddenly fall and draw away, so that the fire leaped into flame and our hearts bounded in our sides. Now the storm in its might would seize and shake the four corners of the roof, roaring like Leviathan in anger. Anon, in a lull, cold eddies of tempest moved shudderingly in the room, lifting the hair upon our heads and passing between us as we sat. And again the wind would break forth in a chorus of melancholy sounds, hooting low in the chimney, wailing with flutelike softness round the house.

It was perhaps eight o'clock when Rorie came in and pulled me mysteriously to the door. My uncle, it appeared, had frightened even his constant comrade; and Rorie, uneasy at his extravagance, prayed me to come out and share the watch. I hastened to do as I was asked; the more readily as, what with fear and horror, and the electrical tension of the night, I was myself restless and disposed for action. I told Mary to be under no alarm, for I should be a safeguard on her father; and wrapping myself warmly in a plaid, I followed Rorie into the open air.

The night, though we were so little past midsummer, was as dark as January. Intervals of a groping twilight alternated with spells of utter blackness; and it was impossible to trace the reason of these changes in the flying horror of the sky. The wind blew the breath out of a man's nostrils; all heaven seemed to thunder overhead like one huge sail; and when there fell a momentary lull on Aros, we could hear the gusts dismally sweeping in the distance. Over all the lowlands of the Ross, the wind must have blown as fierce as on the open sea; and God only knows the uproar that was raging around the head of Ben Kyaw. Sheets of mingled spray and rain were driven in our faces. All round the isle of Aros the surf, with an incessant, hammering thunder, beat upon the reefs and beaches. Now louder in one place, now lower in another, like the combinations of orchestral music, the constant mass of sound was hardly varied for a moment. And loud above all this hurly-burly I could hear the changeful voices of the Roost and the intermittent roaring of the Merry Men. At that hour, there flashed into my mind the reason of the name that they were called. For the noise of them seemed almost mirthful, as it out-topped the other noises of the night; or if not mirthful, yet instinct with a portentous joviality. Nay, and it seemed even human. As when savage men have drunk away their reason, and, discarding speech, bawl together in their madness by the hour; so, to my ears, these deadly breakers shouted by Aros in the night.

Arm in arm, and staggering against the wind, Rorie and I won every yard of ground with conscious effort. We slipped on the wet sod, we fell together sprawling on the rocks. Bruised, drenched, beaten, and breathless, it must have taken us near half an hour to get from the house down to the Head that overlooks the Roost. There, it seemed, was my uncle's favourite observatory. Right in the face of it, where the cliff is highest and most sheer, a hump of earth, like a parapet, makes a place of shelter from the common winds, where a man may sit in quiet and see the tide and the mad billows contending at his feet. As he might look down from the window of a house upon some street disturbance, so, from this post, he looks down upon the tumbling of the Merry Men. On such a night, of course, he peers upon a world of blackness, where the waters wheel and boil, where the waves joust together with the noise of an explosion, and the foam towers and vanishes in the twinkling of an eye. Never before had I seen the Merry Men thus violent. The fury, height, and transiency of their spoutings was a thing to be seen and not recounted. High over our heads on the cliff rose their white columns in the darkness; and the same instant, like phantoms, they were gone. Sometimes three at a time would thus aspire and vanish; sometimes a gust took them, and the spray would fall about us, heavy as a wave. And yet the spectacle was rather maddening in its levity than impressive by its force. Thought was beaten down by the confounding uproar—a gleeful vacancy possessed the brains of men, a state akin to madness; and I found myself at times following the dance of the Merry Men as it were a tune upon a jigging instrument.

I first caught sight of my uncle when we were still some yards away in one of the flying glimpses of twilight that chequered the pitch darkness of the night. He was standing up behind the parapet, his head thrown back and the bottle to his mouth. As he put it down, he saw and recognised us with a toss of one hand fleeringly above his head.

"Has he been drinking?" shouted I to Rorie.

"He will aye be drunk when the wind blaws," returned Rorie in the same high key, and it was all that I could do to hear him.

"Then—was he so—in February?" I inquired.

Rorie's "Ay" was a cause of joy to me. The murder, then, had not sprung in cold blood from calculation; it was an act of madness no more to be condemned than to be pardoned. My uncle was a dangerous madman, if you will, but he was not cruel and base as I had feared. Yet what a scene for a carouse, what an incredible vice, was this that the poor man had chosen! I have always thought drunkenness a wild and almost fearful pleasure, rather demoniacal than human; but drunkenness, out here in the roaring blackness, on the edge of a cliff above that hell of waters, the man's head spinning like the Roost, his foot tottering on the edge of death, his ear watching for the signs of ship-wreck, surely that, if it were credible in any one, was morally impossible in a man like my uncle, whose mind was set upon a damnatory creed and haunted by the darkest superstitions. Yet so it was; and, as we reached the bight of shelter and could breathe again, I saw the man's eyes shining in the night with an unholy glimmer.

"Eh, Charlie, man, it's grand!" he cried. "See to them!" he continued, dragging me to the edge of the abyss from whence arose that deafening clamour and those clouds of spray; "see to them dancin', man! Is that no wicked?"

He pronounced the word with gusto, and I thought it suited with the scene.

"They're yowlin' for thon schooner," he went on, his thin, insane voice clearly audible in the shelter of the bank, "an' she's comin' aye nearer, aye nearer, aye nearer an' nearer an' nearer; an' they ken't, the folk kens it, they ken wool it's by wi' them. Charlie, lad, they're a' drunk in yon schooner, a' dozened wi' drink. They were a' drunk in the Christ-Anna, at the hinder end. There's nane could droon at sea wantin' the brandy. Hoot awa, what do you ken?" with a sudden blast of anger. "I tell ye, it cannae be; they droon withoot it. Ha'e," holding out the bottle, "tak' a sowp."

I was about to refuse, but Rorie touched me as if in warning; and indeed I had already thought better of the movement. I took the bottle, therefore, and not only drank freely myself, but contrived to spill even more as I was doing so. It was pure spirit, and almost strangled me to swallow. My kinsman did not observe the loss, but, once more throwing back his head, drained the remainder to the dregs. Then, with a loud laugh, he cast the bottle forth among the Merry Men, who seemed to leap up, shouting to receive it.

"Ha'e, bairns!" he cried, "there's your han'sel. Ye'll get bonnier nor that, or morning."

Suddenly, out in the black night before us, and not two hundred yards away, we heard, at a moment when the wind was silent, the clear note of a human voice. Instantly the wind swept howling down upon the Head, and the Roost bellowed, and churned, and danced with a new fury. But we had heard the sound, and we knew, with agony, that this was the doomed ship now close on ruin, and that what we had heard was the voice of her master issuing his last command. Crouching together on the edge, we waited, straining every sense, for the inevitable end. It was long, however, and to us it seemed like ages, ere the schooner suddenly appeared for one brief instant, relieved against a tower of glimmering foam. I still see her reefed mainsail flapping loose, as the boom fell heavily across the deck; I still see the black outline of the hull, and still think I can distinguish the figure of a man stretched upon the tiller. Yet the whole sight we had of her passed swifter than lightning; the very wave that disclosed her fell burying her for ever; the mingled cry of many voices at the point of death rose and was quenched in the roaring of the Merry Men. And with that the tragedy was at an end. The strong ship, with all her gear, and the lamp perhaps still burning in the cabin, the lives of so many men, precious surely to others, dear, at least, as heaven to themselves, had all, in that one moment, gone down into the surging waters. They were gone like a dream. And the wind still ran and shouted, and the senseless waters in the Roost still leaped and tumbled as before.

How long we lay there together, we three, speechless and motionless, is more than I can tell, but it must have been for long. At length, one by one, and almost mechanically, we crawled back into the shelter of the bank. As I lay against the parapet, wholly wretched and not entirely master of my mind, I could hear my kinsman maundering to himself in an altered and melancholy mood. Now he would repeat to himself with maudlin iteration, "Sic a fecht as they had—sic a sair fecht as they had, puir lads, puir lads!" and anon he would bewail that "a' the gear was as gude's tint," because the ship had gone down among the Merry Men instead of stranding on the shore; and throughout, the name—the Christ-Anna—would come and go in his divagations, pronounced with shuddering awe. The storm all this time was rapidly abating. In half an hour the wind had fallen to a breeze, and the change was accompanied or caused by a heavy, cold, and plumping rain. I must then have fallen asleep, and when I came to myself, drenched, stiff, and unrefreshed, day had already broken, grey, wet, discomfortable day; the wind blew in faint and shifting capfuls, the tide was out, the Roost was at its lowest, and only the strong beating surf round all the coasts of Aros remained to witness of the furies of the night.

CHAPTER V.
A MAN OUT OF THE SEA.

Rorie set out for the house in search of warmth and breakfast; but my uncle was bent upon examining the shores of Aros, and I felt it a part of duty to accompany him throughout. He was now docile and quiet, but tremulous and weak in mind and body; and it was with the eagerness of a child that he pursued his exploration. He climbed far down upon the rocks; on the beaches, he pursued the retreating breakers. The merest broken plank or rag of cordage was a treasure in his eyes to be secured at the peril of his life. To see him, with weak and stumbling footsteps, expose himself to the pursuit of the surf, or the snares and pitfalls of the weedy rock, kept me in a perpetual terror. My arm was ready to support him, my hand clutched him by the skirt, I helped him to draw his pitiful discoveries beyond the reach of the returning wave; a nurse accompanying a child of seven would have had no different experience.

Yet, weakened as he was by the reaction from his madness of the night before, the passions that smouldered in his nature were those of a strong man. His terror of the sea, although conquered for the moment, was still undiminished; had the sea been a lake of living flames, he could not have shrunk more panically from its touch; and once, when his foot slipped and he plunged to the midleg into a pool of water, the shriek that came up out of his soul was like the cry of death. He sat still for a while, panting like a dog, after that; but his desire for the spoils of shipwreck triumphed once more over his fears; once more he tottered among the curded foam; once more he crawled upon the rocks among the bursting bubbles; once more his whole heart seemed to be set on driftwood, fit, if it was fit for anything, to throw upon the fire. Pleased as he was with what he found, he still incessantly grumbled at his ill-fortune.

"Aros," he said, "is no a place for wrecks ava'—no ava'. A' the years I've dwalt here, this ane maks the second; and the best o' the gear clean tint!"

"Uncle," said I, for we were now on a stretch of open sand, where there was nothing to divert his mind, "I saw you last night, as I never thought to see you—you were drunk."

"Na, na," he said, "no as bad as that. I had been drinking, though. And to tell ye the God's truth, it's a thing I cannae mend. There's nae soberer man than me in my ordnar; but when I hear the wind blaw in my lug, it's my belief that I gang gyte."

"You are a religious man," I replied, "and this is sin'.

"Ou," he returned, "if it wasnae sin, I dinnae ken that I would care for't. Ye see, man, it's defiance. There's a sair spang o' the auld sin o' the warld in you sea; it's an unchristian business at the best o't; an' whiles when it gets up, an' the wind skreights—the wind an' her are a kind of sib, I'm thinkin'—an' thae Merry Men, the daft callants, blawin' and lauchin', and puir souls in the deid thraws warstlin' the leelang nicht wi' their bit ships—weel, it comes ower me like a glamour. I'm a deil, I ken't. But I think naething o' the puir sailor lads; I'm wi' the sea, I'm just like ane o' her ain Merry Men."

I thought I should touch him in a joint of his harness. I turned me towards the sea; the surf was running gaily, wave after wave, with their manes blowing behind them, riding one after another up the beach, towering, curving, falling one upon another on the trampled sand. Without, the salt air, the scared gulls, the widespread army of the sea-chargers, neighing to each other, as they gathered together to the assault of Aros; and close before us, that line on the flat sands that, with all their number and their fury, they might never pass.

"Thus far shalt thou go," said I, "and no farther." And then I quoted as solemnly as I was able a verse that I had often before fitted to the chorus of the breakers:—

But yet the Lord that is on high,
Is more of might by far,
Than noise of many waters is,
As great sea billows are.

"Ay," said my kinsinan, "at the hinder end, the Lord will triumph; I dinnae misdoobt that. But here on earth, even silly men-folk daur Him to His face. It is nae wise; I am nae sayin' that it's wise; but it's the pride of the eye, and it's the lust o' life, an' it's the wale o' pleesures."

I said no more, for we had now begun to cross a neck of land that lay between us and Sandag; and I withheld my last appeal to the man's better reason till we should stand upon the spot associated with his crime. Nor did he pursue the subject; but he walked beside me with a firmer step. The call that I had made upon his mind acted like a stimulant, and I could see that he had forgotten his search for worthless jetsam, in a profound, gloomy, and yet stirring train of thought. In three or four minutes we had topped the brae and begun to go down upon Sandag. The wreck had been roughly handled by the sea; the stem had been spun round and dragged a little lower down; and perhaps the stern had been forced a little higher, for the two parts now lay entirely separate on the beach. When we came to the grave I stopped, uncovered my head in the thick rain, and, looking my kinsman in the face, addressed him.

"A man," said I, "was in God's providence suffered to escape from mortal dangers; he was poor, he was naked, he was wet, he was weary, he was a stranger; he had every claim upon the bowels of your compassion; it may be that he was the salt of the earth, holy, helpful, and kind; it may be he was a man laden with iniquities to whom death was the beginning of torment. I ask you in the sight of heaven: Gordon Darnaway, where is the man for whom Christ died?"

He started visibly at the last words; but there came no answer, and his face expressed no feeling but a vague alarm.

"You were my father's brother," I continued; "You, have taught me to count your house as if it were my father's house; and we are both sinful men walking before the Lord among the sins and dangers of this life. It is by our evil that God leads us into good; we sin, I dare not say by His temptation, but I must say with His consent; and to any but the brutish man his sins are the beginning of wisdom. God has warned you by this crime; He warns you still by the bloody grave between our feet; and if there shall follow no repentance, no improvement, no return to Him, what can we look for but the following of some memorable judgment?"

Even as I spoke the words, the eyes of my uncle wandered from my face. A change fell upon his looks that cannot be described; his features seemed to dwindle in size, the colour faded from his cheeks, one hand rose waveringly and pointed over my shoulder into the distance, and the oft-repeated name fell once more from his lips: "The Christ-Anna!"

I turned; and if I was not appalled to the same degree, as I return thanks to Heaven that I had not the cause, I was still startled by the sight that met my eyes. The form of a man stood upright on the cabin-hutch of the wrecked ship; his back was towards us; he appeared to be scanning the offing with shaded eyes, and his figure was relieved to its full height, which was plainly very great, against the sea and sky. I have said a thousand times that I am not superstitious; but at that moment, with my mind running upon death and sin, the unexplained appearance of a stranger on that sea-girt, solitary island filled me with a surprise that bordered close on terror. It seemed scarce possible that any human soul should have come ashore alive in such a sea as had rated last night along the coasts of Aros; and the only vessel within miles had gone down before our eyes among the Merry Men. I was assailed with doubts that made suspense unbearable, and, to put the matter to the touch at once, stepped forward and hailed the figure like a ship.

He turned about, and I thought he started to behold us. At this my courage instantly revived, and I called and signed to him to draw near, and he, on his part, dropped immediately to the sands, and began slowly to approach, with many stops and hesitations. At each repeated mark of the man's uneasiness I grew the more confident myself; and I advanced another step, encouraging him as I did so with my head and hand. It was plain the castaway had heard indifferent accounts of our island hospitality; and indeed, about this time, the people farther north had a sorry reputation.

"Why," I said, "the man is black!"

And just at that moment, in a voice that I could scarce have recognised, my kinsman began swearing and praying in a mingled stream. I looked at him; he had fallen on his knees, his face was agonised; at each step of the castaway's the pitch of his voice rose, the volubility of his utterance and the fervour of his language redoubled. I call it prayer, for it was addressed to God; but surely no such ranting incongruities were ever before addressed to the Creator by a creature: surely if prayer can be a sin, this mad harangue was sinful. I ran to my kinsman, I seized him by the shoulders, I dragged him to his feet.

"Silence, man," said I, "respect your God in words, if not in action. Here, on the very scene of your transgressions, He sends you an occasion of atonement. Forward and embrace it; welcome like a father yon creature who comes trembling to your mercy."

With that, I tried to force him towards the black; but he felled me to the ground, burst from my grasp, leaving the shoulder of his jacket, and fled up the hillside towards the top of Aros like a deer. I staggered to my feet again, bruised and somewhat stunned; the negro had paused in surprise, perhaps in terror, some halfway between me and the wreck; my uncle was already far away, bounding from rock to rock; and I thus found myself torn for a time between two duties. But I judged, and I pray Heaven that I judged rightly, in favour of the poor wretch upon the sands; his misfortune was at least not plainly of his own creation; it was one, besides, that I could certainly relieve; and I had begun by that time to regard my uncle as an incurable and dismal lunatic. I advanced accordingly towards the black, who now awaited my approach with folded arms, like one prepared for either destiny. As I came nearer, he reached forth his hand with a great gesture, such as I had seen from the pulpit, and spoke to me in something of a pulpit voice, but not a word was comprehensible. I tried him first in English, then in Gaelic, both in vain; so that it was clear we must rely upon the tongue of looks and gestures. Thereupon I signed to him to follow me, which he did readily and with a grave obeisance like a fallen king; all the while there had come no shade of alteration in his face, neither of anxiety while he was still waiting, nor of relief now that he was reassured; if he were a slave, as I supposed, I could not but judge he must have fallen from some high place in his own country, and fallen as he was, I could not but admire his bearing. As we passed the grave, I paused and raised my hands and eyes to heaven in token of respect and sorrow for the dead; and he, as if in answer, bowed low and spread his hands abroad; it was a strange motion, but done like a thing of common custom; and I supposed it was ceremonial in the land from which he came. At the same time he pointed to my uncle, whom we could just see perched upon a knoll, and touched his head to indicate that he was mad.

We took the long way round the shore, for I feared to excite my uncle if we struck across the island; and as we walked, I had time enough to mature the little dramatic exhibition by which I hoped to satisfy my doubts. Accordingly, pausing on a rock, I proceeded to imitate before the negro the action of the man whom I had seen the day before taking bearings with the compass at Sandag. He understood me at once, and, taking the imitation out of my hands, showed me where the boat was, pointed out seaward as if to indicate the position of the schooner, and then down along the edge of the rock with the words "Espirito Santo," strangely pronounced, but clear enough for recognition. I had thus been right in my conjecture; the pretended historical inquiry had been but a cloak for treasure-hunting; the man who had played on Dr. Robertson was the same as the foreigner who visited Grisapol in spring, and now, with many others, lay dead under the Roost of Aros: there had their greed brought them, there should their bones be tossed for evermore. In the meantime the black continued his imitation of the scene, now looking up skyward as though watching the approach of the storm now, in the character of a seaman, waving the rest to come aboard; now as an officer, running along the rock and entering the boat; and anon bending over imaginary oars with the air of a hurried boatman; but all with the same solemnity of manner, so that I was never even moved to smile. Lastly, he indicated to me, by a pantomime not to be described in words, how he himself had gone up to examine the stranded wreck, and, to his grief and indignation, had been deserted by his comrades; and thereupon folded his arms once more, and stooped his head, like one accepting fate.

The mystery of his presence being thus solved for me, I explained to him by means of a sketch the fate of the vessel and of all aboard her. He showed no surprise nor sorrow, and, with a sudden lifting of his open hand, seemed to dismiss his former friends or masters (whichever they had been) into God's pleasure. Respect came upon me and grew stronger, the more I observed him; I saw he had a powerful mind and a sober and severe character, such as I loved to commune with; and before we reached the house of Aros I had almost forgotten, and wholly forgiven him, his uncanny colour.

To Mary I told all that had passed without suppression, though I own my heart failed me; but I did wrong to doubt her sense of justice.

"You did the right," she said. "God's will be done." And she set out meat for us at once.

As soon as I was satisfied, I bade Rorie keep an eye upon the castaway, who was still eating, and set forth again myself to find my uncle. I had not gone far before I saw him sitting in the same place, upon the very topmost knoll, and seemingly in the same attitude as when I had last observed him. From that point, as I have said, the most of Aros and the neighbouring Ross would be spread below him like a map; and it was plain that he kept a bright look-out in all directions, for my head had scarcely risen above the summit of the first ascent before he had leaped to his feet and turned as if to face me. I hailed him at once, as well as I was able, in the same tones and words as I had often used before, when I had come to summon him to dinner. He made not so much as a movement in reply. I passed on a little farther, and again tried parley, with the same result. But when I began a second time to advance, his insane fears blazed up again, and still in dead silence, but with incredible speed, he began to flee from before me along the rocky summit of the hill. An hour before, he had been dead weary, and I had been comparatively active. But now his strength was recruited by the fervour of insanity, and it would have been vain for me to dream of pursuit. Nay, the very attempt, I thought, might have inflamed his terrors, and thus increased the miseries of our position. And I had nothing left but to turn homeward and make my sad report to Mary.

She heard it, as she had heard the first, with a concerned composure, and, bidding me lie down and take that rest of which I stood so much in need, set forth herself in quest of her misguided father. At that age it would have been a strange thing that put me from either meat or sleep; I slept long and deep; and it was already long past noon before I awoke and came downstairs into the kitchen. Mary, Rorie, and the black castaway were seated about the fire in silence; and I could see that Mary had been weeping. There was cause enough, as I soon learned, for tears. First she, and then Rorie, had been forth to seek my uncle; each in turn had found him perched upon the hill-top, and from each in turn he had silently and swiftly fled. Rorie had tried to chase him, but in vain; madness lent a new vigour to his bounds; he sprang from rock to rock over the widest gullies; he scoured like the wind along the hill-tops; he doubled and twisted like a hare before the dogs; and Rorie at length gave in; and the last that he saw, my uncle was seated as before upon the crest of Aros. Even during the hottest excitement of the chase, even when the fleet-footed servant had come, for a moment, very near to capture him, the poor lunatic had uttered not a sound. He fled, and he was silent, like a beast; and this silence had terrified his pursuer.

There was something heart-breaking in the situation. How to capture the madman, how to feed him in the meanwhile, and what to do with him when he was captured, were the three difficulties that we had to solve.

"The black," said I, "is the cause of this attack. It may even be his presence in the house that keeps my uncle on the hill. We have done the fair thing; he has been fed and warmed under this roof; now I propose that Rorie put him across the bay in the coble, and take him through the Ross as far as Grisapol."

In this proposal Mary heartily concurred; and bidding the black follow us, we all three descended to the pier. Certainly, Heaven's will was declared against Gordon Darnaway; a thing had happened, never paralleled before in Aros; during the storm, the coble had broken loose, and, striking on the rough splinters of the pier, now lay in four feet of water with one side stove in. Three days of work at least would be required to make her float. But I was not to be beaten. I led the whole party round to where the gut was narrowest, swam to the other side, and called to the black to follow me. He signed, with the same clearness and quiet as before, that he knew not the art; and there was truth apparent in his signals, it would have occurred to none of us to doubt his truth; and that hope being over, we must all go back even as we came to the house of Aros, the negro walking in our midst without embarrassment.

All we could do that day was to make one more attempt to communicate with the unhappy madman. Again he was visible on his perch; again he fled in silence. But food and a great cloak were at least left for his comfort; the rain, besides, had cleared away, and the night promised to be even warm. We might compose ourselves, we thought, until the morrow; rest was the chief requisite, that we might be strengthened for unusual exertions; and as none cared to talk, we separated at an early hour.

I lay long awake, planning a campaign for the morrow. I was to place the black on the side of Sandag, whence he should head my uncle towards the house; Rorie in the west, I on the east, were to complete the cordon, as best we might. It seemed to me, the more I recalled the configuration of the island, that it should be possible, though hard, to force him down upon the low ground along Aros Bay; and once there, even with the strength of his madness, ultimate escape was hardly to be feared. It was on his terror of the black that I relied; for I made sure, however he might run, it would not be in the direction of the man whom he supposed to have returned from the dead, and thus one point of the compass at least would be secure.

When at length I fell asleep, it was to be awakened shortly after by a dream of wrecks, black men, and submarine adventure; and I found myself so shaken and fevered that I arose, descended the stair, and stepped out before the house. Within, Rorie and the black were asleep together in the kitchen; outside was a wonderful clear night of stars, with here and there a cloud still hanging, last stragglers of the tempest. It was near the top of the flood, and the Merry Men were roaring in the windless quiet of the night. Never, not even in the height of the tempest, had I heard their song with greater awe. Now, when the winds were gathered home, when the deep was dandling itself back into its summer slumber, and when the stars rained their gentle light over land and sea, the voice of these tide-breakers was still raised for havoc. They seemed, indeed, to be a part of the world's evil and the tragic side of life. Nor were their meaningless vociferations the only sounds that broke the silence of the night. For I could hear, now shrill and thrilling and now almost drowned, the note of a human voice that accompanied the uproar of the Roost. I knew it for my kinsman's; and a great fear fell upon me of God's judgments, and the evil in the world. I went back again into the darkness of the house as into a place of shelter, and lay long upon my bed, pondering these mysteries.

It was late when I again woke, and I leaped into my clothes and hurried to the kitchen. No one was there; Rorie and the black had both stealthily departed long before; and my heart stood still at the discovery. I could rely on Rorie's heart, but I placed no trust in his discretion. If he had thus set out without a word, he was plainly bent upon some service to my uncle. But what service could he hope to render even alone, far less in the company of the man in whom my uncle found his fears incarnated? Even if I were not already too late to prevent some deadly mischief, it was plain I must delay no longer. With the thought I was out of the house; and often as I have run on the rough sides of Aros, I never ran as I did that fatal morning. I do not believe I put twelve minutes to the whole ascent.

My uncle was gone from his perch. The basket had indeed been torn open and the meat scattered on the turf; but, as we found afterwards, no mouthful had been tasted; and there was not another trace of human existence in that wide field of view. Day had already filled the clear heavens; the sun already lighted in a rosy bloom upon the crest of Ben Kyaw; but all below me the rude knolls of Aros and the shield of sea lay steeped in the clear darkling twilight of the dawn.

"Rorie!" I cried; and again "Rorie!" My voice died in the silence, but there came no answer back. If there were indeed an enterprise afoot to catch my uncle, it was plainly not in fleetness of foot, but in dexterity of stalking, that the hunters placed their trust. I ran on farther, keeping the higher spurs, and looking right and left, nor did I pause again till I was on the mount above Sandag. I could see the wreck, the uncovered belt of sand, the waves idly beating, the long ledge of rocks, and on either hand the tumbled knolls, boulders, and gullies of the island. But still no human thing.

At a stride the sunshine fell on Aros, and the shadows and colours leaped into being. Not half a moment later, below me to the west, sheep began to scatter as in a panic. There came a cry. I saw my uncle running. I saw the black jump up in hot pursuit; and before I had time to understand, Rorie also had appeared, calling directions in Gaelic as to a dog herding sheep.

I took to my heels to interfere, and perhaps I had done better to have waited where I was, for I was the means of cutting off the madman's last escape. There was nothing before him from that moment but the grave, the wreck, and the sea in Sandag Bay. And yet Heaven knows that what I did was for the best.

My uncle Gordon saw in what direction, horrible to him, the chase was driving him. He doubled, darting to the right and left; but high as the fever ran in his veins, the black was still the swifter. Turn where he would, he was still forestalled, still driven toward the scene of his crime. Suddenly he began to shriek aloud, so that the coast re-echoed; and now both I and Rorie were calling on the black to stop. But all was vain, for it was written otherwise. The pursuer still ran, the chase still sped before him screaming; they avoided the grave, and skimmed close past the timbers of the wreck; in a breath they had cleared the sand; and still my kinsman did not pause, but dashed straight into the surf; and the black, now almost within reach, still followed swiftly behind him. Rorie and I both stopped, for the thing was now beyond the hands of men, and these were the decrees of God that came to pass before our eyes. There was never a sharper ending. On that steep beach they were beyond their depth at a bound; neither could swim; the black rose once for a moment with a throttling cry; but the current had them, racing seaward; and if ever they came up again, which God alone can tell, it would be ten minutes after, at the far end of Aros Roost, where the seabirds hover fishing.

WILL O' THE MILL.

CHAPTER I.
THE PLAIN AND THE STARS.

The Mill here Will lived with his adopted parents stood in a falling valley between pinewoods and great mountains. Above, hill after hill, soared upwards until they soared out of the depth of the hardiest timber, and stood naked against the sky. Some way up, a long grey village lay like a seam or a ray of vapour on a wooded hillside; and when the wind was favourable, the sound of the church bells would drop down, thin and silvery, to Will. Below, the valley grew ever steeper and steeper, and at the same time widened out on either hand; and from an eminence beside the mill it was possible to see its whole length and away beyond it over a wide plain, where the river turned and shone, and moved on from city to city on its voyage towards the sea. It chanced that over this valley there lay a pass into a neighbouring kingdom; so that, quiet and rural as it was, the road that ran along beside the river was a high thoroughfare between two splendid and powerful societies. All through the summer, travelling-carriages came crawling up, or went plunging briskly downwards past the mill; and as it happened that the other side was very much easier of ascent, the path was not much frequented, except by people going in one direction; and of all the carriages that Will saw go by, five-sixths were plunging briskly downwards and only one-sixth crawling up. Much more was this the case with foot-passengers. All the light-footed tourists, all the pedlars laden with strange wares, were tending downward like the river that accompanied their path. Nor was this all; for when Will was yet a child a disastrous war arose over a great part of the world. The newspapers were full of defeats and victories, the earth rang with cavalry hoofs, and often for days together and for miles around the coil of battle terrified good people from their labours in the field. Of all this, nothing was heard for a long time in the valley; but at last one of the commanders pushed an army over the pass by forced marches, and for three days horse and foot, cannon and tumbril, drum and standard, kept pouring downward past the mill. All day the child stood and watched them on their passage—the rhythmical stride, the pale, unshaven faces tanned about the eyes, the discoloured regimentals and the tattered flags, filled him with a sense of weariness, pity, and wonder; and all night long, after he was in bed, he could hear the cannon pounding and the feet trampling, and the great armament sweeping onward and downward past the mill. No one in the valley ever heard the fate of the expedition, for they lay out of the way of gossip in those troublous times; but Will saw one thing plainly, that not a man returned. Whither had they all gone? Whither went all the tourists and pedlars with strange wares? whither all the brisk barouches with servants in the dicky? whither the water of the stream, ever coursing downward and ever renewed from above? Even the wind blew oftener down the valley, and carried the dead leaves along with it in the fall. It seemed like a great conspiracy of things animate and inanimate; they all went downward, fleetly and gaily downward, and only he, it seemed, remained behind, like a stock upon the wayside. It sometimes made him glad when he noticed how the fishes kept their heads up stream. They, at least, stood faithfully by him, while all else were posting downward to the unknown world.

One evening he asked the miller where the river went.

"It goes down the valley," answered he, "and turns a power of mills—six score mills, they say, from here to Unterdeck—and is none the wearier after all. And then it goes out into the lowlands, and waters the great corn country, and runs through a sight of fine cities (so they say) where kings live all alone in great palaces, with a sentry walling up and down before the door. And it goes under bridges with stone men upon them, looking down and smiling so curious it the water, and living folks leaning their elbows on the wall and looking over too. And then it goes on and on, and down through marshes and sands, until at last it falls into the sea, where the ships are that bring parrots and tobacco from the Indies. Ay, it has a long trot before it as it goes singing over our weir, bless its heart!"

"And what is the sea?" asked Will.

"The sea!" cried the miller. "Lord help us all, it is the greatest thing God made! That is where all the water in the world runs down into a great salt lake. There it lies, as flat as my hand and as innocent-like as a child; but they do say when the wind blows it gets up into water-mountains bigger than any of ours, and swallows down great ships bigger than our mill, and makes such a roaring that you can hear it miles away upon the land. There are great fish in it five times bigger than a bull, and one old serpent as long as our river and as old as all the world, with whiskers like a man, and a crown of silver on her head."

Will thought he had never heard anything like this, and he kept on asking question after question about the world that lay away down the river, with all its perils and marvels, until the old miller became quite interested himself, and at last took him by the hand and led him to the hilltop that overlooks the valley and the plain. The sun was near setting, and hung low down in a cloudless sky. Everything was defined and glorified in golden light. Will had never seen so great an expanse of country in his life; he stood and gazed with all his eyes. He could see the cities, and the woods and fields, and the bright curves of the river, and far away to where the rim of the plain trenched along the shining heavens. An over-mastering emotion seized upon the boy, soul and body; his heart beat so thickly that he could not breathe; the scene swam before his eyes; the sun seemed to wheel round and round, and throw off, as it turned, strange shapes which disappeared with the rapidity of thought, and were succeeded by others. Will covered his face with his hands, and burst into a violent fit of tears; and the poor miller, sadly disappointed and perplexed, saw nothing better for it than to take him up in his arms and carry him home in silence.

From that day forward Will was full of new hopes and longings. Something kept tugging at his heart-strings; the running water carried his desires along with it as he dreamed over its fleeting surface; the wind, as it ran over innumerable tree-tops, hailed him with encouraging words; branches beckoned downward; the open road, as it shouldered round the angles and went turning and vanishing fast and faster down the valley, tortured him with its solicitations. He spent long whiles on the eminence, looking down the rivershed and abroad on the fat lowlands, and watched the clouds that travelled forth upon the sluggish wind and trailed their purple shadows on the plain; or he would linger by the wayside, and follow the carriages with his eyes as they rattled downward by the river. It did not matter what it was; everything that went that way, were it cloud or carriage, bird or brown water in the stream, he felt his heart flow out after it in an ecstasy of longing.

We are told by men of science that all the ventures of mariners on the sea, all that countermarching of tribes and races that confounds old history with its dust and rumour, sprang from nothing more abstruse than the laws of supply and demand, and a certain natural instinct for cheap rations. To any one thinking deeply, this will seem a dull and pitiful explanation. The tribes that came swarming out of the North and East, if they were indeed pressed onward from behind by others, were drawn at the same time by the magnetic influence of the South and West. The fame of other lands had reached them; the name of the eternal city rang in their ears; they were not colonists, but pilgrims; they travelled towards wine and gold and sunshine, but their hearts were set on something higher. That divine unrest, that old stinging trouble of humanity that makes all high achievements and all miserable failure, the same that spread wings with Icarus, the same that sent Columbus into the desolate Atlantic, inspired and supported these barbarians on their perilous march. There is one legend which profoundly represents their spirit, of how a flying party of these wanderers encountered a very old man shod with iron. The old man asked them whither they were going; and they answered with one voice: "To the Eternal City!" He looked upon them gravely. "I have sought it," he said, "over the most part of the world. Three such pairs as I now carry on my feet have I worn out upon this pilgrimage, and now the fourth is growing slender underneath my steps. And all this while I have not found the city." And he turned and went his own way alone, leaving them astonished.

And yet this would scarcely parallel the intensity of Will's feeling for the plain. If he could only go far enough out there, he felt as if his eyesight would be purged and clarified, as if his hearing would grow more delicate, and his very breath would come and go with luxury. He was transplanted and withering where he was; he lay in a strange country and was sick for home. Bit by bit, he pieced together broken notions of the world below: of the river, ever moving and growing until it sailed forth into the majestic ocean; of the cities, full of brisk and beautiful people, playing fountains, bands of music and marble palaces, and lighted up at night from end to end with artificial stars of gold; of the great churches, wise universities, brave armies, and untold money lying stored in vaults; of the high-flying vice that moved in the sunshine, and the stealth and swiftness of midnight murder. I have said he was sick as if for home: the figure halts. He was like some one lying in twilit, formless preexistence, and stretching out his hands lovingly towards many-coloured, many-sounding life. It was no wonder he was unhappy, he would go and tell the fish: they were made for their life, wished for no more than worms and running water, and a hole below a falling bank; but he was differently designed, full of desires and aspirations, itching at the fingers, lusting with the eyes, whom the whole variegated world could not satisfy with aspects. The true life, the true bright sunshine, lay far out upon the plain. And O! to see this sunlight once before he died! to move with a jocund spirit in a golden land! to hear the trained singers and sweet church bells, and see the holiday gardens! "And O fish!" he would cry, "if you would only turn your noses down stream, you could swim so easily into the fabled waters and see the vast ships passing over your head like clouds, and hear the great water-hills making music over you all day long!" But the fish kept looking patiently in their own direction, until Will hardly knew whether to laugh or cry.

Hitherto the traffic on the road had passed by Will, like something seen in a picture: he had perhaps exchanged salutations with a tourist, or caught sight of an old gentleman in a travelling cap at a carriage window; but for the most part it had been a mere symbol, which he contemplated from apart and with something of a superstitious feeling. A time came at last when this was to be changed. The miller, who was a greedy man in his way, and never forewent an opportunity of honest profit, turned the mill-house into a little wayside inn, and, several pieces of good fortune falling in opportunely, built stables and got the position of post master on the road. It now became Will's duty to wait upon people, as they sat to break their fasts in the little arbour at the top of the mill garden; and you may be sure that he kept his ears open, and learned many new things about the outside world as he brought the omelette or the wine. Nay, he would often get into conversation with single guests, and by adroit questions and polite attention, not only gratify his own curiosity, but win the goodwill of the travellers. Many complimented the old couple on their serving-boy; and a professor was eager to take him away with him, and have him properly educated in the plain. The miller and his wife were mightily astonished and even more pleased. They thought it a very good thing that they should have opened their inn. "You see," the old man would remark, "he has a kind of talent for a publican; he never would have made anything else!" And so life wagged on in the valley, with high satisfaction to all concerned but Will. Every carriage that left the inn-door seemed to take a part of him away with it; and when people jestingly offered him a lift, he could with difficulty command his emotion. Night after night he would dream that he was awakened by flustered servants, and that a splendid equipage waited at the door to carry him down into the plain; night after night; until the dream, which had seemed all jollity to him at first, began to take on a colour of gravity, and the nocturnal summons and waiting equipage occupied a place in his mind as something to be both feared and hoped for.

One day, when Will was about sixteen, a fat young man arrived at sunset to pass the night. He was a contented-looking fellow, with a jolly eye, and carried a knapsack. While dinner was preparing, he sat in the arbour to read a book; but as soon as he had begun to observe Will, the book was laid aside; he was plainly one of those who prefer living people to people made of ink and paper. Will, on his part, although he had not been much interested in the stranger at first sight, soon began to take a great deal of pleasure in his talk, which was full of good nature and good sense, and at last conceived a great respect for his character and wisdom. They sat far into the night; and about two in the morning Will opened his heart to the young man, and told him how he longed to leave the valley and what bright hopes he had connected with the cities of the plain. The young man whistled, and then broke into a smile.

"My young friend," he remarked, "you are a very curious little fellow to be sure, and wish a great many things which you will never get. Why, you would feel quite ashamed if you knew how the little fellows in these fairy cities of yours are all after the same sort of nonsense, and keep breaking their hearts to get up into the mountains. And let me tell you, those who go down into the plains are a very short while there before they wish themselves heartily back again. The air is not so light nor so pure; nor is the sun any brighter. As for the beautiful men and women, you would see many of them in rags and many of them deformed with horrible disorders; and a city is so hard a place for people who are poor and sensitive that many choose to die by their own hand."

"You must think me very simple," answered Will. "Although I have never been out of this valley, believe me, I have used my eyes. I know how one thing lives on another; for instance, how the fish hangs in the eddy to catch his fellows; and the shepherd, who makes so pretty a picture carrying home the lamb, is only carrying it home for dinner. I do not expect to find all things right in your cities. That is not what troubles me; it might have been that once upon a time; but although I live here always, I have asked many questions and learned a great deal in these last years, and certainly enough to cure me of my old fancies. But you would not have me die like a dog and not see all that is to be seen, and do all that a man can do, let it be good or evil? you would not have me spend all my days between this road here and the river, and not so much as make a motion to be up and live my life?—I would rather die out of hand," he cried, "than linger on as I am doing."

"Thousands of people," said the young man, "live and die like you, and are none the less happy."

"Ah!" said Will, "if there are thousands who would like, why should not one of them have my place?"

It was quite dark; there was a hanging lamp in the arbour which lit up the table and the faces of the speakers; and along the arch, the leaves upon the trellis stood out illuminated against the night sky, a pattern of transparent green upon a dusky purple. The fat young man rose, and, taking Will by the arm, led him out under the open heavens.

"Did you ever look at the stars?" he asked, pointing upwards.

"Often and often," answered Will.

"And do you know what they are?"

"I have fancied many things."

"They are worlds like ours," said the young man. "Some of them less; many of them a million times greater; and some of the least sparkles that you see are not only worlds, but whole clusters of worlds turning about each other in the midst of space. We do not know what there may be in any of them; perhaps the answer to all our difficulties or the cure of all our sufferings: and yet we can never reach them; not all the skill of the craftiest of men can fit out a ship for the nearest of these our neighbours, nor would the life of the most aged suffice for such a journey. When a great battle has been lost or a dear friend is dead, when we are hipped or in high spirits, there they are unweariedly shining overhead. We may stand down here, a whole army of us together, and shout until we break our hearts, and not a whisper reaches them. We may climb the highest mountain, and we are no nearer them. All we can do is to stand down here in the garden and take off our hats; the starshine lights upon our heads, and where mine is a little bald, I dare say you can see it glisten in the darkness. The mountain and the mouse. That is like to be all we shall ever have to do with Arcturus or Aldebaran. Can you apply a parable?" he added, laying his hand upon Will's shoulder. "It is not the same thing as a reason, but usually vastly more convincing."

Will hung his head a little, and then raised it once more to heaven. The stars seemed to expand and emit a sharper brilliancy; and as he kept turning his eyes higher and higher, they seemed to increase in multitude under his gaze.

"I see," he said, turning to the young man. "We are in a rat-trap."

"Something of that size. Did you ever see a squirrel turning in a cage? and another squirrel sitting philosophically over his nuts? I needn't ask you which of them looked more of a fool."

CHAPTER II.
THE PARSON'S MARJORY.

After some years the old people died, both in one winter, very carefully tended by their adopted son, and very quietly mourned when they were gone. People who had heard of his roving fancies supposed he would hasten to sell the property, and go down the river to push his fortunes. But there was never any sign of such in intention on the part of Will. On the contrary, he had the inn set on a better footing, and hired a couple of servants to assist him in carrying it on; and there he settled down, a kind, talkative, inscrutable young man, six feet three in his stockings, with an iron constitution and a friendly voice. He soon began to take rank in the district as a bit of an oddity: it was not much to be wondered at from the first, for he was always full of notions, and kept calling the plainest common-sense in question; but what most raised the report upon him was the odd circumstance of his courtship with the parson's Marjory.

The parson's Marjory was a lass about nineteen, when Will would be about thirty; well enough looking, and much better educated than any other girl in that part of the country, as became her parentage. She held her head very high, and had already refused several offers of marriage with a grand air, which had got her hard names among the neighbours. For all that she was a good girl, and one that would have made any man well contented.

Will had never seen much of her; for although the church and parsonage were only two miles from his own door, he was never known to go there but on Sundays. It chanced, however, that the parsonage fell into disrepair, and had to be dismantled; and the parson and his daughter took lodgings for a month or so, on very much reduced terms, at Will's inn. Now, what with the inn, and the mill, and the old miller's savings, our friend was a man of substance; and besides that, he had a name for good temper and shrewdness, which make a capital portion in marriage; and so it was currently gossiped, among their ill-wishers, that the parson and his daughter had not chosen their temporary lodging with their eyes shut. Will was about the last man in the world to be cajoled or frightened into marriage. You had only to look into his eyes, limpid and still like pools of water, and yet with a sort of clear light that seemed to come from within, and you would understand at once that here was one who knew his own mind, and would stand to it immovably. Marjory herself was no weakling by her looks, with strong, steady eyes and a resolute and quiet bearing. It might be a question whether she was not Will's match in stedfastness, after all, or which of them would rule the roost in marriage. But Marjory had never given it a thought, and accompanied her father with the most unshaken innocence and unconcern.

The season was still so early that Will's customers were few and far between; but the lilacs were already flowering, and the weather was so mild that the party took dinner under the trellice, with the noise of the river in their ears and the woods ringing about them with the songs of birds. Will soon began to take a particular pleasure in these dinners. The parson was rather a dull companion, with a habit of dozing at table; but nothing rude or cruel ever fell from his lips. And as for the parson's daughter, she suited her surroundings with the best grace imaginable; and whatever she said seemed so pat and pretty that Will conceived a great idea of her talents. He could see her face, as she leaned forward, against a background of rising pinewoods; her eyes shone peaceably; the light lay around her hair like a kerchief; something that was hardly a smile rippled her pale cheeks, and Will could not contain himself from gazing on her in an agreeable dismay. She looked, even in her quietest moments, so complete in herself, and so quick with life down to her finger tips and the very skirts of her dress, that the remainder of created things became no more than a blot by comparison; and if Will glanced away from her to her surroundings, the trees looked inanimate and senseless, the clouds hung in heaven like dead things, and even the mountain tops were disenchanted. The whole valley could not compare in looks with this one girl.

Will was always observant in the society of his fellow-creatures; but his observation became almost painfully eager in the case of Marjory. He listened to all she uttered, and read her eyes, at the same time, for the unspoken commentary. Many kind, simple, and sincere speeches found an echo in his heart. He became conscious of a soul beautifully poised upon itself, nothing doubting, nothing desiring, clothed in peace. It was not possible to separate her thoughts from her appearance. The turn of her wrist, the still sound of her voice, the light in her eyes, the lines of her body, fell in tune with her grave and gentle words, like the accompaniment that sustains and harmonises the voice of the singer. Her influence was one thing, not to be divided or discussed, only to be felt with gratitude and joy. To Will, her presence recalled something of his childhood, and the thought of her took its place in his mind beside that of dawn, of running water, and of the earliest violets and lilacs. It is the property of things seen for the first time, or for the first time after long, like the flowers in spring, to reawaken in us the sharp edge of sense and that impression of mystic strangeness which otherwise passes out of life with the coming of years; but the sight of a loved face is what renews a man's character from the fountain upwards.

One day after dinner Will took a stroll among the firs; a grave beatitude possessed him from top to toe, and he kept smiling to himself and the landscape as he went. The river ran between the stepping-stones with a pretty wimple; a bird sang loudly in the wood; the hill-tops looked immeasurably high, and as he glanced at them from time to time seemed to contemplate his movements with a beneficent but awful curiosity. His way took him to the eminence which overlooked the plain; and there he sat down upon a stone, and fell into deep and pleasant thought. The plain lay abroad with its cities and silver river; everything was asleep, except a great eddy of birds which kept rising and falling and going round and round in the blue air. He repeated Marjory's name aloud, and the sound of it gratified his ear. He shut his eyes, and her image sprang up before him, quietly luminous and attended with good thoughts. The river might run for ever; the birds fly higher and higher till they touched the stars. He saw it was empty bustle after all; for here, without stirring a feet, waiting patiently in his own narrow valley, he also had attained the better sunlight.

The next day Will made a sort of declaration across the dinner-table, while the parson was filling his pipe.

"Miss Marjory," he said, "I never knew any one I liked so well as you. I am mostly a cold, unkindly sort of man; not from want of heart, but out of strangeness in my way of thinking; and people seem far away from me. 'Tis as if there were a circle round me, which kept every one out but you; I can hear the others talking and laughing; but you come quite close. Maybe, this is disagreeable to you?" he asked.

Marjory made no answer.

"Speak up, girl," said the parson.

"Nay, now," returned Will, "I wouldn't press her, parson. I feel tongue-tied myself, who am not used to it; and she's a woman, and little more than a child, when all is said. But for my part, as far as I can understand what people mean by it, I fancy I must be what they call in love. I do not wish to be held as committing myself; for I may be wrong; but that is how I believe things are with me. And if Miss Marjory should feel any otherwise on her part, mayhap she would be so kind as shake her head."

Marjory was silent, and gave no sign that she had heard.

"How is that, parson?" asked Will.

"The girl must speak," replied the parson, laying down his pipe. "Here's our neighbour who says he loves you, Madge. Do you love him, ay or no?"

"I think I do," said Marjory, faintly.

"Well then, that's all that could be wished!" cried Will, heartily. And he took her hand across the table, and held it a moment in both of his with great satisfaction.

"You must marry," observed the parson, replacing his pipe in his mouth.

"Is that the right thing to do, think you?" demanded Will.

"It is indispensable," said the parson.

"Very well," replied the wooer.

Two or three days passed away with great delight to Will, although a bystander might scarce have found it out. He continued to take his meals opposite Marjory, and to talk with her and gaze upon her in her father's presence; but he made no attempt to see her alone, nor in any other way changed his conduct towards her from what it had been since the beginning. Perhaps the girl was a little disappointed, and perhaps not unjustly; and yet if it had been enough to be always in the thoughts of another person, and so pervade and alter his whole life, she might have been thoroughly contented. For she was never out of Will's mind for an instant. He sat over the stream, and watched the dust of the eddy, and the poised fish, and straining weeds; he wandered out alone into the purple even, with all the blackbirds piping round him in the wood; he rose early in the morning, and saw the sky turn from grey to gold, and the light leap upon the hill-tops; and all the while he kept wondering if he had never seen such things before, or how it was that they should look so different now. The sound of his own mill-wheel, or of the wind among the trees, confounded and charmed his heart. The most enchanting thoughts presented themselves unbidden in his mind. He was so happy that he could not sleep at night, and so restless, that he could hardly sit still out of her company. And yet it seemed as if he avoided her rather than sought her out.

One day, as he was coming home from a ramble, Will found Marjory in the garden picking flowers, and as he came up with her, slackened his pace and continued walking by her side.

"You like flowers?" he said.

"Indeed I love them dearly," she replied. "Do you?"

"Why, no," said he, "not so much. They are a very small affair, when all is done. I can fancy people caring for them greatly, but not doing as you are just now."

"How?" she asked, pausing and looking up at him.

"Plucking them," said he. "They are a deal better off where they are, and look a deal prettier, if you go to that."

"I wish to have them for my own," she answered, "to carry them near my heart, and keep them in my room. They tempt me when they grow here; they seem to say, 'Come and do something with us;' but once I have cut them and put them by, the charm is laid, and I can look at them with quite an easy heart."

"You wish to possess them," replied Will, "in order to think no more about them. It's a bit like killing the goose with the golden eggs. It's a bit like what I wished to do when I was a boy. Because I had a fancy for looking out over the plain, I wished to go down there—where

I couldn't look out over it any longer. Was not that fine reasoning? Dear, dear, if they only thought of it, all the world would do like me; and you would let your flowers alone, just as I stay up here in the mountains." Suddenly he broke off sharp. "By the Lord!" he cried. And when she asked him what was wrong, he turned the question off and walked away into the house with rather a humorous expression of face.

He was silent at table; and after the night had fallen and the stars had come out overhead, he walked up and down for hours in the courtyard and garden with an uneven pace. There was still a light in the window of Marjory's room: one little oblong patch of orange in a world of dark blue hills and silver starlight. Will's mind ran a great deal on the window; but his thoughts were not very lover-like. "There she is in her room," he thought, "and there are the stars overhead:—a blessing upon both!" Both were good influences in his life; both soothed and braced him in his profound contentment with the world. And what more should he desire with either? The fat young man and his councils were so present to his mind, that he threw back his head, and, putting his hands before his mouth, shouted aloud to the populous heavens. Whether from the position of his head or the sudden strain of the exertion, he seemed to see a momentary shock among the stars, and a diffusion of frosty light pass from one to another along the sky. At the same instant, a corner of the blind was lifted and lowered again at once. He laughed a loud ho-ho! "One and another!" thought Will. "The stars tremble, and the blind goes up. Why, before Heaven, what a great magician I must be! Now if I were only a fool, should not I be in a pretty way?" And he went off to bed, chuckling to himself: "If I were only a fool!"

The next morning, pretty early, he saw her once more in the garden, and sought her out.

"I have been thinking about getting married," he began abruptly; "and after having turned it all over, I have made up my mind it's not worthwhile."

She turned upon him for a single moment; but his radiant, kindly appearance would, under the circumstances, have disconcerted an angel, and she looked down again upon the ground in silence. He could see her tremble.

"I hope you don't mind," he went on, a little taken aback. "You ought not. I have turned it all over, and upon my soul there's nothing in it. We should never be one whit nearer than we are just now, and, if I am a wise man, nothing like so happy."

"It is unnecessary to go round about with me," she said. "I very well remember that you refused to commit yourself; and now that I see you were mistaken, and in reality have never cared for me, I can only feel sad that I have been so far misled."

"I ask your pardon," said Will stoutly; "you do not understand my meaning. As to whether I have ever loved you or not, I must leave that to others. But for one thing, my feeling is not changed; and for another, you may make it your boast that you have made my whole life and character something different from what they were. I mean what I say; no less. I do not think getting married is worth while. I would rather you went on living with your father, so that I could walk over and see you once, or maybe twice a week, as people go to church, and then we should both be all the happier between whiles. That's my notion. But I'll marry you if you will," he added.

"Do you know that you are insulting me?" she broke out.

"Not I, Marjory," said he; "if there is anything in a clear conscience, not I. I offer all my heart's best affection; you can take it or want it, though I suspect it's beyond either your power or mine to change what has once been done, and set me fancy-free. I'll marry you, if you like; but I tell you again and again, it's not worth while, and we had best stay friends. Though I am a quiet man I have noticed a heap of things in my life. Trust in me, and take things as I propose; or, if you don't like that, say the word, and I'll marry you out of hand."

There was a considerable pause, and Will, who began to feel uneasy, began to grow angry in consequence.

"It seems you are too proud to say your mind," he said. "Believe me that's a pity. A clean shrift makes simple living. Can a man be more downright or honourable, to a woman than I have been? I have said my say, and given you your choice. Do you want me to marry you? or will you take my friendship, as I think best? or have you had enough of me for good? Speak out for the dear God's sake! You know your father told you a girl should speak her mind in these affairs."

She seemed to recover herself at that, turned without a word, walked rapidly through the garden, and disappeared into the house, leaving Will in some confusion as to the result. He walked up and down the garden, whistling softly to himself. Sometimes he stopped and contemplated the sky and hill-tops; sometimes he went down to the tail of the weir and sat there, looking foolishly in the water. All this dubiety and perturbation was so foreign to his nature and the life which he had resolutely chosen for himself, that he began to regret Marjory's arrival. "After all," he thought, "I was as happy as a man need be. I could come down here and watch my fishes all day long if I wanted: I was as settled and contented as my old mill."

Marjory came down to dinner, looking very trim and quiet; and no sooner were all three at table than she made her father a speech, with her eyes fixed upon her plate, but showing no other sign of embarrassment or distress.

"Father," she began, "Mr. Will and I have been talking things over. We see that we have each made a mistake about our feelings, and he has agreed, at my request, to give up all idea of marriage, and be no more than my very good friend, as in the past. You see, there is no shadow of a quarrel, and indeed I hope we shall see a great deal of him in the future, for his visits will always be welcome in our house. Of course, father, you will know best, but perhaps we should do better to leave Mr. Will's house for the present. I believe, after what has passed, we should hardly be agreeable inmates for some days."

Will, who had commanded himself with difficulty from the first, broke out upon this into an inarticulate noise, and raised one hand with an appearance of real dismay, as if he were about to interfere and contradict. But she checked him at once looking up at him with a swift glance and an angry flush upon her cheek.

"You will perhaps have the good grace," she said, "to let me explain these matters for myself."

Will was put entirely out of countenance by her expression and the ring of her voice. He held his peace, concluding that there were some things about this girl beyond his comprehension, in which he was exactly right.

The poor parson was quite crestfallen. He tried to prove that this was no more than a true lovers' tiff, which would pass off before night; and when he was dislodged from that position, he went on to argue that where there was no quarrel there could be no call for a separation; for the good man liked both his entertainment and his host. It was curious to see how the girl managed them, saying little all the time, and that very quietly, and yet twisting them round her finger and insensibly leading them wherever she would by feminine tact and generalship. It scarcely seemed to have been her doing—it seemed as if things had merely so fallen out—that she and her father took their departure that same afternoon in a farm-cart, and went farther down the valley, to wait, until their own house was ready for them, in another hamlet. But Will had been observing closely, and was well aware of her dexterity and resolution. When he found himself alone he had a great many curious matters to turn over in his mind. He was very sad and solitary, to begin with. All the interest had gone out of his life, and he might look up at the stars as long as he pleased, he somehow failed to find support or consolation. And then he was in such a turmoil of spirit about Marjory. He had been puzzled and irritated at her behaviour, and yet he could not keep himself from admiring it. He thought he recognised a fine, perverse angel in that still soul which he had never hitherto suspected; and though he saw it was an influence that would fit but ill with his own life of artificial calm, he could not keep himself from ardently desiring to possess it. Like a man who has lived among shadows and now meets the sun, he was both pained and delighted.

As the days went forward he passed from one extreme to another; now pluming himself on the strength of his determination, now despising his timid and silly caution. The former was, perhaps, the true thought of his heart, and represented the regular tenor of the man's reflections; but the latter burst forth from time to time with an unruly violence, and then he would forget all consideration, and go up and down his house and garden or walk among the fir-woods like one who is beside himself with remorse. To equable, steady-minded Will this state of matters was intolerable; and he determined, at whatever cost, to bring it to an end. So, one warm summer afternoon he put on his best clothes, took a thorn switch in his hand, and set out down the valley by the river. As soon as he had taken his determination, he had regained at a bound his customary peace of heart, and he enjoyed the bright weather and the variety of the scene without any admixture of alarm or unpleasant eagerness. It was nearly the same to him how the matter turned out. If she accepted him he would have to marry her this time, which perhaps was, all for the best. If she refused him, he would have done his utmost, and might follow his own way in the future with an untroubled conscience. He hoped, on the whole, she would refuse him; and then, again, as he saw the brown roof which sheltered her, peeping through some willows at an angle of the stream, he was half inclined to reverse the wish, and more than half ashamed of himself for this infirmity of purpose.

Marjory seemed glad to see him, and gave him her hand without affectation or delay.

"I have been thinking about this marriage," he began.

"So have I," she answered. "And I respect you more and more for a very wise man. You understood me better than I understood myself; and I am now quite certain that things are all for the best as they are."

"At the same time—," ventured Will.

"You must be tired," she interrupted. "Take a seat and let me fetch you a glass of wine. The afternoon is so warm; and I wish you not to be displeased with your visit. You must come quite often; once a week, if you can spare the time; I am always so glad to see my friends."

"O, very well," thought Will to himself. "It appears I was right after all." And he paid a very agreeable visit, walked home again in capital spirits, and gave himself no further concern about the matter.

For nearly three years Will and Marjory continued on these terms, seeing each other once or twice a week without any word of love between them; and for all that time I believe Will was nearly as happy as a man can be. He rather stinted himself the pleasure of seeing her; and he would often walk half-way over to the parsonage, and then back again, as if to whet his appetite. Indeed there was one corner of the road, whence he could see the church-spire wedged into a crevice of the valley between sloping firwoods, with a triangular snatch of plain by way of background, which he greatly affected as a place to sit and moralise in before returning homewards; and the peasants got so much into the habit of finding him there in the twilight that they gave it the name of "Will o' the Mill's Corner."

At the end of the three years Marjory played him a sad trick by suddenly marrying somebody else. Will kept his countenance bravely, and merely remarked that, for as little as he knew of women, he had acted very prudently in not marrying her himself three years before. She plainly knew very little of her own mind, and, in spite of a deceptive manner, was as fickle and flighty as the rest of them. He had to congratulate himself on an escape, he said, and would take a higher opinion of his own wisdom in consequence. But at heart, he was reasonably displeased, moped a good deal for a month or two, and fell away in flesh, to the astonishment of his serving-lads.

It was perhaps a year after this marriage that Will was awakened late one night by the sound of a horse galloping on the road, followed by precipitate knocking at the inn-door. He opened his window and saw a farm servant, mounted and holding a led horse by the bridle, who told him to make what haste he could and go along with him; for Marjory was dying, and had sent urgently to fetch him to her bedside. Will was no horseman, and made so little speed upon the way that the poor young wife was very near her end before he arrived. But they had some minutes' talk in private, and he was present and wept very bitterly while she breathed her last.

CHAPTER III.
DEATH

Year after year went away into nothing, with great explosions and outcries in the cities on the plain: red revolt springing up and being suppressed in blood, battle swaying hither and thither, patient astronomers in observatory towers picking out and christening new stars, plays being performed in lighted theatres, people being carried into hospital on stretchers, and all the usual turmoil and agitation of men's lives in crowded centres. Up in Will's valley only the winds and seasons made an epoch; the fish hung in the swift stream, the birds circled overhead, the pine-tops rustled underneath the stars, the tall hills stood over all; and Will went to and fro, minding his wayside inn, until the snow began to thicken on his head. His heart was young and vigorous; and if his pulses kept a sober time, they still beat strong and steady in his wrists. He carried a ruddy stain on either cheek, like a ripe apple; he stooped a little, but his step was still firm; and his sinewy hands were reached out to all men with a friendly pressure. His face was covered with those wrinkles which are got in open air, and which rightly looked at, are no more than a sort of permanent sunburning; such wrinkles heighten the stupidity of stupid faces; but to a person like Will, with his clear eyes and smiling mouth, only give another charm by testifying to a simple and easy life. His talk was full of wise sayings. He had a taste for other people; and other people had a taste for him. When the valley was full of tourists in the season, there were merry nights in Will's arbour; and his views, which seemed whimsical to his neighbours, were often enough admired by learned people out of towns and colleges. Indeed, he had a very noble old age, and grew daily better known; so that his fame was heard of in the cities of the plain; and young men who had been summer travellers spoke together in cafés of Will o' the Mill and his rough philosophy. Many and many an invitation, you may be sure, he had; but nothing could tempt him from his upland valley. He would shake his head and smile over his tobacco-pipe with a deal of meaning. "You come too late," he would answer. "I am a dead man now: I have lived and died already. Fifty years ago you would have brought my heart into my mouth; and now you do not even tempt me. But that is the object of long living, that man should cease to care about life." And again: "There is only one difference between a long life and a good dinner: that, in the dinner, the sweets come last." Or once more: "When I was a boy, I was a bit puzzled, and hardly knew whether it was myself or the world that was curious and worth looking into. Now, I know it is myself, and stick to that."

He never showed any symptom of frailty, but kept stalwart and firm to the last; but they say he grew less talkative towards the end, and would listen to other people by the hour in an amused and sympathetic silence. Only, when he did speak, it was more to the point and more charged with old experience. He drank a bottle of wine gladly; above all, at sunset on the hill-top or quite late at night under the stars in the arbour. The sight of something attractive and unatttainable seasoned his enjoyment, he would say; and he professed he had lived long enough to admire a candle all the more when he could compare it with a planet.

One night, in his seventy-second year, he awoke in bed in such uneasiness of body and mind that he arose and dressed himself and went out to meditate in the arbour. It was pitch dark, without a star; the river was swollen, and the wet woods and meadows loaded the air with perfume. It had thundered during the day, and it promised more thunder for the morrow. A murky, stifling night for a man of seventy-two! Whether it was the weather or the wakefulness, or some little touch of fever in his old limbs, Will's mind was besieged by tumultuous and crying memories. His boyhood, the night with the fat young man, the death of his adopted parents, the summer days with Marjory, and many of those small circumstances, which seem nothing to another, and are yet the very gist of a man's own life to himself—things seen, words heard, looks misconstrued—arose from their forgotten corners and usurped his attention. The dead themselves were with him, not merely taking part in this thin show of memory that defiled before his brain, but revisiting his bodily senses as they do in profound and vivid dreams. The fat young man leaned his elbows on the table opposite; Marjory came and went with an apronful of flowers between the garden and the arbour; he could hear the old parson knocking out his pipe or blowing his resonant nose. The tide of his consciousness ebbed and flowed: he was sometimes half-asleep and drowned in his recollections of the past; and sometimes he was broad awake, wondering at himself. But about the middle of the night he was startled by the voice of the dead miller calling to him out of the house as he used to do on the arrival of custom. The hallucination was so perfect that Will sprang from his seat and stood listening for the summons to be repeated; and as he listened he became conscious of another noise besides the brawling of the river and the ringing in his feverish ears. It was like the stir of horses and the creaking of harness, as though a carriage with an impatient team had been brought up upon the road before the courtyard gate. At such an hour, upon this rough and dangerous pass, the supposition was no better than absurd; and Will dismissed it from his mind, and resumed his seat upon the arbour chair; and sleep closed over him again like running water. He was once again awakened by the dead miller's call, thinner and more spectral than before; and once again he heard the noise of an equipage upon the road. And so thrice and four times, the same dream, or the same fancy, presented itself to his senses: until at length, smiling to himself as when one humours a nervous child, he proceeded towards the gate to set his uncertainty at rest.

From the arbour to the gate was no great distance, and yet it took Will some time; it seemed as if the dead thickened around him in the court, and crossed his path at every step. For, first, he was suddenly surprised by an overpowering sweetness of heliotropes; it was as if his garden had been planted with this flower from end to end, and the hot, damp night had drawn forth all their perfumes in a breath. Now the heliotrope had been Marjory's favourite flower, and since her death not one of them had ever been planted in Will's ground.

"I must be going crazy," he thought. "Poor Marjory and her heliotropes!"

And with that he raised his eyes towards the window that had once been hers. If he had been bewildered before, he was now almost terrified; for there was a light in the room; the window was an orange oblong as of yore; and the corner of the blind was lifted and let fall as on the night when he stood and shouted to the stars in his perplexity. The illusion only endured an instant; but it left him somewhat unmanned, rubbing his eyes and staring at the outline of the house and the black night behind it. While he thus stood, and it seemed as if he must have stood there quite a long time, there came a renewal of the noises on the road: and he turned in time to meet a stranger, who was advancing to meet him across the court. There was something like the outline of a great carriage discernible on the road behind the stranger, and, above that, a few black pine-tops, like so many plumes.

"Master Will?" asked the new-comer, in brief military fashion.

"That same, sir," answered Will. "Can I do anything to serve you?"

"I have heard you much spoken of, Master Will," returned the other; "much spoken of, and well. And though I have both hands full of business, I wish to drink a bottle of wine with you in your arbour. Before I go, I shall introduce myself."

Will led the way to the trellis, and got a lamp lighted and a bottle uncorked. He was not altogether unused to such complimentary interviews, and hoped little enough from this one, being schooled by many disappointments. A sort of cloud had settled on his wits and prevented him from remembering the strangeness of the hour. He moved like a person in his sleep; and it seemed as if the lamp caught fire and the bottle came uncorked with the facility of thought. Still, he had some curiosity about the appearance of his visitor, and tried in vain to turn the light into his face; either he handled the lamp clumsily, or there was a dimness over his eyes; but he could make out little more than a shadow at table with him. He stared and stared at this shadow, as he wiped out the glasses, and began to feel cold and strange about the heart. The silence weighed upon him, for he could hear nothing now, not even the river, but the drumming of his own arteries in his ears.

"Here's to you," said the stranger, roughly.

"Here is my service, sir," replied Will, sipping his wine, which somehow tasted oddly.

"I understand you are a very positive fellow," pursued the stranger.

Will made answer with a smile of some satisfaction and a little nod.

"So am I," continued the other; "and it is the delight of my heart to tramp on people's corns. I will have nobody positive but myself; not one. I have crossed the whims, in my time, of kings and generals and great artists. And what would you say," he went on, "if I had come up here on purpose to cross yours?"

Will had it on his tongue to make a sharp rejoinder; but the politeness of an old innkeeper prevailed; and he held his peace and made answer with a civil gesture of the hand.

"I have," said the stranger. "And if I did not hold you in a particular esteem, I should make no words about the matter. It appears you pride yourself on staying where you are. You mean to stick by your inn. Now I mean you shall come for a turn with me in my barouche; and before this bottle's empty, so you shall."

"That would be an odd thing, to be sure," replied Will, with a chuckle. "Why, sir, I have grown here like an old oak-tree; the Devil himself could hardly root me up: and for all I perceive you are a very entertaining old gentleman, I would wager you another bottle you lose your pains with me."

The dimness of Will's eyesight had been increasing all this while; but he was somehow conscious of a sharp and chilling scrutiny which irritated and yet overmastered him.

"You need not think," he broke out suddenly, in an explosive, febrile manner that startled and alarmed himself, "that I am a stay-at-home, because I fear anything under God. God knows I am tired enough of it all; and when the time comes for a longer journey than ever you dream of, I reckon I shall find myself prepared."

The stranger emptied his glass and pushed it away from him. He looked down for a little, and then, leaning over the table, tapped Will three times upon the forearm with a single finger. "The time has come!" he said solemnly.

An ugly thrill spread from the spot he touched. The tones of his voice were dull and startling, and echoed strangely in Will's heart.

"I beg your pardon," he said, with some discomposure. "What do you mean?"

"Look at me, and you will find your eyesight swim. Raise your hand; it is dead-heavy. This is your last bottle of wine, Master Will, and your last night upon the earth."

"You are a doctor?" quavered Will.

"The best that ever was," replied the other; "for I cure both mind and body with the same prescription. I take away all pain and I forgive all sins; and where my patients have gone wrong in life, I smooth out all complications and set them free again upon their feet."

"I have no need of you," said Will.

"A time comes for all men, Master Will," replied the doctor, "when the helm is taken out of their hands. For you, because you were prudent and quiet, it has been long of coming, and you have had long to discipline yourself for its reception. You have seen what is to be seen about your mill; you have sat close all your days like a hare in its form; but now that is at an end; and," added the doctor, getting on his feet, "you must arise and come with me."

"You are a strange physician," said Will, looking steadfastly upon his guest.

"I am a natural law," he replied, "and people call me Death."

"Why did you not tell me so at first?" cried Will. "I have been waiting for you these many years. Give me your hand, and welcome."

"Lean upon my arm," said the stranger, "for already your strength abates. Lean on me as heavily as you need; for though I am old, I am very strong. It is but three steps to my carriage, and there all your trouble ends. Why, Will," he added, "I have been yearning for you as if you were my own son; and of all the men that ever I came for in my long days, I have come for you most gladly. I am caustic, and sometimes offend people at first sight; but I am a good friend at heart to such as you."

"Since Marjory was taken," returned Will, "I declare before God you were the only friend I had to look for." So the pair went arm-in-arm across the courtyard.

One of the servants awoke about this time and heard the noise of horses pawing before he dropped asleep again; all down the valley that night there was a rushing as of a smooth and steady wind descending towards the plain; and when the world rose next morning, sure enough Will o' the Mill had gone at last upon his travels.

MARKHEIM

"Yes," said the dealer, "our windfalls are of various kinds. Some customers are ignorant, and then I touch a dividend on my superior knowledge. Some are dishonest," and here he held up the candle, so that the light fell strongly on his visitor, "and in that case," he continued, "I profit by my virtue."

Markheim had but just entered from the daylight streets, and his eyes had not yet grown familiar with the mingled shine and darkness in the shop. At these pointed words, and before the near presence of the flame, he blinked painfully and looked aside.

The dealer chuckled. "You come to me on Christmas Day," he resumed, "when you know that I am alone in my house, put up my shutters, and make a point of refusing business. Well, you will have to pay for that; you will have to pay for my loss of time, when I should be balancing my books; you will have to pay, besides, for a kind of manner that I remark in you to-day very strongly. I am the essence of discretion, and ask no awkward questions; but when a customer cannot look me in the eye, he has to pay for it." The dealer once more chuckled; and then, changing to his usual business voice, though still with a note of irony, "You can give, as usual, a clear account of how you came into the possession of the object?" he continued. "Still your uncle's cabinet? A remarkable collector, sir!"

And the little pale, round-shouldered dealer stood almost on tip-toe, looking over the top of his gold spectacles, and nodding his head with every mark of disbelief. Markheim returned his gaze with one of infinite pity, and a touch of horror.

"This time," said he, "you are in error. I have not come to sell, but to buy. I have no curios to dispose of; my uncle's cabinet is bare to the wainscot; even were it still intact, I have done well on the Stock Exchange, and should more likely add to it than otherwise, and my errand to-day is simplicity itself. I seek a Christmas present for a lady," he continued, waxing more fluent as he struck into the speech he had prepared; "and certainly I owe you every excuse for thus disturbing you upon so small a matter. But the thing was neglected yesterday; I must produce my little compliment at dinner; and, as you very well know, a rich marriage is not a thing to be neglected."

There followed a pause, during which the dealer seemed to weigh this statement incredulously. The ticking of many clocks among the curious lumber of the shop, and the faint rushing of the cabs in a near thoroughfare, filled up the interval of silence.

"Well, sir," said the dealer, "be it so. You are an old customer after all; and if, as you say, you have the chance of a good marriage, far be it from me to be an obstacle. Here is a nice thing for a lady now," he went on, "this hand glass—fifteenth century, warranted; comes from a good collection, too; but I reserve the name, in the interests of my customer, who was just like yourself, my dear sir, the nephew and sole heir of a remarkable collector."

The dealer, while he thus ran on in his dry and biting voice, had stooped to take the object from its place; and, as he had done so, a shock had passed through Markheim, a start both of hand and foot, a sudden leap of many tumultuous passions to the face. It passed as swiftly as it came, and left no trace beyond a certain trembling of the hand that now received the glass.

"A glass," he said hoarsely, and then paused, and repeated it more clearly. "A glass? For Christmas? Surely not?"

"And why not?" cried the dealer. "Why not a glass?"

Markheim was looking upon him with an indefinable expression. "You ask me why not?" he said. "Why, look here—look in it—look at yourself! Do you like to see it? No! nor I—nor any man."

The little man had jumped back when Markheim had so suddenly confronted him with the mirror; but now, perceiving there was nothing worse on hand, he chuckled. "Your future lady, sir, must be pretty hard favoured," said he.

"I ask you," said Markheim, "for a Christmas present, and you give me this—this damned reminder of years, and sins and follies—this hand-conscience! Did you mean it? Had you a thought in your mind? Tell me. It will be better for you if you do. Come, tell me about yourself. I hazard a guess now, that you are in secret a very charitable man?"

The dealer looked closely at his companion. It was very odd, Markheim did not appear to be laughing; there was something in his face like an eager sparkle of hope, but nothing of mirth.

"What are you driving at?" the dealer asked.

"Not charitable?" returned the other, gloomily. "Not charitable; not pious; not scrupulous; unloving, unbeloved; a hand to get money, a safe to keep it. Is that all? Dear God, man, is that all?"

"I will tell you what it is," began the dealer, with some sharpness, and then broke off again into a chuckle. "But I see this is a love match of yours, and you have been drinking the lady's health."

"Ah!" cried Markheim, with a strange curiosity. "Ah, have you been in love? Tell me about that."

"I," cried the dealer. "I in love! I never had the time, nor have I the time to-day for all this nonsense. Will you take the glass?"

"Where is the hurry?" returned Markheim. "It is very pleasant to stand here talking; and life is so short and insecure that I would not hurry away from any pleasure—no, not even from so mild a one as this. We should rather cling, cling to what little we can get, like a man at a cliff's edge. Every second is a cliff, if you think upon it—a cliff a mile high—high enough, if we fall, to dash us out of every feature of humanity. Hence it is best to talk pleasantly. Let us talk of each other: why should we wear this mask? Let us be confidential. Who knows, we might become friends?"

"I have just one word to say to you," said the dealer. "Either make your purchase, or walk out of my shop!"

"True true," said Markheim. "Enough, fooling. To business. Show me something else."

The dealer stooped once more, this time to replace the glass upon the shelf, his thin blond hair falling over his eyes as he did so. Markheim moved a little nearer, with one hand in the pocket of his greatcoat; he drew himself up and filled his lungs; at the same time many different emotions were depicted together on his face—terror, horror, and resolve, fascination and a physical repulsion; and through a haggard lift of his upper lip, his teeth looked out.

"This, perhaps, may suit," observed the dealer: and then, as he began to re-arise, Markheim bounded from behind upon his victim. The long, skewerlike dagger flashed and fell. The dealer struggled like a hen, striking his temple on the shelf, and then tumbled on the floor in a heap.

Time had some score of small voices in that shop, some stately and slow as was becoming to their great age; others garrulous and hurried. All these told out the seconds in an intricate, chorus of tickings. Then the passage of a lad's feet, heavily running on the pavement, broke in upon these smaller voices and startled Markheim into the consciousness of his surroundings. He looked about him awfully. The candle stood on the counter, its flame solemnly wagging in a draught; and by that inconsiderable movement, the whole room was filled with noiseless bustle and kept heaving like a sea: the tall shadows nodding, the gross blots of darkness swelling and dwindling as with respiration, the faces of the portraits and the china gods changing and wavering like images in water. The inner door stood ajar, and peered into that leaguer of shadows with a long slit of daylight like a pointing finger.

From these fear-stricken rovings, Markheim's eyes returned to the body of his victim, where it lay both humped and sprawling, incredibly small and strangely meaner than in life. In these poor, miserly clothes, in that ungainly attitude, the dealer lay like so much sawdust. Markheim had feared to see it, and, lo! it was nothing. And yet, as he gazed, this bundle of old clothes and pool of blood began to find eloquent voices. There it must lie; there was none to work the cunning hinges or direct the miracle of locomotion—there it must lie till it was found. Found! ay, and then? Then would this dead flesh lift up a cry that would ring over England, and fill the world with the echoes of pursuit. Ay, dead or not, this was still the enemy. "Time was that when the brains were out," he thought; and the first word struck into his mind. Time, now that the deed was accomplished—time, which had closed for the victim, had become instant and momentous for the slayer.

The thought was yet in his mind, when, first one and then another, with every variety of pace and voice—one deep as the bell from a cathedral turret, another ringing on its treble notes the prelude of a waltz-the clocks began to strike the hour of three in the afternoon.

The sudden outbreak of so many tongues in that dumb chamber staggered him. He began to bestir himself, going to and fro with the candle, beleaguered by moving shadows, and startled to the soul by chance reflections. In many rich mirrors, some of home design, some from Venice or Amsterdam, he saw his face repeated and repeated, as it were an army of spies; his own eyes met and detected him; and the sound of his own steps, lightly as they fell, vexed the surrounding quiet. And still, as he continued to fill his pockets, his mind accused him with a sickening iteration, of the thousand faults of his design. He should have chosen a more quiet hour; he should have prepared an alibi; he should not have used a knife; he should have been more cautious, and only bound and gagged the dealer, and not killed him; he should have been more bold, and killed the servant also; he should have done all things otherwise: poignant regrets, weary, incessant toiling of the mind to change what was unchangeable, to plan what was now useless, to be the architect of the irrevocable past. Meanwhile, and behind all this activity, brute terrors, like the scurrying of rats in a deserted attic, filled the more remote chambers of his brain with riot; the hand of the constable would fall heavy on his shoulder, and his nerves would jerk like a hooked fish; or he beheld, in galloping defile, the dock, the prison, the gallows, and the black coffin.

Terror of the people in the street sat down before his mind like a besieging army. It was impossible, he thought, but that some rumour of the struggle must have reached their ears and set on edge their curiosity; and now, in all the neighbouring houses, he divined them sitting motionless and with uplifted ear—solitary people, condemned to spend Christmas dwelling alone on memories of the past, and now startingly recalled from that tender exercise; happy family parties struck into silence round the table, the mother still with raised finger: every degree and age and humour, but all, by their own hearths, prying and hearkening and weaving the rope that was to hang him. Sometimes it seemed to him he could not move too softly; the clink of the tall Bohemian goblets rang out loudly like a bell; and alarmed by the bigness of the ticking, he was tempted to stop the clocks. And then, again, with a swift transition of his terrors, the very silence of the place appeared a source of peril, and a thing to strike and freeze the passer-by; and he would step more boldly, and bustle aloud among the contents of the shop, and imitate, with elaborate bravado, the movements of a busy man at ease in his own house.

But he was now so pulled about by different alarms that, while one portion of his mind was still alert and cunning, another trembled on the brink of lunacy. One hallucination in particular took a strong hold on his credulity. The neighbour hearkening with white face beside his window, the passer-by arrested by a horrible surmise on the pavement—these could at worst suspect, they could not know; through the brick walls and shuttered windows only sounds could penetrate. But here, within the house, was he alone? He knew he was; he had watched the servant set forth sweet-hearting, in her poor best, "out for the day" written in every ribbon and smile. Yes, he was alone, of course; and yet, in the bulk of empty house above him, he could surely hear a stir of delicate footing—he was surely conscious, inexplicably conscious of some presence. Ay, surely; to every room and corner of the house his imagination followed it; and now it was a faceless thing, and yet had eyes to see with; and again it was a shadow of himself; and yet again behold the image of the dead dealer, reinspired with cunning and hatred.

At times, with a strong effort, he would glance at the open door which still seemed to repel his eyes. The house was tall, the skylight small and dirty, the day blind with fog; and the light that filtered down to the ground story was exceedingly faint, and showed dimly on the threshold of the shop. And yet, in that strip of doubtful brightness, did there not hang wavering a shadow?

Suddenly, from the street outside, a very jovial gentleman began to beat with a staff on the shop-door, accompanying his blows with shouts and railleries in which the dealer was continually called upon by name. Markheim, smitten into ice, glanced at the dead man. But no! he lay quite still; he was fled away far beyond earshot of these blows and shoutings; he was sunk beneath seas of silence; and his name, which would once have caught his notice above the howling of a storm, had become an empty sound. And presently the jovial gentleman desisted from his knocking, and departed.

Here was a broad hint to hurry what remained to be done, to get forth from this accusing neighbourhood, to plunge into a bath of London multitudes, and to reach, on the other side of day, that haven of safety and apparent innocence—his bed. One visitor had come: at any moment another might follow and be more obstinate. To have done the deed, and yet not to reap the profit, would be too abhorrent a failure. The money, that was now Markheim's concern; and as a means to that, the keys.

He glanced over his shoulder at the open door, where the shadow was still lingering and shivering; and with no conscious repugnance of the mind, yet with a tremor of the belly, he drew near the body of his victim. The human character had quite departed. Like a suit half-stuffed with bran, the limbs lay scattered, the trunk doubled, on the floor; and yet the thing repelled him. Although so dingy and inconsiderable to the eye, he feared it might have more significance to the touch. He took the body by the shoulders, and turned it on its back. It was strangely light and supple, and the limbs, as if they had been broken, fell into the oddest postures. The face was robbed of all expression; but it was as pale as wax, and shockingly smeared with blood about one temple. That was, for Markheim, the one displeasing circumstance. It carried him back, upon the instant, to a certain fair-day in a fishers' village: a gray day, a piping wind, a crowd upon the street, the blare of brasses, the booming of drums, the nasal voice of a ballad singer; and a boy going to and fro, buried over head in the crowd and divided between interest and fear, until, coming out upon the chief place of concourse, he beheld a booth and a great screen with pictures, dismally designed, garishly coloured: Brown-rigg with her apprentice; the Mannings with their murdered guest; Weare in the death-grip of Thurtell; and a score besides of famous crimes. The thing was as clear as an illusion; he was once again that little boy; he was looking once again, and with the same sense of physical revolt, at these vile pictures; he was still stunned by the thumping of the drums. A bar of that day's music returned upon his memory; and at that, for the first time, a qualm came over him, a breath of nausea, a sudden weakness of the joints, which he must instantly resist and conquer.

He judged it more prudent to confront than to flee from these considerations; looking the more hardily in the dead face, bending his mind to realise the nature and greatness of his crime. So little a while ago that face had moved with every change of sentiment, that pale mouth had spoken, that body had been all on fire with governable energies; and now, and by his act, that piece of life had been arrested, as the horologist, with interjected finger, arrests the beating of the clock. So he reasoned in vain; he could rise to no more remorseful consciousness; the same heart which had shuddered before the painted effigies of crime, looked on its reality unmoved. At best, he felt a gleam of pity for one who had been endowed in vain with all those faculties that can make the world a garden of enchantment, one who had never lived and who was now dead. But of penitence, no, not a tremor.

With that, shaking himself clear of these considerations, he found the keys and advanced towards the open door of the shop. Outside, it had begun to rain smartly; and the sound of the shower upon the roof had banished silence. Like some dripping cavern, the chambers of the house were haunted by an incessant echoing, which filled the ear and mingled with the ticking of the clocks. And, as Markheim approached the door, he seemed to hear, in answer to his own cautious tread, the steps of another foot withdrawing up the stair. The shadow still palpitated loosely on the threshold. He threw a ton's weight of resolve upon his muscles, and drew back the door.

The faint, foggy daylight glimmered dimly on the bare floor and stairs; on the bright suit of armour posted, halbert in hand, upon the landing; and on the dark wood-carvings, and framed pictures that hung against the yellow panels of the wainscot. So loud was the beating of the rain through all the house that, in Markheim's ears, it began to be distinguished into many different sounds. Footsteps and sighs, the tread of regiments marching in the distance, the chink of money in the counting, and the creaking of doors held stealthily ajar, appeared to mingle with the patter of the drops upon the cupola and the gushing of the water in the pipes. The sense that he was not alone grew upon him to the verge of madness. On every side he was haunted and begirt by presences. He heard them moving in the upper chambers; from the shop, he heard the dead man getting to his legs; and as he began with a great effort to mount the stairs, feet fled quietly before him and followed stealthily behind. If he were but deaf, he thought, how tranquilly he would possess his soul! And then again, and hearkening with ever fresh attention, he blessed himself for that unresting sense which held the outposts and stood a trusty sentinel upon his life. His head turned continually on his neck; his eyes, which seemed starting from their orbits, scouted on every side, and on every side were half-rewarded as with the tail of something nameless vanishing. The four-and-twenty steps to the first floor were four-and-twenty agonies.

On that first storey, the doors stood ajar, three of them like three ambushes, shaking his nerves like the throats of cannon. He could never again, he felt, be sufficiently immured and fortified from men's observing eyes, he longed to be home, girt in by walls, buried among bedclothes, and invisible to all but God. And at that thought he wondered a little, recollecting tales of other murderers and the fear they were said to entertain of heavenly avengers. It was not so, at least, with him. He feared the laws of nature, lest, in their callous and immutable procedure, they should preserve some damning evidence of his crime. He feared tenfold more, with a slavish, superstitions terror, some scission in the continuity of man's experience, some wilful illegality of nature. He played a game of skill, depending on the rules, calculating consequence from cause; and what if nature, as the defeated tyrant overthrew the chess-board, should break the mould of their succession? The like had befallen Napoleon (so writers said) when the winter changed the time of its appearance. The like might befall Markheim: the solid walls might become transparent and reveal his doings like those of bees in a glass hive; the stout planks might yield under his foot like quicksands and detain him in their clutch; ay, and there were soberer accidents that might destroy him: if, for instance, the house should fall and imprison him beside the body of his victim; or the house next door should fly on fire, and the firemen invade him from all sides. These things he feared; and, in a sense, these things might be called the hands of God reached forth against sin. But about God himself he was at ease; his act was doubtless exceptional, but so were his excuses, which God knew; it was there, and not among men, that he felt sure of justice.

When he had got safe into the drawing-room, and shut the door behind him, he was aware of a respite from alarms. The room was quite dismantled, uncarpeted besides, and strewn with packing cases and incongruous furniture; several great pier-glasses, in which he beheld himself at various angles, like an actor on a stage; many pictures, framed and unframed, standing, with their faces to the wall; a fine Sheraton sideboard, a cabinet of marquetry, and a great old bed, with tapestry hangings. The windows opened to the floor; but by great good fortune the lower part of the shutters had been closed, and this concealed him from the neighbours. Here, then, Markheim drew in a packing case before the cabinet, and began to search among the keys. It was a long business, for there were many; and it was irksome, besides; for, after all, there might be nothing in the cabinet, and time was on the wing. But the closeness of the occupation sobered him. With the tail of his eye he saw the door—even glanced at it from time to time directly, like a besieged commander pleased to verify the good estate of his defences. But in truth he was at peace. The rain falling in the street sounded natural and pleasant. Presently, on the other side, the notes of a piano were wakened to the music of a hymn, and the voices of many children took up the air and words. How stately, how comfortable was the melody! How fresh the youthful voices! Markheim gave ear to it smilingly, as he sorted out the keys; and his mind was thronged with answerable ideas and images; church-going children and the pealing of the high organ; children afield, bathers by the brookside, ramblers on the brambly common, kite-flyers in the windy and cloud-navigated sky; and then, at another cadence of the hymn, back again to church, and the somnolence of summer Sundays, and the high genteel voice of the parson (which he smiled a little to recall) and the painted Jacobean tombs, and the dim lettering of the Ten Commandments in the chancel.

And as he sat thus, at once busy and absent, he was startled to his feet. A flash of ice, a flash of fire, a bursting gush of blood, went over him, and then he stood transfixed and thrilling. A step mounted the stair slowly and steadily, and presently a hand was laid upon the knob, and the lock clicked, and the door opened.

Fear held Markheim in a vice. What to expect he knew not, whether the dead man walking, or the official ministers of human justice, or some chance witness blindly stumbling in to consign him to the gallows. But when a face was thrust into the aperture, glanced round the room, looked at him, nodded and smiled as if in friendly recognition, and then withdrew again, and the door closed behind it, his fear broke loose from his control in a hoarse cry. At the sound of this the visitant returned.

"Did you call me?" he asked, pleasantly, and with that he entered the room and closed the door behind him.

Markheim stood and gazed at him with all his eyes. Perhaps there was a film upon his sight, but the outlines of the new comer seemed to change and waver like those of the idols in the wavering candle-light of the shop; and at times he thought he knew him; and at times he thought he bore a likeness to himself; and always, like a lump of living terror, there lay in his bosom the conviction that this thing was not of the earth and not of God.

And yet the creature had a strange air of the commonplace, as he stood looking on Markheim with a smile; and when he added: "You are looking for the money, I believe?" it was in the tones of everyday politeness.

Markheim made no answer.

"I should warn you," resumed the other, "that the maid has left her sweetheart earlier than usual and will soon be here. If Mr. Markheim be found in this house, I need not describe to him the consequences."

"You know me?" cried the murderer.

The visitor smiled. "You have long been a favourite of mine," he said; "and I have long observed and often sought to help you."

"What are you?" cried Markheim: "the devil?"

"What I may be," returned the other, "cannot affect the service I propose to render you."

"It can," cried Markheim; "it does! Be helped by you? No, never; not by you! You do not know me yet; thank God, you do not know me!"

"I know you," replied the visitant, with a sort of kind severity or rather firmness. "I know you to the soul."

"Know me!" cried Markheim. "Who can do so? My life is but a travesty and slander on myself. I have lived to belie my nature. All men do; all men are better than this disguise that grows about and stifles them. You see each dragged away by life, like one whom bravos have seized and muffled in a cloak. If they had their own control—if you could see their faces, they would be altogether different, they would shine out for heroes and saints! I am worse than most; myself is more overlaid; my excuse is known to me and God. But, had I the time, I could disclose myself."

"To me?" inquired the visitant.

"To you before all," returned the murderer. "I supposed you were intelligent. I thought—since you exist—you would prove a reader of the heart. And yet you would propose to judge me by my acts! Think of it; my acts! I was born and I have lived in a land of giants; giants have dragged me by the wrists since I was born out of my mother—the giants of circumstance. And you would judge me by my acts! But can you not look within? Can you not understand that evil is hateful to me? Can you not see within me the clear writing of conscience, never blurred by any wilful sophistry, although too often disregarded? Can you not read me for a thing that surely must be common as humanity—the unwilling sinner?"

"All this is very feelingly expressed," was the reply, "but it regards me not. These points of consistency are beyond my province, and I care not in the least by what compulsion you may have been dragged away, so as you are but carried in the right direction. But time flies; the servant delays, looking in the faces of the crowd and at the pictures on the hoardings, but still she keeps moving nearer; and remember, it is as if the gallows itself was striding towards you through the Christmas streets! Shall I help you; I, who know all? Shall I tell you where to find the money?"

"For what price?" asked Markheim.

"I offer you the service for a Christmas gift," returned the other.

Markheim could not refrain from smiling with a kind of bitter triumph. "No," said he, "I will take nothing at your hands; if I were dying of thirst, and it was your hand that put the pitcher to my lips, I should find the courage to refuse. It may be credulous, but I will do nothing to commit myself to evil."

"I have no objection to a death-bed repentance," observed the visitant.

"Because you disbelieve their efficacy!" Markheim cried.

"I do not say so," returned the other; "but I look on these things from a different side, and when the life is done my interest falls. The man has lived to serve me, to spread black looks under colour of religion, or to sow tares in the wheat-field, as you do, in a course of weak compliance with desire. Now that he draws so near to his deliverance, he can add but one act of service—to repent, to die smiling, and thus to build up in confidence and hope the more timorous of my surviving followers. I am not so hard a master. Try me. Accept my help. Please yourself in life as you have done hitherto; please yourself more amply, spread your elbows at the board; and when the night begins to fall and the curtains to be drawn, I tell you, for your greater comfort, that you will find it even easy to compound your quarrel with your conscience, and to make a truckling peace with God. I came but now from such a deathbed, and the room was full of sincere mourners, listening to the man's last words: and when I looked into that face, which had been set as a flint against mercy, I found it smiling with hope."

"And do you, then, suppose me such a creature?" asked Markheim. "Do you think I have no more generous aspirations than to sin, and sin, and sin, and, at the last, sneak into heaven? My heart rises at the thought. Is this, then, your experience of mankind? or is it because you find me with red hands that you presume such baseness? and is this crime of murder indeed so impious as to dry up the very springs of good?"

"Murder is to me no special category," replied the other. "All sins are murder, even as all life is war. I behold your race, like starving mariners on a raft, plucking crusts out of the hands of famine and feeding on each other's lives. I follow sins beyond the moment of their acting; I find in all that the last consequence is death; and to my eyes, the pretty maid who thwarts her mother with such taking graces on a question of a ball, drips no less visibly with human gore than such a murderer as yourself. Do I say that I follow sins? I follow virtues also; they differ not by the thickness of a nail, they are both scythes for the reaping angel of Death. Evil, for which I live, consists not in action but in character. The bad man is dear to me; not the bad act, whose fruits, if we could follow them far enough down the hurtling cataract of the ages, might yet be found more blessed than those of the rarest virtues. And it is not because you have killed a dealer, but because you are Markheim, that I offer to forward your escape."

"I will lay my heart open to you," answered Markheim. "This crime on which you find me is my last. On my way to it I have learned many lessons; itself is a lesson, a momentous lesson. Hitherto I have been driven with revolt to what I would not; I was a bond-slave to poverty, driven and scourged. There are robust virtues that can stand in these temptations; mine was not so: I had a thirst of pleasure. But to-day, and out of this deed, I pluck both warning and riches—both the power and a fresh resolve to be myself. I become in all things a free actor in the world; I begin to see myself all changed, these hands the agents of good, this heart at peace. Something comes over me out of the past; something of what I have dreamed on Sabbath evenings to the sound of the church organ, of what I forecast when I shed tears over noble books, or talked, an innocent child, with my mother. There lies my life; I have wandered a few years, but now I see once more my city of destination."

"You are to use this money on the Stock Exchange, I think?" remarked the visitor; "and there, if I mistake not, you have already lost some thousands?"

"Ah," said Markheim, "but this time I have a sure thing."

"This time, again, you will lose," replied the visitor quietly.

"Ah, but I keep back the half!" cried Markheim.

"That also you will lose," said the other.

The sweat started upon Markheim's brow. "Well, then, what matter?" he exclaimed. "Say it be lost, say I am plunged again in poverty, shall one part of me, and that the worse, continue until the end to override the better? Evil and good run strong in me, haling me both ways. I do not love the one thing, I love all. I can conceive great deeds, renunciations, martyrdoms; and though I be fallen to such a crime as murder, pity is no stranger to my thoughts. I pity the poor; who knows their trials better than myself? I pity and help them; I prize love, I love honest laughter; there is no good thing nor true thing on earth but I love it from my heart. And are my vices only to direct my life, and my virtues to lie without effect, like some passive lumber of the mind? Not so; good, also, is a spring of acts."

But the visitant raised his finger. "For six-and-thirty years that you have been in this world," said be, "through many changes of fortune and varieties of humour, I have watched you steadily fall. Fifteen years ago you would have started at a theft. Three years back you would have blenched at the name of murder. Is there any crime, is there any cruelty or meanness, from which you still recoil?—five years from now I shall detect you in the fact! Downward, downward, lies your way; nor can anything but death avail to stop you."

"It is true," Markheim said huskily, "I have in some degree complied with evil. But it is so with all: the very saints, in the mere exercise of living, grow less dainty, and take on the tone of their surroundings."

"I will propound to you one simple question," said the other; "and as you answer, I shall read to you your moral horoscope. You have grown in many things more lax; possibly you do right to be so—and at any account, it is the same with all men. But granting that, are you in any one particular, however trifling, more difficult to please with your own conduct, or do you go in all things with a looser rein?"

"In any one?" repeated Markheim, with an anguish of consideration. "No," he added, with despair, "in none! I have gone down in all."

"Then," said the visitor, "content yourself with what you are, for you will never change; and the words of your part on this stage are irrevocably written down."

Markheim stood for a long while silent, and indeed it was the visitor who first broke the silence. "That being so," he said, "shall I show you the money?"

"And grace?" cried Markheim.

"Have you not tried it?" returned the other. "Two or three years ago, did I not see you on the platform of revival meetings, and was not your voice the loudest in the hymn?"

"It is true," said Markheim; "and I see clearly what remains for me by way of duty. I thank you for these lessons from my soul; my eyes are opened, and I behold myself at last for what I am."

At this moment, the sharp note of the door-bell rang through the house; and the visitant, as though this were some concerted signal for which he had been waiting, changed at once in his demeanour.

"The maid!" he cried. "She has returned, as I forewarned you, and there is now before you one more difficult passage. Her master, you must say, is ill; you must let her in, with an assured but rather serious countenance—no smiles, no overacting, and I promise you success! Once the girl within, and the door closed, the same dexterity that has already rid you of the dealer will relieve you of this last danger in your path. Thenceforward you have the whole evening—the whole night, if needful—to ransack the treasures of the house and to make good your safety. This is help that comes to you with the mask of danger. Up!" he cried; "up, friend; your life hangs trembling in the scales: up, and act!"

Markheim steadily regarded his counsellor. "If I be condemned to evil acts," he said, "there is still one door of freedom open—I can cease from action. If my life be an ill thing, I can lay it down. Though I be, as you say truly, at the beck of every small temptation, I can yet, by one decisive gesture, place myself beyond the reach of all. My love of good is damned to barrenness; it may, and let it be! But I have still my hatred of evil; and from that, to your galling disappointment, you shall see that I can draw both energy and courage."

The features of the visitor began to undergo a wonderful and lovely change: they brightened and softened with a tender triumph, and, even as they brightened, faded and dislimned. But Markheim did not pause to watch or understand the transformation. He opened the door and went downstairs very slowly, thinking to himself. His past went soberly before him; he beheld it as it was, ugly and strenuous like a dream, random as chance-medley—a scene of defeat. Life, as he thus reviewed it, tempted him no longer; but on the further side he perceived a quiet haven for his bark. He paused in the passage, and looked into the shop, where the candle still burned by the dead body. It was strangely silent. Thoughts of the dealer swarmed into his mind, as he stood gazing. And then the bell once more broke out into impatient clamour.

He confronted the maid upon the threshold with something like a smile.

"You had better go for the police," said he: "I have killed your master."

THRAWN JANET

The Reverend Murdoch Soulis was long minister of the moorland parish of Balweary, in the vale of Dule. A severe, bleak-faced old man, dreadful to his hearers, he dwelt in the last years of his life, without relative or servant or any human company, in the small and lonely manse under the Hanging Shaw. In spite of the iron composure of his features, his eye was wild, scared, and uncertain; and when he dwelt, in private admonitions, on the future of the impenitent, it seemed as if his eye pierced through the storms of time to the terrors of eternity. Many young persons, coming to prepare themselves against the season of the Holy Communion, were dreadfully affected by his talk. He had a sermon on lst Peter, v. and 8th, "The devil as a roaring lion," on the Sunday after every seventeenth of August, and he was accustomed to surpass himself upon that text both by the appalling nature of the matter and the terror of his bearing in the pulpit. The children were frightened into fits, and the old looked more than usually oracular, and were, all that day, full of those hints that Hamlet deprecated. The manse itself, where it stood by the water of Dule among some thick trees, with the Shaw overhanging it on the one side, and on the other many cold, moorish hilltops rising towards the sky, had begun, at a very early period of Mr. Soulis's ministry, to be avoided in the dusk hours by all who valued themselves upon their prudence; and guidmen sitting at the clachan alehouse shook their heads together at the thought of passing late by that uncanny neighbourhood. There was one spot, to be more particular, which was regarded with especial awe. The manse stood between the high road and the water of Dule, with a gable to each; its back was towards the kirk-town of Balweary, nearly half a mile away; in front of it, a bare garden, hedged with thorn, occupied the land between the river and the road. The house was two stories high, with two large rooms on each. It opened not directly on the garden, but on a causewayed path, or passage, giving on the road on the one hand, and closed on the other by the tall willows and elders that bordered on the stream. And it was this strip of causeway that enjoyed among the young parishioners of Balweary so infamous a reputation. The minister walked there often after dark, sometimes groaning aloud in the instancy of his unspoken prayers; and when he was from home, and the manse door was locked, the more daring schoolboys ventured, with beating hearts, to "follow my leader" across that legendary spot.

This atmosphere of terror, surrounding, as it did, a man of God of spotless character and orthodoxy, was a common cause of wonder and subject of inquiry among the few strangers who were led by chance or business into that unknown, outlying country. But many even of the people of the parish were ignorant of the strange events which had marked the first year of Mr. Soulis's ministrations; and among those who were better informed, some were naturally reticent, and others shy of that particular topic. Now and again, only, one of the older folk would warm into courage over his third tumbler, and recount the cause of the minister's strange looks and solitary life.

Fifty years syne, when Mr. Soulis cam first into Ba'weary, he was still a young man—a callant, the folk said—fu' o' book learnin' and grand at the exposition, but, as was natural in sae young a man, wi' nae leevin' experience in religion. The younger sort were greatly taken wi' his gifts and his gab; but auld, concerned, serious men and women were moved even to prayer for the young man, whom they took to be a self-deceiver, and the parish that was like to be sae ill-supplied. It was before the days o' the moderates—weary fa' them; but ill things are like guid—they baith come bit by bit, a pickle at a time; and there were folk even then that said the Lord had left the college professors to their ain devices, an' the lads that went to study wi' them wad hae done mair and better sittin' in a peat-bog, like their forbears of the persecution, wi' a Bible under their oxter and a speerit o' prayer in their heart. There was nae doubt, onyway, but that Mr. Soulis had been ower lang at the college. He was careful and troubled for many things besides the ae thing needful. He had a feck o' books wi' him—mair than had ever been seen before in a' that presbytery; and a sair wark the carrier had wi' them, for they were a' like to have smoored in the Deil's Hag between this and Kilmackerlie. They were books o' divinity, to be sure, or so they ca'd them; but the serious were o' opinion there was little service for sae mony, when the hail o' God's Word would gang in the neuk of a plaid. Then he wad sit half the day and half the nicht forbye, which was scant decent—writin', nae less; and first, they were feared he wad read his sermons; and syne it proved he was writin' a book himsel', which was surely no fittin' for ane of his years an' sma' experience.

Onyway it behoved him to get an auld, decent wife to keep the manse for him an' see to his bit denners; and he was recommended to an auld limmer—Janet M'Clour, they ca'd her—and sae far left to himsel' as to be ower persuaded. There was many advised him to the contrar, for Janet was mair than suspeckit by the best folk in Ba'weary. Lang or that, she had had a wean to a dragoon; she hadnae come forrit for maybe thretty year; and bairns had seen her mumblin' to hersel' up on Key's Loan in the gloamin', whilk was an unco time an' place for a God-fearin' woman. Howsoever, it was the laird himsel' that had first tauld the minister o' Janet; and in thae days he wad have gane a far gate to pleesure the laird. When folk tauld him that Janet was sib to the deil, it was a' superstition by his way of it; an' when they cast up the Bible to him an' the witch of Endor, he wad threep it doun their thrapples that thir days were a' gane by, and the deil was mercifully restrained.

Weel, when it got about the clachan that Janet M'Clour was to be servant at the manse, the folk were fair mad wi' her an' him thegether; and some o' the guidwives had nae better to dae than get round her door cheeks and chairge her wi' a' that was ken't again her, frae the sodger's bairn to John Tamson's twa kye. She was nae great speaker; folk usually let her gang her ain gate, an' she let them gang theirs, wi', neither Fair-guid-een nor Fair-guid-day; but when she buckled to, she had a tongue to deave the miller. Up she got, an' there wasnae an auld story in Ba'weary but she gart somebody lowp for it that day; they couldnae say ae thing but she could say twa to it; till, at the hinder end, the guidwives up and claught haud of her, and clawed the coats aff her back, and pu'd her doun the clachan to the water o' Dule, to see if she were a witch or no, soum or droun. The carline skirled till ye could hear her at the Hangin' Shaw, and she focht like ten; there was many a guidwife bure the mark of her neist day an' mony a lang day after; and just in the hettest o' the collieshangie, wha suld come up (for his sins) but the new minister.

"Women," said he (and he had a grand voice), "I charge you in the Lord's name to let her go."

Janet ran to him—she was fair wud wi' terror—an' clang to him, an' prayed him, for Christ's sake, save her frae the cummers; an' they, for their pairt, tauld him a' that was ken't, and maybe mair.

"Woman," says he to Janet, "is this true?"

"As the Lord sees me," says she, "as the Lord made me, no a word o't. Forbye the bairn," says she, "I've been a decent woman a' my days."

"Will you," says Mr. Soulis, "in the name of God, and before me, His unworthy minister, renounce the devil and his works?"

Weel, it wad appear that when he askit that, she gave a girn that fairly frichtit them that saw her, an' they could hear her teeth play dirl thegether in her chafts; but there was naething for it but the ae way or the ither; an' Janet lifted up her hand and renounced the deil before them a'.

"And now," says Mr. Soulis to the guidwives, "home with ye, one and all, and pray to God for His forgiveness."

And he gied Janet his arm, though she had little on her but a sark, and took her up the clachan to her ain door like a leddy of the land; an' her scrieghin' and laughin' as was a scandal to be heard.

There were mony grave folk lang ower their prayers that nicht; but when the morn cam' there was sic a fear fell upon a' Ba'weary that the bairns hid theirsels, and even the men folk stood and keekit frae their doors. For there was Janet comin' doun the clachan—her or her likeness, nane could tell—wi' her neck thrawn, and her heid on ae side, like a body that has been hangit, and a girn on her face like an unstreakit corp. By an' by they got used wi' it, and even speered at her to ken what was wrang; but frae that day forth she couldnae speak like a Christian woman, but slavered and played click wi' her teeth like a pair o' shears; and frae that day forth the name o' God cam never on her lips. Whiles she wad try to say it, but it michtnae be. Them that kenned best said least; but they never gied that Thing the name o' Janet M'Clour; for the auld Janet, by their way o't, was in muckle hell that day. But the minister was neither to haud nor to bind; he preached about naething but the folk's cruelty that had gi'en her a stroke of the palsy; he skelpt the bairns that meddled her; and he had her up to the manse that same nicht, and dwalled there a' his lane wi' her under the Hangin' Shaw.

Weel, time gaed by: and the idler sort commenced to think mair lichtly o' that black business. The minister was weel thocht o'; he was aye late at the writing, folk wad see his can'le doon by the Dule water after twal' at e'en; and he seemed pleased wi' himsel' and upsitten as at first, though a' body could see that he was dwining. As for Janet she cam an' she gaed; if she didnae speak muckle afore, it was reason she should speak less then; she meddled naebody; but she was an eldritch thing to see, an' nane wad hae mistrysted wi' her for Ba'weary glebe.

About the end o' July there cam' a spell o' weather, the like o't never was in that country side; it was lown an' het an' heartless; the herds couldnae win up the Black Hill, the bairns were ower weariet to play; an' yet it was gousty too, wi' claps o' het wund that rumm'led in the glens, and bits o' shouers that slockened naething. We aye thocht it but to thun'er on the morn; but the morn cam, an' the morn's morning, and it was aye the same uncanny weather, sair on folks and bestial. Of a' that were the waur, nane suffered like Mr. Soulis; he could neither sleep nor eat, he tauld his elders; an' when he wasnae writin' at his weary book, he wad be stravaguin' ower a' the countryside like a man possessed, when a' body else was blythe to keep caller ben the house.

Abune Hangin' Shaw, in the bield o' the Black Hill, there's a bit enclosed grund wi' an iron yett; and it seems, in the auld days, that was the kirkyaird o' Ba'weary, and consecrated by the Papists before the blessed licht shone upon the kingdom. It was a great howff o' Mr. Soulis's, onyway; there he would sit an' consider his sermons; and indeed it's a bieldy bit. Weel, as he cam ower the wast end o' the Black Hill, ae day, he saw first twa, an syne fower, an' syne seeven corbie craws fleein' round an' round abune the auld kirkyaird. They flew laigh and heavy, an' squawked to ither as they gaed; and it was clear to Mr. Soulis that something had put them frae their ordinar. He wasnae easy fleyed, an' gaed straucht up to the wa's; an' what suld he find there but a man, or the appearance of a man, sittin' in the inside upon a grave. He was of a great stature, an' black as hell, and his e'en were singular to see.[144] Mr. Soulis had heard tell o' black men, mony's the time; but there was something unco about this black man that daunted him. Het as he was, he took a kind o' cauld grue in the marrow o' his banes; but up he spak for a' that; an' says he: "My friend, are you a stranger in this place?" The black man answered never a word; he got upon his feet, an' begude to hirsle to the wa' on the far side; but he aye lookit at the minister; an' the minister stood an' lookit back; till a' in a meenute the black man was ower the wa' an' rinnin' for the bield o' the trees. Mr. Soulis, he hardly kenned why, ran after him; but he was sair forjaskit wi' his walk an' the het, unhalesome weather; and rin as he likit, he got nae mair than a glisk o' the black man amang the birks, till he won doun to the foot o' the hillside, an' there he saw him ance mair, gaun, hap, step, an' lowp, ower Dule water to the manse.

Mr. Soulis wasnae weel pleased that this fearsome gangrel suld mak' sae free wi' Ba'weary manse; an' he ran the harder, an', wet shoon, ower the burn, an' up the walk; but the deil a black man was there to see. He stepped out upon the road, but there was naebody there; he gaed a' ower the gairden, but na, nae black man. At the hinder end, and a bit feared as was but natural, he lifted the hasp and into the manse; and there was Janet M'Clour before his een, wi' her thrawn craig, and nane sae pleased to see him. And he aye minded sinsyne, when first he set his een upon her, he had the same cauld and deidly grue.

"Janet," says he, "have you seen a black man?"

"A black man?" quo' she. "Save us a'! Ye're no wise, minister. There's nae black man in a Ba'weary."

But she didnae speak plain, ye maun understand; but yam-yammered, like a powney wi' the bit in its moo.

"Weel," says he, "Janet, if there was nae black man, I have spoken with the Accuser of the Brethren."

And he sat down like ane wi' a fever, an' his teeth chittered in his heid.

"Hoots," says she, "think shame to yoursel', minister;" an' gied him a drap brandy that she keepit aye by her.

Syne Mr. Soulis gaed into his study amang a' his books. It's a lang, laigh, mirk chalmer, perishin' cauld in winter, an' no very dry even in the tap o' the simmer, for the manse stands near the burn. Sae doun he sat, and thocht of a' that had come an' gane since he was in Ba'weary, an' his hame, an' the days when he was a bairn an' ran daffin' on the braes; and that black man aye ran in his heid like the ower-come of a sang. Aye the mair he thocht, the mair he thocht o' the black man. He tried the prayer, an' the words wouldnae come to him; an' he tried, they say, to write at his book, but he could nae mak' nae mair o' that. There was whiles he thocht the black man was at his oxter, an' the swat stood upon him cauld as well-water; and there was other whiles, when he cam to himsel' like a christened bairn and minded naething.

The upshot was that he gaed to the window an' stood glowrin' at Dule water. The trees are unco thick, an' the water lies deep an' black under the manse; an' there was Janet washin' the cla'es wi' her coats kilted. She had her back to the minister, an' he, for his pairt, hardly kenned what he was lookin' at. Syne she turned round, an' shawed her face; Mr. Soulis had the same cauld grue as twice that day afore, an' it was borne in upon him what folk said, that Janet was deid lang syne, an' this was a bogle in her clay-cauld flesh. He drew back a pickle and he scanned her narrowly. She was tramp-trampin' in the cla'es, croonin' to hersel'; and eh! Gude guide us, but it was a fearsome face. Whiles she sang louder, but there was nae man born o' woman that could tell the words o' her sang; an' whiles she lookit side-lang doun, but there was naething there for her to look at. There gaed a scunner through the flesh upon his banes; and that was Heeven's advertisement. But Mr. Soulis just blamed himsel', he said, to think sae ill of a puir, auld afflicted wife that hadnae a freend forbye himsel'; an' he put up a bit prayer for him and her, an' drank a little caller water—for his heart rose again the meat—an' gaed up to his naked bed in the gloaming.

That was a nicht that has never been forgotten in Ba'weary, the nicht o' the seeventeenth of August, seventeen hun'er' an' twal'. It had been het afore, as I hae said, but that nicht it was hetter than ever. The sun gaed doun amang unco-lookin' clouds; it fell as mirk as the pit; no a star, no a breath o' wund; ye couldnae see your han' afore your face, and even the auld folk cuist the covers frae their beds and lay pechin' for their breath. Wi' a' that he had upon his mind, it was gey and unlikely Mr. Soulis wad get muckle sleep. He lay an' he tummled; the gude, caller bed that he got into brunt his very banes; whiles he slept, and whiles he waukened; whiles he heard the time o' nicht, and whiles a tyke yowlin' up the muir, as if somebody was deid; whiles he thocht he heard bogles claverin' in his lug, an' whiles he saw spunkies in the room. He behoved, he judged, to be sick; an' sick he was—little he jaloosed the sickness.

At the hinder end, he got a clearness in his mind, sat up in his sark on the bed-side, and fell thinkin' ance mair o' the black man an' Janet. He couldnae weel tell how—maybe it was the cauld to his feet—but it cam' in upon him wi' a spate that there was some connection between thir twa, an' that either or baith o' them were bogles. And just at that moment, in Janet's room, which was neist to his, there cam' a stramp o' feet as if men were wars'lin', an' then a loud bang; an' then a wund gaed reishling round the fower quarters of the house; an' then a' was aince mair as seelent as the grave.

Mr. Soulis was feared for neither man nor deevil. He got his tinder-box, an' lit a can'le, an' made three steps o't ower to Janet's door. It was on the hasp, an' he pushed it open, an' keeked bauldly in. It was a big room, as big as the minister's ain, an' plenished wi' grand, auld, solid gear, for he had naething else. There was a fower-posted bed wi' auld tapestry; and a braw cabinet of aik, that was fu' o' the minister's divinity books, an' put there to be out o' the gate; an' a wheen duds o' Janet's lying here and there about the floor. But nae Janet could Mr. Soulis see; nor ony sign of a contention. In he gaed (an' there's few that wad ha'e followed him) an' lookit a' round, an' listened. But there was naethin' to be heard, neither inside the manse nor in a' Ba'weary parish, an' naethin' to be seen but the muckle shadows turnin' round the can'le. An' then a' at aince, the minister's heart played dunt an' stood stock-still; an' a cauld wund blew amang the hairs o' his heid. Whaten a weary sicht was that for the puir man's een! For there was Janat hangin' frae a nail beside the auld aik cabinet: her heid aye lay on her shoother, her een were steeked, the tongue projekit frae her mouth, and her heels were twa feet clear abune the floor.

"God forgive us all!" thocht Mr. Soulis; "poor Janet's dead."

He cam' a step nearer to the corp; an' then his heart fair whammled in his inside. For by what cantrip it wad ill-beseem a man to judge, she was hingin' frae a single nail an' by a single wursted thread for darnin' hose.

It's an awfu' thing to be your lane at nicht wi' siccan prodigies o' darkness; but Mr. Soulis was strong in the Lord. He turned an' gaed his ways oot o' that room, and lockit the door ahint him; and step by step, doon the stairs, as heavy as leed; and set doon the can'le on the table at the stairfoot. He couldnae pray, he couldnae think, he was dreepin' wi' caul' swat, an' naething could he hear but the dunt-dunt-duntin' o' his ain heart. He micht maybe have stood there an hour, or maybe twa, he minded sae little; when a' o' a sudden, he heard a laigh, uncanny steer upstairs; a foot gaed to an' fro in the cha'mer whaur the corp was hingin'; syne the door was opened, though he minded weel that he had lockit it; an' syne there was a step upon the landin', an' it seemed to him as if the corp was lookin' ower the rail and doun upon him whaur he stood.

He took up the can'le again (for he couldnae want the licht), and as saftly as ever he could, gaed straucht out o' the manse an' to the far end o' the causeway. It was aye pit-mirk; the flame o' the can'le, when he set it on the grund, brunt steedy and clear as in a room; naething moved, but the Dule water seepin' and sabbin' doon the glen, an' yon unhaly footstep that cam' ploddin doun the stairs inside the manse. He kenned the foot over weel, for it was Janet's; and at ilka step that cam' a wee thing nearer, the cauld got deeper in his vitals. He commanded his soul to Him that made an' keepit him; "and O Lord," said he, "give me strength this night to war against the powers of evil."

By this time the foot was comin' through the passage for the door; he could hear a hand skirt alang the wa', as if the fearsome thing was feelin' for its way. The saughs tossed an' maned thegether, a lang sigh cam' ower the hills, the flame o' the can'le was blawn aboot; an' there stood the corp of Thrawn Janet, wi' her grogram goun an' her black mutch, wi' the heid aye upon the shouther, an' the girn still upon the face o't—leevin', ye wad hae said—deid, as Mr. Soulis weel kenned—upon the threshold o' the manse.

It's a strange thing that the saul of man should be that thirled into his perishable body; but the minister saw that, an' his heart didnae break.

She didnae stand there lang; she began to move again an' cam' slowly towards Mr. Soulis whaur he stood under the saughs. A' the life o' his body, a' the strength o' his speerit, were glowerin' frae his een. It seemed she was gaun to speak, but wanted words, an' made a sign wi' the left hand. There cam' a clap o' wund, like a cat's fuff; oot gaed the can'le, the saughs skrieghed like folk; an' Mr. Soulis kenned that, live or die, this was the end o't.

"Witch, beldame, devil!" he cried, "I charge you, by the power of God, begone—if you be dead, to the grave—if you be damned, to hell."

An' at that moment the Lord's ain hand out o' the Heevens struck the Horror whaur it stood; the auld, deid, desecrated corp o' the witch-wife, sae lang keepit frae the grave and hirsled round by deils, lowed up like a brunstane spunk and fell in ashes to the grund; the thunder followed, peal on dirling peal, the rairing rain upon the back o' that; and Mr. Soulis lowped through the garden hedge, and ran, wi' skelloch upon skelloch, for the clachan.

That same mornin', John Christie saw the Black Man pass the Muckle Cairn as it was chappin' six; before eicht, he gaed by the change-house at Knockdow; an' no lang after, Sandy M'Lellan saw him gaun linkin' doun the braes frae Kilmackerlie. There's little doubt but it was him that dwalled sae lang in Janet's body; but he was awa' at last; and sinsyne the deil has never fashed us in Ba'weary.

But it was a sair dispensation for the minister; lang, lang he lay ravin' in his bed; and frae that hour to this, he was the man ye ken the day.

OLALLA

"Now," said the doctor, "my part is done, and, I may say, with some vanity, well done. It remains only to get you out of this cold and poisonous city, and to give you two months of a pure air and an easy conscience. The last is your affair. To the first I think I can help you. It falls indeed rather oddly; it was but the other day the Padre came in from the country; and as he and I are old friends, although of contrary professions, he applied to me in a matter of distress among some of his parishioners. This was a family—but you are ignorant of Spain, and even the names of our grandees are hardly known to you; suffice it, then, that they were once great people, and are now fallen to the brink of destitution. Nothing now belongs to them but the residencia, and certain leagues of desert mountain, in the greater part of which not even a goat could support life. But the house is a fine old place, and stands at a great height among the hills, and most salubriously; and I had no sooner heard my friend's tale, than I remembered you. I told him I had a wounded officer, wounded in the good cause, who was now able to make a change; and I proposed that his friends should take you for a lodger. Instantly the Padre's face grew dark, as I had maliciously foreseen it would. It was out of the question, he said. Then let them starve, said I, for I have no sympathy with tatterdemalion pride. There-upon we separated, not very content with one another; but yesterday, to my wonder, the Padre returned and made a submission: the difficulty, he said, he had found upon enquiry to be less than he had feared; or, in other words, these proud people had put their pride in their pocket. I closed with the offer; and, subject to your approval, I have taken rooms for you in the residencia. The air of these mountains will renew your blood; and the quiet in which you will there live is worth all the medicines in the world."

"Doctor," said I, "you have been throughout my good angel, and your advice is a command. But tell me, if you please, something of the family with which I am to reside."

"I am coming to that," replied my friend; "and, indeed, there is a difficulty in the way. These beggars are, as I have said, of very high descent and swollen with the most baseless vanity; they have lived for some generations in a growing isolation, drawing away, on either hand, from the rich who had now become too high for them, and from the poor, whom they still regarded as too low; and even to-day, when poverty forces them to unfasten their door to a guest, they cannot do so without a most ungracious stipulation. You are to remain, they say, a stranger; they will give you attendance, but they refuse from the first the idea of the smallest intimacy."

I will not deny that I was piqued, and perhaps the feeling strengthened my desire to go, for I was confident that I could break down that barrier if I desired. "There is nothing offensive in such a stipulation," said I; "and I even sympathise with the feeling that inspired it."

"It is true they have never seen you," returned the doctor politely; "and if they knew you were the handsomest and the most pleasant man that ever came from England (where I am told that handsome men are common, but pleasant ones not so much so), they would doubtless make you welcome with a better grace. But since you take the thing so well, it matters not. To me, indeed, it seems discourteous. But you will find yourself the gainer. The family will not much tempt you. A mother, a son, and a daughter; an old woman said to be halfwitted, a country lout, and a country girl, who stands very high with her confessor, and is, therefore," chuckled the physician, "most likely plain; there is not much in that to attract the fancy of a dashing officer."

"And yet you say they are high-born," I objected.

"Well, as to that, I should distinguish," returned the doctor. "The mother is; not so the children. The mother was the last representative of a princely stock, degenerate both in parts and fortune.

Her father was not only poor, he was mad: and the girl ran wild about the residencia till his death. Then, much of the fortune having died with him, and the family being quite extinct, the girl ran wilder than ever, until at last she married, Heaven knows whom, a muleteer some say, others a smuggler; while there are some who uphold there was no marriage at all, and that Felipe and Olalla are bastards. The union, such as it was, was tragically dissolved some years ago; but they live in such seclusion, and the country at that time was in so much disorder, that the precise manner of the man's end is known only to the priest—if even to him."

"I begin to think I shall have strange experiences," said I.

"I would not romance, if I were you," replied the doctor; "you will find, I fear, a very grovelling and commonplace reality. Felipe, for instance, I have seen. And what am I to say? He is very rustic, very cunning, very loutish, and, I should say, an innocent; the others are probably to match. No, no, senor commandante, you must seek congenial society among the great sights of our mountains; and in these at least, if you are at all a lover of the works of nature, I promise you will not be disappointed."

The next day Felipe came for me in a rough country cart, drawn by a mule; and a little before the stroke of noon, after I had said farewell to the doctor, the innkeeper, and different good souls who had befriended me during my sickness, we set forth out of the city by the Eastern gate, and began to ascend into the Sierra. I had been so long a prisoner, since I was left behind for dying after the loss of the convoy, that the mere smell of the earth set me smiling. The country through which we went was wild and rocky, partially covered with rough woods, now of the cork-tree, and now of the great Spanish chestnut, and frequently intersected by the beds of mountain torrents. The sun shone, the wind rustled joyously; and we had advanced some miles, and the city had already shrunk into an inconsiderable knoll upon the plain behind us, before my attention began to be diverted to the companion of my drive. To the eye, he seemed but a diminutive, loutish, well-made country lad, such as the doctor had described, mighty quick and active, but devoid of any culture; and this first impression was with most observers final. What began to strike me was his familiar, chattering talk; so strangely inconsistent with the terms on which I was to be received; and partly from his imperfect enunciation, partly from the sprightly incoherence of the matter, so very difficult to follow clearly without an effort of the mind. It is true I had before talked with persons of a similar mental constitution; persons who seemed to live (as he did) by the senses, taken and possessed by the visual object of the moment and unable to discharge their minds of that impression. His seemed to me (as I sat, distantly giving ear) a kind of conversation proper to drivers, who pass much of their time in a great vacancy of the intellect and threading the sights of a familiar country. But this was not the case of Felipe; by his own account, he was a home-keeper; "I wish I was there now," he said; and then, spying a tree by the wayside, he broke off to tell me that he had once seen a crow among its branches.

"A crow?" I repeated, struck by the ineptitude of the remark, and thinking I had heard imperfectly.

But by this time he was already filled with a new idea; hearkening with a rapt intentness, his head on one side, his face puckered; and he struck me rudely, to make me hold my peace. Then he smiled and shook his head.

"What did you hear?" I asked.

"O, it is all right," he said; and began encouraging his mule with cries that echoed unhumanly up the mountain walls.

I looked at him more closely. He was superlatively well-built, light, and lithe and strong; he was well-featured; his yellow eyes were very large, though, perhaps, not very expressive; take him altogether, he was a pleasant-looking lad, and I had no fault to find with him, beyond that he was of a dusky hue, and inclined to hairyness; two characteristics that I disliked. It was his mind that puzzled, and yet attracted me. The doctor's phrase—an innocent—came back to me; and I was wondering if that were, after all, the true description, when the road began to go down into the narrow and naked chasm of a torrent. The waters thundered tumultuously in the bottom; and the ravine was filled full of the sound, the thin spray, and the claps of wind, that accompanied their descent. The scene was certainly impressive; but the road was in that part very securely walled in; the mule went steadily forward; and I was astonished to perceive the paleness of terror in the face of my companion. The voice of that wild river was inconstant, now sinking lower as if in weariness, now doubling its hoarse tones; momentary freshets seemed to swell its volume, sweeping down the gorge, raving and booming against the barrier walls; and I observed it was at each of these accessions to the clamour, that my driver more particularly winced and blanched. Some thoughts of Scottish superstition and the river Kelpie, passed across my mind; I wondered if perchance the like were prevalent in that part of Spain; and turning to Felipe, sought to draw him out.

"What is the matter?" I asked.

"O, I am afraid," he replied.

"Of what are you afraid?" I returned. "This seems one of the safest places on this very dangerous road."

"It makes a noise," he said, with a simplicity of awe that set my doubts at rest.

The lad was but a child in intellect; his mind was like his body, active and swift, but stunted in development; and I began from that time forth to regard him with a measure of pity, and to listen at first with indulgence, and at last even with pleasure, to his disjointed babble.

By about four in the afternoon we had crossed the summit of the mountain line, said farewell to the western sunshine, and began to go down upon the other side, skirting the edge of many ravines and moving through the shadow of dusky woods. There rose upon all sides the voice of falling water, not condensed and formidable as in the gorge of the river, but scattered and sounding gaily and musically from glen to glen. Here, too, the spirits of my driver mended, and he began to sing aloud in a falsetto voice, and with a singular bluntness of musical perception, never true either to melody or key, but wandering at will, and yet somehow with an effect that was natural and pleasing, like that of the of birds. As the dusk increased, I fell more and more under the spell of this artless warbling, listening and waiting for some articulate air, and still disappointed; and when at last I asked him what it was he sang—"O," cried he, "I am just singing!" Above all, I was taken with a trick he had of unweariedly repeating the same note at little intervals; it was not so monotonous as you would think, or, at least, not disagreeable; and it seemed to breathe a wonderful contentment with what is, such as we love to fancy in the attitude of trees, or the quiescence of a pool.

Night had fallen dark before we came out upon a plateau, and drew up a little after, before a certain lump of superior blackness which I could only conjecture to be the residencia. Here, my guide, getting down from the cart, hooted and whistled for a long time in vain; until at last an old peasant man came towards us from somewhere in the surrounding dark, carrying a candle in his hand. By the light of this I was able to perceive a great arched doorway of a Moorish character: it was closed by iron-studded gates, in one of the leaves of which Felipe opened a wicket. The peasant carried off the cart to some out-building; but my guide and I passed through the wicket, which was closed again behind us; and by the glimmer of the candle, passed through a court, up a stone stair, along a section of an open gallery, and up more stairs again, until we came at last to the door of a great and somewhat bare apartment. This room, which I understood was to be mine, was pierced by three windows, lined with some lustrous wood disposed in panels, and carpeted with the skins of many savage animals. A bright fire burned in the chimney, and shed abroad a changeful flicker; close up to the blaze there was drawn a table, laid for supper; and in the far end a bed stood ready. I was pleased by these preparations, and said so to Felipe; and he, with the same simplicity of disposition that I held already remarked in him, warmly re-echoed my praises. "A fine room," he said; "a very fine room. And fire, too; fire is good; it melts out the pleasure in your bones. And the bed," he continued, carrying over the candle in that direction—"see what fine sheets—how soft, how smooth, smooth;" and he passed his hand again and again over their texture, and then laid down his head and rubbed his cheeks among them with a grossness of content that somehow offended me. I took the candle from his hand (for I feared he would set the bed on fire) and walked back to the supper-table, where, perceiving a measure of wine, I poured out a cup and called to him to come and drink of it. He started to his feet at once and ran to me with a strong expression of hope; but when he saw the wine, he visibly shuddered.

"Oh, no," he said, "not that; that is for you. I hate it."

"Very well, Senor," said I; "then I will drink to your good health, and to the prosperity of your house and family. Speaking of which," I added, after I had drunk, "shall I not have the pleasure of laying my salutations in person at the feet of the Senora, your mother?"

But at these words all the childishness passed out of his face, and was succeeded by a look of indescribable cunning and secrecy. He backed away from me at the same time, as though I were an animal about to leap or some dangerous fellow with a weapon, and when he had got near the door, glowered at me sullenly with contracted pupils. "No," he said at last, and the next moment was gone noiselessly out of the room; and I heard his footing die away downstairs as light as rainfall, and silence closed over the house.

After I had supped I drew up the table nearer to the bed and began to prepare for rest; but in the new position of the light, I was struck by a picture on the wall. It represented a woman, still young. To judge by her costume and the mellow unity which reigned over the canvas, she had long been dead; to judge by the vivacity of the attitude, the eyes and the features, I might have been beholding in a mirror the image of life. Her figure was very slim and strong, and of a just proportion; red tresses lay like a crown over her brow; her eyes, of a very golden brown, held mine with a look; and her face, which was perfectly shaped, was yet marred by a cruel, sullen, and sensual expression. Something in both face and figure, something exquisitely intangible, like the echo of an echo, suggested the features and bearing of my guide; and I stood awhile, unpleasantly attracted and wondering at the oddity of the resemblance. The common, carnal stock of that race, which had been originally designed for such high dames as the one now looking on me from the canvas, had fallen to baser uses, wearing country clothes, sitting on the shaft and holding the reins of a mule cart, to bring home a lodger. Perhaps an actual link subsisted; perhaps some scruple of the delicate flesh that was once clothed upon with the satin and brocade of the dead lady, now winced at the rude contact of Felipe's frieze.

The first light of the morning shone full upon the portrait, and, as I lay awake, my eyes continued to dwell upon it with growing complacency; its beauty crept about my heart insidiously, silencing my scruples one after another; and while I knew that to love such a woman were to sign and seal one's own sentence of degeneration, I still knew that, if she were alive, I should love her. Day after day the double knowledge of her wickedness and of my weakness grew clearer. She came to be the heroine of many day-dreams, in which her eyes led on to, and sufficiently rewarded, crimes. She cast a dark shadow on my fancy; and when I was out in the free air of heaven, taking vigorous exercise and healthily renewing the current of my blood, it was often a glad thought to me that my enchantress was safe in the grave, her wand of beauty broken, her lips closed in silence, her philtre spilt. And yet I had a half-lingering terror that she might not be dead after all, but re-arisen in the body of some descendant.

Felipe served my meals in my own apartment; and his resemblance to the portrait haunted me. At times it was not; at times, upon some change of attitude or flash of expression, it would leap out upon me like a ghost. It was above all in his ill tempers that the likeness triumphed. He certainly liked me; he was proud of my notice, which he sought to engage by many simple and childlike devices; he loved to sit close before my fire, talking his broken talk or singing his odd, endless, wordless songs, and sometimes drawing his hand over my clothes with an affectionate manner of caressing that never failed to cause in me an embarrassment of which I was ashamed. But for all that, he was capable of flashes of causeless anger and fits of sturdy sullenness. At a word of reproof, I have seen him upset the dish of which I was about to eat, and this not surreptitiously, but with defiance; and similarly at a hint of inquisition. I was not unnaturally curious, being in a strange place and surrounded by staring people; but at the shadow of a question, he shrank back, lowering and dangerous. Then it was that, for a fraction of a second, this rough lad might have been the brother of the lady in the frame. But these humours were swift to pass; and the resemblance died along with them.

In these first days I saw nothing of any one but Felipe, unless the portrait is to be counted; and since the lad was plainly of weak mind, and had moments of passion, it may be wondered that I bore his dangerous neighbourhood with equanimity. As a matter of fact, it was for some time irksome; but it happened before long that I obtained over him so complete a mastery as set my disquietude at rest.

It fell in this way. He was by nature slothful, and much of a vagabond, and yet he kept by the house, and not only waited upon my wants, but laboured every day in the garden or small farm to the south of the residencia. Here he would be joined by the peasant whom I had seen on the night of my arrival, and who dwelt at the far end of the enclosure, about half a mile away, in a rude out-house; but it was plain to me that, of these two, it was Felipe who did most; and though I would sometimes see him throw down his spade and go to sleep among the very plants he had been digging, his constancy and energy were admirable in themselves, and still more so since I was well assured they were foreign to his disposition and the fruit of an ungrateful effort. But while I admired, I wondered what had called forth in a lad so shuttle-witted this enduring sense of duty. How was it sustained? I asked myself, and to what length did it prevail over his instincts? The priest was possibly his inspirer; but the priest came one day to the residencia. I saw him both come and go after an interval of close upon an hour, from a knoll where I was sketching, and all that time Felipe continued to labour undisturbed in the garden.

At last, in a very unworthy spirit, I determined to debauch the lad from his good resolutions, and, way-laying him at the gate, easily pursuaded him to join me in a ramble. It was a fine day, and the woods to which I led him were green and pleasant and sweet-smelling and alive with the hum of insects. Here he discovered himself in a fresh character, mounting up to heights of gaiety that abashed me, and displaying an energy and grace of movement that delighted the eye. He leaped, he ran round me in mere glee; he would stop, and look and listen, and seem to drink in the world like a cordial; and then he would suddenly spring into a tree with one bound, and hang and gambol there like one at home. Little as he said to me, and that of not much import, I have rarely enjoyed more stirring company; the sight of his delight was a continual feast; the speed and accuracy of his movements pleased me to the heart; and I might have been so thoughtlessly unkind as to make a habit of these wants, had not chance prepared a very rude conclusion to my pleasure. By some swiftness or dexterity the lad captured a squirrel in a tree top. He was then some way ahead of me, but I saw him drop to the ground and crouch there, crying aloud for pleasure like a child. The sound stirred my sympathies, it was so fresh and innocent; but as I bettered my pace to draw near, the cry of the squirrel knocked upon my heart. I have heard and seen much of the cruelty of lads, and above all of peasants; but what I now beheld struck me into a passion of anger. I thrust the fellow aside, plucked the poor brute out of his hands, and with swift mercy killed it. Then I turned upon the torturer, spoke to him long out of the heat of my indignation, calling him names at which he seemed to wither; and at length, pointing toward the residencia, bade him begone and leave me, for I chose to walk with men, not with vermin. He fell upon his knees, and, the words coming to him with more cleanness than usual, poured out a stream of the most touching supplications, begging me in mercy to forgive him, to forget what he had done, to look to the future. "O, I try so hard," he said. "O, commandante, bear with Felipe this once; he will never be a brute again!" Thereupon, much more affected than I cared to show, I suffered myself to be persuaded, and at last shook hands with him and made it up. But the squirrel, by way of penance, I made him bury; speaking of the poor thing's beauty, telling him what pains it had suffered, and how base a thing was the abuse of strength. "See, Felipe," said I, "you are strong indeed; but in my hands you are as helpless as that poor thing of the trees. Give me your hand in mine. You cannot remove it. Now suppose that I were cruel like you, and took a pleasure in pain. I only tighten my hold, and see how you suffer." He screamed aloud, his face stricken ashy and dotted with needle points of sweat; and when I set him free, he fell to the earth and nursed his hand and moaned over it like a baby. But he took the lesson in good part; and whether from that, or from what I had said to him, or the higher notion he now had of my bodily strength, his original affection was changed into a dog-like, adoring fidelity.

Meanwhile I gained rapidly in health. The residencia stood on the crown of a stony plateau; on every side the mountains hemmed it about; only from the roof, where was a bartizan, there might be seen between two peaks, a small segment of plain, blue with extreme distance. The air in these altitudes moved freely and largely; great clouds congregated there, and were broken up by the wind and left in tatters on the hilltops; a hoarse, and yet faint rumbling of torrents rose from all round; and one could there study all the ruder and more ancient characters of nature in something of their pristine force. I delighted from the first in the vigorous scenery and changeful weather; nor less in the antique and dilapidated mansion where I dwelt. This was a large oblong, flanked at two opposite corners by bastion-like projections, one of which commanded the door, while both were loopholed for musketry. The lower storey was, besides, naked of windows, so that the building, if garrisoned, could not be carried without artillery. It enclosed an open court planted with pomegranate trees. From this a broad flight of marble stairs ascended to an open gallery, running all round and resting, towards the court, on slender pillars. Thence again, several enclosed stairs led to the upper storeys of the house, which were thus broken up into distinct divisions. The windows, both within and without, were closely shuttered; some of the stone-work in the upper parts had fallen; the roof, in one place, had been wrecked in one of the flurries of wind which were common in these mountains; and the whole house, in the strong, beating sunlight, and standing out above a grove of stunted cork-trees, thickly laden and discoloured with dust, looked like the sleeping palace of the legend. The court, in particular, seemed the very home of slumber. A hoarse cooing of doves haunted about the eaves; the winds were excluded, but when they blew outside, the mountain dust fell here as thick as rain, and veiled the red bloom of the pomegranates; shuttered windows and the closed doors of numerous cellars, and the vacant arches of the gallery, enclosed it; and all day long the sun made broken profiles on the four sides, and paraded the shadow of the pillars on the gallery floor. At the ground level there was, however, a certain pillared recess, which bore the marks of human habitation. Though it was open in front upon the court, it was yet provided with a chimney, where a wood fire would he always prettily blazing; and the tile floor was littered with the skins of animals.

It was in this place that I first saw my hostess. She had drawn one of the skins forward and sat in the sun, leaning against a pillar. It was her dress that struck me first of all, for it was rich and brightly coloured, and shone out in that dusty courtyard with something of the same relief as the flowers of the pomegranates. At a second look it was her beauty of person that took hold of me. As she sat back—watching me, I thought, though with invisible eyes—and wearing at the same time an expression of almost imbecile good-humour and contentment, she showed a perfectness of feature and a quiet nobility of attitude that were beyond a statue's. I took off my hat to her in passing, and her face puckered with suspicion as swiftly and lightly as a pool ruffles in the breeze; but she paid no heed to my courtesy. I went forth on my customary walk a trifle daunted, her idol-like impassivity haunting me; and when I returned, although she was still in much the same posture, I was half surprised to see that she had moved as far as the next pillar, following the sunshine. This time, however, she addressed me with some trivial salutation, civilly enough conceived, and uttered in the same deep-chested, and yet indistinct and lisping tones, that had already baffled the utmost niceness of my hearing from her son. I answered rather at a venture; for not only did I fail to take her meaning with precision, but the sudden disclosure of her eyes disturbed me. They were unusually large, the iris golden like Felipe's, but the pupil at that moment so distended that they seemed almost black; and what affected me was not so much their size as (what was perhaps its consequence) the singular insignificance of their regard. A look more blankly stupid I have never met. My eyes dropped before it even as I spoke, and I went on my way upstairs to my own room, at once baffled and embarrassed. Yet, when I came there and saw the face of the portrait, I was again reminded of the miracle of family descent. My hostess was, indeed, both older and fuller in person; her eyes were of a different colour; her face, besides, was not only free from the ill-significance that offended and attracted me in the painting; it was devoid of either good or bad—a moral blank expressing literally naught. And yet there was a likeness, not so much speaking as immanent, not so much in any particular feature as upon the whole. It should seem, I thought, as if when the master set his signature to that grave canvas, he had not only caught the image of one smiling and false-eyed woman, but stamped the essential quality of a race.

From that day forth, whether I came or went, I was sure to find the Senora seated in the sun against a pillar, or stretched on a rug before the fire; only at times she would shift her station to the top round of the stone staircase, where she lay with the same nonchalance right across my path. In all these days, I never knew her to display the least spark of energy beyond what she expended in brushing and re-brushing her copious copper-coloured hair, or in lisping out, in the rich and broken hoarseness of her voice, her customary idle salutations to myself. These, I think, were her two chief pleasures, beyond that of mere quiescence. She seemed always proud of her remarks, as though they had been witticisms: and, indeed, though they were empty enough, like the conversation of many respectable persons, and turned on a very narrow range of subjects, they were never meaningless or incoherent; nay, they had a certain beauty of their own, breathing, as they did, of her entire contentment. Now she would speak of the warmth, in which (like her son) she greatly delighted; now of the flowers of the pomegranate trees, and now of the white doves and long-winged swallows that fanned the air of the court. The birds excited her. As they raked the eaves in their swift flight, or skimmed sidelong past her with a rush of wind, she would sometimes stir, and sit a little up, and seem to awaken from her doze of satisfaction. But for the rest of her days she lay luxuriously folded on herself and sunk in sloth and pleasure. Her invincible content at first annoyed me, but I came gradually to find repose in the spectacle, until at last it grew to be my habit to sit down beside her four times in the day, both coming and going, and to talk with her sleepily, I scarce knew of what. I had come to like her dull, almost animal neighbourhood; her beauty and her stupidity soothed and amused me. I began to find a kind of transcendental good sense in her remarks, and her unfathomable good nature moved me to admiration and envy. The liking was returned; she enjoyed my presence half-unconsciously, as a man in deep meditation may enjoy the babbling of a brook. I can scarce say she brightened when I came, for satisfaction was written on her face eternally, as on some foolish statue's; but I was made conscious of her pleasure by some more intimate communication than the sight. And one day, as I set within reach of her on the marble step, she suddenly shot forth one of her hands and patted mine. The thing was done, and she was back in her accustomed attitude, before my mind had received intelligence of the caress; and when I turned to look her in the face I could perceive no answerable sentiment. It was plain she attached no moment to the act, and I blamed myself for my own more uneasy consciousness.

The sight and (if I may so call it) the acquaintance of the mother confirmed the view I had already taken of the son. The family blood had been impoverished, perhaps by long inbreeding, which I knew to be a common error among the proud and the exclusive. No decline, indeed, was to be traced in the body, which had been handed down unimpaired in shapeliness and strength; and the faces of to-day were struck as sharply from the mint, as the face of two centuries ago that smiled upon me from the portrait. But the intelligence (that more precious heirloom) was degenerate; the treasure of ancestral memory ran low; and it had required the potent, plebeian crossing of a muleteer or mountain contrabandista to raise, what approached hebetude in the mother, into the active oddity of the son. Yet of the two, it was the mother I preferred. Of Felipe, vengeful and placable, full of starts and shyings, inconstant as a hare, I could even conceive as a creature possibly noxious. Of the mother I had no thoughts but those of kindness. And indeed, as spectators are apt ignorantly to take sides, I grew something of a partisan in the enmity which I perceived to smoulder between them. True, it seemed mostly on the mother's part. She would sometimes draw in her breath as he came near, and the pupils of her vacant eyes would contract as if with horror or fear. Her emotions, such as they were, were much upon the surface and readily shared; and this latent repulsion occupied my mind, and kept me wondering on what grounds it rested, and whether the son was certainly in fault.

I had been about ten days in the residencia, when there sprang up a high and harsh wind, carrying clouds of dust. It came out of malarious lowlands, and over several snowy sierras. The nerves of those on whom it blew were strung and jangled; their eyes smarted with the dust; their legs ached under the burthen of their body; and the touch of one hand upon another grew to be odious. The wind, besides, came down the gullies of the hills and stormed about the house with a great, hollow buzzing and whistling that was wearisome to the ear and dismally depressing to the mind. It did not so much blow in gusts as with the steady sweep of a waterfall, so that there was no remission of discomfort while it blew. But higher upon the mountain, it was probably of a more variable strength, with accesses of fury; for there came down at times a far-off wailing, infinitely grievous to hear; and at times, on one of the high shelves or terraces, there would start up, and then disperse, a tower of dust, like the smoke of an explosion.

I no sooner awoke in bed than I was conscious of the nervous tension and depression of the weather, and the effect grew stronger as the day proceeded. It was in vain that I resisted; in vain that I set forth upon my customary morning's walk; the irrational, unchanging fury of the storm had soon beat down my strength and wrecked my temper; and I returned to the residencia, glowing with dry heat, and foul and gritty with dust. The court had a forlorn appearance; now and then a glimmer of sun fled over it; now and then the wind swooped down upon the pomegranates, and scattered the blossoms, and set the window shutters clapping on the wall. In the recess the Senora was pacing to and fro with a flushed countenance and bright eyes; I thought, too, she was speaking to herself, like one in anger. But when I addressed her with my customary salutation, she only replied by a sharp gesture and continued her walk. The weather had distempered even this impassive creature; and as I went on upstairs I was the less ashamed of my own discomposure.

All day the wind continued; and I sat in my room and made a feint of reading, or walked up and down, and listened to the riot overhead. Night fell, and I had not so much as a candle. I began to long for some society, and stole down to the court. It was now plunged in the blue of the first darkness; but the recess was redly lighted by the fire. The wood had been piled high, and was crowned by a shock of flames, which the draught of the chimney brandished to and fro. In this strong and shaken brightness the Senora continued pacing from wall to wall with disconnected gestures, clasping her hands, stretching forth her arms, throwing back her head as in appeal to heaven. In these disordered movements the beauty and grace of the woman showed more clearly; but there was a light in her eye that struck on me unpleasantly; and when I had looked on awhile in silence, and seemingly unobserved, I turned tail as I had come, and groped my way back again to my own chamber.

By the time Felipe brought my supper and lights, my nerve was utterly gone; and, had the lad been such as I was used to seeing him, I should have kept him (even by force had that been necessary) to take off the edge from my distasteful solitude. But on Felipe, also, the wind had exercised its influence. He had been feverish all day; now that the night had come he was fallen into a low and tremulous humour that reacted on my own. The sight of his scared face, his starts and pallors and sudden harkenings, unstrung me; and when he dropped and broke a dish, I fairly leaped out of my seat.

"I think we are all mad to-day," said I, affecting to laugh.

"It is the black wind," he replied dolefully. "You feel as if you must do something, and you don't know what it is."

I noted the aptness of the description; but, indeed, Felipe had sometimes a strange felicity in rendering into words the sensations of the body. "And your mother, too," said I; "she seems to feel this weather much. Do you not fear she may be unwell?"

He stared at me a little, and then said, "No," almost defiantly; and the next moment, carrying his hand to his brow, cried out lamentably on the wind and the noise that made his head go round like a millwheel. "Who can be well?" he cried; and, indeed, I could only echo his question, for I was disturbed enough myself.

I went to bed early, wearied with day-long restlessness, but the poisonous nature of the wind, and its ungodly and unintermittent uproar, would not suffer me to sleep. I lay there and tossed, my nerves and senses on the stretch. At times I would doze, dream horribly, and wake again; and these snatches of oblivion confused me as to time. But it must have been late on in the night, when I was suddenly startled by an outbreak of pitiable and hateful cries. I leaped from my bed, supposing I had dreamed; but the cries still continued to fill the house, cries of pain, I thought, but certainly of rage also, and so savage and discordant that they shocked the heart. It was no illusion; some living thing, some lunatic or some wild animal, was being foully tortured. The thought of Felipe and the squirrel flashed into my mind, and I ran to the door, but it had been locked from the outside; and I might shake it as I pleased, I was a fast prisoner. Still the cries continued. Now they would dwindle down into a moaning that seemed to be articulate, and at these times I made sure they must be human; and again they would break forth and fill the house with ravings worthy of hell. I stood at the door and gave ear to them, till at, last they died away. Long after that, I still lingered and still continued to hear them mingle in fancy with the storming of the wind; and when at last I crept to my bed, it was with a deadly sickness and a blackness of horror on my heart.

It was little wonder if I slept no more. Why had I been locked in? What had passed? Who was the author of these indescribable and shocking cries? A human being? It was inconceivable. A beast? The cries were scarce quite bestial; and what animal, short of a lion or a tiger, could thus shake the solid walls of the residencia? And while I was thus turning over the elements of the mystery, it came into my mind that I had not yet set eyes upon the daughter of the house. What was more probable than that the daughter of the Senora, and the sister of Felipe, should be herself insane? Or, what more likely than that these ignorant and half-witted people should seek to manage an afflicted kinswoman by violence? Here was a solution; and yet when I called to mind the cries (which I never did without a shuddering chill) it seemed altogether insufficient: not even cruelty could wring such cries from madness. But of one thing I was sure: I could not live in a house where such a thing was half conceivable, and not probe the matter home and, if necessary, interfere.

The next day came, the wind had blown itself out, and there was nothing to remind me of the business of the night. Felipe came to my bedside with obvious cheerfulness; as I passed through the court, the Senora was sunning herself with her accustomed immobility; and when I issued from the gateway, I found the whole face of nature austerely smiling, the heavens of a cold blue, and sown with great cloud islands, and the mountain-sides mapped forth into provinces of light and shadow. A short walk restored me to myself, and renewed within me the resolve to plumb this mystery; and when, from the vantage of my knoll, I had seen Felipe pass forth to his labours in the garden, I returned at once to the residencia to put my design in practice. The Senora appeared plunged in slumber; I stood awhile and marked her, but she did not stir; even if my design were indiscreet, I had little to fear from such a guardian; and turning away, I mounted to the gallery and began my exploration of the house.

All morning I went from one door to another, and entered spacious and faded chambers, some rudely shuttered, some receiving their full charge of daylight, all empty and unhomely. It was a rich house, on which Time had breathed his tarnish and dust had scattered disillusion. The spider swung there; the bloated tarantula scampered on the cornices; ants had their crowded highways on the floor of halls of audience; the big and foul fly, that lives on carrion and is often the messenger of death, had set up his nest in the rotten woodwork, and buzzed heavily about the rooms. Here and there a stool or two, a couch, a bed, or a great carved chair remained behind, like islets on the bare floors, to testify of man's bygone habitation; and everywhere the walls were set with the portraits of the dead. I could judge, by these decaying effigies, in the house of what a great and what a handsome race I was then wandering. Many of the men wore orders on their breasts and had the port of noble offices; the women were all richly attired; the canvases most of them by famous hands. But it was not so much these evidences of greatness that took hold upon my mind, even contrasted, as they were, with the present depopulation and decay of that great house. It was rather the parable of family life that I read in this succession of fair faces and shapely bodies. Never before had I so realised the miracle of the continued race, the creation and recreation, the weaving and changing and handing down of fleshly elements. That a child should be born of its mother, that it should grow and clothe itself (we know not how) with humanity, and put on inherited looks, and turn its head with the manner of one ascendant, and offer its hand with the gesture of another, are wonders dulled for us by repetition. But in the singular unity of look, in the common features and common bearing, of all these painted generations on the walls of the residencia, the miracle started out and looked me in the face. And an ancient mirror falling opportunely in my way, I stood and read my own features a long while, tracing out on either hand the filaments of descent and the bonds that knit me with my family.

At last, in the course of these investigations, I opened the door of a chamber that bore the marks of habitation. It was of large proportions and faced to the north, where the mountains were most wildly figured. The embers of a fire smouldered and smoked upon the hearth, to which a chair had been drawn close. And yet the aspect of the chamber was ascetic to the degree of sternness; the chair was uncushioned; the floor and walls were naked; and beyond the books which lay here and there in some confusion, there was no instrument of either work or pleasure. The sight of books in the house of such a family exceedingly amazed me; and I began with a great hurry, and in momentary fear of interruption, to go from one to another and hastily inspect their character. They were of all sorts, devotional, historical, and scientific, but mostly of a great age and in the Latin tongue. Some I could see to bear the marks of constant study; others had been torn across and tossed aside as if in petulance or disapproval. Lastly, as I cruised about that empty chamber, I espied some papers written upon with pencil on a table near the window. An unthinking curiosity led me to take one up. It bore a copy of verses, very roughly metred in the original Spanish, and which I may render somewhat thus—

Pleasure approached with pain and shame,
Grief with a wreath of lilies came.
Pleasure showed the lovely sun;
Jesu dear, how sweet it shone!

Grief with her worn hand pointed on,
   Jesu dear, to thee!

Shame and confusion at once fell on me; and, laying down the paper, I beat an immediate retreat from the apartment. Neither Felipe nor his mother could have read the books nor written these rough but feeling verses. It was plain I had stumbled with sacrilegious feet into the room of the daughter of the house. God knows, my own heart most sharply punished me for my indiscretion. The thought that I had thus secretly pushed my way into the confidence of a girl so strangely situated, and the fear that she might somehow come to hear of it, oppressed me like guilt. I blamed myself besides for my suspicions of the night before; wondered that I should ever have attributed those shocking cries to one of whom I now conceived as of a saint, spectral of mien, wasted with maceration, bound up in the practices of a mechanical devotion, and dwelling in a great isolation of soul with her incongruous relatives; and as I leaned on the balustrade of the gallery and looked down into the bright close of pomegranates and at the gaily dressed and somnolent woman, who just then stretched herself and delicately licked her lips as in the very sensuality of sloth, my mind swiftly compared the scene with the cold chamber looking northward on the mountains, where the daughter dwelt.

That same afternoon, as I sat upon my knoll, I saw the Padre enter the gates of the residencia. The revelation of the daughter's character had struck home to my fancy, and almost blotted out the horrors of the night before; but at sight of this worthy man the memory revived. I descended, then, from the knoll, and making a circuit among the woods, posted myself by the wayside to await his passage. As soon as he appeared I stepped forth and introduced myself as the lodger of the residencia. He had a very strong, honest countenance, on which it was easy to read the mingled emotions with which he regarded me, as a foreigner, a heretic, and yet one who had been wounded for the good cause. Of the family at the residencia he spoke with reserve, and yet with respect. I mentioned that I had not yet seen the daughter, whereupon he remarked that that was as it should be, and looked at me a little askance. Lastly, I plucked up courage to refer to the cries that had disturbed me in the night. He heard me out in silence, and then stopped and partly turned about, as though to mark beyond doubt that he was dismissing me.

"Do you take tobacco powder?" said he, offering his snuff-box; and then, when I had refused, "I am an old man," he added, "and I may be allowed to remind you that you are a guest."

"I have, then, your authority," I returned, firmly enough, although I flushed at the implied reproof, "to let things take their course, and not to interfere?"

He said "yes," and with a somewhat uneasy salute turned and left me where I was. But he had done two things: he had set my conscience at rest, and he had awakened my delicacy. I made a great effort, once more dismissed the recollections of the night, and fell once more to brooding on my saintly poetess. At the same time, I could not quite forget that I had been locked in, and that night when Felipe brought me my supper I attacked him warily on both points of interest.

"I never see your sister," said I casually.

"Oh, no," said he; "she is a good, good girl," and his mind instantly veered to something else.

"Your sister is pious, I suppose?" I asked in the next pause.

"Oh!" he cried, joining his hands with extreme fervour, "a saint; it is she that keeps me up."

"You are very fortunate," said I, "for the most of us, I am afraid, and myself among the number, are better at going down."

"Senor," said Felipe earnestly, "I would not say that. You should not tempt your angel. If one goes down, where is he to stop?"

"Why, Felipe," said I, "I had no guess you were a preacher, and I may say a good one; but I suppose that is your sister's doing?"

He nodded at me with round eyes.

"Well, then," I continued, "she has doubtless reproved you for your sin of cruelty?"

"Twelve times!" he cried; for this was the phrase by which the odd creature expressed the sense of frequency. "And I told her you had done so—I remembered that," he added proudly—"and she was pleased."

"Then, Felipe," said I, "what were those cries that I heard last night? for surely they were cries of some creature in suffering."

"The wind," returned Felipe, looking in the fire.

I took his hand in mine, at which, thinking it to be a caress, he smiled with a brightness of pleasure that came near disarming my resolve. But I trod the weakness down. "The wind," I repeated; "and yet I think it was this hand," holding it up, "that had first locked me in." The lad shook visibly, but answered never a word. "Well," said I, "I am a stranger and a guest. It is not my part either to meddle or to judge in your affairs; in these you shall take your sister's counsel, which I cannot doubt to be excellent. But in so far as concerns my own I will be no man's prisoner, and I demand that key." Half an hour later my door was suddenly thrown open, and the key tossed ringing on the floor.

A day or two after I came in from a walk a little before the point of noon. The Senora was lying lapped in slumber on the threshold of the recess; the pigeons dozed below the eaves like snowdrifts; the house was under a deep spell of noontide quiet; and only a wandering and gentle wind from the mountain stole round the galleries, rustled among the pomegranates, and pleasantly stirred the shadows. Something in the stillness moved me to imitation, and I went very lightly across the court and up the marble staircase. My foot was on the topmost round, when a door opened, and I found myself face to face with Olalla. Surprise transfixed me; her loveliness struck to my heart; she glowed in the deep shadow of the gallery, a gem of colour; her eyes took hold upon mine and clung there, and bound us together like the joining of hands; and the moments we thus stood face to face, drinking each other in, were sacramental and the wedding of souls. I know not how long it was before I awoke out of a deep trance, and, hastily bowing, passed on into the upper stair. She did not move, but followed me with her great, thirsting eyes; and as I passed out of sight it seemed to me as if she paled and faded.

In my own room, I opened the window and looked out, and could not think what change had come upon that austere field of mountains that it should thus sing and shine under the lofty heaven. I had seen her—Olalla! And the stone crags answered, Olalla! and the dumb, unfathomable azure answered, Olalla! The pale saint of my dreams had vanished for ever; and in her place I beheld this maiden on whom God had lavished the richest colours and the most exuberant energies of life, whom he had made active as a deer, slender as a reed, and in whose great eyes he had lighted the torches of the soul. The thrill of her young life, strung like a wild animal's, had entered into me; the force of soul that had looked out from her eyes and conquered mine, mantled about my heart and sprang to my lips in singing. She passed through my veins: she was one with me.

I will not say that this enthusiasm declined; rather my soul held out in its ecstasy as in a strong castle, and was there besieged by cold and sorrowful considerations. I could not doubt but that I loved her at first sight, and already with a quivering ardour that was strange to my experience. What then was to follow? She was the child of an afflicted house, the Senora's daughter, the sister of Felipe; she bore it even in her beauty. She had the lightness and swiftness of the one, swift as an arrow, light as dew; like the other, she shone on the pale background of the world with the brilliancy of flowers. I could not call by the name of brother that half-witted lad, nor by the name of mother that immovable and lovely thing of flesh, whose silly eyes and perpetual simper now recurred to my mind like something hateful. And if I could not marry, what then? She was helplessly unprotected; her eyes, in that single and long glance which had been all our intercourse, had confessed a weakness equal to my own; but in my heart I knew her for the student of the cold northern chamber, and the writer of the sorrowful lines; and this was a knowledge to disarm a brute. To flee was more than I could find courage for; but I registered a vow of unsleeping circumspection.

As I turned from the window, my eyes alighted on the portrait. It had fallen dead, like a candle after sunrise; it followed me with eyes of paint. I knew it to be like, and marvelled at the tenacity of type in that declining race; but the likeness was swallowed up in difference. I remembered how it had seemed to me a thing unapproachable in the life, a creature rather of the painter's craft than of the modesty of nature, and I marvelled at the thought, and exulted in the image of Olalla. Beauty I had seen before, and not been charmed, and I had been often drawn to women, who were not beautiful except to me; but in Olalla all that I desired and had not dared to imagine was united.

I did not see her the next day, and my heart ached and my eyes longed for her, as men long for morning. But the day after, when I returned, about my usual hour, she was once more on the gallery, and our looks once more met and embraced. I would have spoken, I would have drawn near to her; but strongly as she plucked at my heart, drawing me like a magnet, something yet more imperious withheld me; and I could only bow and pass by; and she, leaving my salutation unanswered, only followed me with her noble eyes.

I had now her image by rote, and as I conned the traits in memory it seemed as if I read her very heart. She was dressed with something of her mother's coquetry, and love of positive colour. Her robe, which I know she must have made with her own hands, clung about her with a cunning grace. After the fashion of that country, besides, her bodice stood open in the middle, in a long slit, and here, in spite of the poverty of the house, a gold coin, hanging by a ribbon, lay on her brown bosom. These were proofs, had any been needed, of her inborn delight in life and her own loveliness. On the other hand, in her eyes that hung upon mine, I could read depth beyond depth of passion and sadness, lights of poetry and hope, blacknesses of despair, and thoughts that were above the earth. It was a lovely body, but the inmate, the soul, was more than worthy of that lodging. Should I leave this incomparable flower to wither unseen on these rough mountains? Should I despise the great gift offered me in the eloquent silence of her eyes? Here was a soul immured; should I not burst its prison? All side considerations fell off from me; were she the child of Herod I swore I should make her mine; and that very evening I set myself, with a mingled sense of treachery and disgrace, to captivate the brother. Perhaps I read him with more favourable eyes, perhaps the thought of his sister always summoned up the better qualities of that imperfect soul; but he had never seemed to me so amiable, and his very likeness to Olalla, while it annoyed, yet softened me.

A third day passed in vain—an empty desert of hours. I would not lose a chance, and loitered all afternoon in the court where (to give myself a countenance) I spoke more than usual with the Senora. God knows it was with a most tender and sincere interest that I now studied her; and even as for Felipe, so now for the mother, I was conscious of a growing warmth of toleration. And yet I wondered. Even while I spoke with her, she would doze off into a little sleep, and presently awake again without embarrassment; and this composure staggered me. And again, as I marked her make infinitesimal changes in her posture, savouring and lingering on the bodily pleasure of the movement, I was driven to wonder at this depth of passive sensuality. She lived in her body; and her consciousness was all sunk into and disseminated through her members, where it luxuriously dwelt. Lastly, I could not grow accustomed to her eyes. Each time she turned on me these great beautiful and meaningless orbs, wide open to the day, but closed against human inquiry—each time I had occasion to observe the lively changes of her pupils which expanded and contracted in a breath—I know not what it was came over me, I can find no name for the mingled feeling of disappointment, annoyance, and distaste that jarred along my nerves. I tried her on a variety of subjects, equally in vain; and at last led the talk to her daughter. But even there she proved indifferent; said she was pretty, which (as with children) was her highest word of commendation, but was plainly incapable of any higher thought; and when I remarked that Olalla seemed silent, merely yawned in my face and replied that speech was of no great use when you had nothing to say. "People speak much, very much," she added, looking at me with expanded pupils; and then again yawned and again showed me a mouth that was as dainty as a toy. This time I took the hint, and, leaving her to her repose, went up into my own chamber to sit by the open window, looking on the hills and not beholding them, sunk in lustrous and deep dreams, and hearkening in fancy to the note of a voice that I had never heard.

I awoke on the fifth morning with a brightness of anticipation that seemed to challenge fate. I was sure of myself, light of heart and foot, and resolved to put my love incontinently to the touch of knowledge. It should lie no longer under the bonds of silence, a dumb thing, living by the eye only, like the love of beasts; but should now put on the spirit, and enter upon the joys of the complete human intimacy. I thought of it with wild hopes, like a voyager to El Dorado; into that unknown and lovely country of her soul, I no longer trembled to adventure. Yet when I did indeed encounter her, the same force of passion descended on me and at once submerged my mind; speech seemed to drop away from me like a childish habit; and I but drew near to her as the giddy man draws near to the margin of a gulf. She drew back from me a little as I came; but her eyes did not waver from mine, and these lured me forward. At last, when I was already within reach of her, I stopped. Words were denied me; if I advanced I could but clasp her to my heart in silence; and all that was sane in me, all that was still unconquered, revolted against the thought of such an accost. So we stood for a second, all our life in our eyes, exchanging salvos of attraction and yet each resisting; and then, with a great effort of the will, and conscious at the same time of a sudden bitterness of disappointment, I turned and went away in the same silence.

What power lay upon me that I could not speak? And she, why was she also silent? Why did she draw away before me dumbly, with fascinated eyes? Was this love? or was it a mere brute attraction, mindless and inevitable, like that of the magnet for the steel? We had never spoken, we were wholly strangers: and yet an influence, strong as the grasp of a giant, swept us silently together. On my side, it filled me with impatience; and yet I was sure that she was worthy; I had seen her books, read her verses, and thus, in a sense, divined the soul of my mistress. But on her side, it struck me almost cold. Of me, she knew nothing but my bodily favour; she was drawn to me as stones fall to the earth; the laws that rule the earth conducted her, unconsenting, to my arms; and I drew back at the thought of such a bridal, and began to be jealous for myself. It was not thus that I desired to be loved. And then I began to fall into a great pity for the girl herself. I thought how sharp must be her mortification, that she, the student, the recluse, Felipe's saintly monitress, should have thus confessed an overweening weakness for a man with whom she had never exchanged a word. And at the coming of pity, all other thoughts were swallowed up; and I longed only to find and console and reassure her; to tell her how wholly her love was returned on my side, and how her choice, even if blindly made, was not unworthy.

The next day it was glorious weather; depth upon depth of blue over-canopied the mountains; the sun shone wide; and the wind in the trees and the many falling torrents in the mountains filled the air with delicate and haunting music. Yet I was prostrated with sadness. My heart wept for the sight of Olalla, as a child weeps for its mother. I sat down on a boulder on the verge of the low cliffs that bound the plateau to the north. Thence I looked down into the wooded valley of a stream, where no foot came. In the mood I was in, it was even touching to behold the place untenanted; it lacked Olalla; and I thought of the delight and glory of a life passed wholly with her in that strong air, and among these rugged and lovely surroundings, at first with a whimpering sentiment, and then again with such a fiery joy that I seemed to grow in strength and stature, like a Samson.

And then suddenly I was aware of Olalla drawing near. She appeared out of a grove of cork-trees, and came straight towards me; and I stood up and waited. She seemed in her walking a creature of such life and fire and lightness as amazed me; yet she came quietly and slowly. Her energy was in the slowness; but for inimitable strength, I felt she would have run, she would have flown to me. Still, as she approached, she kept her eyes lowered to the ground; and when she had drawn quite near, it was without one glance that she addressed me. At the first note of her voice I started. It was for this I had been waiting; this was the last test of my love. And lo, her enunciation was precise and clear, not lisping and incomplete like that of her family; and the voice, though deeper than usual with women, was still both youthful and womanly. She spoke in a rich chord; golden contralto strains mingled with hoarseness, as the red threads were mingled with the brown among her tresses. It was not only a voice that spoke to my heart directly; but it spoke to me of her. And yet her words immediately plunged me back upon despair.

"You will go away," she said, "to-day."

Her example broke the bonds of my speech; I felt as lightened of a weight, or as if a spell had been dissolved. I know not in what words I answered; but, standing before her on the cliffs, I poured out the whole ardour of my love, telling her that I lived upon the thought of her, slept only to dream of her loveliness, and would gladly forswear my country, my language, and my friends, to live for ever by her side. And then, strongly commanding myself, I changed the note; I reassured, I comforted her; I told her I had divined in her a pious and heroic spirit, with which I was worthy to sympathise, and which I longed to share and lighten. "Nature," I told her, "was the voice of God, which men disobey at peril; and if we were thus humbly drawn together, ay, even as by a miracle of love, it must imply a divine fitness in our souls; we must be made," I said—"made for one another. We should be mad rebels," I cried out—"mad rebels against God, not to obey this instinct."

She shook her head. "You will go to-day," she repeated, and then with a gesture, and in a sudden, sharp note—"no, not to-day," she cried, "to-morrow!"

But at this sign of relenting, power came in upon me in a tide. I stretched out my arms and called upon her name; and she leaped to me and clung to me. The hills rocked about us, the earth quailed; a shock as of a blow went through me and left me blind and dizzy. And the next moment she had thrust me back, broken rudely from my arms, and fled with the speed of a deer among the cork-trees.

I stood and shouted to the mountains; I turned and went back towards the residencia, waltzing upon air. She sent me away, and yet I had but to call upon her name and she came to me. These were but the weaknesses of girls, from which even she, the strangest of her sex, was not exempted. Go? Not I, Olalla—O, not I, Olalla, my Olalla! A bird sang near by; and in that season, birds were rare. It bade me be of good cheer. And once more the whole countenance of nature, from the ponderous and stable mountains down to the lightest leaf and the smallest darting fly in the shadow of the groves, began to stir before me and to put on the lineaments of life and wear a face of awful joy. The sunshine struck upon the hills, strong as a hammer on the anvil, and the hills shook; the earth, under that vigorous insulation, yielded up heady scents; the woods smouldered in the blaze. I felt the thrill of travail and delight run through the earth. Something elemental, something rude, violent, and savage, in the love that sang in my heart, was like a key to nature's secrets; and the very stones that rattled under my feet appeared alive and friendly. Olalla! Her touch had quickened, and renewed, and strung me up to the old pitch of concert with the rugged earth, to a swelling of the soul that men learn to forget in their polite assemblies. Love burned in me like rage; tenderness waxed fierce; I hated, I adored, I pitied, I revered her with ecstasy. She seemed the link that bound me in with dead things on the one hand, and with our pure and pitying God upon the other: a thing brutal and divine, and akin at once to the innocence and to the unbridled forces of the earth.

My head thus reeling, I came into the courtyard of the residencia, and the sight of the mother struck me like a revelation. She sat there, all sloth and contentment, blinking under the strong sunshine, branded with a passive enjoyment, a creature set quite apart, before whom my ardour fell away like a thing ashamed. I stopped a moment, and, commanding such shaken tones as I was able, said a word or two. She looked at me with her unfathomable kindness; her voice in reply sounded vaguely out of the realm of peace in which she slumbered, and there fell on my mind, for the first time, a sense of respect for one so uniformly innocent and happy, and I passed on in a kind of wonder at myself, that I should be so much disquieted.

On my table there lay a piece of the same yellow paper I had seen in the north room; it was written on with pencil in the same hand, Olalla's hand, and I picked it up with a sudden sinking of alarm, and read, "If you have any kindness for Olalla, if you have any chivalry for a creature sorely wrought, go from here to-day; in pity, in honour, for the sake of Him who died, I supplicate that you shall go." I looked at this awhile in mere stupidity, then I began to awaken to a weariness and horror of life; the sunshine darkened outside on the bare hills, and I began to shake like a man in terror. The vacancy thus suddenly opened in my life unmanned me like a physical void. It was not my heart, it was not my happiness, it was life itself that was involved. I could not lose her. I said so, and stood repeating it. And then, like one in a dream, I moved to the window, put forth my hand to open the casement, and thrust it through the pane. The blood spurted from my wrist; and with an instantaneous quietude and command of myself, I pressed my thumb on the little leaping fountain, and reflected what to do. In that empty room there was nothing to my purpose; I felt, besides, that I required assistance. There shot into my mind a hope that Olalla herself might be my helper, and I turned and went down stairs, still keeping my thumb upon the wound.

There was no sign of either Olalla or Felipe, and I addressed myself to the recess, whither the Senora had now drawn quite back and sat dozing close before the fire, for no degree of heat appeared too much for her.

"Pardon me," said I, "if I disturb you, but I must apply to you for help."

She looked up sleepily and asked me what it was, and with the very words I thought she drew in her breath with a widening of the nostrils and seemed to come suddenly and fully alive.

"I have cut myself," I said, "and rather badly. See!" And I held out my two hands from which the blood was oozing and dripping.

Her great eyes opened wide, the pupils shrank into points; a veil seemed to fall from her face, and leave it sharply expressive and yet inscrutable. And as I still stood, marvelling a little at her disturbance, she came swiftly up to me, and stooped and caught me by the hand; and the next moment my hand was at her mouth, and she had bitten me to the bone. The pang of the bite, the sudden spurting of blood, and the monstrous horror of the act, flashed through me all in one, and I beat her back; and she sprang at me again and again, with bestial cries, cries that I recognised, such cries as had awakened me on the night of the high wind. Her strength was like that of madness; mine was rapidly ebbing with the loss of blood; my mind besides was whirling with the abhorrent strangeness of the onslaught, and I was already forced against the wall, when Olalla ran betwixt us, and Felipe, following at a bound, pinned down his mother on the floor.

A trance-like weakness fell upon me; I saw, heard, and felt, but I was incapable of movement. I heard the struggle roll to and fro upon the floor, the yells of that catamount ringing up to Heaven as she strove to reach me. I felt Olalla clasp me in her arms, her hair falling on my face, and, with the strength of a man, raise and half drag, half carry me upstairs into my own room, where she cast me down upon the bed. Then I saw her hasten to the door and lock it, and stand an instant listening to the savage cries that shook the residencia. And then, swift and light as a thought, she was again beside me, binding up my hand, laying it in her bosom, moaning and mourning over it with dove-like sounds. They were not words that came to her, they were sounds more beautiful than speech, infinitely touching, infinitely tender; and yet as I lay there, a thought stung to my heart, a thought wounded me like a sword, a thought, like a worm in a flower, profaned the holiness of my love. Yes, they were beautiful sounds, and they were inspired by human tenderness; but was their beauty human?

All day I lay there. For a long time the cries of that nameless female thing, as she struggled with her half-witted whelp, resounded through the house, and pierced me with despairing sorrow and disgust. They were the death-cry of my love; my love was murdered; was not only dead, but an offence to me; and yet, think as I pleased, feel as I must, it still swelled within me like a storm of sweetness, and my heart melted at her looks and touch. This horror that had sprung out, this doubt upon Olalla, this savage and bestial strain that ran not only through the whole behaviour of her family, but found a place in the very foundations and story of our love—though it appalled, though it shocked and sickened me, was yet not of power to break the knot of my infatuation.

When the cries had ceased, there came a scraping at the door, by which I knew Felipe was without; and Olalla went and spoke to him—I know not what. With that exception, she stayed close beside me, now kneeling by my bed and fervently praying, now sitting with her eyes upon mine. So then, for these six hours I drank in her beauty, and silently perused the story in her face. I saw the golden coin hover on her breaths; I saw her eyes darken and brighter, and still speak no language but that of an unfathomable kindness; I saw the faultless face, and, through the robe, the lines of the faultless body. Night came at last, and in the growing darkness of the chamber, the sight of her slowly melted; but even then the touch of her smooth hand lingered in mine and talked with me. To lie thus in deadly weakness and drink in the traits of the beloved, is to reawake to love from whatever shock of disillusion. I reasoned with myself; and I shut my eyes on horrors, and again I was very bold to accept the worst. What mattered it, if that imperious sentiment survived; if her eyes still beckoned and attached me; if now, even as before, every fibre of my dull body yearned and turned to her? Late on in the night some strength revived in me, and I spoke:—

"Olalla," I said, "nothing matters; I ask nothing; I am content; I love you."

She knelt down awhile and prayed, and I devoutly respected her devotions. The moon had begun to shine in upon one side of each of the three windows, and make a misty clearness in the room, by which I saw her indistinctly. When she rearose she made the sign of the cross.

"It is for me to speak," she said, "and for you to listen. I know; you can but guess. I prayed, how I prayed for you to leave this place. I begged it of you, and I know you would have granted me even this; or if not, O let me think so!"

"I love you," I said.

"And yet you have lived in the world," she said; after a pause, "you are a man and wise; and I am but a child. Forgive me, if I seem to teach, who am as ignorant as the trees of the mountain; but those who learn much do but skim the face of knowledge; they seize the laws, they conceive the dignity of the design—the horror of the living fact fades from their memory. It is we who sit at home with evil who remember, I think, and are warned and pity. Go, rather, go now, and keep me in mind. So I shall have a life in the cherished places of your memory: a life as much my own, as that which I lead in this body."

"I love you," I said once more; and reaching out my weak hand, took hers, and carried it to my lips, and kissed it. Nor did she resist, but winced a little; and I could see her look upon me with a frown that was not unkindly, only sad and baffled. And then it seemed she made a call upon her resolution; plucked my hand towards her, herself at the same time leaning somewhat forward, and laid it on the beating of her heart. "There," she cried, "you feel the very footfall of my life. It only moves for you; it is yours. But is it even mine? It is mine indeed to offer you, as I might take the coin from my neck, as I might break a live branch from a tree, and give it you. And yet not mine! I dwell, or I think I dwell (if I exist at all), somewhere apart, an impotent prisoner, and carried about and deafened by a mob that I disown. This capsule, such as throbs against the sides of animals, knows you at a touch for its master; ay, it loves you! But my soul, does my soul? I think not; I know not, fearing to ask. Yet when you spoke to me your words were of the soul; it is of the soul that you ask—it is only from the soul that you would take me."

"Olalla," I said, "the soul and the body are one, and mostly so in love. What the body chooses, the soul loves; where the body clings, the soul cleaves; body for body, soul to soul, they come together at God's signal; and the lower part (if we can call aught low) is only the footstool and foundation of the highest."

"Have you," she said, "seen the portraits in the house of my fathers? Have you looked at my mother or at Felipe? Have your eyes never rested on that picture that hangs by your bed? She who sat for it died ages ago; and she did evil in her life. But, look again: there is my hand to the least line, there are my eyes and my hair. What is mine, then, and what am I? If not a curve in this poor body of mine (which you love, and for the sake of which you dotingly dream that you love me) not a gesture that I can frame, not a tone of my voice, not any look from my eyes, no, not even now when I speak to him I love, but has belonged to others? Others, ages dead, have wooed other men with my eyes; other men have heard the pleading of the same voice that now sounds in your ears. The hands of the dead are in my bosom; they move me, they pluck me, they guide me; I am a puppet at their command; and I but reinform features and attributes that have long been laid aside from evil in the quiet of the grave. Is it me you love, friend? or the race that made me? The girl who does not know and cannot answer for the least portion of herself? or the stream of which she is a transitory eddy, the tree of which she is the passing fruit? The race exists; it is old, it is ever young, it carries its eternal destiny in its bosom; upon it, like waves upon the sea, individual succeeds to individual, mocked with a semblance of self-control, but they are nothing. We speak of the soul, but the soul is in the race."

"You fret against the common law," I said. "You rebel against the voice of God, which he has made so winning to convince, so imperious to command. Hear it, and how it speaks between us! Your hand clings to mine, your heart leaps at my touch, the unknown elements of which we are compounded awake and run together at a look; the clay of the earth remembers its independent life and yearns to join us; we are drawn together as the stars are turned about in space, or as the tides ebb and flow, by things older and greater than we ourselves."

"Alas!" she said, "what can I say to you? My fathers, eight hundred years ago, ruled all this province: they were wise, great, cunning, and cruel; they were a picked race of the Spanish; their flags led in war; the king called them his cousin; the people, when the rope was slung for them or when they returned and found their hovels smoking, blasphemed their name. Presently a change began. Man has risen; if he has sprung from the brutes, he can descend again to the same level. The breath of weariness blew on their humanity and the cords relaxed; they began to go down; their minds fell on sleep, their passions awoke in gusts, heady and senseless like the wind in the gutters of the mountains; beauty was still handed down, but no longer the guiding wit nor the human heart; the seed passed on, it was wrapped in flesh, the flesh covered the bones, but they were the bones and the flesh of brutes, and their mind was as the mind of flies. I speak to you as I dare; but you have seen for yourself how the wheel has gone backward with my doomed race. I stand, as it were, upon a little rising ground in this desperate descent, and see both before and behind, both what we have lost and to what we are condemned to go farther downward. And shall I—I that dwell apart in the house of the dead, my body, loathing its ways—shall I repeat the spell? Shall I bind another spirit, reluctant as my own, into this bewitched and tempest-broken tenement that I now suffer in? Shall I hand down this cursed vessel of humanity, charge it with fresh life as with fresh poison, and dash it, like a fire, in the faces of posterity? But my vow has been given; the race shall cease from off the earth. At this hour my brother is making ready; his foot will soon be on the stair; and you will go with him and pass out of my sight for ever. Think of me sometimes as one to whom the lesson of life was very harshly told, but who heard it with courage; as one who loved you indeed, but who hated herself so deeply that her love was hateful to her; as one who sent you away and yet would have longed to keep you for ever; who had no dearer hope than to forget you, and no greater fear than to be forgotten."

She had drawn towards the door as she spoke, her rich voice sounding softer and farther away; and with the last word she was gone, and I lay alone in the moonlit chamber. What I might have done had not I lain bound by my extreme weakness, I know not; but as it was there fell upon me a great and blank despair. It was not long before there shone in at the door the ruddy glimmer of a lantern, and Felipe coming, charged me without a word upon his shoulders, and carried me down to the great gate, where the cart was waiting. In the moonlight the hills stood out sharply, as if they were of cardboard; on the glimmering surface of the plateau, and from among the low trees which swung together and sparkled in the wind, the great black cube of the residencia stood out bulkily, its mass only broken by three dimly lighted windows in the northern front above the gate. They were Olalla's windows, and as the cart jolted onwards I kept my eyes fixed upon them till, where the road dipped into a valley, they were lost to my view forever. Felipe walked in silence beside the shafts, but from time to time he would cheek the mule and seem to look back upon me; and at length drew quite near and laid his hand upon my head. There was such kindness in the touch, and such a simplicity, as of the brutes, that tears broke from me like the bursting of an artery.

"Felipe," I said, "take me where they will ask no questions."

He said never a word, but he turned his mule about, end for end, retraced some part of the way we had gone, and, striking into another path, led me to the mountain village, which was, as we say in Scotland, the kirkton of that thinly peopled district. Some broken memories dwell in my mind of the day breaking over the plain, of the cart stopping, of arms that helped me down, of a bare room into which I was carried, and of a swoon that fell upon me like sleep.

The next day and the days following the old priest was often at my side with his snuff-box and prayer book, and after a while, when I began to pick up strength, he told me that I was now on a fair way to recovery, and must as soon as possible hurry my departure; whereupon, without naming any reason, he took snuff and looked at me sideways. I did not affect ignorance; I knew he must have seen Olalla. "Sir," said I, "you know that I do not ask in wantonness. What of that family?"

He said they were very unfortunate; that it seemed a declining race, and that they were very poor and had been much neglected.

"But she has not," I said. "Thanks, doubtless, to yourself, she is instructed and wise beyond the use of women."

"Yes," he said; "the Senorita is well-informed. But the family has been neglected."

"The mother?" I queried.

"Yes, the mother too," said the Padre, taking snuff. "But Felipe is a well-intentioned lad."

"The mother is odd?" I asked.

"Very odd," replied the priest.

"I think, sir, we beat about the bush," said I. "You must know more of my affairs than you allow. You must know my curiosity to be justified on many grounds. Will you not be frank with me?"

"My son," said the old gentleman, "I will be very frank with you on matters within my competence; on those of which I know nothing it does not require much discretion to be silent. I will not fence with you, I take your meaning perfectly; and what can I say, but that we are all in God's hands, and that His ways are not as our ways? I have even advised with my superiors in the church, but they, too, were dumb. It is a great mystery."

"Is she mad?" I asked.

"I will answer you according to my belief. She is not," returned the Padre, "or she was not. When she was young—God help me, I fear I neglected that wild lamb—she was surely sane; and yet, although it did not run to such heights, the same strain was already notable; it had been so before her in her father, ay, and before him, and this inclined me, perhaps, to think too lightly of it. But these things go on growing, not only in the individual but in the race."

"When she was young," I began, and my voice failed me for a moment, and it was only with a great effort that I was able to add, "was she like Olalla?"

"Now God forbid!" exclaimed the Padre. "God forbid that any man should think so slightingly of my favourite penitent. No, no; the Senorita (but for her beauty, which I wish most honestly she had less of) has not a hair's resemblance to what her mother was at the same age. I could not bear to have you think so; though, Heaven knows, it were, perhaps, better that you should."

At this, I raised myself in bed, and opened my heart to the old man; telling him of our love and of her decision, owning my own horrors, my own passing fancies, but telling him that these were at an end; and with something more than a purely formal submission, appealing to his judgment.

He heard me very patiently and without surprise; and when I had done, he sat for some time silent. Then he began: "The church," and instantly broke off again to apologise. "I had forgotten, my child, that you were not a Christian," said he. "And indeed, upon a point so highly unusual, even the church can scarce be said to have decided. But would you have my opinion? The Senorita is, in a matter of this kind, the best judge; I would accept her judgment."

On the back of that he went away, nor was he thenceforward so assiduous in his visits; indeed, even when I began to get about again, he plainly feared and deprecated my society, not as in distaste but much as a man might be disposed to flee from the riddling sphynx. The villagers, too, avoided me; they were unwilling to be my guides upon the mountain. I thought they looked at me askance, and I made sure that the more superstitious crossed themselves on my approach. At first I set this down to my heretical opinions; but it began at length to dawn upon me that if I was thus redoubted it was because I had stayed at the residencia. All men despise the savage notions of such peasantry; and yet I was conscious of a chill shadow that seemed to fall and dwell upon my love. It did not conquer, but I may not deny that it restrained my ardour.

Some miles westward of the village there was a gap in the sierra, from which the eye plunged direct upon the residencia; and thither it became my daily habit to repair. A wood crowned the summit; and just where the pathway issued from its fringes, it was overhung by a considerable shelf of rock, and that, in its turn, was surmounted by a crucifix of the size of life and more than usually painful in design. This was my perch; thence, day after day, I looked down upon the plateau, and the great old house, and could see Felipe, no bigger than a fly, going to and fro about the garden. Sometimes mists would draw across the view, and be broken up again by mountain winds; sometimes the plain slumbered below me in unbroken sunshine; it would sometimes be all blotted out by rain. This distant post, these interrupted sights of the place where my life had been so strangely changed, suited the indecision of my humour. I passed whole days there, debating with myself the various elements of our position; now leaning to the suggestions of love, now giving an ear to prudence, and in the end halting irresolute between the two.

One day, as I was sitting on my rock, there came by that way a somewhat gaunt peasant wrapped in a mantle. He was a stranger, and plainly did not know me even by repute; for, instead of keeping the other side, he drew near and sat down beside me, and we had soon fallen in talk. Among other things he told me he had been a muleteer, and in former years had much frequented these mountains; later on, he had followed the army with his mules, had realised a competence, and was now living retired with his family.

"Do you know that house?" I inquired, at last, pointing to the residencia, for I readily wearied of any talk that kept me from the thought of Olalla.

He looked at me darkly and crossed himself.

"Too well," he said, "it was there that one of my comrades sold himself to Satan; the Virgin shield us from temptations! He has paid the price; he is now burning in the reddest place in Hell!"

A fear came upon me; I could answer nothing; and presently the man resumed, as if to himself: "Yes," he said, "O yes, I know it. I have passed its doors. There was snow upon the pass, the wind was driving it; sure enough there was death that night upon the mountains, but there was worse beside the hearth. I took him by the arm, Senor, and dragged him to the gate; I conjured him, by all he loved and respected, to go forth with me; I went on my knees before him in the snow; and I could see he was moved by my entreaty. And just then she came out on the gallery, and called him by his name; and he turned, and there was she standing with a lamp in her hand and smiling on him to come back. I cried out aloud to God, and threw my arms about him, but he put me by, and left me alone. He had made his choice; God help us. I would pray for him, but to what end? there are sins that not even the Pope can loose."

"And your friend," I asked, "what became of him?"

"Nay, God knows," said the muleteer. "If all be true that we hear, his end was like his sin, a thing to raise the hair."

"Do you mean that he was killed?" I asked.

"Sure enough, he was killed," returned the man. "But how? Ay, how? But these are things that it is sin to speak of."

"The people of that house . . . " I began.

But he interrupted me with a savage outburst. "The people?" he cried. "What people? There are neither men nor women in that house of Satan's! What? have you lived here so long, and never heard?" And here he put his mouth to my ear and whispered, as if even the fowls of the mountain might have over-heard and been stricken with horror.

What he told me was not true, nor was it even original; being, indeed, but a new edition, vamped up again by village ignorance and superstition, of stories nearly as ancient as the race of man. It was rather the application that appalled me. In the old days, he said, the church would have burned out that nest of basilisks; but the arm of the church was now shortened; his friend Miguel had been unpunished by the hands of men, and left to the more awful judgment of an offended God. This was wrong; but it should be so no more. The Padre was sunk in age; he was even bewitched himself; but the eyes of his flock were now awake to their own danger; and some day—ay, and before long—the smoke of that house should go up to heaven.

He left me filled with horror and fear. Which way to turn I knew not; whether first to warn the Padre, or to carry my ill-news direct to the threatened inhabitants of the residencia. Fate was to decide for me; for, while I was still hesitating, I beheld the veiled figure of a woman drawing near to me up the pathway. No veil could deceive my penetration; by every line and every movement I recognised Olalla; and keeping hidden behind a corner of the rock, I suffered her to gain the summit. Then I came forward. She knew me and paused, but did not speak; I, too, remained silent; and we continued for some time to gaze upon each other with a passionate sadness.

"I thought you had gone," she said at length. "It is all that you can do for me—to go. It is all I ever asked of you. And you still stay. But do you know, that every day heaps up the peril of death, not only on your head, but on ours? A report has gone about the mountain; it is thought you love me, and the people will not suffer it."

I saw she was already informed of her danger, and I rejoiced at it. "Olalla," I said, "I am ready to go this day, this very hour, but not alone."

She stepped aside and knelt down before the crucifix to pray, and I stood by and looked now at her and now at the object of her adoration, now at the living figure of the penitent, and now at the ghastly, daubed countenance, the painted wounds, and the projected ribs of the image. The silence was only broken by the wailing of some large birds that circled sidelong, as if in surprise or alarm, about the summit of the hills. Presently Olalla rose again, turned towards me, raised her veil, and, still leaning with one hand on the shaft of the crucifix, looked upon me with a pale and sorrowful countenance.

"I have laid my hand upon the cross," she said. "The Padre says you are no Christian; but look up for a moment with my eyes, and behold the face of the Man of Sorrows. We are all such as He was—the inheritors of sin; we must all bear and expiate a past which was not ours; there is in all of us—ay, even in me—a sparkle of the divine. Like Him, we must endure for a little while, until morning returns bringing peace. Suffer me to pass on upon my way alone; it is thus that I shall be least lonely, counting for my friend Him who is the friend of all the distressed; it is thus that I shall be the most happy, having taken my farewell of earthly happiness, and willingly accepted sorrow for my portion."

I looked at the face of the crucifix, and, though I was no friend to images, and despised that imitative and grimacing art of which it was a rude example, some sense of what the thing implied was carried home to my intelligence. The face looked down upon me with a painful and deadly contraction; but the rays of a glory encircled it, and reminded me that the sacrifice was voluntary. It stood there, crowning the rock, as it still stands on so many highway sides, vainly preaching to passers-by, an emblem of sad and noble truths; that pleasure is not an end, but an accident; that pain is the choice of the magnanimous; that it is best to suffer all things and do well. I turned and went down the mountain in silence; and when I looked back for the last time before the wood closed about my path, I saw Olalla still leaning on the crucifix.

THE TREASURE OF FRANCHARD.

CHAPTER I.
BY THE DYING MOUNTEBANK.

They had sent for the doctor from Bourron before six. About eight some villagers came round for the performance, and were told how matters stood. It seemed a liberty for a mountebank to fall ill like real people, and they made off again in dudgeon. By ten Madame Tentaillon was gravely alarmed, and had sent down the street for Doctor Desprez.

The Doctor was at work over his manuscripts in one corner of the little dining-room, and his wife was asleep over the fire in another, when the messenger arrived.

"Sapristi!" said the Doctor, "you should have sent for me before. It was a case for hurry." And he followed the messenger as he was, in his slippers and skull-cap.

The inn was not thirty yards away, but the messenger did not stop there; he went in at one door and out by another into the court, and then led the way by a flight of steps beside the stable, to the loft where the mountebank lay sick. If Doctor Desprez were to live a thousand years, he would never forget his arrival in that room; for not only was the scene picturesque, but the moment made a date in his existence. We reckon our lives, I hardly know why, from the date of our first sorry appearance in society, as if from a first humiliation; for no actor can come upon the stage with a worse grace. Not to go further back, which would be judged too curious, there are subsequently many moving and decisive accidents in the lives of all, which would make as logical a period as this of birth. And here, for instance, Doctor Desprez, a man past forty, who had made what is called a failure in life, and was moreover married, found himself at a new point of departure when he opened the door of the loft above Tentaillon's stable.

It was a large place, lighted only by a single candle set upon the floor. The mountebank lay on his back upon a pallet; a large man, with a Quixotic nose inflamed with drinking. Madame Tentaillon stooped over him, applying a hot water and mustard embrocation to his feet; and on a chair close by sat a little fellow of eleven or twelve, with his feet dangling. These three were the only occupants, except the shadows. But the shadows were a company in themselves; the extent of the room exaggerated them to a gigantic size, and from the low position of the candle the light struck upwards and produced deformed foreshortenings. The mountebank's profile was enlarged upon the wall in caricature, and it was strange to see his nose shorten and lengthen as the flame was blown about by draughts. As for Madame Tentaillon, her shadow was no more than a gross hump of shoulders, with now and again a hemisphere of head. The chair legs were spindled out as long as stilts, and the boy set perched atop of them, like a cloud, in the corner of the roof.

It was the boy who took the Doctor's fancy. He had a great arched skull, the forehead and hands of a musician, and a pair of haunting eyes. It was not merely that these eyes were large, or steady, or the softest ruddy brown. There was a look in them, besides, which thrilled the Doctor, and made him half uneasy. He was sure he had seen such a look before, and yet he could not remember how or where. It was as if this boy, who was quite a stranger to him, had the eyes of an old friend or an old enemy. And the boy would give him no peace; he seemed profoundly indifferent to what was going on, or rather abstracted from it in a superior contemplation, beating gently with his feet against the bars of the chair, and holding his hands folded on his lap. But, for all that, his eyes kept following the Doctor about the room with a thoughtful fixity of gaze. Desprez could not tell whether he was fascinating the boy, or the boy was fascinating him. He busied himself over the sick man: he put questions, he felt the pulse, he jested, he grew a little hot and swore: and still, whenever he looked round, there were the brown eyes waiting for his with the same inquiring, melancholy gaze.

At last the Doctor hit on the solution at a leap. He remembered the look now. The little fellow, although he was as straight as a dart, had the eyes that go usually with a crooked back; he was not at all deformed, and yet a deformed person seemed to be looking at you from below his brows. The Doctor drew a long breath, he was so much relieved to find a theory (for he loved theories) and to explain away his interest.

For all that, he despatched the invalid with unusual haste, and, still kneeling with one knee on the floor, turned a little round and looked the boy over at his leisure. The boy was not in the least put out, but looked placidly back at the Doctor.

"Is this your father?" asked Desprez.

"Oh, no," returned the boy; "my master."

"Are you fond of him?" continued the Doctor.

"No, sir," said the boy.

Madame Tentaillon and Desprez exchanged expressive glances.

"That is bad, my man," resumed the latter, with a shade of sternness. "Every one should be fond of the dying, or conceal their sentiments; and your master here is dying. If I have watched a bird a little while stealing my cherries, I have a thought of disappointment when he flies away over my garden wall, and I see him steer for the forest and vanish. How much more a creature such as this, so strong, so astute, so richly endowed with faculties! When I think that, in a few hours, the speech will be silenced, the breath extinct, and even the shadow vanished from the wall, I who never saw him, this lady who knew him only as a guest, are touched with some affection."

The boy was silent for a little, and appeared to be reflecting.

"You did not know him," he replied at last, "he was a bad man."

"He is a little pagan," said the landlady. "For that matter, they are all the same, these mountebanks, tumblers, artists, and what not. They have no interior."

But the Doctor was still scrutinising the little pagan, his eyebrows knotted and uplifted.

"What is your name?" he asked.

"Jean-Marie," said the lad.

Desprez leaped upon him with one of his sudden flashes of excitement, and felt his head all over from an ethnological point of view.

"Celtic, Celtic!" he said.

"Celtic!" cried Madame Tentaillon, who had perhaps confounded the word with hydrocephalous. "Poor lad! is it dangerous?"

"That depends," returned the Doctor grimly. And then once more addressing the boy: "And what do you do for your living, Jean-Marie?" he inquired.

"I tumble," was the answer.

"So! Tumble?" repeated Desprez. "Probably healthful. I hazard the guess, Madame Tentaillon, that tumbling is a healthful way of life. And have you never done anything else but tumble?"

"Before I learned that, I used to steal," answered Jean-Marie gravely.

"Upon my word!" cried the doctor. "You are a nice little man for your age. Madame, when my confrère comes from Bourron, you will communicate my unfavourable opinion. I leave the case in his hands; but of course, on any alarming symptom, above all if there should be a sign of rally, do not hesitate to knock me up. I am a doctor no longer, I thank God; but I have been one. Good night, madame. Good sleep to you, Jean-Marie."

CHAPTER II.
MORNING TALK

Doctor Desprez always rose early. Before the smoke arose, before the first cart rattled over the bridge to the day's labour in the fields, he was to be found wandering in his garden. Now he would pick a bunch of grapes; now he would eat a big pear under the trellice; now he would draw all sorts of fancies on the path with the end of his cane; now he would go down and watch the river running endlessly past the timber landing-place at which he moored his boat. There was no time, he used to say, for making theories like the early morning. "I rise earlier than any one else in the village," he once boasted. "It is a fair consequence that I know more and wish to do less with my knowledge."

The Doctor was a connoisseur of sunrises, and loved a good theatrical effect to usher in the day. He had a theory of dew, by which he could predict the weather. Indeed, most things served him to that end: the sound of the bells from all the neighbouring villages, the smell of the forest, the visits and the behaviour of both birds and fishes, the look of the plants in his garden, the disposition of cloud, the colour of the light, and last, although not least, the arsenal of meteorological instruments in a louvre-boarded hutch upon the lawn. Ever since he had settled at Gretz, he had been growing more and more into the local meteorologist, the unpaid champion of the local climate. He thought at first there was no place so healthful in the arrondissement. By the end of the second year, he protested there was none so wholesome in the whole department. And for some time before he met Jean-Marie he had been prepared to challenge all France and the better part of Europe for a rival to his chosen spot.

"Doctor," he would say—"doctor is a foul word. It should not be used to ladies. It implies disease. I remark it, as a flaw in our civilisation, that we have not the proper horror of disease. Now I, for my part, have washed my hands of it; I have renounced my laureation; I am no doctor; I am only a worshipper of the true goddess Hygieia. Ah, believe me, it is she who has the cestus! And here, in this exiguous hamlet, has she placed her shrine: here she dwells and lavishes her gifts; here I walk with her in the early morning, and she shows me how strong she has made the peasants, how fruitful she has made the fields, how the trees grow up tall and comely under her eyes, and the fishes in the river become clean and agile at her presence.—Rheumatism!" he would cry, on some malapert interruption, "O, yes, I believe we do have a little rheumatism. That could hardly be avoided, you know, on a river. And of course the place stands a little low; and the meadows are marshy, there's no doubt. But, my dear sir, look at Bourron! Bourron stands high. Bourron is close to the forest; plenty of ozone there, you would say. Well, compared with Gretz, Bourron is a perfect shambles."

The morning after he had been summoned to the dying mountebank, the Doctor visited the wharf at the tail of his garden, and had a long look at the running water. This he called prayer; but whether his adorations were addressed to the goddess Hygieia or some more orthodox deity, never plainly appeared. For he had uttered doubtful oracles, sometimes declaring that a river was the type of bodily health, sometimes extolling it as the great moral preacher, continually preaching peace, continuity, and diligence to man's tormented spirits. After he had watched a mile or so of the clear water running by before his eyes, seen a fish or two come to the surface with a gleam of silver, and sufficiently admired the long shadows of the trees falling half across the river from the opposite bank, with patches of moving sunlight in between, he strolled once more up the garden and through his house into the street, feeling cool and renovated.

The sound of his feet upon the causeway began the business of the day; for the village was still sound asleep. The church tower looked very airy in the sunlight; a few birds that turned about it, seemed to swim in an atmosphere of more than usual rarity; and the Doctor, walking in long transparent shadows, filled his lungs amply, and proclaimed himself well contented with the morning.

On one of the posts before Tentaillon's carriage entry he espied a little dark figure perched in a meditative attitude, and immediately recognised Jean-Marie.

"Aha!" he said, stopping before him humorously, with a hand on either knee. "So we rise early in the morning, do we? It appears to me that we have all the vices of a philosopher."

The boy got to his feet and made a grave salutation.

"And how is our patient?" asked Desprez.

It appeared the patient was about the same.

"And why do you rise early in the morning?" he pursued.

Jean-Marie, after a long silence, professed that he hardly knew.

"You hardly know?" repeated Desprez. "We hardly know anything, my man, until we try to learn. Interrogate your consciousness. Come, push me this inquiry home. Do you like it?"

"Yes," said the boy slowly; "yes, I like it."

"And why do you like it?" continued the Doctor. "(We are now pursuing the Socratic method.) Why do you like it?"

"It is quiet," answered Jean-Marie; "and I have nothing to do; and then I feel as if I were good."

Doctor Desprez took a seat on the post at the opposite side. He was beginning to take an interest in the talk, for the boy plainly thought before he spoke, and tried to answer truly. "It appears you have a taste for feeling good," said the Doctor. "Now, there you puzzle me extremely; for I thought you said you were a thief; and the two are incompatible."

"Is it very bad to steal?" asked Jean-Marie.

"Such is the general opinion, little boy," replied the Doctor.

"No; but I mean as I stole," explained the other. "For I had no choice. I think it is surely right to have bread; it must be right to have bread, there comes so plain a want of it. And then they beat me cruelly if I returned with nothing," he added. "I was not ignorant of right and wrong; for before that I had been well taught by a priest, who was very kind to me." (The Doctor made a horrible grimace at the word "priest.") "But it seemed to me, when one had nothing to eat and was beaten, it was a different affair. I would not have stolen for tartlets, I believe; but any one would steal for baker's bread."

"And so I suppose," said the Doctor, with a rising sneer, "you prayed God to forgive you, and explained the case to Him at length."

"Why, sir?" asked Jean-Marie. "I do not see."

"Your priest would see, however," retorted Desprez.

"Would he?" asked the boy, troubled for the first time. "I should have thought God would have known."

"Eh?" snarled the Doctor.

"I should have thought God would have understood me," replied the other. "You do not, I see; but then it was God that made me think so, was it not?"

"Little boy, little boy," said Dr. Desprez, "I told you already you had the vices of philosophy; if you display the virtues also, I must go. I am a student of the blessed laws of health, an observer of plain and temperate nature in her common walks; and I cannot preserve my equanimity in presence of a monster. Do you understand?"

"No, sir," said the boy.

"I will make my meaning clear to you," replied the doctor. "Look there at the sky—behind the belfry first, where it is so light, and then up and up, turning your chin back, right to the top of the dome, where it is already as blue as at noon. Is not that a beautiful colour? Does it not please the heart? We have seen it all our lives, until it has grown in with our familiar thoughts. Now," changing his tone, "suppose that sky to become suddenly of a live and fiery amber, like the colour of clear coals, and growing scarlet towards the top—I do not say it would be any the less beautiful; but would you like it as well?"

"I suppose not," answered Jean-Marie.

"Neither do I like you," returned the Doctor, roughly. "I hate all odd people, and you are the most curious little boy in all the world."

Jean-Marie seemed to ponder for a while, and then he raised his head again and looked over at the Doctor with an air of candid inquiry. "But are not you a very curious gentleman?" he asked.

The Doctor threw away his stick, bounded on the boy, clasped him to his bosom, and kissed him on both cheeks. "Admirable, admirable imp!" he cried. "What a morning, what an hour for a theorist of forty-two! No," he continued, apostrophising heaven, "I did not know such boys existed; I was ignorant they made them so; I had doubted of my race; and now! It is like," he added, picking up his stick, "like a lovers' meeting. I have bruised my favourite staff in that moment of enthusiasm. The injury, however, is not grave." He caught the boy looking at him in obvious wonder, embarrassment, and alarm. "Hullo!" said he, "why do you look at me like that? Egad, I believe the boy despises me. Do you despise me, boy?"

"O, no," replied Jean-Marie, seriously; "only I do not understand."

"You must excuse me, sir," returned the Doctor, with gravity; "I am still so young. O, hang him!" he added to himself. And he took his seat again and observed the boy sardonically. "He has spoiled the quiet of my morning," thought he. "I shall be nervous all day, and have a febricule when I digest. Let me compose myself." And so he dismissed his pre-occupations by an effort of the will which he had long practised, and let his soul roam abroad in the contemplation of the morning. He inhaled the air, tasting it critically as a connoisseur tastes a vintage, and prolonging the expiration with hygienic gusto. He counted the little flecks of cloud along the sky. He followed the movements of the birds round the church tower—making long sweeps, hanging poised, or turning airy somersaults in fancy, and beating the wind with imaginary pinions. And in this way he regained peace of mind and animal composure, conscious of his limbs, conscious of the sight of his eyes, conscious that the air had a cool taste, like a fruit, at the top of his throat; and at last, in complete abstraction, he began to sing. The Doctor had but one air—, "Malbrouck s'en va-t-en guerre;" even with that he was on terms of mere politeness; and his musical exploits were always reserved for moments when he was alone and entirely happy.

He was recalled to earth rudely by a pained expression on the boy's face. "What do you think of my singing?" he inquired, stopping in the middle of a note; and then, after he had waited some little while and received no answer, "What do you think of my singing?" he repeated, imperiously.

"I do not like it," faltered Jean-Marie.

"Oh, come!" cried the Doctor. "Possibly you are a performer yourself?"

"I sing better than that," replied the boy.

The Doctor eyed him for some seconds in stupefaction. He was aware that he was angry, and blushed for himself in consequence, which made him angrier. "If this is how you address your master!" he said at last, with a shrug and a flourish of his arms.

"I do not speak to him at all," returned the boy. "I do not like him."

"Then you like me?" snapped Doctor Desprez, with unusual eagerness.

"I do not know," answered Jean-Marie.

The Doctor rose. "I shall wish you a good morning," he said. "You are too much for me. Perhaps you have blood in your veins, perhaps celestial ichor, or perhaps you circulate nothing more gross than respirable air; but of one thing I am inexpugnably assured:—that you are no human being. No, boy"—shaking his stick at him—"you are not a human being. Write, write it in your memory—'I am not a human being—I have no pretension to be a human being—I am a dive, a dream, an angel, an acrostic, an illusion—what you please, but not a human being.' And so accept my humble salutations and farewell!"

And with that the Doctor made off along the street in some emotion, and the boy stood, mentally gaping, where he left him.

CHAPTER III.
THE ADOPTION.

Madame Desprez, who answered to the Christian name of Anastasie, presented an agreeable type of her sex; exceedingly wholesome to look upon, a stout brune, with cool smooth cheeks, steady, dark eyes, and hands that neither art nor nature could improve. She was the sort of person over whom adversity passes like a summer cloud; she might, in the worst of conjunctions, knit her brows into one vertical furrow for a moment, but the next it would be gone. She had much of the placidity of a contented nun; with little of her piety, however; for Anastasie was of a very mundane nature, fond of oysters and old wine, and somewhat bold pleasantries, and devoted to her husband for her own sake rather than for his. She was imperturbably good-natured, but had no idea of self-sacrifice. To live in that pleasant old house, with a green garden behind and bright flowers about the window, to eat and drink of the best, to gossip with a neighbour for a quarter of an hour, never to wear stays or a dress except when she went to Fontainebleau shopping, to be kept in a continual supply of racy novels, and to be married to Doctor Desprez and have no ground of jealousy, filled the cup of her nature to the brim. Those who had known the Doctor in bachelor days, when he had aired quite as many theories, but of a different order, attributed his present philosophy to the study of Anastasie. It was her brute enjoyment that he rationalised and perhaps vainly imitated.

Madame Desprez was an artist in the kitchen, and made coffee to a nicety. She had a knack of tidiness, with which she had infected the Doctor; everything was in its place; everything capable of polish shone gloriously; and dust was a thing banished from her empire. Aline, their single servant, had no other business in the world but to scour and burnish. So Doctor Desprez lived in his house like a fatted calf, warmed and cosseted to his heart's content.

The midday meal was excellent. There was a ripe melon, a fish from the river in a memorable Bearnaise sauce, a fat fowl in a fricassee, and a dish of asparagus, followed by some fruit. The Doctor drank half a bottle plus one glass, the wife half a bottle minus the same quantity, which was a marital privilege, of an excellent Côte-Rôtie, seven years old. Then the coffee was brought, and a flask of Chartreuse for madame, for the Doctor despised and distrusted such decoctions; and then Aline left the wedded pair to the pleasures of memory and digestion.

"It is a very fortunate circumstance, my cherished one," observed the Doctor—"this coffee is adorable—a very fortunate circumstance upon the whole—Anastasie, I beseech you, go without that poison for to-day; only one day, and you will feel the benefit, I pledge my reputation."

"What is this fortunate circumstance, my friend?" inquired Anastasie, not heeding his protest, which was of daily recurrence.

"That we have no children, my beautiful," replied the Doctor. "I think of it more and more as the years go on, and with more and more gratitude towards the Power that dispenses such afflictions. Your health, my darling, my studious quiet, our little kitchen delicacies, how they would all have suffered, how they would all have been sacrificed! And for what? Children are the last word of human imperfection. Health flees before their face. They cry, my dear; they put vexatious questions; they demand to be fed, to be washed, to be educated, to have their noses blown; and then, when the time comes, they break our hearts, as I break this piece of sugar. A pair of professed egoists, like you and me, should avoid offspring, like an infidelity."

"Indeed!" said she; and she laughed. "Now, that is like you—to take credit for the thing you could not help."

"My dear," returned the Doctor, solemnly, "we might have adopted."

"Never!" cried madame. "Never, Doctor, with my consent. If the child were my own flesh and blood, I would not say no. But to take another person's indiscretion on my shoulders, my dear friend, I have too much sense."

"Precisely," replied the Doctor. "We both had. And I am all the better pleased with our wisdom, because—because—" He looked at her sharply.

"Because what?" she asked, with a faint premonition of danger.

"Because I have found the right person," said the Doctor firmly, "and shall adopt him this afternoon."

Anastasie looked at him out of a mist. "You have lost your reason," she said; and there was a clang in her voice that seemed to threaten trouble.

"Not so, my dear," he replied; "I retain its complete exercise. To the proof: instead of attempting to cloak my inconsistency, I have, by way of preparing you, thrown it into strong relief. You will there, I think, recognise the philosopher who has the ecstasy to call you wife. The fact is, I have been reckoning all this while without an accident. I never thought to find a son of my own. Now, last night, I found one. Do not unnecessarily alarm yourself, my dear; he is not a drop of blood to me that I know. It is his mind, darling, his mind that calls me father."

"His mind!" she repeated with a titter between scorn and hysterics. "His mind, indeed! Henri, is this an idiotic pleasantry, or are you mad? His mind! And what of my mind?"

"Truly," replied the Doctor with a shrug, "you have your finger on the hitch. He will be strikingly antipathetic to my ever beautiful Anastasie. She will never understand him; he will never understand her. You married the animal side of my nature, dear and it is on the spiritual side that I find my affinity for Jean-Marie. So much so, that, to be perfectly frank, I stand in some awe of him myself. You will easily perceive that I am announcing a calamity for you. Do not," he broke out in tones of real solicitude—"do not give way to tears after a meal, Anastasie. You will certainly give yourself a false digestion."

Anastasie controlled herself. "You know how willing I am to humour you," she said, "in all reasonable matters. But on this point—"

"My dear love," interrupted the Doctor, eager to prevent a refusal, "who wished to leave Paris? Who made me give up cards, and the opera, and the boulevard, and my social relations, and all that was my life before I knew you? Have I been faithful? Have I been obedient? Have I not borne my doom with cheerfulness? In all honesty, Anastasie, have I not a right to a stipulation on my side? I have, and you know it. I stipulate my son."

Anastasie was aware of defeat; she struck her colours instantly. "You will break my heart," she sighed.

"Not in the least," said he. "You will feel a trifling inconvenience for a month, just as I did when I was first brought to this vile hamlet; then your admirable sense and temper will prevail, and I see you already as content as ever, and making your husband the happiest of men."

"You know I can refuse you nothing," she said, with a last flicker of resistance; "nothing that will make you truly happier. But will this? Are you sure, my husband? Last night, you say, you found him! He may be the worst of humbugs."

"I think not," replied the Doctor. "But do not suppose me so unwary as to adopt him out of hand. I am, I flatter myself, a finished man of the world; I have had all possibilities in view; my plan is contrived to meet them all. I take the lad as stable boy. If he pilfer, if he grumble, if he desire to change, I shall see I was mistaken; I shall recognise him for no son of mine, and send him tramping."

"You will never do so when the time comes," said his wife; "I know your good heart."

She reached out her hand to him, with a sigh; the Doctor smiled as he took it and carried it to his lips; he had gained his point with greater ease than he had dared to hope; for perhaps the twentieth time he had proved the efficacy of his trusty argument, his Excalibur, the hint of a return to Paris. Six months in the capital, for a man of the Doctor's antecedents and relations, implied no less a calamity than total ruin. Anastasie had saved the remainder of his fortune by keeping him strictly in the country. The very name of Paris put her in a blue fear; and she would have allowed her husband to keep a menagerie in the back garden, let alone adopting a stable-boy, rather than permit the question of return to be discussed.

About four of the afternoon, the mountebank rendered up his ghost; he had never been conscious since his seizure. Doctor Desprez was present at his last passage, and declared the farce over. Then he took Jean-Marie by the shoulder and led him out into the inn garden where there was a convenient bench beside the river. Here he sat him down and made the boy place himself on his left.

"Jean-Marie," he said very gravely, "this world is exceedingly vast; and even France, which is only a small corner of it, is a great place for a little lad like you. Unfortunately it is full of eager, shouldering people moving on; and there are very few bakers' shops for so many eaters. Your master is dead; you are not fit to gain a living by yourself; you do not wish to steal? No. Your situation then is undesirable; it is, for the moment, critical. On the other hand, you behold in me a man not old, though elderly, still enjoying the youth of the heart and the intelligence; a man of instruction; easily situated in this world's affairs; keeping a good table:—a man, neither as friend nor host, to be despised. I offer you your food and clothes, and to teach you lessons in the evening, which will be infinitely more to the purpose for a lad of your stamp than those of all the priests in Europe. I propose no wages, but if ever you take a thought to leave me, the door shall be open, and I will give you a hundred francs to start the world upon. In return, I have an old horse and chaise, which you would very speedily learn to clean and keep in order. Do not hurry yourself to answer, and take it or leave it as you judge aright. Only remember this, that I am no sentimentalist or charitable person, but a man who lives rigorously to himself; and that if I make the proposal, it is for my own ends—it is because I perceive clearly an advantage to myself. And now, reflect."

"I shall be very glad. I do not see what else I can do. I thank you, sir, most kindly, and I will try to be useful," said the boy.

"Thank you," said the Doctor warmly, rising at the same time and wiping his brow, for he had suffered agonies while the thing hung in the wind. A refusal, after the scene at noon, would have placed him in a ridiculous light before Anastasie. "How hot and heavy is the evening, to be sure! I have always had a fancy to be a fish in summer, Jean-Marie, here in the Loing beside Gretz. I should lie under a water-lily and listen to the bells, which must sound most delicately down below. That would be a life—do you not think so too?"

"Yes," said Jean-Marie.

"Thank God you have imagination!" cried the Doctor, embracing the boy with his usual effusive warmth, though it was a proceeding that seemed to disconcert the sufferer almost as much as if he had been an English schoolboy of the same age. "And now," he added, "I will take you to my wife."

Madame Desprez sat in the dining-room in a cool wrapper. All the blinds were down, and the tile floor had been recently sprinkled with water; her eyes were half shut, but she affected to be reading a novel as the they entered. Though she was a bustling woman, she enjoyed repose between whiles and had a remarkable appetite for sleep.

The Doctor went through a solemn form of introduction, adding, for the benefit of both parties, "You must try to like each other for my sake."

"He is very pretty," said Anastasie. "Will you kiss me, my pretty little fellow?"

The Doctor was furious, and dragged her into the passage. "Are you a fool, Anastasie?" he said. "What is all this I hear about the tact of women? Heaven knows, I have not met with it in my experience. You address my little philosopher as if he were an infant. He must be spoken to with more respect, I tell you; he must not be kissed and Georgy-porgy'd like an ordinary child."

"I only did it to please you, I am sure," replied Anastasie; "but I will try to do better."

The Doctor apologised for his warmth. "But I do wish him," he continued, "to feel at home among us. And really your conduct was so idiotic, my cherished one, and so utterly and distantly out of place, that a saint might have been pardoned a little vehemence in disapproval. Do, do try—if it is possible for a woman to understand young people—but of course it is not, and I waste my breath. Hold your tongue as much as possible at least, and observe my conduct narrowly; it will serve you for a model."

Anastasie did as she was bidden, and considered the Doctor's behaviour. She observed that he embraced the boy three times in the course of the evening, and managed generally to confound and abash the little fellow out of speech and appetite. But she had the true womanly heroism in little affairs. Not only did she refrain from the cheap revenge of exposing the Doctor's errors to himself, but she did her best to remove their ill-effect on Jean-Marie. When Desprez went out for his last breath of air before retiring for the night, she came over to the boy's side and took his hand.

"You must not be surprised nor frightened by my husband's manners," she said. "He is the kindest of men, but so clever that he is sometimes difficult to understand. You will soon grow used to him, and then you will love him, for that nobody can help. As for me, you may be sure, I shall try to make you happy, and will not bother you at all. I think we should be excellent friends, you and I. I am not clever, but I am very good-natured. Will you give me a kiss?"

He held up his face, and she took him in her arms and then began to cry. The woman had spoken in complaisance; but she had warmed to her own words, and tenderness followed. The Doctor, entering, found them enlaced: he concluded that his wife was in fault; and he was just beginning, in an awful voice, "Anastasie—," when she looked up at him, smiling, with an upraised finger; and he held his peace, wondering, while she led the boy to his attic.

CHAPTER IV.
THE EDUCATION OF A PHILOSOPHER.

The installation of the adopted stable-boy was thus happily effected, and the wheels of life continued to run smoothly in the Doctor's house. Jean-Marie did his horse and carriage duty in the morning; sometimes helped in the housework; sometimes walked abroad with the Doctor, to drink wisdom from the fountain-head; and was introduced at night to the sciences and the dead tongues. He retained his singular placidity of mind and manner; he was rarely in fault; but he made only a very partial progress in his studies, and remained much of a stranger in the family.

The Doctor was a pattern of regularity. All forenoon he worked on his great book, the 'Comparative Pharmacopoeia, or Historical Dictionary of all Medicines," which as yet consisted principally of slips of paper and pins. When finished, it was to fill many personable volumes, and to combine antiquarian interest with professional utility. But the Doctor was studious of literary graces and the picturesque; an anecdote, a touch of manners, a moral qualification, or a sounding epithet was sure to be preferred before a piece of science; a little more, and he would have written the "Comparative Pharmacopoeia' in verse! The article "Mummia," for instance, was already complete, though the remainder of the work had not progressed beyond the letter A. It was exceedingly copious and entertaining, written with quaintness and colour, exact, erudite, a literary article; but it would hardly have afforded guidance to a practising physician of to-day. The feminine good sense of his wife had led her to point this out with uncompromising sincerity; for the Dictionary was duly read aloud to her, betwixt sleep and waning, as it proceeded towards an infinitely distant completion; and the Doctor was a little sore on the subject of mummies, and sometimes resented an allusion with asperity.

After the midday meal and a proper period of digestion, he walked, sometimes alone, sometimes accompanied by Jean-Marie; for madame would have preferred any hardship rather than walk. She was, as I have said, a very busy person, continually occupied about material comforts, and ready to drop asleep over a novel the instant she was disengaged. This was the less objectionable, as she never snored or grew distempered in complexion when she slept. On the contrary, she looked the very picture of luxurious and appetising ease, and woke without a start to the perfect possession of her faculties. I am afraid she was greatly an animal, but she was a very nice animal to have about. In this way, she had little to do with Jean-Marie; but the sympathy which had been established between them on the first night remained unbroken; they held occasional conversations, mostly on household matters; to the extreme disappointment of the Doctor, they occasionally sallied off together to that temple of debasing superstition, the village church; madame and he, both in their Sunday's best, drove twice a month to Fontainebleau and returned laden with purchases; and in short, although the Doctor still continued to regard them as irreconcilably anti-pathetic, their relation was as intimate, friendly, and confidential as their natures suffered.

I fear, however, that in her heart of hearts, madame kindly despised and pitied the boy. She had no admiration for his class of virtues; she liked a smart, polite, forward, roguish sort of boy, cap in hand, light of foot, meeting the eye; she liked volubility, charm, a little vice—the promise of a second Doctor Desprez. And it was her indefeasible belief that Jean-Marie was dull. "Poor dear boy," she had said once, "how sad it is that he should be so stupid!" She had never repeated that remark, for the Doctor had raged like a wild bull, denouncing the brutal bluntness of her mind, bemoaning his own fate to be so unequally mated with an ass, and, what touched Anastasie more nearly, menacing the table china by the fury of his gesticulations. But she adhered silently to her opinion; and when Jean-Marie was sitting, stolid, blank, but not unhappy, over his unfinished tasks, she would snatch her opportunity in the Doctor's absence, go over to him, put her arms about his neck, lay her cheek to his, and communicate her sympathy with his distress. "Do not mind," she would say; "I, too, am not at all clever, and I can assure you that it makes no difference in life."

The Doctor's view was naturally different. That gentleman never wearied of the sound of his own voice, which was, to say the truth, agreeable enough to hear. He now had a listener, who was not so cynically indifferent as Anastasie, and who sometimes put him on his mettle by the most relevant objections. Besides, was he not educating the boy? And education, philosophers are agreed, is the most philosophical of duties. What can be more heavenly to poor mankind than to have one's hobby grow into a duty to the State? Then, indeed, do the ways of life become ways of pleasantness. Never had the Doctor seen reason to be more content with his endowments. Philosophy flowed smoothly from his lips. He was so agile a dialectician that he could trace his nonsense, when challenged, back to some root in sense, and prove it to be a sort of flower upon his system. He slipped out of antinomies like a fish, and left his disciple marvelling at the rabbi's depth.

Moreover, deep down in his heart the Doctor was disappointed with the ill-success of his more formal education. A boy, chosen by so acute an observer for his aptitude, and guided along the path of learning by so philosophic an instructor, was bound, by the nature of the universe, to make a more obvious and lasting advance. Now Jean-Marie was slow in all things, impenetrable in others; and his power of forgetting was fully on a level with his power to learn. Therefore the Doctor cherished his peripatetic lectures, to which the boy attended, which he generally appeared to enjoy, and by which he often profited.

Many and many were the talks they had together; and health and moderation proved the subject of the Doctor's divagations. To these he lovingly returned.

"I lead you," he would say, "by the green pastures. My system, my beliefs, my medicines, are resumed in one phrase—to avoid excess. Blessed nature, healthy, temperate nature, abhors and exterminates excess. Human law, in this matter, imitates at a great distance her provisions; and we must strive to supplement the efforts of the law. Yes, boy, we must be a law to ourselves and for ourselves and for our neighbours—lex armata—armed, emphatic, tyrannous law. If you see a crapulous human ruin snuffing, dash from him his box! The judge, though in a way an admission of disease, is less offensive to me than either the doctor or the priest. Above all the doctor—the doctor and the purulent trash and garbage of his pharmacopoeia! Pure air—from the neighbourhood of a pinetum for the sake of the turpentine—unadulterated wine, and the reflections of an unsophisticated spirit in the presence of the works of nature—these, my boy, are the best medical appliances and the best religious comforts. Devote yourself to these. Hark! there are the bells of Bourron (the wind is in the north, it will be fair). How clear and airy is the sound! The nerves are harmonised and quieted; the mind attuned to silence; and observe how easily and regularly beats the heart! Your unenlightened doctor would see nothing in these sensations; and yet you yourself perceive they are a part of health.—Did you remember your cinchona this morning? Good. Cinchona also is a work of nature; it is, after all, only the bark of a tree which we might gather for ourselves if we lived in the locality.—What a world is this! Though a professed atheist, I delight to bear my testimony to the world. Look at the gratuitous remedies and pleasures that surround our path! The river runs by the garden end, our bath, our fishpond, our natural system of drainage. There is a well in the court which sends up sparkling water from the earth's very heart, clean, cool, and, with a little wine, most wholesome. The district is notorious for its salubrity; rheumatism is the only prevalent complaint, and I myself have never had a touch of it. I tell you—and my opinion is based upon the coldest, clearest processes of reason—if I, if you, desired to leave this home of pleasures, it would be the duty, it would be the privilege, of our best friend to prevent us with a pistol bullet."

One beautiful June day they sat upon the hill outside the village. The river, as blue as heaven, shone here and there among the foliage. The indefatigable birds turned and flickered about Gretz church tower. A healthy wind blew from over the forest, and the sound of innumerable thousands of tree-tops and innumerable millions on millions of green leaves was abroad in the air, and filled the ear with something between whispered speech and singing. It seemed as if every blade of grass must hide a cigale; and the fields rang merrily with their music, jingling far and near as with the sleigh-bells of the fairy queen. From their station on the slope the eye embraced a large space of poplar'd plain upon the one hand, the waving hill-tops of the forest on the other, and Gretz itself in the middle, a handful of roofs. Under the bestriding arch of the blue heavens, the place seemed dwindled to a toy. It seemed incredible that people dwelt, and could find room to turn or air to breathe, in such a corner of the world. The thought came home to the boy, perhaps for the first time, and he gave it words.

"How small it looks!" he sighed.

"Ay," replied the Doctor, "small enough now. Yet it was once a walled city; thriving, full of furred burgesses and men in armour, humming with affairs;—with tall spires, for aught that I know, and portly towers along the battlements. A thousand chimneys ceased smoking at the curfew bell. There were gibbets at the gate as thick as scarecrows. In time of war, the assault swarmed against it with ladders, the arrows fell like leaves, the defenders sallied hotly over the drawbridge, each side uttered its cry as they plied their weapons. Do you know that the walls extended as far as the Commanderie? Tradition so reports. Alas, what a long way off is all this confusion—nothing left of it but my quiet words spoken in your ear—and the town itself shrunk to the hamlet underneath us! By-and-by came the English wars—you shall hear more of the English, a stupid people, who sometimes blundered into good—and Gretz was taken, sacked, and burned. It is the history of many towns; but Gretz never rose again; it was never rebuilt; its ruins were a quarry to serve the growth of rivals; and the stones of Gretz are now erect along the streets of Nemours. It gratifies me that our old house was the first to rise after the calamity; when the town had come to an end, it inaugurated the hamlet."

"I, too, am glad of that," said Jean-Marie.

"It should be the temple of the humbler virtues," responded the Doctor with a savoury gusto. "Perhaps one of the reasons why I love my little hamlet as I do, is that we have a similar history, she and I. Have I told you that I was once rich?"

"I do not think so," answered Jean-Marie. "I do not think I should have forgotten. I am sorry you should have lost your fortune."

"Sorry?" cried the Doctor. "Why, I find I have scarce begun your education after all. Listen to me! Would you rather live in the old Gretz or in the new, free from the alarms of war, with the green country at the door, without noise, passports, the exactions of the soldiery, or the jangle of the curfew-bell to send us off to bed by sundown?"

"I suppose I should prefer the new," replied the boy.

"Precisely," returned the Doctor; "so do I. And, in the same way, I prefer my present moderate fortune to my former wealth. Golden mediocrity! cried the adorable ancients; and I subscribe to their enthusiasm. Have I not good wine, good food, good air, the fields and the forest for my walk, a house, an admirable wife, a boy whom I protest I cherish like a son? Now, if I were still rich, I should indubitably make my residence in Paris—you know Paris—Paris and Paradise are not convertible terms. This pleasant noise of the wind streaming among leaves changed into the grinding Babel of the street, the stupid glare of plaster substituted for this quiet pattern of greens and greys, the nerves shattered, the digestion falsified—picture the fall! Already you perceive the consequences; the mind is stimulated, the heart steps to a different measure, and the man is himself no longer. I have passionately studied myself—the true business of philosophy. I know my character as the musician knows the ventages of his flute. Should I return to Paris, I should ruin myself gambling; nay, I go further—I should break the heart of my Anastasie with infidelities."

This was too much for Jean-Marie. That a place should so transform the most excellent of men transcended his belief. Paris, he protested, was even an agreeable place of residence. "Nor when I lived in that city did I feel much difference," he pleaded.

"What!" cried the Doctor. "Did you not steal when you were there?"

But the boy could never be brought to see that he had done anything wrong when he stole. Nor, indeed, did the Doctor think he had; but that gentleman was never very scrupulous when in want of a retort.

"And now," he concluded, "do you begin to understand? My only friends were those who ruined me. Gretz has been my academy, my sanatorium, my heaven of innocent pleasures. If millions are offered me, I wave them back: Retro, Sathanas!—Evil one, begone! Fix your mind on my example; despise riches, avoid the debasing influence of cities. Hygiene—hygiene and mediocrity of fortune—these be your watchwords during life!"

The Doctor's system of hygiene strikingly coincided with his tastes; and his picture of the perfect life was a faithful description of the one he was leading at the time. But it is easy to convince a boy, whom you supply with all the facts for the discussion. And besides, there was one thing admirable in the philosophy, and that was the enthusiasm of the philosopher. There was never any one more vigorously determined to be pleased; and if he was not a great logician, and so had no right to convince the intellect, he was certainly something of a poet, and had a fascination to seduce the heart. What he could not achieve in his customary humour of a radiant admiration of himself and his circumstances, he sometimes effected in his fits of gloom.

"Boy," he would say, "avoid me to-day. If I were superstitious, I should even beg for an interest in your prayers. I am in the black fit; the evil spirit of King Saul, the hag of the merchant Abudah, the personal devil of the mediæval monk, is with me—is in me," tapping on his breast. "The vices of my nature are now uppermost; innocent pleasures woo me in vain; I long for Paris, for my wallowing in the mire. See," he would continue, producing a handful of silver, "I denude myself, I am not to be trusted with the price of a fare. Take it, keep it for me, squander it on deleterious candy, throw it in the deepest of the river—I will homologate your action. Save me from that part of myself which I disown. If you see me falter, do not hesitate; if necessary, wreck the train! I speak, of course, by a parable. Any extremity were better than for me to reach Paris alive."

Doubtless the Doctor enjoyed these little scenes, as a variation in his part; they represented the Byronic element in the somewhat artificial poetry of his existence; but to the boy, though he was dimly aware of their theatricality, they represented more. The Doctor made perhaps too little, the boy possibly too much, of the reality and gravity of these temptations.

One day a great light shone for Jean-Marie. "Could not riches be used well?" he asked.

"In theory, yes," replied the Doctor. "But it is found in experience that no one does so. All the world imagine they will be exceptional when they grow wealthy; but possession is debasing, new desires spring up; and the silly taste for ostentation eats out the heart of pleasure."

"Then you might be better if you had less," said the boy.

"Certainly not," replied the Doctor; but his voice quavered as he spoke.

"Why?" demanded pitiless innocence.

Doctor Desprez saw all the colours of the rainbow in a moment; the stable universe appeared to be about capsizing with him. "Because," said he—affecting deliberation after an obvious pause—"because I have formed my life for my present income. It is not good for men of my years to be violently dissevered from their habits."

That was a sharp brush. The Doctor breathed hard, and fell into taciturnity for the afternoon. As for the boy, he was delighted with the resolution of his doubts; even wondered that he had not foreseen the obvious and conclusive answer. His faith in the Doctor was a stout piece of goods. Desprez was inclined to be a sheet in the wind's eye after dinner, especially after Rhone wine, his favourite weakness. He would then remark on the warmth of his feeling for Anastasie, and with inflamed cheeks and a loose, flustered smile, debate upon all sorts of topics, and be feebly and indiscreetly witty. But the adopted stable-boy would not permit himself to entertain a doubt that savoured of ingratitude. It is quite true that a man may be a second father to you, and yet take too much to drink; but the best natures are ever slow to accept such truths.

The Doctor thoroughly possessed his heart, but perhaps he exaggerated his influence over his mind. Certainly Jean-Marie adopted some of his master's opinions, but I have yet to learn that he ever surrendered one of his own. Convictions existed in him by divine right; they were virgin, unwrought, the brute metal of decision. He could add others indeed, but he could not put away; neither did he care if they were perfectly agreed among themselves; and his spiritual pleasures had nothing to do with turning them over or justifying them in words. Words were with him a mere accomplishment, like dancing. When he was by himself, his pleasures were almost vegetable. He would slip into the woods towards Acheres, and sit in the mouth of a cave among grey birches. His soul stared straight out of his eyes; he did not move or think; sunlight, thin shadows moving in the wind, the edge of firs against the sky, occupied and bound his faculties. He was pure unity, a spirit wholly abstracted. A single mood filled him, to which all the objects of sense contributed, as the colours of the spectrum merge and disappear in white light.

So while the Doctor made himself drunk with words, the adopted stable-boy bemused himself with silence.

CHAPTER V.
TREASURE TROVE.

The Doctor's carriage was a two-wheeled gig with a hood; a kind of vehicle in much favour among country doctors. On how many roads has one not seen it, a great way off between the poplars!—in how many village streets, tied to a gate-post! This sort of chariot is affected—particularly at the trot—by a kind of pitching movement to and fro across the axle, which well entitles it to the style of a Noddy. The hood describes a considerable arc against the landscape, with a solemnly absurd effect on the contemplative pedestrian. To ride in such a carriage cannot be numbered among the things that appertain to glory; but I have no doubt it may be useful in liver complaint. Thence, perhaps, its wide popularity among physicians.

One morning early, Jean-Marie led forth the Doctor's noddy, opened the gate, and mounted to the driving-seat. The Doctor followed, arrayed from top to toe in spotless linen, armed with an immense flesh-coloured umbrella, and girt with a botanical case on a baldric; and the equipage drove off smartly in a breeze of its own provocation. They were bound for Franchard, to collect plants, with an eye to the "Comparative Pharmacopoeia."

A little rattling on the open roads, and they came to the borders of the forest and struck into an unfrequented track; the noddy yawed softly over the sand, with an accompaniment of snapping twigs. There was a great, green, softly murmuring cloud of congregated foliage overhead. In the arcades of the forest the air retained the freshness of the night. The athletic bearing of the trees, each carrying its leafy mountain, pleased the mind like so many statues; and the lines of the trunk led the eye admiringly upward to where the extreme leaves sparkled in a patch of azure. Squirrels leaped in mid air. It was a proper spot for a devotee of the goddess Hygieia.

"Have you been to Franchard, Jean-Marie?" inquired the Doctor. "I fancy not."

"Never," replied the boy.

"It is ruin in a gorge," continued Desprez, adopting his expository voice; "the ruin of a hermitage and chapel. History tells us much of Franchard; how the recluse was often slain by robbers; how he lived on a most insufficient diet; how he was expected to pass his days in prayer. A letter is preserved, addressed to one of these solitaries by the superior of his order, full of admirable hygienic advice; bidding him go from his book to praying, and so back again, for variety's sake, and when he was weary of both to stroll about his garden and observe the honey bees. It is to this day my own system. You must often have remarked me leaving the 'Pharmacopoeia'—often even in the middle of a phrase—to come forth into the sun and air. I admire the writer of that letter from my heart; he was a man of thought on the most important subjects. But, indeed, had I lived in the Middle Ages (I am heartily glad that I did not) I should have been an eremite myself—if I had not been a professed buffoon, that is. These were the only philosophical lives yet open: laughter or prayer; sneers, we might say, and tears. Until the sun of the Positive arose, the wise man had to make his choice between these two."

"I have been a buffoon, of course," observed Jean-Marie.

"I cannot imagine you to have excelled in your profession," said the Doctor, admiring the boy's gravity. "Do you ever laugh?"

"Oh, yes," replied the other. "I laugh often. I am very fond of jokes."

"Singular being!" said Desprez. "But I divagate (I perceive in a thousand ways that I grow old).

Franchard was at length destroyed in the English wars, the same that levelled Gretz. But—here is the point—the hermits (for there were already more than one) had foreseen the danger and carefully concealed the sacrificial vessels. These vessels were of monstrous value, Jean-Marie—monstrous value—priceless, we may say; exquisitely worked, of exquisite material. And now, mark me, they have never been found. In the reign of Louis Quatorze some fellows were digging hard by the ruins. Suddenly—tock!—the spade hit upon an obstacle. Imagine the men fooling one to another; imagine how their hearts bounded, how their colour came and went. It was a coffer, and in Franchard the place of buried treasure! They tore it open like famished beasts. Alas! it was not the treasure; only some priestly robes, which, at the touch of the eating air, fell upon themselves and instantly wasted into dust. The perspiration of these good fellows turned cold upon them, Jean-Marie. I will pledge my reputation, if there was anything like a cutting wind, one or other had a pneumonia for his trouble."

"I should like to have seen them turning into dust," said Jean-Marie. "Otherwise, I should not have cared so greatly."

"You have no imagination," cried the Doctor. "Picture to yourself the scene. Dwell on the idea—a great treasure lying in the earth for centuries: the material for a giddy, copious, opulent existence not employed; dresses and exquisite pictures unseen; the swiftest galloping horses not stirring a hoof, arrested by a spell; women with the beautiful faculty of smiles, not smiling; cards, dice, opera singing, orchestras, castles, beautiful parks and gardens, big ships with a tower of sailcloth, all lying unborn in a coffin—and the stupid trees growing overhead in the sunlight, year after year. The thought drives one frantic."

"It is only money," replied Jean-Marie. "It would do harm."

"O, come!" cried Desprez, "that is philosophy; it is all very fine, but not to the point just now. And besides, it is not 'only money,' as you call it; there are works of art in the question; the vessels were carved. You speak like a child. You weary me exceedingly, quoting my words out of all logical connection, like a parroquet."

"And at any rate, we have nothing to do with it," returned the boy submissively.

They struck the Route Ronde at that moment; and the sudden change to the rattling causeway combined, with the Doctor's irritation, to keep him silent. The noddy jigged along; the trees went by, looking on silently, as if they had something on their minds. The Quadrilateral was passed; then came Franchard. They put up the horse at the little solitary inn, and went forth strolling. The gorge was dyed deeply with heather; the rocks and birches standing luminous in the sun. A great humming of bees about the flowers disposed Jean-Marie to sleep, and he sat down against a clump of heather, while the Doctor went briskly to and fro, with quick turns, culling his simples.

The boy's head had fallen a little forward, his eyes were closed, his fingers had fallen lax about his knees, when a sudden cry called him to his feet. It was a strange sound, thin and brief; it fell dead, and silence returned as though it had never been interrupted. He had not recognised the Doctor's voice; but, as there was no one else in all the valley, it was plainly the Doctor who had given utterance to the sound. He looked right and left, and there was Desprez, standing in a niche between two boulders, and looking round on his adopted son with a countenance as white as paper.

"A viper!" cried Jean-Marie, running towards him. "A viper! You are bitten!"

The Doctor came down heavily out of the cleft, and, advanced in silence to meet the boy, whom he took roughly by the shoulder.

"I have found it," he said, with a gasp.

"A plant?" asked Jean-Marie.

Desprez had a fit of unnatural gaiety, which the rocks took up and mimicked. "A plant!" he repeated scornfully. "Well—yes—a plant. And here," he added suddenly, showing his right hand, which he had hitherto concealed behind his back—"here is one of the bulbs."

Jean-Marie saw a dirty platter, coated with earth.

"That?" said he. "It is a plate!"

"It is a coach and horses," cried the Doctor. "Boy," he continued, growing warmer, "I plucked away a great pad of moss from between these boulders, and disclosed a crevice; and when I looked in, what do you suppose I saw? I saw a house in Paris with a court and garden, I saw my wife shining with diamonds, I saw myself a deputy, I saw you—well, I—I saw your future," he concluded, rather feebly. "I have just discovered America," he added.

"But what is it?" asked the boy.

"The Treasure of Franchard," cried the Doctor; and, throwing his brown straw hat upon the ground, he whooped like an Indian and sprang upon Jean-Marie, whom he suffocated with embraces and bedewed with tears. Then he flung himself down among the heather and once more laughed until the valley rang.

But the boy had now an interest of his own, a boy's interest. No sooner was he released from the Doctor's accolade than he ran to the boulders, sprang into the niche, and, thrusting his hand into the crevice, drew forth one after another, encrusted with the earth of ages, the flagons, candlesticks, and patens of the hermitage of Franchard. A casket came last, tightly shut and very heavy.

"O what fun!" he cried.

But when he looked back at the Doctor, who had followed close behind and was silently observing, the words died from his lips. Desprez was once more the colour of ashes; his lip worked and trembled; a sort of bestial greed possessed him.

"This is childish," he said. "We lose precious time. Back to the inn, harness the trap, and bring it to yon bank. Run for your life, and remember—not one whisper. I stay here to watch."

Jean-Marie did as he was bid, though not without surprise. The noddy was brought round to the spot indicated; and the two gradually transported the treasure from its place of concealment to the boot below the driving seat. Once it was all stored the Doctor recovered his gaiety.

"I pay my grateful duties to the genius of this dell," he said. "O, for a live coal, a heifer, and a jar of country wine! I am in the vein for sacrifice, for a superb libation. Well, and why not? We are at Franchard. English pale ale is to be had—not classical, indeed, but excellent. Boy, we shall drink ale."

"But I thought it was so unwholesome," said Jean-Marie, "and very dear besides."

"Fiddle-de-dee!" exclaimed the Doctor gaily. "To the inn!"

And he stepped into the noddy, tossing his head, with an elastic, youthful air. The horse was turned, and in a few seconds they drew up beside the palings of the inn garden.

"Here," said Desprez—"here, near the table, so that we may keep an eye upon things."

They tied the horse, and entered the garden, the Doctor singing, now in fantastic high notes, now producing deep reverberations from his chest. He took a seat, rapped loudly on the table, assailed the waiter with witticisms; and when the bottle of Bass was at length produced, far more charged with gas than the most delirious champagne, he filled out a long glassful of froth and pushed it over to Jean-Marie. "Drink," he said; "drink deep."

"I would rather not," faltered the boy, true to his training.

"What?" thundered Desprez.

"I am afraid of it," said Jean-Marie: "my stomach—"

"Take it or leave it," interrupted Desprez fiercely; "but understand it once for all—there is nothing so contemptible as a precisian."

Here was a new lesson! The boy sat bemused, looking at the glass but not tasting it, while the Doctor emptied and refilled his own, at first with clouded brow, but gradually yielding to the sun, the heady, prickling beverage, and his own predisposition to be happy.

"Once in a way," he said at last, by way of a concession to the boy's more rigorous attitude, "once in a way, and at so critical a moment, this ale is a nectar for the gods. The habit, indeed, is debasing; wine, the juice of the grape, is the true drink of the Frenchman, as I have often had occasion to point out; and I do not know that I can blame you for refusing this outlandish stimulant. You can have some wine and cakes. Is the bottle empty? Well, we will not be proud; we will have pity on your glass."

The beer being done, the Doctor chafed bitterly while Jean-Marie finished his cakes. "I burn to be gone," he said, looking at his watch. "Good God, how slow you eat!" And yet to eat slowly was his own particular prescription, the main secret of longevity!

His martyrdom, however, reached an end at last; the pair resumed their places in the buggy, and Desprez, leaning luxuriously back, announced his intention of proceeding to Fontainebleau.

"To Fontainebleau?" repeated Jean-Marie.

"My words are always measured," said the Doctor. "On!"

The Doctor was driven through the glades of paradise; the air, the light, the shining leaves, the very movements of the vehicle, seemed to fall in tune with his golden meditations; with his head thrown back, he dreamed a series of sunny visions, ale and pleasure dancing in his veins. At last he spoke.

"I shall telegraph for Casimir," he said. "Good Casimir! a fellow of the lower order of intelligence, Jean-Marie, distinctly not creative, not poetic; and yet he will repay your study; his fortune is vast, and is entirely due to his own exertions. He is the very fellow to help us to dispose of our trinkets, find us a suitable house in Paris, and manage the details of our installation. Admirable Casimir, one of my oldest comrades! It was on his advice, I may add, that I invested my little fortune in Turkish bonds; when we have added these spoils of the mediæval church to our stake in the Mahometan empire, little boy, we shall positively roll among doubloons, positively roll! Beautiful forest," he cried, "farewell! Though called to other scenes, I will not forget thee. Thy name is graven in my heart. Under the influence of prosperity I become dithyrambic, Jean-Marie. Such is the impulse of the natural soul; such was the constitution of primæval man. And I—well, I will not refuse the credit—I have preserved my youth like a virginity; another, who should have led the same snoozing, countryfied existence for these years, another had become rusted, become stereotype; but I, I praise my happy constitution, retain the spring unbroken. Fresh opulence and a new sphere of duties find me unabated in ardour and only more mature by knowledge. For this prospective change, Jean-Marie—it may probably have shocked you. Tell me now, did it not strike you as an inconsistency? Confess—it is useless to dissemble—it pained you?"

"Yes," said the boy.

"You see," returned the Doctor, with sublime fatuity, "I read your thoughts! Nor am I surprised—your education is not yet complete; the higher duties of men have not been yet presented to you fully. A hint—till we have leisure—must suffice. Now that I am once more in possession of a modest competence; now that I have so long prepared myself in silent meditation, it becomes my superior duty to proceed to Paris. My scientific training, my undoubted command of language, mark me out for the service of my country. Modesty in such a case would be a snare. If sin is a philosophical expression, I should call it sinful. A man must not deny his manifest abilities, for that is to evade his obligations. I must be up and doing; I must be no skulker in life's battle."

So he rattled on, copiously greasing the joint of his inconsistency with words; while the boy listened silently, his eyes fixed on the horse, his mind seething. It was all lost eloquence; no array of words could unsettle a belief of Jean-Marie's; and he drove into Fontainebleau filled with pity, horror, indignation, and despair.

In the town Jean-Marie was kept a fixture on the driving-seat, to guard the treasure; while the Doctor, with a singular, slightly tipsy airiness of manner, fluttered in and out of cafés, where he shook hands with garrison officers, and mixed an absinthe with the nicety of old experience; in and out of shops, from which he returned laden with costly fruits, real turtle, a magnificent piece of silk for his wife, a preposterous cane for himself, and a kepi of the newest fashion for the boy; in and out of the telegraph office, whence he despatched his telegram, and where three hours later he received an answer promising a visit on the morrow; and generally pervaded Fontainebleau with the first fine aroma of his divine good humour.

The sun was very low when they set forth again; the shadows of the forest trees extended across the broad white road that led them home; the penetrating odour of the evening wood had already arisen, like a cloud of incense, from that broad field of tree-tops; and even in the streets of the town, where the air had been baked all day between white walls, it came in whiffs and pulses, like a distant music. Half-way home, the last gold flicker vanished from a great oak upon the left; and when they came forth beyond the borders of the wood, the plain was already sunken in pearly greyness, and a great, pale moon came swinging skyward through the filmy poplars.

The Doctor sang, the Doctor whistled, the Doctor talked. He spoke of the woods, and the wars, and the deposition of dew; he brightened and babbled of Paris; he soared into cloudy bombast on the glories of the political arena. All was to be changed; as the day departed, it took with it the vestiges of an outworn existence, and to-morrow's sun was to inaugurate the new. "Enough," he cried, "of this life of maceration!" His wife (still beautiful, or he was sadly partial) was to be no longer buried; she should now shine before society. Jean-Marie would find the world at his feet; the roads open to success, wealth, honour, and post-humous renown. "And O, by the way," said he, "for God's sake keep your tongue quiet! You are, of course, a very silent fellow; it is a quality I gladly recognise in you—silence, golden silence! But this is a matter of gravity. No word must get abroad; none but the good Casimir is to be trusted; we shall probably dispose of the vessels in England."

"But are they not even ours?" the boy said, almost with a sob—it was the only time he had spoken.

"Ours in this sense, that they are nobody else's," replied the Doctor. "But the State would have some claim. If they were stolen, for instance, we should be unable to demand their restitution; we should have no title; we should be unable even to communicate with the police. Such is the monstrous condition of the law.[263] It is a mere instance of what remains to be done, of the injustices that may yet be righted by an ardent, active, and philosophical deputy."

Jean-Marie put his faith in Madame Desprez; and as they drove forward down the road from Bourron, between the rustling poplars, he prayed in his teeth, and whipped up the horse to an unusual speed. Surely, as soon as they arrived, madame would assert her character, and bring this waking nightmare to an end.

Their entrance into Gretz was heralded and accompanied by a most furious barking; all the dogs in the village seemed to smell the treasure in the noddy. But there was no one in the street, save three lounging landscape painters at Tentaillon's door. Jean-Marie opened the green gate and led in the horse and carriage; and almost at the same moment Madame Desprez came to the kitchen threshold with a lighted lantern; for the moon was not yet high enough to clear the garden walls.

"Close the gates, Jean-Marie!" cried the Doctor, somewhat unsteadily alighting. "Anastasie, where is Aline?"

"She has gone to Montereau to see her parents," said madame.

"All is for the best!" exclaimed the Doctor fervently. "Here, quick, come near to me; I do not wish to speak too loud," he continued. "Darling, we are wealthy!"

"Wealthy!" repeated the wife.

"I have found the treasure of Franchard," replied her husband. "See, here are the first fruits; a pineapple, a dress for my ever-beautiful—it will suit her—trust a husband's, trust a lover's, taste! Embrace me, darling! This grimy episode is over; the butterfly unfolds its painted wings. To-morrow Casimir will come; in a week we may be in Paris—happy at last! You shall have diamonds. Jean-Marie, take it out of the boot, with religious care, and bring it piece by piece into the dining-room. We shall have plate at table! Darling, hasten and prepare this turtle; it will be a whet—it will be an addition to our meagre ordinary. I myself will proceed to the cellar. We shall have a bottle of that little Beaujolais you like, and finish with the Hermitage; there are still three bottles left. Worthy wine for a worthy occasion."

"But, my husband; you put me in a whirl," she cried. "I do not comprehend."

"The turtle, my adored, the turtle!" cried the doctor; and he pushed her towards the kitchen, lantern and all.

Jean-Marie stood dumfounded. He had pictured to himself a different scene—a more immediate protest, and his hope began to dwindle on the spot.

The Doctor was everywhere, a little doubtful on his legs, perhaps, and now and then taking the wall with his shoulder; for it was long since he had tasted absinthe, and he was even then reflecting that the absinthe had been a misconception. Not that he regretted excess on such a glorious day, but he made a mental memorandum to beware; he must not, a second time, become the victim of a deleterious habit. He had his wine out of the cellar in a twinkling; he arranged the sacrificial vessels, some on the white table-cloth, some on the sideboard, still crusted with historic earth. He was in and out of the kitchen, plying Anastasie with vermouth, heating her with glimpses of the future, estimating their new wealth at ever larger figures; and before they sat down to supper, the lady's virtue had melted in the fire of his enthusiasm, her timidity had disappeared; she, too, had begun to speak disparagingly of the life at Gretz; and as she took her place and helped the soup, her eyes shone with the glitter of prospective diamonds.

All through the meal, she and the Doctor made and unmade fairy plans. They bobbed and bowed and pledged each other. Their faces ran over with smiles; their eyes scattered sparkles, as they projected the Doctor's political honours and the lady's drawing-room ovations.

"But you will not be a Red!" cried Anastasie.

"I am Left Centre to the core," replied the Doctor.

"Madame Gastein will present us—we shall find ourselves forgotten," said the lady.

"Never," protested the Doctor. "Beauty and talent leave a mark."

"I have positively forgotten how to dress," she sighed.

"Darling, you make me blush," cried he. "Yours has been a tragic marriage!"

"But your success—to see you appreciated, honoured, your name in all the papers, that will be more than pleasure—it will be heaven!" she cried.

"And once a week," said the Doctor, archly scanning the syllables, "once a week—one good little game of baccarat?"

"Only once a week?" she questioned, threatening him with a finger.

"I swear it by my political honour," cried he.

"I spoil you," she said, and gave him her hand.

He covered it with kisses.

Jean-Marie escaped into the night. The moon swung high over Gretz. He went down to the garden end and sat on the jetty. The river ran by with eddies of oily silver, and a low, monotonous song. Faint veils of mist moved among the poplars on the farther side. The reeds were quietly nodding. A hundred times already had the boy sat, on such a night, and watched the streaming river with untroubled fancy. And this perhaps was to be the last. He was to leave this familiar hamlet, this green, rustling country, this bright and quiet stream; he was to pass into the great city; his dear lady mistress was to move bedizened in saloons; his good, garrulous, kind-hearted master to become a brawling deputy; and both be lost for ever to Jean-Marie and their better selves. He knew his own defects; he knew he must sink into less and less consideration in the turmoil of a city life, sink more and more from the child into the servant. And he began dimly to believe the Doctor's prophecies of evil. He could see a change in both. His generous incredulity failed him for this once; a child must have perceived that the Hermitage had completed what the absinthe had begun. If this were the first day, what would be the last? "If necessary, wreck the train," thought he, remembering the Doctor's parable. He looked round on the delightful scene; he drank deep of the charmed night air, laden with the scent of hay. "If necessary, wreck the train," he repeated. And he rose and returned to the house.

CHAPTER VI.
A CRIMINAL INVESTIGATION, IN TWO PARTS.

The next morning there was a most unusual outcry, in the Doctor's house. The last thing before going to bed, the Doctor had locked up some valuables in the dining-room cupboard; and behold, when he rose again, as he did about four o'clock, the cupboard had been broken open, and the valuables in question had disappeared. Madame and Jean-Marie were summoned from their rooms, and appeared in hasty toilets; they found the Doctor raving, calling the heavens to witness and avenge his injury, pacing the room bare-footed, with the tails of his night-shirt flirting as he turned.

"Gone!" he said; "the things are gone, the fortune gone! We are paupers once more. Boy! what do you know of this? Speak up, sir, speak up. Do you know of it? Where are they?" He had him by the arm, shaking him like a bag, and the boy's words, if he had any, were jolted forth in inarticulate murmurs. The Doctor, with a revulsion from his own violence, set him down again. He observed Anastasie in tears. "Anastasie," he said, in quite an altered voice, "compose yourself, command your feelings. I would not have you give way to passion like the vulgar. This—this trifling accident must be lived down. Jean-Marie, bring me my smaller medicine chest. A gentle laxative is indicated."

And he dosed the family all round, leading the way himself with a double quantity. The wretched Anastasie, who had never been ill in the whole course of her existence, and whose soul recoiled from remedies, wept floods of tears as she sipped, and shuddered, and protested, and then was bullied and shouted at until she sipped again. As for Jean-Marie, he took his portion down with stoicism.

"I have given him a less amount," observed the Doctor, "his youth protecting him against emotion. And now that we have thus parried any morbid consequences, let us reason."

"I am so cold," wailed Anastasie.

"Cold!" cried the Doctor. "I give thanks to God that I am made of fierier material. Why, madam, a blow like this would set a frog into a transpiration. If you are cold, you can retire; and, by the way, you might throw me down my trousers. It is chilly for the legs."

"Oh, no!" protested Anastasie; "I will stay with you."

"Nay, madam, you shall not suffer for your devotion," said the Doctor. "I will myself fetch you a shawl." And he went upstairs and returned more fully clad and with an armful of wraps for the shivering Anastasie. "And now," he resumed, "to investigate this crime. Let us proceed by induction. Anastasie, do you know anything that can help us?" Anastasie knew nothing. "Or you, Jean-Marie?"

"Not I," replied the boy steadily.

"Good," returned the Doctor. "We shall now turn our attention to the material evidences. (I was born to be a detective; I have the eye and the systematic spirit.) First, violence has been employed. The door was broken open; and it may be observed, in passing, that the lock was dear indeed at what I paid for it: a crow to pluck with Master Goguelat. Second, here is the instrument employed, one of our own table-knives, one of our best, my dear; which seems to indicate no preparation on the part of the gang—if gang it was. Thirdly, I observe that nothing has been removed except the Franchard dishes and the casket; our own silver has been minutely respected. This is wily; it shows intelligence, a knowledge of the code, a desire to avoid legal consequences. I argue from this fact that the gang numbers persons of respectability—outward, of course, and merely outward, as the robbery proves. But I argue, second, that we must have been observed at Franchard itself by some occult observer, and dogged throughout the day with a skill and patience that I venture to qualify as consummate. No ordinary man, no occasional criminal, would have shown himself capable of this combination. We have in our neighbourhood, it is far from improbable, a retired bandit of the highest order of intelligence."

"Good heaven!" cried the horrified Anastasie. "Henri, how can you?"

"My cherished one, this is a process of induction," said the Doctor. "If any of my steps are unsound, correct me. You are silent? Then do not, I beseech you, be so vulgarly illogical as to revolt from my conclusion. We have now arrived," he resumed, "at some idea of the composition of the gang—for I incline to the hypothesis of more than one—and we now leave this room, which can disclose no more, and turn our attention to the court and garden. (Jean-Marie, I trust you are observantly following my various steps; this is an excellent piece of education for you.) Come with me to the door. No steps on the court; it is unfortunate our court should be paved. On what small matters hang the destiny of these delicate investigations! Hey! What have we here? I have led on to the very spot," he said, standing grandly backward and indicating the green gate. "An escalade, as you can now see for yourselves, has taken place."

Sure enough, the green paint was in several places scratched and broken; and one of the panels preserved the print of a nailed shoe. The foot had slipped, however, and it was difficult to estimate the size of the shoe, and impossible to distinguish the pattern of the nails.

"The whole robbery," concluded the Doctor, "step by step, has been reconstituted. Inductive science can no further go."

"It is wonderful," said his wife. "You should indeed have been a detective, Henri. I had no idea of your talents."

"My dear," replied Desprez, condescendingly, "a man of scientific imagination combines the lesser faculties; he is a detective just as he is a publicist or a general; these are but local applications of his special talent. But now," he continued, "would you have me go further? Would you have me lay my finger on the culprits—or rather, for I cannot promise quite so much, point out to you the very house where they consort? It may be a satisfaction, at least it is all we are likely to get, since we are denied the remedy of law. I reach the further stage in this way. In order to fill my outline of the robbery, I require a man likely to be in the forest idling, I require a man of education, I require a man superior to considerations of morality. The three requisites all centre in Tentaillon's boarders. They are painters, therefore they are continually lounging in the forest. They are painters, therefore they are not unlikely to have some smattering of education. Lastly, because they are painters, they are probably immoral. And this I prove in two ways. First, painting is an art which merely addresses the eye; it does not in any particular exercise the moral sense. And second, painting, in common with all the other arts, implies the dangerous quality of imagination. A man of imagination is never moral; he outsoars literal demarcations and reviews life under too many shifting lights to rest content with the invidious distinctions of the law!"

"But you always say—at least, so I understood you"—said madame, "that these lads display no imagination whatever."

"My dear, they displayed imagination, and of a very fantastic order, too," returned the Doctor, "when they embraced their beggarly profession. Besides—and this is an argument exactly suited to your intellectual level—many of them are English and American. Where else should we expect to find a thief?—And now you had better get your coffee. Because we have lost a treasure, there is no reason for starving. For my part, I shall break my fast with white wine. I feel unaccountably heated and thirsty to-day. I can only attribute it to the shock of the discovery. And yet, you will bear me out, I supported the emotion nobly."

The Doctor had now talked himself back into an admirable humour; and as he sat in the arbour and slowly imbibed a large allowance of white wine and picked a little bread and cheese with no very impetuous appetite, if a third of his meditations ran upon the missing treasure, the other two-thirds were more pleasingly busied in the retrospect of his detective skill.

About eleven Casimir arrived; he had caught an early train to Fontainebleau, and driven over to save time; and now his cab was stabled at Tentaillon's, and he remarked, studying his watch, that he could spare an hour and a half. He was much the man of business, decisively spoken, given to frowning in an intellectual manner. Anastasie's born brother, he did not waste much sentiment on the lady, gave her an English family kiss, and demanded a meal without delay.

"You can tell me your story while we eat," he observed. "Anything good to-day, Stasie?"

He was promised something good. The trio sat down to table in the arbour, Jean-Marie waiting as well as eating, and the Doctor recounted what had happened in his richest narrative manner. Casimir heard it with explosions of laughter.

"What a streak of luck for you, my good brother," he observed, when the tale was over. "If you had gone to Paris, you would have played dick-duck-drake with the whole consignment in three months. Your own would have followed; and you would have come to me in a procession like the last time. But I give you warning—Stasie may weep and Henri ratiocinate—it will not serve you twice. Your next collapse will be fatal. I thought I had told you so, Stasie? Hey? No sense?"

The Doctor winced and looked furtively at Jean-Marie; but the boy seemed apathetic.

"And then again," broke out Casimir, "what children you are—vicious children, my faith! How could you tell the value of this trash? It might have been worth nothing, or next door."

"Pardon me," said the Doctor. "You have your usual flow of spirits, I perceive, but even less than your usual deliberation. I am not entirely ignorant of these matters."

"Not entirely ignorant of anything ever I heard of," interrupted Casimir, bowing, and raising his glass with a sort of pert politeness.

"At least," resumed the Doctor, "I gave my mind to the subject—that you may be willing to believe—and I estimated that our capital would be doubled." And he described the nature of the find.

"My word of honour!" said Casimir, "I half believe you! But much would depend on the quality of the gold."

"The quality, my dear Casimir, was—" And the Doctor, in default of language, kissed his finger-tips.

"I would not take your word for it, my good friend," retorted the man of business. "You are a man of very rosy views. But this robbery," he continued—"this robbery is an odd thing. Of course I pass over your nonsense about gangs and landscape-painters. For me, that is a dream. Who was in the house last night?"

"None but ourselves," replied the Doctor.

"And this young gentleman?" asked Casimir, jerking a nod in the direction of Jean-Marie.

"He too'—the Doctor bowed.

"Well; and if it is a fair question, who is he?" pursued the brother-in-law.

"Jean-Marie," answered the Doctor, "combines the functions of a son and stable-boy. He began as the latter, but he rose rapidly to the more honourable rank in our affections. He is, I may say, the greatest comfort in our lives."

"Ha!" said Casimir. "And previous to becoming one of you?"

"Jean-Marie has lived a remarkable existence; his experience his been eminently formative," replied Desprez. "If I had had to choose an education for my son, I should have chosen such another. Beginning life with mountebanks and thieves, passing onward to the society and friendship of philosophers, he may be said to have skimmed the volume of human life."

"Thieves?" repeated the brother-in-law, with a meditative air.

The Doctor could have bitten his tongue out. He foresaw what was coming, and prepared his mind for a vigorous defence.

"Did you ever steal yourself?" asked Casimir, turning suddenly on Jean-Marie, and for the first time employing a single eyeglass which hung round his neck.

"Yes, sir," replied the boy, with a deep blush.

Casimir turned to the others with pursed lips, and nodded to them meaningly. "Hey?" said he; "how is that?"

"Jean-Marie is a teller of the truth," returned the Doctor, throwing out his bust.

"He has never told a lie," added madame. "He is the best of boys."

"Never told a lie, has he not?" reflected Casimir. "Strange, very strange. Give me your attention, my young friend," he continued. "You knew about this treasure?"

"He helped to bring it home," interposed the Doctor.

"Desprez, I ask you nothing but to hold your tongue," returned Casimir. "I mean to question this stable-boy of yours; and if you are so certain of his innocence, you can afford to let him answer for himself. Now, sir," he resumed, pointing his eyeglass straight at Jean-Marie. "You knew it could be stolen with impunity? You knew you could not be prosecuted? Come! Did you, or did you not?"

"I did," answered Jean-Marie, in a miserable whisper. He sat there changing colour like a revolving pharos, twisting his fingers hysterically, swallowing air, the picture of guilt.

"You knew where it was put?" resumed the inquisitor.

"Yes," from Jean-Marie.

"You say you have been a thief before," continued Casimir. "Now how am I to know that you are not one still? I suppose you could climb the green gate?"

"Yes," still lower, from the culprit.

"Well, then, it was you who stole these things. You know it, and you dare not deny it. Look me in the face! Raise your sneak's eyes, and answer!"

But in place of anything of that sort Jean-Marie broke into a dismal howl and fled from the arbour. Anastasie, as she pursued to capture and reassure the victim, found time to send one Parthian arrow—"Casimir, you are a brute!"

"My brother," said Desprez, with the greatest dignity, "you take upon yourself a licence—"

"Desprez," interrupted Casimir, "for Heaven's sake be a man of the world. You telegraph me to leave my business and come down here on yours. I come, I ask the business, you say 'Find me this thief!' Well, I find him; I say 'There he is!' You need not like it, but you have no manner of right to take offence."

"Well," returned the Doctor, "I grant that; I will even thank you for your mistaken zeal. But your hypothesis was so extravagantly monstrous—"

"Look here," interrupted Casimir; "was it you or Stasie?"

"Certainly not," answered the Doctor.

"Very well; then it was the boy. Say no more about it," said the brother-in-law, and he produced his cigar-case.

"I will say this much more," returned Desprez: "if that boy came and told me so himself, I should not believe him; and if I did believe him, so implicit is my trust, I should conclude that he had acted for the best."

"Well, well," said Casimir, indulgently. "Have you a light? I must be going. And by the way, I wish you would let me sell your Turks for you. I always told you, it meant smash. I tell you so again. Indeed, it was partly that that brought me down. You never acknowledge my letters—a most unpardonable habit."

"My good brother," replied the Doctor blandly, "I have never denied your ability in business; but I can perceive your limitations."

"Egad, my friend, I can return the compliment," observed the man of business. "Your limitation is to be downright irrational."

"Observe the relative position," returned the Doctor with a smile. "It is your attitude to believe through thick and thin in one man's judgment—your own. I follow the same opinion, but critically and with open eyes. Which is the more irrational?—I leave it to yourself."

"O, my dear fellow!" cried Casimir, "stick to your Turks, stick to your stable-boy, go to the devil in general in your own way and be done with it. But don't ratiocinate with me—I cannot bear it. And so, ta-ta. I might as well have stayed away for any good I've done. Say good-bye from me to Stasie, and to the sullen hang-dog of a stable-boy, if you insist on it; I'm off."

And Casimir departed. The Doctor, that night, dissected his character before Anastasie. "One thing, my beautiful," he said, "he has learned one thing from his lifelong acquaintance with your husband: the word ratiocinate. It shines in his vocabulary, like a jewel in a muck-heap. And, even so, he continually misapplies it. For you must have observed he uses it as a sort of taunt, in the sense of to ergotise, implying, as it were—the poor, dear fellow!—a vein of sophistry. As for his cruelty to Jean-Marie, it must be forgiven him—it is not his nature, it is the nature of his life. A man who deals with money, my dear, is a man lost."

With Jean-Marie the process of reconciliation had been somewhat slow. At first he was inconsolable, insisted on leaving the family, went from paroxysm to paroxysm of tears; and it was only after Anastasie had been closeted for an hour with him, alone, that she came forth, sought out the Doctor, and, with tears in her eyes, acquainted that gentleman with what had passed.

"At first, my husband, he would hear of nothing," she said. "Imagine! if he had left us! what would the treasure be to that? Horrible treasure, it has brought all this about! At last, after he has sobbed his very heart out, he agrees to stay on a condition—we are not to mention this matter, this infamous suspicion, not even to mention the robbery. On that agreement only, the poor, cruel boy will consent to remain among his friends."

"But this inhibition," said the Doctor, "this embargo—it cannot possibly apply to me?"

"To all of us," Anastasie assured him.

"My cherished one," Desprez protested, "you must have misunderstood. It cannot apply to me. He would naturally come to me."

"Henri," she said, "it does; I swear to you it does."

"This is a painful, a very painful circumstance," the Doctor said, looking a little black. "I cannot affect, Anastasie, to be anything but justly wounded. I feel this, I feel it, my wife, acutely."

"I knew you would," she said. "But if you had seen his distress! We must make allowances, we must sacrifice our feelings."

"I trust, my dear, you have never found me averse to sacrifices," returned the Doctor very stiffly.

"And you will let me go and tell him that you have agreed? It will be like your noble nature," she cried.

So it would, he perceived—it would be like his noble nature! Up jumped his spirits, triumphant at the thought. "Go, darling," he said nobly, "reassure him. The subject is buried; more—I make an effort, I have accustomed my will to these exertions—and it is forgotten."

A little after, but still with swollen eyes and looking mortally sheepish, Jean-Marie reappeared and went ostentatiously about his business. He was the only unhappy member of the party that sat down that night to supper. As for the Doctor, he was radiant. He thus sang the requiem of the treasure:—

"This has been, on the whole, a most amusing episode," he said. "We are not a penny the worse—nay, we are immensely gainers. Our philosophy has been exercised; some of the turtle is still left—the most wholesome of delicacies; I have my staff, Anastasie has her new dress, Jean-Marie is the proud possessor of a fashionable kepi. Besides, we had a glass of Hermitage last night; the glow still suffuses my memory. I was growing positively niggardly with that Hermitage, positively niggardly. Let me take the hint: we had one bottle to celebrate the appearance of our visionary fortune; let us have a second to console us for its occultation. The third I hereby dedicate to Jean-Marie's wedding breakfast."

CHAPTER VII.
THE FALL OF THE HOUSE OF DESPREZ.

The Doctor's house has not yet received the compliment of a description, and it is now high time that the omission were supplied, for the house is itself an actor in the story, and one whose part is nearly at an end. Two stories in height, walls of a warm yellow, tiles of an ancient ruddy brown diversified with moss and lichen, it stood with one wall to the street in the angle of the Doctor's property. It was roomy, draughty, and inconvenient. The large rafters were here and there engraven with rude marks and patterns; the handrail of the stair was carved in countrified arabesque; a stout timber pillar, which did duty to support the dining-room roof, bore mysterious characters on its darker side, runes, according to the Doctor; nor did he fail, when he ran over the legendary history of the house and its possessors, to dwell upon the Scandinavian scholar who had left them. Floors, doors, and rafters made a great variety of angles; every room had a particular inclination; the gable had tilted towards the garden, after the manner of a leaning tower, and one of the former proprietors had buttressed the building from that side with a great strut of wood, like the derrick of a crane. Altogether, it had many marks of ruin; it was a house for the rats to desert; and nothing but its excellent brightness—the window-glass polished and shining, the paint well scoured, the brasses radiant, the very prop all wreathed about with climbing flowers—nothing but its air of a well-tended, smiling veteran, sitting, crutch and all, in the sunny corner of a garden, marked it as a house for comfortable people to inhabit. In poor or idle management it would soon have hurried into the blackguard stages of decay. As it was, the whole family loved it, and the Doctor was never better inspired than when he narrated its imaginary story and drew the character of its successive masters, from the Hebrew merchant who had re-edified its walls after the sack of the town, and past the mysterious engraver of the runes, down to the long-headed, dirty-handed boor from whom he had himself acquired it at a ruinous expense. As for any alarm about its security, the idea had never presented itself. What had stood four centuries might well endure a little longer.

Indeed, in this particular winter, after the finding and losing of the treasure, the Desprez' had an anxiety of a very different order, and one which lay nearer their hearts. Jean-Marie was plainly not himself. He had fits of hectic activity, when he made unusual exertions to please, spoke more and faster, and redoubled in attention to his lessons. But these were interrupted by spells of melancholia and brooding silence, when the boy was little better than unbearable.

"Silence," the Doctor moralised—"you see, Anastasie, what comes of silence. Had the boy properly unbosomed himself, the little disappointment about the treasure, the little annoyance about Casimir's incivility, would long ago have been forgotten. As it is, they prey upon him like a disease. He loses flesh, his appetite is variable and, on the whole, impaired. I keep him on the strictest regimen, I exhibit the most powerful tonics; both in vain."

"Don't you think you drug him too much?" asked madame, with an irrepressible shudder.

"Drug?" cried the Doctor; "I drug? Anastasie, you are mad!"

Time went on, and the boy's health still slowly declined. The Doctor blamed the weather, which was cold and boisterous. He called in his confrère from Bourron, took a fancy for him, magnified his capacity, and was pretty soon under treatment himself—it scarcely appeared for what complaint. He and Jean-Marie had each medicine to take at different periods of the day. The Doctor used to lie in wait for the exact moment, watch in hand. "There is nothing like regularity," he would say, fill out the doses, and dilate on the virtues of the draught; and if the boy seemed none the better, the Doctor was not at all the worse.

Gunpowder Day, the boy was particularly low. It was scowling, squally weather. Huge broken companies of cloud sailed swiftly overhead; raking gleams of sunlight swept the village, and were followed by intervals of darkness and white, flying rain. At times the wind lifted up its voice and bellowed. The trees were all scourging themselves along the meadows, the last leaves flying like dust.

The Doctor, between the boy and the weather, was in his element; he had a theory to prove. He sat with his watch out and a barometer in front of him, waiting for the squalls and noting their effect upon the human pulse. "For the true philosopher," he remarked delightedly, "every fact in nature is a toy." A letter came to him; but, as its arrival coincided with the approach of another gust, he merely crammed it into his pocket, gave the time to Jean-Marie, and the next moment they were both counting their pulses as if for a wager.

At nightfall the wind rose into a tempest. It besieged the hamlet, apparently from every side, as if with batteries of cannon; the houses shook and groaned; live coals were blown upon the floor. The uproar and terror of the night kept people long awake, sitting with pallid faces giving ear.

It was twelve before the Desprez family retired. By half-past one, when the storm was already somewhat past its height, the Doctor was awakened from a troubled slumber, and sat up. A noise still rang in his ears, but whether of this world or the world of dreams he was not certain. Another clap of wind followed. It was accompanied by a sickening movement of the whole house, and in the subsequent lull Desprez could hear the tiles pouring like a cataract into the loft above his head. He plucked Anastasie bodily out of bed.

"Run!" he cried, thrusting some wearing apparel into her hands; "the house is falling! To the garden!"

She did not pause to be twice bidden; she was down the stair in an instant. She had never before suspected herself of such activity. The Doctor meanwhile, with the speed of a piece of pantomime business, and undeterred by broken shins, proceeded to rout out Jean-Marie, tore Aline from her virgin slumbers, seized her by the hand, and tumbled downstairs and into the garden, with the girl tumbling behind him, still not half awake.

The fugitives rendezvous'd in the arbour by some common instinct. Then came a bull's-eye flash of struggling moonshine, which disclosed their four figures standing huddled from the wind in a raffle of flying drapery, and not without a considerable need for more. At the humiliating spectacle Anastasie clutched her nightdress desperately about her and burst loudly into tears. The Doctor flew to console her; but she elbowed him away. She suspected everybody of being the general public, and thought the darkness was alive with eyes.

Another gleam and another violent gust arrived together; the house was seen to rock on its foundation, and, just as the light was once more eclipsed, a crash which triumphed over the shouting of the wind announced its fall, and for a moment the whole garden was alive with skipping tiles and brickbats. One such missile grazed the Doctor's ear; another descended on the bare foot of Aline, who instantly made night hideous with her shrieks.

By this time the hamlet was alarmed, lights flashed from the windows, hails reached the party, and the Doctor answered, nobly contending against Aline and the tempest. But this prospect of help only awakened Anastasie to a more active stage of terror.

"Henri, people will be coming," she screamed in her husband's ear.

"I trust so," he replied.

"They cannot. I would rather die," she wailed.

"My dear," said the Doctor reprovingly, "you are excited. I gave you some clothes. What have you done with them?"

"Oh, I don't know—I must have thrown them away! Where are they?" she sobbed.

Desprez groped about in the darkness. "Admirable!" he remarked; "my grey velveteen trousers! This will exactly meet your necessities."

"Give them to me!" she cried fiercely; but as soon as she had them in her hands her mood appeared to alter—she stood silent for a moment, and then pressed the garment back upon the Doctor. "Give it to Aline," she said—"poor girl."

"Nonsense!" said the Doctor. "Aline does not know what she is about. Aline is beside herself with terror; and at any rate, she is a peasant. Now I am really concerned at this exposure for a person of your housekeeping habits; my solicitude and your fantastic modesty both point to the same remedy—the pantaloons." He held them ready.

"It is impossible. You do not understand," she said with dignity.

By this time rescue was at hand. It had been found impracticable to enter by the street, for the gate was blocked with masonry, and the nodding ruin still threatened further avalanches. But between the Doctor's garden and the one on the right hand there was that very picturesque contrivance—a common well; the door on the Desprez' side had chanced to be unbolted, and now, through the arched aperture a man's bearded face and an arm supporting a lantern were introduced into the world of windy darkness, where Anastasie concealed her woes. The light struck here and there among the tossing apple boughs, it glinted on the grass; but the lantern and the glowing face became the centre of the world. Anastasie crouched back from the intrusion.

"This way!" shouted the man. "Are you all safe?" Aline, still screaming, ran to the new comer, and was presently hauled head-foremost through the wall.

"Now, Anastasie, come on; it is your turn," said the husband.

"I cannot," she replied.

"Are we all to die of exposure, madame?" thundered Doctor Desprez.

"You can go!" she cried. "Oh, go, go away! I can stay here; I am quite warm."

The Doctor took her by the shoulders with an oath.

"Stop!" she screamed. "I will put them on."

She took the detested lendings in her hand once more; but her repulsion was stronger than shame. "Never!" she cried, shuddering, and flung them far away into the night.

Next moment the Doctor had whirled her to the well. The man was there and the lantern; Anastasie closed her eyes and appeared to herself to be about to die. How she was transported through the arch she knew not; but once on the other side she was received by the neighbour's wife, and enveloped in a friendly blanket.

Beds were made ready for the two women, clothes of very various sizes for the Doctor and Jean-Marie; and for the remainder of the night, while madame dozed in and out on the borderland of hysterics, her husband sat beside the fire and held forth to the admiring neighbours. He showed them, at length, the causes of the accident; for years, he explained, the fall had been impending; one sign had followed another, the joints had opened, the plaster had cracked, the old walls bowed inward; last, not three weeks ago, the cellar door had begun to work with difficulty in its grooves. "The cellar!" he said, gravely shaking his head over a glass of mulled wine. "That reminds me of my poor vintages. By a manifest providence the Hermitage was nearly at an end. One bottle—I lose but one bottle of that incomparable wine. It had been set apart against Jean-Marie's wedding. Well, I must lay down some more; it will be an interest in life. I am, however, a man somewhat advanced in years. My great work is now buried in the fall of my humble roof; it will never be completed—my name will have been writ in water. And yet you find me calm—I would say cheerful. Can your priest do more?"

By the first glimpse of day the party sallied forth from the fireside into the street. The wind had fallen, but still charioted a world of troubled clouds; the air bit like frost; and the party, as they stood about the ruins in the rainy twilight of the morning, beat upon their breasts and blew into their hands for warmth. The house had entirely fallen, the walls outward, the roof in; it was a mere heap of rubbish, with here and there a forlorn spear of broken rafter. A sentinel was placed over the ruins to protect the property, and the party adjourned to Tentaillon's to break their fast at the Doctor's expense. The bottle circulated somewhat freely; and before they left the table it had begun to snow.

For three days the snow continued to fall, and the ruins, covered with tarpaulin and watched by sentries, were left undisturbed. The Desprez' meanwhile had taken up their abode at Tentaillon's. Madame spent her time in the kitchen, concocting little delicacies, with the admiring aid of Madame Tentaillon, or sitting by the fire in thoughtful abstraction. The fall of the house affected her wonderfully little; that blow had been parried by another; and in her mind she was continually fighting over again the battle of the trousers. Had she done right? Had she done wrong? And now she would applaud her determination; and anon, with a horrid flush of unavailing penitence, she would regret the trousers. No juncture in her life had so much exercised her judgment. In the meantime the Doctor had become vastly pleased with his situation. Two of the summer boarders still lingered behind the rest, prisoners for lack of a remittance; they were both English, but one of them spoke French pretty fluently, and was, besides, a humorous, agile-minded fellow, with whom the Doctor could reason by the hour, secure of comprehension. Many were the glasses they emptied, many the topics they discussed.

"Anastasie," the Doctor said on the third morning, "take an example from your husband, from Jean-Marie! The excitement has done more for the boy than all my tonics, he takes his turn as sentry with positive gusto. As for me, you behold me. I have made friends with the Egyptians; and my Pharaoh is, I swear it, a most agreeable companion. You alone are hipped. About a house—a few dresses? What are they in comparison to the 'Pharmacopoeia'—the labour of years lying buried below stones and sticks in this depressing hamlet? The snow falls; I shake it from my cloak! Imitate me. Our income will be impaired, I grant it, since we must rebuild; but moderation, patience, and philosophy will gather about the hearth. In the meanwhile, the Tentaillons are obliging; the table, with your additions, will pass; only the wine is execrable—well, I shall send for some to-day. My Pharaoh will be gratified to drink a decent glass; aha! and I shall see if he possesses that acme of organisation—a palate. If he has a palate, he is perfect."

"Henri," she said, shaking her head, "you are a man; you cannot understand my feelings; no woman could shake off the memory of so public a humiliation." The Doctor could not restrain a titter. "Pardon me, darling," he said; "but really, to the philosophical intelligence, the incident appears so small a trifle. You looked extremely well—"

"Henri!" she cried.

"Well, well, I will say no more," he replied. "Though, to be sure, if you had consented to indue—À propos," he broke off, "and my trousers! They are lying in the snow—my favourite trousers!" And he dashed in quest of Jean-Marie.

Two hours afterwards the boy returned to the inn with a spade under one arm and a curious sop of clothing under the other.

The Doctor ruefully took it in his hands. "They have been!" he said. "Their tense is past. Excellent pantaloons, you are no more! Stay, something in the pocket," and he produced a piece of paper. "A letter! ay, now I mind me; it was received on the morning of the gale, when I was absorbed in delicate investigations. It is still legible. From poor, dear Casimir! It is as well," he chuckled, "that I have educated him to patience. Poor Casimir and his correspondence—his infinitesimal, timorous, idiotic correspondence!"

He had by this time cautiously unfolded the wet letter; but, as he bent himself to decipher the writing, a cloud descended on his brow.

"Bigre!" he cried, with a galvanic start.

And then the letter was whipped into the fire, and the Doctor's cap was on his head in the turn of a hand.

"Ten minutes! I can catch it, if I run," he cried. "It is always late. I go to Paris. I shall telegraph."

"Henri! what is wrong?" cried his wife.

"Ottoman Bonds!" came from the disappearing Doctor; and Anastasie and Jean-Marie were left face to face with the wet trousers. Desprez had gone to Paris, for the second time in seven years; he had gone to Paris with a pair of wooden shoes, a knitted spencer, a black blouse, a country nightcap, and twenty francs in his pocket. The fall of the house was but a secondary marvel; the whole world might have fallen and scarce left his family more petrified.

CHAPTER VIII.
THE WAGES OF PHILOSOPHY.

On the morning of the next day, the Doctor, a mere spectre of himself, was brought back in the custody of Casimir. They found Anastasie and the boy sitting together by the fire; and Desprez, who had exchanged his toilette for a ready-made rig-out of poor materials, waved his hand as he entered, and sank speechless on the nearest chair. Madame turned direct to Casimir.

"What is wrong?" she cried.

"Well," replied Casimir, "what have I told you all along? It has come. It is a clean shave, this time; so you may as well bear up and make the best of it. House down, too, eh? Bad luck, upon my soul."

"Are we—are we—ruined?" she gasped.

The Doctor stretched out his arms to her. "Ruined," he replied, "you are ruined by your sinister husband."

Casimir observed the consequent embrace through his eyeglass; then he turned to Jean-Marie. "You hear?" he said. "They are ruined; no more pickings, no more house, no more fat cutlets. It strikes me, my friend, that you had best be packing; the present speculation is about worked out." And he nodded to him meaningly.

"Never!" cried Desprez, springing up. "Jean-Marie, if you prefer to leave me, now that I am poor, you can go; you shall receive your hundred francs, if so much remains to me. But if you will consent to stay"—the Doctor wept a little—"Casimir offers me a place—as clerk," he resumed. "The emoluments are slender, but they will be enough for three. It is too much already to have lost my fortune; must I lose my son?"

Jean-Marie sobbed bitterly, but without a word.

"I don't like boys who cry," observed Casimir. "This one is always crying. Here! you clear out of this for a little; I have business with your master and mistress, and these domestic feelings may be settled after I am gone. March!" and he held the door open.

Jean-Marie slunk out, like a detected thief.

By twelve they were all at table but Jean-Marie.

"Hey?" said Casimir. "Gone, you see. Took the hint at once."

"I do not, I confess," said Desprez, "I do not seek to excuse his absence. It speaks a want of heart that disappoints me sorely."

"Want of manners," corrected Casimir. "Heart, he never had. Why, Desprez, for a clever fellow, you are the most gullible mortal in creation. Your ignorance of human nature and human business is beyond belief. You are swindled by heathen Turks, swindled by vagabond children, swindled right and left, upstairs and downstairs. I think it must be your imagination. I thank my stars I have none."

"Pardon me," replied Desprez, still humbly, but with a return of spirit at sight of a distinction to be drawn; "pardon me, Casimir. You possess, even to an eminent degree, the commercial imagination. It was the lack of that in me—it appears it is my weak point—that has led to these repeated shocks. By the commercial imagination the financier forecasts the destiny of his investments, marks the falling house—"

"Egad," interrupted Casimir: "our friend the stable-boy appears to have his share of it."

The Doctor was silenced; and the meal was continued and finished principally to the tune of the brother-in-law's not very consolatory conversation. He entirely ignored the two young English painters, turning a blind eyeglass to their salutations, and continuing his remarks as if he were alone in the bosom of his family; and with every second word he ripped another stitch out of the air balloon of Desprez's vanity. By the time coffee was over the poor Doctor was as limp as a napkin.

"Let us go and see the ruins," said Casimir.

They strolled forth into the street. The fall of the house, like the loss of a front tooth, had quite transformed the village. Through the gap the eye commanded a great stretch of open snowy country, and the place shrank in comparison. It was like a room with an open door. The sentinel stood by the green gate, looking very red and cold, but he had a pleasant word for the Doctor and his wealthy kinsman.

Casimir looked at the mound of ruins, he tried the quality of the tarpaulin. "H'm," he said, "I hope the cellar arch has stood. If it has, my good brother, I will give you a good price for the vines."

"We shall start digging to-morrow," said the sentry. "There is no more fear of snow."

"My friend," returned Casimir sententiously, "you had better wait till you get paid."

The Doctor winced, and began dragging his offensive brother-in-law towards Tentaillon's. In the house there would be fewer auditors, and these already in the secret of his fall.

"Hullo!" cried Casimir, "there goes the stable-boy with his luggage; no, egad, he is taking it into the inn."

And sure enough, Jean-Marie was seen to cross the snowy street and enter Tentaillon's, staggering under a large hamper.

The Doctor stopped with a sudden, wild hope.

"What can he have?" he said. "Let us go and see." And he hurried on.

"His luggage, to be sure," answered Casimir. "He is on the move—thanks to the commercial imagination."

"I have not seen that hamper for—for ever so long," remarked the Doctor.

"Nor will you see it much longer," chuckled Casimir; "unless, indeed, we interfere. And by the way, I insist on an examination."

"You will not require," said Desprez, positively with a sob; and, casting a moist, triumphant glance at Casimir, he began to run.

"What the devil is up with him, I wonder?" Casimir reflected; and then, curiosity taking the upper hand, he followed the Doctor's example and took to his heels.

The hamper was so heavy and large, and Jean-Marie himself so little and so weary, that it had taken him a great while to bundle it upstairs to the Desprez' private room; and he had just set it down on the floor in front of Anastasie, when the Doctor arrived, and was closely followed by the man of business. Boy and hamper were both in a most sorry plight; for the one had passed four months underground in a certain cave on the way to Acheres, and the other had run about five miles as hard as his legs would carry him, half that distance under a staggering weight.

"Jean-Marie," cried the Doctor, in a voice that was only too seraphic to be called hysterical, "is it—? It is!" he cried. "O, my son, my son!" And he sat down upon the hamper and sobbed like a little child.

"You will not go to Paris now," said Jean-Marie sheepishly.

"Casimir," said Desprez, raising his wet face, "do you see that boy, that angel boy? He is the thief; he took the treasure from a man unfit to be entrusted with its use; he brings it back to me when I am sobered and humbled. These, Casimir, are the Fruits of my Teaching, and this moment is the Reward of my Life."

"Tiens," said Casimir.

CPSIA information can be obtained
at www.ICGtesting.com
Printed in the USA
LVHW031323090723
751706LV00031B/201